masculine or feminine	mf	maschile o femminile
military	Mil	militare
music		
noun		
nautical		
pejorative		
personal		
photography		
physics		
plural		
politics		
possessive		
past participle		
prefix	prej	premesso
preposition	prep	preposizione
present tense	pres	presente
pronoun	pron	pronome
psychology	Psych	psicologia
past tense	pt	tempo passato
someone	qcno	qualcuno
something	qcsa	qualcosa
rail	Rail	ferrovia
reflexive	refl	riflessivo
religion	Relig	religione
relative pronoun	rel pron	pronome relativo
somebody	sb	qualcuno
school	Sch	scuola
singular	sg	singolare
something	sth	qualcosa
technical	Techn	tecnico
telephone	Teleph	telefono
theatrical	Theat	teatrale
television	TV	televisione
typography	Typ	tipografia
university	Univ	università
auxiliary verb	v aux	verbo ausiliare
intransitive verb	vi	verbo intransitivo
reflexive verb	vr	verbo riflessivo
transitive verb	vt	verbo transitivo
transitive and intransitive verb	vt/i	verbo transitivo e intransitivo
vulgar	vulg	volgare
familiar	[!]	familiare
slang	[×]	gergo
cultural equivalent	≈	equivalenza culturale

Contents/Indice

Fourth edition/Quarta edizione
Editors/Redazione
Joanna Rubery, Loredana Riu, Pat
Bulhosen

Third Edition/Terza edizione
Editors/Redazione
Nicholas Rollin, Francesca Logi

Second Edition/Seconda edizione
Editors/Redazione
Debora Mazza, Donatella Boi, Sonia
Tinagli-Baxter, Peter Terrell, Jane
Goldie, Francesca Logi, Carla Zipoli

First Edition/Prima edizione
Editor/Redazione
Joyce Andrews

Phrasefinder/Trovafrasi
Colin McIntosh, Francesca Logi
Loredana Riu, Neil and Roswitha
Morris

Proprietary terms

This dictionary includes some words which are or are asserted to be, proprietary names or trademarks. Their inclusion does not imply that they have acquired for legal purposes a non-proprietary or general significance, nor is any other judgement implied concerning their legal status. In cases where the editor has some evidence that a word is used as proprietary name or trade mark this is indicated by the symbol (®), but no judgement concerning the legal status of such words is made or implied thereby.

Marchi registrati

Questo dizionario include alcune parole che sono o vengono considerate marchi registrati. La loro presenza non implica che abbiano acquisito legalmente un significato generale, né si suggerisce alcun altro giudizio riguardo il loro stato giuridico. Qualora il redattore abbia trovato testimonianza dell'uso di una parola come marchio registrato, quest'ultima è stata contrassegnata dal simbolo ®, ma nessun giudizio riguardo lo stato giuridico di tale parola viene espresso o suggerito in tal modo.

Preface/Prefazione

This new edition of the *Oxford Italian Mini Dictionary* has been updated to reflect the changes in English and Italian since the last edition in 2005. Notable additions include terms from the spheres of computing, business and communications, that have become common in modern life. The *Phrasefinder* section has been expanded to provide more useful expressions needed for everyday communication. The section is arranged thematically and covers nine key topics: *going places, keeping in touch, food and drink, places to stay, shopping and money, sport and leisure, good timing, health and beauty* and *weights and measures*.

Questa nuova edizione del *Mini Dizionario Oxford* è stata aggiornata per riflettere i cambiamenti avvenuti nell'inglese e nell'italiano dopo la scorsa edizione del 2005. Tra le voci aggiunte si segnalano in particolare termini del settore informatico, commerciale e delle comunicazioni divenuti ricorrenti nella lingua di tutti i giorni. La sezione *Trovafrasi* è stata infine ampliata per dare maggior spazio alle espressioni necessarie alla comunicazione quotidiana. Tale sezione è presentata per tema e copre nove aree chiave: *in viaggio, comunicazioni, mangiare e bere, dove alloggiare, spese e soldi, sport e tempo libero, l'ora giusta, salute e bellezza*, e *pesi e misure*.

Introduzione

Allo scopo di fornire il maggior numero possibile di informazioni riguardo all'inglese e all'italiano, questo dizionario ricorre ad alcune convenzioni per sfruttare al meglio lo spazio disponibile.

All'interno della voce un trattino ondulato ∼ è utilizzato al posto del lemma.

Qualora il lemma contenga una barra verticale |, il trattino ondulato sostituisce solo la parte del lemma che precede la barra. Ad es.:

dark|en *vt* oscurare. **∼ness** *n* buio *m* (la seconda parola in neretto va letta **darkness**).

Vengono forniti indicatori per indirizzare l'utente verso la traduzione del senso voluto di una parola. I tipi di indicatori sono:

- etichette semantiche, indicanti lo specifico settore d'uso di una parola o di un senso (commercio, informatica, fotografia ecc.);

- indicatori di significato, ad es.: **redazione** *f* (ufficio) editorial office; (di testi) editing;

- soggetti tipici di verbi, ad es.: **trovarsi** *vr* (luogo:) be;

- complementi oggetti tipici di verbi, collocati dopo la traduzione del verbo stesso, ad es.: **superare** *vt* overtake (veicolo); pass (esame);

- sostantivi che ricorrono tipicamete con certi aggettivi, ad es.: **solare** *adj* (energia, raggi) solar; (crema) sun.

Il pallino nero indica che la stessa parola viene tradotta come una diversa parte del discorso, ad es.: **calcolatore** *adj* ... ● *m* ...

La pronuncia inglese è trascritta usando l'Alfabetico Fonetico Internazionale (vedi pag. viii).

L'accento tonico nelle parole italiane è indicato dal segno ' collocato davanti alla sillaba accentata.

Le parentesi quadre racchiudono parti di espressioni che possono essere omesse senza alterazioni di significato.

Introduction

In order to give the maximum information about English and Italian in the space available, this new dictionary uses certain space-saving conventions.

A swung dash ∼ is used to replace the headword within the entry.

Where the headword contains a vertical bar | the swung dash replaces only the part of the headword that comes before the |. For example:

efficien | te *adj* efficient. **∼za** *f* efficiency (the second bold word reads efficienza).

Indicators are provided to guide the user to the best translation for a specific sense of a word. Types of indicator are:

- field labels, which indicate a general area of usage (commercial, computing, photography etc);

- sense indicators, eg: **bore** *n* (of gun) calibro *m*; (person) seccatore, -trice *mf*;

- typical subjects of verbs, eg: **bond** *vt* (glue:) attaccare;

- typical objects of verbs, placed after the translation of the verb, eg: **boost** *vt* stimolare (sales); sollevare (morale);

- nouns that typically go together with certain adjectives, eg: **rich** *adj* ricco; (food) pesante;

A bullet point means that a headword has changed its part of speech within an entry, eg: **partition** *n* ... ● *vt* ...

English pronunciation is given for the Italian user in the International Phonetic Alphabet (see p viii).

Italian stress is shown by a ' placed in front of the stressed syllable in a word.

Square brackets are used around parts of an expression which can be omitted without altering its sense.

Pronuncia inglese

Simboli fonetici

Vocali e dittonghi

i:	see	ɔ:	saw	eɪ	page	ɔɪ	join
ɪ	sit	ʊ	put	əʊ	home	ɪə	near
e	ten	u:	too	aɪ	five	eə	hair
æ	hat	ʌ	cup	aɪə	fire	ʊə	poor
ɑ:	arm	ɜ:	fur	aʊ	now		
ɒ	got	ə	ago	aʊə	flour		

Consonanti

p	pen	tʃ	chin	s	so	n	no
b	bad	dʒ	June	z	zoo	ŋ	sing
t	tea	f	fall	ʃ	she	l	leg
d	dip	v	voice	ʒ	measure	r	red
k	cat	θ	thin	h	how	j	yes
g	got	ð	then	m	man	w	wet

Note: ' precede la sillaba accentata.

Pronunciation of Italian

Vowels

a   is broad like *a* in *father*: **casa**

e   has two sounds: closed like *ey* in *they*: **sera**; open like *e* in *egg*: **sette**

i   is like *ee* in *feet*: **venire**.

o   1. closed like *o* in *show*: **croma**. 2. open like *o* in *dog*: **bocca**.

u   is like *oo* in *moon*: **luna**

When two or more vowels come together each vowel is pronounced separately: **buono; baia**.

Consonants

b, d, f, l, m, n, p, t, v are pronounced as in English. When these are double, they are pronounced as separate sounds: **bello**.

c   before **a, o** or **u** and before consonants is like *k* in *king*: **cane**. Before **e** or **i** it is like *ch* in *church*: **cena**.

ch   is also like *k* in *king*: **chiesa**

g   before **a, o** or **u** is hard like *g* in *got*: **gufo**. Before **e** or **i** it is like *j* in *jelly*: **gentile**.

gh   is like *g* in *gun*: **ghiaccio**.

gl   when followed by **a, e, o** and **u** is like *gl* in *glass*: **gloria**.

gli   is like *lli* in *million*: **figlio**.

gn   is like *ni* in *onion*: **bagno**.

h   is silent.

ng   is like *ng* in *finger*: **ringraziare**.

r   is pronounced distinctly.

s   between two vowels is like *s* in *rose*: **riso**. at the beginning of a word it is like *s* in *soap*: **sapone**.

sc   before **e** or **i** is like *sh* in *shell*: **scienza**.

z   sounds like *ts* within a word: **fazione**; like *dz* at the beginning: **zoo**.

Stress is shown by the sign ' printed before the stressed syllable.

Aa

a (ad before vowel) prep to; (stato in luogo, tempo, età) at; (con mese, città) in; (mezzo, modo) by; dire qcsa a qcno tell sb sth; **alle tre** at three o'clock; **a vent'anni** at the age of twenty; **a Natale** at Christmas; **a dicembre** in December; **ero al cinema** I was at the cinema; **vivo a Londra** I live in London; **a due a due** two by two; **a piedi** on o by foot; **maglia a maniche lunghe** long-sleeved sweater; **casa a tre piani** house with three floors; **giocare a tennis** play tennis; **50 km all'ora** 50 km an hour; **4 euro al chilo** 4 euros a kilo; **al mattino/alla sera** in the morning/evening; **a venti chilometri/due ore da qui** twenty kilometres/two hours away

a'bate m abbot

abbacchi'ato adj downhearted

ab'bacchio m [young] lamb

abbagli'ante adj dazzling ● m headlight, high beam

abbagli'are vt dazzle. **ab'baglio** m blunder; **prendere un ~** make a blunder

abbai'are vi bark

abba'ino m dormer window

abbando'na|re vt abandon; leave (luogo); give up (piani ecc). **~rsi** vr let oneself go; **~rsi a** give oneself up to (ricordi ecc). **~to** adj abandoned. **abban'dono** m abandoning; fig abandon; (stato) neglect

abbassa'mento m (di temperatura, prezzi ecc) drop

abbas'sar|e vt lower; turn down (radio, tv); **~e i fari** dip the headlights. **~si** vr stoop; (sole ecc:) sink; fig demean oneself

ab'basso adv below ● int down with

abba'stanza adv enough; (alquanto) quite

ab'batter|e vt demolish; shoot down (aereo); put down (animale); topple (regime); (fig: demoralizzare) dishearten. **~si** vr (cadere) fall; fig be discouraged

abbatti'mento m (morale) despondency

abbat'tuto adj despondent

abba'zia f abbey

abbel'lir|e vt embellish. **~si** vr adorn oneself

abbeve'ra|re vt water. **~'toio** m drinking trough

abbi'ente adj well-to-do

abbiglia'mento m clothes pl; (industria) clothing industry

abbigli'ar|e vt dress. **~si** vr dress up

abbina'mento m combining

abbi'nare vt combine; match (colori)

abbindo'lare vt cheat

abbocca'mento m interview; (conversazione) talk

abboc'care vi bite; (tubi:) join; fig swallow the bait

abboc'cato adj (vino) fairly sweet

abbof'farsi vr stuff oneself

abbona'mento m subscription; (ferroviario ecc) season-ticket; **fare l'~** take out a subscription

abbo'na|re vt make a subscriber. **~rsi** vr subscribe (a to); take out a season-ticket (a for) (teatro, stadio).

∼to, -a *mf* subscriber

abbon'dan|te *adj* abundant; (quantità) copious; (nevicata) heavy; (vestiario) roomy. ∼**te di** abounding in. ∼**te'mente** *adv* (mangiare) copiously. ∼**za** *f* abundance

abbon'dare *vi* abound

abbor'da|bile *adj* (persona) approachable; (prezzo) reasonable. ∼**ggio** *m* (Mil) boarding. ∼**re** *vt* board (nave); approach (persona); (🎯: attaccar bottone a) chat up; tackle (compito ecc)

abbotto'na|re *vt* button up. ∼**tura** *f* [row of] buttons. ∼**to** *adj fig* tight-lipped

abboz'zare *vt* sketch [out]; ∼ **un sorriso** give a hint of a smile. ab'**bozzo** *m* sketch

abbracci'are *vt* embrace; take up (professione); *fig* include. ab'**braccio** *m* hug

abbrevi'a|re *vt* shorten; (ridurre) curtail; abbreviate (parola). ∼**zi'one** *f* abbreviation

abbron'zante *m* sun-tan lotion

abbron'za|re *vt* bronze; tan (pelle). ∼**rsi** *vr* get a tan. ∼**to** *adj* tanned. ∼**tura** *f* [sun-]tan

abbrusto'lire *vt* toast; roast (caffè ecc)

abbruti'mento *m* brutalization. abbru'**tire** *vt* brutalize. **abbru'tirsi** *vr* become brutalized

abbuf'fa|rsi *vr* 🎯 stuff oneself. ∼**ta** *f* blowout

abbuo'nare *vt* reduce

abbu'ono *m* allowance; *Sport* handicap

abdi'ca|re *vi* abdicate. ∼**zi'one** *f* abdication

aber'rante *adj* aberrant

a'bete *m fir*

abi'etto *adj* despicable

'abi|le *adj* able; (idoneo) fit; (astuto) clever. ∼**ità** *f inv* ability; (idoneità) fitness; (astuzia) cleverness. ∼'**mente** *adv* ably; (con astuzia) cleverly

abili'ta|re *vt* qualify. ∼**to** *adj* qualified. ∼**zi'one** *f* qualification; (titolo) diploma

abis'sale *adj* abysmal. a'**bisso** *m* abyss

abi'tabile *adj* inhabitable

abi'tacolo *m* (Auto) passenger compartment

abi'tante *mf* inhabitant

abi'ta|re *vi* live. ∼**to** *adj* inhabited ● *m* built-up area. ∼**zi'one** *f* house

'abito *m* (da donna) dress; (da uomo) suit. ∼ **da cerimonia/da sera** formal/evening dress

abitu'al|e *adj* usual. ∼'**mente** *adv* usually

abitu'ar|e *vt* accustom. ∼**si a** *vr* get used to

abitudi'nario, -a *adj* of fixed habits ● *mf* person of fixed habits

abi'tudine *f* habit; d'∼ usually; **per** ∼ out of habit; **avere l'**∼ **di fare qcsa** be in the habit of doing sth

abnegazi'one *f* self-sacrifice

ab'norme *adj* abnormal

abo'li|re *vt* abolish; repeal (legge). ∼**zi'one** *f* abolition; repeal

abomi'nevole *adj* abominable

abor'rire *vt* abhor

abor'ti|re *vi* miscarry; (volontariamente) have an abortion; *fig* fail. ∼**vo** *adj* abortive. a'**borto** *m* miscarriage; (volontario) abortion. ∼**sta** *adj* pro-choice

abrasi'|one *f* abrasion. abra'**sivo** *adj* & *m* abrasive

abro'ga|re *vt* repeal. ∼**zi'one** *f* repeal

'abside *f* apse

abu'lia *f* apathy. a'**bulico** *adj* apathetic

abu's|are *vi* ∼ **di** abuse; overindulge in (alcol); (approfittare di) take advantage of; (*violentare*) rape. **∼ivo** *adj* illegal

a'buso *m* abuse. **∼** di confidenza breach of confidence

a.C. *abbr* (avanti Cristo) BC

'acca *f* Ⓘ non ho capito un'∼ I understood damn all

acca'demi|a *f* academy. A∼a di Belle Arti Academy of Fine Arts. **∼co, -a** *adj* academic **∘mf** academician

acca'd|ere *vi* happen; accada quel che accada come what may. **∼uto** *m* event

accalappi'are *vt* catch; *fig* allure

accal'carsi *vr* crowd

accal'da|rsi *vr* get overheated; *fig* get excited. **∼to** *adj* overheated

accalo'rarsi *vr* get excited

accampa'mento *m* camp. accam'pare *vt fig* put forth. **accam'parsi** *vr* camp

accani'mento *m* tenacity; (*odio*) rage

acca'ni|rsi *vr* persist; (*infierire*) rage. **∼to** *adj* persistent; (*odio*) fierce; *fig* inveterate

ac'canto *adv* near; **∼** a *prep* next to

accanto'nare *vt* set aside; (*Mil*) billet

accaparra'mento *m* hoarding; (*Comm*) cornering

accapar'ra|re *vt* hoard. **∼rsi** *vr* grab; corner (*mercato*). **∼tore, ∼trice** *mf* hoarder

accapigli'arsi *vr* scuffle; (*litigare*) squabble

accappa'toio *m* bathrobe; (*per spiaggia*) beachrobe

accappo'nare *vt* fare **∼** la pelle a qcno make sb's flesh creep

accarez'zare *vt* caress; *fig* cherish

accartocci'ar|e *vt* scrunch up. **∼si** *vr* curl up

acca'sarsi *vr* get married

accasci'arsi *vr* flop down; *fig*

lose heart

accata'stare *vt* pile up

accatti'vante *adj* beguiling

accatti'varsi *vr* **∼** le simpatie/la stima/l'affetto di qcno gain sb's sympathy/respect/affection

accatto'naggio *m* begging. accat'tone, -a *mf* beggar

accaval'lar|e *vt* cross (*gambe*). **∼si** *vr* pile up; *fig* overlap

acce'cante *adj* (*luce*) blinding

acce'care *vt* blind **∘vi** go blind

ac'cedere *vi* **∼** a enter; (*acconsentire*) comply with

accele'ra|re *vi* accelerate **∘vt** accelerate. **∼to** *adj* rapid. **∼tore** *m* accelerator. **∼zi'one** *f* acceleration

ac'cender|e *vt* light; turn on (*luce, TV ecc*); *fig* inflame; ha da ∼e? have you got a light? **∼si** *vr* catch fire; (*illuminarsi*) light up; (*TV ecc*:) turn on; *fig* become inflamed

accendi'gas *m inv* gas lighter; (*su cucina*) automatic ignition

accen'dino *m* lighter

accendi'sigari *m* cigar-lighter

accen'nare *vt* indicate; hum (*melodia*) **∘vi ∼** a beckon to; *fig* hint at; (*far l'atto di*) make as if to; accenna a piovere it looks like rain. ac'cenno *m* gesture; (*con il capo*) nod; *fig* hint

accensi'one *f* lighting; (*di motore*) ignition

accen'ta|re *vt* accent; (*con accento tonico*) stress. **∼zi'one** *f* accentuation. ac'cento *m* accent; (*tonico*) stress

accentra'mento *m* centralizing

accen'trare *vt* centralize

accentu'a|re *vt* accentuate. **∼rsi** *vr* become more noticeable. **∼to** *adj* marked

accerchia'mento *m* surrounding

accerchi'are *vt* surround

accerta'mento *m* check

accer'tare *vt* ascertain; (*controllare*) check; assess (*reddito*)

a ac'ceso adj lighted; (radio, TV ecc) on; (colore) bright

acces'sibile adj accessible; (persona) approachable; (spesa) reasonable

ac'cesso m access; (Med: di rabbia) fit; vietato l'∼ no entry

acces'sorio adj accessory; (secondario) of secondary importance ● m accessory; accessori pl (rifiniture) fittings

ac'cetta f hatchet

accet'tabile adj acceptable

accet'tare vt accept; (aderire a) agree to

accettazi'one f acceptance; (luogo) reception. ∼ [bagagli] check-in. [banco] ∼ check-in [desk]

ac'cetto adj agreeable; essere bene ∼ be very welcome

accezi'one f meaning

acchiap'pare vt catch

acchito m di primo ∼ at first

acciac'care vt crush; fig prostrate. ∼to, -a adj essere ∼to ache all over. acci'acco m infirmity; acciacchi pl aches and pains

acciaie'ria f steelworks

acci'aio m steel; ∼ inossidabile stainless steel

acciden'tale adj accidental. ∼l'mente adv accidentally. ∼to adj (terreno) uneven

acci'dente m accident; (Med) stroke; non capisce un ∼ ⚠ he doesn't understand a damn thing. acci'denti! int damn!

accigli'a|rsi vr frown. ∼to adj frowning

ac'cingersi vr ∼ a be about to

acci'picchia int good Lord!

acciuf'fare vt catch

acci'uga f anchovy

accla'ma|re vt applaud; (eleggere) acclaim. ∼zi'one f applause

acclima'ta|re vt acclimatize. ∼si vr get acclimatized

ac'clu|dere vt enclose. ∼so adj enclosed

accoc'co'larsi vr squat

accogli'en|te adj welcoming; (confortevole) cosy. ∼za f welcome

ac'cogliere vt receive; (con piacere) welcome; (contenere) hold

accol'larsi vr take on (responsabilità, debiti, doveri). accol'lato adj high-necked

accoltel'lare vt knife

accomia'tar|e vt dismiss. ∼si vr take one's leave (da of)

accomo'dante adj accommodating

accomo'dar|e vt (riparare) mend; (disporre) arrange. ∼si vr make oneself at home; si accomodi! come in!; (si sieda) take a seat!

accompagna'mento m accompaniment; (seguito) retinue

accompa'gna|re vt accompany; ∼re qcno a casa see sb home; ∼re qcno alla porta show sb out. ∼tore, ∼trice mf companion; (di comitiva) escort; (Mus) accompanist

accomu'nare vt pool

acconci'a|re vt arrange. ∼tura f hair-style; (ornamento) head-dress

accondiscen'den|te adj too obliging. ∼za f excessive desire to please

accondi'scendere vi ∼ a condescend; comply with (desiderio); (acconsentire) consent to

acconsen'tire vi consent

acconten'tar|e vt satisfy. ∼si vr be content (di with)

ac'conto m deposit; in ∼ on account; lasciare un ∼ leave a deposit

accop'pare vt ⚠ bump off

accoppia'mento m coupling; (di animali) mating

accoppi'a|re vt couple; mate (animali). ∼rsi vr pair off; mate. ∼ta f (scommessa) bet on two horses for first *and second place*

acco'rato *adj* sorrowful

accorci'ar|e *vt* shorten. **~si** *vr* get shorter

accor'dar|e *vt* concede; match (colori ecc); (*Mus*) tune. **~si** *vr* agree

ac'cordo *m* agreement; (*Mus*) chord; (armonia) harmony; **andare d'~** get on well; **d'~!** agreed!; **essere d'~** agree; **prendere accordi con qcno** make arrangements with sb

ac'corgersi *vr* **~ di** notice; (capire) realize

accorgi'mento *m* shrewdness; (espediente) device

ac'correre *vi* hasten

accor'tezza *f* (previdenza) forethought

ac'corto *adj* shrewd; **mal ~** incautious

accosta'mento *m* combination

acco'star|e *vt* draw close to; approach (persona); set ajar (porta ecc). **~si** *vr* **~si a** come near to

accovacci'a|rsi *vr* crouch

accoz'zaglia *f* jumble; (di persone) mob

accoz'zare *vt* **~ colori** mix colours that clash

accredita'mento *m* credit; **~ tramite bancogiro** Bank Giro Credit

accredi'tare *vt* confirm (notizia); (*Comm*) credit

ac'cresc|ere *vt* increase. **~ersi** *vr* gtow larger. **~i'tivo** *adj* augmentative

accucci'arsi *vr* (cane:) lie down; (persona:) crouch

accu'dire *vi* **~ a** attend to

accumu'la|re *vt* accumulate. **~rsi** *vr* accumulate. **~tore** *m* accumulator; (*Auto*) battery. **~zi'one** *f* accumulation.

accura'tezza *f* care

accu'rato *adj* careful

ac'cusa *f* accusation; (*Jur*) charge; **essere in stato di ~** have been charged; **la Pubblica A~** the public prosecutor

accu'sa|re *vt* accuse; (*Jur*) charge; complain of (dolore); **~re ricevuta di** acknowledge receipt of. **~to, -a** *mf* accused. **~'tore** *m* prosecutor

a'cerbo *adj* sharp; (non maturo) unripe

'acero *m* maple

a'cerrimo *adj* implacable

a'ceto *m* vinegar

ace'tone *m* nail-polish remover

A.C.I. *abbr* (Automobile Club d'Italia) Italian Automobile Association

acidità *f* acidity. **~ di stomaco** acid stomach

'acido *adj* acid; (persona) sour ● *m* acid

a'cidulo *adj* slightly sour

'acino *m* berry; (chicco) grape

'acne *f* acne

'acqua *f* water; **fare ~** leak; **~ in bocca!** fig mum's the word!; **~ corrente** running water. **~ dolce** fresh water. **~ minerale** mineral water. **~ minerale gassata** fizzy mineral water. **~ naturale** still mineral water. **~ potabile** drinking water. **~ salata** salt water. **~ tonica** tonic water

acqua'forte *f* etching

ac'quaio *m* sink

acquama'rina *adj* aquamarine

acqua'rello *m* = **ACQUERELLO**

ac'quario *m* aquarium; (*Astr*) Aquarius

acqua'santa *f* holy water

acqua'scooter *m inv* water-scooter

ac'quatico *adj* aquatic

acquat'tarsi *vr* crouch

acqua'vite *f* brandy

acquaz'zone *m* downpour

acque'dotto *m* aqueduct

'acqueo *adj* **vapore ~**

water vapour

acque'rello m water-colour

acqui'rente mf purchaser

acqui'si|re vt acquire. ∼to adj acquired. ac'quisto m purchase

acquis't|are vt purchase; (ottenere) acquire. ac'quisto m purchase; uscire per ∼i go shopping; fare ∼i shop

acqui'trino m marsh

acquo'lina f far venire l'∼ in bocca a qcno make sb's mouth water

ac'quoso adj watery

'acre adj acrid; (al gusto) sour; fig harsh

a'crilico m acrylic

a'croba|ta mf acrobat. ∼'zia f acrobatics pl

a'cronimo m acronym

acu'ir|e vt sharpen. ∼si vr become more intense

a'culeo m sting; (Bot) prickle

acumi'nato adj pointed

a'custic|a f acoustics pl. ∼o adj acoustic

acu'tezza f acuteness

acutiz'zarsi vr become worse

a'cuto adj sharp; (suono) shrill; (freddo, odore) intense; (Gram, Math, Med) acute ●m (Mus) high note

ad prep = A (davanti a vocale)

adagi'ar|e vt lay down. ∼si vr lie down

a'dagio adv slowly ●m (Mus) adagio; (proverbio) adage

adattabilità f adaptability

adatta'mento m adaptation; avere spirito di ∼ be adaptable

adat'ta|re vt adapt; (aggiustare) fit. ∼rsi vr adapt. ∼'tore m adaptor. a'datto adj suitable (a for); (giusto) right

addebita'mento m debit. ∼ diretto direct debit

addebi'tare vt debit; ascribe (colpa)

ad'debito m charge

addensa'mento m thickening; (di persone) gathering

adden'sar|e vt thicken. ∼si vr thicken; (affollarsi) gather

adden'tare vt bite

adden'trarsi vr penetrate

ad'dentro adv deeply; essere ∼ be in on

addestra'mento m training

adde'str|are vt train. ∼si vr train

ad'detto, -a adj assigned ●mf employee; (diplomatico) attaché. ∼ stampa press officer

addiaccio m dormire all'∼ sleep in the open

addi'etro adv (indietro) back; (nel passato) before

ad'dio m & int goodbye. ∼ al celibato stag party

addirit'tura adv (perfino) even; (assolutamente) absolutely; ∼! really!

ad'dirsi vr ∼ a suit

addi'tare vt point at; (in mezzo a un gruppo) point out; fig point to

addi'tivo adj & m additive

addizio'nal|e adj additional. ∼'mente adv additionally

addizio'nare vt add [up]. addizi'one f addition

addob'bare vt decorate. ad'dobbo m decoration

addol'cir|e vt sweeten; tone down (colore); fig soften. ∼si vr fig mellow

addolo'rar|e vt grieve. ∼rsi vr be upset (per by). ∼to adj distressed

ad'dom|e m abdomen. ∼'inale adj abdominal; [muscoli] addominali pl abdominals

addomesti'ca|re vt tame. ∼'tore m tamer

addormen'ta|re vt put to sleep. ∼rsi vr go to sleep. ∼to adj asleep; fig slow

addos'sar|e vt ~e a (appoggiare) lean against; (attribuire) lay on. ~**si** vr (ammassarsi) crowd; shoulder (responsabilità ecc)

ad'dosso adv on; ~ a prep on; (molto vicino) right next to; mettere gli occhi ~ a qcno/qcsa hanker after sb/sth; non mettermi le mani ~! keep your hands off me!; stare ~ a qcno fig be on sb's back

ad'durre vt produce (prova, documento); give (pretesto, esempio)

adegua'mento m adjustment

adegu'a|re vt adjust. ~**rsi** vr conform. ~**to** adj adequate; (conforme) consistent

a'dempi|ere vt fulfil. ~'**mento** m fulfilment

ade'noidi fpl adenoids

ade'ren|te adj adhesive; (vestito) tight ● mf follower. ~**za** f adhesion. ~**ze** pl connections

ade'rire vi ~ a adhere to; support (petizione); agree to (richiesta)

adesca'mento m (Jur) soliciting

ade'scare vt bait; fig entice

adesi'one f adhesion; fig agreement

ade'sivo adj adhesive ● m sticker; (Auto) bumper sticker

a'desso adv now; (poco fa) just now; (tra poco) any moment now; da ~ in poi from now on; per ~ for the moment

adia'cente adj adjacent; ~ a next to

adi'bire vt ~ a put to use as

'adipe m adipose tissue

adi'ra|rsi vr get irate. ~**to** adj irate

a'dire vt resort to; ~ le vie legali take legal proceedings

'adito m dare ~ a give rise to

adocchi'are vt eye; (con desiderio) covet

adole'scen|te adj & mf adolescent. ~**za** f adolescence. ~**zi'ale** adj

adolescent

adom'brar|e vt darken; fig veil. ~**si** vr (offendersi) take offence

adope'rar|e vt use. ~**si** vr take trouble

ado'rabile adj adorable

ado'ra|re vt adore. ~**zi'one** f adoration

ador'nare vt adorn

adot'ta|re vt adopt. ~**ivo** adj adoptive. adozi'one f adoption

adrena'lina f adrenalin

adri'atico adj Adriatic ● m l'A~ the Adriatic

adu'la|re vt flatter. ~'**tore**, ~'**trice** mf flatterer. ~**zi'one** f flattery

adulte'ra|re vt adulterate. ~**to** adj adulterated

adul'terio m adultery. a'dultero, -a adj adulterous ● m adulterer ● f adulteress

a'dulto, -a adj & mf adult; (maturo) mature

adu'nanza f assembly

adu'na|re vt gather. ~**ta** f (Mil) parade

a'dunco adj hooked

ae'rare vt air (stanza)

a'ereo adj aerial; (dell'aviazione) air attrib ● m aeroplane, plane

ae'robic|a f aerobics. ~**o** adj aerobic

aerodi'namic|a f aerodynamics sg. ~**o** adj aerodynamic

aero'nautic|a f aeronautics sg; (Mil) Air Force. ~**o** adj aeronautical

aero'plano m aeroplane

aero'porto m airport

aero'scalo m cargo and servicing area

aero'sol m inv aerosol

'afa f sultriness

af'fabil|e adj affable. ~**ità** f affability

affaccen'da|rsi vr busy oneself (a

with). ~to adj busy

affacci'arsi vr show oneself; ~ alla finestra appear at the window

affa'ma|re vt starve [out]. ~to adj starving

affan'na|re vt leave breathless. ~rsi vr busy oneself; (agitarsi) get worked up. ~to adj breathless; dal respiro ~to wheezy. af'fanno m breathlessness; fig worry

af'fare m matter; (Comm) deal; (occasione) bargain; affari pl business; non sono affari tuoi it's none of your business. affa'rista mf wheeler-dealer

affasci'nante adj fascinating; (persona, sorriso) bewitching

affasci'nare vt bewitch; fig charm

affatica'mento m fatigue

affati'ca|re vt tire; (sfinire) exhaust. ~si vr tire oneself out; (affannarsi) strive

af'fatto adv completely; non... ~ not... at all; niente ~! not at all!

affer'ma|re vt affirm; (sostenere) assert. ~rsi vr establish oneself

affermativa'mente adv in the affirmative

afferma'tivo adj affirmative

affermazi'one f assertion; (successo) achievement

affer'rar|e vt seize; catch (oggetto); (capire) grasp; ~e al volo fig be quick on the uptake. ~si vr ~si a grasp at

affet'ta|re vt slice; (ostentare) affect. ~to adj sliced; (maniere) affected ●m cold meat.

affet'tivo adj affective; rapporto ~ emotional tie

af'fetto[1] m affection

af'fetto[2] adj ~ da suffering from

affettuosità f inv (gesto) affectionate gesture

affettu'oso adj affectionate

affezio'na|rsi vr ~rsi a grow fond of. ~to adj devoted (a to)

affian'car|e vt put side by side; (Mil) flank; fig support. ~si vr come side by side; fig stand together; ~si a qcno fig help sb out

affia'ta'mento m harmony

affia'ta|rsi vr get on well together. ~to adj close-knit; una coppia ~ta a very close couple

affibbi'are vt ~ qcsa a qcno saddle sb with sth; ~ un pugno a qcno let fly at sb

affi'dabil|e adj dependable. ~ità f dependability

affida'mento m (Jur: dei minori) custody; fare ~ su qcno rely on sb; non dare ~ not inspire confidence

affi'dar|e vt entrust. ~si vr ~si a rely on

affievo'lirsi vr grow weak

af'figgere vt affix

affi'lare vt sharpen

affili'ar|e vt affiliate. ~si vr become affiliated

affi'nare vt sharpen; (perfezionare) refine

affinché conj so that, in order that

af'fin|e adj similar. ~ità f affinity

affiora'mento m emergence; (Naut) surfacing

affio'rare vi emerge; fig come to light

af'fisso m bill; (Gram) affix

affitta'camere m inv landlord ●f inv landlady

affit'tare vt rent; 'af'fittasi' 'for rent'

af'fitt|o m rent; contratto d'~o lease; dare in ~o let; prendere in ~o rent. ~u'ario, ~a mf (Jur) lessee

af'fligger|e vt torment. ~si vr distress oneself

af'fli|tto adj distressed. ~zi'one f distress; fig affliction

afflosci'arsi vr become floppy; (accasciarsi) flop down; (morale:) decline

afflu'en|te adj & m tributary. ~za f

flow; (*di gente*) crowd

afflu'ire *vi* flow; *fig* pour in

af'flusso *m* influx

affo'gare *vt/i* drown; (*Culin*) poach; ~**re in** *fig* be swamped with. ~**to** *adj* (*persona*) drowned; (*uova*) poached. ~**to al caffè** *m* ice cream with hot espresso poured over it

affol'lare *vt*, ~**rsi** *vr* crowd. ~**to** *adj* crowded

affonda'mento *m* sinking

affon'dare *vt/i* sink

affossa'mento *m* pothole

affran'care *vt* redeem (bene); stamp (lettera); free (schiavo). ~**rsi** *vr* free oneself. ~**trice** *f* franking machine. ~**tura** *f* stamping; (*di spedizione*) postage

af'franto *adj* prostrated; (*esausto*) worn out

af'fresco *m* fresco

affret'tare *vt* speed up. ~**rsi** *vr* hurry. ~**ta'mente** *adv* hastily. ~**to** *adj* hasty

affron'tare *vt* face; confront (nemico); meet (spese). ~**si** *vr* clash

af'fronto *m* affront, insult; **fare un ~ a qcno** insult sb

affumi'care *vt* fill with smoke; (*Culin*) smoke. ~**to** *adj* (*prosciutto, formaggio*) smoked

affuso'lare *vt* taper [off]. ~**to** *adj* tapering

afo'risma *m* aphorism

a'foso *adj* sultry

'Africa *f* Africa. **afri'cano, -a** *agg & mf* African

afrodi'siaco *adj & m* aphrodisiac

a'genda *f* diary

agen'dina *f* pocket-diary

a'gente *m* agent; **agenti** *pl* **atmosferici** atmospheric agents. ~ **di cambio** stockbroker. ~ **di polizia** police officer

agen'zia *f* agency; (*filiale*) branch office; (*di banca*) branch. ~ **di viaggi**

travel agency. ~ **immobiliare** estate agency

agevo'lare *vt* facilitate. ~**zi'one** *f* facilitation

a'gevole *adj* easy; (*strada*) smooth. ~**'mente** *adv* easily

agganci'are *vt* hook up; (*Rail*) couple. ~**si** *vr* (*vestito:*) hook up

ag'geggio *m* gadget

agget'tivo *m* adjective

agghiacci'ante *adj* terrifying

agghiacci'are *vt* *fig* ~ **qcno** make sb's blood run cold. ~**si** *vr* freeze

agghin'dare *vt* ① dress up. ~**rsi** *vr* ① doll oneself up. ~**to** *adj* dressed up

aggiorna'mento *m* up-date

aggior'nare *vt* (*rinviare*) postpone; (*mettere a giorno*) bring up to date. ~**rsi** *vr* get up to date. ~**to** *adj* up-to-date; (*versione*) updated

aggi'rare *vt* surround; (*fig: ingannare*) trick. ~**si** *vr* hang about; ~**si su** (*discorso ecc:*) be about; (*somma:*) be around

aggiudi'care *vt* award; (*all'asta*) knock down. ~**si** *vr* win

aggi'ungere *vt* add. ~**ta** *f* addition. ~**tivo** *m* supplementary. ~**to** *adj* added ● *adj & m* (*assistente*) assistant

aggiu'stare *vt* mend; (*sistemare*) settle; (①: *mettere a posto*) fix. ~**si** *vr* adapt; (*mettersi in ordine*) tidy oneself up; (*decidere*) sort things out; (*tempo:*) clear up

agglomera'mento *m* conglomeration

agglome'rato *m* built-up area

aggrap'parle *vt* grasp. ~**si** *vr* ~**si a** cling to

aggra'vante (*Jur*) *f* aggravation ● *adj* aggravating

aggra'varle *vt* (*peggiorare*) make worse; increase (pena); (*appesantire*)

weigh down. ~**si** vr worsen

aggrazi'ato adj graceful

aggre'dire vt attack

aggre'gare vt add; (associare a un gruppo ecc) admit. ~**rsi** vr ~**rsi a** join. ~**to a** associated ● m aggregate; (di case) block

aggressi'one f aggression; (atto) attack

aggres's|ivo adj aggressive. ~**ività** f aggressiveness. ~**ore** m aggressor

aggrin'zare, aggrin'zire vt wrinkle

aggrot'tare vt ~ **le ciglia/la fronte** frown

aggrovigli'a|re vt tangle. ~**rsi** vr get entangled; fig get complicated. ~**to** adj entangled; fig confused

agguan'tare vt catch

aggu'ato m ambush; (tranello) trap; **stare in** ~ lie in wait

agguer'rito adj fierce

agia'tezza f comfort

agi'ato adj (persona) well off; (vita) comfortable

a'gibil|e adj (palazzo) fit for human habitation. ~**ità** f fitness for human habitation

'agil|e adj agile. ~**ità** f agility

'agio m ease; **mettersi a proprio** ~ make oneself at home

a'gire vi act; (comportarsi) behave; (funzionare) work; ~ **su** affect

agi'tare vt shake; wave (mano); (fig: turbare) trouble. ~**rsi** vr toss about; (essere inquieto) be restless; (mare:) get rough. ~**tore**, ~**trice** mf (persona) agitator. ~**zi'one** f agitation; **mettere in** ~**zione** qcno make sb worried

'agli = A + GLI

'aglio m garlic

a'gnello m lamb

agno'lotti mpl ravioli sg

a'gnostico, -a adj & mf agnostic

'ago m needle

ago'ni|a f agony. ~**zzare** vi be on one's deathbed

ago'nistic|a f competition. ~**o** adj competitive

agopun'tura f acupuncture

a'gosto m August

a'grari|a f agriculture. ~**o** adj agricultural ● m landowner

a'gricol|o adj agricultural. ~**tore** m farmer. ~**tura** f agriculture

agri'foglio m holly

agritu'rismo m farm holidays, agro-tourism

> **Agriturismo** In the 1980s many farmers began to supplement their falling incomes by offering tourists an authentic experience of the Italian countryside. Agriturismo is now a very popular form of tourism in Italy. Guests can learn traditional skills and crafts, such as cooking and wine-making, all of which helps to preserve a threatened way of life.

'agro adj sour

agroalimen'tare adj food attrib

agro'dolce adj bitter-sweet; (Culin) sweet-and-sour; **in** ~ sweet and sour

agrono'mia f agronomy

a'grume m citrus fruit; (pianta) citrus tree

aguz'zare vt sharpen; ~ **le orecchie** prick up one's ears; ~ **la vista** look hard

aguz'zino m slave-driver; (carceriere) jailer

ahimè int alas

'ai = A + I

'aia f threshing-floor

'Aia f L'~ The Hague

Aids *mf* Aids

ai'rone *m* heron

ai'tante *adj* sturdy

aiu'ola *f* flower-bed

aiu'tante *mf* assistant ●*m* (Mil) adjutant. ~ **di campo** aide-decamp

aiu'tare *vt* help

ai'uto *m* help, aid; (*assistente*) assistant

aiz'zare *vt* incite; ~ **contro** set on

al = A+IL

'ala *f* wing; **fare** ~ make way

ala'bastro *m* alabaster

a'lacre *adj* brisk

a'lano *m* Great Dane

'alba *f* dawn

Alba'n|ia *f* Albania. a~**ese** *adj & mf* Albanian

albeggi'are *vi* dawn

albe'ra|to *adj* wooded; (*viale*) treelined. ~'**tura** *f* (*Naut*) masts *pl.* albe'**rello** *m* sapling

al'berg|o *m* hotel. ~**o diurno** *hotel where rooms are rented during the daytime.* ~**a'tore**, ~**a'trice** *mf* hotel-keeper. ~**hi'ero** *adj* hotel *attrib*

'albero *m* tree; (*Naut*) mast; (*Mech*) shaft. ~ **genealogico** family tree. ~ **maestro** (*Naut*) mainmast. ~ **di Na-tale** Christmas tree

albi'cocc|a *f* apricot. ~**o** *m* apricot-tree

al'bino, **-a** *mf* albino

'albo *m* register; (*libro ecc*) album; (*per avvisi*) notice board

'album *m* album. ~ **da disegno** sketch-book

al'bume *m* albumen

'alce *m* elk

'alcol *m* alcohol; (*Med*) spirit; (*liquori forti*) spirits *pl*; **darsi all'**~ take to drink. **al'colici** *mpl* alcoholic drinks. **al'colico** *adj* alcoholic. **alco'lismo** *m* alcoholism. ~**iz'zato**, **-a** *adj & mf* alcoholic

alco'test® *m inv* Breathalyser®

al'cova *f* alcove

al'cun, **al'cuno** *adj & pron* any; **non ha** ~ **amico** he hasn't any/no friends. **alcuni** *pl* some, a few; ~**i suoi amici** some of his friends

alea'torio *adj* unpredictable

a'letta *f* (*Mech*) fin

alfa'betico *adj* alphabetical

alfabetizzazi'one *f* ~ **della popolazione** teaching people to read and write

alfa'beto *m* alphabet

alfi'ere *m* (*negli scacchi*) bishop

al'fine *adv* eventually, in the end

'alga *f* seaweed

'algebra *f* algebra

Alge'ri|a *f* Algeria. a~**no**, **-a** *agg & mf* Algerian

ali'ante *m* glider

'alibi *m inv* alibi

alie'na|re *vt* alienate. ~**rsi** *vr* become estranged; ~**rsi le simpatie di qcno** lose sb's good will. ~**to**, **-a** *adj* alienated ●*mf* lunatic

a'lieno, **-a** *mf* alien ●*adj* **è** ~ **da in-vidia** envy is foreign to him

alimen'ta|re *vt* feed; *fig* foment ●*adj* food *attrib*; (*abitudine*) dietary ●*m* ~**ri** *pl* food-stuffs. ~'**tore** *m* power unit. ~**zi'one** *f* feeding

---

Alimentari *Alimentari* are food shops offering a range of products, from groceries, fruit, and vegetables to prepared foods like cheeses, cured hams, and salamis. Some even bake their own bread. An *alimentari* will also usually prepare *panini* (filled rolls) using their own ingredients. Small villages which have no other shops usually have an *alimentari*.

---

ali'mento *m* food; **alimenti** *pl* food; (*Jur*) alimony

a'liquota *f* share; (*di imposta*) rate

a

ali'scafo m hydrofoil

'alito m breath

'alla = A + LA

allaccia'mento m connection

allacci'ar|e vt fasten (cintura); lace up (scarpe); do up (vestito); (collegare) connect; form (amicizia). ~**si** vr do up, fasten

allaga'mento m flooding

alla'gar|e vt flood. ~**si** vr become flooded

allampa'nato adj lanky

allarga'mento m widening

allar'gar|e vt widen; open (braccia, gambe); let out (vestito ecc); fig extend. ~**si** vr widen

allar'mante adj alarming

allar'ma|re vt alarm. ~**to** adj panicky

al'larme m alarm; dare l'~ raise the alarm; falso ~ fig false alarm. ~ aereo air raid warning

allar'mis|mo m alarmism. ~**ta** mf alarmist

allatta'mento m (di animale) suckling; (di neonato) feeding

allat'tare vt suckle (animale); feed (neonato)

'alle = A + LE

alle'a|nza f alliance. ~**to**, **-a** adj allied ● mf ally

alle'ar|e vt unite. ~**si** vr form an alliance

alle'ga|re¹ vt (Jur) allege

alle'ga|re² vt (accludere) enclose; set on edge (denti). ~**to** adj enclosed ● m enclosure; (Comput) attachment; in ~**to** attached. ~**zi'one** f (Jur) allegation

allegge'rir|e vt lighten; fig alleviate. ~**si** vr become lighter; (vestirsi leggero) put on lighter clothes

allego'ria f allegory. **alle'gorico** adj allegorical

allegra'mente adv breezily

alle'gria f gaiety

al'legro adj cheerful; (colore) bright; (brillo) tipsy ● m (Mus) allegro

alle'luia int hallelujah!

allena'mento m training

alle'na|re vt, ~**rsi** vr train. ~**tore**, ~**'trice** mf trainer, coach

allen'tar|e vt loosen; fig relax. ~**si** vr become loose; (Mech) work loose

aller'gia f allergy. **al'lergico** adj allergic

all'erta f stare ~ be alert

allesti'mento m preparation. ~ scenico (Theat) set

alle'stire vt prepare; stage (spettacolo); (Naut) fit out

allet'tante adj alluring

allet'tare vt entice

alleva'mento m breeding; (processo) bringing up; (luogo) farm; (per piante) nursery; **pollo di** ~ battery chicken

alle'vare vt bring up (bambini); breed (animali); grow (piante)

allevi'are vt alleviate; fig lighten

alli'bito adj astounded

allibra'tore m bookmaker

allie'tar|e vt gladden. ~**si** vr rejoice

alli'evo, -a mf pupil ● m (Mil) cadet

alliga'tore m alligator

allinea'mento m alignment

alline'ar|e vt line up; (Typ) align; Fin adjust. ~**si** vr fall into line

'allo = A + LO

al'locco m Zool tawny owl

al'lodola f [sky]lark

alloggi'are vt put up; (casa:) provide accommodation for; (Mil) billet ● vi stay; (Mil) be billeted. **al'loggio** m apartment; (Mil) billet

allonta'namento m removal

allonta'nar|e vt move away; (licenziare) dismiss; avert (pericolo). ~**si** vr go away

al'lora adv then; (a quel tempo) at that time; (in tal caso) in that case;

d'∼ in poi from then on; e ∼? what now?; (e con ciò?) so what?; fino ∼ until then

al'loro m laurel; (Culin) bay

'alluce m big toe

alluci'na|nte adj ① incredible; sostanza ∼nte hallucinogen. ∼to, -a m/f ① space cadet. ∼zi'one f hallucination

allucino'geno adj (sostanza) hallucinatory

al'ludere vi ∼ a allude to

allu'minio m aluminium

allun'gar|e vt lengthen; stretch [out] (gamba); extend (tavolo); (diluire) dilute; ∼e il collo crane one's neck. ∼e le mani su qcno touch sb up. ∼e il passo quicken one's step. ∼si vr grow longer; (crescere) grow taller; (sdraiarsi) lie down

allusi'one f allusion

allu'sivo adj allusive

alluvio'nale adj alluvial

alluvi'one f flood

al'meno adv at least; [se] ∼ venisse il sole! if only the sun would come out!

a'logeno m halogen ● adj lampada alogena halogen lamp

a'lone m halo

'Alpi fpl le ∼ the Alps

alpi'nis|mo m mountaineering. ∼ta mf mountaineer

al'pino adj Alpine ● m (Mil) gli alpini the Alpine troops

al'quanto adj a certain amount of ● adv rather

alt int stop

alta'lena f swing; (tavola in bilico) see-saw

altale'nare vi fig vacillate

alta'mente adv highly

al'tare m altar

alta'rino m scoprire gli altarini di qcno reveal sb's guilty secrets

alte'ra|re vt alter; adulterate (vino);

(falsificare) falsify. ∼rsi vr be altered; (cibo): go bad; (merci:) deteriorate; (arrabbiarsi) get angry. ∼to adj (vino) adulterated. ∼zi'one f alteration; (di vino) adulteration

al'terco m altercation

alter'nanza f alternation

alter'na|re vt, ∼rsi vr alternate. ∼tiva f alternative. ∼tivo adj alternate. ∼to adj alternating. ∼tore m (Electr) alternator

al'tern|o adj alternate; a giorni ∼i every other day

al'tero adj haughty

al'tezza f height; (profondità) depth; (suono) pitch; (di tessuto) width; (titolo) Highness; essere all'∼ di be on a level with; fig be up to

altezzosa|'mente adv haughtily. ∼ità f haughtiness

altez'zoso adj haughty

al'ticcio adj tipsy, merry

altipi'ano m plateau

alti'tudine f altitude

'alto adj high; (di statura) tall; (profondo) deep; (suono) high-pitched; (tessuto) northern; a notte alta in the middle of the night; avere degli alti e bassi have some ups and downs; ad alta fedeltà high-fidelity; a voce alta, ad alta voce in a loud voice; (leggere) aloud; essere in ∼ mare be on the high seas. alta finanza f high finance. alta moda f high fashion. alta tensione f high voltage ● adv high; in ∼ at the top; (guardare:) up; mani in ∼! hands up!

alto'forno m blast-furnace

altolà int halt there!

altolo'cato adj highly placed

altopar'lante m loudspeaker

altopi'ano m plateau

altret'tanto adj & pron as much; (pl) as many ● adv likewise; buona fortuna! – grazie, ∼ good luck! – thank you, the same to you

a

altri'menti *adv* otherwise

'altro *adj* other; un ~, un'altra another; l'altr'anno last year; domani l'~ the day after tomorrow; l'ho visto l'~ giorno I saw him the other day ●*pron* other [one]; un ~, un'altra another [one]; ne vuoi dell'~? would you like some more?; l'un l'~ one another; nessun ~ nobody else; gli altri (*la gente*) other people ●*m* something else; non fa ~ che lavorare he does nothing but work; desidera ~? (*in negozio*) anything else?; più che ~, sono stanco I'm tired more than anything; se non ~ at least; senz'~ certainly; tra l'~ what's more; ~ che! and how!

altroi'eri *m* l'~ the day before yesterday

al'tronde *adv* d'~ on the other hand

al'trove *adv* elsewhere

al'trui *adj* other people's ●*m* other people's belongings *pl*

al'tura *f* high ground; (*Naut*) deep sea

a'lunno, -a *mf* pupil

alve'are *m* hive

al'za|re *vt* lift; (*costruire*) build; (*Naut*) hoist; ~re le spalle shrug one's shoulders. ~rsi *vr* rise; (*in piedi*) stand up; (*da letto*) get up; ~rsi in piedi get to one's feet. ~ta *f* lifting; (*aumento*) rise; (*da letto*) getting up; (*Archit*) elevation. ~to *adj* up

a'mabile *adj* lovable; (*vino*) sweet

a'maca *f* hammock

amalga'mar|e *vt*, ~si *vr* amalgamate

a'mante *adj* ~ di fond of ●*m* lover ●*f* mistress, lover

a'ma|re *vt* love; like (*musica, ecc*). ~to, -a *adj* loved ●*mf* beloved

ama'rena *f* sour black cherry

ama'retto *m* macaroon

ama'rezza *f* bitterness; (*dolore*) sorrow

a'maro *adj* bitter ●*m* bitterness; (*liquore*) bitters *pl*

ama'rognolo *adj* rather bitter

ama'tore, -'trice *mf* lover

ambasci'a|ta *f* embassy; (*messaggio*) message. ~'tore, ~'trice *m* ambassador ●*f* ambassadress

ambe'due *adj* & *pron* both

ambien'ta|le *adj* environmental. ~'lista *adj* & *mf* environmentalist

ambien'tar|e *vt* acclimatize; set (*personaggio, film ecc*). ~si *vr* get acclimatized

ambi'ente *m* environment; (*stanza*) room; *fig* milieu

ambigu'ità *f inv* ambiguity; (*di persona*) shadiness

am'biguo *adj* ambiguous; (*persona*) shady

am'bire *vi* ~ a aspire to

'ambito *m* sphere

ambiva'len|te *adj* ambivalent. ~za *f* ambivalence

ambizi'o|ne *f* ambition. ~so *adj* ambitious

ambu'lante *adj* wandering; vendi- tore ~ hawker

ambu'lanza *f* ambulance

ambula'torio *m* (*di medico*) surgery; (*di ospedale*) out-patients'

a'meba *f* amoeba

a'meno *adj* pleasant

A'merica *f* America. ~ del Sud South America. ameri'cano, -a *agg* & *mf* American

ami'anto *m* asbestos

ami'chevole *adj* friendly

ami'cizia *f* friendship; fare ~ con qcno make friends with sb; amicizie *pl* (*amici*) friends

a'mico, -a *mf* friend; ~ del cuore bosom friend

'amido *m* starch

ammac'ca|re *vt* dent; bruise

(frutto). **~rsi** vr (metallo:) get dented; (frutto:) bruise. **~to** adj dented; (frutto) bruised. **~'tura** f dent; (livido) bruise

ammae'stra|re vt (istruire) teach; train (animale). **~to** adj trained

ammai'nare vt lower (bandiera); furl (vele)

amma'la|rsi vr fall ill. **~to**, **-a** adj ill ● mf sick person; (paziente) patient

ammali'are vt bewitch

am'manco m deficit

ammanet'tare vt handcuff

ammani'cato adj essere ~ have connections

amma'raggio m splashdown

amma'rare vi put down on the sea; (nave spaziale:) splash down

ammas'sar|e vt amass. **~si** vr crowd together. **am'masso** m mass; (mucchio) pile

ammat'tire vi go mad

ammaz'zar|e vt kill. **~si** vr (suicidarsi) kill oneself; (rimanere ucciso) be killed

am'menda f amends pl; (multa) fine; fare **~ di** qcsa make amends for sth

am'messo pp di ammettere ● conj **~ che** supposing that

am'mettere vt admit; (riconoscere) acknowledge; (supporre) suppose

ammic'care vi wink

ammini'stra|re vt administer; (gestire) run. **~'tivo** adj administrative. **~'tore**, **~'trice** mf administrator; (di azienda) manager; (di società) director. **~'tore delegato** managing director. **~zi'one** f administration; fatti di ordinaria **~zione** fig routine matters

ammi'ragli|o m admiral. **~'ato** m admiralty

ammi'ra|re vt admire. **~to** adj restare/essere **~to** be full of admiration. **~'tore**, **~'trice** mf admirer. **~zi'one** f admiration. **ammi'revole**

adj admirable

ammis'sibile adj admissible

ammissi'one f admission; (approvazione) acknowledgement

ammobili'a|re vt furnish. **~to** adj furnished

am'modo adj proper ● adv properly

am'mollo m in ~ soaking

ammo'niaca f ammonia

ammoni'mento m warning; (di rimprovero) admonishment

ammo'ni|re vt warn; (rimproverare) admonish. **~'tore** adj admonishing. **~zi'one** f Sport warning

ammon'tare vi ~ a amount to ● m amount

ammonticchi'are vt heap up

ammorbi'dente m (per panni) softener

ammorbi'dir|e vt, **~si** vr soften

ammorta'mento m (Comm) amortization

ammor'tare vt pay off (spesa); (Comm) amortize (debito)

ammortiz'za|re vt (Comm) = AM-MORTARE; (Mech) damp. **~'tore** m shock-absorber

ammosci'ar|e vt make flabby. **~si** vi get flabby

ammucchi'a|re vt, **~rsi** vr pile up. **~ta** f ⊞: orgia) orgy

ammuf'fi|re vi go mouldy. **~to** adj mouldy

ammutina'mento m mutiny

ammuti'narsi vr mutiny

ammuto'lire vi be struck dumb

amni'stia f amnesty

'amo m hook; fig bait

a'more m love; fare l'~ make love; per l'amor di Dio/del cielo! for heaven's sake!; andare d'~ e d'accordo get on like a house on fire; amor proprio self-respect; è un ~ (persona) he/she is a darling; per ~ di for the sake of; amori pl love affairs. **~ggi'are** vi flirt.

a

amo'revole *adj* loving

a'morfo *adj* shapeless; (fig) grey

amo'roso *adj* loving; (sguardo ecc) amorous; (lettera, relazione) love

ampi'ezza *f* (di esperienza) breadth; (di stanza) spaciousness; (di gonna) fullness; (importanza) scale

'ampio *adj* ample; (esperienza) wide; (stanza) spacious; (vestito) loose; (gonna) full; (pantaloni) baggy

am'plesso *m* embrace

amplia'mento *m* (di casa, porto) enlargement; (di strada) widening

ampli'are *vt* broaden (conoscenze)

amplifi'ca|re *vt* amplify; *fig* magnify. ~tore *m* amplifier. ~zi'one *f* amplification

am'polla *f* cruet

ampu'ta|re *vt* amputate. ~zi'one *f* amputation

amu'leto *m* amulet

anabbagli'ante *adj* (Auto) dipped ●*mpl* anabbaglianti dipped headlights

anacro'nis|mo *m* anachronism. ~tico *adj* anachronistic

a'nagrafe *f* (ufficio) register office; (registro) register of births, marriages and deaths

ana'grafico *adj* dati *mpl* ana-grafici personal data

ana'gramma *m* anagram

anal'colico *adj* non-alcoholic ●*m* soft drink, non-alcoholic drink

analfa'be|ta *adj* & *mf* illiterate. ~tismo *m* illiteracy

anal'gesico *m* painkiller

a'nalisi *f inv* analysis; (Med) test. ~ grammaticale/del periodo/logica parsing. ~ del sangue blood test

ana'li|sta *mf* analyst. ~tico *adj* analytical. ~z'zare *vt* analyse; (Med) test

anal'lergico *adj* hypoallergenic

analo'gia *f* analogy. a'nalogo *adj* analogous

'ananas *m inv* pineapple

anar'chi|a *f* anarchy. a'narchico, -a *adj* anarchic ●*mf* anarchist. ~smo *m* anarchism

A.N.A.S. *f abbr* (Azienda Nazionale Autonoma delle Strade) national road maintenance authority

anato'mia *f* anatomy. ana'tomico *adj* anatomical; (sedia) contoured

'anatra *f* duck

ana'troccolo *m* duckling

'anca *f* hip; (di animale) flank

ance'strale *adj* ancestral

'anche *conj* also, too; (persino) even; ~ se even if

anchi'losato *adj* fig stiff

an'cora¹ *adv* still, yet; (di nuovo) again; (di più) some more; ~ una volta once more

'anco|ra² *f* anchor; gettare l'~ra drop anchor. ~'raggio *m* anchorage. ~rare *vt* anchor

anda'mento *m* (del mercato, degli affari) trend

an'dante *adj* (corrente) current; (di poco valore) cheap ●*m* (Mus) andante

an'da|re *vi* go; (funzionare) work; ~ via (partire) leave; (macchia) come out; ~ [bene] (confarsi) suit; (taglia:) fit; ti va bene alle tre? does three o'clock suit you?; non mi va di mangiare I don't feel like eating; ~ di fretta be in a hurry; ~ fiero di be proud of; ~ di moda be in fashion; va per i 20 anni he's nearly 20; ma va' [là]! come on!; come va? how are things?; ~ a male go off; ~ a fuoco go up in flames; va spedito [entro] stamattina it must be sent this morning; ne va del mio lavoro my job is at stake; come è andata a finire? how did it turn out?; cosa vai dicendo? what are you talking about?; ~rsene go away; (morire) pass away ●*m* going; a lungo ~re eventually ●

'andito m passage

an'drone m entrance

a'neddoto m anecdote

ane'lare vt ~ a long for. **a'nelito** m longing

a'nello m ring; (di catena) link

ane'mia f anaemia. **a'nemico** adj anaemic

a'nemone m anemone

aneste'si|a f anaesthesia; (sostanza) anaesthetic. **~sta** mf anaesthetist. **ane'stetico** adj & m anaesthetic

an'fibi mpl (stivali) army boots

an'fibio m (animale) amphibian ● adj amphibious

anfite'atro m amphitheatre

'anfora f amphora

an'fratto m ravine

an'gelico adj angelic

'angelo m angel. **~ custode** guardian angel

angli'c|ano adj Anglican. **angli'smo** m Anglicism

an'glofilo, -a adj & mf Anglophile

an'glofono, -a mf English-speaker

anglo'sassone adj & mf Anglo-Saxon

ango'la|re adj angular. **~zi'one** f angle shot

'angolo m corner; (Math) angle. **~ [di] cottura** kitchenette

ango'loso adj angular

an'gosci|a f anguish. **~'are** vt torment. **~'ato** adj agonized. **~'oso** adj (disperato) anguished; (che dà angoscia) distressing

angu'illa f eel

an'guria f water-melon

an'gusti|a f (ansia) anxiety; (penuria) poverty. **~'are** vt distress. **~'arsi** vr be very worried (per about)

an'gusto adj narrow

'anice m anise; (Culin) aniseed; (liquore) anisette

ani'dride f ~ carbonica carbon dioxide

'anima f soul; non c'era ~ viva there was not a soul about; all'~! good grief!; un'~ in pena a soul in torment. ~ **gemella** soul mate

ani'ma|le adj & m animal; **~li domestici** pl pets. **~'lesco** adj animal

ani'ma|re vt give life to; (ravvivare) enliven; (incoraggiare) encourage. **~rsi** vr come to life; (accalorarsi) become animated. **~to** adj animate; (discussione) animated; (paese) lively. **~tore, ~trice** mf leading spirit; Cinema animator. **~zi'one** f animation

'animo m (mente) mind; (indole) disposition; (cuore) heart; perdersi d'~ lose heart; farsi ~ take heart. **~sità** f animosity

ani'moso adj brave; (ostile) hostile

'anitra f = **ANATRA**

annac'qua|re vt water down. **~to** adj watered down

annaffi'a|re vt water. **~toio** m watering-can

an'nali mpl annals

anna'spare vi flounder

an'nata f year; (importo annuale) annual amount; (di vino) vintage

annebbia'mento m fog build-up; fig clouding

annebbi'ar|e vt cloud (vista, mente). **~si** vr become foggy; (vista, mente:) grow dim

annega'mento m drowning

anne'ga|re vt/i drown

anne'rir|e vt/i blacken. **~si** vr become black

annessi'one f (di nazione) annexation

an'nesso pp di **annettere** ● adj attached; (stato) annexed

an'nettere vt add; (accludere) enclose; annex (stato)

annichi'lire vt annihilate

anni'darsi vr nest

annienta'mento m annihilation

a

annien'tar|e vt annihilate. ~si vr abase oneself

anniver'sario adj & m anniversary. ~ di matrimonio wedding anniversary

'anno m year; Buon A~! Happy New Year!; quanti anni ha? how old are you?; Tommaso ha dieci anni Thomas is ten [years old]. ~ bisestile leap year

anno'dar|e vt knot; do up (cintura); fig form. ~si vr become knotted

annoi'a|re vt bore; (recare fastidio) annoy. ~rsi vr get bored; (condizione) be bored. ~to adj bored

anno'ta|re vt note down; annotate (testo). ~zi'one f note

annove'rare vt number

annu'a|le adj annual, yearly. ~rio m year-book

annu'ire vi nod; (acconsentire) agree

annulla'mento m annulment; (di appuntamento) cancellation

annul'lar|e vt annul; cancel (appuntamento); (togliere efficacia a) undo; disallow (gol); (distruggere) destroy. ~si vr cancel each other out

annunci'a|re vt announce; (preannunciare) foretell. ~tore, ~trice f announcer. A~zi'one f Annunciation

an'nuncio m announcement; (pubblicitario) advertisement; (notizia) news. annunci pl economici classified advertisements

'annuo adj annual, yearly

annu'sare vt sniff

annuvo'lar|e vt cloud. ~si vr cloud over

'ano m anus

a'nomalo adj anomalous

anoni'mato m mantenere l'~ remain anonymous

a'nonimo, -a adj anonymous ●m (pittore, scrittore) anonymous painter/writer

ano'ressico, -a mf anorexic

anor'mal|e adj abnormal ●mf deviant. ~ità f inv abnormality

'ansa f handle; (di fiume) bend

an'sare vi pant

'ansia, ansietà f anxiety; stare/essere in ~ per be anxious about

ansi'oso adj anxious

antago'nis|mo m antagonism. ~ta mf antagonist

an'tartico adj & m Antarctic

antece'dente adj preceding ●m precedent

ante'fatto m prior event

ante'guerra adj pre-war ●m pre-war period

ante'nato, -a mf ancestor

an'tenna f (Radio, TV) aerial; (di animale) antenna; (Naut) yard. ~ parabolica satellite dish

ante'porre vt put before

ante'prima f preview; vedere qcsa in ~ have a sneak preview of sth

anteri'ore adj front attrib; (nel tempo) previous

antia'ereo adj anti-aircraft attrib

antial'lergico adj hypoallergenic

antia'tomico adj rifugio ~ fallout shelter

antibi'otico adj & m antibiotic

anti'caglia f (oggetto) piece of old junk

antica'mente adv long ago

anti'camera f ante-room; far ~ be kept waiting

antichità f inv antiquity; (oggetto) antique

antici'clone m anticyclone

antici'pa|re vt advance; (Comm) pay in advance; (prevedere) anticipate; (prevenire) forestall ●vi be early. ~ta'mente adv in advance. ~zi'one f anticipation; (notizia) advance news

an'ticipo m advance; (caparra) deposit; in ~ early; (*nel lavoro*) ahead of schedule

an'tico *adj* ancient; (*mobile ecc*) antique; (*vecchio*) old; all'antica old-fashioned ●*mpl* gli antichi the ancients

anticoncezio'nale *adj & m* contraceptive

anticonfor'mis|mo *m* unconventionality. ~**ta** *mf* nonconformist. ~**tico** *adj* unconventional

anticonge'lante *adj & m* anti-freeze

anticostituzio'nale *adj* unconstitutional

anti'crimine *adj inv* (squadra) crime *attrib*

antidemo'cratico *adj* undemocratic

antidolo'rifico *m* painkiller

an'tidoto *m* antidote

anti'droga *adj inv* (campagna) anti-drugs; (squadra) drug *attrib*

antie'stetico *adj* ugly

antifa'scismo *m* anti-fascism

antifa'scista *adj & mf* anti-fascist

anti'furto *m* anti-theft device; (*allarme*) alarm ●*adj inv* (sistema) anti-theft

anti'gelo *m* antifreeze; (*parabrezza*) defroster

antigi'enico *adj* unhygienic

An'tille *fpl* le ~ the West Indies

an'tilope *f* antelope

antin'cendio *adj inv* allarme ~ fire alarm; porta ~ fire door

anti'nebbia *m inv* (*Auto*) [faro] ~ foglamp

antinfiamma'torio *adj & m* anti-inflammatory

antinucle'are *adj* anti-nuclear

antio'rario *adj* anti-clockwise

anti'pasto *m* hors d'oeuvre

an'tipodi *mpl* antipodes; essere agli ~ *fig* be poles apart

antiquari'ato *m* antique trade

anti'quario, -a *mf* antique dealer

anti'quato *adj* antiquated

anti'ruggine *m inv* rust-inhibitor

anti'rughe *adj inv* anti-wrinkle *attrib*

anti'scippo *adj inv* theft-proof

anti'settico *adj & m* antiseptic

antisoci'ale *adj* anti-social

antista'minico *m* antihistamine

anti'stante *a* *prep* in front of

anti'tarlo *m inv* woodworm treatment

antiterro'ristico *adj* antiterrorist *attrib*

an'titesi *f inv* antithesis

'antivirus *m inv* virus checker

antolo'gia *f* anthology

'antro *m* cavern

antropolo'gia *f* anthropology. antro'pologo, -a *mf* anthropologist

anu'lare *m* ring-finger

'anzi *conj* in fact; (*o meglio*) or better still; (*al contrario*) on the contrary

anzianità *f* old age; (*di servizio*) seniority

anzi'ano, -a *adj* elderly; (*di grado*) senior ●*mf* elderly person

anziché *conj* rather than

anzi'tempo *adv* prematurely

anzi'tutto *adv* first of all

a'orta *f* aorta

apar'titico *adj* unaligned

apa'tia *f* apathy. a'patico *adj* apathetic

'ape *f* bee; nido di api honeycomb

aperi'tivo *m* aperitif

aperta'mente *adv* openly

a'perto *adj* open; all'aria aperta in the open air; all'~ open-air

aper'tura *f* opening; (*inizio*) beginning; (*ampiezza*) spread; (*di arco*) span; (*Pol*) overtures *pl*; (*Phot*) aperture; ~ mentale openness

'apice *m* apex

a

apicol'tura f beekeeping

ap'nea f immersione in ~ free diving

a'polide adj stateless ● mf stateless person

a'postolo m apostle

apostro'fare vt (mettere un apostrofo a) write with an apostrophe; reprimand (persona)

a'postrofo m apostrophe

appaga'mento m fulfilment

appa'gare vt satisfy. ~rsi vr ~rsi di be satisfied with

appai'are vt pair; mate (animali)

appallotto'lare vt roll into a ball

appalta'tore m contractor

ap'palto m contract; dare in ~ to contract

appan'naggio m (in denaro) annuity; fig prerogative

appan'nar|e vt mist (vetro); dim (vista). ~si vr mist over; (vista:) grow dim

appa'rato m apparatus; (pompa) display

apparecchi'a|re vt prepare ● vi lay the table. ~'tura f (impianti) equipment

appa'recchio m apparatus; (congegno) device; (radio, tv ecc) set; (aeroplano) aircraft. ~ acustico hearing aid

appa'ren|te adj apparent. ~te'mente adv apparently. ~za f appearance; in ~za apparently

appa'ri|re vi appear; (sembrare) look. ~'scente adj striking; pej gaudy. ~zi'one f apparition

apparta'mento m apartment

appar'ta|rsi vr withdraw. ~to adj secluded

apparte'nenza f membership

apparte'nere vi belong

appassio'nante adj (storia, argomento) exciting

appassio'nare vt excite; (commuo-

vere). move. ~rsi vr ~rsi a become excited by. ~to adj passionate; ~to di (entusiastico) fond of

appas'sir|e vi wither. ~si vr fade

appel'larsi vr ~ a appeal to

ap'pello m appeal; (chiamata per nome) rollcall; (esami) exam session; fare l'~ call the roll

ap'pena adv just; (a fatica) hardly ● conj [non] ~ as soon as

ap'pendere vt hang [up]

appen'dice f appendix. appendi'cite f appendicitis

Appen'nini mpl gli ~ the Apennines

appesan'tir|e vt weigh down. ~si vr become heavy

ap'peso pp di appendere adj hanging; (impiccato) hanged

appe'ti|to m appetite; aver ~to be hungry; buon ~to! enjoy your meal!. ~'toso adj appetizing; fig tempting

appezza'mento m plot of land

appia'nar|e vt level; fig smooth over. ~si vr improve

appiat'tir|e vt flatten. ~si vr flatten oneself

appic'care vt ~ il fuoco a set fire to

appicci'car|e vt stick; ~e a (fig: appioppare) palm off on ● vi be sticky. ~si vr stick; (cose:) stick together; ~si a qcno fig stick to sb like glue

appiccica'ticcio adj sticky; fig clingy

appicci'coso adj sticky; fig clingy

appie'dato adj sono ~ I don't have the car; sono rimasto ~ I was stranded

appi'eno adv fully

appigli'arsi vr ~ a get hold of; fig stick to. ap'piglio m fingerhold; (per piedi) foothold; fig pretext

appiop'pare vt ~ a palm off on; (⊞: dare) give

appiso'larsi vr doze off

applau'dire vt/i applaud. ap'plauso m applause

appli'cabile adj applicable

appli'ca|re vt apply; enforce (legge ecc). **~rsi** vr apply oneself. **~tore** m applicator. **~zi'one** f application; (di legge) enforcement

appoggi'ar|e vt lean (a against); (mettere) put; (sostenere) back. **~si** a lean against; fig rely on. ap'poggio m support

appollai'arsi vr fig perch

ap'porre vt affix

appor'tare vt bring; (causare) cause. ap'porto m contribution

apposita'mente adv especially

ap'posito adj proper

ap'posta adv on purpose; (espressamente) specially

apposta'mento m ambush; (caccia) lying in wait

appo'star|e vt post (soldati). **~si** vr lie in wait

ap'prend|ere vt understand; (imparare) learn. **~i'mento** m learning

appren'di|sta mf apprentice. **~stato** m apprenticeship

apprensi'one f apprehension; essere in **~** per be anxious about. appren'sivo adj apprehensive

ap'presso adv & prep (vicino) near; (dietro) behind; come **~** as follows

appre'star|e vt prepare. **~si** vr get ready

apprez'za|bile adj appreciable. **~'mento** m appreciation; (giudizio) opinion

apprez'za|re vt appreciate. **~to** adj appreciated

ap'proccio m approach

appro'dare vi land; **~** a fig come to; **non ~** a nulla** come to nothing. ap'prodo m landing; (luogo) landing-stage

approfit'ta|re vi take advantage

(di of), profit (di by). **~tore**, **~'trice** mf chancer

approfondi'mento m deepening; di **~** fig (esame) further

approfon'di|re vt deepen. **~rsi** vr (divario) widen. **~to** adj (studio, ricerca) in-depth

appropri'ar|si vr (essere adatto a) suit; **~rsi di** take possession of. **~to** adj appropriate. **~zi'one** f (Jur) appropriation. **~zione indebita** (Jur) embezzlement

approssi'ma|re vt **~re per eccesso/difetto** round up/down. **~rsi** vr draw near. **~tiva'mente** adv approximately. **~'tivo** adj approximate. **~zi'one** f approximation

appro'va|re vt approve of; approve (legge). **~zi'one** f approval

approvvigiona'mento m supplying; **approvvigionamenti** pl provisions

approvvigio'nar|e vt supply. **~si** vr stock up

appunta'mento m appointment; **fissare un ~** make an appointment; **darsi ~** decide to meet

appun'tar|e vt (annotare) take notes; (fissare) fix; (con spillo) pin; (appuntire) sharpen. **~si** vr **~si su** (teoria:) be based on

appun'ti|re vt sharpen. **~to** adj (mento) pointed

ap'punto¹ m note; (piccola critica) niggle

ap'punto² adv exactly; **per l'~!** exactly!; **stavo ~ dicendo...** I was just saying...

appu'rare vt verify

a'pribile adj that can be opened

apribot'tiglie m inv bottle-opener

a'prile m April; **il primo d'~** April Fools' Day

a'prir|e vt open; turn on (acqua ecc); (con chiave) unlock; open up (ferita ecc). **~si** vr open; (spaccarsi) split; (confidarsi) confide (con in)

apri'scatole *f inv* tin-opener

aqua'planing *m* andare in ∼ aquaplane

'aquila *f* eagle; non è un'∼al he is no genius!. ∼'lino *adj* aquiline

aqui'lone *m* (*giocattolo*) kite

ara'besco *m* arabesque; *hum* scribble

A'rabia Sau'dita *f* l'∼ Saudi Arabia

'arabo, -a *adj* Arab; (*lingua*) Arabic • *mf* Arab • *m* (*lingua*) Arabic

a'rachide *f* peanut

ara'gosta *f* lobster

a'rancia *f* orange. ∼'ata *f* orangeade. ∼o *m* orange-tree; (*colore*) orange. ∼'one *adj & m* orange

a'rare *vt* plough. ∼tro *m* plough

ara'tura *f* ploughing

a'razzo *m* tapestry

arbi'trare *vt* arbitrate in; *Sport* referee. ∼ietà *f* arbitrariness. ∼io *adj* arbitrary

ar'bitrio *m* will; è un ∼ it's very high-handed

'arbitro *m* arbiter; *Sport* referee; (*nel baseball*) umpire

ar'busto *m* shrub

'arca *f* ark; (*cassa*) chest

ar'caico *adj* archaic. ∼'ismo *m* archaism

ar'cangelo *m* archangel

ar'cata *f* arch; (*serie di archi*) arcade

archeolo'gia *f* archaeology. ∼o'logico *adj* archaeological. ∼'ologo, -a *mf* archaeologist

ar'chetto *m* (*Mus*) bow

archi'tet'tare *vt fig* devise; cosa state architettando? *fig* what are you plotting?

archi'tet|to *m* architect. ∼'tonico *adj* architectural. ∼'tura *f* architecture

archivi'are *vt* file; (*Jur*) close

ar'chivio *m* archives *pl*; (*Comput*) file

archi'vista *mf* filing clerk

ar'cigno *adj* grim

arci'pelago *m* archipelago

arci'vescovo *m* archbishop

'arco *m* arch; (*Math*) arc; (*Mus, arma*) bow; nell'∼ di una giornata/due mesi in the space of a day/two months

arcoba'leno *m* rainbow

arcu'a|re *vt* bend. ∼rsi *vr* bend. ∼to *adj* bent, curved

ar'dente *adj* burning; *fig* ardent. ∼'mente *adv* ardently

'ardere *vt/i* burn

ar'desia *f* slate

ar'di|re *vi* dare. ∼to *adj* daring; (*coraggioso*) bold; (*sfacciato*) impudent

ar'dore *m* (*calore*) heat; *fig* ardour

'arduo *adj* arduous; (*ripido*) steep

'area *f* area. ∼ di rigore (*nel calcio*) penalty area. ∼ di servizio service area

a'rena *f* arena

are'narsi *vr* run aground; *fig:* (*trattative*) reach deadlock; mi sono arenato I'm stuck

'argano *m* winch

argen'tato *adj* silver-plated

argente'ria *f* silver[ware]

ar'gento *m* silver

ar'gilla *f* clay. ∼'loso *adj* (*terreno*) clayey

argi'nare *vt* embank; *fig* hold in check, contain

'argine *m* embankment; (*diga*) dike

argomen'tare *vi* argue

argo'mento *m* argument; (*motivo*) reason; (*soggetto*) subject

argu'ire *vt* deduce

ar'gu|to *adj* witty. ∼zia *f* wit; (*battuta*) witticism

'aria *f* air; (*aspetto*) appearance; (*Mus*) tune; andare all'∼ *fig* come to nothing; avere l'∼... look...; corrente d'∼ draught; mandare all'∼ qcsa *fig* ruin sth

aridità *f* aridity, dryness

'arido *adj* arid

arieggi'a|re *vi* air. **~to** *adj* airy

ari'ete *m* ram. A~ (*Astr*) Aries

ari'etta *f* (*brezza*) breeze

a'ringa *f* herring

ari'oso *adj* (*locale*) light and airy

aristo'cra|tico, -a *adj* aristocratic
● *mf* aristocrat. **~zia** *f* aristocracy

arit'metica *f* arithmetic

arlec'chino *m* Harlequin; *fig*
buffoon

'arma *f* weapon; **armi** *pl* arms; (*forze
armate*) [armed] forces; **chiamare
alle armi** call up; **sotto le armi** in
the army; **alle prime armi** *fig* inexperienced. **~ da fuoco** firearm.
armi *mpl* **di distruzione di massa**
weapons of mass destruction.

armadi'etto *m* locker, cupboard

ar'madio *m* cupboard; (*guardaroba*)
wardrobe

armamen'tario *m* tools *pl*; *fig*
paraphernalia

arma'mento *m* armament; (*Naut*)
fitting out

ar'ma|re *vt* arm; (*equipaggiare*) fit
out; (*Archit*) reinforce. **~rsi** *vr* arm
oneself (**di** with). **~ta** *f* army; (*flotta*)
fleet. **~tore** *m* shipowner. **~tura** *f*
framework; (*impalcatura*) scaffolding;
(*di guerriero*) armour

armeggi'are *vi* *fig* manoeuvre

armi'stizio *m* armistice

armo'ni|a *f* harmony. **ar'monica**
f **~** [**a bocca**] mouth organ. **ar'mo-
nico** *adj* harmonic. **~'oso** *adj* harmonious

armoniz'zar|e *vt* harmonize ● *vi*
match. **~si** *vr* (*colori*) match

ar'nese *m* tool; (*oggetto*) thing; (*congegno*) gadget; **male in ~** in bad
condition

'arnia *f* beehive

a'roma *m* aroma; **aromi** *pl* herbs.

~tera'pia *f* aromatherapy

aro'matico *adj* aromatic

aromatiz'zare *vt* flavour

'arpa *f* harp

ar'peggio *m* arpeggio

ar'pia *f* harpy

arpi'one *m* hook; (*pesca*) harpoon

arrab'bia|rsi *vr* get angry. **~to** *adj*
angry. **~tura** *f* rage; **prendersi una
~tura** fly into a rage

arraf'fare *vt* grab

arrampi'ca|rsi *vr* climb [up]. **~ta**
f climb. **~tore**, **~trice** *mf* climber.
~tore sociale social climber

arran'care *vi* limp, hobble

arrangia'mento *m* arrangement

arrangi'ar|e *vt* arrange. **~si** *vr*
manage; **~si alla meglio** get by; ar-
'rangiatil get on with it!

arra'parsi *vr* 🄳 get randy

arre'care *vt* bring; (*causare*) cause

arreda'mento *m* interior decoration; (*l'arredare*) furnishing; (*mobili
ecc*) furnishings *pl*

arre'da|re *vt* furnish. **~tore**,
~trice *mf* interior designer. **ar'redo**
m furnishings *pl*

ar'rendersi *vr* surrender

arren'devo|le *adj* (*persona*) yield-
ing. **~lezza** *f* softness

arre'star|e *vt* arrest; (*fermare*) stop.
~si *vr* halt. **ar'resto** *m* stop; (*Med*,
Jur) arrest; **la dichiaro in** [**stato d'**]
arresto you are under arrest; **mandato di arresto** warrant. **arresti** *pl*
domiciliari (*Jur*) house arrest

arre'tra|re *vt/i* withdraw; pull back
(*giocatore*). **~to** *adj* (*paese ecc*)
backward; (*Mil*: *posizione*) rear; **numero ~to** (*di rivista*) back number;
del lavoro ~to a backlog of work
● *m* (*di stipendio*) back pay

arre'trati *mpl* arrears

arricchi'mento *m* enrichment

arric'chi|re *vt* enrich. **~rsi** *vr* get

a

rich. ~to, -a mf nouveau riche

arricci'are vt curl; ~ il naso turn up one's nose

ar'ringa f harangue; (Jur) closing address

arrischi'a|rsi vr dare. ~to adj risky; (imprudente) rash

arri'va|re vi arrive; ~re a (raggiungere) reach; (ridursi) be reduced to. ~to, -a adj successful; ben ~to! welcome! ●mf successful person

arrive'derci int goodbye; ~ a domani see you tomorrow

arri'vi|smo m social climbing; (nel lavoro) careerism. ~ta mf social climber; (nel lavoro) careerist

ar'rivo m arrival; Sport finish

arro'gan|te adj arrogant. ~za f arrogance

arro'garsi vr ~ il diritto di fare qcsa take it upon oneself to do sth

arrossa'mento m reddening

arros'sa|re vt make red (occhi). ~si vr go red

arros'sire vi blush, go red

arro'stire vt roast; toast (pane); (ai ferri) grill. **ar'rosto** adj & m roast

arroto'lare vt roll up

arroton'dar|e vt round; (Math ecc) round off. ~si vr become round; (persona): get plump

arrovel'larsi vr ~ il cervello rack one's brains

arroven'ta|re vt make red-hot. ~rsi vr become red-hot. ~to adj red-hot

arruf'fa|re vt ruffle; fig confuse. ~to adj (capelli) ruffled

arruffianarsi vr ~ qcno fig butter sb up

arruggi'ni|re vt rust. ~rsi vr go rusty; fig (fisicamente) stiffen up; (conoscenze): go rusty. ~to adj rusty

arruola'mento m enlistment

arruo'lar|e vt/i, ~si vr enlist

arse'nale m arsenal; (cantiere)

[naval] dockyard

ar'senico m arsenic

'arso pp di ardere ●adj burnt; (arido) dry. **ar'sura** f burning heat; (sete) parching thirst

'arte f art; (abilità) craftsmanship; le belle arti the fine arts. **arti figurative** figurative arts

arte'fa|re vt adulterate (vino); disguise (voce). ~tto adj fake; (vino) adulterated

ar'tefice mf craftsman; craftswoman; fig author

ar'teria f artery. ~ [stradale] arterial road

arterioscle'rosi f arteriosclerosis

'artico adj & m Arctic

artico'la|re adj articular ●vt articulate; (suddividere) divide. ~rsi vr fig ~rsi in consist of. ~to adj (Auto) articulated; fig well-constructed. ~zi'one f (Anat) articulation

ar'ticolo m article. ~ di fondo leader

artifici'ale adj artificial

arti'fici|o m artifice; (affettazione) affectation. ~'oso adj artful; (affettato) affected

artigia'nal|e adj made by hand; hum amateurish. ~'mente adv with craftsmanship; hum amateurishly

artigia'nato m craftsmanship; (ceto) craftsmen pl. ~'ano, -a m craftsman ●f craftswoman

artigli'ere m artilleryman. ~e'ria f artillery

ar'tiglio m claw; fig clutch

ar'tist|a mf artist. ~ica'mente adv artistically. ~ico adj artistic

'arto m limb

ar'trite f arthritis

ar'trosi f rheumatism

arzigogo'lato adj bizarre

ar'zillo adj sprightly

a'scella f armpit

ascen'den|te adj ascending ●m

(*antenato*) ancestor; (*influenza*) ascendancy; (*Astr*) ascendant

ascensi'one *f* ascent; **l'A~** the Ascension

ascen'sore *m* lift, elevator *Am*

a'scesa *f* ascent; (*al trono*) accession; (*al potere*) rise

a'scesso *m* abscess

a'sceta *mf* ascetic

'**ascia** *f* axe

asciugabianche'ria *m inv* (*stenditoio*) clothes horse

asciugaca'pelli *m inv* hair dryer

asciuga'mano *m* towel

asciu'gar|e *vt* dry. **~si** *vr* dry oneself; (*diventare asciutto*) dry up

asci'utto *adj* dry; (*magro*) wiry; (*risposta*) curt; **essere all'~** *fig* be hard up

ascol'ta|re *vt* listen to ● *vi* listen. **~'tore**, **~'trice** *mf* listener

a'scolto *m* listening; **dare ~** a listen to; **mettersi in ~** *Radio* tune in

asfal'tare *vt* asphalt

a'sfalto *m* asphalt

asfis'si|a *f* asphyxia. **~'ante** *adj* oppressive; *fig* (*persona*) annoying. **~'are** *vt* asphyxiate; *fig* annoy

'**Asia** *f* Asia. **asi'atico**, **-a** *agg & mf* Asian

a'silo *m* shelter; (*d'infanzia*) nursery school. **~ nido** day nursery. **~ politico** political asylum

asim'metrico *adj* asymmetrical

'**asino** *m* donkey; (*fig: persona stupida*) ass

'**asma** *f* asthma. **a'smatico** *adj* asthmatic

asoci'ale *adj* asocial

'**asola** *f* buttonhole

a'sparagi *mpl* asparagus *sg*

a'sparago *m* asparagus spear

asperità *f inv* harshness; (*di terreno*) roughness

aspet'ta|re *vt* wait for; (*prevedere*)

expect; **~re un bambino** be expecting [a baby]; **fare ~re qcno** keep sb waiting ● *vi* wait. **~rsi** *vr* expect. **~'tiva** *f* expectation

a'spetto[1] *m* appearance; (*di problema*) aspect; **di bell'~** good-looking

a'spetto[2] *m* **sala** *f* **d'~** waiting room

aspi'rante *adj* aspiring; (*pompa*) suction *attrib* ● *mf* (*a un posto*) applicant; (*al trono*) aspirant; **gli aspiranti al titolo** the contenders for the title

aspira'polvere *m inv* vacuum cleaner

aspi'ra|re *vt* inhale; (*Mech*) suck in ● *vi* **~re** a aspire to. **~'tore** *m* extractor fan. **~zi'one** *f* inhalation; (*Mech*) suction; (*ambizione*) ambition

aspi'rina *f* aspirin

aspor'tare *vt* take away

aspra'mente *adv* (*duramente*) severely

a'sprezza *f* (*al gusto*) sourness; (*di clima*) severity; (*di suono*) harshness; (*di odore*) pungency

'**aspro** *adj* (*al gusto*) sour; (*clima*) severe; (*suono, parole*) harsh; (*odore*) pungent; (*litigio*) bitter

assag|gi'are *vt* taste. **~'gini** *mpl* (*Culin*) samples. **as'saggio** *m* tasting; (*piccola quantità*) taste

as'sai *adv* very; (*moltissimo*) very much; (*abbastanza*) enough

assa'li|re *vt* attack. **~'tore**, **~'trice** *mf* assailant

as'salto *m* attack; **prendere d'~** storm (*città*); *fig* mob (*persona*); hold up (*banca*)

assapo'rare *vt* savour

assassi'nare *vt* murder, assassinate

assas'sin|io *m* murder, assassination. **~o**, **-a** *adj* murderous ● *m* murderer ● *f* murderess

'**asse** *f* board ● *m* (*Techn*) axle; (*Math*) axis. **~ da stiro** ironing board

a

asseconˈdare vt satisfy; (favorire) support

assediˈare vt besiege. **asˈsedio** m siege

assegnaˈmento m allotment; fare ~ su rely on

asseˈgnaˌre vt allot; award (premio). **~ˈtario** mf recipient. **~ziˈone** f (di alloggio, borsa di studio) allocation; (di premio) award

asˈsegno m allowance; (bancario) cheque; contro ~ cash on delivery. ~ circolare bank draft. assegni pl familiari family allowance. ~ non trasferibile non-transferable cheque.

assemˈblea f assembly; (adunanza) gathering

assembraˈmento m gathering

assenˈnato adj sensible

asˈsenso m assent

assenˈtarsi vr go away; (da stanza) leave the room

asˈsenˌte adj absent; (distratto) absent-minded ● mf absentee. **~teˈismo** m absenteeism. **~teˈista** mf frequent absentee. **~za** f absence; (mancanza) lack

asseˈrire vt assert. **~ˈtivo** adj assertive. **~ziˈone** f assertion

assesˈsorato m department

assesˈsore m councillor

assestaˈmento m settlement

asseˈstarˌe vt arrange; ~e un colpo deal a blow. **~si** vr settle oneself

asseˈtato adj parched

asˈsetto m order; (Aeron, Naut) trim

assicuˈraˌre vt assure; (Comm) insure; register (posta); (fissare) secure; (accertare) ensure. **~rsi** vr (con contratto) insure oneself; (legarsi) fasten oneself; **~rsi** che make sure that. **~ˈtivo** adj insurance attrib. **~ˈtore**, **~ˈtrice** mf insurance agent ● adj insurance attrib. **~ziˈone** f assurance; (contratto) insurance

assideraˈmento m exposure. **asˌsideˈrato** adj (Med) suffering from exposure; ▣ frozen

assiduaˈmente adv assiduously. **~ità** f assiduity

asˈsiduo adj assiduous; (cliente) regular

assilˈlante adj (persona, pensiero) nagging

assilˈlare vt pester

asˈsillo m worry

assimiˈlaˌre vt assimilate. **~ziˈone** f assimilation

asˈsise fpl assizes; Corte d'A~ Court of Assize[s]

assisˈtenˌte mf assistant. **~te soˈciale** social worker. **~te di volo** flight attendant. **~za** f assistance; (presenza) presence. **~za soˈciale** social work

assistenziˈaˌlle adj welfare attrib. **~ˈlismo** m welfare

asˈsistere vt assist; (curare) nurse ● vi ~ a (essere presente) be present at; watch (spettacolo ecc)

ˈasso m ace; piantare in ~ leave in the lurch

associˈaˌre vt join; (collegare) associate. **~rsi** vr join forces; (Comm) enter into partnership. **~rsi** a join. **~ziˈone** f association

assogˈgetˌtarˌe vt subject. **~si** vr submit

assoˈlato adj sunny

assolˈdare vt recruit

asˈsolo m (Mus) solo

asˈsolto pp di assolvere

assolutaˈmente adv absolutely

assoluˈtismo m absolutism

assoˈluˌto adj absolute. **~ziˈone** f acquittal; (Relig) absolution

asˈsolvere vt perform (compito); (Jur) acquit; (Relig) absolve

assomigliˈaˌre vi ~e a resemble. **~si** vr resemble each other

assom'marsi vr combine; ~ a qcsa add to sth

asso'nanza f assonance

asson'nato adj drowsy

asso'pirsi vr doze off

assor'bente adj & m absorbent. ~ igienico sanitary towel

assor'bire vt absorb

assor'da|re vt deafen. ~nte adj deafening

assorti'mento m assortment

assor'ti|re vt match (colori). ~to adj assorted; (colori, persone) matched

as'sorto adj engrossed

assottigli'ar|e vt make thin; (aguzzare) sharpen; (ridurre) reduce. ~si vr grow thin; (finanze): be whittled away

assue'fa|re vt accustom. ~rsi vr ~rsi a get used to. ~tto adj (a caffè, aspirina) immune to the effects; (a droga) addicted. ~zi'one f (a caffè, aspirina) immunity to the effects; (a droga) addiction

as'sumere vt assume; take on (impiegato); ~ informazioni make inquiries

as'sunto pp di assumere ● m task. assunzi'one f (di impiegato) employment

assurdità f inv absurdity; ~ pl nonsense

as'surdo adj absurd

asta f pole; (Mech) bar; (Comm) auction; a mezz'~ at half-mast

a'stemio adj abstemious

aste'n|ersi vr abstain (da from). ~si'one f abstention

aste'nuto, -a mf abstainer

aste'risco m asterisk

astig'ma|tico adj astigmatic. ~'tismo m astigmatism

asti|o m rancour; avere ~o contro qcno bear sb a grudge. ~'oso adj resentful

a'stratto adj abstract

astrin'gente adj & m astringent

'astro m star

astrolo'gia f astrology. a'strologo, -a mf astrologer

astro'nauta mf astronaut

astro'nave f spaceship

astro|no'mia f astronomy. ~o'nomico adj astronomical. a'stronomo m astronomer

astrusità f abstruseness

a'stuccio m case

a'stu|to adj shrewd; (furbo) cunning. ~zia f shrewdness; (azione) trick

ate'ismo m atheism

A'tene f Athens

'ateo, -a adj & mf atheist

a'tipico adj atypical

at'lan|te m atlas. ~tico adj Atlantic; l' [Oceano] A~ico the Atlantic [Ocean]

at'let|a mf athlete. ~ica f athletics sg. ~ica leggera track and field events. ~ica pesante weight-lifting, boxing, wrestling, etc. ~ico adj athletic

atmo'sfer|a f atmosphere. ~ico adj atmospheric

a'tomic|a f atom bomb. ~o adj atomic

'atomo m atom

'atrio m entrance hall

a'troc|e adj atrocious; (terrible) dreadful. ~ità f inv atrocity

atrofiz'zarsi vr atrophy

attaccabot'toni mf inv [crashing] bore

attacca'brighe mf inv troublemaker

attacca'mento m attachment

attacca'panni m inv [coat-]hanger; (a muro) clothes hook

attac'car|e vt attach; (legare) tie; (appendere) hang; (cucire) sew on; (contagiare) pass on; (assalire) attack; (iniziare) start ● vi stick; (diffondersi) catch

a on. ~si vr cling; (affezionarsi) become attached; (litigare) quarrel

attacca'ticcio adj sticky

at'tacco m attack; (punto d'unione) junction

attar'darsi vr stay late; (indugiare) linger

attec'chire vi take; (moda ecc:) catch on

atteggia'mento m attitude

atteggi'ar|e vt assume. ~si vr ~si a pose as

attem'pato adj elderly

at'tender|e vt wait for ● vi ~e a attend to. ~si vr expect

atten'dibil|e adj reliable. ~ità f reliability

atte'nersi vr ~ a stick to

attenta'mente adv attentively

atten'ta|re vi ~re a make an attempt on. ~to m act of violence; (contro politico ecc) assassination attempt. ~'tore, ~'trice mf (a scopo politico) terrorist

at'tento adj attentive; (accurato) careful; ~! look out!; stare ~ pay attention

attenu'ante f extenuating circumstance

attenu'a|re vt attenuate; (minimizzare) minimize; subdue (colori ecc); calm (dolore); soften (colpo). ~rsi vr diminish. ~zi'one f lessening

attenzi'one f attention; ~! watch out!

atter'ra|ggio m landing. ~re vt knock down ● vi land

atter'rire vt terrorize. ~si vr be terrified

at'tesa f waiting; (aspettativa) expectation; in ~a di waiting for. ~o pp di attendere

atte'sta|re vt state; (certificare) certify. ~to m certificate. ~zi'one f certificate; (dichiarazione) declaration

'attico m attic

at'tiguo adj adjacent

attil'lato adj (vestito) close-fitting

'attimo m moment

atti'nente adj ~ a pertaining to

at'tingere vt draw; fig obtain

atti'rare vt attract

atti'tudine f (disposizione) aptitude; (atteggiamento) attitude

atti'v|are vt activate. ~ismo m activism. ~ista mf activist. attività f inv activity; (Comm) assets pl. ~o adj active; (Comm) productive ● m assets pl.

attiz'za|re vt poke; fig stir up. ~'toio m poker

'atto m act; (azione) action; (Comm, Jur) deed; (certificato) certificate; atti pl (di società ecc) proceedings; mettere in ~ put into effect

at'tonito adj astonished

attorcigli'ar|e vt twist. ~si vr get twisted

at'tore m actor

attorni'ar|e vt surround. ~si vr ~si di surround oneself with

at'torno adv around, about ● prep ~ a around, about

attrac'care vt/i dock

attra'ente adj attractive

at'tra|rre vt attract. ~rsi vr be attracted to each other. ~t'tiva f charm

attraversa'mento m crossing. ~ pedonale crossing, crosswalk Am

attraver'sare vt cross; (passare) go through

attra'verso prep through; (obliquamente) across

attrazi'on|e f attraction. ~i pl turistiche tourist attractions

attrez'za|re vt equip; (Naut) rig. ~rsi vr kit oneself out; ~'tura f equipment; (Naut) rigging

at'trezzo m tool; attrezzi pl equipment; Sport appliances pl; (Theat) props pl

attribu'ir|e vt attribute. ~si vr

ascribe to oneself; ∼**si il merito di** claim credit for

attri'bu|to m attribute. ∼**zi'one** f attribution

at'trice f actress

at'trito m friction

attu'abile adj feasible

attu'al|e adj present; (di attualità) topical; (effettivo) actual. ∼**ità** f topicality; (avvenimento) news; **programma di** ∼**ità** current affairs programme. ∼**iz'zare** vt update. ∼**'mente** adv at present

attu'a|re vt carry out. ∼**rsi** vr be realized. ∼**zi'one** f carrying out

attu'tire vt deaden; ∼ **il colpo** soften the blow

au'dac|e adj audacious;. ∼**ia** f boldness; (insolenza) audacity

'**audience** f inv (telespettatori) audience

'**audio** m audio

audiovi'sivo adj audiovisual

audi'torio m auditorium

audizi'one f audition; (Jur) hearing

'**auge** m height; **essere in** ∼ be popular

augu'rar|e vt wish. ∼**si** vr hope. **au'gurio** m wish; (presagio) omen; **auguri!** all the best!; (a Natale) Happy Christmas!; **tanti auguri** best wishes

'**aula** f classroom; (università) lecture-hall; (sala) hall. ∼ **magna** (in università) great hall. ∼ **del tribunale** courtroom

aumen'tare vt/i increase. **au'mento** m increase; (di stipendio) [pay] rise

au'reola f halo

au'rora f dawn

auscul'tare vt (Med) auscultate

ausili'are adj & mf auxiliary

auspi'cabile adj **è** ∼ **che...** it is to be hoped that...

auspi'care vt hope for

au'spicio m omen; **auspici** (pl: pro-

tezione) auspices

austerità f austerity

au'stero adj austere

Au'strali|a f Australia. **a**∼**'ano, -a** adj & mf Australian

'**Austria** f Austria. **au'striaco, -a** agg & mf Austrian

autar'chia f autarchy. **au'tarchico** adj autarchic

autenti'c|are vt authenticate. ∼**ità** f authenticity

au'tentico adj authentic; (vero) true

au'tista m driver

'**auto+** pref self +; auto-

autoabbron'zante m self-tan
 ● adj self-tanning

autoambu'lanza f ambulance

autoartico'lato m articulated lorry

autobio|gra'fia f autobiography. ∼**'grafico** adj autobiographical

auto'botte f tanker

'**autobus** m inv bus

auto'carro m lorry

autocommiserazi'one f self-pity

auto'critica f self-criticism

autodi'fesa f self-defence

auto'gol m inv own goal

au'tografo adj & m autograph

autolesio'nis|mo m fig self-destruction. ∼**tico** adj self-destructive

auto'linea f bus line

au'toma m robot

automatica'mente adv automatically

auto'matico adj automatic ● m (bottone) press-stud; (fucile) automatic

automatiz'za|re vt automate. ∼**zi'one** f automation

auto'mezzo m motor vehicle

a

auto'mobi|le f [motor] car. ~**lismo** m motoring. ~**lista** mf motorist. ~**listico** adj (industria) automobile attrib

autonoma'mente adv autonomously

autono'mia f autonomy; (Auto) range; (di laptop, cellulare) battery life. au'**tonomo** adj autonomous

auto'psia f autopsy

auto'radio f inv car radio; (veicolo) radio car

au'tore, -'trice mf author; (di pittura) painter; (di furto ecc) perpetrator; quadro d'~ genuine master

auto'revo|le adj authoritative; (che ha influenza) influential. ~**lezza** f authority

autori'carica f mobile phone tariff where users' accounts are credited depending on usage

autori'messa f garage

autori'tà f inv authority. ~**'tario** adj autocratic. ~**ta'rismo** m authoritarianism

autori'tratto m self-portrait

autoriz'za|re vt authorize. ~**zi'one** f authorization

auto'scontro m inv bumper car

autoscu'ola f driving school

auto'stop m hitch-hiking; fare l'~ hitch-hike. ~**'pista** f hitch-hiker

auto'strada f motorway

autostra'dale adj motorway attrib

autosuffici'en|te adj self-sufficient. ~**za** f self-sufficiency

autotrasporta'|tore, -'trice mf haulier, carrier

auto'treno m articulated lorry

autove'icolo m motor vehicle

Auto'velox® m inv speed camera

autovet'tura f motor vehicle

autun'nale adj autumn[al]

au'tunno m autumn

aval'lare vt endorse

a'vallo m endorsement

avam'braccio m forearm

avangu'ardia f vanguard; fig avant-garde; essere d'~ be in the forefront

a'vanti adv (in avanti) forward; (davanti) in front; (prima) before; ~! (entrate) come in!; (suvvia) come on!; (su semaforo) cross now; va' ~! go ahead!; andare ~ (precedere) go ahead; (orologio:) be fast; ~ e indietro backwards and forwards ● adj before ● prep ~ a before; (in presenza di) in the presence of

avanti'eri adv the day before yesterday

avanza'mento m progress; (promozione) promotion

avan'za|re vi advance; (progredire) progress; (essere d'avanzo) be left [over] ● vt advance; (superare) surpass; (promuovere) promote. ~**rsi** vr advance; (avvicinarsi) approach. ~**ta** f advance. ~**to** adj advanced; (nella notte) late; in età ~**ta** elderly. a'**vanzo** m remainder; (Comm) surplus; avanzi pl (rovine) remains; (di cibo) left-overs

ava'ri|a f (di motore) engine failure. ~**'ato** adj (frutta, verdura) rotten; (carne) tainted

ava'rizia f avarice. a'**varo, -a** adj stingy ● mf miser

a'vena f oats pl

a'vere

Si può usare have o have got per parlare di ciò che si possiede. have got non si usa nell'inglese americano

● vt have; (ottenere) get; (indossare) wear; (provare) feel; ho trent'anni I'm thirty; ha avuto il posto he got the job; ~ fame/freddo be hungry/cold; ho mal di denti I've got toothache; cos'ha a che fare con lui? what has it got to do with him?; ~ **da fare** be busy; **che hai?** what's the matter with you?; **nei hai per molto?** will you be long?; **quanti ne abbiamo oggi?** what date is it today?; **avercela con qcno** have it in for sb

● *v aux* have; (**non l'ho visto I haven't seen him; lo hai visto?** have you seen him?; **l'ho visto ieri I** saw him yesterday

● *m* **averi** *pl* wealth *sg*

avia|'tore *m* flyer, aviator. **~zi'one** *f* aviation; (*Mil*) Air Force

avidità *f* avidness. **'avido** *adj* avid

avio'getto *m* jet

'avo, -a *mf* ancestor

avo'cado *m inv* avocado

a'vorio *m* ivory

Avv. *abbr* avvocato

avva'lersi *vr* avail oneself (**di** of)

avvalla'mento *m* depression

avvalo'rare *vt* bear out (*tesi*); endorse (*documento*); (*accrescere*) enhance

avvam'pare *vi* flare up; (*arrossire*) blush

avvantaggi'ar|e *vt* favour. **~si** *vr* **~si di** benefit from; (*approfittare*) take advantage of

avve'd|ersi *vr* (*accorgersi*) notice; (*capire*) realize. **~uto** *adj* shrewd

avvelena'mento *m* poisoning

avvele'na|re *vt* poison. **~rsi** *vr* poison oneself. **~to** *adj* poisoned

avve'nente *adj* attractive

avveni'mento *m* event

avve'nire[1] *vi* happen; (*aver luogo*) take place

avve'ni|re[2] *m* future. **~'ristico** *adj* futuristic

avven'ta|rsi *vr* fling oneself. **~to** *adj* (*decisione*) rash

av'vento *m* advent; (*Relig*) Advent

avven'tore *m* regular customer

avven'tu|ra *f* adventure; (*amorosa*) affair; **d'~** (*film*) adventure *attrib*. **~'rarsi** *vr* venture. **~ri'ero, -a** *m* adventurer ●*f* adventur-ess. **~'roso** *adj* adventurous

avve'ra|bile *adj* (*previsione*) that may come true. **~rsi** *vr* come true

av'verbio *m* adverb

avver'sar|e *vt* oppose. **~io, -a** *adj* opposing ●*mf* opponent

avversi'one *f* aversion. **~tà** *f inv* adversity

av'verso *adj* (*sfavorevole*) adverse; (*contrario*) averse

avver'tenza *f* (*cura*) care; (*avvertimento*) warning; (*avviso*) notice; (*premessa*) foreword; **avvertenze** *pl* (*istruzioni*) instructions

avverti'mento *m* warning

avver'tire *vt* warn; (*informare*) inform; (*sentire*) feel

avvez'zar|e *vt* accustom. **~si** *vr* accustom oneself. **av'vezzo** *adj* **avvezzo a** used to

avvia'mento *m* starting; (*Comm*) goodwill

avvi'a|re *vt* start. **~rsi** *vr* set out. **~to** *adj* under way; **bene ~to** thriving

avvicenda'mento *m* (*in agricoltura*) rotation; (*nel lavoro*) replacement

avvicen'darsi *vr* alternate

avvici'namento *m* approach

avvici'nar|e *vt* bring near; approach (*persona*). **~si** *vr* approach; **~si a** a approach

avvi'lente *adj* demoralizing; (*umiliante*) humiliating

avvili'mento *m* despondency; (*degradazione*) degradation

avvi'li|re *vt* dishearten; (*degradare*) degrade. **~rsi** *vr* lose heart; (*degradarsi*) degrade oneself. **~to** *adj* disheartened; (*degradato*) degraded

avvilup'par|e *vt* envelop. **~si** *vr*

wrap oneself up; (aggrovigliarsi) get entangled

avvinaz'zato adj drunk

avvin'cente adj (libro ecc) enthralling. av'vincere vt enthral

avvinghi'ar|e vt clutch. ∼si vr cling

av'vio m start-up; dare l'∼ a qcsa get sth under way; prendere l'∼ get under way

avvi'sare vt inform; (mettere in guardia) warn

av'viso m notice; (annuncio) announcement; (avvertimento) warning; (pubblicitario) advertisement; a mio ∼ in my opinion. ∼ di garanzia (Jur) notification that one is to be the subject of a legal enquiry

avvi'stare vt catch sight of

avvi'tare vt screw in; screw down (coperchio)

avviz'zire vi wither

avvo'ca|to m lawyer; fig advocate. ∼'tura f legal profession

av'volger|e vt wrap [up]. ∼si vr wrap oneself up

avvol'gibile m roller blind

avvol'toio m vulture

aza'lea f azalea

azi'en|da f business. ∼ agricola farm. ∼ di soggiorno tourist bureau. ∼'dale agj (politica) corporate; (giornale) in-house

aziona'mento m operation

azio'nare vt operate

azio'nario adj share attrib

azi'one f action; Fin share; d'∼ (romanzo, film) action[-packed]. azio'nista mf shareholder

a'zoto m nitrogen

azzan'nare vt seize with its teeth; sink its teeth into (gamba)

azzar'd|are vt risk; (precipitoso) rash. azzardo m hazard; gioco d'azzardo game of chance

azzec'care vt hit; (indovinare) guess

azzuf'farsi vr come to blows

az'zur|ro adj & m blue; il principe ∼ Prince Charming. ∼'rognolo adj bluish

Bb

bab'beo adj foolish ● m idiot

'babbo m ① dad, daddy. B∼ Natale Father Christmas

bab'buccia f slipper

babbu'ino m baboon

ba'bordo m (Naut) port side

baby 'sitter mf inv baby-sitter; fare la ∼ babysit

ba'cato adj wormeaten

'bacca f berry

baccalà m inv dried salted cod

bac'cano m din

bac'cello m pod

bac'chetta f rod; (magica) wand; (di direttore d'orchestra) baton; (di tamburo) drumstick

ba'checa f showcase; (in ufficio) notice board. ∼ elettronica (Comput) bulletin board

bacia'mano m kiss on the hand; fare il ∼ a qcno kiss sb's hand

baci'ar|e vt kiss. ∼si vr kiss [each other]

ba'cillo m bacillus

baci'nella f basin

ba'cino m basin; (Anat) pelvis; (di porto) dock; (di minerali) field

'bacio m kiss

'baco m worm. ∼ da seta silkworm

ba'cucco adj un vecchio ∼ a senile old man

'bada f tenere qcno a ∼ keep sb at bay

ba'dante mf carer

ba'dare vi take care (a of); (*fare attenzione*) look out; **bada ai fatti tuoi!** mind your own business!

ba'dia f abbey

ba'dile m shovel

'badminton m badminton

'baffi mpl moustache sg; (*di animale*) whiskers; **mi fa un baffo** I don't give a damn; **ridere sotto i ~** laugh up one's sleeve

baf'futo adj moustached

ba'gagli mpl baggage. **~aio** m (*Rail*) baggage car; (*Auto*) boot

ba'gaglio m baggage; **un ~** a piece of baggage. **~ a mano** hand baggage

baggia'nata f **non dire baggianate** don't talk nonsense

bagli'ore m glare; (*improvviso*) flash; (*fig: di speranza*) glimmer

ba'gnante mf bather

ba'gna|re vt wet; (*inzuppare*) soak; (*immergere*) dip; (*innaffiare*) water; (*mare:*) wash; (*fiume:*) flow through. **~rsi** vr get wet; (*al mare ecc*) bathe

ba'gnato adj wet

ba'gnino, -a mf life guard

'bagno m bath; (*stanza*) bathroom; (*gabinetto*) toilet; (*in casa*) toilet; (*al mare*) bathe; **bagni** m (*stabilimento*) lido; **fare il ~** have a bath; (*nel mare ecc*) [have a] swim; **andare in ~** go to the toilet; **mettere a ~** soak. **~ turco** Turkish bath

bagnoma'ria m bain marie

bagnoschi'uma m inv bubble bath

'baia f bay

baio'netta f bayonet

'baita f mountain chalet

bala'ustra, balaus'trata f balustrade

balbet't|are vt/i stammer; (*bambino:*) babble. **~io** m stammering; babble

bal'buzi|e f stutter. **~ente** adj stuttering ● mf stutterer

Bal'can|i mpl Balkans. **b~ico** adj Balkan

balco'nata f (*Theat*) balcony

balcon'cino m **reggiseno a ~** underwired bra

bal'cone m balcony

baldac'chino m canopy; **letto a ~** four-poster bed

bal'dan|za f boldness. **~'zoso** adj bold

bal'doria f revelry; **far ~** have a riotous time

ba'lena f whale

bale'nare vi lighten; *fig* flash; **mi è balenata un'idea** I've just had an idea

bale'niera f whaler

ba'leno m **in un ~** in a flash

ba'lera f dance hall

ba'lia f **in ~ di** at the mercy of

'balla f bale; (**fam**: *frottola*) tall story

bal'labile adj good for dancing to

bal'la|re vi dance. **~ta** f ballad

balla'toio m (*nelle scale*) landing

balle'rino, -a mf dancer; (*classico*) ballet dancer; **ballerina** (*classica*) ballet dancer, ballerina

bal'letto m ballet

'ballo m dance; (*il ballare*) dancing; **sala da ~** ballroom; **essere in ~** (*lavoro, vita:*) be at stake; (*persona:*) be committed; **tirare qcno in ~** involve sb

ballonzo'lare vi skip about

ballot'taggio m second count (*of votes*)

balne'a|re adj bathing attrib. **stagione ~** swimming season. **stazione ~** seaside resort. **~zi'one** f **è vietata la ~zione** no swimming

ba'lordo adj foolish; (*stordito*) stunned; **tempo ~** nasty weather

'balsamo m balsam; (*per capelli*) conditioner; (*lenitivo*) remedy

'baltico *adj* Baltic. il [mar] B~ the Baltic [Sea]

ba'luardo *m* bulwark

'balza *f* crag; *(di abito)* flounce

bal'zano *adj (idea)* weird

bal'zare *vi* bounce; *(saltare)* jump; ~ in piedi leap to one's feet. **'balzo** *m* bounce; *(salto)* jump; prendere la palla al ~ seize an opportunity

bam'bagia *f* cotton wool

bambi'naio *m* childish thing to do/say

bam'bi|no, -a *mf* child; *(appena nato)* baby; avere un ~no have a baby. ~'none, -a *mf pej* big or overgrown child

bam'boccio *m* chubby child; *(sciocco)* simpleton; *(fantoccio)* rag doll

'bambo|la *f* doll. ~'lotto *m* male doll

bambù *m* bamboo

ba'nal|e *adj* banal; ~ità *f inv* banality; ~iz'zare *vt* trivialize

ba'nan|a *f* banana. ~o *m* banana-tree

'banca *f* bank. ~ [di] dati databank

banca'rella *f* stall

ban'cario, -a *adj* banking *attrib*; trasferimento ~ bank transfer ●*mf* bank employee

banca'rotta *f* bankruptcy; fare ~ go bankrupt

banchet'tare *vi* banquet. **ban'chetto** *m* banquet

banchi'ere *m* banker

ban'china *f (Naut)* quay; *(in stazione)* platform; *(di strada)* path; ~ non transitabile soft verge

ban'chisa *f* floe

'banco *m (di scuola)* desk; *(di negozio)* counter; *(di officina)* bench; *(di gioco, banca)* bank; *(di mercato)* stall; *(degli imputati)* dock; sotto ~ under the counter; medicinale da ~ over the counter medicines. ~ informazioni information desk. ~ di nebbia fog bank

'bancomat® *m inv* cashpoint, ATM; *(carta)* bank card

ban'cone *m* counter; *(in bar)* bar

banco'nota *f* banknote, bill *Am*; banco'note *pl* paper currency

'banda *f* band; *(di delinquenti)* gang. ~ d'atterraggio landing strip. ~ larga broad band. ~ rumorosa rumble strip

banderu'ola *f* weathercock; *(Naut)* pennant

bandi'e|ra *f* flag. ~'rina *f (nel calcio)* corner flag. ~'rine *pl* bunting *sg*

ban'di|re *vt* banish; *(pubblicare)* publish; *fig* dispense with *(formalità, complimenti)*. ~to *m* bandit. ~'tore *m (di aste)* auctioneer

'bando *m* proclamation; ~ di concorso job advertisement *(published in an official gazette for a job for which a competitive examination has to be taken)*

bar *m inv* bar

> **Bar** In Italy a bar is first and foremost a place where coffee is drunk, although alcoholic and soft drinks are also served. Italians tend to drink their coffee standing up at the bar, and there is usually an additional charge for sitting at a table.

'bara *f* coffin

ba'rac|ca *f* hut; *(catapecchia)* hovel; mandare avanti la ~ca keep the ship afloat. ~'cato *m* person living in a makeshift shelter. ~'chino *m (di gelati, giornali)* kiosk; *Radio* CB radio. ~'cone *m (roulotte)* circus caravan; *(in luna park)* booth. ~'copoli *f inv* shanty town

bara'onda *f* chaos

ba'rare *vi* cheat

'baratro *m* chasm

barat'tare *vt* barter. **ba'ratto** *m* barter

ba'rattolo *m* jar; *(di latta)* tin

'barba f beard; (⬜: noia) bore; farsi la ~ shave; è una ~ (noia) it's boring

barbabi'etola f beetroot. ~ da zucchero sugar-beet

bar'barico adj barbaric. **bar'barie** f barbarity. **'barbaro** adj barbarous ●m barbarian

barbecue m inv barbecue

barbi'ere m barber; (negozio) barber's

barbi'turico m barbiturate

bar'bone m (vagabondo) vagrant; (cane) poodle

bar'boso adj boring

barbu'gliare vi mumble

bar'buto adj bearded

'barca f boat. ~ a motore motorboat. ~ da pesca fishing boat. ~ a remi rowing boat. ~ di salvataggio lifeboat. ~ a vela sailing boat. ~i'olo m boatman

barcame'narsi vr manage

barcol'lare vi stagger

bar'cone m barge; (di ponte) pontoon

bar'dar|e vt harness. ~**si** vr hum dress up

ba'rel|la f stretcher. ~**li'ere** m stretcher-bearer

'Barents il mare di ~ the Barents Sea

bari'centro m centre of gravity

ba'ri|le m barrel. ~'**lotto** m fig tub of lard

ba'rista m barman ●f barmaid

ba'ritono m baritone

bar'lume m glimmer; un ~ di speranza a glimmer of hope

'barman m inv barman

'baro m cardsharper

ba'rocco adj & m baroque

ba'rometro m barometer

ba'rone m baron; i baroni fig the top brass. **baro'nessa** f baroness

'barra f bar; (lineetta) oblique; (Naut) tiller. ~ spazio (Comput) space bar. ~ strumenti (Comput) tool bar

bar'rare vt block off (strada)

barri'ca|re vt barricade. ~**ta** f barricade

barri'era f barrier; (stradale) road-block; (Geol) reef. ~ razziale colour bar

bar'ri|re vi trumpet. ~**to** m trumpeting

barzel'letta f joke; ~ sporca o spinta dirty joke

basa'mento m base

ba'sar|e vt base. ~**si** vr ~**si** su be based on; mi baso su ciò che ho visto I'm going on [the basis of] what I saw

'basco, -a mf & adj Basque ●m (copricapo) beret

'base f basis; (fondamento) foundation; (Mil) base; (Pol) rank and file; a ~ di containing; in ~ a on the basis of. ~ **dati** database

'baseball m baseball

ba'setta f sideburn

basi'lare adj basic

ba'silica f basilica

ba'silico m basil

ba'sista m grass roots politician; (di un crimine) mastermind

'basket m basketball

bas'sezza f lowness; (di statura) shortness; (viltà) vileness

bas'sista mf bassist

'basso adj low; (di statura) short; (acqua) shallow; (televisione) quiet; (vile) despicable; parlare a bassa voce speak in a low voice; la bassa Italia southern Italy ●m lower part; (Mus) bass. guardare in ~ look down

basso'fondo m (pl bassifondi) shallows pl; bassifondi pl (quartieri poveri) slums

bassorili'evo m bas-relief

bas'sotto m dachshund

ba'stardo, -a adj bastard; (di animale) mongrel ●mf bastard; (animale) mongrel

ba'stare vi be enough; (durare) last; basta! that's enough!; basta che (purché) provided that; basta così that's enough; basta così? is that enough?; (in negozio) anything else?; basta andare alla posta you only have to go to the post office

Basti'an con'trario m contrary old so-and-so

basti'one m bastion

basto'nare vt beat

baston'cino m ski pole. ~ **di pesce** fish finger, fish stick Am

ba'stone m stick; (da golf) club; (da passeggio) walking stick

ba'tosta f blow

bat'taglia f battle; (lotta) fight. ~'**are** vi battle; fig fight

bat'taglio m (di campana) clapper; (di porta) knocker

battagli'one m battalion

bat'tello m boat; (motonave) steamer

bat'tente m (di porta) wing; (di finestra) shutter; (battaglio) knocker

'batter|e vt beat; (percorrere) scour; thresh (grano); break (record) ●vi (bussare, urtare) knock; (cuore) beat; (ali ecc) flap; Tennis serve; ~**e a macchina** type; ~**e le palpebre** blink; ~**e le mani** clap [one's hands]; ~**e le ore** strike the hours. ~**si** vr fight

bat'teri mpl bacteria

batte'ria f battery; (Mus) drums pl

bat'terio m bacterium. ~'**logico** adj bacteriological

batte'rista mf drummer

bat'tesimo m baptism

battez'zare vt baptize

battiba'leno m in un ~ in a flash

batti'becco m squabble

batticu'ore m palpitation; **mi venne il** ~ I was scared

bat'tigia f water's edge

batti'mano m applause

batti'panni m inv carpetbeater

batti'stero m baptistery

batti'strada m inv outrider; (di pneumatico) tread; Sport pacesetter

battitap'peto m inv carpet sweeper

'battito m [heart]beat; (alle tempie) throbbing; (di orologio) ticking; (della pioggia) beating

bat'tuta f beat; (colpo) knock; (spiritosaggine) wisecrack; (osservazione) remark; (Mus) bar; Tennis service; (Theat) cue; (dattilografia) stroke

ba'tuffolo m flock

ba'ule m trunk

'bava f dribble; (di cane ecc) slobber; **aver la** ~ **alla bocca** foam at the mouth

bava'glino m bib

ba'vaglio m gag

'bavero m collar

ba'zar m inv bazaar

baz'zecola f trifle

bazzi'care vt/i haunt

be'arsi vr delight (di in)

beati'tudine f bliss. **be'ato** adj blissful; (Relig) blessed; **beato te!** lucky you!

beauty-'case m inv toilet bag

bebè m inv baby

bec'caccia f woodcock

bec'ca|re vt peck; fig catch. ~**rsi** vr (litigare) quarrel. ~**ta** f peck

becheggi'are vi pitch

bec'chino m grave-digger

'bec|co m beak; (di caffettiera ecc) spout. ~'**cuccio** m spout

be'fana f Epiphany; (donna brutta) old witch

Befana *La Befana*, whose name is derived from *Epifania* (Epiphany) who is an old woman who is said to visit children on 6 January, bringing presents and sweets. *Befana* is also the name for the Epiphany holiday and usually signals the end of the Christmas celebrations and the return to school.

'beffa *f* hoax; farsi beffe di qcno mock sb. bef'fardo *adj* derisory; (persona) mocking

bef'far|e *vt* mock. ∼si *vr* ∼si di make fun of

'bega *f* quarrel; è una bella ∼ it's really annoying

'beige *adj* & *m* beige

be'lare *vi* bleat. ∼to *m* bleating

'belga *adj* & *mf* Belgian

'Belgio *m* Belgium

'bella *f* (in carte, Sport) decider

bel'lezza *f* beauty; che ∼! how lovely!; chiudere/finire in ∼ end on a high note

'belli|co *adj* war *attrib*. ∼'coso *adj* warlike. ∼ge'rante *adj* & *mf* belligerent

'bello *adj* nice; (di aspetto) beautiful; (uomo) handsome; (moralmente) good; cosa fai di ∼ stasera? what are you up to tonight?; oggi fa ∼ it's a nice day; una bella cifra a lot; un bel piatto di pasta a big plate of pasta; nel bel mezzo right in the middle; un bel niente absolutely nothing; bell'e fatto over and done with; bell'amico [a] fine friend he is/you are!; questa è bella! that's a good one!; scamparla bella have a narrow escape ● *m* (bellezza) beauty; (innamorato) sweetheart; sul più ∼ at the crucial moment; il ∼ è che... the funny thing is that...

'belva *f* wild beast

be'molle *m* (Mus) flat

ben ▷BENE

benché *conj* though, although

'benda *f* bandage; (per occhi) blindfold. ben'dare *vt* bandage; blindfold (occhi)

'bene *adv* well; ben ∼ thoroughly; ∼! good!; star ∼ (di salute) be well; (vestito, stile:) suit; (finanziariamente) be well off; non sta ∼ (non è educato) it's not nice; sta/va ∼! all right!; ti sta ∼! [it] serves you right!; ti auguro ogni ∼ I wish you well; di ∼ in meglio better and better; fare ∼ (aver ragione) do the right thing; fare ∼ a (cibo:) be good for; una persona per ∼ a good person; per ∼ (fare) properly; è ben difficile it's very difficult; come tu ben sai as you well know; lo credo ∼! I can well believe it! ● *m* good; per il tuo ∼ for your own good. beni *mpl* (averi) property *sg*; un ∼ di famiglia a family heirloom

bene'detto *adj* blessed

bene'di|re *vt* bless. ∼zi'one *f* blessing

benedu'cato *adj* well-mannered

benefat'tore, -'trice *m* benefactor ● *f* benefactress

benefi'care *vt* help

benefi'cenza *f* charity

benefici'ar|e *vi* ∼e di profit by. ∼io, -a *adj* & *mf* beneficiary. bene'ficio *m* benefit. be'nefico *adj* beneficial; (di beneficenza) charitable

bene'placito *m* approval

be'nessere *m* well-being

bene'stante *adj* well-off ● *mf* well-off person

bene'stare *m* consent

be'nevolo *adj* benevolent

ben'fatto *adj* well-made

'beni *mpl* property *sg*; Fin assets; ∼ di consumo consumer goods

benia'mino *m* favourite

be'nigno *adj* kindly; (Med) benign

benin·for'mato adj well-informed

benintenzio'nato, -a adj well-meaning ● m'f well-meaning person

benin'teso adv of course

benpen'sante adj selfrighteous

benser'vito m dare il ~ a qcno fire sb

bensì conj but rather

benve'nuto adj & m welcome

ben'visto adj essere ~ go down well (da with)

benvo'lere vt farsi ~ da qcno win sb's affection; prendere qcno in ~ take a liking to sb; essere benvoluto da tutti to be well-liked by everyone

ben'zina f petrol, gas Am; far ~ get petrol. ~ **verde** unleaded petrol. benzi'naio, -a mf petrol station attendant

'bere vt drink; (assorbire) absorb; fig swallow ● m drinking; (bevande) drinks pl

berga'motto m bergamot

ber'lina f (Auto) saloon

Ber'lino m Berlin

ber'muda mpl (pantaloni) Bermuda shorts

ber'noccolo m bump; (disposizione) flair

ber'retto m beret, cap

bersagli'are vt fig bombard. ber-'saglio m target

be'stemmi·a f swear-word; (maledizione) oath; (spropositо) blasphemy. ~**are** vi swear

'besti·a f animal; (persona brutale) beast; (persona sciocca) fool; andare in ~a 🆃 blow one's top. ~**ale** agg bestial; (espressione, violenza) brutal; 🆃: (freddo, fame) terrible. ~**alità** f inv bestiality; fig nonsense. ~**ame** m livestock

'bettola f fig dive

be'tulla f birch

be'vanda f drink

bevi'tore, -'trice mf drinker

be'vut·a f drink. ~**o** pp di bere

bi'ada f fodder

bianche'ria f linen. ~ **intima** underwear

bi'anco adj white; (foglio, pagina ecc) blank ● m white; mangiare in ~ not eat rich food; in ~ e nero (film, fotografia) black and white; passare una notte in ~ have a sleepless night

bian'core m whiteness

bianco'spino m hawthorn

biasci'care vt (mangiare) eat noisily; (parlare) mumble

biasi'mare vt blame. bi'asimo m blame

'Bibbia f Bible

bibe'ron m inv [baby's] bottle

'bibita f [soft] drink

'biblico adj biblical

bibliogra'fia f bibliography

biblio'te·ca f library; (mobile) bookcase. ~**cario, -a** mf librarian

bicarbo'nato m bicarbonate

bicchi'ere m glass

bicchie'rino m 🆃 tipple

bici'cletta f bicycle; andare in ~ ride a bicycle

bico'lore adj two-coloured

bidè m inv bidet

bi'dello, -a mf janitor

bido'nata f 🆃 swindle

bi'done m bin; (🆃: truffa) swindle; fare un ~ a qcno 🆃 stand sb up

bien'nale adj biennial

bi'ennio m two-year period

bi'etola f beet

bifo'cale adj bifocal

bi'folco, -a mf fig boor

bifor'car·si vr fork. ~**azi'one** f fork. ~**uto** adj forked

biga'mia f bigamy. 'bigamo, -a adj bigamous ● m'f bigamist

bighello'nare vi loaf around. bighel'lone m loafer

bigiotte'ria f costume jewellery; (negozio) jeweller's

bigliet'taio m booking clerk; (sui treni) ticket-collector. ~e'ria f ticket-office; (Theat) box-office

bigli'et|to m ticket; (lettera breve) note; (cartoncino) card; (di banca) bank-note. ~to da visita business card. ~'tone m (🆒: soldi) big one

bignè m inv cream puff

bigo'dino m roller

bi'gotto m bigot

bi'kini m inv bikini

bi'lanci|a f scales pl; (Comm) balance; B~a (Astr) Libra. ~'are vt balance; fig weigh. ~o m budget; (Comm) balance sheet; fare il ~o balance the books; fig take stock

'bil|e f bile; fig rage

bili'ardo m billiards sg

bi'lico m equilibrium; in ~ in the balance

bi'lingue adj bilingual

bili'one m billion

bilo'cale adj two-room

'bimbo, -a mf child

bimen'sile adj fortnightly

bime'strale adj bimonthly

bi'nario m track; (piattaforma) platform

bi'nocolo m binoculars pl

bio'chimica f biochemistry

biodegra'dabile adj biodegradable

bio'etica f bioethics

bio'fisica f biophysics

biogra'fia f biography. bio'grafico adj biographical. bi'ografo, -a mf biographer

biolo'gia f biology. bio'logico adj biological; (alimento, agricoltura) organic. bi'ologo, -a mf biologist

bi'ond|a f blonde. ~o adj blond ●m fair colour; (uomo) fair-haired man

bio'sfera f biosphere

bi'ossido m ~ di carbonio carbon dioxide

bioterro'rismo m bioterrorism

biparti'tismo m two-party system

'birba f, **bir'bante** m rascal, rogue. bir'bone adj wicked

biri'chino, -a adj naughty ●mf little devil

bi'rillo m skittle

'birr|a f beer; a tutta ~a fig flat out. ~a chiara lager. ~a scura brown ale. ~e'ria f beer-house; (fabbrica) brewery

bis m inv encore

bi'saccia f haversack

bi'sbetic|a f shrew. ~o adj bad-tempered

bisbigli'are vt/i whisper. bi'sbiglio m whisper

'bisca f gambling-house

'biscia f snake

bi'scotto m biscuit

bisessu'ale adj & mf bisexual

bi'se'stile adj anno ~ leap year

bisettima'nale adj fortnightly

bi'slacco adj peculiar

bis'nonno, -a mf great-grandfather; great-grandmother

biso'gn|are vi ~a agire subito we must act at once; ~a farlo it is necessary to do it; non ~a venire you don't have to come. ~o m need; (povertà) poverty; aver ~o di need. ~oso adj needy; (povero) poor; ~oso di in need of

bi'sonte m bison

bi'stecca f steak

bisticci'are vi quarrel. bi'sticcio m quarrel; (gioco di parole) pun

bistrat'tare vt mistreat

bi'torzolo m lump

'bitter m inv (bitter) aperitif

bi'vacco m bivouac

'bivio m crossroads; (di strada) fork

bizan'tino adj Byzantine

'bizza f tantrum; fare le bizze (bambini:) play up

biz'zarro adj bizarre

biz'zeffe adv a ~ galore

blan'dire vt soothe; (allettare) flatter. 'blando adj mild

bla'sone m coat of arms

'blatta f cockroach

blin'da|re vt armour-plate. ~to adj armoured

blitz m inv blitz

bloc'car|e vt block; (isolare) cut off; (Mil) blockade; (Comm) freeze. ~si vi or (Mech) jam

blocca'sterzo m steering lock

'blocco m block; (Mil) blockade; (dei fitti) restriction; (di carta) pad; (unione) coalition; in ~ (Comm) in bulk. ~ stradale road-block

bloc-'notes m writing pad

blog'gista mf blogger

blu adj & m blue

blue-'jeans mpl jeans

bluff m inv (carte, fig) bluff

'blusa f blouse

'boa m boa [constrictor]; (sciarpa) [feather] boa • f (Naut) buoy

bo'ato m rumbling

bo'bina f spool; (di film) reel; (Electr) coil

'bocca f mouth; a ~ aperta fig dumbfounded; in ~ al lupo! 🔢 break a leg!; fare la respirazione a ~ a ~ a qcno give sb mouth to mouth resuscitation or the kiss of life

boc'caccia f grimace; far boccacce make faces

boc'caglio m nozzle

boc'cale m jug; (da birra) tankard

bocca'porto m (Naut) hatch

boc'cata f (di fumo) puff; prendere una ~ d'aria get a breath of

fresh air

boc'cetta f small bottle

boccheggi'are vi gasp

boc'chino m cigarette holder; (Mus, di pipa) mouthpiece

'bocc|ia f (palla) bowl; ~e pl (gioco) bowls sg

bocci'a|re vt (agli esami) fail; (respingere) reject; (alle bocce) hit; essere ~to fail; (ripetere) repeat a year. ~tura f failure

bocci'olo m bud

boccon'cino m morsel

boc'cone m mouthful; (piccolo pasto) snack

boc'coni adv face downwards

'boia m executioner

bol'ata f 🔢 rubbish

boicot'tare vt boycott

bo'lero m bolero

'bolgia f (caos) bedlam

'bolide m meteor; passare come un ~ shoot past [like a rocket]

Bo'livi|a f Bolivia. b~'ano, -a agg & mf Bolivian

'bolla f bubble; (pustola) blister

bol'la|re vt stamp; fig brand. ~to adj fig branded; carta ~ta paper with stamp showing payment of duty

bol'lente adj boiling [hot]

bol'let|ta f bill; essere in ~ta be hard up. ~tino m bulletin; (Comm) list

bol'lino m coupon

bol'li|re vt/i boil. ~to m boiled meat. ~tore m boiler; (per l'acqua) kettle. ~tura f boiling

'bollo m stamp

bol'lore m boil; (caldo) intense heat; fig ardour

'bomba f bomb; a prova di ~ bomb-proof

bombarda'mento m shelling; (con aerei) bombing; fig bombard- ment. ~ aereo air raid

bombar'd|are vt shell; (con aerei) bomb; fig bombard. **~i'ere** m bomber

bom'betta f bowler [hat]

'bombola f cylinder. **~ di gas** gas cylinder

bombo'lone m doughnut

bomboni'era f wedding keep-sake

bo'naccia f (Naut) calm

bonacci'one, -a mf goodnatured person • adj good-natured

bo'nario adj kindly

bo'nifica f land reclamation. **bonifi-'care** vt reclaim

bo'nifico m (Comm) discount; (banca-rio) [credit] transfer

bontà f goodness; (gentilezza) kindness

'bora f bora (cold north-east wind in the upper Adriatic)

'borchi|a f stud. **~'ato** adj studded

bor'da|re vt border. **~'tura** f border

bor'deaux adj inv maroon

bor'dello m brothel; fig bedlam; (disordine) mess

'bordo m border; (estremità) edge; **a ~** (Aeron, Naut) on board

bor'gata f hamlet

bor'ghese adj bourgeois; (abito) civilian; **in ~** in civilian dress; (poliziotto) in plain clothes

borghe'sia f middle classes pl

'borgo m village

'bori|a f conceit. **~'oso** adj conceited

bor'lotto m [fagiolo] **~** borlotto bean

boro'talco m talcum powder

bor'raccia f flask

'bors|a f bag; (borsetta) handbag; (valori) Stock Exchange. **~a dell'acqua calda** hot-water bottle. **~a frigo** cool-box. **~a della spesa** shopping bag. **~a di studio** scholarship. **~ai'olo** m pickpocket. **~el'lino** m

purse. **bor'sista** mf Fin speculator; (Sch) scholarship holder

bor'se|llo m purse; (borsetto) man's handbag. **~tta** f handbag. **~tto** m man's handbag

bo'scaglia f woodlands pl

boscai'olo m woodman; (guardaboschi) forester

'bosco m wood. **bo'scoso** adj wooded

'Bosnia f Bosnia

'bossolo m cartridge case

bo'tanic|a f botany. **~o** adj botanical • m botanist

'botta f blow; (rumore) bang; **fare a botte** come to blows. **~ e risposta** fig thrust and counter-thrust

'botte f barrel

bot'te|ga f shop; (di artigiano) workshop. **~gaio, -a** mf shopkeeper. **~ghino** m Theatr boxoffice; (del lotto) lottery-shop

bot'tiglia f bottle; **in ~a** bottled. **~e'ria** f wine shop

bot'tino m loot; (Mil) booty

'botto m bang; **di ~** all of a sudden

bot'tone m button; (Bot) bud

bo'vino adj bovine; **bovini** pl cattle

box m inv (per cavalli) loosebox; (recinto per bambini) play-pen

'boxe f boxing

'bozza f draft; (Typ) proof; (bernoc-colo) bump. **boz'zetto** m sketch

'bozzolo m cocoon

brac'care vt hunt

brac'cetto m **a ~** arm in arm

bracci'a|le m bracelet; (fascia) arm-band. **~'letto** m bracelet; (di orologio) watch-strap

bracci'ante m day labourer

bracci'ata f (nel nuoto) stroke

'bracci|o m (pl f braccia) arm; (di fiume, di braccio) arm; (di strada, di sedia) arm[rest]; (da nuoto) armband

'bracco m hound

bracconi'ere m poacher

'brac|e f embers pl; **alla ~e** chargrilled. **~i'ere** m brazier. **~i'ola** f chop

'brado adj **allo stato ~** in the wild

'brama f longing. **bra'mare** vt long for. **bramo'sia** f yearning

'branca f branch

'branchia f gill

'branco m (di cani) pack; (pej: di persone) gang

branco'lare vi grope

'branda f camp-bed

bran'dello m scrap; **a brandelli in tatters**

bran'dire vt brandish

'brano m piece; (di libro) passage

Bra'sil|e m Brazil. **b~i'ano, -a** agg & mf Brazilian

bra'vata f bragging

'bravo adj good; (abile) clever; (coraggioso) brave; **~! well done!. bra'vura** f skill

'breccia f breach; **sulla ~** fig very successful, at the top

bre'saola f dried, salted beef sliced thinly and eaten cold

bre'tella f shoulder-strap; **bretelle** pl (di calzoni) braces

'breve adj brief; **in ~** briefly; **tra ~** shortly

brevet'tare vt patent. **bre'vetto** m patent; (attestato) licence

brevità f shortness

'brezza f breeze

'bricco m jug

bric'cone m blackguard; hum rascal

'briciol|a f crumb; fig grain. **~o** m fragment

'briga f (fastidio) trouble; (lite) quarrel; **attaccar ~** pick a quarrel; **prendersi la ~ di fare qcsa** go to the trouble of doing sth

brigadi'ere m (dei carabinieri) sergeant

bri'gante m bandit; hum rogue

bri'gare vi intrigue

bri'gata f brigade; (gruppo) group

briga'tista mf (Pol) member of the Red Brigades

'briglia f rein; **a ~ sciolta** at breakneck speed

bril'lante adj brilliant; (scintillante) sparkling ●m diamond

bril'lare vi shine; (metallo:) glitter; (scintillare) sparkle

'brillo adj tipsy

'brina f hoar-frost

brin'dare vi toast; **~ a qcno** drink a toast to sb

'brindisi m inv toast

bri'tannico adj British

'brivido m shiver; (di paura ecc) shudder; (di emozione) thrill

brizzo'lato adj greying

'brocca f jug

broc'cato m brocade

'broccoli mpl broccoli sg

'brodo m broth; (per cucinare) stock. **~ ristretto** consommé

'broglio m **~ elettorale** gerrymandering

bron'chite f bronchitis

'broncio m sulk; **fare il ~** sulk

bronto'l|are vi grumble; (tuono ecc.) rumble. **~io** m grumbling; (di tuono) rumbling. **~one, -a** mf grumbler

'bronzo m bronze

bros'sura f **edizione in ~** paperback

bru'care vt (pecora:) graze

bruciacchi'are vt scorch

brucia'pelo adv **a ~** point-blank

bruci'a|re vt burn; (scottare) scald; (incendiare) set fire to ●vi burn; (scottare) scald. **~rsi** vr burn oneself. **~to** adj burnt; fig burnt-out. **~tore** m burner. **~'tura** f burn. **bruci'ore** m burning sensation

'bruco m grub

'brufolo m spot

brugh'iera f heath

bruli'c|are vi swarm

'brullo adj bare

'bruma f mist

'bruno adj brown; (occhi, capelli) dark

brusca'mente adv (di colpo) suddenly

bru'schetta f toasted bread rubbed with garlic and sprinkled with olive oil

'brusco adj sharp; (persona) brusque; (improvviso) sudden

bru'sio m buzzing

bru'tal|e adj brutal. ~ità f inv brutality. ~iz'zare vt brutalize. 'bruto adj & m brute

brut'tezza f ugliness

'brut|to adj ugly; (tempo, tipo, situazione, affare) nasty; (cattivo) bad; ~ta copia rough copy; ~to tiro dirty trick. ~'tura f ugly thing

'buca f hole; (avvallamento) hollow. ~ delle lettere (a casa) letter-box

buca'neve m inv snowdrop

bu'car|e vt make a hole in; (pungere) prick; (punch (biglietti) • vi have a puncture. ~si vr prick oneself; (con droga) shoot up

'bucato m washing

'buccia f peel, skin

bucherel'lare vt riddle

'buco m hole

bu'dello m (pl f budella) bowel

bu'dino m pudding

'bue m (pl buoi) ox; carne di ~ beef

'bufalo m buffalo

bu'fera f storm; (di neve) blizzard

buf'fetto m cuff

'buffo adj funny; (Theat) comic • m funny thing. ~'nata f (scherzo) joke. buf'fone m buffoon; fare il buffone play the fool

bu'gi|a f lie; ~a pietosa white lie. ~'ardo, -a adj lying • mf liar

bugi'gattolo m cubby-hole

'buio adj dark • m darkness; al ~ in the dark; ~ pesto pitch dark

'bulbo m bulb; (dell'occhio) eyeball

Bulga'ria f Bulgaria. 'bulgaro, -a adj & mf Bulgarian

'bullo m bully

bul'lone m bolt

'bunker m inv bunker

buona'fede f good faith

buona'notte int good night

buona'sera int good evening

buon'giorno int good morning; (di pomeriggio) good afternoon

buon'grado: di ~ adv willingly

buongu'staio, -a mf gourmet. buon'gusto m good taste

bu'ono adj good; (momento) right; dar ~ (convalidare) accept; alla buona easy-going; (cena) informal; buona notte/sera good night/evening; buon compleanno/Natale! happy birthday/merry Christmas!; buon senso common sense; di buon'ora early; una buona volta once and for all; buona parte di the best part of; tre ore buone three good hours • m good; (in film) goody; (tagliando) voucher; (titolo) bond; con le buone gently; ~ sconto money-off coupon • mf buono, -a a nulla dead loss

buontem'pone, -a mf happy-go-lucky person

buonu'more m good temper

buonu'scita f retirement bonus; (di dirigente) golden handshake

burat'tino m puppet

'burbero adj surly; (nei modi) rough

bu'rocra|te m bureaucrat. buro-'cratico adj bureaucratic. ~'zia f bureaucracy

bur'ra|sca f storm. ~'scoso adj stormy

'burro m butter

bur'rone *m* ravine
bu'scar|e *vt*, **~si** *vr* catch
bus'sare *vt* knock
'bussola *f* compass; **perdere la ~** lose one's bearings
'busta *f* envelope; *(astuccio)* case. **~ paga** pay packet. **~rella** *f* bribe. **bu'stina** *f (di tè)* tea bag; *(per medicine)* sachet
'busto *m* bust; *(indumento)* girdle
but'tar|e *vt* throw; **~e giù** *(demolire)* knock down; *(inghiottire)* gulp down; scribble down *(scritto)*; 🅣 put on *(pasta)*; *(scoraggiare)* dishearten; **~e via** throw away. **~si** *vr* throw oneself; *(saltare)* jump
butte'rato *adj* pock-marked

Cc

caba'ret *m inv* cabaret
ca'bina *f (Aeron, Naut)* cabin; *(balneare)* beach hut. **~ elettorale** polling booth. **~ di pilotaggio** cockpit. **~ telefonica** telephone box. **cabi'nato** *m* cabin cruiser
ca'cao *m* cocoa
'cacca *f* 🅣 pooh
'caccia *f* hunt; *(con fucile)* shooting; *(inseguimento)* chase; *(selvaggina)* game ● *m inv (Aeron)* fighter; *(Naut)* destroyer
cacciabombardi'ere *m* fighter-bomber
cacciagi'one *f* game
cacci'a|re *vt* hunt; *(mandar via)* chase away; *(scacciare)* drive out; *(ficcare)* shove ● *vi* go hunting. **~rsi** *vr (nascondersi)* hide; *(andare a finire)* get to; **~rsi nei guai** get into trouble; **alla ~'tora** *adj (Culin)* chasseur. **~tore, ~trice** *mf* hunter. **~tore di frodo**

poacher
caccia'vite *m inv* screwdriver
ca'chet *m inv (Med)* capsule; *(colorante)* colour rinse; *(stile)* cachet
'cachi *m inv (albero, frutta)* persimmon
'cacio *m (formaggio)* cheese
'cactus *m inv* cactus
ca'da|vere *m* corpse. **~'verico** *adj fig* deathly pale
ca'dente *adj* falling; *(casa)* crumbling
ca'denza *f* cadence; *(ritmo)* rhythm; *(Mus)* cadenza
ca'dere *vi* fall; *(capelli ecc.)* fall out; *(capitombolare)* tumble; *(vestito ecc.)* hang; **far ~** *(di mano)* drop; **~ dal sonno** feel very sleepy; **lasciar ~** drop; **~ dalle nuvole** *fig* be taken aback
ca'detto *m* cadet
ca'duta *f* fall; *(di capelli)* loss; *fig* downfall
caffè *m inv* coffee; *(locale)* café. **~ corretto** espresso coffee with a dash of liqueur. **~ lungo** weak black coffee. **~ macchiato** coffee with a dash of milk. **~ ristretto** strong espresso coffee. **~ solubile** instant coffee. **caffe'ina** *f* caffeine. **caffe l'latte** *m inv* white coffee.

> **Caffè** If you ask for a *caffè* in an Italian bar you will be served an *espresso*, a small amount of very strong coffee in a small cup. A *macchiato* is the same, but with the addition of a little frothy milk. *Cappuccino* is drunk in the morning or afternoon, never at the end of a meal. A *corretto* has a dash of spirits in it.

caffetti'era *f* coffee-pot
cafo'naggine *f* boorishness
cafo'nata *f* boorishness
ca'fone, -a *mf* boor

ca'gare vi 🔲 crap

cagio'nare vt cause

cagio'nevole adj delicate

cagli'ar|e vi, **~si** vr curdle

'cagna f bitch

ca'gnara f 🔲 din

ca'gnesco adj guardare qcno in ~ scowl at sb

'cala f creek

cala'brone m hornet

cala'maio m inkpot

cala'mari mpl squid sg

cala'mita f magnet

calamità f inv calamity

ca'lar|e vi come down; (vento:) drop; (diminuire) fall; (tramontare) set ●vt (abbassare) lower; (nei lavori a maglia) decrease ●m (di luna) waning. **~si** vr lower oneself

'calca f throng

cal'cagno m heel

cal'care[1] m limestone

cal'care[2] vt tread; (premere) press [down]; ~ **la mano** fig exaggerate; ~ **le orme di qcno** fig follow in sb's footsteps

'calce[1] f lime

'calce[2] m in ~ at the foot of the page

calce'struzzo m concrete

cal'cetto m Sport five-a-side [football]

calci'a|re vt kick. **~tore** m footballer

cal'cina f mortar

calci'naccio m (pezzo di intonaco) flake of plaster

'calcio[1] m kick; (Sport) football; (di arma da fuoco) butt; **dare un ~ a** kick. **~ d'angolo** corner [kick]

'calcio[2] m (chimica) calcium

'calco m tracing; (arte) cast

calco'la|re vt calculate; (considerare) consider. **~tore** adj calculating ●m calculator; (macchina elettronica)

computer

'calcolo m calculation; (Med) stone

cal'daia f boiler

caldar'rosta f roast chestnut

caldeggi'are vt support

'caldo adj warm; (molto caldo) hot ●m heat; **avere** ~ be warm/hot; **fa** ~ it is warm/hot

calen'dario m calendar

ca'libro m calibre; (strumento) callipers pl; **di grosso** ~ (persona) top attrib

'calice m goblet; (Relig) chalice

ca'ligine m fog; (industriale) smog

'call centre m inv call centre

calligra'fia f handwriting; (cinese) calligraphy

cal'lista mf chiropodist. **'callo** m corn; **fare il callo a** become hardened to. **cal'loso** adj callous

'calma f calm. **cal'mante** adj calming ●m sedative. **cal'mare** vt calm [down]; (lenire) soothe. **cal'marsi** vr calm down; (vento:) drop; (dolore:) die down. **'calmo** adj calm

'calo m (Comm) fall; (di volume) shrinkage; (di peso) loss

ca'lore m heat; (moderato) warmth; **in** ~ (animale) on heat. **calo'roso** adj warm

calo'ria f calorie

ca'lorico adj calorific

calo'rifero m radiator

calorosa'mente adv (cordialmente) warmly

calpe'stare vt trample [down]; fig trample on (diritti, sentimenti); **vietato** ~ **l'erba** keep off the grass

calpe'stio m (passi) footsteps

ca'lunni|a f slander. **~are** vt slander. **~oso** adj slanderous

ca'lura f heat

cal'vario m Calvary; fig trial

cal'vizie f baldness. **'calvo** adj bald

'calz|a f (da donna) stocking; (da uomo)

sock. ~a'maglia f tights pl; (per danza) leotard

cal'zante adj fig fitting

cal'za|re vt (indossare) wear; (mettersi) put on ● vi fit

calza'scarpe m inv shoehorn

calza'tura f footwear

calzaturi'ficio m shoe factory

cal'zetta f è una mezza ~ fig he's no use

calzet'tone m knee-length woollen sock. cal'zino m sock

calzo'l|aio m shoemaker. ~e'ria f (negozio) shoe shop

calzon'cini mpl shorts. ~ da bagno swimming trunks

cal'zone m folded pizza with tomato and mozzarella or ricotta

cal'zoni mpl trousers, pants Am

camale'onte m chameleon

cambi'ale f bill of exchange

cambia'mento m change. ~ climatico climate change

cambi'ar|e vt/i change; move (casa); (fare cambio di) exchange. ~si vr change. 'cambio m change; (Comm, scambio) exchange; (Mech) gear; dare il ~ a qcno relieve sb; in ~ di in exchange for

'camera f room; (mobili) [bedroom] suite; (Phot) camera; C~ (Comm, Pol) Chamber. ~ ardente funeral parlour. ~ d'aria inner tube. C~ di Commercio Chamber of Commerce. C~ dei Deputati (Pol) ~House of Commons. ~ doppia double room. ~ da letto bedroom. ~ matrimoniale double room. ~ oscura darkroom. ~ singola single room

came'rata¹ f (dormitorio) dormitory; (Mil) barrack room

came'ra|ta² mf (amico) mate; (Pol) comrade. ~'tismo m comradeship

cameri'era f maid; (di ristorante) waitress; (in albergo) chamber-maid; (di bordo) stewardess

cameri'ere m manservant; (di ristorante) waiter; (di bordo) steward

came'rino m dressing-room

'camice m overall. cami'cetta f blouse. ca'micia f shirt; uovo in ~ poached egg. camicia da notte nightdress

cami'netto m fireplace

ca'mino m chimney; (focolare) fireplace

'camion m inv truck, lorry Br

camion'cino m van

camio'netta f jeep

camio'nista mf truck driver

cam'mello m camel; (tessuto) camel-hair ● adj inv (colore) camel

cam'meo m cameo

cammi'na|re vi walk; (auto, orologio): go. ~ta f walk; fare una ~ta go for a walk. cam'mino m way; essere in ~ be on the way; mettersi in ~ set out

camo'milla f camomile; (bevanda) camomile tea

ca'morra f local mafia

ca'moscio m chamois; (pelle) suede

cam'pagna f country; (paesaggio) countryside; (Comm, Mil) campaign; in ~ in the country. ~ elettorale election campaign. ~ pubblicitaria marketing campaign. campa'gnolo, -a adj rustic ● m countryman ● f countrywoman

cam'pale adj field attrib; giornata ~ fig strenuous day

cam'pa|na f bell; (di vetro) belljar. ~'nella f (di tenda) curtain ring. ~'nello m door-bell; (cicalino) buzzer

campa'nile m belfry

campani'lismo m parochialism

campani'lista mf person with a parochial outlook

cam'panula f (Bot) campanula

cam'pare vi live; (a stento) get by

cam'pato adj ~ in aria unfounded

campeggi'a|re vi camp; (spiccare)

stand out. ~'**tore**, ~'**trice** mf camper. **cam'peggio** m camping; (terreno) campsite

cam'pestre adj rural

'**camping** m inv campsite

campio'nari|o m [set of] samples ●adj samples; **fiera** ~**a** trade fair

campio'nato m championship

campiona'tura f (di merce) range of samples

campi'on|e m champion; (Comm) sample; (esemplare) specimen. ~'**essa** f ladies' champion

'**campo** m field; (accampamento) camp. ~ **da calcio** football pitch. ~ **di concentramento** concentration camp. ~ **da golf** golf course. ~ **da tennis** tennis court. ~ **profughi** refugee camp

campo'santo m cemetery

camuf'far|e vt disguise. ~**si** vr disguise oneself

'**Cana|da** m Canada. ~'**dese** agg & mf Canadian

ca'naglia f scoundrel; (plebaglia) rabble

ca'nal|e m channel; (artificiale) canal. ~**iz'zare** vt channel (acque). ~**izza-zi'one** f channelling; (rete) pipes pl

'**canapa** f hemp

cana'rino m canary

cancel'la|re vt cross out; (con la gomma) rub out; (annullare) cancel; (Comput) delete. ~'**tura** f erasure. ~**zi'one** f cancellation; (Comput) deletion

cancelle'ria f chancellery; (articoli per scrivere) stationery

cancelli'ere m chancellor; (di tribunale) clerk

can'cello m gate

cance'ro|geno m carcinogen ●adj carcinogenic. ~'**so** adj cancerous

can'crena f gangrene

'**cancro** m cancer. **C**~ (Astr) Cancer

candeg'gi|na f bleach. ~'**are** vt

bleach. **can'deggio** m bleaching

can'de|la f candle; (Auto) spark plug. ~**li'ere** m candlestick

candi'da|rsi vr stand as a candidate. ~**to**, -**a** mf candidate. ~'**tura** f (Pol) candidacy; (per lavoro) application

'**candido** adj snow-white; (sincero) candid; (puro) pure

can'dito adj candied

can'dore m whiteness; fig innocence

'**cane** m dog; (di arma da fuoco) cock; **un tempo da cani** foul weather. ~ **da caccia** hunting dog

ca'nestro m basket

cangi'ante adj iridescent; **seta** ~ shot silk

can'guro m kangaroo

ca'nile m kennel; (di allevamento) kennels pl. ~ **municipale** dog pound

ca'nino adj & m canine

'**canna** f reed; (da zucchero) cane; (di fucile) barrel; (bastone) stick; (di bicicletta) crossbar; (asta) rod; (🇮 : hascish) joint; **povero in** ~ destitute. ~ **da pesca** fishingrod

can'nella f cinnamon

can'neto m bed of reeds

canni'bal|e m cannibal. ~'**lismo** m cannibalism

cannocchi'ale m telescope

canno'nata f cannon shot; **è una** ~ fig it's brilliant

cannon'cino m (dolce) cream horn

can'none m cannon; fig ace

can'nuccia f [drinking] straw; (di pipa) stem

ca'noa f canoe

ca'none m canon; (affitto) rent; **equo** ~ fair rents act

canoniz'za|re vt canon. ~**z'zare** canonize. ~**zzazi'one** f canonization

ca'noro adj melodious

ca'notta f (estiva) vest top

canot'taggio *m* canoeing; (*voga*) rowing

canotti'era *f* singlet

canotti'ere *m* oarsman

ca'notto *m* [rubber] dinghy

cano'vaccio *m* (*trama*) plot; (*straccio*) duster

can'tante *mf* singer

can'ta|re *vt/i* sing. **~au'tore, ~au'trice** *mf* singer-songwriter. **~icchi'are** *vt* sing softly; (*a bocca chiusa*) hum

canti'ere *m* yard; (*Naut*) shipyard; (*di edificio*) construction site. **~ navale** naval dockyard

canti'lena *f* singsong; (*ninna-nanna*) lullaby

can'tina *f* cellar; (*osteria*) wine shop

'canto[1] *m* singing; (*canzone*) song; (*Relig*) chant; (*poesia*) poem

'canto[2] *m* (*angolo*) corner; (*lato*) side; **dal ~** for my part; **d'altro ~** on the other hand

canto'nata *f* **prendere una ~** *fig* be sadly mistaken

can'tone *m* canton; (*angolo*) corner

can'tuccio *m* nook

canzo'na|re *vt* tease. **~'torio** *adj* teasing. **~'tura** *f* teasing

can'zo|ne *f* song. **~'netta** *f* 🔲 pop song. **~ni'ere** *m* songbook

---

'caos *m* chaos. **ca'otico** *adj* chaotic

C.A.P. *m* abbr (Codice di Avviamento Postale) post code, zip code *Am*

ca'pac|e *adj* able; (*esperto*) skilled; (*stadio, contenitore*) big; **~e di** (*disposto a*) capable of. **~ità** *f inv* ability; (*attitudine*) skill; (*capienza*) capacity

capaci'tarsi *vr* **~ di** (*rendersi conto*) understand; (*accorgersi*) realize

ca'panna *f* hut

capan'nello *m* **fare ~ intorno a** qcno/qcsa gather round sb/sth

capan'none *m* shed; (*Aeron*) hangar

ca'parbio *adj* obstinate

ca'parra *f* deposit

capa'tina *f* short visit; **fare una ~ in città/da** qcno pop into town/in on sb

ca'pel|lo *m* hair; **~li** *pl* (*capigliatura*) hair *sg*. **~'lone** *m* hippie. **~'luto** *adj* hairy

capez'zale *m* bolster; *fig* bedside

ca'pezzolo *m* nipple

capi'en|te *adj* capacious. **~za** *f* capacity

capiglia'tura *f* hair

ca'pire *vt* understand; **~ male** misunderstand; **si capisce!** naturally!; **sì, ho capito** yes, I see

capi'ta|le *adj* (*Jur*) capital; (*principale*) main ● *f* (*città*) capital ● *m* (*Comm*) capital. **~'lismo** *m* capitalism. **~'lista** *mf* capitalist. **~'listico** *adj* capitalist

capitane'ria *f* **~ di porto** port authorities *pl*

capi'tano *m* captain

capi'tare *vi* (*giungere per caso*) come; (*accadere*) happen

capi'tello *m* (*Archit*) capital

capito'la|re *vi* capitulate. **~zi'one** *f* capitulation

ca'pitolo *m* chapter

capi'tombolo *m* headlong fall; **fare un ~** tumble down

'capo *m* head; (*chi comanda*) boss 🔲; (*di vestiario*) item; (*Geog*) cape; (*in tribù*) chief; (*parte estrema*) top; **a ~ new** paragraph; **da ~** over again; **in ~ a**

un mese within a month; gira-mento di ~ dizziness; mal di ~ headache; ~ d'abbigliamento item of clothing. ~ d'accusa (Jur) charge. ~ di bestiame head of cattle

capo'banda m (Mus) bandmaster; (di delinquenti) ringleader

ca'poccia m (🔲: testa) nut

capocci'one, -a mf 🔲 brainbox

capo'danno m New Year's Day

capofa'miglia m head of the family

capo'fitto m a ~ headlong

capo'giro m giddiness

capola'voro m masterpiece

capo'linea m terminus

capo'lino m fare ~ peep in

capolu'ogo m main town

capo'rale m lance-corporal

capo'squadra mf Sport team captain

capo'stipite m (di famiglia) pro-genitor

capo'tavola mf head of the table

capo'treno m guard

capouf'ficio m head clerk

capo'verso m first line

capo'vol|gere vt overturn; fig re-verse. ~**gersi** vr overturn; (barca:) capsize; fig be reversed. ~**to** pp di capovolgere ● adj upside-down

'cappa f cloak; (di camino) cowl; (di cucina) hood

cap'pel|la f chapel. ~'**lano** m chaplain

cap'pello m hat. ~ a cilindro top hat

'cappero m caper

'cappio m noose

cap'pone m capon

cap'potto m [over]coat

cappuc'cino m (frate) Capuchin; (bevanda) white coffee

cap'puccio m hood; (di penna stilo-grafica) cap

'capra f goat. **ca'pretto** m kid

ca'pricci|o m whim; (bizzarria) freak; fare i capricci have tantrums. ~**oso** adj capricious; (bambino) naughty

Capri'corno m (Astr) Capricorn

capri'ola f somersault

capri'olo m roe-deer

'capro m [billy-]goat. ~ espiatorio scapegoat.

ca'prone m [billy] goat

'capsula f capsule; (di proiettile) cap; (di dente) crown

cap'tare vt (Radio, TV) pick up; catch (attenzione)

carabini'ere m carabiniere; carabi-ni'eri pl Italian police

Carabinieri The Carabinieri are a national Italian police force which is part of the army. They deal with issues of pub-lic order and serious crimes, but there is a certain amount of over-lap with the duties of the Polizia di Stato, which is not part of the army and is controlled by the Interior Ministry. Carabinieri wear a distinct-ive dark uniform with a red stripe.

---

ca'raffa f carafe

Ca'raibi mpl (zona) Caribbean sg; (isole) Caribbean Islands; il mar dei ~ the Caribbean [Sea]

cara'mella f sweet

cara'mello m caramel

ca'rato m carat

ca'ratte|re m character; (caratteri-stica) characteristic; (Typ) type; di buon ~re good-natured. ~'**ristico, -a** adj characteristic; (pittoresco) quaint ● f characteristic. ~**riz'zare** vt char-acterize

carbon'cino m charcoal

car'bone m coal

car'bonio m carbon

carbu'rante m fuel

carbura'tore m carburettor

car'cassa f carcass; fig old wreck

carce'ra|rio adj prison attrib. ~to, -a mf prisoner. ~zi'one f imprisonment. ~zione preventiva preventive detention

'carcere m prison; (punizione) imprisonment. ~i'ere, -a mf gaoler

carci'ofo m artichoke

cardi'nale adj & m cardinal

'cardine m hinge

cardio|chi'rurgo m heart surgeon. ~lo'gia f cardiology. cardi'ologo m heart specialist. ~'tonico m heart stimulant

'cardo m thistle

ca'rena f (Naut) bottom

ca'ren|te adj ~te di lacking in. ~za f lack; (scarsità) scarcity

care'stia f famine; (mancanza) dearth

ca'rezza f caress

cari'a|rsi vi decay. ~to adj decayed

'carica f office; (Electr, Mil) charge; fig drive. cari'care vt load; (Electr, Mil) charge; wind up (orologio). ~tore m (per proiettile) magazine

carica'tu|ra f caricature. ~'rale adj grotesque. ~'rista mf caricaturist

'carico adj loaded (di with); (colore) strong; (orologio) wound [up]; (batteria) charged ● m load; (di nave) cargo; (il caricare) loading; a ~ di (Comm) to be charged to; (persona) dependent on

'carie f [tooth] decay

ca'rino adj pretty; (piacevole) agreeable

ca'risma m charisma

carit|à f charity; per ~à! (come rifiuto) God forbid!. ~a'tevole adj charitable

carnagi'one f complexion

car'naio m fig shambles

car'nale adj carnal; cugino ~ first cousin

'carne f flesh; (alimento) meat; ~ di manzo/maiale/vitello beef/pork/veal

car'nefi|ce m executioner. ~'cina f slaughter

carne'va|le m carnival. ~'lesco adj carnival

car'noso adj fleshy

'caro, -a adj dear; cari saluti kind regards ● mf 🔢 darling, dear; i miei cari my nearest and dearest

ca'rogna f carcass; fig bastard

caro'sello m merry-go-round

ca'rota f carrot

caro'vana f caravan; (di veicoli) convoy

caro'vita m high cost of living

'carpa f carp

carpenti'ere m carpenter

car'pire vt seize; (con difficoltà) extort

car'poni adv on all fours

car'rabile adj suitable for vehicles; passo ~ ▷CARRAIO

car'raio adj passo ~ entrance to driveway, garage etc where parking is forbidden

carreggi'ata f roadway; doppia ~ dual carriageway, divided highway Am

carrel'lata f (TV) pan

car'rello m trolley; (di macchina da scrivere) carriage; (Aeron) undercarriage; (Cinema, TV) dolly. ~ d'atterraggio (Aeron) landing gear

car'retto m cart

carri'e|ra f career; di gran ~ra at full speed; fare ~ra get on. ~'rismo m careerism

carri'ola f wheelbarrow

'carro m cart. ~ armato tank. ~ attrezzi breakdown vehicle. ~ funebre hearse. ~ merci truck

car'rozza f carriage; (Rail) car. ~ cuccette sleeping car. ~ ristorante restaurant car

carroz'zella f (per bambini) pram;

(*per disabili*) wheelchair

carrozze'ria *f* bodywork; (*officina*) bodyshop

carro'zzina *f* pram; (*pieghevole*) push-chair, stroller *Am*

carroz'zone *m* (*di circo*) caravan

'**carta** *f* paper; (*da gioco*) card; (*statuto*) charter; (*Geog*) map. ~ d'argento ≈ senior citizens' railcard. ~ assorbente blotting-paper. ~ di credito credit card. ~ geografica map. ~ d'identità identity card. ~ igienica toilet-paper. ~ d'imbarco boarding card *or* pass. ~ da lettere writing-paper. ~ da parati wallpaper. ~ SIM SIM card. ~ stagnola silver paper; (*Culin*) aluminium foil. ~ straccia waste paper. ~ stradale road map. ~ velina tissue-paper. ~ verde (*Auto*) green card. ~ vetrata sandpaper

cartacar'bone *f* carbon paper

car'taccia *f* waste paper

carta'modello *m* pattern

cartamo'neta *f* paper money

carta'pesta *f* papier mâché

carta'straccia *f* waste paper

cartave'trare *vt* sand [down]

car'tella *f* briefcase; (*di cartone*) folder; (*di scolaro*) satchel. ~la clinica medical record. ~'lina *f* folder

cartel'lino *m* (*etichetta*) label; (*dei prezzi*) price-tag; (*di presenza*) timecard; timbrare il ~ clock in; (*all'uscita*) clock out

car'tello *m* sign; (*pubblicitario*) poster; (*stradale*) road sign; (*di protesta*) placard; (*Comm*) cartel. ~'lone *m* poster; (*Theat*) bill

carti'era *f* paper-mill

car'tina *f* map

car'toccio *m* paper bag; al ~ (*Culin*) baked in foil

carto'laio, -a *mf* stationer. ~le'ria *f* stationer's. ~libre'ria *f* stationer's and book shop

carto'lina *f* postcard. ~ postale postcard

carto'mante *mf* fortune-teller

carton'cino *m* (*materiale*) card

car'tone *m* cardboard; (*arte*) cartoon. ~ animato [animated] cartoon

car'tuccia *f* cartridge

'**casa** *f* house; (*abitazione propria*) home; (*ditta*) firm; amico di ~ family friend; andare a ~ go home; essere di ~ be like one of the family; fatto in ~ home-made; padrone di ~ (*di pensione ecc*) landlord; (*proprietario*) house owner. ~ di cura nursing home. ~ popolare council house. ~ dello studente hall of residence

ca'sacca *f* military coat; (*giacca*) jacket

ca'saccio *adv* a ~ at random

casa'linga *f* housewife. ~o *adj* domestic; (*fatto in casa*) home-made; (*amante della casa*) home-loving; (*semplice*) homely

ca'scante *adj* falling; (*floscio*) flabby

ca'sca|**re** *vi* fall [down]. ~ta *f* (*di acqua*) waterfall

ca'schetto *m* [capelli a] ~ bob

ca'scina *f* farm building

'**casco** *m* crash-helmet; (*asciugacapelli*) [hair-]drier; ~ di banane bunch of bananas

caseggi'ato *m* apartment block

ca'seificio *m* dairy

ca'sella *f* pigeon-hole. ~ postale post office box; (*Comput*) mailbox

casel'lante *m* (*per treni*) signalman

casel'lario *m* ~ giudiziario record of convictions; avere il ~ giudiziario vergine have no criminal record

ca'sello **[autostra'dale]** *m* [motorway] toll booth

case'reccio *adj* home-made

ca'serma *f* barracks *pl*; (*dei carabinieri*) [police] station

casi'nista *mf* 🔲 muddler. ca'sino *m* 🔲 (*bordello*) brothel; (*fig: confusione*) racket; (*disordine*) mess; **un casino di loads of

casinò *m inv* casino

ca'sistica *f* (*classificazione*) case records *pl*

'caso *m* chance; (*Gram, Med*), (*fatto, circostanza*) case; **a ~** at random; **~ mai** if need be; **far ~ a** pay attention to; **non far ~ a** take no account of; **per ~** by chance. **~ [giudiziario] [legal] case

caso'lare *m* farmhouse

'caspita *int* good gracious!

'cassa *f* till; cash; (*luogo di pagamento*) cash desk; (*mobile*) chest; (*istituto bancario*) bank. **~ automatica prelievi** cash dispenser, ATM. **~ da morto** coffin. **~ toracica** ribcage

cassa'forte *f* safe

cassa'panca *f* linen chest

casseru'ola *f* saucepan

cas'setta *f* case; (*per registratore*) cassette. **~ delle lettere** letterbox. **~ di sicurezza** strong-box

cas'set|to *m* drawer. **~'tone** *m* chest of drawers

cassi'ere, -a *mf* cashier; (*di supermercato*) checkout assistant; (*di banca*) teller

'casta *f* caste

ca'stagn|a *f* chestnut. **casta'gneto** *m* chestnut grove. **~o** *m* chestnut[-tree]

ca'stano *adj* chestnut

ca'stello *m* castle; (*impalcatura*) scaffold

casti'gare *vt* punish

casti'gato *adj* (*casto*) chaste

ca'stigo *m* punishment

castità *f* chastity. **'casto** *adj* chaste

ca'storo *m* beaver

ca'strare *vt* castrate

casu'al|e *adj* chance *attrib*. **~'mente** *adv* by chance

ca'supola *f* little house

cata'clisma *m fig* upheaval

cata'comba *f* catacomb

cata'fascio *m* **andare a ~** go to rack and ruin

cata'litico *adj* **marmitta catalitica** (*Auto*) catalytic converter

cataliz'za|re *vt* heighten. **~'tore** *m* (*Auto*) catalytic converter

catalo'gare *vt* catalogue. **ca'talogo** *m* catalogue

catama'rano *m* (*da diporto*) catamaran

cata'pecchia *f* hovel; ⊞ dump

catapul'tar|e *vt* eject. **~si** *vr* (*precipitarsi*) dive

catarifran'gente *m* reflector

ca'tarro *m* catarrh

ca'tasta *f* pile

ca'tasto *m* land register

ca'tastrofe *f* catastrophe. **cata-'strofico** *adj* catastrophic

cate'chismo *m* catechism

cate'go|ria *f* category. **~'gorico** *adj* categorical

ca'tena *f* chain. **~ montuosa** mountain range. **catene** *pl* **da neve** tyre-chains. **cate'naccio** *m* bolt

cate'|nella *f* (*collana*) chain. **~'nina** *f* chain

cate'ratta *f* cataract

ca'terva *f* **una ~ di** heaps of

cati'nell|a *f* basin; **piovere a ~e** bucket down

ca'tino *m* basin

ca'trame *m* tar

'cattedra *f* (*tavolo di insegnante*) desk; (*di università*) chair

catte'drale *f* cathedral

catti'veria *f* wickedness; (*azione*) wicked action

cattività *f* captivity

cat'tivo *adj* bad; (*bambino*)

naughty

cattoli'cesimo m Catholicism

cat'tolico, -a adj & mf [Roman] Catholic

cat'tura f capture. **~rare** vt capture

cauc'ciù m rubber

'causa f cause; (*Jur*) lawsuit; far **~ a** qcno sue sb. **cau'sare** vt cause

'caustico adj caustic

cauta'mente adv cautiously

cau'tela f caution

caute'lar|e vt protect. **~si** vr take precautions

cauteriz'z|are vt cauterize. **cauterizzazi'one** f cauterization

'cauto adj cautious

cauzi'one f security; (*per libertà provvisoria*) bail

'cava f quarry; *fig* mine

caval'ca|re vt ride; (*stare a cavalcioni*) sit astride. **~ta** f ride; (*corteo*) cavalcade. **~'via** m flyover

cavalci'oni: a ~ adv astride

cavali'ere m rider; (*titolo*) knight; (*accompagnatore*) escort; (*al ballo*) partner

cavalle'resco adj chivalrous. **~'ria** f chivalry; (*Mil*) cavalry. **~'rizzo, -a** m horseman •f horsewoman

caval'letta f grasshopper

caval'letto m trestle; (*di macchina fotografica*) tripod; (*di pittore*) easel

caval'lina f (*ginnastica*) horse

ca'vallo m horse; (*misura di potenza*) horsepower; (*scacchi*) knight; (*dei pantaloni*) crotch; a **~** on horseback; andare a **~** go horse-riding. **~ a dondolo** rocking-horse

caval'lone m (*ondata*) roller

caval'luccio ma'rino m sea horse

ca'var|e vt take out; (*di dosso*) take

off; **~sela** get away with it; se la **cava bene** he's doing all right

cava'tappi m inv corkscrew

ca'ver|na f cave. **~'noso** adj (*voce*) deep

'cavia f guinea-pig

cavi'ale m caviar

ca'viglia f ankle

cavil'lare vi quibble. **ca'villo** m quibble

cavità f inv cavity

'cavo adj hollow •m cavity; (*di metallo*) cable; (*Naut*) rope

cavo'lata f 🔟 rubbish

cavo'letto m **~ di Bruxelles** Brussels sprout

cavolfi'ore m cauliflower

'cavolo m cabbage; **~!** 🔟 sugar!

caz'zo int vulg fuck!

caz'zott|o m punch; prendere qcno a **~i** beat sb up

cazzu'ola f trowel

c/c abbr (*conto corrente*) c/a

CD-Rom m inv CD-Rom

ce pers pron (*a noi*) (to) us •adv there; **~ ne sono molti** there are many

'cece m chick-pea

cecità f blindness

'ceco, -a adj & mf Czech; la Repubblica Ceca the Czech Republic

'cedere vi (*arrendersi*) surrender; (*concedere*) yield; (*sprofondare*) subside •vt give up; make over (*proprietà ecc*). **ce'devole** adj (*terreno ecc*) soft; *fig* yielding. **cedi'mento** m (*di terreno*) subsidence

'cedola f coupon

'cedro m (*albero*) cedar; (*frutto*) citron

'ceffo m (*muso*) snout; (*pej: persona*) mug

cef'fone m slap

ce'lar|e vt conceal. **~si** vr hide

cele'bra|re vt celebrate. **~zi'one** f

celebration

'celebr|e *adj* famous. **~ità** *f inv* celebrity

'celere *adj* swift

ce'leste *adj* (*divino*) heavenly ● *agg* & *m* (*colore*) sky-blue

celi'bato *m* celibacy

'celibe *adj* single ● *m* bachelor

'cella *f* cell

cello'fan *m inv* cellophane; (*Culin*) cling film

'cellula *f* cell. **~ fotoelettrica** electronic eye

cellu'lare *m* (*telefono*) cellular phone ● *adj* [furgone] **~** *m* police van. [telefono] **~** *m* cellular phone

cellu'lite *f* cellulite

cellu'loide *adj* celluloid

cellu'losa *f* cellulose

'Celt|i *mpl* Celts. **~ico** *adj* Celtic

cemen'tare *vt* cement. **ce'mento** *m* cement. **cemento armato** reinforced concrete

'cena *f* dinner; (*leggera*) supper

i **Cena** *Cena* is the evening meal, traditionally a lighter meal than *pranzo*, although it too may start with a *primo* (often small pasta shapes in broth). A *cena* can also be a dinner party or a dinner at a restaurant, two of the principal ways in which Italians socialize.

ce'nacolo *m* circle

ce'nare *vi* have dinner

'cenci|o *m* rag; (*per spolverare*) duster. **~oso** *adj* in rags

'cenere *f* ash; (*di carbone ecc*) cinders

ce'netta *f* (*cena semplice*) informal dinner

'cenno *m* sign; (*col capo*) nod; (*con la mano*) wave; (*allusione*) hint; (*breve resoconto*) mention

ce'none *m* il **~ di Capodanno/ Natale** special New Year's Eve/Christmas Eve dinner

censi'mento *m* census

cen's|ore *m* censor. **~ura** *f* censorship. **~u'rare** *vt* censor

'cent *m inv* cent

centelli'nare *vt* sip

cente'n|ario, -a *adj* & *mf* centenarian ● *m* centenary. **~'nale** *adj* centennial

cen'tesimo *adj* hundredth ● *m* (*di moneta*) cent; **non avere un ~** be penniless

cen'ti|grado *adj* centigrade. **~metro** *m* centimetre

centi'naio *m* hundred

'cento *adj* & *m inv* one or a hundred; **per ~** per cent

centome'trista *mf* *Sport* one hundred metres runner

cento'mila *m* one or a hundred thousand

cen'trale *adj* central ● *f* (*di società ecc*) head office. **~ atomica** atomic power station. **~ elettrica** power station. **~ nucleare** nuclear power station. **~ telefonica** [telephone] exchange

centra'li|na *f* (*Teleph*) switchboard. **~'nista** *mf* operator

centra'lino *m* (*Teleph*) exchange; (*di albergo ecc*) switchboard

centra'li|smo *m* centralism. **~z'zare** *vt* centralize

cen'trare *vt* **~ qcsa** hit sth in the centre; (*fissare nel centro*) centre; *fig* hit on the head (*idea*)

cen'trifu|ga *f* spin-drier. **centrifuga** [asciugaverdure] shaker. **~'gare** *vt* centrifuge; (*lavatrice*) spin

'centro *m* centre. **~** [città] city centre. **~ commerciale** mall. **~ di accoglienza** reception centre. **~ sociale** community centre

ceppo | che

Centro storico The layout and much of the fabric of most Italian town and city centres derive from medieval or even Roman times, with the result that the *centro storico* is a place of narrow streets. Some (like Lucca) are surrounded by city walls. This makes life difficult for the motorist, and cars have been banned from many city centres.

'**ceppo** m (di albero) stump; (da ardere) log; (fig: gruppo) stock

'**cera** f wax; (aspetto) look. ~ **per il pavimento** floor-polish

ce'**ramica** f (arte) ceramics; (materia) pottery; (oggetto) pot

ce'**rato** adj (tela) waxed

cerbi'**atto** m fawn

'**cerca** f **andare in ~ di** look for

cercaper'**sone** m inv beeper

cer'**care** vt look for ● vi ~ **di** try to

'**cerchi|a** f circle. ~'**are** vt circle (parola). ~'**ato** adj (occhi) black-ringed. ~'**etto** m (per capelli) hairband

'**cerchio** m circle; (giocattolo) hoop. ~'**one** m alloy wheel

cere'**ale** m cereal

cere'**brale** adj cerebral

'**cereo** adj waxen

ce'**retta** f depilatory wax

ceri'**moni|a** f ceremony. ~'**ale** m ceremonial. ~'**oso** adj ceremonious

ce'**rino** m [wax] match

cerni'**era** f hinge; (di borsa) clasp. ~ **lampo** zip[-fastener], zipper Am

'**cernita** f selection

'**cero** m candle

ce'**rone** m grease-paint

ce'**rotto** m [sticking] plaster

certa'**mente** adv certainly

cer'**tezza** f certainty

certifi'**ca|re** vt certify. ~to m certificate

'**certo** adj certain; (notizia) definite; (indeterminativo) some; **sono ~ di riuscire** I am certain to succeed; **certi giorni** some days; **un ~ signor Giardini** a Mr Giardini; **una certa Anna** somebody called Anna; **certa gente** pej some people; **ho certi dolori!** I'm in such pain!. **certi** pron pl some; (alcune persone) some people ● adv of course; **sapere per ~** know for certain; **di ~** surely; **~ che sì!** of course!

cer'**vello** m brain.

'**cervo** m deer

ce'**sareo** adj (Med) Caesarean

cesel'**la|re** vt chisel. ~to adj chiselled. ce'**sello** m chisel

ce'**soie** fpl shears

ce'**spuglio** m bush. ~'**oso** adj (terreno) bushy

ces'**sa|re** vi stop, cease ● vt stop. ~te **il fuoco** ceasefire

cessi'**one** f handover

'**cesso** m 🗙 (gabinetto) bog, john Am; (fig: locale, luogo) dump

'**cesta** f [large] basket. ce'**stello** m (di lavatrice) drum

cesti'**nare** vt throw away. ce'**stino** m [small] basket; (per la carta straccia) waste-paper basket. '**cesto** m basket

'**ceto** m [social] class

'**cetra** f lyre

cetrio'**lino** m gherkin. cetri'**olo** m cucumber

cfr abbr (confronta) cf.

chat'**tare** vi (Comput) chat

che

● pron rel (persona: soggetto) who; (persona: oggetto) that, who, whom fml; (cosa, animale) that, which; **questa è la casa ~ ho comprato** this is the house [that] I've bought; **il ~ mi sorprende** which surprises me; **dal**

~ **deduco che...** from which I gather that...; **avere di ~ vivere** have enough to live on; **grazie! - non c'è di ~!** thank you! - don't mention it!; **il giorno ~ ti ho visto** ① the day I saw you

● *adj inter* which, what; (*esclamativo: con aggettivo*) how; (*con nome*) what a; ~ **macchina prendiamo, la tua o la mia?** which car are we taking, yours or mine?; ~ **bello!** how nice!; ~ **idea!** what an idea!; ~ **bella giornata!** what a lovely day!

● *pron inter* what; **a ~ pensi?** what are you thinking about?

● *conj* that; (*con comparazioni*) than; **credo ~ abbia ragione** I think [that] he is right; **era così commosso ~ non riusciva a parlare** he was so moved [that] he couldn't speak; **aspetto ~ telefoni** I'm waiting for him to phone; **è da un po' ~ non lo vedo** it's been a while since I saw him; **mi piace più Roma ~ Milano** I like Rome better than Milan; ~ **ti piaccia o no** whether you like it or not; ~ **io sappia** as far as I know

checché *indef pron* whatever
chemiotera'pia *f* chemotherapy
chero'sene *m* paraffin
cheti'chella: alla ~ *adv* silently
'cheto *adj* quiet

chi
● *rel pron* whoever; (*coloro che*) people who; **ho trovato ~ ti può aiutare** I found somebody who can help you; **c'è ~ dice che...** some people say that...; **senti ~ parla!** listen to who's talking!

● *inter pron* (*soggetto*) who; (*oggetto,

con preposizione*) who, whom *fml*; (*possessivo*) di ~ whose; ~ **sei?** who are you?; ~ **hai incontrato?** who did you meet?; **di ~ sono questi libri?** whose books are these?; **con ~ parli?** who are you talking to?; **a ~ lo dici!** tell me about it!

chi'acchie|ra *f* chat; (*pettegolezzo*) gossip. ~'**rare** *vi* chat; (*far pettegolezzi*) gossip. ~'**rato** *adj* **essere** ~**rato** (*persona*): be the subject of gossip; ~**re** *pl* chitchat; **far quattro** ~**re** have a chat. ~'**rone, -a** *adj* talkative ● *mf* chatterer

chia'ma|re *vt* call; (*far venire*) send for; **come ti chiami?** what's your name?; **mi chiamo Roberto** my name is Robert; ~**re alle armi** call up. ~**rsi** *vr* be called. ~**ta** *f* call; (*Mil*) call-up

chi'appa *f* ① cheek
chiara'mente *adv* clearly
chia'rezza *f* clarity; (*limpidezza*) clearness
chiarifi'ca|re *vt* clarify. ~'**tore** *adj* clarificatory. ~**zi'one** *f* clarification
chiari'mento *m* clarification
chia'rir|e *vt* make clear; (*spiegare*) clear up. ~**si** *vr* become clear
chi'aro *adj* clear; (*luminoso*) bright; (*colore*) light. **chia'rore** *m* glimmer
chiaroveg'gente *adj* clear-sighted ● *mf* clairvoyant
chi'as|so *m* din. ~'**soso** *adj* rowdy
chi'av|e *f* key; **chiudere a ~e** lock. ~**e inglese** spanner. ~**i'stello** *m* latch
chiaz'za *f* stain. ~'**zare** *vt* stain
chic *adj* *inv* chic
chicches'sia *pron* anybody
'chicco *m* grain; (*di caffè*) bean; (*d'uva*) grape
chi'eder|e *vt* ask; (*per avere*) ask for; (*esigere*) demand. ~**si** *vr* wonder
chi'esa *f* church

chi'esto pp di chiedere

'**chiglia** f keel

'**chilo** m kilo

chilo'grammo m kilogram[me]

chilome'traggio m (Auto) mileage

chilo'metrico adj in kilometres

chi'lometro m kilometre

chi'mera f fig illusion

'**chimic|a** f chemistry. ~o, -a adj chemical ● mf chemist

'**china** f (declivio) slope; inchiostro di ~ Indian ink

chi'nar|e vt lower. ~si vr stoop

chincaglie'rie fpl knick-knacks

chinesitera'pia f physiotherapy

chi'nino m quinine

'**chino** adj bent

chi'notto m sparkling soft drink

chi'occia f sitting hen

chi'occiola f snail; (Comput) at sign; scala a ~ spiral staircase

chi'odo m nail; (idea fissa) obsession. ~ di garofano clove

chi'oma f head of hair; (fogliame) foliage

chi'osco m kiosk

chi'ostro m cloister

chiro'man|te mf palmist. ~'zia f palmistry

chirur'gia f surgery. chi'rurgico adj surgical. chi'rurgo m surgeon

chissà adv who knows; ~ quando arriverà I wonder when he will arrive

chi'tar|ra f guitar. ~'rista mf guitarist

chi'uder|e vt close; (con la chiave) lock; turn off (luce, acqua); (per sempre) close down (negozio ecc); (recingere) enclose ● vi shut, close. ~si vr shut; (tempo:) cloud over; (ferita:) heal up.

chi'unque pron anyone, anybody ● rel pron whoever

chi'usa f enclosure; (di canale) lock;

(conclusione) close

chi'uso pp di chiudere ● adj shut; (tempo) overcast; (persona) reserved. ~sura f closing; (sistema) lock; (allacciatura) fastener. ~sura lampo zip, zipper Am

ci

● pron (personale) us; (riflessivo) ourselves; (reciproco) each other; (a ciò, di ciò ecc) about it; non ci disturbare don't disturb us; aspettateci wait for us; ci ha detto tutto he told us everything; ce lo manderanno they'll send it to us; ci consideriamo... we consider ourselves...; ci laviamo le mani we wash our hands; ci odiamo we hate each other; non ci penso mai I never think about it; pensaci! think about it!

● adv (qui) here; (lì) there; (moto per luogo) through it; ci siamo we are here; ci siete? are you there?; ci siamo passati tutti we all went through it; c'è there is; ce ne sono molti there are many; ci vuole pazienza it takes patience; non ci vedo/sento I can't see/hear

cia'bat|ta f slipper. ~'tare vi shuffle

ciabat'tino m cobbler

ci'alda f wafer

cial'trone m scoundrel

ciam'bella f (Culin) ring-shaped cake; (salvagente) lifebelt; (gonfiabile) rubber ring

cianci'are vi gossip

cia'notico adj (colorito) puce

ci'ao int 🔵 (all'arrivo) hello!, hi!; (alla partenza) bye-bye!

ciar'la|re vi chat. ~'tano m charlatan

cias'cuno adj each ● pron everyone,

everybody; (*distributivo*) each [one]; per ~ each

ci'bar|e *vt* feed. ~ie *fpl* provisions ~ **si** *vr* eat; ~si di live on

ciber'netico *adj* cybernetic

'cibo *m* food

ci'cala *f* cicada

cica'lino *m* buzzer

cica'tri|ce *f* scar. ~z'ante *m* ointment

cicatriz'zarsi *vr* heal [up]. **cicatriz-zazi'one** *f* healing

'cicca *f* cigarette end; (Ⅱ: *sigaretta*) fag; (Ⅱ: *gomma*) [chewing] gum

cic'chetto *m* Ⅱ (*bicchierino*) nip; (*rimprovero*) telling-off

'ciccia *f* fat, flab

cice'rone *m* guide

cicla'mino *m* cyclamen

ci'clis|mo *m* cycling. ~ta *mf* cyclist

'ciclo *m* cycle; (*di malattia*) course

ciclomo'tore *m* moped

ci'clone *m* cyclone

ci'cogna *f* stork

ci'coria *f* chicory

ci'eco, -a *adj* blind ●*m* blind man ●*f* blind woman

ci'elo *m* sky; (*Relig*) heaven; santo ~! good heavens!

'cifra *f* figure; (*somma*) sum; (*monogramma*) monogram; (*codice*) code

ci'fra|re *vt* embroider with a monogram; (*codificare*) code. ~to *adj* monogrammed; coded

'ciglio *m* (*bordo*) edge; (*pl f* ciglia: *delle palpebre*) eyelash

'cigno *m* swan

cigo'l|are *vi* squeak. ~io *m* squeak

'Cile *m* Chile

ci'lecca *f* far ~ miss

ci'leno, -a *adj* & *mf* Chilean

cili'egi|a *f* cherry. ~o *m* cherry [tree]

cilin'drata *f* cubic capacity; macchina di alta ~ highpowered car

ci'lindro *m* cylinder; (*cappello*) top hat

'cima *f* top; (*fig: persona*) genius; da ~ a fondo from top to bottom

ci'melio *m* relic

cimen'tar|e *vt* put to the test. ~si *vr* (*provare*) try one's hand

'cimice *f* bug; (*puntina*) drawing pin, thumbtack *Am*

cimi'niera *f* chimney; (*Naut*) funnel

cimi'tero *m* cemetery

ci'murro *m* distemper

'Cina *f* China

cin cin! *int* cheers!

cincischi'are *vi* fiddle

'cine Ⅱ cinema

cine'asta *mf* film maker

'cinema *m inv* cinema. cine'presa *f* cine-camera

ci'nese *adj* & *mf* Chinese

cine'teca *f* film collection

'cingere *vt* (*circondare*) surround

cinghia *f* strap; (*cintura*) belt

cinghi'ale *m* wild boar; pelle di ~ pigskin

cinguet't|are *vi* twitter. ~io *m* twittering

'cinico *adj* cynical

ci'niglia *f* (*tessuto*) chenille

ci'nismo *m* cynicism

ci'nofilo *adj* dog-loving

cin'quanta *adj* & *m* fifty. cinquan-'tenne *adj* & *mf* fifty-year-old. cin-quan'tesimo *adj* fiftieth. cinquan-'tina *f* una cinquantina di about fifty

'cinque *adj* & *m* five

cinquecen'tesco *adj* sixteenth-century

cinque'cento *adj* five hundred ●*m* il C~ the sixteenth century

cinque'mila *adj* & *m* five thousand

'cinta *f* (*di pantaloni*) belt; muro di ~ [boundary] wall. cin'tare *vt* enclose

'cintola *f* (*di pantaloni*) belt

cin'tura f belt. ~ **di salvataggio** lifebelt. ~ **di sicurezza** (Aeron), (Auto) seat-belt

cintu'rino m ~ **dell'orologio** watch-strap

ciò pron this; that; ~ **che** what; ~ **nondimeno** nevertheless

ci'occa f lock

ciocco'la|ta f chocolate; (bevanda) [hot] chocolate. ~**tino** m chocolate. ~**to** m chocolate. ~**to al latte/fondente** milk/plain chocolate

cioè adv that is

ciondo'lare vi dangle. **ci'ondolo** m pendant

cionono'stante adv nonetheless

ci'otola f bowl

ci'ottolo m pebble

ci'polla f onion; (bulbo) bulb

ci'presso m cypress

'**cipria** f [face] powder

'**Cipro** m Cyprus. **cipri'ota** adj & mf Cypriot

'**circa** adv & prep about

'**circo** m circus

circo'la|re adj circular • f circular; (di metropolitana) circle line • vi circulate. ~**torio** m (Med) circulatory. ~**zi'one** f circulation; (traffico) traffic

'**circolo** m circle; (società) club

circon'ci|dere vt circumcise. ~**si'one** f circumcision

circon'dare vt surround. ~**io** m (amministrativo) administrative district. ~**si di** vr surround oneself with

circonfe'renza f circumference. ~ **dei fianchi** hip measurement

circonvallazi'one f ring road

circo'scritto adj limited

circoscrizi'one f area. ~ **elettorale** constituency

circo'spetto adj wary

circospezi'one f con ~ warily

circo'stante adj surrounding

circo'stanza f circumstance; (occa-** **

sione) occasion

circu'ire vt (ingannare) trick

cir'cuito m circuit

circumnavi'ga|re vt circumnavigate. ~**zi'one** f circumnavigation

ci'sterna f cistern; (serbatoio) tank

'**cisti** f inv cyst

ci'ta|re vt quote; (come esempio) cite; (Jur) summons. ~**zi'one** f quotation; (Jur) summons sg

cito'fonare vt buzz. **ci'tofono** m entry phone; (in ufficio, su aereo ecc) intercom

ci'trullo, -a mf 🔢 dimwit

città f inv town; (grande) city

citta'della f citadel

citta|di'nanza f citizenship; (popolazione) citizens pl. ~**'dino, -a** mf citizen; (abitante di città) city dweller

ciucci'are vt 🔢 suck. **ci'uccio** m 🔢 dummy

ci'uffo m tuft

ci'urma f (Naut) crew

ci'vet|ta f owl; (fig: donna) flirt; [auto] ~**ta** unmarked police car. ~**'tare** vi flirt. ~**te'ria** f coquettishness

'**civico** adj civic

ci'vil|e adj civil. ~**iz'zare** vt civilize. ~**iz'zato** adj (paese) civilized. ~**izzazi'one** f civilization. ~**'mente** adv civilly

civiltà f inv civilization; (cortesia) civility

'**clacson** m inv (car) horn

clacso'nare vi hoot; honk

cla'mo|re m clamour; **fare** ~**re** cause a sensation. ~**rosa'mente** adv (sbagliare) sensationally. ~**'roso** adj noisy; (sbaglio) sensational

clan m inv clan; fig clique

clandestinità f secrecy

clande'stino adj secret; **movimento** ~ underground movement; **passeggero** ~ stowaway

clari'netto m clarinet

'**classe** f class. ~ **turistica** tourist class

classi'cis|mo m classicism. ~ta mf classicist

'**classico** adj classical; (tipico) classic ● m classic

clas'sifi|ca f classification; Sport results pl. ~'**care** vt classify. ~'**carsi** vr be placed. ~**ca'tore** m (cartella) folder. ~**cazi'one** f classification

clas'sista mf class-conscious person

'**clausola** f clause

claustro'fo|bia f claustrophobia. ~'**fobico** adj claustrophobic

clau'sura f (Relig) enclosed order

clavi'cembalo m harpsichord

cla'vicola f collar-bone

cle'men|te adj merciful; (tempo) mild. ~**za** f mercy

cleri'cale adj clerical. '**clero** m clergy

clic m (Comput) click; **fare ~ su** click on; **fare doppio ~ su** double-click on

clic'care vi click (su on)

cli'en|te mf client; (di negozio) customer. ~**tela** f customers pl

'**clima** m climate. **cli'matico** adj climatic; **stazione climatica** health resort

'**clinica** f clinic. **clinico** adj clinical ● m clinician

clo'na|re vt clone. ~'**zione** f cloning

'**cloro** m chlorine

clou adj inv **i momenti ~** the highlights

coabi'ta|re vi live together. ~**zi'one** f cohabitation

coagu'la|re vt, ~**rsi** vr coagulate. ~**zi'one** f coagulation

coalizi'one f coalition. ~'**zarsi** vr unite

co'atto adj (Jur) compulsory

'**cobra** m inv cobra

coca'ina f cocaine. **coca'inomane** mf cocaine addict

cocci'nella f ladybird

'**coccio** m earthenware; (frammento) fragment

cocciu'taggine f stubbornness. ~'**uto** adj stubborn

'**cocco** m coconut palm; ⚀ love; **noce di ~** coconut

cocco'drillo m crocodile

cocco'lare vt cuddle

co'cente adj (sole) burning

cock'tail m inv (ricevimento) cocktail party

co'comero m watermelon

co'cuzzolo m top; (di testa, capello) crown

'**coda** f tail; (di abito) train; (fila) queue; **fare la ~** queue [up], stand in line Am. ~ **di cavallo** (acconciatura) ponytail.

co'dardo, -a adj cowardly ● mf coward

'**codice** m code. ~ **di avviamento postale** postal code, zip code Am. ~ **a barre** bar-code. ~ **fiscale** tax code. ~ **della strada** highway code.

codifi'care vt codify

coe'ren|te adj consistent. ~**za** f consistency

coesi'one f cohesion

coe'taneo, -a adj & mf contemporary

cofa'netto m casket. '**cofano** m chest; (Auto) bonnet, hood Am

'**cogliere** vt pick; (sorprendere) catch; (afferrare) seize; (colpire) hit

co'gnato, -a mf brother-in-law; sister-in-law

cognizi'one f knowledge

co'gnome m surname

'**coi** = CON + 1

coinci'denza f coincidence; (di treno ecc) connection

coin'cidere vi coincide

coinqui'lino m flatmate

coin'vol|gere vt involve. **~gi-
'mento** m involvement. **~to** adj involved

'coito m coitus

col = CON + IL

colà adv there

cola|'brodo m inv strainer; ridotto
a un **~brodo** 🔲 full of holes.
~pasta m inv colander

co'la|re vt strain; (versare lentamente)
drip ● vi (gocciolare) drip; (perdere)
leak; **~re a picco** (Naut) sink. **~ta** f
(di metallo) casting; (di lava) flow

colazi'one f (del mattino) breakfast;
(di mezzogiorno) lunch; **prima ~**
breakfast; **far ~** have breakfast/
lunch. **~ al sacco** packed lunch

co'lei pron f the one

co'lera m cholera

coleste'rolo m cholesterol

colf f abbr (collaboratrice familiare)
home help

'colica f colic

co'lino m [tea] strainer

'colla f glue; (di farina) paste. **~ di
pesce** gelatine

collabo'ra|re vi collaborate.
~tore, **~trice** mf collaborator.
~zi'one f collaboration

col'lana f necklace; (serie) series

col'lant m inv tights pl

col'lare m collar

col'lasso m collapse

collau'dare vt test. **col'laudo**
m test

'colle m hill

col'lega mf colleague

collega'mento m connection;
(Mil) liaison; Radio link; **~ iperte-
stuale** hypertext link. **colle'gar|e** vt
connect. **~rsi** vr link up

collegi'ale mf boarder ● adj (responsabilità, decisione) collective

col'legio m (convitto) boarding-
school. **~ elettorale** constituency

'collera f anger; **andare in ~** get

angry. **col'lerico** adj irascible

col'letta f collection

collet'tività f inv community.
~tivo adj collective; (interesse) general; **biglietto ~tivo** group ticket

col'letto m collar

collezi|o'nare vt collect. **~'one** f
collection. **~o'nista** mf collector

colli'mare vi coincide

col'li|na f hill. **~'noso** adj (ter-
reno) hilly

col'lirio m eyewash

collisi'one f collision

'collo m neck; (pacco) package; **a ~
alto** high-necked. **~ del piede**
instep

colloca'mento m placing; (impiego)
employment

collo'ca|re vt place. **~rsi** vr take
one's place. **~zi'one** f placing

colloqui'ale adj (termine) colloquial. **col'loquio** m conversation;
(udienza ecc) interview; (esame) oral
[exam]

collusi'one f collusion

collut'tazi'one f scuffle

col'mare vt fill [to the brim];
bridge (divario); **~ qcno di genti-
lezze** overwhelm sb with kindness.
'colmo adj full ● top; fig height; **al
colmo della disperazione** in the
depths of despair; **questo è il
colmo!** (con indignazione) this is the
last straw!; (con stupore) I don't believe it!

co'lomb|a f dove. **~o** m pigeon

co'lonia¹ f colony; **~a** [estiva]
(per bambini) holiday camp. **~'ale** adj
colonial

co'lonia² f [acqua di] ~ [eau de]
Cologne

co'lonico adj (terreno, casa) farm

coloniz'za|re vt colonize. **~tore**,
~trice mf colonizer

co'lon|na f column. **~ sonora**
sound-track. **~ vertebrale** spine.

~'nato m colonnade

colon'nello m colonel

co'lono m tenant farmer

colo'rante m colouring

colo'rare vt colour; colour in (disegno)

co'lore m colour; a colori in colour; di ~ coloured. colo'rito adj coloured; (viso) rosy; (racconto) colourful ● m complexion

co'loro pron pl the ones

colos'sale adj colossal. co'losso m colossus

'colpa f fault; (biasimo) blame; (colpevolezza) guilt; (peccato) sin; dare la ~ a blame; essere in ~ be at fault; per ~ di because of me. col'pevole adj guilty ● mf culprit

col'pire vt hit, strike

'colpo m blow; (di arma da fuoco) shot; (urto) knock; (emozione) shock; (Med, Sport) stroke; (furto) raid; di ~ suddenly; far ~ make a strong impression; far venire un ~ a qcno fig give sb a fright; perdere colpi (motore:) keep missing; a ~ d'occhio at a glance; a ~ sicuro for certain. ~ d'aria chill. ~ di sole sunstroke; colpi di sole (su capelli) highlights. ~ di stato coup [d'état]. ~ di telefono ring; dare un ~ di telefono a qn give sb a ring. ~ di testa [sudden] impulse. ~ di vento gust of wind

col'poso adj omicidio ~ manslaughter

coltel'lata f stab. col'tello m knife

colti'va|re vt cultivate. ~'tore, ~'trice mf farmer. ~zi'one f farming; (di piante) growing

'colto pp di cogliere ● adj cultured

'coltre f blanket

col'tura f cultivation

co'lui pron inv m the one

'coma m coma; in ~ in a coma

comanda'mento m

commandment

coman'dante m commander; (Aeron, Naut) captain

coman'dare vt command; (Mech) control ● vi be in charge. co'mando m command; (di macchina) control

co'mare f godmother

combaci'are vi fit together; (testimonianze:) concur

combat'tente adj fighting ● m combatant. ex ~ ex-serviceman

com'bat|tere vt/i fight. ~ti'mento m fight; (Mil) battle; fuori ~timento (pugilato) knocked out. ~'tuto adj (gara) hard fought

combi'na|re vt/i arrange; (mettere insieme) combine; (🇮🇹: fare) do; cosa stai ~ndo? what are you doing? ~rsi vr combine; (mettersi d'accordo) come to an agreement. ~zi'one f combination; (caso) coincidence; per ~zione by chance

com'briccola f gang

combu'sti|bile adj combustible ● m fuel. ~one f combustion

com'butta f gang; in ~ in league

'come
● adv like; (in qualità di) as; (interrogativo, esclamativo) how; questo vestito è ~ il tuo this dress is like yours; ~ stai? how are you?; ~ va? how are things?; ~ mai? how come?; ~? what?; non sa ~ fare he doesn't know what to do; ~ sta bene! how well he looks!; ~ no! that will be right!; ~ tu sai as you know; fa ~ vuoi do as you like; ~ se as if
● conj (non appena) as soon as

co'meta f comet

'comico, -a adj comic ● m funny side ● mf (attore) comedian ● f (a torte in faccia) slapstick sketch

co'mignolo m chimney-pot

cominci'are vt/i begin, start; a ~ da oggi from today.

comi'tato m committee

comi'tiva f party, group

co'mizio m meeting

com'mando m inv commando

com'medi|a f comedy; (opera teatrale) play; fig sham. ~a musicale musical. ~'ante mf comedian; fig pej phoney. ~'ografo, -a mf playwright

commemora're vt commemorate. ~zi'one f commemoration

commen'sale mf fellow diner

commen't|are vt comment on; (annotare) annotate. ~'ario m commentary. ~a'tore, ~a'trice mf commentator. com'mento m comment

commerci'a|le adj commercial; (relazioni, trattative) trade; (attività) business. centro ~le shopping centre. ~'lista mf business consultant; (contabile) accountant. ~liz'zare vt market. ~lizzazi'one f marketing

commerci'ante mf trader; (negoziante) shopkeeper. ~ all'ingrosso wholesaler

commerci'are vi ~ in deal in

com'mercio m commerce; (internazionale) trade; (affari) business; in ~ (prodotto) on sale. ~ equo e solidale fair trade. ~ all'ingrosso wholesale trade. ~ al minuto retail trade

com'messo, -a pp di commettere ● mf shop assistant. ~ viaggiatore commercial traveller ● f (ordine) order

comme'stibile adj edible. commestibili mpl groceries

com'mettere vt commit; make (sbaglio)

commi'ato m leave; prendere ~ da take leave of

commise'rar|e vt commiserate with. ~si vr feel sorry for oneself

commissari'ato m (di polizia) police station

commis's|ario m [police] superin-

tendent; (membro di commissione) commissioner; Sport steward; (Comm) commission agent. ~'ario d'esame examiner. ~'one f (incarico) errand; (comitato ecc) commission; (Comm: di merce) order; ~ioni pl (acquisti) fare ~ioni go shopping. ~ione d'esame board of examiners. C~ione Europea European Commission

commit'tente mf purchaser

com'mo|sso pp di commuovere ● adj moved. ~'vente adj moving

commozi'one f emotion. ~ cerebrale concussion

commu'over|e vt touch, move. ~si vr be touched

commu'tare vt change; (Jur) commute

comò m inv chest of drawers

comoda'mente adv comfortably

como'dino m bedside table

comodità f inv comfort; (convenienza) convenience

'comodo adj comfortable; (conveniente) convenient; (spazioso) roomy; (facile) easy; stia ~! don't get up!; far ~ be useful ● m comfort; fare il proprio ~ do as one pleases

compae'sano, -a mf fellow countryman

com'pagine f (squadra) team

compa'gnia f company; (gruppo) party; fare ~ a qcno keep sb company; essere di ~ be sociable. ~ aerea airline

com'pagno, -a mf companion; (Comm, Sport, in coppia) partner; (Pol) comrade. ~ di scuola schoolmate

compa'rabile adj comparable

compa'ra|re vt compare. ~'tivo adj & m comparative. ~zi'one f comparison

com'pare m (padrino) godfather; (testimone di matrimonio) witness

compa'rire vi appear; (spiccare) stand out; ~ in giudizio appear in court

com'parso, -a *pp di* comparire • *f* appearance; *Cinema* extra

compartecipazi'one *f* sharing; (*quota*) share

comparti'mento *m* compartment; (*amministrativo*) department

compas'sato *adj* calm and collected

compassi'o|ne *f* compassion; aver ∼ne per feel pity for; far ∼ne arouse pity. ∼'nevole *adj* compassionate

com'passo *m* [pair of] compasses *pl*

compa'tibil|e *adj* (*conciliabile*) compatible; (*scusabile*) excusable. ∼ità *f* compatibility. ∼'mente *adv* ∼mente con i miei impegni if my commitments allow

compa'tire *vt* pity; (*scusare*) make allowances for

compat'tezza *f* (*di materia*) compactness. com'patto *adj* compact; (*denso*) dense; (*solido*) solid; *fig* united

compene'trare *vt* pervade

compen'sar|e *vt* compensate; (*supplire*) make up for. ∼si *vr* balance each other out

compen'sato *m* (*legno*) plywood

compensazi'one *f* compensation

com'penso *m* compensation; (*retribuzione*) remuneration; in ∼ (*in cambio*) in return; (*d'altra parte*) on the other hand; (*invece*) instead

'comper|a *f* purchase; far ∼e do some shopping

compe'rare *vt* buy

compe'ten|te *adj* competent. ∼za *f* competence; (*responsabilità*) responsibility

com'petere *vi* compete; ∼ a (*compito*) be the responsibility of

competi|tività *f* competitiveness. ∼'tivo *adj* (*prezzo, carattere*) competitive. ∼'tore, ∼'trice *mf* competitor. ∼zi'one *f* competition

compia'cen|te *adj* obliging. ∼za *f* obligingness

compia'c|ere *vt/i* please. ∼ersi *vr* (*congratularsi*) congratulate. ∼ersi di (*degnarsi*) condescend. ∼i'mento *m* satisfaction; *pej* smugness. ∼i'uto *adj* satisfied; (*aria, sorriso*) smug

compi'an|gere *vt* pity; (*per lutto ecc*) sympathize with. ∼to *adj* lamented • *m* grief

'compier|e *vt* (*concludere*) complete; commit (*delitto*); ∼e gli anni have one's birthday. ∼si *vr* end; (*avverarsi*) come true

compi'la|re *vt* compile; fill in (*modulo*). ∼zi'one *f* compilation

compi'mento *m* portare a ∼ qcsa conclude sth

com'pire *vt* = COMPIERE

compi'tare *vt* spell

com'pito[1] *adj* polite

com'pito[2] *m* task; (*Sch*) homework

compi'ut|o *adj* avere 30 anni ∼i be over 30

comple'anno *m* birthday

complemen'tare *adj* complementary; (*secondario*) subsidiary

comple'mento *m* complement; (*Mil*) draft. ∼ oggetto direct object

comples|sità *f* complexity. ∼siva'mente *adv* on the whole. ∼'sivo *adj* comprehensive; (*totale*) total. com'plesso *adj* complex; (*difficile*) complicated • *m* complex; (*di cantanti ecc*) group; (*di circostanze, fattori*) combination; in ∼so on the whole

completa'mente *adv* completely

comple'tare *vt* complete

com'pleto *adj* complete; (*pieno*) full [up]; essere al ∼ (*teatro:*) be sold out; la famiglia al ∼ the whole family • *m* (*vestito*) suit; (*insieme di cose*) set

compli'ca|re *vt* complicate. ∼rsi *vr* become more complicated. ∼to *adj* complicated. ∼zi'one *f* complication; salvo ∼zioni all being well

'complic|e *mf* accomplice ● *adj* (sguardo) knowing. **~ità** *f* complicity

complimen'tar|e *vt* compliment. **~si** *vr* **~si con** congratulate

compli'menti *mpl* (ossequi) regards; (congratulazioni) congratulations; **far ~** stand on ceremony

compli'mento *m* compliment

complot'tare *vi* plot

compo'nente *adj & m* component ● *mf* member

compo'nibile *adj* (cucina) fitted; (mobili) modular

componi'mento *m* composition; (letterario) work

com'por|re *vt* compose; (ordinare) put in order; (Typ) set. **~si** *vr* **~si di** be made up of

comporta'mento *m* behaviour

compor'tar|e *vt* involve; (consentire) allow. **~si** *vr* behave

composi|'tore, -'trice *mf* composer; (Typ) compositor. **~zi'one** *f* composition

com'posta *f* stewed fruit; (concime) compost

compo'stezza *f* composure

com'posto *pp di* **comporre** ● *adj* composed; (costituito) comprising; **stai ~!** sit properly! ● *m* (Chem) compound

com'pra|re *vt* buy. **~'tore, ~'trice** *mf* buyer

compra'vendita *f* buying and selling

com'pren|dere *vt* understand; (includere) comprise. **~'sibile** *adj* understandable. **~sibil'mente** *adv* understandably. **~si'one** *f* understanding. **~'sivo** *adj* understanding; (che include) inclusive. **com'preso** *pp di* **comprendere** ● *adj* included; **tutto ~** all included; **tutto compreso (prezzo)** all-in

com'pressa *f* compress; (pastiglia) tablet

---

complice | con

compressi'one *f* compression. **com'presso** *pp di* **comprimere** ● *adj* compressed

com'primere *vt* press; (reprimere) repress

compro'me|sso *pp di* **compromettere** ● *m* compromise. **~t'tente** *adj* compromising. **~ttere** *vt* compromise

comproprietà *f* multiple ownership

compro'vare *vt* prove

compu'tare *vt* calculate

com'puter *m inv* computer. **~iz-'zare** *vt* computerize. **~iz'zato** *adj* computerized

computiste'ria *f* book-keeping. **'computo** *m* calculation

comu'nale *adj* municipal

co'mune *adj* common; (condiviso) mutual; (ordinario) ordinary ● *m* borough; (amministrativo) commune; **fuori del ~** extraordinary. **~'mente** *adv* commonly

comuni'ca|re *vt* communicate; pass on (malattia); (Relig) administer Communion to. **~rsi** *vr* receive Communion. **~'tiva** *f* communicativeness. **~'tivo** *adj* communicative. **~to** *m* communiqué. **~to stampa** press release. **~zi'one** *f* communication; (Teleph) [phone] call; **avere la ~zione** get through; **dare la ~zione a qcno** put sb through

comuni'one *f* communion; (Relig) [Holy] Communion

comu'nis|mo *m* communism. **~ta** *adj & mf* communist

comunità *f inv* community. **C~ [Economica] Europea** European [Economic] Community

co'munque *conj* however ● *adv* anyhow

con *prep* with; (mezzo) by; **~ facilità** easily; **~ mia grande gioia** to my great delight; **è gentile ~ tutti** he is kind to everyone; col treno by train; ~ questo tempo in this weather

co'nato m ~ di vomito retching

'conca f basin; (valle) dell

concate'na|re vt link together. ~zi'one f connection

'concavo adj concave

con'ceder|e vt grant; award (premio); (ammettere) admit. ~si vr allow oneself (pausa)

concentra'mento m concentration

concen'tra|re vt, ~rsi vr concentrate. ~to adj concentrated ● m ~to di pomodoro tomato pureé. ~zi'one f concentration

concepi'mento m conception

conce'pire vt conceive (bambino); (capire) understand; (figurarsi) conceive of; devise (piano ecc)

con'cernere vt concern

concer'tar|e vt (Mus) harmonize; (organizzare) arrange. ~si vr agree

concer'tista mf concert performer. **con'certo** m concert; (composizione) concerto

concessio'nario m agent

concessi'one f concession

con'cesso pp di concedere

con'cetto m concept; (opinione) opinion

concezi'one f conception; (idea) concept

con'chiglia f [sea] shell

'concia f tanning; (di tabacco) curing

conci'a|re vt tan; cure (tabacco); ~re qcno per le feste give sb a good hiding. ~rsi vr (sporcarsi) get dirty; (vestirsi male) dress badly. ~to adj (pelle, cuoio) tanned

concili'abile adj compatible

concili'a|re vt reconcile; settle (contravvenzione); (favorire) induce. ~rsi vr go together; (mettersi d'accordo) become reconciled. ~zi'one f

reconciliation; (Jur) settlement

con'cilio m (Relig) council; (riunione) assembly

conci'mare vt feed (pianta). con'cime m fertilizer; (chimico) fertilizer

concisi'one f conciseness. con'ciso adj concise

conci'tato adj excited

concitta'dino, -a mf fellow citizen

con'clu|dere vt conclude; (finire con successo) achieve. ~dersi vr come to an end. ~si'one f conclusion; in ~si'one (insomma) in short. ~si'vo adj conclusive. ~so pp di concludere

concomi'tanza f (di circostanze, fatti) combination

concor'da|nza f agreement. ~re vt agree; (Gram) make agree. ~to m agreement; (Comm, Jur) arrangement

con'corde adj in agreement; (unanime) unanimous

concor'ren|te adj concurrent; (rivale) competing ● mf (Comm, Sport) competitor; (candidato) candidate. ~za f competition. ~zi'ale adj competitive

con'cor|rere vi (contribuire) concur; (andare insieme) go together; (competere) compete. ~so pp di concorrere ● m competition; fuori ~so not in the official competition. ~so di bellezza beauty contest

concreta'mente adv specifically

concre'|tare vt (concludere) achieve. ~tiz'zare vt put into concrete form (idea, progetto)

con'creto adj concrete; in ~ in concrete terms

concussi'one f extortion

con'danna f sentence; pronunziare una ~ pass a sentence. con'dan'nare vt condemn; (Jur) sentence. condan'nato, -a mf convict

conden'sa|re vt, ~rsi vr condense. ~zi'one f condensation

condi'mento m seasoning; (salsa) dressing. **con'dire** vt flavour; dress (insalata)

condiscen'den|te adj indulgent; pej condescending. **~za** f indulgence; pej condescension

condi'videre vt share

condizio'na|le adj & m conditional • f (Jur) suspended sentence

condizio'na|re vt condition. **~to** adj conditional. **~tore** m air conditioner

condizi'one f condition; a **~** che on condition that

condogli'anze fpl condolences; fare le **~** a offer condolences to

condomini'ale adj (spese) common. **condo'minio** m joint ownership; (edificio) condominium

condo'nare vt remit. **con'dono** m remission

con'dotta f conduct, (circoscrizione di medico) district; (di gara ecc) management; (tubazione) piping

con'dotto pp di condurre • adj medico **~** district doctor • m pipe; (Anat) duct

condu'cente m driver

con'du|rre vt lead; drive (veicoli); (accompagnare) take; conduct (gas, elettricità ecc); (gestire) run. **~rsi** vr behave. **~t'tore**, **~t'trice** mf (TV) presenter; (di veicolo) driver • m (Electr) conductor. **~t'tura** f duct

confabu'lare vi have a confab

confa'cente adj suitable. **con'farsi** vr confarsi a suit

confederazi'one f confederation

confe'renz|a f (discorso) lecture; (congresso) conference. **~** a stampa news conference. **~i'ere**, **-a** mf lecturer

confe'rire vt (donare) give • vi confer

con'ferma f confirmation. **confer'mare** vt confirm

confes'sare vt, **~arsi** vr confess. **~io'nale** adj & m confessional. **~i'one** f confession. **~ore** m confessor

con'fetto m sugared almond

confet'tura f jam

confezio'na|re vt manufacture; make (abiti); package (merci). **~to** adj (vestiti) off-the-peg; (gelato) wrapped

confezi'one f manufacture; (di abiti) tailoring; (di pacchi) packaging; confezioni pl clothes. **~** regalo gift pack

confic'car|e vt thrust. **~si** vr run into

confi'd|are vi **~are** in trust • vt confide. **~arsi** vr **~arsi con** confide in. **~ente** adj confident • mf confidant

confi'denz|a f confidence; (familiarità) familiarity; prenderci delle **~e** take liberties. **~i'ale** adj confidential; (rapporto, tono) familiar

configu'ra|re vt (Comput) configure. **~zi'one** f configuration

confi'nante adj neighbouring

confi'na|re vi (relegare) confine • vi **~re con** border on. **~rsi** vr withdraw. **~to** adj confined

con'fin|e m border; (tra terreni) boundary. **~o** m political exile

con'fisca f (di proprietà) forfeiture. **~'scare** vt confiscate

con'flitt|o m conflict. **~u'ale** adj adversarial

conflu'enza f confluence; (di strade) junction

conflu'ire vi (fiumi:) flow together; (strade:) meet

con'fonder|e vt confuse; (turbare) confound; (imbarazzare) embarrass. **~si** vr (mescolarsi) mingle; (turbarsi) become confused; (sbagliarsi) be mistaken

confor'ma|re vt adapt. **~rsi** vr conform. **~zi'one** f conformity (a

with); (del terreno) composition
con'forme adj according. ~'mente adv accordingly
confor'mismo m conformity. ~sta mf conformist. ~tà f (a norma) conformity
confor'tante adj comforting
confor't|are vt comfort. ~evole adj (comodo) comfortable. con'forto m comfort
confron'tare vt compare
con'fronto m comparison; **in** ~ **a** by comparison with; **nei tuoi confronti** towards you; **senza** ~ far and away
confusio'nario adj (persona) muddle-headed. ~'one f confusion; (baccano) racket; (disordine) mess; (imbarazzo) embarrassment. con'fuso pp di confondere ● adj confused; (indistinto) indistinct; (imbarazzato) embarrassed
conge'dar|e vt dismiss; (Mil) discharge. ~si vr take one's leave
con'gedo m leave; **essere in** ~ be on leave. ~ **malattia** sick leave. ~ **maternità** maternity leave
conge'gnare vt devise; (mettere insieme) assemble. con'gegno m device
congela'mento m freezing; (Med) frost-bite
conge'la|re vt freeze. ~to adj (cibo) deep-frozen. ~'tore m freezer
congeni'ale adj congenial
con'genito adj congenital
congestio'na|re vt congest. ~to adj (traffico) congested. conge'stione f congestion
conget'tura f conjecture
congi'unger|e vt join; combine (sforzi). ~si vr join
congiunti'vite f conjunctivitis
congiun'tivo m subjunctive
congi'unto pp di congiungere ● adj joined ● m relative
congiun'tu|ra f joint; (circostanza)

juncture; (situazione) situation. ~'rale adj economic
congiunzi'one f conjunction
congi'u|ra f conspiracy. ~'rare vi conspire
conglome'rato m conglomerate; fig conglomeration; (da costruzione) concrete
congratu'la|rsi vr ~rsi con qcno per congratulate sb on. ~zi'oni fpl congratulations
con'grega f band
congre'ga|re vt, ~rsi vr congregate. ~zi'one f congregation
con'gresso m congress
'congruo adj proper; (giusto) fair
conguagli'are vt balance. congu'aglio m balance
coni'are vt coin
'conico adj conical
co'nifera f conifer
co'niglio m rabbit
coniu'gale adj marital; (vita) married
coniu'ga|re vt conjugate. ~rsi vr get married. ~zi'one f conjugation
'coniuge mf spouse
connessi'one f connection. con'nesso pp di connettere
con'netter|e vt connect ● vi think rationally. ~rsi vr go online
conni'vente adj conniving
conno'ta|re vt connote. ~to m distinguishing feature; ~ti pl description
con'nubio m fig union
'cono m cone
cono'scen|te mf acquaintance. ~za f knowledge; (persona) acquaintance; (sensi) consciousness; **perdere** ~za lose consciousness; **riprendere** ~za regain consciousness
co'nosc|ere vt know; (essere a conoscenza di) be acquainted with; (fare la conoscenza di) meet. ~i'tore, ~i'trice mf connoisseur. ~i'uto pp di cono-

scere ● *adj* well-known

con'quist|a *f* conquest. conqui'stare *vt* conquer; *fig* win

consa'cra|re *vt* consecrate; ordain (*sacerdote*); (*dedicare*) dedicate. ~rsi *vr* devote oneself

consangu'ineo, -a *mf* bloodrelation

consa'pevo|le *adj* conscious. ~'lezza *f* consciousness. ~l'mente *adv* consciously

'conscio *adj* conscious

consecu'tivo *adj* consecutive; (*seguente*) next

con'segna *f* delivery; (*merce*) consignment; (*custodia*) care; (*di prigioniero*) handover; (*Mil: ordine*) orders *pl*; (*Mil: punizione*) confinement; pagamento alla ~ cash on delivery

conse'gnare *vt* deliver; (*affidare*) give in charge; (*Mil*) confine to barracks

consegu'en|te *adj* consequent. ~za *f* consequence; di ~za (*perciò*) consequently

consegui'mento *m* achievement

consegu'ire *vt* achieve ● *vi* follow

con'senso *m* consent

consensu'ale *adj* consensus-based

consen'tire *vi* consent ● *vt* allow

con'serva *f* preserve; (*di frutta*) jam; (*di agrumi*) marmalade. ~ di pomodoro tomato sauce

conser'var|e *vt* preserve; (*mantenere*) keep. ~si *vr* keep; (*di persona*) keep well

conserva'tore, -'trice *mf* (*Pol*) conservative

conserva'torio *m* conservatory

conservazi'one *f* preservation; a lunga ~ long-life

conside'ra|re *vt* consider; (*stimare*) regard. ~to *adj* (*stimato*) esteemed. ~zi'one *f* consideration; (*osservazione, riflessione*) remark

conside'revole *adj* considerable

consigli'abile *adj* advisable

consigli'|are *vt* advise; (*raccomandare*) recommend. ~arsi *vr* ~arsi con qcno ask sb's advice. ~'ere, -a *mf* adviser; (*membro di consiglio*) councillor

con'siglio *m* advice; (*ente*) council. ~ d'amministrazione board of directors. C~ dei Ministri Cabinet

consi'sten|te *adj* substantial; (*spesso*) thick; (*fig: argomento*) valid

con'sistere *vi* ~ in consist of

consoci'ata *f* associate company

conso'lar|e¹ *vt* console; (*rallegrare*) cheer. ~si *vr* console oneself

conso'lare² *adj* consular. ~to *m* consulate

consolazi'one *f* consolation; (*gioia*) joy

'console *m* consul

consoli'dar|e *vt, ~si *vr* consolidate

conso'nante *f* consonant

con'sono *adj* consistent

con'sorte *mf* consort

con'sorzio *m* consortium

con'stare *vi* ~ di consist of; (*risultare*) appear; a quanto mi consta as far as I know; mi consta che it appears that

consta'tare *vt* ascertain. ~zi'one *f* observation

consu'e|to *adj* & *m* usual. ~tudi'nario *adj* (*diritto*) common; (*persona*) set in one's ways. ~'tudine *f* habit; (*usanza*) custom

consu'len|te *mf* consultant. ~za *f* consultancy

consul'ta|re *vt* consult. ~rsi con consult with. ~zi'one *f* consultation

consul't|ivo *adj* consultative. ~orio *m* clinic

consu'ma|re *vt* (*usare*) consume; wear out (*abito, scarpe*); consummate (*matrimonio*); commit (*delitto*). ~rsi *vr* consume; (*abito,* scarpe:) wear out; *(struggersi)* pine

consu'mato adj *(politico)* seasoned; *(scarpe, tappeto)* worn

consuma'tore, -'trice m consumer. ~zi'one f *(bibita)* drink; *(spuntino)* snack

consu'mis|mo m consumerism. ~ta mf consumerist

con'sumo m consumption; *(di abito, scarpe)* wear; *(uso)* use; generi di ~ consumer goods or items. ~ [di carburante] [fuel] consumption

consun'tivo m [bilancio] ~ final statement

conta'balle mf 🔢 storyteller

con'tabil|e adj book-keeping • mf accountant. ~ità f accounting; tenere la ~ità keep the accounts

contachi'lometri m inv mileometer, odometer Am

conta'dino, -a mf farm-worker; *(medievale)* peasant

contagi|'are vt infect. con'tagio m infection. ~'oso adj infectious

conta'gocce m inv dropper

contami'na|re vt contaminate. ~zi'one f contamination

con'tante m cash; pagare in contanti pay cash

con'tare vt/i count; *(tenere conto di)* take into account; *(proporsi)* intend

conta'scatti m inv *(Teleph)* time-unit counter

conta'tore m meter

contat'tare vt contact. con'tatto m contact

'conte m count

conteggi'are vt put on the bill • vi calculate. con'teggio m calculation. conteggio alla rovescia countdown

con'te|gno m behaviour; *(atteggiamento)* attitude. ~'gnoso adj dignified

contem'pla|re vt contemplate; *(fissare)* gaze at. ~zi'one f contemplation

con'tempo m nel ~ in the meantime

contempo|ranea'mente adv at once. ~'raneo, -a adj & mf contemporary

conten'dente mf competitor. con-'tendere vi compete; *(litigare)* quarrel • vt contend

conte'n|ere vt contain; *(reprimere)* repress. ~ersi vr contain oneself. ~i'tore m container

conten'tarsi vr ~ di be content with

conten'tezza f joy

conten'tino m placebo

con'tento adj glad; *(soddisfatto)* contented

conte'nuto m contents pl; *(soggetto)* content

contenzi'oso m legal department

con'tes|a f disagreement; *Sport* contest. ~o pp di contendere • adj contested

con'tessa f countess

conte'sta|re vt contest; *(Jur)* notify. ~'tario adj anti-establishment. ~'tore, ~'trice mf protester. ~zi'one f *(disputa)* dispute

con'testo m context

con'tiguo adj adjacent

continen'tale adj continental. conti'nente m continent

conti'nenza f continence

contin'gen|te m contingent; *(quota)* quota. ~za f contingency

continua'mente adv *(senza interruzione)* continuously; *(frequentemente)* continually

continu|'are vt/i continue; *(riprendere)* resume. ~a'tivo adj permanent. ~azi'one f continuation. ~ità f continuity

con'tinuo adj continuous; *(molto frequente)* continual. corrente ~a direct current; di ~o continually

'conto m calculation; *(Comm)* account; (*di ristorante ecc*) bill; (*stima*) consideration; a conti fatti all things considered; far ~ di (*supporre*) suppose; (*proporsi*) intend; far ~ su rely on; in fin dei conti when all is said and done; per ~ di on behalf of; per ~ mio (*a mio parere*) in my opinion; (*da solo*) on my own; starsene per ~ proprio be on one's own; rendersi ~ di qcsa realize sth; sul ~ di qcno (*voci, informazioni*) about sb; tener ~ di qcsa take sth into account; tenere da ~ qcsa look after sth. ~ corrente current account, checking account *Am*. ~ alla rovescia countdown

con'torcer|e *vt* twist. ~**si** *vr* twist about

contor'nare *vt* surround

con'torno *m* contour; (*Culin*) vegetables *pl*

contorsi'one *f* contortion. **con-'torto** *pp di* contorcere ● *adj* twisted

contrabban|'dare *vt* smuggle. ~**di'ere, -a** *mf* smuggler. **contrab-'bando** *m* contraband

contrab'basso *m* double bass

contraccambi'are *vt* return. **contrac'cambio** *m* return

contracce|t'tivo *m* contraceptive. ~**zi'one** *f* contraception

contrac'col|po *m* rebound; (*di arma da fuoco*) recoil; *fig* repercussion

con'trada *f* (*rione*) district

contrad'detto *pp di* contraddire

contrad'di|re *vt* contradict. ~**t'to-rio** *adj* contradictory. ~**zi'one** *f* contradiction

contraddi'stin|guere *vt* differentiate. ~**to** *adj* distinct

contra'ente *mf* contracting party

contra'ereo *adj* anti-aircraft

contraf'fa|re *vt* disguise; (*imitare*) imitate; (*falsificare*) forge. ~**tto** *adj* forged. ~**zi'one** *f* disguising; (*imitazione*) imitation; (*falsificazione*) forgery

con'tralto *m* countertenor ● *f*

contralto

contrap'peso *m* counterbalance

contrap'por|re *vt* counter; (*confrontare*) compare. ~**si** *vr* contrast; ~**si a** be opposed to

contraria'mente *adv* contrary (a to)

contrari'a|re *vt* oppose; (*infastidire*) annoy. ~**arsi** *vr* get annoyed. ~**età** *f inv* adversity; (*ostacolo*) set-back

con'trario *adj* contrary; (*direzione*) opposite; (*sfavorevole*) unfavourable ● *m* contrary; al ~ on the contrary

con'trarre *vt* contract

contras|se'gnare *vt* mark. ~**'segno** *m* mark; [in] ~**segno** (*spedizione*) cash on delivery

contra'stare *vt* oppose; (*contestare*) contest ● *vi* clash. **con'trasto** *m* contrast; (*litigio*) dispute

contrat'tacca're *vt* counterattack. **contrat'tacco** *m* counter-attack

contrat'ta|re *vt/i* negotiate; (*mercanteggiare*) bargain. ~**zi'one** *f* (*salariale*) bargaining

contrat'tempo *m* hitch

con'tratt|o *pp di* contrarre ● *m* contract. ~**o a termine** fixed-term contract. ~**u'ale** *adj* contractual

contravve'n|ire *vi* contravene. ~**zi'one** *f* (*contravvention*); (*multa*) fine

contrazi'one *f* contraction; (*di prezzi*) reduction

contribu'ente *mf* contributor; (*del fisco*) taxpayer

contribu'ire *vi* contribute. **contri-'buto** *m* contribution

'contro *prep* against; ~ di me against me ● *m* i pro e i ~ the pros and cons

contro'battere *vt* counter

controbilanci'are *vt* counterbalance

controcor'rente *adj* nonconformist ● *adv* upriver; *fig* upstream

controffen'siva *f* counteroffensive

controfi'gura f stand-in

controindicazi'one f (Med) contraindication

control'la|re vt control; (verificare) check; (collaudare) test. ~**rsi** vr have self-control. ~**to** adj controlled

con'trol|lo m control; (verifica) check; (Med) check-up. ~**lo delle nascite** birth control. ~**lore** m controller; (sui treni ecc) [ticket] inspector. ~**lore di volo** air-traffic controller

contro'mano adv in the wrong direction

contromi'sura f countermeasure

contropi'ede m **prendere in** ~ catch off guard

controprodu'cente adj self-defeating

con'trordin|e m counter order; **salvo** ~**i** unless I/you hear to the contrary

contro'senso m contradiction in terms

controspio'naggio m counterespionage

contro'vento adv against the wind

contro'vers|ia f controversy; (Jur) dispute. ~**o** adj controversial

contro'voglia adv unwillingly

contu'macia f default; **in** ~ in one's absence

contun'dente adj (corpo, arma) blunt

contur'ba|nte adj perturbing

contusi'one f bruise

convale'scen|te adj convalescent

con'vali|da f validation. ~**'dare** vt confirm; validate (atto, biglietto)

con'vegno m meeting; (congresso) congress

conve'nevol|e adj suitable; ~**i** pl pleasantries

conveni'en|te adj convenient; (prezzo) attractive; (vantaggioso) advantageous. ~**za** f convenience; (interesse) advantage; (di prezzo) attractiveness

conve'nire vi (riunirsi) gather; (concordare) agree; (ammettere) admit; (essere opportuno) be convenient ● vt agree on; **ci conviene andare** it is better to go; **non mi conviene stancarmi** I'd better not tire myself out

con'vento m (di suore) convent; (di frati) monastery

conve'nuto adj fixed

convenzi|o'nale adj conventional. ~**'one** f convention

conver'gen|te adj converging. ~**za** f fig confluence

con'vergere vi converge

conver'sa|re vi converse. ~**zi'one** f conversation

conversi'one f conversion

con'verso pp di convergere

conver'tibile f (Auto) convertible

conver'ti|re vt convert. ~**rsi** vr be converted. ~**to, -a** mf convert

con'vesso adj convex

convin'cente adj convincing

con'vin|cere vt convince. ~**to** adj convinced. ~**zi'one** f conviction

con'vitto m boarding school

convi'ven|te m common-law husband ● f common-law wife. ~**za** f cohabitation. **con'vivere** vi live together

convivi'ale adj convivial

convo'ca|re vt convene. ~**zi'one** f convening

convogli'are vt convey; convoy (navi) con'voglio m convoy; (ferroviario) train

convulsi'one f convulsion. **con-'vulso** adj convulsive; (febbrile) feverish

coope'ra|re vi co-operate. ~**'tiva** f co-operative. ~**zi'one** f co-operation

coordina'mento m co-ordination

coordi'na|re vt co-ordinate. ~ta f (Math) coordinate. ~te bancarie bank (account) details. ~zi'one f co-ordination

co'perchio m lid; (copertura) cover

co'perta f blanket; (copertura) cover; (Naut) deck

coper'tina f cover; (di libro) dust-jacket

co'perto pp di coprire ● adj covered; (cielo) overcast ● m (a tavola) place; (prezzo del coperto) cover charge; al ~ under cover

coper'tone m tarpaulin; (gomma) tyre

coper'tura f covering; (Comm, Fin) cover

copia f copy; **bella/brutta ~** fair/rough copy; **~ su carta** hardcopy. **copi'are** vt copy

copi'one m script

copi'oso adj plentiful

coppa f (calice) goblet; (per gelato ecc) dish; Sport cup. ~ **[di]** gelato ice-cream (served in a dish)

cop'petta f bowl; (di gelato) small tub

coppia f couple; (in carte) pair

co'prente adj (cipria, vernice) covering

coprifu'oco m curfew

copri'letto m bedspread

copripiu'mino m duvet cover

co'prir|e vt cover; drown (suono); hold (carica). ~si vr (vestirsi) cover up; fig cover oneself; (cielo:) become overcast

coque f alla ~ (uovo) soft-boiled

co'raggi|o m courage; (sfacciataggine) nerve; ~o! come on. ~oso adj courageous

co'rale adj choral

co'rallo m coral

Co'rano m Koran

co'raz|za f armour; (di animali) shell. ~zata f battleship. ~zato adj (nave) armour-clad

corbelle'ria f nonsense; (sproposito) blunder

corda f cord; (Mus, spago) string; (fune) rope; (cavo) cable; **essere giù di ~** be depressed; **dare ~ a qcno** encourage sb. **corde vocali** vocal cords

cordi'al|e adj cordial ● m (bevanda) cordial; **~i saluti** best wishes. ~**ità** f cordiality

'cordless m inv cordless phone

cor'doglio m grief; (lutto) mourning

cor'done m cord; (schieramento) cordon

core|ogra'fia f choreography. ~'ografo, ~'ografa mf choreographer

cori'andoli mpl confetti sg

cori'andolo m (spezia) coriander

cori'car|e vt put to bed. ~si vr go to bed

co'rista mf choir member

corna ▷CORNO

cor'nacchia f crow

corna'musa f bagpipes pl

cor'nett|a f (Mus) cornet; (del telefono) receiver. ~o m (brioche) croissant

cor'ni|ce f frame. ~ci'one m cornice

'corno m (pl f corna) horn; **fare le corna a qcno** be unfaithful to sb; **fare le corna** (per scongiuro) touch wood. **cor'nuto** adj horned ● m (I): marito tradito) cuckold; (insulto) bastard

'coro m chorus; (Relig) choir

co'rolla f corolla

co'rona f crown; (di fiori) wreath; (rosario) rosary. ~'mento m (di impresa) crowning. **coro'nare** vt crown; (sogno) fulfil

cor'petto m bodice

'corpo m body; (Mil, diplomatico) corps inv; **~ a ~** man to man; **andare**

di ∼ move one's bowels. ∼ di ballo corps de ballet. ∼ insegnante teaching staff. ∼ del reato incriminating item

corpo'rale adj corporal

corporati'vismo m corporatism

corpora'tura f build

corporazi'one f corporation

cor'poreo adj bodily

cor'poso adj full-bodied

corpu'lento adj stout

cor'puscolo m corpuscle

corre'dare vt equip

corre'dino m (per neonato) layette

cor'redo m (nuziale) trousseau

cor'reggere vt correct; lace (bevanda)

corre'lare vt correlate

cor'rente adj running; (in vigore) current; (frequente) everyday; (inglese ecc) fluent ● f current; (d'aria) draught; essere al ∼ be up to date. ∼'mente adv (parlare) fluently

'correre vi run; (affrettarsi) hurry; Sport race; (notizie:) circulate; ∼ dietro a run after ● vt run; ∼ un pericolo run a risk; lascia ∼! don't bother!

corret'tamente adv correctly. cor'retto pp di correggere ● adj correct; (caffè) with a drop of alcohol. ∼zi'one f correction

cor'rida f bullfight

corri'doio m corridor; (Aeron) aisle

corri|dore, **-'trice** mf racer; (a piedi) runner

corri'era f coach, bus

corri'ere m courier; (posta) mail; (spedizioniere) carrier

corri'mano m bannister

corrispet'tivo m amount due

corrispon'den|te adj corresponding ● mf correspondent. ∼za f correspondence; scuola/corsi per ∼za correspondence course; vendite per ∼za mail-order [shopping]. corri-

'spondere vi correspond; (stanza:) communicate; corrispondere a (contraccambiare) return

corri'sposto adj (amore) reciprocated

corrobo'rare vt strengthen; fig corroborate

cor'roder|e vt, ∼si vr corrode

cor'rompere vt corrupt; (con denaro) bribe

corrosi'one f corrosion. corro'sivo adj corrosive

cor'roso pp di corrodere

cor'rotto pp di corrompere ● adj corrupt

corrucci'a|rsi vr be vexed. ∼to adj upset

corru'gare vt wrinkle; ∼ la fronte knit one's brows

corruzi'one f corruption; (con denaro) bribery

'corsa f running; (rapida) dash; Sport race; (di treno ecc) journey; di ∼ at a run; fare una ∼ run

cor'sia f gangway; (di ospedale) ward; (Auto) lane; (di supermercato) aisle

cor'sivo m italics pl

'corso pp di correre ● m course; (strada) main street; (Comm) circulation; lavori in ∼ work in progress; nel ∼ di during. ∼ d'acqua watercourse

'corte f [court]yard; (Jur, regale) court; fare la ∼ a a qcno court sb. ∼ d'appello court of appeal

cor'teccia f bark

corteggia'mento m courtship

corteggi'a|re vt court. ∼tore m admirer

cor'teo m procession

cor'te|se adj courteous. ∼'sia f courtesy; per ∼sia please

cortigi'ano, -a mf courtier ● f courtesan

cor'tile m courtyard

cor'tina f curtain; (schermo) screen

corto *adj* short; essere a ~ di be short of. ~ **circuito** *m* short [circuit]

cortome'traggio *m* Cinema short

cor'vino *adj* jet-black

corvo *m* raven

cosa *f* thing; (*faccenda*) matter; *inter, rel* what; [che] ~ what; nessuna ~ nothing; ogni ~ everything; per prima ~ first of all; tante cose so many things; (*augurio*) all the best

cosca *f* clan

coscia *f* thigh; (*Culin*) leg

cosci'en|te *adj* conscious. ~za *f* conscience; (*consapevolezza*) consciousness

cu'scritto *m* conscript. ~zi'one *f* conscription

così *adv* so; (*in questo modo*) like this, like that; (*perciò*) therefore; le cose stanno ~ that's how things stand; ~ **fermo** ~! hold it; proprio ~! exactly!; basta ~! that will do!; ah, è ~? it's like that, is it?; ~ ~ so-so; ~ **via** and so on; per ~ **dire** so to speak; più di ~ any more; una ~ **cara ragazza!** such a nice girl!; è stato ~ **generoso** da aiutarti he was kind enough to help you ● *conj* (*allora*) so ● *adj inv* (*tale*) like that; una **ragazza** ~ a girl like that

cosicché *conj* and so

cosid'detto *adj* so-called

co'smesi *f* cosmetics

co'smetico *adj & m* cosmetic

cosmico *adj* cosmic

cosmo *m* cosmos

cosmopo'lita *adj* cosmopolitan

co'spargere *vt* sprinkle; (*disseminare*) scatter

co'spetto *m* al ~ di in the presence of

co'spicuo *adj* conspicuous; (*somma ecc*) considerable

cospi'ra|re *vi* conspire. ~**tore**, ~**trice** *mf* conspirator. ~zi'one *f* conspiracy

'**costa** *f* coast; (*Anat*) rib

costà *adv* there

co'stan|te *adj & f* constant. ~za *f* constancy

co'stare *vi* cost; quanto costa? how much is it?

co'stata *f* chop

costeggi'are *vt* (*per mare*) coast; (*per terra*) skirt

co'stei *pers pron* ▷COSTUI

costellazi'one *f* constellation

coster'na|to *adj* dismayed. ~zi'one *f* consternation

costi'er|a *f* stretch of coast. ~o *adj* coastal

costi'pa|to *adj* constipated. ~zi'one *f* constipation; (*raffreddore*) bad cold

costitu'ir|e *vt* constitute; (*formare*) form; (*nominare*) appoint. ~**si** *vr* (*Jur*) give oneself up

costituzio'nale *adj* constitutional. costituzi'one *f* constitution; (*fondazione*) setting up

'**costo** *m* cost; ad ogni ~ at all costs; a nessun ~ on no account

'**costola** *f* rib; (*di libro*) spine

costo'letta *f* cutlet

co'storo *pron* ▷COSTUI

co'stoso *adj* costly

co'stretto *pp di* costringere

co'strin|gere *vt* compel; (*stringere*) constrict. ~**t'tivo** *adj* coercive

costru'ir|e *vt* build. ~**t'tivo** *adj* constructive. ~zi'one *f* construction

co'stui, co'stei, *pl* **co'storo** *pron* (*soggetto*) he, she, *pl* they; (*complemento*) him, her, *pl* them

co'stume *m* (*usanza*) custom; (*condotta*) morals *pl*; (*indumento*) costume. ~ **da bagno** swim-suit; (*da uomo*) swimming trunks

co'tenna *f* pigskin; (*della pancetta*) rind

coto'letta *f* cutlet

co'tone m cotton. ∼ idrofilo cotton wool, absorbent cotton Am

'cottimo m lavorare a ∼ do piece-work

'cotto pp di cuocere ● adj done; (①: infatuato) in love; (①: sbronzo) drunk; ben ∼ (carne) well done

'cotton fi'oc® m inv cotton bud

cot'tura f cooking

co'vare vt hatch; sicken for (malattia); harbour (odio) ● vi smoulder

'covo m den

co'vone m sheaf

'cozza f mussel

coz'zare vi ∼ contro bump into. **'cozzo** m fig clash

C.P. abbr (Casella Postale) PO Box

'crampo m cramp

'cranio m skull

cra'tere m crater

cra'vatta f tie; (a farfalla) bow-tie

cre'anza f politeness; mala ∼ bad manners

cre'a|re vt create; (causare) cause. ∼tività f creativity. ∼'tivo adj creative. ∼to m creation. ∼'tore, ∼'trice mf creator. ∼zi'one f creation

crea'tura f creature; (bambino) baby; povera ∼! poor thing!

cre'den|te mf believer. ∼za f belief; (Comm) credit; (mobile) sideboard. ∼zi'ali fpl credentials

cre'der|e vt believe; (pensare) think ● vi ∼e in believe in; credo di sì I think so; non ti credo I don't believe you. ∼si vr think oneself to be. cre'dibile adj credible. credibilità f credibility

'credi|to m credit; (stima) esteem; comprare a ∼to buy on credit. ∼tore, ∼'trice mf creditor

credulità f credulity

'credu|lo adj credulous. ∼'lone, -a mf simpleton

'crema f cream; (di uova e latte) cus-

---

tard. ∼ idratante moisturizer. ∼ pasticciera egg custard. ∼ solare suntan lotion

cre'ma|re vt cremate. ∼'torio m crematorium. ∼zi'one f cremation

'crème cara'mel f crème caramel

creme'ria f dairy (also selling ice cream and cakes)

'crepa f crack

cre'paccio m cleft; (di ghiacciaio) crevasse

crepacu'ore m heart-break

crepa'pelle: a ∼ adv fit to burst; ridere a ∼ split one's sides with laughter

cre'pare vi crack; (①: morire) kick the bucket; ∼ dal ridere laugh fit to burst

crepa'tura f crevice

crêpe f inv pancake

crepi'tare vi crackle

cre'puscolo m twilight

cre'scendo m crescendo

'cresc|ere vi grow; (aumentare) increase ● vt (allevare) bring up; (aumentare) increase. ∼'ita f growth; (aumento) increase. ∼'iuto pp di crescere

'cresi|ma f confirmation. ∼'mare** confirm

'crespo adj frizzy ● m crêpe

'cresta f crest; (cima) peak

'creta f clay

'Creta f Crete

cre'tino, -a adj stupid ● mf idiot

cric m inv jack

cri'ceto m hamster

crimi'nal|e adj & mf criminal. ∼ità f crime. **'crimine** m crime

crimi'noso adj criminal

crin|e m horsehair. ∼i'era f mane

'cripta f crypt

crisan'temo m chrysanthemum

'crisi f inv crisis; (Med) fit

cristal'lino m crystalline

cristalliz'zar|e vt, ∼si vr crystal-

77

cri'stallo m crystal

Cristia'nesimo m Christianity

cristi'ano, -a adj & mf Christian

Cristo m Christ; un povero c~ a poor beggar

cri'terio m criterion; (buon senso) [common] sense

criti|ca f criticism; (recensione) review. criti'care vt criticize. ~co adj critical ● m critic. ~cone, -a mf faultfinder

rivel'lare vt riddle (di with)

ri'vello m sieve

ro'azia f Croatia

roc'cante adj crisp ● m type of crunchy nut biscuit

roc'chetta f croquette

croce f cross; a occhio e ~ roughly. C~ Rossa Red Cross

roce'via m inv crossroads sg

roci'ata f crusade

ro'cicchio m crossroads sg

roci'era f cruise; (Archit) crossing

roci'fi|ggere vt crucify. ~ssi'one f crucifixion. ~sso pp di crocifiggere ● adj crucified ● m crucifix

rogio'larsi vr bask

rogi[u]'olo m crucible; fig melting pot

rol'lare vi collapse; (prezzi:) slump. crollo m collapse; (dei prezzi) slump

ro'mato adj chromium-plated. cromo m chrome. cromo'soma m chromosome

ronaca f chronicle; (di giornale) news; (Radio, TV) commentary; fatto di ~ news item. ~ nera crime news

ronico adj chronic

ro'nista mf reporter

rono'logico adj chronological

ronome'trare vt time

ro'nometro m chronometer

'crosta f crust; (di formaggio) rind; (di ferita) scab; (quadro) daub

cro'staceo m shellfish

cro'stata f tart

cro'stino m croûton

crucci'arsi vr worry. 'cruccio m worry

cruci'ale adj crucial

cruci'verba m inv crossword [puzzle]

cru'del|e adj cruel. ~tà f inv cruelty

'crudo adj raw; (rigido) harsh

cru'ento adj bloody

cru'miro m blackleg, scab

'crusca f bran

cru'scotto m dashboard

'Cuba f Cuba

cu'betto m ~ di ghiaccio ice cube

'cubico adj cubic

cubi'tal|e adj a caratteri ~i in enormous letters

'cubo m cube

cuc'cagna f abundance; (baldoria) merry-making; paese della ~ land of plenty

cuc'cetta f (su un treno) couchette; (Naut) berth

cucchia'ino m teaspoon

cucchi'a|io m spoon; al ~io (dolce) creamy. ~i'ata f spoonful

'cuccia f dog's bed; fa la ~! lie down!

cuccio'lata f litter

'cucciolo m puppy

cu'cina f kitchen; (il cucinare) cooking; (cibo) food; (apparecchio) cooker; far da ~ cook; libro di ~ cook[ery] book. ~ a gas gas cooker

cuci'n|are vt cook. ~ino m kitchenette

cu'ci|re vt sew; macchina per ~re sewing-machine. ~to m sewing. ~'tura f seam

cucù m inv cuckoo

'cuculo m cuckoo

'cuffia f bonnet; (da bagno) bathing-cap; (ricevitore) headphones pl

cu'gino, -a mf cousin

'cui pron rel (persona: con prep) who, whom fml; (cose, animali: con prep) which; (tra articolo e nome) whose; la persona con ~ ho parlato the person [who] I spoke to; la ditta per ~ lavoro the company I work for, the company for which I work; l'amico per ~ libro è stato pubblicato the friend whose book was published; in ~ (dove) where; (quando) that; per ~ (perciò) so; la città in ~ vivo the city I live in, the city where I live; il giorno in ~ l'ho visto the day [that] I saw him

culi'nari|a f cookery. **~o** adj culinary

'culla f cradle. **cul'lare** vt rock

culmi'na|nte adj culminating. **~re** vi culminate. **'culmine** m peak

'culto m cult; (Relig) religion; (adorazione) worship

cul'tu|ra f culture. **~ra generale** general knowledge. **~'rale** adj cultural

cultu'ris|mo m body-building

cumula'tivo adj cumulative; biglietto ~ group ticket

'cumulo m pile; (mucchio) heap; (nuvola) cumulus

'cuneo m wedge

cu'netta f gutter

cu'ocere vt/i cook; fire (ceramica)

cu'oco, -a mf cook

cu'oio m leather. ~ **capelluto** scalp

cu'ore m heart; cuori pl (carte) hearts; nel profondo del ~ in one's heart of hearts; di [buon] ~ (persona) kind-hearted; nel ~ della notte in the middle of the night; stare a ~ a qcno be very important to sb

cupi'digia f greed

'cupo adj gloomy; (suono) deep

'cupola f dome

'cura f care; (amministrazione) management; (Med) treatment; a ~ di edited by; in ~ under treatment. ~ dimagrante slimming cure. cu'rante adj medico curante GP, doctor

cu'rar|e vt take care of; (Med) treat; (guarire) cure; edit (testo). **~si** vr take care of oneself; (Med) follow a treatment; **~si di** (badare a) mind

cu'rato m parish priest

cura'to|re, -'trice mf trustee; (di testo) editor

'curia f curia

curio's|are vi be curious; (mettere il naso) pry (in into); (nei negozi) look around. **~ità** f inv curiosity. **curi'oso** adj curious; (strano) odd

cur'sore m (Comput) cursor

'curva f curve; (stradale) bend. ~ a gomito U-bend. **cur'vare** vt/i curve; (strada:) bend. **cur'varsi** vr bend. **'curvo** adj curved; (piegato) bent

cusci'netto m pad; (Mech) bearing

cu'scino m cushion; (guanciale) pillow. ~ **d'aria** air cushion

'cuspide f spire

cu'stod|e m caretaker. **~e giudiziario** official receiver. **~ia** f care; (Jur) custody; (astuccio) case. **custo'dire** vt keep; (badare) look after

cu'taneo adj skin attrib

'cute f skin

Dd

da prep from; (con verbo passivo) by (moto a luogo) to; (moto per luogo) through; (stato in luogo) at; (continuativo) for; (causale) with; (in qualità di) as; (con caratteristica) with; (come) like; (temporale) since, for

da si traduce con for quando si tratta di un periodo di tempo e con since quando si riferisce al momento in cui qualcosa è cominciato. Nota che in inglese si usa il passato prossimo invece del presente: aspetto da mesi I've been waiting for months; aspetto da lunedì I've been waiting since Monday

••••> da Roma a Milano from Rome to Milan; staccare un quadro dalla parete take a picture off the wall; i bambini dai 5 ai 10 anni children between 5 and 10; vedere qcsa da vicino/lontano see sth from up close/from a distance; scritto da written by; andare dal panettiere go to the baker's; passo da te più tardi I'll come over to your place later; passiamo da qui let's go this way; un appuntamento dal dentista an appointment at the dentist's; il treno passa da Venezia the train goes through Venice; dall'anno scorso since last year; vivo qui da due anni I've been living here for two years; da domani from tomorrow; piangere dal dolore cry with pain; ho molto da fare I have a lot to do; occhiali da sole sunglasses; qualcosa da mangiare something to eat; un uomo dai capelli scuri a man with dark hair; è un oggetto da poco it's not worth much; l'ho fatto da solo I did it by myself; sì è fatto da sé he is a self-made man; non è da lui it's not like him

dac'capo adv again; (dall'inizio) from the beginning

dacché conj since

'dado m dice; (Culin) stock cube; (Techn) nut

daf'fare m work

'dagli = DA + GLI. **'dai** = DA + I

'dai int come on!

'daino m deer; (pelle) buckskin

dal = DA + IL. **'dalla** = DA + LA. **'dalle** = DA + LE. **'dallo** = DA + LO

'dalia f dahlia

dal'tonico adj colour-blind

'dama f lady; (nei balli) partner; (gioco) draughts sg

dami'gella f (di sposa) bridesmaid

damigi'ana f demijohn

dam'meno adv non essere ~ (di qcno) be no less good (than sb)

da'naro m = DENARO

dana'roso adj (fam: ricco) loaded

da'nese adj Danish ●mf Dane ●m (lingua) Danish

Dani'marca f Denmark

dan'na|re vt damn; far ~re qcno drive sb mad. ~to adj damned. ~zi'one f damnation

danneggi|a'mento m damage. ~'are vt damage; (nuocere) harm

'danno m damage; (a persona) harm. dan'noso adj harmful

'danza f dance; (il danzare) dancing. dan'zare vi dance

dapper'tutto adv everywhere

dap'poco adj worthless

dap'prima adv at first

'dardo m dart

'dar|e vt give; take (esame); have (festa); ~ qcsa a qcno give sb sth; ~ da mangiare a qcno give sb something to eat; ~ il benvenuto a qcno welcome sb; ~ la buonanotte a qcno say good night to sb; ~ del tu/del lei a qcno address sb as "tu"/ "lei"; ~ del cretino a qcno call sb an idiot; ~ qcsa per scontato take sth for granted; **cosa danno alla TV stasera?** what's on TV tonight? ●vi **∼ nell'occhio** be conspicuous; **∼ alla testa** go to one's head; **∼ su** (finestra, casa:) look on to; **∼ su o ai nervi a qcno** get on sb's nerves ●m (Comm) debit. **∼si** vr (scambiarsi) give each other; **∼si da fare** get down to it; **si è dato tanto da fare!** he went to so much trouble!; **∼si a** (cominciare) take up; **∼si al bere** take to drink; **∼si per** (malato) pretend to be; **∼si per vinto** give up; **può ∼si** maybe

'**darsena** f dock

'**data** f date. **∼ di emissione** date of issue. **∼ di nascita** date of birth. **∼ di scadenza** cut-off date

da'ta|re vt date; **a ∼re da** as from. **∼to** adj dated

'**dato** adj given; (dedito) addicted; **∼ che** given that ●m datum. **∼ di fatto** well-established fact; **dati** pl data. **da'tore** m giver. **datore, datrice** mf **di lavoro** employer

'**dattero** m date

dattilogra'f|are vt type. **∼ia** f typing. **datti'lografo, -a** mf typist

dat'torno adv **togliersi ∼** clear off

da'vanti adv before; (dirimpetto) opposite; (di fronte) in front ●adj inv front ●m front; **∼ a** prep in front of

da'vanzo adv more than enough

dav'vero adv really; **per ∼** in earnest; **dici ∼?** honestly?

'**dazio** m duty; (ufficio) customs pl

d.C. abbr (dopo Cristo) AD

'**dea** f goddess

debel'lare vt defeat

debili'ta|nte adj weakening. **∼re** vt weaken. **∼rsi** vr become weaker

debita'mente adv duly

'**debi|to** adj due; **a tempo ∼to** in due course ●m debt. **∼'tore, ∼'trice** mf debtor

'**debo|le** adj weak; (luce) dim; (suono) faint ●m weak point; (prefe-

renza) weakness. **∼'lezza** f weakness

debor'dare vi overflow

debosci'ato adj debauched

debut'ta|nte m (attore) actor making his début ●f actress making her début. **∼re** vi make one's début. **de'butto** m début

deca'den|te adj decadent. **∼'tismo** m decadence. **∼za** f decline; (Jur) loss. **deca'dere** vi lapse. **deca'dimento** m (delle arti) decline

decaffei'nato adj decaffeinated ●m decaffeinated coffee

decan'tare vt (lodare) praise

decapi'ta|re vt decapitate; behead (condannato). **∼zi'one** f decapitation; beheading

decappot'tabile adj convertible

de'ce|dere vi (morire) die. **∼'duto** adj deceased

dece'lerare vt decelerate

decen'nale adj ten-yearly. **de'cennio** m decade

de'cen|te adj decent. **∼te'mente** adv decently. **∼za** f decency

decentra'mento m decentralization

de'cesso m death; **atto di ∼** death certificate

de'cider|e vt decide; settle (questione). **∼si** vr make up one's mind

deci'frare vt decipher; (documenti cifrati) decode

deci'male adj decimal

deci'mare vt decimate

'decimo adj tenth

de'cina f (Math) ten; **una ∼ di** (circa dieci) about ten

decisa'mente adv definitely

decisio'nale adj decision-making

deci'si'one f decision. **∼'sivo** adj decisive. **de'ciso** pp di **decidere** ●adj decided

decla'ma|re vt/i declaim. **∼'torio** adj (stile) declamatory

declas'sare vt downgrade

decli'na|re vt decline; ~re ogni responsabilità disclaim all responsibility ● vi go down; (tramontare) set. ~zi'one f declension. de'clino m decline; in declino on the decline

decodificazi'one f decoding

decol'lare vi take off

décolle'té m inv décolleté

de'collo m take-off

decolo'ra|nte m bleach. ~re vt bleach

decolorazi'one f bleaching

decom'po|rre vt, ~rsi vr decompose. ~sizi'one f decomposition

deconcen'trarsi vr become distracted

deconge'lare vt defrost

decongestio'nare vt relieve congestion in

deco'ra|re vt decorate. ~'tivo adj decorative. ~to adj (ornato) decorated. ~'tore, ~'trice mf decorator. ~zi'one f decoration

de'coro m decorum

decorosa'mente adv decorously. decoroso adj dignified

decor'renza f ~ dal... starting from...

de'correre vi pass; a ~ da with effect from. de'corso pp di decorrere ● m passing; (Med) course

de'crepito adj decrepit

decre'scente adj decreasing. de'crescere vi decrease; (prezzi:) go down; (acque:) subside

decre'tare vt decree. de'creto m decree. decreto legge decree which has the force of law

dedalo m maze

dedica f dedication

dedi'car|e vt dedicate. ~si vr dedicate oneself

dedi'to adj ~ a given to; (assorto) engrossed in; (addicted to (vizi). ~zi'one f dedication

de'dotto pp di dedurre

dedu'cibile adj (tassa) allowable

de'du|rre vt deduce; (sottrarre) deduct. ~t'tivo adj deductive. ~zi'one f deduction

defal'care vt deduct

defe'rire vt (Jur) remit

defezi|o'nare vi (abbandonare) defect. ~'one f defection

defici'en|te adj (mancante) deficient; (Med) mentally deficient ● mf mental defective ~za f deficiency; (lacuna) gap; (Med) mental deficiency

'defici|t m inv deficit. ~'tario adj (bilancio) deficit attrib

defi'larsi vr (scomparire) slip away

defi'lé m inv fashion show

defi'ni|re vt define; (risolvere) settle. ~tiva'mente adv for good. ~'tivo adj definitive. ~to adj definite. ~zi'one f definition; (soluzione) settlement

deflazi'one f deflation

deflet'tore m (Auto) quarterlight

deflu'ire vi (liquidi:) flow away; (persone:) stream out

de'flusso m (di marea) ebb

defor'mar|e vt deform (arto); fig distort. ~si vr lose its shape. de-'form|e adj deformed. ~ità f deformity

defor'ma|to adj warped. ~one f (di fatti) distortion

defrau'dare vt defraud

de'funto, -a adj & mf deceased

degene'ra|re vi degenerate. ~to adj degenerate. ~zi'one f degeneration. de'genere adj degenerate

de'gen|te mf patient. ~za f confinement

'degli = DI + GLI

deglu'tire vt swallow

de'gnare vt ~ qcno di uno sguardo deign to look at sb

'degno adj worthy; (meritevole) deserving

degrada'mento m degradation

degra'da|re vt degrade. ~**rsi** vr lower oneself; (città:) fall into disrepair. ~**zi'one** f degradation

de'grado m damage; ~ **ambientale** m environmental damage

degu'sta|re vt taste. ~**zi'one** f tasting

'**dei** = DI + I. '**del** = DI + IL

dela|'tore, -'**trice** mf [police] informer. ~**zi'one** f informing

delega f proxy

dele'ga|re vt delegate. ~**to** m delegate. ~**zi'one** f delegation

dele'terio adj harmful

del'fino m dolphin; (stile di nuoto) butterfly [stroke]

de'libera f bylaw

delibe'ra|re vt/i deliberate; ~ **su/in** rule on/in. ~**to** adj deliberate

delicata'mente adv delicately

delica'tezza f delicacy; (fragilità) frailty; (tatto) tact

deli'cato adj delicate

delimi'tare vt delimit

deline'a|re vt outline. ~**rsi** vr be outlined; fig take shape. ~**to** adj defined

delin'quen|te mf delinquent. ~**za** f delinquency

deli'rante adj (Med) delirious; (assurdo) insane

deli'rare vi be delirious. **de'lirio** m delirium; fig frenzy

de'litt|o m crime. ~**u'oso** adj criminal

de'lizi|a f delight. ~'**are** vt delight. ~'**oso** adj delightful; (cibo) delicious

'**della** = DI + LA. '**delle** = DI + LE. '**dello** = DI + LO

delocaliz'zare vt relocate

'**delta** m inv delta

delta'piano m hang-glider; fare ~ go hang-gliding

delucidazi'one f clarification

delu'dente adj disappointing

delu'de|re vt disappoint. ~**si'one** f disappointment. **de'luso** adj disappointed

demar'ca|re vt demarcate. ~**zi'one** f demarcation

de'men|te adj demented. ~**za** f dementia. ~**zi'ale** adj (assurdo) zany

demilitariz'za|re vt demilitarize. ~**zi'one** f demilitarization

demistificazi'one f debunking

demo'cra|tico adj democratic. ~**zia** f democracy

democristi'ano, -**a** adj & mf Christian Democrat

demogra'fia f demography. **demo'grafico** adj demographic

demo'li|re vt demolish. ~**zi'one** f demolition

'**demone** m demon. **de'monio** m demon

demoraliz'zar|e vt demoralize. ~**si** vr become demoralized

de'mordere vi give up

demoti'vato adj demotivated

de'nari mpl (nelle carte) diamonds

de'naro m money

deni'gra|re vt denigrate. ~'**torio** adj denigratory

denomi'na|re vt name. ~'**tore** m denominator. ~**zi'one** f denomination; ~**zione di origine controllata** guarantee of a wine's quality

deno'tare vt denote

densità f inv density. '**denso** adj dense

den'tale adj dental. ~**rio** adj dental. ~**ta** f bite. ~**tura** f teeth pl

'**dente** m tooth; (di forchetta) prong; **al** ~ (Culin) slightly firm. ~ **del giudizio** wisdom tooth. ~ **di latte** milk tooth. **denti'era** f false teeth pl

denti'fricio m toothpaste

den'tista mf dentist

'**dentro** adv in, inside; (in casa) indoors; **da** ~ from within; **qui** ~ in here ● prep in, inside; (di tempo) within, by ● m inside

de|nu'dar|e vt bare. **~si** vr strip

le'nunci|a, de'nunzia f denunciation; (alla polizia) report; (dei redditi) [income] tax return. **~'are** vt denounce; (accusare) report

denutri'zione f malnutrition

deodo'rante adj & m deodorant

épendance f inv outbuilding

depe'ribile adj perishable. **~mento** m wasting away; (di merci) deterioration. **~re** vi waste away

depi'lare vt depilate. **~rsi** vr shave (gambe); pluck (sopracciglia). **~torio** m depilatory

deplo'rabile adj deplorable

deplo'r|are vt deplore; (dolersi di) grieve over. **~evole** adj deplorable

de'porre vt put down; lay (uova); (togliere da una carica) depose; (testimoniare) testify

depor'ta|re vt deport. **~to, -a** mf deportee. **~zione** f deportation

deposi'tar|e vt deposit; (lasciare in custodia) leave; (in magazzino) store. **~io, -a** mf (di segreto) repository. **~si** vr settle

de'posito m deposit; (luogo) warehouse; (Mil) depot. **~to bagagli** left-luggage office. **~zione** f deposition; (da una carica) removal

depra'va|re vt deprave. **~to** adj depraved

depre'cabile adj appalling. **~re** vt deprecate

depre'dare vt plunder

depres'sione f depression. depresso pp di deprimere ● adj depressed

deprez'zar|e vt depreciate. **~si** vr depreciate

depri'mente adj depressing

de'primer|e vt depress. **~si** vr become depressed

depu'ra|re vt purify. **~'tore** m purifier

depu'ta|re vt delegate. **~to, -a** mf Member of Parliament, MP

deraglia'mento m derailment

deragli'are vi go off the lines; far **~** derail

'derby m inv Sport local Derby

deregolamentazi'one f deregulation

dere'litto adj derelict

dere'tano m backside, bottom

de'ri|dere vt deride. **~si'one** f derision. **~'sorio** adj derisory

deri'va|re vi **~re da** (provenire) derive from ● vt derive; (sviare) divert. **~zi'one** f derivation; (di fiume) diversion

dermato|lo'gia f dermatology. derma'tologo, -a mf dermatologist

'deroga f dispensation. dero'gare a **~** derogare a depart from

der'rat|a f merchandise. **~e alimentari** foodstuffs

deru'bare vt rob

descrit'tivo adj descriptive. de-s'critto pp di descrivere

des'cri|vere vt describe. **~'vibile** adj describable. **~zi'one** f description

de'serto adj uninhabited ● m desert

eside'rabile adj desirable

eside'rare vt wish; (volere) want; (intensamente) long for; desidera? can I help you?; lasciare a **~** leave a lot to be desired

desi'de|rio m wish; (brama) desire; (intenso) longing. **~'roso** adj desirous; (bramoso) longing

desi'gnare vt designate; (fissare) fix

de'sistere vi **~ da** desist from

'desktop 'publishing m desktop publishing

deso'la|re vt distress. **~to** adj desolate; (spiacente) sorry. **~zi'one** f desolation

'despota m despot

de'star|e vt waken; fig awaken. **~si**

vr waken; *fig* awaken

desti'na|re vt destine; (*nominare*) appoint; (*assegnare*) assign; (*indirizzare*) address. ∼**tario** *m* addressee. ∼**zi'one** *f* destination; *fig* purpose

de'stino *m* destiny; (*fato*) fate

destitu'ire vt dismiss. ∼**zi'one** *f* dismissal

'desto *adj liter* awake

'destra *f* (*parte*) right; (*mano*) right hand; prendere a ∼ turn right

destreggi'ar|e vi, ∼**si** vr manoeuvre

de'strezza *f* dexterity, skill

'destro *adj* right; (*abile*) skilful

dete'nato *adj* tannin-free

dete'n|ere vt hold; (*polizia*): detain. ∼**uto, -a** *mf* prisoner. ∼**zi'one** *f* detention

deter'gente *adj* cleaning; (*latte, crema*) cleansing ● *m* detergent; (*per la pelle*) cleanser

deteriora'mento *m* deterioration

deterio'rar|e vt deteriorate. ∼**si** vr deteriorate

determi'nante *adj* determining

determi'na|re vt determine. ∼**rsi** vr ∼**rsi** a resolve to. ∼**tezza** *f* determination. ∼**tivo** *adj* (*Gram*) definite. ∼**to** *adj* (*risoluto*) determined; (*particolare*) specific. ∼**zi'one** *f* determination; (*decisione*) decision

deter'rente *adj* & *m* deterrent

deter'sivo *m* detergent; ∼ per i piatti washing-up liquid

dete'stare vt detest, hate

deto'nare vi detonate

de'tra|rre vt deduct (da from). ∼**zi'one** *f* deduction

detri'mento *m* detriment; a ∼ di to the detriment of

de'trito *m* debris

'detta *f* a ∼ di according to

dettagli'ante *mf* retailer

dettagli'a|re vt detail. ∼**ta'mente** *adv* in detail

det'taglio *m* detail; al ∼ (*Comm*) retail

det'ta|re vt dictate. ∼**to** *m*, ∼**tura** *f* dictation

'detto *adj* said; (*chiamato*) called; (*soprannominato*) nicknamed; ∼ fatto no sooner said than done ● *m* saying

detur'pare vt disfigure

deva'sta|re vt devastate. ∼**to** *adj* devastated

devi'a|re vi deviate ● vt divert. ∼**zi'one** *f* deviation; (*stradale*) diversion

devitaliz'zare vt deaden (*dente*)

devo'lu|to *pp di* devolvere ● *adj* devolved. ∼**zi'one** *f* devolution

de'volvere vt devolve

de'vo|to *adj* devout; (*affezionato*) devoted. ∼**zi'one** *f* devotion

di *prep* of; (*partitivo*) some; (*scritto da*) by; (*parlare, pensare ecc*) about; (*con causa, mezzo*) with; (*con provenienza*) from; (*in comparazioni*) than; (*con infinito*) to; la casa di mio padre/dei miei genitori my father's house/my parents' house; compra del pane buy some bread; hai del pane? do you have any bread?; un film di guerra a war film; piangere di dolore cry with pain; coperto di neve covered with snow; sono di Genova I'm from Genoa; uscire di casa leave one's house; più alto di te taller than you; è ora di partire it's time to go; crede di aver ragione he thinks he's right; dire di sì say yes; di domenica on Sundays; di sera in the evening; una pausa di un'ora an hour's break; un corso di due mesi a two-month course

dia'bet|e *m* diabetes. ∼**ico, -a** *adj* & *mf* diabetic

dia'bolico adj diabolical

dia'dema m diadem; (di donna) tiara

di'afano adj diaphanous

dia'framma m diaphragm; (divisione) screen

di'agnos|i f inv diagnosis. ~ti'care vt diagnose

diago'nale adj & f diagonal

dia'gramma m diagram

dia'letto m dialect

Dialetto As Italy was not unified until 1861, standard Italian was slow to become widely used except by the cultural elite. As a result dialects are used by many Italians, with 60% using their dialect regularly. Ranging from Neapolitan and Sicilian to Milanese and Venetian, they vary considerably from each other. Tuscan dialects are the closest to standard Italian.

di'alogo m dialogue

dia'mante m diamond

di'ametro m diameter

di'amine int che ~... what on earth...

diaposi'tiva f slide

di'ario m diary

diar'rea f diarrhoea

di'avolo m devil

di'batt|ere vt debate. ~ersi vr struggle. ~ito m debate; (meno formale) discussion

ica'stero m office

di'cembre m December

di'ceria f rumour

ichia'ra|re vt state; (ufficialmente) declare. ~rsi vr si dichiara innocente he says he's innocent. ~zi'one f statement; (documento, di guerra) declaration

ician'nove adj & m nineteen

icias'sette adj & m seventeen

dici'otto adj & m eighteen

dici'tura f wording

didasca'lia f (di film) subtitle; (di illustrazione) caption

di'dattico adj didactic; (televisione) educational

di'dentro adv inside

didi'etro adv behind ● m hum hindquarters pl

di'eci adj & m ten

die'cina = DECINA

'diesel adj & f inv diesel

di'esis m inv sharp

di'eta f diet; essere a ~ be on a diet. die'tetico adj diet. die'tista mf dietician. die'tologo, -a mf dietician

di'etro adv behind ● prep behind; (dopo) after ● adj back; (di zampe) hind ● m back; le stanze di ~ the back rooms

dietro'front m inv about-turn; fig U-turn

di'fatti adv in fact

di'fen|dere vt defend. ~dersi vr defend oneself. ~siva f stare sulla ~siva be on the defensive. ~sivo adj defensive. ~sore m defender; avvocato ~sore defence counsel

di'fes|a f defence; prendere le ~ di qcno come to sb's defence. ~o pp di difendere

difet't|are vi be defective; ~are di lack. ~ivo adj defective

di'fet|to m (morale) fault, flaw; (mancanza) lack; (in tessuto, abito) flaw; essere in ~to be at fault; far ~to be lacking. ~'toso adj defective; (abito) flawed

diffa'ma|re vt (con parole) slander; (per iscritto) libel. ~'torio adj slanderous; (per iscritto) libellous. ~zi'one f slander; (scritta) libel

diffe'ren|te adj different. ~za f difference; a ~za di unlike; non fare ~za make no distinction (fra between). ~zi'ale adj & m differential

differenzi'ar|e vt differentiate. ~**si** vr ~**si da** differ from

diffe'ri|re vt postpone •vi be different. ~**ta** f in ~**ta** (TV) prerecorded

dif'ficil|e adj difficult; (duro) hard; (improbabile) unlikely •**m** difficulty. ~**'mente** adv with difficulty

difficoltà f inv difficulty

dif'fida f warning

diffi'd|are vi ~**are di** distrust • warn. ~**ente** adj mistrustful. ~**enza** f mistrust

dif'fonder|e vt spread; diffuse (calore, luce ecc). ~**si** vr spread. diffusi'one f diffusion; (di giornale) circulation

diffi'lato adv straight; (subito) straightaway

'**diga** f dam; (argine) dike

dige'ribile adj digestible

dige|'rire vt digest; ⊞ stomach. ~**sti'one** f digestion. ~**'stivo** adj digestive •**m** digestive; (dopo cena) liqueur

digi'tale adj digital; (delle dita) finger attrib •f (fiore) foxglove

digitaliz'zare vt digitize

digi'tare vt key in

digiu'nare vi fast

digi'uno adj essere ~ have an empty stomach •**m** fast; a ~ (bere ecc) on an empty stomach

dignità f dignity. ~'**tario** m dignitary. ~'**toso** adj dignified

digressi'one f digression

digri'gnare vi ~ i denti grind one's teeth

dila'gare vi flood; fig spread

dila'niare vt tear to pieces

dilapi'dare vt squander

dila'ta|re vt, ~**rsi** vr dilate; (metallo, gas:) expand

dilazio'nabile adj postponable

dilazio'nare vt delay. ~'**one** f delay

dilegu'ar|e vt disperse. ~**si** vr disappear

di'lemma m dilemma

dilet'tante mf amateur

dilet'tare vt delight

di'letto, -a adj beloved •**m** delight •mf (persona) beloved

dili'gen|te adj diligent; (lavoro) accurate. ~**za** f diligence

dilu'ire vt dilute

dilun'gar|e vt prolong. ~**si** vr ~**si su** dwell on (argomento)

diluvi'are vi pour [down]. di'luvio m downpour; fig flood

dima'gr|ante adj slimming. ~**i'mento** m weight loss. ~**ire** vi slim

dime'nar|e vt wave; wag (coda). ~**si** vr be agitated

dimensi'one f dimension; (misura) size

dimenti'canza f forgetfulness; (svista) oversight

dimenti'car|e vt, ~**si** vr ~ [di] forget. dimentico adj dimentico di (che non ricorda) forgetful of

di'messo pp di dimettere •adj humble; (trasandato) shabby; (voce) low

domesti'chezza f familiarity

di'metter|e vt dismiss; (da ospedale ecc) discharge. ~**si** vr resign

dimez'zare vt halve

diminu'ire vt/i diminish; (in maglia) decrease. ~'**tivo** adj & m diminutive. ~**zi'one** f decrease; (riduzione) reduction

dimissi'oni fpl resignation sg; dare le ~ resign

di'mo|ra f residence. ~'**rare** vi reside

dimo'strante mf demonstrator

dimo'stra|re vt demonstrate; (pro-

vare) prove; (*mostrare*) show. ∼**rsi** vr prove [to be]. ∼'**tivo** adj demonstrative. ∼**zi'one** f demonstration; (Math) proof

di'namico, -a adj dynamic. dina-'**mismo** m dynamism

dinami'tardo adj attentato ∼ bomb attack

dina'mite f dynamite

di'namo f inv dynamo

di'nanzi adv in front ● prep ∼ **a** in front of

dina'stia f dynasty

dini'ego m denial

dinocco'lato adj lanky

dino'sauro m dinosaur

din'torn|i mpl outskirts; nei ∼**i di** in the vicinity of. ∼**o** adv around

'dio m (pl **'dei**) god; **D**∼ God

di'ocesi f inv diocese

dipa'nare vt wind into a ball; fig unravel

diparti'mento m department

dipen'den|te adj depending ● mf employee. ∼**za** f dependence; (*edificio*) annexe

di'pendere vi ∼ **da** depend on; (*provenire*) derive from; **dipende** it depends

di'pinger|e vt paint; (*descrivere*) describe. ∼**si** vr (*truccarsi*) make up. di-'**pinto** pp di **dipingere** ● adj painted ● m painting

di'plo|ma m diploma. ∼'**marsi** vr graduate

diplo'matico adj diplomatic ● m diplomat; (*pasticcino*) millefeuille (*with alcohol*)

diplo'mato mf person with school-leaving qualification ● adj qualified

diploma'zia f diplomacy

di'porto m imbarcazione da ∼ pleasure craft

dira'dar|e vt thin out; make less frequent (*visite*). ∼**si** vr thin out; (*nebbia:*) clear

dira'ma|re vt issue ● vi, ∼**rsi** vr branch out; (*diffondersi*) spread. ∼**zi'one** f (*di strada*) fork

'**dire** vt say; (*raccontare, riferire*) tell; ∼ quello che si pensa speak one's mind; **voler** ∼ mean; **volevo ben** ∼! I wondered!; ∼ **di sì/no** say yes/no; **si dice che...** rumour has it that...; **come si dice "casa" in in-glese?** what's the English for "casa"?; **che ne dici di...?** how about...?; **non c'è che** ∼ there's no disputing that; **e** ∼ **che...** to think that...; **a dir poco/tanto** at least; **most** ● **vi** ∼ **bene/male di** speak highly/ill of; **dica pure** how can I help you?; **dici sul serio?** are you serious?

diretta'mente adv directly

diret'tissima f per ∼ (Jur) omit-ting normal procedure

diret'tissimo m fast train

diret'tiva f directive

di'retto pp di **dirigere** ● adj direct. ∼ **a** (*inteso*) meant for. **essere** ∼ **a** be heading for. **in diretta** (trasmis-sione) live ● vi (*treno*) through train

diret'tor|e, -'trice m manager; manageress; (*di scuola*) headmaster; headmistress. ∼**tore d'orchestra** conductor

direzi'one f direction; (*di società*) management; (Sch) headmaster's/headmistress's office (*primary school*)

diri'gen|te adj ruling ● mf execu-tive; (Pol) leader. ∼**za** f manage-ment. ∼**zi'ale** adj managerial

di'riger|e vt direct; conduct (orche-stra); run (impresa). ∼**si** vr ∼**si verso** head for

dirim'petto adv opposite ● prep ∼ **a** facing

di'ritto[1], dritto adj straight; (*de-stro*) right ● adv straight; **andare** ∼ go straight on ● m right side; (Tennis) forehand

di'ritt|o[2] m right; (Jur) law. ∼**i** pl

d'autore royalties

dirit'tura f straight line; *fig* honesty. ~ d'arrivo *Sport* home straight

diroc'cato adj tumbledown

dirom'pente adj fig explosive

dirot'ta|re vt reroute (treno, aereo); (illegalmente) hijack; divert (traffico) •vi alter course. ~'tore, ~'trice mf hijacker

di'rotto adj (pioggia) pouring; (pianto) uncontrollable; piovere a ~ rain heavily

di'rupo m precipice

dis'abile mf disabled person

disabi'tato adj uninhabited

disabitu'arsi vr ~ a get out of the habit of

disac'cordo m disagreement

disadat'tato, -a adj maladjusted •mf misfit

disa'dorno adj unadorned

disa'gevole adj (scomodo) uncomfortable

disagi'ato adj poor; (vita) hard

di'sagio m discomfort; (difficoltà) inconvenience; (imbarazzo) embarrassment; sentirsi a ~ feel uncomfortable; disagi pl (privazioni) hardships

disappro'va|re vt disapprove of. ~zi'one f disapproval

disap'punto m disappointment

disar'mante adj fig disarming

disar'mare vt/i disarm. **di'sarmo** m disarmament

disa'strato, -a adj devastated

di'sastro m disaster; (🔒: grande confusione) mess; (🔒: persona) disaster area. **disa'stroso** adj disastrous

disat'ten|to adj inattentive. ~zi'one f inattention; (svista) oversight

disatti'vare vt de-activate

disa'vanzo m deficit

disavven'tura f misadventure

dis'brigo m dispatch

dis'capito m a ~ di to the detriment of

dis'carica f scrap-yard

discen'den|te adj descending •mf descendant. ~za f descent; (discendenti) descendants pl

di'scendere vt/i descend; (dal treno) get off; (da cavallo) dismount; (sbarcare) land. ~ da (trarre origine da) be a descendant of

di'scepolo, -a mf disciple

di'scernere vt discern

di'sces|a f descent; (pendio) slope; ~a in picchiata (di aereo) nosedive; essere in ~a (strada:) go downhill. ~a libera (in sci) downhill race. **disce'sista** mf (sciatore) downhill skier. ~o pp di discendere

dis'chetto m (Comput) diskette

dischi'uder|e vt open; (svelare) disclose. ~si vr open up

disci'ogliere vt, ~si vr dissolve; (fondersi) melt. **disci'olto** pp di disciogliere

disci'pli|na f discipline. ~'nare adj disciplinary ~'nato adj disciplined

'disco m disc; (Comput) disk; *Sport* discus; (Mus) record; ernia del ~ slipped disc. ~ fisso (Comput) hard disk. ~ volante flying saucer

disco'gra'fia f (insieme di incisioni) discography. **disco'grafico** adj (industria) recording; casa discografica recording company

'discolo mf rascal •adj unruly

discol'par|e vt clear. ~si vr clear oneself

disconnet'tersi vr go offline

disco'noscere vt disown (figlio)

discontinuità f (nel lavoro) irregularity. **discon'tinuo** adj intermittent; (rendimento) uneven

discor'dan|te adj discordant. ~za f mismatch

discor'dare vi (opinioni:) conflict. **dis'corde** adj clashing. **dis'cordia** f discord; (*dissenso*) dissension

dis'cor|rere *vi* talk (di about). ~'**sivo** *adj* colloquial. **dis'corso** *pp di* **discorrere** ● *m* speech; (*conversazione*) talk

dis'costo *adj* distant ● *adv* far away; **stare** ~ stand apart

disco'te|ca *f* disco; (*raccolta*) record library

discre'pan|te *adj* contradictory. ~**za** *f* discrepancy

dis'cre|to *adj* discreet; (*moderato*) moderate; (*abbastanza buono*) fairly good. ~**zi'one** *f* discretion; (*giudizio*) judgement; **a** ~**zione di** at the discretion of

discrimi'nante *adj* extenuating

discrimi'na|re *vt* discriminate. ~**torio** *adj* (*atteggiamento*) discriminatory. ~**zi'one** *f* discrimination

discussi'one *f* discussion; (*alterco*) argument. **dis'cusso** *pp di* **discutere** ● *adj* controversial

dis'cutere *vt* discuss; (*formale*) debate; (*litigare*) argue; ~ **sul prezzo** bargain. **discu'tibile** *adj* debatable; (*gusto*) questionable

disde'gnare *vt* disdain. **dis'degno** *m* disdain

dis'dett|a *f* retraction; (*sfortuna*) bad luck; (*Comm*) cancellation. ~**o** *pp di* **disdire**

disdi'cevole *adj* unbecoming

dis'dire *vt* retract; (*annullare*) cancel

diseduca'tivo *adj* boorish

dise'gna|re *vt* draw; (*progettare*) design. ~**tore**, ~**trice** *mf* designer. **di'segno** *m* drawing; (*progetto, linea*) design

diser'bante *m* herbicide ● *adj* herbicidal

disere'da|re *vt* disinherit ● *mf* **i** ~**ti** the dispossessed

diser|'tare *vt/i* desert; ~**tare la scuola** stay away from school. ~**'tore** *m* deserter. ~**zi'one** *f* desertion

disfaci'mento *m* decay

dis'fa|re *vt* undo; strip (*letto*); (*smantellare*) take down; (*annientare*) defeat; ~**re le valigie** unpack [one's bags]. ~**rsi** *vr* fall to pieces; (*sciogliersi*) melt; ~**rsi di** (*liberarsi di*) get rid of; ~**rsi in lacrime** dissolve into tears. ~**tta** *f* defeat. ~**tto** *adj fig* worn out

disfat'tis|mo *m* defeatism. ~**ta** *adj & mf* defeatist

disfunzi'one *f* disorder

dis'gelo *m* thaw

dis'grazi|a *f* misfortune; (*incidente*) accident; (*sfavore*) disgrace. ~**ata'mente** *adv* unfortunately. ~**'ato, -a** *adj* unfortunate ● *mf* wretch

disgre'gare *vt* break up. ~**si** *vr* disintegrate

disgu'ido *m* ~ **postale** mistake in delivery

disgu'st|are *vt* disgust. ~**arsi** *vr* ~**arsi di** be disgusted by. **dis'gusto** *m* disgust. ~**oso** *adj* disgusting

disidra'ta|re *vt* dehydrate. ~**to** *adj* dehydrated

disil'lu|dere *vt* disenchant. ~**si'one** *f* disenchantment. ~**so** *adj* disillusioned

disimbal'lare *vt* unpack

disimpa'rare *vt* forget

disimpe'gnar|e *vt* release; (*compiere*) fulfil; redeem (*oggetto dato in pegno*). ~**si** *vr* disengage oneself; (*cavarsela*) manage. **disim'pegno** *m* (*locale*) vestibule

disincan'tato *adj* (*disilluso*) disillusioned

disinfe'sta|re *vt* disinfest. ~**zi'one** *f* disinfestation

disinfet'tante *adj & m* disinfectant

disinfe|t'tare *vt* disinfect. ~**zi'one** *f* disinfection

disinfor'mato *adj* uninformed

disini'bito *adj* uninhibited

disinne'scare *vt* defuse (*mina*). disin'nesco m *(di bomba)* bomb disposal

disinse'rire *vt* disconnect

disinte'gra|re *vt*, ~**rsi** *vr* disintegrate. ~**zi'one** *f* disintegration

disinteres'sarsi *vr* ~ di take no interest in. disinte'resse *m* indifference; *(oggettività)* disinterestedness

disintossi'ca|re *vt* detoxify. ~**rsi** *vr* come off drugs. ~**zi'one** *f* giving up alcohol/drugs

disin'volto *adj* natural. disinvol'tura *f* confidence

disles'sia *f* dyslexia

disli'vello *m* difference in height; *fig* inequality

dislo'care *vt (Mil)* post

dismi'sura *f* excess; a ~ excessively

disobbedi'ente *adj* disobedient

disobbe'dire *vt* disobey

disoccu'pa|to, -a *adj* unemployed ● *mf* unemployed person. ~**zi'o-ne** *f* unemployment

disonestà *f* dishonesty. diso'nesto *adj* dishonest

disono'rare *vt* dishonour. diso'nore *m* dishonour

di'sopra *adv* above ● *adj* upper ● *m* top

disordi'na|re *vt* disarrange. ~**ta-'mente** *adv* untidily. ~**to** *adj* untidy; *(sregolato)* immoderate. di'sordine *m* disorder

disorganiz'za|re *vt* disorganize. ~**to** *adj* disorganized. ~**zi'one** *f* disorganization

disorienta'mento *m* disorientation

disorien'ta|re *vt* disorientate. ~**rsi** *vr* lose one's bearings. ~**to** *adj fig* bewildered

di'sotto *adv* below ● *adj* lower ● *m* bottom

dis'paccio *m* dispatch

dispa'rato *adj* disparate

'dispari *adj* odd. ~**tà** *f inv* disparity

dis'parte *adv* in ~ apart; stare in ~ stand aside

dis'pendi|o *m (spreco)* waste. ~**'oso** *adj* expensive

dis'pen|sa *f* pantry; *(distribuzione)* distribution; *(mobile)* cupboard; *(Jur)* exemption; *(Relig)* dispensation; *(pubblicazione periodica)* number. ~**'sare** *vt* distribute; *(esentare)* exonerate

dispe'ra|re *vi* despair (di of). ~**rsi** *vr* despair. ~**ta'mente** *(piangere)* desperately. ~**to** *adj* desperate. ~**zi'one** *f* despair

dis'per|dere *vt*, ~**dersi** *vr* disperse. ~**si'one** *f* dispersion; *(di truppe)* dispersal. ~**sivo** *adj* disorganized. ~**so** *pp di* **disperdere** ● *adj* scattered; *(smarrito)* lost ● *m* missing soldier

dis'pet|to *m* spite; a ~ di in spite of. ~**'toso** *adj* spiteful

dispia'c|ere *m* upset; *(rammarico)* regret; *(dolore)* sorrow; *(preoccupazione)* worry ● *vi* mi dispiace I'm sorry; non mi dispiace I don't dislike it; se non ti dispiace if you don't mind. ~**i'uto** *adj* upset; *(dolente)* sorry

dispo'nibil|e *adj* available; *(gentile)* helpful. ~**ità** *f* availability; *(gentilezza)* helpfulness

dis'por|re *vt* arrange ● *vi* dispose; *(stabilire)* order; ~**re** di have at one's disposal. ~**si** *vr* line up

disposi'tivo *m* device

disposizi'one *f* disposition; *(ordine)* order; *(libera disponibilità)* disposal. di-s'posto *pp di* disporre ● *adj* ready; *(incline)* disposed; essere ben disposto verso a favourably disposed towards

di'spotico *adj* despotic

dispregia'tivo *adj* disparaging

disprez'zare *vt* despise. dis'prezzo *m* contempt

'disputa *f* dispute

dispu'tar|e *vi* dispute; *(gareggiare)*

d

compete. ~si vr ~si qcsa contend for sth

dissacra'torio adj debunking

dissangua'mento m loss of blood

dissangu'a|re vt, ~rsi vr bleed. ~rsi vr fig become impoverished. ~to adj bloodless; fig impoverished

dissa'pore m disagreement

dissec'car|e vt, ~si vr dry up

dissemi'nare vt disseminate; (notizie) spread

dis'senso m dissent; (disaccordo) disagreement

dissente'ria f dysentery

dissen'tire vi disagree (da with)

dissertazi'one f dissertation

disser'vizio m poor service

disse'sta|re vt upset; (Comm) damage. ~to adj (strada) uneven. dis'sesto m ruin

disse'tante adj thirst-quenching

disse'ta|re vt ~re qcno quench sb's thirst

dissi'dente adj & mf dissident

dis'sidio m disagreement

dis'simile adj unlike, dissimilar

dissimu'lare vt conceal; (fingere) dissimulate

dissi'pa|re vt dissipate; (sperperare) squander. ~rsi vr (nebbia:) clear; (dubbio:) disappear. ~to adj dissipated. ~zi'one f squandering

dissoci'ar|e vt, ~si vr dissociate

disso'dare vt till

dis'solto pp di dissolvere

disso'luto adj dissolute

dis'solver|e vt, ~si vr dissolve; (disperdere) dispel

disso'nanza f dissonance

dissua'de|re vt dissuade. ~si'one f dissuasion. ~sivo adj dissuasive

distac'car|e vt detach; Sport leave behind. ~si vr be detached. di'stacco m detachment; (separazione)

separation; Sport lead

di'stan|te adj far away; fig: (persona) detached ● adv far away ~za f distance. ~zi'are vt space out; Sport outdistance

di'stare vi be distant; quanto dista? how far is it?

di'sten|dere vt stretch out (parte del corpo); (spiegare) spread; (deporre) lay. ~dersi vr stretch; (sdraiarsi) lie down; (rilassarsi) relax. ~si'one f stretching; (rilassamento) relaxation; (Pol) détente. ~sivo adj relaxing

di'steso, -a pp di distendere ●f expanse

distil'l|are vt/i distil. ~azi'one f distillation. ~e'ria f distillery

di'stinguer|e vt distinguish. ~si vr distinguish oneself. distin'guibile adj distinguishable

di'stinta f (Comm) list. ~ di pagamento receipt. ~ di versamento paying-in slip

distinta'mente adv individually; (chiaramente) clearly

distin'tivo adj distinctive ● m badge

di'stin|to, -a pp di distinguere ● adj distinct; (signorile) distinguished. ~ti saluti Yours faithfully. ~zi'one f distinction

di'stogliere vt ~ da remove from; (dissuadere) dissuade from. di'stolto pp di distogliere

di'storcere vt twist

distorsi'one f (Med) sprain; (alterazione) distortion

di'stra|rre vt distract; (divertire) amuse. ~rsi vr get distracted; (svagarsi) amuse oneself; non ti distrarre! pay attention!. ~tta'mente adv absently. ~tto pp di distrarre ● adj absent-minded; (disattento) inattentive. ~zi'one f absent-mindedness; (errore) inattention; (svago) amusement

di'stretto m district

distribu|'ire vt distribute; (disporre) arrange; deal (carte). ~'tore m distributor; (di benzina) petrol pump; (automatico) slot-machine. ~zi'one f distribution

distri'car|e vt disentangle; ~si vr fig get out of it

di'stru|ggere vt destroy. ~t'tivo adj destructive; (critica) negative. ~tto pp di distruggere. ~zi'one f destruction

distur'bar|e vt disturb; (sconvolgere) upset. ~si vr trouble oneself. di'sturbo m bother; (indisposizione) trouble; (Med) problem; (Radio, TV) interference; disturbi pl (Radio, TV) static. disturbi di stomaco stomach trouble

disubbidi'en|te adj disobedient. ~za f disobedience

disubbi'dire vi ~ a disobey

disugu|agli'anza f disparity. ~'ale adj unequal; (irregolare) irregular

di'suso m cadere in ~ fall into disuse

di'tale m thimble

di'tata f poke; (impronta) finger-mark

'dito m (pl f dita) finger; (di vino) finger. ~ del piede toe

'ditta f firm

ditt'afono m dictaphone

ditta'tor|e m dictator. ~i'ale adj dictatorial. ditta'tura f dictatorship

ditt'ongo m diphthong

di'urno adj daytime; spettacolo ~ matinée

'diva f diva

diva'ga|re vi digress. ~zi'one f digression

divam'pare vi burst into flames; fig spread like wildfire

di'vano m sofa. ~ letto sofa bed

divari'care vt open

di'vario m discrepancy; un ~ di

opinioni a difference of opinion

dive'n|ire vi = DIVENTARE. ~uto pp di divenire

diven'tare vi become; (lentamente) grow; (rapidamente) turn

di'verbio m squabble

diver'gen|te adj divergent. ~za f divergence; ~za di opinioni difference of opinion. di'vergere vi diverge

diversa'mente adv otherwise; (in modo diverso) differently

diversifi'ca|re vt diversify. ~rsi vr differ. ~zi'one f diversification

diver'si|one f diversion. ~tà f inv difference. ~sivo m diversion. diverso adj different; diversi pl (parecchi) several • pron several [people]

diver'tente adj amusing. diverti'mento m amusement

diver'tir|e vt amuse. ~si vr enjoy oneself

divi'dendo m dividend

di'vider|e vt divide; (condividere) share. ~si vr (separarsi) separate

divi'eto m prohibition; ~ di sosta no parking

divinco'larsi vr wriggle

divinità f inv divinity. di'vino adj divine

di'visa f uniform; (Comm) currency

divisi'one f division

di'vismo m worship; (atteggiamento) superstar mentality

di'vi|so pp di dividere. ~'sore m divisor. ~'sorio adj dividing

'divo, -a mf star

divo'rar|e vt devour. ~si vr ~si da be consumed with

divorzi'a|re vi divorce. ~to, -a mf divorcee. di'vorzio m divorce

divul'ga|re vt divulge; (rendere popolare) popularize. ~rsi vr spread. ~'tivo adj popular. ~zi'one f popularization

dizio'nario m dictionary

dizi'one f diction

do m (Mus) C

DOC Italian wines which are grown in certain specified areas and which conform to certain regulations may be styled DOC (*Denominazione di Origine Controllata*). The classification *DOCG* (*Denominazione di Origine Controllata e Garantita*) is awarded to DOC wines of particular quality. Wines must conform to the DOC criteria for at least five years before they can be classified as DOCG.

doccia f shower; (*grondaia*) gutter; fare la ~ have a shower

do'cen|te adj teaching • mf teacher; (*Univ*) lecturer. ~za f (*Univ*) lecturer's qualification

docile adj docile

documen'tar|e vt document. ~si vr gather information (su about)

documen'tario adj & m documentary

documen'ta|to adj well-documented; (*persona*) well-informed. ~zi'one f documentation

docu'mento m document

dodi'cesimo adj & m twelfth. 'do-dici adj & m twelve

do'gan|a f customs pl; (*dazio*) duty. doga'nale adj customs. ~i'ere m customs officer

doglie fpl labour pains

dogma m dogma. dog'matico adj dogmatic. ~'tismo m dogmatism

dolce adj sweet; (*clima*) mild; (*voce*, *consonante*) soft; (*acqua*) fresh • m (*portata*) dessert; (*torta*) cake; non mangio dolci I don't eat sweet things. ~'mente adv sweetly. dol-'cezza f sweetness; (*di clima*) mildness

dolce'vita adj inv (*maglione*) rollneck

dolci'ario adj confectionery

dolci'astro adj sweetish

dolcifi'cante m sweetener • adj sweetening

dolci'umi mpl sweets

do'lente adj painful; (*spiacente*) sorry

do'le|re vi ache, hurt; (*dispiacere*) regret. ~rsi vr regret; (*protestare*) complain; ~rsi di be sorry for

'dollaro m dollar

'dolo m (*Jur*) malice; (*truffa*) fraud

Dolo'miti fpl le ~ the Dolomites

do'lore m pain; (*morale*) sorrow. do-lo'roso adj painful

do'loso adj malicious

do'manda f question; (*richiesta*) request; (*scritta*) application; (*Comm*) demand; fare una ~ (a qcno) ask (sb) a question. ~ di impiego job application

doman'dar|e vt ask; (*esigere*) demand; ~e qcsa a qcno ask sb for sth. ~si vr wonder

do'mani adv tomorrow; ~ sera tomorrow evening • m il ~ the future; a ~ see you tomorrow

do'ma|re vt tame; fig control (emozioni). ~'tore m tamer

domat'tina adv tomorrow morning

do'meni|ca f Sunday. ~'cale adj Sunday attrib

do'mestico, -a adj domestic • m servant • f maid

domicili'are adj arresti domiciliari (*Jur*) house arrest

domicili'arsi vr settle

domi'cilio m domicile; (*abitazione*) home; recapitiamo a ~ we do home deliveries

domi'na|re vt dominate; (*controllare*) control • vi rule over; (*prevalere*) be dominant. ~rsi vr control oneself. ~'tore, ~'trice mf ruler; ~zi'one f domination

do'minio m control; (Pol) dominion; (ambito) field; di ~ pubblico common knowledge

don m inv (ecclesiastico) Father

do'na|re vt give; donate (sangue, organo) ●vi ~re a (giovare esteticamente) suit. ~'tore, ~'trice mf donor. ~zi'one f donation

dondo'l|are vi swing; (cullare) rock ●vi sway. ~arsi vr swing. ~lo m rocking. 'dondolo m swing; cavallo/sedia a dondolo rocking-horse/chair

dongio'vanni m inv Romeo

'donna f woman. ~ di servizio domestic help

don'naccia f pej whore

'dono m gift

'dopo prep after; (a partire da) since ●adv afterwards; (più tardi) later; (in seguito) later on; ~ di me after me

dopo'barba m inv aftershave

dopo'cena m inv evening

dopodi'ché adv after which

dopodo'mani adv the day after tomorrow

dopogu'erra m inv post-war period

dopo'pranzo m inv afternoon

dopo'sci ● nm inv après-ski

doposcu'ola m inv after-school activities pl

dopo-'shampoo m inv conditioner ●adj inv conditioning

dopo'sole m inv aftersun cream ●adj inv aftersun

dopo'tutto adv after all

doppi'aggio m dubbing

doppia'mente adv doubly

doppi'a|re vt double; Sport lap; Cinema dub. ~'tore, ~'trice mf dubber

'doppio adj & adv double. ~ clic m (Comput) double click. ~ fallo m Tennis double fault. ~ gioco m double-dealing. ~ mento m double chin. ~ senso m double entendre. doppi

vetri mpl double glazing. ●m double; Tennis doubles pl. ~ misto Tennis mixed doubles

doppi'one m duplicate

doppio'petto adj double-breasted

dop'pista mf doubles player

do'ra|re vt gild; (Culin) brown. ~to adj gilt; (color oro) golden. ~'tura f gilding

dormicchi'are vi doze

dormigli'one, -a mf sleepyhead; fig lazy-bones

dor'mi|re vi sleep; (essere addormentato) be asleep; fig be asleep. ~ta f good sleep. ~'tina f nap. ~'torio m dormitory

dormi'veglia m essere in ~ be half asleep

dor'sale adj dorsal ●f (di monte) ridge

'dorso m back; (di libro) spine; (di monte) crest; (nel nuoto) backstroke

do'saggio m dosage

do'sare vt dose; fig measure; ~ le parole weigh one's words

dosa'tore m measuring jug

'dose f dose; in buona ~ fig in good measure. ~ eccessiva overdose

dossi'er m inv file

'dosso m (dorso) back; levarsi di ~ gli abiti take off one's clothes

do'ta|re vt endow; (di accessori) equip. ~to adj (persona) gifted; (fornito) equipped. ~zi'one f (attrezzatura) equipment; in ~zione at one's disposal

'dote f dowry; (qualità) gift

'dotto adj learned ●m scholar; (Anat) duct

dotto'rato m doctorate. dot'tore, ~'ressa mf doctor

dot'trina f doctrine

'dove adv where; di ~ sei? where do you come from; fin ~? how far?

per ~? which way?

do'vere vi (obbligo) have to, must; devo andare I have to go, I must go; devo venire anch'io? do I have to come too?; avresti dovuto dirmelo you should have told me, you ought to have told me; devo sedermi un attimo I must sit down for a minute, I need to sit down for a minute; dev'essere successo qualcosa something must have happened; come si deve properly • vt (essere debitore di, derivare) owe; essere dovuto a be due to • m duty; per ~ out of duty. dove'roso adj only right and proper

do'vunque adv (dappertutto) everywhere; (in qualsiasi luogo) anywhere • conj wherever

do'vuto adj due; (debito) proper

doz'zina f dozen. ~'nale adj cheap

dra'gare vt dredge

'drago m dragon

'dramm|a m drama. dram'matico adj dramatic. ~atiz'zare vt dramatize. ~a'turgo m playwright. dram-'mone m (film) tear-jerker

drappeggi'are vt drape. drap-'peggio m drapery

drap'pello m (Mil) squad; (gruppo) band

'drastico adj drastic

dre'nare vt drain

drib'blare vt (in calcio) dribble

'dritta f (mano destra) right hand; (Naut) starboard; (informazione) pointer, tip; a ~ e a manca left, right and centre

'dritto adj = DIRITTO[1] • mf [1] crafty so-and-so

driz'zar|e vt straighten; (rizzare) prick up. ~si vi straighten [up]; (alzarsi) raise

'dro|ga f drug. ~'gare vt drug. ~'garsi vr take drugs. ~'gato, -a mf drug addict

drogh|e'ria f grocery. ~'iere, -a mf grocer

'dubbi|o adj doubtful; (ambiguo) dubious • m doubt; (sospetto) suspicion; mettere in ~o doubt; essere fuori ~o be beyond doubt; essere in ~o be doubtful. ~'oso adj doubtful

dubi'ta|re vi doubt; ~re di doubt; (diffidare) mistrust; dubito che venga I doubt whether he'll come. ~'tivo adj ambiguous

'duca, du'chessa mf duke; duchess

'due adj & m two

due'cento adj & m two hundred

du'ello m duel

due'mila adj & m two thousand

due'pezzi m inv (bikini) bikini

du'etto m duo; (Mus) duet

'duna f dune

'dunque conj therefore; (allora) well [then]

'duo m inv duo; (Mus) duet

du'omo m cathedral

dupli'ca|re vt duplicate. ~to m duplicate. 'duplice adj double; in duplice in duplicate

dura'mente adv (lavorare) hard; (rimproverare) harshly

du'rante prep during

du'r|are vi last; (cibo:) keep; (resistere) hold out. ~ata f duration. ~a'turo, ~evole adj lasting, enduring

du'rezza f hardness; (di carne) toughness; (di voce, padre) harshness

'duro, -a adj hard; (persona, carne) tough; (voce) harsh; (pane) stale • mf tough person

du'rone m hardened skin

'duttile adj (materiale) ductile; (carattere) malleable

DVD m inv DVD

Ee

e, ed *conj* and

'ebano *m* ebony

eb'bene *conj* well [then]

eb'brezza *f* inebriation; (*euforia*) elation; **guida in stato di ~** drink-driving; **'ebbro** *adj* inebriated; (*di gioia*) ecstatic

'ebete *adj* stupid

ebollizi'one *f* boiling

e'braico *adj* Hebrew ●*m* (*lingua*) Hebrew. **e'breo, -a** *adj* Jewish ●*mf* Jew

eca'tombe *f* **fare un'~** wreak havoc

ecc *abbr* (*eccetera*) etc

ecce'den|te *adj* (peso, bagaglio) excess. **~za** *f* excess; (*d'avanzo*) surplus; **avere qcsa in ~za** have an excess of sth; **bagagli in ~za** excess baggage. **~za di cassa** surplus. **ec'cedere** *vt* exceed ●*vi* go too far; **eccedere nel bere** drink too much

eccel'len|te *adj* excellent. **~za** *f* excellence; (*titolo*) Excellency; **per ~za** par excellence. **ec'cellere** *vi* excel (**in** at)

ec'centrico, -a *adj* & *mf* eccentric. **eccess'ivo** *adj* excessive

ec'cesso *m* excess; **andare agli eccessi** go to extremes; **all'~** to excess. **~ di velocità** speeding

ec'cetera *adv* et cetera

ec'cetto *prep* except; **~ che** (*a meno che*) unless. **eccettu'are** *vt* except

eccezio'nal|e *adj* exceptional. **~'mente** *adv* exceptionally; (*contrariamente alla regola*) as an exception

eccezi'one *f* exception; (*jur*) objection; **a ~ di** with the exception of

eccita'mento *m* excitement. **ecci-**

'tante *adj* exciting; (*sostanza*) stimulant ●*m* stimulant

ecci'ta|re *vt* excite. **~rsi** *vr* get excited. **~to** *adj* excited

eccitazi'one *f* excitement

ecclesi'astico *adj* ecclesiastical ●*m* priest

'ecco *adv* (*qui*) here; (*là*) there; **~!** exactly!; **~ fatto** there we are; **~ la tua borsa** here is your bag; **~ [il] mio figlio** there is my son; **~mi** here I am; **~ tutto** that is all

ec'come *adv* & *int* and how!

echeggi'are *vi* echo

e'clissi *f inv* eclipse

'eco *f* (*pl m* **echi**) echo

ecogra'fia *f* scan

ecolo'gia *f* ecology. **eco'logico** *adj* ecological; (*prodotto*) environmentally friendly

e commerci'ale *f* ampersand

econo'm|ia *f* economy; (*scienza*) economics; **fare ~ia** economize (**di** on). **eco'nomico** *adj* economic; (*a buon prezzo*) cheap. **~ista** *mf* economist. **~iz'zare** *vt/i* economize; save (tempo, denaro). **e'conomo, -a** *adj* thrifty ●*mf* (*di collegio*) bursar

é'cru *adj inv* raw

ec'zema *m* eczema

ed *conj vedi* **e**

'edera *f* ivy

e'dicola *f* [newspaper] kiosk

edifi'cabile *adj* (area, terreno) *classified as* suitable for development

edifi'cante *adj* edifying

edifi'care *vt* build

edi'ficio *m* building; *fig* structure

e'dile *adj* building *attrib*

edi'lizi|a *f* building trade. **~o** *adj* building *attrib*

edi'tore, -'trice *adj* publishing ●*mf* publisher; (*curatore*) editor. **~to'ria** *f* publishing. **~tori'ale** *adj* publishing ●*m* editorial

edizi'one *f* edition; (*di manifestazione*)

performance. ~ ridotta abridg[e]ment. ~ della sera (di telegiornale) evening news

edu'ca|re vt educate; (allevare) bring up. ~**'tivo** adj educational. ~**to** adj polite. ~**tore**, ~**trice** mf educator. ~**zi'one** f education; (di bambini) upbringing; (buone maniere) [good] manners pl. ~**zione fisica** physical education

e'felide f freckle

effemi'nato adj effeminate

efferve'scente adj effervescent; (frizzante) fizzy; (aspirina) soluble

effettiva'mente adv è troppo tardi – ~ it's too late – so it is

effet'tivo adj actual; (efficace) effective; (personale) permanent; (Mil) regular •m sum total

ef'fett|o m effect; (impressione) impression; in ~ i in fact; ~ i personali personal belongings. ~**u'are** vt carry out (controllo, sondaggio). ~**u'arsi** vr take place

effi'cac|e adj effective. ~**ia** f effectiveness

effici'en|te adj efficient. ~**za** f efficiency

ef'fimero adj ephemeral

effusi'one f effusion

E'geo m l'~ the Aegean [Sea]

E'gitto m Egypt. **egizi'ano, -a** agg & mf Egyptian

'egli pers pron he; ~ **stesso** he himself

ego'centrico, -a adj egocentric

ego'is|mo m selfishness. ~**ta** adj selfish •mf selfish person. ~**tico** adj selfish

e'gregio adj distinguished; E~ **Signore** Dear Sir

eiaculazi'one f ejaculation

elabo'ra|re vt elaborate; process (dati). ~**to** adj elaborate. ~**zi'one** f elaboration; (di dati) processing. ~**zione [di] testi** word processing

elar'gire vt lavish

elastici'tà f elasticity. ~**z'zato** adj (stoffa) elasticated. **e'lastico** adj elastic; (tessuto) stretch; (orario, mente) flexible; (persona) easygoing •m elastic; (fascia) rubber band

ele'fante m elephant

ele'gan|te adj elegant. ~**za** f elegance

e'leggere vt elect. **eleg'gibile** adj eligible

elemen'tare adj elementary; **scuola** ~ primary school

ele'mento m element; **elementi** pl (fatti) data; (rudimenti) elements

ele'mosina f charity; **chiedere l'**~ beg. **elemosi'nare** vt/i beg

elen'care vt list

e'lenco m list. ~ **abbonati** telephone directory. ~ **telefonico** telephone directory

elet'tivo adj (carica) elective. **e'letto, -a** pp di **eleggere** •adj chosen •mf elected member

eletto'ra|le adj electoral. ~**to** m electorate

elet'|tore, -'trice mf voter

elet'trauto m inv garage for electrical repairs

elettri'cista m electrician

elettri|cità f electricity. **e'lettrico** adj electric. ~**z'zante** adj (notizia, gara) electrifying. ~**z'zare** vt fig electrify. ~**z'zato** adj fig electrified

elettrocardio'gramma m electrocardiogram

e'lettrodo m electrode

elettrodo'mestico m [electrical] household appliance

elet'trone m electron

elet'tronico, -a adj electronic •f electronics

ele'va|re vt raise; (promuovere) promote; (erigere) erect; (fig: migliorare) better; ~ **al quadrato/cubo** square/cube. ~**rsi** vr rise; (edificio:) stand.

~**to** adj high. ~**zi|one** f elevation

elezi'one f election

'elica f (Aeron, Naut) propeller; (del ventilatore) blade

eli'cottero m helicopter

elimi'na|re vt eliminate. ~**toria** f Sport preliminary heat. ~**zi'one** f elimination

é'li|te f inv élite. ~**tista** adj élitist

'ella pers pron she

el'metto m helmet

elogi'are vt praise

elo'quen|te adj eloquent; fig telltale. ~**za** f eloquence

e'lu|dere vt elude; evade (sorveglianza). ~**sivo** adj elusive

el'vetico adj Swiss

emaci'ato adj emaciated

'e-mail f e-mail; indirizzo ~ e-mail address. ~ **spazzatura** junk e-mail

ema'na|re vt give off; pass (legge) ● vi emanate

emanci'pa|re vt emancipate. ~**rsi** vr become emancipated. ~**to** adj emancipated. ~**zi'one** f emancipation

emargi'na|to m marginalized person. ~**zi'one** f marginalization

em'bargo m embargo

em'ble|ma m emblem. ~**'matico** adj emblematic

embrio'nale adj embryonic. **em-bri'one** m embryo

emen'da|mento m amendment. ~**'dare** vt amend

emer'gen|te adj emergent. ~**za** f emergency; in caso di ~**za** in an emergency

e'mergere vi emerge; (sottomarino:) surface; (distinguersi) stand out

e'merso pp di emergere

e'messo pp di emettere

e'mettere vt emit; give out (luce, suono); let out (grido); (mettere in circolazione) issue

emi'crania f migraine

emi'gra|re vi emigrate. ~**to, -a** mf immigrant. ~**zi'one** f emigration

emi'nen|te adj eminent. ~**za** f eminence

e'miro m emir

emis'fero m hemisphere

emis'sario m emissary

emissi'one f emission; (di denaro) issue; (trasmissione) broadcast

emit'ten|te adj issuing; (trasmittente) broadcasting ● f transmitter

emor'ra'gia f haemorrhage

emor'roidi fpl piles

emoti'vità f emotional make-up. **emo'tivo** adj emotional

emozio'na|nte adj exciting; (commovente) moving. ~**re** vt excite; (commuovere) move. ~**rsi** vr become excited; (commuoversi) be moved. ~**to** adj excited; (commosso) moved. **emo-zi'one** f emotion; (agitazione) excitement

'empio adj impious; (spietato) pitiless; (malvagio) wicked

em'pirico adj empirical

em'porio m emporium; (negozio) general store

emu'la|re vt emulate. ~**zi'one** f emulation

emulsi'one f emulsion

en'ciclica f encyclical

enciclo'pe'dia f encyclopaedia

encomi'are vt commend. **en'co-mio** m commendation

en'demico adj endemic

endo've|na f intravenous injection. ~**noso** adj intravenous; per via ~**nosa** intravenously

ener'getico adj (risorse, crisi) energy attrib; (alimento) energy-giving

ener'gia f energy. **e'nergico** adj energetic; (efficace) strong

'enfasi f emphasis

en'fati|co adj emphatic. ~**z'zare** vt emphasize

e'nigma m enigma. **enig'matico** adj enigmatic. **enig'mistica** f puzzles pl

E.N.I.T. m abbr (Ente Nazionale Italiano per il Turismo) Italian State Tourist Office

en'nesimo adj (Math) nth; ⊡ umpteenth

e'norm|e adj enormous. **~e'mente** adv massively. **~ità** f inv enormity; (assurdità) absurdity

eno'teca f wine-tasting shop

'ente m board; (società) company; (filosofia) being

en'tità f inv entity; (gravità) seriousness; (dimensione) extent

entou'rage m inv entourage

en'trambi adj & pron both

en'tra|re vi go in, enter; **~re** in go into; (stare in, trovar posto in) fit into; (arruolarsi) join; **~rci** (avere a che fare) have to do with; tu che c'entri? what has it got to do with you? **~ta** f entrance; **~te** pl (Comm) takings; (reddito) income sg

'entro prep (tempo) within

entro'terra m inv hinterland

entusias'mante adj fascinating

entusias'mar|e vt arouse enthusiasm in. **~si** vr be enthusiastic (per about)

entusi'as|mo m enthusiasm. **~ta** adj enthusiastic ● mf enthusiast. **~tico** adj enthusiastic

enume'ra|re vt enumerate. **~zi'one** f enumeration

enunci'a|re vt enunciate. **~zi'one** f enunciation

epa'tite f hepatitis

'epico adj epic

epide'mia f epidemic

epi'dermide f epidermis

epifa'nia f Epiphany

epi'gramma m epigram

epiles'sia f epilepsy. **epi'lettico, -a** adj & mf epileptic

e'pilogo m epilogue

epi'sodi|co adj episodic; caso **~co** one-off case. **~o** m episode

'epoca f age; (periodo) period; a quell'**~** in those days; auto d'**~** vintage car

ep'pure conj [and] yet

epu'rare vt purge

equa'tore m equator. **equatori'ale** adj equatorial

equazi'one f equation

e'questre adj equestrian; circo **~** circus

equili'bra|re vt balance. **~to** adj well-balanced. **equi'librio** m balance; (buon senso) common sense; (di bilancia) equilibrium

equili'brismo m fare **~** do a balancing act

e'quino m horse attrib

equi'nozio m equinox

equipaggia'mento m equipment

equipaggi'are vt equip; (di persone) man

equi'paggio m crew; (Aeron) cabin crew

equipa'rare vt make equal

é'quipe f inv team

equità f equity

equitazi'one f riding

equiva'len|te adj & m equivalent. **~za** f equivalence

equiva'lere vi **~** a be equivalent to

equivo'care vi misunderstand

e'quivoco adj equivocal; (sospetto) suspicious ● m misunderstanding

'equo adj fair, just

'era f era

'erba f grass; (aromatica, medicinale) herb. **~** cipollina chives pl. **er'baccia** f weed. **er'baceo** adj herbaceous

erbi'cida m weed-killer

erbo'rist|a mf herbalist. **∼e'ria** f herbalist's shop

er'boso adj grassy

er'culeo adj (forza) herculean

e'red|e mf heir; heiress. **∼ità** f inv inheritance; (Biol) heredity. **∼i'tare** vt inherit. **∼itarietà** f heredity. **∼i'tario** adj hereditary

ere'sia f heresy. **e'retico, -a** adj heretical ● m f heretic

e're|tto pp di erigere ● adj erect. **∼zi'one** f erection; (costruzione) building

er'gastolo m life sentence; (luogo) prison

'erica f heather

e'rigere vt erect; (fig: fondare) found

eri'tema m (cutaneo) inflammation; (solare) sunburn

er'metico adj hermetic; (a tenuta d'aria) airtight

'ernia f hernia

e'rodere vt erode

e'ro|e m hero. **∼ico** adj heroic. **∼ismo** m heroism

ero'gare vt distribute; (fornire) supply. **∼zi'one** f supply

ero'ina f heroine; (droga) heroin

erosi'one f erosion

e'rotico adj erotic

er'rante adj wandering. **er'rare** vi wander; (sbagliare) be mistaken

er'rato adj (sbagliato) mistaken

erronea'mente adv mistakenly

er'rore m error; (di stampa) misprint; essere in **∼** be wrong

'erta f stare all'**∼** be on the alert

eru'di|rsi vr get educated. **∼to** adj learned

erut'tare vt (vulcano:) erupt ● vi (ruttare) belch. **eruzi'one** f eruption; (Med) rash

esage'ra|re vt exaggerate ● vi exaggerate; (nel comportamento) go over

the top; **∼re nel mangiare** eat too much. **∼ta'mente** adv excessively. **∼to** adj exaggerated; (prezzo) exorbitant ● m **è un ∼to** he exaggerates **∼zi'one** f exaggeration; **è costato un'∼zione** it cost the earth

esa'lare vt/i exhale

esal'ta|re vt exalt; (entusiasmare) elate. **∼to** adj (fanatico) fanatical ● m fanatic. **∼zi'one** f exaltation; (in discorso) fervour

e'same m examination, exam; **dare un ∼** take an exam; **prendere in ∼** examine. **∼ del sangue** blood test. **esami** pl **di maturità** ≈ A-levels

esami'na|re vt examine. **∼tore, ∼trice** mf examiner

e'sangue adj bloodless

e'sanime adj lifeless

esaspe'rante adj exasperating

esaspe'ra|re vt exasperate. **∼rsi** vr get exasperated. **∼zi'one** f exasperation

esat|ta'mente adv exactly. **∼tezza** f exactness; (precisione) precision; (di risultato) accuracy

e'satto pp di esigere ● adj exact; (risposta, risultato) correct; (orologio) right; **hai l'ora esatta?** do you have the right time?; **sono le due esatte** it's two o'clock exactly

esat'tore m collector

esau'dire vt grant; fulfil (speranze)

esau'riente adj exhaustive

esau'ri|re vt exhaust. **∼rsi** vr exhaust oneself; (merci ecc:) run out. **∼to** adj exhausted; (merci) sold out; (libro) out of print; **fare il tutto ∼to** (spettacolo:) play to a full house

'esca f bait

escande'scenz|a f outburst; **dare in ∼e** lose one's temper

escla'ma|re vi exclaim. **∼tivo** adj exclamatory. **∼zi'one** f exclamation

es'clu|dere vt exclude (possibilità,

ipotesi). ~si'one f exclusion. ~'siva f exclusive right; in ~siva exclusive. ~'siva'mente adv exclusively. ~'sivo adj exclusive. e'so pp di escludere ● adj non è ~so che ci sia il's not out of the question that he'll be there

escogi'tare vt contrive

escursi'one f excursion; (scorreria) raid; (di temperatura) range

ese'crabile adj abominable. ~re vt abhor

esecu'tivo adj & m executive. ~'tore, ~'trice mf executor; (Mus) performer. ~zi'one f execution; (Mus) performance

esegu'ire vt carry out; (Jur) execute; (Mus) perform

e'sempio m example; ad o per ~ for example; dare l'~ a qcno set sb an example; fare un ~ give an example

esem'plare m specimen; (di libro) copy

esen'tar|e vt exempt. ~si vr free oneself. e'sente adj exempt. esente da imposta duty-free. esente da IVA VAT-exempt

esen'tasse adj duty-free

e'sequie fpl funeral rites

eser'cente mf shopkeeper

eserci'ta|re vt exercise; (addestrare) train; (fare uso di) exert; (professione) practise. ~rsi vr practise. ~zi'one f exercise; (Mil) drill

e'sercito m army

eser'cizio m exercise; (pratica) practice; (Comm) financial year; (azienda) business; essere fuori ~ be out of practice

esi'bi|re vt show off; produce (documenti). ~rsi vr (Theat) perform; fig show off. ~zi'one f (Theat) performance; (di documenti) production

esibizio'nis|mo m showing off

esi'gen|te adj exacting; (pignolo) fastidious. ~za f demand; (bisogno) need. e'sigere vt demand; (riscuotere) collect

e'siguo adj meagre

esila'rante adj exhilarating

'esile adj slender; (voce) thin

esili'a|re vt exile. ~rsi vr go into exile. ~to, -a adj exiled ● mf exile. e'silio m exile

e'simer|e vt release. ~si vr ~si da get out of

esi'sten|te adj existing. ~za f existence.

e'sistere vi exist

esi'tante adj hesitating; (voce) faltering

esi'ta|re vi hesitate. ~zi'one f hesitation

'esito m result; avere buon ~ be a success

'esodo m exodus

e'sofago m oesophagus

eso'ne|rare vt exempt. e'sonero m exemption

esorbi'tante adj exorbitant

esorciz'zare vt exorcize

esordi'ente mf person making his/her début. e'sordio m opening; (di attore) début. esor'dire vi début

esor'tare vt (pregare) beg; (incitare) urge

e'sotico adj exotic

espa'drillas fpl espadrilles

es'pan|dere vt expand. ~dersi vr expand; (diffondersi) extend. ~si'one f expansion. ~'sivo adj expansive; (persona) friendly

espatri'are vi leave one's country. es'patrio m expatriation

espedi'ente m expedient; vivere di ~i live by one's wits

es'pellere vt expel

esperi'enza f experience; parlare per ~enza speak from experience. ~'mento m experiment

es'perto, -a adj & mf expert

espi'a|re vt atone for. ~'torio adj expiatory

espi'rare vt/i breathe out

espli'care vt carry on

esplicita'mente adv explicitly. es'plicito adj explicit

es'plodere vi explode ● vt fire

esplo'ra|re vt explore. ~'tore, ~'trice mf explorer; giovane ~tore boy scout. ~zi'one f exploration

esplosi'one f explosion. ~'sivo adj & m explosive

es'por|re vt expose; display (merci); (spiegare) expound; exhibit (quadri ecc). ~**si** vr (compromettersi) compromise oneself; (al sole) expose oneself

espor'ta|re vt export. ~'tore, ~'trice mf exporter. ~zi'one f export

esposizi'one f (mostra) exhibition; (in vetrina) display; (spiegazione ecc) exposition; (posizione, fotografia) exposure. es'posto pp di esporre ● adj exposed; esposto a (rivolto) facing ● m (Jur) statement

espressa'mente adv expressly; non l'ha detto ~ he didn't put it in so many words

espres'si|one f expression. ~'sivo adj expressive

es'presso pp di esprimere ● adj express ● m (lettera) express letter; (treno) express train; (caffè) espresso; per ~ (spedire) [by] express [post]

es'prime|re vt express. ~**si** vr express oneself

espropri'a|re vt dispossess. ~zi'one f (Jur) expropriation. es'proprio m expropriation

espulsi'one f expulsion. es'pulso pp di espellere

es'senz|a f essence. ~i'ale adj essential ● m important thing. ~ial'mente adj essentially

'essere

● vi be; c'è there is; ci sono there are; che ora è? – sono le dieci what time is it? – it's ten o'clock; chi è? – sono io who is it? – it's me; ci sono! (ho capito) I've got it!; ci siamo! (siamo arrivati) here we are at last!; siamo in due there are two of us; questa camicia è da lavare this shirt is to be washed; non è da te it's not like you; ~ di (provenire da) be from; ~ per (favorevole) be in favour of; se fossi in te,... if I were you,...; sarà! if you say so!; come sarebbe a dire? what are you getting at?

● v aux have; (in passivi) be; siamo arrivati we have arrived; ci sono stato ieri I was there yesterday; sono nato a Torino I was born in Turin; è riconosciuto come... he is recognized as...; è stato detto che it has been said that

● m being. ~ umano human being. ~ vivente living creature

essic'cato adj dried

'esso, -a pers pron he, she; (cosa, animale) it

est m east

'estasi f ecstasy; andare in ~ per go into raptures over

e'state f summer

e'sten|dere vt extend. ~**dersi** vr spread; (allungarsi) stretch. ~si'one f extension; (ampiezza) expanse; (Mus) range. ~'sivo adj extensive

estenu'ante adj exhausting

estenu'a|re vt wear out; deplete (risorse, casse). ~**rsi** vr wear oneself out

esteri'or|e adj & m exterior. ~'mente adv externally; (di persone) outwardly

esterna'mente adv on the outside

ester'nare vt express, show

e'sterno adj external; per uso ~ for external use only ● m (allievo) day-boy; (Archit) exterior; (in film) location shot

'estero adj foreign ● m foreign countries pl; all'~ abroad

esterre'fatto adj horrified

e'steso pp di estendere ● adj extensive; (diffuso) widespread; per ~ (scrivere) in full

e'stetic|a f aesthetics sg. ~a'mente adv aesthetically. ~o, -a adj aesthetic; (chirurgia, chirurgo) plastic. este'tista f beautician

'estimo m estimate

e'stin|guere vt extinguish. ~guersi vr die out. ~to, -a pp di estinguere ● mf deceased. ~tore m [fire] extinguisher. ~zi'one f extinction; (di incendio) putting out

estir'pa|re vt uproot; extract (dente); fig eradicate (crimine, malattia). ~zi'one f eradication; (di dente) extraction

e'stivo adj summer

e'stor|cere vt extort. ~si'one f extortion. ~to pp di estorcere

estradizi'one f extradition

e'straneo, -a adj extraneous; (straniero) foreign ● mf stranger

estrani'ar|e vt estrange. ~si vr become estranged

e'stra|rre vt extract; (sorteggiare) draw. ~tto pp di estrarre ● m extract; (brano) excerpt; (documento) abstract. ~tto conto statement [of account], bank statement. ~zi'one f extraction; (sorte) draw

estrema'mente adv extremely

estre'mis|mo m extremism. ~ta mf extremist

estremità f inv extremity; (di una corda) end ● fpl (Anat) extremities

e'stremo adj extreme; (ultimo) last; misure estreme drastic measures; l'E~ Oriente the Far East ● m (limite) extreme. estremi pl (di documento) main points; (di reato) essential elements; essere agli estremi be at the end of one's tether

'estro m (disposizione artistica) talent; (ispirazione) inspiration; (capriccio) whim. e'stroso adj talented; (capriccioso) unpredictable

estro'mettere vt expel

estro'verso adj extroverted ● m extrovert

estu'ario m estuary

esube'ran|te adj exuberant. ~za f exuberance

'esule mf exile

esul'tante adj exultant

esul'tare vi rejoice

esu'mare vt exhume

età f inv age; raggiungere la maggiore ~ come of age; un uomo di mezz'~ a middle-aged man

'etere m ether. e'tereo adj ethereal

eterna'mente adv eternally

eternità f eternity; è un'~ che non la vedo I haven't seen her for ages

e'terno adj eternal; (questione, problema) age-old; in ~ 🄸 for ever

eterosessu'ale mf heterosexual

'etica f ethics

eti'chetta[1] f label; price-tag

eti'chetta[2] f etiquette

etichet'tare vt label

'etico adj ethical

eti'lometro m Breathalyzer®

Eti'opia f Ethiopia

'etnico adj ethnic

e'trusco adj & mf Etruscan

'ettaro m hectare

'etto, etto'grammo m hundred grams, ≈ quarter pound

eucari'stia f Eucharist

eufe'mismo *m* euphemism
eufo'ria *f* elation; (*Med*) euphoria. **eu'forico** *adj* elated; (*Med*) euphoric
'euro *m inv Fin* euro
Euro'city *m* international Intercity
eurodepu'tato *m* Euro MP, MEP
Eu'ropa *f* Europe. **euro'peo, -a** *agg & mf* European
eutana'sia *f* euthanasia
evacu'a|re *vt* evacuate. **~zi'one** *f* evacuation
e'vadere *vt* evade; (*sbrigare*) deal with ●*vi* **~ da** escape from
evane'scente *adj* vanishing
evan'gel|ico *adj* evangelical. **evange'lista** *m* evangelist
evapo'ra|re *vi* evaporate. **~zi'one** *f* evaporation
evasi'one *f* escape; (*fiscale*) evasion; *fig* escapism. **eva'sivo** *adj* evasive
e'vaso *pp di* evadere ●*m* fugitive
eva'sore *m* **~ fiscale** tax evader
eveni'enza *f* eventuality
e'vento *m* event
eventu'al|e *adj* possible. **~ità** *f inv* eventuality
evi'den|te *adj* evident; **è ~te che** it is obvious that. **~te'mente** *adv* evidently. **~za** *f* evidence; **mettere in ~za** emphasize; **mettersi in ~za** make oneself conspicuous
evidenzi'a|re *vt* highlight. **~'tore** *m* (*penna*) highlighter
evi'tare *vt* avoid; (*risparmiare*) spare
evo'care *vt* evoke
evo'lu|to *pp di* evolvere ●*adj* evolved; (*progredito*) progressive; (*civiltà, nazione*) advanced; **una donna evoluta** a modern woman. **~zi'one** *f* evolution; (*di ginnasta, aereo*) circle
e'volver|e *vt* develop. **~si** *vr* evolve
ev'viva *int* hurray; **~ il Papa!** long live the Pope!; **gridare ~** cheer
ex+ *pref* ex+, former

'extra *adj inv* extra; (*qualità*) first-class ●*m inv* extra
extracomuni'tario *adj* non-EU
extrater'restre *mf* extra-terrestrial

Extravergine Olive oil which is obtained from the first pressing of the olives is called *extravergine* (extra virgin). It has a distinctive peppery flavour and is often a cloudy greenish colour. A less refined grade, suitable for cooking, is obtained by using chemical methods. This is called simply *olio d'oliva*.

Ff

fa[1] *m inv* (*Mus*) F
fa[2] *adv* ago; **due mesi ~** two months ago
fabbi'sogno *m* requirements *pl*
'fabbrica *f* factory
fabbri'cabile *adj* (*area, terreno*) that can be built on
fabbri'cante *m* manufacturer
fabbri'ca|re *vt* build; (*produrre*) manufacture; (*fig: inventare*) fabricate. **~to** *m* building. **~zi'one** *f* manufacturing; (*costruzione*) building
'fabbro *m* blacksmith
fac'cend|a *f* matter; **~e** *pl* (*lavori domestici*) housework *sg*. **~i'ere** *m* wheeler-dealer
fac'chino *m* porter
'facci|a *f* face; (*di foglio*) side; **~a a ~a** face to face; **~a tosta** cheek; **voltar ~a** change sides; **di ~a** (*palazzo*) opposite; **alla ~a di** (**I**: *a dispetto di*) in spite of. **~'ata** *f* façade; (*di foglio*) side; (*fig: esteriorità*) outward

appearance

fa'ceto adj facetious; tra il serio e il ~ half joking

fa'chiro m fakir

facil|e adj easy; (affabile) easygoing; essere ~e alle critiche be quick to criticize; essere ~e al riso laugh a lot; ~e a farsi easy to do; è ~e che piova it's likely to rain. ~ità f ease; (disposizione) aptitude; avere ~ità di parola express oneself well

facili'ta|re vt facilitate. ~zi'one f facility; ~zioni pl special terms

facil'mente adv (con facilità) easily; (probabilmente) probably

faci'lone adj slapdash. ~'ria f slapdash attitude

faci'noroso adj violent

facoltà f inv faculty; (potere) power. facolta'tivo adj optional; fermata facoltativa request stop

facol'toso adj wealthy

'faggio m beech

fagi'ano m pheasant

fagio'lino m French bean

fagi'olo m bean; a ~ (arrivare, capitare) at the right time

fagoci'tare vt gobble up (società)

fa'gotto m bundle; (Mus) bassoon

'falda f feud

fai da te m do-it-yourself, DIY

fal'cata f stride

'falc|e f scythe. fal'cetto m sickle. ~i'are vt cut; fig mow down. ~ia'trice f [lawn-]mower

'falco m hawk

fal'cone m falcon

'falda f stratum; (di neve) flake; (di cappello) brim; (pendio) slope

fale'gname m carpenter. ~'ria f carpentry

'falla f leak

fal'lace adj deceptive

fallimen'tare adj disastrous; (Jur) bankruptcy. falli'mento m Fin bank-

ruptcy; fig failure

fal'li|re vi Fin go bankrupt; fig fail ● vt miss (colpo). ~to, -a adj unsuccessful; Fin bankrupt ● mf failure; Fin bankrupt

'fallo m fault; (errore) mistake; Sport foul; (imperfezione) flaw; senza ~ without fail

falò m inv bonfire

fal'sar|e vt alter; (falsificare) falsify. ~io, -a mf forger; (di documenti) counterfeiter

falsifi'ca|re vt fake; (contraffare) forge. ~zi'one f (di documento) falsification

falsità f falseness

'falso adj false; (sbagliato) wrong; (opera d'arte ecc) fake; (gioielli, oro) imitation ● m forgery; giurare il ~ commit perjury

'fama f fame; (reputazione) reputation

'fame f hunger; aver ~ be hungry; fare la ~ barely scrape a living. fa-'melico adj ravenous

famige'rato adj infamous

fa'miglia f family

famili'ar|e adj family attrib; (ben noto) familiar; (senza cerimonie) informal ● mf relative, relation. ~ità f familiarity; (informalità) informality. ~iz'zarsi vr familiarize oneself

fa'moso adj famous

fa'nale m lamp; (Auto) light. fanali pl posteriori (Auto) rear lights

fa'natico, -a adj fanatical; essere ~ di calcio be a football fanatic ● mf fanatic. fana'tismo m fanaticism

fanci'ul|la f young girl. ~'lezza f childhood. ~lo m young boy

fan'donia f lie; fandonie! nonsense!

fan'fara f fanfare; (complesso) brass band

fanfaro'nata f brag. fanfa'rone, -a mf braggart

fan'ghiglia f mud. 'fango m mud.

fan'goso *adj* muddy

fannul'lone, -a *mf* idler

fantasci'enza *f* science fiction

fanta'si|a *f* fantasy; (*immaginazione*) imagination; (*capriccio*) fancy; (*di tessuto*) pattern. ∼'oso *adj* (stilista, ragazzo) imaginative; (*resoconto*) improbable

fan'tasma *m* ghost

fantasti'c|are *vi* day-dream. ∼he'ria *f* day-dream. fan'tastico *adj* fantastic; (*racconto*) fantasy

'fante *m* infantryman; (*nelle carte*) jack. ∼'ria *m* infantry

fan'tino *m* jockey

fan'toccio *m* puppet

fanto'matico *adj* phantom *attrib*

fara'butto *m* trickster

fara'ona *f* (*uccello*) guinea-fowl

far'ci|re *vt* stuff; fill (torta). ∼to *adj* stuffed; (*dolce*) filled

far'dello *m* bundle; *fig* burden

'fare
- *vt* do; make (dolce, letto ecc); (*recitare la parte di*) play; (*trascorrere*) spend; ∼ una pausa/un sogno have a break/a dream; ∼ colpo su impress; ∼ paura a frighten; ∼ piacere a please; farla finita put an end to it; ∼ l'insegnante be a teacher; ∼ lo scemo play the idiot; ∼ una settimana al mare spend a week at the seaside; 3 più 3 fa 6 3 and 3 makes 6; quanto fa? - fanno 10 000 euro how much is it? - it's 10,000 euros; far ∼ qcsa a qcno get sb to do sth; (*costringere*) make sb do sth; ∼ vedere show; fammi parlare let me speak; niente a che ∼ con nothing to do with; non c'è niente da ∼ (*per problema*) there is nothing we/you/etc. can do; fa caldo/buio it's

warm/dark; non fa niente it doesn't matter; strada facendo on the way; farcela (*riuscire*) manage
- *vi* fai in modo di venire try and come; ∼ da act as; ∼ per make as if to; ∼ presto be quick; non fa per me it's not for me
- *m* way; sul far del giorno at daybreak.
- **farsi** *vr* (*diventare*) get; farsi avanti come forward; farsi i fatti propri mind one's own business; farsi la barba shave; farsi il ragazzo 🄴 find a boyfriend; farsi male hurt oneself; farsi strada (*aver successo*) make one's way in the world

fa'retto *m* spot[light]

far'falla *f* butterfly

farfal'lino *m* (cravatta) bow tie

farfugli'are *vt* mutter

fa'rina *f* flour. fari'nacei *mpl* starchy food *sg*

fa'ringe *f* pharynx

fari'noso *adj* (neve) powdery; (mela) soft; (patata) floury

farma|'ceutico *adj* pharmaceutical. ∼'cia *f* pharmacy; (*negozio*) chemist's [shop]. ∼cia di turno duty chemist. ∼'cista *mf* chemist. **'farmaco** *m* drug

---

Farmacia A *farmacia* in Italy sells medicines and health-related products, whereas a *profumeria* sells not only perfume, but also beauty and personal hygiene products. For film and developing services it is necessary to go to a shop specializing in photographic equipment.

i

'faro *m* (*Auto*) headlight; (*Aeron*) beacon; (*costruzione*) lighthouse

'farsa *f* farce

'fasci|a *f* band; (*zona*) area; (*ufficiale*)

sash; (benda) bandage. ~'are vt bandage; cling to (fianchi). ~a'tura f dressing; (azione) bandaging

fa'scicolo m file; (di rivista) issue; (libretto) booklet

fascino m fascination

fascio m bundle; (di fiori) bunch

fa'scis|mo m fascism. ~ta mf fascist

fase f phase

fa'stidi|o m nuisance; (scomodo) inconvenience; dar ~o a qcno bother sb; ~i pl (preoccupazioni) worries; (disturbi) troubles. ~oso adj tiresome

fasto m pomp. fa'stoso adj sumptuous

fa'sullo adj bogus

fata f fairy

fa'tale adj fatal; (inevitabile) fated

fata'lis|mo m fatalism. ~ista mf fatalist. ~ità f inv fate; (caso sfortunato) misfortune. ~'mente adv inevitably

fa'tica f effort; (lavoro faticoso) hard work; (stanchezza) fatigue; a ~ with great difficulty; è ~ sprecata it's a waste of time; fare ~ a fare qcsa find it difficult to do sth; fare ~ a finire qcsa struggle to finish sth. fa-ti'caccia f pain

fati'ca|re vi toil; ~re a (stentare) find it difficult to. ~ta f effort; (sfacchinata) grind. fati'coso adj tiring; (difficile) difficult

fato m fate

at'taccio m hum foul deed

at'tezze fpl features

at'tibile adj feasible

fatto pp di fare ●adj done, made; ~ a mano hand-made ●m fact; (azione) action; (avvenimento) event; bada ai fatti tuoi mind your own business; di ~ in fact; in ~ di as regards

at'to|re m (Math, causa) factor; (di fattoria) farm manager. ~'ria f farm; (casa) farmhouse

atto'rino m messenger [boy]

fattucchi'era f witch

fat'tura f (stile) cut; (lavorazione) workmanship; (Comm) invoice

fattu'ra|re vt invoice; (adulterare) adulterate. ~to m turnover, sales pl. ~zi'one f invoicing, billing

'fatuo adj fatuous

fau'tore m supporter

'fava f broad bean

fa'vella f speech

fa'villa f spark

'favo|la f fable; (fiaba) story; (oggetto di pettegolezzi) laughing-stock; (meraviglia) dream. ~'loso adj fabulous

fa'vore m favour; essere a ~ di be in favour of; per ~ please; di ~ (condizioni, trattamento) preferential. ~ggia'mento m (Jur) aiding and abetting. favo'revole adj favourable. ~vol'mente adv favourably

favo'ri|re vt favour; (promuovere) promote; vuol ~re? will you have some? (entrare) will you come in?. ~to, -a adj & mf favourite

fax m inv fax. fa'xare vt fax

fazi'one f faction

faziosità f bias. fazi'oso m sectarian

fazzo'let|tino m ~ [di carta] [paper] tissue

fazzo'letto m handkerchief; (da testa) headscarf

feb'braio m February

'febbre f fever; avere la ~ have o run a temperature. ~ da fieno hay fever. feb'brile adj feverish

feccia f dregs pl

fecola f potato flour

fecon'da|re vt fertilize. ~'tore m fertilizer. ~zi'one f fertilization. ~zione artificiale artificial insemination. fe'condo adj fertile

fede f faith; (fiducia) trust; (anello) wedding-ring; in buona/mala ~ in good/bad faith; prestar ~ a believe; tener ~ alla parola keep one's word. fe'dele adj faithful • mf believer; (seguace) follower. ~l'mente adv faithfully. ~ltà f faithfulness

'federa f pillowcase

fede'ra|le adj federal. ~lismo m federalism. ~zi'one f federation

fe'dina f avere la ~ penale sporca/pulita have a no criminal record

'fegato m liver; fig guts pl

'felce f fern

fe'lic|e adj happy; (fortunato) lucky. ~ità f happiness

felici'ta|rsi vr ~rsi con congratulate. ~zi'oni fpl congratulations

'felpa f (indumento) sweatshirt

fel'pato adj brushed; (passo) stealthy

'feltro m felt; (cappello) felt hat

'femmin|a f female. femmi'nile adj feminine; (abbigliamento) women's; (sesso) female • m feminine. ~ilità f femininity. femmi'nismo m feminism

'femore m femur

fend|ere vt split. ~i'tura f split; (in roccia) crack

feni'cottero m flamingo

fenome'nale adj phenomenal. fe'nomeno m phenomenon

feretro m coffin

feri'ale adj weekday; giorno ~ weekday

'ferie fpl holidays; (di università, tribunale ecc) vacation sg; andare in ~ go on holiday

feri'mento m wounding

fe'ri|re vt wound; (in incidente) injure; fig hurt. ~rsi vr injure oneself. ~ta f wound. ~to adj wounded • m wounded person; (Mil) casualty

'ferma f (Mil) period of service

ferma'capelli m inv hairslide

ferma'carte m inv paperweight

fermacra'vatta m inv tiepin

fer'maglio m clasp; (spilla) brooch; (per capelli) hair slide

ferma'mente adv firmly

fer'ma|re vt stop; (fissare) fix; (Jur) detain • vi stop. ~rsi vr stop. ~ta f stop. ~ta dell'autobus bus-stop. ~ta a richiesta request stop

fermen'ta|re vi ferment. ~zi'one f fermentation. fer'mento m ferment; (lievito) yeast

fer'mezza f firmness

'fermo adj still; (veicolo) stationary; (stabile) steady; (orologio) not working • m (Jur) detention; (Mech) catch; in stato di ~ in custody

fe'roc|e adj ferocious; (bestia) wild; (dolore) unbearable. ~e'mente adv fiercely. ~ia f ferocity

fer'raglia f scrap iron

ferra'gosto m 15 August (bank holiday in Italy); (periodo) August holidays pl

ferra'menta fpl ironmongery sg; negozio di ~ ironmonger's

fer'ra|re vt shoe (cavallo). ~to adj ~to in (preparato in) well up in

'ferreo adj iron

'ferro m iron; (attrezzo) tool; (di chirurgo) instrument; bistecca ai ferri grilled steak; di ~ (memoria) excellent; (alibi) cast-iron; salute di ~ iron constitution. ~ battuto wrought iron. ~ da calza knitting needle. ~ di cavallo horseshoe. ~ da stiro iron

ferro'vecchio m scrap merchant

ferro'vi|a f railway. ~'ario adj railway. ~'ere m railwayman

fer'tille adj fertile. ~ità f fertility. ~iz'zante m fertilizer

fer'vente adj blazing; fig fervent

'ferv|ere vi (preparativi:) be well under way

'fervido adj fervent; ~i auguri best wishes

fer'vore m fervour

fesse'ria f nonsense

'fesso pp di fendere ● adj cracked; (🔟: sciocco) foolish ● m 🔟 (idiota) fool; far ~ qcno con sb

fes'sura f crack; (per gettone ecc) slot

festa f feast; (giorno festivo) holiday; (compleanno) birthday; (ricevimento) party; fig joy; fare ~ a qcno welcome sb; essere in ~ be on holiday; far ~ celebrate. ~i'olo adj festive

festeggia'mento m celebration; (manifestazione) festivity

festeggi'are vt celebrate; (accogliere festosamente) give a hearty welcome to

fe'stino m party

festività fpl festivities. fe'stivo adj holiday; (lieto) festive. festivi mpl public holidays

fe'stoso adj merry

fe'tente adj evil smelling; fig revolting ● mf 🔟 bastard

fe'ticcio m fetish

feto m foetus

fe'tore m stench

fetta f slice; a fette sliced. ~ bi-scottata slices of crispy toast-like bread

fet'tuccia f tape; (con nome) name tape

eu'dale adj feudal. 'feudo m feud

FSS abbr (Ferrovie dello Stato) Italian state railways

i'aba f fairy-tale. fia'besco adj fairy-tale

i'acca f weariness; (indolenza) laziness; battere la ~a be sluggish. fiac'care vt weaken. ~o adj weak; (indolente) slack; (stanco) weary; (partita) dull

i'acco|la f torch. ~lata f torchlight procession

i'ala f phial

i'amma f flame; (Naut) pennant; in fiamme aflame. andare in fiamme go up in flames. ~ ossidrica blowtorch

fiam'mante adj flaming; nuovo ~nte brand new. ~ta f blaze

fiammeggi'are vi blaze

fiam'mifero m match

fiam'mingo, -a adj Flemish ● mf Fleming ● m (lingua) Flemish

fiancheggi'are vt border; fig support

fi'anco m side; (di persona) hip; (di animale) flank; (Mil) wing; al mio ~ by my side; ~ a ~ (lavorare) side by side

fi'asco m flask; fig fiasco; fare ~ be a fiasco

fia'tare vi breathe; (parlare) breathe a word

fi'ato m breath; (vigore) stamina; strumenti a ~ wind instruments; senza ~ breathlessly; tutto d'un ~ (bere, leggere) all in one go

'fibbia f buckle

'fibra f fibre; fibre pl (alimentari) roughage. ~ ottica optical fibre

ficca'naso m nosey parker

fic'car|e vt thrust; drive (chiodo ecc); (🔟: mettere) shove. ~si vr thrust oneself; (nascondersi) hide; ~si nei guai get oneself into trouble

fiche f inv (gettone) chip

'fico m (albero) fig-tree; (frutto) fig. ~ d'India prickly pear

'fico, -a 🔟 mf cool sort ● adj cool

fidanza'mento m engagement

fidan'za|rsi vr get engaged. ~to, -a mf (ufficiale) fiancé; fiancée

fi'dar|si vr ~rsi di trust. ~to adj trustworthy

'fido m devoted follower; (Comm) credit

fi'duci|a f confidence; degno di ~a trustworthy; persona di ~a reliable person; di ~a (fornitore) usual. ~'oso adj trusting

fi'ele m bile; fig bitterness

fie'nile m barn. 'fieno m hay

fi'era f fair

fie'rezza f (dignità) pride. **fi'ero** adj proud

fi'evole adj faint; (luce) dim

'fifa f 🔲 jitters; aver ~ have the jitters

'figli|a f daughter; ~a unica only child. ~'astra f stepdaughter. ~'astro m stepson. ~o m son; (generico) child. ~o unico only child

Figlio di papà With the rapid rise in living standards which took place in Italy after 1945, many more children grew up in affluent families than was previously the case, and figli unici (only children) are often the norm. Children, both young and grown-up, are often given considerable financial help by their parents, and are sometimes termed figli di papà, implying that they are also spoilt.

figli'occia f goddaughter. ~o m godson

figli'o|la f girl. ~'lanza f offspring. ~lo m boy

'figo, -a ▷ FICO, -A

fi'gura f figure; (aspetto esteriore) shape; (illustrazione) illustration; far bella/brutta ~ make a good/bad impression; mi hai fatto fare una brutta ~ you made me look a fool; che ~! how embarrassing!. figu'raccia f bad impression

figu'ra|re vt represent; (simboleggiare) symbolize; (immaginare) imagine ●vi (far figura) cut a dash; (in lista) appear. ~rsi vr (immaginarsi) imagine; ~ti! imagine that!; posso? – [ma] ~ti may I? – of course!. ~'tivo adj figurative

figu'rina f ≈ cigarette card

figu|ri'nista mf dress designer. ~'rino m fashion sketch. ~'rone m fare un ~rone make an excellent impression

'fila f line; (di soldati ecc) file; (di oggetti) row; (coda) queue; di ~ in succession; fare la ~ queue [up], stand in line Am

fi'lare vt spin; (Naut) pay out ●vi (andarsene) run away; (liquido) trickle; filal 🔲 scram!; ~ con (🔲 amoreggiare) go out with

filar'monica f (orchestra) orchestra

fila'strocca f rigmarole; (per bambini) nursery rhyme

fi'la|to adj spun; (ininterrotto) running; (continuato) uninterrupted; di ~to (subito) immediately ●m yarn

fil di 'ferro m wire

fi'letto m (bordo) border; (di vite) thread; (Culin) fillet

fili'ale adj filial ●f (Comm) branch

fili'grana f filigree; (su carta) watermark

film m inv film. ~ giallo thriller. ~ a lungo metraggio feature film

fil'ma|re vt film. ~to m short film. fil'mino m cine film

'filo m thread; (tessile) yarn; (metallico) wire; (di lama) edge; (venatura) grain; (di perle) string; (d'erba) blade; (di luce) ray; con un ~ di voce in a whisper; fare il ~ a qcno fancy sb; perdere il ~ lose the thread. ~ spinato barbed wire

'filobus m inv trolleybus

filodiffusi'one f rediffusion

fi'lone m vein; (di pane) long loaf

filoso'fia f philosophy. fi'losofo, -a mf philosopher

fil'trare vt filter. 'filtro m filter

'filza f string

fin ▷ FINE, FINO

fi'nal|e adj final ●m end ●f Sport final. fina'lista mf finalist. ~ità f inv finality; (scopo) aim. ~'mente adv at last; (in ultimo) finally

fi'nanza f finance; ~i'ario adj financial. ~'ere m financier; (guardia di finanza) customs officer. ~ia'mento finanziare | fisima

_m_ funding

finanzi'a|re _vt_ fund, finance. ~'**tore**, ~'**trice** _mf_ backer

finché _conj_ until; (_per tutto il tempo che_) as long as

'**fine** _adj_ fine; (_sottile_) thin; (_udito, vista_) keen; (_raffinato_) refined ● _f_ end; alla ~ in the end; alla fin ~ after all; in fin dei conti when all's said and done; senza ~ endless ● _m_ aim. ~ **settimana** weekend

fi'**nestra** _f_ window. fine'**strella** _f_ aiuto (_Comput_) help box. fine'**strino** _m_ (_Auto, Rail_) window

fi'**nezza** _f_ fineness; (_sottigliezza_) thinness; (_raffinatezza_) refinement

'**finger|e** _vt_ pretend; feign (_affetto ecc_). ~**si** _vr_ pretend to be

fini'**menti** _mpl_ finishing touches; (_per cavallo_) harness _sg_

fini'**mondo** _m_ end of the world; _fig_ pandemonium

fi'**ni|re** _vt/i_ finish, end; (_smettere_) stop; (_diventare, andare a finire_) end up; ~**scila!** stop it!. ~**to** _adj_ finished; (_abile_) accomplished. ~'**tura** _f_ finish

finlan'**dese** _adj_ Finnish ● _mf_ Finn ● _m_ (_lingua_) Finnish

Fin'**landia** _f_ Finland

'**fino**[^1] _prep_ ~ a till, until; (_spazio_) as far as; ~ all'ultimo to the last; fin da (_tempo_) since; (_spazio_) from; fin qui as far as here; fin troppo too much; ~ a che punto how far

'**fino**[^2] _adj_ fine; (_acuto_) subtle; (_puro_) pure

fi'**nocchio** _m_ fennel; (🔲: _omosessuale_) poof

fi'**nora** _adv_ so far, up till now

'**finta** _f_ sham; _Sport_ feint; far ~ di pretend to; far ~ di niente act as if nothing had happened; per ~ (_per scherzo_) for a laugh

'**fint|o, -a** _pp di_ fingere ● _adj_ false; (_artificiale_) artificial; fare il ~**o** tonto act dumb

finzi'**one** _f_ pretence

fi'**occo** _m_ bow; (_di neve_) flake; (_nappa_) tassel; coi fiocchi _fig_ excellent. ~ **di neve** snowflake

fi'**ocina** _f_ harpoon

fi'**oco** _adj_ weak; (_luce_) dim

fi'**onda** _f_ catapult

fio'**raio, -a** _mf_ florist

fiorda'**liso** _m_ cornflower

fi'**ordo** _m_ fiord

fi'**ore** _m_ flower; (_parte scelta_) cream; fiori _pl_ (_nelle carte_) clubs; a fior d'acqua on the surface of the water; fior di (_abbondanza_) a lot of; ha i nervi a fior di pelle his nerves are on edge; a fiori flowery

fioren'**tino** _adj_ Florentine

fio'**retto** _m_ (_scherma_) foil; (_Relig_) act of mortification

fio'**rire** _vi_ flower; (_albero:_) blossom; _fig_ flourish

fio'**rista** _mf_ florist

fiori'**tura** _f_ (_di albero_) blossoming

fi'**otto** _m_ scorrere a fiotti gush out; piove a fiotti the rain is pouring down

Fi'**renze** _f_ Florence

'**firma** _f_ signature; (_nome_) name

fir'**ma|re** _vt_ sign. ~'**tario, -a** _mf_ signatory. ~**to** _adj_ (_abito, borsa_) designer _attrib_

fisar'**monica** _f_ accordion

fi'**scale** _adj_ fiscal

fischi'**are** _vi_ whistle ● _vt_ whistle; (_in segno di disapprovazione_) boo

fischiet'**t|are** _vt_ whistle. ~**io** _m_ whistling

fischi'**etto** _m_ whistle. '**fischio** _m_ whistle

'**fisco** _m_ treasury; (_tasse_) taxation; il ~ the taxman

'**fisica** _f_ physics

'**fisico, -a** _adj_ physical ● _mf_ physicist ● _m_ physique

'**fisima** _f_ whim

[^1]:
[^2]:

fisio|lo'gia f physiology. ~'logico adj physiological

fisiono'mia f features, face; (di paesaggio) appearance

fisiotera'pi|a f physiotherapy. ~sta mf physiotherapist

fis'sa|re vt fix, fasten; (guardare fissamente) stare at; arrange (appuntamento, ora). ~rsi vr (stabilirsi) settle; (fissare lo sguardo) stare; ~rsi su (ostinarsi) set one's mind on; ~rsi di fare qcsa become obsessed with doing sth. ~to m obsessive. ~zi'one f fixation; (ossessione) obsession

'fisso adj fixed; un lavoro ~ a regular job; senza fissa dimora of no fixed abode

fit'tizio adj fictitious

'fitto[1] adj thick; ~ di full of ● m depth

'fitto[2] m (affitto) rent; dare a ~ let; prendere a ~ rent; (noleggiare) hire

fiu'mana f swollen river; fig stream

fi'ume m river; fig stream

fiu'tare vt smell. fi'uto m [sense of] smell; fig nose

'flaccido adj flabby

fla'cone m bottle

fla'gello m scourge

fla'grante adj flagrant; in ~ in the act

fla'nella f flannel

'flash m inv Journ newsflash

'flauto m flute

'flebile adj feeble

'flemma f calm; (Med) phlegm

fles'sibil|e adj flexible. ~ità f flexibility

flessi'one f (del busto in avanti) forward bend

'flesso pp di flettere

flessu'oso adj supple

'flettere vt bend

flir'tare vi flirt

F.lli abbr (fratelli) Bros

'floppy disk m inv floppy disk

'florido adj flourishing

'floscio adj limp; (flaccido) flabby

'flotta f fleet. flot'tiglia f flotilla

flu'ente adj fluent

flu'ido m fluid

flu'ire vi flow

fluore'scente adj fluorescent

fluo'ro m fluorine

'flusso m flow; (Med) flux; (del mare) flood[-tide]; ~ e riflusso ebb and flow

fluttu'ante adj fluctuating

fluttu'a|re vi (prezzi, moneta:) fluctuate. ~zi'one f fluctuation

fluvi'ale adj river

fo'bia f phobia

'foca f seal

fo'caccia f (pane) flat bread; (dolce) ≈ raisin bread

fo'cale adj (distanza, punto) focal. focaliz'zare vt get into focus (fotografia); focus (attenzione); define (problema)

'foce f mouth

foco'laio m (Med) focus; fig centre

foco'lare m hearth; (caminetto) fireplace; (Techn) furnace

fo'coso adj fiery

'foder|a f lining; (di libro) dust-jacket; (di poltrona ecc) loose cover. fode'rare vt line; cover (libro). ~o m sheath

'foga f impetuosity

foggi|a f fashion; (maniera) manner; (forma) shape. ~are vt mould

'foglia f leaf; (di metallo) foil

fogli'etto m (pezzetto di carta) piece of paper

'foglio m sheet; (pagina) leaf. ~ elettronico (Comput) spreadsheet. ~ rosa (Auto) provisional licence

'fogna f sewer. ~'tura f sewerage

fo'lata f gust

fol'clo|re m folklore. ~'ristico adj

folk; (*bizzarro*) weird

folgo'ra|re *vi* (*splendere*) shine ●*vt* (*con un fulmine*) strike. ~**zi'one** *f* (*da fulmine, elettrica*) electrocution; (*idea*) brainwave

'**folgore** *f* thunderbolt

'**folla** *f* crowd

'**folle** *adj* mad; in ~ (*Auto*) in neutral

folle'mente *adv* madly

fol'lia *f* madness; alla ~ (*amare*) to distraction

'**folto** *adj* thick

fomen'tare *vt* stir up

fon'dale *m* (*Theat*) backcloth

fonda'men|ta *fpl* foundations. ~'**tale** *adj* fundamental. ~**to** *m* (*di principio, teoria*) foundation

fon'da|re *vt* establish; base (*ragionamento, accusa*). ~**to** *adj* (*ragionamento*) well-founded. ~**zi'one** *f* establishment; ~**zioni** *pl* (*di edificio*) foundations

fon'delli *mpl* prendere qcno per i ~ 🇮🇹 pull sb's leg

fon'dente *adj* (*cioccolato*) dark

'**fonder|e** *vt/i* melt; (*colori*) blend. ~**si** *vr* melt; (*Comm*) merge

'**fondi** *mpl* (*denaro*) funds; (*di caffè*) grounds

'**fondo** *adj* deep; è notte fonda it's the middle of the night ●*m* bottom; (*fine*) end; (*sfondo*) background; (*indole*) nature; (*somma di denaro*) fund; (*feccia*) dregs *pl*; andare a ~ (*nave*:) sink; da cima a ~ from beginning to end; in ~ after all; in ~ a ~ deep down; fino in ~ right to the end; (*capire*) thoroughly. ~ **d'investimento** investment trust

fondo'tinta *m* foundation cream

fon'duta *f* ≈ fondue

fo'netic|a *f* phonetics. ~**o** *adj* phonetic

fon'tana *f* fountain

'**fonte** *f* spring; *fig* source ●*m* font

fo'raggio *m* forage

fo'rar|e *vt* pierce; punch (*biglietto*) ●*vi* puncture. ~**si** *vr* (*gomma, pallone*:) go soft

'**forbici** *fpl* scissors

forbi'cine *fpl* (*per le unghie*) nail scissors

'**forca** *f* fork; (*patibolo*) gallows *pl*

for'**cella** *f* fork; (*per capelli*) hairpin

for'**chet|ta** *f* fork. ~'**tata** *f* (*quantità*) forkful

for'**cina** *f* hairpin

'**forcipe** *m* forceps *pl*

for'**cone** *m* pitchfork

fo'**resta** *f* forest. fore'stale *adj* forest *attrib*

foresti'**ero, -a** *adj* foreign ●*mf* foreigner

for'**fait** *m inv* fixed price; dare ~ (*abbandonare*) give up

for'**fora** *f* dandruff

for'**gi|a** *f* forge. ~**are** *vt* forge

'**forma** *f* form; (*sagoma*) shape; (*Culin*) mould; (*da calzolaio*) last; essere in ~ be in good form; a ~ di in the shape of; forme *pl* (*del corpo*) figure *sg*; (*convenzioni*) appearances

formag'**gino** *m* processed cheese. for'**maggio** *m* cheese

for'**mal|e** *adj* formal. ~**ità** *f inv* formality. ~**izzarsi** *vr* stand on ceremony. ~'**mente** *adv* formally

for'**ma|re** *vt* form. ~**rsi** *vr* form; (*svilupparsi*) develop. ~**to** *m* size; (*di libro*) format; ~**to tessera** (*fotografia*) passportsize

format'**tare** *vt* format

formazi'**one** *f* formation; *Sport* line-up. ~ **professionale** vocational training

formico'l|**are** *vi* (*braccio ecc*:) tingle; ~**are di** be swarming with; mi ~**a la mano** I have pins and needles in my hand. ~**io** *m* swarming; (*di braccio ecc*) pins and needles *pl*

formi'**dabile** *adj* (*tremendo*) formidable; (*eccezionale*) tremendous

for'mina f mould

for'moso adj shapely

'formula f formula. **formu'lare** vt formulate; (esprimere) express

for'nace f furnace; (per laterizi) kiln

for'naio m baker; (negozio) bakery

for'nello m stove; (di pipa) bowl

for'ni|re vt supply (di with). ~**tore** m supplier. ~**tura** f supply

'forno m oven; (panetteria) bakery; al ~ roast. ~ a microonde microwave [oven]

'foro m hole; (romano) forum; (tribunale) [law] court

'forse adv perhaps, maybe; essere in ~ be in doubt

forsen'nato, -a adj mad ●mf madman; madwoman

'forte adj strong; (colore) bright; (suono) loud; (resistente) tough; (spesa) considerable; (dolore) severe; (pioggia) heavy; (a tennis, calcio) good; (fam: simpatico) great; (taglia) large ● adv strongly; (parlare) loudly; (velocemente) fast; (piovere) heavily ●m (fortezza) fort; (specialità) strong point

for'tezza f fortress; (forza morale) fortitude

fortifi'care vt fortify

for'tino m (Mil) blockhouse

for'tuito adj fortuitous; incontro ~ chance encounter

for'tuna f fortune; (successo) success; (sorte) luck. atterraggio di ~ forced landing; aver ~ be lucky; buona ~! good luck!; di ~ makeshift; per ~ luckily. fortu'nato adj lucky, fortunate; (impresa) successful. ~ta'mente adv fortunately

fo'runcolo m pimple; (grosso) boil

'forza f strength; (potenza) power; (fisica) force; di ~ by force; a ~ di by dint of; con ~ hard; ~! come on!; ~ di volontà will-power; ~ maggiore circumstances beyond one's control; la ~ pubblica the police; per ~ against one's will; (natu-

raimente) of course; farsi ~ bear up; mare ~ 8 force 8 gale; bella ~! [i] big deal!. **le forze armate** the armed forces

for'za|re vt force; (scassare) break open; (sforzare) strain. ~**to** adj forced; (sorriso) strained ●m convict

forzi'ere m coffer

for'zuto adj strong

fo'schia f haze

'fosco adj dark

fo'sfato m phosphate

'fosforo m phosphorus

'fossa f pit; (tomba) grave. ~ biologica cesspool. **fos'sato** m (di fortificazione) moat

fos'setta f dimple

'fossile m fossil

'fosso m ditch; (Mil) trench

'foto f inv [i] photo; fare delle ~ take some photos

foto'camera f camera

foto'cellula f photocell

fotocomposizi'one f filmsetting, photocomposition

foto'copia f photocopy. ~**are** vt photocopy. ~**a'trice** f photocopier

foto'finish m inv photo finish

fotogra'fare vt photograph. ~**fia** f (arte) photography; (immagine) photograph; fare ~**fie** take photographs. **foto'grafico** adj photographic; **macchina fotografica** camera. **fo'tografo, -a** mf photographer

foto'gramma m frame

fotomo'dello, -a mf [photographer's] model

foto'romanzo m photo story

fou'lard m inv scarf

fra prep (in mezzo a due) between; (in un insieme) among; (tempo, distanza) in; detto ~ noi between you and me; ~ sé e sé to oneself; ~ l'altro what's more; ~ breve soon; ~ quindici giorni in two weeks' time;

~ **tutti**, siamo in venti there are twenty of us altogether

fracas'sar|e vt smash. ~**si** vr shatter

fra'casso m din; (di cose che cadono) crash

'fradicio adj (bagnato) soaked; (guasto) rotten; ubriaco ~ blind drunk

'fragil|e adj fragile; fig frail. ~**ità** f fragility; fig frailty

'fragola f strawberry

fra'go|re m uproar; (di cose rotte) clatter; (di tuono) rumble. ~**roso** adj uproarious; (tuono) rumbling; (suono) clanging

fra'gran|te adj fragrant. ~**za** f fragrance

frain'te|ndere vt misunderstand. ~**ndersi** vr be at cross-purposes. ~**so** pp di **fraintendere**

frammen'tario adj fragmentary

'frana f landslide. **fra'nare** vi slide down

franca'mente adv frankly

fran'cese adj French ● mf Frenchman; Frenchwoman ● m (lingua) French

fran'chezza f frankness

'Francia f France

'franco¹ adj frank; (Comm) free; farla franca get away with sth

'franco² m (moneta) franc

franco'bollo m stamp

fran'gente m (onda) breaker; (scoglio) reef; (fig: momento difficile) crisis; in quel ~ given the situation

'frangia f fringe

fra'noso adj subject to landslides

fran'toio m olive-press

frantu'mar|e vt, ~**si** vr shatter. **fran'tumi** mpl splinters; andare in frantumi be smashed to pieces

frappé m inv milkshake

frap'por|re vt interpose. ~**si** vr intervene

fra'sario m vocabulary; (libro)

phrase book

'frase f sentence; (espressione) phrase. ~ **fatta** cliché

'frassino m ash[-tree]

frastagli'a|re vt make jagged. ~**to** adj jagged

frastor'na|re vt daze. ~**to** adj dazed

frastu'ono m racket

'frate m friar; (monaco) monk

fratel'la|nza f brotherhood. ~**stro** m half-brother

fra'tell|i mpl (fratello e sorella) brother and sister. ~**o** m brother

fraterniz'zare vi fraternize. **fra'terno** adj brotherly

frat'taglie fpl (di pollo ecc) giblets

frat'tanto adv in the meantime

frat'tempo m nel ~ meanwhile, in the meantime

frat'tu|ra f fracture. ~**rare** vt, ~**rarsi** vr break

fraudo'lento adj fraudulent

frazi'one f fraction; (borgata) hamlet

'frecci|a f arrow; (Auto) indicator. ~**ata** f (osservazione pungente) cutting remark

fredda'mente adv coldly

fred'dare vt cool; (fig: con sguardo, battuta) cut down; (uccidere) kill

fred'dezza f coldness

'freddo adj ● m cold; aver ~ be cold; fa ~ it's cold

freddo'loso adj sensitive to cold

fred'dura f pun

fre'gare vt rub; (🔲: truffare) cheat; (🔲: rubare) swipe. ~**rsene** 🔲 not give a damn; chi se ne fregal what the heck!. ~**si** vr rub (occhi). ~**ta** f rub. ~**tura** f (🔲 (truffa) swindle; (delusione) letdown

'fregio m (Archit) frieze; (ornamento) decoration

'frem|ere vi quiver. ~**ito** m quiver

fre'na|re vt brake; (fig) restrain; hold back (lacrime) ●vi brake. **~rsi** vr check oneself. **~ta** f fare una **~ta brusca** brake sharply

frene'sia f frenzy; (desiderio smodato) craze. **fre'netico** adj frenzied

'freno m brake; (fig) check; togliere il **~** release the brake; usare il **~** apply the brake; tenere a **~** restrain. **~ a mano** handbrake

frequen'tare vt frequent; attend (scuola ecc); mix with (persone)

fre'quen|te adj frequent; di **~te** frequently. **~za** f frequency; (assiduità) attendance

fre'schezza f freshness; (di temperatura) coolness

'fresco adj fresh; (temperatura) cool; stai **~**! you're for it! ●m coolness; far **~** be cool; mettere/tenere in **~** put/keep in a cool place

'fretta f hurry, haste; aver **~** be in a hurry; far **~** a qcno hurry sb; in **~ e furia** in a great hurry. **frettolosa'mente** adv hurriedly. **fretto'loso** adj (persona) in a hurry; (lavoro) rushed, hurried

fri'abile adj crumbly

'friggere vt fry; vai a farti **~**! get lost! ●vi sizzle

friggi'trice f chip pan

frigidità f frigidity. **'frigido** adj frigid

fri'gnare vi whine

'frigo m inv fridge

frigo'bar m inv minibar

frigo'rifero adj refrigerating ●m refrigerator

frit'tata f omelette

frit'tella f fritter; (▣: macchia d'unto) grease stain

'fritto pp di friggere ●adj fried; essere **~** be done for ●m fried food. **~ misto** mixed fried fish/vegetables. **frit'tura** f fried dish

frivo'lezza f frivolity. **'frivolo** adj frivolous

frizio'nare vt rub. **frizi'one** f friction; (Mech) clutch; (di pelle) rub

friz'zante adj fizzy; (vino) sparkling; (aria) bracing

'frizzo m gibe

fro'dare vt defraud

'frode f fraud. **~ fiscale** tax evasion

'frollo adj tender; (selvaggina) high; (persona) spineless; **pasta frolla** short[crust] pastry

'fronda f [leafy] branch; (fig) rebellion. **fron'doso** adj leafy

fron'tale adj frontal; (scontro) head-on

'fronte f forehead; (di edificio) front; di **~** opposite; di **~ a** opposite, facing; (a paragone) compared with; far **~ a** face ●m (Mil, Pol) front. **~ggi'are** vt face

fronti'era f frontier, border

fron'tone m pediment

fronzolo m frill

'frotta f swarm; (di animali) flock

'frottola f fib; **frottole** pl nonsense sg

fru'gale adj frugal

fru'gare vi rummage ●vt search

frul'la|re vt (Culin) whisk ●vi (ali:) whirr. **~to** m **~to di frutta** fruit drink with milk and crushed ice. **~'tore** m [electric] mixer. **frul'lino** m whisk

fru'mento m wheat

frusci'are vi rustle

fru'scio m rustle; (radio, giradischi) background noise; (di acque) murmur

'frusta f whip; (frullino) whisk

fru'sta|re vt whip. **~ta** f lash. **fru'stino** m riding crop

fru'stra|re vt frustrate. **~to** adj frustrated. **~zi'one** f frustration

frutt|a f fruit; (portata) dessert. **frut'tare** vi bear fruit ●vt yield. **frut'teto**

m orchard. ~i'**vendolo**, -a *mf* green-grocer. ~o *m* fruit; *Fin* yield; ~i **di bosco** fruits of the forest. ~i **di mare** seafood *sg*. ~u'**oso** *adj* profitable

f.to *abbr* (firmato) signed

fu *adj* (defunto) late; **il ~ signor Rossi** the late Mr Rossi

fuci'la|re *vt* shoot. ~**ta** *f* shot

fu'cile *m* rifle

fu'cina *f* forge

'**fuga** *f* escape; (perdita) leak; (Mus) fugue; **darsi alla ~** escape

fu'gace *adj* fleeting

fug'gevole *adj* short-lived

fuggi'asco, -**a** *mf* fugitive

fuggi'fuggi *m* stampede

fug'gi|re *vi* flee; (innamorati:) elope; *fig* fly. ~'**tivo**, -**a** *mf* fugitive

fulcro *m* fulcrum

ful'gore *m* splendour

fu'liggine *f* soot

fulmi'nar|e *vt* strike by lightning; (con sguardo) look daggers at; (con scarica elettrica) electrocute. ~**si** *vr* burn out. '**fulmine** *m* lightning. **ful'mineo** *adj* rapid

'**fulvo** *adj* tawny

fumai'olo *m* funnel; (di casa) chimney

fu'ma|re *vt/i* smoke; (in ebollizione) steam. ~'**tore**, ~'**trice** *mf* smoker; **non fumatori** non-smoker, non-smoking

fu'metto *m* comic strip; **fumetti** *pl* comics

'**fumo** *m* smoke; (vapore) steam; *fig* hot air; **andare in ~** vanish. **fu'moso** *adj* smoky; (discorso) vague

fu'nambolo, -**a** *mf* tightrope walker

'**fune** *f* rope; (cavo) cable

'**funebre** *adj* funeral; (cupo) gloomy

fune'rale *m* funeral

fu'nesto *adj* sad

'**fungere** *vi* **~ da** act as

Funghi Wild mushrooms are an Italian passion, and the most prized is the *porcino* (cep), which can be bought fresh or dried. However, many Italians are also avid mushroom-pickers and are expert at differentiating edible mushrooms (*funghi commestibili*) from poisonous ones. Local authorities often have a department controlling the picking and selling of mushrooms.

'**fungo** *m* mushroom; (Bot) fungus

funico'lare *f* funicular [railway]

funi'via *f* cableway

funzio'nal|e *adj* functional. ~**ità** *f* functionality

funziona'mento *m* functioning

funzio'nare *vi* work, function; **~ da** (fungere da) act as

funzio'nario *m* official

funzi'one *f* function; (carica) office; (Relig) service; **entrare in ~** take up office

fu'oco *m* fire; (fisica, fotografia) focus; **far ~** fire; **dar ~ a** set fire to; **prendere ~** catch fire. **fuochi** *pl* **d'artificio** fireworks

fuorché *prep* except

fu'ori *adv* out; (all'esterno) outside; (all'aperto) outdoors; **andare di ~** (traboccare) spill over; **essere ~ di sé** be beside oneself; **essere in ~** (sporgere) stick out; **far ~** 🔟 do in; **~ luogo** (inopportuno) out of place; **~ mano** out of the way; **~ moda** old-fashioned; **~ pasto** between meals; **~ pericolo** out of danger; **~ questione** out of the question; **~ uso** out of use ●**m** outside

fuori'bordo *m* speedboat (with outboard motor)

fuori'classe mf champion

fuorigi'oco m & adv offside

fuori'legge mf outlaw

fuori'serie adj custom-made • f (Auto) custom-built model

fuori'strada m off-road vehicle

fuorvi'are vt lead astray • vi go astray

fur'beria f cunning. fur'bizia f cunning

'furbo adj cunning; (intelligente) clever; (astuto) shrewd; bravo ∼! nice one!; fare il ∼ try to be clever

fu'rente adj furious

fur'fante m scoundrel

furgon'cino m delivery van. fur-'gone m van

'furi|a f fury; (fretta) haste; a ∼a di by dint of. ∼'bondo, ∼'oso adj furious

fu'rore m fury; (veemenza) frenzy; far ∼ be all the rage. ∼ggi'are vi be a great success

furtiva'mente adv covertly. fur-'tivo adj furtive

'furto m theft; (con scasso) burglary; commettere un ∼ steal. ∼ d'iden-tità identity theft

'fusa fpl fare le ∼ purr

fu'scello m (di legno) twig; (di paglia) straw; sei un ∼ you're as light as a feather

fu'seaux mpl leggings

fu'sibile m fuse

fusi'one f fusion; (Comm) merger

'fuso pp di fondere • adj melted • m spindle. ∼ orario time zone

fusoli'era f fuselage

fu'stagno m corduroy

fu'stino m (di detersivo) box

'fusto m stem; (tronco) trunk; (reci-piente di metallo) drum; (di legno) barrel

'futile adj futile

fu'turo adj & m future

Gg

gab'bar|e vt cheat. ∼si vr ∼si di make fun of

'gabbia f cage; (da imballaggio) crate. ∼ degli imputati dock. ∼ toracica rib cage

gabbi'ano m [sea]gull

gabi'netto m consulting room; (Pol) cabinet; (bagno) lavatory; (labora-torio) laboratory

'gaffe f inv blunder

gagli'ardo adj vigorous

gai'ezza f gaiety. 'gaio adj cheerful

'gala f gala

ga'lante adj gallant. ∼'ria f gal-lantry. galantu'omo m (pl galantuo-mini) gentleman

ga'lassia f galaxy

gala'teo m [good] manners pl; (trat-tato) book of etiquette

gale'otto m (rematore) galley-slave; (condannato) convict

ga'lera f (nave) galley; 🔒 prison

'galla f (Bot) gall; a ∼ adv afloat; ve-nire a ∼ surface

galleggi'are vi float

galle'ria f tunnel; (d'arte) gallery; (Theat) circle; (arcata) arcade. ∼ d'arte art gallery

'Galles m Wales. gal'lese adj welsh • m Welshman; (lingua) Welsh • f Welshwoman

gal'letto m cockerel; fare il ∼ show off

gal'lina f hen

gal'lismo m machismo

'gallo m cock

gal'lone m stripe; (misura) gallon

galop'pare vi gallop. ga'loppo m gallop; al galoppo at a gallop

'gamba f leg; (di lettera) stem; a

quattro gambe on all fours; essere in ∼ (*essere forte*) be strong; (*capace*) be smart

gamba'letto *m* pop sock

gambe'retto *m* shrimp. 'gambero *m* prawn; (*di fiume*) crayfish

'**gambo** *m* stem; (*di pianta*) stalk

'**gamma** *f* (Mus) scale; *fig* range

ga'nascia *f* jaw; ganasce *pl* del freno brake shoes

'**gancio** *m* hook

'**ganghero** *m* uscire dai gangheri *fig* get into a temper

'**gara** *f* competition; (*di velocità*) race; fare i ∼ compete

ga'rage *m inv* garage

ga'ran|te *m* guarantor. ∼'tire *vt* guarantee; (*rendersi garante*) vouch for; (*assicurare*) assure. ∼'zia *f* guarantee; in ∼zia under guarantee

gar'ba|re *vi* like; non mi garba I don't like it. ∼to *adj* courteous

'**garbo** *m* courtesy; (*grazia*) grace; con ∼ graciously

gareggi'are *vi* compete

garga'nella *f* a ∼ from the bottle

garga'rismo *m* gargle; fare i gargarismi gargle

ga'rofano *m* carnation

'**garza** *f* gauze

gar'zone *m* boy. ∼ di stalla stable-boy

gas *m inv* gas; (*Auto*) accelerate; a tutto ∼ flat out. ∼ lacrimogeno tear gas. ∼ *pl* di scarico exhaust fumes

gas'dotto *m* natural gas pipeline

ga'solio *m* diesel oil

ga'sometro *m* gasometer

gas's|are *vt* aerate; (*uccidere col gas*) gas. ∼ato *adj* gassy. ∼oso, -a *adj* gassy; (*bevanda*) fizzy ● *f* lemonade

'**gastrico** *adj* gastric. ga'strite *f* gastritis

gastro|no'mia *f* gastronomy. ∼'nomico *adj* gastronomic. ga'stro-

nomo, -a *mf* gourmet

'**gatta** *f* una ∼ da pelare a headache

gatta'buia *f* *hum* clink

gat'tino, -a *mf* kitten

'**gatto, -a** *mf* cat. ∼ delle nevi snowmobile

gat'toni *adv* on all fours

gay *adj inv* gay

'**gazza** *f* magpie

gaz'zarra *f* racket

gaz'zella *f* gazelle; (Auto) police car

gaz'zetta *f* gazette

gaz'zosa *f* clear lemonade

'**geco** *m* gecko

ge'la|re *vt/i* freeze. ∼ta *f* frost

gela't|aio, -a *mf* ice-cream seller; (*negozio*) ice-cream shop. ∼e'ria *f* ice-cream parlour. ∼'era *f* ice-cream maker

gela'ti|na *f* gelatine; (*dolce*) jelly. ∼na di frutta fruit jelly.

ge'lato *adj* frozen ● *m* ice-cream

'**gelido** *adj* freezing

'**gelo** *m* (*freddo intenso*) freezing cold; (*brina*) frost; *fig* chill

ge'lone *m* chilblain

gelosa'mente *adv* jealously

gelo'sia *f* jealousy. ge'loso *adj* jealous

'**gelso** *m* mulberry[-tree]

gelso'mino *m* jasmine

gemel'laggio *m* twinning

ge'mello, -a *adj* & *mf* twin; (*di polsino*) cuff-link; Gemelli *pl* (Astr) Gemini *sg*

gem|ere *vi* groan; (*tubare*) coo. ∼ito *m* groan

'**gemma** *f* gem; (Bot) bud

'**gene** *m* gene

genealo'gia *f* genealogy

gene'rale[^1] *adj* general; spese ∼i overheads

gene'rale[^2] *m* (Mil) general

generalità *f* (*qualità*) generality, ge-

[^1]: 1
[^2]: 2

neral nature; ∼ pl (dati personali) particulars

generaliz'za|re vt generalize. ∼**zi'one** f generalization. general'mente adv generally

gene'ra|re vt give birth to; (causare) breed; (Techn) generate. ∼**'tore** m (Techn) generator. ∼**zi'one** f generation

'**genere** m kind; (Biol) genus; (Gram) gender; (letterario, artistico) genre; (prodotto) product; il ∼ umano mankind; in ∼ generally. generi pl alimentari provisions

ge'nerico adj generic; medico generico general practitioner

'**genero** m son-in-law

generosità f generosity. gene'roso adj generous

'**genesi** f inv genesis

ge'netico, -a adj genetic ●f genetics

gen'giva f gum

geni'ale adj ingenious; (congeniale) congenial

'**genio** m genius; andare a ∼ be to one's taste. ∼ civile civil engineering. ∼ [militare] Engineers

geni'tale adj genital. genitali mpl genitals

geni'tore m parent

gen'naio m January

'**Genova** f Genoa

gen'taglia f rabble

'**gente** f people pl

gen'til|e adj kind; G∼e Signore (in lettere) Dear Sir. genti'lezza f kindness; per gentilezza (per favore) please. ∼**'mente** adv kindly. ∼**u'omo** (pl ∼**u'omini**) m gentleman

genu'ino adj genuine; (cibo, prodotto) natural

geogra'fia f geography. geo'grafico adj geographical. ge'ografo, -a mf geographer

geolo'gia f geology. geo'logico adj geological. ge'ologo, -a mf geologist

ge'ometra mf surveyor

geome'tria f geometry

ge'ranio m geranium

gerar'chia f hierarchy

ge'rente m manager ●f manageress

'**gergo** m slang; (di professione ecc) jargon

geria'tria f geriatrics sg

Ger'mania f Germany

'**germe** m germ; (fig: principio) seed

germogli'are vi sprout. ger'moglio m sprout

gero'glifico m hieroglyph

'**gesso** m chalk; (Med, scultura) plaster

gestazi'one f gestation

gestico'lare vi gesticulate

gesti'one f management

ge'stir|e vi manage. ∼**si** vr budget one's time and money

'**gesto** m gesture; (azione pl f gesta) deed

ge'store m manager

Gesù m Jesus. ∼ bambino baby Jesus

gesu'ita m Jesuit

get'ta|re vt throw; (scagliare) fling; (emettere) spout; (Techn, fig) cast; ∼**re** via throw away. ∼**rsi** vr throw oneself; ∼**rsi** in (fiume:) flow into. ∼**ta** f throw

'**getto** m throw; (di liquidi, gas) jet; a ∼ continuo in a continuous stream; di ∼ straight off

getto'nato adj popular. get'tone m token; (per giochi) counter

'**ghetto** m ghetto

ghiacci'aio m glacier

ghiacci'a|re vt/i freeze. ∼**to** adj frozen; (freddissimo) ice-cold

ghi'acci|o m ice; (Auto) black ice. ∼**'olo** m icicle; (gelato) ice lolly

ghi'aia f gravel

ghi'anda f acorn

ghi'andola f gland

ghigliot'tina f guillotine

ghi'gnare vi sneer

ghi'ot|to adj greedy; (*appetitoso*) appetizing. ~'tone, -a mf glutton. ~tone'ria f (*qualità*) gluttony; (*cibo*) tasty morsel

ghir'landa f (*corona*) wreath; (*di fiori*) garland

'ghiro m dormouse; dormire come un ~ sleep like a log

'ghisa f cast iron

già adv already; (*un tempo*) formerly; ~! indeed!; ~ da ieri since yesterday

gi'acca f jacket. ~ a vento windcheater

giacché conj since

giac'cone m jacket

gia'cere vi lie

giaci'mento m deposit. ~ di petrolio oil deposit

gia'cinto m hyacinth

gi'ada f jade

giag'giolo m iris

giagu'aro m jaguar

gial'lastro adj yellowish

gi'allo adj & m yellow; [*libro*] ~ thriller

Giap'pone m Japan. **giappo'nese** adj & mf Japanese

giardi'n|aggio m gardening. ~'iere, -a mf gardener ● f (*Auto*) estate car; (*sottaceti*) pickles pl

giar'dino m garden. ~ d'infanzia kindergarten. ~ pensile roofgarden. ~ zoologico zoo

giarretti'era f garter

giavel'lotto m javelin

gi'gan|te adj gigantic ● m giant. ~'tesco adj gigantic

gigantogra'fia f blow-up

'giglio m lily

gilè m inv waistcoat

gin m inv gin

gineco|lo'gia f gynaecology. ~lo'gico adj gynaecological. gine'cologo, -a mf gynaecologist

gi'nepro m juniper

gingil'larsi vr fiddle; (*perder tempo*) potter. **gin'gillo** m plaything; (*ninnolo*) knick-knack

gin'nasio m ≈ grammar school

gin'nast|a mf gymnast. ~ica f gymnastics; (*esercizi*) exercises pl

ginocchi'ata f prendere una ~ bang one's knee

gi'nocchio m (pl m ginocchi o f ginocchia) knee; in ~ on one's knees; mettersi in ~ kneel down; (*per supplicare*) go down on one's knees. ~'oni adv kneeling

gio'ca|re vt/i play; (*giocherellare*) toy; (*d'azzardo*) gamble; (*puntare*) stake; (*ingannare*) trick. ~rsi la carriera throw one's career away. ~'tore, ~'trice mf player; (*d'azzardo*) gambler

gio'cattolo m toy

giocherel'l|are vi toy; (*nervosamente*) fiddle. ~one adj skittish

gi'oco m game; (*Techn*) play; (*d'azzardo*) gambling; (*scherzo*) joke; (*insieme di pezzi ecc*) set; fare il doppio ~ con qcno double-cross sb

giocoli'ere m juggler

gio'coso adj playful

gi'oia f joy; (*gioiello*) jewel; (*appellativo*) sweetie

gioiel|le'ria f jeweller's [shop]. ~'iere, -a mf jeweller; (*negozio*) jeweller's. gioi'ello m jewel; gioielli pl jewellery

gioi'oso adj joyous

gio'ire vi ~ per rejoice at

Gior'dania f Jordan

giorna'laio, -a mf newsagent

gior'nale m [news]paper; (*diario*) journal. ~ di bordo logbook. ~ radio news bulletin

giornali'ero adj daily ●m (per sciare) day pass

giorna'lino m comic

giorna'lis|mo m journalism. ~ta mf journalist

giornal'mente adv daily

gior'nata f day; in ~ today

gi'orno m day; al ~ per day; al ~ d'oggi nowadays; di ~ by day; un ~ si, un ~ no every other day

gi'ostra f merry-go-round

giova'mento m trarre ~ da derive benefit from

gi'ova|ne adj young; (giovanile) youthful ●m young man ●f young woman. ~'nile adj youthful. ~'notto m young man

gio'var|e vi ~e a be useful to; (far bene a) be good for. ~si vr ~si di avail oneself of

giovedì m inv Thursday. ~ grasso last Thursday before Lent

gioventù f youth; (i giovani) young people pl

giovi'ale adj jovial

giovi'nezza f youth

gira'dischi m inv record-player

gi'raffa f giraffe; Cinema boom

gi'randola f (fuoco d'artificio) Catherine wheel; (giocattolo) windmill; (banderuola) weathercock

gi'ra|re vt turn; (andare intorno, visitare) go round; (Comm) endorse; Cinema shoot ●vi turn; (aerei, uccelli) circle; (andare in giro) wander; ~re al largo steer clear. ~rsi vr turn [round]; mi gira la testa I'm dizzy

girar'rosto m spit

gira'sole m sunflower

gi'rata f turn; (Comm) endorsement; (in macchina ecc) ride; fare una ~ (a piedi) go for a walk; (in macchina) go for a ride

gira'volta f spin; fig U-turn

gi'rello m (per bambini) babywalker; (Culin) topside

gi'revole adj revolving

gi'rino m tadpole

'giro m turn; (circolo) circle; (percorso) round; (viaggio) tour; (passeggiata) short walk; (in macchina) drive; (in bicicletta) ride; (circolazione di denaro) circulation; nel ~ di un mese within a month; senza giri di parole without beating about the bush; a ~ di posta by return mail. ~ d'affari (Comm) turnover. giri pl al minuto rpm. ~ turistico sightseeing tour. ~ vita waist measurement

giro'collo m choker; a ~ crewneck

gi'rone m round

gironzo'lare vi wander about

girova'gare vi wander about. gi'rovago m wanderer

'gita f trip; andare in ~ go on a trip. ~ scolastica school trip. gi'tante mf tripper

giù adv down; (sotto) below; (dabbasso) downstairs; a testa in ~ (a capofitto) headlong; essere ~ be down; (di salute) be run down; ~ di corda down; ~ di lì, su per ~ more or less; non andare ~ a qcno stick in sb's craw

gi'ub|ba f jacket; (Mil) tunic. ~'botto m bomber jacket

giudi'care vt judge; (ritenere) consider

gi'udice m judge. ~ conciliatore justice of the peace. ~ di gara umpire. ~ di linea linesman

giu'dizi|o m judg[e]ment; (opinione) opinion; (senno) wisdom; (processo) trial; (sentenza) sentence; mettere ~o become wise. ~'oso adj sensible

gi'ugno m June

giu'menta f mare

giu'nger|e vi arrive; ~ a (riuscire) succeed ●vt (unire) join

gi'ungla f jungle

gi'unta f addition; (Mil) junta; per ~ in addition. ~ comunale district council

gi'unto pp di giungere ● m (Mech) joint

giun'tura f joint

giuo'care, **giu'oco** = GIO-CARE, GIOCO

giura'mento m oath; prestare ~ take the oath

giu'ra|re vt/i swear. ~to, -a adj sworn ● mf juror

giu'ria f jury

giu'ridico adj legal

giurisdizi'one f jurisdiction

giurispru'denza f jurisprudence

giu'rista mf jurist

giustifi'ca|re vt justify. ~zi'one f justification

giu'stizi|a f justice. ~'are vt execute. ~'ere m executioner

gi'usto adj just, fair; (adatto) right; (esatto) exact ● m (uomo retto) just man; (cosa giusta) right ● adv exactly; ~ ora just now

glaci'ale adj glacial

gla'diolo m gladiolus

'glassa f (Culin) icing

gli def art mpl (before vowel and s + consonant, gn, ps, z) the; ▸IL ● pron (a lui) [to] him; (a esso) [to] it; (a loro) [to] them

glice'rina f glycerine

gli'cine m wisteria

gli'e|llo, -a pron [to] him/her/them; (forma di cortesia) [to] you; ~ chiedo I'll ask him/her/them/you; glielʼho prestato I've lent it to him/her/them/you. ~ne (di ció) [of] it; ~ne ho dato un poʼ I gave him/her/them/you some

glo'bal|e adj global; fig overall. ~izza'zione f globalization. ~'mente adv globally

'globo m globe. ~ oculare eyeball. ~ terrestre globe

'globulo m globule; (Med) corpuscle. ~ bianco white corpuscle. ~ rosso red corpuscle

'glori|a f glory. ~'arsi vr ~arsi di be proud of. ~'oso adj glorious

glos'sario m glossary

glu'cosio m glucose

'gluteo m buttock

'gnorri m fare lo ~ play dumb

'gobb|a f hump. ~o, -a adj hunchbacked ● mf hunchback

'gocc|ia f drop; (di sudore) bead; è stata l'ultima ~a it was the last straw. ~o'lare vi drip. ~o'lio m dripping

go'der|e vi (sessualmente) come; ~e di enjoy. ~sela have a good time. ~si vr ~si qcsa enjoy sth

godi'mento m enjoyment

goffa'mente adv awkwardly. **'goffo** adj awkward

'gola f throat; (ingordigia) gluttony; (Geog) gorge; (di camino) flue; avere mal di ~ have a sore throat; far ~ a qcno tempt sb

golf m inv jersey; Sport golf

'golfo m gulf

golosità f inv greediness; (cibo) tasty morsel. go'loso adj greedy

'golpe m inv coup

gomi'tata f nudge

'gomito m elbow; alzare il ~ raise one's elbow

go'mitolo m ball

'gomma f rubber; (colla, da masticare) gum; (pneumatico) tyre. ~ da masticare chewing gum

gommapi'uma f foam rubber

gom'mista m tyre specialist

gom'mone m [rubber] dinghy

'gondol|a f gondola. ~i'ere m gondolier

gonfa'lone m banner

gonfi'abile adj inflatable

gonfi'ar|e vi swell ● vt blow up; pump up (pneumatico); (esagerare) exaggerate. ~si vr swell; (acque): rise. **'gonfio** adj swollen; (pneumatico) inflated. **gonfi'ore** m swelling

gongo'la|nte adj overjoyed. ~re vi be overjoyed

'**gonna** f skirt. ~ pantalone culottes pl

goo'glare vt/i google

gorgogli'are vi gurgle

go'rilla m inv gorilla; (guardia del corpo) bodyguard

'**gotico** adj & m Gothic

gover'nante f housekeeper

gover'na|re vt govern; (dominare) rule; (dirigere) manage; (curare) look after. ~'tore m governor

go'verno m government; (dominio) rule; al ~ in power

gps m gps

gracchi'are vi caw; fig: (persona:) screech

graci'dare vi croak

'**gracile** adj delicate

gra'dasso m braggart

gradata'mente adv gradually

gradazi'one f gradation. ~ alcolica alcohol[ic] content

gra'devol|e adj agreeable.

gradi'mento m liking; indice di ~ (Radio, TV) popularity rating; non è di mio ~ it's not to my liking

gradi'nata f flight of steps; (di stadio) stand; (di teatro) tiers pl

gra'dino m step

gra'di|re vt like; (desiderare) wish. ~to adj pleasant; (bene accetto) welcome

'**grado** m degree; (rango) rank; di buon ~ willingly; essere in ~ di fare qcsa be in a position to do sth; (essere capace a) be able to do sth

gradu'ale adj gradual

gradu'a|re vt graduate. ~to adj graded; (provvisto di scala graduata) graduated ●m (Mil) non-commissioned officer. ~'toria f list. ~zi'one f graduation

'**graffa** f clip

graf'fetta f staple

graffi'a|re vt scratch. ~'tura f scratch

'**graffio** m scratch

gra'fia f [hand]writing; (ortografia) spelling

'**grafic|a** f graphics; ~a pubblicitaria commercial art. ~a'mente adv graphically. ~o adj graphic ●m graph; (persona) graphic designer

gra'migna f weed

gram'matica f grammar

'**grammo** m gram[me]

gran adj ▷GRANDE

'**grana** f grain; (formaggio) parmesan; (I): seccatura) trouble; (I): soldi) readies pl

gra'naio m barn

gra'nat|a f (Mil) grenade; (frutto) pomegranate. ~i'ere m (Mil) grenadier

Gran Bre'tagna f Great Britain

gran'chio m crab; (errore) blunder; prendere un ~ make a blunder

grandango'lare m wide-angle lens

'**grande** (a volte gran) adj (ampio) large; (grosso) big; (alto) tall; (largo) wide; (fig: senso morale) great; (grandioso) grand; (adulto) grown-up; ho una gran fame I'm very hungry; fa un gran caldo it is very hot; in ~ on a large scale; in gran parte to a great extent; in un gran ballo a grand ball ●mf (persona adulta) grown-up; (persona eminente) great man/woman. ~ggi'are vi ~ggiare su tower over; (darsi arie) show off

gran'dezza f greatness; (ampiezza) largeness; (larghezza) width, breadth; (dimensione) size; (fasto) grandeur; (prodigalità) lavishness; a ~ naturale life-size

grandi'nare vi hail; grandina it's hailing. '**grandine** f hail

grandiosità f grandeur. **gran-di'oso** adj grand

gran'duca m grand duke

gra'nello m grain; (di frutta) pip

gra'nita f crushed ice drink

gra'nito m granite

'grano m grain; (frumento) wheat

gran'turco m maize

'granulo m granule

'grappa f grappa; (morsa) cramp

'grappolo m bunch. ~ d'uva bunch of grapes

gras'setto m bold [type]

gras'sezza f fatness

'gras|so adj fat; (cibo) fatty; (unto) greasy; (terreno) rich; (grossolano) coarse ●m fat; (sostanza) grease. ~'soccio adj plump

'grata f grating. **gra'tella**, **gra'ticola** f (Culin) grill

gra'tifica f bonus. ~zi'one f satisfaction

grati'na|re vt cook au gratin. ~to adj au gratin

grati'tudine f gratitude. **'grato** adj grateful; (gradito) pleasant

gratta'capo m trouble

gratta'cielo m skyscraper

grat'tar|e vt scratch; (raschiare) scrape; (grattugiare) grate; (🔲: rubare) pinch ●vi grate. ~**si** vr scratch oneself

grat'tugi|a f grater. ~'are vt grate

gratuita'mente adv free [of charge]. **gra'tuito** adj free [of charge]; (ingiustificato) gratuitous

gra'vare vt burden ●vi ~ su weigh on

'grave adj (pesante) heavy; (serio) serious; (difficile) hard; (voce, suono) low; (fonetica) grave; essere ~ (ammalato) be seriously ill. ~'mente adv seriously

gravi'danza f pregnancy. **'gravido** adj pregnant

gravità f seriousness; (Phys) gravity

gra'voso adj onerous

grazi|a f grace; (favore) favour; (Jur)

pardon; entrare nelle ~e di qcno get into sb's good books. ~'are vt pardon

'grazie int thank you!, thanks!; ~ mille! many thanks!

grazi'oso adj charming; (carino) pretty

'Grec|ia f Greece. g~o, -a agg & mf Greek

'gregge m flock

'greggio adj raw ●m crude oil

grembi'ale, **grembi'ule** m apron

'grembo m lap; (utero) womb; fig bosom

gre'mi|re vt pack. ~**rsi** vr become crowded (di with). ~to adj packed

'gretto adj stingy; (di vedute ristrette) narrow-minded

'grezzo adj = GREGGIO

gri'dare vi shout; (di dolore) scream; (animale:) cry ●vt shout

'grido m (pl m gridi o f grida) shout; (di animale) cry; l'ultimo ~ the latest fashion

'grigio adj & m grey

'griglia f grill; alla ~ grilled

gril'letto m trigger

'grillo m cricket; (fig: capriccio) whim

grin'fia f fig clutch

'grin|ta f grit. ~'toso adj determined

'grinza f wrinkle; (di stoffa) crease

grip'pare vi (Mech) seize

gris'sino m bread-stick

'gronda f eaves pl

gron'daia f gutter

gron'dare vi pour; (essere bagnato fradicio) be dripping

'groppa f back

'groppo m knot

gros'sezza f size; (spessore) thickness

gros'sista mf wholesaler

'grosso adj big, large; (spesso) thick;

(*grossolano*) coarse; (*grave*) serious ● *m* big part; (*massa*) bulk; farla grossa do a stupid thing

grosso|lanità *f inv* (*qualità*) coarseness; (*di errore*) grossness; (*azione, parola*) coarse thing. ~**lano** *adj* coarse; (*errore*) gross

grosso'modo *adv* roughly

'grotta *f* cave, grotto

grovi'era *m* Gruyère

gro'viglio *m* tangle; *fig* muddle

gru *f inv* (*uccello, edilizia*) crane

gruccia *f* (*stampella*) crutch; (*per vestito*) hanger

gru'gni|re *vi* grunt. ~**to** *m* grunt

'grugno *m* snout

'grullo *adj* silly

'grumo *m* clot; (*di farina ecc*) lump. **gru'moso** *adj* lumpy

'gruppo *m* group; (*comitiva*) party. ~ **sanguigno** blood group

gruvi'era *m* Gruyère

'gruzzolo *m* nest-egg

guada'gnare *vt* earn; gain (*tempo, forza ecc*). **gua'dagno** *m* gain; (*profitto*) profit; (*entrate*) earnings *pl*

gu'ado *m* ford; passare a ~ ford

gua'ina *f* sheath; (*busto*) girdle

gu'aio *m* trouble; che ~! that's just brilliant!; essere nei guai be in a fix; guai a te se lo tocchi! don't you dare touch it!

gu'anci|a *f* cheek. ~**ale** *m* pillow

gu'anto *m* glove. guantoni *pl* [da boxe] boxing gloves

guarda'coste *m inv* coastguard

guarda'linee *m inv* *Sport* linesman

guar'dar|e *vt* look at; (*osservare*) watch; (*badare a*) look after; (*dare su*) look out on ● *vi* look; (*essere orientato verso*) face. ~**si** *vr* look at oneself; ~**si da** be aware of; (*astenersi*) refrain from

guarda'rob|a *m inv* wardrobe; (*di locale pubblico*) cloakroom. ~**i'ere, -a**

mf cloakroom attendant

gu'ardia *f* guard; (*poliziotto*) policeman; (*vigilanza*) watch; essere di ~ be on guard; (*medico*:) be on duty; fare la ~ a keep guard over; mettere in ~ qcno warn sb. ~ **carceraria** prison warder. ~ **del corpo** bodyguard. ~ **di finanza** ≈ Fraud Squad. ~ **forestale** forest ranger. ~ **medica** duty doctor

guardi'ano, -a *mf* caretaker. ~ **notturno** night watchman

guar'dingo *adj* cautious

guardi'ola *f* gatekeeper's lodge

guarigi'one *f* recovery

gua'rire *vt* cure ● *vi* recover; (*ferita*:) heal [up]

guarnigi'one *f* garrison

guar'ni|re *vt* trim; (*Culin*) garnish. ~**zi'one** *f* trimming; (*Culin*) garnish; (*Mech*) gasket

gua'star|e *vt* spoil; (*rovinare*) ruin; break (*meccanismo*). ~**si** *vr* spoil; (*andare a male*) go bad; (*tempo*:) change for the worse; (*meccanismo*:) break down. **gu'asto** *adj* broken; (*ascensore, telefono*) out of order; (*auto*) broken down; (*cibo, dente*) bad ● *m* breakdown; (*danno*) damage

guazza'buglio *m* muddle

guaz'zare *vi* wallow

gu'ercio *adj* cross-eyed

gu'err|a *f* war; (*tecnica bellica*) warfare. ~ **mondiale** world war. ~**eggi'are** *vi* wage war. **guer'resco** *adj* (*di guerra*) war; (*bellicoso*) warlike. ~**i'ero** *m* warrior

guer'rigli|a *f* guerrilla warfare. ~**'ero, -a** *mf* guerrilla

'gufo *m* owl

'guglia *f* spire

gu'id|a *f* guide; (*direzione*) guidance; (*comando*) leadership; (*Auto*) driving; (*tappeto*) runner; ~ **a destra/sinistra** right-/left-hand drive. ~ **a telefonica** telephone directory. ~**a**

turistica tourist guide. **gui'dare** vt guide; (*Auto*) drive; steer (nave). ~a'tore, ~a'trice mf driver

guin'zaglio m leash

quiz'zare vi dart; (luce:) flash. **qu'izzo** m dart; (di luce) flash

'guscio m shell

gu'stare vt taste ●vi like. 'gusto m taste; (piacere) liking; **mangiare di gusto** eat well; **prenderci gusto** develop a taste for. **gu'stoso** adj tasty; fig delightful

guttu'rale adj guttural

Hh

habitué mf inv regular
ham'burger m inv hamburger
'handicap m inv handicap
handicap'pa|re vt handicap. ~to, -a mf disabled person ●adj disabled
'hascisc m hashish
henné m henna
hi-fi m inv hi-fi
'hippy adj hippy
hockey m hockey. ~ **su ghiaccio** ice hockey. ~ **su prato** hockey
hollywoodi'ano adj Hollywood
ho'tel m inv hotel

Ii

i def art mpl the; ▷**IL**
iber'na|re vi hibernate. ~zi'one f hibernation
i'bisco m hibiscus
'ibrido adj & m hybrid

'iceberg m inv iceberg
i'cona f icon
Id'dio m God
i'dea f idea; (opinione) opinion; (ideale) ideal; (indizio) inkling; (piccola quantità) hint; (intenzione) intention; **cambiare** ~ change one's mind; **neanche per** ~**!** not on your life!; **chiarirsi le idee** get one's ideas straight. ~ **fissa** obsession
ide'a|le adj & m ideal. ~'lista mf idealist. ~liz'zare vt idealize. ~'tore, ~'trice mf originator
'idem adv the same
i'dentico adj identical
identifi'cabile adj identifiable
identifi'ca|re vt identify. ~zi'one f identification
identità f inv identity
ideolo'gia f ideology. **ideo'logico** adj ideological
idi'oma m idiom. **idio'matico** adj idiomatic
idi'ota adj idiotic ●mf idiot. **idio'zia** f (cosa stupida) idiocy
idola'trare vt worship
idoleggi'are vt idolize. **'idolo** m idol
idoneità f suitability; (Mil) fitness; **esame di** ~ qualifying examination. **i'doneo** adj **idoneo a** suitable for; (Mil) fit for
i'drante m hydrant
idra'ta|nte adj (crema, gel) moisturizing. ~zi'one f moisturizing
i'draulico adj hydraulic ●m plumber
'idrico adj water attrib
idrocar'buro m hydrocarbon
idroe'lettrico adj hydroelectric
i'drofilo adj ▷**COTONE**
i'drogeno m hydrogen
i'ella f 🔢 bad luck; **portare** ~ **be bad luck**. **iel'lato** adj 🔢 jinxed, plagued by bad luck

i'ena f hyena

i'eri adv yesterday; ~ l'altro, l'altro ~ the day before yesterday; ~ pomeriggio yesterday afternoon; il giornale di ~ yesterday's paper

ietta'tore, -'trice mf jinx. ~tura f (sfortuna) bad luck

igi'ene f hygiene. ~ico adj hygienic. igie'nista mf hygienist

i'gnaro adj unaware

i'gnobile adj base; (non onorevole) dishonourable

igno'ran|te adj ignorant • mf ignoramus. ~za f ignorance

igno'rare vt (non sapere) be unaware of; (trascurare) ignore

i'gnoto adj unknown

---

il def art m the

L'articolo determinativo in inglese non si usa quando si parla in generale: Il latte fa bene milk is good for you

····▸ il signor Magnetti Mr Magnetti; il dottor Piazza Dr Piazza; ha il naso storto he has a bent nose; mettiti il cappello put your hat on; il lunedì on Mondays; il 1986 1986; 5 euro il chilo 5 euros a kilo

---

'ilar|e adj merry. ~ità f hilarity

illazi'one f inference

illecita'mente adv illicitly. il'lecito adj illicit

ille'gal|e adj illegal. ~ità f illegality. ~'mente adv illegally

illeg'gibile adj illegible; (libro) unreadable

illegittimità f illegitimacy. ille'gittimo adj illegitimate

il'leso adj unhurt

illette'rato, -a adj & mf illiterate

illimi'tato adj unlimited

illivi'dire vt bruise • vi (per rabbia)

become livid

il'logico adj illogical

il'luder|e vt deceive. ~si vr deceive oneself

illumi'na|re vt light [up]; fig enlighten; ~re a giorno floodlight. ~rsi vr light up. ~zi'one f lighting; fig enlightenment

illumi'nismo m Enlightenment

illusi'one f illusion; farsi illusioni delude oneself

il'luso, -a pp di illudere • adj deluded • mf day-dreamer.

illu'stra|re vt illustrate. ~'tivo adj illustrative. ~'tore, -'trice mf illustrator. ~zi'one f illustration

il'lustre adj distinguished

imbacuc'ca|re vt, ~rsi vr wrap up. ~to adj wrapped up

imbal'laggio m packing. ~re vt pack; (Auto) race

imbalsa'ma|re vt embalm; stuff (animale). ~to adj embalmed; (animale) stuffed

imbambo'lato adj vacant

imbaraz'zante adj embarrassing

imbaraz'za|re vt embarrass; (ostacolare) encumber. ~to adj embarrassed

imba'razzo m embarrassment; (ostacolo) hindrance; trarre qcno d'~ help sb out of a difficulty. ~ di stomaco indigestion

imbarca'dero m landing-stage

imbar'ca|re vt embark; (□: rimorchiare) score. ~rsi vr embark. ~zi'one f boat. ~zione di salvataggio lifeboat. im'barco m embarkation; (banchina) landing-stage

imba'sti|re vt tack; fig sketch. ~'tura f tacking, basting

im'battersi vr ~ in run into

imbat'tibile adj unbeatable. ~'uto adj unbeaten

imbavagli'are vt gag

imbe'cille adj stupid • mf imbecile

imbel'lire vt embellish

imbestia'lir|e vi, ~**rsi** vr fly into a rage. ~**to** adj enraged

im'bever|e vt imbue (di with). ~**si** vr absorb

imbe'v|ibile adj undrinkable. ~**uto** adj ~**uto di** (acqua) soaked in; (nozioni) imbued with

imbian'c|are vt whiten • vi turn white. ~**hino** m house painter

imbizzar'rir|e vi, ~**si** vr become restless; (arrabbiarsi) get angry

imboc'ca|re vt feed; (entrare) enter; fig prompt. ~**tura** f opening; (ingresso) entrance; (Mus: di strumento) mouthpiece. im'bocco m entrance

imbo'scar|e vt hide. ~**si** vr (Mil) shirk military service

imbo'scata f ambush

imbottigli'a|re vt bottle. ~**rsi** vr get snarled up in a traffic jam. ~**to** adj (vino, acqua) bottled

imbot'ti|re vt stuff; pad (giacca); (Culin) fill. ~**rsi** vr stuff di (fig: di pasticche) stuff oneself with. ~**ta** f quilt. ~**to** adj (spalle) padded; (cuscino) stuffed; (panino) filled. ~**tura** f stuffing; (di giacca) padding; (Culin) filling

imbra'nato adj clumsy

imbrat'tar|e vt mark. ~**si** vr dirty oneself

imbroc'car|e vt hit; ~**la giusta** hit the nail on the head

imbrogli'|are vt muddle; (raggirare) cheat. im'broglio m tangle; (pasticcio) mess; (inganno) trick. ~**one, -a** mf cheat

imbronci'a|re vi, ~**rsi** vr sulk. ~**to** adj sulky

imbru'nire vi get dark; all'~ at dusk

imbrut'tire vt make ugly • vi become ugly

imbu'care vt post, mail; (nel biliardo) pot

imbur'rare vt butter

im'buto m funnel

IMC m abbr (indice di massa corporea) BMI

imi'ta|re vt imitate. ~**tore**, ~**trice** mf imitator. ~**zi'one** f imitation

immaco'lato adj immaculate

immagazzi'nare vt store

immagi'na|re vt imagine; (supporre) suppose; s'immagini! imagine that!. ~**rio** adj imaginary. ~**zi'one** f imagination. im'magine f image

imman'cabile adj unfailing. ~**mente** adv without fail

im'mane adj huge; (orribile) terrible

imma'nente adj immanent

immangi'abile adj inedible

immatrico'la|re vt register. ~**rsi** vr (studente) matriculate. ~**zi'one** f registration; (di studente) matriculation

immaturità f immaturity. imma-'turo adj unripe; (persona) immature; (precoce) premature

immedesi'ma|rsi vr ~**rsi in** identify oneself with. ~**zi'one** f identification

immedia|ta'mente adv immediately. ~**tezza** f immediacy. imme-di'ato adj immediate

immemo'rabile adj immemorial

immens|a'mente adv enormously. ~**ità** f immensity. im-'menso adj immense

immensu'rabile adj immeasurable

im'merger|e vt immerse. ~**si** vr plunge; (sommergibile) dive; ~**si in** immerse oneself in

immersi'one f immersion; (di sommergibile) dive. im'merso pp di immergere

immi'gra|nte adj & mf immigrant. ~**re** vi immigrate. ~**to, -a** mf immigrant. ~**zi'one** f immigration

immi'nen|te adj imminent. ~**za** f imminence

immischi'ar|e vt involve. ~**si** vr ~**si in** meddle in

immis'sario m tributary

immissi'one f insertion

im'mobile adj motionless

im'mobili mpl real estate. ~'**are** adj società ~**are** building society, savings and loan Am

immobili|tà f immobility. ~**z'zare** vt immobilize; (Comm) tie up

immo'lare vt sacrifice

immondez'zaio m rubbish tip. **immon'dizia** f filth; (spazzatura) rubbish. **im'mondo** adj filthy

immo'ral|e adj immoral. ~**ità** f immorality

immorta'lare vt immortalize. **immor'tale** adj immortal

immoti'vato adj (gesto) unjustified

im'mun|e adj exempt; (Med) immune. ~**ità** f immunity. ~**iz'zare** vt immunize. ~**izzazi'one** f immunization

immunodefici'enza f immunodeficiency

immuso'ni|rsi vr sulk. ~**to** adj sulky

immu'ta|bile adj unchangeable. ~**to** adj unchanging

impacchet'tare vt wrap up

impacci'a|re vt hamper; (disturbare) inconvenience; (imbarazzare) embarrass. ~**to** adj embarrassed; (goffo) awkward. **im'paccio** m embarrassment; (ostacolo) hindrance; (situazione difficile) awkward situation

im'pacco m compress

impadro'nirsi vr ~ **di** take possession of; (fig: imparare) master

impa'gabile adj priceless

impagi'na|re vt paginate. ~**zi'one** f pagination

impagli'are vt stuff (animale)

impa'lato adj fig stiff

impalca'tura f scaffolding; fig

structure

impalli'dire vi turn pale; (fig: perdere d'importanza) pale into insignificance

impa'nare vt roll in breadcrumbs

impanta'narsi vr get bogged down

impape'rarsi, impappi'narsi vr falter, stammer

impa'rare vt learn

impareggi'abile adj incomparable

imparen'ta|rsi vr ~ **con** become related to. ~**to** adj related

'impari adj unequal; (dispari) odd

impar'tire vt impart

imparzi'al|e adj impartial. ~**ità** f impartiality

impas'sibile adj impassive

impa'sta|re vt (Culin) knead; blend (colori). **im'pasto** m (Culin) dough; (miscuglio) mixture

im'patto m impact

impau'rir|e vt frighten. ~**si** vr become frightened

im'pavido adj fearless

impazi'en|te adj impatient; ~**te di fare qcsa** eager to do sth. ~**tirsi** vr lose patience. ~**za** f impatience

impaz'zata f **all**'~ full speed

impaz'zire vi go mad; (maionese:) separate; **far** ~ **qcno** drive sb mad; ~ **per** be crazy about; **da** ~ (mal di testa) blinding

impec'cabile adj impeccable

impedi'mento m hindrance; (ostacolo) obstacle

impe'dire vt ~ **di** prevent from; (impacciare) hinder; (ostruire) obstruct; ~ **a qcno di fare qcsa** prevent sb [from] doing sth

impe'gna|re vt (dare in pegno) pawn; (vincolare) bind; (prenotare) reserve; (assorbire) take up. ~**rsi** vt apply oneself; ~**rsi a fare qcsa** commit oneself to doing sth. ~'**tiva**

f referral. ∼'tivo adj binding; (lavoro) demanding. ∼ato adj engaged; (Pol) committed. im'pegno m engagement; (Comm) commitment; (zelo) care

impel'lente adj pressing

impen'na|rsi vr (cavallo:) rear; fig bristle. ∼ta f sharp rise; (di cavallo) rearing; (di moto) wheelie

impen'sa|bile adj unthinkable. ∼to adj unexpected

impensie'rir|e vt, ∼si vr worry

impe'ra|nte adj prevailing. ∼re vi reign; (tendenza:) prevail

impera'tivo adj & m imperative

impera'tore, -'trice m emperor ● f empress

impercet'tibile adj imperceptible

imperdo'nabile adj unforgivable

imper'fe|tto adj & m imperfect. ∼zi'one f imperfection

imperi'a|le adj imperial. ∼'lismo m imperialism

imperi'oso adj imperious; (impellente) urgent

impe'rizia f lack of skill

imperme'abile adj waterproof ● m raincoat

imperni'are vt pivot; (fondare) base. ∼si vr ∼si su be based on

im'pero m empire; (potere) rule

imperscru'tabile adj inscrutable

imperso'nale adj impersonal

imperso'nare vt personify; (interpretare) act [the part of]

imper'territo adj undaunted

imperti'nen|te adj impertinent. ∼za f impertinence

imperver'sare vi rage

im'pervio adj inaccessible

'impet|o m impetus; (impulso) impulse; (slancio) transport. ∼u'oso adj impetuous; (vento) blustering

impet'tito adj stiff

impian'tare vt install; set up

(azienda)

impi'anto m plant; (sistema) system; (operazione) installation. ∼ radio (Auto) car stereo system

impia'strare vt plaster; (sporcare) dirty. impi'astro m poultice; (persona noiosa) bore; (pasticcione) cack-handed person

impic'car|e vt hang. ∼si vr hang oneself

impicci|'arsi vr meddle. im'piccio m hindrance; (seccatura) bother. ∼'one, -a mf nosey parker

impie'ga|re vt employ; (usare) use; spend (tempo, denaro); Fin invest; l'autobus ha ∼to un'ora it took the bus an hour. ∼rsi vr get [oneself] a job

impie'gatizio adj clerical

impie'gato, -a mf employee. ∼ di banca bank clerk. impi'ego m employment; (posto) job; Fin investment

impieto'sir|e vt move to pity. ∼si vr be moved to pity

impie'trito adj petrified

impigli'ar|e vt entangle. ∼si vr get entangled

impi'grir|e vt make lazy. ∼si vr get lazy

impli'car|e vt implicate; (sottintendere) imply. ∼rsi vr become involved. ∼zi'one f implication

implicita'mente adv implicitly. im'plicito adj implicit

implo'ra|re vt implore. ∼zi'one f entreaty

impolve'ra|re vt cover with dust. ∼rsi vr get covered with dust. ∼to adj dusty

impon'derabile adj imponderable; (causa, evento) unpredictable

impo'nen|te adj imposing. ∼za f impressiveness

impo'nibile adj taxable ● m taxable income

impopo'lar|e adj unpopular. ~**ità** f unpopularity

im'por|re vt impose; (ordinare) order. ~**si** vr assert oneself; (aver successo) be successful; ~**si di** (prefiggersi di) set oneself the task of

impor'tan|te adj important ● m important thing. ~**za** f importance

impor'ta|re vt import; (comportare) cause ● vi matter; (essere necessario) be necessary. **non** ~**!** it doesn't matter!; **non me ne** ~ **niente!** I couldn't care less! ~**tore**, ~**'trice** mf importer. ~**zi'one** f importation; (merce importata) import

im'porto m amount

importu'nare vt pester. **impor'tuno** adj troublesome; (inopportuno) untimely

imposizi'one f imposition; (imposta) tax

imposses'sarsi vr ~ **di** seize

impos'sibil|e adj impossible ● m **fare l'**~ do absolutely all one can. ~**ità** f impossibility

im'posta[1] f tax; ~ **sul reddito** income tax; ~ **sul valore aggiunto** value added tax

im'posta[2] f (di finestra) shutter

impo'sta|re vt (progettare) plan; (basare) base; (Mus) pitch; (imbucare) post, mail; set out (domanda, problema). ~**zi'one** f planning; (di voce) pitching

im'posto pp di **imporre**

impo'store, **-a** mf impostor

impo'ten|te adj powerless; (Med) impotent. ~**za** f powerlessness; (Med) impotence

impove'rir|e vt impoverish. ~**si** vr become poor

imprati'cabile adj impracticable; (strada) impassable

imprati'chir|e vt train. ~**si** vr ~**si in** o **a** get practice in

impre'care vi curse

impreci's|abile adj indeterminable. ~**ato** adj indeterminate. ~**i'one** f inaccuracy. **impre'ciso** adj inaccurate

impre'gnar|e vt impregnate; (imbevere) soak; fig imbue. ~**si** vr become impregnated with

imprendi'tor|e, **-'trice** mf entrepreneur. ~**i'ale** adj entrepreneurial

imprepa'rato adj unprepared

im'presa f undertaking; (gesta) exploit; (azienda) firm

impre'sario m impresario; (appaltatore) contractor

imprescin'dibile adj inescapable

impressio'na|bile adj impressionable. ~**nte** adj impressive; (spaventoso) frightening

impressio'nare vt impress; (spaventare) frighten; expose (foto). ~**rsi** vr be affected; (spaventarsi) be frightened. ~**one** f impression; (sensazione) sensation; (impronta) mark; **far** ~**one a qcno** upset sb

impressio'nis|mo m impressionism. ~**ta** mf impressionist

im'presso pp di **imprimere** ● adj printed

impre'stare vt lend

impreve'dibile adj unexpected

imprevi'dente adj improvident

impre'visto adj unforeseen ● m unforeseen event

imprigio'na|mento m imprisonment. ~**nare** vt imprison

im'primere vt impress; (stampare) print; (comunicare) impart

impro'babil|e adj unlikely, improbable. ~**ità** f improbability

improdut'tivo adj unproductive

im'pronta f impression; fig mark. ~ **digitale** fingerprint. ~ **ecologica** carbon footprint. ~ **del piede** footprint

impro'perio m insult; **improperi**

pl abuse *sg*

im'proprio *adj* improper

improvvi'sa|re *vt/i* improvise. **~rsi** *vr* turn oneself into a. **~ta** *f* surprise. **~zi'one** *f* improvisation

improv'viso *adj* sudden; all'**~** unexpectedly

impru'den|te *adj* imprudent. **~za** *f* imprudence

impu'gna|re *vt* grasp; (*Jur*) contest. **~tura** *f* grip; (*manico*) handle

impulsività *f* impulsiveness. **im·pul'sivo** *adj* impulsive

im'pulso *m* impulse; agire d'**~** act on impulse

impune'mente *adv* with impunity. **impu'nito** *adj* unpunished

impun'tura *f* stitching

impurità *f inv* impurity. **im'puro** *adj* impure

impu'tabile *adj* attributable (a to)

impu'ta|re *vt* attribute; (*accusare*) charge. **~to, -a** *mf* accused. **~zi'one** *f* charge

imputri'dire *vi* rot

in *prep* in; (*moto a luogo*) to; (*su*) on; (*entro*) within; (*mezzo*) by; (*con materiale*) made of; essere in casa/ufficio be at home/at the office; in mano/ tasca in one's hand/pocket; andare in Francia/campagna go to France/ the country; salire in treno get on the train; versa la birra nel bicchiere pour the beer into the glass; in alto up there; in giornata within the day; nel 1997 in 1997; una borsa in pelle a bag made of leather, a leather bag; in macchina (*viaggiare, venire*) by car; in contanti [in] cash; in vacanza on holiday; se fossi in te if I were you; siamo in sette there are seven of us

inabbor'dabile *adj* unapproachable

i'nabi|le *adj* incapable; (*fisicamente*) unfit. **~ità** *f* incapacity

inabi'tabile *adj* uninhabitable

inacces'sibile *adj* inaccessible; (persona) unapproachable

inaccet'tabi|le *adj* unacceptable. **~ità** *f* unacceptability

inacer'bi|re *vt* embitter; exacerbate (rapporto). **~si** *vr* grow bitter

inaci'dire *vt* turn sour. **~si** *vr* go sour; (persona:) become bitter

ina'datto *adj* unsuitable

inadegu'ato *adj* inadequate

inadempi'ente *mf* defaulter. **~'mento** *m* nonfulfilment

inaffer'rabile *adj* elusive

ina'la|re *vt* inhale. **~'tore** *m* inhaler. **~zi'one** *f* inhalation

inalbe'rar|e *vt* hoist. **~si** *vr* (cavallo:) rear [up]; (*adirarsi*) lose one's temper

inalte'ra|bile *adj* unchangeable; (colore) fast. **~to** *adj* unchanged

inami'da|re *vt* starch. **~to** *adj* starched

inammis'sibile *adj* inadmissible

inamovi'bile *adj* irremovable

inani'mato *adj* inanimate; (*senza vita*) lifeless

inappa'gabile *adj* unsatisfiable. **~to** *adj* unfulfilled

inappe'tenza *f* lack of appetite

inappli'cabile *adj* inapplicable

inappun'tabile *adj* faultless

inar'car|e *vt* arch; raise (sopracciglia). **~si** *vr* (legno:) warp; (ripiano:) sag; (linea:) curve

inari'dir|e *vt* parch; empty of feelings (persona). **~si** *vr* dry up; (persona:) become empty of feelings

inartico'lato *adj* inarticulate

inaspettata'mente *adv* unexpectedly. **inaspet'tato** *adj* unexpected

inaspri'mento *m* embitterment; (*di conflitto*) worsening

ina'sprir|e *vt* embitter. **~si** *vr* become embittered

inattac'cabile *adj* unassailable; (ir-

reprensibile) irreproachable

inatten'dibile *adj* unreliable. inat-'teso *adj* unexpected

inattività *f* inactivity. inat'tivo *adj* inactive

inattu'abile *adj* impracticable

inau'dito *adj* unheard of

inaugu'rale *adj* inaugural; viaggio ∼ maiden voyage

inaugu'rare *vt* inaugurate; open (mostra); unveil (statua); christen (lavastoviglie ecc). ∼zi'one *f* inauguration; (di mostra) opening; (di statua) unveiling

inavver't|enza *f* inadvertence. ∼ita'mente *adv* inadvertently

incagli'ar|e *vt* ground • *vi* hinder. ∼si *vr* run aground

incalco'labile *adj* incalculable

incal'li|rsi *vr* grow callous; (abituarsi) become hardened. ∼to *adj* callous; (abituato) hardened

incal'za|nte *adj* (ritmo) driving; (richiesta) urgent. ∼re *vt* pursue; *fig* press

incame'rare *vt* appropriate

incammi'nar|e *vt* get going; (*fig*: guidare) set off. ∼si *vr* set out

incana'lar|e *vt* canalize; *fig* channel. ∼si *vr* converge on

incande'scen|te *adj* incandescent; (discussione) burning

incan'ta|re *vt* enchant. ∼rsi *vr* stand spellbound; (incepparsi) jam. ∼tore *m*, ∼'trice *f* enchanter • *f* enchantress

incan'tesimo *m* spell

incan'tevole *adj* enchanting

in'canto *m* spell; *fig* delight; (asta) auction; come per ∼ as if by magic

incanu'ti|re *vt* turn white. ∼to *adj* white

inca'pac|e *adj* incapable. ∼ità *f* incapability

incapo'nirsi *vr* be set (a fare on doing)

incap'pare *vi* ∼ in run into

incappucci'arsi *vr* wrap up

incapricci'arsi *vr* ∼ di take a fancy to

incapsu'lare *vt* seal; crown (dente)

incarce'ra|re *vt* imprison. ∼zi'one *f* imprisonment

incari'ca|re *vt* charge. ∼rsi *vr* take upon oneself; me ne incarico io I will see to it. ∼to, -a *adj* in charge • *mf* representative. in'carico *m* charge; per incarico di on behalf of

incar'na|re *vt* embody. ∼rsi *vr* become incarnate

incarta'mento *m* documents *pl.* incar'tare *vt* wrap [in paper]

incas'sa|re *vt* pack; (*Mech*) embed; box in (mobile, frigo); (riscuotere) cash; take (colpo). ∼to *adj* set; (fiume) deeply embanked. in'casso *m* collection; (introito) takings *pl*

incasto'na|re *vt* set. ∼tura *f* setting. ∼to *adj* embedded; (anello) inset (di with)

inca'strar|e *vt* fit in; (□: in situazione) corner. ∼si *vr* fit. in'castro *m* joint; a incastro (pezzi) interlocking

incate'nare *vt* chain

incatra'mare *vt* tar

incatti'vire *vt* turn nasty

in'cauto *adj* imprudent

inca'va|re *vt* hollow out. ∼to *adj* hollow. ∼tura *f* hollow. in'cavo *m* hollow; (scanalatura) groove

incendi'ar|e *vt* set fire to; *fig* inflame. ∼si *vr* catch fire. ∼io, -a *adj* incendiary; (*fig*: discorso) inflammatory; *fig*: (bellezza) sultry • *mf* arsonist. in'cendio *m* fire. incendio doloso arson

incene'ri|re *vt* burn to ashes; (cremare) cremate. ∼rsi *vr* be burnt to ashes. ∼'tore *m* incinerator

in'censo *m* incense

incensu'rato *adj* blameless; essere ∼ (*Jur*) have a clean record

incenti'vare vt motivate. incen'tivo m incentive

incen'trarsi vr ~ su centre on

incep'par|e vt block; fig hamper. **~si** vr jam

ince'rata f oilcloth

incerot'tato adj with a plaster on

incer'tezza f uncertainty. in'certo adj uncertain ●m uncertainty

inces'sante adj unceasing. **~mente** adv incessantly

in'cest|o m incest. **~u'oso** adj incestuous

in'cetta f buying up; fare ~ di stockpile

in'chiesta f investigation

inchi'nar|e vt, **~si** vr bow. in'chino m bow; (di donna) curtsy

inchio'dare vt nail; nail down (coperchio); ~ a letto (malattia:) confine to bed

inchi'ostro m ink

inciam'pare vi stumble; ~ in (imbattersi) run into. inci'ampo m hindrance

inciden'tale adj incidental

inci'den|te m (episodio) incident; (infortunio) accident. **~za** f incidence

in'cidere vt cut; (arte) engrave; (registrare) record ●vi ~ su (gravare) weigh upon

in'cinta adj pregnant

incipi'ente adj incipient

incipri'ar|e vt powder. **~si** vr powder one's face

in'circa adv all'~ more or less

incisi'one f incision; (arte) engraving; (acquaforte) etching; (registrazione) recording

inci'sivo adj incisive ●m (dente) incisor

in'ciso m per ~ incidentally

incita'mento m incitement. inci'tare vt incite

inci'vil|e adj uncivilized; (maleducato) impolite. **~tà** f barbarism; (maleducazione) rudeness

incle'men|te adj harsh

incli'nabile adj reclining

incli'nar|e vt tilt ●vi ~re a be inclined to. **~rsi** vr list. **~to** adj tilted; (terreno) sloping. **~zi'one** f slope, inclination. in'cline adj inclined

in'clu|dere vt include; (allegare) enclose. **~si'one** f inclusion. **~'sivo** adj inclusive. **~so** pp di includere ●adj included; (compreso) inclusive; (allegato) enclosed

incoe'ren|te adj (contraddittorio) inconsistent. **~za** f inconsistency

in'cognit|a f unknown quantity. **~o** adj unknown ●m in ~o incognito

incol'lar|e vt stick; (con colla liquida) glue. **~si** vr stick to; (con si) a qcno stick close to sb

incolle'ri|rsi vr lose one's temper. **~to** adj enraged

incol'mabile adj (differenza) unbridgeable; (vuoto) unfillable

incolon'nare vt line up

inco'lore adj colourless

incol'pare vt blame

in'colto adj uncultivated; (persona) uneducated

in'colume adj unhurt

incom'ben|te adj impending. **~za** f task

in'combere vi ~ su hang over; ~ a (spettare) be incumbent on

incominci'are vt/i begin, start

incomo'dar|e vt inconvenience. **~si** vr trouble. in'comodo adj uncomfortable; (inopportuno) inconvenient ●m inconvenience

incompa'rabile adj incomparable

incompe'ten|te adj incompetent. **~za** f incompetence

incompi'uto adj unfinished

incom'pleto adj incomplete

incompren'si|bile adj incomprehensible. **~'one** f lack of understanding; *(malinteso)* misunderstanding. **incom'preso** *adj* misunderstood

inconce'pibile *adj* inconceivable

inconclu'dente *adj* inconclusive; (persona) ineffectual

incondizio|nata'mente *adv* unconditionally. **~'nato** *adj* unconditional

inconfes'sabile *adj* unmentionable

inconfon'dibile *adj* unmistakable

incongru'ente *adj* inconsistent

in'congruo *adj* inadequate

inconsa'pevole *adj* unaware; *(inconscio)* unconscious. **~'mente** *adv* unwittingly

inscia'mente *adv* unconsciously. **in'conscio** *adj* & *m (Psych)* unconscious

inconsi'stente *adj* insubstantial; *(notizia ecc)* unfounded. **~za** *f (di ragionamento, prove)* flimsiness

inconsu'eto *adj* unusual

incon'sulto *adj* rash

incontami'nato *adj* uncontaminated

inconte'nibile *adj* irrepressible

inconten'tabile *adj* insatiable; *(esigente)* hard to please

inconti'nen|te *adj* incontinent. **~za** *f* incontinence

incon'trare *vt* meet; encounter, meet with (difficoltà). **~si** *vr* meet (con qcno sb)

incon'trario: all'**~** *adv* the other way around; *(in modo sbagliato)* the wrong way around

incontrasta'bile *adj* incontrovertible. **~to** *adj* undisputed

in'contro *m* meeting; *Sport* match. **~** al vertice summit meeting ● *prep* **~** a towards; andare **~** a qcno go to meet sb; *fig* meet sb half way

inconveni'ente *m* drawback

incoraggia|'mento *m* encouragement. **~'ante** *adj* encouraging.

~'are *vt* encourage

incornici'a|re *vt* frame. **~'tura** *f* framing

incoro'na|re *vt* crown. **~zi'one** *f* coronation

incorpo'rar|e *vt* incorporate; *(mescolare)* blend. **~si** *vr* blend; *(territori:)* merge

incorreg'gibile *adj* incorrigible

in'correre *vi* **~** in incur; **~** nel pericolo di... run the risk of...

incorrut'tibile *adj* incorruptible

incosci'en|te *adj* unconscious; *(irresponsabile)* reckless ● *mf* irresponsible person. **~za** *f* unconsciousness; recklessness

inco'stan|te *adj* changeable; *(persona)* fickle. **~za** *f* changeableness; *(di persona)* fickleness

incre'dibile *adj* unbelievable, incredible

incredulità *f* incredulity. **in'credulo** *adj* incredulous

incre'mentare *vt* increase; *(intensificare)* step up. **incre'mento** *m* increase. incremento demografico population growth

incresci'oso *adj* regrettable

incre'spar|e *vt* ruffle; wrinkle (tessuto); make frizzy (capelli); **~e** la fronte frown. **~si** *vr* (acqua:) ripple; (tessuto:) wrinkle; (capelli:) go frizzy

incrimi'na|re *vt* indict; *fig* incriminate. **~zi'one** *f* indictment

incri'na|re *vt* crack; *fig* affect (amicizia). **~rsi** *vr* crack; (amicizia:) be affected. **~'tura** *f* crack

incroci'a|re *vt* cross ● *vi (Aeron, Naut)* cruise. **~rsi** *vr* cross. **~'tore** *m* cruiser

in'crocio *m* crossing; *(di strade)* crossroads *sg*

incrol'labile *adj* indestructible

incro'sta|re *vt* encrust. **~zi'one** *f* encrustation

incuba|'trice *f* incubator. **~zi'one**

f incubation

'incubo *m* nightmare

in'cudine *f* anvil

incu'rabile *adj* incurable

incu'rante *adj* careless

incurio'sir|e *vt* make curious. ~**si** *vr* become curious

incursi'one *f* raid. ~ **aerea** air raid

incurva'mento *m* bending

incur'va|re *vt*, ~**rsi** *vr* bend. ~**tura** *f* bending

in'cusso *pp di* incutere

incusto'dito *adj* unguarded

in'cutere *vt* arouse

'indaco *m* indigo

indaffa'rato *adj* busy

inda'gare *vt/i* investigate

in'dagine *f* research; (*giudiziaria*) investigation. ~ **di mercato** market survey

indebi'tar|e *vt*, ~**si** *vr* get into debt

in'debito *adj* undue

indeboli'mento *m* weakening

indebo'lir|e *vt*, ~**si** *vr* weaken

inde'cen|te *adj* indecent. ~**za** *f* indecency; (*vergogna*) disgrace

indeci'frabile *adj* indecipherable

indecisi'one *f* indecision. **inde-'ciso** *adj* undecided

inde'fesso *adj* tireless

indefi'ni|bile *adj* indefinable. ~**to** *adj* indefinite

indefor'mabile *adj* crushproof

in'degno *adj* unworthy

indelica'tezza *f* indelicacy; (*azione*) tactless act. **indeli'cato** *adj* indiscreet; (*grossolano*) indelicate

in'denn|e *adj* uninjured; (*da malattia*) unaffected. ~**ità** *f inv* allowance; (*per danni*) compensation. ~**ità di trasferta** travel allowance. ~**iz'zare** *vt* compensate. **inden'nizzo** *m* compensation

indero'gabile *adj* binding

indeside'ra|bile *adj* undesirable. ~**to** *adj* (*figlio, ospite*) unwanted

indetermi'na|bile *adj* indeterminable. ~**tezza** *f* vagueness. ~**to** *adj* indeterminate

'Indi|a *f* India. **i~'ano, -a** *adj & mf* Indian; **in fila i~'ana** in single file

indiavo'lato *adj* possessed; (*vivace*) wild

indi'ca|re *vt* show, indicate; (*col dito*) point at; (*far notare*) point out; (*consigliare*) advise. ~**tivo** *adj* indicative ● *m* (*Gram*) indicative. ~**tore** *m* indicator; (*Techn*) gauge; (*prontuario*) directory. ~**zi'one** *f* indication; (*istruzione*) direction

'indice *m* forefinger; (*lancetta*) pointer; (*di libro, statistica*) index; (*fig: segno*) sign

indietreggi'are *vi* draw back; (*Mil*) retreat

indi'etro *adv* back, behind; **all'**~ backwards; **avanti e** ~ back and forth; **essere** ~ be behind; (*mentalmente*) be backward; (*con pagamenti*) be in arrears; (*di orologio*) be slow; **fare marcia** ~ reverse; **rimandare** ~ send back; **rimanere** ~ be left behind; **torna** ~! come back!

indi'feso *adj* undefended; (*inerme*) helpless

indiffe'ren|te *adj* indifferent; **mi è** ~**te** it is all the same to me. ~**za** *f* indifference

in'digeno, -a *adj* indigenous ● *mf* native

indi'gen|te *adj* needy. ~**za** *f* poverty

indigesti'one *f* indigestion. **indi'gesto** *adj* indigestible

indi'gna|re *vt* make indignant. ~**rsi** *vr* be indignant. ~**to** *adj* indignant. ~**zi'one** *f* indignation

indimenti'cabile *adj* unforgettable

indipen'den|te *adj* independent.

∼te'mente adv independently; ∼te-mente dal tempo regardless of the weather, whatever the weather. ∼za f independence

in'dire vt announce

indiretta'mente adv indirectly. indi'retto adj indirect

indiriz'zar|e vt address; (mandare) send; (dirigere) direct. ∼si vr direct one's steps. indi'rizzo m address; (direzione) direction

indisci'pli|na f lack of discipline. ∼'nato adj undisciplined

indi'scre|to adj indiscreet. ∼zi'one f indiscretion

indi'scusso adj unquestioned

indiscu'tibil|e adj unquestionable. ∼'mente adv unquestionably

indispen'sabile adj essential, indispensable

indispet'tir|e vt irritate. ∼si vr get irritated

indi'spo|rre vt antagonize. ∼sto pp di indisporre • adj indisposed. ∼sizi'one f indisposition

indisso'lubile adj indissoluble

indistin'guibile adj indiscernible

indistinta'mente adv without exception. indi'stinto adj indistinct

indistrut'tibile adj indestructible

indistur'bato adj undisturbed

in'divia f endive

individu'a|le adj individual. ∼'lista mf individualist. ∼lità f individuality. ∼re vt individualize; (localizzare) locate; (riconoscere) single out

indi'viduo m individual

indivi'sibile adj indivisible. indi-'viso adj undivided

indizi'a|re vt throw suspicion on. ∼to, -a adj suspected • mf suspect. in'dizio m sign; (Jur) circumstantial evidence

'indole f nature

indolenzi'mento m stiffness

indolen'zi|rsi vr go stiff.

∼to adj stiff

indo'lore adj painless

indo'mani m l'∼ the following day

Indo'nesia f Indonesia

indo'rare vt gild

indos'sa|re vt wear; (mettere addosso) put on. ∼'tore, ∼'trice mf model

in'dotto pp di indurre

indottri'nare vt indoctrinate

indovi'n|are vt guess; (predire) foretell. ∼ato adj successful; (scelta) well-chosen. ∼ello m riddle. indo-'vino, -a mf fortune-teller

indubbia'mente adv undoubtedly. in'dubbio adj undoubted

indugi'ar|e vi, ∼si vr linger. in'dugio m delay

indul'gen|te adj indulgent. ∼za f indulgence

in'dul|gere vi ∼gere a indulge in. ∼to pp di indulgere • m (Jur) pardon

indu'mento m garment; indumenti pl clothes

induri'mento m hardening

indu'rir|e vt, ∼si vr harden

in'durre vt induce

in'dustri|a f industry. ∼'ale adj industrial • mf industrialist

industrializ'za|re vt industrialize. ∼to adj industrialized. ∼zi'one f industrialization

industri'arsi vr try one's hardest. ∼'oso adj industrious

induzi'one f induction

inebe'tito adj stunned

inebri'ante adj intoxicating, exciting

i'nedia f starvation

i'nedito adj unpublished

ineffi'cace adj ineffective

ineffici'en|te adj inefficient. ∼za f inefficiency

ineguagli'abile adj incomparable

inegu'ale adj unequal;

(superficie) uneven

inelut'tabile adj inescapable

ine'rente adj ~ a concerning

i'nerme adj unarmed; fig defenceless

inerpi'carsi vr ~ su clamber up; (pianta:) climb up

i'ner|te adj inactive; (Phys) inert. ~zia f inactivity; (Phys) inertia

inesat'tezza f inaccuracy. ine-'satto adj inaccurate; (erroneo) incorrect; (non riscosso) uncollected

inesau'ribile adj inexhaustible

inesi'sten|te adj non-existent. ~za f non-existence

inesperi'enza f inexperience. ine-'sperto adj inexperienced

inespli'cabile adj inexplicable

ine'sploso adj unexploded

inesti'mabile adj inestimable

inetti'tudine f ineptitude. i'netto adj inept; inetto a unsuited to

ine'vaso adj (pratiche) pending; (corrispondenza) unanswered

inevi'tabil|e adj inevitable. ~'mente adv inevitably

i'nezia f trifle

infagot'tar|e vt wrap up. ~si vr wrap [oneself] up

infal'libile adj infallible

infa'ma|re vt defame. ~'torio adj defamatory

in'fam|e adj infamous; (🅸: orrendo) awful, shocking. ~ia f infamy

infan'garsi vr get muddy

infan'tile adj children's; (ingenuità) childlike; pej childish

in'fanzia f childhood; (bambini) children pl; prima ~ infancy

infar'cire vt pepper (discorso) (di with)

infari'na|re vt flour; ~re di sprinkle with. ~'tura f fig smattering

in'farto m coronary

infasti'dir|e vt irritate. ~si vr get irritated

infati'cabile adj untiring

in'fatti conj as a matter of fact; (veramente) indeed

infatu'a|rsi vr become infatuated (di with). ~to adj infatuated. ~zi'one f infatuation

infe'condo adj infertile

infe'del|e adj unfaithful. ~tà f unfaithfulness; ~ pl affairs

infe'lic|e adj unhappy; (inappropriato) unfortunate; (cattivo) bad. ~ità f unhappiness

infel'tri|rsi vr get matted. ~to adj matted

inferi'or|e adj (più basso) lower; (qualità) inferior ● mf inferior. ~ità f inferiority

inferme'ria f infirmary; (di nave) sick-bay

infermi'er|a f nurse. ~e m [male] nurse

infermità f sickness. ~ mentale mental illness. in'fermo, -a adj sick ● mf invalid

infer'nale adj infernal; (spaventoso) hellish

in'ferno m hell; va all'~! go to hell!

infero'cirsi vr become fierce

inferri'ata f grating

infervo'rar|e vt arouse enthusiasm in. ~si vr get excited

infe'stare vt infest

infet'tar|e vt infect. ~arsi vr become infected. ~ivo adj infectious. in'fetto adj infected. infezi'one f infection

infiac'chir|e vt/i, ~si vr weaken

infiam'mabile adj [in]flammable

infiam'ma|re vt set on fire; (Med, fig) inflame. ~rsi vr catch fire; (Med) become inflamed. ~zi'one f (Med) inflammation

in'fido adj treacherous

infie'rire vi (imperversare) rage; ~ su

attack furiously

in'figger|e vt drive. ~**si** vr ~**si in** penetrate

infi'lar|e vt thread; (mettere) insert; (indossare) put on. ~**si** vr slip on (vestito); ~**si in** (introdursi in) slip into

infil'tra|rsi vr infiltrate. ~**zi'one** f infiltration; (d'acqua) seepage; (Med: iniezione) injection

infil'zare vt pierce; (infilare) string; (conficcare) stick

'infimo adj lowest

in'fine adv finally; (insomma) in short

infinità f infinity; un'~ di masses of. **infi'nito** adj infinite; (Gram) infinitive ● m infinite; (Gram) infinitive; (Math) infinity; all'~ endlessly

infinocchi'are vt 🔲 hoodwink

infischi'ars|i vr ~ di not care about; me ne infischio 🔲 I couldn't care less

in'fisso pp di infiggere ● m fixture; (di porta, finestra) frame

infit'tir|e vt/i, ~**si** vr thicken

inflazi'one f inflation

infles'sibil|e adj inflexible. ~**ità** f inflexibility

inflessi'one f inflexion

in'flig|gere vt inflict. ~**tto** pp di infliggere

influ'en|te adj influential. ~**za** f influence; (Med) influenza

influen'za|bile adj (mente, opinione) impressionable. ~**re** vt influence. ~**to** adj (malato) with the flu

influ'ire vi ~ **su** influence

in'flusso m influence

info'carsi vr catch fire; (viso:) go red; (discussione:) become heated

infol'tire vt/i thicken

in'fondere vt instil

infor'care vt fork up; get on (bici); put on (occhiali)

infor'male adj informal

infor'ma|re vt inform. ~**rsi** vr inquire (di about).

infor'matica f computing, IT. ~**o** adj computer attrib

infor'ma|tivo adj informative. **infor'mato** adj informed; male informato ill-informed. ~**tore**, ~**trice** mf (di polizia) informer. ~**zi'one** f information (solo sg); un'~**zione** a piece of information

in'forme adj shapeless

infor'nare vt put into the oven

infortu'narsi vr have an accident. ~**nio sul lavoro** industrial accident

infos'sa|rsi vr sink; (guance, occhi:) become hollow. ~**to** adj sunken, hollow

infradici'ar|e vt drench. ~**si** vr get drenched; (diventare marcio) rot

infra'dito m pl (scarpe) flip-flops

in'frang|ere vt break; (in mille pezzi) shatter. ~**ersi** vr break. ~**gibile** adj unbreakable

in'franto pp di infrangere ● adj shattered; (cuore) broken

infra'rosso adj infra-red

infrastrut'tura f infrastructure

infrazi'one f offence

infredda'tura f cold

infreddo'li|rsi vr feel cold. ~**to** adj cold

infruttu'oso adj fruitless

infuo'ca|re vt make red-hot. ~**to** adj burning

infu'ori adv all'~ outwards; all'~ **di** except

infuri'a|re vi rage. ~**rsi** vr fly into a rage. ~**to** adj blustering

infusi'one f infusion. **in'fuso** pp di infondere ● m infusion

Ing. abbr ingegnere

ingabbi'are vt cage; (fig: mettere in prigione) jail

ingaggi'are vt engage; sign up

(calciatori ecc); begin (lotta, battaglia). in'gaggio *m* engagement; (*di calciatore*) signing [up]

ingan'nar|e *vt* deceive; (*essere infedele a*) be unfaithful to. ~si *vr* deceive oneself; se non m'inganno if I am not mistaken

ingan'nevole *adj* deceptive. in'ganno *m* deceit; (*frode*) fraud

ingarbugli'a|re *vt* entangle; (*confondere*) confuse. ~rsi *vr* get entangled; (*confondersi*) become confused. ~to *adj* confused

inge'gnarsi *vr* do one's best

in'gegnere *m* engineer. ingegne'ria *f* engineering

in'gegno *m* brains *pl*; (*genio*) genius; (*abilità*) ingenuity. ~sa'mente *adv* ingeniously

ingelo'sir|e *vt* make jealous. ~si *vr* become jealous

in'gente *adj* huge

ingenu|a'mente *adv* naïvely. ~ità *f* naïvety. in'genuo *adj* ingenuous; (*credulone*) naïve

inge'renza *f* interference

inge'rire *vt* swallow

inges'sa|re *vt* put in plaster. ~tura *f* plaster

Inghil'terra *f* England

inghiot'tire *vt* swallow

in'ghippo *m* trick

ingial'li|re *vi*, ~rsi *vr* turn yellow. ~to *adj* yellowed

ingigan'tire *vt* magnify •*vi*, ~si *vr* grow to enormous proportions

inginocchi'a|rsi *vr* kneel [down]. ~to *adj* kneeling. ~'toio *m* prie-dieu

ingiù *adv* down; all'~ downwards; a testa ~ head downwards

ingi'un|gere *vt* order. ~zi'one *f* injunction. ~zione di pagamento final demand

ingi'uri|a *f* insult; (*torto*) wrong; (*danno*) damage. ~'are *vt* insult; (*fare*

un torto a*) wrong. ~'oso *adj* insulting

ingiu'stizia *f* injustice. ingi'usto *adj* unjust, unfair

in'glese *adj* English •*m* Englishman; (*lingua*) English •*f* Englishwoman

ingoi'are *vt* swallow

ingol'far|e *vt* flood (motore). ~si *vr fig* get involved; (*motore:*) flood

ingom'bra|nte *adj* cumbersome. ~re *vt* clutter up; *fig* cram (mente)

in'gombro *m* encumbrance; essere d'~ be in the way

in'gordigia *f* greed. in'gordo *adj* greedy

ingor'gar|e *vt* block. ~si *vr* be blocked [up]. in'gorgo *m* blockage; (*del traffico*) jam

ingoz'zar|e *vt* gobble up; (*nutrire eccessivamente*) stuff; fatten (animali)

ingra'na|ggio *m* gear; *fig* mechanism. ~re *vt* engage •*vi* be in gear

ingrandi'mento *m* enlargement

ingran'dir|e *vt* enlarge; (*esagerare*) magnify. ~rsi *vr* become larger; (*aumentare*) increase

ingras'sar|e *vt* fatten up; (*Mech*) grease •*vi*, ~si *vr* put on weight

ingrati'tudine *f* ingratitude. in'grato *adj* ungrateful; (*sgradevole*) thankless

ingredi'ente *m* ingredient

in'gresso *m* entrance; (*accesso*) admittance; (*sala*) hall; ~ gratuito/libero admission free; vietato l'~ no entry; no admittance

ingros'sar|e *vt* make big; (*gonfiare*) swell •*vi*, ~si *vr* grow big; (*gonfiare*) swell

in'grosso: all'~ *adv* wholesale; (*pressappoco*) roughly

ingua'ribile *adj* incurable

'inguine *m* groin

ingurgi'tare *vt* gulp down

ini'bi|re *vt* inhibit; (*vietare*) forbid.

~to adj inhibited. **~zi'one** f inhibition; (divieto) prohibition

iniet'tar|e vt inject. **~si** vr ~si di sangue (occhi:) become bloodshot. **iniezi'one** f injection

inimic'arsi vr make an enemy of. **inimi'cizia** f enmity

inimi'tabile adj inimitable

ininter|rotta'mente adv continuously. **~'rotto** adj continuous

iniquità f iniquity. **i'niquo** adj iniquitous

inizi'are vt begin; (avviare) open; ~ qcno a qcsa initiate sb in sth • vi begin

inizia'tiva f initiative; prendere l'~ take the initiative

inizi'a|to, -a adj initiated • mf initiate; gli ~ti the initiated. **~'tore, ~'trice** mf initiator. **~zi'one** f initiation

i'nizio m beginning, start; dare ~ a start; avere ~ get under way

innaffi'a|re vt water. **~'toio** m watering-can

innal'zar|e vt raise; (erigere) erect. **~si** vr rise

innamo'ra|rsi vr fall in love (di with). **~ta** f girl-friend. **~to** adj in love • m boy-friend

in'nanzi adv (stato in luogo) in front; (di tempo) ahead; (avanti) forward; (prima) before; d'ora ~ from now on • prep (prima) before; ~ a in front of. **~'tutto** adv first of all; (soprattutto) above all

in'nato adj innate

innatu'rale adj unnatural

inne'gabile adj undeniable

innervo'sir|e vt make nervous. **~si** vr get irritated

inne'scare vt prime. **in'nesco** m primer

inne'stare vt graft; (Mech) engage; (inserire) insert. **in'nesto** m graft; (Mech) clutch; (Electr) connection

inne'vato adj covered in snow

'inno m hymn. ~ **nazionale** national anthem

inno'cen|te adj innocent **~te'mente** adv innocently

in'nocuo adj innocuous

inno'va|re vt make changes in. **~'tivo** adj innovative. **~'tore** adj trail-blazing. **~zi'one** f innovation

innume'revole adj innumerable

ino'doro adj odourless

inoffen'sivo adj harmless

inol'trar|e vt forward. **~si** vr advance

inol'trato adj late

i'noltre adv besides

inon'da|re vt flood. **~zi'one** f flood

inope'roso adj idle

inoppor'tuno adj untimely

inorgo'glir|e vt make proud. **~si** vr become proud

inorri'dire vt horrify • vi be horrified

inosser'vato adj unobserved; (non rispettato) disregarded; passare ~ go unnoticed

inossi'dabile adj stainless

'inox adj inv (acciaio) stainless

inqua'dra|re vt frame; fig put in context (scrittore, problema). **~rsi** vr fit into. **~'tura** f framing

inquali'ficabile adj unspeakable

inquie'tar|e vt worry. **~si** get worried; (impazientirsi) get cross. inqui'eto adj restless; (preoccupato) worried. **inquie'tudine** f anxiety

inqui'lino, -a mf tenant

inquina'mento m pollution

inqui'na|re vt pollute. **~to** adj polluted

inqui'rente adj (Jur) (magistrato) examining; commissione ~ commission of enquiry

inqui'si|re vt/i investigate. **~to** adj under investigation. **~'tore, ~'trice**

adj inquiring ●*mf* inquisitor. ~zi'one *f* inquisition

insabbi'are *vt* shelve

insa'lata *f* salad. ~a belga endive. ~i'era *f* salad bowl

insa'lubre *adj* unhealthy

insa'nabile *adj* incurable

insangui'na|re *vt* cover with blood. ~to *adj* bloody

insa'po|re *adj* tasteless. ~rire *vt* flavour

insa'puta *f* all'~ di unknown to

insazi'abile *adj* insatiable

insce'nare *vt* stage

inscin'dibile *adj* inseparable

insedia'mento *m* installation

insedi'ar|e *vt* install. ~si *vr* install oneself

in'segna *f* sign; (*bandiera*) flag; (*decorazione*) decoration; (*emblema*) insignia *pl*; (*stemma*) symbol. ~ luminosa neon sign

insegna'mento *m* teaching. inse'gnante *adj* teaching ●*mf* teacher

inse'gnare *vt/i* teach; ~ qcsa a qcno teach sb sth

insegui'mento *m* pursuit

insegu'i|re *vt* pursue. ~tore, ~'trice *mf* pursuer

insemi'na|re *vt* inseminate. ~zi'one *f* insemination. ~zione artificiale artificial insemination

insena'tura *f* inlet

insen'sato *adj* senseless; (*folle*) crazy

insen'sibil|e *adj* insensitive; (*braccio ecc*) numb. ~ità *f* insensitivity

inseri'mento *m* insertion

inse'ri|re *vt* insert; place (*annuncio*); (*Electr*) connect. ~si *vr* ~si in get into. in'serto *m* file; (*in un film ecc*) insert

inservi'ente *mf* attendant

inserzi'o|ne *f* insertion; (*avviso*) advertisement. ~'nista *mf* advertiser

insetti'cida *m* insecticide

in'setto *m* insect

insicu'rezza *f* insecurity. insi'curo *adj* insecure

in'sidi|a *f* trick; (*tranello*) snare. ~'are *vt/i* lay a trap for. ~'oso *adj* insidious

insi'eme *adv* together; (*contemporaneamente*) at the same time ●*prep* ~ a [together] with ●*m* whole; (*completo*) outfit; (*Theat*) ensemble; (*Math*) set; nell'~ as a whole; tutto ~ all together; (*bere*) at one go

in'signe *adj* renowned

insignifi'cante *adj* insignificant

insi'gnire *vt* decorate

insinda'cabile *adj* final

insinu'ante *adj* insinuating

insinu'a|re *vt* insinuate. ~rsi *vr* penetrate; ~rsi in *fig* creep into

in'sipido *adj* insipid

insi'sten|te *adj* insistent. ~te'mente *adv* repeatedly. ~za *f* insistence. in'sistere *vi* insist; (*perseverare*) persevere

insoddisfa'cente *adj* unsatisfactory

insoddi'sfa|tto *adj* unsatisfied; (*scontento*) dissatisfied. ~zi'one *f* dissatisfaction

insoffe'ren|te *adj* intolerant. ~za *f* intolerance

insolazi'one *f* sunstroke

inso'len|te *adj* rude, insolent. ~za *f* rudeness, insolence; (*commento*) insolent remark

in'solito *adj* unusual

inso'lubile *adj* insoluble

inso'luto *adj* unsolved; (*non pagato*) unpaid

insol'venza *f* insolvency

in'somma *adv* in short; (*dunque*) well reallyǃ; (*così così*) so so

in'sonn|e *adj* sleepless. ~ia *f* insomnia

insonno'lito *adj* sleepy

insonoriz'zato adj soundproofed

insoppor'tabile adj unbearable

insor'genza f onset

in'sorgere vi revolt, rise up; (sorgere) arise; (difficoltà) crop up

insormon'tabile adj (ostacolo, difficoltà) insurmountable

in'sorto pp di insorgere● adj rebellious ● m rebel

insospet'tabile adj unsuspected

insospet'tir|e vt make suspicious ● vi, ~si vr become suspicious

insoste'nibile adj untenable; (insopportabile) unbearable

insostitu'ibile adj irreplaceable

inspe'ra|bile adj una sua vittoria è ~bile there is no hope of him winning. ~to adj unhoped-for

inspie'gabile adj inexplicable

inspi'rare vt breathe in

in'stabil|e adj unstable; (tempo) changeable. ~ità f instability; (di tempo) changeability

instal'la|re vt install. ~rsi vr settle in. ~zi'one f installation

instau'ra|re vt found. ~rsi vr become established. ~zi'one f foundation

instra'dare vt direct

insù adv all'~ upwards

insuc'cesso m failure

insudici'ar|e vt dirty. ~si vr get dirty

insuffici'en|te adj insufficient; (inadeguato) inadequate ● m (Sch) fail. ~za f insufficiency; (inadeguatezza) inadequacy; (Sch) fail. ~za cardiaca heart failure. ~za di prove lack of evidence

insu'lare adj insular

insu'lina f insulin

in'sulso adj insipid; (sciocco) silly

insul'tare vt insult. in'sulto m insult

insupe'rabile adj insuperable; (eccezionale) incomparable

insussi'stente adj groundless

intac'care vt nick; (corrodere) corrode; draw on (capitale); (danneggiare) damage

intagli'are vt carve. in'taglio m carving

intan'gibile adj untouchable

in'tanto adv meanwhile; (per ora) for the moment; (avversativo) but; ~ che while

intarsi'a|re vt inlay. ~to adj ~to di inset with. in'tarsio m inlay

inta'sa|re vt clog; block (traffico). ~rsi vr get blocked. ~to adj blocked

inta'scare vt pocket

in'tatto adj intact

intavo'lare vt start

inte'gra|le adj whole; edizione ~le unabridged edition; pane ~le wholemeal bread. ~nte adj integral. 'integro adj complete; (retto) upright

inte'gra|re vt integrate; (aggiungere) supplement. ~rsi vr integrate. ~'tivo adj (corso) supplementary. ~zi'one f integration

integrità f integrity

intelaia'tura f framework

intel'letto m intellect

intellettu'al|e adj & mf intellectual. ~'mente adv intellectually

intelli'gen|te adj intelligent. ~te'mente adv intelligently. ~za f intelligence

intelli'gibile adj intelligible

intempe'ranza f intemperance

intem'perie fpl bad weather

inten'den|te m superintendent. ~za f ~za di finanza inland revenue office

in'tender|e vt (comprendere) understand; (udire) hear; (avere intenzione) intend; (significare) mean. ~sela can have an understanding with; ~si vr (capirsi) understand each other; ~si di (essere esperto) have a good knowledge of

intendi'mento m understanding; (*intenzione*). intention. ∼tore, ∼'trice mf connoisseur

intene'rir|e vt soften; (*commuovere*) touch. ∼si vr be touched

intensifi'car|e vt, ∼si vr intensify

intensità f intensity. inten'sivo adj intensive. in'tenso adj intense

inten'tare vt start up; ∼ causa contro qcno bring o institute proceedings against sb

in'tento adj engrossed (a in) ● m purpose

intenzio'nale adj intentional. intenzi'one f intention; senza ∼ne unintentionally; avere ∼ne di fare qcsa intend to do sth, have the intention of doing sth

intenzio'nato adj essere ∼ a fare qcsa have the intention of doing sth

intera'gire vi interact

intera'mente adv completely

intera|t'tivo adj interactive. ∼zi'one f interaction

interca'lare[1] m stock phrase

interca'lare[2] vt insert

intercambi'abile adj interchangeable

interca'pedine f cavity

inter'ce|dere vi intercede. ∼ssi'one f intercession

intercet'ta|re vt intercept; tap (telefono). ∼zi'one f interception. ∼zione telefonica telephone tapping

inter'city m inv inter-city

intercontinen'tale adj intercontinental

inter'correre vi (tempo:) elapse; (esistere) exist

inter'detto pp di interdire ● adj astonished; (proibito) forbidden; rimanere ∼ be taken aback

inter'di|re vt forbid; (Jur) deprive of civil rights. ∼zi'one f prohibition

interessa'mento m interest

interes'sante adj interesting; essere in stato ∼ be pregnant

interes'sa|re vt interest; (riguardare) concern ● vi ∼re a matter to. ∼rsi vr ∼rsi a take an interest in. ∼rsi di take care of. ∼to, -a mf interested party ● adj interested; essere ∼to pej have an interest

inte'resse m interest; fare qcsa per ∼ do sth out of self-interest

inter'faccia f (Comput) interface

interfe'renza f interference

interfe'r|ire vi interfere

interiezi'one f interjection

interi'ora fpl entrails

interi'ore adj interior

inter'ludio m interlude

intermedi'ario, -a adj & mf intermediary

inter'medio adj in-between

inter'mezzo m (Mus, Theat) intermezzo

intermit'ten|te adj intermittent; (luce) flashing. ∼za f luce a ∼za flashing light

interna'mento m internment; (in manicomio) committal

inter'nare vt intern; (in manicomio) commit [to a mental institution]

internazio'nale adj international

'Internet f Internet, internet

in'terno adj internal; (Geog) inland; (interiore) inner; (politica) national; alunno ∼ boarder ● m interior; (di condominio) flat; (Teleph) extension; Cinema interior shot; all'∼ inside

in'tero adj whole, entire; (intatto) intact; (completo) complete; per ∼ in full

interpel'lare vt consult

inter'por|re vt place (ostacolo). ∼si vr come between

interpre'ta|re vt interpret; (Mus) perform. ∼zi'one f interpretation;

(Mus) performance. in'terprete mf interpreter; (Mus) performer

inter'ra|re vt (seppellire) bury; plant (pianta). ~to m basement

interro'ga|re vt question; (Sch) test; examine (studenti). ~'tivo adj interrogative; (sguardo) questioning; punto ~'tivo question mark ●m question. ~'torio adj & m quèstioning. ~zi'one f question; (Sch) oral [test]

inter'romper|e vt interrupt; (sospendere) stop; cut off (collegamento). ~si vr break off

interrut'tore m switch

interruzi'one f interruption; senza ~ non-stop. ~ di gravidanza termination of pregnancy

interse'care vt, ~'carsi vr intersect. ~zi'one f intersection

interur'ban|a f long-distance call. ~o adj inter-city; telefonata ~a long-distance call

interval'lare vt space out. inter-'vallo m interval; (spazio) space; (Sch) break. intervallo pubblicitario commercial break

interve'nire vi intervene; (Med: operare) operate; ~ a take part in. inter'vento m intervention; (presenza) presence; (chirurgico) operation; pronto intervento emergency services

inter'vista f interview

intervi'sta|re vt interview. ~'tore, ~'trice mf interviewer

in'tes|a f understanding; cenno d'~a acknowledgement. ~o pp di intendere ●adj resta ~o che...; needless to say,...; ~il agreed!; ~o a meant to

inte'sta|re vt head; write one's name and address at the top of (lettera); (Comm) register. ~rsi vr si fare qcsa take it into one's head to do sth. ~'tario, -a mf holder. ~zi'one f heading; (su carta da lettere)

letterhead

inte'stino adj (lotte) internal ●m intestine

intima'mente adv intimately

inti'ma|re vt order; ~re l'alt a qcno order sb to stop. ~zi'one f order

intimida|'torio adj threatening. ~zi'one f intimidation

intimi'dire vt intimidate

intimità f cosiness. 'intimo adj intimate; (interno) innermost; (amico) close ●m (amico) close friend; (dell'animo) heart

intimo'ri|re vt frighten. ~rsi vr get frightened. ~to adj frightened

in'tingere vt dip

in'tingolo m sauce; (pietanza) stew

intiriz'zi|re vt numb. ~rsi vr grow numb. ~to adj essere ~ to (dal freddo) be perished

intito'lar|e vt entitle; (dedicare) dedicate. ~si vr be called

intolle'rabile adj intolerable

intona'care vt plaster. in'tonaco m plaster

into'na|re vt start to sing; tune (strumento); (accordare) match. ~rsi vr match. ~to adj (persona) able to sing in tune; (colore) matching

intonazi'one f (inflessione) intonation; (ironica) tone

inton'ti|re vt daze; (gas:) make dizzy ●vi be dazed. ~to adj dazed

intop'pare vi ~ in run into

in'toppo m obstacle

in'torno adv around ●prep ~ a around; (circa) about

intorpi'di|re vt numb. ~rsi vr become numb. ~to adj torpid

intossi'ca|re vt poison. ~rsi vr be poisoned. ~zi'one f poisoning

intralci'are vt hamper

in'tralcio m hitch; essere d'~ be a hindrance (a to)

intrallaz'zare vi intrigue. intral-'lazzo m racket

intramon'tabile adj timeless

intransi'gente adj uncompromising. ∼za f intransigence

intransi'tivo adj intransitive

intrappo'lato adj rimanere ∼ be trapped

intrapren'dente adj enterprising. ∼za f initiative

intra'prendere vt undertake

intrat'tabile adj very difficult

intratte'ner|e vt entertain. ∼ersi vr linger. ∼i'mento m entertainment

intrave'dere vt catch a glimpse of; (presagire) foresee

intrecci'ar|e vt interweave; plait (capelli, corda). ∼si vr intertwine; (aggrovigliarsi) become tangled; ∼e le mani clasp one's hands

in'treccio m (trama) plot

intri'cato adj tangled

intri'gante adj scheming; (affascinante) intriguing

intri'ga|re vt entangle; (incuriosire) intrigue ● vi intrigue, scheme. ∼rsi vr meddle. in'trigo m plot; intrighi pl intrigues

in'triso adj ∼ di soaked in

intri'stirsi vr grow sad

intro'du|rre vt introduce; (inserire) insert; ∼rre a (iniziare a) introduce to. ∼rsi vr get in (in to). ∼t'tivo adj (pagine, discorso) introductory. ∼zi'one f introduction

in'troito m income, revenue; (incasso) takings pl

intro'metter|e vt introduce. ∼si vr interfere; (interporsi) intervene. in-tromissi'one f intervention

intro'vabile adj that can't be found; (prodotto) unobtainable

intro'verso, -a adj introverted ● mf introvert

intrufo'larsi vr sneak in

in'truglio m concoction

intrusi'one f intrusion. in'truso, -a mf intruder

intu'i|re vt perceive

intui'tivo adj intuitive. in'tuito m intuition. ∼zi'one f intuition

inuguagli'anza f inequality

inu'mano adj inhuman

inu'mare vt inter

inumi'dir|e vt dampen; moisten (labbra). ∼si vr become damp

i'nutil|e adj useless; (superfluo) unnecessary. ∼ità f uselessness

inutiliz'za|bile adj unusable. ∼to adj unused

inva'dente adj intrusive

in'vadere vt invade; (affollare) overrun

invali'd|are vt invalidate. ∼ità f disability; (Jur) invalidity. in'valido, -a adj invalid; (handicappato) disabled ● mf disabled person

in'vano adv in vain

invari'abile adj invariable

invari'ato adj unchanged

invasi'one f invasion. in'vaso pp di invadere. inva'sore adj invading ● m invader

invecchia'mento m (di vino) maturation

invecchi'are vt/i age

in'vece adv instead; (anzi) but; ∼ di instead of

inve'ire vi ∼ contro inveigh against

inven'dibile adj unsaleable. ∼uto adj unsold

inven'tare vt invent

inventari'are vt make an inventory of. inven'tario m inventory

inven'tivo, -a adj inventive ● f inventiveness. ∼'tore, -'trice mf inventor. ∼zi'one f invention

inver'nale adj wintry. in'verno m winter

invero'simile adj improbable

inversi'one f inversion; (Mech) reversal. in'verso adj inverse; (opposto) opposite ● m opposite

inverte'brato adj & m invertebrate

inver'ti|re vt reverse; (capovolgere) turn upside down.

investi'ga|re vt investigate. ∼'tore m investigator. ∼zi'one f investigation

investi'mento m investment; (incidente) crash

inve'sti|re vt invest; (urtare) collide with; (travolgere) run over; ∼re qcno di invest sb with; ∼'tura f investiture

invi'a|re vt send. ∼to, -a mf envoy; (di giornale) correspondent

invidi|a f envy. ∼'are vt envy. ∼'oso adj envious

invigo'rir|e vt invigorate. ∼si vr become strong

invin'cibile adj invincible

in'vio m dispatch; (Comput) enter

invipe'ri|rsi vr get nasty. ∼to adj furious

invi'sibil|e adj invisible. ∼ità f invisibility

invi'tante adj (piatto, profumo) enticing

invi'ta|re vt invite. ∼to, -a mf guest. in'vito m invitation

invo'ca|re vt invoke; (implorare) beg. ∼zi'one f invocation

invogli'ar|e vt tempt; (indurre) induce. ∼si vr ∼si di take a fancy to

involon|taria'mente adv involuntarily. ∼'tario adj involuntary

invol'tino m (Culin) beef olive

in'volto m parcel; (fagotto) bundle

in'volucro m wrapping

invulne'rabile adj invulnerable

inzacche'rare vt splash with mud

inzup'par|e vt soak; (intingere) dip. ∼si vr get soaked

'io pers pron l; chi è? - [sono] io who is it? - [it's] me; l'ho fatto io

[stesso] I did it myself ● m l'∼ the ego

i'odio m iodine

l'onio m lo ∼ the Ionian [Sea]

i'osa: a ∼ adv in abundance

iperat'tivo adj hyperactive

ipermer'cato m hypermarket

iper'metrope adj long-sighted

ipertensi'one f high blood pressure

ip'no|si f hypnosis. ∼tico adj hypnotic. ∼'tismo m hypnotism. ∼tiz'zare vt hypnotize

ipoca'lorico adj low-calorie

ipocon'driaco, -a adj & mf hypochondriac

ipocri'sia f hypocrisy. i'pocrita adj hypocritical ● mf hypocrite

ipo'te|ca f mortgage. ∼'care vt mortgage

i'potesi f inv hypothesis; (caso, eventualità) eventuality. ipo'tetico adj hypothetical. ipotiz'zare vt hypothesize

'ippico, -a adj horse attrib ● f riding

ippoca'stano m horse-chestnut

ip'podromo m racecourse

ippo'potamo m hippopotamus

'ira f anger. ∼'scibile adj irascible

i'rato adj irate

'iride f (Anat) iris; (arcobaleno) rainbow

Ir'lan|da f Ireland. ∼da del Nord Northern Ireland. i∼'dese adj Irish ● m Irishman; (lingua) Irish ● f Irishwoman

iro'nia f irony. i'ronico adj ironic[al]

irradi'a|re vt/i radiate. ∼zi'one f radiation

irraggiun'gibile adj unattainable

irragio'nevole adj unreasonable; (speranza, timore) irrational; (assurdo) absurd

irrazio'nal|e adj irrational. ∼ità adj irrationality

irre'alle adj unreal. ~'listico adj unrealistic. ~lizza'bile adj unattainable. ~ltà f unreality

irrecupe'rabile adj irrecoverable

irrego'larle adj irregular. ~ità f inv irregularity

irremo'vibile adj fig adamant

irrepa'rabile adj irreparable

irrepe'ribile adj not to be found; sarò ~ I won't be contactable

irrepren'sibile adj irreproachable

irrepri'mibile adj irrepressible

irrequi'eto adj restless

irresi'stibile adj irresistible

irrespon'sabille adj irresponsible. ~ità f irresponsibility

irrever'sibile adj irreversible

irricono'scibile adj unrecognizable

irri'garle vt irrigate; (fiume:) flow through. ~zi'one f irrigation

irrigidi'mento m stiffening

irrigi'dirle vt, ~si vr stiffen

irrile'vante adj unimportant

irrime'diabile adj irreparable

irripe'tibile adj unrepeatable

irri'sorio adj derisive; (differenza, particolare, somma) insignificant

irri'tabile adj irritable. ~nte adj aggravating

irri'tarle vt irritate. ~rsi vr get annoyed. ~to adj irritated; (gola) sore. ~zi'one f irritation

irrobu'stirle vt fortify. ~si vr get stronger

ir'rompere vi burst (in into)

irro'rare vt sprinkle

irru'ente adj impetuous

irruzi'one f fare ~ in burst into

i'scritto, -a pp di iscrivere ● adj registered ● mf member; per ~ in writing

i'scriverle vt register. ~si vr ~si a

register at, enrol at (scuola); join (circolo ecc.) iscrizi'one f registration; (epigrafe) inscription

I'slanda f Iceland. i~'dese adj Icelandic ●mf Icelander

i'sla|mico adj Islamic. ~'mismo m Islam

'isola f island. le isole britanniche the British Isles. ~ pedonale pedestrian precinct. ~ spartitraffico traffic island

iso'lante adj insulating ● m insulator

iso'la|re vt isolate; (Electr, Mech) insulate; (acusticamente) soundproof. ~to adj isolated ● m (di appartamenti) block

ispes'sir|e vt, ~si vr thicken

ispetto'rato m inspectorate. ispet'tore m inspector. ispezio'nare vt inspect. ispezi'one f inspection

'ispido adj bristly

ispi'ra|re vt inspire; suggest (idea, soluzione). ~rsi vr ~rsi a be based on. ~to adj inspired. ~zi'one f inspiration; (idea) idea

Isra'el|e m Israel. i~i'ano, -a agg & mf Israeli

istan'taneo, -a adj instantaneous ●f snapshot

i'stante m instant; all'~ instantly

i'stanza f petition

i'sterico adj hysterical. iste'rismo m hysteria

isti'ga|re vt instigate; ~re qcno al male incite sb to evil. ~zi'one f instigation

istin'tivo adj instinctive. i'stinto m instinct; d'istinto instinctively

istitu'ire vt institute; (fondare) found; initiate (manifestazione)

isti'tu|to m institute; (universitario) department; (Sch) secondary school. ~to di bellezza beauty salon. ~'tore, ~'trice mf (insegnante) tutor;

(*fondatore*) founder

istituzio'nale *adj* institutional. **istituzi'one** *f* institution

'istrice *f* porcupine

istru'i|re *vt* instruct; (*addestrare*) train; (*informare*) inform; (*Jur*) prepare. **~to** *adj* educated

istrut'tivo *adj* instructive. **~ore**, **~rice** *mf* instructor; **giudice ~ore** examining magistrate. **~oria** *f* (*Jur*) investigation. **istruzi'one** *f* education; (*indicazione*) instruction

l'tali|a *f* Italy. **i~'ano, -a** *adj* & *mf* Italian

Italo- Descendants of those who emigrated from Italy are often referred to as *italo-americani*, *italo-brasiliani*, etc. Massive emigration started in the 1870s, mainly from the north of Italy to South America. Buenos Aires and Sao Paulo have the highest concentrations of Italians outside Italy. Subsequently more and more southern Italians emigrated to the United States.

itine'rario *m* route, itinerary

itte'rizia *f* jaundice

'ittico *adj* fishing *attrib*

I.V.A. *f abbr* (imposta sul valore aggiunto) VAT

Jj

jack *m inv* jack

jazz *m* jazz. **jaz'zista** *mf* jazz player

jeep *f inv* jeep

'jolly *m inv* (carta da gioco) joker

ju'niores *mfpl* Sport juniors

Kk

ka'jal *m inv* kohl

kara'oke *m inv* karaoke

kara'te *m* karate

kg *abbr* (chilogrammo) kg

km *abbr* (chilometro) km

Ll

l' *def art m* (before vowel) the; ▶IL

la *def art f* the; ▶IL ● *pron* (oggetto, riferito a persona) her; (riferito a cosa, animale) it; (forma di cortesia) you ● *m inv* (Mus) A

là *adv* there; **di là** (in quel luogo) in there; (da quella parte) that way; **eccolo là!** there he is!; **farsi più in là** (far largo) make way; **là dentro** in there; **là fuori** out there; **[ma] va là!** come off it!; **più in là** (nel tempo) later on; (nello spazio) further on

'labbro *m* (pl f (Anat) labbra) lip

labi'rinto *m* labyrinth; (di sentieri ecc) maze

labora'torio *m* laboratory; (di negozio, officina ecc) workshop

labori'oso *adj* industrious; (faticoso) laborious

labu'rista *adj* Labour ● *mf* member of the Labour Party

'lacca *f* lacquer; (per capelli) hairspray. **lac'care** *vt* lacquer

'laccio *m* noose; (lazo) lasso; (trappola) snare; (stringa) lace

lace'rante *adj* (grido) earsplitting

lace'ra|re *vt* tear; lacerate (carne).

~**rsi** vr tear. ~**zi'one** f laceration. '**lacero** adj torn; (cencioso) ragged
'**lacri|ma** f tear; (goccia) drop. ~'**mare** vi weep. ~'**mevole** adj tear-jerking
lacri'mogeno adj gas ~ tear gas
la'cuna f gap. **lacu'noso** adj (preparazione, resoconto) incomplete
la'custre adj lake attrib

> *i* **Ladino** Ladin (*ladino* in Italian) is a direct descendant of the Latin spoken in the valleys in north-eastern Italy. Western Ladin is spoken in Alto Adige alongside German, and Eastern Ladin (also called Friulian) in Friuli-Venezia Giulia. Numbers of speakers are shrinking as gradually German or Italian predominate.

'**ladro, -a** mf thief; **al ~l stop thief!**; ~'**cinio** m theft. **la'druncolo** m petty thief
'**lager** m inv concentration camp
aggiù adv down there; (lontano) over there
'**agna** f (🔟: persona) moaning Minnie; (film) bore
a'gna|nza f complaint. ~**rsi** vr moan; (protestare) complain (di about)
'**ago** m lake
a'guna f lagoon
'**aico, -a** adj lay; (vita) secular ● m layman ● f laywoman
'**ama** f blade ● m inv llama
ambic'carsi vr ~ **il cervello** rack one's brains
am'bire vt lap
amé m inv lamé
amen'tar|e vt lament. ~**si** vi moan. ~**si di** complain about
amen'te|la f complaint. ~'**vole** adj mournful; (pietoso) pitiful. **la'mento** m moan
'**ametta** f ~ [da barba]

razor blade
laml'era f sheet metal
'**lamina** f foil. ~ **d'oro** gold leaf
lami'na|re vt laminate. ~**to** adj laminated ● m laminate; (tessuto) lamé
'**lampa|da** f lamp. ~**da abbronzante** sunlamp. ~**da a pila** torch. ~'**dario** m chandelier. ~'**dina** f light bulb
lam'pante adj clear
lampeggi'a|re vi flash. ~'**tore** m (Auto) indicator
lampi'one m street lamp
'**lampo** m flash of lightning; (luce) flash; **lampi** pl lightning sg. ~ **di genio** stroke of genius. [cerniera] ~ **zip** [fastener], zipper Am
lam'pone m raspberry
'**lana** f wool; **di** ~ woollen. ~ **d'acciaio** steel wool. ~ **vergine** new wool. ~ **di vetro** glass wool
lan'cetta f (pointer); (di orologio) hand
'**lancia** f spear; (Naut) launch
lanci'ar|e vt throw; (da un aereo) drop; launch (missile, prodotto); give (grido); ~**e uno sguardo a** glance at. ~**si** vr fling oneself; (intraprendere) launch out
lanci'nante adj piercing
'**lancio** m throwing; (da aereo) drop; (di missile, prodotto) launch. ~ **del disco discus** [throwing]. ~ **del giavellotto javelin** [throwing]
'**landa** f heath
lani'ero adj wool
lani'ficio m woollen mill
lan'terna f lantern; (faro) lighthouse
la'nugine f down
lapi'dare vt stone; fig demolish
lapi'dario adj (conciso) terse
'**lapide** f tombstone; (commemorativa) memorial tablet
'**lapis** m inv pencil
'**lapsus** m inv lapse, error

'lardo *m* lard
larga'mente *adv* widely
lar'ghezza *f* breadth; *fig* liberality. **~ di vedute** broadmindedness
'largo *adj* wide; (*ampio*) broad; (abito) loose; (*liberale*) liberal; (*abbondante*) generous; **stare alla larga** keep away; **~ di manica** *fig* generous; **~ di spalle/vedute** broad-shouldered/-minded ● *m* width; **andare al ~** (*Naut*) go out to sea; **fare ~** make room; **farsi ~** make one's way; **al ~ di** off the coast of
'larice *m* larch
la'ringe *f* larynx. **larin'gite** *f* laryngitis
'larva *f* larva; (*persona emaciata*) shadow
la'sagne *fpl* lasagna *sg*
lasciapas'sare *m inv* pass
l **lasci'ar|e** *vt* leave; (*rinunciare*) give up; (*rimetterci*) lose; (*smettere di tenere*) let go [of]; (*concedere*) let; **~e di fare qcsa** (*smettere*) stop doing sth; **lascia perdere!** forget it!; **lascialo venire** let him come. **~si** *vr* (*reciproco*) leave each other; **~si andare** let oneself go
'lascito *m* legacy
'laser *adj & m inv* **[raggio] ~** laser [beam]
lassa'tivo *adj & m* laxative
'lasso *m* **~ di tempo** period of time
lassù *adv* up there
'lastra *f* slab; (*di ghiaccio*) sheet; (*Phot, di metallo*) plate; (*radiografia*) X-ray [plate]
lastri'ca|re *vt* pave. **~to, 'lastrico** *m* pavement
la'tente *adj* latent
late'rale *adj* side *attrib*; (*Med, Techn ecc*) lateral; **via ~** side street
late'rizi *mpl* bricks
lati'fondo *m* large estate
la'tino *adj & m* Latin
lati'tan|te *adj* in hiding ● *mf* fugitive [from justice]
lati'tudine *f* latitude
'lato *adj* (*ampio*) broad; **in senso ~** broadly speaking ● *m* side; (*aspetto*) aspect; **a ~ di** beside; **dal ~ mio** (*punto di vista*) for my part; **d'altro ~** *fig* on the other hand
la'tra|re *vi* bark. **~to** *m* barking
la'trina *f* latrine
'latta *f* tin, can
lat'taio, -a *m* milkman ● *f* milkwoman
lat'tante *adj* breast-fed ● *mf* suckling
'latt|e *m* milk. **~e acido** sour milk. **~e condensato** condensed milk. **~e detergente** cleansing milk. **~e in polvere** powdered milk. **~e scre**mato skimmed milk. **~eo** *adj* milky. **~e'ria** *f* dairy. **~i'cini** *mpl* dairy products. **~i'era** *f* milk jug
lat'tina *f* can
lat'tuga *f* lettuce
'laure|a *f* degree; **prendere la ~a** graduate. **~'ando, -a** *mf* final-year student
laure'a|rsi *vr* graduate. **~to, -a** *agg & mf* graduate
'lauro *m* laurel
'lauto *adj* lavish; **~ guadagno** hand some profit
'lava *f* lava
la'vabile *adj* washable
la'vabo *m* wash-basin
la'vaggio *m* washing. **~ automatico** (*per auto*) carwash. **~ a secco** dry-cleaning
la'vagna *f* slate; (*Sch*) blackboard
la'van|da *f* wash; (*Bot*) lavender; **fare una ~da gastrica** have one's stomach pumped. **~'daia** *f* washerwoman. **~de'ria** *f* laundry. **~deria automatica** launderette
lavan'dino *m* sink; (🄸 *persona*) bottomless pit
lavapi'atti *mf inv* dishwasher

la'var|e vt wash; ~e i piatti wash up. ~si vr wash, have a wash; ~si i denti brush one's teeth; ~si le mani wash one's hands

lava'secco mf inv dry-cleaner's

lavasto'viglie f inv dishwasher

la'vata f wash; darsi una ~ have a wash; ~ di capo fig scolding

lava'tivo, -a mf idler

lava'trice f washing-machine

lavo'rante mf worker

lavo'ra|re vi work ● vt work; knead (pasta ecc); till (la terra); ~re a maglia knit. ~tivo adj working. ~to adj (pietra, legno) carved; (cuoio) tooled; (metallo) wrought. ~'tore, ~'trice mf worker ● adj working. ~zi'one f manufacture; (di terra) working; (artigianale) workmanship; (del terreno) cultivation. lavo'rio m intense activity

la'voro m work; (faticoso, sociale) labour; (impiego) job; (Theat, piece) met-tersi al ~ set to work (su on). ~ a maglia knitting. ~ straordinario overtime. ~ a tempo pieno full-time job. lavori pl di casa housework. lavori pl in corso roadworks. lavori pl stradali roadworks

le def art fpl the; ▶IL ● pers pron (oggetto) them; (a lei) her; (forma di cortesia) you

le'al|e adj loyal. ~'mente adv loyally. ~tà f loyalty

lebbra f leprosy

lecca 'lecca m inv lollipop

leccapi'edi mf inv pej bootlicker

lec'ca|re vt lick; fig suck up to. ~rsi vr lick; (fig: agghindarsi) doll oneself up; da ~rsi i baffi mouth-watering. ~ta f lick

leccor'nia f delicacy

lecito adj lawful; (permesso) permissible

ledere vt damage; (Med) injure

lega f league; (di metalli) alloy; far ~ con qcno take up with sb

le'gaccio m string; (delle scarpe) shoelace

le'gal|e adj legal ● m lawyer. ~ità f legality. ~iz'zare vt authenticate; (rendere legale) legalize. ~'mente adv legally

le'game m tie; (amoroso) liaison; (connessione) link

lega'mento m (Med) ligament

le'gar|e vt tie; tie up (persona); tie together (due cose); (unire, rilegare) bind; alloy (metalli); (connettere) connect ● vi (far lega) get on well. ~si vr bind oneself; ~si a qcno become attached to sb

le'gato m legacy; (Relig) legate

lega'tura f tying; (di libro) binding

le'genda f legend

'legge f law; (parlamentare) act; a norma di ~ by law

leg'genda f legend; (didascalia) caption. leg'dario adj legendary

'leggere vt/i read

legge'r|ezza f lightness; (frivolezza) frivolity; (incostanza) fickleness. ~'mente adv slightly

leg'gero adj light; (bevanda) weak; (lieve) slight; (frivolo) frivolous; (incostante) fickle

leg'gibile adj (scrittura) legible; (stile) readable

leg'gio m lectern; (Mus) music stand

legife'rare vi legislate

legio'nario m legionary. legio'ne f legion

legisla|'tivo adj legislative. ~'tore m legislator. ~'tura f legislature. ~zi'one f legislation

legittimità f legitimacy. le'gittimo adj legitimate; (giusto) proper; legit-tima difesa self-defence

'legna f firewood

le'gname m timber

'legno m wood; di ~ wooden. ~ compensato plywood. le'gnoso

adj woody

le'gume m pod

'lei pers pron (soggetto) she; (oggetto, con prep) her; (forma di cortesia) you; lo ha fatto ~ **stessa** she did it herself

'lembo m edge; (di terra) strip

'lena f vigour

le'nire vt soothe

lenta'mente adv slowly

'lente f lens. ~ **a contatto** contact lens. ~ **d'ingrandimento** magnifying glass

len'tezza f slowness

len'ticchia f lentil

len'tiggine f freckle

'lento adj slow; (allentato) slack; (abito) loose

'lenza f fishing-line

len'zuolo m (pl f **lenzuola**) m sheet

le'one m lion; (Astr) Leo

leo'pardo m leopard

'lepre f hare

'lercio adj filthy

'lesbica f lesbian

lesi'nare vt grudge ● vi be stingy

lesio'nare vt damage. **lesi'one** f lesion

'leso pp di **ledere** ● adj injured

les'sare vt boil

'lessico m vocabulary

'lesso adj boiled ● m boiled meat

'lesto adj quick; (mente) sharp

le'tale adj lethal

le'targico adj lethargic. ~o m lethargy; (di animali) hibernation

le'tizia f joy

'lettera f letter; **alla** ~ literally; ~ **maiuscola** capital letter; ~ **minuscola** small letter; **lettere** pl (letteratura) literature sg; (Univ) Arts; **dottore in lettere** BA, Bachelor of Arts

lette'rale adj literal

lette'rario adj literary

lette'rato adj well-read

lettera'tura f literature

let'tiga f stretcher

let'tino m cot; (Med) couch

'letto m bed. ~ **a castello** bunkbed. ~ **a una piazza** single bed. ~ **a due piazze** double bed. ~ **matrimoniale** double bed

letto'rato m (corso) ≈ tutorial

let'tore, **-'trice** mf reader; (Univ) language assistant ● m (Comput) disk drive. ~ **CD-ROM** CD-Rom drive. ~ **MP3** MP3 player

let'tura f reading

leuce'mia f leukaemia

'leva f lever; (Mil) call-up; **far** ~ lever. ~ **del cambio** gear lever

le'vante m East; (vento) east wind

le'va|re vt (alzare) raise; (togliere) take away; (rimuovere) take off; (estrarre) pull out; ~**re di mezzo qcsa** get sth out of the way. ~**rsi** vr rise; (da letto) get up; ~**rsi di mezzo**, ~**rsi dai piedi** get out of the way. ~**ta** f rising; (di posta) collection

leva'taccia f **fare una** ~ get up at the crack of dawn

leva'toio adj **ponte** ~ drawbridge

levi'ga|re vt smooth; (con carta vetro) rub down. ~**to** adj (superficie) polished

levri'ero m greyhound

lezi'one f lesson; (Univ) lecture; (rimprovero) rebuke

lezi'oso adj (stile, modi) affected

li pers pron mpl them

lì adv there; **fin lì** as far as there; **giù di lì** thereabouts; **lì per lì** there and then

Li'bano m Lebanon

'libbra f (peso) pound

li'beccio m south-west wind

li'bellula f dragon-fly

libe'rale adj liberal; (generoso) generous ● mf liberal

libe'ra|re vt free; release (prigioniero); vacate (stanza); (salvare) rescue. ~**rsi** vr (stanza:) become vacant; (*Teleph*) become free; (*da impegno*) get out of it; **~rsi** di get rid of. **~'tore**, **~'trice** *adj* liberating ●*mf* liberator. **~zi'one** *f* liberation; la L~zione Liberation Day

liber|o *adj* free; (*strada*) clear. **~o docente** qualified university lecturer. **~o professionista** selfemployed person. **~tà** *f inv* freedom; (*di prigioniero*) release. **~tà provvisoria** (*Jur*) bail; **~tà** *pl* (*confidenze*) liberties

liberty *m & adj inv* Art Nouveau

Libia *f* Libya. **l~co**, -a *adj & mf* Libyan

libra'io *m* bookseller

libre'ria *f* (*negozio*) bookshop; (*mobile*) bookcase; (*biblioteca*) library

li'bretto *m* booklet; (*Mus*) libretto. **~ degli assegni** cheque book. **~ di circolazione** logbook. **~ d'istruzioni** instruction booklet. **~ di risparmio** bankbook. **~ universitario** student record of exam results

'libro *m* book. **~ giallo** thriller. **~ paga** payroll

li'ce'ale *mf* secondary-school student ● *adj* secondary-school *attrib*

li'cenza *f* licence; (*permesso*) permission; (*Mil*) leave; (*Sch*) school-leaving certificate; **essere in ~** be on leave

licenzia'mento *m* dismissal

licenzi'a|re *vt* dismiss, sack 🔲. **~rsi** *vr* (*da un impiego*) resign; (*accomiatarsi*) take one's leave

li'ceo *m* secondary school. **~ classico** secondary school emphasizing humanities. **~ scientifico** secondary school emphasizing science

li'ceo There are two main types of secondary school in Italy: the *licei*, which offer an academic syllabus, and the *istituti*, which have a more vocational syllabus, offering subjects like accountancy, electronics, and catering. *Licei* may specialize in particular

subjects such as science, languages or classical studies.

'lido *m* beach

li'eto *adj* glad; (*evento*) happy; **molto ~!** pleased to meet you!

li'eve *adj* light; (*debole*) faint; (*trascurabile*) slight

lievi'tare *vi* rise ● *vt* leaven. **lie'vito** *m* yeast. **lievito in polvere** baking powder

'lifting *m inv* face-lift

'ligio *adj* essere **~ al dovere** have a sense of duty

'lilla¹ (*colore*) lilac

'lillà² *m inv* (*Bot*) lilac

'lima *f* file

limacci'oso *adj* slimy

li'mare *vt* file

li'metta *f* nail-file

limi'ta|re *m* threshold ● *vt* limit. **~rsi** *vr* **~rsi a fare qcsa** restrict oneself to doing sth; **~rsi in qcsa** cut down on sth. **~'tivo** *adj* limiting. **~zi'one** *f* limitation

'limite *m* limit; (*confine*) boundary. **~ di velocità** speed limit

li'mitrofo *adj* neighbouring

limo'nata *f* (*bibita*) lemonade; (*succo*) lemon juice

li'mone *m* lemon; (*albero*) lemon tree

'limpido *adj* clear; (*occhi*) limpid

'lince *f* lynx

linci'are *vt* lynch

'lindo *adj* neat; (*pulito*) clean

'linea *f* line; (*di autobus, aereo*) route; (*di metro*) line; (*di abito*) cut; (*di auto, mobile*) design; (*fisico*) figure; **è caduta la ~** i've been cut off; **in ~** (*Comput*) on line; **mantenere la ~** keep one's figure; **mettersi in ~** line up; **nave di ~** liner; **volo di ~** scheduled flight. **~ d'arrivo** finishing line. **~ continua** unbroken line

linea'menti *mpl* features

line'are adj linear; (discorso) to the point; (ragionamento) consistent

line'etta f (tratto lungo) dash; (d'unione) hyphen

lin'gotto m ingot

'lingua f tongue; (linguaggio) language. ~'accia f (persona) backbiter. ~'aggio m language. ~'etta f (di scarpa) tongue; (di strumento) reed; (di busta) flap

lingu'ist|a mf linguist. ~ica f linguistics sg. ~ico adj linguistic

'lino m (Bot) flax; (tessuto) linen

li'noleum m linoleum

liofiliz'za|re vt freeze-dry. ~to adj freeze-dried

liposuzi'one f liposuction

lique'far|e vt, ~si vr liquefy; (sciogliersi) melt

liqui'dare vt liquidate; settle (conto); pay off (debiti); clear (merce); (🗲: uccidere) get rid of. ~zi'one f liquidation; (di conti) settling; (di merce) clearance sale

'liquido adj & m liquid

liqui'rizia f liquorice

li'quore m liqueur; **liquori** pl (bevande alcoliche) liquors

'lira f lira; (Mus) lyre

'lirico, -a adj lyrical (poesia) lyric; (cantante, musica) opera attrib ● f lyric poetry; (Mus) opera

lisci'are vt smooth; (accarezzare) stroke. **'liscio** adj smooth; (capelli) straight; (liquore) neat; (acqua minerale) still; passarla liscia get away with it

'liso adj worn [out]

'lista f list; (striscia) strip. ~ di attesa waiting list; in ~ di attesa (Aeron) stand-by. ~ elettorale electoral register. ~ nera blacklist. ~ di nozze wedding list. li'stare vt edge; (Comput) list

li'stino m list. ~ prezzi price list

Lit. abbr (lire italiane) Italian lire

'lite f quarrel; (baruffa) row; (Jur) lawsuit

liti'gare vi quarrel. **li'tigio** m quarrel. **litigi'oso** adj quarrelsome

lito'rale adj coastal ● m coast

'litro m litre

li'turgico adj liturgical

li'vella f level. ~ a bolla d'aria spirit level

livel'lar|e vt level. ~si vr level out

li'vello m level; passaggio a ~ level crossing; sotto/sul ~ del mare below/above sea level

'livido adj livid; (per il freddo) blue; (per una botta) black and blue ● m bruise

Li'vorno f Leghorn

'lizza f lists pl; essere in ~ per qcs be in the running for sth

lo def art m (before s + consonant, gn, ps, z) the; ▷IL ● pron (riferito a persona) him; (riferito a cosa) it; non lo so l don't know

'lobo m lobe

lo'cale adj local ● m (stanza) room; (treno) local train; ~i pl (edifici) premises. ~e notturno night-club. ~ità f inv locality

localiz'zare vt localize; (trovare) locate

localizza'zione f localization

lo'canda f inn

locan'dina f bill, poster

loca'|tario, -a mf tenant. ~'tore m landlord ● f landlady. ~zi'one f tenancy

locomo'|tiva f locomotive. ~zi'one f locomotion; mezzi di ~zione means of transport

'loculo m burial niche

lo'custa f locust

locuzi'one f expression

lo'dare vt praise. **'lode** f praise; laurea con lode first-class degree

'loden m inv (cappotto) loden coat

'lodola f lark

loggia f loggia; (massonica) lodge

loggione m gallery, the gods

logica f logic

logica'mente adv (in modo logico) logically; (ovviamente) of course

logico adj logical

logistica f logistics sg

logo'ra|re vt wear out; (sciupare) waste. **~rsi** vr wear out; (persona:) wear oneself out. **logo'rio** m wear and tear. **logoro** adj worn-out

lom'baggine f lumbago

lombar'dia f Lombardy

lom'bata f loin. **lombo** m (Anat) loin

lom'brico m earthworm

Londra f London

lon'gevo adj long-lived

longi'lineo adj tall and slim

longi'tudine f longitude

lontana'mente adv distantly; (vagamente) vaguely; **neanche ~** not for a moment

lonta'nanza f distance; (separazione) separation; **in ~** in the distance

lon'tano adj far; (distante) distant; (nel tempo) far-off, distant; (parente) distant; (vago) vague; (assente) absent; **più ~** further ● adv far [away]; **da ~** from a distance

lontra f otter

lo'quace adj talkative

lordo adj dirty; (somma, peso) gross

loro¹ pron pl (soggetto) they; (oggetto) them; (forma di cortesia) you; **sta a ~** it is up to them

loro² (**il ~** m, **la ~** f, **i ~** mpl, **le ~** fpl) poss adj their; (forma di cortesia) your; **un ~ amico** a friend of theirs; (forma di cortesia) a friend of yours ● poss pron theirs; (forma di cortesia) yours; **i ~** (famiglia) their folk

lo'sanga f lozenge; **a losanghe** diamond-shaped

losco adj suspicious

lotta f fight, struggle; (contrasto) conflict; Sport wrestling. **lot'tare** vi fight, struggle; Sport, fig wrestle. **~a'tore** m wrestler

lotte'ria f lottery

lotto m [national] lottery; (porzione) lot; (di terreno) plot

lozi'one f lotion

lubrifi'ca|nte adj lubricating ● m lubricant. **~re** vt lubricate

luc'chetto m padlock

lucci'ca|nte adj sparkling. **~re** vi sparkle. **lucci'chio** m sparkle

luccio m pike

lucciola f glow-worm

luce f light; far **~** su shed light on; **dare alla ~** give birth to. **~ della luna** moonlight. **luci** pl di posizione sidelights. **~ del sole** sunlight

lu'cente adj shining. **~'tezza** f shine

lucer'nario m skylight

lu'certola f lizard

lucida'labbra m inv lip gloss

luci'da|re vt polish. **~'trice** f [floor-]polisher. **lucido** adj shiny; (pavimento, scarpe) polished; (chiaro) clear; (persona, mente) lucid; (occhi) watery ● m shine. **lucido [da scarpe]** [shoe] polish

lucra'tivo adj lucrative

luglio m July

lugubre adj gloomy

lui pron (soggetto) he; (oggetto, con prep) him; **lo ha fatto ~ stesso** he did it himself

lu'maca f (mollusco) snail; fig slowcoach

lume m lamp; (luce) light; **a ~ di candela** by candlelight

luminosità f brightness. **lumi'noso** adj luminous; (stanza, cielo ecc) bright

luna f moon; **chiaro di ~** moonlight. ~ di miele honeymoon

luna park m inv fairground

lu'nario m almanac; sbarcare il ~ make both ends meet

lu'natico a moody

lunedì m inv Monday

lu'netta f half-moon [shape]

lun'gaggine f slowness

lun'ghezza f length. ~ d'onda wavelength

'lungi adv ero [ben] ~ dall'imma-ginare che... I never dreamt for a moment that...

lungimi'rante adj far-sighted

'lungo adj long; (diluito) weak; (lento) slow; saperla lunga be shrewd •m length; di gran lunga by far; andare per le lunghe drag on •prep (durante) throughout; (per la lunghezza di) along

lungofi'ume m riverside

lungo'lago m lakeside

lungo'mare m sea front

lungome'traggio m feature film

lu'notto m rear window

lu'ogo m place; (punto preciso) spot; (passo d'autore) passage; aver ~ take place; dar ~ a give rise to; del ~ (usanze) local. ~ pubblico pub-lic place

luogote'nente m (Mil) lieutenant

lu'petto m Cub [Scout]

'lupo m wolf

'luppolo m hop

'lurido adj filthy. luri'dume m filth

lusin'g|are vt flatter. ~arsi vr flat-ter oneself; (illudersi) fool oneself. ~hi'ero a flattering

lus'sa|re vt, ~rsi vr dislocate. ~zi'one f dislocation

Lussem'burgo m Luxembourg

'lusso m luxury; di ~ luxury attrib

lussu'oso adj luxurious

lus'suria f lust

lu'strare vt polish

'lustro adj shiny •m sheen; fig pres-tige; (quinquennio) five-year period

'lutt|o m mourning; ~o stretto deep mourning. ~u'oso a a mournful

Mm

m abbr (metro) m

ma conj but; (eppure) yet; mai (dubbio) I don't know; (indignazione) really!; ma davvero? really?; ma sì why not!; (certo che sì) of course!

'macabro adj macabre

macché int of course not!

macche'roni mpl macaroni sg

macche'ronico a (italiano) broken

'macchia¹ f stain; (di diverso colore) spot; (piccola) speck; senza ~ spotless

'macchia² f (boscaglia) scrub

macchi'a|re vt, ~rsi vr stain. ~to adj (caffè) with a dash of milk; ~to di (sporco) stained with

'macchina f machine; (motore) en-gine; (automobile) car. ~ da cucire sewing machine. ~ da presa cine camera. ~ da scrivere typewriter. ~ fotografica (digitale) (digital) camera

macchinal'mente adv mechan-ically

macchi'nare vt plot

macchi'nario m machinery

macchi'netta f (per i denti) brace

macchi'nista m (Rail) engine-driver; (Naut) engineer; (Theat) stagehand

macchi'noso adj complicated

mace'donia f fruit salad

Mace'donia f Macedonia

macel·la|io m butcher. ~re vt slaughter, butcher. macelle'ria f butcher's [shop]. ma'cello m (*mattatoio*) slaughterhouse; *fig* shambles sg; andare al macello *fig* go to the slaughter

mace'rar|e vt macerate; *fig* distress. ~si vr be consumed

ma'cerie fpl rubble sg; (*rottami*) debris sg

ma'cigno m boulder

'macina f millstone

macinacaffè m inv coffee mill

macina'pepe m inv pepper mill

maci'na|re vt mill. ~to adj ground ● m (*carne*) mince. maci'nino m mill; (*hum*) old banger

maciul'lare vt (*stritolare*) crush

macrobiotic|a f negozio di ~a health-food shop. ~o adj macrobiotic

macu'lato adj spotted

'madido adj ~ di moist with

Ma'donna f Our Lady

mador'nale adj gross

madre f mother. ~lingua adj inv inglese ~lingua English native speaker. ~patria f native land. ~perla f mother-of-pearl

ma'drina f godmother

maestà f majesty

maestosità f majesty. mae'stoso adj majestic

mae'strale m northwest wind

mae'stranza f workers pl

nae'stria f mastery

ma'estro, -a mf teacher ● m master; (*Mus*) maestro. ~ di cerimonie master of ceremonies ● adj (*principale*) chief; (*di grande abilità*) skilful

mafi|a f Mafia. ~'oso adj of the Mafia ● m member of the Mafia, Mafioso

---

Mafia The Mafia developed in Sicily in the nineteenth century, where it continues to wield considerable power in opposition to the authorities. Strictly speaking, the term Mafia applies only to Sicily, and its equivalents in other regions (*Camorra* in Naples and '*ndrangheta* in Calabria) are separate organizations, although often working in collaboration with each other.   *i*

---

ma'gagna f fault

ma'gari adv (*forse*) maybe ● int I wish! ● conj (*per esprimere desiderio*) if only; (*anche se*) even if

magazzini'ere m storesman, warehouseman. magaz'zino m warehouse; (*emporio*) shop; grande magazzino department store

'maggio m May

maggio'lino m May bug

maggio'rana f marjoram

maggio'ranza f majority

maggio'rare vt increase

maggior'domo m butler

maggi'ore adj (*di dimensioni, numero*) bigger, larger; (*superlativo*) biggest, largest; (*di età*) older; (*superlativo*) oldest; (*di importanza, musica*) major; (*superlativo*) greatest; la maggior parte di most; la maggior parte del tempo most of the time ● pron (*di dimensioni*) the bigger, the larger; (*superlativo*) the biggest, the largest; (*di età*) the older; (*superlativo*) the oldest; (*di importanza*) the major; (*superlativo*) the greatest ● m (*Mil*) major; (*Aeron*) squadron leader. maggio'renne adj of age ● mf adult

maggiori'tario adj (*sistema*) first-past-the-post attrib. ~'mente adv [all] the more; (*più di tutto*) most

'Magi mpl i re ~ the Magi

ma'gia f magic; (*trucco*) magic trick. magica'mente adv magically. 'magico *adj* magic

magi'stero *m* (*insegnamento*) teaching; (*maestria*) skill; **facoltà di ~ arts** faculty

magi'stra|le *adj* masterly; **istituto ~e** teachers' training college

magi'stra|to *m* magistrate. **~'tura** *f* magistrature. **la ~tura** the Bench

'magli|a *f* stitch; (*lavoro ai ferri*) knitting; (*tessuto*) jersey; (*di rete*) mesh; (*di catena*) link; (*indumento*) vest; **fare la ~a** knit. **~a diritta** knit. **~a rosa** (*ciclismo*) ≈ yellow jersey. **~a rovescia** purl. **~e'ria** *f* knitwear. **~'etta** *f* **~etta [a maniche corte]** tee-shirt. **~'ficio** *m* knitwear factory. **ma'glina** *f* (*tessuto*) jersey

magli'one *m* sweater

'magma *m* magma

ma'gnanimo *adj* magnanimous

ma'gnate *m* magnate

ma'gnesi|a *f* magnesia. **~o** *m* magnesium

ma'gne|te *m* magnet. **~tico** *adj* magnetic. **~tismo** *m* magnetism

magne'tofono *m* tape recorder

magnifi|ca'mente *adv* magnificently. **~'cenza** *f* magnificence; (*generosità*) munificence. **ma'gnifico** *adj* magnificent; (*generoso*) munificent

ma'gnolia *f* magnolia

ma'gone *m* **avere il ~** be down; **mi è venuto il ~** I've got a lump in my throat

'magr|a *f* low water. **ma'grezza** *f* thinness. **~o** *adj* thin; (*carne*) lean; (*scarso*) meagre

'mai *adv* never; (*inter, talvolta*) ever; **caso ~** if anything; **caso ~ tornasse** in case he comes back; **come ~?** why?; **cosa ~?** what on earth?; **~ più** never again; **più che ~** more than ever; **quando ~?** whenever?; **quasi ~** hardly ever

mai'ale *m* pig; (*carne*) pork

mai'olica *f* majolica

maio'nese *f* mayonnaise

'mais *m* maize

mai'uscol|a *f* capital [letter]. **~o** *adj* capital

mal ▷**MALE**

'mala *f* **la ~** ⊠ the underworld

mala'fede *f* bad faith

malaf'fare *m* **gente di ~** shady characters *pl*

mala'lingua *f* backbiter

mala'mente *adv* (*ridotto*) badly

malan'dato *adj* in bad shape; (*di salute*) in poor health

ma'lanimo *m* ill will

ma'lanno *m* misfortune; (*malattia*) illness; **prendersi un ~** catch something

mala'pena: **a ~** *adv* hardly

ma'laria *f* malaria

mala'ticcio *adj* sickly

ma'lato, -a *adj* ill, sick; (*pianta*) diseased ● *mf* sick person. **~ di mente** mentally ill person. **malat'tia** *f* disease, illness; **ho preso due giorni di malattia** I had two days off sick. **malattia venerea** venereal disease

malaugu'rato *adj* ill-omened. **ma-lau'gurio** *m* **di ~** bad o ill omen

mala'vita *f* underworld

mala'voglia *f* unwillingness; **di ~** unwillingly

malcapi'tato *adj* wretched

malce'lato *adj* ill-concealed

mal'concio *adj* battered

malcon'tento *m* discontent

malco'stume *m* immorality

mal'destro *adj* awkward; (*inesperto*) inexperienced

maldi'cen|te *adj* slanderous. **~za** *f* slander

maldi'sposto *adj* ill-disposed

'male *adv* badly; **funzionare ~** not work properly; **star ~** be ill; **star ~ a qcno** (*vestito ecc.*) not suit sb; **ri-**

manerci ∼ be hurt; non c'è ∼! not bad at all ●m evil; (dolore) pain; (malattia) illness; (danno) harm. distinguere il bene dal ∼ know right from wrong; andare a ∼ go off; aver ∼ a have a pain in; dove hai ∼? where does it hurt?; far ∼ a qcno (provocare dolore) hurt sb; (cibo:) be bad for sb; le cipolle mi fanno ∼ onions don't agree with me; mi fa ∼ la schiena my back is hurting; mal d'auto car-sickness. mal di denti toothache. mal di gola sore throat. mal di mare sea-sickness; avere il mal di mare be sea-sick. mal di pancia stomach ache. mal di testa headache

male'detto adj cursed; (orribile) awful

male'di|re vt curse. ∼zi'one f curse; ∼zione! damn!

maledu|'cato adj ill-mannered. ∼cazi'one f rudeness

male'fatta f misdeed

ma'lefico adj (azione) evil; (nocivo) harmful

maleodo'rante adj foul-smelling

ma'lessere m indisposition; fig uneasiness

ma'levolo adj malevolent

malfa'mato adj of ill repute

mal'fat|to adj badly done; (malformato) ill-shaped. ∼'tore m wrongdoer

mal'fermo adj unsteady; (salute) poor

malfor'ma|to adj misshapen. ∼zi'one f malformation

mal'grado prep in spite of ●conj although

ma'lia f spell

mali'gn|are vi malign. ∼ità f malice; (Med) malignancy. ma'ligno adj malicious; (perfido) evil; (Med) malignant

malinco'ni|a f melancholy. malin'conico adj melancholy

malincu'ore: a ∼ adv reluctantly

malinfor'mato adj misinformed

malintenzio'nato, -a mf miscreant

malin'teso adj mistaken ●m misunderstanding

ma'lizi|a f malice; (astuzia) cunning; (espediente) trick. ∼'oso adj malicious; (birichino) mischievous

malle'abile adj malleable

malme'nare vt ill-treat

mal'messo adj (vestito male) shabbily dressed; (casa) poorly furnished; (fig: senza soldi) hard up

malnu'tri|to adj undernourished. ∼zi'one f malnutrition

'malo adj in ∼ modo badly

ma'locchio m evil eye

ma'lora f ruin; della ∼ awful; andare in ∼ go to ruin

ma'lore m illness; essere colto da ∼ be suddenly taken ill

malri'dotto adj (persona) in a sorry state

mal'sano adj unhealthy

'malta f mortar

mal'tempo m bad weather

'malto m malt

maltrat|ta'mento m illtreatment. ∼'tare vt ill-treat

malu'more m bad mood; di ∼ in a bad mood

mal'vag|io adj wicked. ∼tà f wickedness

malversazi'one f embezzlement

mal'visto adj unpopular (da with)

malvi'vente m criminal

malvolenti'eri adv unwillingly

malvo'lere vt farsi ∼ make oneself unpopular

'mamma f mummy, mum; ∼ mia! good gracious!

mam'mella f breast

mam'mifero m mammal

'mammola f violet

ma'nata f handful; (colpo) slap

'manca f ▷MANCO

manca'mento m avere un ~ faint

man'can|te adj missing. ~za f lack; (assenza) absence; (insufficienza) shortage; (fallo) fault; (imperfezione) defect; sento la sua ~za I miss him

man'care vi be lacking; (essere assente) be missing; (venir meno) fail; (morire) pass away; ~ di be lacking in; ~ a fail to keep (promessa); mi manca casa I miss home; mi manchi I miss you; mi è mancato il tempo I didn't have [the] time; mi manca un euro I'm one euro short; quanto manca alla partenza? how long before we leave?; è mancata la corrente there was a power failure; sentirsi ~ feel faint; sentirsi ~ il respiro be unable to breathe [properly] ● vt miss (bersaglio); è mancato poco che cadesse he nearly fell

'manche f inv heat

man'chevole adj defective

'mancia f tip

manci'ata f handful

man'cino adj left-handed

'manco, -a adj left ● f left hand ● adv (nemmeno) not even

man'dante mf (di delitto) instigator

manda'rancio m clementine

man'dare vt send; (emettere) give off; utter (suono); ~ a chiamare send for; ~ avanti la casa run the house; ~ giù (ingoiare) swallow

manda'rino m (Bot) mandarin

man'data f consignment; (di serratura) turn; chiudere a doppia ~ double lock

man'dato m (incarico) mandate; (Jur) warrant; (di pagamento) money order. ~ di comparizione [in giudizio] subpoena. ~ di perquisizione search warrant

man'dibola f jaw

mando'lino m mandolin

'mandor|la f almond; a ~la (occhi) almond-shaped. ~lato m nut brittle (type of nougat). ~lo m almond[-tree]

'mandria f herd

maneg'gevole adj easy to handle. **maneggi'are** vt handle

ma'neggio m handling; (intrigo) plot; (scuola di equitazione) riding school

ma'netta f hand lever; **manette** pl handcuffs

man'forte m dare ~ a qcno support sb

manga'nello m truncheon

manga'nese m manganese

mange'reccio adj edible

mangia'dischi® m inv type of portable record player

mangia'fumo adj inv candela ~ air-purifier in the form of candle

mangia'nastri m inv cassette player

mangi'a|re vt/i eat; (consumare) eat up; (corrodere) eat away; take (scacchi, carte ecc) ● m eating; (cibo) food; (pasto) meal. ~rsi vt eat up; ~rsi le parole mumble; ~rsi le unghie bite one's nails

mangi'ata f big meal; farsi una bella ~ di... feast on...

man'gime m fodder

mangiuc'chiare vt nibble

'mango m mango

ma'nia f mania. ~ di grandezza delusions of grandeur ● mf maniac

'manica f sleeve; (🗆: gruppo) band; a maniche lunghe long-sleeved; essere in maniche di camicia be in shirt sleeves

'Manica f la ~ the [English] Channel

manica'retto m tasty dish

mani'chetta f hose

mani'chino m dummy

manico | **marchio**

manico m handle; (*Mus*) neck

mani'comio m mental home; (🔟: *confusione*) tip

mani'cotto m muff; (*Mech*) sleeve

mani'cure f manicure ● *mf inv* (*persona*) manicurist

mani'e|ra f manner; in ~ra che so that. ~'rato adj affected; (*stile*) mannered. ~'rismo m mannerism

manifat'tura f manufacture; (*fabbrica*) factory

manife'stante mf demonstrator

manife'sta|re vt show; (*esprimere*) express ● vi demonstrate. ~rsi vr show oneself. ~zi'one f show; (*espressione*) expression; (*sintomo*) manifestation; (*dimostrazione pubblica*) demonstration

mani'festo adj evident ● m poster; (*dichiarazione pubblica*) manifesto

ma'niglia f handle; (*sostegno, in autobus ecc*) strap

manipo'la|re vt handle; (*massaggiare*) massage; (*alterare*) adulterate; *fig* manipulate. ~'tore, ~'trice mf manipulator. ~zi'one f handling; (*massaggio*) massage; (*alterazione*) adulteration; *fig* manipulation

mani'scalco m smith

man'naia f axe; (*da macellaio*) cleaver

man'naro adj lupo m ~ werewolf

mano f hand; (*strato di vernice ecc*) coat; alla ~ informal; fuori ~ out of the way; man ~ little by little; man ~ che as; sotto ~ to hand

mano'dopera f labour

ma'nometro m gauge

mano'mettere vt tamper with; (*violare*) violate

ma'nopola f knob; (*guanto*) mitten; (*su pullman*) handle

mano'scritto adj handwritten ● m manuscript

mano'vale m labourer

mano'vella f handle; (*Techn*) crank

ma'no|vra f manoeuvre; (*Rail*)

shunting; fare le ~vre (*Auto*) manoeuvre. ~'vrabile adj *fig* easy to manipulate. ~'vrare vt operate; *fig* manipulate (*persona*) ● vi manoeuvre

man'rovescio m slap

man'sarda f attic

mansi'one f task; (*dovere*) duty

mansu'eto adj meek; (*animale*) docile

man'tell|a f cape. ~o m cloak; (*soprabito, di animale*) coat; (*di neve*) mantle

mante'ner|e vt keep; (*in buono stato, sostentare*) maintain. ~si vr ~si in forma keep fit. manteni'mento m maintenance

'mantice m bellows pl; (*di automobile*) hood

'manto m cloak; (*coltre*) mantle

manto'vana f (*di tende*) pelmet

manu'al|e adj & m manual. ~e d'uso user manual. ~'mente adv manually

ma'nubrio m handle; (*di bicicletta*) handlebars pl; (*per ginnastica*) dumb-bell

manu'fatto adj manufactured

manutenzi'one f maintenance

'manzo m steer; (*carne*) beef

'mappa f map

mappa'mondo m globe

mar ▷MARE

ma'rasma m *fig* decline

mara'to|na f marathon. ~'neta mf marathon runner

'marca f mark; (*Comm*) brand; (*fabbricazione*) make; (*scontrino*) ticket. ~ da bollo revenue stamp

mar'ca|re vt mark; *Sport* score. ~ta'mente adv markedly. ~to adj (*tratto, accento*) strong. ~'tore m (*nel calcio*) scorer

mar'chese, -a m marquis ● f marchioness

marchi'are vt brand

'marchio m brand; (*caratteristica*) mark. ~ di fabbrica trademark. ~

registrato registered trademark

'marcia f march; (Auto) gear; Sport walk; mettere in ~ put into gear; mettersi in ~ start off; fare ~ indietro reverse; fig back-pedal. ~ funebre funeral march. ~ nuziale wedding march

marciapi'ede m pavement; (di stazione) platform

marci'a|re vi march; (funzionare) go, work. ~'tore, ~'trice mf walker

'marcio adj rotten ● m rotten part; fig corruption. **mar'cire** vi go bad, rot

'marco m (moneta) mark

'mare m sea; (luogo di mare) seaside; sul ~ (casa) at the seaside; (città) on the sea; in alto ~ on the high seas. ~ Adriatico Adriatic Sea. mar Ionio Ionian Sea. mar Mediterraneo Mediterranean. mar Tirreno Tyrrhenian Sea

ma'rea f tide; una ~ di hundreds of; alta ~ high tide; bassa ~ low tide

mareggi'ata f [sea] storm

mare'moto m tidal wave, seaquake

maresci'allo m marshal; (sottufficiale) warrantofficer

marga'rina f margarine

marghe'rita f marguerite. **margheri'tina** f daisy

margi'nale adj marginal

'margine m margin; (orlo) brink; (bordo) border. ~ di errore margin of error. ~ di sicurezza safety margin

ma'rina f navy; (costa) seashore; (quadro) seascape. ~ mercantile merchant navy. ~ militare navy

mari'naio m sailor

mari'na|re vt marinate. ~ta f marinade. ~to adj (Culin) marinated

ma'rino adj sea attrib, marine

mario'netta f puppet

ma'rito m husband

ma'rittimo adj maritime

mar'maglia f rabble

marmel'lata f jam; (di agrumi) marmalade

mar'mitta f pot; (Auto) silencer. ~ catalitica catalytic converter

'marmo m marble

mar'mocchio m 🅸 brat

mar'mor|eo adj marble. ~iz'zato adj marbled

mar'motta f marmot

Ma'rocco m Morocco

ma'roso m breaker

mar'rone adj brown ● m brown; (castagna) chestnut; **marroni** pl canditi marrons glacés

mar'sina f tails pl

mar'supio m (borsa) bumbag

martedì m inv Tuesday. ~ grasso Shrove Tuesday

martel'la|re vt hammer ● vi throb. ~ta f hammer blow

martel'letto m (di giudice) gavel

mar'tello m hammer; (di battente) knocker. ~ pneumatico pneumatic drill

marti'netto m (Mech) jack

'martire mf martyr. **mar'tirio** m martyrdom

'martora f marten

martori'are vt torment

mar'xis|mo m Marxism. ~ta agg & mf Marxist

marza'pane m marzipan

marzi'ale adj martial

marzi'ano, -a mf Martian

'marzo m March

mascal'zone m rascal

ma'scara m inv mascara

mascar'pone m full-fat cream cheese

ma'scella f jaw

'mascher|a f mask; (costume) fancy dress; (Cinema,Theat) usher m, usherette f; (nella commedia dell'arte) stock character. ~a antigas gas mask. ~

di bellezza face pack. ~a ad ossigeno oxygen mask. ~a'mento m masking; (*Mil*) camouflage. masche'rare *vt* mask. ~arsi *vr* put on a mask; ~arsi da dress up as. ~ata *f* masquerade

naschi'accio *m* tomboy

na'schi|le *adj* masculine; (*sesso*) male ● *m* masculine [gender]. ~'lista *adj* sexist. 'maschio *adj* male; (*virile*) manly ● *m* male; (*figlio*) son.

masco'lino *adj* masculine

na'scotte *f inv* mascot

naso'chis|mo *m* masochism. ~ta *adj* & *m/f* masochist

massa *f* mass; (*Electr*) earth, ground *Am*; comunicazioni di ~ mass media

nassa'crare *vt* massacre. mas'sacro *m* massacre; *fig* mess

nassaggi'a|re *vt* massage. mas'saggio *m* massage. ~tore, ~trice *m* masseur ● *f* masseuse

nas'saia *f* housewife

nasse'rizie *fpl* household effects

nas'siccio *adj* massive; (*oro ecc*) solid; (*corporatura*) heavy ● *m* massif

nassim|a *f* maxim; (*temperatura*) maximum. ~o *adj* greatest; (*quantità*) maximum, greatest ● *m* il ~o the maximum; al ~o at [the] most, as a maximum

nasso *m* rock

nas'sone *m* [Free]mason. ~'ria Freemasonry

aa'stello *m* wooden box for the grape or olive harvest

aasteriz'zare *vt* (*Comput*) burn

aasterizza'tore *m* (*Comput*) burner

nasti'care *vt* chew; (*borbottare*) mumble

nastice *m* mastic; (*per vetri*) putty

aa'stino *m* mastiff

aasto'dontico *adj* gigantic

nastro *m* master; libro ~ ledger

mastur'ba|rsi *vr* masturbate. ~zi'one *f* masturbation

ma'tassa *f* skein

mate'matic|a *f* mathematics, maths. ~o, -a *adj* mathematical ● *mf* mathematician

mate'rasso *m* ~ gonfiabile air bed

mate'rasso *m* mattress. ~ a molle spring mattress

ma'teria *f* matter; (*materiale*) material; (*di studio*) subject. ~ prima raw material

materi'a|le *adj* material; (*grossolano*) coarse ● *m* material. ~'lismo *m* materialism. ~'lista *adj* materialistic ● *mf* materialist. ~liz'zarsi *vr* materialize. ~l'mente *adv* physically

mater'nità *f* motherhood; ospedale di ~ maternity hospital

ma'terno *adj* maternal; lingua materna mother tongue

ma'tita *f* pencil

ma'trice *f* matrix; (*origini*) roots *pl*; (*Comm*) counterfoil

ma'tricola *f* (*registro*) register; (*Univ*) fresher

ma'trigna *f* stepmother

matrimoni'ale *adj* matrimonial; vita ~ married life. matri'monio *m* marriage; (*cerimonia*) wedding

ma'trona *f* matron

'matta *f* (*nelle carte*) joker

matta'toio *m* slaughterhouse

matte'rello *m* rolling-pin

mat'ti|na *f* morning; la ~na in the morning. ~'nata *f* morning; (*Theat*) matinée. ~no *m* morning

'matto, -a *adj* mad, crazy; (*Med*) insane; (*falso*) false; (*opaco*) matt; ~ da legare barking mad; avere una voglia matta di be dying for ● *mf* madman; madwoman

mat'tone *m* brick; (*libro*) bore

matto'nella *f* tile

mattu'tino *adj* morning *attrib*

matu'rare vt ripen. **maturità** f maturity; (Sch) school-leaving certificate. **ma'turo** adj mature; (frutto) ripe

---

> **Maturità** The Italian secondary school-leaving exam is called the *Esame di Maturità*. Candidates are examined by a committee consisting of external examiners and their own teachers, and the exams may be oral or written, depending on the subject. Candidates are tested on a wide range of subjects, including philosophy and history of art.

---

mauso'leo m mausoleum

maxi+ pref maxi+

'**mazza** f club; (martello) hammer; (da baseball, cricket) bat. ~ **da golf** golf-club. **maz'zata** f blow

maz'zetta f (di banconote) bundle

'**mazzo** m bunch; (carte da gioco) pack

me pers pron me; me lo ha dato ne gave it to me; fai come me do as I do; è più veloce di me he is faster than me o faster than I am

me'andro m meander

M.E.C. m abbr (Mercato Comune Europeo) EEC

mec'canica f mechanics sg

meccanica'mente adv mechanically

mec'canico adj mechanical ●m mechanic. **mecca'nismo** m mechanism

mèche fpl [farsi] fare le ~ have one's hair streaked

me'daglia f medal. ~'one m medallion; (gioiello) locket

me'desimo adj same

'**media** f average; (Sch) average mark; (Math) mean; essere nella ~a be in the mid-range. ~'ano adj middle ●m (calcio) half-back

medi'ante prep by

medi'a|re vt act as intermediary in. ~'tore, ~'trice mf mediator; (Comm) middleman

medica'mento m medicine

medi'ca|re vt treat; dress (ferita). ~zi'one f medication; (di ferita) dressing

medi'c|ina f medicine. ~**ina legale** forensic medicine. ~**i'nale** adj medicinal ●m medicine

'**medico** adj medical ●m doctor. ~ **generico** general practitioner. ~ **legale** forensic scientist. ~ **di turno** duty doctor

medie'vale adj medieval

'**medio** adj average; (punto) middle (statura) medium ●m (dito) middle finger

medi'ocre adj mediocre; (scadente) poor

medio'evo m Middle Ages pl

medi'ta|re vt meditate; (progettare) plan; (considerare attentamente) think over ●vi meditate. ~zi'one f meditation

mediter'raneo adj Mediterranean il [mar] M~ the Mediterranean [Sea]

me'dusa f jellyfish

me'gafono m megaphone

mega'lomane mf megalomaniac

me'gera f hag

'**meglio** adv better; tanto ~, ~ così so much the better ●adj better (superlativo) best ●mf best ●f avere ~ su have the better of; fare qcsa alla [bell'e] ~ do sth as best one can ●m fare del proprio ~ do one's best; fare qcsa il ~ possibile make an excellent job of sth; al ~ to the best of one's ability

'**mela** f apple. ~ **cotogna** quince

mela'grana f pomegranate

mela'nina f melanin

melan'zana f aubergine,

melassa | mercato

eggplant *Am*

me'lassa *f* molasses *sg*

me'lenso *adj* (persona, film) dull

mel'lifluo *adj* (parole) honeyed; (voce) sugary

'melma *f* slime. mel'moso *adj* slimy

'melo *m* apple[-tree]

melo'di|a *f* melody. me'lodico *adj* melodic. ~'oso *adj* melodious

melo'dram|ma *m* melodrama. ~'matico *adj* melodramatic

melo'grano *m* pomegranate tree

me'lone *m* melon

'membro *m* member; (*pl f* membra (*Anat*)) limb

memo'rabile *adj* memorable

'memore *adj* mindful; (riconoscente) grateful

me'mori|a *f* memory; (oggetto ricordo) souvenir. imparare a ~ learn by heart. ~a tampone (*Comput*) buffer. ~a volatile (*Comput*) volatile memory. memorie *pl* (biografiche) memoirs. ~'ale *m* memorial. ~z'zare *vt* memorize; (*Comput*) save, store

mena'dito: a ~ adv perfectly

me'nare *vt* lead; (fam: picchiare) hit

mendi'ca|nte *mf* beggar. ~re *vt/i* beg

me'ningi *fpl* spremersi le ~ rack one's brains

menin'gite *f* meningitis

'meno *adv* less; (superlativo) least; (in operazioni, con temperatura) minus; far qcsa alla ~ peggio do sth as best one can; fare a ~ di qcsa do without sth; non posso fare a ~ di ridere I can't help laughing; ~ male! thank goodness!; sempre ~ less and less; venir ~ (svenire) faint; venir ~ a qcno (coraggio:) fail sb; sono le tre ~ un quarto it's a quarter to three; che tu venga o ~ whether you're coming or not; quanto ~ at least • *adj inv* less; (con

nomi plurali) fewer • *m* least; (*Math*) minus sign; il ~ possibile as little as possible; per lo ~ at least • *prep* except [for] • *conj* a ~ che unless

meno'ma|re *vt* (incidente:) maim. ~to *adj* disabled

meno'pausa *f* menopause

'mensa *f* table; (*Mil*) mess; (*Sch, Univ*) refectory

men'sil|e *adj* monthly • *m* (stipendio) [monthly] salary; (rivista) monthly. ~ità *f inv* monthly salary. ~'mente *adv* monthly

'mensola *f* bracket; (scaffale) shelf

'menta *f* mint. ~ peperita peppermint

men'tal|e *adj* mental. ~ità *f inv* mentality

'mente *f* mind; a ~ fredda in cold blood; venire in ~ a qcno occur to sb

men'tina *f* mint

men'tire *vi* lie

'mento *m* chin

'mentre *conj* (temporale) while; (invece) whereas

menu *m inv* menu. ~ fisso set menu. ~ a tendina (*Comput*) pull-down menu

menzio'nare *vt* mention. menzi'one *f* mention

men'zogna *f* lie

mera'viglia *f* wonder; a ~ marvellously; che ~! how wonderful!; con mia grande ~ much to my amazement; mi fa ~ che... I am surprised that...

meravigli'ar|e *vt* surprise. ~si *vr* ~si di be surprised at

meravigli'oso *adj* marvellous

mer'can|te *m* merchant. ~teggi'are *vi* trade; (sul prezzo) bargain. ~'zia *f* merchandise, goods *pl* • *m* merchant ship

mer'cato *m* market; *Fin* market[-place]. a buon ~ (comprare)

m

cheap[ly]; (articolo) cheap. ~ dei cambi foreign exchange market. ~ coperto covered market. ~ libero free market. ~ nero black market

'**merce** f goods pl

mercé f alla ~ di at the mercy of

merce'nario adj & m mercenary

merce'ria f haberdashery; (negozio) haberdasher's

mercoledì m inv Wednesday. ~ delle Ceneri Ash Wednesday

mer'curio m mercury

me'renda f afternoon snack; far ~ have an afternoon snack

meridi'ana f sundial

meridi'ano adj midday ●m meridian

meridio'nale adj southern ●mf southerner. meridi'one m south

me'rin|ga f meringue. ~'gata f meringue pie

meri'tare vt deserve. meri'tevole adj deserving

'**meri|to** m merit; (valore) worth; in ~to a as to; per ~to di thanks to. ~'torio adj meritorious

mer'letto m lace

'**merlo** m blackbird

mer'luzzo m cod

'**mero** adj mere

meschine'ria f meanness. me'schino adj wretched; (gretto) mean ●m wretch

mesco'la|mento m mixing. ~'lanza f mixture

mesco'la|re vt mix; shuffle (carte); (confondere) mix up; blend (tè, tabacco ecc). ~rsi vr mix; (immischiarsi) meddle. ~ta f (a carte) shuffle; (Culin) stir

'**mese** m month

me'setto m un ~ about a month

'**messa**[1] f Mass

'**messa**[2] f (il mettere) putting. ~ in moto (Auto) starting. ~ in piega (di capelli) set. ~ a punto adjustment.

~ in scena production. ~ a terra earthing, grounding Am

messag'gero m messenger. mes'saggio m message

'**messe** f harvest

Mes'sia m Messiah

messi'cano, -a adj & mf Mexican

'**Messico** m Mexico

messin'scena f staging; fig act

'**messo** pp di mettere ●m messenger

mesti'ere m trade; (lavoro) job; essere del ~ be an expert

'**mesto** adj sad

'**mestola** f (di cuoco) ladle

mestru'a|le adj menstrual. ~zi'one f menstruation. ~zi'oni pl period

'**meta** f destination; fig aim

metà f inv half; (centro) middle; a ~ strada half-way; fare a ~ con qcno go halves with sb

metabo'lismo m metabolism

meta'done m methadone

me'tafora f metaphor. meta'forico adj metaphorical

me'talli|co adj metallic. ~z'zato adj (grigio) metallic

me'tal|lo m metal. ~ur'gia f metallurgy

metalmec'canico adj engineering ●m engineering worker

me'tano m methane. ~'dotto m methane pipeline

meta'nolo m methanol

me'teora f meteor. meteo'rite m meteorite

meteoro'lo'gia f meteorology. ~'logico adj meteorological

me'ticcio, -a mf half-caste

metico'loso adj meticulous

me'tod|ico adj methodical. 'metodo m method. ~olo'gia f methodology

me'traggio m length (in metres)

'metrico, -a adj metric; (in poesia) metrical ●f metrics sg

'metro m metre; (nastro) tape measure ●f inv (🔁: metropolitana) tube Br, subway

me'tronomo m metronome

metro'notte mf inv night security guard

me'tropoli f inv metropolis. ~'tana f subway, underground Br. ~'tano adj metropolitan

'metter|e vt put; (indossare) put on; (🔁: installare) put in; ~e al mondo bring into the world; ~e da parte set aside; ~e fiducia inspire trust; ~e qcsa in chiaro make sth clear; ~e in mostra display; ~e a posto tidy up; ~e in vendita put up for sale; ~e su set up (casa, azienda); ci ho messo un'ora it took me an hour; mettiamo che... let's suppose that... ~si vr (indossare) put on; (diventare) turn out; ~si a start to; ~si con qcno (🔁: formare una coppia) start to go out with sb; ~si a letto go to bed; ~si a sedere sit down; ~si in viaggio set out

'mezza f è la ~ it's half past twelve; sono le quattro e ~ it's half past four

mezza'luna f half moon; (simbolo islamico) crescent; (coltello) two-handled chopping knife

mezza'manica f a ~ (maglia) short-sleeved

mez'zano adj middle

mezza'notte f midnight

mezz'asta a ~ adv at half mast

mezzo adj half; di mezza età middle-aged; ~ bicchiere half a glass; una mezza idea a vague idea; sono le quattro e ~ it's half past four. mezz'ora f half an hour. mezza pensione f half board. mezza stagione f una giacca di mezza stagione a spring/autumn jacket ●adv (a metà) half ●m (metà) half; (centro)

middle; (per raggiungere un fine) means sg; uno e ~ one and a half; tre anni e ~ three and a half years; in ~ a in the middle of; il giusto ~ the happy medium; levare di ~ clear away; per ~ di by means of; a ~ posta by mail; via di ~ fig halfway house; (soluzione) middle way. mezzi pl (denaro) means pl. mezzi pubblici public transport. mezzi di trasporto [means of] transport

mezzo'busto a ~ adj (foto, ritratto) half-length

mezzo'fondo m middle-distance running

mezzogi'orno m midday; (sud) South. il M~ Southern Italy. ~ in punto high noon

mi¹ pers pron me; (refl) myself; mi ha dato un libro he gave me a book; mi lavo le mani I wash my hands; eccomi here I am

mi² m (Mus) E

'mica¹ f mica

'mica² adv 🔁 (per caso) by any chance; hai ~ visto Paolo? have you seen Paul, by any chance?; non è ~ bello it is not at all nice; ~ male not bad

'miccia f fuse

micidi'ale adj deadly

'micio m pussy-cat

'microbo m microbe

micro'cosmo m microcosm

micro'fiche f inv microfiche

micro'film m inv microfilm

mi'crofono m microphone

microorga'nismo m microorganism

microproces'sore m microprocessor

micro'scopi|o m microscope

micro'solco m (disco) long-playing record

mi'dollo m (pl f midolla, (Anat)) marrow; fino al ~ through and

m

through. ~ **spinale** spinal cord

mi'ele m honey

'mie, mi'ei ▷ MIO

mi'et|ere vt reap. ~**i'trice** f (Mech) harvester. ~**i'tura** f harvest

migli'aio m (pl f migliaia) thousand. **a migliaia** in thousands

'miglio m (Bot) millet; (misura: pl f miglia) mile

migliora'mento m improvement

miglio'rare vt/i improve

migli'ore adj better; (superlativo) the best ● mf il/la ~ the best

'mignolo m little finger; (del piede) little toe

mi'gra|re vi migrate. ~**zi'one** f migration

'mila ▷ MILLE

Mi'lano f Milan

miliar'dario, -a m millionaire; (plurimiliardario) billionaire ● f millionairess; billionairess. **mili'ardo** m billion

mili'are adj **pietra** f ~ milestone

milio'nario, -a m millionaire ● f millionairess

mili'one m million

milio'nesimo adj millionth

mili'tante adj & mf militant

mili'tare vi ~ **in** be a member of (partito ecc) ● adj military ● m soldier; **fare il** ~ do one's military service. ~ **di leva** national serviceman

'milite m soldier. **mil'izia** f militia

'mille adj & m (pl f mila) a one thousand; **due/tre mila** two/three thousand; ~ **grazie!** thanks a lot!

mille'foglie m inv (Culin) vanilla slice

mil'lennio m millennium

millepi'edi m inv centipede

mil'lesimo adj & m thousandth

milli'grammo m milligram

mil'limetro m millimetre

mi'mare vt mimic (persona)

● vi mime

mi'metico adj camouflage attrib

mimetiz'zar|e vt camouflage. ~**si** vr camouflage oneself

'mim|ica f mime. ~**ico** adj mimic. ~**o** m mime

mi'mosa f mimosa

'mina f mine; (di matita) lead

mi'naccia f threat

minacci'|are vt threaten. ~**'oso** adj threatening

mi'nare vt mine; fig undermine

mina'tor|e m miner. ~**io** adj threatening

mine'ra|le adj & m mineral. ~**rio** adj mining attrib

mi'nestra f soup. **mine'strone** m vegetable soup; (🅸: insieme confuso) hotchpotch

mini+ pref mini+

minia'tura f miniature. **miniaturiz-'zato** adj miniaturized

mini'era f mine

mini'golf m miniature golf

mini'gonna f miniskirt

minima'mente adv minimally

mini'market m inv minimarket

minimiz'zare vt minimize

'minimo adj least, slightest; (il più basso) lowest; (salario, quantità ecc) minimum ● m minimum

mini'stero m ministry; (governo) government

mi'nistro m minister. M~ **del Te-soro** Finance Minister

mino'ranza f minority attrib

---

i

Minoranza linguistica Mi-noranze linguistiche (linguistic minorities) are protected by the Italian constitution. As well as dialects of Italian, and the re-lated languages Sardinian and Ladin, other languages spoken.

They include German in Alto Adige; French in Valdaosta; Greek, Albanian, and Serbo-Croat in the rural south; Slovenian in the north-east and Catalan in Alghero.

mino'rato, -a adj disabled ● mf disabled person

mi'nore adj (gruppo, numero) smaller; (superlativo) smallest; (distanza) shorter; (superlativo) shortest; (prezzo) lower; (superlativo) lowest; (di età) younger; (superlativo) youngest; (di importanza) minor; (superlativo) least important ● mf younger; (superlativo) youngest; (Jur) minor; **i minori di 14 anni** children under 14. **mino·'renne** adj under age ● mf minor

minori'tario adj minority attrib

ninu'etto m minuet

ni'nuscolo, -a adj tiny ● f small letter

ni'nuta f rough copy

ni'nuto[1] adj minute; (persona) delicate; (ricerca) detailed; (pioggia, neve) fine; **al ~** (Comm) retail

ni'nuto[2] m (di tempo) minute; **spaccare il ~ be** dead on time

nl'nuzi|a f trifle. **~'oso** adj detailed; (persona) meticulous

mio (il mio m, la mia f, i miei mpl, le mie fpl) adj poss my; **questa macchina è mia** this car is mine; **~ padre** my father; **un ~ amico** a friend of mine ● poss pron mine; **i miei** (genitori ecc) my folks

mlope adj short-sighted. **mio'pia** f short-sightedness

nira f aim; (bersaglio) target; **prendere la ~** take aim

ni'racolo m miracle. **~sa'mente** adv miraculously. **miraco'loso** adj miraculous

ni'raggio m mirage

ni'rar|e vi [take] aim. **~si** vr (guardarsi) look at oneself

ni'riade f myriad

mi'rino m sight; (Phot) view-finder

mir'tillo m blueberry

mi'santropo, -a mf misanthropist

mi'scela f mixture; (di caffè, tabacco ecc) blend. **~'tore** m (di acqua) mixer tap

miscel'lanea f miscellany

'mischia f scuffle; (nel rugby) scrum

mischi'ar|e vt mix; shuffle (carte da gioco). **~si** vr (immischiarsi) interfere

misco'noscere vt not appreciate

mi'scuglio m mixture

mise'rabile adj wretched

misera'mente adv (finire) miserably; (vivere) in abject poverty

mi'seria f poverty; (infelicità) misery; **guadagnare una ~** earn a pittance; **porca ~!** hell!

miseri'cordi|a f mercy. **~'oso** adj merciful

'misero adj (miserabile) wretched; (povero) poor; (scarso) paltry

mi'sfatto m misdeed

mi'sogino m misogynist

mis'saggio m vision mixer

'missile m missile

missio'nario, -a mf missionary. **missi'one** f mission

misteri|'oso adj mysterious. **mi·'stero** m mystery

'misti|ca f mysticism. **~'cismo** m mysticism. **~co** adj mystic[al] ● m mystic

mistifi'car|e vt distort (verità). **~zi'one** f (della verità) distortion

'misto adj mixed; **scuola mista** mixed or co-educational school ● m mixture; **~ lana/cotone** wool/cotton mix

mi'sura f measure; (dimensione) measurement; (taglia) size; (limite) limit; **su ~** (abiti) made to measure; (mobile) custom-made; **a ~** (andare, calzare) perfectly. **~ di sicurezza** safety measure. **mi-**

su'rare vt measure; try on (indumenti); (limitare) limit. **misu'rarsi** vr misurarsi con (gareggiare) compete with. **misu'rato** adj measured. misu-'rino m measuring spoon

'mite adj mild; (prezzo) moderate

'mitico adj mythical

miti'gare vt mitigate. ~si vr calm down; (clima:) become mild

'mito m myth. ~lo'gia f mythology. ~'logico adj mythological

'mitra f (Relig) mitre ● m inv (Mil) machine-gun

mitragli'are vt machine-gun; ~re di domande fire questions at. ~'trice f machine-gun

mit'tente mf sender

mo' m a ~ di by way of (esempio, consolazione)

'mobbing m harassment

'mobile[1] adj mobile; (volubile) fickle; (che si può muovere) movable; beni mobili personal estate; squadra ~ flying squad

'mobi|le[2] m piece of furniture; mobili pl furniture sg. **mo'bilia** f furniture. ~li'ficio m furniture factory

mo'bilio m furniture

mobilità f mobility

mobili'tare vt mobilize. ~zi'one f mobilization

mocas'sino m moccasin

'moccolo m candle-end; (moccio) snot

'moda f fashion; di ~ in fashion; alla ~ (musica, vestiti) up-to-date; fuori ~ unfashionable

modalità f inv formality; ~ d'uso instruction

mo'della f model. model'lare vt model

model'li|no m model. ~sta mf designer

mo'dello m model; (stampo) mould; (di carta) pattern; (modulo) form

'modem m inv modem

mode'ra|re vt moderate; (diminuire) reduce. ~rsi vr control oneself. ~ta'mente adv moderately ~to adj moderate. ~'tore, ~'trice mf (in tavola rotonda) moderator. ~zi'one f moderation

modern|a'mente adv (in modo moderno) in a modern style. ~iz'zare vt modernize. **mo'derno** adj modern

mo'dest|ia f modesty. ~o adj modest

'modico adj reasonable

mo'difica f modification

modifi'care vt modify. ~zi'one f modification

mo'dista f milliner

'modo m way; (garbo) manners pl; (occasione) chance; (Gram) mood; ad ogni ~ anyhow; di ~ che so that; fare in ~ di try to; in che ~ (inter) how; in qualche ~ somehow; in questo ~ like this; ~ di dire idiom per ~ di dire so to speak

modu'lare vt modulate. ~zi'one f modulation. ~zione di frequenza frequency modulation

'modulo m form; (lunare, di comando) module. ~ continuo continuous paper

'mogano m mahogany

'mogio adj dejected

'moglie f wife

'mola f millstone; (Mech) grindstone

mo'lare m molar

'mole f mass; (dimensione) size

mo'lecola f molecule

mole'stare vt bother; (più forte) molest. **mo'lestia** f nuisance. **mo'lesto** adj bothersome

'molla f spring; molle pl tongs

mol'lare vt let go; (I: lasciare) leave; I give (ceffone); (Naut) cast off ● vi cease; mollala! I stop that

'molle adj soft; (bagnato) wet

mol'letta f (per capelli) hair-grip; (per bucato) clothes-peg; mollette pl

(*per ghiaccio ecc*) tongs

mol'lezz|a *f* softness; **~e** *pl fig* luxury

mol'lica *f* crumb

molo *m* pier; (*banchina*) dock

mol'teplice *adj* manifold; (*numeroso*) numerous. **~ità** *f* multiplicity

molti pli'ca|re *vt*, **~rsi** *vr* multiply. **~'tore** *m* multiplier. **~'trice** *f* calculating machine. **~zi'one** *f* multiplication

molti'tudine *f* multitude

'molto

● *adj* a lot of; (*con negazione e interrogazione*) much, a lot of; (*con nomi plurali*) many, a lot of; **non ~ tempo** not much time, not a lot of time

● *adv* very; (*con verbi*) a lot; (*con avverbi*) much; **~ stupido** very stupid; **mangiare ~** eat a lot; **~ più veloce** much faster; **non mangiare ~** not eat much

● *pron* a lot; (*molto tempo*) a lot of time; (*con negazione e interrogazione*) much, a lot; (*plurale*) many; **non ne ho ~** I don't have much; **non ne ho molti** I don't have many, I don't have a lot; **non ci metterò ~** I won't be long; **fra non ~** before long; **molti** (*persone*) a lot of people; **eravamo in molti** there were a lot of us

momentanea'mente *adv* momentarily; **è ~ assente** he's not here at the moment. **momen'taneo** *adj* momentary

mo'mento *m* moment; **a momenti** (*a volte*) sometimes; (*fra un momento*) in a moment; **dal ~ che** since; **per il ~** for the time being; **da un ~ all'altro** (cambiare idea ecc) from one moment to the next; (*aspettare qcno ecc*) at any moment

'monac|a *f* nun. **~o** *m* monk

mollezza | monotonia

'Monaco *m* Monaco ● *f* (*di Baviera*) Munich

mo'narc|a *m* monarch. **monar'chia** *f* monarchy

mona'stero *m* (*di monaci*) monastery; (*di monache*) convent. **mo'nastico** *adj* monastic

monche'rino *m* stump

'monco *adj* maimed; (*fig: troncato*) truncated; **~ di un braccio** one-armed

mon'dano *adj* worldly; **vita mondana** social life

mondi'ale *adj* world *attrib*; **di fama ~** world-famous

'mondo *m* world; **il bel ~** fashionable society; **un ~** (*molto*) a lot

mondovisi'one *f* **in ~** transmitted worldwide

mo'nello, -a *mf* urchin

mo'neta *f* coin; (*denaro*) money; (*denaro spicciolo*) [small] change. **~ estera** foreign currency. **~ legale** legal tender. **~ unica** single currency. **mone'tario** *adj* monetary

mongolfi'era *f* hot air balloon

mo'nile *m* jewel

'monito *m* warning

moni'tore *m* monitor

monoco'lore *adj* (Pol) one-party

mono'dose *adj inv* individually packaged

monogra'fia *f* monograph

mono'gramma *m* monogram

mono'kini *m inv* monokini

mono'lingue *adj* monolingual

monolo'cale *m* studio apartment

mo'nologo *m* monologue

mono'pattino *m* [child's] scooter

mono'poli|o *m* monopoly. **~o di Stato** state monopoly. **~z'zare** *vt* monopolize

mono'sci *m inv* monoski

monosil'labico *adj* monosyllabic. **mono'sillabo** *m* monosyllable

monoto'nia *f* monotony. **mo'nono-**

tono adj monotonous
mono'uso adj disposable
monsi'gnore m monsignor
mon'sone m monsoon
monta'carichi m inv hoist
mon'taggio m (Mech) assembly; Cinema editing; catena di ~ production line
mon'tagna f mountain; (zona) mountains pl. montagne pl russe big dipper. ~'gnoso adj mountainous. ~'naro, -a mf highlander. ~no adj mountain attrib
mon'tante m (di finestra, porta) upright
mon'ta|re vt/i mount; get on (veicolo); (aumentare) rise; (Mech) assemble; frame (quadro); (Culin) whip; edit (film); (a cavallo) ~ la blow up; ~rsi la testa get big-headed. ~to, -a mf poser. ~'tura f (Mech) assembling; (di occhiali) frame; (di gioiello) mounting; fig exaggeration
'monte m mountain; a ~ up-stream; andare a ~ be ruined; mandare a ~ qcsa ruin sth. ~ di pietà pawnshop
Monte'negro m Montenegro
monte'premi m inv jackpot
mon'tone m ram; carne di ~ mutton
montu'oso adj mountainous
monumen'tale adj monumental. monu'mento m monument
mo'quette f fitted carpet
'mora f (del gelso) mulberry; (del rovo) blackberry
mo'ra|le adj moral ● f morals pl; (di storia) moral ● m morale. mora'lista mf moralist. ~ità f morality; (condotta) morals pl. ~iz'zare vt/i moralize. ~'mente adv morally
morbi'dezza f softness
'morbido adj soft
mor'billo m measles sg
'morbo m disease. ~sità f (qualità)

morbidity
mor'boso adj morbid
mor'dente adj biting. 'mordere vt bite; (corrodere) bite into. mordicchi'are vt gnaw
mor'fina f morphine. morfi'nomane mf morphine addict
mori'bondo adj dying; (istituzione) moribund
morige'rato adj moderate
mo'rire vi die; fig die out; fa un freddo da ~ it's freezing cold, it's perishing; ~ di noia be bored to death
mor'mone mf Mormon
mormo'r|are vt/i murmur; (brontolare) mutter. ~io m murmuring; (lamentela) grumbling
'moro adj dark ● m Moor
mo'roso adj in arrears
'morsa f vice; fig grip
'morse adj alfabeto ~ Morse code
mor'setto m clamp
morsi'care vt bite. 'morso m bite; (di cibo, briglia) bit; i morsi della fame hunger pangs
morta'della f mortadella (type of salted pork)
mor'taio m mortar
mor'ta|le adj mortal; (simile a morte) deadly; di una noia ~e deadly. ~ità f mortality. ~'mente adv (ferito) fatally; (offeso) mortally
morta'retto m firecracker
'morte f death
mortifi'ca|re vt mortify. ~rsi vr be mortified. ~to adj mortified. ~zi'one f mortification
'morto, -a pp di morire ● adj dead ~ di freddo frozen to death; stanc ~ dead tired ● m dead man ● f dead woman
mor'torio m funeral
mo'saico m mosaic
'mosca f fly. ~ cieca blindman's buff

'**Mosca** f Moscow

mo'**scato** adj muscat; noce moscata nutmeg ● m muscatel

mosce'**rino** m midge

mo'**schea** f mosque

moschi'**cida** adj fly attrib

'**moscio** adj limp; avere l'erre moscia not be able to say one's r's properly

mo'**scone** m bluebottle; (barca) pedalo

'**moss|a** f movement; (passo) move. ~o pp di **muovere** ● adj (mare) rough; (capelli) wavy; (fotografia) blurred

mo'**starda** f mustard

'**mostra** f show; (d'arte) exhibition; far ~ di pretend; in ~ on show; mettersi in ~ make oneself conspicuous

mo'**stra|re** vt show; (indicare) point out; (spiegare) explain. ~rsi vr show oneself; (apparire) appear

'**mostro** m monster; (fig: persona) genius; ~ sacro fig sacred cow

mostru**osa'mente** adv tremendously. ~**oso** adj monstrous; (incredibile) enormous

mo'**tel** m inv motel

moti'**va|re** vt cause; (Jur) justify. ~to adj (persona) motivated. ~zi'**one** f motivation; (giustificazione) justification

mo'**tivo** m reason; (movente) motive; (in musica, letteratura) theme; (disegno) motif

'**moto** m motion; (esercizio) exercise; (gesto) movement; (sommossa) rising ● f inv (motocicletta) motor bike; mettere in ~ start (motore)

moto'**carro** m three-wheeler

motoci'**cl|etta** f motor cycle. ~**ismo** m motorcycling. ~**ista** mf motor-cyclist

moto'**cros|s** m motocross. ~**sista** mf scrambler

moto'**lancia** f motor launch

moto'**nave** f motor vessel

mo'**tore** adj motor ● m motor, engine. ~ di ricerca (Comput) search engine. moto'**retta** f motor scooter. moto'**rino** m moped. motorino d'avviamento starter

motoriz'**za|to** adj (Mil) motorized. ~**zi'one** f (ufficio) vehicle licensing office

moto'**scafo** m motorboat

moto'**vedetta** f patrol vessel

'**motto** m motto; (facezia) witticism; (massima) saying

mouse m inv (Comput) mouse

mo'**vente** m motive

movimen'**ta|re** vt enliven. ~**to** adj lively. movi'**mento** m movement; essere sempre in movimento be always on the go

mozi'**one** f motion

mozzafi'**ato** adj inv nail-biting

moz'**zare** vt cut off; dock (coda); ~ il fiato a qcno take sb's breath away

mozza'**rella** f mozzarella (mild, white cheese)

mozzi'**cone** m (di sigaretta) stub

'**mozzo** m (Mech) hub; (Naut) ship's boy ● adj (coda) truncated; (testa) severed

'**mucca** f cow. morbo della ~ pazza mad cow disease

'**mucchio** m heap, pile; un ~ di fig lots of

'**muco** m mucus

'**muffa** f mould; fare la ~ go mouldy. muf'**fire** vi go mouldy

muf'**fole** fpl mittens

mug'**gi|re** vi (mucca:) moo, low; (toro:) bellow

mu'**ghetto** m lily of the valley

mugo'**lare** vi whine; (persona:) moan. mugo'**lio** m whining

mulat'**tiera** f mule track

mu'**latto, -a** mf mulatto

muli'**nello** m (d'acqua) whirl-pool;

(di vento) eddy; (giocattolo) windmill
mu'lino m mill. ~ **a vento** windmill
'**mulo** m mule
'**multa** f fine. **mul'tare** vt fine
multico'lore adj multicoloured
multi'lingue adj multilingual
multi'media mpl multimedia
multimedi'ale adj multimedia attrib
multimiliar'dario, -a mf multimillionaire
multinazio'nale f multinational
'**multiplo** adj & m multiple
multiproprietà f inv time-share
multi'uso adj (utensile) all-purpose
'**mummia** f mummy
'**mungere** vt milk
munici'palle adj municipal. ~**ità** f inv town council. **muni'cipio** m town hall
mu'nifico adj munificent
mu'nire vt fortify; ~ **di** (provvedere) supply with
munizi'oni fpl ammunition sg
'**munto** pp di **mungere**
mu'over|e vt move; (suscitare) arouse. ~**si** vr move
mura fpl (cinta di città) walls
mu'raglia f wall
mu'rale adj mural; (pittura) wall attrib
mur'a|re vt wall up. ~**tore** m bricklayer; (con pietre) mason; (operaio edile) builder. ~**tura** f (di pietra) masonry, stonework; (di mattoni) brickwork
mu'rena f moray eel
'**muro** m wall; (di nebbia) bank; a ~ (armadio) built-in. ~ **portante** load-bearing wall. ~ **del suono** sound barrier
'**muschio** m (Bot) moss
musco'la|re adj muscular. ~**tura** f muscles pl. '**muscolo** m muscle
mu'seo m museum
museru'ola f muzzle

'**musi|ca** f music. ~**cal** m inv musical. ~**cale** adj musical. ~**cista** mf musician.
'**muso** m (pej: di persona) mug; (di aeroplano) nose; fare il ~ sulk. **mu'sone, -a** mf sulker
mussola f muslin
musul'mano, -a mf Moslem
'**muta** f (cambio) change; (di penne) moult; (di cani) pack; (per immersione subacquea) wetsuit
muta'mento m change
mu'tan|de fpl pants; (da donna) knickers. ~**doni** mpl (da uomo) long johns; (da donna) bloomers
mu'tare vt change
mu'tevole adj changeable
muti'la|re vt mutilate. ~**to, -a** mf disabled person. ~**to di guerra** disabled ex-serviceman
mu'tismo m dumbness; fig obstinate silence
'**muto** adj dumb; (silenzioso) silent; (fonetica) mute
'**mutu|a** f [cassa f] ~ sickness benefit fund. ~'**ato, -a** mf ≈ NHS patient
mutuo¹ adj mutual
mutuo² m loan; (per la casa) mortgage; fare un ~ take out a mortgage. ~ **ipotecario** mortgage

Nn

n° abbr (numero) No
'**nacchera** f castanet
'**nafta** f naphtha; (per motori) diesel oil
'**naia** f cobra; (🅇: servizio militare) national service
'**nailon** m nylon
'**nano, -a** adj & mf dwarf

napole'tano, -a *adj & mf* Neapolitan

'Napoli *f* Naples

'nappa *f* tassel; (*pelle*) soft leather

nar'ciso *m* narcissus

nar'cotico *adj & m* narcotic

na'rice *f* nostril

nar'ra|re *vt* tell. ~**tivo, -a** *adj* narrative ●*f* fiction. ~**tore, ~trice** *mf* narrator. ~**zi'one** *f* narration; (*racconto*) story

na'sale *adj* nasal

'nasc|ere *vi* (*venire al mondo*) be born; (*germogliare*) sprout; (*sorgere*) rise; ~**ere da** *fig* arise from. ~**ita** *f* birth. ~**i'turo** *m* unborn child

na'scondere *vt* hide. ~**si** *vr* hide

nascon'di|glio *m* hiding-place. ~**no** *m* hide-and-seek. **na'scosto** *pp di* **nascondere** ●*adj* hidden; **di nascosto** secretly

na'sello *m* (*pesce*) hake

'naso *m* nose

'nastro *m* ribbon; (*di registratore ecc*) tape. ~ **adesivo** adhesive tape. ~ **isolante** insulating tape. ~ **trasportatore** conveyor belt

na'tal|e *adj* (*paese*) of one's birth. **N~e** *m* Christmas; ~**i** *pl* parentage. ~**ità** *f* [number of] births. **nata'lizio** *adj* (*del Natale*) Christmas *attrib*; (*di nascita*) of one's birth

na'tante *adj* floating ●*m* craft

natica *f* buttock

na'tio *adj* native

Nativita *f* Nativity. **na'tivo, -a** *agg & mf* native

nato *pp di* **nascere** ●*adj* born; **uno scrittore ~** a born writer; **nata Rossi** née Rossi

NATO *f* Nato, NATO

na'tura *f* nature; **pagare in ~** pay in kind. ~ **morta** still life

natu'ra|le *adj* natural; **al ~le** (*alimento*) plain, natural; ~**lei** naturally, of course. ~**lezza** *f* naturalness. ~**liz'zare** *vt* naturalize. ~**l'mente** *adv*
naturally

natu'rista *mf* naturalist

naufra'gare *vi* be wrecked; (*persona:*) be shipwrecked. **nau'fragio** *m* shipwreck; *fig* wreck. **'naufrago, -a** *mf* survivor

'nause|a *f* nausea; **avere la ~a** feel sick. ~**ante** *adj* nauseating. ~**are** *vt* nauseate

'nautic|a *f* navigation. ~**o** *adj* nautical

na'vale *adj* naval

na'vata *f* nave; (*laterale*) aisle

'nave *f* ship. ~ **cisterna** tanker. ~ **da guerra** warship. ~ **spaziale** spaceship

na'vetta *f* shuttle

navi'cella *f* ~ **spaziale** nose cone

navi'gabile *adj* navigable

navi'ga|re *vi* sail; ~**re in Internet** surf the Net. ~**tore, ~trice** *mf* navigator. ~**zi'one** *f* navigation

na'viglio *m* fleet; (*canale*) canal

nazio'na|le *adj* national ●*f* Sport national team. ~**lismo** *m* nationalism. ~**lista** *mf* nationalist ~**lità** *f inv* nationality.

nazionaliz'zare *vt* nationalize. **nazi'one** *f* nation

na'zista *adj & mf* Nazi

N.B. *abbr* (nota bene) N.B.

---

ne

Spesso non si traduce: **Ne ho cinque** I've got five (of them)

● *pers pron* (*di lui*) about him; (*di lei*) about her; (*di loro*) about them; (*di ciò*) about it; (*da ciò*) from that; (*di un insieme*) of it; (*di un gruppo*) of them

⤵ **non ne conosco nessuno** I don't know any of them; **ne ho**

I have some; **non ne ho più** I don't have any left

● *adv* from there; **ne vengo ora** I've just come from there; **me ne vado** I'm off

né *conj* **né... né...** neither... nor...; **non ne ho il tempo né la voglia** I don't have either the time or the inclination; **né tu né io vogliamo andare** neither you nor I want to go; **né l'uno né l'altro** neither [of them/us]

ne'anche *adv* (*neppure*) not even; (*senza neppure*) without even ● *conj* (*e neppure*) neither... nor; **non parlo inglese, e lui ~** I don't speak English, neither does he **o** and he doesn't either

'nebbi|a *f* mist; (*in città, su strada*) fog. **~'oso** *adj* misty; foggy

necessaria'mente *adv* necessarily. **neces'sario** *adj* necessary

necessità *f inv* necessity; (*bisogno*) need

necessi'tare *vi* **~ di** need; (*essere necessario*) be necessary

necro'logio *m* obituary

ne'fando *adj* wicked

ne'fasto *adj* ill-omened

ne'ga|re *vt* deny; (*rifiutare*) refuse; **essere ~to per qcsa** be no good at sth. **~'tivo, -a** *adj* negative ● *f neg*ative. **~zi'one** *f* negation; (*diniego*) denial; (*Gram*) negative

ne'gletto *adj* neglected

'negli = IN + GLI

negli'gen|te *adj* negligent. **~za** *f* negligence

negozi'abile *adj* negotiable

negozi'ante *mf* dealer; (*bottegaio*) shopkeeper

negozi'a|re *vt* negotiate ● *vi* **~re in** trade in. **~ti** *mpl* negotiations

ne'gozio *m* shop

'negro, -a *adj* black ● *mf* black; (*scrittore*) ghost writer

'nei = IN + I. **nel** = IN + IL. **'nella** = IN + LA. **'nelle** = IN + LE. **'nello** = IN + LO

'nembo *m* nimbus

ne'mico, -a *adj* hostile ● *mf* enemy

nem'meno *conj* not even

'nenia *f* dirge; (*per bambini*) lullaby; (*piagnucolio*) wail

'neo+ *pref* neo+

neofa'scismo *m* neofascism

neo'litico *adj* Neolithic

'neon *m* neon

neo'nato, -a *adj* newborn ● *mf* newborn baby

neozelan'dese *adj* New Zealand ● *mf* New Zealander

nep'pure *conj* not even

'nerb|o *m* (*forza*) strength; *fig* backbone. **~o'ruto** *adj* brawny

ne'retto *m* (*Typ*) bold [type]

'nero *adj* black; (⊞: *arrabbiato*) fuming ● *m* black; **mettere ~ su bianco** put in writing

nerva'tura *f* nerves *pl*; (*Bot*) veining; (*di libro*) band

'nervo *m* nerve; (*Bot*) vein; **avere i nervi** be bad-tempered; **dare ai nervi a qcno** get on sb's nerves. **~'sismo** *m* nerviness

ner'voso *adj* nervous; (*irritabile*) bad-tempered; **avere il ~** be irritable; **esaurimento** *m* **~** nervous breakdown

'nespo|la *f* medlar. **~o** *m* medlar[-tree]

'nesso *m* link

nes'suno *adj* no, not... any; (*qualche*) any; **non ho nessun problema** I don't have any problems, I have no problems; **non lo trovo da nessuna parte** I can't find it anywhere; **in nessun modo** on no account ● *pron* nobody, no one, not... anybody, not... anyone; (*qualcuno*) anybody, anyone; **hai delle domande? - nessuna** do you have any questions? -

none; ~ di voi none of you; ~ dei due (di voi due) neither of you; non ho visto ~ dei tuoi amici I haven't seen any of your friends; c'è ~? is anybody there?

net'tare vt clean

net'tezza f cleanliness. ~ urbana cleansing department

netto adj clean; (chiaro) clear; (Comm) net; di ~ just like that

nettur'bino m dustman

neu'tral|e adj & m neutral. ~ità f neutrality. ~iz'zare vt neutralize. 'neutro adj neutral; (Gram) neuter • m (Gram) neuter

neu'trone m neutron

neve f snow

nevi'care vi snow; ~ca it is snowing. ~'cata f snowfall. ne'vischio m sleet. ne'voso adj snowy

nevral'gia f neuralgia

ne'vro|si f inv neurosis. ~tico adj neurotic

nibbio m kite

nicchia f niche

nicchi'are vi shilly-shally

nichel m nickel

nichi'lista adj & mf nihilist

nico'tina f nicotine

nidi'ata f brood. 'nido m nest; (giardino d'infanzia) crèche

ni'ente pron nothing, not... anything; (qualcosa) anything; non ho fatto ~ di male I didn't do anything wrong, I did nothing wrong; grazie! – di ~! thank you! – don't mention it!; non serve a ~ it is no use; vuoi ~? do you want anything?; da ~ (di poco importante) minor; (di poco valore) worthless • adj inv 🅣 non ho ~ fame I'm not the slightest bit hungry • adv non fa ~ (non importa) it doesn't matter; per ~ at all; (litigare) over nothing; ~ af'fatto! no way! • m un bel ~ absolutely nothing

nientedi'meno, niente'meno adv ~ che no less than • int fancy that!

'ninfa f nymph

nin'fea f water-lily

'ninnolo m plaything; (fronzolo) knick-knack

ni'pote m (di zii) nephew; (di nonni) grandson, grandchild • f (di zii) niece; (di nonni) granddaughter, grandchild

'nitido adj neat; (chiaro) clear

ni'trato m nitrate

ni'tri|re vi neigh. ~to m (di cavallo) neigh

no adv no; (con congiunzione) not; dire di no say no; credo di no I don't think so; perché no? why not?; io no not me; fa freddo, no? it's cold, isn't it?

'nobil|e adj noble • m noble, nobleman • f noble, noblewoman. ~'are adj noble. ~tà f nobility

'nocca f knuckle

nocci'ol|a f hazelnut. ~o m (albero) hazel

'nocciolo m stone; fig heart

'noce f walnut • m (albero, legno) walnut. ~ moscata nutmeg. ~'pesca f nectarine

no'civo adj harmful

'nodo m knot; fig lump; (Comput) node; fare il ~ della cravatta do up one's tie. no'doso adj knotty

'noi pers pron (soggetto) we; (oggetto, con prep) us; chi è? – siamo ~ who is it? – it's us

'noia f boredom; (fastidio) bother; (persona) bore; dar ~ annoy

nol'altri pers pron we

noi'oso adj boring; (fastidioso) tiresome

noleggi'are vt hire; (dare a noleggio) hire out; charter (nave, aereo). no'leggio m hire; (di nave, aereo) charter. 'nolo m hire; (Naut) freight; a nolo for hire

'nomade adj nomadic ● mf nomad

'nome m name; (Gram) noun; a ~ di in the name of; di ~ by name. ~ di famiglia surname. ~ da ragazza maiden name. no'mea f reputation

nomencla'tura f nomenclature

no'mignolo m nickname

'nomina f appointment. **nomi'nale** adj nominal; (Gram) noun attrib

nomi'na|re vt name; (menzionare) mention; (eleggere) appoint. ~'tivo adj nominative; (Comm) registered ● m nominative; (nome) name

---

non adv not; ~ ti amo I do not love you; ~ c'è di che not at all

> Per formare il negativo dei verbi regolari si usa l'ausiliare *do*: Non mi piace il don't like it

---

nonché conj (tanto meno) let alone; (e anche) as well as

noncu'ran|te adj nonchalant; (negligente) indifferent. ~za f nonchalance; (negligenza) indifference

nondi'meno conj nevertheless

'nonna f grandmother

'nonno m grandfather; **nonni** pl grandparents

non'nulla m inv trifle

'nono adj & m ninth

nono'stante prep in spite of ● conj although

nonvio'lento adj nonviolent

nord m north; del ~ northern

nor'd-est m northeast; a ~ northeasterly

'nordico adj northern

nordocciden'tale adj northwestern

nordorien'tale adj northeastern

nor'd-ovest m northwest; a ~ northwesterly

'norma f rule; (istruzione) instruction; a ~ di legge according to law; è

buona ~ it's advisable

nor'mal|e adj normal. ~ità f normality. ~iz'zare vt normalize. ~'mente adv normally

norve'gese adj & mf Norwegian. Nor'vegia f Norway

nossi'gnore adv no way

nostal'gia f (di casa, patria) homesickness; (del passato) nostalgia; aver ~ be homesick; aver ~ di qcno miss sb. no'stalgico, -a adj nostalgic ● mf reactionary

no'strano adj local; (fatto in casa) home-made

'nostro (il nostro m, la nostra f, i nostri mpl, le nostre fpl) poss adj our quella macchina è nostra that car is ours; ~ padre our father; un ~ amico a friend of ours ● poss pron ours

'nota f (segno) sign; (comunicazione, commento, musica) note; (conto) bill; (lista) list; degno di ~ noteworthy; prendere ~ take note. note pl caratteristiche distinguishing marks

no'tabile adj & m notable

no'taio m notary

no'ta|re vt (segnare) mark; (annotare) note down; (osservare) notice; far ~re qcsa point sth out. ~zi'one f marking; (annotazione) notation

'notes m inv notepad

no'tevole adj (degno di nota) remarkable; (grande) considerable

no'tifica f notification. notifi'care notify; (Comm) advise. ~zi'one f notification

no'tizi|a f una ~a a piece of news (informazione) a piece of information; le ~e the news sg. ~'ario m news sg

'noto adj [well-]known; rendere ~ (far sapere) announce

notorietà f fame; raggiungere la ~ become famous. no'torio adj well-known; pej notorious

not'tambulo m night-bird

not'tata f night; far ∼ stay up all night

notte f night; **di** ∼ at night; ∼ **bianca** sleepless night. ∼**tempo** adv at night

not'turno adj nocturnal; (servizio ecc) night

no'vanta adj & m ninety

novan't|enne adj & m ninety-year-old. ∼**esimo** adj ninetieth. ∼**ina** f about ninety. **'nove** adj & m nine. no've'cento adj & m nine hundred. **il Novecento** the twentieth century

no'vella f short story

novel'lino, -a adj inexperienced ● mf novice, beginner. **no'vello** adj new

no'vembre m November

novità f inv novelty; (notizie) news sg; **l'ultima** ∼ (moda) the latest fashion

novizi'ato m (Relig) novitiate; (tirocinio) apprenticeship

nozi'one f notion; **nozioni** pl rudiments

nozze fpl marriage sg; (cerimonia) wedding-sg. ∼ **d'argento** silver wedding [anniversary]. ∼ **d'oro** golden wedding [anniversary]

nub|e f cloud. ∼**e tossica** toxic cloud. ∼**i'fragio** m cloudburst

nubile adj unmarried ● f unmarried woman

nuca f nape

nucle'are adj nuclear

nucleo m nucleus; (unità) unit

nu'di|sta mf nudist. ∼**tà** f inv nudity

nudo adj naked; (spoglio) bare; **a occhio** ∼ to the naked eye

nugolo m large number

nulla pron = NIENTE

nulla'osta m inv permit

nul|lità f inv (persona) nonentity. ∼**lo** adj (Jur) null and void

nume'ra|bile adj countable. ∼**le** adj & m numeral

nume'ra|re vt number. ∼**zi'one** f numbering. **nu'merico** adj numerical

'numero m number; (romano, arabo) numeral; (di scarpe ecc) size; **dare i numeri** be off one's head. ∼ **cardinale** cardinal [number]. ∼ **decimale** decimal. ∼ **ordinale** ordinal [number]. ∼ **di telefono** phone number. ∼ **verde** Freephone®. **nume'roso** adj numerous

'nunzio m nuncio

nu'ocere vi ∼ **a** harm

nu'ora f daughter-in-law

nuo'ta|re vi swim; fig wallow. **nuo'to** m swimming. ∼**tore**, ∼**trice** mf swimmer

nu'ov|a f (notizia) news sg. ∼**a'mente** adv again. ∼**o** adj new; **di** ∼**o** again; **rimettere a** ∼**o** give a new lease of life to

nutri'ente adj nourishing. ∼**mento** m nourishment

nu'tri|re vt nourish; harbour (sentimenti). ∼**rsi** eat; ∼**rsi di** fig live on. ∼**tivo** adj nourishing. ∼**zi'one** f nutrition

'nuvola f cloud. **nuvo'loso** adj cloudy

nuzi'ale adj nuptial; (vestito, anello ecc) wedding attrib

n
o

Oo

o conj or; ∼ **l'uno** ∼ **l'altro** one or the other, either

O abbr (ovest) W

'oasi f inv oasis

obbedi'ente ecc = UBBIDIENTE ecc

obbli'ga|re vt force, oblige; ∼**rsi** vr ∼**rsi a** undertake to. ∼**to** adj obliged. ∼**torio** adj compulsory. ∼**zi'one** f obligation; (Comm) bond. **'obbligo** m obligation; (dovere) duty;

avere obblighi verso be under an obligation to; **d'obbligo** obligatory

obbligatoria'mente *adv* **fare qcsa ~** be obliged to do sth

ob'bro|brio *m* disgrace. **~'brioso** *adj* disgraceful

obe'lisco *m* obelisk

obe'rare *vt* overburden

obesità *f* obesity. **o'beso** *adj* obese

obiet'tare *vt/i* object; **~ su** object to

obiettivi'tà *f* objectivity. **obiet'tivo** *adj* objective ● *m* objective; (*scopo*) object

obie|t'tore *m* objector. **~t'tore di coscienza** conscientious objector. **~zi'one** *f* objection

obi'torio *m* mortuary

o'blio *m* oblivion

o'bliquo *adj* oblique; *fig* underhand

oblite'rare *vt* obliterate

oblò *m inv* porthole

'oboe *m* oboe

obso'leto *adj* obsolete

'oca *f* (*pl* **oche**) goose

occasio'nal|e *adj* occasional. **~'mente** *adv* occasionally

occasi'one *f* occasion; (*buon affare*) bargain; (*motivo*) cause; (*opportunità*) chance; **d'~** secondhand

occhi'aia *f* eye socket; **occhiaie** *pl* shadows under the eyes

occhi'ali *mpl* glasses, spectacles. **~ da sole** sunglasses. **~ da vista** glasses, spectacles

occhi'ata *f* look; **dare un'~** have a look at

occhieggi'are *vt* ogle ● *vi* peep

occhi'ello *m* buttonhole; (*asola*) eyelet

'occhio *m* eye; **~!** watch out!; **a quattr'occhi** in private; **tenere d'~** qcno keep an eye on sb; **a ~ [e croce]** roughly; **chiudere un'~** turn a blind eye; **dare nell'~** attract attention; **pagare o spendere un ~**

pay an arm and a leg. **~ nero** (*pesto*) black eye. **~ di pernice** (*callo*) corn. **~'lino** *m* **fare l'~lino a** qcno wink at sb

occiden'tale *adj* western ● *mf* westerner. **occi'dente** *m* west

oc'clu|dere *vt* obstruct. **~si'one** *f* occlusion

occor'ren|te *adj* necessary ● *m* the necessary. **~za** *f* need; **all'~za** if need be

oc'correre *vi* be necessary

occulta'mento *m* **~ di prove** concealment of evidence

occul't|are *vt* hide. **~ismo** *m* occult. **oc'culto** *adj* hidden; (*magico*) occult

occu'pante *mf* occupier; (*abusivo*) squatter

occu'pa|re *vt* occupy; spend (*tempo*); take up (*spazio*); (*dar lavoro a*) employ. **~rsi** *vr* occupy oneself; (*trovare lavoro*) find a job; **~rsi di** (*badare*) look after. **~to** *adj* engaged; (*persona*) busy; (*posto*) taken. **~zi'one** *f* occupation

o'ceano *m* ocean. **~ Atlantico** Atlantic [Ocean]. **~ Pacifico** Pacific [Ocean]

'ocra *f* ochre

ocu'lare *adj* ocular; (*testimone*, *bagno*) eye *attrib*

ocula'tezza *f* care. **ocu'lato** *adj* (*scelta*) wise

ocu'lista *mf* optician; (*per malattie*) ophthalmologist

od *conj* or

'ode *f* ode

odi'are *vt* hate

odi'erno *adj* of today; (*attuale*) present

'odi|o *m* hatred; **avere in ~o** hate. **~'oso** *adj* hateful

odo'ra|re *vt* smell; (*profumare*) perfume ● *vi* **~re di** smell of. **~to** *m* sense of smell. **o'dore** *m* smell; (*pro-*

fumo) scent; c'è odore di... there's a smell of...; **sentire odore di** smell; **odori** *pl* (*Culin*) herbs. **odo'roso** *adj* fragrant

of'fender|e *vt* offend; (*ferire*) injure. **~si** *vr* take offence

offen'siv|a *f* (*Mil*) offensive. **~o** *adj* offensive

offe'rente *mf* offerer; (*in aste*) bidder

of'fert|a *f* offer; (*donazione*) donation; (*Comm*) supply; (*nelle aste*) bid; **in ~a speciale** on special offer. **~o** *pp di* **offrire**

of'fes|a *f* offence. **~o** *pp di* **offendere** ● *adj* offended

offi'ciare *vt* officiate

offi'cina *f* workshop; **~** [**mecca-nica**] *garage*

of'frir|e *vt* offer. **~si** *vr* offer oneself; (*occasione:*) present itself; **~si di fare qcsa** offer to do sth

offu'scar|e *vt* darken; *fig* dull (*memoria, bellezza*); blur (*vista*). **~si** *vr* darken; *fig*: (*memoria, bellezza:*) fade away; (*vista:*) become blurred

of'talmico *adj* ophthalmic

oggettività *f* objectivity. **ogget-'tivo** *adj* objective

og'getto *m* object; (*argomento*) subject; **oggetti** *pl* **smarriti** lost property, lost and found *Am*

oggi *adv & m* today; (*al giorno d'oggi*) nowadays; **da ~ in poi** from today on; **~ a otto** a week today; **dall'~ al domani** overnight; **al giorno d'~** nowadays. **~gi'orno** *adv* nowadays

ogni *adj* any; (*qualsiasi*) any; **~ tre giorni** every three days; **ad ~ costo** at any cost; **ad ~ modo** anyway; **~ cosa** everything; **~ tanto** now and then; **~ volta che** whenever

o'gnuno *pron* everyone, everybody; **~ di voi** each of you

ola *f inv* Mexican wave

O'lan|da *f* Holland. **o~'dese** *adj*

Dutch ● *m* Dutchman; (*lingua*) Dutch ● *f* Dutchwoman

ole'andro *m* oleander

ole'at|o *adj* oiled; **carta ~a** grease-proof paper

oleo'dotto *m* oil pipeline. **ole'oso** *adj* oily

ol'fatto *m* sense of smell

oli'are *vt* oil

oli'era *f* cruet

olim'piadi *fpl* Olympic Games. **o'limpico** *adj* Olympic. **olim'pionico** *adj* (*primato, squadra*) Olympic

'olio *m* oil; **sott'~** in oil; **colori a ~** oils; **quadro a ~** oil painting. **~ di mais** corn oil. **~ d'oliva** olive oil. **~ di semi** vegetable oil. **~ solare** suntan oil

o'liv|a *f* olive. **oli'vastro** *adj* olive. **oli'veto** *m* olive grove. **~o** *m* olive tree

'olmo *m* elm

oltraggi'are *vt* offend. **ol'traggio** *m* offence

ol'tranza *f* **ad ~** to the bitter end

'oltre *adv* (*di luogo*) further; (*di tempo*) longer ● *prep* (*di luogo*) over; (*di tempo*) later than; (*più di*) more than; (*in aggiunta*) besides; **~ a** (*eccetto*) except, apart from; **per ~ due settimane** for more than two weeks. **~'mare** *adv* overseas. **~'modo** *adv* extremely

oltrepas'sare *vt* go beyond; (*eccedere*) exceed

o'maggio *m* homage; (*dono*) gift; **in ~ con** free with; **omaggi** *pl* (*saluti*) respects

ombeli'cale *adj* umbilical. **ombe-'lico** *m* navel

'ombr|a *f* (*zona*) shade; (*immagine oscura*) shadow; **all'~a** in the shade. **~eggi'are** *vt* shade

om'brello *m* umbrella. **ombrel-'lone** *m* beach umbrella

om'bretto *m* eye-shadow

om'broso *adj* shady

o

ome'lette f inv omelette

ome'lia f (Relig) sermon

omeopa'tia f homoeopathy. **omeo'patico** adj homoeopathic. **●m** homoeopath

omertà f conspiracy of silence

o'messo pp di omettere

o'mettere vt omit

OMG m abbr (organismo modificato geneticamente) GMO

omi'cid|a adj murderous. **●mf** murderer. **~io** m murder. **~io colposo** manslaughter

omissi'one f omission

omogeneiz'zato adj homogenized. **omo'geneo** adj homogeneous

omolo'gare vt approve

o'monimo, -a mf namesake. **●m** (parola) homonym

omosessu'al|e adj & mf homosexual. **~ità** f homosexuality

On. abbr (onorevole) MP

'oncia f ounce

'onda f wave; andare in ~ Radio go on the air. **onde** pl corte short wave. **onde** pl lunghe long wave. **onde** pl medie medium wave. **on'data** f wave

ondeggi'are vi wave; (barca:) roll

ondula|'torio adj undulating. **~zi'one** f undulation; (di capelli) wave

'oner|e m burden. **~'oso** adj onerous

onestà f honesty; (rettitudine) integrity. **o'nesto** adj honest; (giusto) just

'onice f onyx

onnipo'tente adj omnipotent

onnipre'sente adj ubiquitous; Rel omnipresent

ono'mastico m name-day

ono'ra|bile adj honourable. **~re** vt (fare onore a) be a credit to; honour (promessa). **~rio** adj honorary **●m** fee. **~rsi** vr **~rsi di** be proud of

o'nore m honour; in ~ di (festa, ri-

cevimento) in honour of; fare ~ a do justice to (pranzo); farsi ~ in excel in

ono'revole adj honourable. **●mf** Member of Parliament

onorifi'cenza f honour; (decorazione) decoration. **ono'rifico** adj honorary

O.N.U. f abbr (Organizzazione delle Nazioni Unite) UN

o'paco adj opaque; (colori ecc) dull; (fotografia, rossetto) matt

o'pale f opal

'opera f (lavoro) work; (azione) deed; (Mus) opera; (teatro) opera house; (ente) institution; mettere in ~ put into effect; mettersi all'~ get to work; opere pl pubbliche public works. **~ d'arte** work of art. **~ lirica** opera

ope'ra|io, -a adj working **●mf** worker; ~ **specializzato** skilled worker

ope'ra|re vt (Med) operate on; farsi **~re** have an operation **●vi** operate; (agire) work. **~'tivo, ~'torio** adj operating attrib. **~'tore, ~'trice** mf operator; (TV) cameraman. **~'tore turistico** tour operator. **~zi'one** f operation; (Comm) transaction

ope'retta f operetta

ope'roso adj industrious

opini'one f opinion. **~ pubblica** public opinion, vox pop

'oppio m opium

oppo'nente adj opposing **●mf** opponent

op'por|re vt oppose; (obiettare) object; **~re resistenza** offer resistance. **~si** vr **~si a** oppose

opportu'ni|smo m expediency. **~sta** mf opportunist. **~tà** f inv opportunity; (essere opportuno) timeliness. **oppor'tuno** adj opportune; (adeguato) appropriate; il momento opportuno the right moment

opposi'tore m opposer. **~zi'one** f

opposition; **d'~zione** (giornale, partito) opposition

op'posto pp di **opporre** ● adj opposite; (opinioni) opposing ● m opposite; **all'~** on the contrary

oppres|si'one f oppression. **~'sivo** adj oppressive. **op'presso** pp di **opprimere** ● adj oppressed. **~'sore** m oppressor

oppri'me|nte adj oppressive. **op-'primere** vt oppress; (gravare) weigh down

op'pure conj otherwise, or [else]; **lunedì ~ martedì** Monday or Tuesday

op'tare vi **~ per** opt for

opu'lento adj opulent

o'puscolo m booklet; (pubblicitario) brochure

opzio'nale adj optional. **opzi'one** f option

ora[1] f time; (unità) hour; **di buon'~** early; **che ~ è?, che ore sono?** what time is it?; **mezz'~** half an hour; **a ore** (lavorare, pagare) by the hour; **50 km all'~** 50 km an hour; **un'~ di macchina** one hour by car. **~ d'arrivo** arrival time. **l'~ esatta** (Teleph) speaking clock. **~ legale** daylight saving time. **~ di punta, ore** pl **di punta** peak time; (per il traffico) rush hour

ora[2] adv now; (tra poco) presently; **come ~** at the moment; **d'~ in poi** from now on; **per ~** for the time being, for now; **è ~ di finirla!** that's enough now! ● conj (dunque) now **che**; **~ che ci penso,...** now that I come to think about it,...

orafo m goldsmith

o'rale adj & m oral; **per via ~** by mouth

ora'mai adv = ORMAI

o'rario adj (tariffa) hourly; (segnale) time attrib; (velocità) per hour ● m time; (tabella dell'orario) timetable, schedule Am; **essere in ~** be on

time; **in senso ~** clockwise. **~ di chiusura** closing time. **~ flessibile** flexitime. **~ di sportello** banking hours. **~ d'ufficio** business hours. **~ di visita** (Med) consulting hours

o'rata f gilthead

ora'tore, -'trice mf speaker

ora'torio, -a adj oratorical ● m (Mus) oratorio ● f oratory. **orazi'one** f (Relig) prayer

'orbita f orbit; (Anat) [eye-]socket

or'chestra f orchestra; (parte del teatro) pit

orche'stra|le adj orchestral ● mf member of an/the orchestra. **~re** vt orchestrate

orchi'dea f orchid

'orco m ogre

'orda f horde

or'digno m device; (arnese) tool. **~ esplosivo** explosive device

ordi'nale adj & m ordinal

ordina'mento m order; (leggi) rules pl.

ordi'nanza f bylaw; **d'~** (soldato) on duty

ordi'nare vt (sistemare) arrange; (comandare) order; (prescrivere) prescribe; (Relig) ordain

ordi'nario adj ordinary; (grossolano) common; (professore) with tenure; **di ordinaria amministrazione** routine ● m ordinary; (Univ) professor

ordi'nato adj (in ordine) tidy

ordinazi'one f order; **fare un'~** place an order

'ordine m order; (di avvocati, medici) association; **mettere in ~** put in order; **di prim'~** first-class; **di terz'~e** (film, albergo) third- rate; **di ~ pratico/economico** of a practical/economic nature; **fino a nuovo ~** until further notice; **parola d'~** password. **~ del giorno** agenda. **ordini sacri** pl Holy Orders

or'dire vt (tramare) plot

orec'chino m ear-ring

o'recchi|o m (pl f **orecchie**) ear; avere ~o have a good ear; mi è giunto all'~o che... I've heard that...; ~'oni pl (Med) mumps sg

o'refice m jeweller. ~'ria f (arte) goldsmith's art; (negozio) goldsmith's [shop]

'orfano, -a adj orphan • mf orphan. ~'trofio m orphanage

orga'netto m barrel-organ; (a bocca) mouth-organ; (fisarmonica) accordion

or'ganico adj organic • m personnel

orga'nismo m organism; (corpo umano) body

orga'nista mf organist

organiz'za|re vt organize. ~rsi vr get organized. ~tore, ~'trice mf organizer. ~zi'one f organization

'organo m organ

or'gasmo m orgasm

'orgia f orgy

or'gogli|o m pride. ~'oso adj proud

orien'tale adj eastern; (cinese ecc) oriental

orienta'mento m orientation; perdere l'~ lose one's bearings; senso dell'~ sense of direction

orien'ta|re vt orientate. ~rsi vr find one's bearings; (tendere) tend

ori'ente m east. l'Estremo O~ the Far East. il Medio O~ the Middle East

o'rigano m oregano

origi'na|le adj original; (eccentrico) odd • m original. ~lità f originality. ~re vt/i originate. ~rio adj (nativo) native

o'rigine f origin; in ~ originally; aver ~ da originate from; dare ~ a give rise to

o'rina f urine. ori'nale m chamber-pot. ori'nare vi urinate

ori'undo adj native

oriz'zontale adj horizontal

orizzon'tare vt = ORIENTARE. oriz'zonte m horizon

or'la|re vt hem. ~'tura f hem. 'orlo m edge; (di vestito ecc) hem

'orma f track; (di piede) footprint; (impronta) mark

or'mai adv by now; (passato) by then; (quasi) almost

ormeggi'are vt moor

ormo'nale adj hormonal. or'mone m hormone

ornamen'tale adj ornamental. orna'mento m ornament

or'na|re vt decorate. ~rsi vr deck oneself. ~to adj (stile) ornate

ornitolo'gia f ornithology

'oro m gold; d'~ gold; fig golden

orologi'aio, -a mf clockmaker, watchmaker

oro'logio m watch; (da tavolo, muro ecc) clock. ~ a pendolo grandfather clock. ~ da polso wrist-watch. ~ a sveglia alarm clock

o'roscopo m horoscope

or'rendo adj awful, dreadful

or'ribile adj horrible

orripi'lante adj horrifying

or'rore m horror; avere qcsa in ~ hate sth

orsacchi'otto m teddy bear

'orso m bear; (persona scontrosa) hermit. ~ bianco polar bear

or'taggio m vegetable

or'tensia f hydrangea

or'tica f nettle

orticol'tura f horticulture. 'orto m vegetable plot

orto'dosso adj orthodox

ortogo'nale adj perpendicular

orto|gra'fia f spelling. ~'grafico adj spelling attrib

ortolano | ottanta

orto'lano *m* market gardener; (*negozio*) greengrocer's

orto|pe'dia *f* orthopaedics *sg*. ∼'pedico *adj* orthopaedic ● *m* orthopaedist

or'zaiolo *m* sty

or'zata *f* barley-water

o'sare *vt/i* dare; (*avere audacia*) be daring

osce'nità *f inv* obscenity. o'sceno *adj* obscene

oscil'lare *vi* swing; (*prezzi ecc*:) fluctuate; *Tech* oscillate; (*fig: essere indeciso*) vacillate. ∼zi'one *f* swinging; (*di prezzi*) fluctuation; *Tech* oscillation

oscura'mento *m* darkening; (*di vista, mente*) dimming; (*totale*) black-out

oscu'r|are *vt* darken; *fig* obscure. ∼arsi *vr* get dark. ∼ità *f* darkness. o'scuro *adj* dark; (*triste*) gloomy; (*incomprensibile*) obscure

spe'dal|e *m* hospital. ∼i'ero *adj* hospital *attrib*

spi'tale *adj* hospitable. ∼lità *f* hospitality. ∼re *vt* give hospitality to. 'ospite *m* (*chi ospita*) host; (*chi viene ospitato*) guest ● *f* hostess; guest

o'spizio *m* [old people's] home

ossa'tura *f* bone structure; (*di romanzo*) structure, framework. 'osseo *adj* bone *attrib*

ossequi'are *vt* pay one's respects to. os'sequio *m* homage; ossequi *pl* respects. ∼'oso *adj* obsequious

osser'van|te *adj* (*cattolico*) practising. ∼za *f* observance

osser'va|re *vt* observe; (*notare*) notice; keep (*ordine, silenzio*). ∼'tore, ∼'trice *mf* observer. ∼'torio *m* (*Astr*) observatory; (*Mil*) observation post. ∼zi'one *f* observation; (*rimprovero*) reproach

osses'sio'na|nte *adj* haunting; (*persona*) nagging. ∼re *vt* obsess; (*infastidire*) nag. ossessi'one *f* obses-

sion. osses'sivo *adj* obsessive. os-'sesso *adj* obsessed

os'sia *conj* that is

ossi'dabile *adj* liable to tarnish

ossi'dar|e *vt*, ∼si *vr* oxidize

'ossido *m* oxide. ∼ di carbonio carbon monoxide

os'sidrico *adj* fiamma ossidrica blowlamp

ossige'nar|e *vt* oxygenate; (*decolorare*) bleach; *fig* put back on its feet (*azienda*). ∼si *vr* ∼si i capelli day one's hair blonde. os'sigeno *m* oxygen

'osso *m* ((*Anat*): *pl f* ossa) bone; (*di frutto*) stone

osso'buco *m* marrowbone

os'suto *adj* bony

osta'cola|re *vt* hinder, obstruct. o'stacolo *m* obstacle; *Sport* hurdle

o'staggio *m* hostage; prendere in ∼ take hostage

o'stello *m* ∼ della gioventù youth hostel

osten'ta|re *vt* show off; ∼re indifferenza pretend to be indifferent. ∼zi'one *f* ostentation

oste'ria *f inn*

o'stetrico, -a *adj* obstetric ● *mf* obstetrician

'ostia *f* host; (*cialda*) wafer

'ostico *adj* tough

o'stil|e *adj* hostile. ∼ità *f inv* hostility

osti'na|rsi *vr* persist (a in). ∼to *adj* obstinate. ∼zi'one *f* obstinacy

'ostrica *f* oyster

ostru'|ire *vt* obstruct. ∼zi'one *f* obstruction

otorinolaringoi'atra *mf* ear, nose and throat specialist

ottago'nale *adj* octagonal. ot'tagono *m* octagon

ot'tan|ta *adj* & *m* eighty. ∼'tenne

adj & mf eighty-year-old. ~'tesimo adj eightieth. ~'tina f about eighty

ot'tav|a f octave. ~o adj eighth

otte'nere vt obtain; (più comune) get; (conseguire) achieve

'ottico, -a adj optic[al] ● mf optician ● f (scienza) optics sg; (di lenti ecc) optics pl

otti'ma|le adj optimum. ~'mente adv very well

otti'mis|mo m optimism. ~ta mf optimist. ~tico adj optimistic

'ottimo adj very good ● m optimum

'otto adj & m eight

ot'tobre m October

otto'cento adj & m eight hundred; l'O~ the nineteenth century

ot'tone m brass

ottu'ra|re vt block; fill (dente). ~rsi vr clog. ~tore m (Phot) shutter. ~zi'one f stopping; (di dente) filling

ot'tuso pp di ottundere ● adj obtuse

o'vaia f ovary

o'vale adj & m oval

o'vatta f cotton wool

ovazi'one f ovation

over'dose f inv overdose

'ovest m west

o'vi|le m sheep-fold. ~no adj sheep attrib

ovo'via f two-seater cable car

ovulazi'one f ovulation

o'vunque adv = DOVUNQUE

ov'vero conj or; (cioè) that is

ovvia'mente adv obviously

ovvi'are vi ~ a qcsa counter sth. 'ovvio adj obvious

ozi'are vi laze around. 'ozio m idleness. ozi'oso adj idle; (questione) pointless

o'zono m ozone; buco nell'~ hole in the ozone layer

Pp

pa'ca|re vt quieten. ~to adj quiet

pac'chetto m packet; (postale) parcel, package; (di sigarette) pack, packet. ~ software software package

'pacchia f ① bed of roses

pacchi'ano adj garish

'pacco m parcel; (involto) bundle. ~ regalo gift-wrapped package

paccot'tiglia f junk, rubbish

'pace f peace; darsi ~ forget it; fare ~ con qcno make it up with sb; lasciare in ~ qcno leave sb in peace

pachi'stano, -a mf & adj Pakistani

pacifi'ca|re vt reconcile; (mettere pace) pacify. ~zi'one f reconciliation

pa'cifico adj pacific; (calmo) peaceful; il P~ the Pacific

paci'fis|mo m pacifism. ~ta mf pacifist

pa'dano adj pianura padana Po Valley

pa'del|la f frying-pan; (per malati) bedpan

padigli'one m pavilion

'padr|e m father; ~i pl (antenati) forefathers. pa'drino m godfather. ~e'nostro m il ~enostro the Lord's Prayer. ~e'terno m God Almighty

padro'nanza f mastery. ~ di sé self-control

pa'drone, -a mf master; mistress; (datore di lavoro) boss; (proprietario) owner. ~ggi'are vt master

pae'saggio m scenery; (pittura) landscape. ~gista mf landscape architect

pae'sano, -a adj country ● mf villager

pa'ese m (*nazione*) country; (*territorio*) land; (*villaggio*) village; **il Bel P~** Italy; **va' a quel ~!** get lost!; **Paesi** pl **Bassi** Netherlands

paf'futo adj plump

paga f pay, wages pl

pa'gabile adj payable

pa'gaia f paddle

paga'mento m payment; **a ~** (*parcheggio*) which you have to pay to use. **~ anticipato** (*Comm*) advance payment. **~ alla consegna** cash on delivery, COD

pa'gano, -a adj & mf pagan

pa'gare vt/i pay; **~ da bere a qcno** buy sb a drink

pa'gella f [school] report

pagina f page. **Pagine** pl **Gialle®** Yellow Pages. **~ web** (*Comput*) web page

paglia f straw

pagliac'cetto m (*per bambini*) rompers pl

pagliac'ciata f farce

pagli'accio m clown

pagli'aio m haystack

paglie'riccio m straw mattress

pagli'etta f (*cappello*) boater; (*per pentole*) steel wool

pagli'uzza f wisp of straw; (*di metallo*) particle

pa'gnotta f [round] loaf

pail'lette f inv sequin

paio m (pl *paia* f *pala*) pair; **un ~** (*circa due*) a couple; **un ~ di** (*scarpe, forbici*) a pair of

pakistan m Pakistan

pakistano m Pakistani

pala f shovel; (*di remo, elica*) blade; (*di ruota*) paddle

pala'fitta f pile-dwelling

pala'sport m inv indoor sports arena

pa'late fpl **a ~** (*fare soldi*) hand over fist

pa'lato m palate

palaz'zetto m **~ dello sport** indoor sports arena

palaz'zina f villa

pa'lazzo m palace; (*edificio*) building. **~ delle esposizioni** exhibition centre. **~ di giustizia** law courts pl, courthouse. **~ dello sport** indoor sports arena

'palco m (*pedana*) platform; (*Theat*) box. **~'[scenico]** m stage

pale'sar|e vt disclose. **~si** vr reveal oneself. **pa'lese** adj evident

Pale'sti|na f Palestine. **~nese** mf Palestinian

pa'lestra f gymnasium, gym; (*ginnastica*) gymnastics pl

pa'letta f spade; (*per focolare*) shovel. **~ [della spazzatura]** dustpan

pa'letto m peg

'palio m (*premio*) prize. **il P~** horse-race held at Siena

paliz'zata f fence

'palla f ball; (*proiettile*) bullet; (🔲: *bugia*) porkie; **che palle!** 🔲 this is a pain in the arse!. **~ di neve** snowball. **~ al piede** fig millstone round one's neck

pallaca'nestro f basketball

palla'mano f handball

pallanu'oto f water polo

palla'volo f volley-ball

palleg'giare vi (*calcio*) practise ball control; *Tennis* knock up

pallia'tivo m palliative

'pallido adj pale

pal'lina f (*di vetro*) marble

pal'lino m **avere il ~ del calcio** be crazy about football

pallon'cino m balloon; (*lanterna*) Chinese lantern; (🔲: *etilometro*) Breathalyzer®

pal'lone m ball; (*calcio*) football; (*aerostato*) balloon

pal'lore m pallor

pal'loso adj 🔲 boring

pal'lottola f pellet; (proiettile) bullet

'palm|a f (Bot) palm. ~o m (Anat) palm; (misura) hand's-breadth; restare con un ~o di naso feel disappointed

pal'mare m palmtop

'palo m pole; (di sostegno) stake; (in calcio) goalpost; fare il ~ (ladro:) keep a lookout. ~ della luce lamppost

palom'baro m diver

pal'pare vt feel

'palpebra f eyelid

palpi'ta|re vi throb; (fremere) quiver. ~zi'one f palpitation. 'palpito m throb; (del cuore) beat

pa'lude f marsh, swamp

palu'doso adj marshy

pa'lustre adj marshy; (piante, uccelli) marsh attrib

'pampino m vine leaf

'panca f bench; (in chiesa) pew

pancar'rè m sliced bread

pan'cetta f (Culin) bacon; (di una certa età) paunch

pan'chetto m [foot]stool

pan'china f garden seat; (in calcio) bench

'pancia f belly; mal di ~ stomachache; metter su ~ develop a paunch; a ~ in giù lying face down

panci'olle: stare in ~ lounge about

panci'one m (persona) pot belly

panci'otto m waistcoat

pande'monio m pandemonium

pan'doro m sponge cake eaten at Christmas

'pane m bread; (pagnotta) loaf; (di burro) block. ~ a cassetta sliced bread. pan grattato breadcrumbs pl. ~ di segale rye bread. pan di Spagna sponge cake. ~ tostato toast

panet'te|ria f bakery; (negozio) baker's [shop]. ~i'ere, -a mf baker

panet'tone m kind of Christmas cake

'panfilo m yacht

pan'forte m nougat-like delicacy from Siena

'panico m panic; lasciarsi prendere dal ~ panic

pani'ere m basket; (cesta) hamper

pani'ficio m bakery; (negozio) baker's [shop]

pa'nino m [bread] roll. ~ imbottito filled roll. ~ al prosciutto ham roll. ~'teca f sandwich bar

'panna f cream. ~ da cucina [single] cream. ~ montata whipped cream

'panne f (Mech) in ~ broken down; restare in ~ break down

pan'nello m panel. ~ solare solar panel

'panno m cloth; panni pl (abiti) clothes

pan'nocchia f (di granoturco) cob

panno'lino m (per bambini) nappy; (da donna) sanitary towel

pano'ram|a m panorama; fig overview. ~ico adj panoramic

pantacol'lant mpl leggings

pantalon'cini mpl ~ [corti] short

panta'loni mpl trousers, pants Am

pan'tano m bog

pan'tera f panther; (auto della polizia) high-speed police car

pan'tofo|la f slipper

pan'zana f fib

pao'nazzo adj purple

'papa m Pope

papà m inv dad[dy]

pa'pale adj papal

papa'lina f skull-cap

papa'razzo m paparazzo

pa'pato m papacy

pa'pavero m poppy

'paper|a f (errore) slip of the tongue. ~o m gosling

papil'lon m inv bow tie

pa'piro m papyrus

'pappa f (per bambini) pap

pappa'gallo m parrot

pappa'molle mf wimp

'para f suole fpl di ~ crêpe soles

pa'rabola f parable; (curva) parabola. ~ satellitare satellite dish

para'bolico adj parabolic

para'brezza m inv windscreen, windshield Am

paracadu'tar|e vt parachute. ~ si vr parachute

paraca'du|te m inv parachute. ~ 'tista mf parachutist

para'carro m roadside post

paradi'siaco adj heavenly

para'diso m paradise. ~ terrestre Eden, earthly paradise

parados'sale adj paradoxical. pa-ra'dosso m paradox

para'fango m mudguard

paraf'fina f paraffin

parafra'sare vt paraphrase

para'fulmine m lightning-conductor

pa'raggi mpl neighbourhood sg

parago'na|bile adj comparable (a to). ~ re vt compare. para'gone m comparison; a paragone di in comparison with

pa'ragrafo m paragraph

pa'ra|lisi f inv paralysis. ~ 'litico, -a adj & mf paralytic. ~ liz'zare vt paralyse

paral'lel|a f parallel line. ~ a'mente adv in parallel. ~ o agg & m parallel; ~ e pl parallel bars. ~ o'gramma m parallelogram

para'lume m lampshade

para'medico m paramedic

pa'rametro m parameter

para'noia f paranoia

parao'cchi mpl blinkers. parao'recchie mpl earmuffs

Paralim'piadi fpl Paralympic Games

para'petto m parapet

para'piglia m turmoil

para'plegico, -a adj & mf paraplegic

pa'rar|e vt (addobbare) adorn; (riparare) shield; save (tiro, pallone); ward off, parry (schiaffo, pugno) ● vi (mirare) lead up to. ~ si vr (abbigliarsi) dress up; (da pioggia, pugni) protect oneself; ~ si dinanzi a qcno appear in front of sb

para'sole m inv parasol

paras'sita adj parasitic ● m parasite

parasta'tale adj government-controlled

pa'rata f parade; (in calcio) save; (in scherma, pugilato) parry

para'urti m inv (Auto) bumper, fender Am

para'vento m screen

par'cella f bill

parcheggi'a|re vt park. par'cheg-gio m parking; (posteggio) carpark, parking lot Am. ~ 'tore, ~ 'trice mf parking attendant. ~ tore abusivo person extorting money for guarding cars

par'chimetro m parking-meter

'parco¹ adj sparing; (moderato) moderate

'parco² m park. ~ a tema theme park. ~ di divertimenti fun-fair. ~ giochi playground. ~ naturale wildlife park. ~ nazionale national park. ~ regionale [regional] wildlife park

pa'recchi adj a good many ● pron several

pa'recchio adj quite a lot of ● pron quite a lot ● adv rather; (parecchio tempo) quite a time

pareggi'are vt level; (eguagliare) equal; (Comm) balance ● vi draw

pa'reggio m (Comm) balance; Sport draw

paren'tado m relatives pl; (vincolo di sangue) relationship

pa'rente mf relative. ~ stretto

close relation

paren'tela f relatives pl; (vincolo di sangue) relationship

pa'rentesi f inv parenthesis; (segno grafico) bracket; (fig: pausa) break. ∼ pl graffe curly brackets. ∼ quadre square brackets. ∼ tonde round brackets

pa'reo m sarong

pa'rere[1] m opinion; a mio ∼ in my opinion

pa'rere[2] vi seem; (pensare) think; che te ne pare? what do you think of it?; pare di sì it seems so

pa'rete f wall; (in alpinismo) face. ∼ divisoria partition wall

'pari adj inv equal; (numero) even; andare di ∼ passo keep pace; arrivare ∼ draw; (copiare, ripetere) word for word ● mf inv equal; ragazza alla ∼ au pair [girl] ● m (titolo nobiliare) peer

Pa'rigi f Paris

pa'riglia f pair

pari'tà f equality; Tennis deuce. ∼tario adj parity attrib

parlamen'tare adj parliamentary ● mf Member of Parliament ● vi discuss. **parla'mento** m Parliament. il Parlamento europeo the European Parliament

par'la|re vt/i speak, talk; (confessare) talk; ∼ bene/male di qcno speak well/ill of somebody; non parliamone più let's forget about it; non se ne parla nemmeno! don't even mention it!. ∼to adj (lingua) spoken. ∼torio m parlour; (in prigione) visiting room

parlot'tare vi mutter. **parlot'tio** m muttering

parmigi'ano m Parmesan

paro'dia f parody

pa'rola f word; (facoltà) speech; parole pl (di canzone) words, lyrics; rivolgere la ∼ a address; dare a qcno la propria ∼ give sb one's

word; in parole povere crudely speaking. parole pl incrociate crossword [puzzle] sg. ∼ d'ordine password. paro'laccia f swear-word

par'quet m inv (pavimento) parquet flooring

par'rocchi|a f parish. ∼'ale adj parish attrib; ∼'ano, -a mf parishioner. 'parr'oco m parish priest

par'rucca f wig

parrucchi'ere, -a mf hairdresser

parruc'chino m toupée, hairpiece

parsi'moni|a f thrift

'parso pp di parere

'parte f part; (lato) side; (partito) party; (porzione) share; a ∼ apart from; in ∼ in part; la maggior ∼ di of; d'altra ∼ on the other hand; da ∼ aside; (in disparte) to one side; farsi da ∼ stand aside; da ∼ di from; (per conto di) on behalf of; è gentile da ∼ tua it is kind of you; fare una brutta ∼ a qcno behave badly towards sb; da che ∼ è...? whereabouts is...?; da una ∼..., dall'altra... on the one hand..., on the other hand...; dall'altra ∼ di on the other side of; da nessuna ∼ nowhere; da questa ∼ (in questa direzione) this way; da un anno a questa ∼ for about a year now; essere dalla ∼ di qcno be on sb's side; essere in ∼ in causa be involved; prendere ∼ a take part in. ∼ civile plaintiff

parteci'pante mf participant

parteci'pa|re vi ∼re a participate in, take part in; (condividere) share in. ∼zi'one f participation; (annuncio) announcement; Fin shareholding; (presenza) presence. **par'tecipe** adj participating

parteggi'are vi ∼ per side with

par'tenza f departure; Sport start; in ∼ per leaving for

parti'cella f particle

parti'cipio m participle

partico'lar|e adj particular; (*privato*) private ● m detail, particular; **fin nei minimi ~i** down to the smallest detail. **~eggi'ato** adj detailed. **~ità** f inv particularity; (*dettaglio*) detail

partigi'ano, -a adj & mf partisan

par'tire vi leave; (*aver inizio*) start; **a ~ da** [beginning] from

par'tita f game; (*incontro*) match; (*Comm*) lot; (*contabilità*) entry. **~ di calcio** football match. **~ a carte** game of cards

par'tito m party; (*scelta*) choice; (*occasione di matrimonio*) match

'parto m childbirth; **un ~ facile** an easy birth o labour; **dolori** pl **del ~** labour pains. **~ cesareo** Caesarian section. **~rire** vt give birth to

par'venza f appearance

parzi'al|e adj partial. **~ità** f partiality. **~'mente** adv (*non completamente*) partially; **~'mente scremato** semi-skimmed

pasco'lare vt graze. **'pascolo** m pasture

'Pasqua f Easter. **pa'squale** adj Easter attrib

'passa: **e ~** adv (*e oltre*) plus

pas'sabile adj passable

pas'saggio m passage; (*traversata*) crossing; *Sport* pass; (*su veicolo*) lift; **essere di ~** be passing through. **~ a livello** level crossing, grade crossing *Am*. **~ pedonale** pedestrian crossing

pas'sante mf passer-by ● m (*di cintura*) loop ● adj *Tennis* passing

passa'porto m passport

pas'sa|re vi pass; (*attraversare*) pass through; (*far visita*) call; (*andare*) go; (*essere approvato*) be passed; **~re alla storia** go down in history; **mi è ~to di mente** it slipped my mind; **~re per un genio/idiota** be taken for a genius/an idiot ● vt (*far scorrere*) pass over; (*sopportare*) go through; (*al tele-*

fono) put through; (*Culin*) strain; **~re di moda** go out of fashion; **le passo il signor Rossi** I'll put you through to Mr Rossi; **~rsela bene** be well off; **come te la passi?** how are you doing?. **~ta** f (*di vernice*) coat; (*spolverata*) dusting; (*occhiata*) look

passa'tempo m pastime

pas'sato adj past; **l'anno ~** last year; **sono le tre passate** it's past o after three o'clock ● m past; (*Culin*) purée; (*Gram*) past tense. **~ prossimo** (*Gram*) present perfect. **~ remoto** (*Gram*) [simple] past. **~ di verdure** cream of vegetable soup

passa'verdure m inv food mill

passeg'gero, -a adj passing ● mf passenger

passeggi'a|re vi walk, stroll. **~ta** f walk, stroll; (*luogo*) public walk; (*in bicicletta*) ride; **fare una ~ta** go for a walk

passeg'gino m pushchair, stroller *Am*

pas'seggio m walk; (*luogo*) promenade; **andare a ~** go for a walk; **scarpe da ~** walking shoes

passe-partout m inv master-key

passe'rella f gangway; (*Aeron*) boarding bridge; (*per sfilate*) catwalk

'passero m sparrow. **passe'rotto** m (*passero*) sparrow

pas'sibile adj **~ di** liable to

passio'nale adj passionate. **passi'one** f passion

pas'sivo adj passive ● m passive; (*Comm*) liabilities pl; **in ~** (*bilancio*) loss-making

pass magnetico m inv swipe card

'passo m step; (*orma*) footprint; (*andatura*) pace; (*brano*) passage; (*valico*) pass; **a due passi da qui** a stone's throw away; **a ~ d'uomo** at walking pace; **fare due passi** go for a stroll; **di pari ~** fig hand in hand. **~ carrabile**, **~ carraio** driveway

'past|a f (impasto per pane ecc) dough; (per dolci, pasticcini) pastry; (pastasciutta) pasta; (massa molle) paste; fig nature. ~a **frolla** shortcrust pastry. **pa'stella** f batter

Pasta A popular myth says that Marco Polo brought pasta back from China. Italians like to make their own pasta for special occasions (pasta fatta in casa), usually with eggs and sometimes with various fillings. Traditional pasta varies enormously from region to region, and sometimes the same name can be used for different types.

pastasci'utta f pasta
pa'stello m pastel
pa'sticca f pastille; (🔲: pastiglia) pill
pasticc|e'ria f cake shop, patisserie; (pasticcini) pastries pl; (arte) confectionery
pasticci'are vi make a mess ● vt make a mess of
pasticci'ere, -a mf confectioner
pastic'cino m little cake
pa'sticci|o m (Culin) pie; (lavoro disordinato) mess. ~'one, -a m f bungler ● adj bungling
pasti'ficio m pasta factory
pa'stiglia f (Med) pill, tablet; (di menta) sweet. ~ **dei freni** brake pad
'pasto m meal
pasto'rale adj pastoral. **pa'store** m shepherd; (Relig) pastor. **pastore tedesco** German shepherd
pastoriz'za|re vt pasteurize. ~zi'one f pasteurization
pa'stoso adj doughy; fig mellow
pa'stura f pasture; (per pesci) bait
pa'tacca f (macchia) stain; (fig: oggetto senza valore) piece of junk
pa'tata f potato. **patate pl fritte** chips Br, French fries. **pata'tine** fpl [potato] crisps, chips Am

pata'trac m inv (crollo) crash
pâté m inv pâté
pa'tella f limpet
pa'tema m anxiety
pa'tente f licence. ~ **di guida** driving licence
pater'na|le f scolding. ~'lista m paternalist
paternità f paternity. **pa'terno** adj paternal; (affetto ecc) fatherly
pa'tetico adj pathetic. **'pathos** m pathos
pa'tibolo m gallows sg
'patina f patina; (sulla lingua) coating
pa'ti|re vt/i suffer. ~to, -a adj suffering ● mf fanatic. ~to **della musica** music lover
patolo'gia f pathology. **pato'lo-gico** adj pathological
'patria f native land
patri'arca m patriarch
pa'trigno m stepfather
patrimoni'ale adj property attrib. **patri'monio** m estate
patri'o|ta mf patriot
pa'trizio, -a adj & mf patrician
patro|ci'nare vt support. ~'cinio m support
patro'nato m patronage. **pa'trono** m (Relig) patron saint; (Jur) counsel
'patta¹ f (di tasca) flap
'patta² f (pareggio) draw
patteggia'mento m bargaining. ~'are vt/i negotiate
patti'naggio m skating. ~ **su ghiaccio** ice skating. ~ **a rotelle** roller skating
patti'na|re vi skate; (auto:) skid. ~'tore, ~'trice mf skater. **'pattino** m skate; (Aeron) skid. **pattino da ghiaccio** iceskate. **pattino a rotelle** roller skate; **pattini mpl in linea** roller blades®.
'patto m deal; (Pol) pact; **a ~ che** on condition that

pat'tuglia f patrol. ~ **stradale** patrol car; highway patrol

pattu'ire vt negotiate

pattumi'era f dustbin, trashcan Am

pa'ura f fear; (spavento) fright; aver ~ be afraid; mettere ~ a frighten. pau'roso adj (che fa paura) frightening; (che ha paura) fearful; (❏: enorme) awesome

'pausa f pause; (nel lavoro) break; fare una ~ pause; (nel lavoro) have a break

pavimen'ta|re vt pave (strada). ~zi'one f (operazione) paving. pavi'mento m floor

pa'vone m peacock

pazien'tare vi be patient

pazi'ente adj & mf patient. ~'mente adv patiently. pazi'enza f patience

'pazza f madwoman. ~'mente adv madly

paz'z|esco adj foolish; (esagerato) crazy. ~ia f madness; (azione) [act of] folly. 'pazzo adj mad; fig crazy ● m madman; essere pazzo di/per be crazy about; darsi alla pazza gioia live it up. paz'zoide adj whacky

'pecca f fault; senza ~ flawless. peccami'noso adj sinful

pec'ca|re vi sin; ~re di be guilty of (ingratitudine). ~to m sin; ~to che... it's a pity that...; [che] ~to! [what a] pity!. ~tore, ~'trice mf sinner

'pece f pitch

peco|ra f sheep. ~ra nera black sheep. ~'raio m shepherd. ~'rella f cielo a ~relle sky full of fluffy white clouds. ~'rino m (formaggio) sheep's milk cheese

peculi'ar|e adj ~ di peculiar to. ~ità f inv peculiarity

pe'daggio m toll

pedago'gia f pedagogy. peda'gogico adj pedagogical

peda'lare vi pedal. pe'dale m pedal. pedalò m inv pedalo

pe'dana f footrest; Sport springboard

pe'dante adj pedantic. ~'ria f pedantry. pedan'tesco adj pedantic

pe'data f (in calcio) kick; (impronta) footprint

pede'rasta m pederast

pe'destre adj pedestrian

pedi'atra mf paediatrician. pedia'tria f paediatrics sg

pedi'cure mf inv chiropodist, podiatrist Am ● m pedicure

pedi'gree m inv pedigree

pe'dina f (nella dama) piece; fig pawn. ~'mento m shadowing. pedi'nare vt shadow

pe'dofilo, -a mf paedophile

pedo'nale adj pedestrian. pe'done, -a mf pedestrian

peeling m inv exfoliation treatment

'peggio adv worse; ~ per te! too bad!; la persona ~ vestita the worst dressed person ● adj worse; niente di ~ nothing worse ● m il ~ è che... the worst of it is that...; pensare al ~ think the worst ● f alla ~ at worst; avere la ~ get the worst of it; alla meno ~ as best I can

peggiora'mento m worsening

peggio'ra|re vt make worse, worsen ● vi get worse. ~'tivo adj pejorative

peggi'ore adj worse; (superlativo) worst ● adj mf il/la ~ the worst

'pegno m pledge; (nei giochi di società) forfeit; fig token

pelan'drone m slob

pe'la|re vt (spennare) pluck; (spellare) skin; (sbucciare) peel; (❏: spillare denaro) fleece. ~rsi vr (❏: lose one's hair. ~to adj bald. ~ti mpl (pomodori) peeled tomatoes

pel'lame m skins pl

p

'**pelle** f skin; (cuoio) leather; (buccia) peel; avere la ~ d'oca have goose-flesh

pellegri'naggio m pilgrimage. **pelle'grino, -a** mf pilgrim.

pelle'rossa mf Red Indian

pellette'ria f leather goods pl

pelli'cano m pelican

pellicce'ria f furrier's [shop]. **pel-'licc'ia** f fur; (indumento) fur coat. ~i'aio, -a mf furrier

pel'licola f film. ~ (trasparente) cling film

'**pelo** m hair; (di animale) coat; (di lana) pile; per un ~ by the skin of one's teeth. **pe'loso** adj hairy

'**peltro** m pewter

pe'luche m: giocattolo di ~ soft toy

pe'luria f down

'**pelvico** adj pelvic

'**pena** f (punizione) punishment; (sofferenza) pain; (dispiacere) sorrow; (disturbo) trouble; a mala ~ hardly; mi fa ~ I pity him; vale la ~ andare it is worth [while] going. ~ di morte death sentence

pe'nale adj criminal; diritto m ~e criminal law. ~**ità** f inv penalty

penaliz'za're vt penalize. ~**zi'one** f (penalità) penalty

pe'nare vi suffer; (faticare) find it difficult

pen'daglio m pendant

pen'dant m inv fare ~ [con] match

pen'den|te adj hanging; (Comm) outstanding ● m (ciondolo) pendant; ~ti pl drop earrings. ~**za** f slope; (Comm) outstanding account

'**pendere** vi hang; (superficie:) slope; (essere inclinato) lean

pen'dio m slope; in ~ sloping

pendo'llare adj pendulum ● m f commuter. ~**ino** m (treno) special, first class only, fast train

'**pendolo** m pendulum

'**pene** m penis

pene'trante adj penetrating; (freddo) biting

pene'tra|re vt/i penetrate; (trafiggere) pierce ● vt (odore:) get into ● vi (entrare furtivamente) steal in. ~**zi'one** f penetration

penicil'lina f penicillin

pe'nisola f peninsula

peni'ten|te adj & mf penitent. ~**za** f penitence; (in gioco) forfeit. ~**zi'ario** m penitentiary

'**penna** f pen; (di uccello) feather. ~ a feltro felt-tip[ped pen]. ~ a sfera ball-point [pen]

pen'nacchio m plume

penna'rello m felt-tip[ped pen]

pennel'la|re vt paint. ~**ta** f brushstroke. **pen'nello** m brush; a pennello (alla perfezione) perfectly

pen'nino m nib

pen'none m flagpole

pen'nuto adj feathered

pe'nombra f half-light

pe'noso adj (🔲: pessimo) painful

pen'sa|re vi think; penso di sì I think so; ~e a think of; remember to (chiudere il gas ecc); ci penso io I'll take care of it; ~re la pensi qcsa think of doing sth; ~re tra sé e sé think to oneself ● vt think. ~**ta** f idea

pensi'e|ro m thought; (mente) mind; (preoccupazione) worry; stare in ~ro per be anxious about. ~**roso** adj pensive

'**pensi|le** adj hanging; giardino ~le roof-garden ● m (mobile) wall unit. ~**lina** f bus shelter

pensio'nante mf boarder; (ospite pagante) lodger

pensio'nato, -a mf pensioner ● m (per anziani) [old folks'] home; (per studenti) hostel. **pensi'one** f pension; (albergo) boarding-house; (vitto e alloggio) board and lodging; andare in

pensione retire; **mezza pensione** half board. **pensione completa** full board

pen'soso adj pensive

pen'tagono m pentagon

Pente'coste f Whitsun

penti'tirsi vr ~rsi di repent of; (rammaricarsi) regret. ~'tismo m turning informant. ~to m Mafioso turned informant

pentola f saucepan; (contenuto) potful. ~ **a pressione** pressure cooker

pe'nultimo adj penultimate

pe'nuria f shortage

penzo'l|are vi dangle. ~oni adv dangling

pe'pa|re vt pepper. ~to adj peppery

pepe m pepper; **grano di** ~ peppercorn. ~ **in grani** whole peppercorns. ~ **macinato** ground pepper

pepero'n|ata f peppers cooked in olive oil with onion, tomato and garlic. ~'cino m chilli pepper. **pepe'rone** m pepper. **peperone verde** green pepper

pe'pita f nugget

per prep for; (attraverso) through; (stato in luogo) in, on; (distributivo) per; (mezzo, entro) by; (causa) with; (in qualità di) as; ~ **strada** on the street; ~ **la fine del mese** by the end of the month; **in fila** ~ **due** in double file; **l'ho sentito** ~ **telefono** I spoke to him on the phone; ~ **iscritto** in writing; ~ **caso** by chance; **ho aspettato** ~ **ore** I've been waiting for hours; ~ **tempo** in time; ~ **sempre** forever; ~ **scherzo** as a joke; **gridare** ~ **il dolore** scream with pain; **vendere** ~ **10 milioni** sell for 10 million; **uno** ~ **volta** one at a time; **uno** ~ **uno** one by one; **venti** ~ **cento** twenty per cent; ~ **fare qcsa** [in order to] do sth; **stare** ~ be about to

pera f pear; **farsi una** ~ (🅧: di eroina) shoot up

per'cento adv per cent. **percen'tu'ale** f percentage

perce'pibile adj perceivable; (somma) payable

perce'pi|re vt perceive; (riscuotere) cash

perce|t'tibile adj perceptible. ~zi'one f perception

perché conj (in interrogazioni) why; (per il fatto che) because; (affinché) so that; ~ **non vieni?** why don't you come?; **dimmi** ~ tell me why; ~ **no/sì** because!; **la ragione** ~ **l'ho fatto** the reason [that] I did it, the reason why I did it; **è troppo difficile** ~ **lo possa capire** it's too difficult for me to understand ●m inv reason [why]; **senza un** ~ without any reason

perciò conj so

per'correre vt cover (distanza); (viaggiare) travel. **per'corso** pp di **percorrere** ●m (distanza) distance; (viaggio) journey

per'coss|a f blow. ~o pp di **percuotere**. **percu'otere** vt strike

percussi'o|ne f percussion; **strumenti** pl **a** ~**ne** percussion instruments. ~'nista mf percussionist

per'dente mf loser

'**perder|e** vt lose; (sprecare) waste; (non prendere) miss; fig: ruin (vizio): ~e **tempo** waste time ●vi lose; (recipiente): leak; **lascia** ~el forget it!. ~si vr get lost; (reciproco) lose touch

perdi'giorno mf inv idler

'**perdita** f loss; (spreco) waste; (falla) leak; **a** ~ **d'occhio** as far as the eye can see. ~ **di tempo** waste of time. **perdi'tempo** m time-waster

perdo'nare vt forgive; (scusare) excuse. **per'dono** m forgiveness; (Jur) pardon

perdu'rare vi last; (perseverare) persist

perduta'mente adv hopelessly. **per'duto** pp di **perdere** ●adj lost; (rovinato) ruined

pe'renne adj everlasting; (Bot) perennial. ~'mente adv perpetually

peren'torio adj peremptory

per'fetto adj perfect ● m (Gram) perfect [tense]

perfezio'nar|e vt perfect; (migliorare) improve. ~**si** vr improve oneself; (specializzarsi) specialize

perfezi'o|ne f perfection; **alla ~ne** to perfection. ~**nista** mf perfectionist

per'fidia f wickedness; (atto) wicked act. **'perfido** adj treacherous; (malvagio) perverse

per'fino adv even

perfo'ra|re vt pierce; punch (schede); (Mech) drill. ~**'tore,** ~**'trice** mf punch-card operator ● m perforator. ~**zi'one** f perforation; (di schede) punching

per'formance f inv performance

perga'mena f parchment

perico'lante adj precarious; (azienda) shaky

pe'rico|lo m danger; (rischio) risk; **mettere in ~lo** endanger. ~**loso** adj dangerous

perife'ria f periphery; (di città) outskirts pl, fig fringes pl

peri'feric|a f peripheral; (strada) ring road. ~**o** adj (quartiere) outlying

pe'rifrasi f inv circumlocution

pe'rimetro m perimeter

peri'odico adj periodical ● adj periodical; (vento, mal di testa) (Math) recurring. **pe'riodo** m period; (Gram) sentence. **periodo di prova** trial period

peripe'zie fpl misadventures

pe'rire vi perish

pe'ri|to, -a adj skilled ● mf expert

perito'nite f peritonitis

pe'rizia f skill; (valutazione) survey

'perla f pearl. **per'lina** f bead

perlo'meno adv at least

perlu'stra|re vt patrol. ~**zi'one** f patrol; **andare in ~zione** go on patrol

perma'loso adj touchy

perma'ne|nte adj permanent ● f perm; **farsi [fare] la ~nte** have a perm. ~**nza** f permanence; (soggiorno) stay; **in ~nza** permanently. ~**re** vi remain

perme'are vt permeate

per'messo pp di **permettere** ● m permission; (autorizzazione) permit; (Mil) leave; [**è**] **~?** (posso entrare?) may I come in?; (posso passare?) excuse me. **~ di lavoro** work permit

per'mettere vt allow, permit; **potersi ~** qcsa (finanziariamente) afford sth; **come si permette?** how dare you?

permutazi'one f exchange; (Math) permutation

per'nic|e f partridge. ~**i'oso** adj pernicious

'perno m pivot

pernot'tare vi stay overnight

'pero m pear-tree

però conj but; (tuttavia) however

pero'rare vt plead

perpendico'lare adj & f perpendicular

perpe'trare vt perpetrate

perpetu'are vt perpetuate. **per'petuo** adj perpetual

perplessità f inv perplexity; (dubbio) doubt. **per'plesso** adj perplexed

perqui'si|re vt search. ~**zi'one** f search. ~**zione domiciliare** search of the premises

persecu'tore, -'trice mf persecutor. ~**zi'one** f persecution

persegu'ire vt pursue

persegui'tare vt persecute

perseve'ra|nza f perseverance. ~**re** vi persevere

persi'ano, -a adj Persian ● f (di finestra) shutter. **'persico** adj Persian

per'sino adv = PERFINO

persi'sten|te *adj* persistent. **~za** *f* persistence. **per'sistere** *vi* persist

'perso *pp di* perdere ●*adj* lost; **a tempo ~** in one's spare time

per'sona *f* person; (*un tale*) somebody; **di ~, in ~** in person, personally; **per ~** per person, a head; **per interposta ~** through an intermediary; **persone** *pl* people

perso'naggio *m* personality; (*Theat*) character

perso'nal|e *adj* personal ●*m* staff. **~e di terra** ground crew. **~ità** *f inv* personality. **~iz'zare** *vt* customize (auto ecc); personalize (penna ecc)

personifi'ca|re *vt* personify. **~zi'one** *f* personification

perspi'cace *adj* shrewd

persua'dere *vt* convince; impress (critici); **~dere qcno a fare qcsa** persuade sb to do sth. **~si'one** *f* persuasion. **~sivo** *adj* persuasive. **persu'aso** *pp di* persuadere

per'tanto *conj* therefore

'pertica *f* pole

perti'nente *adj* relevant

per'tosse *f* whooping cough

pertur'ba|re *vt* perturb. **~rsi** *vr* be perturbed. **~zi'one** *f* disturbance. **~zione atmosferica** atmospheric disturbance

per'va|dere *vt* pervade. **~so** *pp di* pervadere

perve'nire *vi* reach; **far ~ qcsa a qcno** send sth to sb

pervers|i'one *f* perversion. **~ità** *f* perversity. **per'verso** *adj* perverse

perver'ti|re *vt* pervert. **~to** *adj* perverted ●*m* pervert

per'vinca *f* (*colore*) blue with a touch of purple

p.es. *abbr* (*per esempio*) e.g.

pesa *f* weighing; (*bilancia*) weighing machine; (*per veicoli*) weighbridge

pe'sante *adj* heavy; (*stomaco*) overfull ●*adv* (*vestirsi*) warmly. **~'mente** *adv* (*cadere*) heavily. **pesan'tezza** *f* heaviness

pe'sar|e *vt/i* weigh; **~e su** *fig* lie heavy on; **~e le parole** weigh one's words. **~si** *vr* weigh oneself

'pesca¹ *f* (*frutto*) peach

'pesca² *f* fishing; **andare a ~** go fishing. **~ subacquea** underwater fishing. **pe'scare** *vt* fish for; (*prendere*) catch; (*fig: trovare*) fish out. **~'tore** *m* fisherman

'pesce *m* fish. **~ d'aprile!** April Fool!. **~ grosso** *fig* big fish. **~ piccolo** *fig* small fry. **~ rosso** goldfish. **~ spada** swordfish. **Pesci** *pl* (*Astr*) Pisces

pesce'cane *m* shark

pesche'reccio *m* fishing boat

pesc|he'ria *f* fishmonger's [shop]. **~hi'era** *f* fish-pond. **~i'vendolo** *m* fishmonger

'pesco *m* peach-tree

'peso *m* weight; **essere di ~ per qcno** be a burden to sb; **di poco ~** (*senza importanza*) not very important

pessi'mis|mo *m* pessimism. **~ta** *mf* pessimist ●*adj* pessimistic. **'pessimo** *adj* very bad

pe'staggio *m* beating-up. **pe'stare** *vt* tread on; (*schiacciare*) crush; (*pigiare*) beat; crush (aglio, prezzemolo)

'peste *f* plague; (*persona*) pest

pe'stello *m* pestle

pesti'cida *m* pesticide

pesti'len|za *f* pestilence; (*fetore*) stench. **~zi'ale** *adj* noxious

'pesto *adj* ground; **occhio ~** black eye ●*m* basil and garlic sauce

'petalo *m* petal

pe'tardo *m* banger

petizi'one *f* petition; **fare una ~** draw up a petition

petro'li|era *f* (*oil*) tanker. **~lifero** *adj* oil-bearing. **pe'trolio** *m* oil

pettego'lare *vi* gossip. **~'lezzo** *m* piece of gossip; **far ~lezzi** gossip

pet'tegolo, -a *adj* gossipy ●*mf*

P

gossip

petti'na|re vt comb. **~rsi** vr comb one's hair. **~'tura** f combing; (acconciatura) hair-style. **'pettine** m comb

'petting m petting

petti'nino m (fermaglio) comb

petti'rosso m robin

'petto m chest; (seno) breast; a doppio ~ double-breasted

petto'rale m (in gare sportive) number. **~rina** f (di salopette) bib. **~ruto** adj (donna) full-breasted; (uomo) broad-chested

petu'lante adj impertinent

'pezza f cloth; (toppa) patch; (rotolo di tessuto) roll

pez'zente mf tramp; (avaro) miser

'pezzo m piece; (parte) part; un ~ (di tempo) some time; (di spazio) a long way; al ~ (costare) each; fare a pezzi tear to shreds. ~ grosso bigwig

pia'cente adj attractive

---

pia'ce|re

● m pleasure; (favore) favour; a ~re as much as one likes; per ~re! please!; ~re [di conoscerla]! pleased to meet you!; con ~re with pleasure

● vi la Scozia mi piace I like Scotland; mi piacciono i dolci I like sweets; ti piace? do you like it?; faccio come mi pare e piace I do as I please; lo spettacolo è piaciuto the show was a success.

Nota che il soggetto in italiano corrisponde al complemento oggetto in inglese, mentre il complemento indiretto in italiano corrisponde al soggetto in inglese: Non mi piace I don't like it

---

pia'vole adj pleasant

piaci'mento m a ~ as much as you like

pia'dina f unleavened bread

pi'aga f sore; scourge; (persona noiosa) pain; (fig: ricordo doloroso) wound

piagni'steo m whining

piagnuco'lare vi whimper

pi'alla f plane. **pial'lare** vt plane

pi'ana f plane. **pianeggi'ante** adj level

piane'rottolo m landing

pia'neta m planet

pi'angere vi cry; (disperatamente) weep ● vt (lamentare) lament; (per un lutto) mourn

pianifi'ca|re vt plan. **~zi'one** f planning

pia'nista mf (Mus) pianist

pi'ano adj flat; (a livello) flush; (regolare) smooth; (facile) easy ● adv slowly; (con cautela) gently; andarci ~ go carefully ● m plain; (di edificio) floor; (livello) plane; (progetto) plan; (Mus) piano; di primo ~ first-rate; primo ~ (Phot) close-up; in primo ~ in the foreground. ~ regolatore town plan. ~ di studi syllabus

piano'forte m piano. ~ a coda grand piano

piano'terra m inv ground floor

pi'anta f plant; (del piede) sole; (disegno) plan; di sana ~ (totalmente) entirely; in ~ stabile permanently. ~ stradale road map. ~gl'one f plantation

pian'tar|e vt plant; (conficcare) drive; (🔲: abbandonare) dump; **piantala!** 🔲 stop it!. **~si** vr plant oneself; (🔲: lasciarsi) leave each other

pianter'reno m ground floor

pi'anto pp di piangere ● m crying; (disperato) weeping; (lacrime) tears pl

pian|to'nare vt guard. **~'tone** m guard

pia'nura f plain

p'iastra f plate; (*lastra*) slab; (*Culin*) griddle. ~ **madre** (*Comput*) motherboard

pia'strella f tile

pia'strina f (*Mil*) identity disc; (*Med*) platelet; (*Comput*) chip

piatta'forma f platform. ~ **di lancio** launch pad

piat'tino m saucer

pi'atto adj flat ● m plate; (*da portata, vivanda*) dish; (*portata*) course; (*parte piatta*) flat; (*di giradischi*) turntable; **piatti** pl (*Mus*) cymbals; **lavare i piatti** do the washing-up; ~ **fondo** soup plate. ~ **piano** [ordinary] plate

pi'azza f square; (*Comm*) market; **letto a una** ~ single bed; **letto a due piazze** double bed; **far** ~ **pulita** make a clean sweep. ~ **forte** m stronghold. **piaz'zale** m large square. ~ **'mento** m (*in classifica*) placing

piaz'za|re vt place. ~**rsi** vr Sport be placed; ~**rsi secondo** come second. ~**to** adj (*cavallo*) placed; **ben** ~ **to** (*robusto*) well built

piaz'zista m salesman

piaz'zuola f ~ **di sosta** pull-in

pic'cante adj hot; (*pungente*) sharp; (*salace*) spicy

pic'carsi vr (*risentirsi*) take offence; ~ **di** (*vantarsi di*) claim to

'picche fpl (*in carte*) spades

picchet'tare vt stake; (*scioperanti:*) picket. **pic'chetto** m picket

picchi'a|re vt beat, hit ● vi (*bussare*) knock; (*Aeron*) nosedive; ~**re in testa** (*motore:*) knock. ~**ta** f beating; (*Aeron*) nosedive; **scendere in** ~**ta** nosedive

picchiet'tare vt tap; (*punteggiare*) spot

'picchio m woodpecker

pic'cino adj tiny; (*gretto*) mean; (*di poca importanza*) petty ● m little one, child

picci'one m pigeon

'picco m peak; **a** ~ vertically; **colare a** ~ sink

'piccolo, -a adj small, little; (*di età*) young; (*di statura*) short; (*gretto*) petty ● mf child; **da** ~ as a child

pic'cone m pickaxe. ~**zza** f ice axe

pic'nic m inv picnic

pi'docchio m louse

piè m inv **a** ~ **di pagina** at the foot of the page; **saltare a** ~ **pari** skip

pi'ede m foot; **a piedi** on foot; **andare a piedi** walk; **a piedi nudi** barefoot; **in** ~ free; **in piedi** standing; **alzarsi in piedi** stand up; **ai piedi di** (*montagna*) at the foot of; **prendere** ~ **fig** gain ground; (*moda:*) catch on; **mettere in piedi** (*allestire*) set up

piedi'stallo m pedestal

pi'ega f (*piegatura*) fold; (*di gonna*) pleat; (*di pantaloni*) crease; (*grinza*) wrinkle; (*andamento*) turn; **non fare una** ~ (*ragionamento:*) be flawless

pie'ga|re vt fold; (*flettere*) bend ● vi bend. ~**rsi** vr bend. ~**rsi** a fig yield to. ~**'tura** f folding

pieghet'ta|re vt pleat. ~**to** adj pleated. **pie'ghevole** adj pliable; (*tavolo*) folding ● m leaflet

piemon'tese adj Piedmontese

pi'en|a f (*di fiume*) flood; (*folla*) crowd. ~**o** adj full; (*massiccio*) solid; **in** ~**a estate** in the middle of summer; **a** ~**i voti** (*diplomarsi*) ≈ with A-grades, with first class honours ● m (*colmo*) height; (*carico*) full load; **in** ~**o** (*completamente*) fully; **fare il** ~**o** (*di benzina*) fill up

pie'none m **c'era il** ~ the place was packed

'piercing m inv body piercing

pietà f pity; (*misericordia*) mercy; **senza** ~ (*persona*) pitiless; (*spietatamente*) pitilessly; **avere** ~ **di qcno** take pity on sb; **far** ~ (*far pena*) be pitiful

pie'tanza f dish

pie'toso adj pitiful, merciful; (~pessimo~) terrible

pi'etra f stone. ~a dura semi-precious stone. ~a preziosa precious stone. ~a dello scandalo cause of the scandal. **pie'trame** m stones pl. ~ifi'care vt petrify. pie'trina f flint. **pie'troso** adj stony

pigi'ama m pyjamas pl

'pigia 'pigia m inv crowd, crush. **pigi'are** vt press

pigi'one f rent; dare a ~ let, rent out; prendere a ~ rent

pigli'are vt (□: afferrare) catch. **'piglio** m air

pig'mento m pigment

'pigna f cone

pi'gnolo adj pedantic

pigo'lare vi chirp. **pigo'lio** m chirping

pi'grizia f laziness. **'pigro** adj lazy; (intelletto) slow

'pila f pile; (Electr) battery; (□: lampadina tascabile) torch; (vasca) basin; a pile battery powered

pi'lastro m pillar

'pillola f pill; prendere la ~ be on the pill

pi'lone m pylon; (di ponte) pier

pi'lota mf pilot ● m (Auto) driver. **pi'lotare** vt pilot; drive (auto)

pinaco'teca f art gallery

pi'neta f pine-wood

ping-'pong m table tennis, ping-pong □

'pingue adj fat. ~'edine f fatness

pingu'ino m penguin; (gelato) choc ice on a stick

'pinna f fin; (per nuotare) flipper

'pino m pine[-tree]; ~ marittimo cluster pine. **pi'nolo** m pine kernel

'pinta f pint

'pinza f pliers pl; (Med) forceps pl

pin'za|re vt (con pinzatrice) staple. ~'trice f stapler

pin'zette fpl tweezers pl

pinzi'monio m sauce for crudités

'pio adj pious; (benefico) charitable

pi'oggia f rain; (fig: di pietre, insulti) hail, shower; sotto la ~ in the rain. ~ acida acid rain

pi'olo m (di scala) rung

piom'ba|re vi fall heavily; ~re su fall upon ● vt fill (dente). ~'tura f (di dente) filling. **piom'bino** m (sigillo) [lead] seal; (da pesca) sinker; (in gonne) weight

pi'ombo m lead; (sigillo) [lead] seal; a ~ plumb; senza ~ (benzina) lead-free

pioni'ere, -a mf pioneer

pi'oppo m poplar

pio'vano adj acqua piovana rainwater

pi'ove|re vi rain; ~e it's raining; ~iggi'nare vi drizzle. **pio'voso** adj rainy

'pipa f pipe

pipì f fare [la] ~ pee

pipi'strello m bat

pi'ramide f pyramid

pi'ranha m inv piranha

pi'ra|ta m pirate. ~a della strada road-hog ● adj inv pirate. ~e'ria f piracy

piro'fil|a f (tegame) oven-proof dish. ~o adj heat-resistant

pi'romane mf pyromaniac

pi'roscafo m steamer. ~ di linea liner

pi'scina f swimming pool. ~ coperta indoor swimming pool. ~ scoperta outdoor swimming pool

pi'sello m pea; (□: pene) willie

piso'lino m nap; fare un ~ have a nap

'pista f track; (Aeron) runway; (orma) footprint; (sci) slope, piste. ~ d'atterraggio airstrip. ~ da ballo dance floor. ~ ciclabile cycle track

pi'stacchio m pistachio

pi'stola f pistol; (*per spruzzare*) spray-gun. ∼ **a spruzzo** paint spray

pi'stone m piston

pi'tone m python

pit'to|re, -'trice mf painter. ∼'**resco** adj picturesque. **pit'torico** adj pictorial

pit'tu|ra f painting. ∼'**rare** vt paint

---

più

● adv more; (*superlativo*) most

Il comparativo e il superlativo di aggettivi di una sillaba che terminano in -y si formano con i suffissi -er e -est: più breve shorter il più giovane the youngest

∼ **importante** more important; **il** ∼ **importante** the most important; ∼ **caro** more expensive; **il** ∼ **caro** the most expensive; **di** ∼ more; **una coperta in** ∼ an extra blanket; **non ho** ∼ **soldi** I don't have any more money; **non vive** ∼ **a Milano** he doesn't live in Milan any longer; ∼ **o meno** more or less; **il** ∼ **lentamente possibile** as slowly as possible; **per di** ∼ what's more; **mai** ∼**!** never again!; ∼ **di** more than; **sempre** ∼ more and more; (*Math*) plus

● adj more; (*superlativo*) most; ∼ **tempo** more time; **la classe con** ∼ **alunni** the class with most pupils; ∼ **volte** several times

● m most; (*Math*) plus sign; **il** ∼ **è fatto** the worst is over; **parlare del** ∼ **e del meno** make small talk; **i** ∼ the majority

---

piuccheper'fetto m pluperfect

pi'uma f feather. **piu'maggio** m plumage. **piu'mino** m (*di cigni*) down; (*copriletto*) eiderdown; (*per cipria*) powder-puff; (*per spolverare*) feather duster; (*giacca*) down jacket. **piu-'mone**® m duvet

piut'tosto adv rather; (*invece*) instead

pi'vello m 🔲 greenhorn

'pizza f pizza; *Cinema* reel.

pizza'iola f slices of beef in tomato sauce, oregano and anchovies

pizze'ria f pizza restaurant

pizzi'c|are vt pinch; (*pungere*) sting; (*di sapore*) taste sharp; (🔲: *sorprendere*) catch; (*Mus*) pluck ● vi scratch; (*cibo*:) be spicy '**pizzico** m, ∼**otto** m pinch

'pizzo m lace; (*di montagna*) peak

pla'car|e vt placate; assuage (*fame, dolore*). ∼**si** vr calm down

'placca f plate; (*commemorativa, dentale*) plaque; (*Med*) patch

plac'ca|re vt plate. ∼**to** adj ∼**to d'argento** silver-plated. ∼**to d'oro** gold-plated. ∼**tura** f plating

pla'centa f placenta

'placido adj placid

plagi'are vt plagiarize; pressure (*persona*). '**plagio** m plagiarism

plaid m inv tartan rug

pla'nare vi glide

'plancia f (*Naut*) bridge; (*passerella*) gangplank

pla'smare vt mould

'plastic|a f (*arte*) plastic art; (*Med*) plastic surgery; (*materia*) plastic. ∼**o** adj plastic ● m plastic model

'platano m plane[-tree]

pla'tea f stalls pl; (*pubblico*) audience

'platino m platinum

plau'sibil|e adj plausible. ∼**ità** f plausibility

ple'baglia f pej mob

pleni'lunio m full moon

'plettro m plectrum

pleu'rite f pleurisy

'plico m packet; **in** ∼ **a parte** under separate cover

plissé adj inv plissé; (gonna) accordeon-pleated

plo'tone m platoon; (di ciclisti) group. ~ d'esecuzione firing-squad

plumbeo adj leaden

plu'ral|e adj & m plural; al ~e in the plural. ~ità f majority

pluridiscipli'nare adj multidisciplinary

plurien'nale adj ~ esperienza many years' experience

pluripar'titico adj (Pol) multi-party

plu'tonio m plutonium

pluvi'ale adj rain attrib

pneu'matico adj pneumatic ● m tyre

pneu'monia f pneumonia

po' ▷POCO

po'chette f inv clutch bag

po'chino m un ~ a little bit

'poco

● adj little; (tempo) short; (con nomi plurali) few

● adv (con verbi) not much; (con avverbi) not very; parla ~ he doesn't speak much; lo conosco ~ I don't know him very well

poco + aggettivo spesso si traduce con un aggettivo specifico: ~ probabile unlikely, ~ profondo shallow

● pron little; (poco tempo) a short time; (plurale) few

● m little; un po' a little [bit]; un po' di a little; some; a ~ a ~ little by little; fra ~ soon; per ~ (a poco prezzo) cheap; (quasi) nearly; ~ fa a little while ago; sono arrivato da ~ I have just arrived; un bel po' quite a lot

---

po'dere m farm

pode'roso adj powerful

'podio m dais; (Mus) podium

po'dis|mo m walking. ~ta mf walker

po'e|ma m poem. ~'sia f poetry; (componimento) poem. ~ta m poet. ~'tessa f poetess. ~tico adj poetic

poggiapi'edi m inv footrest

poggi'a|re vt lean; (posare) place ● vi ~re su be based on. ~testa m inv head-rest

poggi'olo m balcony

poi adv (dopo) then; (più tardi) later [on]; (finalmente) finally. d'ora in ~ from now on; questa ~! well!

poiché conj since

pois m inv a ~ polka-dot

'poker m poker

po'lacco, -a adj Polish ● mf Pole ● m (lingua) Polish

po'lar|e adj polar. ~iz'zare vt polarize

'polca f polka

po'lemi|ca f controversy. ~ca-'mente adv controversially. ~co adj controversial. ~z'zare vi engage in controversy

po'lenta f cornmeal porridge

poli'clinico m general hospital

poli'estere m polyester

polio[mie'lite] f polio[myelitis]

'polipo m polyp

polisti'rolo m polystyrene

poli'tecnico m polytechnic

po'litic|a f politics sg; (linea di condotta) policy; fare ~a be in politics. ~iz'zare vt politicize. ~o, -a adj political ● mf politician

poliva'lente adj catch-all

poli'zi|a f police. ~a giudiziaria ≈ Criminal Investigation Department. ~a stradale traffic police. ~'esco adj police attrib; (romanzo, film) detective attrib. ~'otto m policeman 'po**lizza** f policy

pol'la**io** m chicken run; (🔲: *luogo chiassoso*) mad house. ~**me** m poultry. ~**strello** m spring chicken. ~**stro** m cockerel

'pollice m thumb; (*unità di misura*) inch

pol'line m pollen; allergia al ~ hay fever

polli'vendolo, -a *mf* poulterer

'pollo m chicken; (🔲: *sempliciotto*) simpleton

polmo|'nare *adj* pulmonary. pol-'mone m lung. ~'nite f pneumonia

'polo m pole; Sport polo; (*maglietta*) polo top. ~ nord North Pole. ~ sud South Pole

Po'lonia f Poland

'polpa f pulp

pol'paccio m calf

polpa'strello m fingertip

pol'pet|ta f meatball. ~'tone m meat loaf

'polpo m octopus

pol'sino m cuff

'polso m pulse; (*Anat*) wrist; *fig* authority; avere ~ be strict

pol'tiglia f mush

pol'trire *vi* lie around

pol'tron|a f armchair; (*Theat*) seat in the stalls. ~e *adj* lazy

'polve|re f dust; (*sostanza polverizzata*) powder; in ~re powdered; sapone in ~re soap powder. ~'rina f (*medicina*) powder. ~'riz'zare *vt* pulverize; (*nebulizzare*) atomize. ~'rone m cloud of dust. ~'roso *adj* dusty

po'mata f ointment, cream

po'mello m knob; (*guancia*) cheek

pomeridi'ano *adj* afternoon *attrib*; alle tre pomeridiane at three in the afternoon. pome'riggio m afternoon

'pomice f pumice

'pomo m (*oggetto*) knob. ~ d'Adamo Adam's apple

pomo'doro m tomato

'pompa f pump; (*sfarzo*) pomp. pompe (*pl funebri*) (*funzione*) funeral. pom'pare *vt* pump; (*gonfiare d'aria*) pump up; (*fig: esagerare*) exaggerate; pompare fuori pump out

pom'pelmo m grapefruit

pompi'ere m fireman; i pompieri the fire brigade

pom'poso *adj* pompous

ponde'rare *vt* ponder

po'nente m west

'ponte m bridge; (*Naut*) deck; (*impalcatura*) scaffolding; fare il ~ make a long weekend of it

pon'tefice m pontiff

pontifi'ca|re *vi* pontificate. ~to m pontificate

ponti'ficio *adj* papal

pon'tile m jetty

popò *f inv* 🔲 pooh

popo'lano *adj* of the people

popo'la|re *adj* popular; (*comune*) common ● *vt* populate. ~rsi *vr* get crowded. ~rità f popularity. ~zi'one f population. 'popolo m people. popo'loso *adj* populous

'poppa f (*Naut*) stern; (*mammella*) breast; a ~ astern

pop'pa|re *vt* suck. ~ta f (*pasto*) feed. ~toio m [feeding-]bottle

popu'lista *mf* populist

por'cata f load of rubbish; porcate *pl* (🔲: *cibo*) junk food

porcel'lana f porcelain

porcel'lino m piglet. ~ d'India guinea-pig

porche'ria f dirt; (*cosa orrenda*) piece of filth; (*robaccia*) rubbish

por'ci|le m pigsty. ~no *adj* pig *attrib* ● m (*fungo*) edible mushroom. 'porco m pig; (*carne*) pork

'porgere *vt* give; (*offrire*) offer; porgo distinti saluti (*in lettera*) I remain, yours sincerely

porno|gra'fia f pornography. ~'grafico *adj* pornographic

'poro m pore. **po'roso** adj porous

'porpora f purple

'por|re vt put; (collocare) place; (supporre) suppose; ask (domanda); present (candidatura); poniamo il caso che... let us suppose that...; ~re fine o termine a put an end to. ~si vr put oneself; ~si a sedere sit down; ~si in cammino set out

'porro m (Bot) leek; (verruca) wart

'porta f door; Sport goal; (di città) gate; (Comput) port. ~ a ~ door-to-door; mettere alla ~ show sb the door. ~ di servizio tradesmen's entrance

porta'bagagli m inv porter; (di treno ecc) luggage rack; (Auto) boot, trunk Am; (sul tetto di un'auto) roof rack

porta'bottiglie m inv bottle rack, wine rack

porta'cenere m inv ashtray

portachi'avi m inv keyring

porta'cipria m inv compact

portadocu'menti m inv document wallet

porta'erei f inv aircraft carrier

portafi'nestra f French window

porta'foglio m wallet; (per documenti) portfolio; (ministero) ministry

portafor'tuna m inv lucky charm ● adj inv lucky

portagi'oie m inv jewellery box

por'tale m door

porta'matite m inv pencil case

porta'mento m carriage; (condotta) behaviour

porta'mina m inv propelling pencil

portamo'nete m inv purse

portaom'brelli m inv umbrella stand

porta'pacchi m inv roof rack; (su bicicletta) luggage rack

porta'penne m inv pencil case

por'ta|re vt (verso chi parla) bring; (lontano da chi parla) take; (sorreggere) (Math) carry; (condurre) lead; (indossare) wear; (avere) bear. ~**rsi** vr (trasferirsi) move; (comportarsi) behave; ~**rsi bene/male** gli anni look young/old for one's age

portari'viste m inv magazine rack

porta'sci m inv ski rack

portasiga'rette m inv cigarette-case

por'ta|ta f (di pranzo) course; (Auto) carrying capacity; (di arma) range; (fig: abilità) capability; a ~**ta di mano** within reach. **por'tatile** agg & m portable. ~**to** adj (indumento) worn; (dotato) gifted; essere ~**to per qcsa** have a gift for sth; essere ~**to a** (tendere a) be inclined to. ~**tore, ~trice** mf bearer; al ~**tore** to the bearer. ~**tore di handicap** disabled person

portatovagli'olo m napkin ring

portau'ovo m inv egg-cup

porta'voce m inv spokesman ●f inv spokeswoman

por'tento m marvel; (persona dotata) prodigy

'portico m portico

porti'er|a f door; (tendaggio) door curtain. ~**e** m porter, doorman; Sport goalkeeper. ~**e di notte** night porter

porti'n|aio, -a mf caretaker. ~**e'ria** f concierge's room; (di ospedale) porter's lodge

'porto pp di porgere ● m harbour; (complesso) port; (vino) port [wine]; (spesa di trasporto) carriage; andare in ~ succeed. ~ **d'armi** gun licence

Porto'gallo m Portugal. p~**hese** adj & mf Portuguese

por'tone m main door

portu'ale m docker

porzi'one f portion

'posa f laying; (riposo) rest; (Phot) exposure; (atteggiamento) pose; mettersi in ~ pose

po'sa|re vt put; (giù) put [down] ● vi (poggiare) rest; (per un ritratto) pose.

~rsi vr alight; (*sostare*) rest; (*Aeron*) land. **~ta** f piece of cutlery; (*~te* pl cutlery sg. **~to** sed sedate

po'scritto m postscript

posi'tivo adj positive

posizio'nare vt position

posizi'one f position; farsi una ~ get ahead

posolo'gia f dosage

po'sporre vt place after; (*posticipare*) postpone. **~sto** pp di posporre

posse'dere vt possess, own. **~i'mento** m possession

posses'sivo adj possessive. **posses'sore** m ownership; (*bene*) possession. **~sore** m owner

pos'sibil|e adj possible; il più presto ~e as soon as possible ●m fare [tutto] il ~e do one's best. **~ità** f inv possibility; (*occasione*) chance ●fpl (*mezzi*) means

possi'dente mf land-owner

'posta f post, mail; (*ufficio postale*) post office; (*al gioco*) stake; spese di ~ postage; per ~ by post, by mail; a bella ~ on purpose; **Poste e Telecomunicazioni** pl [Italian] Post Office. **~ elettronica** e-mail. **~ prioritaria** ≈ first-class mail. **~ vocale** voice-mail

posta'giro m postal giro

po'stale adj postal

postazi'one f position

postda'tare vt postdate (*assegno*)

posteggi'a|re vt/i park. **~tore**, **~trice** mf parking attendant. **po'steggio** m car-park, parking lot Am; (*di taxi*) taxi-rank

'posteri mpl descendants. **~ore** adj rear; (*nel tempo*) later **~tà** f posterity

po'sticcio adj artificial; (*baffi, barba*) false ●m hair-piece

postici'pare vt postpone

po'stilla f note; (*Jur*) rider

po'stino m postman, mailman Am

'posto pp di porre ●m place; (*spazio*)

---

poscritto | pralinato

room; (*impiego*) job; (*Mil*) post; (*sedile*) seat; a/fuori ~ in/out of place; prendere ~ take up room; sul ~ on-site; essere a ~ (*casa, libri*) be tidy; fare ~ a make room for; al ~ di (*invece di*) in place of, instead of. **~ di blocco** checkpoint. **~ di guida** driving seat. **~ di lavoro** workstation. **posti** pl in piedi standing room. **~ di polizia** police station

post-'partum adj post-natal

'postumo adj posthumous ●m after-effect

po'tabile adj drinkable; acqua ~ drinking water

po'tare vt prune

po'tassio m potassium

po'ten|te adj powerful; (*efficace*) potent. **~za** f power; (*efficacia*) potency. **~zi'ale** adj & m potential

po'tere m power; al ~ in power ●vi can, be able to; posso entrare? may I come in?; posso fare qualche cosa? can I do something?; che tu possa essere felice! may you be happy!; non ne posso più (*sono stanco*) I can't go on; (*sono stufo*) I can't take any more; può darsi perhaps; può darsi che sia vero perhaps it's true; potrebbe aver ragione he could be right, he might be right; avresti potuto telefonare you could have phoned, you might have phoned; spero di poter venire I hope to be able to come

potestà f inv power

'pover|o, -a adj poor; (*semplice*) plain ●m poor man ●f poor woman; i ~i the poor. **~tà** f poverty

'pozza f pool. **poz'zanghera** f puddle

'pozzo m well; (*minerario*) pit. **~ petrolifero** oil-well

PP.TT. abbr (Poste e Telegrafi) [Italian] Post Office

prali'nato adj (*mandorla, gelato*)

praline-coated

pram'matica *f* essere di ~ be customary

pran'zare *vi* dine; *(a mezzogiorno)* lunch. **'pranzo** *m* dinner; *(a mezzogiorno)* lunch. **pranzo di nozze** wedding breakfast

Pranzo *Pranzo* is traditionally the day's main meal and school timetables and hours of business are geared to a break between one and four o'clock. It starts with a *primo* (usually pasta), followed by a *secondo* (main course). Gradually Italians, especially city-dwellers, are adopting a more northern European timetable and making less of *pranzo*.

'prassi *f* standard procedure

prate'ria *f* grassland

'prati|ca *f* practice; *(esperienza)* experience; *(documentazione)* file; **avere** ~**ca di qcsa** be familiar with sth; **far** ~**ca** gain experience. ~**cabile** *adj* practicable; *(strada)* passable. ~**ca'mente** *adv* practically. ~**cante** *mf* apprentice; *(Relig)* [regular] church-goer

prati'ca|re *vt* practise; *(frequentare)* associate with; *(fare)* make

praticità *f* practicality. **'pratico** *adj* practical; *(esperto)* experienced; **essere pratico di qcsa** know about sth

'prato *m* meadow; *(di giardino)* lawn

pre'ambolo *m* preamble

preannunci'are *vt* give advance notice of

preavvi'sare *vt* forewarn. **preav-'viso** *m* warning

pre'cario *adj* precarious

precauzi'one *f* precaution; *(cautela)* care

prece'den|te *adj* previous ● *m* precedent. ~**te'mente** *adv* previously.

~**za** *f* precedence; *(di veicoli)* right of way; **dare la** ~**za** give way. **pre'cedere** *vt* precede

pre'cetto *m* precept

precipi'ta|re *vt* ~**re le cose** precipitate events ● *vi* fall headlong; *(situazione, eventi:)* come to a head. ~**rsi** *vr* *(gettarsi)* throw oneself; *(affrettarsi)* rush; ~**rsi a fare qcsa** rush to do sth. ~**zi'one** *f (fretta)* haste; *(atmosferica)* precipitation. **precipi-'toso** *adj* hasty; *(avventato)* reckless; *(caduta)* headlong

preci'pizio *m* precipice; **a** ~ headlong

precisa'mente *adv* precisely

preci'sa|re *vt* specify; *(spiegare)* clarify. ~**zi'one** *f* clarification

precisi'one *f* precision. **pre'ciso** *adj* precise; *(ore)* sharp; *(identico)* identical

pre'clu|dere *vt* preclude. ~**so** *pp di* precludere

pre'coc|e *adj* precocious; *(prematuro)* premature

precon'cetto *adj* preconceived ● *m* prejudice

pre'corr|ere *vt* ~**ere i tempi** be ahead of one's time

precur'sore *m* precursor

'preda *f* prey; *(bottino)* booty; **essere in** ~ **al panico** be panic-stricken; **in** ~ **alle fiamme** engulfed in flames. **pre'dare** *vt* plunder. ~**tore** *m* predator

predeces'sore *mf* predecessor

pre'del|la *f* platform. ~**lino** *m* step

predesti'na|re *vt* predestine. ~**to** *adj* *(Relig)* predestined, preordained

predetermi'nato *adj* predetermined, preordained

pre'detto *pp di* predire

'predica *f* sermon; *fig* lecture

predi'care *vt* preach

predi'le|tto, -a *pp di* prediligere ● *adj* favourite ● *mf* pet. ~**zi'one** *f* predilection. **predi'ligere** vt prefer

pre'dire vt foretell

predi'spo|rre vt arrange. **~rsi** vr **~rsi a** prepare oneself for. **~si-zi'one** f predisposition; (al disegno ecc) bent (a for). **~sto** pp di **predisporre**

predizi'one f prediction

predomi'na|nte adj predominant. **~re** vi predominate. **predo'minio** m predominance

pre'done m robber

prefabbri'cato adj prefabricated ● m prefabricated building

prefazi'one f preface

prefe'ren|za f preference; di **~a** preferably. **~i'ale** adj preferential; **corsia ~iale** bus and taxi lane

prefe'ribil|e adj preferable. **~'mente** adv preferably

prefe'ri|re vt prefer. **~to, -a** agg & mf favourite

pre'fet|to m prefect. **~'tura** f prefecture

pre'figgersi vr be determined

pre'fisso pp di **prefiggere** ● m prefix; (Teleph) [dialling] code

pre'ga|re vt/i pray; (supplicare) beg; **farsi ~** need persuading

preghi'era f prayer; (richiesta) request

pregi'ato adj esteemed; (prezioso) valuable. **'pregio** m esteem; (valore) value; (di persona) good point; di **pregio** valuable

pregiudi'ca|re vt prejudice; (danneggiare) harm. **~to** adj prejudiced ● m (Jur) previous offender

pregiu'dizio m prejudice; (danno) detriment

'prego int (non c'è di che) don't mention it!; (per favore) please; **~?** I beg your pardon?

pregu'stare vt look forward to

pre'lato m prelate

prela'vaggio m prewash

preleva'mento m withdrawal.

prele'vare vt withdraw (denaro); collect (merci); (Med) take. **preli'evo** m (di soldi) withdrawal. **prelievo di sangue** blood sample

prelimi'nare adj preliminary ● m **preliminari** pl preliminaries

pre'ludio m prelude

prema'man m inv maternity dress ● adj maternity attrib

prema'turo, -a adj premature ● mf premature baby

premedi'ta|re vt premeditate. **~zi'one** f premeditation

'premere vt press; (Comput) hit (tasto) ● vi **~ a** (importare) matter to; **mi preme sapere** I need to know; **~ su** press on; push (pulsante)

pre'messa f introduction

pre'me|sso pp di **premettere**. **~sso che** bearing in mind that. **~ttere** vt put forward; (mettere prima) put before.

premi'a|re vt give a prize to; (ricompensare) reward. **~zi'one** f prize giving

premi'nente adj pre-eminent

'premio m prize; (ricompensa) reward; (Comm) premium. **~ di consolazione** booby prize

premoni'tore adj (sogno, segno) premonitory. **~zi'one** f premonition

premu'nir|e vt fortify. **~si** vr take protective measures; **~si di** provide oneself with; **~si contro** protect oneself against

pre'mu|ra f (fretta) hurry; (cura) care. **~roso** adj thoughtful

prena'tale adj antenatal

'prender|e vt take; (afferrare) seize; catch (treno, malattia, ladro, pesce); have (cibo, bevanda); (far pagare) charge; (assumere) take on; (ottenere) get; (occupare) take up; **~e informazioni** make inquiries; **~e a calci/**

p

pugni kick/punch; **quanto prende?** what do you charge?; ~**e una persona per un'altra** mistake a person for someone else ● *vi* (*voltare*) turn; (*attecchire*) take root; (*rapprendersi*) set; ~**e a destra/sinistra** turn right/left; ~**e a fare qcsa** start doing sth. ~**si** *vr* ~**si a pugni** come to blows; ~**si cura di** take care of (*ammalato*)

prendi'sole *m inv* sundress

preno'ta|re *vt* book, reserve. ~**to** *adj* booked, reserved ~**zi'one** *f* booking, reservation

preoccu'pante *adj* alarming

preoccu'pa|re *vt* worry. ~**rsi** *vr* ~**rsi** worry (**di** about); ~**rsi di fare qcsa** take the trouble to do sth. ~**to** *adj* (*ansioso*) worried. ~**zi'one** *f* worry; (*apprensione*) concern

prepa'gato *adj* prepaid

prepa'ra|re *vt* prepare. ~**rsi** *vr* get ready. ~**tivi** *mpl* preparations. ~**to** *m* (*prodotto*) preparation. ~**torio** *adj* preparatory. ~**zi'one** *f* preparation

prepensiona'mento *m* early retirement

preponde'ran|te *adj* predominant. ~**za** *f* prevalence

pre'porre *vt* place before

preposizi'one *f* preposition

pre'posto *pp di* **preporre** ● *adj* ~ **a** (*addetto a*) in charge of

prepo'ten|te *adj* overbearing ● *mf* bully

preroga'tiva *f* prerogative

'presa *f* taking; (*conquista*) capture; (*stretta*) hold; (*di cemento ecc*) setting; (*Electr*) socket; (*pizzico*) pinch; **essere alle prese con** be struggling with; **a ~ rapida** (*cemento, colla*) quick-setting; **far ~ su qcno** influence sb. ~ **d'aria** air vent. ~ **multipla** adaptor

pre'sagio *m* omen. **presa'gire** *vt* foretell

'presbite *adj* long-sighted

presbi'terio *m* presbytery

pre'scelto *adj* selected

pre'scindere *vi* ~ **da** leave aside; **a ~ da** apart from

presco'lare *adj* **in età ~** pre-school

pre'scri|tto *pp di* **prescrivere**

pre'scri|vere *vt* prescribe. ~**zi'one** *f* prescription; (*norma*) rule

preselezi'one *f* **chiamare qcno in ~** call sb via the operator

presen'ta|re *vt* present; (*far conoscere*) introduce; show (*documento*); (*inoltrare*) submit. ~**rsi** *vr* present oneself; (*farsi conoscere*) introduce oneself; (*a ufficio*) attend; (*alla polizia ecc*) report; (*come candidato*) stand, run; (*occasione:*) occur; ~**rsi bene/male** (*persona:*) make a good/bad impression; (*situazione:*) look good/bad. ~**tore**, ~**trice** *mf* presenter; (*di notizie*) announcer. ~**zi'one** *f* presentation; (*per conoscersi*) introduction

pre'sente *adj* present; (*attuale*) current; (*questo*) this; **aver ~** remember ● *m* present; **i presenti** those present ● *f* **allegato alla ~** (*in lettera*) enclosed

presenti'mento *m* foreboding

pre'senza *f* presence; (*aspetto*) appearance; **in ~ di, alla ~ di** in the presence of; **di bella ~** personable. ~ **di spirito** presence of mind

presenzi'are *vi* ~ **a** attend

pre'sepe *m*, **pre'sepio** *m* crib

> **Presepe** The *presepe* (also called *presepio*) is a traditional nativity scene made with ceramic or wooden figures. Most homes have small ones and large-scale models are assembled in churches during Advent. *Presepi* from Naples, sometimes made of porcelain, are particularly prized.   *i*

preser'va|re vt preserve; (*proteggere*) protect (da from). ~**tivo** m condom. ~**zi'one** f preservation

'preside m headmaster; (*Univ*) dean ●f headmistress; (*Univ*) dean

presi'den|te m chairman; (*Pol*) president ● chairwoman; (*Pol*) president. ~ **del consiglio [dei ministri]** Prime Minister. ~ **della repubblica** President of the Republic. ~**za** f presidency; (*di assemblea*) chairmanship

presidi'are vt garrison. **pre'sidio** m garrison

presi'edere vt preside over

'preso pp di **prendere**

'pressa f (*Mech*) press

pres'sante adj urgent

pressap'poco adv about

pres'sare vt press

pressi'one f pressure. ~ **del sangue** blood pressure

'presso prep near; (*a casa di*) with; (*negli indirizzi*) care of, c/o; (*lavorare*) for ●**pressi** mpl: **nei pressi di...** in the neighbourhood o vicinity of...

pressoché adv almost

pressuriz'za|re vt pressurize. ~**to** adj pressurized

prestabi'li|re vt arrange in advance. ~**to** adj agreed

prestam'pato adj printed ● m (*modulo*) form

pre'stante adj good-looking

pre'star|e vt lend; ~**e attenzione** pay attention; ~**e aiuto** lend a hand; **farsi** ~**e** borrow (da from). ~**si** vr (*frase:*) lend itself; (*persona:*) offer

prestazi'one f performance; **prestazioni** pl (*servizi*) services

prestigia'tore, -'trice mf conjurer

pre'stigi|o m prestige; **gioco di** ~**o** conjuring trick. ~**oso** m prestigious

tigious

'prestito m loan; **dare in** ~ lend; **prendere in** ~ borrow

'presto adv soon; (*di buon'ora*) early; (*in fretta*) quickly; **a** ~ see you soon; **al più** ~ as soon as possible; ~ **o tardi** sooner or later

pre'sumere vt presume; (*credere*) think

presu'mibile adj è ~ **che...** presumably,...

pre'sunto adj (*colpevole*) presumed

presun'tu'oso adj presumptuous. ~**zi'one** f presumption

presup'po|rre vt suppose; (*richiedere*) presuppose. ~**sizi'one** f presupposition. ~**sto** m essential requirement

'prete m priest

preten'dente mf pretender ● m (*corteggiatore*) suitor

pre'ten|dere vt (*sostenere*) claim; (*esigere*) demand ● vi ~**dere a** claim to; ~**dere di** (*esigere*) demand to. ~**si'one** f pretension. ~**zi'oso** adj pretentious

pre'tes|a f pretension; (*esigenza*) claim; **senza** ~**e** unpretentious. ~**o** pp di **pretendere**

pre'testo m pretext

pre'tore m magistrate

pre'tura f magistrate's court

preva'le|nte adj prevalent. ~**nte-'mente** adv primarily. ~**nza** f prevalence. ~**re** vi prevail

pre'valso pp di **prevalere**

preve'dere vt foresee; forecast (*tempo*); (*legge ecc:*) provide for

preve'nire vt precede; (*evitare*) prevent; (*avvertire*) forewarn

preven'ti'vare vt estimate; (*aspettarsi*) budget for. ~**tivo** adj preventive ● m (*Comm*) estimate

preve'n'uto adj forewarned; (*mal*

disposto) prejudiced. ~zi'one f prevention; (*.preconcetto*) prejudice

previ'den|te *adj* provident. ~za f foresight. ~za sociale social security, welfare *Am.* ~zi'ale *adj* provident

'previo *adj* ~ pagamento on payment

previsi'one f forecast; in ~ di in anticipation of

pre'visto *pp di* prevedere ● *adj* foreseen ● *m* più/meno/prima del ~ more/less/earlier than expected

prezi'oso *adj* precious

prez'zemolo *m* parsley

'prezzo *m* price. ~ di fabbrica factory price. ~ all'ingrosso wholesale price. [a] metà ~ half price

prigi'on|e f prison; (*pena*) imprisonment. prigio'nia f imprisonment. ~i'ero, -a *adj* imprisoned ● *mf* prisoner

'prima *adv* before; (*più presto*) earlier; (*in primo luogo*) first; ~, finiamo questo let's finish this first; ~ o poi sooner or later; quanto ~ as soon as possible ● *prep* ~ di before; ~ d'ora before ● *conj* ~ che before ● *f* first class; (*Theat*) first night; (*Auto*) first [gear]

pri'mario *adj* primary; (*principale*) principal

pri'mat|e *m* primate. ~o *m* supremacy; *Sport* record

prima've|ra f spring. ~rile *adj* spring *attrib*

primeggi'are *vi* excel

primi'tivo *adj* primitive; (*originario*) original

pri'mizie *fpl* early produce *sg*

'primo *adj* first; (*fondamentale*) principal; (*precedente di due*) former; (*iniziale*) early; (*migliore*) best ● *m* first; primi *pl* (*i primi giorni*) the beginning; in un ~ tempo at first. prima copia master copy

primordi'ale *adj* primordial

'primula f primrose

princi'pale *adj* main ● *m* head, boss ⓘ

princi'p|ato *m* principality. 'principe *m* prince. ~'pessa f princess

princi'piante ● *mf* beginner

prin'cipio *m* beginning; (*concetto*) principle; (*causa*) cause; per ~ on principle

pri'ore *m* prior

priori|tà f inv priority. ~'tario *adj* having priority

'prisma *m* prism

pri'va|re *vt* deprive. ~rsi *vr* deprive oneself

privatizzazi'one f privatization. pri'vato, -a *adj* private ● *mf* private citizen

privazi'one f deprivation

privilegi'are *vt* privilege; (*considerare più importante*) favour. privi'legio *m* privilege

'privo *adj* ~ di devoid of; (*mancante*) lacking in

pro *prep* for ● *m* advantage; a che ~? what's the point?

pro'babil|e *adj* probable. ~ità f inv probability. ~'mente *adv* probably

pro'ble|ma *m* problem. ~'matico *adj* problematic

pro'boscide f trunk

procacci'ar|e *vt*, ~si *vr* obtain

pro'cace *adj* (*ragazza*) provocative

pro'ced|ere *vi* proceed; (*iniziare*)

start; **∼ere contro** (*Jur*) start legal proceedings against. **∼i'mento** *m* process; (*Jur*) proceedings *pl.* **proce'dura** *f* procedure

proces'sare *vt* (*Jur*) try

processi'one *f* procession

pro'cesso *m* process; (*Jur*) trial

proces'sore *m* processor

processu'ale *adj* trial

pro'cinto *m* essere in ∼ di be about to

pro'clama *m* proclamation

procla'ma|re *vt* proclaim. **∼zi'one** *f* proclamation

procreazi'one *f* procreation

pro'cura *f* power of attorney; per ∼ by proxy

procu'ra|re *vt/i* procure; (*causare*) cause; (*cercare*) try. **∼tore** *m* attorney. **P∼tore Generale** Attorney General. **∼tore legale** lawyer. **∼tore della repubblica** public prosecutor

'**prode** *adj* brave. **pro'dezza** *f* bravery

prodi'ga|re *vt* lavish. **∼si** *vr* do one's best

pro'digi|o *m* prodigy. **∼oso** *adj* prodigious

pro'dotto *pp di* **produrre** ● *m* product. **prodotti agricoli** farm produce *sg.* ∼ **derivato** by-product. ∼ **interno lordo** gross domestic product. ∼ **nazionale lordo** gross national product

pro'du|rre *vt* produce. **∼rsi** *vr* (*attore*) play; (*accadere*) happen. **∼ttività** *f* productivity. **∼t'tivo** *adj* productive. **∼t'tore, ∼t'trice** *mf* producer. **∼zi'one** *f* production

Prof. *abbr* (**Professore**) Prof.

profa'na|re *vt* desecrate

profe'rire *vt* utter

Prof.essa *abbr* (**Professoressa**) Prof.

profes'sare *vt* profess; practise (*professione*)

professio'nale *adj* professional

professi'o|ne *f* profession; **libera ∼ne** profession. **∼'nismo** *m* professionalism. **∼'nista** *mf* professional

profes'sor|e, -'essa *mf* (*Sch*) teacher; (*Univ*) lecturer; (*titolare di cattedra*) professor

pro'feta *m* prophet

pro'ficuo *adj* profitable

profi'lare *vt* outline; (*ornare*) border; (*Aeron*) streamline. **∼si** *vr* stand out

profi'lattico *adj* prophylactic ● *m* condom

pro'filo *m* profile; (*breve studio*) outline; di ∼ in profile

profit'tare *vi* ∼ **di** (*avvantaggiarsi*) profit by; (*approfittare*) take advantage of. **pro'fitto** *m* profit; (*vantaggio*) advantage

profond|a'mente *adv* deeply, profoundly. **∼ità** *f inv* depth

pro'fondo *adj* deep; *fig* profound; (*cultura*) great

'**profugo, -a** *mf* refugee

profu'ma|re *vt* perfume. **∼si** *vr* put on perfume

profu'mato *adj* (*fiore*) fragrant; (*fazzoletto ecc*) scented

profume'ria *f* perfumery. **pro'fumo** *m* perfume, scent

profusi'one *f* profusion; a ∼ in profusion. **pro'fuso** *pp di* **profondere** ● *adj* profuse

proget'tare *vt* plan. **∼'tista** *mf* designer. **pro'getto** *m* plan; (*di lavoro importante*) project. **progetto di legge** bill

prog'nosi *f inv* prognosis; in ∼ riservata on the danger list

pro'gramma *m* programme; (*Comput*) program. ∼ **scolastico** syllabus

program'ma|re *vt* programme; (*Comput*) program. **∼tore, ∼trice** *mf* [computer] programmer. **∼zi'one** *f* programming

progre'dire *vi* [make] progress

progres|si'one *f* progression.

∼sivo adj progressive. pro'gresso m progress

proi'bi|re vt forbid. ∼tivo adj prohibitive. ∼to adj forbidden. ∼zi'one f prohibition

proiet'tare vt project; show (film). ∼tore m projector; (Auto) headlight

proi'ettile m bullet

proiezi'one f projection

'prole f offspring. prole'tario agg & m proletarian

prolife'rare vi proliferate. pro'lifico adj prolific

pro'lisso adj verbose, prolix

'prologo m prologue

pro'lunga f (Electr) extension

prolun'gar|e vt prolong; (allungare) lengthen; extend (contratto, scadenza). ∼si vr continue; (nello spazio) stretch; ∼si su (dilungarsi) dwell upon

prome'moria m memo; (per se stessi) reminder, note; (formale) memorandum

pro'mes|sa f promise. ∼sso pp di promettere. ∼ttere vt/i promise

promet'tente adj promising

promi'nente adj prominent

promiscuità f promiscuity. pro'miscuo adj promiscuous

promon'torio m promontory

pro'mos|so pp di promuovere ● adj (Sch) who has gone up a year; (Univ) who has passed an exam. ∼tore, ∼trice mf promoter

promozio'nale adj promotional. promozi'one f promotion

promul'gare vt promulgate

promu'overe vt promote; (Sch) move up a class

proni'pote m (di bisnonno) great-grandson; (di prozio) great-nephew ● f (di bisnonno) great-granddaughter; (di prozio) great-niece

pro'nome m pronoun

pronosti'care vt forecast. pro'nostico m forecast

pron'tezza f readiness; (rapidità) quickness

'pronto adj ready; (rapido) quick; ∼! (Teleph) hello!; tenersi ∼ be ready (per for); pronti, via! (in gare) ready! steady! go!. ∼ soccorso first aid; (in ospedale) accident and emergency

prontu'ario m handbook

pro'nuncia f pronunciation

pronunci'a|re vt pronounce; (dire) utter; deliver (discorso). ∼rsi vr (su un argomento) give one's opinion. ∼to adj pronounced; (prominente) prominent

pro'nunzia ecc = PRONUNCIA ecc

propa'ganda f propaganda

propa'ga|re vt propagate. ∼rsi vr spread. ∼zi'one f propagation

prope'deutico adj introductory

pro'pen|dere vi ∼dere per be in favour of. ∼so pp di propendere ● adj essere ∼so a fare qcsa be inclined to do sth

propi'nare vt administer

pro'pizio adj favourable

proponi'mento m resolution

pro'por|re vt propose; (suggerire) suggest. ∼si vr set oneself (obiettivo, meta); ∼si di intend to

proporzio'na|le adj proportional. ∼re vt proportion. proporzi'one f proportion

pro'posito m purpose; a ∼ by the way; a ∼ with regard to; di ∼ (apposta) on purpose

proposizi'one f clause; (frase) sentence

pro'post|a f proposal. ∼o pp di proporre

proprietà f inv property; (diritto) ownership; (correttezza) propriety. ∼ immobiliare property. ∼ privata private property. proprie'taria f owner; (di casa affittata) landlady. proprie'tario m owner; (di casa affittata) landlord

proprio | provider

'**proprio** adj one's [own]; (caratteristico) typical; (appropriato) proper ● adv just; (veramente) really; **non** ~ not really, not exactly; (affatto) not... at all ● pron one's own ● m one's [own]; **lavorare in** ~ be one's own boss; **mettersi in** ~ set up on one's own

propul|si'one f propulsion. ~'**sore** m propeller

'**proroga** f extension

proro'ga|bile adj extendable. ~**re** vt extend

pro'rompere vi burst out

'**prosa** f prose. **pro'saico** adj prosaic

pro'scio|gliere vt release; (Jur) acquit. ~**lto** pp di **prosciogliere**

prosciu'gar|e vt dry up; (bonificare) reclaim. ~**si** vr dry up

prosci'utto m ham. ~ **cotto** cooked ham. ~ **crudo** Parma ham

pro'scri|tto, -a pp di **proscrivere** ● mf exile

prosecuzi'one f continuation

prosegui'mento m continuation; **buon** ~**!** (viaggio) have a good journey!; (festa) enjoy the rest of the party!

prosegu'ire vt continue ● vi go on, continue

prospe'r|are vi prosper. ~**ità** f prosperity. '**prospero** adj prosperous; (favorevole) favourable. ~**oso** adj flourishing; (ragazza) buxom

prospet'tar|e vt show. ~**si** vr seem

prospet'tiva f perspective; (panorama) view; fig prospect. **pro'spetto** m (vista) view; (facciata) façade; (tabella) table

prospici'ente adj facing

prossima'mente adv soon

prossimità f proximity

'**prossimo, -a** adj near; (seguente) next; (molto vicino) close; **l'anno** ~ next year ● mf neighbour

prosti'tu|ta f prostitute. ~**zi'one** f prostitution

protago'nista mf protagonist

pro'teggere vt protect; (favorire) favour

prote'ina f protein

pro'tender|e vt stretch out. ~**si** vr (in avanti) lean out. **pro'teso** pp di **protendere**

pro'te|sta f protest; (dichiarazione) protestation. ~**stante** adj & mf Protestant. ~**stare** vt/i protest

prote|t'tivo adj protective. ~**tto** pp di **proteggere**. ~**t'tore**, ~**t'trice** mf protector; (sostenitore) patron ● m (di prostituta) pimp. ~**zi'one** f protection

protocol'lare adj (visita) protocol ● vt register

proto'collo m protocol; (registro) register; **carta** ~ official stamped paper

pro'totipo m prototype

pro'tra|rre vt protract; (differire) postpone. ~**rsi** vr go on, continue. ~**tto** pp di **protrarre**

protube'ran|te adj protuberant. ~**za** f protuberance

'**prova** f test; (dimostrazione) proof; (tentativo) try; (di abito) fitting; Sport heat; (Theat) rehearsal; (bozza) proof; **in** ~ (assumere) for a trial period; **mettere alla** ~ put to the test. ~ **generale** dress rehearsal

pro'var|e vt test; (dimostrare) prove; (tentare) try; try on (abiti ecc); (sentire) feel; (Theat) rehearse. ~**si** vr try

proveni'enza f origin. **prove'nire** vi provenire da come from

pro'vento m proceeds pl

prove'nuto pp di **provenire**

pro'verbio m proverb

pro'vetta f test-tube; **bambino in** ~ test-tube baby

pro'vetto adj skilled

'**provider** m inv ISP, Internet Service Provider

P

pro'vinci|a f province; (strada) B road, secondary road. ~**ale** adj provincial; **strada** ~**ale** B road

pro'vino m specimen; Cinema screen test

provo'ca|nte adj provocative. ~**re** vt provoke; (causare) cause. ~**tore**, ~**trice** mf trouble-maker. ~**torio** adj provocative. ~**zi'one** f provocation

provve'd|ere vi ~**ere** a provide for. ~**i'mento** m measure; (previdenza) precaution

provvi'denz|a f providence. ~**i'ale** adj providential

provvigi'one f commission

provvi'sorio adj provisional

prov'vista f supply

pro'zio, -a m great-uncle • f great-aunt

'prua f prow

pru'den|te adj prudent. ~**za** f prudence; **per** ~**za** as a precaution

'prudere vi itch

'prugn|a f plum. ~**a secca** prune. ~**o** m plum[-tree]

pru'rito m itch.

pseu'donimo m pseudonym

psica'na|lisi f psychoanalysis. ~**lista** mf psychoanalyst. ~**liz'zare** vt psychoanalyse

'psiche f psyche

psichi'a|tra mf psychiatrist. ~**tria** f psychiatry. ~**trico** adj psychiatric

'psichico adj mental

psico|lo'gia f psychology. ~**lo'gico** adj psychological. **psi'cologo, -a** mf psychologist

psico'patico, -a mf psychopath

PT abbr (Posta e Telecomunicazioni) PO

pubbli'ca|re vt publish. ~**zi'one** f publication. ~**zioni** pl (di matrimonio) banns

pubbli'cista mf Journ correspondent

pubblici'tà f inv publicity; (annuncio) advertisement, advert; **fare** ~ **a qcsa** advertise sth; **piccola** ~ small advertisements. **pubblici'tario** adj advertising

'pubblico adj public; **scuola pubblica** state school • m public; (spettatori) audience; **grande** ~ general public. **Pubblica Sicurezza** Police. ~ **ufficiale** civil servant

'pube m pubis

puber'tà f puberty

pu'dico adj modest

pue'rile adj children's; pej childish

pugi'lato m boxing. **'pugile** m boxer

pugna'la|re vt stab. ~**ta** f stab. **pu'gnale** m dagger

'pugno m fist; (colpo) punch; (manciata) fistful; (numero limitato) handful; **dare un** ~ **a** punch

'pulce f flea; (microfono) bug

pul'cino m chick; (nel calcio) junior

pu'ledra f filly

pu'ledro m colt

pu'li|re vt clean. ~**re a secco** dry-clean. ~**to** adj clean. ~**tura** f cleaning. ~**zia** f (il pulire) cleaning; (l'essere pulito) cleanliness; ~**zie** pl housework; **fare le** ~**zie** do the cleaning

'pullman m inv bus, coach; (urbano) bus

pul'mino m minibus

'pulpito m pulpit

pul'sante m button; (Electr) [push-]button. ~ **di accensione** on-/off switch

pul'sa|re vi pulsate. ~**zi'one** f pulsation

pul'viscolo m dust

'puma m inv puma

pun'gente adj prickly; (insetto) stinging; (odore ecc) sharp

'punger|e vt prick; (insetto:) sting

pungigli'one m sting

pu'ni|re vt punish. ~**'tivo** adj punitive. ~zi'one f punishment; Sport free kick

'**punta** f point; (estremità) tip; (di monte) peak; (un po') pinch; Sport forward; **doppie punte** (di capelli) split ends

pun'tare vt point; (spingere con forza) push; (scommettere) bet; ([Ⅰ]: appuntare) fasten ● vi. ~ su fig rely on; ~ verso (dirigersi) head for; ~ a aspire to

punta'spilli m inv pincushion

pun'tat|a f (di una storia) instalment; (televisiva) episode; (al gioco) stake, bet; (breve visita) flying visit; a ~e serialized, in instalments

punteggia'tura f punctuation

pun'teggio m score

puntel'lare vt prop. **pun'tello** m prop

pun'tiglio m spite; (ostinazione) obstinacy. ~'oso adj punctilious, pernickety pej

pun'tin|a f (da disegno) drawing pin, thumb tack Am; (di giradischi) stylus. ~o m dot; a ~o perfectly; (cotto) to a T

'**punto** m point; (Med, in cucito,) stitch; (in punteggiatura) full stop; in che ~? where, exactly?; **due punti** colon; in ~ sharp; **mettere a** ~ put right; fig fine tune; tune up (motore); **essere sul** ~ **di fare qcsa** be about to do sth, be on the point of doing sth. ~ **esclamativo** exclamation mark. ~ **interrogativo** interrogation mark. ~ **nero** (Med) blackhead. ~ **di riferimento** landmark; (per la qualità) benchmark. ~ **di vendita** point of sale. ~ **e virgola** semicolon. ~ **di vista** point of view

puntu'al|e adj punctual. ~ità f punctuality. ~'mente adv punctually

pun'tura f (di insetto) sting; (di ago ecc) prick; (Med) puncture; (iniezione) injection; (fitta) stabbing pain

punzecchi'are vt prick; fig tease

pupa f doll. **pu'pazzo** m puppet.

pupazzo di neve snowman

pup'illa f (Anat) pupil

pu'pillo, -a mf (di professore) favourite

purché conj provided

'**pure** adv too, also; (concessivo) fate ~! please do! ● conj (tuttavia) yet; (anche se) even if; **pur di** just to

purè m inv purée. ~ **di patate** creamed potatoes

pu'rezza f purity

'**purga** f purge. **pur'gante** m laxative. **pur'gare** vt purge

purga'torio m purgatory

purifi'care vt purify

puri'tano, -a adj & mf Puritan

'**puro** adj pure; (vino ecc) undiluted; **per** ~ **caso** purely by chance

puro'sangue adj & m thoroughbred

pur'troppo adv unfortunately

pus m pus. '**pustola** f pimple

puti'ferio m uproar

putre'far|e, ~si vt putrefy

'**putrido** adj putrid

'**puzza** f = PUZZO

puz'zare vi stink; ~ **di bruciato** fig smell fishy

'**puzzo** m stink, bad smell. ~**la** f polecat. ~**lente** adj stinking

p.zza abbr (piazza) Sq.

Qq

qua adv here; **da un anno in** ~ for the last year; **da quando in** ~? since when?; **di** ~ this way; **di** ~ **di** on this side of; ~ **dentro** in here; ~ **sotto** under here; ~ **vicino** near here; ~ **e là** here and there

qua'derno m exercise book; (per

appunti) notebook

quadrango'lare *adj* (forma) quadrangular. qua'drangolo *m* quadrangle

qua'drante *m* quadrant; *(di orologio)* dial

qua'dra|re *vt* square; *(contabilità)* balance ● *vi* fit in. ~to *adj* square; *(equilibrato)* level-headed ● *m* square; *(pugilato)* ring; al ~to squared

quadret'tato *adj* squared; *(carta)* graph *attrib.* qua'dretto *m* square; *(piccolo quadro)* small picture; a quadretti *(tessuto)* check

quadrien'nale *adj* (che dura quattro anni) four-year

quadri'foglio *m* four-leaf clover

quadri'latero *m* quadrilateral

quadri'mestre *m* four-month period

'**quadro** *m* picture, painting; *(quadrato)* square; *(fig: scena)* sight; *(tabella)* table; *(Theat)* scene; *(Comm)* executive quadri *pl (carte)* diamonds; a quadri *(tessuto, giacca, motivo)* check. quadri *pl* direttivi senior management

quaggiù *adv* down here

'**quaglia** *f* quail

'**qualche** *adj (alcuni)* a few, some; *(un certo)* some; *(in interrogazioni)* any; ho ~ problema I have a few problems, I have some problems; ~ tempo fa some time ago; hai ~ libro italiano? have you any Italian books?; posso pren-dere ~ libro? can I take some books?; in ~ modo somehow; in ~ posto somewhere; ~ volta sometimes; ~ cosa = QUALCOSA

qual'cos|a *pron* something, *(in interrogazioni)* anything; ~'altro something else; vuoi ~'altro? would you like anything else?; ~a di strano something strange; vuoi ~a da mangiare? would you like something to eat?

qual'cuno *pron* someone, somebody; *(in interrogazioni)* anyone, anybody; *(alcuni)* some; *(in interrogazioni)* any; c'è ~? is anybody in?; qualcun altro someone else, somebody else; c'è qualcun altro che aspetta? is anybody else waiting?; ho letto ~ dei suoi libri I've read some of his books; conosci ~ dei suoi amici? do you know any of his friends?

'**quale** *adj* which; *(indeterminato)* what; *(come)* as, like; ~ macchina è la tua? which car is yours?; ~ motivo avrà di parlare così? what reason would he have to speak like that?; ~ onore! what an honour!; città quali Venezia towns like Venice; ~ che sia la tua opinione whatever you may think ● *pron inter* which [one]; ~ preferisci? which [one] do you prefer? ● *pron rel* il/la ~ *(persona)* who; *(animale, cosa)* that, which; *(oggetto: con prep)* whom; *(animale, cosa)* which; hai incontrato tua madre, la ~ mi ha detto... I met your mother, who told me...; l'ufficio nel ~ lavoro the office in which I work; l'uomo con il ~ parlavo the man to whom I was speaking ● *adv (come)* as

qua'lifica *f* qualification; *(titolo)* title

qualifi'ca|re *vt* qualify; *(definire)* define. ~rsi *vr* be placed. ~tivo *adj* qualifying; *(lavoro)* qualifying; *(operaio)* semi-skilled. ~zi'one *f* qualification

qualità *f inv* quality; *(specie)* kind; in ~ di in one's capacity as. qualita'tivo *adj* qualitative

qua'lora *conj* in case

qual'siasi, qua'lunque *adj* any; *(non importa quale)* whatever; *(ordinario)* ordinary; dammi una penna ~ give me any pen [whatsoever]; farei ~ cosa I would do anything; ~ cosa io faccia whatever I do; ~ persona anyone; in ~ caso in any case; uno ~ any one, whichever; l'uomo qualunque the man in the street

qualunqu'ismo m lack of political views

'quando conj & adv when; da ~ ti ho visto since I saw you; da ~ esci con lui? how long have you been going out with him?; da ~ in qua? since when?; ~...~... sometimes..., sometimes...

quantifi'care vt quantify

quantità f inv quantity; una ~ di (gran numero) a great deal of. quanti'tativo m amount ● adj quantitative

'quanto
● adj inter how much; (con nomi plurali) how many; (in esclamazione) what a lot of; ~ tempo? how long?; quanti anni hai? how old are you?
● adj rel as much... as; (con nomi plurali) as many... as; prendi ~ denaro ti serve take as much money as you need; prendi quanti libri vuoi take as many books as you like
● pron inter how much; (quanto tempo) how long; (plurale) how many; quanti ne abbiamo oggi? what date is it today?, what's the date today?
● pron rel as much as; (quanto tempo) as long as; (plurale) as many as; prendine ~/quanti ne vuoi take as much/as many as you like; stai ~ vuoi stay as long as you like; questo è ~ that's it
● adv inter how long; (quanto tempo) how long; ~ sei alto? how tall are you?; ~ hai aspettato? how long did you wait for?; ~ costa? how much is it?; ~ mi dispiace! I'm so sorry!; ~ è bello! how nice!
● adv rel as much as; lavoro ~ posso I work as much as I can; è tanto intelligente ~ bello

he's as intelligent as he's good-looking; in ~ (in qualità di) as; (poiché) since; in ~ a me as far as I'm concerned; per ~ however; per ~ ne sappia as far as I know; per ~ mi riguarda as far as I'm concerned; ~ a as for; ~ prima (al più presto) as soon as possible

quan'tunque conj although

qua'ranta adj & m forty

quaran'tena f quarantine

quaran'tenn|e adj forty-year-old. ~io m period of forty years

quaran't|esimo adj fortieth. ~ina f una ~ina about forty

qua'resima f Lent

quar'tetto m quartet

quarti'ere m district; (Mil) quarters pl. ~ generale headquarters

'quarto adj fourth ● m fourth; (quarta parte) quarter; le sette e un ~ a quarter past seven. quarti pl di finale quarterfinals. ~ d'ora quarter of an hour. quar'tultimo, -a mf fourth from the end

'quarzo m quartz

'quasi adv almost, nearly; ~ mai hardly ever ● conj (come se) as if; ~ sto a casa I'm tempted to stay home

quas'sù adv up here

'quatto adj crouching; (silenzioso) silent

quat'tordici adj & m fourteen

quat'trini mpl money sg

'quattro adj & m four; dirne ~ a qcno give sb a piece of one's mind; farsi in ~ (per qcno/per fare qcsa) go to a lot of trouble for sb/to do sth); in ~ e quattr'otto in a flash. ~ per ~ m inv (Auto) four-wheel drive [vehicle]

quat'trocchi: a ~ adv in private

quattro|'cento adj & m four hundred; il Q~cento the

q

fifteenth century

quattro'mila adj & m four thousand

'quell|o adj that (pl those); quell'albero that tree; quegli alberi those trees; quel cane that dog; quei cani those dogs ● pron that [one] (pl those [ones]); ~o lì that one over there; ~o che the one that; (ciò che) what; quelli che the ones that, those that; ~o a destra the one on the right

'quercia f oak

que'rela f [legal] action

quere'lare vt bring an action against

que'sito m question

questio'nario m questionnaire

quest'ione f question; (faccenda) matter; (litigio) quarrel; in ~ in doubt; è fuori ~ it's out of the question

'quest|o adj this (pl these) ● pron this [one] (pl these [ones]); ~o qui, ~o qua this one here; ~o è quello che ha detto that's what he said; per ~o for this or that reason. que'st'oggi today

que'store m chief of police

que'stura f police headquarters

qui adv here; da ~ in poi from now on; fin ~ (di tempo) up till now, until now; ~ dentro in here; ~ sotto under here; ~ vicino near here ● m ~ pro quo misunderstanding

quie'scienza f trattamento di ~ retirement package

quie'tanza f receipt

quie'tare vt calm. ~si vr quieten down

quie'te f quiet; disturbo della ~e pubblica breach of the peace. ~o adj quiet

'quindi adv then ● conj therefore

'quindici adj & m fifteen. ~'cina f una ~cina about fifteen; una ~cina di giorni two weeks pl

quinquen'nale adj (che dura cinque anni) five-year. quin'quennio m [period of] five years

quin'tale m a hundred kilograms

'quinte fpl (Theat) wings

quin'tetto m quintet

'quinto adj fifth

quin'tuplo adj quintuple

'quota f quota; (rata) instalment; (altitudine) height; (Aeron) altitude, height; (ippica) odds pl; perdere ~ lose altitude; prendere ~ gain altitude. ~ di iscrizione entry fee

quo'tare vt (Comm) quote. ~to adj quoted; essere ~to in Borsa be quoted on the Stock Exchange. ~zi'one f quotation

quotidiana'mente adv daily. ~'ano adj daily; (ordinario) everyday ● m daily [paper]

quozi'ente m quotient. ~ d'intelligenza intelligence quotient, IQ

Rr

ra'barbaro m rhubarb

'rabbia f rage; (ira) anger; (Med) rabies sg; che ~! what a nuisance!; mi fa ~ it makes me angry

rab'bino m rabbi

rabbiosa'mente adv furiously. rabbi'oso adj hot-tempered; (Med) rabid; (violento) violent

rabbo'nire vt pacify. ~si vr calm down

rabbrivi'dire vi shudder; (di freddo) shiver

rabbui'arsi vr become dark

raccapez'zare vt put together. ~si vr see one's way ahead

raccapricci'ante adj horrifying

raccatta'palle *m inv* ball boy •*f inv* ball girl

raccat'tare *vt* pick up

rac'chetta *f* racket. ~ **da ping pong** table-tennis bat. ~ **da sci** ski pole. ~ **da tennis** tennis racket

racchi'udere *vt* contain

rac'cogli|ere *vt* pick; (*da terra*) pick up; (*mietere*) harvest; (*collezionare*) collect; (*radunare*) gather; win (*voti ecc*); (*dare asilo a*) take in. ~**ersi** *vr* gather; (*concentrarsi*) collect one's thoughts. ~**'mento** *m* concentration. ~**tore**, ~**'trice** *mf* collector •*m* (*di fieno*) binder

rac'colto, -a *pp di* **raccogliere** •*a* (*rannicchiato*) hunched; (*intimo*) cosy; (*concentrato*) engrossed •*m* (*mietitura*) harvest •*f* collection; (*di scritti*) compilation; (*del grano ecc*) harvesting; (*adunata*) gathering

raccoman'dabile *adj* recommendable; **poco** ~ (*persona*) shady

raccoman'da|re *vt* recommend; (*affidare*) entrust. ~**rsi** *vr* (*implorare*) beg. ~**ta** *f* registered letter; ~**ta con ricevuta di ritorno** recorded delivery. ~**espresso** *f* next-day delivery of recorded items. ~**zi'one** *f* recommendation

raccon'tare *vt* tell. **rac'conto** *m* story

raccorci'are *vt* shorten

raccor'dare *vt* join. **rac'cordo** *m* connection; (*stradale*) feeder. **raccordo anulare** ring road. **raccordo ferroviario** siding

ra'chitico *adj* rickety; (*poco sviluppato*) stunted

racimo'lare *vt* scrape together

'racket *m inv* racket

'radar *m inv* radar

raddol'cir|e *vt* sweeten; *fig* soften. ~**si** *vr* become milder; (*carattere:*) mellow

raddoppi'are *vt* double. **rad'doppio** *m* doubling

raddriz'zare *vt* straighten

'rader|e *vt* shave; graze (*muro*); ~**e al suolo** raze. ~**si** *vr* shave

radi'are *vt* strike off; ~ **dall'albo** strike off

radia|'tore *m* radiator. ~**zi'one** *f* radiation

'radica *f* briar

radi'cale *adj* radical •*m* (*Gram*) root; (*Pol*) radical

ra'dicchio *m* chicory

ra'dice *f* root

'radio *f inv* radio; **via** ~ by radio. ~ **a transistor** transistor radio •*m* (*Chem*) radium.

radioama'tore, -'trice *mf* [radio] ham

radioascolta'tore, -'trice *mf* listener

radioat|tività *f* radioactivity. ~**'tivo** *adj* radioactive

radio'cro|naca *f* radio commentary; **fare la** ~**naca di** commentate on. ~**'nista** *mf* radio reporter

radiodiffusi'one *f* broadcasting

radio'fonico *adj* radio *attrib*

radiogra|'fare *vt* X-ray. ~**'fia** *f* X-ray [photograph]; (*radiologia*) radiography; **fare una** ~**fia** (*paziente:*) have an X-ray; (*dottore:*) take an X-ray

radio'lina *f* transistor

radi'ologo, -a *mf* radiologist

radi'oso *adj* radiant

radio'sveglia *f* radio alarm

radio'taxi *m inv* radio taxi

radiote'lefono *m* radiotelephone; (*privato*) cordless [phone]

radiotelevi'sivo *adj* broadcasting *attrib*

'rado *adj* sparse; (*non frequente*) rare; **di** ~ seldom

radu'nar|e *vt*, ~**si** *vr* gather [together]. **ra'duno** *m* meeting; *Sport* rally

ra'dura *f* clearing

'rafano m horseradish

raf'fermo adj stale

'raffica f gust; (di armi da fuoco) burst; (di domande) barrage

raffigu'ra|re vt represent. ~zi'one f representation

raffi'na|re vt refine. ~ta'mente adv elegantly. ~to adj refined. raffine'ria f refinery

rafforza|'mento m reinforcement; (di muscolatura) strengthening. ~re vt reinforce. ~tivo m (Gram) intensifier

raffredda'mento m (processo) cooling

raffred'd|are vt cool. ~arsi vr get cold; (prendere un raffreddore) catch a cold. ~ore m cold. ~ore da fieno hay fever

raf'fronto m comparison

'rafia f raffia

Rag. abbr ragioniere

ra'gaz|za f girl; (fidanzata) girlfriend. ~za alla pari au pair [girl]. ~'zata f prank. ~zo m boy; (fidanzato) boyfriend

ragge'lar|e vt fig freeze. ~si vr fig turn to ice

raggi'ante adj radiant; ~ di successo flushed with success

raggi'a|re fa ~ with a pattern like spokes radiating from a centre

'raggio m ray; (Math) radius; (di ruota) spoke; ~ d'azione range. ~ laser laser beam

raggi'rare vt trick. rag'giro m trick

raggi'un|gere vt reach; (conseguire) achieve. ~'gibile adj (luogo) within reach

raggomito'lar|e vt wind. ~si vr curl up

raggranel'lare vt scrape together

raggrin'zir|e vt, ~si vr wrinkle

raggrup|pa'mento m (gruppo) group; (azione) grouping. ~'pare vt group together

ragguagli'are vt compare; (informare) inform. raggu'aglio m comparison; (informazione) information

ragguar'devole adj considerable

'ragia f resin; acqua ~ turpentine

ragiona'mento m reasoning; (discussione) discussion. ragio'nare vi reason; (discutere) discuss

ragi'one f reason; (ciò che è giusto) right; a ~ o a torto rightly or wrongly; aver ~ be right; perdere la ~ go out of one's mind

ragione'ria f accountancy

ragio'nevol|e adj reasonable. ~'mente adv reasonably

ragioni'ere, -a mf accountant

ragli'are vi bray

ragna'tela f cobweb. 'ragno m spider

ragù m inv meat sauce

RAI f abbr (Radio Audizioni Italiane) Italian public broadcasting company

ralle'gra|re vt gladden. ~rsi vr rejoice; ~rsi con qcno congratulate sb. ~'menti mpl congratulations

rallenta'mento m slowing down

rallen'ta|re vt/i slow down; (allentare) slacken. ~rsi vr slow down. ~'tore m speed bump; al ~tore in slow motion

raman'zina f reprimand

ra'marro m type of lizard

ra'mato adj copper[-coloured]

'rame m copper

ramifi'ca|re vi, ~rsi vr branch out; (strada:) branch. ~zi'one f ramification

rammari'carsi vr ~ di regret; (lamentarsi) complain (di about). ram'marico m regret

rammen'dare vt darn. ram'mendo m darning

rammen'tar|e vt remember; ~e qcsa a qcno (richiamare alla memoria) remind sb of sth. ~si vr remember

rammol'li|re vt soften. ~rsi vr go

soft. ~to, -a *mf* wimp

'**ramo** *m* branch. ~'scello *m* twig

'**rampa** *f* (*di scale*) flight. ~ d'accesso slip road. ~ di lancio launch[ing] pad

ram'**pante** *adj* giovane ~ yuppie

rampi'**cante** *adj* climbing ●*m* (*Bot*) creeper

ram'**pollo** *m hum* brat; (*discendente*) descendant

ram'**pone** *m* harpoon; (*per scarpe*) crampon

'**rana** *f* frog; (*nel nuoto*) breaststroke; uomo ~ frogman

ran'**core** *m* resentment

ran'**dagio** *adj* stray

'**rango** *m* rank

rannicchi'**arsi** *vr* huddle up

rannuvo'**larsi** *vr* cloud over

ra'**nocchio** *m* frog

ranto'**lare** *vi* wheeze. '**rantolo** *m* wheeze; (*di moribondo*) deathrattle

'**rapa** *f* turnip

ra'**pace** *adj* rapacious; (*uccello*) predatory

ra'**pare** *vt* crop

'**rapida** *f* rapids *pl*. ~'mente *adv* rapidly

rapidità *f* speed

'**rapido** *adj* swift ●*m* (*treno*) express [train]

rapi'**mento** *m* kidnapping

ra'**pina** *f* robbery; ~ a mano armata armed robbery. ~ in banca bank robbery. rapi'nare *vt* rob. ~'tore *m* robber

ra'**pi|re** *vt* abduct; (*a scopo di riscatto*) kidnap; (*estasiare*) ravish. ~'tore, ~'trice *mf* kidnapper

rappacifi'**ca|re** *vt* pacify. ~rsi *vr* be reconciled. ~zi'one *f* reconciliation

rappor'**tare** *vt* reproduce (*disegno*); (*confrontare*) compare

rap'**porto** *m* report; (*connessione*) relation; (*legame*) relationship; (*Math, Techn*) ratio; rapporti *pl* relationship; essere in buoni rapporti be on good terms. ~ di amicizia friendship. ~ di lavoro working relationship. rapporti *pl* sessuali sexual intercourse

rap'**prendersi** *vr* set; (*latte:*) curdle

rappre'**saglia** *f* reprisal

rappresen'**tan|te** *mf* representative. ~te di commercio sales representative. ~za *f* delegation; (*Comm*) agency; spese *pl* di ~za entertainment expenses; di ~za (appartamento ecc) company

rappresen'**ta|re** *vt* represent; (*Theat*) perform. ~'tivo *adj* representative. ~zi'one *f* representation; (*spettacolo*) performance

rap'**preso** *pp di* rapprendersi

rapso'**dia** *f* rhapsody

'**raptus** *m inv* fit of madness

rara'**mente** *adv* rarely, seldom

rare'**fa|re** *vt*, ~rsi *vr* rarefy. ~tto *adj* rarefied

rarità *f inv* rarity. 'raro *adj* rare

ra'**sar|e** *vt* shave; trim (*siepe ecc*). ~si *vr* shave

raschi'**are** *vt* scrape; (*togliere*) scrape off

rasen'**tare** *vt* go close to. ra'sente *prep* very close to

'**raso** *pp di* radere ●*adj* smooth; (*colmo*) full to the brim; (*barba*) close-cropped; ~ terra close to the ground; un cucchiaio ~ a level spoonful ●*m* satin

ra'**soio** *m* razor

ras'**segna** *f* review; (*mostra*) exhibition; (*musicale, cinematografica*) festival; passare in ~ review; (*Mil*) inspect

rasse'**gna|re** *vt* present. ~rsi *vr* resign oneself. ~to *adj* (*persona, aria, tono*) resigned. ~zi'one *f* resignation

rassere'**nar|e** *vt* clear; *fig* cheer up.

~si vr become clear; *fig* cheer up

rasset'tare vt tidy up; (*ripa-rare*) mend

rassicu'ra|nte *adj* reassuring. **~re** vt reassure. **~zi'one** f reassurance

rasso'dare vt harden; *fig* strengthen

rassomigli'a|nza f resemblance. **~re** vi **~re a** resemble

rastrella'mento m (*di fieno*) raking; (*perlustrazione*) combing. **rastrel'lare** vt rake; (*perlustrare*) comb

rastrelli'era f rack; (*per biciclette*) bicycle rack; (*scolapiatti*) [plate] rack. **ra'strello** m rake

'rata f instalment; pagare a rate pay by instalments; rate'ale *adj* by instalments; pagamento rateale payment by instalments

rate'are, rateiz'zare vt divide into instalments

ra'tifica f (*Jur*) ratification

ratifi'care vt (*Jur*) ratify

'ratto m abduction; (*roditore*) rat

rattop'pare vt patch. **rat'toppo** m patch

rattrap'pir|e vt make stiff. **~si** vr become stiff

rattri'star|e vt sadden. **~si** vr become sad

rau'cedine f hoarseness. **'rauco** *adj* hoarse

rava'nello m radish

ravi'oli *mpl* ravioli *sg*

ravve'dersi vr mend one's ways

ravvicina'mento m reconciliation; (*Pol*) rapprochement

ravvici'nar|e vt bring closer; (*riconciliare*) reconcile. **~si** vr be reconciled

ravvi'sare vt recognize

ravvi'var|e vt revive; *fig* brighten up. **~si** vr revive

'rayon m rayon

razio'cinio m rational thought; (*buon senso*) common sense

razio'nal|e *adj* rational. **~ità** f (*ra-*

ziocinio) rationality; (*di ambiente*) functional nature. **~iz'zare** vt rationalize (programmi, metodi, spazio). **~'mente** *adv* rationally

razio'nare vt ration. **razi'one** f ration

'razza f race; (*di cani ecc*) breed; (*genere*) kind; che **~ di idiota!** [f] what an idiot!

raz'zia f raid

razzi'ale *adj* racial

raz'zis|mo m racism. **~ta** *adj & mf* racist

'razzo m rocket. **~ da segnalazione** flare

razzo'lare vi (*polli*) scratch about

re m *inv* king; (*Mus*) D

rea'gire vi react

re'ale *adj* real; (*di re*) royal

rea'lis|mo m realism. **~ta** *mf* realist; (*fautore del re*) royalist

realistica'mente *adv* realistically. **rea'listico** *adj* realistic

'reality tv f reality tv

realiz'zabile *adj* feasible

realiz'zar|e vt (*attuare*) carry out, realize; (*Comm*) make; score (gol, canestro); (*rendersi conto di*) realize. **~rsi** vr come true; (*nel lavoro ecc*) fulfil oneself. **~zi'one** f realization; (*di sogno, persona*) fulfilment. **~zione scenica** production

rea'lizzo m (*vendita*) proceeds *pl*; (*riscossione*) yield

real'mente *adv* really

realtà f *inv* reality. **~ virtuale** virtual reality

re'ato m crime

reat'tivo *adj* reactive

reat'tore m reactor; (*Aeron*) jet [aircraft]

reazio'nario, -a *adj & mf* reactionary

reazi'one f reaction. **~ a catena** chain reaction

'rebus m *inv* rebus; (*enigma*) puzzle

recapi'tare vt deliver. **re'capito** m address; (*consegna*) delivery. **recapito a domicilio** home delivery. **recapito telefonico** contact telephone number

re'car|e vt bear; (*produrre*) cause. **~si** vr go

re'cedere vi recede; fig give up

recensi'one f review

recen's|ire vt review. **~ore** m reviewer

re'cente adj recent; **di ~** recently. **~mente** adv recently

recessi'one f recession

re'cesso m recess

re'cidere vt cut off

reci'divo, -a adj (*Med*) recurrent ● mf repeat offender

recin|'tare vt close off. **re'cinto** m enclosure; (*per animali*) pen; (*per bambini*) play-pen. **~zi'one** f (*muro*) wall; (*rete*) wire fence; (*cancellata*) railings pl

recipi'ente m container

re'ciproco adj reciprocal

re'ciso pp di recidere

'recita f performance. **reci'tare** vt recite; (*Theat*) act; play (ruolo). **~zi'one** f recitation; (*Theat*) acting

recla'mare vi protest ● vt claim

ré'clame f inv advertising; (*avviso pubblicitario*) advertisement

re'clamo m complaint; **ufficio reclami** complaints department

recli'na|bile adj reclining; **sedile ~bile** reclining seat. **~re** vt tilt (sedile); lean (capo)

reclusi'one f imprisonment. **re'cluso, -a** adj secluded ● mf prisoner

'recluta f recruit

reclu|ta'mento m recruitment. **~'tare** vt recruit

'record m inv record ● adj inv (*cifra*) record attrib

recrimi'na|re vi recriminate

recupe'rare vt recover. **re'cupero** m recovery; **corso di recupero** additional classes; **minuti di recupero** Sport injury time

redargu'ire vt rebuke

re'datto, -pp di redigere

redat'tore, -'trice mf editor; (*di testo*) writer

redazi'one f (*ufficio*) editorial office; (*di testi*) editing

reddi'tizio adj profitable

'reddito m income. **~ imponibile** taxable income

re'den|to pp di redimere. **~'tore** m redeemer. **~zi'one** f redemption

re'digere vt write; draw up (documento)

re'dimer|e vt redeem. **~si** vr redeem oneself

'redini fpl reins

'reduce adj **~ da** back from ● mf survivor

refe'rendum m inv referendum

refe'renza f reference

refet'torio m refectory

refrat'tario adj refractory; **essere ~ a** have no aptitude for

refrige'ra|re vt refrigerate. **~zi'one** f refrigeration

refur'tiva f stolen goods pl

rega'lare vt give

re'galo m present, gift

re'gata f regatta

reg'gen|te mf regent. **~za** f regency

'regger|e vt (*sorreggere*) bear; (*tenere in mano*) hold; (*dirigere*) run; (*governare*) govern; (*Gram*) take ● vi (*resistere*) hold out; (*durare*) last; fig stand. **~si** vr stand

'reggia f royal palace

reggi'calze m inv suspender belt

reggi'mento m regiment

reggi'petto, reggi'seno m bra

re'gia f Cinema direction; (*Theat*) production

re'gime m regime; (*dieta*) diet;

(Mech) speed

re'gina f queen

'regio adj royal

regio'na|le adj regional. ~'lismo m (parola) regionalism

regi'one f region

re'gista mf (Cinema) director; (Theat, TV) producer

regi'stra|re vt register; (Comm) enter; (incidere su nastro) tape, record; (su disco) record. ~'tore m recorder; (magnetofono) tape-recorder. ~tore di cassa cash register. ~zi'one f registration; (Comm) entry; (di programma) recording

re'gistro m register; (ufficio) registry. ~ di cassa ledger

re'gnare vi reign

'regno m kingdom; (sovranità) reign. R~ Unito United Kingdom

'regola f rule; essere in ~ be in order; (persona:) have one's papers in order. rego'labile adj (meccanismo) adjustable. ~'mento m regulation; (Comm) settlement

rego'lar|e adj regular • vt regulate; (ridurre, moderare) limit; (sistemare) settle. ~si vr (agire) act; (moderarsi) control oneself. ~ità f regularity. ~iz-'zare vt settle (debito)

rego'la|ta f darsi una ~ta pull oneself together. ~'tore, ~'trice adj piano ~tore urban development plan

'regolo m ruler

regres'sivo adj regressive. re-'gresso m decline

reinseri'mento m (di persona) re-integration

reinser'irsi vr (in ambiente) re-integrate

reinte'grare vt restore

relativa'mente adv relatively; ~ a as regards. rela'tivo adj relative

rela'tore, -'trice mf (in una conferenza) speaker

re'lax m relaxation

relazi'one f relation[ship]; (rapporto amoroso) [love] affair; (resoconto) report; pubbliche relazioni pl public relations

rele'gare vt relegate

religi'o|ne f religion. ~so, -a adj religious • m monk • f nun

re'liqui|a f relic. ~'ario m reliquary

re'litto m wreck

re'ma|re vi row. ~'tore, ~'trice mf rower

remini'scenza f reminiscence

remissi'one f remission; (sottomissione) submissiveness. remis'sivo adj submissive

'remo m oar

'remora f senza remore without hesitation

re'moto adj remote

remune'ra|re vt remunerate. ~zi'one f remuneration

'render|e vt (restituire) return; (esprimere) render; (fruttare) yield; (far diventare) make. ~si vr become; ~si conto di qcsa realize sth; ~si utile make oneself useful

rendi'conto m report

rendi'mento m rendering; (produzione) yield

'rendita f income; (dello Stato) revenue

'rene m kidney. ~ artificiale kidney machine

'reni fpl (schiena) back

reni'tente adj essere ~ a (consigli di qcno) be unwilling to accept

'renna f reindeer (pl inv); (pelle) buckskin

'reo, -a adj guilty • mf offender

re'parto m department; (Mil) unit

repel'lente adj repulsive

repen'taglio m mettere a ~ risk

repen'tino adj sudden

reper'ibile adj available; non è ~

(*perduto*) it's not to be found

repe'rire vt trace (*fondi*)

re'perto m ~ archeologico find

reper'torio m repertory; (*elenco*) index; **immagini** pl **di** ~ archive footage

'replica f reply; (*obiezione*) objection; (*copia*) replica; (*Theat*) repeat performance. **repli'care** vt reply; (*Theat*) repeat

repor'tage m inv report

repres|si'one f repression. ~'si-vo adj repressive. **re'presso** pp di re-primere. **re'primere** vt repress

re'pubbli|ca f republic. ~'cano, -a adj & mf republican

repu'tare vt consider

reputazi'one f reputation

requi'sito m requirement

requisi'toria f (*arringa*) closing speech

'resa f surrender; (*Comm*) rendering. ~ **dei conti** rendering of accounts

'residence m inv residential hotel

resi'den|te adj & mf resident. ~za f residence; (*soggiorno*) stay. ~zi'ale adj residential; **zona** ~zi'ale residential district

re'siduo adj residual ● m remainder

'resina f resin

resi'sten|te adj resistant; ~te al-l'acqua water-resistant. ~za f resistance; (*fisica*) stamina; (*Electr*) resistor; **la R~za** the Resistance

re'sistere vi ~ [a] resist; (*a colpi, scosse*) stand up to; ~ **alla pioggia/al vento** be rain-/wind-resistant

'reso pp di rendere

reso'conto m report

re'spin|gere vt repel; (*rifiutare*) reject; (*bocciare*) fail. ~**to** pp di re-spingere

respi'ra|re vt/i breathe. ~'tore m respirator. ~'tore [a tubo] snorkel; ~'torio adj respiratory. ~zi'one f breathing; (*Med*) respiration. ~zione

bocca a bocca mouth-to-mouth re-suscitation, kiss of life. **re'spiro** m breath; (*il respirare*) breathing; fig respite

respon'sabil|e adj responsible (**di** for); (*Jur*) liable ● mf person responsible. ~**e della produzione** production manager. ~**ità** f inv responsibility; (*Jur*) liability. ~**iz'zare** vt give responsibility to

re'sponso m response

'ressa f crowd

re'stante adj remaining ● m remainder

re'stare vi = RIMANERE

restau'ra|re vt restore. ~'tore, ~'trice mf restorer. ~zi'one f restoration. (*riparazione*) repair

re'stio adj restive; ~ **a** reluctant to

resti'tu|'ire vt return; (*reintegrare*) re-store. ~zi'one f return; (*Jur*) restitution

'resto m remainder; (*saldo*) balance; (*denaro*) change; **resti** pl (*avanzi*) re-mains; **del** ~ besides

re'string|ere vt contract; take in (*vestiti*); (*limitare*) restrict; shrink (*stoffa*). ~**si** vt contract; (*farsi più vi-cini*) close up; (*stoffa*): shrink. re-stringi'mento m (*di tessuto*) shrinkage

restri|t'tivo adj restrictive. ~zi'one f restriction

resurrezi'one f resurrection

resusci'tare vt/i revive

re'tata f round-up

'rete f net; (*sistema*) network; (*televi-siva*) channel; (*in calcio*) goal; fig trap; (*per la spesa*) string bag. ~ **locale** (*Comput*) local [area] network. ~ **stradale** road network. ~ **televisiva** television channel

reti'cen|te adj reticent. ~za f reticence

retico'lato m grid; (*rete metallica*) wire netting. **re'ticolo** m network

re'torico, -a adj rhetorical; **do-manda retorica** rhetorical question

● *f* rhetoric

retribu'ire *vt* remunerate. **∼zio'ne** *f* remuneration

'**retro** *adv* behind; vedi ∼ see over ● *m inv* back. ∼ **di copertina** outside back cover

retroat'tivo *adj* retroactive

retro'ce|dere *vi* retreat ● *vt* (*Mil*) demote; *Sport* relegate. ∼**ssi'one** *f Sport* relegation

retroda'tare *vt* backdate

re'trogrado *adj* retrograde; *fig* old-fashioned; (*Pol*) reactionary

retrogu'ardia *f* (*Mil*) rearguard

retro'marcia *f* reverse [gear]

retro'scena *m inv* (*Theat*) backstage; *fig* background details *pl*

retrospet'tivo *adj* retrospective

retro'stante *adj* **il palazzo** ∼ **the** building behind

retrovi'sore *m* rear-view mirror

'**retta**[1] *f* (*Math*) straight line; (*di collegio, pensionato*) fee

'**retta**[2] *f* **dar** ∼ **a qcno** take sb's advice

rettango'lare *adj* rectangular. **ret-'tangolo** *m* rectangle

ret'tifi|ca *f* rectification. ∼'**care** *vt* rectify

'**rettile** *m* reptile

retti'lineo *adj* rectilinear; (*retto*) upright ● *m Sport* back straight

'**retto** *pp di reggere* ● *adj* straight; (*giusto*) correct; **angolo** ∼ right angle

ret'tore *m* (*Relig*) rector; (*Univ*) principal, vice-chancellor

reu'matico *adj* rheumatic

reuma'tismi *mpl* rheumatism

reve'rendo *adj* reverend

rever'sibile *adj* reversible

revisio'nare *vt* revise; (*Comm*) audit; (*Auto*) overhaul. **revisi'one** *f* revision; (*Comm*) audit; (*Auto*) overhaul. **revi'sore** *m* (*di conti*) auditor; (*di bozze*) proof-reader; (*di traduzioni*) revisor

re'vival *m inv* revival

'**revoca** *f* repeal. **revo'care** *vt* repeal

riabili'ta|re *vt* rehabilitate. ∼**zio'ne** *f* rehabilitation

riabitu'ar|e *vt* reaccustom. ∼**si** *vr* reaccustom oneself

riac'cender|e *vt* rekindle (fuoco). ∼**si** *vr* (luce:) come back on

riacqui'stare *vt* buy back; regain (libertà, prestigio); recover (vista, udito)

riagganci'are *vt* replace (ricevitore); ∼ **la cornetta** hang up ● *vi* hang up

riallac'ciare *vt* refasten; reconnect (corrente); renew (amicizia)

rial'zare *vt* raise ● *vi* rise. **ri'alzo** *m* rise

riani'mar|e *vt* (*Med*) resuscitate; (*dare forza a*) revive; (*ridare coraggio a*) cheer up. ∼**si** *vr* regain consciousness; (*riprendere forza*) revive; (*riprendere coraggio*) cheer up

riaper'tura *f* reopening

ria'prir|e *vt*, ∼**si** *vr* reopen

rias'sumere *vt* summarize

riassun'tivo *adj* summarizing. **rias'sunto** *pp di riassumere* ● *m* summary

ria'ver|e *vt* get back; regain (salute, vista). ∼**si** *vr* recover

riavvici'namento *m* reconciliation

riavvici'nar|e *vt* reconcile (paesi, persone). ∼**si** *vr* (riconciliarsi) be reconciled, make it up

riba'dire *vt* (confermare) reaffirm

ri'balta *f* flap; (*Theat*) footlights *pl*; *fig* limelight

ribal'tar|e *vt*/*i*, ∼**si** *vr* tip over; (*Naut*) capsize

ribas'sare *vt* lower ● *vi* fall. **ri'basso** *m* fall; (*sconto*) discount

ri'battere *vt* (*a macchina*) retype; (*controbattere*) deny ● *vi* answer back

ribel'l|arsi *vr* rebel. **ri'belle** *adj*

rebellious ●*mf* rebel. ~'ione *f* rebellion

'**ribes** *m inv* (*rosso*) redcurrant; (*nero*) blackcurrant

ribol'lire *vi* ferment; *fig* seethe

ri'brezzo *m* disgust; far ~ a disgust

rica'dere *vi* fall back; (*nel peccato ecc*) lapse; (*pendere*) hang [down]; ~ su (*riversarsi*) fall on. **rica'duta** *f* relapse

rical'care *vt* trace

rica'ma|re *vt* embroider. ~to *adj* embroidered

ri'cambi *mpl* spare parts

ricambi'are *vt* return; reciprocate (*sentimento*); ~ qcsa a qcno repay sb for sth. **ri'cambio** *m* replacement; (*Biol*) metabolism; pezzo di ricambio spare [part]

ri'camo *m* embroidery

ricapito'la|re *vt* sum up. ~zi'one *f* summary, recap 🔟

ri'carica *f* (*di sveglia*) rewinding; (*Teleph*) top-up card

ricari'care *vt* reload (macchina fotografica, fucile, camion); recharge (batteria); (*Comput*) reboot

ricat'ta|re *vt* blackmail. ~tore, ~'trice *mf* blackmailer. **ri'catto** *m* blackmail

rica'va|re *vt* get; (*ottenere*) obtain; (*dedurre*) draw. ~to *m* proceeds *pl*. **ri'cavo** *m* proceeds *pl*

'ricca *f* rich woman. ~'mente *adv* lavishly

ric'chezza *f* wealth; *fig* richness

'riccio *adj* curly ●*m* curl; (*animale*) hedgehog. ~ di mare sea-urchin. ~lo *m* curl. ~'luto *adj* curly. **ric'ciuto** *adj* (*barba*) curly

'**ricco** *adj* rich ●*m* rich man

ri'cerca *f* search; (*indagine*) investigation; (*scientifica*) research; (*Sch*) project

ricer'ca|re *vt* search for; (*fare ricer-*

che su) research. ~**ta** *f* wanted woman. ~'**tezza** *f* refinement. ~**to** *adj* sought-after; (*raffinato*) refined; (*affettato*) affected ●*m* (*dalla polizia*) wanted man

ricetrasmit'tente *f* transceiver

ri'cetta *f* prescription; (*Culin*) recipe

ricet'tacolo *m* receptacle

ricet'tario *m* (*di cucina*) recipe book

ricetta'|tore, -'trice *mf* fence, receiver of stolen goods. ~zi'one *f* receiving [stolen goods]

rice'vente *adj* (apparecchio, stazione) receiving ●*mf* receiving

ri'cev|ere *vt* receive; (*dare il benvenuto*) welcome; (*di albergo*) accommodate. ~i'mento *m* receiving; (*accoglienza*) welcome; (*trattenimento*) reception

ricevi'tor|e *m* receiver. ~'ia *f* ~ia del lotto agency authorized to sell lottery tickets

rice'vuta *f* receipt

ricezi'one *f* (*Radio, TV*) reception

richia'mare *vt* (*al telefono*) call back; (*far tornare*) recall; (*rimproverare*) rebuke; (*attirare*) draw; ~ alla mente call to mind. **richi'amo** *m* recall; (*attrazione*) call

richi'edere *vt* ask for; (*di nuovo*) ask again for; ~ a qcno di fare qcsa ask o request sb to do sth. **richi'esta** *f* request; (*Comm*) demand

ri'chiuder|e *vt* close again. ~**si** *vr* (*ferita:*) heal

rici'claggio *m* recycling

rici'clare *vt* recycle (carta, vetro); launder (denaro sporco)

'**ricino** *m* olio di ~ castor oil

ricognizi'one *f* reconnaissance

ri'colmo *adj* full

ricominci'are *vt/i* start again

ricom'parire *vi* reappear

ricom'pen|sa *f* reward. ~'sare *vt* reward

ricom'por|re *vt* (*riscrivere*) rewrite;

(ricostruire) reform; (Typ) reset. **~si** vr regain one's composure

riconcili'a|re vt reconcile. **~rsi** vr be reconciled. **~zi'one** f reconciliation

ricono'scen|te adj grateful. **~za** f gratitude

rico'nosc|ere vt recognize; (ammettere) acknowledge. **~i'mento** m recognition; (ammissione) acknowledgement; (per la polizia) identification. **~i'uto** adj recognized

riconside'rare vt rethink

rico'prire vt re-cover; (rivestire) coat; (di insulti) shower (di with); hold (carica)

ricor'dar|e vt remember; (richiamare alla memoria) recall; (far ricordare) remind; (rassomigliare) look like. **~si** vr **~si [di]** remember. ri'cordo m memory; (oggetto) memento; (di viaggio) souvenir; ricordi pl (memorie) memoirs

ricor'ren|te adj recurrent. **~za** f recurrence; (anniversario) anniversary

ri'correre vi recur; (accadere) occur; (data:) fall; **~ a** have recourse to; (rivolgersi a) turn to. ri'corso pp di ricorrere ● m recourse; (Jur) appeal

ricostitu'ente m tonic

ricostitu'ire vt re-establish

ricostru|'ire vt reconstruct. **~zi'one** f reconstruction

ricove'ra|re vt give shelter to; **~re in ospedale** admit to hospital, hospitalize. **~to, -a** mf hospital patient. ri'covero m shelter; (ospizio) home

ricre'a|re vt re-create; (ristorare) restore. **~rsi** vr amuse oneself. **~'tivo** adj recreational. **~zi'one** f recreation; (Sch) break

ri'credersi vr change one's mind

ricupe'rare vt recover; rehabilitate (tossicodipendente); **~ il tempo perduto** make up for lost time. ri'cupero m recovery; (di tossicodipendente) rehabilitation; (salvataggio) res-

cue; **[minuti mpl di] ricupero** injury time

ri'curvo adj bent

ri'dare vt give back, return

ri'dente adj (piacevole) pleasant

'ridere vi laugh; **~ di** (deridere) laugh at

ri'detto pp di ridire

ridicoliz'zare vt ridicule. ri'dicolo adj ridiculous

ridimensio'nare vt reshape; fig see in the right perspective

ri'dire vt repeat; (criticare) find fault with

ridon'dante adj redundant

ri'dotto pp di ridurre ● m (Theat) foyer ● adj reduced

ri'du|rre vt reduce. **~rsi** vr diminish. **~rsi a** be reduced to. **~t'tivo** adj reductive. **~zi'one** f reduction; (per cinema, teatro) adaptation

rieducazi'one f (di malato) rehabilitation

riem'pi|re vt fill [up]; fill in (moduli ecc). **~rsi** vr fill [up]. **~'tivo** adj filling ● m filler

rien'tranza f recess

rien'trare vi go/come back in; (tornare) return; (piegare indentro) recede; **~ in** (far parte) fall within. ri'entro m return; (di astronave) re-entry

riepilo'gare vt recapitulate. rie'pilogo m roundup

riesami'nare vt reappraise

riesu'mare vt exhume

rievo'ca|re vt commemorate. **~zi'one** f commemoration

rifaci'mento m remake

ri'fa|re vt do again; (creare) make again; (riparare) repair; (imitare) imitate; make (letto). **~rsi** vr (rimettersi) recover; (vendicarsi) get even; **~rsi una vita/carriera** make a new life/career for oneself; **~rsi** di make up for. **~tto** pp di rifare

riferi'mento m reference

riferire | rilasciare

rife'rir|e vt report; ~e a attribute to ● vi make a report. ~si vr ~si a refer to

rifi'lare vt (tagliare a filo) trim; (🔲: affibbiare) saddle

rifi'ni|re vt finish off. ~'tura f finish

rifiu'tare vt refuse. rifi'uto m refusal; rifiuti pl (immondizie) rubbish sg. rifiuti pl urbani urban waste sg

riflessi'one f reflection; (osservazione) remark. rifles'sivo adj thoughtful; (Gram) reflexive

ri'flesso pp di riflettere ● m (luce) reflection; (Med) reflex; per ~ indirectly

ri'fletter|e vt reflect ● vi think. ~si vr be reflected

iflet'tore m reflector; (proiettore) searchlight

ri'flusso m ebb

ifocil'lar|e vt restore. ~si vr liter, hum take some refreshment

i'fondere vt refund

ri'forma f reform; (Relig) reformation; (Mil) medical exemption

ifor'ma|re vt re-form; (migliorare) reform; (Mil) declare unfit for military service. ~to adj (chiesa) Reformed. ~'tore, ~'trice mf reformer. ~'torio m reformatory. rifor'mista adj reformist

forni'mento m supply; (scorta) stock; (di combustibile) refuelling; stazione f di ~ petrol station

ifor'nir|e vt ~e di provide with. ~si vr restock, stock up (di with)

i'fra|ngere vt refract. ~tto pp di rifrangere. ~zi'one f refraction

ifug'gire vi ~ da fig shun

ifugi'a|rsi vr take refuge. ~to, -a mf refugee. ~to economico economic refugee

i'fugio m shelter; (nascondiglio) hideaway

iga f line; (fila) row; (striscia) stripe; (scriminatura) parting; (regolo) rule; a

righe (stoffa) striped; (quaderno) ruled; mettersi in ~ line up

ri'gagnolo m rivulet

ri'gare vt rule (foglio) ● vi ~ dritto behave well

rigatti'ere m junk dealer

rigene'rare vt regenerate

riget'tare vt throw back; (respingere) reject; (vomitare) throw up. ri'getto m rejection

ri'ghello m ruler

rigida|'mente adv rigidly. ~ità f rigidity; (di clima) severity; (severità) strictness. 'rigido adj rigid; (freddo) severe (severo) strict

rigi'rar|e vt turn again; (ripercorrere) go round; fig twist (argomentazione) ● vi walk about. ~si vr turn round; (nel letto) turn over. ri'giro m (imbroglio) trick

'rigo m line; (Mus) staff

ri'gogli|o m bloom. ~'oso adj luxuriant

ri'gonfio adj swollen

ri'gore m rigours pl; a ~ strictly speaking; calcio di ~ penalty [kick]; area di ~ penalty area; essere di ~ be compulsory

rigo'roso adj (severo) strict; (scrupoloso) rigorous

riguada'gnare vt regain (quota, velocità)

riguar'dar|e vt look at again; (considerare) regard; (concernere) concern; per quanto riguarda with regard to. ~si vr take care of oneself. ri'guardo m care; (considerazione) consideration; nei riguardi di towards; riguardo a with regard to

ri'gurgito m regurgitation

rilanci'are vt throw back (palla); (di nuovo) throw again; increase (offerta); revive (moda); relaunch (prodotto) ● vi (a carte) raise the stakes

rilasci'ar|e vt (concedere) grant; (liberare) release; issue (documento). ~si vr relax. ri'lascio m release; (di *documento*) issue

rilassa'mento *m* relaxation

rilas'sa|re *vt*, **~rsi** *vr* relax. **~to** *adj* (*ambiente*) relaxed

rile'ga|re *vt* bind (*libro*). **~to** *adj* bound. **~tura** *f* binding

ri'leggere *vt* reread

ri'lento: a **~** *adv* slowly

rileva'mento *m* survey; (*Comm*) buyout

rile'van|te *adj* considerable

rile'va|re *vt* (*trarre*) get; (*mettere in evidenza*) point out; (*notare*) notice; (*topografia*) survey; (*Comm*) take over; (*Mil*) relieve. **~zio'ne** *f* (*statistica*) survey

rili'evo *m* relief; (*Geog*) elevation; (*topografia*) survey; (*importanza*) importance; (*osservazione*) remark; **mettere in ~** qcsa point sth out

rilut'tan|te *adj* reluctant. **~za** *f* reluctance

'rima *f* rhyme

riman'dare *vt* (*posporre*) postpone; (*mandare indietro*) send back; (*mandare di nuovo*) send again; (*far ridare un esame*) make resit an examination. **ri'mando** *m* return; (*in un libro*) cross-reference

rima'nen|te *adj* remaining **•m** remainder. **~za** *f* remainder

rima'ne|re *vi* stay, remain; (*essere d'avanzo*) be left; (*venirsi a trovare*) be; (*restare stupito*) be astonished; (*restare d'accordo*) agree

rimar'chevole *adj* remarkable

ri'mare *vt/i* rhyme

rimargi'nar|e *vt*, **~si** *vr* heal

ri'masto *pp di* rimanere

rimbal'zare *vi* rebound; (*proiettile*) ricochet; far **~** bounce. **rim'balzo** *m* rebound; (*di proiettile*) ricochet

rimbam'bi|re *vi* be in one's dotage **•vt** stun. **~to** *adj* in one's dotage

rimboc'care *vt* turn up; roll up (*maniche*); tuck in (*coperte*)

rimbom'bare *vi* resound

rimbor'sare *vt* reimburse, repay. **rim'borso** *m* reimbursement, repayment. **rimborso spese** reimbursement of expenses

rimedi'are *vi* **~** a remedy; make up for (*errore*); (*procurare*) scrape up. **ri'medio** *m* remedy

rimesco'lare *vt* mix [up]; shuffle (*carte*); (*rivangare*) rake up

ri'messa *f* (*locale per veicoli*) garage; (*per aerei*) hangar; (*per autobus*) depot; (*di denaro*) remittance; (*di merci*) consignment

ri'messo *pp di* rimettere

ri'metter|e *vt* put back; (*restituire*) return; (*affidare*) entrust; (*perdonare*) remit; (*rimandare*) put off; (*vomitare*) bring up. **~si** *vr* (*ristabilirsi*) recover; (*tempo*) clear up; **~si** a start again

'rimmel® *m inv* mascara

rimoder'nare *vt* modernize

rimon'tare *vt* (*risalire*) go up; (*Mech*) reassemble **•vi** remount; **~** a (*risalire*) go back to

rimorchi'a|re *vt* tow; Ⓕ pick up (*ragazza*). **~'tore** *m* tug[boat]. **ri'morchio** *m* tow; (*veicolo*) trailer

ri'morso *m* remorse

rimo'stranza *f* complaint

rimozi'one *f* removal; (*da un incarico*) dismissal. **~** forzata illegally parked vehicles removed at owner's expense

rim'pasto *m* (*Pol*) reshuffle

rimpatri'are *vt/i* repatriate. **rim'patrio** *m* repatriation

rim'pian|gere *vt* regret. **~to** *pp di* rimpiangere **•m** regret

rimpiaz'zare *vt* replace

rimpiccio'lire *vi* become smaller

rimpinzar'|e *vt* **~e di** stuff with. **~si** *vr* stuff oneself

rimprove'rare *vt* reproach; **~** qcsa a qcno reproach sb for sth.

|

rim'provero m reproach

rimune'ra|re vt remunerate. ~tivo adj remunerative. ~zi|one f remuneration

ri'muovere vt remove

ri'nascere vi be reborn

rinascimen'tale adj Renaissance. Rinasci'mento m Renaissance

ri'nascita f rebirth

rincal'zare vt (sostenere) support; (rimboccare) tuck in. rin'calzo m support; rincalzi pl (Mil) reserves

rincantucci'arsi vr hide oneself away in a corner

rinca'rare vt increase the price of ● vi become more expensive. rin'caro m price increase

rinca'sare vi return home

rinchi'ud|ere vt shut up. ~si vr shut oneself up

rin'correre vt run after

rin'cors|a f run-up. ~o pp di rincorrere

rin'cresc|ere vi mi rincresce di non... I'm sorry o I regret that I can't...; se non ti ~e if you don't mind. ~i'mento m regret. ~i'uto pp di rincrescere

increti'nire vi be stupid

rincu'lare vi (arma:) recoil; (cavallo:) shy. rin'culo m recoil

rincuo'rar|e vt encourage. ~si vr take heart

infacci'are vt ~ qcsa a qcno throw sth in sb's face

infor'zar|e vt strengthen; (rendere più saldo) reinforce. ~si vr become stronger. rin'forzo m reinforcement; fig support

infran'care vt reassure

infre'scante adj cooling

infre'scar|e vt cool; (rinnovare) freshen up ● vi get cooler. ~si vr freshen [oneself] up. rin'fresco m light refreshment; (ricevimento) party

in'fusa f alla ~ at random

ringhi'era f railing; (di scala) banisters pl

ringiova'nire vt rejuvenate (pelle, persona); (vestito:) make look younger ● vi become young again; (sembrare) look young again

ringrazi|a'mento m thanks pl. ~'are vt thank

rinne'ga|re vt disown. ~to, -a mf renegade

rinnova'mento m renewal; (di edifici) renovation

rinno'var|e vt renew; renovate (edifici). ~si vr be renewed; (ripetersi) recur, happen again. rin'novo m renewal

rinoce'ronte m rhinoceros

rino'mato adj renowned

rinsal'dare vt consolidate

rinsa'vire vi come to one's senses

rinsec'chi|re vi shrivel up. ~to adj shrivelled up

rinta'narsi vr hide oneself away; (animale:) retreat into its den

rintoc'care vi (campana:) toll; (orologio:) strike. rin'tocco m toll; (di orologio) stroke

rinton'ti|re vt stun. ~to adj dazed

rintracci'are vt trace

rintro'nare vt stun ● vi boom

ri'nuncia f renunciation

rinunci'a|re vi ~re a renounce, give up. ~'tario adj defeatist

ri'nunzia, rinunzi'are = RINUNCIA, RINUNCIARE

rinveni'mento m (di reperti) discovery; (di refurtiva) recovery. rinve'nire vt find ● vi (riprendere i sensi) come round; (ridiventare fresco) revive

rinvi'are vt put off; (mandare indietro) return; (in libro) refer; ~ a giudizio indict

rin'vio m Sport goal kick; (in libro) cross-reference; (di appuntamento) postponement; (di merce) return

rio'nale adj local. ri'one m district

riordi'nare vt tidy [up]; (*ordinare di nuovo*) reorder; (*riorganizzare*) reorganize

riorganiz'zare vt reorganize

ripa'gare vt repay

ripa'ra|re vt protect; (*aggiustare*) repair; (*porre rimedio*) remedy ● vi ~a make up for. ~**rsi** vr take shelter. ~to adj (*luogo*) sheltered. ~**zi'one** f repair; fig reparation. **ri'paro** m shelter; (*rimedio*) remedy

ripar'ti|re vt (*dividere*) divide ● vi leave again. ~**zi'one** f division

ripas'sa|re vt (*rivedere*) revise ● vi pass again. **ri'passo** m (*di lezione*) revision

ripensa'mento m second thoughts pl

ripen'sare vi change one's mind; ~ a think of; ripensaci! think again!

riper'correre vt go back over

riper'cosso pp di ripercuotere

ripercu'oter|e vt strike again. ~**si** vr (*suono*) reverberate; ~**si su** (*avere conseguenze*) impact on. ripercussi'one f repercussion

ripe'scare vt fish out (*oggetto*)

ripe'tente mf student repeating a year

ri'pet|ere vt repeat. ~**ersi** vr (*evento*) recur. ~**izi'one** f repetition; (*di lezione*) revision; (*lezione privata*) private lesson. ~**uta'mente** adv repeatedly

ri'piano m (*di scaffale*) shelf; (*terreno pianeggiante*) terrace

ri'picc|a f fare qcsa per ~**a** do sth out of spite. ~**o** m spite

'ripido adj steep

ripie'ga|re vt refold; (*abbassare*) lower ● vi (*indietreggiare*) retreat. ~**rsi** vr bend; (*sedile*) fold. **ripi'ego** m expedient; (*via d'uscita*) way out

ripi'eno adj full; (*Culin*) stuffed ● m filling; (*Culin*) stuffing

ri'porre vt put back; (*mettere da parte*) put away; (*collocare*) place; repeat (*domanda*)

ripor'tar|e vt (*restituire*) bring/take back; (*riferire*) report; (*subire*) suffer; (*Math*) carry; win (*vittoria*); transfer (*disegno*). ~**si** vr go back; (*riferirsi*) refer

ripo'sante adj (*colore*) restful, soothing

ripo'sa|re vi rest ● vt put back. ~**rsi** vr rest. ~**to** adj (*mente*) fresh. **ri'poso** m rest; andare a riposo retire; riposo! (*Mil*) at ease!; giorno di riposo day off

ripo'stiglio m cupboard

ri'posto pp di riporre

ri'prend|ere vt take again; (*prendere indietro*) take back; (*riconquistare*) recapture; (*ricuperare*) recover; (*ricominciare*) resume; (*rimproverare*) reprimand; take in (*in cucitura*); Cinema shoot. ~**ersi** vr recover; (*correggersi*) correct oneself

ri'presa f resumption; (*ricupero*) recovery; (*Theat*) revival; Cinema shot; (*Auto*) acceleration; (*Mus*) repeat. ~ **aerea** bird's-eye view

ripresen'tar|e vt resubmit (*domanda, certificato*). ~**si** vr go back again; (*come candidato*) run again (*occasione*) arise again

ri'preso pp di riprendere

ripristi'nare vt restore

ripro'dotto pp di riprodurre

ripro'du|rre vt, ~**rsi** vr reproduce. ~**t'tivo** adj reproductive. ~**zi'one** f reproduction

ripro'mettersi vr intend

ri'prova f confirmation

ripudi'are vt repudiate

ripu'gnan|te adj repugnant. ~**za** f disgust. ripu'gnare vi disgust a disgust

ripu'li|re vt clean [up]; fig polish

ripuls|i'one f repulsion. ~'ivo adj repulsive

ri'quadro m square; (*pannello*) pane

ri'sacca f undertow

risa'lire vt go back up ● vi ~ a (nel tempo) go back to; (essere datato a) date back to, go back to

risal'tare vi stand out. ri'salto m prominence; (rilievo) relief

risa'nare vt heal; (bonificare) reclaim

risa'puto adj well-known

risarci'mento m compensation. risar'cire vt indemnify

ri'sata f laugh

riscalda'mento m heating. ~ autonomo central heating (for one flat)

iscal'dar|e vt heat; warm (persona). ~si vr warm up

iscat'tar|e vt ransom. ~si vr redeem oneself. ri'scatto m ransom; (morale) redemption

ischia'rar|e vt light up; brighten (colore). ~si vr light up; (cielo:) clear up

ischi'are vt risk ● vi run the risk. 'rischio m risk. ~'oso adj risky

isciac'quare vt rinse

iscon'trare vt (confrontare) compare; (verificare) check; (rilevare) find. ri'scontro m comparison; check; (Comm: risposta) reply

i'scossa f revolt; (riconquista) recovery

iscossi'one f collection

i'scosso pp di riscuotere

iscu'oter|e vt shake; (percepire) draw; (ottenere) gain; cash (assegno). ~si vr rouse oneself

isen'tir|e vt hear again; (provare) feel ● vi ~re di feel the effect of. ~rsi vr (offendersi) take offence. ~to adj resentful

i'serbo m reserve; mantenere il ~ remain tight-lipped

i'serva f reserve; (di caccia, pesca) preserve; Sport substitute, reserve. ~ di caccia game reserve. ~ naturale wildlife reserve

iser'va|re vt reserve; (prenotare)

book; (per occasione) keep. ~rsi vr (ripromettersi) plan for oneself (cambiamento). ~'tezza f reserve. ~to adj reserved

ri'siedere vi ~ a live in/at

'riso[1] m (cereale) rice

'riso[2] pp di ridere ● m (pl f risa) laughter; (singolo) laugh. ~'lino m giggle

ri'solto pp di risolvere

risolu'tezza f determination. riso'luto adj resolute, determined. ~zi'one f resolution

ri'solver|e vt resolve; (Math) solve. ~si vr (decidersi) decide; ~si in turn into

riso'na|nza f resonance; aver ~nza arouse great interest. ~re vi resound; (rimbombare) echo

ri'sorgere vi rise again

risorgi'mento m revival; (storico) Risorgimento

ri'sorsa f resource; (espediente) resort

ri'sorto pp di risorgere

ri'sotto m risotto

ri'sparmi mpl (soldi) savings

risparmi'a|re vt save; (salvare) spare. ~'tore, ~'trice mpl saver ri'sparmio m saving

rispecchi'are vt reflect

rispet'tabil|e adj respectable. ~ità f respectability

rispet'tare vt respect; farsi ~ command respect

rispet'tivo adj respective

ri'spetto m respect; ~ a as regards; (in confronto a) compared to

rispet'tosa'mente adv respectfully. ~'toso adj respectful

risplen'dente adj shining. ri'splendere vi shine

rispon'den|te adj in a keeping with. ~za f correspondence

ri'spondere vi answer; (rimbeccare) answer back; (obbedire) respond; ~ a reply to; ~ **di** (*rendersi responsabile*) answer for

ri'spost|a *f* answer, reply; (*reazione*) response. ~**o** *pp* di **rispondere**

'**rissa** *f* brawl. **ris'soso** *adj* pugnacious

ristabi'lir|e *vt* re-establish. ~**si** *vr* (*in salute*) recover

rista'gnare *vi* stagnate; (*sangue:*) coagulate. **ri'stagno** *m* stagnation

ri'stampa *f* reprint; (*azione*) reprinting. **ristam'pare** *vt* reprint

risto'rante *m* restaurant

risto'ra|re *vt* refresh. ~**rsi** *vr* liter take some refreshment; (*riposarsi*) take a rest. ~**tore**, ~**trice** *mf* (*proprietario di ristorante*) restaurateur; (*fornitore*) caterer ● *adj* refreshing. **ri'storo** *m* refreshment; (*sollievo*) relief

ristret'tezza *f* narrowness; (*povertà*) poverty

ri'stretto *pp* di **restringere** ● *adj* narrow; (*condensato*) condensed; (*limitato*) restricted; **di idee ristrette** narrow-minded

ristruttu'rare *vt* restructure (*ditta*); refurbish (*casa*)

risucchi'are *vt* suck in. **ri'succhio** *m* whirlpool; (*di corrente*) undertow

risul'ta|re *vi* result; (*riuscire*) turn out. ~**to** *m* result

risuo'nare *vi* echo; (*Phys*) resonate

risurrezi'one *f* resurrection

risusci'tare *vt* resuscitate; *fig* revive ● *vi* return to life

risvegli'ar|e *vt* reawaken (*interesse*). ~**si** *vr* wake up; (*natura:*) awake; (*desiderio:*) be aroused. **ri'sveglio** *m* waking up; (*dell'interesse*) revival; (*del desiderio*) arousal

ri'svolto *m* lapel; (*di pantaloni*) turn-up, cuff *Am*; (*di manica*) cuff; (*di tasca*) flap; (*di libro*) inside flap

ritagli'are *vt* cut out. **ri'taglio** *m* cutting; (*di stoffa*) scrap

ritar'da|re *vi* be late; (*orologio:*) be slow ● *vt* delay; slow down (*progresso*); (*differire*) postpone. ~**tario**, -**a** *mf* late-comer

ri'tardo *m* delay; **essere in** ~ **be** late; (*volo:*) be delayed

ri'tegno *m* reserve

rite'n|ere *vt* retain; deduct (*somma*); (*credere*) believe. ~**uta** *f* deduction

riti'ra|re *vt* throw back (*palla*); (*prelevare*) withdraw; (*riscuotere*) draw; collect (*pacco*). ~**rsi** *vr* withdraw; (*stoffa:*) shrink; (*da attività*) retire; (*marea:*) recede. ~**ta** *f* retreat; (*WC*) toilet. **ri'tiro** *m* withdrawal; (*Relig*) retreat; (*da attività*) retirement. **ritiro bagagli** baggage reclaim

'**ritmo** *m* rhythm

'**rito** *m* rite; **di** ~ customary

ritoc'care *vt* touch up

ritor'nare *vi* return; (*andare venire indietro*) go/come back; (*ricorrere*) recur; (*ridiventare*) become again

ritor'nello *m* refrain

ri'torno *m* return

ritorsi'one *f* retaliation

ri'tra|rre *vt* withdraw; (*distogliere*) turn away; (*rappresentare*) portray

ritrat'ta|re *vt* deal with again; retract (*dichiarazione*). ~**zi'one** *f* withdrawal, retraction

ritrat'tista *mf* portrait painter. **ri'tratto** *pp* di **ritrarre** ● *m* portrait

ritro'sia *f* shyness. **ri'troso** *adj* backward; (*timido*) shy; **a ritroso** backwards; **ritroso a** reluctant to

ritro'va|re *vt* find [again]; regain (*salute*). ~**rsi** *vr* meet; (*di nuovo*) meet again; (*capitare*) find oneself; (*raccapezzarsi*) see one's way. ~**to** *m* discovery. **ri'trovo** *m* meeting-place; (*notturno*) night-club

'**ritto** *adj* upright; (*diritto*) straight

ritu'ale *adj* & *m* ritual

riunifi'ca|re *vt* reunify. ~**rsi** *vr* be reunited. ~**zi'one** *f* reunification

riuni'one f meeting; (fra amici) reunion

riu'nir|e vt (unire) join together; (radunare) gather. ~**si** vr be re-united; (adunarsi) meet

rius'ci|re vi (aver successo) succeed; (in matematica ecc) be good (in at); (aver esito) turn out; **le è riuscito simpatico** she found him likeable. ~**ta** f result; (successo) success

'riva f shore; (di fiume) bank

ri'val|e mf rival. ~**ità** f inv rivalry

rivalutazi'one f revaluation

rive'dere vt see again; (verificare) check

rive'la|re vt reveal. ~**rsi** vr (dimostrarsi) turn out. ~**'tore** adj revealing ● m (Techn) detector. ~**zi'one** f revelation

ri'vendere vt resell

rivendi'ca|re vt claim. ~**zi'one** f claim

ri'vendi|ta f (negozio) shop. ~**tore**, **~'trice** mf retailer. ~**tore autorizzato** authorized dealer

ri'verbero m reverberation; (bagliore) glare

rive'renza f reverence; (inchino) curtsy; (di uomo) bow

rive'rire vt respect; (ossequiare) pay one's respects to

river'sar|e vt pour. ~**si** vr (fiume:) flow

rivesti'mento m covering

rive'sti|re vt (rifornire di abiti) clothe; (ricoprire) cover; (internamente) line; hold (carica). ~**rsi** vr get dressed again; (per una festa) dress up

rivi'era f coast; **la ~ ligure** the Italian Riviera

ri'vincita f Sport return match; (vendetta) revenge

rivis'suto pp di rivivere

ri'vista f review; (pubblicazione) magazine; (Theat) revue; **passare in ~** review

ri'vivere vi come to life again; (riprendere le forze) revive ● vt relive

ri'volger|e vt turn; (indirizzare) address; **~e da** (distogliere) turn away from. ~**si** vr turn round; ~**si a** (indirizzarsi) turn to

ri'volta f revolt

rivol'tante adj disgusting

rivol'tar|e vt turn [over]; (mettendo l'interno verso l'esterno) turn inside out; (sconvolgere) upset. ~**si** vr (ribellarsi) revolt

rivol'tella f revolver

ri'volto pp di rivolgere

rivoluzio'nare vt revolutionize. ~**io, -a** adj & mf revolutionary. **rivoluzi'one** f revolution; (fig: disordine) chaos

riz'zar|e vt raise; (innalzare) erect; prick up (orecchie). ~**si** vr stand up; (capelli:) stand on end; (orecchie:) prick up

'roaming m inv (Teleph) ~ **[internazionale]** roaming

'roba f stuff; (personale) belongings pl, stuff; (faccenda) things pl; (▣: droga) drugs pl. ~ **da mangiare** things to eat

ro'baccia f rubbish

ro'bot m inv robot. ~ **da cucina** food processor

robu'stezza f sturdiness, robustness; (forza) strength. **ro'busto** adj sturdy, robust; (forte) strong

'rocca f fortress. ~**forte** f stronghold

roc'chetto m reel

'roccia f rock

ro'da|ggio m running in. ~**re** vt run in

'roder|e vt gnaw; (corrodere) corrode. ~**si** vr ~**si da** be consumed with. **rodi'tore** m rodent

rodo'dendro m rhododendron

ro'gnone m (Culin) kidney

'rogo m (supplizio) stake; (per

cadaveri) pyre

'**Roma** f Rome

Roma'nia f Romania

ro'manico adj Romanesque

ro'mano, -a adj & mf Roman

romanti'cismo m romanticism. **ro'mantico** adj romantic

ro'man|za f romance. **~'zato** adj romanticized. **~'zesco** adj fictional; (*stravagante*) wild, unrealistic. **~zi'ere** m novelist

ro'manzo adj Romance ●m novel. **~ giallo** thriller

'**rombo** m rumble; (*Math*) rhombus; (*pesce*) turbot

'**romper|e** vt break; break off (*relazione*); non **~e** [le scatole]! (🔲: *seccare*) don't be a pain [in the neck]!. **~si** vr break; **~si una gamba** break one's leg

rompi'capo m nuisance; (*indovinello*) puzzle

rompi'collo m daredevil; **a ~** at breakneck speed

rompighi'accio m ice-breaker

rompi'scatole mf inv 🔲 pain

'**ronda** f rounds pl

ron'della f (*Mech*) washer

ron'dine f swallow

ron'done m swift

ron'fare vi snore

ron'zino m jade

ron'zio m buzz

'**rosa** f rose. **~ dei venti** wind rose ●adj & m pink. **ro'saio** m rose-bush

ro'sario m rosary

ro'sato adj rosy ●m (*vino*) rosé

'**roseo** adj pink

ro'seto m rose garden

rosma'rino m rosemary

'**roso** pp di **rodere**

roso'lare vt brown

roso'lia f German measles

ro'sone m rosette; (*apertura*) rose-window

'**rospo** m toad

ros'setto m (*per labbra*) lipstick

'**rosso** adj & m red; **passare con il ~** jump a red light. **~ d'uovo** [egg] yolk. **ros'sore** m redness; (*della pelle*) flush

rostice'ria f shop selling cooked meat and other prepared food

ro'tabile adj strada **~** carriageway

ro'taia f rail; (*solco*) rut

ro'ta|re vt/i rotate. **~zi'one** f rotation

rote'are vt/i roll

ro'tella f small wheel; (*di mobile*) castor

roto'lar|e vt/i roll. **~si** vr roll [about]. '**rotolo** m roll; **andare a ~toli** go to rack and ruin

rotondità f roundness; (*curve femminili*) curves. **ro'tondo, -a** adj round ●f (*spiazzo*) terrace

ro'tore m rotor

'**rotta**[1] f (*Naut*), (*Aeron*) course; **far ~ per** make course for; **fuori ~** off course

'**rotta**[2] f **a ~ di collo** at breakneck speed; **essere in ~ con** be on bad terms with

rot'tame m scrap; fig wreck

'**rotto** pp di **rompere** ●adj broken; (*stracciato*) torn

rot'tura f break

'**rotula** f kneecap

rou'lette f inv roulette

rou'lotte f inv caravan, trailer Am

rou'tine f inv routine; **di ~** (*operazioni, controlli*) routine

ro'vente adj scorching

'**rovere** m (*legno*) oak

rovesci'ar|e vt knock over; (*sottosopra*) turn upside down; (*rivoltare*) turn inside out; spill (*liquido*); overthrow (*governo*); reverse (*situazione*). **~si** vr (*capovolgersi*) overturn; (*riversarsi*) pour. **ro'vescio** adj (*contrario*) reverse **alla rovescia** (*capovolto*) upside dow (con l'interno all'esterno) inside out ● *m* reverse; (nella maglia) purl; (di pioggia) downpour; Tennis backhand

ro'vina *f* ruin; (crollo) collapse

rovi'na|re *vt* ruin; (guastare) spoil ● *vi* crash. **~rsi** *vr* be ruined. **~to** *adj* (oggetto) ruined. **rovi'noso** *adj* ruinous

rovi'stare *vt* ransack

'rovo *m* bramble

'rozzo *adj* rough

R.R. *abbr* (ricevuta di ritorno) return receipt for registered mail

'ruba *f* andare a ~ sell like hot cakes

ru'bare *vt* steal

rubi'netto *m* tap, faucet Am

ru'bino *m* ruby

ru'brica *f* column; (in programma televisivo) TV report; (quaderno con indice) address book. ~ **telefonica** telephone and address book

rude *adj* rough

rudere *m* ruin

rudimen'tale *adj* rudimentary. **rudi'menti** *mpl* rudiments

ruffi'an|a *f* procuress. **~o** *m* pimp; (adulatore) bootlicker

ruga *f* wrinkle

ruggine *f* rust; fare la ~ go rusty

ug'gire *vi* roar. **~to** *m* roar

ugi'ada *f* dew

'u'goso *adj* wrinkled

ul'lare *vi* roll; (Aeron) taxi

ul'lino *m* film

ul'lio *m* rolling; (Aeron) taxiing

'um *m* rum

u'meno, -a *adj* & *mf* Romanian

u'mor|e *m* noise; fig rumour. **~eg-gi'are** *vi* rumble. **rumo'roso** *adj* noisy; (sonoro) loud

u'olo *m* roll; (Theat) role; di ~ on the staff

u'ota *f* wheel; andare a ~ libera free-wheel. ~ **di scorta** spare wheel

'rupe *f* cliff

ru'rale *adj* rural

ru'scello *m* stream

'ruspa *f* bulldozer

rus'sare *vi* snore

'Russ|ia *f* Russia. **r~o**, **-a** *adj* & *mf* Russian; (lingua) Russian

'rustico *adj* rural; (carattere) rough

rut'tare *vi* belch. **'rutto** *m* belch

'ruvido *adj* coarse

ruzzo'l|are *vi* tumble down. **~one** *m* tumble; cadere ruzzoloni tumble down

- - - - - - - - - - - - - - - - - -

Ss

- - - - - - - - - - - - - - - - - -

'sabato *m* Saturday

'sabbi|a *f* sand. **~e** *pl* mobili quicksand. **~oso** *a* sandy

sabo'ta|ggio *m* sabotage. **~re** *vt* sabotage. **~'tore**, **~'trice** *mf* saboteur

'sacca *f* bag. ~ **da viaggio** travelling-bag

sacca'rina *f* saccharin

sac'cente *adj* pretentious ● *mf* know-all

saccheggi'a|re *vt* sack; hum raid (frigo)

sac'chetto *m* bag

'sacco *m* sack; (Anat) sac; mettere nel ~ fig swindle; un ~ (moltissimo) a lot; un ~ di (gran quantità) lots of. ~ **a pelo** sleeping-bag

sacer'do|te *m* priest

sacra'mento *m* sacrament

sacrifi'ca|re *vt* sacrifice. **~rsi** *vr* sacrifice oneself. **~to** *adj* (non valorizzato) wasted. **sacri'ficio** *m* sacrifice

sa'crilego *adj* sacrilegious

'sacro *adj* sacred ● *m* (Anat) sacrum

sacro'santo *adj* sacrosanct

'sadico, -a *adj* sadistic ●*mf* sadist. **sa'dismo** *m* sadism

sa'etta *f* arrow

sa'fari *m inv* safari

'saga *f* saga

sa'gace *adj* shrewd

sag'gezza *f* wisdom

saggi'are *vt* test

'saggio¹ *m* (*scritto*) essay; (*prova*) proof; (*di metallo*) assay; (*campione*) sample; (*esempio*) example

'saggio² *adj* wise

sag'gistica *f* non-fiction

Sagit'tario *m* (*Astr*) Sagittarius

sa'goma *f* shape; (*profilo*) outline. **sago'mato** *adj* shaped

'sagra *f* festival

sagre'stano *m* sacristan. ~**'stia** *f* sacristy

'sala *f* hall; (*stanza*) room; (*salotto*) living room. ~ **d'attesa** waiting room. ~ **da ballo** ballroom. ~ **macchine** engine room. ~ **operatoria** operating theatre. ~ **parto** delivery room. ~ **da pranzo** dining room

sa'lame *m* salami

sala'moia *f* brine

sa'lare *vt* salt

sa'lario *m* wages *pl*

sa'lasso *m* essere un ~ *fig* cost a fortune

sala'tini *mpl* savouries (*eaten with aperitifs*)

sa'lato *adj* salty; (*costoso*) dear

sal'ciccia *f* = SALSICCIA

sal'dar|e *vt* weld; set (*osso*); pay off (*debito*); settle (*conto*); ~**e a stagno** solder. ~**si** *vr* (*Med: osso*) knit

salda'trice *f* welder; (*a stagno*) soldering iron

salda'tura *f* weld; (*azione*) welding; (*di osso*) knitting

'saldo *adj* firm; (*resistente*) strong ●*m* settlement; (*svendita*) sale; (*Comm*) balance

'sale *m* salt. ~ **fine** table salt. ~ **grosso** cooking salt. **sali** *pl* e **tabacchi** tobacconist's shop

'salice *m* willow. ~ **piangente** weeping willow

sali'ente *adj* outstanding; **i punti salienti di un discorso** the main points of a speech

sali'era *f* salt-cellar

sa'lina *f* salt-works *sg*

sa'li|re *vi* go/come up; (*levarsi*) rise; (*su treno ecc*) get on; (*in macchina*) get in ●*vt* go/come up (*scale*). ~**ta** *f* climb; (*aumento*) rise; **in** ~**ta** uphill

sa'liva *f* saliva

'salma *f* corpse

'salmo *m* psalm

sal'mone *m* & *adj inv* salmon

sa'lone *m* hall; (*salotto*) living room; (*di parrucchiere*) salon. ~ **di bellezza** beauty parlour

salo'pette *f inv* dungarees *pl*

salot'tino *m* bower

sa'lotto *m* drawing room; (*soggiorno*) sitting room; (*mobili*) [three-piece] suite

sal'pare *vt/i* sail; ~ **l'ancora** weigh anchor

'salsa *f* sauce

sal'sedine *f* saltiness

sal'siccia *f* sausage

sal'ta|re *vi* jump; (*venir via*) come off; (*balzare*) leap; (*esplodere*) blow up; ~**r fuori** spring from nowhere; (*oggetto cercato*): turn up; **è** ~**to fuori che...** it emerged that...; ~**re fuori con...** come out with...; ~**re in mente** spring to mind ●*vt* jump [over]; skip (*pasti, lezioni*); (*Culin*) sauté. ~**to** *adj* (*Culin*) sautéed

saltel'lare *vi* hop; (*di gioia*) skip

saltim'banco *m* acrobat

'salto *m* jump; (*balzo*) leap; (*dislivello*) drop; (*omissione, lacuna*) gap; fare un

saltuariamente | Sardegna

~ da drop in on. ~ in alto high jump. ~ con l'asta pole-vault. ~ in lungo long jump. ~ pagina (Comput) page down

saltuaria'mente adv occasionally. **saltu'ario** adj desultory; lavoro saltuario casual work

sa'lubre adj healthy

salume'ria f delicatessen. **sa'lumi** mpl cold cuts

salu'tare vt greet; (congedandosi) say goodbye to; (portare i saluti a) give one's regards to; (Mil) salute ● adj healthy

sa'lute f health; ~! (dopo uno starnuto) bless you!; (a un brindisi) your health!

sa'luto m greeting; (di addio) goodbye; (Mil) salute; **saluti** pl (ossequi) regards

salva f salvo; sparare a salve fire blanks

salvada'naio m money box

salva'gente m lifebelt; (a giubbotto) life-jacket; (ciambella) rubber ring; (spartitraffico) traffic island

salvaguar'dare vt safeguard. **salvagu'ardia** f safeguard

sal'var|e vt save; (proteggere) protect. ~si vr save oneself

salva'slip m inv panty-liner

salva|'taggio m rescue; (Naut) salvage; (Comput) saving; battello di ~taggio lifeboat

sal'vezza f safety; (Relig) salvation

salvia f sage

salvi'etta f serviette

salvo adj safe ● prep except [for] ● conj ~ che (a meno che) unless; (eccetto che) except that

samari'tano, -a adj & mf Samaritan

sam'buco m elder

san m S~ Francesco Saint Francis

sa'nare vt heal

sana'torio m sanatorium

san'cire vt sanction

'sandalo m sandal

'sangu|e m blood; al ~e (carne) rare; farsi cattivo ~e per worry about. ~e freddo composure; a ~e freddo in cold blood. ~'igno adj blood

sangui'naccio m (Culin) black pudding

sangui'nante adj bleeding

sangui'nar|e vi bleed. ~io adj bloodthirsty

sangui'noso adj bloody

sangui'suga f leech

sanità f soundness; (salute) health. ~ mentale mental health

sani'tario adj sanitary; Servizio S~ Health Service

'sano adj sound; (salutare) healthy; ~ di mente sane; ~ come un pesce as fit as a fiddle

San Sil'vestro m New Year's Eve

santifi'care vt sanctify

'santo adj holy; (con nome proprio) saint ● m saint. **san'tone** m guru. **santu'ario** m sanctuary

sanzi'one f sanction

sa'pere vt know; (essere capace di) be able to; (venire a sapere) hear; saperla lunga know a thing or two ● vi ~ di know about; (aver sapore di) taste of; (aver odore di) smell of; saperci fare have the know-how ● m knowledge

sapi'en|te adj wise; (esperto) expert ● m (uomo colto) sage. ~za f wisdom

sa'pone m soap. ~ da bucato washing soap. **sapo'netta** f bar of soap

sa'pore m taste. **sapo'rita'mente** adv soundly. **sapo'rito** adj tasty

sapu'tello, -a adj & m [x] know-all, know-it-all Am

saraci'nesca f roller shutter

sar'cas|mo m sarcasm. ~tico adj sarcastic

Sar'degna f Sardinia

sar'dina f sardine

'sardo, -a adj & mf Sardinian

> *i* Sardo *Sardo* is Sardinia's traditional language. It is considered to be an independent language because of its many differences from Italian and its long independent history. Sardinian preserves many features derived from Latin which were lost in Italian, e.g. the k-sound in words like *chelu* (Italian *cielo*).

sar'donico adj sardonic

'sarto, -a m tailor • f dressmaker. ~'ria f tailor's; dressmaker's; (*arte*) couture

'sasso m stone; (*ciottolo*) pebble

sassofo'nista mf saxophonist. sas'sofono m saxophone

sas'soso adj stony

sa'tellite adj inv & nm satellite

sati'nato adj glossy

'satira f satire. sa'tirico adj satirical

satu'rare vt saturate. ~zi'one f saturation. 'saturo adj saturated; (*pieno*) full

'sauna f sauna

savoi'ardo m (*biscotto*) sponge finger

sazi'ar|e vt satiate. ~si vr si di fig grow tired of

sazietà f mangiare a ~ eat one's fill. 'sazio adj satiated

sbaciucchi'ar|e vt smother with kisses. ~si vr kiss and cuddle

sbada'ta|ggine f carelessness; è stata una ~ggine it was careless. ~'mente adv carelessly. sba'dato adj careless

sbadigli'are vi yawn. sba'diglio m yawn

sba'fare vt sponge

'sbafo m sponging; a ~ without paying

sbagli'ar|e vi make a mistake; (*aver torto*) be wrong • vt make a mistake in; ~e strada go the wrong way; ~e numero get the number wrong; (*Teleph*) dial the wrong number. ~si vr make a mistake. 'sbaglio m mistake; per sbaglio by mistake

sbal'l|are vt unpack; ▣ screw up (*conti*) • vi ▣ go crazy. ~ato adj (*squilibrato*) unbalanced

sballot'tare vt toss about

sbalor'di|re vt stun • vi be stunned. ~'tivo adj amazing. ~to adj stunned

sbal'zare vt throw; (*da una carica*) dismiss • vi bounce; (*saltare*) leap. 'sbalzo m bounce; (*sussulto*) jolt; (*di temperatura*) sudden change; a sbalzi in spurts; a sbalzo (*lavoro a rilievo*) embossed

sban'care vt bankrupt; ~ il banco break the bank

sbanda'mento m (*Auto*) skid; (*Naut*) list; fig going off the rails

sban'da|re vi (*Auto*) skid; (*Naut*) list. ~rsi vr (*disperdersi*) disperse. ~ta f skid; (*Naut*) list. ~to, -a adj mixed-up • mf mixed-up person

sbandie'rare vt wave; fig display

sbaracc'are vt/i clear up

sbaragli'ar|e vt rout. sba'raglio m rout; mettere allo sbaraglio rout

sbaraz'zar|e vt clear. ~si vr ~si di get rid of

sbaraz'zino, -a adj mischievous • mf scamp

sbar'bar|e vt, ~si vr shave

sbar'care vt/i disembark; ~ il lunario make ends meet. 'sbarco m landing; (*di merci*) unloading

'sbarra f bar; (*di passaggio a livello*) barrier. ~'mento m barricade. sbar'rare vt bar; (*ostruire*) block; cross (*assegno*); (*spalancare*) open wide

sbatacchi'are vt/i ⊠ bang

'sbatter|e vt bang; slam, bang (*porta*); (*urtare*) knock; (*Culin*) beat;

flap (ali); shake (tappeto) • vi bang; (porta:) slam, bang. ~si vr ⊠ rush around; ~sene di qcsa not give a damn about sth. sbat'tuto adj tossed; (Culin) beaten; fig run down

sba'va|re vi dribble; (colore:) smear. ~tura f smear; senza ~tura fig faultless

sbel'li|carsi vr ~ dalle risa split one's sides [with laughter]

sberla f slap

sbia'di|re vt/i, ~rsi vr fade. ~to adj faded; fig colourless

sbian'car|e vt/i, ~si vr whiten

sbi'eco adj slanting; di ~ on the slant; (guardare) sidelong; guardare qcno di ~ look askance at sb; tagliare di ~ cut on the bias

bigot'ti|re vt dismay • vt/i, ~rsi vr be dismayed. ~to adj dismayed

sbilanci'ar|e vt unbalance • vi (perdere l'equilibrio) overbalance. ~si vr lose one's balance

bizzar'rirsi vr satisfy one's whims

bloc'care vt unblock; (Mech) release; decontrol (prezzi)

boc'care vi ~ in (fiume:) flow into; (strada:) lead to; (folla:) pour into

boc'cato adj foul-mouthed

bocci'are vi blossom

sbocco m flowing; (foce) mouth; (Comm) outlet

bolo'gnare vt ① get rid of

sbornia f prendere una ~ get drunk

bor'sare vi pay out

bot'tare vi burst out

botto'nar|e vt unbutton. ~si vr (①: confidarsi) open up; ~si la camicia unbutton one's shirt

bra'carsi vr put on something more comfortable; ~ dalle risate ① kill oneself laughing

bracci'a|rsi vr wave one's arms. ~to adj bare-armed; (abito)

sleeveless

sbrai'tare vi bawl

sbra'nare vt tear to pieces

sbricio'lar|e vt, ~si vr crumble

sbri'ga|re vt expedite; (occuparsi di) attend to. ~rsi vr be quick. ~'tivo adj quick

sbrindel'lare vt tear to shreds. ~to adj in rags

sbrodo'l|are vt stain

'sbronz|a f prendersi una ~a get tight. sbron'zarsi vr get tight. ~o adj (ubriaco) tight

sbruffo'nata f boast. sbruf'fone, -a mf boaster

sbu'care vi come out

sbucci'ar|e vt peel; shell (piselli). ~si vr graze oneself

sbuf'fare vi snort; (per impazienza) fume. 'sbuffo m puff

'scabbia f scabies sg

sca'broso adj rough; fig difficult; (scena) indecent

scacci'are vt chase away

scacc|o m check; ~hi pl (gioco) chess; (pezzi) chessmen; dare ~o matto a checkmate; a ~hi (tessuto) checked. ~hi'era f chess-board

sca'dente adj shoddy

sca'de|nza f expiry; (Comm) maturity; (di progetto) deadline; a breve/lunga ~nza short-/long-term. ~re vi expire; (valore:) decline; (debito:) be due. sca'duto adj out-of-date

sca'fandro m diving suit; (di astronauta) spacesuit

scaf'fale m shelf; (libreria) bookshelf

'scafo m hull

scagio'nare vt exonerate

'scaglia f scale; (di sapone) flake; (scheggia) chip

scagli'ar|e vt fling. ~si vr fling oneself; ~si contro fig rail against

scaglio|'nare vt space out. ∼'one m group; a ∼oni in groups. ∼one di reddito tax bracket

'**scala** f staircase; (*portatile*) ladder; (*Mus, misura, fig*) scale; scale di stairs. ∼ mobile escalat-or; (*dei salari*) cost of living index

sca'la|re vt climb; layer (*capelli*); (*detrarre*) deduct. ∼ta f climb; (*dell'E-verest ecc*) ascent; fare delle ∼te go climbing. ∼'tore, -'trice mf climber

scalca'gnato adj down at heel

scalci'are vi kick

scalci'nato adj shabby

scalda'bagno m water heater

scalda'muscoli m inv leg-warmer

scal'dar|e vt heat. ∼si vr warm up; (*eccitarsi*) get excited

scal'fi|re vt scratch. ∼t'tura f scratch

scali'nata f flight of steps. sca'lino m step; (*di scala a pioli*) rung

scalma'narsi vr get worked up

'**scalo** m slipway; (*Aeron, Naut*) port of call; fare ∼ a call at; (*Aeron*) land a

scalo'gna f bad luck. ∼'gnato adj unlucky

scalop'pina f escalope

scal'pello m chisel

'**scalpo** m scalp

scal'pore m noise; far ∼ fig cause a sensation

scal'trezza f shrewdness. 'scaltro adj shrewd

scal'zare vt bare the roots of (*albero*); fig undermine; (*da una carica*) oust

'**scalzo** adj & adv barefoot

scambi|'are vt exchange; ∼are qcno per qualcun altro mistake sb for somebody else. ∼'evole adj reciprocal

'**scambio** m exchange; (*Comm*) trade; libero ∼ free trade

scamosci'ato adj suede

scampa'gnata f trip to the country

scampa'nato adj (*gonna*) flared

scampanel'lata f [loud] ring

scam'pare vt save; (*evitare*) escape. '**scampo** m escape

'**scampolo** m remnant

scanala'tura f groove

scandagli'are vt sound

scanda'listico adj sensational

scandaliz'zare vt scandalize. ∼**'zarsi** vr be scandalized

'**scanda|lo** m scandal. ∼'loso adj (*somma*) ecc scandalous; (*fortuna*) outrageous

Scandi'navia f Scandinavia. scan-di'navo, -a adj & mf Scandi-navian

scan'dire vt scan (*verso*); pronounce clearly (*parole*)

scan'nare vt slaughter

'**scanner** m inv scanner

scanneriz'zare vt (*Comput*) scan

scan'sar|e vt shift; (*evitare*) avoid. ∼si vr get out of the way

scansi'one f (*Comput*) scanning

'**scanso** m a ∼ di in order to avoid; a ∼ di equivoci to avoid any misunderstanding

scanti'nato m basement

scanto'nare vi turn the corner; (*svignarsela*) sneak off

scanzo'nato adj easy-going

scapacci'one m smack

scape'strato adj dissolute

'**scapito** m loss

'**scapola** f shoulder-blade

'**scapolo** m bachelor

scappa'mento m (*Auto*) exhaust

scap'pare vi escape; (*andarsene*) dash [off]; (*sfuggire*) slip; mi ∼ da ridere! I want to burst out laughing. ∼ta f short visit. ∼'tella f escapade (*infedeltà*) fling. ∼'toia f way out

scappel'lotto m cuff

scarabocchi'are vt scribble

scara'bocchio m scribble

scara'faggio m cockroach

scara'muccia f skirmish

scaraven'tare vt hurl

scar'cerare vt release [from prison]

scardi'nare vt unhinge

'scarica f discharge; (di arma da fuoco) volley; fig shower

scari'ca|re vt discharge; unload (arma, merci); (Comput) download; fig unburden. ~rsi vr (fiume:) flow; (orologio, batteria:) run down; fig unwind. ~'tore m loader; (di porto) docker. 'scarico adj unloaded; (vuoto) empty; (orologio) run-down; (batteria) flat; fig untroubled ● m unloading; (di rifiuti) dumping; (di acqua) draining; (di sostanze inquinanti) discharge; (luogo) [rubbish] dump; (Auto) exhaust; (idraulico) drain; (tubo) waste pipe

scarlat'tina f scarlet fever

car'latto adj scarlet

'scarno adj thin; (stile) bare

ca'ro|gna f ☐ bad luck. ~'gnato adj ☐ unlucky

'scarpa f shoe. scarpe pl da ginnastica trainers, gym shoes

car'pata f slope; (burrone) escarpment

carpi'nare vi hike

car'pone m boot. scarponi pl da sci ski boot. scarponi pl da trekking walking boots

carroz'zare vt/i drive around

carseggi'are vi be scarce; ~ di (mancare) be short of

car'sezza f scarcity, shortage. scarsità f shortage. 'scarso adj scarce; (manchevole) short

carta'mento m (Rail) gauge. ~ ridotto narrow gauge

car'tare vt discard; unwrap (pacco); (respingere) reject ● vi (deviare) swerve. 'scarto m scrap; (in carte) discard; (deviazione) swerve; (distacco) gap

scas'sa|re vt break. ~to adj ☐ clapped out

scassi'nare vt force open

scassina'tore, -'trice mf burglar. 'scasso m (furto) house-breaking

scate'na|re vt fig stir up. ~rsi vr break out; fig: (temporale:) break; (☐: infiammarsi) get excited. ~to adj crazy

'scatola f box; (di latta) can, tin Br; in ~ (cibo) canned, tinned Br

scat'tare vi go off; (balzare) spring up; (adirarsi) lose one's temper; take (foto). 'scatto m (balzo) spring; (d'ira) outburst; (di telefono) unit; (dispositivo) release; a scatti jerkily; di scatto suddenly

scatu'rire vi spring

scaval'care vt jump over (muretto); climb over (muro); (fig: superare) overtake

sca'vare vt dig (buca); dig up (tesoro); excavate (città sepolta). 'scavo m excavation

'scegliere vt choose, select

scelle'rato adj wicked

'scelt|a f choice; (di articoli) range; ...a ~a (in menu) choice of...; prendine uno a ~a take your choice o pick; di prima ~a a top-grade, choice. ~o pp di scegliere ● adj select; (merce ecc) choice

sce'mare vt/i diminish

sce'menza f silliness; (azione) silly thing to do/say. 'scemo adj silly

'scempio m havoc; (fig: di paesaggio) ruination; fare ~ di play havoc with

'scena f scene; (palcoscenico) stage; entrare in ~ go/come on; fig enter the scene; fare ~ put on an act; fare una ~ make a scene; andare in ~ (Theat) be staged, be put on. sce'nario m scenery

sce'nata f row, scene

'scendere vi go/come down; (da treno, autobus) get off; (da macchina) get out; (strada:) slope; (notte, prezzi:)

fall ●vt go/come down (scale)

sceneggia're vt dramatize. ~**to** m television serial. ~**tura** f screenplay

'scenico adj scenic

scervel'larsi vr rack one's brains. ~**to** adj brainless

'sceso pp di **scendere**

scetti'cismo m scepticism. **'scettico, -a** adj sceptical ●mf sceptic

'scheda f card. ~ **elettorale** ballot-paper. ~ **di espansione** (*Comput*) expansion card. ~ **telefonica** phone-card. **sche'dare** vt file. **sche'dario** m file; (*mobile*) filing cabinet

sche'dina f ≈ pools coupon; giocare la ~ do the pools

'scheggia|a f fragment; (*di legno*) splinter. ~**arsi** vr chip; (legno:) splinter

'scheletro m skeleton

'schema m diagram; (*abbozzo*) outline. **sche'matico** adj schematic

'scherma f fencing

scher'mirsi vr protect oneself

'schermo m screen; **grande ~** big screen

scher'nire vt mock. **'scherno** m mockery

scher'zare vt joke; (*giocare*) play

'scherzo m joke; (*trucco*) trick; (*effetto*) play; (*Mus*) scherzo; **fare uno ~ a qcno** play a joke on sb. **scher'zoso** adj playful

schiaccia'noci m inv nutcrackers pl

schiacci'ante adj damning

schiacci'are vt crush; *Sport* smash; press (pulsante); crack (noce)

schiaffeggi'are vt slap. **schi'affo** m slap; **dare uno schiaffo a** slap

schiamaz'zare vi make a racket; (galline:) cackle

schian'tar|e vt break. ~**si** vr crash ●vi schianto dalla fatica I'm wiped out. **'schianto** m crash; Ⓣ knock-out; (*divertente*) scream

schia'rir|e vt clear; (*sbiadire*) fade ●vi, ~**si** vr brighten up; ~**si la gola** clear one's throat

schiavitù f slavery. **schi'avo, -a** mf slave

schi'ena f back; **mal di ~** backache. **schie'nale** m (*di sedia*) back

schi'er|a f (*Mil*) rank; (*moltitudine*) crowd. ~**a'mento** m lining up

schie'rar|e vt draw up. ~**si** vr draw up; ~**si con** (*parteggiare*) side with

schiet'tezza f frankness. **schi'etto** adj frank; (*puro*) pure

schi'fezza f **una ~** rubbish. **schifil'toso** adj fussy. **'schifo** m disgust; **mi fa schifo** it makes me sick. **schi'fos** adj disgusting; (*di cattiva qualità*) rubbishy

schioc'care vt crack; snap (dita). **schi'occo** m (*di frusta*) crack; (*di bacio*) smack; (*di dita, lingua*) click

schi'uder|e vt, ~**si** vr open

schi'u|ma f foam; (*di sapone*) lather; (*feccia*) scum. ~**ma da barba** shaving foam. ~'**mare** vt skim ●vi foam

schi'uso pp di **schiudere**

schi'vare vt avoid. **'schivo** adj bashful

schizo'frenico adj schizophrenic

schiz'zare vt squirt; (*inzaccherare*) splash; (*abbozzare*) sketch ●vi spurt; ~ **via** scurry away

schizzi'noso adj squeamish

'schizzo m squirt; (*di fango*) splash; (*abbozzo*) sketch

sci m inv ski; (*sport*) skiing. ~ **d'acqua** water-skiing

'scia f wake; (*di fumo ecc*) trail

sci'abola f sabre

scia'callo m jackal; *fig* profiteer

sciac'quar|e vt rinse. ~**si** vr rinse oneself. **sci'acquo** m mouthwash

scia'gur|a f disaster. ~'**rato** adj un fortunate; (*scellerato*) wicked

scialac'quare vt squander

scia'lare vi squander

sci'albo adj pale; *fig* dull

sci'alle *m* shawl

scia'luppa *f* dinghy. ~ di salvataggio lifeboat

sci'ame *m* swarm

sci'ampo *m* shampoo

scian'cato *adj* lame

sci'are *vi* ski

sci'arpa *f* scarf

sci'atica *f* (Med) sciatica

scia'tore, -'trice *mf* skier

sci'atto *adj* slovenly; (stile) careless. sciat'tone, -a *mf* slovenly person

scienti'fico *adj* scientific

sci'enz|a *f* science; (sapere) knowledge. ~i'ato, -a *mf* scientist

'scimmi|a *f* monkey. ~ot'tare *vt* ape

scimpanzé *m inv* chimpanzee, chimp

scimu'nito *adj* idiotic

'scin|dere *vt*, ~**si** *vr* split

scin'tilla *f* spark. scintil'lante *adj* sparkling. scintil'lare *vi* sparkle

scioc'ca|nte *adj* shocking. ~**re** *vt* shock

scioc'chezza *f* foolishness; (assurdità) nonsense. sci'occo *adj* foolish

sci'oglier|e *vt* untie; (liberare) release; (liquefare) melt; dissolve (contratto, qcsa nell'acqua); loosen up (muscoli). ~**si** *vr* release oneself; (liquefarsi) melt; (contratto:) be dissolved; (pastiglia:) dissolve

sciogli'lingua *m inv* tongue-twister

scio'lina *f* wax

sciol'tezza *f* agility; (disinvoltura) ease

sci'olto *pp di* sciogliere ● *adj* loose; (agile) agile; (disinvolto) easy; versi sciolti blank verse *sg*

sciope'ra|nte *mf* striker. ~**re** *vi* go on strike, strike. sci'opero *m* strike. sciopero a singhiozzo on-off strike

sciori'nare *vt fig* show off

sci'pito *adj* insipid

scip'pa|re *vt* 🄵 snatch. ~**tore, ~'trice** *mf* bag snatcher. 'scippo *m* bag-snatching

sci'rocco *m* sirocco

scirop'pato *adj* (frutta) in syrup. sci'roppo *m* syrup

'scisma *m* schism

scissi'one *f* division

'scisso *pp di* scindere

sciu'par|e *vt* spoil; (sperperare) waste. ~**si** *vr* get spoiled; (deperire) wear oneself out. sciu'pio *m* waste

scivo'l|are *vi* slide; (involontariamente) slip. **'scivolo** *m* slide; (Techn) chute. ~**oso** *adj* slippery

scoc'care *vt* shoot ● *vi* (scintilla:) shoot out; (ora:) strike

scocci'a|re *vt* (dare noia a) bother. ~**rsi** *vr* be bothered. ~**to** *adj* 🄵 narked. ~**tore, ~'trice** *mf* bore. ~**tura** *f* nuisance

sco'della *f* bowl

scodinzo'lare *vi* wag its tail

sco'gli|era *f* cliff; (a fior d'acqua) reef. 'scoglio *m* rock; (fig: ostacolo) stumbling block

scoi'attolo *m* squirrel

scola'|pasta *m inv* colander. ~**pi'atti** *m inv* dish drainer

sco'lara *f* schoolgirl

sco'lare *vt* drain; strain (pasta, verdura) ● *vi* drip

sco'la|ro *m* schoolboy. ~**'resca** *f* pupils *pl*. ~**stico** *adj* school *attrib*

scol'la|re *vt* cut away the neck of (abito); (staccare) unstick. ~**to** *adj* low-necked. ~**'tura** *f* neckline

'scolo *m* drainage

scolo'ri|re *vt*, ~**rsi** *vr* fade. ~**to** *adj* faded

scol'pire *vt* carve; (imprimere) engrave

scombi'nare *vt* upset

scombusso'lare *vt* muddle up

scom'mess|a *f* bet. ~**o** *pp di*

scommettere. scom'mettere vt bet

scomo'dar|e vt, ~**si** vr trouble. **scomodità** f discomfort. **'scomodo** adj uncomfortable

scompa'rire vi disappear; (morire) pass on. **scom'parsa** f disappearance; (morte) passing, death. **scom'parso**, -a pp di **scomparire** ●mf departed

scomparti'mento m compartment. **scom'parto** m compartment

scom'penso m imbalance

scompigli'are vt disarrange. **scom'piglio** m confusion

scom'po|rre vt take to pieces; (fig: turbare) upset. ~**rsi** vr get flustered. ~**sto** pp di **scomporre** ●adj (sguaiato) unseemly; (disordinato) untidy

sco'muni|ca f excommunication. ~'**care** vt excommunicate

sconcer'ta|re vt disconcert; (rendere perplesso) bewilder. ~**to** adj disconcerted; bewildered

scon'cezza f obscenity. **'sconcio** adj dirty ●m è uno sconcio che... it's a disgrace that...

sconclusio'nato adj incoherent

scon'dito adj unseasoned; (insalata) with no dressing

sconfes'sare vt disown

scon'figgere vt defeat

sconfi'na|re vi cross the border; (in proprietà privata) trespass. ~**to** adj unlimited

scon'fitt|a f defeat. ~**o** pp di **sconfiggere**

scon'forto m dejection

sconge'lare vt thaw out (cibo), defrost

scongiu'rare vt beseech; (evitare) avert. ~'**uro** m **fare gli scongiuri** touch wood, knock on wood Am

scon'nesso pp di **sconnettere** ●adj fig incoherent. **scon'nettere** vt disconnect

sconosci'uto, -a adj unknown ●mf stranger

sconquas'sare vt smash; (sconvolgere) upset

sconside'rato adj inconsiderate

sconsigli'a|bile adj not advisable. ~**re** vt advise against

sconso'lato adj disconsolate

scon'ta|re vt discount; (dedurre) deduct; (pagare) pay off; serve (pena). ~**to** adj discount; (ovvio) expected; ~**to del 10%** with 10% discount

scon'tento adj displeased ●m discontent

'sconto m discount; **fare uno ~** give a discount

scon'trarsi vr clash; (urtare) collide

scon'trino m ticket; (di cassa) receipt

'scontro m clash; (urto) collision

scon'troso adj unsociable

sconveni'ente adj unprofitable; (scorretto) unseemly

sconvol'gente adj mind-blowing

scon'vol|gere vt upset; (mettere in disordine) disarrange. ~**gi'mento** m upheaval. ~**to** pp di **sconvolgere** ●adj distraught

'scopa f broom. **sco'pare** vt sweep

scoperchi'are vt take the lid off (pentola); take the roof off (casa)

sco'pert|a f discovery. ~**o** pp di **scoprire** ●adj uncovered; (senza riparo) exposed; (conto) overdrawn; (spoglio) bare

'scopo m aim; **allo ~ di** in order to

scoppi'are vi burst; fig break out. **scoppiet'tare** vi crackle. **'scoppio** m burst; (di guerra) outbreak; (esplosione) explosion

sco'prire vt discover; (togliere la copertura a) uncover

scoraggi'a|re vt discourage. ~**rsi** vr lose heart

scor'butico adj peevish

scorcia'toia f short cut

'scorcio m (di epoca) end; (di cielo)

patch; (*in arte*) foreshortening; di ~ (vedere) from an angle. ~ panora**mico** panoramic view

scor'da|re *vt*, ~**rsi** *vr* forget. ~**to** *adj* (*Mus*) out of tune

'**scorgere** *vt* make out; (*notare*) notice

'**scoria** *f* waste; (*di metallo, carbone*) slag; **scorie** *pl* radioattive radio-active waste

scor'**nato** *adj fig* hangdog. '**scorno** *m* humiliation

scorpi'**one** *m* scorpion; (*Astr*) S ~ Scorpio

scorraz'**zare** *vi* run about

'**scorrere** *vt* (*dare un'occhiata*) glance through ● *vi* run; (*scivolare*) slide; (*fluire*) flow; (*Comput*) scroll. scor're**vole** *adj* scrolling ~ **porta scorrevole** sliding door

scor're'**ria** *f* raid

scorret'**tezza** *f* (*mancanza di educazione*) bad manners *pl.* scor'**retto** *adj* incorrect; (*sconveniente*) improper

scorri'**banda** *f* raid; *fig* excursion

'**scorsa** *f* glance. ~**o** *pp di* scorrere ● *adj* last

scor'**soio** *adj* nodo ~ noose

'**scorta** *f* escort; (*provvista*) supply. ~'**tare** *vt* escort

scor'te|**se** *adj* discourteous. ~**sia** *f* discourtesy

scorti'**ca|re** *vt* skin. ~'**tura** *f* graze

'**scorto** *pp di* scorgere

'**scorza** *f* peel; (*crosta*) crust; (*corteccia*) bark

sco'**sceso** *adj* steep

'**scossa** *f* shake; (*Electr, fig*) shock; prendere la ~ get an electric shock. ~ **elettrica** electric shock. ~ **sismica** earth tremor

'**scosso** *pp di* scuotere ● *adj* shaken; (*sconvolto*) upset

sco'**stante** *adj* off-putting

sco'**sta|re** *vt* push away. ~**rsi** *vr* stand aside

scostu'**mato** *adj* dissolute; (*maleducato*) ill-mannered

scot'**tante** *adj* dangerous

scot'**ta|re** *vt* scald ● *vi* burn; (*bevanda*:) be too hot; (*sole, pentola*:) be very hot. ~**rsi** *vr* burn oneself; (*al sole*) get sunburnt; *fig* get one's fingers burnt. ~'**tura** *f* burn; (*da liquido*) scald; ~'**tura solare** sunburn; *fig* painful experience

'**scotto** *adj* overcooked

sco'**vare** *vt* (*scoprire*) discover

'**Scoz|ia** *f* Scotland. ~'**zese** *adj* Scottish ● *mf* Scot

scredi'**tare** *vt* discredit

scre'**mare** *vt* skim

screpo'**la|re** *vt*, ~**rsi** *vr* crack. ~**to** *adj* (*labbra*) chapped. ~'**tura** *f* crack

screzi'**ato** *adj* speckled

'**screzio** *m* disagreement

scribac'**chi|are** *vt* scribble. ~'**chino**, -**a** *mf* scribbler; (*impiegato*) penpusher

scric'**chio'l|are** *vi* creak. ~**io** *m* creaking

'**scricciolo** *m* wren

'**scrigno** *m* casket

scrimina'**tura** *f* parting

'**scrit'ta** *f* writing; (*su muro*) graffiti. ~**to** *pp di* scrivere ● *adj* written ● *m* writing; (*lettera*) letter. ~'**toio** *m* writing-desk. ~'**tore**, -'**trice** *mf* writer. ~'**tura** *f* writing; (*Relig*) scripture

scrittu'**rare** *vt* engage

scriva'**nia** *f* desk

'**scrivere** *vt* write; (*descrivere*) write about; ~ **a macchina** type

scroc'**c|are** *vt* ~**are a sponge off**. '**scrocco** *m* **a scrocco** **b** without paying. ~**one**, -**a** *mf* sponger

'**scrofa** *f* sow

scrol'**lar|e** *vt* shake; ~**e le spalle** shrug one's shoulders. ~**si** *vr* shake oneself; ~**si qcsa di dosso** shake sth off

scrosci'are vi roar; (pioggia): pelt down. **'scroscio** m roar; (di pioggia) pelting

scro'star|e vt scrape. **~si** vr peel off

'scrupo|lo m scruple; (diligenza) care; **senza scrupoli** unscrupulous, without scruples. **~'loso** adj scrupulous

scru'ta|re vt scan; (indagare) search. **~'tore** m (alle elezioni) returning officer

scruti'nare vt scrutinize. **scru'tinio** m (di voti alle elezioni) poll; (Sch) assessment of progress

scu'cire vt unstitch

scude'ria f stable

scu'detto m Sport championship shield

'scudo m shield

sculacci'|are vt spank. **~'ata** f spanking. **~'one** m spanking

sculet'tare vi wiggle one's hips

scul'to|re, -'trice m sculptor • f sculptress. **~'tura** f sculpture

scu'ola f school. **~ elementare** primary school. **~ guida** driving school. **~ materna** day nursery. **~ media [inferiore]** secondary school (10-13). **~ [media] superiore** secondary school (13-18)

scu'oter|e vt shake. **~si** vr (destarsi) rouse oneself; **~si di dosso** shake off

'scure f axe

scu'reggia f ① fart. **scureggi'are** vi ① fart

scu'rire vt/i darken

'scuro adj dark • m darkness; (imposta) shutter

'scusa f excuse; (giustificazione) apology; **chiedere ~** apologize; **chiedo ~!** I'm sorry!

scu'sar|e vt excuse. **~si** vr **~si** apologize (di for); **[mi] scusi!** excuse me!; (chiedendo perdono) [I'm] sorry!

sdebi'tarsi vr repay a kindness

sde'gna|re vt despise. **~rsi** vr get angry. **~to** adj indignant. **'sdegno** m disdain. **sde'gnoso** adj disdainful

sdolci'nato adj sentimental

sdoppi'are vt halve

sdrai'arsi vr lie down. **'sdraio** m **[sedia a]** sdraio deckchair

sdrammatiz'zare vi provide some comic relief

sdruccio'levole adj slippery

---

se

● conj if; (interrogativo) whether, if; **se mai** (caso mai) if need be; **se mai telefonasse,...** should he call,...; **se ti chiede,...** if he calls,...; **se no** otherwise, or else; **se non altro** at least, if nothing else; **se pure** (sebbene) even though; (anche se) even if; **non so se sia vero** I don't know whether it's true, I don't know if it's true; **come se** as if; **se lo avessi saputo prima!** if only I had known before!; **e se andassimo fuori a cena?** how about going out for dinner?

● m inv if

sé pers pron oneself; (lui) himself; (lei) herself; (esso, essa) itself; (loro) themselves; **l'ha fatto da sé** he did it himself; **ha preso i soldi con sé** he took the money with him; **si sono tenuti le notizie per sé** they kept the news to themselves

seb'bene conj although

'secca f shallows pl; **in ~** (nave) aground

sec'cante adj annoying

sec'ca|re vt dry; (importunare) annoy • vi dry up. **~rsi** vr dry up; (irritarsi) get annoyed; (annoiarsi) get bored. **~'tore, -'trice** m/f nuisance. **~'tura** f bother

secchi'ello m pail

'**secchio** m bucket. ~ della spazzatura rubbish bin, trash can Am

secco, -a adj dry; (dissecato) dried; (magro) thin; (brusco) curt; (preciso) sharp ● m (siccità) drought; lavare a ~ dry-clean

secessi'one f secession

seco'lare adj age-old; (laico) secular. '**secolo** m century; (epoca) age

se'cond|a f (Rail, Sch) second class; (Auto) second [gear]. ~o adj second ● m second; (secondo piatto) main course ● prep according to; ~o me in my opinion

secrezi'one f secretion

sedano m celery

seda'tivo adj & m sedative

sede f seat; (centro) centre; (Relig) see; (Comm) head office. ~ sociale registered office

seden'tario adj sedentary

se'der|e vi sit. ~si vr sit down ● m (deretano) bottom

sedia f chair. ~ a dondolo rocking chair. ~ a rotelle wheelchair

edi'cente adj self-styled

'**e'dile** m seat

edizi'o|ne f sedition. ~so adj seditious

se'dotto pp di sedurre

e'durre vt seduce

e'duta f session; (di posa) sitting. ~ stante adv here and now

eduzi'one f seduction

sega f saw

segala f rye

'**e'gare** vt saw

seggio m seat. ~ elettorale polling station

eg'gio|la f chair. ~'lino m seat; (da bambino) child's seat. ~'lone m (per bambini) high chair

seggio'via f chair lift

seghe'ria f sawmill

se'ghetto m hacksaw

seg'mento m segment

segna'lar|e vt signal; (annunciare) announce; (indicare) point out. ~si vr distinguish oneself

se'gnale m signal; (stradale) sign. ~le acustico beep. ~le orario time signal. ~'letica f signs pl. ~'letica stradale road signs pl

se'gnare vt mark; (prendere nota) note; (indicare) indicate; Sport score. ~si vr cross oneself. '**segno** m sign; (traccia, limite) mark; (bersaglio) target; far segno (col capo) nod; (con la mano) beckon. segno zodiacale birth sign

segre'ga|re vt segregate. ~zi'one f segregation

segretari'ato m secretariat

segre'tario, -a mf secretary. ~ comunale town clerk

segrete'ria f [administrative] office; (segretariato) secretariat. ~ telefonica answering machine

segre'tezza f secrecy

se'greto adj & m secret; in ~ in secret

segu'ace mf follower

segu'ente adj following, next

se'gugio m bloodhound

segu'ire vt/i follow; (continuare) continue

segui'tare vt/i continue

'**seguito** m retinue; (sequela) series; (continuazione) continuation; di ~ in succession; in ~ later on; in ~ a following; al ~ owing to; fare ~ a follow up

'**sei** adj & m six. sei'cento adj & m six hundred; il Seicento the seventeenth century. sei'mila adj & m six thousand

sel'ciato m paving

selet'tivo adj selective. selezio'nare vt select. selezi'one f selection

'sella f saddle. **sel'lare** vt saddle

seltz m soda water

'selva f forest

selvag'gina f game

sel'vaggio, -a adj wild; (*primitivo*) savage ● mf savage

sel'vatico adj wild

se'maforo m traffic lights pl

sem'brare vi seem; (*assomigliare*) look like; **che te ne sembra?** what do you think?; **mi sembra che...** I think...

'seme m seed; (*di mela*) pip; (*di carte*) suit; (*sperma*) semen

se'mestre m half-year

semi'cerchio m semicircle

semifi'nale f semifinal

semi'freddo m ice cream and sponge dessert

'semina f sowing

semi'nare vt sow; [T] shake off (inseguitori)

semi'nario m seminar; (*Relig*) seminary

seminter'rato m basement

se'mitico adj Semitic

sem'mai conj in case ● adv **è lui,** ~, **che...** if anyone, it's him who...

'semola f bran. **semo'lino** m semolina

'semplic|e adj simple; **in parole semplici** in plain words. ~'**cemente** adv simply. ~**cità** f simplicity. ~**fi-'care** vt simplify

'sempre adv always; (*ancora*) still; **per** ~ for ever

sempre'verde adj & m evergreen

'senape f mustard

se'nato m senate. **sena'tore** m senator

se'nil|e adj senile. ~**ità** f senility

'senno m sense

'seno m breast; (*Math*) sine

sen'sato adj sensible

sensazi|o'nale adj sensational. ~**'one** f sensation

sen'sibil|e adj sensitive; (*percepibile*) perceptible; (*notevole*) considerable. ~**ità** f sensitivity. ~**iz'zare** vt make more aware (a of)

sensi'tivo, -a adj sensory ● mf sensitive person; (*medium*) medium

'senso m sense; (*significato*) meaning; (*direzione*) direction; **non ha** ~ it doesn't make sense; **perdere i sensi** lose consciousness. ~ **dell'umorismo** sense of humour. ~ **unico** (*strada*) one-way; ~ **vietato** no entry

sensu'al|e adj sensual. ~**ità** f sensuality

sen'tenz|a f sentence; (*massima*) saying. ~**i'are** vi pass judgment

senti'ero m path

sentimen'tale adj sentimental. **senti'mento** m feeling

senti'nella f sentry

sen'ti|re vt feel; (*udire*) hear; (*ascoltare*) listen to; (*gustare*) taste; (*odorare*) smell ● vi feel; (*udire*) hear; ~**re caldo/freddo** feel hot/cold. ~**rsi** vr feel; ~**rsi di fare qcsa** feel like doing sth; ~**rsi bene** feel well; ~**rsi poco bene** feel unwell; ~**to** adj sincere

sen'tore m inkling

'senza prep without; ~ **correre** without running; **senz'altro** certainly; ~ **ombrello** without an umbrella

senza'tetto m inv **i** ~ **the** homeless

sepa'rar|e vt separate. ~**rsi** vr separate; (*amici:*) part; ~**rsi da** be separated from. ~**ta'mente** adv separately. ~**zi'one** f separation

se'pol|cro m sepulchre. ~**to** pp di seppellire. ~**tura** f burial

seppel'lire vt bury

'seppia f cuttle fish; **nero di** ~ sepia

sep'pure *conj* even if

se'quenza *f* sequence

seque'strare *vt* (*rapire*) kidnap; (*Jur*) impound; (*confiscare*) confiscate. **se'questro** *m* impounding; (*di persona*) kidnap[ping]

sera *f* evening; **di** ~ in the evening. **se'rale** *adj* evening. **se'rata** *f* evening; (*ricevimento*) party

ser'bare *vt* keep; harbour (*odio*); cherish (*speranza*)

serba'toio *m* tank. ~ **d'acqua** water tank; (*per una città*) reservoir

Serbia *f* Serbia

serbo, -a *adj* & *mf* Serbian ● *m* (*lingua*) Serbian

sere'nata *f* serenade

serenità *f* serenity. **se'reno** *adj* serene; (*cielo*) clear

ser'gente *m* sergeant

seria'mente *adv* seriously

serie *f inv* series; (*complesso*) set; *Sport* division; **fuori** ~ custom-built; **produzione in** ~ mass production; **di** ~ B second-rate

serietà *f* seriousness. **serio** *adj* serious; (*degno di fiducia*) reliable; **sul serio** seriously; (*davvero*) really

er'mone *m* sermon

serpe *f filter* viper. ~**ggi'are** *vi* meander; (*diffondersi*) spread

er'pente *m* snake

serra *f* greenhouse; **effetto** ~ greenhouse effect

er'randa *f* shutter

er'ra|re *vt* shut; (*stringere*) tighten; (*incalzare*) press on. ~**tura** *f* lock

server *m inv* (*Comput*) server

er'vir|e *vt* serve; (*al ristorante*) wait on ● *vi* serve; (*essere utile*) be of use; **non serve** it's no good. ~**si** *vr* (*di cibo*) help oneself; ~**si a** buy from; ~**si di** use

ervitù *f* servitude; (*personale di servizio*) servants *pl*

er'vizio *m* service; (*da caffè ecc*) set;

(*di cronaca, sportivo*) report; **servizi** *pl* bathroom; **essere di** ~ be on duty; **fare** ~ (*autobus ecc*.) run; **fuori** ~ (*bus*) not in service; (*ascensore*) out of order; ~ **compreso** service charge included. ~ **in camera** room service. ~ **civile** civilian duties done instead of national service. ~ **militare** military service. ~ **pubblico** utility company. ~ **al tavolo** waiter service

'servo, -a *mf* servant

servo'sterzo *m* power steering

ses'san|ta *adj* & *m* sixty. ~**'tina** *f* **una** ~**tina** about sixty

sessi'one *f* session

'sesso *m* sex

sessu'ale *adj* sexual. ~**ità** *f* sexuality

'sesto¹ *adj* sixth

'sesto² *m* (*ordine*) order

'seta *f* silk

setacci'are *vt* sieve. **se'taccio** *m* sieve

'sete *f* thirst; **avere** ~ be thirsty

'setta *f* sect

set'tan|ta *adj* & *m* seventy. ~**'tina** *f* **una** ~**tina** about seventy

'sette *adj* & *m* seven. ~**'cento** *agg* & *m* seven hundred; **il S**~**cento** the eighteenth century

set'tembre *m* September

settentri|o'nale *adj* northern ● *mf* northerner. ~**'one** *m* north

setti'ma|na *f* week. ~**'nale** *agg* & *m* weekly

'settimo *adj* seventh

set'tore *m* sector

severità *f* severity. **se'vero** *adj* severe; (*rigoroso*) strict

se'vizi|a *f* torture; **se'vizie** *pl* torture *sg*. ~**'are** *vt* torture

sezio'nare *vt* divide; (*Med*) dissect. **sezi'one** *f* section; (*reparto*) department; (*Med*) dissection

sfaccen'dato *adj* idle

sfacchi'na|re *vi* toil. ~**ta** *f*

drudgery

sfaccia|taggine f insolence. **~'ato** adj cheeky, fresh Am

sfa'celo m ruin; in **~** in ruins

sfal'darsi vr flake off

sfa'mare vt feed. **~si** vr satisfy one's hunger

sfar'zoso adj sumptuous

sfa'sato adj 🄵 confused; (motore) which needs tuning

sfasci'a|re vt unbandage; (fracassare) smash. **~rsi** vr fall to pieces. **~to** adj beat-up

sfa'tare vt explode

sfati'cato adj lazy

sfavil'lare vi sparkle

sfavo'revole adj unfavourable

sfavo'rire vt disadvantage

'sfer|a f sphere. **~ico** adj spherical

sfer'rare vt unshoe (cavallo); (scagliare) land

sfer'zare vt whip

sfian'carsi vr wear oneself out

sfi'bra|re vt exhaust. **~to** adj exhausted

'sfida f challenge. **sfi'dare** vt challenge

sfi'duci|a f mistrust. **~ato** adj discouraged

sfigu'rare vt disfigure ● vi (far cattiva figura) look out of place

sfilacci'ar|e vt, **~si** vr fray

sfi'la|re vt unthread; (togliere di dosso) take off ● vi (truppe:) march past; (in parata) parade. **~rsi** vr come unthreaded; (collant:) ladder; take off (pantaloni). **~ta** f parade; (sfilza) series. **~ta di moda** fashion show

'sfilza f (di errori) string

'sfinge f sphinx

sfi'nito adj worn out

sfio'rare vt skim; touch on (argomento)

sfio'rire vi wither; (bellezza:) fade

'sfitto adj vacant

'sfizio m whim, fancy; **togliersi uno ~** satisfy a whim

sfo'cato adj out of focus

sfoci'are vi **~ in** flow into

sfode'ra|re vt draw (pistola, spada). **~to** adj unlined

sfo'gar|e vt vent. **~si** vr give vent to one's feelings

sfoggi'are vt/i show off. **'sfoggio** m show, display; **fare sfoggio di** show off

'sfoglia f sheet of pastry; **pasta ~** puff pastry

sfogli'are vt leaf through

'sfogo m outlet; fig outburst; (Med) rash; **dare ~ a** give vent to

sfolgo'rare vi blaze

sfol'la|re vt clear ● vi (Mil) be evacuated

sfol'tire vt thin [out]

sfon'dare vt break down ● vi (aver successo) make a name for oneself

'sfondo m background

sfor'ma|re vt pull out of shape (tasche). **~rsi** vr lose its shape; (persona:) lose one's figure. **~to** m (Culin) flan

sfor'nito adj **~ di** (negozio) out of

sfor'tuna f bad luck. **~ta'mente** adv unfortunately. **sfortu'nato** adj unlucky

sfor'zar|e vt force. **~si** vr try hard. **'sforzo** m effort; (tensione) strain

sfottere vt 🄴 tease

sfracel'larsi vr smash

sfrat'tare vt evict. **'sfratto** m eviction

sfrecci'are vi flash past

sfregi'a|re vt slash. **~to** adj scarred. **'sfregio** m slash

sfre'na|rsi vr run wild. **~to** adj wild

sfron'tato adj shameless

sfrutta'mento m exploitation.

sfrut'tare vt exploit

sfug'gente adj elusive; (mento) receding

sfug'gi|re vi escape; ~re a escape [from]; mi sfugge it escapes me; mi è sfuggito di mano I lost hold of it ● vt avoid. ~ta f di ~ta in passing

sfu'ma|re vi (svanire) vanish; (colore:) shade off ● vt soften (colore). ~'tura f shade

sfuri'ata f outburst [of anger]

sga'bello m stool

sgabuz'zino m cupboard

sgam'bet'tare vi kick one's legs; (camminare) trot. sgam'betto m fare lo sgambetto a qcno trip sb up

sganasci'arsi vr ~ dalle risa roar with laughter

sganci'ar|e vt unhook; (Rail) uncouple; drop (bombe); 🗓 cough up (denaro). ~si vr become unhooked; fig get away

sganghe'rato adj ramshackle

sgar'bato adj rude. 'sgarbo m discourtesy

sgargi'ante adj garish

sgar'rare vi be wrong; (da regola) stray from the straight and narrow. 'sgarro m mistake, slip

sgattaio'lare vi sneak away; ~ via decamp

sghignaz'zare vi laugh scornfully, sneer

sgoccio'lare vi drip

sgo'larsi vr shout oneself hoarse

sgomb[e]'rare vt clear [out]. 'sgombro adj clear ● m (trasloco) removal; (pesce) mackerel

sgomen'tar|e vt dismay. ~si vr be dismayed. sgo'mento m dismay

sgomi'nare vt defeat

sgom'mata f screech of tyres

sgonfi'ar|e vt deflate. ~si vr go down. 'sgonfio adj flat

sgorbio m scrawl; (fig: vista sgradevole) sight

sgor'gare vi gush [out] ● vt flush out, unblock (lavandino)

sgoz'zare vt ~ qcno cut sb's throat

sgra'd|evole adj disagreeable. ~ito adj unwelcome

sgrammati'cato adj ungrammatical

sgra'nare vt shell (piselli); open wide (occhi)

sgran'chir|e vt, ~si vr stretch

sgranocchi'are vt munch

sgras'sare vt remove the grease from

sgrazi'ato adj ungainly

sgreto'lar|e vt, ~si vr crumble

sgri'da|re vt scold. ~ta f scolding

sgros'sare vt rough-hew (marmo); fig polish

sgu'ai'ato adj coarse

sgual'cire vt crumple

sgu'ardo m look; (breve) glance

sguaz'zare vi splash; (nel fango) wallow

sguinzagli'are vt unleash

sgusci'ar|e vt shell ● vi (sfuggire) slip away; ~ fuori slip out

shake'rare vt shake

si

● pers pron (riflessivo) oneself; (lui) himself; (lei) herself; (esso, essa) itself; (loro) themselves; (reciproco) each other; (tra più di due) one another; (impersonale) you, one; lavarsi si wash [oneself]; si è lavata he washed [herself]; lavarsi le mani wash one's hands; si è lavata le mani she washed her hands; si è mangiato un pollo intero he ate an entire chicken by himself; incontrarsi meet each other; la gente si aiuta a vicenda people help one another; non si sa mai you never know, one never knows *fml*; **queste cose si dimenticano facilmente** these things are easily forgotten

● *m* (chiave, nota) B

sì *adv* yes

'sia[1] ▷ ESSERE

'sia[2] *conj* ~...~... (entrambi) both...and...; (o l'uno o l'altro) either...or...; ~ **che venga**, ~ **che non venga** whether he comes or not; **scegli** ~ **questo** o **quello** choose either this one or that one; **voglio** ~ **questo** che **quello** I want both this one and that

sia'mese *adj* Siamese

sibi'lare *vi* hiss

si'cario *m* hired killer

sicché *conj* (perciò) so [that]; (allora) then

siccità *f* drought

sic'come *conj* as

Si'cili|a *f* Sicily. **s~'ano, -a** *adj & mf* Sicilian

si'cura *f* safety catch; (di portiera) child-proof lock. **~'mente** *adv* definitely

sicu'rezza *f* certainty; (salvezza) safety; **uscita di** ~ emergency exit. **~ delle frontiere** homeland security

si'curo *adj* safe; (certo) sure; (saldo) steady; (Comm) sound ● *adv* certainly ● *m* safety; **al** ~ safe; **andare sul** ~ play [it] safe; **di** ~ definitely; **di** ~, **sarà arrivato** he must have arrived

siderur'gia *f* iron and steel industry

'sidro *m* cider

si'epe *f* hedge

si'ero *m* serum

sieroposi'tivo *adj* HIV positive

si'esta *f* afternoon nap

si'fone *m* siphon

Sig. *abbr* (signore) Mr

Sig.a *abbr* (signora) Mrs, Ms

siga'retta *f* cigarette

'sigaro *m* cigar

Sigg. *abbr* (signori) Messrs

sigil'lare *vt* seal. **si'gillo** *m* seal

'sigla *f* initials *pl*. ~ **musicale** programme signature tune. **si'glare** *vt* initial

Sig.na *abbr* (signorina) Miss, Ms

signifi'ca|re *vt* mean. **~'tivo** *adj* significant. **~to** *m* meaning

si'gnora *f* lady; (davanti a nome proprio) Mrs; (non sposata) Miss; (in lettere ufficiali) Dear Madam; **il signor Vené e** ~ **Mr and Mrs Vené**

si'gnore *m* gentleman; (Relig) lord; (davanti a nome proprio) Mr; (in lettere ufficiali) Dear Sir. **signo'rile** *adj* gentlemanly; (di lusso) luxury

signo'rina *f* young lady; (seguito da nome proprio) Miss

silenzia'tore *m* silencer

si'lenzi|o *m* silence. **~'oso** *adj* silent

silhou'ette *f* silhouette

si'licio *m* piastrina di ~ silicon chip

sili'cone *m* silicone

'sillaba *f* syllable

silu'rare *vt* torpedo. **si'luro** *m* torpedo

simboleggi'are *vt* symbolize

sim'bolico *adj* symbolic[al]

'simbolo *m* symbol

similarità *f inv* similarity

'simil|e *adj* similar; (tale) such; ~**e a** like ● *m* (il prossimo) fellow man. **~'mente** *adv* similarly. **~'pelle** *f* Leatherette®

simme'tria *f* symmetry. **sim'metrico** *adj* symmetric[al]

simpa'ti|a *f* liking; (compenetrazione) sympathy; **prendere qcno in** ~**a** take a liking to sb. **sim'patico** *adj* nice. **~iz'zante** *mf* well-wisher. **~iz'zare** *vi* ~**izzare con** take a liking to; **~izzare per qcsa/qcno** lean towards sth/sb

sim'posio m symposium

simu'la|re vt simulate; feign (amicizia, interesse). **~zi'one** f simulation

simul'taneo adj simultaneous

sina'goga f synagogue

sincerità f sincerity. **sin'cero** adj sincere

'sincope f syncopation; (Med) fainting fit

sincro'nia f synchronization

sincroniz'zare vt synchronize

sinda'ca|le adj [trade] union, [labor] union Am. **~'lista** mf trade unionist, labor union member Am. **~re** vt inspect. **~to** m [trade] union, [labor] union Am; (associazione) syndicate

'sindaco m mayor

'sindrome f syndrome

sinfo'nia f symphony. **sin'fonico** adj symphonic

singhi|oz'zare vi (di pianto) sob. **~'ozzo** m hiccup; (di pianto) sob

singo'lar|e adj singular ●m singular. **~'mente** adv individually; (stranamente) peculiarly

'singolo adj single ●m individual; (Tennis) singles pl

si'nistra f left; a ~ on the left; girare a ~ turn to the left; con la guida a ~ (auto) with left-hand drive

sini'strato adj injured

si'nistr|o, -a adj left[-hand]; (avverso) sinister ●m accident ●f left [hand]; (Pol) left [wing]

'sino prep = **FINO**

si'nonimo adj synonymous ●m synonym

sin'tassi f syntax

'sintesi f inv synthesis; (riassunto) summary

sin'teti|co adj synthetic; (conciso) summary. **~z'zare** vt summarize

sintetizza'tore m synthesizer

sinto'matico adj symptomatic.

'sintomo m symptom

sinto'nia f tuning; in ~ on the same wavelength

sinu'oso adj (strada) winding

si'pario m curtain

si'rena f siren

'Siri|a f Syria. **s~ano, -a** adj & mf Syrian

si'ringa f syringe

'sismico adj seismic

si'stem|a m system. **~a operativo** (Comput) operating system **siste'ma|re** vt (mettere) put; tidy up (casa, camera); (risolvere) sort out; (procurare lavoro a) fix up with a job; (trovare alloggio a) find accommodation for; (sposare) marry off; (亚: punire) sort out. **~rsi** vr settle down; (trovare un lavoro) find a job; (trovare alloggio) find accommodation; (sposarsi) marry. **~tico** adj systematic. **~zi'one** f arrangement; (di questione) settlement; (lavoro) job; (alloggio) accommodation; (matrimonio) marriage

'sito m site. ~ **web** web site

situ'are vt place

situazi'one f situation

ski-'lift m inv ski tow

slacci'are vt unfasten

slanci'a|rsi vr hurl oneself. **~to** adj slender. **'slancio** m impetus; (impulso) impulse

sla'vato adj fair

'slavo adj Slav[onic]

sle'ale adj disloyal. **~tà** f disloyalty

sle'gare vt untie

'slitta f sledge, sleigh. **~'mento** m (di macchina) skid; (fig: di riunione) postponement

slit'ta|re vi (Auto) skid; (riunione:) be put off. **~ta** f skid

slit'tino m toboggan

'slogan m inv slogan

slo'ga|re vt dislocate. **~rsi** vr **~rsi una caviglia** sprain one's ankle. **~'tura** f dislocation

sloggi'are vi move out

Slo'vacchia f Slovakia

Slo'venia f Slovenia

smacchi'a|re vt clean. ~**tore** m stain remover

'smacco m humiliating defeat

smagli'ante adj dazzling

smagli'a|rsi vr (calza:) run. ~**tura** f run

smalizi'ato adj cunning

smal'ta|re vt enamel; glaze (ceramica); varnish (unghie). ~**to** adj enamelled

smalti'mento m disposal; (di merce) selling off. ~ **rifiuti** waste disposal; (di grassi) burning off

smal'tire vt burn off; (merce) sell off; fig get through (corrispondenza); ~ **la sbornia** sober up

'smalto m enamel; (di ceramica) glaze; (per le unghie) nail varnish

smantella'mento m dismantling. ~**lare** vt dismantle

smarri'mento m loss; (psicologico) bewilderment

smar'ri|re vt lose; (temporaneamente) mislay. ~**rsi** vr get lost; (turbarsi) be bewildered

smasche'rar|e vt unmask. ~**si** (tradirsi) give oneself away

smemo'rato, -a adj forgetful • mf scatterbrain

smen'ti|re vt deny. ~**ta** f denial

sme'raldo m & adj emerald

smerci'are vt sell off

smerigli'ato adj emery; vetro ~ frosted glass. **smeriglio** m emery

'smesso pp di smettere • adj (abiti) cast-off

'smett|ere vt stop; stop wearing (abiti); ~**ila!** stop it!

smidol'lato adj spineless

sminu'ir|e vt diminish. ~**si** vr fig belittle oneself

sminuz'zare vt crumble; (fig: analizzare) analyse in detail

smista'mento m clearing; (postale) sorting. **smi'stare** vt sort; (Mil) post

smisu'rato adj boundless; (esorbitante) excessive

smobili'ta|re vt demobilize. ~**zi'one** f demobilization

smo'dato adj immoderate

smog m smog

'smoking m inv dinner jacket, tuxedo Am

smon'ta|re vt take to pieces; (scoraggiare) dishearten • vi (da veicolo) get off; (da cavallo) dismount; (dal servizio) go off duty. ~**si** vr lose heart

'smorfi|a f grimace; (moina) simper; **fare** ~**e** make faces. ~**oso** adj affected

'smorto adj pale; (colore) dull

smor'zare vt dim (luce); tone down (colori); deaden (suoni); quench (sete)

'smosso pp di smuovere

smotta'mento m landslide

sms m inv (short message service) text message

'smunto adj emaciated

smu'over|e vt shift; (commuovere) move. ~**si** vr move; (commuoversi) be moved

smus'sar|e vt round off; (fig: attenuare) tone down. ~**si** vr go blunt

snatu'rato adj inhuman

snel'lir|e vt slim down. ~**si** vr slim [down]. '**snello** adj slim

sner'va|re vt enervate. ~**rsi** vr get exhausted

sni'dare vt drive out

snif'fare vt snort

snob'bare vt snub. **sno'bismo** m snobbery

snoccio'lare vt stone; fig blurt out

sno'da|re vt untie; (sciogliere) loosen. ~**rsi** vr come untied; (strada:) wind. ~**to** adj (persona) double-jointed; (dita) flexible

so'ave adj gentle

sobbal'zare vi jerk; (trasalire) start. sob'balzo m jerk; (trasalimento) start

sobbar'carsi vr ~ a undertake

sob'borgo m suburb

sobil'la|re vt stir up

'sobrio adj sober

soc'chiu|dere vt half-close. ~so pp di socchiudere ● adj (occhi) half-closed; (porta) ajar

soc'cor|rere vt assist. ~so pp di soccorrere ● m assistance; soccorsi pl rescuers; (dopo disastro) relief workers. ~so stradale breakdown service

socialdemo'cra|tico, -a adj Social Democratic ● mf Social Democrat. ~zia f Social Democracy

soci'ale adj social

socia'li|smo m Socialism. ~sta agg & mf Socialist. ~z'zare vi socialize

società f inv society; (Comm) company. ~ per azioni plc. ~ a responsabilità limitata limited liability company

soci'evole adj sociable

socio, -a mf member; (Comm) partner

sociolo'gia f sociology. socio'logico adj sociological

soda f soda

soddisfa'cente adj satisfactory

soddi'sfa|re vt/i satisfy; meet (richiesta); make amends for (offesa). ~tto pp di soddisfare ● adj satisfied. ~zi'one f satisfaction

sodo adj hard; fig firm; (uovo) hard-boiled ● adv hard; dormire ~ sleep soundly

sofà m inv sofa

soffe'ren|te adj ill

soffer'marsi vr pause; ~ su dwell on

of'ferto pp di soffrire

offi'a|re vt blow; reveal (segreto); (rubare) pinch Ⅱ ● vi blow. ~ta f fig ⊠ tip-off

'soffice adj soft

'soffio m puff; (Med) murmur

sof'fitt|a f attic. ~o m ceiling

soffo'ca|nte adj suffocating. ~re vt/i suffocate; (con cibo) choke; fig stifle

sof'friggere vt fry lightly

sof'frire vt/i suffer; (sopportare) bear; ~ di suffer from

sof'fritto pp di soffriggere

sof'fuso adj (luce) soft

sofisti'ca|re vt (adulterare) adulterate ● vi (sottilizzare) quibble. ~to adj sophisticated

sogget'tivo adj subjective

sog'getto m subject ● adj subject; essere ~ a be subject to

soggezi'one f subjection; (rispetto) awe

sogghi'gnare vi sneer

soggio'gare vt subdue

soggior'nare vi stay. soggi'orno m stay; (stanza) living room

soggi'ungere vt add

'soglia f threshold

sogli'ola f sole

so'gna|re vt/i dream; ~re a occhi aperti daydream. ~tore, ~'trice mf dreamer. 'sogno m dream; fare un sogno have a dream; neanche per sogno! not at all!

'soia f soya

sol m (Mus) G

so'laio m attic

sola'mente adv only

so'lar|e adj (energia, raggi) solar; (crema) sun attrib. ~ium m inv solarium

sol'care vt plough. 'solco m furrow; (di ruota) track; (di nave) wake; (di disco) groove

sol'dato m soldier

'soldo m non ha un ~ he hasn't got a penny; senza un ~ penniless;

soldi pl (denaro) money sg

'sole m sun; (luce del sole) sun[light]; al ~ in the sun; prendere il ~ sunbathe

soleggi'ato adj sunny

so'lenn|e adj solemn. ~ità f solemnity

so'lere vi be in the habit of; come si suol dire as they say

sol'fato m sulphate

soli'da|le adj in agreement. ~rietà f solidarity

solidifi'car|e vt/i, ~si vr solidify

solidità f solidity; (di colori) fastness. 'solido adj solid; (robusto) sturdy; (colore) fast ● m solid

so'lista adj solo ● mf soloist

solita'mente adv usually

soli'tario adj solitary; (isolato) lonely ● m (brillante) solitaire; (gioco di carte) patience, solitaire

'solito adj usual; essere ~ fare qcsa be in the habit of doing sth ● m usual; di ~ usually

soli'tudine f solitude

solleci'tar|e vt speed up; urge (persona); ~zi'one f (richiesta) request; (preghiera) entreaty

sol'lecito adj prompt ● m reminder. ~'tudine f promptness; (interessamento) concern

solle'one m noonday sun; (periodo) dog days of summer

solleti'care vt tickle

solleva'mento m ~ pesi weight-lifting

solleva'r|e vt lift; (elevare) raise; (confortare) comfort. ~si vr rise; (riaversi) recover

solli'evo m relief

'solo, -a adj alone; (isolato) lonely; (unico) only; (Mus) solo; da ~ by myself/yourself/himself etc ● mf il ~, la sola the only one ● m (Mus) solo ● adv only

sol'stizio m solstice

sol'tanto adv only

so'lubile adj soluble; (caffè) instant

soluzi'one f solution; (Comm) payment

sol'vente adj & m solvent; ~ per unghie nail polish remover

so'maro m ass; (Sch) dunce

so'matico adj somatic

somigli'an|te adj similar. ~za f resemblance

somigli'ar|e vi ~e a resemble. ~si vr be alike

'somma f sum; (Math) addition

som'mare vt add; (totalizzare) add up

som'mario adj & m summary

som'mato adj tutto ~ all things considered

somme'li'er m inv wine waiter

som'mer|gere vt submerge. ~'gibile m submarine. ~so pp di sommergere

som'messo adj soft

sommini'stra|re vt administer. ~zi'one f administration

sommità f inv summit

'sommo adj highest; fig supreme ● m summit

som'mossa f rising

sommozza'tore m frogman

so'naglio m bell

so'nata f sonata; fig 🔟 beating

'sonda f (Mech) drill; (Med, spaziale). son'daggio m drilling; (Med, spaziale) probe; (indagine) survey. sondaggio d'opinioni opinion poll. son'dare vt sound; (investigare) probe

sonnam'bulismo m sleepwalking. son'nambulo, -a mf sleepwalker

sonnecchi'are vi doze

son'nifero m sleeping-pill

'sonno m sleep; aver ~ be sleepy. ~'lenza f sleepiness

so'noro adj resonant; (rumoroso) loud; (onde, scheda) sound attrib

sontuoso | sornione

sontu'oso adj sumptuous
sopo'rifero adj soporific
sop'palco m platform
soppe'rire vi ~ a qcsa provide for sth
soppe'sare vt weigh up
soppor'ta|re vt support; (tollerare) stand; bear (dolore)
soppressi'one f removal; (di legge) abolition; (di diritti, pubblicazione) suppression; (annullamento) cancellation. sop'presso pp di sopprimere
sop'primere vt get rid of; abolish (legge); suppress (diritti, pubblicazione); (annullare) cancel
sopra adv on top; (più in alto) higher [up]; (al piano superiore) upstairs; (in testo) above; mettilo lì ~ put it up there; di ~ upstairs; pensarci ~ think about it; vedi ~ see above ● prep ~ [a] on; (senza contatto, oltre) over; (riguardo a) about; è ~ al tavolo, è ~ il tavolo it's on the table; il quadro è appeso ~ al camino the picture is hanging over the fireplace; il ponte passa ~ all'autostrada the bridge crosses over the motorway; è caduto ~ il tetto it fell on the roof; l'uno ~ l'altro one on top of the other; (senza contatto) one above the other; abita ~ di me he lives upstairs from me; i bambini ~ i dieci anni children over ten; 20° ~ lo zero 20° above zero; ~ il livello del mare above sea level; rifletti ~ quello che è successo think about what happened ● m il [di] ~ the top
o'prabito m overcoat
oprac'ciglio m (pl sopracciglia) eyebrow
opracco'per|ta f bedspread; (di libro) [dust-]jacket. ~'tina f book jacket
oprad'detto adj above-mentioned
opraele'vata f elevated railway

sopraf'fa|re vt overwhelm. ~tto pp di sopraffare. ~zi'one f abuse of power
sopraf'fino adj excellent; (gusto, udito) highly refined
sopraggi'ungere vi (persona:) turn up; (accadere) happen
soprallu'ogo m inspection
sopram'mobile m ornament
soprannatu'rale adj & m supernatural
sopran'nome m nickname
so'prano mf soprano
soprappensi'ero adv lost in thought
sopras'salto m di ~ with a start
soprasse'dere vi ~ a postpone
soprat'tutto adv above all
sopravvalu'tare vt overvalue
soprav|ve'nire vi turn up; (accadere) happen. ~'vento m fig upper hand
sopravvi'|s'suto pp di sopravvivere. ~'venza f survival. sopravvi'vere vi survive; sopravvivere a outlive (persona)
soprinten'den|te mf supervisor; (di museo ecc) keeper. ~za f supervision; (ente) board
so'pruso m abuse of power
soq'quadro m mettere a ~ turn upside down
sor'betto m sorbet
'sordido adj sordid; (avaro) stingy
sor'dina f mute; in ~ on the quiet
sordità f deafness. 'sordo, -a adj deaf; (rumore, dolore) dull ● mf deaf person. sordo'muto, -a adj deaf-and-dumb
so'rel|la f sister. ~'lastra f stepsister
sor'gente f spring; (fonte) source
'sorgere vi rise; fig arise
sormon'tare vt surmount
sorni'one adj sly

sorpas'sa|re vt surpass; (eccedere) exceed; overtake (veicolo). ~**to** adj old-fashioned. **sor'passo** m overtaking

sorpren'dente adj surprising; (straordinario) remarkable

sor'prendere vt surprise; (cogliere in flagrante) catch

sor'pres|a f surprise; di ~**a** by surprise. ~**o** pp di **sorprendere**

sor're|ggere vt support; (tenere) hold up. ~**ggersi** vr support oneself. ~**tto** pp di **sorreggere**

sor'ri|dere vi smile. ~**so** pp di **sorridere** ●m smile

sorseggi'are vt sip. **'sorso** m sip; (piccola quantità) drop

'sorta f sort; di ~ whatever; ogni ~ di all sorts of

'sorte f fate; (caso imprevisto) chance; tirare a ~ draw lots. **sor'teggio** m draw

sorti'legio m witchcraft

sor'ti|re vi come out. ~**ta** f (Mil) sortie; (battuta) witticism

'sorto pp di **sorgere**

sorvegli'an|te mf keeper; (controllore) overseer. ~**za** f watch; (Mil ecc) surveillance

sorvegli'are vt watch over; (controllare) oversee; (polizia) keep under surveillance

sorvo'lare vt fly over; fig skip

'sosia m inv double

so'spen|dere vt hang; (interrompere) stop; (privare di una carica) suspend. ~**si'one** f suspension

so'speso pp di **sospendere** ●adj (impiegato, alunno) suspended; ~ **a** hanging from; ~ **a un filo** fig hanging by a thread ●m in ~ pending; (emozionato) in suspense

sospet'tare vt suspect. **so'spetto** adj suspicious; **persona sospetta** suspicious person ●m suspicion; (persona) suspect. ~**oso** adj suspicious

so'spin|gere vt drive. ~**to** pp di **sospingere**

sospi'rare vi sigh ●vt long for. **so'spiro** m sigh

'sosta f stop; (pausa) pause; **senza** ~ non-stop; **"divieto di** ~**"** "no parking"

sostan'tivo m noun

so'stanz|a f substance; ~**e** pl (patrimonio) property sg. ~**i'oso** adj substantial; (cibo) nourishing

so'stare vi stop; (fare una pausa) pause

so'stegno m support

soste'ner|e vt support; (sopportare) bear; (resistere) withstand; (affermare) maintain; (nutrire) sustain; sit (esame); ~**e le spese** meet the costs. ~**si** vr support oneself

sosteni'tore, -'trice mf supporter

sostenta'mento m maintenance

soste'nuto adj (stile) formal; (prezzi, velocità) high

sostitu'ir|e vt substitute (a for), replace (con with). ~**si** vr ~**si a** replace

sosti'tu|to, -ta mf replacement, stand-in ●m (surrogato) substitute. ~**zi'one** f substitution

sot'tana f petticoat; (di prete) cassock

sotter'raneo adj underground ●m cellar

sotter'rare vt bury

sottigli'ezza f slimness; fig subtlety

sot'til|e adj thin; (udito, odorato) keen; (osservazione, distinzione) subtle. ~**iz'zare** vi split hairs

sottin'te|ndere vt imply. ~**so** pp di **sottintendere** ●m allusion; **senza** ~**si** openly ●adj implied

'sotto adv below; (più in basso) lower [down]; (al di sotto) underneath; (al piano di sotto) downstairs; **è lì** ~ it's underneath; ~ ~ deep down; (di nascosto) on the quiet; di ~ downstairs; mettersi ~ fig get down to it; mettere ~ (〓: investire) knock down ● prep ~ [a] under; (al di sotto di) under[neath]; abita ~ di me he lives downstairs from me; i bambini ~ i dieci anni children under ten; 20° ~ zero 20° below zero; ~ il livello del mare below sea level; ~ la pioggia in the rain; ~ calmante under sedation; ~ condizione che... on condition that...; ~ giuramento under oath; ~ sorveglianza under surveillance; ~ Natale/gli esami around Christmas/exam time; al di ~ di under; andare ~ i 50 all'ora do less than 50km an hour ● m il [di] ~ the bottom

sotto'banco adv under the counter

sottobicchi'ere m coaster

sotto'bosco m undergrowth

sotto'braccio adv arm in arm

sotto'fondo m background

sottoline'are vt underline; fig stress

sot'tolio adv in oil

sotto'mano adv within reach

sottoma'rino adj & m submarine

sotto'messo pp di sottomettere

sotto'metter|e vt submit; subdue (popolo). ~si vr submit. sottomissi'one f submission

sottopas'saggio m underpass; (pedonale) subway

sotto'por|re vt submit; (costringere) subject. ~si vr submit oneself; ~si a undergo. sotto'posto pp di sottoporre

sotto'scala m cupboard under the stairs

sotto'scritto pp di sottoscrivere ● m undersigned

sotto'scri|vere vt sign; (approvare) sanction, subscribe to. ~zi'one f (petizione) petition; (approvazione) sanction; (raccolta di denaro) appeal

sotto'sopra adv upside down

sotto'stante adj la strada ~ the road below

sottosu'olo m subsoil

sottosvilup'pato adj underdeveloped

sotto'terra adv underground

sotto'titolo m subtitle

sottovalu'tare vt underestimate

sotto'veste f slip

sotto'voce adv in a low voice

sottovu'oto adj vacuum-packed

sot'tra|rre vt remove; embezzle (fondi); (Math) subtract. ~rsi vr ~rsi a escape from; avoid (responsabilità). ~tto pp di sottrarre. ~zi'one f removal; (di fondi) embezzlement; (Math) subtraction

sottuffici'ale m non-commissioned officer; (Naut) petty officer

sou'brette f inv showgirl

so'vietico, -a adj & mf Soviet

sovraccari'care vt overload. sovrac'carico adj overloaded (di with) ● m overload

sovrannatu'rale adj & m = SOPRANNATURALE

so'vrano, -a adj sovereign; fig supreme ● mf sovereign

sovrap'por|re vt superimpose. ~si vr overlap

sovra'stare vt dominate; fig: (pericolo) hang over

sovrinten'den|te, ~za = SOPRINTENDENTE, SOPRINTENDENZA

sovru'mano adj superhuman

sovvenzi'one f subsidy

sovver'sivo adj subversive

'sozzo adj filthy

S.p.A. abbr (società per azioni) plc

spac'care vt split; chop (legna). ~rsi vr split. ~'tura f split

spacci'a|re vt deal in, push (droga); ~re qcsa per qcsa pass sth off as

s

sth. **∼rsi** vr ∼**rsi per** pass oneself off as. ∼**tore**, ∼**trice** mf (di droga) pusher; (di denaro falso) distributor of forged bank notes. **'spaccio** m (di droga) dealing; (negozio) shop

'spacco m split

spac'cone, -a mf boaster

'spada f sword. ∼**c'cino** m swordsman

spae'sato adj disorientated

spa'ghetti mpl spaghetti sg

spa'ghetto m (🔲: spavento) fright

'Spagna f Spain

spa'gnolo, -a adj Spanish ●mf Spaniard ●m (lingua) Spanish

'spago m string; dare ∼ a qcno encourage sb

spai'ato adj odd

spalan'ca|re vt, ∼**rsi** vr open wide. ∼**to** adj wide open

spa'lare vt shovel

'spall|a f shoulder; (di comico) straight man; ∼**e** pl (schiena) back; alle ∼**e di** qcno (ridere) behind sb's back. ∼**eggi'are** vt back up

spal'letta f parapet

spalli'era f back; (di letto) headboard; (ginnastica) wall bars pl

spal'lina f strap; (imbottitura) shoulder pad

spal'mare vt spread

'spander|e vt spread; (versare) spill. ∼**si** vr spread

spappo'lare vt crush

spa'ra|re vt/i shoot; ∼**rle** grosse talk big. ∼**toria** f shooting

sparecchi'are vt clear

spa'reggio m (Comm) deficit; Sport play-off

'sparg|ere vt scatter; (diffondere) spread; shed (lacrime, sangue). ∼**ersi** vr spread. ∼**imento** m scattering; ∼**imento di sangue** bloodshed

spa'ri|re vi disappear; ∼**scil** get lost!. ∼**zi'one** f disappearance

spar'lare vi ∼ **di** run down

'sparo m shot

sparpagli'ar|e vt, ∼**si** vr scatter

'sparso pp di spargere ●adj scattered; (sciolto) loose

spar'tire vt share out; (separare) separate

sparti'traffico m inv traffic island; (di autostrada) central reservation, median strip Am

spartizi'one f division

spa'ruto adj gaunt; (gruppo) small; (peli, capelli) sparse

sparvi'ero m sparrow-hawk

'spasimo m spasm

spa'smodico adj spasmodic

spas'sar|si vr amuse oneself; ∼**sela** have a good time

spassio'nato adj dispassionate

'spasso m fun; essere uno ∼ be hilarious; andare a ∼ go for a walk. **spas'soso** adj hilarious

'spatola f spatula

spau'racchio m scarecrow; fig bugbear. **spau'rire** vt frighten

spa'valdo adj defiant

spaventa'passeri m inv scarecrow

spaven'tar|e vt frighten. ∼**si** vr be frightened. **spa'vento** m fright. **spaven'toso** adj frightening. **spa** (🔲: enorme) incredible

spazi'ale adj spatial; (cosmico) space attrib

spazi'are vt space out ●vi range

spazien'tirsi vr lose patience

'spazi|o m space. ∼**oso** adj spacious

spaz'z|are vt sweep; ∼**are via** sweep away; (🔲: mangiare) devour. ∼**atura** f rubbish. ∼**ino** m road sweeper; (netturbino) dustman

'spazzo|la f brush; (di tergicristallo) blade. ∼**'lare** vt brush. ∼**lino** m small brush. ∼**lino da denti** toothbrush. ∼**lone** m scrubbing brush

specchi'arsi vr look at oneself in the mirror; (*riflettersi*) be mirrored; ~ in qcno model oneself on sb

specchi'etto m ~ retrovisore driving mirror

'specchio m mirror

speci'a|le adj special ●m (TV) special [programme]. ~lista mf specialist. ~lità f inv specialty

specializ'za|re vt, ~rsi vr specialize. ~to adj skilled

special'mente adv especially

'specie f inv species; (*tipo*) kind; fare ~ a surprise

specifi'care vt specify. **spe'cifico** adj specific

specu'lare[1] vi speculate; ~ su (*indagare*) speculate on; (Fin) speculate in

specu'lare[2] adj mirror attrib

specula'tore, -'trice mf speculator. ~zi'one f speculation

spe'di|re vt send. ~to pp di spedire ●adj quick; (*parlata*) fluent. ~zi'one f dispatch; (Comm) consignment; (*scientifica*) expedition

spegner|e vt put out; turn off (gas, luce); switch off (motore); slake (sete). ~si vr go out; (*morire*) pass away

spelacchi'ato adj (*tappeto*) threadbare; (cane) mangy

spe'lar|e vt skin (coniglio). ~si vr (cane) moult

speleolo'gia f potholing

spel'lar|e vt skin; fig fleece. ~si vr peel off

spe'lonca f cave; fig hole

spendacci'one, -a mf spendthrift

spendere vt spend; ~ fiato waste one's breath

spen'nare vt pluck; Ⅱ fleece (cliente)

spennel'lare vt brush

spensie|ra'tezza f lightheartedness. ~'rato adj carefree

'spento pp di spegnere ●adj off; (gas) out; (*smorto*) dull

spe'ranza f hope; pieno di ~ hopeful; senza ~ hopeless

spe'rare vt hope for; (*aspettarsi*) expect ●vi ~ in trust in; spero di sì I hope so

sper|'dersi vr get lost. ~'duto adj lost; (*isolato*) secluded

spergi'uro, -a mf perjurer ●m perjury

sperimen'ta|le adj experimental. ~re vt experiment with; test (*resistenza, capacità, teoria*). ~zi'one f experimentation

'sperma m sperm

spe'rone m spur

sperpe'rare vt squander. **'sperpero** m waste

'spes|a f expense; (*acquisto*)-purchase; andare a far ~e go shopping; fare la ~a do the shopping; fare il ~e di pay for. ~e pl bancarie bank charges. ~e a carico del destinatario carriage forward. spe'sato adj all-expenses-paid. ~o pp di spendere

'spesso[1] adj thick

'spesso[2] adv often

spes'sore m thickness; (*fig: consistenza*) substance

spet'tabile adj (Comm) abbr (Spett.) S~ ditta Rossi Messrs Rossi

spettaco'lare adj spectacular. **spet'tacolo** m spectacle; (*rappresentazione*) show. ~'loso adj spectacular

spet'tare vi ~ a be up to; (*diritto*) be due to

spetta'tore, -'trice mf spectator; spettatori pl audience sg

spettego'lare vi gossip

spet'trale adj ghostly. **'spettro** m ghost; (Phys) spectrum

'spezie fpl spices

spez'zar|e vt, ~si vr break

spezza'tino m stew

spez'zato m coordinated jacket and trousers

spezzet'tare vt break into small pieces

spia f spy; (della polizia) informer; (di porta) peep-hole; fare la ~ sneak. ~ [luminosa] light. ~ dell'olio oil [warning] light

spiacci'care vt squash

spia'ce|nte adj sorry. ~vole adj unpleasant

spi'aggia f beach

spia'nare vt level; (rendere liscio) smooth; roll out (pasta); raze to the ground (edificio)

spian'tato adj fig penniless

spi'are vt spy on; wait for (occasione ecc)

spiattel'lare vt blurt out; shove (oggetto)

spi'azzo m (radura) clearing

spic'ca|re vt ~re un salto jump; ~re il volo take flight ● vi stand out. ~to adj marked

'spicchio m (di agrumi) segment; (di aglio) clove

spicci'a|rsi vr hurry up. ~'tivo adj speedy

spicciolo adj (comune) banal; spi'cciolo m change. spiccioli (denaro, 5 euro) in change. spiccioli pl change sg

'spicco m relief; fare ~ stand out

'spider f inv open-top sports car

spie'dino m kebab. spi'edo m spit; allo spiedo on a spit, spit-roasted

spie'ga|re vt explain; open out (cartina); unfurl (vele). ~rsi vr explain oneself; (vele, bandiere:) unfurl. ~zi'one f explanation

spiegaz'zato adj crumpled

spie'tato adj ruthless

spiffe'rare vt blurt out ● vi (vento:) whistle. 'spiffero m draught

'spiga f spike; (Bot) ear

spigli'ato adj self-possessed

'spigolo m edge; (angolo) corner

'spilla f brooch. ~ da balia safety pin. ~ di sicurezza safety pin

spil'lare vt tap

'spillo m pin. ~ di sicurezza safety pin; (in arma) safety catch

spi'lorcio adj stingy

'spina f thorn; (di pesce) bone; (Electr) plug. ~ dorsale spine

spi'naci mpl spinach

spi'nale adj spinal

spi'nato adj (filo) barbed; (pianta) thorny

spi'nello m ① joint

'spinger|e vt push; fig drive. ~si vr (andare) proceed

spi'noso adj thorny

spint|a f push; (violenta) thrust; fig spur. ~o pp di spingere

spio'naggio m espionage

spio'vente adj sloping

spi'overe vi litter stop raining; (ricadere) fall; (scorrere) flow down

'spira f coil

spi'raglio m small opening; (soffio d'aria) breath of air; (raggio di luce) gleam of light

spi'rale adj spiral ● f spiral; (negli orologi) hairspring; (anticoncezionale) coil

spi'rare vi (soffiare) blow; (morire) pass away

spiri'tato adj possessed; (espressione) wild. 'spirito m spirit; (arguzia) wit; (intelletto) mind; fare dello spirito be witty; sotto spirito in brandy. ~o'saggine f witticism. spi'ritoso adj witty

spiritu'ale adj spiritual

'splen|dere vi shine. ~dido adj splendid. ~'dore m splendour

'spoglia f (di animale) skin; spoglie pl (salma) mortal remains; (bottino) spoils

spogli'a|re vt strip; (svestire) undress; (fare lo spoglio di) go through. ~'rello m strip-tease. ~rsi vr strip, undress. ~'toio m dressing room; Sport changing room; (guardaroba) spola | spuntare

cloakroom, checkroom Am. 'spoglio adj undressed; (albero, muro) bare ● m (scrutinio) perusal

spola f shuttle; fare la ~ shuttle

spol'pare vt flesh; fig fleece

spolve'rare vt dust; 🔟 devour (cibo)

sponda f shore; (di fiume) bank; (bordo) edge

sponsoriz'zare vt sponsor

spon'taneo adj spontaneous

spopo'lar|e vt depopulate ● vi (avere successo) draw the crowds. ~si vr become depopulated

spora'dica'mente adv sporadically. spo'radico adj sporadic

spor'c|are vt dirty; (macchiare) soil. ~arsi vr get dirty. ~izia f dirt. 'sporco adj dirty; avere la coscienza sporca have a guilty conscience ● m dirt

spor'gen|te adj jutting. ~za f projection

sporger|e vt stretch out; ~e querela contro take legal action against ● vi jut out. ~si vr lean out

sport m inv sport

sporta f shopping basket

por'tello m door; (di banca ecc) window. ~ automatico cash dispenser

por'tivo, -a adj sports attrib; (persona) sporty ● m sportsman ● f sportswoman

sporto pp di sporgere

sposa f bride. ~lizio m wedding

po'sa|re vt marry; fig espouse. ~rsi vr get married; (vino:) go (con with). ~to adj married. 'sposo m bridegroom; sposi pl [novelli] newlyweds

possa'tezza f exhaustion. spos'sato adj exhausted, worn out

po'sta|re vt move; (differire) postpone; (cambiare) change. ~rsi vr move. ~to, -a adj ill-adjusted ● mf

(disadattato) misfit

'spranga f bar. spran'gare vt bar

'sprazzo m (di colore) splash; (di luce) flash; fig glimmer

spre'care vt waste. 'spreco m waste

spre'g|evole adj despicable. ~ia'tivo adj pejorative. 'spregio m contempt

spregiudi'cato adj unscrupulous

'spremer|e vt squeeze. ~si vr ~si le meningi rack one's brains

spremia'grumi m lemon squeezer

spre'muta f juice. ~ d'arancia fresh orange [juice]

sprez'zante adj contemptuous

sprigio'nar|e vt emit. ~si vr burst out

spriz'zare vt/i spurt; be bursting with (salute, gioia)

sprofon'dar|e vi sink; (crollare) collapse. ~si vr ~si in sink into; fig be engrossed in

'sprone m spur; (sartoria) yoke

sproporzi|o'nato adj disproportionate. ~'one f disproportion

sproposi'tato adj full of blunders; (enorme) huge. spro'posito m blunder; (eccesso) excessive amount

sprov've'duto adj unprepared; ~ di lacking in

sprov'visto adj ~ di out of; lacking in (fantasia, pazienza); alla sprovvista unexpectedly

spruz'za|re vt sprinkle; (vaporizzare) spray; (inzaccherare) spatter. ~'tore m spray; 'spruzzo m spray; (di fango) splash

spudo'ra'tezza f shamelessness. ~'rato adj shameless

'spugna f sponge; (tessuto) towelling. spu'gnoso adj spongy

'spuma f foam; (schiuma) froth; (Culin) mousse. spu'mante m sparkling wine. spumeggi'are vi foam

spun'tare vt break the point of;

trim (capelli); ~**rla** *fig* win ● *vi*
(pianta:) sprout; (capelli:) begin to
grow; (sorgere) rise; (apparire) appear.
~**rsi** *vr* get blunt. ~**ta** *f* trim

spun'tino *m* snack

'**spunto** *m* cue; *fig* starting point;
dare ~ a give rise to

spur'gar|e *vt/i* purge. ~**si** *vr* (Med)
expectorate

spu'tare *vt/i* spit; ~ sentenze pass
judgment. '**sputo** *m* spit

'**squadra** *f* team, squad; (di polizia
ecc) squad; (da disegno) square. squa-
'**drare** *vt* square; (guardare) look up
and down

squa'**driglia** *f*, ~**one** *m* squadron

squagli'ar|e *vt*, ~**si** *vr* melt; ~**sela**
(Ⅱ: svignarsela) steal out

squa'**lifica** *f* disqualification.
~'**care** *vt* disqualify

'**squallido** *adj* squalid. squal'**lore** *m*
squalor

'**squalo** *m* shark

'**squama** *f* scale; (di pelle) flake

squa'**mar|e** *vt* scale. ~**arsi** *vr*
(pelle:) flake off. ~'**moso** *adj* scaly;
(pelle) flaky

squarcia'**gola**: a ~ *adv* at the top
of one's voice

squarci'**ar|e** *vt* rip. '**squarcio** *m* rip;
(di ferita, in nave) gash; (di cielo) patch

squattri'**nato** *adj* penniless

squilib'**rar|e** *vt* unbalance. ~**to**, ~**ta**
adj unbalanced ● *mf* lunatic. squi'**li-**
brio *m* imbalance

squil'**lan|te** *adj* shrill. ~**re** *vi* (cam-
pana:) peal; (tromba:) blare; (tele-
fono:) ring. '**squillo** *m* blare; (Teleph)
ring ● *f* (ragazza) call girl

squi'**sito** *adj* exquisite

sradi'**care** *vt* uproot; eradicate
(vizio, male)

sragio'**nare** *vi* rave

srego'**lato** *adj* inordinate; (dissoluto)
dissolute

s.r.l. *abbr* (società a responsabilità li-

mitata) Ltd

sroto'**lare** *vt* uncoil

SS *abbr* (strada statale) national road

'**stabile** *adj* stable; (permanente) lasting; (saldo) steady; compagnia ~
(Theat) repertory company ● *m* (edificio) building

stabili'**mento** *m* factory; (industriale) plant; (edificio) establishment.
~ balneare lido

stabi'**li|re** *vt* establish; (decidere) de-
cide. ~**rsi** *vr* settle. ~**tà** *f* stability

stabiliz'**za|re** *vt* stabilize. ~**rsi** *vr*
stabilize. ~**tore** *m* stabilizer

stac'**car|e** *vt* detach; pronounce
clearly (parole); (separare) separate;
turn off (corrente) ● *vi* (Ⅱ: finire di lavorare) knock off. ~**si** *vr* come off;
~**si da** break away from (partito, famiglia)

staccio'**nata** *f* fence

'**stacco** *m* gap

'**stadio** *m* stadium

'**staffa** *f* stirrup

staf'**fetta** *f* dispatch rider

stagio'**nale** *adj* seasonal

stagio'**na|re** *vt* season (legno);
mature (formaggio). ~**to** *adj* (legno)
seasoned; (formaggio) matured

stagi'**one** *f* season; alta/bassa ~
high/low season

stagli'**arsi** *vr* stand out

sta'**gnan|te** *adj* stagnant. ~**re** *vt*
(saldare) solder; (chiudere ermeticamente)
seal ● *vi* stagnate. '**stagno** *adj* water-
tight ● *m* pond; (metallo) tin

sta'**gnola** *f* tinfoil

'**stall|a** *f* stable; (per buoi) cowshed.
~**i'ere** *m* groom

stal'**lone** *m* stallion

sta'**mani, stamat'tina** *adv* this
morning

stam'**becco** *m* ibex

stam'**berga** *f* hovel

'**stampa** *f* (Typ) printing; (giornali,
giornalisti) press; (riproduzione) print

stam'pa|nte f printer. ~**nte laser** laser printer. ~**re** vt print. ~**tello** m block letters pl

stam'pella f crutch

stampo m mould; **di vecchio** ~ (persona) of the old school

sta'nare vt drive out

stan'car|e vt tire; (annoiare) bore. ~**si** vr get tired

stan'chezza f tiredness. **'stanco** adj tired; **stanco di** fed up with. **stanco morto** dead tired, exhausted

standard adj & m inv standard. ~**iz'zare** vt standardize

stan|ga f bar; (persona) beanpole. ~**'gata** f fig blow; (🖼: nel calcio) big kick. **stan'ghetta** f (di occhiali) leg

sta'notte adv tonight; (la notte scorsa) last night

stante prep on account of; **a se** ~ separate

stan'tio adj stale

stan'tuffo m piston

stanza f room; (metrica) stanza

stanzi'are vt allocate

tap'pare vt uncork

'stare
● vi (rimanere) stay; (abitare) live; (con gerundio) be; **sto solo cinque minuti** I'll stay only five minutes; **sto in piazza Peyron** I live in Peyron Square; **sta dormendo** he's sleeping; ~ **a** (attenersi) keep to; (spettare) be up to; ~ **bene** (economicamente) be well off; (di salute) be well; (addirsi) suit; ~ **dietro a** (seguire) follow; (sorvegliare) keep an eye on; (corteggiare) run after; ~ **in piedi** stand; ~ **per** be about to; **come stai/sta?** how are you?; **lasciar** ~ leave alone; **starci** (essere contento) go into; (essere d'accordo) agree; **il 3 nel 12 ci sta 4 volte** 3 into 12

stampante | stelo

goes 4; **non sa** ~ **agli scherzi** he can't take a joke; ~ **sulle proprie** keep oneself to oneself.
● **starsene** vr (rimanere) stay

starnu'tire vi sneeze. **star'nuto** m sneeze

sta'sera adv this evening, tonight

sta'tale adj state attrib ● mf state employee ● f main road

'statico adj static

sta'tista m statesman

sta'tistic|a f statistics sg. ~**o** adj statistical

'stato pp di essere, stare ● m state; (posizione sociale) position; (Jur) status. ~ **d'animo** frame of mind. ~ **civile** marital status. **S~ Maggiore** (Mil) General Staff. **Stati** pl **Uniti [d'America]** United States [of America]

'statua f statue

statuni'tense adj United States attrib, US attrib ● mf citizen of the United States, US citizen

sta'tura f height; **di alta** ~ tall; **di bassa** ~ short

sta'tuto m statute

stazio'nario adj stationary

stazi'one f station; (città) resort. ~ **balneare** seaside resort. ~ **ferroviaria** train station. ~ **di servizio** service station. ~ **termale** spa

'stecca f stick; (di ombrello) rib; (da biliardo) cue; (Med) splint; (di sigaretta) carton; (di reggiseno) stiffener

stec'cato m fence

stec'chito adj skinny; (rigido) stiff; (morto) stone cold dead

'stella f star; **salire alle stelle** (prezzi) rise sky-high. ~ **alpina** edelweiss. ~ **cadente** shooting star. ~ **filante** streamer. ~ **di mare** starfish

stel'lare adj stellar

'stelo m stem; **lampada** f **a** ~

standard lamp

'**stemma** m coat of arms

stempi'ato adj bald at the temples

sten'dardo m standard

'**stender|e** vt spread out; (appendere) hang out; (distendere) stretch [out]; (scrivere) write down. ~si vr stretch out

stendibianche'ria f inv, **stendi'toio** m clothes horse

stenodatti|logra'fia f shorthand typing

stenogra'f|are vt take down in shorthand. ~ia f shorthand

sten'ta|re vi ~re a find it hard to. ~to adj laboured. '**stento** m effort; a stento with difficulty; **stenti** pl hardships, privations

'**sterco** m dung

'**stereo['fonico]** adj stereo[phonic]

stereoti'pato adj stereotyped; (sorriso) insincere. **stere'otipo** m stereotype

'**steril|e** adj sterile; (terreno) barren. ~ità f sterility. ~iz'zare vt sterilize. ~izzazi'one f sterilization

ster'lina f pound; lira ~ [pound] sterling

stermi'nare vt exterminate

stermi'nato adj immense

ster'minio m extermination

ste'roide m steroid

ster'zare vi steer. '**sterzo** m steering

'**steso** pp di stendere

'**stesso** adj same; io ~ myself; tu ~ yourself; me ~ myself; se ~ himself; in quel momento ~ at that very moment; dalla stessa regina by the Queen herself; coi miei stessi occhi with my own eyes ●pron lo ~ the same one; (la stessa cosa) the same; fa lo ~ it's all the same; ci vado lo ~ I'll go just the same

ste'sura f drawing up; (documento) draft

stick m colla a ~ glue stick; deodorante a ~ stick deodorant

'**stigma** m stigma. ~te fpl stigmata

sti'lare vt draw up

'**still|e** m style. **sti'lista** mf stylist. ~iz'zato adj stylized

stil'lare vi ooze

stilo'grafic|a f fountain pen. ~o adj penna ~a fountain pen

'**stima** f esteem; (valutazione) estimate. **sti'mare** vt esteem; (valutare) estimate; (ritenere) consider

stimo'la|nte adj stimulating ●m stimulant. ~re vt stimulate; (incitare) incite

'**stimolo** m stimulus; (fitta) pang

'**stinco** m shin

'**stinger|e** vt/i fade. ~si vr fade. '**stinto** pp di stingere

sti'par|e vt cram. ~si vr crowd together

stipendi'ato adj salaried ●m salaried worker. **sti'pendio** m salary

'**stipite** m doorpost

stipu'la|re vt stipulate. ~zi'one f stipulation; (accordo) agreement

stira'mento m sprain

sti'ra|re vt iron; (distendere) stretch. ~rsi vr (distendersi) stretch; pull (muscolo). ~'tura f ironing. '**stiro** m ferro da stiro iron

'**stirpe** f stock

stiti'chezza f constipation. '**stitico** adj constipated

'**stiva** f (Naut) hold

sti'vale m boot. **stivali** pl di gomma Wellington boots

'**stizza** f anger

stiz'zi|re vt irritate. ~rsi vr become irritated. ~to ad irritated. **stiz'zoso** adj peevish

stocca'fisso m stockfish

stoc'cata f stab; (battuta pungente) gibe

'stoffa f material; fig stuff

'stola f stole

'stolto adj foolish

stoma'chevole adj revolting

'stomaco m stomach; mal di ∼ stomach-ache

sto'na|re vt/i sing/play out of tune ●vi (non intonarsi) clash. ∼to adj out of tune; (discordante) clashing; (confuso) bewildered. ∼'tura f false note; (discordanza) clash

'stoppia f stubble

stop'pino m wick

stop'poso adj tough

'storcer|e vt, ∼si vr twist

stor'di|re vt stun; (intontire) daze. ∼rsi vr dull one's senses. ∼to adj stunned; (intontito) dazed; (sventato) heedless

'storia f history; (racconto, bugia) story; (pretesto) excuse; fare [delle] storie make a fuss

'storico, -a adj historical; (di importanza storica) historic ●mf historian

stori'one m sturgeon

'stormo m flock

'storno m starling

storpi'a|re vt cripple; mangle (parole). ∼'tura f deformation. 'stor-pio, -a adj crippled ●mf cripple

'stort|a f (distorsione) sprain; prendere una ∼a alla caviglia sprain one's ankle. ∼o pp di storcere ●adj crooked; (ritorto) twisted; (gambe) bandy; fig wrong

sto'viglie fpl crockery sg

'strabico adj cross-eyed

strabili'ante adj astonishing

stra'bismo m squint

strabocc'care vi overflow

stra'carico adj overloaded

stracci'a|re vt tear; (I: vincere) thrash. ∼ato adj torn; (persona) in rags; (prezzi) slashed; a un prezzo ∼ato dirt cheap. 'straccio m torn ●m rag; (strofinaccio) cloth. ∼'one m tramp

stra'cotto adj overdone; (I: innamorato) head over heels ●m stew

'strada f road; (di città) street; essere fuori ∼ be on the wrong track; fare ∼ lead the way; farsi ∼ make one's way. ∼ maestra main road. ∼ a senso unico one-way street. ∼ senza uscita blind alley. stra'dale adj road attrib

strafalci'one m blunder

stra'fare vi overdo things

stra'foro: di ∼ adv on the sly

strafot'ten|te adj arrogant. ∼za f arrogance

'strage f slaughter

'stralcio m (parte) extract

stralu'na|re vt ∼re gli occhi open one's eyes wide. ∼to adj (occhi) staring; (persona) distraught

stramaz'zare vi fall heavily

strambe'ria f oddity. 'strambo adj strange

strampa'lato adj odd

stra'nezza f strangeness

strango'lare vt strangle

strani'ero, -a adj foreign ●mf foreigner

'strano adj strange

straordi|naria'mente adv extraordinarily. ∼'nario adj extraordinary; (notevole) remarkable; (edizione) special; lavoro ∼nario overtime; treno ∼nario special train

strapaz'zar|e vt ill-treat; scramble (uova). ∼si vr tire oneself out. stra-'pazzo m strain; da strapazzo fig worthless

strapi'eno adj overflowing

strapi'ombo m projection; a ∼ sheer

strap'par|e vt tear; (per distruggere) tear up; pull out (dente, capelli); (sradicare) pull up; (estorcere) wring. ∼si vr get torn; (allontanarsi) tear oneself away. 'strappo m tear; (strattone) jerk; (⊞: *passaggio*) lift; fare uno strappo alla regola make an exception to the rule. ~ muscolare muscle strain

strapun'tino *m* folding seat

strari'pare *vi* flood

strasci'c|are *vt* trail; shuffle (*piedi*); drawl (*parole*). 'strascico *m* train; *fig* after-effect

strass *m inv* rhinestone

strata'gemma *m* stratagem

strate'gia *f* strategy. stra'tegico *adj* strategic

'strato *m* layer; (*di vernice ecc*) coat; (*rocioioso, sociale*) stratum. ~'sfera *f* stratosphere. ~'sferico *adj* stratospheric

stravac'carsi *vr* ⊞ slouch

strava'gan|te *adj* extravagant; (*eccentrico*) eccentric. ~za *f* extravagance; (*eccentricità*) eccentricity

stra'vecchio *adj* ancient

stra've'dere *vt* ~ per worship

stravi'zi|are *vi* indulge oneself. stra'vizio *m* excess

stra'volg|ere *vt* twist; (*turbare*) upset. ~i'mento *m* twisting. stra-'volto *adj* distraught; (⊞: *stanco*) done in

strazi'a|nte *adj* heartrending; (*dolore*) agonizing. ~re *vt* grate on (*orecchie*); break (*cuore*). 'strazio *m* agony; che strazio! ⊞ it's awful!

'strega *f* witch. stre'gare *vt* bewitch. stre'gone *m* wizard

stre'gua *f* alla ~ di like

stre'ma|re *vt* exhaust. ~to *adj* exhausted

'strenuo *adj* strenuous

strepi'ta|re *vi* make a din. 'strepito *m* noise. ~'toso *adj* noisy; *fig* resounding

strito'lare *vt* grind

striz'zare *vt* squeeze; (*torcere*) wring [out]; ~ l'occhio wink

'strofa *f* strophe

strofi'naccio *m* cloth; (*per spolverare*) duster

strofi'nare *vt* rub

~ di mano handshake

stret'tezza *f* narrowness; stret'tezze *pl* (*difficoltà finanziarie*) financial difficulties

'stret|to *pp di* stringere ● *adj* narrow; (*serrato*) tight; (*vicino*) close; (*dialetto*) broad; (*rigoroso*) strict; lo ~to necessario the bare minimum ● *m* (*Geog*) strait. ~'toia *f* bottleneck; (⊞: *difficoltà*) tight spot

stri'ato *adj* striped. ~'tura *f* streak

stri'dente *adj* strident

'stridere *vi* squeak; *fig* clash. stri-'dore *m* screech

'stridulo *adj* shrill

strigli'a|re *vt* groom. ~ta *f* grooming; *fig* dressing down

stril'l|are *vi t* scream. 'strillo *m* scream

strimin'zito *adj* skimpy; (*magro*) skinny

strimpel'lare *vt* strum

'strin|ga *f* lace; (*Comput*) string. ~'gato *adj fig* terse

'stringer|e *vt* press; (*serrare*) squeeze; (*tenere stretto*) hold tight; take in (*abito*); (*comprimere*) be tight; (*restringere*) tighten; ~ la mano a shake hands with ● *vi* (*premere*) press. ~si *vr* (*accostarsi*) draw close (a to); (*avvicinarsi*) squeeze up

'striscia *f* strip; (*riga*) stripe. strisce *pl* [pedonali] zebra crossing *sg*

strisci'ar|e *vi* crawl; (*sfiorare*) graze ● *vt* drag (*piedi*). ~si *vr* ~si a rub against. 'striscio *m* graze; (*Med*) smear; colpire di striscio graze

strisci'one *m* banner

strombaz'zare vt boast about ●vi hoot

strombaz'zata f hoot

stron'care vt cut off; (reprimere) crush; (criticare) tear to shreds

stropicci'are vt rub; crumple (vestito)

stroz'za|re vt strangle. ~'tura f strangling; (di strada) narrowing

strozzi'naggio m loan-sharking

stroz'zino m pej usurer; (truffatore) shark

strug'gente adj all-consuming

strumen'tale adj instrumental

strumentaliz'zare vt make use of

stru'mento m instrument; (arnese) tool. ~ a corda string instrument. ~ musicale musical instrument

strusci'are vt rub

'strutto m lard

strut'tura f structure. struttu'rale adj structural

struttu'rare vt structure

strutturazi'one f structuring

'struzzo m ostrich

stuc'ca|re vt stucco

stuc'chevole adj nauseating

'stucco m stucco

stu'den|te, -'tessa mf student; (di scuola) schoolboy; schoolgirl. ~'tesco adj student; (di scolaro) school attrib

studi'ar|e vt study. ~si vr ~si di try to

'studi|o m studying; (stanza, ricerca) study; (di artista, TV ecc) studio; (di professionista) office. ~'oso, -a adj studious ●mf scholar

'stufa f stove. ~ elettrica electric fire

stu'fa|re vt (Culin) stew; (dare fastidio) bore. ~rsi vr get bored. ~to m stew

'stufo adj bored; essere ~ di be fed up with

stu'oia f mat

stupefa'cente adj amazing ●m drug

stu'pendo adj stupendous

stupi'd|aggine f (azione) stupid thing; (cosa da poco) nothing. ~ata f stupid thing. ~ità f stupidity. 'stupido adj stupid

stu'pir|e vt astonish ●vi, ~si vr be astonished. stu'pore m amazement

stu'pra|re vt rape. ~'tore m rapist. 'stupro m rape

sturalavan'dini m inv plunger

stu'rare vt uncork; unblock (lavandino)

stuzzi'care vt prod [at]; pick (denti); poke (fuoco); (molestare) tease; whet (appetito)

stuzzi'chino m (Culin) appetizer

su prep on; (senza contatto) over; (riguardo a) about; (circa, intorno a) about, around; le chiavi sono sul tavolo the keys are on the table; il quadro è appeso sul camino the picture is hanging over the fireplace; un libro sull'antico Egitto a book on o about Ancient Egypt; costa sui 25 euro it costs about 25 euros; decidere sul momento decide at the time; su commissione on commission; su due piedi on the spot; uno su dieci one out of ten ●adv (sopra) up; (al piano di sopra) upstairs; (addosso) on; ho su il cappotto I've got my coat on; in su (guardare) up; dalla vita in su from the waist up; su! come on!

su'bacqueo adj underwater

subaffit'tare vt sublet. subaf'fitto m sublet

subal'terno adj & m subordinate

sub'buglio m turmoil

sub'conscio adj & m subconscious

'subdolo adj devious

suben'trare vi (circostanze:) come up; ~ a take the place of

su'bire vt undergo; (patire) suffer

subis'sare vt fig ∼ di overwhelm with

'subito adv at once; ∼ dopo straight after

su'blime adj sublime

subodo'rare vt suspect

subordi'nato, -a adj & mf subordinate

subur'bano adj suburban

suc'ceder|e vi (accadere) happen; ∼a succeed; (venire dopo) follow; ∼al trono succeed to the throne. ∼si vr happen one after the other

successi'one f succession; in ∼ in succession

succes|siva'mente adv subsequently. ∼'sivo adj successive

suc'ces|so pp di succedere ●m success; (esito) outcome; (disco ecc) hit

succes'sore m successor

succhi'are vt suck [up]

suc'cinto adj (conciso) concise; (abito) scanty

'succo m juice; fig essence; ∼ di frutta fruit juice. suc'coso adj juicy

succu'lento adj succulent

succur'sale f branch [office]

sud m south; del ∼ southern

su'dar|e vi sweat; (faticare) sweat blood; ∼re freddo be in a cold sweat. ∼ta f sweat. ∼'ticcio adj sweaty. ∼to adj sweaty

sud'detto adj above-mentioned

'suddito, -a m & f subject

suddi'vid|ere vt subdivide. ∼si'one f subdivision

su'd-est m southeast

'sudici|o adj filthy. ∼'ume m filth

su'dore m sweat; fig sweat

su'd-ovest m southwest

suffi'ci|ente adj sufficient; (presuntuoso) conceited ●m bare essentials pl; (Sch) pass mark. ∼za f sufficiency; (presunzione) conceit; (Sch) pass; a ∼za enough

suf'fisso m suffix

suf'fragio m vote. ∼ universale universal suffrage

suggeri'mento m suggestion

sugge'ri|re vt suggest; (Theat) prompt. ∼'tore, ∼'trice mf (Theat) prompter

suggestiona'bile adj suggestible

suggestio'na|re vt influence suggestioni'one f influence

sugge'stivo adj suggestive; (musica ecc) evocative

'sughero m cork

'sugli = su + GLI

'sugo m (di frutta) juice; (di carne) gravy; (salsa) sauce; (sostanza) substance

'sui = su + I

sui'cida adj suicidal ●mf suicide. suici'darsi vr commit suicide. ∼io m suicide

su'ino adj carne suina pork ●m swine

sul = su + IL. **'sullo** = su + LO. **'sulla** = su + LA. **'sulle** = su + LE

sul'ta|na f sultana. ∼'nina adj uva ∼nina sultana. ∼no m sultan

'sunto m summary

'suo, -a poss adj il ∼, i suoi his; (di cosa, animale) its; (forma di cortesia) your; la sua, le sue her; (di cosa, animale) its; (forma di cortesia) your; questa macchina è sua this car is his/hers; ∼ padre his/her/your father; un ∼ amico a friend of his/hers/yours ●poss pron il ∼, i suoi his; (di cosa, animale) its; (forma di cortesia) yours; la sua, le sue hers; (di cosa animale) its; (forma di cortesia) yours; i suoi his/her folk

su'ocera f mother-in-law

su'ocero m father-in-law

su'ola f sole

su'olo m ground; (terreno) soil

suo'na|re vt/i (Mus) play; ring (campanello); sound (allarme, clacson);

(orologio:) strike. **~'tore**, **~'trice** *mf*
player. **suone'ria** *f* alarm; (*di cellulare*)
ringtone. **su'ono** *m* sound
su'ora *f* nun; Suor Maria Sister Maria
superal'colico *m* spirit ● *adj* bevande *pl* superalcoliche spirits
supera'mento *m* (*di timidezza*)
overcoming; (*di esame*) success (*di* in)
supe'rare *vt* surpass; (*eccedere*) exceed; (*vincere*) overcome; overtake
(*veicolo*); pass (*esame*)
su'perbo *adj* haughty; (*magnifico*)
superb
superdo'tato *adj* highly gifted
superfici'al|e *adj* superficial ● *mf*
superficial person. **~ità** *f* superficial-
ity. **super'ficie** *f* surface; (*area*) area
su'perfluo *adj* superfluous
superi'or|e *adj* superior; (*di grado*)
senior; (*più elevato*) higher; (*sovrastante*)
upper; (*al di sopra*) above ● *mf* superior. **~ità** *f* superiority
superla'tivo *adj* & *m* superlative
supermer'cato *m* supermarket
super'sonico *adj* supersonic
su'perstite *adj* surviving ● *mf*
survivor
superstizi'o|ne *f* superstition.
~so *adj* superstitious
super'strada *f* toll-free motorway
supervi|si'one *f* supervision.
~'sore *m* supervisor
su'pino *adj* supine
suppel'lettili *fpl* furnishings
suppergiù *adv* about
supplemen'tare *adj* supplementary
supple'mento *m* supplement; **~**
rapido express train supplement
sup'plen|te *adj* temporary ● *mf*
(*Sch*) supply teacher. **~za** *f* temporary post
suppli|ca *f* plea; (*domanda*) petition.
~care *vt* beg
sup'plire *vt* replace ● *vi* **~** a (*com-*

**pensare*) make up for
sup'plizio *m* torture
sup'porre *vt* suppose
sup'porto *m* support
supposizi'one *f* supposition
sup'posta *f* suppository
sup'posto *pp di* **supporre**
suprema'zia *f* supremacy. **su-
'premo** *adj* supreme
sur'fare *vi* **~** in Internet surf
the Net
surge'la|re *vt* deep-freeze. **~ti** *mp*
frozen food *sg*. **~to** *adj* frozen
surrea'lis|mo *m* surrealism. **~ta**
mf surrealist
surriscal'dare *vt* overheat
surro'gato *m* substitute
suscet'tibil|e *adj* touchy. **~ità** *f*
touchiness
susci'tare *vt* stir up; arouse (*ammirazione ecc*)
su'sin|a *f* plum. **~o** *m* plumtree
su'spense *f* suspense
sussegu'|ente *adj* subsequent.
~'irsi *vr* follow one after the other
sussidi'ar|e *vt* subsidize. **~io** *adj*
subsidiary. **sus'sidio** *m* subsidy; (*aiuto*)
aid. sussidio di disoccupazione unemployment benefit
sus'siego *m* haughtiness
sussi'stenza *f* subsistence. **sus'sistere** *vi* subsist; (*essere valido*)
hold good
sussul'tare *vi* start. **sus'sulto**
m start
sussur'rare *vi* whisper. **sus'surro** *m*
whisper
sva'gar|e *vt* amuse. **~si** *vr* amuse
oneself. **'svago** *m* relaxation; (*divertimento*) amusement
svaligi'are *vt* rob; burgle (*casa*)
svalu'ta|re *vt* devalue; *fig* underesti-
mate. **~rsi** *vr* lose value. **~zi'one** *f*
devaluation
svam'pito *adj* absent-minded

s

sva'nire vi vanish

svantaggi'ato adj at a disadvantage; (bambino, paese) disadvantaged. **svan'taggio** m disadvantage; essere in svantaggio Sport be losing; ~oso adj disadvantageous

svapo'rare vi evaporate

svari'ato adj varied

sva'sato adj flared

'svastica f swastika

sve'dese adj & m (lingua) Swedish ● mf Swede

'sveglia f (orologio) alarm [clock]; ~! get up!; mettere la ~ set the alarm [clock]

svegli'are vt wake up; fig awaken. ~si vr wake up. **'sveglio** adj awake; (di mente) quick-witted

sve'lare vt reveal

svel'tezza f speed; fig quick-wittedness

svel'tire vt quicken. ~si vr (persona:) liven up. **'svelto** adj quick; (slanciato) svelte; alla svelta quickly

'svendere vt undersell. ~ita f [clearance] sale

sve'nire vi faint

sven'tare vt foil. ~to adj thoughtless ● mf thoughtless person

'sventola f slap

svento'lare vt/i wave

sven'trare vt disembowel; fig demolish (edificio)

sven'tura f misfortune. sventu-'rato adj unfortunate

sve'nuto pp di svenire

svergo'gnato adj shameless

sver'nare vi winter

sve'stire vt undress

'Svezia f Sweden

svez'zare vt wean

svi'are vt divert; (corrompere) lead astray. ~si vr fig go astray

svico'lare vi turn down a side street; (dalla questione ecc) evade the issue; (da una persona) dodge out of the way

svi'gnarsela vr slip away

svi'lire vt debase

svilup'par|e vt, ~si vr develop. svi'luppo m development; paese in via di sviluppo developing country

svinco'lar|e vt release; clear (merce). ~si vr free oneself. 'svincolo m clearance; (di autostrada) exit

svisce'ra|re vt gut; fig dissect. ~to adj passionate; (ossequioso) obsequious

'svista f oversight

svi'ta|re vt unscrew. ~to adj (🔢: matto) cracked, nutty

'Svizzer|a f Switzerland. s~o, -a adj & mf Swiss

svogli|a'tezza f half-hearted-ness. ~'ato adj lazy

svolaz'za|nte adj (capelli) windswept. ~re vi flutter

'svolger|e vt unwind; unwrap (pacco); (risolvere) solve; (portare a termine) carry out; (sviluppare) develop. ~si vr (accadere) take place. svolgi-'mento m course; (sviluppo) development

'svolta f turning; fig turning-point. svol'tare vi turn

'svolto pp di svolgere

svuo'tare vt empty [out]

Tt

tabac'c|aio, -a *mf* tobacconist. **∼he'ria** *f* tobacconist's. **ta'bacco** *m* tobacco

>
> **Tabaccheria** By law, cigarettes and other tobacco products can be sold only in *tabaccherie*, which must be licensed by the State. They can be recognized by a sign with a large T. As well as tobacco, *tabaccherie* have a monopoly on postage stamps, lottery tickets, and other items controlled by the State.

ta'bel|la *f* table; (*lista*) list. **∼la dei prezzi** price list. **∼'lina** *f* (*Math*) multiplication table. **∼'lone** *m* wall chart. **∼lone del canestro** backboard

taber'nacolo *m* tabernacle

tabù *adj & m inv* taboo

tabu'lato *m* [data] printout

'tacca *f* notch; **di mezza ∼** (*attore, giornalista*) second-rate

tac'cagno *adj* [T] stingy

tac'cheggio *m* shoplifting

tac'chetto *m* Sport stud

tac'chino *m* turkey

tacci'are *vt* **∼ qcno di qcsa** accuse sb of sth

'tacco *m* heel; **alzare i tacchi** take to one's heels; **scarpe senza ∼** flat shoes; **tacchi pl a spillo** stiletto heels

taccu'ino *m* notebook

ta'cere *vi* be silent ●*vt* say nothing about; **mettere a ∼ qcsa** (*scandalo*) hush sth up

ta'chimetro *m* speedometer

'tacito *adj* silent; (*inespresso*) tacit.

taci'turno *adj* taciturn

ta'fano *m* horsefly

taffe'ruglio *m* scuffle

'taglia *f* (*riscatto*) ransom; (*ricompensa*) reward; (*statura*) height; (*misura*) size. **∼ unica** one size

taglia'carte *m inv* paperknife

taglia'erba *m inv* lawn-mower

tagliafu'oco *adj inv* **porta ∼** fire door; **striscia ∼** fire break

tagli'ando *m* coupon; **fare il ∼ ≈** put one's car in for its MOT

tagli'ar|e *vt* cut; (*attraversare*) cut across; (*interrompere*) cut off; (*togliere*) cut out; carve (*carne*); mow (*erba*); **farsi ∼ i capelli** have a haircut ●*vi* cut. **∼si** *vr* cut oneself; **∼si i capelli** have a haircut

taglia'telle *fpl* tagliatelle *sg*, thin, flat strips of egg pasta

taglieggi'are *vt* extort money from

tagli'e|nte *adj* sharp ●*m* cutting edge. **∼re** *m* chopping board

'taglio *m* cut; (*il tagliare*) cutting; (*di stoffa*) length; (*parte tagliente*) edge. **∼ cesareo** Caesarean section

tagli'ola *f* trap

tagliuz'zare *vt* cut

tail'leur *m inv* [lady's] suit

'talco *m* talcum powder

'tale *adj* such a; (*con nomi plurali*) such; **c'è un ∼ disordine** there is such a mess; **non accetto tali scuse** I won't accept such excuses; **il rumore era ∼ che non si sentiva nulla** there was so much noise you couldn't hear yourself think; **il ∼ giorno** on such and such a day; **quel tal signore** that gentleman; **quel ∼** *quale* just like ●*pron* **un ∼** someone; **quel ∼** that man; **il tal dei tali** such and such a person

ta'lento *m* talent

tali'smano *m* talisman

tallo'nare *vt* be hot on the heels of

tallon'cino m coupon

tal'lone m heel

tal'mente adv so

ta'lora adv = TALVOLTA

'talpa f mole

tal'volta adv sometimes

tamburel'lare vi (con le dita) drum; (pioggia): beat, drum. tambu'rello m tambourine. tambu'rino m drummer. tam'buro m drum

tampona'mento m (Auto) collision; (di ferita) dressing; (di falla) plugging. ~ a catena pile-up. tampo'nare vt (urtare) crash into; (otturare) plug. tam'pone m swab; (per timbri) pad; (per mestruazioni) tampon; (Comput) (per treni) buffer

'tana f den

'tanfo m stench

'tanga m inv tanga

tan'gente adj tangent • f tangent; (somma) bribe. ~'topoli f widespread corruption in Italy in the early 90s. ~zi'ale f orbital road

tan'gibile adj tangible

'tango m tango

tan'tino: un ~ adv a little [bit]

'tanto adj [so] much; (con nomi plurali) [so] many, [such] a lot of; ~ tempo [such] a long time; non ha tanta pazienza he doesn't have much patience; ~ tempo quanto ti serve as much time as you need; non è ~ intelligente quanto suo padre he's not as intelligent as his father; tanti amici quanti parenti as many friends as relatives • pron much; (tanto tempo) many; (tanto tempo) a long time; è un uomo come tanti he's just an ordinary man; tanti (molte persone) many people; non ci vuole così ~ it doesn't take that long; ~ quanto as much as; tanti quanti as many as • adv (così) so; (con verbi) so much; ~ debole so weak; è ~ ingenuo da crederlo he's naive enough to be-

lieve her; di ~ in ~ every now and then; ~ l'uno come l'altro both; ~ quanto as much as; tre volte ~ three times as much; una volta ~ once in a while; tant'è so much so; ~ per cambiare for a change

'tappa f stop; (parte di viaggio) stage

tappa'buchi m inv stopgap

tap'par|e vt plug; cork (bottiglia); ~e la bocca a qcno 🔢 shut sb up. ~si vr ~si gli occhi cover one's eyes; ~si il naso hold one's nose

tappa'rella f 🔢 roller blind

tappe'tino m mat; (Comput) mouse mat

tap'peto m carpet; (piccolo) rug; mandare qcno al ~ knock sb down

tappez'zar|e vt paper (pareti); (rivestire) cover. ~e'ria f tapestry; (di carta) wallpaper; (arte) upholstery. ~i'ere m upholsterer; (imbianchino) decorator

'tappo m plug; (di sughero) cork; (di metallo, per penna) top; (🔢: persona piccola) dwarf. ~ di sughero cork

'tara f (difetto) flaw; (ereditaria) hereditary defect; (peso) tare

ta'rantola f tarantula

ta'rar|e vt calibrate (strumento). ~to adj (Comm) discounted; (Techn) calibrated; (Med) with a hereditary defect; 🔢 crazy

tarchi'ato adj stocky

tar'dare vi be late • vt delay

'tard|i adv late; al più ~i at the latest; più ~i later [on]; sul ~i late in the day; far ~i (essere in ritardo) be late; (con gli amici) stay up late; a più ~i see you later. tar'divo adj late; (bambino) retarded. ~o adj slow; (tempo) late

'targ|a f plate; (Auto) numberplate. ~a di circolazione numberplate. tar'gato adj un'auto targata... a car with the registration number.... ~'hetta f (su porta) nameplate; (sulla *valigia*) name tag

ta'rif|fa f tariff. ~'fario m price list

'**tarlo** m woodworm

'**tarma** f moth

ta'rocco m tarot; ta'rocchi pl tarot

tarta'gliare vi stutter

'**tartaro** adj & m tartar

tarta'ruga f tortoise; (*di mare*) turtle; (*per pettine ecc*) tortoiseshell

tartas'sare vt harass

tar'tina f canapé

tar'tufo m truffle

'**tasca** f pocket; (*in borsa*) compartment; da ~ pocket attrib. ~ da pasticciere icing bag

ta'scabile adj pocket attrib ●m paperback

tasca'pane m inv haversack

ta'schino m breast pocket

'**tassa** f tax; (*d'iscrizione ecc*) fee; (*doganale*) duty. ~ di circolazione road tax. ~ d'iscrizione registration fee

tas'sametro m taximeter

tas'sare vt tax

tassa|tiva'mente adv without question

tassazi'one f taxation

tas'sello m wedge; (*di stoffa*) gusset

tassì m inv taxi. tas'sista mf taxi driver

'**tasso**[1] m yew; (*animale*) badger

'**tasso**[2] m rate. ~ di cambio exchange rate. ~ di interesse interest rate

ta'stare vt feel; (*sondare*) sound; ~ il terreno fig test the water

tasti'e|ra f keyboard. ~'rista mf keyboarder

'**tasto** m key; (*tatto*) touch. ~ delicato fig touchy subject. ~ funzione (*Comput*) function key. ~ tabulatore tab key

'**tattica** f tactics pl

'**tattico** adj tactical

'**tatto** m (*senso*) touch; (*accortezza*)

tact; aver ~ be tactful

tatu'a|ggio m tattoo. ~re vt tattoo

'**tavola** f table; (*illustrazione*) plate; (*asse*) plank. ~ calda snackbar

tavo'lato m boarding; (*pavimento*) wood floor

tavo'letta f bar; (*medicinale*) tablet; andare a ~ (*Auto*) drive flat out

tavo'lino m small table

'**tavolo** m table. ~ operatorio (*Med*) operating table

tavo'lozza f palette

'**tazza** f cup; (*del water*) bowl. ~ da caffè/tè coffee-cup/teacup

taz'zina f ~ da caffè espresso coffee cup

T.C.I. abbr (Touring Club Italiano) Italian Touring Club

te pers pron you; te l'ho dato I gave it to you

tè m inv tea

TEAM f abbr (Tessera Europea di Assicurazione Malattia) EHIC

tea'trale adj theatrical

te'atro m theatre. ~ all'aperto open-air theatre. ~ di posa Cinema set. ~ tenda marquee for theatre performances

'**tecnico**, **-a** adj technical ●mf technician ●f technique

tecno|lo'gia f technology. ~'logico adj technological

te'desco, **-a** adj & mf German

te'dioso adj tedious

'**teglia** f baking tin

'**tegola** f tile; fig blow

tei'era f teapot

tek m teak

'**tela** f cloth; (*per quadri, vele*) canvas; (*Theat*) curtain. ~ cerata oilcloth. ~ di lino linen

te'laio m (*di bicicletta, finestra*) frame; (*Auto*) chassis; (*per tessere*) loom

t (margin tab)

tele'camera f television camera

teleco|man'dato adj remote-controlled, remote control attrib. ~'mando m remote control

Telecom Italia f Italian State telephone company

telecomunicazi'oni fpl telecommunications

tele'cro|naca f [television] commentary. ~naca diretta live [television] coverage. ~'nista mf television commentator

tele'ferica f cableway

telefo'na|re vt/i [tele]phone, ring. ~ta f call. ~ta interurbana long-distance call

telefonica'mente adv by [tele]phone

tele'fo|nico adj [tele]phone attrib. ~'nino m mobile [phone]. ~'nista mf operator

te'lefono m [tele]phone. ~ senza filo cordless [phone]. ~ interno internal telephone. ~ satellitare satphone. ~ a schede cardphone

telegior'nale m television news sg

tele'grafico adj telegraphic; (risposta) monosyllabic; sii telegrafico keep it brief

tele'gramma m telegram

telela'voro m teleworking

tele'matica f data communications, telematics

teleno'vela f soap opera

teleobiet'tivo m telephoto lens

telepa'tia f telepathy

telero'manzo m television serial

tele'scopio m telescope

teleselezi'one f subscriber trunk dialling, STD; chiamare in ~ dial direct

telespetta'tore, -'trice mf viewer

tele'text® m Teletext®

televisi'one f television; guardare la ~ watch television

televi'sivo adj television attrib; operatore ~ television cameraman; apparecchio ~ television set

televi'sore m television [set]

'tema m theme; (Sch) essay. te'matica f main theme

teme'rario adj reckless

te'mere vt be afraid of, fear ● vi be afraid, fear

temperama'tite m inv pencil-sharpener

tempera'mento m temperament

tempe'ra|re vt temper; sharpen (matita). ~to adj temperate. ~tura f temperature. ~tura ambiente room temperature

tempe'rino m penknife

tem'pe|sta f storm. ~sta di neve snowstorm. ~sta di sabbia sandstorm

tempe'stiva'mente adv quickly. ~'stivo adj timely. ~'stoso adj stormy

'tempia f (Anat) temple

'tempio m (Relig) temple

tem'pismo m timing

'tempo m time; (atmosferico) weather; (Mus) tempo; (Gram) tense; (di film) part; (di partita) half; a suo ~ in due course; ~ fa some time ago; un ~ once; ha fatto il suo ~ it's superannuated. ~ supplementare Sport extra time, overtime Am. ~'rale adj temporal ● m [thunder] storm. ~ranea'mente adv temporarily. ~'raneo adj temporary. ~reg-gi'are vi play for time

tem'prare vt temper

te'nac|e adj tenacious. ~ia f tenacity

te'naglia f pincers pl

'tenda f curtain; (per campeggio) tent; (tendone) awning. ~ a ossigeno oxygen tent

ten'denz|a f tendency. ~ial'mente adv by nature

'**tendere** vt (allargare) stretch [out]; (tirare) tighten; (porgere) hold out; fig lay (trappola) ● vi ~ a aim at; (essere portato a) tend to

ten'**dine** m tendon

ten'do|ne m awning; (di circo) tent. ~**poli** f inv tent city

tene'broso adj gloomy

te'nente m lieutenant

tenera'mente adv tenderly

te'ner|e vt hold; (mantenere) keep; (gestire) run; (prendere) take; (seguire) follow; (considerare) consider ● vi hold; ~**ci a**, ~**e a** be keen on; ~**e per** support (squadra). ~**si** vr hold on (a to); (in una condizione) keep oneself; (seguire) stick to; ~**si indietro** stand back

tene'rezza f tenderness. '**tenero** adj tender

'**tenia** f tapeworm

'**tennis** m tennis. ~ **da tavolo** table tennis. **ten'nista** mf tennis player

te'nore m standard; (Mus) tenor; a ~ **di legge** by law. ~ **di vita** standard of living

tensi'one f tension; (Electr) voltage; **alta** ~ high voltage

ten'tacolo m tentacle

ten'ta|re vt attempt; (sperimentare) try; (indurre in tentazione) tempt. ~**tivo** m attempt. ~**zi'one** f temptation

tenten'nare vi waver

te'nue adj fine; (debole) weak; (esiguo) small; (leggero) slight

te'nuta f (capacità) capacity; (Sport: resistenza) stamina; (possedimento) estate; (divisa) uniform; (abbigliamento) clothes pl; a ~ **d'aria** airtight. ~ **di strada** road holding

teolo'gia f theology. **teo'logico** adj theological. **te'ologo** m theologian

teo'rema m theorem

teo'ria f theory

teorica'mente adv theoretically.

te'orico adj theoretical

te'pore m warmth

'**teppa** f mob. **tep'pismo** m hooliganism. **tep'pista** m hooligan

tera'peutico adj therapeutic. tera'pia f therapy

tergicri'stallo m windscreen wiper, windshield wiper Am

tergilu'notto m rear windscreen wiper

tergiver'sare vi hesitate

'**tergo** m a ~ behind

ter'male adj thermal; **stazione** ~ spa. '**terme** fpl thermal baths

'**termico** adj thermal

termi'na|le adj & m terminal; **malato** ~**le** terminally ill person. ~**re** vt/i finish, end. '**termine** m (limite) limit; (fine) end; (condizione, espressione) term

terminolo'gia f terminology

'**termite** f termite

termoco'perta f electric blanket

ter'mometro m thermometer

'**termos** m inv thermos®

termosi'fone m radiator; (sistema) central heating

ter'mostato m thermostat

'**terra** f earth; (regione) land; (terreno) ground; (argilla) clay; (cosmetico) dark face powder (for impression of tan); a ~ (sulla costa) ashore; (installazioni) onshore; per ~ on the ground; **sotto** ~ underground. ~**cotta** f terracotta; **vasellame di** ~**cotta** earthenware. ~**pi'eno** m embankment

ter'razz|a f, ~**o** m balcony

terremo'tato, -a adj (zona) affected by an earthquake ● mf earthquake victim. **terre'moto** m earthquake

ter'reno adj earthly ● m ground; (suolo) soil; (proprietà terriera) land; **perdere/guadagnare** ~ lose/gain ground. ~ **di gioco** playing field

t

ter'restre adj terrestrial; esercito ~ land forces pl

ter'ribil|e adj terrible. ~'mente adv terribly

ter'riccio m potting compost

terrifi'cante adj terrifying

territori'ale adj territorial. terri'torio m territory

ter'rore m terror

terro'ris|mo m terrorism. ~ta m/f terrorist

terroriz'zare vt terrorize

'terso adj clear

ter'zetto m trio

terzi'ario adj tertiary

'terzo adj third; di terz'ordine (locale, servizio) third-rate; la terza età the third age • m third; terzi pl (Jur) third party sg. ter'zultimo, -a agg & m/f third from last

'tesa f brim

'teschio m skull

'tesi f inv thesis

'teso pp di tendere • adj taut; fig tense

tesor|e'ria f treasury. ~i'ere m treasurer

te'soro m treasure; (tesoreria) treasury

'tessera f card; (abbonamento all'autobus) season ticket

'tessere vt weave; hatch (complotto)

tesse'rino m travel card

'tessile adj textile. tessili mpl textiles; (operai) textile workers

tessi'tore, -'trice m/f weaver

tes'suto m fabric; (Anat) tissue

'testa f head; (cervello) brain; essere in ~ a be ahead of; in ~ Sport in the lead; ~ o croce? heads or tails?

'testa-'coda m inv fare un ~ spin right round

testa'mento m will; T~ (Relig) Testament

testar'daggine f stubbornness. te'stardo adj stubborn

te'stata f head; (intestazione) heading; (colpo) butt

'teste m/f witness

te'sticolo m testicle

testi'mon|e m/f witness. ~e oculare eye witness

testi'monial m/f inv celebrity promoting brand of cosmetics

testimoni'anza f testimony. ~'are vt testify to • vi give evidence

'testo m text; far ~ be an authority

te'stone, -a m/f blockhead

testu'ale adj textual

'tetano m tetanus

'tetro adj gloomy

tetta'rella f teat

'tetto m roof. ~ apribile sunshine roof. tet'toia f roofing. tet'tuccio m tettuccio apribile sun-roof

'Tevere m Tiber

ti pers pron you; (riflessivo) yourself; ti ha dato un libro he gave you a book; lavati le mani wash your hands; eccoti! here you are!; sbrigati! hurry up!

ti'ara f tiara

ticchet't|are vi tick. ~io m ticking

'ticchio m tic; (ghiribizzo) whim

'ticket m inv (per farmaco, esame) amount paid by National Health patients

tiepida'mente adv half-heartedly. ti'epido adj lukewarm

ti'fare vi ~ per shout for. 'tifo m (Med) typhus; fare il tifo per fig be a fan of

tifo'idea f typhoid

ti'fone m typhoon

ti'foso, -a m/f fan

'tiglio m lime

ti'grato adj gatto ~ tabby [cat]

'tigre f tiger

'tilde m/f tilde

tim'ballo m (Culin) pie

tim'brare vt stamp; ~ il cartellino clock in/out

'timbro m stamp; (di voce) tone

timida'mente adv timidly, shyly. **timi'dezza** f timidity, shyness. **'timido** adj timid, shy

'timo m thyme

ti'mon|e m rudder. **~i'ere** m helmsman

ti'more m fear; (soggezione) awe

'timpano m eardrum; (Mus) kettledrum

ti'nello m dining-room

'tinger|e vt dye; (macchiare) stain. **~si** vi (viso, cielo:) be tinged (di with); **~si i capelli** have one's hair dyed; (da solo) dye one's hair

'tino m, **ti'nozza** f tub

'tint|a f dye; (colore) colour; in **~a unita** plain. **~a'rella** f suntan

tintin'nare vi tinkle

'tinto pp di tingere. **~'ria** f (negozio) cleaner's. **tin'tura** f dyeing; (colorante) dye.

'tipico adj typical

'tipo m type; (individuo) guy

tipogra'fia f printery; (arte) typography. **tipo'grafico** adj typographic[al]. **ti'pografo** m printer

tip tap m tap dancing

ti'raggio m draught

tiramisù m inv dessert made of coffee-soaked sponge, eggs, Marsala, cream and cocoa powder

tiran'nia f tyranny. **ti'ranno, -a** adj tyrannical ● mf tyrant

ti'rar|e vt pull; (gettare) throw; kick (palla); (sparare) fire; (tracciare) draw; (stampare) print ● vi pull; (vento:) blow; (abito:) be tight; (sparare) fire; **~e avanti** get by; **~e su** (crescere) bring up; (da terra) pick up. **~si** vr **~si indietro** fig back out

tiras'segno m target shooting; (alla fiera) rifle range

ti'rata f tug; in una **~** in one go

tira'tore m shot. **~ scelto** marksman

tira'tura f printing; (di giornali) circulation; (di libri) [print] run

'tirchio adj mean

tiri'tera f spiel

'tiro m (traino) draught; (lancio) throw; (sparo) shot; (scherzo) trick. **~ con l'arco** archery. **~ alla fune** tug-of-war. **~ a segno** rifle-range

tiro'cinio m apprenticeship

ti'roide f thyroid

Tir'reno m il [mar] **~** the Tyrrhenian Sea

ti'sana f herb[al] tea

tito'lare adj regular ● mf principal; (proprietario) owner; (calcio) regular player

'titolo m title; (accademico) qualification; (Comm) security; a **~** di as; a **~** di favore as a favour. **titoli** pl di studio qualifications

titu'ba|nte adj hesitant. **~nza** f hesitation. **~re** vi hesitate

tivù f inv ⊤ TV, telly

'tizio m fellow

tiz'zone m brand

toc'cante adj touching

toc'ca|re vt touch; touch on (argomento); (tastare) feel; (riguardare) concern ● vi **~re a** (capitare) happen to; mi tocca aspettare I'll have to wait; tocca a te it's your turn; (pagare da bere) it's your round

tocca'sana m inv cure-all

'tocco m touch; (di pennello, orologio) stroke; (di pane ecc) chunk ● adj ⊤ crazy, touched

'toga f toga; (accademica, di magistrato) gown

'toglier|e vt take off (coperta); take away (bambino da scuola, sете); (Math); take out, remove (dente); **~e qcsa di dosso a qcno** take sth away from sb; **~e qcno dei guai** get sb out of trouble; ciò non toglie

t

che... nevertheless... **~si** *vr* take off (abito); **~si la vita** take one's [own] life

toilette *f inv*, **to'letta** *f* toilet; (*mobile*) dressing table

tolle'ra|nte *adj* tolerant. **~nza** *f* tolerance. **~re** *vt* tolerate

'**tolto** *pp di* togliere

to'**maia** *f* upper

'**tomba** *f* grave, tomb

tom'**bino** *m* manhole cover

'**tombola** *f* bingo; (*caduta*) tumble

'**tomo** *m* tome

'**tonaca** *f* habit

tonalità *f inv* (*Mus*) tonality

'**tondo** *adj* round ● *m* circle

'**tonico** *adj & m* tonic

tonifi'**care** *vt* brace

tonnel'la|ggio *m* tonnage. **~ta** *f* ton

'**tonno** *m* tuna [fish]

'**tono** *m* tone

ton'sil|la *f* tonsil. **~'lite** *f* tonsillitis

'**tonto** *adj* 🆃 thick

top *m inv* (*indumento*) sun-top

to'**pazio** *m* topaz

'**topless** *m inv* in **~ topless**

'**topo** *m* mouse. **~ di biblioteca** *fig* bookworm

to'**ponimo** *m* place name

'**toppa** *f* patch; (*serratura*) keyhole

to'**race** *m* chest

'**torba** *f* peat

'**torbido** *adj* cloudy; *fig* troubled

'**torcer|e** *vt* twist; wring [out] (*biancheria*). **~si** *vr* twist

'**torchio** *m* press

'**torcia** *f* torch

torci'**collo** *m* stiff neck

'**tordo** *m* thrush

to'**rero** *m* bullfighter

To'**rino** *m* Turin

tor'**menta** *f* snowstorm

tormen'**tare** *vt* torment.

tor'**mento** *m* torment

torna'**conto** *m* benefit

tor'**nado** *m* tornado

tor'**nante** *m* hairpin bend

tor'**nare** *vi* return, go/come back; (*ridiventare*) become again; (*conto:*) add up; **~ a sorridere** become happy again

tor'**neo** *m* tournament

'**tornio** *m* lathe

'**torno** **togliersi di ~** get out of the way

'**toro** *m* bull; (*Astr*) **T~** Taurus

tor'**pedine** *f* torpedo

tor'**pore** *m* torpor

'**torre** *f* tower; (*scacchi*) castle. **~ di controllo** control tower

torrefazi'**one** *f* roasting

tor'**ren|te** *m* torrent, mountain stream; (*fig: di lacrime*) flood. **~zi'ale** *adj* torrential

tor'**retta** *f* turret

'**torrido** *adj* torrid

torri'**one** *m* keep

tor'**rone** *m* nougat

'**torso** *m* torso; (*di mela, pera*) core; **a ~ nudo** bare-chested

'**torsolo** *m* core

'**torta** *f* cake; (*crostata*) tart

tortel'**lini** *mpl* tortellini, *small packets of pasta stuffed with pork, ham, Parmesan and nutmeg*

torti'**era** *f* baking tin

tor'**tino** *m* pie

'**torto** *pp di* torcere ● *adj* twisted ● *m* wrong; (*colpa*) fault; **aver ~** be wrong; **a ~** wrongly

tor'**tora** *f* turtle-dove

tortu'**oso** *adj* winding; (*ambiguo*) tortuous

tor'**tu|ra** *f* torture. **~'rare** *vt* torture

'**torvo** *adj* grim

to'**sare** *vt* shear

tosa'**tura** *f* shearing

To'**scana** *f* Tuscany

'tosse f cough

'tossico adj toxic ●m poison. **tossi-'comane** mf drug addict

tos'sire vi cough

tosta'pane m inv toaster

to'stare vt toast (pane); roast (caffè)

'tosto adv (subito) soon ●adj 🇬🇧 cool

tot adj inv una cifra ~ such and such a figure ●m un ~ so much

to'tale adj & m total. **~ità** f entirety; la **~ità dei presenti** all those present

totali'tario adj totalitarian

totaliz'zare vt total; score (punti)

total'mente adv totally

'totano m squid

toto'calcio m ≈ [football] pools pl

tournée f inv tour

to'vagli|a f tablecloth. **~etta** f **~etta [all'americana]** place mat. **~olo** m napkin

'tozzo adj squat

tra = FRA

trabal'la|nte adj staggering; (sedia) rickety. **~re** vi stagger; (veicolo:) jolt

tra'biccolo m 🇬🇧 contraption; (auto) jalopy

traboc'care vi overflow

traboc'chetto m trap

tracan'nare vt gulp down

'traccia f track; (orma) footstep; (striscia) trail; (residuo) trace; fig sign. **~'are** vt trace; sketch out (schema); draw (linea). **~'ato** m (schema) layout

tra'chea f windpipe

tra'colla f shoulder-strap; borsa a ~ shoulder-bag

tra'collo m collapse

tradi'mento m betrayal

tra'di|re vt betray; be unfaithful to (moglie, marito). **~tore**, **~trice** mf traitor

tradizio'na|le adj traditional.

~'lista mf traditionalist. **~l'mente** adv traditionally. **tradizi'one** f tradition

tra'dotto pp di tradurre

tra'du|rre vt translate. **~t'tore**, **~t'trice** mf translator. **~ttore elet-tronico** electronic phrasebook. **~zi'one** f translation

tra'ente mf (Comm) drawer

trafe'lato adj breathless

traffi'ca|nte mf dealer. **~nte di droga** [drug] pusher. **~re** vi (affaccendarsi) busy oneself; **~re in** pej traffic in. **'traffico** m traffic; (Comm) trade

tra'figgere vt stab; (straziare) pierce

tra'fila f fig rigmarole

trafo'rare vt bore, drill. **tra'foro** m boring; (galleria) tunnel

trafu'gare vt steal

tra'gedia f tragedy

traghet'tare vt ferry. **tra'ghetto** m ferrying; (nave) ferry

tragica'mente adv tragically. **'tra-gico** adj tragic

tra'gitto m journey; (per mare) crossing

tragu'ardo m finishing post; (meta) goal

traiet'toria f trajectory

trai'nare vt drag; (rimorchiare) tow

tralasci'are vt interrupt; (omettere) leave out

'tralcio m (Bot) shoot

tra'liccio m trellis

tram m inv tram, streetcar Am

'trama f weft; (di film ecc) plot

traman'dare vt hand down

tra'mare vt weave; (macchinare) plot

tram'busto m turmoil

trame'stio m bustle

tramez'zino m sandwich

tra'mezzo m partition

'tramite prep through ●m link; fare da ~ act as go-between

tramon'tana f north wind

tramon'tare vi set; (declinare) decline. **tra'monto** m sunset; (declino) decline

tramor'tire vt stun ● vi faint

trampo'lino m springboard; (per lo sci) ski-jump

'trampolo m stilt

tramu'tare vt transform

'trancia f shears pl; (fetta) slice

tra'nello m trap

trangugi'are vt gulp down

'tranne prep except

tranquilla'mente adv peacefully

tranquil'lante m tranquillizer

tranquilli'tà f calm; (di spirito) tranquillity. ~z'zare vt reassure. tran'quillo adj quiet; (pacifico) peaceful; (coscienza) easy

transat'lantico adj transatlantic ● m ocean liner

tran'satto pp di transigere. ~zi'one f (Comm) transaction

tran'senna f (barriera) barrier

trans'genico adj genetically modified, transgenic

tran'sigere vi reach an agreement; (cedere) yield

transi'tabile adj passable. ~re vi pass

transi'tivo adj transitive

'transito m transit; diritto di ~to right of way; "divieto di ~to" "no thoroughfare". ~'torio adj transitory. ~zi'one f transition

tranvi'ere m tram driver

'trapano m drill

trapas'sare vt go [right] through ● vi (morire) pass away

tra'passo m passage

tra'pezio m trapeze; (Math) trapezium

trapi an'tare vt transplant. ~'anto m transplant

'trappola f trap

tra'punta f quilt

'trarre vt draw; (ricavare) obtain; ~ in inganno deceive

trasa'lire vi start

trasan'dato adj shabby

trasbor'dare vt transfer; (Naut) tran[s]ship ● vi change. tra'sbordo m trans[s]hipment

tra'scendere vt transcend ● vi (eccedere) go too far

trasci'nar|e vt drag; (entusiasmo:) carry away. ~si vr drag oneself

tra'scorrere vt spend ● vi pass

tra'scri|tto pp di trascrivere. ~vere vt transcribe. ~zi'one f transcription

trascu'ra|bile adj negligible. ~re vt neglect; (non tenere conto di) disregard. ~'tezza f negligence. ~to adj negligent; (curato male) neglected; (nel vestire) slovenly

traseco'lato adj amazed

trasferi'mento m transfer; (trasloco) move

trasfe'ri|re vt transfer. ~rsi vr move

tra'sferta f transfer; (indennità) subsistence allowance; Sport away match; giocare in ~ play away

trasfigu'rare vt transfigure

trasfor'ma|re vt transform; (in rugby) convert. ~'tore m transformer. ~zi'one f transformation; (in rugby) conversion

trasfor'mista mf quick-change artist

trasfusi'one f transfusion

trasgre'dire vt disobey; (Jur) infringe

trasgredi'trice f transgressor

trasgres|si'one f infringement. ~'sore m transgressor

tra'slato adj metaphorical

traslo'car|e vi, ~si vr move; move house. tra'sloco m removal

tra'smesso pp di trasmettere

tra'smett|ere *vt* pass on; (*Radio, TV*) broadcast; (*Med, Techn*) transmit. ~l'tore *m* transmitter

trasmis'si|bile *adj* transmissible. ~'one *f* transmission; (*Radio, TV*) programme

trasmit'tente *m* transmitter •*f* broadcasting station

traso'gna|re *vi* day-dream

traspa'ren|te *adj* transparent. ~za *f* transparency; in ~za against the light. traspa'rire *vi* show [through]

traspi'ra|re *vi* perspire; *fig* transpire. ~zi'one *f* perspiration

tra'sporre *vt* transpose

traspor'tare *vt* transport; lasciarsi ~ da get carried away by. tra'sporto *m* transport; (*passione*) passion

trastul'la|re *vt* amuse. ~si *vr* amuse oneself

trasu'dare *vt* ooze with •*vi* sweat

trasver'sale *adj* transverse

trasvo'la|re *vt* fly over •*vi* ~re su *fig* skim over. ~ta *f* crossing [by air]

'tratta *f* illegal trade; (*Comm*) draft

tratta'mento *m* treatment. ~ di riguardo special treatment

trat'ta|re *vt* treat; (*commerciare in*) deal in; (*negoziare*) negotiate •*vi* ~re di deal with. ~rsi *vr* di che si tratta? what is it about? si tratta di... it's about.... ~'tive *fpl* negotiations. ~to *m* treaty; (*opera scritta*) treatise

tratteggi'are *vt* outline; (*descrivere*) sketch

tratte'ner|e *vt* (*far restare*) keep; hold (*respiro, in questura*); hold back (*lacrime, riso*); (*frenare*) restrain; (*da paga*) withhold; sono stato trattenuto (*ritardato*) I got held up. ~si *vr* restrain oneself; (*fermarsi*) stay; ~si su (*indugiare*) dwell on. tratteni'mento *m* entertainment; (*ricevimento*) party

tratte'nuta *f* deduction

trat'tino *m* dash; (*in parole composte*) hyphen

'tratto *pp di* trarre •*m* (*di spazio, tempo*) stretch; (*di penna*) stroke; (*linea*) line; (*brano*) passage; tratti *pl* features; a tratti at intervals; ad un ~ suddenly

trat'tore *m* tractor

tratto'ria *f* restaurant

'trauma *m* trauma. trau'matico *adj* traumatic

tra'vaglio *m* labour; (*angoscia*) anguish

trava'sare *vt* decant

'trave *f* beam

tra'versa *f* crossbar; è una ~ di Via Roma it's off Via Roma

traver'sa|re *vt* cross. ~ta *f* crossing

traver'sie *fpl* misfortunes

traver'sina *f* (*Rail*) sleeper

tra'vers|o *adj* crosswise •*adv* di ~o crossways; andare di ~o (*cibo:*) go down the wrong way; camminare di ~o not walk in a straight line. ~one *m* (*in calcio*) cross

travesti'mento *m* disguise

trave'sti|re *vt* disguise. ~rsi *vr* disguise oneself. ~to *adj* disguised •*m* transvestite

travi'are *vt* lead astray

travi'sare *vt* distort

tra'vol|gere *vt* sweep away; (*sopraffare*) overwhelm. ~to *pp di* travolgere

trazi'one *f* traction. ~ anteriore/posteriore front-/rear-wheel drive

tre *adj* & *m* three

trebbi'a|re *vt* thresh

'treccia *f* plait, braid

tre'cento *adj* & *m* three hundred; il T~ the fourteenth century

tredi'cesima *f* Christmas bonus of one month's pay

'tredici adj & m thirteen

'tregua f truce; fig respite

tre'mare vi tremble; (di freddo) shiver

tremenda'mente adv terribly. tre'mendo adj terrible; ho una fame tremenda I'm very hungry

tremen'tina f turpentine

tre'mila adj & m three thousand

'tremito m tremble

tremo'lare vi shake; (luce:) flicker. tre'more m trembling

tre'nino m miniature railway

'treno m train

'tren|ta adj & m thirty; ~ta e lode top marks. ~tatré giri m inv LP. ~'tenne adj & mf thirty-year-old. ~'tesimo adj & m thirtieth. ~'tina f una ~tina di about thirty

trepi'dare vi be anxious. 'trepido adj anxious

treppi'ede m tripod

'tresca f intrigue; (amorosa) affair

tri'angolo m triangle

tri'bale adj tribal

tribo'la|re vi suffer; (fare fatica) go through trials and tribulations. ~zi'one f tribulation

tribù f inv tribe

tri'buna f tribune; (per uditori) gallery; Sport stand. ~ coperta stand

tribu'nale m court

tribu'tare vt bestow

tribu'tario adj tax attrib. tri'buto m tribute; (tassa) tax

tri'checo m walrus

tri'ciclo m tricycle

trico'lore adj three-coloured ● m (bandiera) tricolour

tri'dente m trident

trien'nale adj (ogni tre anni) three-yearly; (lungo tre anni) three-year. tri'ennio m three-year period

tri'foglio m clover

trifo'lato adj sliced and cooked with olive oil, parsley and garlic

'triglia f mullet

trigonome'tria f trigonometry

tri'mestre m quarter; (Sch) term

'trina f lace

trin'cea f trench

trincia'pollo m inv poultry shears pl

trinci'are vt cut up

Trinità f Trinity

'trio m trio

trion'fa|le adj triumphal. ~nte adj triumphant. ~re vi triumph; ~re su triumph over. tri'onfo m triumph

tripli'care vt triple. 'triplice adj triple; in triplice [copia] in triplicate. 'triplo adj triple ● m il triplo (di) three times as much (as)

'trippa f tripe; ([✗]: pancia) belly

'trist|e adj sad; (luogo) gloomy. tri'stezza f sadness. ~o adj wicked; (meschino) miserable

trita'carne m inv mincer

tri'ta|re vt mince. 'trito adj trito e ritrito well-worn, trite

'trittico m triptych

tritu'rare vt chop finely

triumvi'rato m triumvirate

tri'vella f drill. trivel'lare vt drill

trivi'ale adj vulgar

tro'feo m trophy

'trogolo m (per maiali) trough

'troia f sow; ([✗] donna) whore

'tromba f trumpet; (Auto) horn; (delle scale) well. ~ d'aria whirlwind

trom'b|etta m toy trumpet. ~one m trombone

trom'bosi f thrombosis

tron'care vt sever; truncate (parola)

'tronco adj truncated; licenziare in ~ fire on the spot ● m trunk; (di strada) section. tron'cone m stump

troneggi'are vi ~ su tower over

'trono m throne

tropi'cale adj tropical. **'tropico** m tropic

'troppo adj too much; (con nomi plurali) too many ●pron too much; (plurale) too many; (troppo tempo) too long; **troppi** (troppa gente) too many people ●adv too; (con verbi) too much; ~ **stanco** too tired; **ho mangiato** ~ I ate too much; **hai fame? - non** ~ are you hungry? - not very

'trota f trout

trot'tare vi trot. **trotterel'lare** vi trot along; (bimbo:) toddle

'trotto m trot; andare al ~ trot

'trottola f [spinning] top; (movimento) spin

troupe f inv televisiva camera crew

tro'va|re vt find; (scoprire) find out; (incontrare) meet; (ritenere) think; andare a ~re go and see, meet oneself; (luogo:) be; (sentirsi) feel. ~**ta** f bright idea. ~**ta pubblicitaria** advertising gimmick

truc'ca|re vt make up; (falsificare) fix ⊠. ~**rsi** vr make up

'trucco m (cosmetico) make-up; (imbroglio) trick

'truce adj fierce; (delitto) appalling

truci'dare vt slay

'truciolo m shaving

tru'cu'lento adj truculent

'truffa f fraud. **truf'fare** vt swindle. ~**'tore**, ~**'trice** mf swindler

'truppa f troops pl; (gruppo) group

tu pers pron you; **sei tu?** is that you?; **l'hai fatto tu?** did you do it yourself?; **a tu per tu** in private; **darsi del tu** use the familiar tu

'tuba f tuba; (cappello) top hat

tuba'tura f piping

tubazi'oni fpl piping sg, pipes

tuberco'losi f tuberculosis

tu'betto m tube

tu'bino m (vestito) shift

'tubo m pipe; (Anat) canal; non ho

capito un ~ ⓘ I understood zilch. ~ **di scappamento** exhaust [pipe]

tuf'fa|re vt plunge. ~**rsi** vr dive. ~**'tore**, ~**'trice** mf diver

'tuffo m dive; (bagno) dip; **ho avuto un** ~ **al cuore** my heart missed a beat. ~ **di testa** dive

'tufo m tufa

tu'gurio m hovel

tuli'pano m tulip

'tulle m tulle

tume'fa|tto adj swollen. ~**zi'one** f swelling. **'tumido** adj swollen

tu'more m tumour

tumulazi'one f burial

tu'mult|o m turmoil; (sommossa) riot. ~**u'oso** adj uproarious

'tunica f tunic

Tuni'sia f Tunisia

'tunnel m inv tunnel

'tuo (il ~ m, la tua f, i ~i mpl, le tue fpl) poss adj your; **è tua questa macchina?** is this car yours?; **un** ~ **amico** a friend of yours; ~ **padre** your father ●poss pron yours; **i tuoi** your folks

tuo'nare vi thunder. **tu'ono** m thunder

tu'orlo m yolk

tu'racciolo m stopper; (di sughero) cork

tu'rar|e vt stop; cork (bottiglia). ~**si** vr become blocked; ~**si il naso** hold one's nose

'turba f crowd

turba'mento m disturbance; (sconvolgimento) upsetting. ~ **della quiete pubblica** breach of the peace

tur'bante m turban

tur'ba|re vt upset. ~**rsi** vr get upset. ~**to** adj upset

tur'bina f turbine

turbi'nare vi whirl. **'turbine** m whirl. **turbine di vento** whirlwind

turbo'lenza f turbulence

turboreat'tore m turbo-jet

t

tur'chese *adj & mf* turquoise

Tur'chia *f* Turkey

tur'chino *adj & m* deep blue

'turco, -a *adj* Turkish • *mf* Turk • *m* (*lingua*) Turkish; *fig* double Dutch; fumare come un ~ smoke like a chimney

tu'ris|mo *m* tourism. ~ culturale heritage tourism. ~ta *mf* tourist. ~tico *adj* tourist *attrib*

'turno *m* turn; a ~ in turn; di ~ on duty; fare a ~ take turns. ~ di notte night shift

'turpe *adj* base

'tuta *f* overalls *pl*; *Sport* tracksuit. ~ da lavoro overalls *pl*. ~ mimetica camouflage. ~ spaziale spacesuit. ~ subacquea wetsuit

tu'tela *f* (*Jur*) guardianship; (*protezione*) protection. tute'lare *vt* protect

tu'tina *f* sleepsuit; (*da danza*) leotard

tu'tore, -'trice *mf* guardian

'tutta *f* mettercela ~ per fare qcsa go flat out for sth

tutta'via *conj* nevertheless

'tutto *adj* whole; (*con nomi plurali*) all; (*ogni*) every; tutta la classe the whole class, all the class; tutti gli alunni all the pupils; a tutta velocità at full speed; ho aspettato ~ il giorno I waited all day [long]; in ~ il mondo all over the world; noi tutti all of us; era tutta contenta she was delighted; tutti e due both; tutti e tre all three • *pron* all; (*tutta la gente*) everybody; (*tutte le cose*) everything; (*qualunque cosa*) anything; l'ho mangiato ~ I ate it all; le ho lavate tutte I washed them all; raccontami ~ tell me everything; lo sanno tutti everybody knows; è capace di ~ he's capable of anything; ~ compreso all in; del ~ quite; in ~ altogether • *adv* completely; tutt'a un tratto all at once; tutt'altro not at all; tutt'altro che anything but • *m* whole. ~'fare *a inv & nmf* [impiegato] ~ general handyman; donna

~ general maid

tut'tora *adv* still

tutù *m inv* tutu, ballet dress

tv *f inv* TV

Uu

ubbidi'en|te *adj* obedient. ~za *f* obedience. ubbi'dire *vi* ~ (a) obey

ubi'ca|to *adj* located. ~zi'one *f* location

ubria'car|e *vt* get drunk. ~si *vr* get drunk; ~si di *fig* become intoxicated with

ubria'chezza *f* drunkenness; in stato di ~ inebriated

ubri'aco, -a *adj* drunk • *mf* drunk

ubria'cone *m* drunkard

uccel'lliera *f* aviary. uc'cello *m* bird; (➤: *pene*) cock

uc'cider|e *vt* kill. ~si *vr* kill oneself

ucci|si'one *f* killing. uc'ciso *pp di* uccidere. ~'sore *m* killer

u'dente *adj* i non udenti the hearing-impaired

u'dibile *adj* audible

udi'enza *f* audience; (*colloquio*) interview; (*Jur*) hearing

u'di|re *vt* hear. ~'tivo *adj* auditory. ~to *m* hearing. ~'tore, ~'trice *mf* listener; (*Sch*) unregistered student (*allowed to attend lectures*). ~'torio *m* audience

uffici'al|e *adj* official • *m* officer; (*funzionario*) official; pubblico ~ public official. ~iz'zare *vt* make official

uf'ficio *m* office; (*dovere*) duty. ~ di collocamento employment office. ~ informazioni information office. ~ del personale personnel department. ~sa'mente *adv* unofficially

uffici'oso adj unofficial

'**ufo**[1] m inv ufo

'**ufo**[2]: a ~ adv without paying

uggi'oso adj boring

uguagli'a|nza f equality. ~**re** vt make equal; (essere uguale) equal; (livellare) level. ~**rsi** vr ~**rsi** a compare oneself to

ugu'al|e adj equal; (lo stesso) the same; (simile) like. ~**mente** adv equally; (malgrado tutto) all the same

'**ulcera** f ulcer

ulteri'or|e adj further. ~'**mente** adv further

uli'veto m olive grove

ultima'mente adv lately

ulti'ma|re vt complete. ~**tum** m inv ultimatum

ulti'missime fpl stop press sg

'**ultimo** adj last; (notizie ecc) latest; (più lontano) farthest; fig ultimate ● m last; fino all'~ to the last; per ~ at the end; l'~ **piano** the top floor

ultrà mf inv Sport fanatical supporter

ultra'moderno adj ultramodern

ultra'rapido adj extra-fast

ultrasen'sibile adj ultrasensitive

ultra's|onico adj ultrasonic. ~**u'ono** m ultrasound

ultravio'letto adj ultraviolet

ulu'la|re vi howl. ~**to** m howling

umana'mente adv (trattare) humanely; ~ **impossibile** not humanly possible

uma'nesimo m humanism

umanità f humanity. **umani'tario** adj humanitarian. u'**mano** adj human; (benevolo) humane

umidifica'tore m humidifier

umidità f dampness; (di clima) humidity. '**umido** adj damp; (clima) humid; (mani, occhi) moist ● m dampness; **in umido** (Culin) stewed

'**umile** adj humble

umili'a|nte adj humiliating. ~**re** vt humiliate. ~**rsi** vr humble oneself.

~**zi'one** f humiliation. **umil'mente** adv humbly. **umiltà** f humility

u'**more** m humour; (stato d'animo) mood; **di cattivo/buon** ~ **in** a bad/good mood

umo'ri|smo m humour. ~**ta** mf humorist. ~**tico** adj humorous

> **un** in def art
>
> Un/una si traduce con one
> quando si tratta di un numero
>
> a;
>
> ····➤ (davanti a vocale o h muta)
> an; ▷**UN**

'**una** indef art f a; ▷**UN**

u'**nanim|e** adj unanimous. ~**e'mente** adv unanimously. ~**ità** f unanimity; **all'~ità** unanimously

unci'nato adj hooked; (parentesi) angle

un'**cino** m hook

'**undici** adj & m eleven

'**unger|e** vt grease; (sporcare) get greasy; (Relig) anoint; (blandire) flatter. ~**si** vr (con olio solare) oil oneself; ~**si le mani** get one's hands greasy

un'**ghe|rese** adj & mf Hungarian. **Unghe'ria** f Hungary

'**unghi|a** f nail; (di animale) claw. ~**'ata** f (graffio) scratch

ungu'ento m ointment

unica'mente adv only. '**unico** adj only; (singolo) single; (incomparabile) unique

unifi'ca|re vt unify. ~**zi'one** f unification

unifor'mar|e vt level. ~**si** vr conform (a to)

uni'form|e adj & f uniform. ~**ità** f uniformity

unilate'rale adj unilateral

uni'one f union; (armonia) unity. U~ **Europea** European Union. U~ **Mo-**

netaria Europea European Monetary Union. ~ sindacale trade union

u'ni|re vt unite; (collegare) join; blend (colori ecc.). ~**rsi** vr unite; (collegarsi) join

'**unisex** adj inv unisex

unità f inv unity; (Math, Mil) unit; (Comput) drive. ~**rio** adj unitary

u'nito adj united; (tinta) plain

univer'sal|e adj universal. ~'**mente** adv universally

univer'sità f inv university. ~**rio, -a** adj university attrib ● mf (insegnante) university lecturer; (studente) undergraduate

> **Università** Italy's first university was founded in Bologna in 1088, and they are still run on traditional lines. Oral exams are the norm. Students study for a number of exams, which can be taken in a flexible order. For this reason Italian students often combine study with a job. The drop-out rate is high. *i*

uni'verso m universe

> **uno, -a** indef art (before s + consonant, gn, ps, z) a
>
> ● pron one; a ~ a ~ one by one; l'~ e l'altro both [of them]; né l'~ né l'altro neither [of them]; ~ di noi one of us; ~ fa quello che può you do what you can
>
> ● adj a, one
>
> ● m (numerale) one; (un tale) some man;
>
> ● f some woman

'**unt|o** pp di ungere ● adj greasy ● m grease. ~'**uoso** adj greasy. unzi'one f l'Estrema Unzione Extreme Unction

u'omo m (pl uomini) man. ~ d'affari business man. ~ di fiducia right-hand man. ~ di Stato statesman

u'ovo m (pl f uova) egg. ~ in camicia poached egg. ~ alla coque boiled egg. ~ di Pasqua Easter egg. ~ sodo hard-boiled egg. ~ strapazzato scrambled egg

ura'gano m hurricane

u'ranio m uranium

urba'n|esimo m urbanization. ~**ista** mf town planner. ~**istica** f town planning. ~**istico** adj urban. urbanizzazi'one f urbanization. ur'bano adj urban; (cortese) urbane

ur'gen|te adj urgent. ~**te'mente** adv urgently. ~**za** f urgency; in caso d'~**za** in an emergency; d'~**za** (misura, chiamata) emergency

'**urgere** vi be urgent

u'rina f urine. **u'ri'nare** vi urinate

ur'lare vi yell; (cane, vento:) howl. '**urlo** m (pl m urli, f urla) shout; (di cane, vento) howling

'**urna** f urn; (elettorale) ballot box; andare alle urne go to the polls

urrà int hurrah!

ur'tar|e vt knock against; (scontrarsi) bump into; fig irritate. ~**si** vr collide; fig clash

'**urto** m knock; (scontro) crash; (contrasto) conflict; fig clash; d'~ (misure, terapia) shock

usa e getta adj inv (rasoio, siringa) disposable

u'sanza f custom; (moda) fashion

u'sa|re vt use; (impiegare) employ; (esercitare) exercise; ~**re** fare qcsa be in the habit of doing sth ● vi (essere di moda) be fashionable; non si usa più it is out of fashion; it's not used any more. ~**to** adj used; (non nuovo) second-hand

u'scente adj (presidente) outgoing

usci'ere m usher. '**uscio** m door

u'sci|re vi come out; (andare fuori) go out; (sfuggire) get out; (essere sorteggiato) come up; (giornale:) come out; ~**re da** (Comput) exit from, quit; ~**re di strada** leave the road. ~**ta** f exit, way out; (spesa) outlay; (di autostrada) junction; (*battuta*) witty remark; essere in libera ~ta be in free fall. ~ta di servizio back door. ~ta di sicurezza emergency exit

usi'gnolo *m* nightingale

'uso *m* use; (*abitudine*) custom; (*usanza*) usage; fuori ~ out of use; per ~ esterno for external use only

U.S.S.L. *f abbr* (Unità Socio-Sanitaria Locale) local health centre

ustio'nar|si *vr* burn oneself ●*adj* burnt. usti'one *f* burn

usu'ale *adj* usual

usufru'ire *vi* ~ di take advantage of

u'sura *f* usury

usur'pare *vt* usurp

u'tensile *m* tool; (*Culin*) utensil; cassetta degli utensili tool box

u'tente *mf* user. ~ finale end user

u'tenza *f* use; (*utenti*) users *pl.* ~ finale end users

ute'rino *adj* uterine. 'utero *m* womb

'util|e *adj* useful ●*m* (*Comm*) profit. ~ità *f* usefulness; (*Comput*) utility. ~i'taria *f* (*Auto*) small car. ~i'tario *adj* utilitarian

utiliz'za|re *vt* utilize. ~zi'one *f* utilization. uti'lizzo *m* use

uto'pistico *adj* Utopian

'uva *f* grapes *pl*; chicco d'~ grape. ~ passa raisins *pl.* ~ sultanina currants *pl*

. . . .

Vv

va'cante *adj* vacant

va'canza *f* holiday; (*posto vacante*) vacancy. essere in ~ be on holiday

'vacca *f* cow. ~ da latte dairy cow

vacci'nare *vt* vaccinate. ~ina-zi'one *f* vaccination. vac'cino *m*

vaccine

vacil'la|nte *adj* tottering; (*oggetto*) wobbly; (*luce*) flickering; *fig* wavering. ~re *vi* totter; (*oggetto*) wobble; (*luce*) flicker; *fig* waver

'vacuo *adj* (*vano*) vain; *fig* empty ●*m* vacuum

vagabon'dare *vi* wander. vaga-'bondo, -a *adj* (*cane*) stray; gente vagabonda tramps *pl* ●*mf* tramp

va'gare *vi* wander

vagheggi'are *vt* long for

va'gi|na *f* vagina. ~'nale *adj* vaginal

va'gire *vi* whimper

'vaglia *m inv* money order. ~ ban-cario bank draft. ~ postale postal order

vagli'are *vt* sift; *fig* weigh

'vago *adj* vague

vagon'cino *m* (*di funivia*) car

va'gone *m* (*per passeggeri*) carriage; (*per merci*) wagon. ~ letto sleeper. ~ ristorante restaurant car

vai'olo *m* smallpox

va'langa *f* avalanche

va'lente *adj* skilful

va'ler|e *vi* be worth; (*contare*) count; (*regola*) apply (per to); (*essere valido*) be valid; far ~ i propri diritti assert one's rights; farsi ~ assert oneself; non vale! that's not fair! ●*vt* ~re qcsa a qcno (*procurare*) earn sb sth; ~ne la pena be worth it; vale la pena di vederlo it's worth seeing; ~si di avail oneself of

valeri'ana *f* valerian

va'levole *adj* valid

vali'care *vt* cross. 'valico *m* pass

validità *f* validity; con ~ illimitata valid indefinitely

'valido *adj* valid; (*efficace*) efficient; (*contributo*) valuable

valige'ria *f* (*fabbrica*) leather factory; (*negozio*) leather goods shop

va'ligia f suitcase; fare le valigie pack one's bags. ~ diplomatica diplomatic bag

val'lata f valley. 'valle f valley; a valle downstream

val'lett|a f (TV) assistant. ~o m valet; (TV) assistant

val'lone m (valle) deep valley

va'lor|e m value; (merito) merit; (coraggio) valour; ~i pl (Comm) securities; di ~e (oggetto) valuable; oggetti di ~e valuables; senza ~e worthless. ~iz'zare vt (mettere in valore) use to advantage; (aumentare di valore) increase the value of; (migliorare l'aspetto di) enhance

valo'roso adj courageous

'valso pp di valere

va'luta f currency. ~ estera foreign currency

valu'ta|re vt value; weigh up (situazione). ~rio adj (mercato, norme) currency. ~zi'one f valuation

'valva f valve. 'valvola f valve; (Electr) fuse

vam'pata f blaze; (di calore) blast; (al viso) flush

vam'piro m vampire

vana'mente adv in vain

van'dal|ico adj atto ~lico act of vandalism. ~'lismo m vandalism. 'vandalo m vandal

vaneggi'are vi rave

'vanga f spade. van'gare vt dig

van'gelo m Gospel; (🔲: verità) gospel [truth]

vanifi'care vt nullify

va'nigli|a f vanilla. ~'ato adj (zucchero) vanilla attrib

vanità f vanity. vani'toso adj vain

'vano adj vain ● m (stanza) room; (spazio vuoto) hollow

van'taggi|o m advantage; Sport lead; Tennis advantage; trarre ~o da qcsa derive benefit from sth. ~'oso adj advantageous

van'ta|re vt praise; (possedere) boast. ~arsi vr boast. ~e'ria f boasting. 'vanto m boast

'vanvera f a ~ at random; parlare a ~ talk nonsense

va'por|e m steam; (di benzina, cascata) vapour; a ~e steam attrib; al ~e (Culin) steamed. ~e acqueo steam, water vapour; battello a ~e steamboat. vapo'retto m ferry. ~i'era f steam engine

vaporiz'za|re vt vaporize. ~'tore m spray

vapo'roso adj (vestito) filmy; capelli vaporosi big hair sg

va'rare vt launch

var'care vt cross. 'varco m passage; aspettare al varco lie in wait

vari'abil|e adj variable. ● f variable. ~ità f variability

vari'a|nte f variant. ~re vt/i vary; ~re di umore change one's mood. ~zi'one f variation

va'rice f varicose vein

vari'cella f chickenpox

vari'coso adj varicose

varie'gato adj variegated

varietà f inv variety ● m inv variety show

'vario adj varied; (al pl, parecchi) various; vari pl (molti) several; varie ed eventuali any other business

vario'pinto adj multicoloured

'varo m launch

va'saio m potter

'vasca f (per piscina) pool; (lunghezza) length. ~ da bagno bath

va'scello m vessel

va'schetta f tub

vase'lina f Vaseline®

vasel'lame m china. ~ d'oro/d'argento gold/silver plate

'vaso m pot; (da fiori) vase; (Anat) vessel; (per cibi) jar. ~ da notte chamber pot

vas'soio m tray

vastità f vastness. **'vasto** adj vast; di vaste vedute broad-minded

Vati'cano m Vatican

ve pers pron you; ve l'ho dato I gave it to you

vecchia f old woman. vecchi'aia f old age. **'vecchio** adj old ●mf old man; i vecchi old people

'vece f in ~ di in place of; fare le veci di qcno take sb's place

ve'dente adj i non vedenti the visually handicapped

ve'der|e vt/i see; far ~e show; farsi ~e show one's face; non vedo l'ora di... I can't wait to.... ~**si** vr see oneself; (reciproco) see each other

ve'detta f lookout; (Naut) patrol vessel

vedovo, -a m widower ●f widow

ve'duta f view

vee'mente adj vehement

vege'ta|le adj & m vegetable. ~**li'ano** adj & mf vegan. ~**re** vi vegetate. ~**ri'ano, -a** adj & mf vegetarian. ~**zi'one** f vegetation

'vegeto adj ▶vivo

veg'gente mf clairvoyant

'veglia f watch; fare la ~ keep watch. ~ funebre vigil

vegli|'are vi be awake; ~**are** su watch over. ~**ta'mente** una ~ di Capodanno New Year's Eve celebration

ve'icolo m vehicle

'vela f sail; (Sport) sailing; far ~ set sail

ve'la|re vt veil; (fig: nascondere) hide. ~**rsi** vr (vista:) mist over; (voce:) go husky. ~**ta'mente** adv indirectly. ~**to** adj veiled; (occhi) misty; (collant) sheer

'velcro® m velcro®

veleggi'are vi sail

ve'leno m poison. vele'noso adj poisonous

vell'ero m sailing ship

vel'lina f (carta) ~ tissue paper;

(copia) carbon copy

ve'lista m yachtsman ●f yachtswoman

ve'livolo m aircraft

velle'itario adj unrealistic

'vello m fleece

vellu'tato adj velvety. vel'luto m velvet. velluto a coste corduroy

'velo m veil; (di zucchero, cipria) dusting; (tessuto) voile

ve'loc|e adj fast. ~**emente** adv quickly. velo'cista mf (Sport) sprinter. ~**ità** f inv speed; (Auto: marcia) gear. ~**iz'zare** vt speed up

ve'lodromo m cycle track

'vena f vein; essere in ~ di be in the mood for

ve'nale adj venal; (persona) mercenary, venal

ve'nato adj grainy

vena'torio adj hunting attrib

ve'na|tura f (di legno) grain; (di foglia, marmo) vein

ven'demmi|a f grape harvest. ~**'are** vt harvest

'vender|e vt sell. ~**si** vr sell oneself; "vendesi" "for sale"

ven'detta f revenge

vendi'ca|re vt avenge. ~**rsi** vr get one's revenge. ~**tivo** adj vindictive

'vendi|ta f sale; in ~**ta** on sale. ~**ta all'asta** sale by auction. ~**ta al dettaglio** retailing. ~**ta all'ingrosso** wholesaling. ~**ta al minuto** retailing. ~**tore, ~trice** mf seller. ~**tore ambulante** hawker, pedlar

vene'ra|bile, ~ndo adj venerable

vene'ra|re vt revere

venerdì m inv Friday. V~ Santo Good Friday

'Venere f Venus. ve'nereo adj venereal

Ve'nezi|a f Venice. v~**'ano, -a** agg & mf Venetian ●f (persiana) Venetian blind; (Culin) sweet bun

veni'ale adj venial

ve'nire vi come; (riuscire) turn out; (costare) cost; (in passivi) be; ~ a sapere learn; ~ in mente occur; ~ meno (svenire) faint; ~ meno a un contratto go back on a contract; ~ via come away; (staccarsi) come off; vieni a prendermi come and pick me up

ven'taglio m fan

ven'tata f gust [of wind]; fig breath

ven'te|nne adj & mf twenty-year-old. ~simo adj & m twentieth. 'venti adj & m twenty

venti'la|re vt air. ~'tore m fan. ~zi'one f ventilation

ven'tina f una ~ (circa venti) about twenty

ventiquat'trore f inv (valigia) overnight case

'vento m wind; farsi ~ fan oneself

ven'tosa f sucker

ven'toso adj windy

'ventre m stomach. ven'triloquo m ventriloquist

ven'tura f fortune

ven'turo adj next

ve'nuta f coming

vera'mente adv really

ve'randa f veranda

ver'bal|e adj verbal ● m (di riunione) minutes pl. ~'mente adv verbally

'verbo m verb. ~ ausiliare auxiliary [verb]

'verde adj green ● m green; (vegetazione) greenery; (semaforo) green light. ~ oliva olive green. ~'rame m verdigris

ver'detto m verdict

ver'dura f vegetables pl; una ~ a vegetable

'verga f rod

vergi'n|ale adj virginal. 'vergine f virgin; (Astr) V~ Virgo ● adj virgin; (cassetta) blank. ~ità f virginity

ver'gogna f shame; (timidezza) shyness

vergo'gn|arsi vr feel ashamed; (essere timido) feel shy. ~oso adj ashamed; (timido) shy; (disonorevole) shameful

ve'rifica f check. verifi'cabile adj verifiable

verifi'car|e vt check. ~si vr come true

ve'rismo m realism

verit|à f truth. ~i'ero adj truthful

'verme m worm. ~ solitario tapeworm

ver'miglio adj & m vermilion

'vermut m inv vermouth

ver'nacolo m vernacular

ver'nic|e f paint; (trasparente) varnish; (pelle) patent leather; fig veneer; "vernice fresca" "wet paint". ~i'are vt paint; (con vernice trasparente) varnish. ~ia'tura f painting; (strato) paintwork; fig veneer

'vero adj true; (autentico) real; (perfetto) perfect; è ~? is that so?; sei stanca, ~? you're tired, aren't you ● m truth; (realtà) life

verosimigli'anza f probability. vero'simile adj probable

ver'ruca f wart; (sotto la pianta del piede) verruca

versa'mento m payment; (in banca) deposit

ver'sante m slope

ver'sa|re vt pour; (spargere) shed; (rovesciare) spill; pay (denaro). ~rsi vr spill; (sfociare) flow

ver'satil|e adj versatile. ~ità f versatility

ver'setto m verse

versi'one f version; (traduzione) translation; "~ integrale" "unabridged version"

'verso[1] m verse; (grido) cry; (gesto) gesture; (senso) direction; (modo) manner; non c'è ~ di there is no way of

'verso[2] prep towards; (nei pressi di)

round about; ~ dove? which way?

'vertebra f vertebra

'vertere vi ~ su focus on

verti'cal|e adj vertical; (in parole crociate) down ● m vertical ● f handstand. ~'mente adv vertically

'vertice m summit; (Math) vertex; conferenza al ~ summit conference

ver'tigine f dizziness; (Med) vertigo. vertigini f pl giddy spells

vertigi|nosa'mente adv dizzily. ~'noso adj dizzy; (velocità) breakneck; (prezzi) sky-high; (scollatura) plunging

ve'scica f bladder; (sulla pelle) blister

'vescovo m bishop

'vespa f wasp

vespasi'ano m urinal

'vespro m vespers pl

ves'sillo m standard

ve'staglia f dressing gown

'vest|e f dress; (rivestimento) covering; in ~e di in the capacity of. ~i'ario m clothing

ve'stibolo m hall

ve'stigio m (pl m vestigi, pl f vestigia) trace

ve'sti|re vt dress. ~rsi vr get dressed. ~ti pl clothes. ~to adj dressed ● m (da uomo) suit; (da donna) dress

vete'rano, -a adj & mf veteran

veteri'naria f veterinary science

veteri'nario adj veterinary ● m veterinary surgeon

'veto m inv veto

ve'tra|io m glazier. ~ta f big window; (in chiesa) stained-glass window; (porta) glass door. ~to adj glazed. vetre'ria f glass works

ve'tri|na f [shop-]window; (mobile) display cabinet. ~'nista mf window dresser

vetri'olo m vitriol

'vetro m glass; (di finestra, porta) pane. ~'resina f fibreglass

'vetta f peak

vet'tore m vector

vetto'vaglie fpl provisions

vet'tura f coach; (ferroviaria) carriage; (Auto) car. vettu'rino m coachman

vezzeggi'a|re vt fondle. ~'tivo m pet name. 'vezzo m habit; (attrattiva) charm; vezzi pl (moine) affectation sg. vez'zoso adj charming; pej affected

vi pers pron you; (riflessivo) yourselves; (reciproco) each other; (tra pl persone) one another; vi ho dato un libro I gave you a book; lavatevi le mani wash your hands; eccovi here you are! ● adv = ci

'via¹ f street, road; fig way; (Anat) tract; in ~ di in the course of; per ~ di on account of; ~ ~ che as; per ~ aerea by airmail

'via² adv away; (fuori) out; andar ~ go away; e così ~ and so on; e ~ dicendo and whatnot ● int ~! go away!; Sport go!; (andiamo) come on! ● m starting signal

viabilità f road conditions pl; (rete) road network; (norme) road and traffic laws pl

'via'card f inv motorway card

viaggi'a|re vi travel. ~'tore, ~'trice mf traveller

vi'aggio m journey; (breve) trip; buon ~! safe journey!, have a good trip!; fare un ~ go on a journey. ~ di nozze honeymoon

vi'ale m avenue; (privato) drive

vi'bra|nte adj vibrant. ~re vi vibrate; (fremere) quiver. ~zi'one f vibration

vi'cario m vicar

'vice mf deputy. ~diret'tore m assistant manager

vi'cenda f event; a ~ (fra due) each other; (a turno) in turn[s]

vice'versa adv vice versa

vici'na|nza f nearness; ~nze pl (paraggi) neighbourhood. ~to m

v

neighbourhood; (*vicini*) neighbours *pl*

vi'cino, -a *adj* near; (*accanto*) next ● *adv* near, close. ~ a *prep* near [to] ● *mf* neighbour. ~ di casa nextdoor neighbour

'**vicolo** *m* alley

'**video** *m* video. ~'camera *f* camcorder. ~cas'setta *f* video cassette

videoci'tofono *m* video entry phone

video'clip *m inv* video clip

videogi'oco *m* video game

videoregistra'tore *m* video-recorder

video'teca *f* video library

video'tel® *m* ≈ Videotex®

videote'lefono *m* videophone

videotermi'nale *m* visual display unit, VDU

vidi'mare *vt* authenticate

vie'tare *vt* forbid; sosta ~ta no parking; ~to fumare no smoking

vi'gente *adj* in force. 'vigere *vi* be in force

vigi'lante *adj* vigilant. ~nza *f* vigilance. ~re *vt* keep an eye on ● *vi* keep watch

'**vigile** *adj* watchful ● *m* ≈ [urbano] policeman. ~ del fuoco fireman

vi'gilia *f* eve

vigliacche'ria *f* cowardice. vigli'acco, -a *adj* cowardly ● *mf* coward

'**vigna** *f*, **vi'gneto** *m* vineyard

vi'gnetta *f* cartoon

vi'gore *m* vigour; entrare in ~ come into force. vigo'roso *adj* vigorous

'**vile** *adj* cowardly; (*abietto*) vile

'**villa** *f* villa

vil'laggio *m* village. ~ turistico holiday village

vil'lano *adj* rude ● *m* boor; (*contadino*) peasant

villeggi'ante *mf* holiday-maker. ~re *vi* spend one's holidays. ~'tura *f* holiday[s] [*pl*]

vil'letta *f* small detached house. ~ino *m* detached house

viltà *f* cowardice

'**vimine** *m* wicker

'**vincere** *vt* win; (*sconfiggere*) beat; (*superare*) overcome. ~ita *f* win; (*somma vinta*) winnings *pl*. ~i'tore, ~i'trice *mf* winner

vinco'lante *adj* binding. ~re *vt* bind; (*Comm*) tie up. 'vincolo *m* bond

vi'nicolo *adj* wine *attrib*

vinil'pelle® *f* Leatherette®

'**vino** *m* wine. ~ spumante sparkling wine. ~ da taglio blending wine. ~ da tavola table wine

'**vinto** *pp di* vincere

vi'ola *f* (*Bot*) violet; (*Mus*) viola. viola *adj & m inv* purple

vio'lare *vt* violate. ~zi'one *f* violation. ~zione di domicilio breaking and entering

violen'tare *vt* rape

vio'lento *adj* violent. ~za *f* violence. ~za carnale rape

vio'letta *f* violet

vio'letto *adj & m* (*colore*) violet

vio'linista *mf* violinist. vio'lino *m* violin. violon'cello *m* cello

vi'ottolo *m* path

'**vipera** *f* viper

vi'raggio *m* (*Phot*) toning; (*Aeron, Naut*) turn. ~re *vi* turn

vir'gola *f* comma. ~ette *fpl* inverted commas

vi'rile *adj* virile; (*da uomo*) manly. ~ità *f* virility; manliness

virtù *f inv* virtue; in ~ di (*legge*) under. virtu'ale *adj* virtual. virtu'oso *adj* virtuous ● *m* virtuoso

viru'lento *adj* virulent

'**virus** *m inv* virus

visa'gista *mf* beautician

visce'rale *adj* visceral; (*odio*) deep-seated; (*reazione*) gut

'**viscere** m internal organ ● fpl guts

'**vischi**|**o** m mistletoe. ~'**oso** adj viscous; (appiccicoso) sticky

vi'**scont**|**e** m viscount. ~'**essa** f viscountess

vi'**scoso** adj viscous

vi'**sibile** adj visible

visi'**bilio** m profusion; andare in ~ go into ecstasies

visibilità f visibility

visi'**era** f (di elmo) visor; (di berretto) peak

visio'**nare** vt examine; Cinema screen. **visi**'**one** f vision; **prima visione** Cinema first showing

'**visit**|**a** f visit; (breve) call; (Med) examination. ~**a di controllo** (Med) checkup. **visi**'**tare** vt visit; (brevemente) call on; (Med) examine; ~'**a**'**tore**, ~'**a**'**trice** mf visitor

vi'**sivo** adj visual

'**viso** m face

vi'**sone** m mink

'**vispo** adj lively

vis'**suto** pp di vivere ● adj experienced

'**vist**|**a** f sight; (veduta) view; a ~**a d'occhio** (crescere) visibly; (estendersi) as far as the eye can see; in ~**a di** in view of. ~**o** pp di vedere ● m visa. **vi**'**stoso** adj showy; (notevole) considerable

visu'**ale** adj visual. ~**izza**'**tore** m (Comput) display, VDU. ~**izzazi**'**one** f (Comput) display

'**vita** f life; (durata della vita) lifetime; (Anat) waist; a ~ for life; essere in ~ be alive

vi'**tale** adj vital. ~**ità** f vitality

vita'**lizio** adj life attrib ● m [life] annuity

vita'**min**|**a** f vitamin. ~**iz**'**zato** adj vitamin-enriched

'**vite** f (Mech) screw; (Bot) vine

vi'**tello** m calf; (Culin) veal; (pelle) calfskin

vi'**ticcio** m tendril

viticol'**t**|**ore** m wine grower. ~**ura** f wine growing

'**vitreo** adj vitreous; (sguardo) glassy

'**vittima** f victim

'**vitto** m food; (pasti) board. ~ **e alloggio** board and lodging

vit'**toria** f victory

vittori'**oso** adj victorious

vi'**uzza** f narrow lane

'**viva** int hurrah!; ~ **la Regina!** long live the Queen!

vi'**vac**|**e** adj vivacious; (mente) lively; (colore) bright. ~**ità** f vivacity; (di mente) liveliness; (di colore) brightness. ~**iz**'**zare** vt liven up

vi'**vaio** m nursery; (per pesci) pond; fig breeding ground

viva'**mente** adv (ringraziare) warmly

vi'**vanda** f food; (piatto) dish

vi'**vente** adj living ● mpl i **viventi** the living

'**vivere** vi live; ~ **di** live on ● vt (passare) go through ● m life

vi'**veri** mpl provisions

'**vivido** adj vivid

vivisezi'**one** f vivisection

'**vivo** adj alive; (vivente) living; (vivace) lively; (colore) bright; ~ **e vegeto** alive and kicking; farsi ~ keep in touch; (arrivare) turn up ● m dal ~ (trasmissione) live; (disegnare) from life; i vivi the living

vizi'**are** vt spoil (bambino ecc); (guastare) vitiate. ~'**ato** adj spoilt; (aria) stale. '**vizio** m vice; (cattiva abitudine) bad habit; (difetto) flaw. ~'**oso** adj dissolute; (difettoso) faulty; **circolo** ~**oso** vicious circle

vocabo'**lario** m dictionary; (lessico) vocabulary. **vo**'**cabolo** m word

vo'**cale** adj vocal ● f vowel. **vo**'**calico** adj (corde) vocal; (suono) vowel attrib

vocazi'one f vocation

'voce f voice; (*diceria*) rumour; (*di bilancio, dizionario*) entry

voci'are vi (*spettegolare*) gossip ● m buzz of conversation

vocife'rare vi shout

'vog|a f rowing; (*lena*) enthusiasm; (*moda*) vogue; essere in ~a be in fashion. vo'gare vi row. ~'tore m oarsman; (*attrezzo*) rowing machine

'vogli|a f desire; (*volontà*) will; (*della pelle*) birthmark; aver ~a di fare qcsa feel like doing sth

'voi pers pron you; siete ~? is that you?; l'avete fatto ~? did you do it yourself?. ~'altri pers pron you

vo'lano m shuttlecock; (*Mech*) flywheel

vo'lante adj flying; (*foglio*) loose ● m steering-wheel

volan'tino m leaflet

vo'la|re vi fly. ~ta f Sport final sprint; di ~ta in a rush

vo'latile adj (*liquido*) volatile ● m bird

volée f inv Tennis volley

vo'lente adj ~ o nolente whether you like it or not

volenti'eri adv willingly; ~! with pleasure!

vo'lere vt want; (*chiedere di*) ask for; (*aver bisogno di*) need; vuole che lo faccia io he wants me to do it; fai come vuoi do as you like; se tuo padre vuole, ti porto al cinema if your father agrees, I'll take you to the cinema; vorrei un caffè I'd like a coffee; la vuoi smettere? will you stop that!; senza ~ without meaning to; voler bene/male a qcb love/have something against sb; voler dire mean; ci vuole il latte we need milk; ci vuole tempo/pazienza it takes time/patience; volerne a have a grudge against; vuoi ... vuoi... either... or... ● m will; vo'leri pl wishes

vol'gar|e adj vulgar; (*popolare*) common. ~ità f inv vulgarity. ~iz'zare vt popularize. ~'mente adv (*grossolanamente*) vulgarly, coarsely; (*comunemente*) commonly

'volger|e vt/i turn. ~si vr turn [round]; ~si a (*dedicarsi*) take up

voli'era f aviary

voli'tivo adj strong-minded

'volo m flight; al ~ (fare qcsa) quickly; (prendere qcsa) in mid-air; alzarsi in ~ (uccello:) take off; in ~ airborne. ~ di linea scheduled flight. ~ nazionale domestic flight. ~ a vela gliding.

volontà f inv (*desiderio*) wish; a ~ (mangiare) as much as you like. volontaria'mente adv voluntarily. volon'tario adj voluntary ● m volunteer

volonte'roso adj willing

'volpe f fox

volt m inv volt

'volta f time; (*turno*) turn; (*curva*) bend; (*Archit*) vault; 4 volte 4 4 times 4; a volte sometimes; c'era una ~... once upon a time, there was...; una ~ once; due volte twice; tre/ quattro volte three/four times; una ~ per tutte once and for all; uno per ~ one at a time; uno alla ~ one at a time; alla ~ di in the direction of

volta'faccia m inv volte-face

vol'taggio m voltage

vol'ta|re vt/i turn; (*rigirare*) turn round; (*rivoltare*) turn over. ~rsi vr turn [round]

volta'stomaco m nausea

volteggi'are vi circle; (*ginnastica*) vault

'volto pp di volgere ● m face; mi ha mostrato il suo vero ~ he revealed his true colours

vo'lubile adj fickle

vo'lum|e m volume. ~i'noso adj voluminous

voluta'mente *adv* deliberately
voluttu|osità *f* voluptuousness.
~**'oso** *adj* voluptuous
vomi'tare *vt* vomit, be sick. '**vo-mito** *m* vomit
'vongola *f* clam
vo'race *adj* voracious
vo'ragine *f* abyss
'vortice *m* whirl; (*gorgo*) whirlpool;
(*di vento*) whirlwind
'vostro (il ~ *m*, la vostra *f*, i vostri
mpl, le vostre *fpl*) *poss adj* your; è vo-stra questa macchina? is this car
yours?; un ~ amico a friend of
yours; ~ padre your father ●*poss
pron* yours; i vostri your folks
vo'ta|nte *mf* voter. ~**re** *vi* vote.
~**zi'one** *f* voting; (*Sch*) marks *pl*.
'**voto** *m* vote; (*Sch*) mark; (*Relig*) vow
vs. *abbr* (*Comm*) (vostro) yours
vul'canico *adj* volcanic. **vul'cano** *m*
volcano
vulne'rabil|e *adj* vulnerable. ~**ità** *f*
vulnerability
vuo'tare *vt*, **vuo'tarsi** *vr* empty
vu'oto *adj* empty; (*non occupato*) va-cant; ~ di (*sprovvisto*) devoid of ●*m*
empty space; (*Phys*) vacuum; *fig* void;
assegno a ~ dud cheque; sotto ~
(*prodotto*) vacuum-packed; ~ a
perdere no deposit. ~ **d'aria** air
pocket

W *abbr* (viva) long live
'wafer *m inv* (*biscotto*) wafer
walkie-'talkie *m inv* walkie-talkie
watt *m inv* watt
WC *m* WC
'Web *m inv* Web

'webmaster *m* webmaster
'western *adj inv* cowboy *attrib* ●*m Ci-nema* western

X, x *adj* raggi *pl* X X-rays; il giorno
X D-day
xeno'fo'bia *f* xenophobia. **xe'no-fobo, -a** *adj* xenophobic ●*mf*
xenophobe
xi'lofono *m* xylophone

Yy

yacht *m inv* yacht
yen *m inv* Fin yen
'yoga *m* yoga; (*praticante*) yogi
'yogurt *m inv* yoghurt. ~**i'era** *f*
yoghurt-maker

Zz

zaba[gli]'one *m* zabaglione (*des-sert made from eggs, wine or marsala and
sugar*)
zaf'fata *f* whiff; (*di fumo*) cloud
zaffe'rano *m* saffron
zaf'firo *m* sapphire
'zaino *m* rucksack
'zampa *f* leg; a quattro zampe
(*animale*) four-legged; (*carponi*) on

v
w
x
y
z

all fours

zampil'la|nte *adj* spurting. ~re *vi* spurt. zam'pillo *m* spurt

zam'pogna *f* bagpipe

zam'pone *fpl* stuffed pig's trotter with lentils

'zanna *f* fang; (*di elefante*) tusk

zan'zar|a *f* mosquito. ~i'era *f* (*velo*) mosquito net; (*su finestra*) insect screen

'zappa *f* hoe. zap'pare *vt* hoe

'zattera *f* raft

zatte'roni *mpl* (*scarpe*) wedge shoes

za'vorra *f* ballast; *fig* dead wood

'zazzera *f* mop of hair

'zebra *f* zebra; zebre *pl* (*passaggio pedonale*) zebra crossing

'zecca¹ *f* mint; nuovo di ~ brand-new

'zecca² *f* (*parassita*) tick

zec'chino *m* sequin; oro ~ pure gold

ze'lante *adj* zealous. **'zelo** *m* zeal

'zenit *m* zenith

'zenzero *m* ginger

'zeppa *f* wedge

'zeppo *adj* packed full; pieno ~ di crammed up o packed with

zer'bino *m* doormat

'zero *m* zero, nought; (*in calcio*) nil; *Tennis* love; due a ~ (*in partite*) two nil

'zeta *f* zed, zee *Am*

'zia *f* aunt

zibel'lino *m* sable

'zigomo *m* cheek-bone

zig'zag *m inv* zigzag; andare a ~ zigzag

zim'bello *m* decoy; (*oggetto di scherno*) laughing-stock

'zinco *m* zinc

'zingaro, -a *mf* gypsy

'zio *m* uncle

zi'tel|la *f* spinster; *pej* old maid. ~'lona *f pej* old maid

zit'tire *vi* fall silent ● *vt* silence. **'zitto** *adj* silent; sta' zitto! keep quiet!

ziz'zania *f* (*discordia*) discord

'zoccolo *m* clog; (*di cavallo*) hoof; (*di terra*) clump; (*di parete*) skirting board, baseboard *Am*; (*di colonna*) base

zodia'cale *adj* of the zodiac. zo'diaco *m* zodiac

'zolfo *m* sulphur

'zolla *f* clod; (*di zucchero*) lump

zol'letta *f* sugar lump

'zombi *mf inv* fig zombie

'zona *f* zone; (*area*) area. ~ di depressione area of low pressure. ~ disco area for parking discs only. ~ pedonale pedestrian precinct. ~ verde green belt

'zonzo *adv* andare a ~ stroll about

'zoo *m inv* zoo

zoolo'gia *f* zoology. zoo'logico *adj* zoological. zo'ologo, -a *mf* zoologist

zoo sa'fari *m inv* safari park

zoppi'ca|nte *adj* limping; *fig* shaky. ~re *vi* limp; (*essere debole*) be shaky. **'zoppo, -a** *adj* lame ● *mf* cripple

zoti'cone *m* boor

'zucca *f* marrow; (🔲: *testa*) head; (🔲: *persona*) thickie

zucche'r|are *vt* sugar. ~i'era *f* sugar bowl. ~i'ficio *m* sugar refinery. zucche'rino *adj* sugary ● *m* sugar lump

'zucchero *m* sugar. ~ di canna cane sugar. ~ vanigliato vanilla sugar. ~ a velo icing sugar. zucche-'roso *adj* honeyed

zuc'chin|a *f*, ~o *m* courgette, zucchini *Am*

'zuffa *f* scuffle

zufo'lare *vt/i* whistle

zu'mare *vi* zoom

'zuppa *f* soup. ~ inglese trifle

zup'petta *f* fare ~ [con] dunk

zuppi'era *f* soup tureen

'zuppo *adj* soaked

Phrasefinder/Frasi utili

Key phrases Frasi chiave

yes, please	sì, grazie
no, thank you	no, grazie
sorry!	scusa
excuse me	mi scusi
you're welcome	prego
I'm sorry, I don't understand	scusi, non capisco

Meeting people Incontri

hello/goodbye	ciao/arrivederci
how do you do?	come sta?
how are you?	come stai?
nice to meet you	piacere

Asking questions	Fare domande
do you speak English/Italian?	parli inglese/italiano?
what's your name?	come ti chiami?
where are you from?	di dove sei?
where is...?	dov'è...?
can I have...?	posso avere...?
would you like...?	vuoi...?
do you mind if...?	le dispiace se...?

About you	Presentarsi
my name is...	mi chiamo...
I'm English/Italian/American	sono inglese/italiano/-a/ americano/-a
I don't speak Italian/English very well	non parlo molto bene l'italiano/ l'inglese
I'm here on holiday	sono qui in vacanza
I live near York/Pisa	abito vicino a York/Pisa

Emergencies	Emergenze
can you help me, please?	mi può aiutare, per favore?
I'm lost	mi sono perso/-a
I'm ill	sto male
call an ambulance	chiami un'ambulanza
watch out!	attenzione!

Reading signs	Segnali e cartelli
no entry	vietato l'ingresso
no smoking	vietato fumare
fire exit	uscita di sicurezza
for sale	in vendita/vendesi
push	spingere
pull	tirare
press	premere

Going Places/In viaggio

By rail and underground — In treno e sul metrò

where can I buy a ticket?	dove si fanno i biglietti?
what time is the next train to Milan/New York?	a che ora è il prossimo treno per Milano/New York?
do I have to change?	devo cambiare?
can I take my bike on the train?	posso portare la bicicletta sul treno?
which platform for the train to Bath/Florence?	da quale binario parte il treno per Bath/Firenze?
a single/return, (*Amer*) round trip to Baltimore/Turin, please	un biglietto di sola andata/di andata e ritorno per Baltimora/Torino, per favore
I'd like an all-day ticket	vorrei un biglietto giornaliero
I'd like to reserve a seat	vorrei prenotare un posto
is there a student/senior citizen discount?	c'è uno sconto per studenti/anziani?
is this the train for Rome/Manchester?	è questo il treno per Roma/Manchester?
what time does the train arrive in Naples/London?	a che ora arriva il treno a Napoli/Londra?
have I missed the train?	ho perso il treno?
which line do I need to take for the Colosseum/London Eye?	che linea si prende per il Colosseo/London Eye?

YOU WILL HEAR: SENTIRAI:

il treno è in arrivo sul binario 2	the train is arriving at platform 2
c'è un treno per Roma alle 10	there's a train to Rome at 10 o'clock
il treno è in ritardo/orario	the train is delayed/on time
la prossima fermata è ...	the next stop is...
il suo biglietto non è valido	your ticket isn't valid

MORE USEFUL WORDS: ALTRE PAROLE UTILI:

underground station, (*Amer*) subway station	stazione di metropolitana
timetable	orario
connection	coincidenza
express train	treno espresso
local train	treno locale
high-speed train	treno ad alta velocità

DID YOU KNOW...? LO SAPEVI...?

In an Italian train station, before you get on the train you must validate your ticket, i.e. have it stamped in the special yellow machine on the platform to make it valid for your journey. You risk a fine if you forget to do this.

Dall'aeroporto di Heathrow è possibile raggiungere il centro di Londra in meno di venti minuti grazie all'Heathrow Express.

At the airport   All'aeroporto

when's the next flight to Paris/ Rome?	quand'è il prossimo volo per Parigi/Roma?
what time do I have to check in?	a che ora si fa il check-in?
where do I check in?	dov'è il check-in?
I'd like to confirm my flight	vorrei confermare il mio volo
I'd like a window seat/an aisle seat	vorrei un posto accanto al finestrino/di corridoio
I want to change/cancel my reservation	vorrei cambiare/annullare la mia prenotazione
can I carry this in my hand luggage, (Amer) carry-on luggage?	posso portare questo nel bagaglio a mano?
my luggage hasn't arrived	il mio bagaglio non è arrivato

YOU WILL HEAR:	SENTIRAI:
il volo BA7057 è in ritardo/ cancellato	flight BA7057 is delayed/ cancelled
presentarsi all'uscita 29	please go to gate 29
la sua carta d'imbarco, per favore	your boarding card, please

MORE USEFUL WORDS:	ALTRE PAROLE UTILI:
arrivals	arrivi
departures	partenze
baggage claim	ritiro bagagli

Asking how to get there   Chiedere e dare indicazioni

how do I get to the airport?	come si arriva all'aeroporto?
how long will it take to get there?	quanto ci vuole per arrivarci?
how far is it from here?	quanto dista da qui?
which bus do I take for the cathedral?	quale autobus devo prendere per andare al duomo?
where does this bus go?	dove va questo autobus?
does this bus/train go to...?	questo autobus/treno va a...?
where should I get off?	può dirmi dove devo scendere?
how much is it to the town centre?	quant'è la tariffa per il centro?
what time is the last bus?	che ora è l'ultimo autobus?
where's the nearest underground station, (*Amer*) subway station?	dov'è la metropolitana più vicina?
is this the turning for...?	si svolta qui per...?
can you call me a taxi?	può chiamarmi un taxi, per favore?

YOU WILL HEAR: SENTIRAI:

prenda la prima a destra	take the first turning on the right
dopo il semaforo/la chiesa svolti a sinistra	turn left at the traffic lights/just past the church

---

Disabled travellers   Viaggiatori disabili

I'm disabled	sono disabile
is there wheelchair access?	c'è l'accesso per sedia a rotelle?
are guide dogs permitted?	sono ammessi i cani guida per non vedenti?

On the road | Sulla strada

where's the nearest petrol station, (Amer) gas station?	dov'è la stazione di servizio più vicina?
what's the best way to get there?	qual è la strada migliore per arrivarci?
I've got a puncture, (Amer) flat tire	ho bucato
I'd like to hire, (Amer) rent a bike/car	vorrei noleggiare una bicicletta/una macchina
where can I park around here?	c'è un parcheggio qui vicino?
there's been an accident	c'è stato un incidente
my car's broken down	ho la macchina in panne
the car won't start	la macchina non parte
where's the nearest garage?	dov'è l'officina più vicina?
pump number six, please	pompa numero sei, grazie
fill it up, please	il pieno, per favore
can I wash my car here?	c'è l'autolavaggio?
can I park here?	posso parcheggiare qui?
there's a problem with the brakes/lights	i freni/fari hanno qualcosa che non va
the clutch/gearstick isn't working	la frizione/leva del cambio non funziona
take the third exit off the roundabout, (Amer) traffic circle	alla rotatoria prenda la terza uscita
turn right at the next junction	al prossimo incrocio svolti a destra
slow down	rallenta
I can't drink – I'm driving	non posso bere, devo guidare
can I buy a road map here?	vendete cartine stradali?

YOU WILL HEAR: SENTIRAI:

favorisca la patente	can I see your driving licence?
deve compilare la denuncia di sinistro	you need to fill out an accident report
questa strada è a senso unico	this road is one-way
qui non si può parcheggiare	you can't park here

MORE USEFUL WORDS: ALTRE PAROLE UTILI:

diesel	gasolio
unleaded	senza piombo/verde
motorway, (*Amer*) expressway	autostrada
toll	pedaggio
satnav, (*Amer*) GPS	navigatore satellitare
speed camera	autovelox
roundabout	rotatoria
crossroads	crocevia
dual carriageway, (*Amer*) divided highway	strada a due carreggiate
exit	uscita
traffic lights	semaforo
driver	conducente

DID YOU KNOW...? LO SAPEVI...?

In Italy, all drivers are required to wear a reflective vest and to use a reflective triangle warning sign if they need to stop at the roadside.

Il pedaggio per circolare e sostare in auto nel centro di Londra, nei giorni lavorativi, si può pagare presso le stazioni di servizio o le edicole.

COMMON ITALIAN ROAD SIGNS

Alt polizia	Stop for police check
Consentito ai soli mezzi autorizzati	Authorized vehicles only
Passo carrabile	No blocking of passageway
Lavori in corso	Roadworks ahead
Zona pedonale	Pedestrian zone
Rallentare	Slow down
Zona rimozione	Tow-away zone
ZTL (Zona traffico limitato)	Traffic restricted area
Postazione fissa di misuratore della velocità	Speed cameras ahead
Passaggio a livello	Train crossing

SEGNALI STRADALI COMUNI NEI PAESI ANGLOFONI

Cattle	Animali domestici vaganti
Contraflow	Doppio senso di circolazione
Ford	Guado
Get in lane	Immettersi in corsia
Give way	Dare precedenza
Keep clear	Lasciare libero il passaggio
No overtaking, (*Amer*) Do not pass	Divieto di sorpasso
Pedestrians crossing	Attraversamento pedonale
Red route – no stopping	Divieto di sosta e fermata
Reduce speed now	Rallentare
Stop	Stop

Keeping in touch/Comunicazioni

On the phone   Al telefono

where can I buy a phone card?	dove si comprano le schede telefoniche?
may I use your phone?	posso usare il telefono?
do you have a mobile, (*Amer*) cell phone?	hai il cellulare?
what is your phone number?	qual è il tuo numero di telefono?
what is the area code for Venice/Sheffield?	qual è il prefisso di Venezia/Sheffield?
I want to make a phone call	vorrei fare una telefonata
I'd like to reverse the charges, (*Amer*) call collect	vorrei fare una telefonata a carico del destinatario
the line's engaged/busy	è occupato
there's no answer	non risponde nessuno
hello, this is Natalie	pronto, sono Natalie
is Riccardo there, please?	c'è Riccardo, per favore?
who's calling?	chi parla?
sorry, wrong number	ha sbagliato numero
just a moment, please	un attimo, prego
would you like to hold?	vuole attendere in linea?
it's a business/personal call	è una chiamata di lavoro/personale
I'll put you through to him/her	le passo la comunicazione
s/he cannot come to the phone at the moment	in questo momento non può venire al telefono
please tell him/her I called	gli/le dica che ho chiamato
I'd like to leave a message for him/her	vorrei lasciare un messaggio

I'll try again later	riproverò più tardi
please tell him/her that Maria called	gli/le dica ha chiamato Maria
can he/she ring me back?	mi può richiamare?
my home number is...	il mio numero è...
my business number is...	il mio numero al lavoro è...
my fax number is...	il mio numero di fax è...
we were cut off	è caduta la linea
I'll call you later	ti chiamo più tardi
I need to top up my phone	mi serve una ricarica per il cellulare
the battery's run out	ho la batteria scarica
I'm running low on credit	sto esaurendo il credito
send me a text	mandami un sms/messaggino
there's no signal here	non c'è campo
you're breaking up	la linea è molto disturbata
could you speak a little louder?	puoi parlare più forte?

YOU WILL HEAR:	SENTIRAI:
pronto?	hello
chiamami sul cellulare	call me on my mobile, (*Amer*) cell phone
vuole lasciare un messaggio?	would you like to leave a message?

MORE USEFUL WORDS:	ALTRE PAROLE UTILI:
text message	SMS/messaggino
top-up card	ricarica
phone box, (*Amer*) phone booth	cabina telefonica
dial	comporre il numero
directory enquiries	elenco abbonati

11

Writing   Corrispondenza

what's your address?	qual è il tuo indirizzo?
where is the nearest post office?	dov'è l'ufficio postale più vicino?
could I have a stamp for the UK/ Italy, please?	mi dà un francobollo per la Gran Bretagna/l'Italia, per favore?
I'd like to send a parcel	vorrei spedire un pacco
where is the nearest postbox, (Amer) mailbox?	dov'è la buca delle lettere più vicina?
dear Isabella/Fred	cara Isabella/caro Fred
dear Sir or Madam	gentili Signori
yours sincerely	distinti saluti
yours faithfully	cordialmente
best wishes	cari saluti

YOU WILL HEAR:	SENTIRAI:
vuole spedirla per posta prioritaria?	would you like to send it first class?
c'è qualcosa di valore?	is it valuable?

MORE USEFUL WORDS:	ALTRE PAROLE UTILI:
letter	lettera
postcode, (Amer) ZIP code	codice di avviamento postale/CAP
airmail	posta aerea
postcard	cartolina
fragile	fragile
urgent	urgente
registered post, (Amer) mail	raccomandata

On line   Internet

are you on the Internet?	siete su Internet?
what's your e-mail address?	qual è il tuo indirizzo email?
I'll e-mail it to you on Tuesday	te lo mando per email martedì
I looked it up on the Internet	l'ho cercato su Internet
the information is on their website	le informazioni si trovano sul sito web
my e-mail address is anna dot rossi at rapido dot com	il mio indirizzo email è: anna punto rossi chiocciola rapido punto com
can I check my e-mail here?	posso controllare l'email qui?
I have broadband/dial-up	ho la linea veloce/connessione dial-up
do you have wireless internet access?	avete accesso internet wireless?
I'll send you the file as an attachment	ti mando il file in allegato

YOU WILL SEE: VEDRAI:

ricerca	search
fare doppio click sull'icona	double-click on the icon
apri l'applicazione	open (up) the application
scarica il file	download file

MORE USEFUL WORDS: ALTRE PAROLE UTILI:

subject (*of an email*)	oggetto
password	password
social networking site	sito di social network
search engine	motore di ricerca
mouse	mouse
keyboard	tastiera

Meeting up   Appuntamenti

what shall we do this evening?	cosa facciamo stasera?
do you want to go out tonight?	ti va di uscire stasera?
where shall we meet?	dove ci diamo appuntamento?
I'll see you outside the café at 6 o'clock	ci vediamo davanti al bar alle 6
see you later	a più tardi
I can't today, I'm busy	oggi non posso, sono impegnato
I'm sorry, I've got something planned	mi dispiace, ho già altri programmi
let's meet for a coffee in town	troviamoci al centro per un caffè
would you like to see a show/film, (Amer) movie?	ti va di andare a teatro/al cinema?
what about next week instead?	che ne dici se facciamo la prossima settimana?
shall we go for something to eat?	andiamo a mangiare qualcosa?

YOU WILL HEAR:	SENTIRAI:
piacere	nice to meet you
posso offrirti qualcosa da bere?	can I buy you a drink?

MORE USEFUL WORDS:	ALTRE PAROLE UTILI:
bar	bar
bar (serving counter in a bar/pub)	banco
meal	pasto
snack	spuntino
date	appuntamento
cigarette	sigaretta

Food and Drink/Mangiare e bere

Booking a table — Prenotare un ristorante

can you recommend a good restaurant?	può consigliarmi un buon ristorante?
I'd like to reserve a table for four	vorrei prenotare un tavolo per quattro
a reservation for tomorrow evening at eight o'clock	una prenotazione per domani sera alle otto
I booked a table for two	ho prenotato un tavolo per due

Ordering — Per Ordinare

could we see the menu/wine list, please?	possiamo avere il menù/la carta dei vini, per favore?
do you have a vegetarian menu?	avete un menù vegetariano?
could we have some more bread?	possiamo avere dell'altro pane?
could I have the bill, (*Amer*) check?	il conto, per favore
what would you recommend?	che cosa consiglia?
I'd like a black/white coffee	vorrei un caffè/un caffè macchiato

YOU WILL HEAR:	IL CAMERIERE CHIEDE ...
Volete ordinare?	Are you ready to order?
Prendete un antipasto?	Would you like a starter?
Che cosa prendete come secondo?	What will you have for the main course?
Posso consigliare ...	I can recommend ...
Altro?	Anything else?
Buon appetito!	Enjoy your meal!
Il servizio non è compreso	Service is not included.

The menu Il menu

starters	antipasti	antipasti	starters
melon	melone	antipasto di mare	seafood starter
omelette	frittata	antipasto di terra	assorted hams etc
soup	zuppa		
salad	insalata	prosciutto crudo	cured ham
		zuppa	soup

fish	pesce	pesce	fish
cod	merluzzo	acciughe	anchovies
hake	nasello	calamari	squid
halibut	ippoglosso	cozze	mussels
herring	aringa	dentice	sea bream
monk fish	squadro	frutti di mare	seafood
mussels	cozze	gamberetti	shrimp
oysters	ostriche	gamberi	prawns
plaice	platessa	merluzzo	cod
prawns	gamberi	nasello	hake
red mullet	triglie	ostriche	oysters
salmon	salmone	pesce spada	swordfish
seafood	frutti di mare	platessa	plaice
sea bass	spigola	rombo	turbot
shrimp	gamberetti	salmone	salmon
sole	sogliola	sogliola	sole
squid	calamari	spigola	sea bass
trout	trota	tonno	tuna
tuna	tonno	triglie	red mullet
turbot	rombo	trota	trout

meat	carne	carne	meat
beef	manzo	agnello	lamb
chicken	pollo	anatra	duck

duck	anatra	bistecca	steak
goose	oca	cinghiale	wild boar
hare	lepre	coniglio	rabbit
lamb	agnello	fegato	liver
liver	fegato	lepre	hare
pork	maiale	maiale	pork
rabbit	coniglio	manzo	beef
steak	bistecca	oca	goose
veal	vitello	pollo	chicken
wild boar	cinghiale	vitello	veal

vegetables	**verdure**	**verdure**	**vegetables**
artichokes	carciofi	asparagi	asparagus
asparagus	asparagi	carciofi	artichokes
aubergines	melanzane	carote	carrots
beans	fagioli	cavolfiore	cauliflower
cabbage	cavolo	cavolo	cabbage
carrots	carote	cipolle	onions
cauliflower	cavolfiore	fagioli	beans
celery	sedano	fagiolini	green beans
courgettes	zucchini	funghi	mushrooms
green beans	fagiolini	insalata	salad
mushrooms	funghi	melanzane	aubergines
onions	cipolle	patate	potatoes
peas	piselli	peperoni	peppers
peppers	peperoni	piselli	peas
potatoes	patate	sedano	celery
salad	insalata	zucchini	courgettes

the way it's cooked	**cottura**	**cottura**	**the way it's cooked**
boiled	lesso	al forno	cooked in the oven
fried	fritto		
grilled	alla griglia	al pomodoro	in tomato sauce

17

griddled	alla piastra	al ragù	in a meat sauce
puree	purè	al sangue	rare
roast	arrosto	alla griglia	grilled
stewed	in umido	arrosto	roast
rare	al sangue	ben cotta	well done
medium	cotta al punto giusto	cotta al punto giusto	medium
well done	ben cotta	fritto	fried
		in umido	stewed
		lesso	boiled

desserts	dolci	dolci	desserts
cream	panna	crostata	tart
fruit	frutta	frutta	fruit
ice cream	gelato	gelato	ice cream
pie	torta	panna	cream
tart	crostata	torta	pie

sundries	contorni, salse, ecc.	contorni, salse, ecc.	sundries
bread	pane	aceto	vinegar
butter	burro	burro	butter
cheese	formaggio	condimento	seasoning
herbs	erbe	erbe	herbs
mayonnaise	maionese	formaggio	cheese
mustard	senape	maionese	mayonnaise
olive oil	olio d'oliva	olio d'oliva	olive oil
pepper	pepe	pane	bread
rice	riso	pepe	pepper
salt	sale	riso	rice
sauce	salsa	sale	salt
seasoning	condimento	salsa	sauce
vinegar	aceto	senape	mustard

18

drinks	bevande		bevande	drinks
beer	birra		acqua minerale	mineral water
bottle	bottiglia		bibite analcoliche	soft drinks
carbonated	gassato		birra	beer
coffee	caffè		bottiglia	bottle
decaffeinated coffee	decaffeinato		caffè	coffee
espresso	espresso		decaffeinato	decaffeinated coffee
half-bottle	mezza bottiglia		espresso	espresso
liqueur	liquore		gassato	carbonated
mineral water	acqua minerale		liquore	liqueur
red wine	vino rosso		mezza bottiglia	half-bottle
soft drinks	bibite analcoliche		naturale	still
sparkling wine	spumante		spumante	sparkling wine
still	naturale		vino	wine
table wine	vino da tavola		vino bianco	white wine
white wine	vino bianco		vino da tavola	table wine
wine	vino		vino rosso	red wine

Places to stay/Dove alloggiare

Camping — In campeggio

can we pitch our tent here?	possiamo montare la tenda qui?
can we park our caravan here?	possiamo parcheggiare la roulotte qui?
what are the facilities like?	che attrezzature ci sono?
how much is it per night?	quant'è a notte?
where do we park the car?	dov'è il parcheggio?
we're looking for a campsite	stiamo cercando un campeggio
this is a list of local campsites	questo è l'elenco dei campeggi della zona
we go on a camping holiday every year	andiamo in campeggio tutti gli anni

At the hotel — In albergo

I'd like a double/single room with bath	vorrei una camera doppia/singola con bagno
we have a reservation in the name of Morris	abbiamo prenotato a nome Morris
we'll be staying three nights, from Friday to Sunday	ci fermiamo tre notti, da venerdì a domenica
how much does the room cost?	quant'è la camera?
I'd like to see the room, please	vorrei vedere la camera, per favore
what time is breakfast?	a che ora è la colazione?
can I leave this in your safe?	posso lasciare questo nella cassaforte?
bed and breakfast	camera e prima colazione
we'd like to stay another night	vorremmo fermarci un'altra notte
please call me at 7:30	mi chiami alle 7:30, per favore
are there any messages for me?	ci sono messaggi per me?

★★★

20

Hostels | Ostelli

could you tell me where the youth hostel is?	mi sa dire dov'è l'ostello della gioventù?
what time does the hostel close?	a che ora chiude l'ostello?
I'm staying in a hostel	alloggio in un ostello
the hostel we're staying in is great value	l'ostello in cui alloggiamo è molto conveniente
I know a really good hostel in Dublin	conosco un ottimo ostello a Dublino
I'd like to go backpacking in Australia	mi piacerebbe girare l'Australia con zaino e sacco a pelo

Rooms to let | In affitto

I'm looking for a room with a reasonable rent	vorrei affittare una camera a prezzo modico
I'd like to rent an apartment for a few weeks	vorrei affittare un appartamento per qualche settimana
where do I find out about rooms to let?	dove posso informarmi su camere in affitto?
what's the weekly rent?	quant'è l'affitto alla settimana?
I'm staying with friends at the moment	al momento alloggio presso amici
I rent an apartment on the outskirts of town	affitto un appartamento in periferia
the room's fine—I'll take it	la camera mi piace, la prendo
the deposit is one month's rent in advance	la caparra è di un mese d'affitto

Shopping and money/Spese e soldi

At the bank | In banca

I'd like to change some money	vorrei cambiare dei soldi
I want to change some euros into pounds	vorrei cambiare degli euro in sterline
do you take Eurocheques?	accettate Eurochèque?
what's the exchange rate today?	quant'è il tasso di cambio oggi?
I prefer traveller's cheques, (Amer) traveler's checks to cash	preferisco i traveller's cheque al contante
I'd like to transfer some money from my account	vorrei fare un bonifico
I'll get some money from the cash machine	prenderò dei soldi dal bancomat®
I'm with another bank	ho il conto in un'altra banca

Finding the right shop | Il negozio giusto

where's the main shopping district?	dov'è la zona commerciale principale?
where's a good place to buy sunglasses/shoes?	qual è il posto migliore per comprare occhiali da sole/scarpe?
where can I buy batteries/ postcards?	dove posso comprare pile/ cartoline?
where's the nearest chemist/ bookshop?	dov'è la farmacia/libreria più vicina?
is there a good food shop around here?	c'è un buon negozio di generi alimentari qui vicino?
what time do the shops open/ close?	a che ora aprono/chiudono i negozi?
where can I hire a car?	dove posso noleggiare una macchina?
where did you get those?	dove le/li hai comprate/-i?
I'm looking for presents for my family	sto cercando dei regalini per la mia famiglia
we'll do all our shopping on Saturday	faremo la spesa sabato
I love shopping	adoro fare spese

Are you being served? Nei negozi

how much does that cost?	quanto costa quello?
can I try it on?	posso provarlo?
can you keep it for me?	me lo mette da parte?
could you wrap it for me, please?	me lo incarta, per favore?
can I pay by credit card/cheque, (Amer) check?	posso pagare con la carta di credito/un assegno?
do you have this in another colour, (Amer) color?	c'è in altri colori?
could I have a bag, please?	mi dà un sacchetto, per favore?
I'm just looking	sto solo dando un'occhiata
I'll think about it	ci devo pensare
I'd like a receipt, please	mi dà lo scontrino, per favore?
I need a bigger/smaller size	mi serve la taglia più grande/piccola
I take a size 10/a medium	porto la 42/la media
it doesn't suit me	non mi sta bene
I'm sorry, I don't have any change/anything smaller	mi dispiace, non ho spiccioli/biglietti più piccoli
that's all, thank you	nient'altro, grazie

Changing things Cambiare un acquisto

can I have a refund?	rimborsate i soldi?
can you mend it for me?	può ripararlo?
can I speak to the manager?	posso parlare con il direttore?
it doesn't work	non funziona
I'd like to change it, please	vorrei cambiarlo, per favore
I bought this here yesterday	l'ho comprato qui ieri

Currency Convertor Convertitore di valute

€/$	£/$	£/$	€/$
0.25		0.25	
0.50		0.50	
0.75		0.75	
1		1	
1.5		1.5	
2		2	
3		3	
5		5	
10		10	
20		20	
30		30	
40		40	
50		50	
100		100	
200		200	
1000		1000	

Sport and leisure/Sport e tempo libero

Keeping fit Tenersi in forma

where can we play tennis/badminton?	dove si può giocare a tennis/badminton?
I'm looking for a swimming pool/golf course	sto cercando una piscina/un campo da golf
is there a hotel gym?	c'è una palestra in albergo?
are there any yoga/pilates classes here?	ci sono corsi di yoga/pilates?
I would like to go cycling/riding	mi piacerebbe andare in bici/a cavallo
I love swimming/football	mi piace nuotare/il calcio
where can I get tickets for the match, (*Amer*) game on Saturday?	dove si comprano i biglietti per la partita di sabato?

Going out Uscire

what's on at the theatre/cinema?	cosa danno a teatro/al cinema?
how much are the tickets?	quanto costano i biglietti?
what time does the concert/performance start?	a che ora inizia il concerto/lo spettacolo?
I'd like to book tickets for tonight	vorrei prenotare dei biglietti per stasera
we'd like to go to a club	vorremmo andare in qualche locale

25

Good timing/L'Ora giusta

Telling the time Dire l'ora

could you tell me the time?	mi dica che ore sono?
what time is it?	che ora è?
it's 2 o'clock	sono le due
at about 8 o'clock	verso le otto
at 9 o'clock tomorrow	domani mattina alle nove
from 10 o'clock onwards	dalle dieci in poi
at 8 a.m./p.m.	alle otto di mattina/di sera
at 5 o'clock in the morning/afternoon	alle cinque del mattino/di sera
it's five past/quarter past/half past one	è l'una e cinque/e un quarto/e mezza
it's twenty-five to/quarter to/five to one	è l'una meno venticinque/meno un quarto/meno cinque
a quarter /three quarters of an hour	un quarto/tre quarti d'ora

Days and dates Giorni, mesi e date

Sunday, Monday, Tuesday, Wednesday, Thursday, Friday, Saturday	domenica, lunedì, martedì, mercoledì, giovedì, venerdì, sabato
January, February, March, April, May, June, July, August, September, October, November, December	gennaio, febbraio, marzo, aprile, maggio, giugno, luglio, agosto, settembre, ottobre, novembre, dicembre
what's the date?	quanti ne abbiamo oggi?
it's the second of June	è il due giugno
we meet up every Monday	ci incontriamo ogni lunedì
she comes on Tuesdays	viene di martedì
we're going away in August	saremo via ad agosto
it was the first of April	era il primo aprile
on November 8th	l'otto novembre

Public holidays and special days / Festività

Bank holiday	festa civile
Bank holiday Monday	festa civile che cade di lunedì
long weekend	ponte
New Year's Day (Jan 1)	Capodanno (1 gennaio)
Epiphany (Jan 6)	Epifania (la Befana: 6 gennaio)
St Valentine's Day (Feb 14)	San Valentino (14 febbraio)
Shrove Tuesday/Pancake Day	martedì grasso
Ash Wednesday	mercoledì delle Ceneri
St Joseph's Day (Mar 19)	San Giuseppe (19 marzo)
Mother's Day	Festa della mamma
Palm Sunday	domenica delle Palme
Maundy Thursday	giovedì grasso
Good Friday	venerdì santo
Easter Day	Pasqua
Easter Monday	lunedì dell'Angelo (pasquetta)
Anniversary of the liberation of Italy in 1945	anniversario della Liberazione (25 aprile)
May Day (May 1)	Festa del lavoro (1 maggio)
Father's Day	Festa del papà
Independence Day (Jul 4)	anniversario dell'Indipendenza (4 luglio)
Assumption (Aug 15)	Assunzione (ferragosto: 15 agosto)
Halloween (Oct 31)	vigilia d'Ognissanti
All Saints' Day (Nov 1)	Ognissanti (1 novembre)
Thanksgiving	giorno del Ringraziamento
Christmas Eve (Dec 24)	vigilia di Natale (24 dicembre)
Christmas Day (Dec 25)	Natale (25 dicembre)
Boxing Day (Dec 26)	Santo Stefano (26 dicembre)
New Year's Eve (Dec 31)	San Silvestro (31 dicembre)

Health and Beauty/Salute e bellezza

At the doctor's Dal medico

can I see a doctor?	potrei vedere un medico?
I don't feel well	non mi sento bene
it hurts here	mi fa male qui
I have a migraine/stomachache	ho l'emicrania/il mal di stomaco
are there any side effects?	ci sono effetti collaterali?
I have a sore ankle/wrist/knee	mi fa male la caviglia/il polso/il ginocchio

YOU WILL HEAR: SENTIRAI:

deve prendere un appuntamento	you need to make an appointment
si accomodi	please take a seat
ha la Tessera Europea di Assicurazione Malattia (TEAM)?	do you have a European Health Insurance Card (EHIC)?
ha l'assistenza medica?	do you have Health Insurance?
devo misurarle la pressione	I need to take your blood pressure

MORE USEFUL WORDS: ALTRE PAROLE UTILI:

nurse	infermiere/a
antibiotics	antibiotici
medicine	medicina
infection	infezione
treatment	cura
rest	riposo

At the pharmacy | In farmacia

can I have some painkillers?	mi dà un antidolorifico/analgesico?
I have asthma/hay fever/eczema	soffro d'asma/di rinite allergica/d'eczema
I've been stung by a wasp/bee	mi ha punto una vespa/un'ape
I've got a cold/cough/the flu	ho il raffreddore/la tosse/l'influenza
I need something for diarrhoea/stomachache	vorrei qualcosa per la diarrea/il mal di stomaco
I'm pregnant	sono incinta

YOU WILL HEAR: | SENTIRAI

ha già preso questo farmaco?	have you taken this medicine before?
le sue medicine sono pronte tra dieci minuti	your prescription will be ready in ten minutes
da assumere durante i pasti/tre volte al giorno?	take at mealtimes/three times a day?
è allergico/-a a qualcosa?	are you allergic to anything?
sta prendendo qualche altro farmaco?	are you taking any other medication?

MORE USEFUL WORDS: | ALTRE PAROLE UTILI:

plasters, (Amer) Band-Aid™	cerotti
insect repellent	insettifugo
contraception	anticoncezionali
sun cream	solare
aftersun	doposole
dosage	dosi

At the hairdresser's/beauty salon — Dal parrucchiere/dall'estetista

I'd like a cut and blow dry	taglio e asciugatura spazzola e phon
just a trim please	solo una spuntatina, per favore
a grade 3 back and sides	9 mm sia sui lati che dietro
I'd like my hair washed first please	mi faccia lo shampoo prima, per favore
can I have a manicure/pedicure/facial?	fate la manicure/pedicure/pulizia del viso?
how much is a head/back massage?	quant'è il massaggio alla testa/schiena?
can I see a price list?	potrei vedere il listino prezzi?
do you offer reflexology/aromatherapy treatments?	fate riflessologia/aromaterapia?

YOU WILL HEAR: SENTIRAI:

vuole l'asciugatura a spazzola e phon?	would you like your hair blow-dried?
da che lato porta la riga?	where is your parting?
le faccio un taglio scalato?	would you like your hair layered?

MORE USEFUL WORDS: ALTRE PAROLE UTILI:

dry/greasy/fine/flyaway/frizzy hair	capelli secchi/grassi/sottili/sfibrati/crespi
highlights	colpi di sole
extensions	allungamento capelli/extensions
sunbed	lettino solare
leg/arm/bikini wax	ceretta gambe/braccia/inguine

At the dentist's | Dal dentista

I have toothache	ho mal di denti
I'd like an emergency appointment	vorrei un appuntamento d'urgenza
I have cracked a tooth	mi si è spezzato un dente
my gums are bleeding	mi sanguinano le gengive

YOU WILL HEAR:	SENTIRAI:
apra bene la bocca	open your mouth
bisogna fare un'otturazione	you need a filling
devo farle una radiografia	we need to take an X-ray
sciacqui bene	please rinse

MORE USEFUL WORDS:	ALTRE PAROLE UTILI:
anaesthetic	anestesia
root canal treatment	devitalizzazione del dente
injection	iniezione
floss	filo interdentale

Weights & measures/ Pesi e misure

Length/Lunghezza

inches/pollici	0.39	3.9	7.8	11.7	15.6	19.7	39
cm/centimetri	1	10	20	30	40	50	100

Distance/Distanze

miles/miglia	0.62	6.2	12.4	18.6	24.9	31	62
km/chilometri	1	10	20	30	40	50	100

Weight/Pesi

pounds/libbre	2.2	22	44	66	88	110	220
kg/chilogrammi	1	10	20	30	40	50	100

Capacity/Capacità

gallons/galloni	0.22	2.2	4.4	6.6	8.8	11	22
litres/litri	1	10	20	30	40	50	100

Temperature/Temperatura

°C	0	5	10	15	20	25	30	37	38	40
°F	32	41	50	59	68	77	86	98.4	100	104

Clothing and shoe sizes/Taglie e numeri di scarpe

Women's clothing sizes/Abbigliamento femminile

UK	8	10	12	14	16	18
US	6	8	10	12	14	16
Continent	36	38	40	42	44	46

Men's clothing sizes/Abbigliamento maschile

UK/US	36	38	40	42	44	46
Continent	46	48	50	52	54	56

Men's and women's shoes/Scarpe da uomo e da donna

UK women	4	5	6	7	7.5	8			
UK men			6	7	8	9	10	11	
US	6.5	7.5	8.5	9.5	10.5	11.5	12.5	13.5	14.5
Continent	37	38	39	40	41	42	43	44	45

a /ə/, accentato /eɪ/ *indef art*; *davanti a una vocale* **an**

···> un *m*, una *f*; (*before s + consonant, gn, ps and z*) uno; (*before feminine noun starting with a vowel*) un'; a tiger is a feline la tigre è un felino; a knife and fork un coltello e una forchetta; a Mr Smith is looking for you un certo signor Smith ti sta cercando

···> (*each*) a; £2 a kilo/a head due sterline al chilo/a testa

when a refers to professions, it is not translated: I am a lawyer sono avvocato

A /eɪ/ *n* (*Mus*) la *m inv*

aback /ə'bæk/ *adv* be taken ~ essere preso in contropiede

abandon /ə'bændən/ *vt* abbandonare; (*give up*) rinunciare a ●*n* abbandono *m*. ~**ed** *adj* abbandonato

abashed /ə'bæʃt/ *adj* imbarazzato

abate /ə'beɪt/ *vi* calmarsi

abattoir /'æbətwɑː(r)/ *n* mattatoio *m*

abbey /'æbɪ/ *n* abbazia *f*

abbreviat|e /ə'briːvɪeɪt/ *vt* abbreviare. ~**ion** *n* abbreviazione *f*

abdicat|e /'æbdɪkeɪt/ *vt* abdicare ●*vt* rinunciare a. ~**ion** *n* abdicazione *f*

abdom|en /'æbdəmən/ *n* addome *m*. ~**inal** *adj* addominale

abduct /əb'dʌkt/ *vt* rapire. ~**ion** *n* rapimento *m*

abhor /əb'hɔː(r)/ *vt* (*pt/pp* abhorred*) aborrire. ~**rence** *n* orrore *m*

abid|e /ə'baɪd/ *vt* (*pt/pp* abided) (*tolerate*) sopportare ●abide by *vi* rispettare. ~**ing** *adj* perpetuo

ability /ə'bɪlətɪ/ *n* capacità *f inv*

abject /'æbdʒekt/ *adj* (*poverty*) degradante; (*apology*) umile; (*coward*) abietto

ablaze /ə'bleɪz/ *adj* in fiamme; be ~ with light risplendere di luci

able /'eɪbl/ *adj* capace, abile; be ~ to do sth poter fare qcsa; were you ~ to...? sei riuscito a...? ~-'bodied *adj* robusto; (*Mil*) abile

ably /'eɪblɪ/ *adv* abilmente

abnormal /æb'nɔːml/ *adj* anormale. ~**ity** *n* anormalità *f inv*. ~**ly** *adv* in modo anormale

aboard /ə'bɔːd/ *adv* & *prep* a bordo

abolish /ə'bɒlɪʃ/ *vt* abolire. ~**ition** *n* abolizione *f*

abominable /ə'bɒmɪnəbl/ *adj* abominevole

abort /ə'bɔːt/ *vt* fare abortire; *fig* annullare. ~**ion** *n* aborto *m*; have an ~ion abortire. ~**ive** *adj* (*attempt*) infruttuoso

abound /ə'baʊnd/ *vi* abbondare; ~ in abbondare di

about /ə'baʊt/ *adv* (*here and there*) [di] qua e [di] là; (*approximately*) circa; be ~ (*illness, tourists*:) essere in giro; be up and ~ essere alzato; leave sth lying ~ lasciare in giro qcsa ●*prep* (*concerning*) su; (*in the region of*) intorno a; (*here and there*) per; what is the book/the film ~? di cosa parla il libro/il film?; he wants to see you – what ~? ti vuole vedere – a che proposito?; talk/know ~ parlare/sapere di; I know nothing ~ it non ne so niente; ~ 5 o'clock intorno alle 5; travel ~ the world viaggiare per il mondo; be ~ to do sth stare per fare qcsa; how ~ going to the cinema? e se andassimo al cinema?

about: ~-'face n, ~-'turn n dietro front m inv

above /ə'bʌv/ adv & prep sopra; ~ all soprattutto

above: ~-'board adj onesto. ~-'mentioned adj suddetto

abrasive /ə'breɪsɪv/ adj abrasivo; (remark) caustico ● n abrasivo m

abreast /ə'brest/ adv fianco a fianco; come ~ of allinearsi con; keep ~ of tenersi al corrente di

abroad /ə'brɔːd/ adv all'estero

abrupt /ə'brʌpt/ adj brusco

abscess /'æbsɪs/ n ascesso m

abscond /əb'skɒnd/ vi fuggire

absence /'æbsəns/ n assenza f; (lack) mancanza f

absent¹ /'æbsənt/ adj assente

absent² /æb'sent/ vt ~ oneself essere assente

absentee /æbsən'tiː/ n assente mf

absent-minded /æbsənt'maɪndɪd/ adj distratto

absolute /'æbsəluːt/ adj assoluto; an ~ idiot un perfetto idiota. ~ly adv assolutamente; (fam: indicating agreement) esattamente

absolve /əb'zɒlv/ vt assolvere

absorb /əb'sɔːb/ vt assorbire; ~ed in assorto in. ~ent adj assorbente

absorption /əb'sɔːpʃn/ n assorbimento m; (in activity) concentrazione f

abstain /əb'steɪn/ vi astenersi (from da)

abstemious /əb'stiːmɪəs/ adj moderato

abstention /əb'stenʃn/ n (Pol) astensione f

abstract /'æbstrækt/ adj astratto ● n astratto m; (summary) estratto m

absurd /əb'sɜːd/ adj assurdo. ~ity n

assurdità f inv

abundan|ce /ə'bʌndəns/ n abbondanza f. ~t adj abbondante

abuse¹ /ə'bjuːz/ vt (misuse) abusare di; (insult) insultare; (ill-treat) maltrattare

abus|e² /ə'bjuːs/ n abuso m; (verbal) insulti mpl; (ill-treatment) maltrattamento m. ~ive adj offensivo

abysmal /ə'bɪzml/ adj (fam) pessimo; (ignorance) abissale

abyss /ə'bɪs/ n abisso m

academic /ækə'demɪk/ adj teorico; (qualifications, system) scolastico; be ~ (person): avere predisposizione allo studio ● n docente mf universitario, -a

academy /ə'kædəmɪ/ n accademia f; (of music) conservatorio m

accelerat|e /ək'seləreɪt/ vt/i accelerare. ~ion n accelerazione f. ~or n (Auto) acceleratore m

accent /'æksənt/ n accento m

accept /ək'sept/ vt accettare. ~able adj accettabile. ~ance n accettazione f

access /'ækses/ n accesso m. ~ible adj accessibile

accession /ək'seʃn/ n (to throne) ascesa f al trono

accessory /ək'sesərɪ/ n accessorio m; (Jur) complice mf

accident /'æksɪdənt/ n incidente m; (chance) caso m; by ~ per caso; (unintentionally) senza volere; I'm sorry, it was an ~ mi dispiace, non l'ho fatto apposta. ~al adj (meeting) casuale; (death) incidentale; (unintentional) involontario. ~ally adv per caso; (unintentionally) inavvertitamente

acclaim /ə'kleɪm/ n acclamazione f ● vt acclamare (as come)

accolade /'ækəleɪd/ n riconoscimento m

accommodat|e /ə'kɒmədeɪt/ vt ospitare; (oblige) favorire. ~ing adj accomodante. ~ion n (place to stay) sistemazione f

accompan|iment /əˈkʌmpənɪmənt/ n accompagnamento m. ~ist n (Mus) accompagnatore, -trice f

accompany /əˈkʌmpənɪ/ vt (pt/pp -ied) accompagnare

accomplice /əˈkʌmplɪs/ n complice mf

accomplish /əˈkʌmplɪʃ/ vt (achieve) concludere; realizzare (aim). ~ed adj dotato; (fact) compiuto. ~ment n realizzazione f; (achievement) risultato m; (talent) talento m

accord /əˈkɔːd/ n (treaty) accordo m; with one ~ tutti d'accordo; of his own ~ di sua spontanea volontà. ~ance n in ~ance with in conformità to o a

according /əˈkɔːdɪŋ/ adv ~ to secondo. ~ly adv di conseguenza

accordion /əˈkɔːdɪən/ n fisarmonica f

accost /əˈkɒst/ vt abbordare

account /əˈkaʊnt/ n conto m; (report) descrizione f; (of eye-witness) resoconto m; ~s pl (Comm) conti mpl; on ~ of a causa di; on no ~ per nessun motivo; on this ~ per questo motivo; on my ~ per causa mia; of no ~ di nessuna importanza; take into ~ tener conto di ● account for vi (explain) spiegare; (person:) render conto di; (constitute) costituire. ~ability n responsabilità f inv. ~able adj responsabile (for di)

accountant /əˈkaʊntənt/ n (book-keeper) contabile mf; (consultant) commercialista mf

accumulat|e /əˈkjuːmjʊleɪt/ vt accumulare ● vi accumularsi. ~ion n accumulazione f

accura|cy /ˈækjʊrəsɪ/ n precisione f. ~te adj preciso. ~tely adv con precisione

accusation /ækjʊˈzeɪʃn/ n accusa f

accuse /əˈkjuːz/ vt accusare; ~ sb of doing sth accusare qcno di fare

qcsa. ~d n the ~d l'accusato m, l'accusata f

accustom /əˈkʌstəm/ vt abituare (to a); grow o get ~ed to abituarsi a. ~ed adj abituato

ace /eɪs/ n (Cards) asso m; (tennis) ace m inv

ache /eɪk/ n dolore m ● vi dolere, far male; ~ all over essere tutto indolenzito

achieve /əˈtʃiːv/ vt ottenere (success); realizzare (goal, ambition). ~ment n (feat) successo m

acid /ˈæsɪd/ adj acido ● n acido m. ~ity n acidità f. ~ ˈrain n pioggia f acida

acknowledge /əkˈnɒlɪdʒ/ vt riconoscere; rispondere a (greeting); far cenno di aver notato (sb's presence); ~ receipt of accusare ricevuta di. ~ment n riconoscimento m; send an ~ment of a letter confermare il ricevimento di una lettera

acne /ˈæknɪ/ n acne f

acorn /ˈeɪkɔːn/ n ghianda f

acoustic /əˈkuːstɪk/ adj acustico. ~s n acustica fsg

acquaint /əˈkweɪnt/ vt ~ sb with metter qcno al corrente di; be ~ed with conoscere (person); essere a conoscenza di (fact). ~ance n (person) conoscente mf; make sb's ~ance fare la conoscenza di qcno

acquiesce /ækwɪˈes/ vi acconsentire (to, in a). ~nce n acquiescenza f

acquire /əˈkwaɪə(r)/ vt acquisire

acquisit|ion /ækwɪˈzɪʃn/ n acquisizione f. ~ive adj avido

acquit /əˈkwɪt/ vt (pt/pp acquitted) assolvere; ~ oneself well cavarsela bene. ~tal n assoluzione f

acre /ˈeɪkə(r)/ n acro m (= 4 047 m²)

acrid /ˈækrɪd/ adj acre

acrimon|ious /ækrɪˈməʊnɪəs/ adj aspro. ~y n asprezza f

acrobat /ˈækrəbæt/ n acrobata mf. ~ic adj acrobatico

a

across /əˈkrɒs/ adv dall'altra parte; (wide) in larghezza; (not lengthwise) attraverso; (in crossword) orizzontale; come ~ sth imbattersi in qcsa o; ~ attraversare ● prep (crosswise) di traverso su; (on the other side of) dall'altra parte di

act /ækt/ n atto m; (in variety show) numero m; put on an ~ ⊞ fare scena ● vi agire; (behave) comportarsi; (Theat) recitare; (pretend) fingere; ~ as fare da ● vt recitare (role). ~ing adj (deputy) provvisorio ● n (Theat) recitazione f; (profession) teatro m. ~ing profession n professione f dell'attore

action /ˈækʃn/ n azione f; (Mil) combattimento m; (Jur) azione f legale; out of ~ (machine:) fuori uso; take ~ agire. ~ 'replay n replay m inv

active /ˈæktɪv/ adj attivo. ~ely adv attivamente. ~ity n attività f inv

act|or /ˈæktə(r)/ n attore m. ~ress n attrice f

actual /ˈæktʃʊəl/ adj (real) reale. ~ly adv in realtà

acute /əˈkjuːt/ adj acuto; (shortage, hardship) spaventoso

ad /æd/ n ⊞ pubblicità f inv

AD abbr (Anno Domini) d.C.

adapt /əˈdæpt/ vt adattare (play) ● vi adattarsi. ~ability n adattabilità f. ~able adj adattabile

adaptation /ædæpˈteɪʃn/ n (Theat) adattamento m

adapter, adaptor /əˈdæptə(r)/ n adattatore m; (two-way) presa f multipla

add /æd/ vt aggiungere; (Math) addizionare ● vi addizionare; ~ to (fig: increase) aggravare. □ ~ **up** vt addizionare (figures) ● vi addizionare; ~ up to ammontare a; it doesn't ~ up fig non quadra

adder /ˈædə(r)/ n vipera f

addict /ˈædɪkt/ n tossicodipendente

mf; fig fanatico, -a mf

addict|ed /əˈdɪktɪd/ adj assuefatto (to a); ~ed to drugs tossicodipendente; he's ~ed to television è videodipendente. ~ion n dipendenza f; (to drugs) tossicodipendenza f. ~ive adj be ~ive dare assuefazione

addition /əˈdɪʃn/ n (Math) addizione f; (thing added) aggiunta f; in ~ in aggiunta. ~al adj supplementare. ~ally adv in più

additive /ˈædɪtɪv/ n additivo m

address /əˈdres/ n indirizzo m; (speech) discorso m; form of ~ formula f di cortesia ● vt indirizzare; (speak to) rivolgersi a (person); tenere un discorso a (meeting). ~ee n destinatario, -a mf

adept /ˈædept/ adj & n esperto, -a mf (at in)

adequate /ˈædɪkwət/ adj adeguato. ~ly adv adeguatamente

adhere /ədˈhɪə(r)/ vi aderire; ~ to attenersi a (principles, rules)

adhesive /ədˈhiːsɪv/ adj adesivo ● n adesivo m

adjacent /əˈdʒeɪsənt/ adj adiacente

adjective /ˈædʒɪktɪv/ n aggettivo m

adjourn /əˈdʒɜːn/ vt/i aggiornare (until a). ~ment n aggiornamento m

adjust /əˈdʒʌst/ vt modificare; regolare (focus, sound etc) ● vi adattarsi. ~able adj regolabile. ~ment n adattamento m; (Techn) regolamento m

administer /ədˈmɪnɪstə(r)/ vt amministrare; somministrare (medicine)

administrat|ion /ədmɪnɪˈstreɪʃn/ n amministrazione f; (Pol) governo m. ~or n amministratore, -trice mf

admirable /ˈædmərəbl/ adj ammirevole

admiral /ˈædmərəl/ n ammiraglio m

admiration /ædməˈreɪʃn/ n ammirazione f

admire /ədˈmaɪə(r)/ vt ammirare

~r n ammiratore, -trice mf

admission /əd'mɪʃn/ n ammissione f; (to hospital) ricovero m; (entry) ingresso m

admit /əd'mɪt/ vt (pt/pp admitted) (let in) far entrare; (to hospital) ricoverare; (acknowledge) ammettere • vi ~ to sth ammettere qcsa. **~tance** n ammissione f; 'no ~tance' 'vietato l'ingresso'. **~tedly** adv bisogna riconoscerlo

admonish /əd'mɒnɪʃ/ vt ammonire

ado /ə'duː/ n without more ~ senza ulteriori indugi

adolescen|ce /ædə'lesns/ n adolescenza f. **~t** adj & n adolescente mf

adopt /ə'dɒpt/ vt adottare; (Pol) scegliere (candidate). **~ion** n adozione f. **~ive** adj adottivo

ador|able /ə'dɔːrəbl/ adj adorabile. **~ation** n adorazione f

adore /ə'dɔː(r)/ vt adorare

adrenalin /ə'drenəlɪn/ n adrenalina f

Adriatic /eɪdrɪ'ætɪk/ adj & n the ~ [Sea] il mare Adriatico, l'Adriatico m

adrift /ə'drɪft/ adj alla deriva; be ~ andare alla deriva; come ~ staccarsi

adult /'ædʌlt/ n adulto, -a mf

adultery /ə'dʌltəri/ n adulterio m

advance /əd'vɑːns/ n avanzamento m; (Mil) avanzata f; (payment) anticipo m; in ~ in anticipo • vi avanzare; (make progress) fare progressi • vt avanzare (theory); promuovere (cause); anticipare (money). ~ booking n prenotazione f [in anticipo]. **~d** adj avanzato. **~ment** n promozione f

advantage /əd'vɑːntɪdʒ/ n vantaggio m; take ~ of approfittare di. **~ous** adj vantaggioso

advent /'ædvent/ n avvento m

adventur|e /əd'ventʃə(r)/ n avventura f. **~ous** adj avventuroso

adverb /'ædvɜːb/ n avverbio m

adversary /'ædvəsəri/ n avversario, -a mf

advers|e /'ædvɜːs/ adj avverso. **~ity** n avversità f

advert /'ædvɜːt/ n 🗓 = advertisement

advertise /'ædvətaɪz/ vt reclamizzare; mettere un annuncio per (job, flat) • vi fare pubblicità; (for job, flat) mettere un annuncio

advertisement /əd'vɜːtɪsmənt/ n pubblicità f inv; (in paper) inserzione f, annuncio m

advertis|er /'ædvətaɪzə(r)/ n (in newspaper) inserzionista mf. **~ing** n pubblicità f • attrib pubblicitario

advice /əd'vaɪs/ n consigli mpl; piece of ~ consiglio m

advisable /əd'vaɪzəbl/ adj consigliabile

advis|e /əd'vaɪz/ vt consigliare; (inform) avvisare; ~e sb to do sth consigliare a qcno di fare qcsa; ~e sb against sth sconsigliare qcsa a qcno. **~er** n consulente mf. **~ory** adj consultivo

advocate[1] /'ædvəkət/ n (supporter) fautore, -trice mf

advocate[2] /'ædvəkeɪt/ vt propugnare

aerial /'eərɪəl/ adj aereo • n antenna f

aerobics /eə'rəʊbɪks/ n aerobica fsg

aero|drome /'eərədrəʊm/ n aerodromo m. **~plane** n aeroplano m

aerosol /'eərəsɒl/ n bomboletta f spray

aesthetic /iːs'θetɪk/ adj estetico

afar /ə'fɑː(r)/ adv from ~ da lontano

affable /'æfəbl/ adj affabile

affair /ə'feə(r)/ n affare m; (scandal) caso m; (sexual) relazione f

affect /ə'fekt/ vt influire su; (emotionally) colpire; (concern) riguardare.

a

~ation n affettazione f. ~ed adj affettato

affection /əˈfekʃn/ n affetto m. ~ate adj affettuoso

affirm /əˈfɜːm/ vt affermare; (Jur) dichiarare solennemente

affirmative /əˈfɜːmətɪv/ adj affermativo ● n in the ~ affermativamente

afflict /əˈflɪkt/ vt affliggere. ~ion n afflizione f

affluen|ce /ˈæfluəns/ n agiatezza f. ~t adj agiato

afford /əˈfɔːd/ vt be able to ~ sth potersi permettere qcsa. ~able adj abbordabile

affront /əˈfrʌnt/ n affronto m

afield /əˈfiːld/ adv further ~ più lontano

afloat /əˈfləʊt/ adj a galla

afraid /əˈfreɪd/ adj be ~ aver paura; I'm ~ not troppo no; I'm ~ so temo di sì; I'm ~ I can't help you mi dispiace, ma non posso esserle d'aiuto

afresh /əˈfreʃ/ adv da capo

Africa /ˈæfrɪkə/ n Africa f. ~n adj & n africano, -a mf

after /ˈɑːftə(r)/ adv dopo; the day ~ il giorno dopo; be ~ cercare ● prep dopo; ~ all dopotutto; the day ~ tomorrow dopodomani ● conj dopo che

after: ~-effect n conseguenza f. ~math /-mæθ/ n conseguenze fpl; the ~math of war il dopoguerra; in the ~math of nel periodo successivo a. ~noon n pomeriggio m; good ~noon! buon giorno!. ~shave n [lozione f.] dopobarba m inv. ~thought n added as an ~thought aggiunto in un secondo momento; ~wards adv in seguito

again /əˈgem/ adv di nuovo; [then] ~ (besides) inoltre; (on the other hand) d'altra parte; ~ and ~ conti-

nuamente

against /əˈgemst/ prep contro

age /eɪdʒ/ n età f inv; (era) era f; ~s 🛽 secoli; what ~ are you? quanti anni hai?; be under ~ non avere l'età richiesta; he's two years of ~ ha due anni ● vt/i (pres p ageing) invecchiare

aged[1] /eɪdʒd/ adj ~ two di due anni

aged[2] /ˈeɪdʒɪd/ adj anziano ● n the ~ pl gli anziani

agency /ˈeɪdʒənsɪ/ n agenzia f; have the ~ for essere un concessionario di

agenda /əˈdʒendə/ n ordine m del giorno; on the ~ all'ordine del giorno; fig in programma

agent /ˈeɪdʒənt/ n agente mf

aggravat|e /ˈæɡrəveɪt/ vt aggravare; (annoy) esasperare. ~ion n aggravamento m; (annoyance) esasperazione f

aggress|ion /əˈɡreʃn/ n aggressione f. ~ive adj aggressivo. ~iveness n aggressività f. ~or n aggressore m

aghast /əˈɡɑːst/ adj inorridito

agil|e /ˈædʒaɪl/ adj agile. ~ity n agilità f

agitat|e /ˈædʒɪteɪt/ vt mettere in agitazione; (shake) agitare ● vi fig ~e for creare delle agitazioni per. ~ed adj agitato. ~ion n agitazione f. ~or n agitatore, -trice mf

ago /əˈɡəʊ/ adv fa; a long time/a month ~ molto tempo/un mese fa

agonize /ˈæɡənaɪz/ vi angosciarsi (over per). ~ing adj angosciante

agony /ˈæɡənɪ/ n agonia f; (mental) angoscia f; be in ~ avere dei dolori atroci

agree /əˈɡriː/ vt accordarsi su; ~ to do sth accettare di fare qcsa; ~ that essere d'accordo [sul fatto] che ● vi essere d'accordo; (figures:) concordare; (reach agreement) mettersi d'accordo; (get on) andare d'accordo; (consent) acconsentire (to a); it doesn't ~ with me mi fa male; ~ with sth (approve of) approvare qcsa

agreeable /əˈgriːəbl/ adj gradevole; (willing) d'accordo

agreed /əˈgriːd/ adj convenuto

agreement /əˈgriːmənt/ n accordo m; in ~ d'accordo

agricultur|al /ægrɪˈkʌltʃərəl/ adj agricolo. ~e n agricoltura f

aground /əˈgraʊnd/ adv run ~ (ship:) arenarsi

ahead /əˈhed/ adv avanti; be ~ of essere davanti a; fig essere avanti rispetto a; draw ~ passare davanti (of a); get ~ (in life) riuscire; go ~! fai pure!; look ~ pensare all'avvenire; plan ~ fare progetti per l'avvenire

aid /eɪd/ n aiuto m; in ~ of a favore di ● vt aiutare

Aids /eɪdz/ n AIDS m

aim /eɪm/ n mira f; fig scopo m; take ~ prendere la mira ● vt puntare (gun) (at contro) ● vi mirare; ~ to do sth aspirare a fare qcsa. ~less adj, ~lessly adv senza scopo

air /eə(r)/ n aria f; be on the ~ (programme:) essere in onda; put on ~s darsi delle arie; by ~ in aereo; (airmail) per via aerea ● vt arieggiare; far conoscere (views)

air: ~-conditioned adj con aria condizionata. ~-conditioning n aria f condizionata. ~craft n aereo m. ~craft carrier n portaerei f inv. ~field n campo m d'aviazione. ~force n aviazione f. ~ freshener n deodorante m per l'ambiente. ~gun n fucile m pneumatico. ~ hostess n hostess f inv. ~line n compagnia f aerea. ~mail n posta f aerea. ~plane n Am aereo m. ~port n aeroporto m. ~tight adj ermetico. ~-traffic controller n controllore m

di volo

airy /ˈeərɪ/ adj (-ier, -iest) arieggiato; (manner) noncurante

aisle /aɪl/ n corridoio m; (in supermarket) corsia f; (in church) navata f

ajar /əˈdʒɑː(r)/ adj socchiuso

alarm /əˈlɑːm/ n allarme m; set the ~ (of alarm clock) mettere la sveglia ● vt allarmare. ~ clock n sveglia f

Albania /ælˈbeɪnɪə/ n Albania f

album /ˈælbəm/ n album m inv

alcohol /ˈælkəhɒl/ n alcol m. ~ic /-ˈhɒlɪk/ adj alcolico ● n alcolizzato, -a mf. ~ism n alcolismo m

alcove /ˈælkəʊv/ n alcova f

alert /əˈlɜːt/ adj sveglio; (watchful) vigile ● n segnale m d'allarme; be on the ~ stare allerta ● vt allertare

algebra /ˈældʒɪbrə/ n algebra f

Algeria /ælˈdʒɪərɪə/ n Algeria f. ~n adj & n algerino, -a mf

alias /ˈeɪlɪəs/ n pseudonimo m ● adv alias

alibi /ˈælɪbaɪ/ n alibi m inv

alien /ˈeɪlɪən/ adj straniero; fig estraneo ● n straniero, -a mf; (from space) alieno, -a mf

alienat|e /ˈeɪlɪəneɪt/ vt alienare. ~ion n alienazione f

alight[1] /əˈlaɪt/ vi scendere; (bird:) posarsi

alight[2] adj be ~ essere in fiamme; set ~ dar fuoco a

align /əˈlaɪn/ vt allineare. ~ment n allineamento m; out of ~ment non allineato

alike /əˈlaɪk/ adj simile; be ~ rassomigliarsi ● adv in modo simile; look ~ rassomigliarsi; summer and winter ~ sia d'estate che d'inverno

alimony /ˈælɪmənɪ/ n alimenti mpl

alive /əˈlaɪv/ adj vivo; ~ with brulicante di; ~ to sensibile a; ~ and kicking vivo e vegeto

alkali /ˈælkəlaɪ/ n alcali m

a **all** /ɔːl/
- adj tutto; ~ the children, ~ children tutti i bambini; ~ day tutto il giorno; he refused ~ help ha rifiutato qualsiasi aiuto; for ~ that (nevertheless) ciononostante; in ~ sincerity in tutta sincerità; be ~ for essere favorevole a
- pron tutto; ~ of you/them tutti voi/loro; ~ of it tutto; ~ of the town tutta la città; in ~ in tutto; ~ in ~ tutto sommato; most of ~ più di ogni altra cosa; once and for ~ una volta per tutte
- adv completamente; ~ but quasi; ~ at once (at the same time) tutto in una volta; ~ at once, ~ of a sudden all'improvviso; ~ too soon troppo presto; ~ the same (nevertheless) ciononostante; ~ the better meglio ancora; she's not ~ that good un'attrice non è poi così brava come attrice; ~ in tutto; ⚽ esausto; thirty/three ~ (in sport) trenta/tre pari; ~ over (finished) tutto finito; (everywhere) dappertutto; it's ~ right (I don't mind) non fa niente; I'm ~ right (not hurt) non ho niente; ~ right! va bene!

allay /ə'leɪ/ vt placare (suspicions, anger)

allegation /ælɪ'geɪʃn/ n accusa f

allege /ə'ledʒ/ vt dichiarare. ~d adj presunto. ~dly adv a quanto si dice

allegiance /ə'liːdʒəns/ n fedeltà f

allerg|ic /ə'lɜːdʒɪk/ adj allergico. ~y n allergia f

alleviate /ə'liːvɪeɪt/ vt alleviare

alley /'ælɪ/ n vicolo m; (for bowling) corsia f

alliance /ə'laɪəns/ n alleanza f

alligator /'ælɪgeɪtə(r)/ n alligatore m

allocat|e /'æləkeɪt/ vt assegnare; distribuire (resources). ~ion n assegnazione f; (of resources) distribuzione f

allot /ə'lɒt/ vt (pt/pp allotted) distribuire. ~ment n distribuzione f; (share) parte f; (land) piccolo lotto m di terreno

allow /ə'laʊ/ vt permettere; (grant) accordare; (reckon on) contare; (agree) ammettere; ~ for tener conto di; ~ sb to do sth permettere a qcno di fare qcsa; you are not ~ed to... è vietato...

allowance /ə'laʊəns/ n sussidio m; (Am: pocket money) paghetta f; (for petrol etc) indennità f inv; (of luggage, duty free) limite m; make ~s for essere indulgente verso (sb); tener conto di (sth)

alloy /'ælɔɪ/ n lega f

allusion /ə'luːʒn/ n allusione f

ally¹ /'ælaɪ/ n alleato, -a mf

ally² /ə'laɪ/ vt (pt/pp -ied) alleare; ~ oneself with allearsi con

almighty /ɔːl'maɪtɪ/ adj (🔲: big) mega inv • the A~ l'Onnipotente m

almond /'ɑːmənd/ n mandorla f; (tree) mandorlo m

almost /'ɔːlməʊst/ adv quasi

alone /ə'ləʊn/ adj solo; leave me ~! lasciami in pace!; let ~ (not to mention) figurarsi • adv da solo

along /ə'lɒŋ/ prep lungo • adv ~ with assieme a; all ~ tutto il tempo; come ~! (hurry up) vieni qui!; I'll be ~ in a minute arrivo tra un attimo; move ~ spostarsi; move ~! circolare!

along'side adv lungo bordo • prep lungo; work ~ sb lavorare fianco a fianco con qcno

aloof /ə'luːf/ adj distante

aloud /ə'laʊd/ adv ad alta voce

alphabet /'ælfəbet/ n alfabeto m. ~ical adj alfabetico

Alps /ælps/ *npl* Alpi *fpl*

already /ɔːl'redɪ/ *adv* già

Alsatian /æl'seɪʃn/ *n* (*dog*) pastore *m* tedesco

also /'ɔːlsəʊ/ *adv* anche; ∼, I need... [e] inoltre, ho bisogno di...

altar /'ɔːltə(r)/ *n* altare *m*

alter /'ɔːltə(r)/ *vt* cambiare; aggiustare (*clothes*) ● *vi* cambiare. ∼ation *n* modifica *f*

alternate[1] /'ɔːltəneɪt/ *vi* alternarsi ● *vt* alternare

alternate[2] /ɔːl'tɜːnət/ *adj* alterno; on ∼ days a giorni alterni

alternative /ɔːl'tɜːnətɪv/ *adj* alternativo ● *n* alternativa *f*. ∼ly *adv* alternativamente

although /ɔːl'ðəʊ/ *conj* benché, sebbene

altitude /'æltɪtjuːd/ *n* altitudine *f*

altogether /ɔːltə'geðə(r)/ *adv* (*in all*) in tutto; (*completely*) completamente; I'm not ∼ sure non sono del tutto sicuro

aluminium /æljʊ'mɪnɪəm/ *n*, Am **aluminum** /ə'luːmɪnəm/ *n* alluminio *m*

always /'ɔːlweɪz/ *adv* sempre

am /æm/ ▷BE

a.m. *abbr* (ante meridiem) del mattino

amalgamate /ə'mælgəmeɪt/ *vt* fondere ● *vi* fondersi

amass /ə'mæs/ *vt* accumulare

amateur /'æmətə(r)/ *n* non professionista *mf*; *pej* dilettante *mf* ● *attrib* dilettante; ∼ dramatics filodrammatica *f*. ∼ish *adj* dilettantesco

amaze /ə'meɪz/ *vt* stupire. ∼d *adj* stupito. ∼ment *n* stupore *m*

amazing /ə'meɪzɪŋ/ *adj* incredibile

ambassador /æm'bæsədə(r)/ *n* ambasciatore, -trice *mf*

ambigu|ity /æmbɪ'gjuːətɪ/ *n* ambiguità *f inv*. ∼ous *adj* ambiguo

ambiti|on /æm'bɪʃn/ *n* ambizione

f; (*aim*) aspirazione *f*. ∼ous *adj* ambizioso

ambivalent /æm'bɪvələnt/ *adj* ambivalente

amble /'æmbl/ *vi* camminare senza fretta

ambulance /'æmbjʊləns/ *n* ambulanza *f*

ambush /'æmbʊʃ/ *n* imboscata *f* ● *vt* tendere un'imboscata a

amend /ə'mend/ *vt* modificare. ∼ment *n* modifica *f*. ∼s *npl* make ∼s fare ammenda (for, per)

amenities /ə'miːnətɪz/ *npl* comodità *fpl*

America /ə'merɪkə/ *n* America *f*. ∼n *adj* & *n* americano, -a *mf*

> **American dream** Il cosiddetto 'sogno americano' è la convinzione che negli Stati Uniti chiunque sia disposto a lavorare sodo possa migliorare la propria posizione economica e sociale. Per gli immigrati e le minoranze il concetto di *American dream* significa anche libertà e uguaglianza di diritti.
> *i*

amiable /'eɪmɪəbl/ *adj* amabile

amicable /'æmɪkəbl/ *adj* amichevole

ammonia /ə'məʊnɪə/ *n* ammoniaca *f*

ammunition /æmjʊ'nɪʃn/ *n* munizioni *fpl*

amnesty /'æmnəstɪ/ *n* amnistia *f*

among[st] /ə'mʌŋ[st]/ *prep* tra, fra

amount /ə'maʊnt/ *n* quantità *f inv*; (*sum of money*) importo *m* ● *vi* ∼ to ammontare a; *fig* equivalere a

amphibi|an /æm'fɪbɪən/ *n* anfibio *m*. ∼ous *adj* anfibio

amphitheatre /'æmfɪ-/ *n* anfiteatro *m*

ample /'æmpl/ *adj* (*large*) grande; (*proportions*) ampio; (*enough*)

a

largamente sufficiente

amplif|ier /'æmplɪfaɪə(r)/ n amplificatore m. ~y vt (pt/pp -ied) amplificare (sound)

amputat|e /'æmpjʊteɪt/ vt amputare. ~ion n amputazione f

amuse /ə'mju:z/ vt divertire. ~ment n divertimento m. ~ment arcade n sala f giochi

amusing /ə'mju:zɪŋ/ adj divertente

an /ən/, accentato /æn/ ▸ A

anaem|ia /ə'ni:mɪə/ n anemia f. ~ic adj anemico

anaesthetic /ænəs'θetɪk/ n anestesia f

anaesthet|ist /ə'ni:sθətɪst/ n anestesista mf

analogy /ə'nælədʒɪ/ n analogia f

analyse /'ænəlaɪz/ vt analizzare

analysis /ə'næləsɪs/ n analisi f inv

analyst /'ænəlɪst/ n analista m

analytical /ænə'lɪtɪkl/ adj analitico

anarch|ist /'ænəkɪst/ n anarchico, -a mf. ~y n anarchia f

anatom|ical /ænə'tɒmɪkl/ adj anatomico. ~ically adv anatomicamente. ~y n anatomia f

ancest|or /'ænsestə(r)/ n antenato, -a mf. ~ry n antenati mpl

anchor /'æŋkə(r)/ n ancora f • vi gettar l'ancora • vt ancorare

anchovy /'æntʃəvɪ/ n acciuga f

ancient /'eɪnʃənt/ adj antico; ⒤ vecchio

ancillary /æn'sɪlərɪ/ adj ausiliario

and /ænd/, accentato /ænd/ conj e; two ~ two due più due; six hundred ~ two seicentodue; more ~ more sempre più; nice ~ warm bello caldo; try ~ come cerca di venire; go ~ get vai a prendere

anecdote /'ænɪkdəʊt/ n aneddoto m

anew /ə'nju:/ adv di nuovo

angel /'eɪndʒl/ n angelo m. ~ic adj angelico

anger /'æŋgə(r)/ n rabbia f • vt far arrabbiare

angle¹ /'æŋgl/ n angolo m; fig angolazione f; at an ~ storto

angle² vi pescare con la lenza; ~ for fig cercare di ottenere; ~r n pescatore, -trice mf

Anglican /'æŋglɪkən/ adj & n anglicano, -a mf

angr|y /'æŋgrɪ/ adj (-ier, -iest) arrabbiato; get ~y arrabbiarsi; ~y with or at sb arrabbiato con qcno; ~y at or about sth arrabbiato per qcsa. ~ily adv rabbiosamente

anguish /'æŋgwɪʃ/ n angoscia f

animal /'ænɪml/ adj & n animale m

animate¹ /'ænɪmət/ adj animato

animat|e² /'ænɪmeɪt/ vt animare. ~ed adj animato; (person) vivace. ~ion n animazione f

animosity /ænɪ'mɒsətɪ/ n animosità f inv

ankle /'æŋkl/ n caviglia f

annihilat|e /ə'naɪəleɪt/ vt annientare. ~ion n annientamento m

anniversary /ænɪ'vɜːsərɪ/ n anniversario m

announce /ə'naʊns/ vt annunciare. ~ment n annuncio m. ~r n annunciatore, -trice mf

annoy /ə'nɔɪ/ vt dare fastidio a; get ~ed essere infastidito. ~ance n seccatura f; (anger) irritazione f. ~ing adj fastidioso

annual /'ænjʊəl/ adj annuale; (income) annuo • n (Bot) pianta f annua; (children's book) almanacco m

annul /ə'nʌl/ vt (pt/pp annulled) annullare

anonymous /ə'nɒnɪməs/ adj anonimo

anorak /'ænəræk/ n giacca f a vento

another /ə'nʌðə(r)/ adj & pron; ~ [one] un altro, un'altra; in ~ way diversamente; one ~ l'un l'altro

answer /'ɑːnsə(r)/ n risposta f; (*solution*) soluzione f • vt rispondere a (person, question, letter); esaudire (prayer); ~ the door aprire la porta; ~ the telephone rispondere al telefono • vi rispondere; ~ back ribattere; ~ for rispondere di. ~able adj responsabile; be ~able to sb rispondere a qcno. ~ing machine n (Teleph) segreteria f telefonica

ant /ænt/ n formica f

antagonis|m /æn'tægənɪzm/ n antagonismo m. ~tic adj antagonistico

antagonize /æn'tægənaɪz/ vt provocare l'ostilità di

Antarctic /æn'tɑːktɪk/ n Antartico m • adj antartico

antenatal /æntɪ'neɪtl/ adj prenatale

antenna /æn'tenə/ n antenna f

anthem /'ænθəm/ n inno m

anthology /æn'θɒlədʒɪ/ n antologia f

anthropology /ænθrə'pɒlədʒɪ/ n antropologia f

anti-'aircraft /æntɪ-/ adj antiaerea

antibiotic /æntɪbaɪ'ɒtɪk/ n antibiotico m

anticipat|e /æn'tɪsɪpeɪt/ vt prevedere; (*forestall*) anticipare. ~ion n anticipo m; (*excitement*) attesa f

anti'climax n delusione f

anti'clockwise adj & adv in senso antiorario

antidote /'æntɪdəʊt/ n antidoto m

antifreeze /'æntɪfriːz/ n antigelo m

antiquated /'æntɪkweɪtɪd/ adj antiquato

antique /æn'tiːk/ adj antico • n antichità f inv. ~ dealer n antiquario, -a mf

antiquity /æn'tɪkwətɪ/ n antichità f

anti'septic adj & n antisettico m

anti'social adj (behaviour) antisociale; (person) asociale

antlers /'æntləz/ npl corna fpl

anus /'eɪnəs/ n ano m

anxiety /æŋ'zaɪətɪ/ n ansia f

anxious /'æŋkʃəs/ adj ansioso. ~ly adv con ansia

any /'enɪ/
● adj (no matter which) qualsiasi, qualunque; ~ colour/number you like qualsiasi colore/numero ti piaccia; we don't have ~ wine/biscuits non abbiamo vino/biscotti; for ~ reason per qualsiasi ragione

any is often not translated: have we ~ wine/biscuits? abbiamo del vino/dei biscotti?

● pron (some) ne; (no matter which) uno qualsiasi; I don't want ~ [of it] non ne voglio [nessuno]; there aren't ~ non ce ne sono; have we ~? ne abbiamo?; have you read ~ of her books? hai letto qualcuno dei suoi libri?

● adv I can't go ~ quicker non posso andare più in fretta; is it ~ better? va un po' meglio?; would you like ~ more? ne vuoi ancora?; I can't eat ~ more non posso mangiare più niente

'anybody pron chiunque; (after negative) nessuno; I haven't seen ~ non ho visto nessuno

'anyhow adv ad ogni modo, comunque; (badly) non importa come

'anyone pron = anybody

'anything pron qualche cosa, qualcosa; (no matter what) qualsiasi cosa; (after negative) niente; take/buy ~ you like prendi/compra quello che vuoi; I don't remember ~ non mi ricordo niente; he's ~ but stupid è tutto, ma non stupido; I'll do ~ but that farò qualsiasi cosa, tranne quello

'anyway adv ad ogni modo, comunque

'anywhere adv dovunque; (after negative) da nessuna parte; put it ~ mettilo dove vuoi; I can't find it ~ non lo trovo da nessuna parte; ~ else da qualch'altra parte; (after negative) da nessun'altra parte; I don't want to go ~ else non voglio andare da nessun'altra parte

apart /ə'pɑːt/ adv lontano; live ~ vivere separati; 100 miles ~ lontani 100 miglia; ~ from a parte; you can't tell them ~ non si possono distinguere; joking ~ scherzi a parte

apartment /ə'pɑːtmənt/ n (Am: flat) appartamento m; in my ~ a casa mia

apathy /'æpəθɪ/ n apatia f

ape /eɪp/ n scimmia f • vt scimmiottare

aperitif /ə'perətiːf/ n aperitivo m

aperture /'æpətʃə(r)/ n apertura f

apex /'eɪpeks/ n vertice m

apologetic /əpɒlə'dʒetɪk/ adj (air, remark) di scusa; be ~ essere spiacente

apologize /ə'pɒlədʒaɪz/ vi scusarsi (for per)

apology /ə'pɒlədʒɪ/ n scusa f; fig an ~ for a dinner una sottospecie di cena

apostle /ə'pɒsl/ n apostolo m

apostrophe /ə'pɒstrəfɪ/ n apostrofo m

appal /ə'pɔːl/ vt (pt/pp appalled) sconvolgere. ~ling adj sconvolgente

apparatus /æpə'reɪtəs/ n apparato m

apparent /ə'pærənt/ adj evidente; (seeming) apparente. ~ly adv apparentemente

apparition /æpə'rɪʃn/ n apparizione f

appeal /ə'piːl/ n appello m; (attraction) attrattiva f • vi fare appello;

to (be attractive to) attrarre. ~ing adj attraente

appear /ə'pɪə(r)/ vi apparire; (seem) sembrare; (publication:) uscire; (Theat) esibirsi. ~ance n apparizione f; (look) aspetto m; to all ~ances a giudicare dalle apparenze; keep up ~ances salvare le apparenze

appease /ə'piːz/ vt placare

appendicitis /əpendɪ'saɪtɪs/ n appendicite f

appendix /ə'pendɪks/ n (pl -ices /-ɪsiːz/) (of book) appendice f; (pl -es) (Anat) appendice f

appetite /'æpɪtaɪt/ n appetito m

applaud /ə'plɔːd/ vt/i applaudire. ~se n applauso m

apple /'æpl/ n mela f. ~-tree n melo m

appliance /ə'plaɪəns/ n attrezzo m; [electrical] ~ elettrodomestico m

applicable /'æplɪkəbl/ adj be ~ to essere valido per; not ~ (on form) non applicabile

applicant /'æplɪkənt/ n candidato, -a mf

application /æplɪ'keɪʃn/ n applicazione f; (request) domanda f; (for job) candidatura f. ~ form n modulo m di domanda

applied /ə'plaɪd/ adj applicato

apply /ə'plaɪ/ vt (pt/pp -ied) applicare; ~ oneself applicarsi • vi applicarsi; (law:) essere applicabile; ~ to (ask) rivolgersi a; ~ for fare domanda per (job etc)

appoint /ə'pɔɪnt/ vt nominare; fissare (time). ~ment n appuntamento m; (to job) nomina f; (job) posto m

appraisal /ə'preɪz(ə)l/ n valutazione f

appreciable /ə'priːʃəbl/ adj sensibile

appreciat|e /ə'priːʃɪeɪt/ vt apprezzare; (understand) comprendere • vi (increase in value) aumentare di valore.

~ion n (gratitude) riconoscenza f; (enjoyment) apprezzamento m; (understanding) comprensione f; (in value) aumento m. ~ive adj riconoscente

apprehens|ion /æprɪ'henʃn/ n arresto m; (fear) apprensione f. ~ive adj apprensivo

apprentice /ə'prentɪs/ n apprendista mf. ~ship n apprendistato m

approach /ə'prəʊtʃ/ n avvicinamento m; (to problem) approccio m; (access) accesso m; make ~es to fare degli approcci con ● vi avvicinarsi ● vt avvicinarsi a; (with request) rivolgersi a; affrontare (problem). ~able adj accessibile

appropriate¹ /ə'prəʊprɪət/ adj appropriato

appropriate² /ə'prəʊprɪeɪt/ vt appropriarsi di

approval /ə'pruːvl/ n approvazione f; on ~ in prova

approv|e /ə'pruːv/ vt approvare ● vi ~e of approvare (sth); avere una buona opinione di (sb). ~ing adj (smile, nod) d'approvazione

approximate /ə'prɒksɪmət/ adj approssimativo. ~ly adv approssimativamente

approximation /əprɒksɪ'meɪʃn/ n approssimazione f

apricot /'eɪprɪkɒt/ n albicocca f

April /'eɪprəl/ n aprile m; ~ Fool's Day il primo d'aprile

apron /'eɪprən/ n grembiule m

apt /æpt/ adj appropriato; be ~ to do sth avere tendenza a fare qcsa

aptitude /'æptɪtjuːd/ n disposizione f. ~ test n test m inv attitudinale

aquarium /ə'kweərɪəm/ n acquario m

Aquarius /ə'kweərɪəs/ n (Astr) Acquario m

aquatic /ə'kwætɪk/ adj acquatico

Arab /'ærəb/ adj & n arabo, -a mf. ~ian adj arabo

Arabic /'ærəbɪk/ adj arabo; ~ numerals numeri mpl arabici ● n arabo m

arable /'ærəbl/ adj coltivabile

arbitrary /'ɑːbɪtrərɪ/ adj arbitrario

arbitrat|e /'ɑːbɪtreɪt/ vi arbitrare. ~ion n arbitraggio m

arc /ɑːk/ n arco m

arcade /ɑːˈkeɪd/ n portico m; (shops) galleria f

arch /ɑːtʃ/ n arco m; (of foot) dorso m del piede

archaeological /ɑːkɪəˈlɒdʒɪkl/ adj archeologico

archaeolog|ist /ɑːkɪˈɒlədʒɪst/ n archeologo, -a mf. ~y n archeologia f

archaic /ɑːˈkeɪɪk/ adj arcaico

arch'bishop /ɑːtʃ-/ n arcivescovo m

architect /'ɑːkɪtekt/ n architetto m. ~ural adj architettonico

architecture /'ɑːkɪtektʃə(r)/ n architettura f

archives /'ɑːkaɪvz/ npl archivi mpl

archway /'ɑːtʃweɪ/ n arco m

Arctic /'ɑːktɪk/ adj artico ● n the ~ l'Artico

ardent /'ɑːdənt/ adj ardente

arduous /'ɑːdjʊəs/ adj arduo

are /ɑː(r)/ ▷ BE

area /'eərɪə/ n area f; (region) zona f; (fig: field) campo m. ~ code n prefisso m [telefonico]

arena /əˈriːnə/ n arena f

Argentina /ɑːdʒənˈtiːnə/ n Argentina f

Argentinian /-ˈtɪnɪən/ adj & n argentino, -a mf

argue /'ɑːgjuː/ vi litigare (about su); (debate) dibattere; don't ~! non discutere! ● vt (debate) dibattere; (reason) ~ that sostenere che

argument /'ɑːgjʊmənt/ n argomento m; (reasoning) ragionamento m; have an ~ litigare. ~ative adj polemico

arid /'ærɪd/ adj arido

Aries /'eəriːz/ n (Astr) Ariete m

arise /ə'raɪz/ vi (pt arose, pp arisen) (opportunity, need, problem:) presentarsi; (result) derivare

aristocracy /ærɪ'stɒkrəsɪ/ n aristocrazia f

aristocrat /'ærɪstəkræt/ n aristocratico, -a mf. ~ic adj aristocratico

arithmetic /ə'rɪθmətɪk/ n aritmetica f

arm /ɑːm/ n braccio m; (of chair) bracciolo m; ~s pl (weapons) armi fpl; ~ in ~ a braccetto; up in ~s ① furioso (about per) ● vt armare

'armchair n poltrona f

armed /ɑːmd/ adj armato; ~ forces forze fpl armate; ~ robbery rapina f a mano armata

armour /'ɑːmə(r)/ n armatura f. ~ed adj (vehicle) blindato

'armpit n ascella f

army /'ɑːmɪ/ n esercito m; join the ~ arruolarsi

aroma /ə'rəʊmə/ n aroma f. ~tic adj aromatico

arose /ə'rəʊz/ ▷ ARISE

around /ə'raʊnd/ adv intorno; all ~ tutt'intorno; I'm not from ~ here non sono di qui; he's not ~ non c'è ● prep intorno a; in giro per (room, shops, world)

arouse /ə'raʊz/ vt svegliare; (sexually) eccitare

arrange /ə'reɪndʒ/ vt sistemare (furniture, books); organizzare (meeting); fissare (date, time); ~ to do sth combinare di fare qcsa. ~ment n (of furniture) sistemazione f; (Mus) arrangiamento m; (agreement) accordo; (of flowers) composizione f; make ~ments prendere disposizioni

arrears /ə'rɪəz/ npl arretrati mpl; be in ~ essere in arretrato; paid in ~ pagato a lavoro eseguito

arrest /ə'rest/ n arresto m; under ~ in stato d'arresto ● vt arrestare

arrival /ə'raɪvl/ n arrivo m; new ~s pl nuovi arrivati mpl

arrive /ə'raɪv/ vi arrivare; ~ at fig raggiungere

arrogan|ce /'ærəgəns/ n arroganza f. ~t adj arrogante

arrow /'ærəʊ/ n freccia f

arse /ɑːs/ n ① culo m

arsenic /'ɑːsənɪk/ n arsenico m

arson /'ɑːsn/ n incendio m doloso. ~ist n incendiario, -a mf

art /ɑːt/ n arte f; ~s and crafts pl artigianato m; the A~s pl l'arte f; A~s degree (Univ) laurea f in Lettere

artery /'ɑːtərɪ/ n arteria f

'art gallery n galleria f d'arte

arthritis /ɑː'θraɪtɪs/ n artrite f

artichoke /'ɑːtɪtʃəʊk/ n carciofo m

article /'ɑːtɪkl/ n articolo m; ~ of clothing capo m d'abbigliamento

articulate¹ /ɑː'tɪkjʊlət/ adj (speech) chiaro; be ~ esprimersi bene

articulate² /ɑː'tɪkjʊleɪt/ vt scandire (words). ~d lorry n autotreno m

artificial /ɑːtɪ'fɪʃl/ adj artificiale. ~ly adv artificialmente; (smile) artificiosamente

artillery /ɑː'tɪlərɪ/ n artiglieria f

artist /'ɑːtɪst/ n artista m

as /æz/ conj come; (since) siccome; (while) mentre; as he grew older diventando vecchio; as you get to know her conoscendola meglio; young as she is per quanto sia giovane ● prep come; as a friend come amico; as a child da bambino; as a foreigner in quanto straniero; disguised as travestito da ● adv as well (also) anche; as soon as I get home [non] appena arrivo a casa; as quick as you veloce quanto te; as quick as you can più veloce che puoi; as far as (distance) fino a; as far as I'm concerned per quanto mi riguarda; as long as finché; (provided that) purché

asbestos /æz'bestɒs/ n amianto m

ascend /ə'send/ vi salire ● vt salire a (throne)

Ascension /ə'senʃn/ n (Relig) Ascensione f

ascent /ə'sent/ n ascesa f

ascertain /æsə'teɪn/ vt accertare

ash¹ /æʃ/ n (tree) frassino m

ash² n cenere f

ashamed /ə'ʃeɪmd/ adj be/feel ~ vergognarsi

ashore /ə'ʃɔː(r)/ adv a terra; go ~ sbarcare

ash: ~tray n portacenere m. A~ 'Wednesday n mercoledì m inv delle Ceneri

Asia /'eɪʒə/ n Asia f. ~n adj & n asiatico, -a mf. ~tic adj asiatico

aside /ə'saɪd/ adv take sb ~ prendere qcno a parte; put sth ~ mettere qcsa da parte; ~ from you a parte te

ask /ɑːsk/ vt fare (question); (invite) invitare; ~ sb sth domandare or chiedere qcsa a qcno; ~ sb to do sth domandare or chiedere a qcno di fare qcsa ● vi ~ about sth informarsi su qcsa; ~ after chiedere [notizie] di; ~ for chiedere (sth); chiedere di (sb); ~ for trouble 🖵 andare in cerca di guai. □ ~ in vt ~ sb in invitare qcno ad entrare. □ ~ out vt ~ sb out chiedere a qcno di uscire

askew /ə'skjuː/ adj & adv di traverso

asleep /ə'sliːp/ adj be ~ dormire; fall ~ addormentarsi

asparagus /ə'spærəgəs/ n asparagi mpl

aspect /'æspekt/ n aspetto m

asphalt /'æsfælt/ n asfalto m

aspire /ə'spaɪə(r)/ vi ~ to aspirare a

ass /æs/ n asino m

assassin /ə'sæsɪn/ n assassino, -a mf. ~ate vt assassinare. ~ation n as-

sassinio m

assault /ə'sɔːlt/ n (Mil) assalto m; (Jur) aggressione f ● vt aggredire

assemble /ə'sembl/ vi radunarsi ● vt radunare; (Techn) montare

assembly /ə'semblɪ/ n assemblea f; (Sch) assemblea f giornaliera di alunni e professori di una scuola; (Techn) montaggio m. ~ line n catena f di montaggio

assent /ə'sent/ n assenso m ● vi acconsentire

assert /ə'sɜːt/ vt asserire; far valere (one's rights); ~ oneself farsi valere. ~ion n asserzione f. ~ive adj be ~ive farsi valere

assess /ə'ses/ vt valutare; (for tax purposes) stabilire l'imponibile di. ~ment n valutazione f; (of tax) accertamento m

asset /'æset/ n (advantage) vantaggio m; (person) elemento m prezioso. ~s pl inv beni mpl; (on balance sheet) attivo msg

assign /ə'saɪn/ vt assegnare. ~ment n (task) incarico m

assimilate /ə'sɪmɪleɪt/ vt assimilare; integrare (person)

assist /ə'sɪst/ vt/i assistere; ~ sb to do sth assistere qcno nel fare qcsa. ~ance n assistenza f. ~ant adj ~ant manager vicedirettore, -trice mf ● n assistente mf; (in shop) commesso, -a mf

associate¹ /ə'səʊʃɪeɪt/ vt associare (with a); be ~ed with sth (involved in) essere coinvolto in qcsa ● vi ~e with frequentare. ~ion n associazione f. A~ion 'Football n [gioco m del] calcio m

associate² /ə'səʊʃɪət/ adj associato ● n collega mf; (member) socio, -a

assorted /ə'sɔːtɪd/ adj assortito. ~ment n assortimento m

assume /ə'sjuːm/ vt presumere; assumere (control); ~e office entrare in carica; ~ing that you're right,...

a

ammettendo che tu abbia ragione,...

assumption /əˈsʌmpʃn/ n supposizione f; on the ~ that partendo dal presupposto che; the A~ (Relig) l'Assunzione f

assurance /əˈʃʊərəns/ n assicurazione f; (confidence) sicurezza f

assure /əˈʃʊə(r)/ vt assicurare. ~d adj sicuro

asterisk /ˈæstərɪsk/ n asterisco m

asthma /ˈæsmə/ n asma f. ~tic adj asmatico

astonish /əˈstɒnɪʃ/ vt stupire. ~ing adj stupefacente. ~ment n stupore m

astound /əˈstaʊnd/ vt stupire

astray /əˈstreɪ/ adv go ~ smarrirsi; (morally) uscire dalla retta via; lead ~ traviare

astronaut /ˈæstrənɔːt/ n astronauta mf

astronom|er /əˈstrɒnəmə(r)/ n astronomo, -a mf. ~ical adj astronomico. ~y n astronomia f

astute /əˈstjuːt/ adj astuto

asylum /əˈsaɪləm/ n [political] ~ asilo m politico; [lunatic] ~ manicomio m

at /ət/, accentato /æt/ prep a; at the station/the market alla stazione/al mercato; at the office/the bank in ufficio/banca; at the beginning all'inizio; at John's da John; at the hairdresser's dal parrucchiere; at home a casa; at work al lavoro; at school a scuola; at a party/wedding a una festa/un matrimonio; at 1 o'clock all'una; at 50 km an hour a 50 all'ora; at Christmas/Easter a Natale/Pasqua; at times talvolta; two at a time due alla volta; good at languages bravo nelle lingue; at sb's request su richiesta di qcno; are you at all worried? sei preoccupato?

ate /et/ ▷EAT

atheist /ˈeɪθɪɪst/ n ateo, -a mf

athlet|e /ˈæθliːt/ n atleta mf. ~ic adj atletico. ~ics n atletica fsg

Atlantic /ətˈlæntɪk/ adj & n the ~ [Ocean] l'[Oceano m] Atlantico m

atlas /ˈætləs/ n atlante m

atmospher|e /ˈætməsfɪə(r)/ n atmosfera f. ~ic adj atmosferico

atom /ˈætəm/ n atomo m. ~ bomb n bomba f atomica

atomic /əˈtɒmɪk/ adj atomico

atrocious /əˈtrəʊʃəs/ adj atroce; (meal, weather) abominevole

atrocity /əˈtrɒsəti/ n atrocità f inv

attach /əˈtætʃ/ vt attaccare; attribuire (importance); be ~ed to (fig) essere attaccato a

attachment /əˈtætʃmənt/ n (affection) attaccamento m; (accessory) accessorio m; (to email) allegato m

attack /əˈtæk/ n attacco m; (physical) aggressione f ● vt attaccare; (physically) aggredire. ~er n assalitore, -trice mf; (critic) detrattore, -trice mf

attain /əˈteɪn/ vt realizzare (ambition); raggiungere (success, age, goal)

attempt /əˈtempt/ n tentativo m ● vt tentare

attend /əˈtend/ vt essere presente a; (go regularly to) frequentare; (doctor:) avere in cura ● vi essere presente; (pay attention) prestare attenzione. □ ~ to vt occuparsi di; (in shop) servire. ~ance n presenza f. ~ant n guardiano, -a mf

attention /əˈtenʃn/ n attenzione f; ~! (Mil) attenti; pay ~ prestare attenzione; need ~ aver bisogno di attenzioni; (skin, hair, plant:) dover essere curato; (car, tyres:) dover essere riparato; for the ~ of all'attenzione di

attentive /əˈtentɪv/ adj (pupil, audience) attento

attic /ˈætɪk/ n soffitta f

attitude /ˈætɪtjuːd/ n atteggiamento m

attorney /əˈtɜːnɪ/ n (Am: lawyer) avvocato m; power of ~ delega f

attract /əˈtrækt/ vt attirare. ~**ion** n attrazione f; (feature) attrattiva f. ~**ive** adj (person) attraente; (proposal, price) allettante

attribute[1] /ˈætrɪbjuːt/ n attributo m

attribute[2] /əˈtrɪbjuːt/ vt attribuire

aubergine /ˈəʊbəʒiːn/ n melanzana f

auction /ˈɔːkʃn/ n asta f ● vt vendere all'asta. ~**eer** n banditore m

audaci|ous /ɔːˈdeɪʃəs/ adj sfacciato; (daring) audace. ~**ty** n sfacciataggine f; (daring) audacia f

audible /ˈɔːdəbl/ adj udibile

audience /ˈɔːdɪəns/ n (Theat) pubblico m; (TV) telespettatori mpl; (Radio) ascoltatori mpl; (meeting) udienza f

audit /ˈɔːdɪt/ n verifica f del bilancio ● vt verificare

audition /ɔːˈdɪʃn/ n audizione f ● vi fare un'audizione

auditor /ˈɔːdɪtə(r)/ n revisore m di conti

auditorium /ɔːdɪˈtɔːrɪəm/ n sala f

augment /ɔːɡˈment/ vt aumentare

augur /ˈɔːɡə(r)/ vi ~ well/ill essere di buon/cattivo augurio

August /ˈɔːɡəst/ n agosto m

aunt /ɑːnt/ n zia f

au pair /əʊˈpeə(r)/ n ~ [girl] ragazza f alla pari

aura /ˈɔːrə/ n aura f

auster|e /ɒˈstɪə(r)/ adj austero. ~**ity** n austerità f

Australia /ɒˈstreɪlɪə/ n Australia f. ~**n** adj & n australiano, -a mf

Austria /ˈɒstrɪə/ n Austria f. ~**n** adj & n austriaco, -a mf

authentic /ɔːˈθentɪk/ adj autentico. ~**ate** vt autenticare. ~**ity** n autenticità f

author /ˈɔːθə(r)/ n autore m

authoritative /ɔːˈθɒrɪtətɪv/ adj autorevole; (manner) autoritario

authority /ɔːˈθɒrətɪ/ n autorità f; (permission) autorizzazione f; be in ~ over avere autorità su

authorization /ɔːθəraɪˈzeɪʃn/ n autorizzazione f

authorize /ˈɔːθəraɪz/ vt autorizzare

autobi'ography /ɔːtə-/ n autobiografia f

autograph /ˈɔːtə-/ n autografo m

automate /ˈɔːtəmeɪt/ vt automatizzare

automatic /ɔːtəˈmætɪk/ adj automatico ● n (car) macchina f col cambio automatico; (washing machine) lavatrice f automatica. ~**ally** adv automaticamente

automation /ɔːtəˈmeɪʃn/ n automazione f

automobile /ˈɔːtəməbiːl/ n automobile f

autonom|ous /ɔːˈtɒnəməs/ adj autonomo. ~**y** n autonomia f

autopsy /ˈɔːtɒpsɪ/ n autopsia f

autumn /ˈɔːtəm/ n autunno m. ~**al** adj autunnale

auxiliary /ɔːɡˈzɪlɪərɪ/ adj ausiliario ● n ausiliare m

avail /əˈveɪl/ n to no ~ invano ● vi ~ oneself of approfittare di

available /əˈveɪləbl/ adj disponibile; (book, record etc) in vendita

avalanche /ˈævəlɑːnʃ/ n valanga f

avarice /ˈævərɪs/ n avidità f

avenue /ˈævənjuː/ n viale m; fig strada f

average /ˈævərɪdʒ/ adj medio; (mediocre) mediocre ● n media f; on ~ in media ● vt (sales, attendance) etc: raggiungere una media di. □ ~ **out at** vt risultare in media

avers|e /əˈvɜːs/ adj not be ~e to sth non essere contro qcsa. ~**ion** n avversione f (to per)

avert /əˈvɜːt/ vt evitare (crisis); di-

a

stogliere (eyes)

aviation /ɪevɪˈeɪʃn/ n aviazione f

b

avid /ˈævɪd/ adj avido (for di); (reader) appassionato

avocado /ævəˈkɑːdəʊ/ n avocado m

avoid /əˈvɔɪd/ vt evitare. ~**able** adj evitabile

await /əˈweɪt/ vt attendere

awake /əˈweɪk/ adj sveglio; **wide** ~ completamente sveglio ● vi (pt awoke, pp awoken) svegliarsi

awaken /əˈweɪkən/ vt svegliare. ~**ing** n risveglio m

award /əˈwɔːd/ n premio m; (medal) riconoscimento m; (of prize) assegnazione f ● vt assegnare; (hand over) consegnare

aware /əˈweə(r)/ adj be ~ of (sense) percepire; (know) essere conscio di; become ~ of accorgersi di; (learn) venire a sapere di; be ~ that rendersi conto che. ~**ness** n percezione f; (knowledge) consapevolezza f

awash /əˈwɒʃ/ adj inondato (with di)

away /əˈweɪ/ adv via; go/stay ~ andare/stare via; he's ~ from his desk/the office non è alla sua scrivania/in ufficio; far ~ lontano; four kilometres ~ a quattro chilometri; play ~ (Sport) giocare fuori casa. ~ **game** n partita f fuori casa

awe /ɔː/ n soggezione f

awful /ˈɔːfl/ adj terribile. ~**ly** adv terribilmente; (pretty) estremamente

awkward /ˈɔːkwəd/ adj (movement) goffo; (moment, situation) imbarazzante; (time) scomodo. ~**ly** adv (move) goffamente; (say) con imbarazzo

awning /ˈɔːnɪŋ/ n tendone m

awoke(n) /əˈwəʊk (ən)/ ▷ **AWAKE**

axe /æks/ n scure f ● vt (pres p axing) fare dei tagli a (budget); sopprimere (jobs); annullare (project)

axis /ˈæksɪs/ n (pl axes -siːz/) asse m

axle /ˈæksl/ n (Techn) asse m

Bb

BA n abbr Bachelor of Arts

babble /ˈbæbl/ vi farfugliare; (stream:) gorgogliare

baby /ˈbeɪbɪ/ n bambino, -a mf; (🔢: darling) tesoro m

baby: ~ **carriage** n Am carrozzina f. ~**ish** adj bambinesco. ~-**sit** vi fare da baby-sitter. ~-**sitter** n baby-sitter mf

bachelor /ˈbætʃələ(r)/ n scapolo m; B~ of Arts/Science laureato, -a mf in lettere/in scienze

back /bæk/ n schiena f; (of horse, hand) dorso m; (of chair) schienale m; (of house, cheque, page) retro m; (in football) difesa f; at the ~ in fondo; in the ~ (Auto) dietro; ~ to front (sweater) il davanti di dietro; at the ~ of beyond in un posto sperduto ● adj posteriore; (taxes, payments) arretrato ● adv indietro; (returned) di ritorno; turn/move ~ tornare/ spostarsi indietro; put it ~ here; there rimettilo qui/là; ~ at home di ritorno a casa; I'll be ~ in five minutes torno fra cinque minuti; I'm just ~ sono appena tornato; when do you want the book ~? quando rivuoi il libro?; pay ~ ripagare (sb); restituire (money); ~ **in power** di nuovo al potere ● vt (support) sostenere; (with money) finanziare; puntare su (horse); (cover the back of) rivestire il retro di ● vi (Auto) fare retromarcia. □ ~ **down** vi battere in ritirata. □ ~ **in** vi (Auto) entrare in retromarcia; (person:) entrare camminando all'indietro. □ ~ **out** vi (Auto) uscire in retromarcia; (person:) uscire camminando all'indietro; *fig* tirarsi indietro (of da). □ ~ **up** *vt* sostenere; confermare (person's alibi); (*Comput*) fare una copia di salvataggio di; be ~ed up (traffic): essere congestionato ● *vi* (*Auto*) fare retromarcia

back: ~**ache** *n* mal *m* di schiena. ~**bone** *n* spina *f* dorsale. ~**date** *vt* retrodatare (cheque). ~ '**door** *n* porta *f* di servizio

backer /ˈbækə(r)/ *n* sostenitore, -trice *mf*; (*with money*) finanziatore, -trice *mf*

back: ~ '**fire** *vi* (*Auto*) avere un ritorno di fiamma; (*fig: plan*) fallire. ~**ground** *n* sfondo *m*; (*environment*) ambiente *m*. ~**hand** *n* (*tennis*) rovescio *m*

backing /ˈbækɪŋ/ *n* (*support*) supporto *m*; (*material*) riserva *f*; (*Mus*) accompagnamento *m*. ~ **group** gruppo *m* d'accompagnamento

back: ~**lash** *n fig* reazione *f* opposta. ~**log** *n* log of work lavoro *m* arretrato. ~**side** *n* 🅸 fondoschiena *m inv*. ~**slash** *n* (*Typ*) barra *f* retroversa. ~**stage** *adj* & *adv* dietro le quinte. ~**stroke** *n* dorso *m*. ~ '**up** *n* rinforzi *mpl*; (*Comput*) riserva *f*

backward /ˈbækwəd/ *adj* (step) indietro; (child) lento nell'apprendimento; (country) arretrato ● *adv* ~**s** (*also Am:*) indietro; (fall, walk) all'indietro; ~**s** and forwards avanti e indietro

back: ~**water** *n fig* luogo *m* allo scarto. ~ '**yard** *n* cortile *m*

bacon /ˈbeɪkn/ *n* ≈ pancetta *f*

bacteria /bækˈtɪərɪə/ *npl* batteri *mpl*

bad /bæd/ *adj* (worse, worst) cattivo; (weather, habit, news, accident) brutto; (apple etc) marcio; the light is ~ non c'è una buona luce; use ~ language dire delle parolacce; feel ~ sentirsi male; (*feel guilty*) sentirsi in colpa; have a ~ back avere dei problemi alla schiena; smoking is ~ for you fumare fa male; go ~ an-

dare a male; that's just too ~! pazienza!; not ~ niente male

bade /bæd/ ▷**BID**

badge /bædʒ/ *n* distintivo *m*

badger /ˈbædʒə(r)/ *n* tasso *m* ● *vt* tormentare

badly /ˈbædlɪ/ *adv* male; (hurt) gravemente; ~ off povero; ~ behaved maleducato; need ~ aver estremamente bisogno di

bad-'mannered *adj* maleducato

badminton /ˈbædmɪntən/ *n* badminton *m*

bad-'tempered *adj* irascibile

baffle /ˈbæfl/ *vt* confondere

bag /bæg/ *n* borsa *f*; (*of paper*) sacchetto *m*; old ~ 🅸 megera *f*; ~s under the eyes occhiaie *fpl*; ~s of 🅸 un sacco di

baggage /ˈbægɪdʒ/ *n* bagagli *mpl*

baggy /ˈbægɪ/ *adj* (clothes) ampio

'bagpipes *npl* cornamusa *fsg*

bail /beɪl/ *n* cauzione *f*; on ~ su cauzione ● bail out *vt* (*Naut*) aggottare; ~ sb out (*Jur*) pagare la cauzione per qcno ● *vi* (*Aeron*) paracadutarsi

bait /beɪt/ *n* esca *f* ● *vt* innescare; (*fig: torment*) tormentare

bake /beɪk/ *vt* cuocere al forno; (*make*) fare ● *vi* cuocersi al forno

baker /ˈbeɪkə(r)/ *n* fornaio, -a *mf*, panettiere, -a *mf*; ~'s [shop] panetteria *f*. ~y *n* panificio *m*, forno *m*

balance /ˈbæləns/ *n* equilibrio *m*; (*Comm*) bilancio *m*; (*outstanding sum*) saldo *m*; [bank] ~ saldo *m*; be or hang in the ~ *fig* essere in sospeso ● *vt* bilanciare; equilibrare (budget); (*Comm*) fare il bilancio di (books) ● *vi* bilanciarsi; (*Comm*) essere in pareggio. ~d *adj* equilibrato. ~ sheet *n* bilancio *m* [d'esercizio]

balcony /ˈbælkənɪ/ *n* balcone *m*

bald /bɔːld/ *adj* (person) calvo; (tyre) liscio; (statement) nudo e crudo; go ~

~ perdere i capelli

bale /beɪl/ n balla f

ball[1] /bɔːl/ n palla f; (football) pallone m; (of yarn) gomitolo m; on the ~ 🄵 sveglio

ball[2] n (dance) ballo m

ballad /ˈbæləd/ n ballata f

ballast /ˈbæləst/ n zavorra f

ball-'bearing n cuscinetto m a sfera

ballerina /bæləˈriːnə/ n ballerina f [classica]

ballet /ˈbæleɪ/ n balletto m; (art form) danza f; ~ **dancer** n ballerino, -a mf [classico, -a]

balloon /bəˈluːn/ n pallone m; (Aeron) mongolfiera f

ballot /ˈbælət/ n votazione f. ~-**box** n urna f. ~-**paper** n scheda f di votazione

ball: ~-**point** ['pen] n penna f a sfera. ~**room** n sala f da ballo

Baltic /ˈbɔːltɪk/ adj & the ~ [Sea] il [mar] Baltico

bamboo /bæmˈbuː/ n bambù m inv

ban /bæn/ n proibizione f ● vt (pt/pp banned) proibire; ~ **from** espellere da (club); she was ~**ned** from driving le hanno ritirato la patente

banal /bəˈnɑːl/ adj banale. ~**ity** n banalità f inv

banana /bəˈnɑːnə/ n banana f

band /bænd/ n banda f; (stripe) nastro m; (Mus: pop group) complesso m; (Mus: brass ~) banda f; (Mil) fanfara f ● **band together** vi riunirsi

bandage /ˈbændɪdʒ/ n benda f ● vt fasciare (limb)

b. & b. abbr bed and breakfast

bandit /ˈbændɪt/ n bandito m

band: ~**stand** n palco m coperto [dell'orchestra]. ~**wagon** n jump on the ~**wagon** fig seguire la corrente

bandy[1] /ˈbændɪ/ vt (pt/pp -ied)

scambiarsi (words). □ ~ **about** vt far circolare

bandy[2] adj (-ier, -iest) be ~ avere le gambe storte

bang /bæŋ/ n (noise) fragore m; (of gun, firework) scoppio m; (blow) colpo m ● adv ~ **in the middle of** 🄵 proprio nel mezzo di; go ~ (gun): sparare; (balloon): esplodere ● int bum! ● vt battere (fist); battere su (table); sbattere (door, head) ● vi scoppiare; (door): sbattere

banger /ˈbæŋə(r)/ n (firework) petardo m; (🄵: sausage) salsiccia f; old ~ (🄵: car) macinino m

bangle /ˈbæŋgl/ n braccialetto m

banish /ˈbænɪʃ/ vt bandire

banisters /ˈbænɪstəz/ npl ringhiera fsg

bank[1] /bæŋk/ n (of river) sponda f; (slope) scarpata f ● vi (Aeron) inclinarsi in virata

bank[2] n banca f ● vt depositare in banca ● vi ~ **with** avere un conto [bancario] presso. □ ~ **on** vt contare su

'bank card n carta f assegno.

banker /ˈbæŋkə(r)/ n banchiere m

bank: ~ **'holiday** n giorno m festivo. ~**ing** n bancario m. ~**note** n banconota f

bankrupt /ˈbæŋkrʌpt/ adj fallito; go ~ fallire ● n persona f che ha fatto fallimento ● vt far fallire. ~**cy** n bancarotta f

banner /ˈbænə(r)/ n stendardo m; (of demonstrators) striscione m

banquet /ˈbæŋkwɪt/ n banchetto m

banter /ˈbæntə(r)/ n battute fpl di spirito

baptism /ˈbæptɪzm/ n battesimo m

Baptist /ˈbæptɪst/ adj & n battista mf

baptize /bæpˈtaɪz/ vt battezzare

bar /bɑː(r)/ n sbarra f; (Jur) ordine m degli avvocati; (of chocolate) tavoletta f f; (café) bar m inv; (counter) banco m; (Mus) battuta f; (fig: obstacle) ostacolo m; ~ of soap/gold saponetta f/lingotto m; behind ~s 🔲 dietro le sbarre ● vt (pt/pp barred) sbarrare (way); sprangare (door); escludere (person) ● prep tranne; ~ none in assoluto

barbarian /baːˈbeərɪən/ n barbaro, -a mf

barbar|ic /baːˈbærɪk/ adj barbarico. ~ity n barbarie f inv. ~ous adj barbaro

barbecue /ˈbaːbɪkjuː/ n barbecue m inv, (party) grigliata f, barbecue m inv ● vt arrostire sul barbecue

barber /ˈbaːbə(r)/ n barbiere m

bare /beə(r)/ adj nudo; (tree, room) spoglio; (floor) senza moquette ● vt scoprire; mostrare (teeth)

bare: ~**back** adv senza sella. ~**faced** adj sfacciato. ~**foot** adv scalzo. ~**headed** adj a capo scoperto

barely /ˈbeəlɪ/ adv appena

bargain /ˈbaːgɪn/ n (agreement) patto m; (good buy) affare m; into the ~ per di più ● vi contrattare; (haggle) trattare. □ ~ **for** vt (expect) aspettarsi

barge /baːdʒ/ n barcone m ● **barge in** vi 🔲 (to room) piombare dentro; (into conversation) interrompere bruscamente. ~ **into** vt piombare dentro a (room); venire addosso a (person)

baritone /ˈbærɪtəʊn/ n baritono m

bark[1] /baːk/ n (of tree) corteccia f

bark[2] n abbaiamento m ● vi abbaiare

barley /ˈbaːlɪ/ n orzo m

bar: ~**maid** n barista f. ~**man** n barista m

barmy /ˈbaːmɪ/ adj 🔲 strampalato

barn /baːn/ n granaio m

barometer /bəˈrɒmɪtə(r)/ n barometro m

baron /ˈbærn/ n barone m. ~**ess** n

baronessa f

baroque /bəˈrɒk/ adj & n barocco m

barracks /ˈbærəks/ npl caserma fsg

barrage /ˈbæraːʒ/ n (Mil) sbarramento m; (fig: of criticism) sfilza f

barrel /ˈbærl/ n barile m, botte f; (of gun) canna f. ~**organ** n organetto m [a cilindro]

barren /ˈbærən/ adj sterile; (landscape) brullo

barricade /bærɪˈkeɪd/ n barricata f ● vt barricare

barrier /ˈbærɪə(r)/ n barriera f; (Rail) cancello m; fig ostacolo m

barrister /ˈbærɪstə(r)/ n avvocato m

barter /ˈbaːtə(r)/ vi barattare (for con)

base /beɪs/ n base f ● adj vile ● vt basare; be ~**d on** basarsi su

base: ~**ball** n baseball m. ~**ment** n seminterrato m

bash /bæʃ/ n colpo m [violento] ● vt colpire [violentemente]; (dent) ammaccare; ~**ed in** ammaccato

bashful /ˈbæʃfl/ adj timido

basic /ˈbeɪsɪk/ adj di base; (condition, requirement) basilare; (living conditions) povero; my Italian is pretty ~ il mio italiano è abbastanza rudimentale; the ~s (of language, science) i rudimenti; (essentials) l'essenziale m. ~**ally** adv fondamentalmente

basil /ˈbæzɪl/ n basilico m

basin /ˈbeɪsn/ n bacinella f; (washhand ~) lavabo m; (for food) recipiente m; (Geog) bacino m

basis /ˈbeɪsɪs/ n (pl -ses /-siːz/) base f

bask /baːsk/ vi crogiolarsi

basket /ˈbaːskɪt/ n cestino m. ~**ball** n pallacanestro f

bass /beɪs/ adj basso; ~ voice voce f di basso ● n basso m

bastard /'bɑːstəd/ n (illegitimate child) bastardo, -a mf; ✗ figlio m di puttana

bat[1] /bæt/ n mazza f; (for table tennis) racchetta f; off one's own ~ 🗓 tutto da solo ● vt (pt/pp batted) battere; she didn't ~ an eyelid fig non ha battuto ciglio

bat[2] n (Zool) pipistrello m

batch /bætʃ/ n gruppo m; (of goods) partita f; (of bread) infornata f

bated /'beɪtɪd/ adj with ~ breath col fiato sospeso

bath /bɑːθ/ n (pl ~s /bɑːðz/) bagno m; (tub) vasca f da bagno; ~s pl piscina f; have a ~ fare un bagno ● vt fare il bagno a

bathe /beɪð/ n bagno m ● vi fare il bagno ● vt lavare (wound). ~r n bagnante mf

bathing /'beɪðɪŋ/ n bagni mpl. ~-cap n cuffia f. ~-costume n costume m da bagno

bathroom n bagno m

battalion /bə'tæliən/ n battaglione m

batter /'bætə(r)/ n (Culin) pastella f; ~ed adj (car) malandato; (wife, baby) maltrattato

battery /'bætərɪ/ n batteria f; (of torch, radio) pila f

battle /'bætl/ n battaglia f; fig lotta f ● vi fig lottare

battle: ~field n campo m di battaglia. ~ship n corazzata f

bawl /bɔːl/ vt/i urlare

bay[1] /beɪ/ n (Geog) baia f

bay[2] n keep at ~ tenere a bada

bay[3] n (Bot) alloro m. ~-leaf n foglia f d'alloro

bayonet /'beɪənɪt/ n baionetta f

bay 'window n bay window f inv (grande finestra sporgente)

bazaar /bə'zɑː(r)/ n bazar m inv

BC abbr (before Christ) a.C.

be /biː/
● vi (pres am, are, is, are; pt was, were; pp been) essere; he is a teacher è insegnante, fa l'insegnante; what do you want to be? cosa vuoi fare?; be quiet! sta' zitto!; I am cold/hot ho freddo/caldo; it's cold/hot, isn't it? fa freddo/caldo, vero?; how are you? come stai?; I am well sto bene; there is c'è; there are ci sono; I have been to Venice sono stato a Venezia; has the postman been? è passato il postino?; you're coming too, aren't you? vieni anche tu, no?; it's yours, is it? è tuo, vero?; was John there? – yes, he was c'era John? – sì, John wasn't there – yes he was! John non c'era – sì che c'era!; three and three are six tre più tre fanno sei; he is five ha cinque anni; that will be £10, please fanno 10 sterline, per favore; how much is it? quanto costa?; that's £5 you owe me mi devi 5 sterline

● v aux I am coming/reading sto venendo/leggendo; I'm staying (not leaving) resto; I am being lazy sono pigro; I was thinking of you stavo pensando a te; you are not to tell him non devi dirgielo; you are to do that immediately devi farlo subito

● passive essere; I have been robbed sono stato derubato

beach /biːtʃ/ n spiaggia f. ~wear n abbigliamento m da spiaggia

bead /biːd/ n perlina f

beak /biːk/ n becco m

beaker /'biːkə(r)/ n coppa f

beam /biːm/ n trave f; (of light) raggio m ● vi irradiare; (person:) essere raggiante. ~ing adj raggiante

bean /biːn/ n fagiolo m; (of coffee) chicco m

bear¹ /beə(r)/ n orso m

bear² v (pt bore, pp borne) vt (endure) sopportare; mettere al mondo (child); (carry) portare; ~ in mind tenere presente ● vi ~ left/right andare a sinistra/a destra. □ ~ with v aver pazienza con. ~able adj sopportabile

beard /bɪəd/ n barba f. ~ed adj barbuto

bearer /'beərə(r)/ n portatore, -trice mf; (of passport) titolare mf

bearing /'beərɪŋ/ n portamento m; (Techn) cuscinetto m (a sfera); have a ~ on avere attinenza con; get one's ~s orientarsi

beast /biːst/ n bestia f; (I: person) animale m

beat /biːt/ n battito m; (rhythm) battuta f; (of policeman) giro m d'ispezione ● v (pt beat, pp beaten) ● vt battere; picchiare (person); ~ it! I darsela a gambe!; ~ s me why... I non capisco proprio perché... beat up vt picchiare

beating /'biːtɪŋ/ n bastonata f; get a ~ing (with fists) essere preso a pugni; (team, player:) prendere una batosta

beautician /bjuː'tɪʃn/ n estetista mf

beauti|ful /'bjuːtɪfl/ adj bello. ~fully adv splendidamente

beauty /'bjuːtɪ/ n bellezza f. ~ parlour n istituto m di bellezza. ~ spot n neon m; (place) luogo m pittoresco

beaver /'biːvə(r)/ n castoro m

became /bɪ'keɪm/ ▷BECOME

because /bɪ'kɒz/ conj perché; ~ you didn't tell me, I... poiché non me lo hai detto,... ● adv ~ of a causa di

beckon /'bekn/ vt/i ~ [to] chiamare con un cenno

become /bɪ'kʌm/ v (pt became, pp become) ● vt diventare ● vi diventare; what has ~e of her? che ne è di lei? ~ing adj (clothes) bello

bed /bed/ n letto m; (of sea, lake) fondo m; (layer) strato m; (of flowers) aiuola f; in ~ a letto; go to ~ andare a letto; ~ and breakfast pensione f familiare in cui il prezzo della camera comprende la prima colazione. ~clothes npl lenzuola fpl e coperte fpl. ~ding n biancheria f per il letto, materasso e guanciali

bed: ~room n camera f da letto. ~sitter n camera f ammobiliata fornita di cucina. ~spread n copriletto m. ~time n l'ora f di andare a letto

bee /biː/ n ape f

beech /biːtʃ/ n faggio m

beef /biːf/ n manzo m. ~burger n hamburger m inv

bee: ~hive n alveare m. ~-line n make a ~line for I precipitarsi verso

been /biːn/ ▷BE

beer /bɪə(r)/ n birra f

beetle /'biːtl/ n scarafaggio m

beetroot /'biːtruːt/ n barbabietola f

before /bɪ'fɔː(r)/ prep prima di; the day ~ yesterday ieri l'altro; ~ long fra poco ● adv prima; never ~ have I seen... non ho mai visto prima...; ~ that prima; ~ going prima di andare ● conj (time) prima che; ~ you go prima che tu vada. ~hand adv in anticipo

befriend /bɪ'frend/ vt trattare da amico

beg /beg/ v (pt/pp begged) ● vi mendicare ● vt pregare; chiedere (favour, forgiveness)

began /bɪ'gæn/ ▷BEGIN

beggar /'begə(r)/ n mendicante mf; poor ~! I povero cristo!

begin /bɪ'gɪn/ vt/i (pt began, pp begun, pres p beginning) cominciare. ~ner n principiante mf. ~ning n principio m

begrudge /brɪˈɡrʌdʒ/ vt (envy) essere invidioso di; dare malvolentieri (money)

begun /brɪˈɡʌn/ ▷BEGIN

behalf /brɪˈhɑːf/ n on ~ of a nome di; on my ~ a nome mio

behave /brɪˈheɪv/ vi comportarsi; ~ [oneself] comportarsi bene

behaviour /brɪˈheɪvjə(r)/ n comportamento m; (of prisoner, soldier) condotta f

behead /brɪˈhed/ vt decapitare

behind /brɪˈhaɪnd/ prep dietro; be ~ sth fig stare dietro a qcsa ● adv dietro, indietro; (late) in ritardo; a long way ~ molto indietro ● n (fam) dietro m. ~hand adv indietro

beige /beɪʒ/ adj & n beige m inv

being /ˈbiːɪŋ/ n essere m; come into ~ nascere

belated /brɪˈleɪtɪd/ adj tardivo

belch /beltʃ/ vi ruttare ● vt ~ [out] eruttare (smoke)

belfry /ˈbelfrɪ/ n campanile m

Belgian /ˈbeldʒən/ adj & n belga mf

Belgium /ˈbeldʒəm/ n Belgio m

belief /brɪˈliːf/ n fede f; (opinion) convinzione f

believe /brɪˈliːv/ vt/i credere. ~r n (Relig) credente mf; be a great ~r in credere fermamente in

belittle /brɪˈlɪtl/ vt sminuire (person, achievements)

bell /bel/ n campana f; (on door) campanello m

belligerent /brɪˈlɪdʒərənt/ adj belligerante; (aggressive) bellicoso

bellow /ˈbeləʊ/ vi gridare a squarciagola; (animal:) muggire

bellows /ˈbeləʊz/ npl (for fire) soffietto msg

belly /ˈbelɪ/ n pancia f

belong /brɪˈlɒŋ/ vi appartenere (to a); (be member) essere socio (to di). ~ings npl cose fpl

beloved /brɪˈlʌvɪd/ adj & n amato, -a mf

below /brɪˈləʊ/ prep sotto; (with numbers) al di sotto di ● adv sotto, di sotto; (Naut) sotto coperta; see ~ guardare qui di seguito

belt /belt/ n cintura f; (area) zona f; (Techn) cinghia f ● vi ~ along (fam: rush) filare velocemente ● vt (fam: hit) picchiare

bench /bentʃ/ n panchina f; (work-) piano m da lavoro; the B~ (Jur) la magistratura

bend /bend/ n curva f; (of river) ansa f ● v (pt/pp bent) ● vt piegare ● vi piegarsi; (road:) curvare; ~ [down] chinarsi. □ ~ over vi inchinarsi

beneath /brɪˈniːθ/ prep sotto, al di sotto di; he thinks it ~ him fig pensa che sia sotto il suo livello ● adv giù

beneficial /benɪˈfɪʃl/ adj benefico

beneficiary /benɪˈfɪʃərɪ/ n beneficiario, -a mf

benefit /ˈbenɪfɪt/ n vantaggio m; (allowance) indennità f inv ● v (pt/pp -fited, pres p -fiting) ● vt giovare a ● vi trarre vantaggio (from da)

benign /brɪˈnaɪn/ adj benevolo; (Med) benigno

bent /bent/ ▷BEND ● adj (person) ricurvo; (distorted) curvato; (fam: dishonest) corrotto; be ~ on doing sth essere ben deciso a fare qcsa ● n predisposizione f

bereave|d /brɪˈriːvd/ n the ~d pl i familiari del defunto. ~ment n lutto m

beret /ˈbereɪ/ n berretto m

berry /ˈberɪ/ n bacca f

berserk /bəˈsɜːk/ adj go ~ diventare una belva

berth /bɜːθ/ n (bed) cuccetta f; (anchorage) ormeggio m ● vi ormeggiare

beside /brɪˈsaɪd/ prep accanto a; ~ oneself fuori di sé

besides /brɪˈsaɪdz/ prep oltre a

• adv inoltre

besiege /bɪˈsiːdʒ/ vt assediare

best /best/ adj migliore; the ~ part of a year la maggior parte dell'anno; ~ before (Comm) preferibilmente prima di • n the ~ il meglio; (person) il/la migliore; at ~ tutt'al più; all the ~! tanti auguri!; do one's ~ fare del proprio meglio; to the ~ of my knowledge per quel che ne so; make the ~ of it cogliere il lato buono della cosa • adv meglio, nel modo migliore; as ~ I could meglio che potevo. ~ 'man n testimone m

bestow /bɪˈstəʊ/ vt conferire (on a)

best'seller n bestseller m inv

bet /bet/ n scommessa f • vt/i (pt/pp bet or betted) scommettere

betray /bɪˈtreɪ/ vt tradire. ~al n tradimento m

better /ˈbetə(r)/ adj migliore, meglio; get ~ migliorare; (after illness) rimettersi • adv meglio; ~ off meglio; (wealthier) più ricco; all the ~ tanto meglio; the sooner the ~ prima è, meglio è; I've thought of it ci ho ripensato; you'd ~ stay faresti meglio a restare; I'd ~ not è meglio che non lo faccia • vt migliorare; ~ oneself migliorare le proprie condizioni

between /bɪˈtwiːn/ prep fra, tra; ~ you and me detto fra di noi; ~ us (together) tra me e te • adv [in] ~ in mezzo; (time) frattempo

beverage /ˈbevərɪdʒ/ n bevanda f

beware /bɪˈweə(r)/ vi guardarsi (of da); ~ of the dog! attenti al cane

bewilder /bɪˈwɪldə(r)/ vt disorientare; ~ed perplesso. ~ment n perplessità f

beyond /bɪˈjɒnd/ prep oltre; ~ reach irraggiungibile; ~ doubt senza alcun dubbio; ~ belief da non credere; it's ~ me 🔢 non riesco proprio a capire • adv più in là

bias /ˈbaɪəs/ n (preference) preferenza f; pej pregiudizio m • vt (pt/pp biased) (influence) influenzare. ~ed adj parziale

bib /bɪb/ n bavaglino m

Bible /ˈbaɪbl/ n Bibbia f

biblical /ˈbɪblɪkl/ adj biblico

biceps /ˈbaɪseps/ n bicipite m

bicker /ˈbɪkə(r)/ vi litigare

bicycle /ˈbaɪsɪkl/ n bicicletta f • vi andare in bicicletta

bid¹ /bɪd/ n offerta f; (attempt) tentativo m • vt/i (pt/pp bid, pres p bidding) offrire; (in cards) dichiarare

bid² vt (pt bade or bid, pp bidden or bid, pres p bidding) liter (command) comandare; ~ sb welcome dare il benvenuto a qcno

bidder /ˈbɪdə(r)/ n offerente mf

bide /baɪd/ vt ~ one's time aspettare il momento buono

bifocals /baɪˈfəʊklz/ npl occhiali mpl bifocali

big /bɪg/ adj (bigger, biggest) grande; (brother, sister) più grande; (🔢: generous) generoso • adv talk ~ 🔢 sparar le grosse

bigam|ist /ˈbɪgəmɪst/ n bigamo, -a mf. ~y n bigamia f

big-'headed adj 🔢 gasato

bigot /ˈbɪgət/ n fanatico, -a mf. ~ed adj di mentalità ristretta

bike /baɪk/ n 🔢 bici f inv

bikini /bɪˈkiːni/ n bikini m inv

bile /baɪl/ n bile f

bilingual /baɪˈlɪŋgwəl/ adj bilingue

bill¹ /bɪl/ n fattura f; (in restaurant etc) conto m; (poster) manifesto m; (Pol) progetto m di legge; (Am: note) biglietto m di banca • vt fatturare

bill² n (beak) becco m

'billfold n Am portafoglio m

billiards /ˈbɪljədz/ n biliardo m

billion /ˈbɪljən/ n (thousand million) miliardo m; (old-fashioned Br: million million) mille miliardi mpl

bin /bɪn/ n bidone m

bind /baɪnd/ vt (pt/pp bound) legare (to a); (bandage) fasciare; (Jur) obbligare. ~ n (promise, contract) vincolante ● n (of book) rilegatura f; (on ski) attacco m [di sicurezza]

binge /bɪndʒ/ n 🎧 have a ~ fare baldoria; (eat a lot) abbuffarsi ● vi abbuffarsi (on di)

binoculars /bɪˈnɒkjʊləz/ npl [pair of] ~ binocolo msg

biograph|er /baɪˈɒɡrəfə(r)/ n biografo, -a mf. ~y n biografia f

biological /baɪəˈlɒdʒɪkl/ adj biologico

biolog|ist /baɪˈɒlədʒɪst/ n biologo, -a mf. ~y n biologia f

birch /bɜːtʃ/ n (tree) betulla f

bird /bɜːd/ n uccello m; (🎧: girl) ragazza f

Biro® /ˈbaɪrəʊ/ n biro® f inv

birth /bɜːθ/ n nascita f

birth: ~ **certificate** n certificato di nascita. ~**control** n controllo m delle nascite. ~**day** n compleanno m. ~**mark** n voglia f. ~**rate** n natalità f

biscuit /ˈbɪskɪt/ n biscotto m

bisect /baɪˈsekt/ vt dividere in due [parti]

bishop /ˈbɪʃəp/ n vescovo m; (in chess) alfiere m

bit¹ /bɪt/ n pezzo m; (smaller) pezzetto m; (for horse) morso m; (Comput) bit m inv; a ~ of un pezzo di (cheese, paper); un po' di (time, rain, silence); ~ by ~ poco a poco; do one's ~ fare la propria parte

bit² ▷ BITE

bitch /bɪtʃ/ n cagna f; 🎧 stronza f. ~y adj velenoso

bit|e /baɪt/ n morso m; (insect ~) puntura f; (mouthful) boccone m ● vt (pt bit, pp bitten) mordere; (insect:) pungere; ~e one's nails mangiarsi le unghie ● vi mordere; (insect:) pungere. ~ing adj (wind, criticism) pun-

gente; (remark) mordace

bitter /ˈbɪtə(r)/ adj amaro ● n Br birra f amara. ~ly adv amaramente; it's ~ly cold c'è un freddo pungente. ~ness n amarezza f

bizarre /bɪˈzɑː(r)/ adj bizzarro

black /blæk/ adj nero; be ~ and blue essere pieno di lividi ● n negro, -a mf ● vt boicottare (goods). □ ~ **out** vt cancellare ● vi (lose consciousness) perdere coscienza

black: ~**berry** n mora f. ~**bird** n merlo m. ~**board** n (Sch) lavagna f. ~**currant** n ribes m inv nero; ~ **eye** n occhio m nero. ~ **ice** n ghiaccio m (sulla strada). ~**leg** n Br crumiro m. ~**list** vt mettere sulla lista nera. ~**mail** n ricatto m ● vt ricattare. ~**mailer** n ricattatore, -trice mf. ~**out** n blackout m inv; have a ~**out** (Med) perdere coscienza. ~**smith** n fabbro m

bladder /ˈblædə(r)/ n (Anat) vescica f

blade /bleɪd/ n lama f; (of grass) filo m

blame /bleɪm/ n colpa f ● vt dare la colpa a; ~ sb for doing sth dare la colpa a qcno per aver fatto qcsa; no one is to ~ non è colpa di nessuno. ~**less** adj innocente

bland /blænd/ adj (food) insipido; (person) insulso

blank /blæŋk/ adj bianco; (look) vuoto ● n spazio m vuoto; (cartridge) a salve. ~ '**cheque** n assegno m in bianco

blanket /ˈblæŋkɪt/ n coperta f

blare /bleə(r)/ vi suonare a tutto volume. □ ~ **out** vt far risuonare ● vi (music, radio:) strillare

blaspheme /blæsˈfiːm/ vi bestemmiare

blasphem|ous /ˈblæsfəməs/ adj blasfemo. ~y n bestemmia f

blast /blɑːst/ n (gust) raffica f; (sound) scoppio m ● vt (with explosive) far saltare • int 🔲 maledizione!. •ed adj 🔲 maledetto

blast-off n (of missile) lancio m

blatant /'bleɪtənt/ adj sfacciato

blaze /bleɪz/ n incendio m; a ~ of colour un'esplosione f di colori • vi ardere

blazer /'bleɪzə(r)/ n blazer m inv

bleach /bliːtʃ/ n decolorante m; (for cleaning) candeggina f • vt sbiancare; ossigenare (hair)

bleak /bliːk/ adj desolato; (fig: prospects, future) tetro

bleat /bliːt/ vi belare • n belato m

bleed /bliːd/ v (pt/pp bled) • vi sanguinare • vt spurgare (brakes, radiator)

bleep /bliːp/ n bip m • vi suonare • vt chiamare (col cercapersone) (doctor). •er n cercapersone m inv

blemish /'blemɪʃ/ n macchia f

blend /blend/ n (of tea, coffee, whisky) miscela f; (of colours) insieme m • vt mescolare • vi (colours, sounds:) fondersi (with con). •er n (Culin) frullatore m

bless /bles/ vt benedire. •ed adj also 🔲 benedetto. •ing n benedizione f

blew /bluː/ ▷BLOW²

blight /blaɪt/ n (Bot) ruggine f • vt far avvizzire (plants)

blind¹ /blaɪnd/ adj cieco; the ~ npl i ciechi mpl; ~ man/woman cieco/cieca • vt accecare

blind² n (roller) ~ avvolgibile m; [Venetian] ~ veneziana f

blind: ~ 'alley n vicolo m cieco. ~fold adj be ~fold avere gli occhi bendati • n benda f • vt bendare gli occhi a. ~ly adv ciecamente. ~ness n cecità f

blink /blɪŋk/ vi battere le palpebre; (light:) tremolare

blinkers /'blɪŋkəz/ npl paraocchi mpl

bliss /blɪs/ n (Rel) beatitudine f; (happiness) felicità f. ~ful adj beato;

(happy) meraviglioso

blister /'blɪstə(r)/ n (Med) vescica f; (in paint) bolla f • vi (paint:) formare una bolla/delle bolle

blizzard /'blɪzəd/ n tormenta f

bloated /'bləʊtɪd/ adj gonfio

blob /blɒb/ n goccia f

bloc /blɒk/ n (Pol) blocco m

block /blɒk/ n blocco m; (building) isolato m; (building:) cubo m (per giochi di costruzione); ~ of flats palazzo m • vt bloccare. ~ up vt bloccare

blockade /blɒ'keɪd/ n blocco m • vt bloccare

blockage /'blɒkɪdʒ/ n ostruzione f

block: ~head n 🔲 testone, -a mf. ~ 'letters npl stampatello m

bloke /bləʊk/ n 🔲 tizio m

blonde /blɒnd/ adj biondo • n bionda f

blood /blʌd/ n sangue m

blood: ~ bath n bagno m di sangue. ~ group n gruppo m sanguigno. ~hound n segugio m. ~ pressure n pressione f del sangue. ~shed n spargimento m di sangue. ~shot adj iniettato di sangue. ~stream n sangue m. ~thirsty adj assetato di sangue

bloody /'blʌdɪ/ adj (-ier, -iest) insanguinato; 🔲 maledetto • adv 🔲 ~ easy/difficult facile/difficile da matti. ~-'minded adj scorbutico

bloom /bluːm/ n fiore m; in ~ (flower:) sbocciato; (tree:) in fiore • vi fiorire; fig essere in forma smagliante

blossom /'blɒsəm/ n fiori mpl (d'albero); (single one) fiore m • vi sbocciare

blot /blɒt/ n also fig macchia f • blot out vt (pt/pp blotted) fig cancellare

blotch /blɒtʃ/ n macchia f. ~y adj chiazzato

'blotting-paper n carta f assorbente

blouse /blaʊz/ n camicetta f

blow[1] /bləʊ/ n colpo m

blow[2] v (pt blew, pp blown) • vi (wind:) soffiare; (fuse:) saltare • vt ([F]: squander) sperperare; ~ one's nose soffiarsi il naso. □ ~ **away** vt far volar via (papers) • vi (papers:) volare via. □ ~ **down** vt abbattere • vi abbattersi al suolo. □ ~ **out** vt (extinguish) spegnere. □ ~ **over** vi (storm:) passare; (fuss, trouble:) dissiparsi. □ ~ **up** vt (inflate) gonfiare; (enlarge) ingrandire (photograph); (by explosion) far esplodere • vi esplodere

blow: ~**-dry** vt asciugare col fon. ~**lamp** n fiamma f ossidrica

'blowtorch n fiamma f ossidrica

blue /bluː/ adj (pale) celeste; (navy) blu inv; (royal) azzurro; ~ **with cold** livido per il freddo ● n blu m inv; **have the** ~s essere giù [di tono]; **out of the** ~ inaspettatamente

blue: ~**bell** n giacinto m di bosco. ~**berry** n mirtillo m. ~**bottle** n moscone m. ~**film** n film m inv a luci rosse. ~**print** n fig riferimento m

bluff /blʌf/ n bluff m inv ● vi bluffare

blunder /'blʌndə(r)/ n gaffe f inv ● vi fare una/delle gaffe

blunt /blʌnt/ adj spuntato; (person) reciso. ~**ly** adv schiettamente

blur /blɜː(r)/ n **it's all a** ~ fig è tutto un insieme confuso ● vt (pt/pp blurred) rendere confuso. ~**red** adj (vision, photo) sfocato

blurb /blɜːb/ n soffietto m editoriale

blurt /blɜːt/ vt ~ **out** spifferare

blush /blʌʃ/ n rossore m ● vi arrossire

BMI n abbr (body mass index) IMC m

boar /bɔː(r)/ n cinghiale m

board /bɔːd/ n tavola f; (for notices) tabellone m; (committee) assemblea f; (of directors) consiglio m; **full** ~ Br pensione f completa; **half** ~ Br mezza pensione f; ~ **and lodging** vitto e alloggio m; **go by the** ~ [F]

andare a monte ● vt (Naut, Aeron) salire a bordo di ● vi (passengers:) salire a bordo. □ ~ **up** vt sbarrare con delle assi. □ ~ **with** vt stare a pensione da.

boarder /'bɔːdə(r)/ n pensionante m/f; (Sch) convittore, -trice m/f

board: ~**ing-house** n pensione f. ~**ing-school** n collegio m

boast /bəʊst/ vi vantarsi (about di). ~**ful** adj vanaglorioso

boat /bəʊt/ n barca f; (ship) nave f

bob /bɒb/ n (hairstyle) caschetto m ● v (pt/pp bobbed) (also ~ **up and down**) andare su e giù

'bob-sleigh n bob m inv

bode /bəʊd/ vi ~ **well/ill** essere di buono/cattivo augurio

bodily /'bɒdɪlɪ/ adj fisico ● adv (forcibly) fisicamente

body /'bɒdɪ/ n corpo m; (organization) ente m; (amount: of poems etc) quantità f. ~**-guard** n guardia f del corpo. ~**part** n pezzo m del corpo. ~**work** n (Auto) carrozzeria f

bog /bɒg/ n palude f ● vt (pt/pp bogged) **get** ~**ged down** impantanarsi

boggle /'bɒgl/ vi **the mind** ~s non posso neanche immaginarlo

bogus /'bəʊgəs/ adj falso

boil[1] /bɔɪl/ n (Med) foruncolo m

boil[2] n **bring/come to the** ~ portare/arrivare ad ebollizione ● vt [far] bollire ● vi bollire; (fig: with anger) ribollire; **the water or kettle's** ~**ing** l'acqua bolle. **boil down to** vt fig ridursi a. □ ~ **over** vi straboccare (bollendo). □ ~ **up** vt far bollire

boiler /'bɔɪlə(r)/ n caldaia f. ~**suit** n tuta f

boisterous /'bɔɪstərəs/ adj chiassoso

bold /bəʊld/ adj audace ● n (Typ) neretto m. ~**ness** n audacia f

bolster /'bəʊlstə(r)/ n cuscino m (lungo e rotondo) ● vt ~ [**up**] sostenere

bolt /bəʊlt/ n (for door) catenaccio m; (for fixing) bullone m ● vt fissare (con i bulloni) (to a); chiudere col chiavistello (door); ingurgitare (food) ● vi svignarsela; (horse): scappar via ● adv ~ **upright** diritto come un fuso

bomb /bɒm/ n bomba f ● vt bombardare

bombard /bɒm'bɑːd/ vt also bomb bombardare

bomb|er /'bɒmə(r)/ n (Aeron) bombardiere m; (person) dinamitardo m. ~**er jacket** giubbotto m, bomber m inv. ~**shell** n (fig: news) bomba f

bond /bɒnd/ n fig legame m; (Comm) obbligazione f ● vt (glue): attaccare

bondage /'bɒndɪdʒ/ n schiavitù f

bone /bəʊn/ n osso m; (of fish) spina f ● vt disossare (meat); togliere le spine da (fish). ~-**dry** adj secco

bonfire /'bɒn-/ n falò m inv. ~ **night** festa celebrata la notte del 5 novembre con fuochi d'artificio e falò

bonnet /'bɒnɪt/ n cuffia f; (of car) cofano m

bonus /'bəʊnəs/ n (individual) gratifica f; (production ~) premio m; (life insurance) dividendo m; a ~ fig qualcosa in più

bony /'bəʊnɪ/ adj (-ier, -iest) ossuto; (fish) pieno di spine

boo /buː/ interj (to surprise or frighten) bu! ● vt/i fischiare

boob /buːb/ n 🔢 (mistake) gaffe f inv; (breast) tetta f ● vi 🔢 fare una gaffe

book /bʊk/ n libro m; (of tickets) blocchetto m; keep the ~s (Comm) tenere la contabilità; in sb's bad/good ~s essere nel libro nero/nelle grazie di qcno ● vt (reserve) prenotare; (for offence) multare ● vi (reserve) prenotare

book: ~**case** n libreria f. ~**ing-office** n biglietteria f. ~**keeping** n contabilità f. ~**let** n opuscolo m. ~**maker** n allibratore m. ~**mark** n segnalibro m. ~**seller** n libraio, -a mf.

~**shop** n libreria f. ~**worm** n topo m di biblioteca

boom /buːm/ n (Comm) boom m inv; (upturn) impennata f; (of thunder, gun) rimbombo m ● vi (thunder, gun:) rimbombare; fig prosperare

boost /buːst/ n spinta f ● vt stimolare (sales); sollevare (morale); far crescere (hopes). ~**er** n (Med) dose f supplementare

boot /buːt/ n stivale m; (up to ankle) stivaletto m; (football) scarpetta f; (climbing) scarpone m; (Auto) portabagagli m inv ● vt (Comput) inizializzare

booth /buːð/ n (telephone, voting) cabina f; (at market) bancarella f

booze /buːz/ 🔢 n alcolici mpl. ~-**up** n bella bevuta f

border /'bɔːdə(r)/ n bordo m; (frontier) frontiera f; (in garden) bordura f ● vi ~ **on** confinare con; fig essere ai confini di (madness). ~**line** n linea f di demarcazione; ~**line case** m di dubbio

bore[1] /bɔː(r)/ ▷ **BEAR**[2]

bore[2] vt (Techn) forare

bor|e[3] n (of gun) calibro m; (person) seccatore, -trice mf; (thing) seccatura f ● vt annoiare. ~**edom** n noia f. be ~**ed** (to tears or to death) annoiarsi (da morire). ~**ing** adj noioso

born /bɔːn/ pp be ~ nascere; I was ~ in 1966 sono nato nel 1966 ● adj nato; a ~ liar/actor un bugiardo/ attore nato

borne /bɔːn/ ▷ **BEAR**[2]

borough /'bʌrə/ n municipalità f inv

borrow /'bɒrəʊ/ vt prendere a prestito (from da); can I ~ your pen? mi presti la tua penna?

boss /bɒs/ n direttore, -trice mf (also ~ about) comandare a bacchetta. ~**y** adj autoritario

botanical /bə'tænɪkl/ adj botanico

botan|ist /'bɒtənɪst/ n botanico, -a mf. ~**y** n botanica f

both /bəʊθ/ adj & pron tutti e due,

entrambi ● adv ∼ men and women entrambi uomini e donne; ∼ [of] the children tutti e due i bambini; they are ∼ dead sono morti entrambi; ∼ of them tutti e due

bother /'bɒðə(r)/ n preoccupazione f; (minor trouble) fastidio m; it's no ∼ non c'è problema ● int 1 che seccatura! ● vt (annoy) dare fastidio a; (disturb) disturbare ● vi preoccuparsi (about di); don't ∼ lascia perdere

bottle /'bɒtl/ n bottiglia f; (baby's) biberon m inv ● vt imbottigliare. □ ∼ **up** vt fig reprimere

bottle: ∼-**neck** n fig ingorgo m. ∼-**opener** n apribottiglie m inv

bottom /'bɒtm/ adj ultimo; the ∼ shelf l'ultimo scaffale in basso ● n (of container) fondo m; (of river) fondale m; (of hill) piedi mpl; (buttocks) sedere m; at the ∼ of the page in fondo alla pagina; get to the ∼ of fig vedere cosa c'è sotto. ∼-**less** adj senza fondo

bough /baʊ/ n ramoscello m

bought /bɔːt/ ▷ BUY

boulder /'bəʊldə(r)/ n masso m

bounce /baʊns/ vi rimbalzare; (fam: cheque) essere respinto ● vt far rimbalzare (ball)

bound[1] /baʊnd/ n balzo m ● vi balzare

bound[2] ▷BIND ● adj ∼ for (ship) diretto a; be ∼ to do (likely) dovere fare per forza; (obliged) essere costretto a fare

boundary /'baʊndərɪ/ n limite m

bouquet /bʊ'keɪ/ n mazzo m di fiori; (of wine) bouquet m

bout /baʊt/ n (Med) attacco m; (Sport) incontro m

bow[1] /bəʊ/ n (weapon) arco m; (Mus) archetto m; (knot) nodo m

bow[2] /baʊ/ n inchino m ● vi inchinarsi ● vt piegare (head)

bow[3] /baʊ/ n (Naut) prua f

bowl[1] /bəʊl/ n (for soup, cereal) scodella f; (of pipe) fornello m

bowl[2] n (ball) boccia f ● vt lanciare ● vi (Cricket) servire; (in bowls) lanciare. □ ∼ **over** vt buttar giù; (fig: leave speechless) lasciar senza parole

bowler[1] /'bəʊlə(r)/ n (Cricket) lanciatore m; (Bowls) giocatore m di bocce

bowler[2] n ∼ [**hat**] bombetta f

bowling /'bəʊlɪŋ/ n gioco m delle bocce. ∼-**alley** n pista f da bowling

bow-'tie /bəʊ-/ n cravatta f a farfalla

box[1] /bɒks/ n scatola f; (Theat) palco m

box[2] vi (Sport) fare il pugile ● vt ∼ sb's ears dare uno scappaccione a qcno

box|er /'bɒksə(r)/ n pugile m. ∼**ing** n pugilato m. B∼**ing Day** n [giorno m di] Santo Stefano m

box: ∼-**office** n (Theat) botteghino m. ∼-**room** n Br sgabuzzino m

boy /bɔɪ/ n ragazzo m; (younger) bambino m

'**boy band** n boy band f inv

boycott /'bɔɪkɒt/ n boicottaggio m ● vt boicottare

boy: ∼-**friend** n ragazzo m. ∼**ish** adj da ragazzino

bra /brɑː/ n reggiseno m

brace /breɪs/ n sostegno m; (dental) apparecchio m; ∼s npl bretelle fpl ● vt ∼ oneself fig farsi forza (for per affrontare)

bracelet /'breɪslɪt/ n braccialetto m

bracken /'brækn/ n felce f

bracket /'brækɪt/ n mensola f; (group) categoria f; (Typ) parentesi f inv ● vt mettere fra parentesi

brag /bræg/ vi (pt/pp **bragged**) vantarsi (about di)

braid /breɪd/ n (edging) passamano m

brain /breɪn/ n cervello m; ∼s pl fig testa fsg

brain: ∼**child** n invenzione f personale. ∼**wash** vt fare il lavaggio del cervello a. ∼**wave** n lampo m di genio

brainy /ˈbreɪnɪ/ adj (-ier, -iest) intelligente

brake /breɪk/ n freno m ● vi frenare. ~**light** n stop m inv

bramble /ˈbræmbl/ n rovo m; (fruit) mora f

bran /bræn/ n crusca f

branch /brɑːntʃ/ n ramo m; (Comm) succursale f ● vi (road:) biforcarsi. □ ~ **off** vi biforcarsi. □ ~ **out** vi ~ out into allargare le proprie attività nel ramo di

brand /brænd/ n marca f; (on animal) marchio m ● vt marcare (animal); fig tacciare (as di)

brandish /ˈbrændɪʃ/ vt brandire

brandy /ˈbrændɪ/ n brandy m inv

brash /bræʃ/ adj sfrontato

brass /brɑːs/ n ottone m; the ~ (Mus) gli ottoni mpl; top ~ 🔲 pezzi mpl grossi. ~ **band** n banda f (di soli ottoni)

brassiere /ˈbræzɪə(r)/ n fml, Am reggipetto m

brat /bræt/ n pej marmocchio, -a mf

bravado /brəˈvɑːdəʊ/ n bravata f

brave /breɪv/ adj coraggioso ● vt affrontare. ~**ry** n coraggio m

brawl /brɔːl/ n rissa f ● vi azzuffarsi

brazen /ˈbreɪzn/ adj sfrontato

Brazil /brəˈzɪl/ n Brasile m. ~**ian** adj & n brasiliano, -a mf. ~ **nut** n noce f del Brasile

breach /briːtʃ/ n (of law) violazione f; (gap) breccia f; (fig: in party) frattura f; ~ **of contract** inadempienza f di contratto; ~ **of the peace** violazione f della quiete pubblica ● vt recedere (contract)

bread /bred/ n pane m; a slice of ~ **and butter** una fetta di pane imburrato

breadcrumbs npl briciole fpl; (Culin) pangrattato m

breadth /bredθ/ n larghezza f

'bread-winner n quello, -a mf che porta i soldi a casa

break /breɪk/ n rottura f; (interval) intervallo m; (interruption) interruzione f; (🔲: chance) opportunità f inv ● v (pt broke, pp broken) ● vt rompere; ~ **one's arm** rompersi un braccio ● vi rompersi; (day:) spuntare; (storm:) scoppiare; (news:) diffondersi; (boy's voice:) cambiare. □ ~ **away** vi scappare; fig chiudere (from con). □ ~ **down** vi (machine, car:) guastarsi; (emotionally) cedere (psicologicamente) ● vt sfondare (door); ripartire (figures). □ ~ **into** vt introdursi (con la forza) in; forzare (car). □ ~ **off** vt rompere (engagement) ● vi (part of whole:) rompersi. □ ~ **out** vi (fight, war:) scoppiare. □ ~ **up** vt far cessare (fight); disperdere (crowd) ● vi (crowd:) disperdersi; (couple:) separarsi; (Sch) iniziare le vacanze

'break|able /ˈbreɪkəbl/ adj fragile. ~**age** n rottura f. ~**down** n (of car, machine) guasto m; (Med) esaurimento m nervoso; (of figures) analisi f inv. ~**er** n (wave) frangente m

breakfast /ˈbrekfəst/ n [prima] colazione f

break:~through n scoperta f. ~**water** n frangiflutti m inv

breast /brest/ n seno m. ~**feed** vt allattare [al seno]. ~**stroke** n nuoto m a rana

breath /breθ/ n respiro m, fiato m; out of ~ senza fiato. ~**taking** adj mozzafiato. ~ **test** n prova f [etilica] / del palloncino

breathalyse /ˈbreθəlaɪz/ vt sottoporre alla prova [etilica] del palloncino. ~**r®** n Br alcoltest m inv

breathe /briːð/ vt/i respirare. □ ~ **in** vi inspirare ● vt respirare (scent, air). □ ~ **out** vt/i espirare

breath|er /ˈbriːðə(r)/ n pausa f. ~**ing** n respirazione f

bred /bred/ ▷ BREED

breed /briːd/ n razza f ● v (pt/pp

bred) ● vt allevare; (give rise to) generare ● vi riprodursi. ~er n allevatore, -trice mf. ~ing n allevamento m; fig educazione f

breez|e /briːz/ n brezza f. ~y adj ventoso

brew /bruː/ n infuso m ● vt mettere in infusione (tea); produrre (beer) ● vi fig (trouble): essere nell'aria. ~er n birraio m. ~ery n fabbrica f di birra

bribe /braɪb/ n (money) bustarella f; (large sum of money) tangente f ● vt corrompere. ~ry n corruzione f

brick /brɪk/ n mattone m. '~layer n muratore ● **brick up** vt murare

bridal /ˈbraɪdl/ adj nuziale

bride /braɪd/ n sposa f. ~groom n sposo m. ~smaid n damigella f d'onore

bridge[1] /brɪdʒ/ n ponte m; (of nose) dorso m; (of spectacles) ponticello m ● vt fig colmare (gap)

bridge[2] n (Cards) bridge m

bridle /ˈbraɪdl/ n briglia f

brief[1] /briːf/ adj breve

brief[2] n istruzioni fpl; (Jur: case) causa f ● vt dare istruzioni a; (Jur) affidare la causa a. ~case n cartella f

briefs /briːfs/ npl slip m inv

brigad|e /brɪˈɡeɪd/ n brigata f. ~ier n generale m di brigata

bright /braɪt/ adj (metal, idea) brillante; (day, room, future) luminoso; (clever) intelligente; ~ red rosso m acceso

bright|en /ˈbraɪtn/ v ~en [up] ● vt ravvivare; rallegrare (person) ● vi (weather): schiararisi; (face:) illuminarsi; (person:) rallegrarsi. ~ly adv (shine) intensamente; (smile) allegramente. ~ness n luminosità f; (intelligence) intelligenza f

brilliance /ˈbrɪljəns/ n luminosità f; (of person) genialità f

brilliant /ˈbrɪljənt/ adj (very good) eccezionale; (very intelligent) brillante; (sunshine) splendente

brim /brɪm/ n bordo m; (of hat) tesa f ● **brim over** vi (pt/pp brimmed) traboccare

brine /braɪn/ n salamoia f

bring /brɪŋ/ vt (pt/pp brought) portare (person, object). □ ~ **about** vt causare. □ ~ **along** vt portare [con sé]. □ ~ **back** vt restituire (sth borrowed); reintrodurre (hanging); fare ritornare in mente (memories). □ ~ **down** vt portare giù; fare cadere (government); fare abbassare (price). □ ~ **off** vt ~ sth off riuscire a fare qcsa. □ ~ **on** vt (cause) provocare. □ ~ **out** vt (emphasize) mettere in evidenza; pubblicare (book). □ ~ **round** vt portare; (persuade) convincere; far rinvenire (unconscious person). □ ~ **up** vt (vomit) rimettere; allevare (children); tirare fuori (question, subject)

brink /brɪŋk/ n orlo m

brisk /brɪsk/ adj svelto; (person) sbrigativo; (trade, business) redditizio; (walk) a passo spedito

bristl|e /ˈbrɪsl/ n setola f ● vi ~ling with pieno di. ~ly adj (chin) ispido

Brit|ain /ˈbrɪtn/ n Gran Bretagna f. ~ish adj britannico; (ambassador) della Gran Bretagna ● npl the ~ish il popolo britannico. ~on n cittadino, -a britannico, -a mf

brittle /ˈbrɪtl/ adj fragile

broach /brəʊtʃ/ vt toccare (subject)

broad /brɔːd/ adj ampio; (hint) chiaro; (accent) marcato. two metres ~ largo due metri; in ~ daylight in pieno giorno. ~ band n banda f larga. ~ beans npl fave fpl

'broadcast n trasmissione f ● vt/i (pt/pp -cast) trasmettere. ~er n giornalista mf radiotelevisivo, -a. ~ing n diffusione f radiotelevisiva; be on the ~ing lavorare per la televisione/radio

broaden /ˈbrɔːdn/ vt allargare ● vi allargarsi

broadly /'brɔːdlɪ/ adv largamente; ~ [speaking] generalmente

broad'minded adj di larghe vedute

broccoli /'brɒkəlɪ/ n inv broccoli mpl

brochure /'brəʊʃə(r)/ n opuscolo m; (travel ~) dépliant m inv

broke /brəʊk/ ▷**BREAK** ● adj 🆃 al verde

broken /'brəʊkn/ ▷**BREAK** ● adj rotto; (fig: marriage) fallito. ~ English inglese m stentato. ~-hearted adj affranto

broker /'brəʊkə(r)/ n broker m inv

brolly /'brɒlɪ/ n 🆃 ombrello m

bronchitis /brɒŋ'kaɪtɪs/ n bronchite f

bronze /brɒnz/ n bronzo m ● attrib di bronzo

brooch /brəʊtʃ/ n spilla f

brood /bruːd/ n covata f; (hum: children) prole f ● vi fig rimuginare

brook /brʊk/ n ruscello m

broom /bruːm/ n scopa f. ~stick n manico m di scopa

broth /brɒθ/ n brodo m

brothel /'brɒθl/ n bordello m

brother /'brʌðə(r)/ n fratello m

brother: ~-**in-law** n (pl ~s-**in-law**) cognato m. ~**ly** adj fraterno

brought /brɔːt/ ▷**BRING**

brow /braʊ/ n fronte f; (of hill) cima f

'browbeat vt (pt -beat, pp -beaten) intimidire

brown /braʊn/ adj marrone; castano (hair) ● n marrone m ● vt rosolare (meat) ● vi (meat:) rosolarsi. ~ 'paper n carta f da pacchi

browse /braʊz/ vi (read) leggicchiare; (in shop) curiosare

bruise /bruːz/ n livido m; (on fruit) ammaccatura f ● vt ammaccare (fruit); ~ one's arm farsi un livido sul braccio. ~**d** adj contuso

brunette /bruː'net/ n bruna f

brunt /brʌnt/ n bear the ~ of sth subire maggiormente qcsa

brush /brʌʃ/ n spazzola f; (with long handle) spazzolone m; (for paint) pennello m; (bushes) boscaglia f; (fig: conflict) breve scontro m ● vt spazzolare (hair); lavarsi (teeth); scopare (stairs, floor). □ ~ **against** vt sfiorare. □ ~ **aside** vt fig ignorare. □ ~ **off** vt spazzolare; (with hands) togliere; ignorare (criticism). □ ~ **up** vt/i fig ~ **up** [on] rinfrescare

brusque /brʊsk/ adj brusco

Brussels /'brʌslz/ n Bruxelles f. ~ **sprouts** npl cavoletti mpl di Bruxelles

brutal /'bruːtl/ adj brutale. ~**ity** f brutalità f inv

brute /bruːt/ n bruto m. ~ **force** n forza f bruta

BSc n abbr Bachelor of Science

BSE n abbr (bovine spongiform encephalitis) encefalite f bovina spongiforme

bubble /'bʌbl/ n bolla f; (in drink) bollicina f

buck[1] /bʌk/ n maschio m del cervo; (rabbit) maschio m del coniglio ● vi (horse:) saltare a quattro zampe. □ ~ **up** vi 🆃 tirarsi su; (hurry) sbrigarsi

buck[2] n Am 🆃 dollaro m

buck[3] n pass the ~ scaricare le responsabilità

bucket /'bʌkɪt/ n secchio m

buckle /'bʌkl/ n fibbia f ● vt allacciare ● vi (shelf:) piegarsi; (wheel:) storcersi

bud /bʌd/ n bocciolo m

Buddhism /'bʊdɪzm/ n buddismo m. ~**t** adj & n buddista mf

buddy /'bʌdɪ/ n 🆃 amico, -a mf

budge /bʌdʒ/ vt spostare ● vi spostarsi

budgerigar /'bʌdʒərɪɡɑː(r)/ n cocorita f

budget /'bʌdʒɪt/ n bilancio m; (allotted to specific activity) budget m inv ● vi (pt/pp budgeted) prevedere le spese; ~ for sth includere qcsa nelle spese previste

buffalo /'bʌfələʊ/ n (inv or pl -es) bufalo m

buffer /'bʌfə(r)/ n (Rail) respingente m; old ~ ① vecchio bacucco m; ~ zone n zona f cuscinetto

buffet¹ /'bʊfeɪ/ n buffet m inv

buffet² /'bʌfɪt/ vt (pt/pp buffeted) sferzare

bug /bʌg/ n (insect) insetto m; (Comput) bug m inv; (②: device) cimice f ● vt (pt/pp bugged) ① installare delle microspie in (room); mettere sotto controllo (telephone); (①: annoy) scocciare

buggy /'bʌgɪ/ n [baby] ~ passeggino m

bugle /'bjuːgl/ n tromba f

build /bɪld/ n (of person) corporatura f ● vt/i (pt/pp built) costruire. □~ on vt aggiungere (extra storey); sviluppare (previous work). □~ up vt ~ up one's strength rimettersi in forza ● vi (pressure, traffic:) aumentare; (excitement, tension:) crescere

builder /'bɪldə(r)/ n (company) costruttore m; (worker) muratore m

building /'bɪldɪŋ/ n edificio m. ~ site n cantiere m [di costruzione]. ~ society n istituto m di credito immobiliare

build-up n (of gas etc) accumulo m; fig battage m inv pubblicitario

built /bɪlt/ ▶BUILD. ~-in adj (unit) a muro; (fig: feature) incorporato. ~-up area n (Auto) centro m abitato

bulb /bʌlb/ n bulbo m; (Electr) lampadina f

Bulgaria /bʌl'geərɪə/ n Bulgaria f

bulge /bʌldʒ/ n rigonfiamento m ● vi esser gonfio (with di); (stomach, wall:) sporgere; (with surprise:) uscire dalle orbite. ~ing adj gonfio; (eyes:) sporgente

bulk /bʌlk/ n volume m; (greater part) grosso m; in ~ in grande quantità; (loose) sfuso. ~y adj voluminoso

bull /bʊl/ n toro m

bulldog n bulldog m inv

bulldozer /'bʊldəʊzə(r)/ n bulldozer m inv

bullet /'bʊlɪt/ n pallottola f

bulletin /'bʊlɪtɪn/ n bollettino m. ~ board n (Comput) bacheca f elettronica

bullet-proof adj antiproiettile inv; (vehicle) blindato

bullfight n corrida f. ~er n torero m

bull: ~ring n arena f. ~'s-eye n centro m del bersaglio; score a ~'s-eye fare centro

bully /'bʊlɪ/ n prepotente mf ● vt fare il/la prepotente con. ~ing n prepotenze fpl

bum¹ /bʌm/ n ⊠ sedere m

bum² n Am ① vagabondo, -a mf ● bum around vi ① vagabondare

bumble-bee /'bʌmbl-/ n calabrone m

bump /bʌmp/ n botta f; (swelling) bozzo m, gonfiore m; (in road) protuberanza f ● vt sbattere. □~ into vt sbattere contro; (meet) imbattersi in. □~ off vt ① far fuori

bumper /'bʌmpə(r)/ n (Auto) paraurti m inv ● adj abbondante

bun /bʌn/ n focaccina f (dolce); (hair) chignon m inv

bunch /bʌntʃ/ n (of flowers, keys) mazzo m; (of bananas) casco m; (of people) gruppo m; ~ of grapes grappolo m d'uva

bundle /'bʌndl/ n fascio m; (of money) mazzetta f; a ~ of nerves ① un fascio di nervi ● vt ~ [up] affastellare

bungalow /'bʌŋgələʊ/ n bungalow m inv

bungle /'bʌŋgl/ vt fare un

pasticcio di

bunk /bʌŋk/ n cuccetta f. ~-beds npl letti mpl a castello

bunny /'bʌnɪ/ n 🔢 coniglietto m

buoy /bɔɪ/ n boa f

burden /'bɜːdn/ n carico m • vt caricare. ~some adj gravoso

bureau /'bjʊərəʊ/ n (pl -x /-əʊz/ or ~s) (desk) scrivania f; (office) ufficio m

bureaucracy /bjʊə'rɒkrəsɪ/ n burocrazia f

bureaucrat /'bjʊərəkræt/ n burocrate m. ~ic adj burocratico

burger /'bɜːgə(r)/ n hamburger m inv

burglar /'bɜːglə(r)/ n svaligiatore, -trice mf. ~ alarm n antifurto m inv

burgle /'bɜːgl/ vt svaligiare

burial /'berɪəl/ n sepoltura f. ~ ground cimitero m

burly /'bɜːlɪ/ adj (-ier, -iest) corpulento

burn /bɜːn/ n bruciatura f • v (pt/pp burnt or burned) • vt bruciare • vi bruciare. ▫ ~ down vt/i bruciare. ▫ ~ out vi fig esaurirsi. ~er n • (on stove) bruciatore m • (Comput) masterizzatore m

burnt /bɜːnt/ ▷BURN

burp /bɜːp/ n 🔢 rutto m • vi 🔢 ruttare

burrow /'bʌrəʊ/ n tana f • vt scavare (hole)

bursar /'bɜːsə(r)/ n economo, -a mf. ~y n borsa f di studio

burst /bɜːst/ n (of gunfire, energy, laughter) scoppio m; (of speed) scatto m • v (pt/pp burst) • vt far scoppiare • vi scoppiare; ~ into tears scoppiare in lacrime; she ~ into the room ha fatto irruzione nella stanza. ▫ ~ out vi ~ out laughing/crying scoppiare a ridere/piangere

bury /'berɪ/ vt (pt/pp -ied) seppellire; (hide) nascondere

bus /bʌs/ n autobus m inv, pullman m

inv; (long distance) pullman m inv, corriera f

bush /bʊʃ/ n cespuglio m; (land) boscaglia f. ~y adj (-ier, -iest) folto

business /'bɪznɪs/ n affare m; (Comm) affari mpl; (establishment) attività f di commercio; on ~ per affari; he has no ~ to non ha alcun diritto di; mind one's own ~ farsi gli affari propri; that's none of your ~ non sono affari tuoi. ~like adj efficiente. ~man n uomo m d'affari. ~woman n donna f d'affari

busker /'bʌskə(r)/ n suonatore, -trice mf ambulante

'bus station n stazione f degli autobus

'bus-stop n fermata f d'autobus

bust¹ /bʌst/ n busto m; (chest) petto m

bust² adj 🔢 rotto; go ~ fallire • v (pt/pp busted or bust) 🔢 • vt far scoppiare • vi scoppiare

'bust-up n 🔢 lite f

busy /'bɪzɪ/ adj (-ier, -iest) occupato; (day, time) intenso; (street) affollato; (with traffic) pieno di traffico; be ~ doing essere occupato a fare • vt ~ oneself darsi da fare

'busybody n ficcanaso m inv

but /bʌt/, atono /bət/ conj ma • prep eccetto, tranne; nobody ~ you nessuno tranne te; ~ for (without) se non fosse stato per; the last ~ one il penultimo; the next ~ one il secondo • adv (only) soltanto; there were ~ two ce n'erano soltanto due

butcher /'bʊtʃə(r)/ n macellaio m; ~'s [shop] macelleria f • vt macellare; fig massacrare

butler /'bʌtlə(r)/ n maggiordomo m

butt /bʌt/ n (of gun) calcio m; (of cigarette) mozzicone m; (for water) barile m; (fig: target) bersaglio m • vt dare una testata a; (goat:) dare una cornata a. ▫ ~ in vi interrompere

butter /'bʌtə(r)/ n burro m • vt imburrare. □ ~ **up** vt 🔢 arruffianarsi

butter: ~**cup** n ranuncolo m. ~**fingers** nsg 🔢 be a ~**fingers** avere le mani di pasta frolla. ~**fly** n farfalla f

button /'bʌtn/ n bottone m • vt ~ [up] abbottonare • vi abbottonarsi. ~**hole** n occhiello m, asola f

buy /baɪ/ n good/bad ~ buon/cattivo acquisto m • vt (pt/pp bought) comprare; ~ sb a drink pagare da bere a qcno; I'll ~ this one (drink) questo, lo offro io. ~**er** n compratore, -trice mf

buzz /bʌz/ n ronzio m; give sb a ~ 🔢 (on phone) dare un colpo di telefono a qcno; (excite) mettere in fermento qcno • vi ronzare • vt ~ sb chiamare qcno col cicalino. □ ~ **off** vi 🔢 levarsi di torno

buzzer /'bʌzə(r)/ n cicalino m

by /baɪ/
● prep (near, next to) vicino a; (at the latest) per; by Mozart di Mozart; he was run over by a bus è stato investito da un autobus; by oneself da solo; by the sea al mare; by sea via mare; by car/bus in macchina/autobus; by day/night di giorno/notte; by the hour/metre a ore/metri; six metres by four sei metri per quattro; he won by six metres ha vinto di sei metri; I missed the train by a minute ho perso il treno per un minuto; I'll be home by six sarò a casa per le sei; by this time next week a quest'ora tra una settimana; he rushed by me mi è passato accanto di corsa
● adv she'll be here by and by sarà qui fra poco; by and large in complesso

bye[-bye] /baɪ['baɪ]/ int 🔢 ciao

by: ~**-election** n elezione f straordinaria indetta per coprire una carica rimasta vacante in Parlamento. ~**-law** n legge f locale. ~**pass** n circonvallazione f; (Med) by-pass m inv • vt evitare. ~**-product** n sottoprodotto m. ~**stander** n spettatore, -trice mf

Cc

cab /kæb/ n taxi m inv; (of lorry, train) cabina f

cabaret /'kæbəreɪ/ n cabaret m inv

cabbage /'kæbɪdʒ/ n cavolo m

cabin /'kæbɪn/ n (of plane, ship) cabina f; (hut) capanna f

cabinet /'kæbɪnɪt/ n armadietto m; (display) ~ vetrina f; C~ (Pol) consiglio m dei ministri. ~**-maker** n ebanista mf

cable /'keɪbl/ n cavo m. ~ **railway** n funicolare f. ~ '**television** n televisione f via cavo

cackle /'kækl/ vi ridacchiare

cactus /'kæktəs/ n (pl -ti /-taɪ/ or -tuses) cactus m inv

caddie /'kædɪ/ n portabastoni m inv

caddy /'kædɪ/ n [tea-]~ barattolo m del tè

cadet /kə'det/ n cadetto m

cadge /kædʒ/ vt/i 🔢 scroccare

café /'kæfeɪ/ n caffè m inv

cafeteria /kæfə'tɪərɪə/ n tavola f calda

caffeine /'kæfiːn/ n caffeina f

cage /keɪdʒ/ n gabbia f

cake /keɪk/ n torta f; (small) pasticcino m. ~**d** adj incrostato (with di)

calamity /kə'læmətɪ/ n calamità f inv

calcium /'kælsɪəm/ n calcio m

calculat|e /'kælkjʊleɪt/ vt calcolare. ~**ing** adj fig calcolatore. ~**ion** n calcolo m. ~**or** n calcolatrice f

calendar /'kælɪndə(r)/ n calendario m

calf¹ /kɑːf/ n (pl **calves**) vitello m

calf² n (pl **calves**) (Anat) polpaccio m

calibre /'kælɪbə(r)/ n calibro m

call /kɔːl/ n grido m; (Teleph) telefonata f; (visit) visita f; be on ~ (doctor:) essere di guardia • vt chiamare; indire (strike); be ~ed chiamarsi • vi chiamare; ~ **[in** or **round]** passare. □ ~ **back** vt/i richiamare. □ ~ **for** vt (ask for) chiedere; (require) richiedere; (fetch) passare a prendere. □ ~ **off** vt richiamare (dog); disdire (meeting); revocare (strike). □ ~ **on** vt chiamare; (appeal to) fare un appello a; (visit) visitare. □ ~ **out** vt chiamare ad alta voce (names) • vi chiamare ad alta voce. □ ~ **together** vt riunire. □ ~ **up** vt (Mil) chiamare alle armi; (Teleph) chiamare

call: ~**-box** n cabina f telefonica. ~**-centre** n call centre m inv. ~**er** n visitatore, -trice mf; (Teleph) persona f che telefona. ~**ing** n vocazione f

callous /'kæləs/ adj insensibile

calm /kɑːm/ adj calmo • n calma f. □ ~ **down** vt calmare • vi calmarsi. ~**ly** adv con calma

calorie /'kælərɪ/ n caloria f

calves /kɑːvz/ npl see **calf1 &2**

camcorder /'kæmkɔːdə(r)/ n videocamera f

came /keɪm/ ▷**come**

camel /'kæml/ n cammello m

camera /'kæmərə/ n macchina f fotografica; (TV) telecamera f. ~**man** n operatore m [televisivo], cameraman m inv

camouflage /'kæməflɑːʒ/ n mimetizzazione f • vt mimetizzare

camp /kæmp/ n campeggio f; (Mil) campo m • vi campeggiare; (Mil) accamparsi

campaign /kæm'peɪn/ n campagna f • vi fare una campagna

camp: ~**-bed** n letto m da campo. ~**er** n campeggiatore, -trice mf; (Auto) camper m inv. ~**ing** n campeggio m. ~**site** n campeggio m

campus /'kæmpəs/ n (pl **-puses**) (Univ) città f universitaria, campus m inv

can¹ /kæn/ n (for petrol) latta f; (tin) scatola f; ~ **of beer** lattina f di birra • vt mettere in scatola

can² /kæn/, atono /kən/ v aux (pres **can**; pt **could**) (be able to) potere; (know how to) sapere; I **cannot** or **can't** go non posso andare; he **could not** or **couldn't** go non poteva andare; she **can't** swim non sa nuotare; I ~ **smell** something **burning** sento odore di bruciato

Canad|a /'kænədə/ n Canada m. ~**ian** adj & n canadese mf

canal /kə'næl/ n canale m

Canaries /kə'neərɪz/ npl Canarie fpl

canary /kə'neərɪ/ n canarino m

cancel /'kænsl/ v (pt/pp **cancelled**) • vt disdire (meeting, newspaper); revocare (contract, order); annullare (reservation, appointment, stamp). ~**lation** n (of meeting, contract) revoca f; (in hotel, restaurant, for flight) cancellazione f

cancer /'kænsə(r)/ n cancro m; C~ (Astr) Cancro m. ~**ous** adj canceroso

candid /'kændɪd/ adj franco

candidate /'kændɪdət/ n candidato, -a mf

candle /'kændl/ n candela f. ~**stick** n portacandele m inv

candour /'kændə(r)/ n franchezza f

candy /'kændɪ/ n Am caramella f; a [piece of] ~ una caramella. ~**floss** n zucchero m filato

cane /keɪn/ n (stick) bastone m; (Sch)

bacchetta f ● vt prendere a bacchettate (pupil)

canister /'kænɪstə(r)/ n barattolo m (di metallo)

cannabis /'kænəbɪs/ n cannabis f

cannibal /'kænɪbl/ n cannibale mf. **~ism** n cannibalismo m

cannon /'kænən/ n inv cannone m. **~-ball** n palla f di cannone

cannot /'kænɒt/ ▷**CAN²**

canoe /kə'nu:/ n canoa f ● vi andare in canoa

'can-opener n apriscatole m inv

canopy /'kænəpɪ/ n baldacchino f; (of parachute) calotta f

cantankerous /kæn'tæŋkərəs/ adj stizzoso

canteen /kæn'ti:n/ n mensa f; **~ of cutlery** servizio m di posate

canter /'kæntə(r)/ vi andare a piccolo galoppo

canvas /'kænvəs/ n tela f; (painting) dipinto m su tela

canvass /'kænvəs/ vi (Pol) fare propaganda elettorale. **~ing** n sollecitazione f di voti

canyon /'kænjən/ n canyon m inv

cap /kæp/ n berretto m; (nurse's) cuffia f; (top, lid) tappo m ● vt (pt/pp capped) (fig: do better than) superare

capability /keɪpə'bɪlətɪ/ n capacità f

capable /'keɪpəbl/ adj capace; (skilful) abile; **be ~e of** doing essere capace di fare qcsa. **~y** adv con abilità

capacity /kə'pæsətɪ/ n capacità f; (function) qualità f; **in my ~** as **in** qualità di

cape¹ /keɪp/ n (cloak) cappa f

cape² n (Geog) capo m

capital /'kæpɪtl/ n (town) capitale f; (money) capitale m; (letter) lettera f maiuscola. **~ city** n capitale f

capitalism /'kæpɪtəlɪzm/ n capitalismo m. **~ist** adj & n capitalista mf.

~ize vi **~ize on** fig trarre vantaggio da. **~ 'letter** n lettera f maiuscola. **~ 'punishment** n pena f capitale

capitulate /kə'pɪtjʊleɪt/ vi capitolare. **~ion** n capitolazione f

Capricorn /'kæprɪkɔ:n/ n (Astr) Capricorno m

capsize /kæp'saɪz/ vi capovolgersi ● vt capovolgere

capsule /'kæpsjʊl/ n capsula f

captain /'kæptɪn/ n capitano m ● vt comandare (team)

caption /'kæpʃn/ n intestazione f; (of illustration) didascalia f

captivate /'kæptɪveɪt/ vt incantare

captive /'kæptɪv/ adj prigioniero; hold/take **~e** tenere/fare prigioniero ● n prigioniero, -a mf. **~ity** n prigionia f; (animals) cattività f

capture /'kæptʃə(r)/ n cattura f ● vt catturare; attirare (attention)

car /kɑ:(r)/ n macchina f; **by ~** in macchina

carafe /kə'ræf/ n caraffa f

caramel /'kærəmel/ n (sweet) caramella f al mou; (Culin) caramello m

caravan /'kærəvæn/ n roulotte f inv (horse-drawn) carovana f

carbohydrate /kɑ:bə'haɪdreɪt/ n carboidrato m

carbon /'kɑ:bən/ n carbonio m. **~ di'oxide** n anidride f carbonica. **~ 'footprint** n impronta f ecologica

carburettor /kɑ:bjʊ'retə(r)/ n carburatore m

carcass /'kɑ:kəs/ n carcassa f

card /kɑ:d/ n (for birthday, Christmas etc) biglietto m di auguri; (playing ~)

carta f [da gioco]; (membership ~) tessera f; (business ~) biglietto m da visita; (credit ~) carta f di credito; (Comput) scheda f

cardboard n cartone m. ~ **'box** n scatola f di cartone; (large) scatolone m

cardigan /'kɑːdɪgən/ n cardigan m inv

cardinal /'kɑːdɪnl/ adj cardinale; ~ **number** numero m cardinale • n (Relig) cardinale m

care /keə(r)/ n cura f; (caution) attenzione f; (worry) preoccupazione f; ~ **of** (on letter abbr c/o) presso; **take** ~ (be cautious) fare attenzione; **bye, take** ~ ciao, stammi bene; **take** ~ **of** occuparsi di; **be taken into** ~ essere preso in custodia da un ente assistenziale • vi ~ **about** interessarsi di; ~ **for** (feel affection for) volere bene a; (look after) aver cura di; **I don't** ~ **for chocolate** non mi piace il cioccolato; **I don't** ~ non me ne importa; **who** ~**s?** chi se ne frega?

career /kə'rɪə(r)/ n carriera f; (profession) professione f • vi andare a tutta velocità

care: ~**free** adj spensierato. ~**ful** adj attento; (driver) prudente. ~**fully** adv con attenzione. ~**less** adj irresponsabile; (in work) trascurato; (work) fatto con poca cura; (driver) distratto. ~**lessly** adv negligentemente. ~**lessness** n trascuratezza f. ~**r** n persona f che accudisce a un anziano o a un malato

caress /kə'res/ n carezza f • vt accarezzare

'caretaker n custode mf; (in school) bidello m

'car ferry n traghetto m (per il trasporto di auto)

cargo /'kɑːgəʊ/ n (pl -es) carico m

Caribbean /kærɪ'biːən/ n the ~ (sea) il Mar dei Caraibi • adj caraibico

caricature /'kærɪkətjʊə(r)/ n caricatura f

carnage /'kɑːnɪdʒ/ n carneficina f

carnation /kɑː'neɪʃn/ n garofano m

carnival /'kɑːnɪvl/ n carnevale m

carol /'kærəl/ n [Christmas] ~ canzone f natalizia

carp¹ /kɑːp/ n inv carpa f

carp² vi ~ **at** trovare da ridire su

'car park n parcheggio m

carpent|er /'kɑːpɪntə(r)/ n falegname m. ~**ry** n falegnameria f

carpet /'kɑːpɪt/ n tappeto m; (wall-to-wall) moquette f inv • vt mettere la moquette in (room)

carriage /'kærɪdʒ/ n carrozza f; (of goods) trasporto m; (cost) spese fpl di trasporto; (bearing) portamento m; ~**way** n strada f carrozzabile; **northbound** ~**way** carreggiata f nord

carrier /'kærɪə(r)/ n (company) impresa f di trasporti; (Aeron) compagnia f di trasporto aereo; (of disease) portatore m. ~ **bag** n borsa f [per la spesa]

carrot /'kærət/ n carota f

carry /'kærɪ/ v (pt/pp -ied) • vt portare; (transport) trasportare; **get carried away** 🗆 lasciarsi prender la mano • vi (sound): trasmettersi. □ ~ **off** vt portare via; vincere (prize). □ ~ **on** vi continuare; (🗆: make scene) fare delle storie; ~ **on with sth** continuare qcsa; ~ **on with sb** 🗆 intendersela con qcno • vt mantenere (business). □ ~ **out** vt portare fuori; eseguire (instructions, task); mettere in atto (threat); effettuare (experiment, survey)

'carry-cot n porte-enfant m inv

cart /kɑːt/ n carretto m • vt (🗆: carry) portare

carton /'kɑːtn/ n scatola f di cartone; (for drink) cartone m; (of cream, yoghurt) vasetto m; (of cigarettes) stecca f

cartoon /kɑːˈtuːn/ n vignetta f; (strip) vignette fpl; (film) cartone m animato; (in art) bozzetto m. ~ist n vignettista m/f; (for films) disegnatore, -trice m/f di cartoni animati

cartridge /ˈkɑːtrɪdʒ/ n cartuccia f; (for film) bobina f; (of record player) testina f

carve /kɑːv/ vt scolpire; tagliare (meat)

case[1] /keɪs/ n caso m; in any ~ in ogni caso; in that ~ in questo caso; just in ~ per sicurezza; in ~ he comes nel caso in cui venisse

case[2] n (container) scatola f; (crate) cassa f; (for spectacles) astuccio m; (suitcase) valigia f; (for display) vetrina f

cash /kæʃ/ n denaro m contante; (🅸: money) contanti mpl; pay [in] ~ pagare in contanti; ~ on delivery pagamento alla consegna ● vt incassare (cheque). ~ desk n cassa f

cashier /kæˈʃɪə(r)/ n cassiere, -a m/f

casino /kəˈsiːnəʊ/ n casinò m inv

casket /ˈkɑːskɪt/ n scrigno m; (Am: coffin) bara f

casserole /ˈkæsərəʊl/ n casseruola f; (stew) stufato m

cassette /kəˈset/ n cassetta f. ~ recorder n registratore m (a cassette)

cast /kɑːst/ n (mould) forma f; (Theat) cast m; (plaster) ~ (Med) ingessatura f ● vt (pt/pp cast) dare (vote); (Theat) assegnare le parti di (play); fondere (metal); (throw) gettare; ~ an actor as dare a un attore il ruolo di; ~ a glance at lanciare uno sguardo a. □ ~ off vi (Naut) sganciare gli ormeggi ● vt (in knitting) diminuire. □ ~ on vt (in knitting) avviare

castaway /ˈkɑːstəweɪ/ n naufrago, -a m/f

caster /ˈkɑːstə(r)/ n (wheel) rotella f. ~ sugar n zucchero m raffinato

cast iron n ghisa f

cast-iron adj di ghisa; fig solido

castle /ˈkɑːsl/ n castello m;

(in chess) torre f

'cast-offs npl abiti mpl smessi

castrat|e /kæˈstreɪt/ vt castrare. ~ion n castrazione f

casual /ˈkæʒʊəl/ adj (chance) casuale; (remark) senza importanza; (glance) di sfuggita; (attitude, approach) disinvolto; (chat) informale; (clothes) casual inv; (work) saltuario; ~ wear abbigliamento m casual. ~ly adv (dress) casual; (meet) casualmente

casualty /ˈkæʒʊəltɪ/ n (injured person) ferito m; (killed) vittima f. ~ [department] n pronto soccorso m

cat /kæt/ n gatto m; pej arpia f

catalogue /ˈkætəlɒg/ n catalogo m ● vt catalogare

catalyst /ˈkætəlɪst/ n (Chem) & fig catalizzatore m

catapult /ˈkætəpʌlt/ n catapulta f; (child's) fionda f ● vt fig catapultare

catarrh /kəˈtɑː(r)/ n catarro m

catastroph|e /kəˈtæstrəfɪ/ n catastrofe f. ~ic adj catastrofico

catch /kætʃ/ n (of fish) pesca f; (fastener) fermaglio m; (on door) fermo m; (on window) gancio m; (🅸: snag) tranello m ● v (pt/pp caught) ● vt acchiappare (ball); (grab) afferrare; prendere (illness, fugitive, train); ~ a cold prendersi un raffreddore; ~ sight of scorgere; I caught him stealing l'ho sorpreso mentre rubava; ~ one's finger in the door chiudersi il dito nella porta; ~ sb's eye or attention attirare l'attenzione di qcno ● vi (fire): prendere; (get stuck) impigliarsi. □ ~ on vi (🅸 (understand) afferrare; (become popular) diventare popolare. □ ~ up vt raggiungere ● vi recuperare; (runner:) riguadagnare terreno; ~ up with raggiungere (sb); mettersi in pari con (work)

catching /ˈkætʃɪŋ/ adj contagioso

catchphrase n tormentone m

catchy /ˈkætʃɪ/ adj (-ier, -iest)

orecchiabile

categor|ical /ˌkætɪˈɡɒrɪkl/ adj categorico. ~y n categoria f

cater /ˈkeɪtə(r)/ vi ~ for provvedere a (needs); fig venire incontro alle esigenze di. ~ing n (trade) ristorazione f; (food) rinfresco m

caterpillar /ˈkætəpɪlə(r)/ n bruco m

cathedral /kəˈθiːdrl/ n cattedrale f

Catholic /ˈkæθəlɪk/ adj & n cattolico, -a mf. ~ism n cattolicesimo m

cat's eyes npl catarifrangente msg (inserito nell'asfalto)

cattle /ˈkætl/ npl bestiame msg

catwalk /ˈkætwɔːk/ n passerella f

caught /kɔːt/ ▷CATCH

cauliflower /ˈkɒlɪ-/ n cavolfiore m

cause /kɔːz/ n causa f ● vt causare; ~ sb to do sth far fare qcsa a qcno

caution /ˈkɔːʃn/ n cautela f; (warning) ammonizione f ● vt mettere in guardia; (Jur) ammonire

cautious /ˈkɔːʃəs/ adj cauto

cavalry /ˈkævəlrɪ/ n cavalleria f

cave /keɪv/ n caverna f ● cave in vi (roof:) crollare; (fig: give in) capitolare

cavern /ˈkævən/ n caverna f

caviare /ˈkævɪɑː(r)/ n caviale m

cavity /ˈkævətɪ/ n cavità f inv; (in tooth) carie f inv

CD n CD m inv. ~ player n lettore m [di] compact

CD-Rom /siːdiːˈrɒm/ n CD-Rom m inv. ~ drive n lettore m [di] CD-Rom

cease /siːs/ n without ~ incessantemente vt/i cessare. ~-fire n cessate il fuoco m inv. ~less adj incessante

cedar /ˈsiːdə/ n cedro m

ceiling /ˈsiːlɪŋ/ n soffitto m; fig tetto m [massimo]

celebrat|e /ˈselɪbreɪt/ vt festeggiare (birthday, victory) ● vi far festa. ~ed adj celebre (for per). ~ion n celebrazione f

celebrity /sɪˈlebrətɪ/ n celebrità f inv

celery /ˈselərɪ/ n sedano m

cell /sel/ n cella f; (Biol) cellula f

cellar /ˈselə(r)/ n scantinato m; (for wine) cantina f

cello /ˈtʃeləʊ/ n violoncello m

Cellophane® /ˈseləfeɪn/ n cellofan m inv

cellphone /ˈselfəʊn/ n cellulare m

cellular phone /seljʊləˈfəʊn/ n [telefono m] cellulare m

celluloid /ˈseljʊlɔɪd/ n celluloide f

Celsius /ˈselsɪəs/ adj Celsius

cement /sɪˈment/ n cemento m; (adhesive) mastice m ● vt cementare; fig consolidare

cemetery /ˈsemətrɪ/ n cimitero m

censor /ˈsensə(r)/ n censore m ● vt censurare. ~ship n censura f

censure /ˈsenʃə(r)/ vt biasimare

census /ˈsensəs/ n censimento m

cent /sent/ n (of dollar) centesimo m; (of euro) cent m inv, centesimo m

centenary /senˈtiːnərɪ/ n, Am **centennial** /senˈtenɪəl/ n centenario m

center /ˈsentə(r)/ n Am = centre

centigrade /ˈsentɪ-/ adj centigrado. ~metre n centimetro m. ~pede n centopiedi m inv

central /ˈsentrl/ adj centrale. ~ heating n riscaldamento m autonomo. ~ize vt centralizzare. ~ly adv al centro; ~ly heated con riscaldamento autonomo. ~ reservation n (Auto) banchina f spartitraffico

centre /ˈsentə(r)/ n centro m ● v (pt/pp centred) ● vt centrare ● vi ~ on fig incentrarsi su. ~-forward n centravanti m inv

century /ˈsentʃərɪ/ n secolo m

cereal /ˈsɪərɪəl/ n cereale m

ceremon|ial /serɪˈməʊnɪəl/ adj da cerimonia ● n cerimoniale m. ~ious adj cerimonioso

ceremony /ˈserɪmənɪ/ n

cerimonia f

certain /'sɜːtn/ adj certo; for ~ di sicuro; make ~ accertarsi di; he is ~ to win è certo di vincere; it's not ~ whether he'll come non è sicuro che venga. **~ly** adv certamente; **~ly not!** no di certo! **~ty** n certezza f; it's a ~ty è una cosa certa

certificate /sə'tɪfɪkət/ n certificato m

certify /'sɜːtɪfaɪ/ vt (pt/pp -ied) certificare; (declare insane) dichiarare malato di mente

chafe /tʃeɪf/ vt irritare

chain /tʃeɪn/ n catena f ● vt incatenare (prisoner); attaccare con la catena (dog) (to a). □ ~ **up** vt legare alla catena (dog)

chain: ~ re'action n reazione f a catena. ~**smoker** n fumatore, -trice mf accanito, -a. ~ **store** n negozio m appartenente a una catena

chair /tʃeə(r)/ n sedia f; (Univ) cattedra f ● vt presiedere. ~**lift** n seggiovia f. ~**man** n presidente m

chalet /'ʃæleɪ/ n chalet m inv; (in holiday camp) bungalow m inv

chalk /tʃɔːk/ n gesso m. ~**y** adj gessoso

challenge /'tʃælɪndʒ/ n sfida f; (Mil) intimazione f ● vt sfidare; (Mil) intimare il chi va là a; fig mettere in dubbio (statement). ~**er** n sfidante mf. ~**ing** adj (job) impegnativo

chamber /'tʃeɪmbə(r)/ n C~ of Commerce camera f di commercio

chambermaid n cameriera f [d'albergo]

champagne /ʃæm'peɪn/ n champagne m inv

champion /'tʃæmpɪən/ n (Sport) campione m; (of cause) difensore, difenditrice mf ● vt (defend) difendere; (fight for) lottare per. ~**ship** n (Sport) campionato m

chance /tʃɑːns/ n caso m; (possibility) possibilità f inv; (opportunity) occasione

f; by ~ per caso; take a ~ provarci; give sb a second ~ dare un'altra possibilità a qcno ● attrib fortuito ● vt I'll ~ it I corro il rischio

chancellor /'tʃɑːnsələ(r)/ n cancelliere m; (Univ) rettore m; C~ of the Exchequer ≈ ministro m del tesoro

chandelier /ʃændə'lɪə(r)/ n lampadario m

change /tʃeɪndʒ/ n cambiamento m; (money) resto m; (small coins) spiccioli mpl; for a ~ tanto per cambiare; a ~ of clothes un cambio di vestiti; the ~ [of life] la menopausa ● vt cambiare; (substitute) scambiare (for one); ~ one's clothes cambiarsi [i vestiti]; ~ trains cambiare treno ● vi cambiare; (~ clothes) cambiarsi; all ~! stazione terminale!

changeable /'tʃeɪndʒəbl/ adj mutevole; (weather) variabile

'changing-room n camerino m; (for sports) spogliatoio m

channel /'tʃænl/ n canale m; the [English] C~ la Manica; the C~ Islands le Isole del Canale ● vt (pt/pp channelled) ~ one's energies into sth convogliare le proprie energie in qcsa

chant /tʃɑːnt/ n cantilena f; (of demonstrators) slogan m inv di protesta ● vt cantare; (demonstrators:) gridare

chao|s /'keɪɒs/ n caos m. ~**tic** adj caotico

chap /tʃæp/ n I tipo m

chapel /'tʃæpl/ n cappella f

chaperon /'ʃæpərəʊn/ n chaperon f inv ● vt fare da chaperon a (sb)

chapter /'tʃæptə(r)/ n capitolo m

char¹ /tʃɑː(r)/ n I donna f delle pulizie

char² vt (pt/pp charred) (burn) carbonizzare

character /'kærɪktə(r)/ n carattere m; (in novel, play) personaggio m; quite a ~ I un tipo particolare

characteristic /kærɪktə'rɪstɪk/ adj

caratteristico ● *n* **caratteristica** *f.* **~ally** *adv* tipicamente

characterize /'kærɪktəraɪz/ *vt* caratterizzare

charade /ʃəˈrɑːd/ *n* farsa *f*

charcoal /ˈtʃɑː-/ *n* carbonella *f*

charge /tʃɑːdʒ/ *n* (cost) prezzo *m*; (Electr, Mil) carica *f*; (Jur) accusa *f*; free of ~ gratuito; be in ~ essere responsabile (of di); take ~ assumersi la responsibilità; take ~ of occuparsi di ● *vt* far pagare (fee); far pagare a (person); (Electr, Mil) caricare; (Jur) accusare (with di); ~ sb for sth far pagare qcsa a qcno; ~ it to my account lo addebiti sul mio conto □ *vi* (attack) caricare

charitable /ˈtʃærɪtəbl/ *adj* caritatevole; (kind) indulgente

charity /ˈtʃærɪtɪ/ *n* carità *f*; (organization) associazione *f* di beneficenza; concert given for ~ concerto *m* di beneficenza; live on ~ vivere di elemosina

charm /tʃɑːm/ *n* fascino *m*; (object) ciondolo *m* ● *vt* affascinare. **~ing** *adj* affascinante

chart /tʃɑːt/ *n* carta *f* nautica; (table) tabella *f*

charter /ˈtʃɑːtə(r)/ *n* ~ [flight] [volo *m*] charter *m inv* ● *vt* noleggiare. **~ed accountant** *n* commercialista *mf*

chase /tʃeɪs/ *n* inseguimento *m* ● *vt* inseguire. **chase away** or **off** *vt* cacciare via

chassis /ˈʃæsɪ/ *n* (*pl* chassis /-sɪz/) telaio *m*

chastity /ˈtʃæstətɪ/ *n* castità *f*

chat /tʃæt/ *n* chiacchierata *f*; have a ~ with fare quattro chiacchere con ● *vi* (*pt/pp* chatted) chiacchierare; (Comput) chattare. **~ show** *n* talk show *m inv*

chatter /ˈtʃætə(r)/ *n* chiacchiere *fpl* ● *vi* chiacchierare; (teeth:) battere. **~box** *n* 🔢 chiacchierone, -a *mf*

chauffeur /ˈʃəʊfə(r)/ *n* autista *mf*

chauvin|ism /ˈʃəʊvɪnɪzm/ *n* sciovinismo *m.* **~ist** *n* sciovinista *mf.* male **~ist** *n* 🔢 maschilista *m*

cheap /tʃiːp/ *adj* a buon mercato; (rate) economico; (vulgar) grossolano; (of poor quality) scadente ● **cheap** a buon mercato. **~ly** *adv* a buon mercato

cheat /tʃiːt/ *n* imbroglione, -a *mf*; (at cards) baro *m* ● *vt* imbrogliare; ~ sb out of sth sottrarre qcsa a qcno con l'inganno ● *vi* imbrogliare; (at cards) barare. □ ~ **on** *vt* 🔢 tradire (wife)

check¹ /tʃek/ *adj* (pattern) a quadri ● *n* disegno *m* a quadri

check² *n* verifica *f*; (of tickets) controllo *m*; (in chess) scacco *m*; (Am: bill) conto *m*; (Am: cheque) assegno *m*; (Am: tick) segnetto *m*; keep a ~ on controllare; keep in ~ tenere sotto controllo ● *vt* verificare; controllare (tickets); (restrain) contenere; (stop) bloccare ● *vi* controllare; ~ on sth controllare qcsa. □ ~ **in** *vi* registrarsi all'arrivo (in albergo); (Aeron) fare il check-in ● *vt* registrare all'arrivo (in albergo). □ ~ **out** *vi* (of hotel) saldare il conto ● *vt* (🔢: investigate) controllare. □ ~ **up** *vi* accertarsi; ~ **up on** prendere informazioni su

check: **~in** *n* (in airport: place) banco *m* accettazione, check-in *m inv*; **~mate** *int* scacco matto! **~out** *n* (in supermarket) cassa *f.* **~up** *n* (Med) visita *f* di controllo, check-up *m inv*

cheek /tʃiːk/ *n* guancia *f*; (impudence) sfacciataggine *f.* **~y** *adj* sfacciato

cheep /tʃiːp/ *vi* pigolare

cheer /tʃɪə(r)/ *n* evviva *m inv*; three **~s** tre urrà; **~s!** salute!; (goodbye) arrivederci!; (thanks) grazie! ● *vt* acclamare. □ ~ **up** *vt* tirarsi su [di morale] ● *vi* tirarsi su [di morale]; **up!** su con la vita!. **~ful** *adj* allegro. **~fulness** *n* allegria *f.* **~ing** *n* acclamazione *f*

cheerio /tʃɪərɪˈəʊ/ *int* 🔢 arrivederci

'**cheerless** adj triste, tetro

cheese /tʃiːz/ n formaggio m. ~**cake** n dolce m al formaggio

chef /ʃef/ n cuoco, -a mf, chef mf inv

chemical /ˈkemɪkl/ adj chimico ● n prodotto m chimico

chemist /ˈkemɪst/ n (pharmacist) farmacista mf; (scientist) chimico, -a mf; ~'s [shop] farmacia f. ~ry n chimica f

cheque /tʃek/ n assegno m. ~**-book** n libretto m degli assegni. ~ card n carta f assegni

cherish /ˈtʃerɪʃ/ vt curare teneramente; (love) avere caro; nutrire (hope)

cherry /ˈtʃerɪ/ n ciliegia f; (tree) ciliegio m

chess /tʃes/ n scacchi mpl

chessboard n scacchiera f

chest /tʃest/ n petto m; (box) cassapanca f

chestnut /ˈtʃesnʌt/ n castagna f; (tree) castagno m

chest of 'drawers n cassettone m

chew /tʃuː/ vt masticare. ~**ingum** n gomma f da masticare

chic /ʃiːk/ adj chic inv

chick /tʃɪk/ n pulcino m; (⊥: girl) ragazza f

chicken /ˈtʃɪkɪn/ n pollo m ● adj attrib (soup) di pollo ● **chicken out** vi ⊥ he ~ed out gli è venuta fifa. ~**pox** n varicella f

chicory /ˈtʃɪkərɪ/ n cicoria f

chief /tʃiːf/ adj principale ● n capo m. ~**ly** adv principalmente

chilblain /ˈtʃɪlbleɪn/ n gelone m

child /tʃaɪld/ n (pl ~ren) bambino, -a mf; (son/daughter) figlio, -a mf

child: ~**birth** n parto m. ~**hood** n infanzia f. ~**ish** adj infantile. ~**less** adj senza figli. ~**like** adj ingenuo

Chile /ˈtʃɪlɪ/ n Cile m. ~**an** adj & n cileno, -a mf

chill /tʃɪl/ n freddo m; (illness) infreddatura f ● vt raffreddare

chilli /ˈtʃɪlɪ/ n (pl -es) ~ [pepper] peperoncino m

chilly /ˈtʃɪlɪ/ adj freddo

chime /tʃaɪm/ vi suonare

chimney /ˈtʃɪmnɪ/ n camino m. ~**-pot** n comignolo m. ~**-sweep** n spazzacamino m

chimpanzee /tʃɪmpænˈziː/ n scimpanzé m inv

chin /tʃɪn/ n mento m

china /ˈtʃaɪnə/ n porcellana f

China a /ˈtʃaɪnə/ n Cina f. ~**ese** adj & n cinese mf; (language) cinese m; the ~ese pl i cinesi

chink[1] /tʃɪŋk/ n (slit) fessura f

chink[2] n (noise) tintinnio m

chip /tʃɪp/ n (fragment) scheggia f; (in china, paintwork) scheggiatura f; (Comput) chip m inv; (in gambling) fiche f inv; ~s pl Br (Culin) patatine fpl fritte; Am (Culin) patatine fpl ● vt (pt/pp chipped) (damage) scheggiare. ~ in vi ⊥ intromettersi; (with money) contribuire. ~**ped** adj (damaged) scheggiato

chiropodist /kɪˈrɒpədɪst/ n podiatra mf inv. ~y n podiatria f

chirp /tʃɜːp/ vi cinguettare; (cricket:) fare cri cri. ~y adj ⊥ pimpante

chisel /ˈtʃɪzl/ n scalpello m

chivalr|ous /ˈʃɪvlrəs/ adj cavalleresco. ~ry n cavalleria f

chives /tʃaɪvz/ npl erba f cipollina

chlorine /ˈklɔːriːn/ n cloro m

chock-a-block /ˈtʃɒkəblɒk/, **chock-full** /tʃɒkˈfʊl/ adj pieno zeppo

chocolate /ˈtʃɒkələt/ n cioccolato m; (drink) cioccolata f; a ~ un cioccolatino

choice /tʃɔɪs/ n scelta f ● adj scelto

choir /ˈkwaɪə(r)/ n coro m. ~**boy** n corista m

choke /tʃəʊk/ n (Auto) aria f ● vt/i soffocare

cholera /ˈkɒlərə/ n colera m

cholesterol /kəˈlestərɒl/ n colesterolo m

choose /tʃuːz/ vt/i (pt chose, pp chosen) scegliere; as you ~ come vuoi

chop /tʃɒp/ n (blow) colpo m (d'ascia); (Culin) costata f ● vt (pt/pp chopped) tagliare. ~ **down** vt abbattere (tree). □ ~ **off** vt spaccare

chop|per /ˈtʃɒpə(r)/ n accetta f; 🗊 elicottero m. ~**py** adj increspato

chord /kɔːd/ n (Mus) corda f

chore /tʃɔː(r)/ n corvé f inv; [household] ~s faccende fpl domestiche

chorus /ˈkɔːrəs/ n coro m; (of song) ritornello m

chose, chosen /tʃəʊz/, /ˈtʃəʊzn/. ▷CHOOSE

Christ /kraɪst/ n Cristo m

christen /ˈkrɪsn/ vt battezzare. ~**ing** n battesimo m

Christian /ˈkrɪstʃən/ adj & n cristiano, -a mf. ~**ity** n cristianesimo m. ~ **name** n nome m di battesimo

Christmas /ˈkrɪsməs/ n Natale m ● attrib di Natale. '~ **card** n biglietto m d'auguri di Natale. ~ 'Day n il giorno di Natale. ~ 'Eve n la vigilia di Natale. ~ **present** n regalo m di Natale. '~ **pudding** dolce m natalizio a base di frutta candita e liquore. '~ **tree** n albero m di Natale

chrome /krəʊm/ n, **chromium** /ˈkrəʊmɪəm/ n cromo m

chromosome /ˈkrəʊməsəʊm/ n cromosoma m

chronic /ˈkrɒnɪk/ adj cronico

chronicle /ˈkrɒnɪkl/ n cronaca f

chronological /krɒnəˈlɒdʒɪkl/ adj cronologico. ~**ly** adv (ordered) in ordine cronologico

chubby /ˈtʃʌbɪ/ adj (-ier, -iest) paffuto

chuck /tʃʌk/ vt 🗊 buttare. □ ~ **out**

vt 🗊 buttare via (object); buttare fuori (person)

chuckle /ˈtʃʌkl/ vi ridacchiare

chug /tʃʌg/ vi (pt/pp chugged) the train ~ged out of the station il treno è uscito dalla stazione sbuffando

chum /tʃʌm/ n amico, -a mf. ~my adj 🗊 be ~my with essere amico di

chunk /tʃʌŋk/ n grosso pezzo m

church /tʃɜːtʃ/ n chiesa f. ~**yard** n cimitero m

churn /tʃɜːn/ vt churn out sfornare

chute /ʃuːt/ n scivolo m; (for rubbish) canale m di scarico

cider /ˈsaɪdə(r)/ n sidro m

cigar /sɪˈɡɑː(r)/ n sigaro m

cigarette /sɪɡəˈret/ n sigaretta f

cine-camera /ˈsɪnɪ-/ n cinepresa f

cinema /ˈsɪnɪmə/ n cinema m inv

cinnamon /ˈsɪnəmən/ n cannella f

circle /ˈsɜːkl/ n cerchio m; (Theat) galleria f; in a ~ in cerchio ● vt girare intorno a; cerchiare (mistake) ● vi descrivere dei cerchi

circuit /ˈsɜːkɪt/ n circuito m; (lap) giro m; ~ **board** n circuito m stampato. ~**ous** adj ~**ous route** percorso m lungo e indiretto

circular /ˈsɜːkjʊlə(r)/ adj circolare ● n circolare f

circulat|e /ˈsɜːkjʊleɪt/ vt far circolare ● vi circolare. ~**ion** n circolazione f; (of newspaper) tiratura f

circumcis|e /ˈsɜːkəmsaɪz/ vt circoncidere. ~**ion** n circoncisione f

circumference /səˈkʌmfərəns/ n conconferenza f

circumstance /ˈsɜːkəmstəns/ n circostanza f; ~s pl (financial) condizioni fpl finanziarie

circus /ˈsɜːkəs/ n circo m

cistern /ˈsɪstən/ n (tank) cisterna f; (of WC) serbatoio m

cite /saɪt/ vt citare

citizen /ˈsɪtɪzn/ n cittadino, -a mf;

(of town) abitante mf. ~ship n cittadinanza f

citrus /'sɪtrəs/ n ~ [fruit] agrume m

city /'sɪtɪ/ n città f inv; the C~ la City (di Londra)

> **City** La City è quella parte del centro di Londra dove un tempo si trovava l'antica città. Oggi è il centro finanziario della capitale britannica dove numerose banche e istituti finanziari hanno la propria sede centrale; molto spesso the City indica infatti le istituzioni finanziarie oltre che la zona della città.

civic /'sɪvɪk/ adj civico

civil /'sɪvl/ adj civile

civilian /sɪ'vɪljən/ adj civile; in ~ clothes in borghese • n civile mf

civiliz|ation /sɪvɪlaɪ'zeɪʃn/ n civiltà f inv. ~e vt civilizzare

civil: ~ 'servant n impiegato, -a mf statale. C~ 'Service n pubblica amministrazione f

clad /klæd/ adj vestito (in di)

claim /kleɪm/ n richiesta f; (right) diritto m; (assertion) dichiarazione f; lay ~ to sth rivendicare qcsa • vt richiedere; reclamare (lost property); rivendicare (ownership); ~ that sostenere che. ~ant n richiedente mf

clairvoyant /kleə'vɔɪənt/ n chiaroveggente mf

clam /klæm/ n (Culin) vongola f • clam up vi (pt/pp clammed) zittirsi

clamber /'klæmbə(r)/ vi arrampicarsi

clammy /'klæmɪ/ adj (-ier, -iest) appiccicaticcio

clamour /'klæmə(r)/ n (protest) rimostranza f • vi ~ for chiedere a gran voce

clamp /klæmp/ n morsa f • vt am-

morsare; (Auto) mettere i ceppi bloccaruote a. □ ~ **down** vi 🄵 essere duro; ~ **down on** reprimere

clan /klæn/ n clan m inv

clang /klæŋ/ n suono m metallico. ~er n 🄵 gaffe f inv

clap /klæp/ n give sb a ~ applaudire qcno; ~ **of thunder** tuono m • vt/i (pt/pp clapped) applaudire; ~ one's hands applaudire. ~ping n applausi mpl

clari|fication /klærɪfɪ'keɪʃn/ n chiarimento m. ~fy vt/i (pt/pp -ied) chiarire

clarinet /klærɪ'net/ n clarinetto m

clarity /'klærətɪ/ n chiarezza f

clash /klæʃ/ n scontro m; (noise) fragore m • vi scontrarsi; (colours:) stonare; (events:) coincidere

clasp /klɑːsp/ n chiusura f • vt agganciare; (hold) stringere

class /klɑːs/ n classe f; (lesson) corso m • vt classificare

classic /'klæsɪk/ adj classico • n classico m; ~s pl (Univ) lettere fpl classiche. ~al adj classico

classi|fication /klæsɪfɪ'keɪʃn/ n classificazione f. ~fy vt (pt/pp -ied) classificare

classroom n aula f

classy /'klɑːsɪ/ adj (-ier, -iest) 🄵 d'alta classe

clatter /'klætə(r)/ n fracasso m • vi far fracasso

clause /klɔːz/ n clausola f; (Gram) proposizione f

claustrophob|ia /klɔːstrə'fəʊbɪə/ n claustrofobia f

claw /klɔː/ n artiglio m; (of crab, lobster & Techn) tenaglia f • vt (cat:) graffiare

clay /kleɪ/ n argilla f

clean /kliːn/ adj pulito, lindo • adv completamente • vt pulire (shoes, windows); ~ one's teeth lavarsi i denti; have a coat ~ed portare un cappotto in lavanderia. **clean up** vt pulire ● vi far pulizia

cleaner /'kliːnə(r)/ n uomo m/donna f delle pulizie; (substance) detersivo m; [dry] ~'s lavanderia f, tintoria f

cleanliness /'klenlmɪs/ n pulizia f

cleanse /klenz/ vt pulire. ~r n detergente m

cleansing cream /'klenz-/ n latte m detergente

clear /klɪə(r)/ adj chiaro; (conscience) pulito; (road) libero; (profit, majority) netto; (sky) sereno; (water) limpido; (glass) trasparente; **make sth ~** mettere qcsa in chiaro; **have I made myself ~?** mi sono fatto capire?; **five ~ days** cinque giorni buoni ● adv **stand ~ of** allontanarsi da; **keep ~ of** tenersi alla larga da ● vt sgombrare (room, street); passare (Customs); scavalcare senza toccare (fence, wall); guadagnare (sum of money); **~ one's throat** schiarirsi la gola ● vi (face, sky): rasserenarsi; (fog): dissiparsi. □ **~ away** vt metter via. □ **~ off** vi 🖫 filar via. □ **~ out** vt sgombrare ● vi 🖫 filar via. □ **~ up** vt (tidy) mettere a posto; chiarire (mystery) ● vi (weather): schiarirsi

clearance /'klɪərəns/ n (space) spazio m libero; (authorization) autorizzazione f; (Customs) sdoganamento m. **~ sale** n liquidazione f

clear|ing /'klɪərɪŋ/ n radura f. **~ly** adv chiaramente. **~way** n (Auto) strada f con divieto di sosta

cleavage /'kliːvɪdʒ/ n (woman's) décolleté m inv

clench /klentʃ/ vt serrare

clergy /'klɜːdʒɪ/ npl clero m. **~man** n ecclesiastico m

cleric /'klerɪk/ n ecclesiastico m. **~al** adj impiegatizio; (Relig) clericale

clerk /klɑːk/, Am /klɜːk/ n impie-

gato, -a mf; (Am: shop assistant) commesso, -a mf

clever /'klevə(r)/ adj intelligente; (skilful) abile

cliché /'kliːʃeɪ/ n cliché m inv

click /klɪk/ vi scattare; (Comput) cliccare ● n (Comput) click m. **click on** vt (Comput) cliccare su

client /'klaɪənt/ n cliente mf

cliff /klɪf/ n scogliera f

climat|e /'klaɪmət/ n clima f. **~e change** n cambiamento m climatico. **~ic** adj climatico

climax /'klaɪmæks/ n punto m culminante

climb /klaɪm/ n salita f ● vt scalare (mountain); arrampicarsi su (ladder, tree) ● vi arrampicarsi; (rise) salire; (road): salire. **~ down** vi scendere; (from ladder, tree) scendere; fig tornare sui propri passi

climber /'klaɪmə(r)/ n alpinista mf; (plant) rampicante m

clinch /klɪntʃ/ vt 🖫 concludere (deal) ● n (in boxing) clinch m inv

cling /klɪŋ/ vi (pt/pp clung) aggrapparsi; (stick) aderire. **~ film** n pellicola f trasparente

clinic /'klɪnɪk/ n ambulatorio m. **~al** adj clinico

clink /klɪŋk/ n tintinnio m; (🖫: prison) galera f ● vi tintinnare

clip¹ /klɪp/ n fermaglio m; (jewellery) spilla f ● vt (pt/pp **clipped**) attaccare

clip² /klɪp/ n (extract) taglio m ● vt obliterare (ticket). **~board** n fermabloc m inv. **~pers** npl (for hair) rasoio m; (for hedge) tosasiepi m inv; (for nails) tronchesina f. **~ping** n (from newspaper) ritaglio m

cloak /kləʊk/ n mantello m. **~room** n guardaroba m inv; (toilet) bagno m

clock /klɒk/ n orologio m; (🖫: speedometer) tachimetro m. **~ in** vi attaccare. □ **~ out** vi staccare

clock: ~wise adj & adv in senso orario. **~work** n meccanismo m

clog /klɒg/ n zoccolo m ● vt (pt/pp clogged) ~ [up] intasare (drain); inceppare (mechanism) ● vi (drain:) intasarsi

cloister /'klɔɪstə(r)/ n chiostro m

clone /kləʊn/ n clone m

close¹ /kləʊs/ adj vicino; (friend) intimo; (weather) afoso; have a ~ shave 🄴 scamparla bella; be ~ to sb essere unito a qcno ● adv vicino; ~ by vicino; ~ on five o'clock quasi le cinque

close² /kləʊz/ n fine f ● vt chiudere ● vi chiudersi; (shop:) chiudere. □ ~ **down** vt chiudere ● vi (TV station:) interrompere la trasmissione; (factory:) chiudere

closely /'kləʊslɪ/ adv da vicino; (watch, listen) attentamente

closet /'klɒzɪt/ n Am armadio m

close-up /'kləʊs-/ n primo piano m

closure /'kləʊʒə(r)/ n chiusura f

clot /klɒt/ n grumo m, (🄴: idiot) tonto, -a mf ● vi (pt/pp clotted) (blood:) coagularsi

cloth /klɒθ/ n (fabric) tessuto m; (duster etc) straccio m

clothe /kləʊð/ vt vestire

clothes /kləʊðz/ npl vestiti mpl, abiti mpl. ~-brush n spazzola f per abiti. ~-line n corda f stendibiancheria

clothing /'kləʊðɪŋ/ n abbigliamento m

cloud /klaʊd/ n nuvola f ● cloud over vi rannuvolarsi. ~burst n acquazzone m

cloudy /'klaʊdɪ/ adj (-ier, -iest) nuvoloso; (liquid) torbido

clout /klaʊt/ n 🄴 colpo m; (influence) impatto m (with su) ● vt 🄴 colpire

clove /kləʊv/ n chiodo m di garofano; ~ of garlic spicchio m d'aglio

clover /'kləʊvə(r)/ n trifoglio m

clown /klaʊn/ n pagliaccio m ● vi ~ [about] fare il pagliaccio

club /klʌb/ n club m inv; (weapon)

clava f; (Sport) mazza f; ~s pl (Cards) fiori mpl ● vt (pt/pp clubbed) ● vi bastonare. □ ~ **together** vi unirsi

cluck /klʌk/ vi chiocciare

clue /kluː/ n indizio m; (in crossword) definizione f; I haven't a ~ 🄴 non ne ho idea

clump /klʌmp/ n gruppo m

clumsiness /'klʌmzɪnɪs/ n goffaggine f

clumsy /'klʌmzɪ/ adj (-ier, -iest) maldestro; (tool) scomodo; (remark) senza tatto

clung /klʌŋ/ ▷CLING

cluster /'klʌstə(r)/ n gruppo m ● vi raggrupparsi (round intorno a)

clutch /klʌtʃ/ n stretta f; (Auto) frizione f; be in sb's ~es essere in balia di qcno ● vt stringere; (grab) afferrare ● vi ~ at afferrare

clutter /'klʌtə(r)/ n caos m ● vt ~ [up] ingombrare

coach /kəʊtʃ/ n pullman m inv; (Rail) vagone m; (horse-drawn) carrozza f; (Sport) allenatore, -trice f ● vt fare esercitare; (Sport) allenare

coal /kəʊl/ n carbone m

coalition /kəʊə'lɪʃn/ n coalizione f

coarse /kɔːs/ adj grossolano; (joke) spinto

coast /kəʊst/ n costa f ● vi (freewheel) scendere a ruota libera ~al adj costiero. ~er n (mat) sottobicchiere m inv

coast: ~**guard** n guardia f costiera. ~**line** n litorale m

coat /kəʊt/ n cappotto m; (of animal) manto m; (of paint) mano f; ~ of arms stemma f ● vt coprire; (with paint) ricoprire. ~-hanger n gruccia f. ~-hook n gancio m [appendiabiti]

coating /'kəʊtɪŋ/ n rivestimento m; (of paint) stato m

coax /kəʊks/ vt convincere con le moine

cobweb /'kɒb-/ n ragnatela f

cocaine /kəˈkeɪn/ n cocaina f

cock /kɒk/ n gallo m; (any male bird) maschio m ● vt sollevare il grilletto di (gun); ~ its ears (animal:) drizzare le orecchie

cockerel /ˈkɒkərəl/ n galletto m

cock-'eyed adj 🛈 storto; (absurd) assurdo

cockney /ˈkɒknɪ/ n (dialect) dialetto m londinese; (person) abitante mf dell'est di Londra

cock: ~**pit** n (Aeron) cabina f. ~**roach** /-rəʊtʃ/ n scarafaggio m. ~**tail** n cocktail m inv. ~**-up** n ⊠ make a ~**-up** fare un casino (of sth)

cocky /ˈkɒkɪ/ adj (-ier, -iest) 🛈 presuntuoso

cocoa /ˈkəʊkəʊ/ n cacao m

coconut /ˈkəʊkənʌt/ n noce f di cocco

cocoon /kəˈkuːn/ n bozzolo m

cod /kɒd/ n inv merluzzo m

COD abbr (cash on delivery) pagamento m alla consegna

code /kəʊd/ n codice m. ~**d** adj codificato

coedu'cational /kəʊ-/ adj misto

coerc|e /kəʊˈɜːs/ vt costringere. ~**ion** n coercizione f

coffee /ˈkɒfɪ/ n caffè m inv

coffeepot n caffettiera f

coffin /ˈkɒfɪn/ n bara f

cog /kɒg/ n (Techn) dente m (di ruota)

coherent /kəʊˈhɪərənt/ adj coerente; (when speaking) lucido

coil /kɔɪl/ n rotolo m; (Electr) bobina f; ~**s** pl spire fpl ● vt ~ [up] avvolgere

coin /kɔɪn/ n moneta f ● vt coniare (word)

coincide /kəʊɪnˈsaɪd/ vi coincidere

coinciden|ce /kəʊˈɪnsɪdəns/ n coincidenza f. ~**tal** adj casuale. ~**tally** adv casualmente

coke /kəʊk/ n (carbone m) coke m

Coke® /kəʊk/ n Coca[-cola]® f

cold /kəʊld/ adj freddo; I'm ~ ho freddo ● n freddo m; (Med) raffreddore m

cold-'blooded adj spietato

coleslaw /ˈkəʊlslɔː/ n insalata f di cavolo crudo, cipolle e carote in maionese

collaborat|e /kəˈlæbəreɪt/ vi collaborare; ~**e** on sth collaborare in qcsa. ~**ion** n collaborazione f; (with enemy) collaborazionismo m. ~**or** n collaboratore, -trice f; (with enemy) collaborazionista mf

collapse /kəˈlæps/ n crollo m ● vi (person:) svenire; (roof, building:) crollare. ~**ible** adj pieghevole

collar /ˈkɒlə(r)/ n colletto m; (for animal) collare m. ~**-bone** n clavicola f

colleague /ˈkɒliːg/ n collega mf

collect /kəˈlekt/ vt andare a prendere (person); ritirare (parcel, tickets); riscuotere (taxes); raccogliere (rubbish); (as hobby) collezionare ● vi riunirsi ● adv call ~ Am telefonare a carico del destinatario. ~**ed** adj controllato

collection /kəˈlekʃn/ n collezione f; (in church) questua f; (of rubbish) raccolta f; (of post) levata f

collector /kəˈlektə(r)/ n (of stamps etc) collezionista mf

college /ˈkɒlɪdʒ/ n istituto m parauniversitario; C~ of... Scuola f di...

collide /kəˈlaɪd/ vi scontrarsi

collision /kəˈlɪʒn/ n scontro m

colloquial /kəˈləʊkwɪəl/ adj colloquiale. ~**ism** n espressione f colloquiale

colon /ˈkəʊlən/ n due punti mpl; (Anat) colon m inv

colonel /ˈkɜːnl/ n colonnello m

colonial /kəˈləʊnɪəl/ adj coloniale

colon|ize /ˈkɒlənaɪz/ vt colonizzare. ~**y** n colonia f

colossal /kəˈlɒsl/ adj colossale

colour /ˈkʌlə(r)/ n colore m; (comc

plexion) colorito *m*; ∼s *pl* (*flag*) bandiera *fsg*; off ∼ 🔲 giù di tono ●*vt* colorare; ∼ [in] colorare ●*vi* (*blush*) arrossire

colour· ∼-**blind** *adj* daltonico. ∼**ed** *adj* colorato; (*person*) di colore ●*n* (*person*) persona *f* di colore. ∼**ful** *adj* pieno di colore. ∼**less** *adj* incolore

column /ˈkɒləm/ *n* colonna *f*. ∼**ist** *n* giornalista *mf* che cura una rubrica

coma /ˈkəʊmə/ *n* coma *m inv*

comb /kəʊm/ *n* pettine *m*; (*for wearing*) pettinino *m* ●*vt* pettinare; (*fig: search*) setacciare; ∼ **one's hair** pettinarsi i capelli

combat /ˈkɒmbæt/ *n* combattimento *m* ●*vt* (*pt/pp* combated) combattere

combination /kɒmbɪˈneɪʃn/ *n* combinazione *f*

combine[1] /kəmˈbaɪn/ *vt* unire; ∼ **a job with being a mother** conciliare il lavoro con il ruolo di madre ●*vi* (*chemical elements*) combinarsi

combine[2] /ˈkɒmbaɪn/ *n* (*Comm*) associazione *f*. ∼ **harvester** *n* mietitrebbia *f*

combustion /kəmˈbʌstʃn/ *n* combustione *f*

come /kʌm/ *vi* (*pt* came, *pp* come) venire; **where do you** ∼ **from?** da dove vieni? ∼ **to** (*reach*) arrivare a; **that** ∼**s to £10** fanno 10 sterline; ∼ **into money** ricevere dei soldi; ∼ **true/open** verificarsi/aprirsi; ∼ **first** arrivare primo; *fig* venire prima di tutto; ∼ **in two sizes** esistere in due misure; **the years to** ∼ gli anni a venire; **how** ∼? 🔲 come mai? **come about** *vi* succedere. □ ∼ **across** *vi* ∼ **across as being** dare l'impressione di essere ●*vt* (*find*) imbattersi in. □ ∼ **along** *vi* venire; (*job, opportunity*) presentarsi; (*progress*) andare bene. □ ∼ **apart** *vi* smontarsi; (*break*) rompersi. □ ∼ **away** *vi* venir via; (*button, fastener*) staccarsi. □ ∼ **back** *vi* ritornare. □ ∼ **by** *vi* passare ●*vt* (*obtain*) avere. □ ∼ **down** *vi* scendere; ∼ **down to** (*reach*) arrivare a. come **in** *vi* entrare; (*in race*) arrivare; (*tide:*) salire. □ ∼ **in for** *vt* ∼ **in for criticism** essere criticato. □ ∼ **off** *vi* staccarsi; (*take place*) esserci; (*succeed*) riuscire. □ ∼ **on** *vi* (*make progress*) migliorare; ∼ **on!** (*hurry*) dai!; (*indicating disbelief*) ma va là!. □ ∼ **out** *vi* venir fuori; (*book, sun:*) uscire; (*stain:*) andar via. □ ∼ **over** *vi* venire. □ ∼ **round** *vi* venire; (*after fainting*) riaversi; (*change one's mind*) farsi convincere. □ ∼ **to** *vi* (*after fainting*) riaversi. □ ∼ **up** *vi* salire; (*sun:*) sorgere; (*plant:*) crescere; **something came up** (*I was prevented*) ho avuto un imprevisto. □ ∼ **up with** *vt* tirar fuori

'**come-back** *n* ritorno *m*

comedian /kəˈmiːdɪən/ *n* comico *m*

comedy /ˈkɒmədɪ/ *n* commedia *f*

comet /ˈkɒmɪt/ *n* cometa *f*

comfort /ˈkʌmfət/ *n* benessere *m*; (*consolation*) conforto *m* ●*vt* confortare

comfortabl·e /ˈkʌmfətəbl/ *adj* comodo; **be** ∼**e** (*person:*) stare comodo; (*fig: in situation*) essere a proprio agio; (*financially*) star bene. ∼**y** *adv* comodamente

'**comfort station** *n Am* bagno *m* pubblico

comic /ˈkɒmɪk/ *adj* comico ●*n* comico, -a *mf*; (*periodical*) fumetto *m*. ∼**al** *adj* comico. ∼ **strip** *n* striscia *f* di fumetti

coming /ˈkʌmɪŋ/ *n* venuta *f*; ∼**s and goings** viavai *m*

comma /ˈkɒmə/ *n* virgola *f*

command /kəˈmɑːnd/ *n* comando *m*; (*order*) ordine *m*; (*mastery*) padronanza *f* ●*vt* ordinare; comandare (*army*)

commandeer /kɒmənˈdɪə(r)/ *vt* requisire

command·er /kəˈmɑːndə(r)/ *n* comandante *m*. ∼**ing** *adj* (*view*) imponente; (lead) dominante. ∼ing officer *n* comandante *m*. ∼ment *n* comandamento *m*

commemorat|e /kə'meməreɪt/ *vt* commemorare. ∼ion *n* commemorazione *f*. ∼ive *adj* commemorativo

commence /kə'mens/ *vt/i* cominciare. ∼ment *n* inizio *m*

commend /kə'mend/ *vt* complimentarsi con (on per); (*recommend*) raccomandare (to a). ∼able *adj* lodevole

comment /'kɒment/ *n* commento *m* ● *vi* fare commenti (on su)

commentary /'kɒməntrɪ/ *n* commento *m*; [running] ∼ (on radio, (TV)) cronaca *f* diretta

commentat|e /'kɒmənteɪt/ *vt* ∼e on (TV, Radio) fare la cronaca di. ∼or *n* cronista *mf*

commerce /'kɒmɜ:s/ *n* commercio *m*

commercial /kə'mɜ:ʃl/ *adj* commerciale ● *n* (TV) pubblicità *f inv*. ∼ize *vt* commercializzare

commiserate /kə'mɪzəreɪt/ *vi* esprimere il proprio rincrescimento (with a)

commission /kə'mɪʃn/ *n* commissione *f*; receive one's ∼ (Mil) essere promosso ufficiale; out of ∼ fuori uso ● *vt* commissionare

commissionaire /kəmɪʃə'neə(r)/ *n* portiere *m*

commit /kə'mɪt/ *vt* (*pt/pp* committed) commettere; (*to prison, hospital*) affidare (to a); impegnare (funds); ∼ oneself impegnarsi. ∼ment *n* impegno *m*; (*involvement*) compromissione *f*. ∼ted *adj* impegnato

committee /kə'mɪtɪ/ *n* comitato *m*

commodity /kə'mɒdətɪ/ *n* prodotto *m*

common /'kɒmən/ *adj* comune; (*vulgar*) volgare ● *n* prato *m* pubblico; have in ∼ avere in comune; House of C∼s Camera *f* dei Comuni. ∼er *n*

persona *f* non nobile

common: ∼ law *n* diritto *m* consuetudinario. ∼ly *adv* comunemente. C∼ 'Market *n* Mercato *m* Comune. ∼place *adj* banale. ∼room *n* sala *f* dei professori/degli studenti. ∼ 'sense *n* buon senso *m*

Commonwealth Il *Commonwealth*, fondato nel 1931, è l'insieme delle ex colonie e possedimenti dell'ex impero britannico. I paesi membri, oggi stati indipendenti, sono legati da legami economici e culturali. I vari capi di stato si incontrano con scadenza biennale, e progetti educativi internazionali vengono promossi regolarmente. Ogni quattro anni, inoltre, si tengono i *Commonwealth Games*, manifestazioni sportive cui partecipano atleti dei vari paesi.

commotion /kə'məʊʃn/ *n* confusione *f*

communicate /kə'mju:nɪkeɪt/ *vt/i* comunicare

communication /kəmju:nɪ'keɪʃn/ *n* comunicazione *f*; (*of disease*) trasmissione *f*; be in ∼ with sb essere in contatto con qcno; ∼s *pl* (*technology*) telecomunicazioni *fpl*. ∼ cord *n* fermata *f* d'emergenza

communicative /kə'mju:nɪkətɪv/ *adj* comunicativo

Communion /kə'mju:nɪən/ *n* [Holy] ∼ comunione *f*

Communis|m /'kɒmjʊnɪzm/ *n* comunismo *m*. ∼t *adj* & *n* comunista *mf*

community /kə'mju:nətɪ/ *n* comunità *f*. ∼ centre *n* centro *m* sociale

commute /kə'mju:t/ *vi* fare il pendolare ● *vt* (*Jur*) commutare. ∼r *n* pendolare *mf*

compact¹ /kəm'pækt/ *adj* compatto

compact² /'kɒmpækt/ *n* portacipria *m* inv. ~ disc *n* compact disc *m* inv

companion /kəmˈpænjən/ *n* compagno, -a *mf*. ~ship *n* compagnia *f*

company /ˈkʌmpənɪ/ *n* compagnia *f*; (*guests*) ospiti *mpl*. ~ car *n* macchina *f* della ditta

comparable /ˈkɒmpərəbl/ *adj* paragonabile

comparative /kəmˈpærətɪv/ *adj* comparativo; (*relative*) relativo ● *n* (*Gram*) comparativo *m*. ~**ly** *adv* relativamente

compare /kəmˈpeə(r)/ *vt* paragonare (with/to *a*) ● *vi* essere paragonato

comparison /kəmˈpærɪsn/ *n* paragone *m*

compartment /kəmˈpɑːtmənt/ *n* compartimento *m*; (*Rail*) scompartimento *m*

compass /ˈkʌmpəs/ *n* bussola *f*. ~**es** *npl*, pair of ~**es** compasso *msg*

compassion /kəmˈpæʃn/ *n* compassione *f*. ~**ate** *adj* compassionevole

compatible /kəmˈpætəbl/ *adj* compatibile

compel /kəmˈpel/ *vt* (*pt/pp* compelled) costringere. ~**ling** *adj* (*reason*) inconfutabile

compensat|e /ˈkɒmpənseɪt/ *vt* risarcire ● *vi* ~**e** for *fig* compensare di. ~**ion** *n* risarcimento *m*; (*fig*: *comfort*) consolazione *f*

compère /ˈkɒmpeə(r)/ *n* presentatore, -trice *mf*

compete /kəmˈpiːt/ *vi* competere; (*take part*) gareggiare

competen|ce /ˈkɒmpɪtəns/ *n* competenza *f*. ~**t** *adj* competente

competition /kɒmpəˈtɪʃn/ *n* concorrenza *f*; (*contest*) gara *f*

competitive /kəmˈpetɪtɪv/ *adj* competitivo; ~ **prices** prezzi *mpl* concorrenziali

competitor /kəmˈpetɪtə(r)/ *n*

concorrente *mf*

complacen|cy /kəmˈpleɪsənsɪ/ *n* compiacimento *m*. ~**t** *adj* compiaciuto

complain /kəmˈpleɪn/ *vi* lamentarsi (about *di*); (*formally*) reclamare; ~ of (*Med*) accusare. ~**t** *n* lamentela *f*; (*formal*) reclamo *m*; (*Med*) disturbo *m*

complement¹ /ˈkɒmplɪmənt/ *n* complemento *m*

complement² /ˈkɒmplɪment/ *vt* complementare; ~ each other complementarsi a vicenda. ~**ary** *adj* complementare

complete /kəmˈpliːt/ *adj* completo; (*utter*) finito ● *vt* completare; compilare (*form*). ~**ly** *adv* completamente

completion /kəmˈpliːʃn/ *n* fine *f*

complex /ˈkɒmpleks/ *adj* complesso ● *n* complesso *m*

complexion /kəmˈplekʃn/ *n* carnagione *f*

complexity /kəmˈpleksətɪ/ *n* complessità *f* inv

complicat|e /ˈkɒmplɪkeɪt/ *vt* complicare. ~**ed** *adj* complicato. ~**ion** *n* complicazione *f*

compliment /ˈkɒmplɪmənt/ *n* complimento *m*; ~**s** *pl* omaggi *mpl* ● *vt* complimentare. ~**ary** *adj* complimentoso; (*given free*) in omaggio

comply /kəmˈplaɪ/ *vi* (*pt/pp* -ied) ~ with conformarsi a

component /kəmˈpəʊnənt/ *adj* & *n* ~ [part] componente *m*

compose /kəmˈpəʊz/ *vt* comporre; ~ oneself ricomporsi; be ~**d** of essere composto da. ~**d** *adj* (*calm*) composto. ~**r** *n* compositore, -trice *mf*

composition /kɒmpəˈzɪʃn/ *n* composizione *f*; (*essay*) tema *m*

compost /ˈkɒmpɒst/ *n* composta *f*

composure /kəmˈpəʊʒə(r)/ *n* calma *f*

compound /ˈkɒmpaʊnd/ *adj* composto. ~ fracture *n* frattura *f* esposta. ~ 'interest n interesse m composto ●n (Chem) composto m; (Gram) parola f composta; (enclosure) recinto m

comprehen|d /ˌkɒmprɪ'hend/ vt comprendere. ~sible adj comprensibile. ~sion n comprensione f

comprehensive /ˌkɒmprɪ'hensɪv/ adj & n comprensivo; ~ [school] scuola f media in cui gli allievi hanno capacità d'apprendimento diverse. ~ insurance n (Auto) polizza f casco

compress[1] /'kɒmpres/ n compressa f

compress[2] /kəm'pres/ vt comprimere; ~ed air aria f compressa

comprise /kəm'praɪz/ vt comprendere; (form) costituire

compromise /'kɒmprəmaɪz/ n compromesso m ● vt compromettere ● vi fare un compromesso

compuls|ion /kəm'pʌlʃn/ n desiderio m irresistibile. ~ive adj (Psych) patologico. ~ive eating voglia f ossessiva di mangiare. ~ory adj obbligatorio

compute /kəm'pjuːt/ vt calcolare

comput|er /kəm'pjuːtə(r)/ n computer m inv. ~erize vt computerizzare. ~ing n informatica f

comrade /'kɒmreɪd/ n camerata m; (Pol) compagno, -a mf. ~ship n cameratismo m

con[1] /kɒn/ ▷ PRO

con[2] n Ⓕ fregatura f ● vt (pt/pp conned) Ⓕ fregare

concave /'kɒnkeɪv/ adj concavo

conceal /kən'siːl/ vt nascondere

concede /kən'siːd/ vt (admit) ammettere; (give up) rinunciare a; lasciar fare (goal)

conceit /kən'siːt/ n presunzione f. ~ed adj presuntuoso

conceivable /kən'siːvəbl/ adj concepibile

conceive /kən'siːv/ vt (Biol) concepire ● vi aver figli. □~ of vt fig

concepire

concentrat|e /'kɒnsəntreɪt/ vt concentrare ● vi concentrarsi. ~ion n concentrazione f. ~ion camp n campo m di concentramento

concept /'kɒnsept/ n concetto m. ~ion n concezione f; (idea) idea f

concern /kən'sɜːn/ n preoccupazione f; (Comm) attività f inv ● vt (be about, affect) riguardare; (worry) preoccupare; be ~ed about essere preoccupato per; ~ oneself with preoccuparsi di; as far as I am ~ed per quanto mi riguarda. ~ing prep riguardo a

concert /'kɒnsət/ n concerto m. ~ed adj collettivo

concertina /kɒnsə'tiːnə/ n piccola fisarmonica f

concerto /kən'tʃeətəʊ/ n concerto m

concession /kən'seʃn/ n concessione f; (reduction) sconto m. ~ary adj (reduced) scontato

concise /kən'saɪs/ adj conciso

conclu|de /kən'kluːd/ vt concludere ● vi concludersi. ~ding adj finale

conclusion /kən'kluːʒn/ n conclusione f; in ~ per concludere

conclusive /kən'kluːsɪv/ adj definitivo. ~ly adv in modo definitivo

concoct /kən'kɒkt/ vt confezionare; fig inventare. ~ion n mistura f; (drink) intruglio m

concrete /'kɒnkriːt/ adj concreto ●n calcestruzzo m

concussion /kən'kʌʃn/ n commozione f cerebrale

condemn /kən'dem/ vt condannare; dichiarare inagibile (building). ~ation n condanna f

condensation /kɒndenˈseɪʃn/ n condensazione f

condense /kən'dens/ vt condensare; (Phys) condensare ● vi condensarsi. ~d milk n latte m condensato

condescend /kɒndɪˈsend/ vi degnarsi. ~ing adj condiscendente

condition /kənˈdɪʃn/ n condizione f; on ~ that a condizione che ● vt (Psych) condizionare. ~al adj (acceptance) condizionato; (Gram) condizionale ● n (Gram) condizionale m. ~er n balsamo m; (for fabrics) ammorbidente m

condolences /kənˈdəʊlənsɪz/ npl condoglianze fpl

condom /ˈkɒndəm/ n preservativo m

condo[minium] /ˈkɒndə (ˈmɪnɪəm)/ n Am condominio m

condone /kənˈdəʊn/ vt passare sopra a

conduct¹ /ˈkɒndʌkt/ n condotta f

conduct² /kənˈdʌkt/ vt condurre; dirigere (orchestra). ~or n direttore m d'orchestra; (of bus) bigliettaio m; (Phys) conduttore m. ~ress n bigliettaia f

cone /kəʊn/ n cono m; (Bot) pigna f; (Auto) birillo m ● cone off vt be ~d off (Auto) essere chiuso da birilli

confederation /kənfedəˈreɪʃn/ n confederazione f

conference /ˈkɒnfərəns/ n conferenza f

confess /kənˈfes/ vt confessare ● vi confessare; (Relig) confessarsi. ~ion n confessione f. ~ional n confessionale m. ~or n confessore m

confetti /kənˈfetɪ/ n coriandoli mpl

confide /kənˈfaɪd/ vt confidare. □ ~ in vt ~ in sb fidarsi di qcno

confidence /ˈkɒnfɪdəns/ n (trust) fiducia f; (self-assurance) sicurezza f di sé; (secret) confidenza f; in ~ in confidenza. ~ trick n truffa f

confident /ˈkɒnfɪdənt/ adj fiducioso; (self-assured) sicuro di sé. ~ly adv con aria fiduciosa

confidential /kɒnfɪˈdenʃl/ adj confidenziale

configur|ation /kənfɪgəˈreɪʃn/ n configurazione f. ~e vt configurare

confine /kənˈfaɪn/ vt rinchiudere; (limit) limitare; be ~d to bed essere confinato a letto. ~d adj (space) limitato. ~ment n detenzione f; (Med) parto m

confirm /kənˈfɜːm/ vt confermare; (Relig) cresimare. ~ation n conferma f; (Relig) cresima f. ~ed adj incallito; ~ed bachelor scapolo m impenitente

confiscat|e /ˈkɒnfɪskeɪt/ vt confiscare. ~ion n confisca f

conflict¹ /ˈkɒnflɪkt/ n conflitto m

conflict² /kənˈflɪkt/ vi essere in contraddizione. ~ing adj contraddittorio

conform /kənˈfɔːm/ vi (person:) conformarsi; (thing:) essere conforme (to a). ~ist n conformista mf

confounded /kənˈfaʊndɪd/ adj 🄸 maledetto

confront /kənˈfrʌnt/ vt confrontare; the problems ~ing us i problemi che dobbiamo affrontare. ~ation n confronto m

confus|e /kənˈfjuːz/ vt confondere. ~ing adj che confonde. ~ion n confusione f

congeal /kənˈdʒiːl/ vi (blood:) coagularsi

congest|ed /kənˈdʒestɪd/ adj congestionato. ~ion n congestione f

congratulat|e /kənˈɡrætjʊleɪt/ vt congratularsi con (on per). ~ions npl radunarsi

congregat|e /ˈkɒŋɡrɪɡeɪt/ vi radunarsi. ~ion n (Relig) assemblea f

congress /ˈkɒŋɡres/ n congresso m. ~man n Am (Pol) membro m del congresso

conifer /ˈkɒnɪfə(r)/ n conifera f

conjugat|e /ˈkɒndʒʊɡeɪt/ vt coniugare. ~ion n coniugazione f

conjunction /kənˈdʒʌŋkʃn/ n congiunzione f; in ~ with insieme a

conjur|e /ˈkʌndʒə(r)/ vi ~ing

tricks *npl* giochi *mpl* di prestigio. ~or *n* prestigiatore, -trice *mf*. o ~ up *vt* evocare (image); tirar fuori dal nulla (meal)

conk /kɒŋk/ *vi* ~ out 🔟 (machine:) guastarsi; (person:) crollare

'con-man *n* 🔟 truffatore *m*

connect /kə'nekt/ *vt* collegare; be ~ed with avere legami con; (be related to) essere imparentato con; be well ~ed aver conoscenze influenti ● *vi* essere collegato (with a); (train:) fare coincidenza

connection /kə'nekʃn/ *n* (between ideas) nesso *m*; (in travel) coincidenza *f*; (Electr) collegamento *m*; in ~ with con riferimento a. ~s *pl* (people) conoscenze *fpl*

connoisseur /kɒnə'sɜ:(r)/ *n* intenditore, -trice *mf*

conquer /'kɒŋkə(r)/ *vt* conquistare; *fig* superare (fear). ~or *n* conquistatore *m*

conquest /'kɒŋkwest/ *n* conquista *f*

conscience /'kɒnʃəns/ *n* coscienza *f*

conscientious /kɒnʃɪ'enʃəs/ *adj* coscienzioso. ~ ob'jector *n* obiettore *m* di coscienza

conscious /'kɒnʃəs/ *adj* conscio; (decision) meditato; [fully] ~ cosciente; be/become ~ of sth rendersi conto di qcsa. ~ly *adv* consapevolmente. ~ness *n* consapevolezza *f*; (Med) conoscenza *f*

conscript¹ /'kɒnskrɪpt/ *n* coscritto *m*

conscript² /kən'skrɪpt/ *vt* (Mil) chiamare alle armi. ~ion *n* coscrizione *f*, leva *f*

consecrat|e /'kɒnsɪkreɪt/ *vt* consacrare. ~ion *n* consacrazione *f*

consecutive /kən'sekjʊtɪv/ *adj* consecutivo

consensus /kən'sensəs/ *n* consenso *m*

consent /kən'sent/ *n* consenso *m* ● *vi* acconsentire

consequen|ce /'kɒnsɪkwəns/ *n* conseguenza *f*; (importance) importanza *f*. ~t *adj* conseguente. ~tly *adv* di conseguenza

conservation /kɒnsə'veɪʃn/ *n* conservazione *f*. ~ist *n* fautore, -trice *mf* della tutela ambientale

conservative /kən'sɜ:vətɪv/ *adj* conservativo; (estimate) ottimistico. C~ (Pol) *adj* conservatore ● *n* conservatore, -trice *mf*

conservatory /kən'sɜ:vətrɪ/ *n* spazio *m* chiuso da vetrate adiacente alla casa

conserve /kən'sɜ:v/ *vt* conservare

consider /kən'sɪdə(r)/ *vt* considerare; ~ doing sth considerare la possibilità di fare qcsa. ~able *adj* considerevole. ~ably *adv* considerevolmente

consider|ate /kən'sɪdərət/ *adj* pieno di riguardo. ~ately *adv* con riguardo. ~ation *n* considerazione *f*; (thoughtfulness) attenzione *f*; (respect) riguardo *m*; (payment) compenso *m*; take sth into ~ation prendere qcsa in considerazione. ~ing *prep* considerando

consign /kən'saɪn/ *vt* affidare. ~ment *n* consegna *f*

consist /kən'sɪst/ *vi* ~ of consistere di

consisten|cy /kən'sɪstənsɪ/ *n* coerenza *f*; (density) consistenza *f*. ~t *adj* coerente; (loyalty) costante. ~tly *adv* coerentemente; (late, loyal) costantemente

consolation /kɒnsə'leɪʃn/ *n* consolazione *f*. ~ prize *n* premio *m* di consolazione

console /kən'səʊl/ *vt* consolare

consolidate /kən'sɒlɪdeɪt/ *vt* consolidare

consonant /'kɒnsənənt/ *n* consonante *f*

conspicuous /kən'spɪkjʊəs/ adj facilmente distinguibile

conspiracy /kən'spɪrəsɪ/ n cospirazione f

conspire /kən'spaɪə(r)/ vi cospirare

constable /'kʌnstəbl/ n agente m [di polizia]

constant /'kɒnstənt/ adj costante. **~ly** adv costantemente

constellation /kɒnstə'leɪʃn/ n costellazione f

consternation /kɒnstə'neɪʃn/ n costernazione f

constipat|ed /'kɒnstɪpeɪtɪd/ adj stitico. **~ion** n stitichezza f

constituency /kən'stɪtjʊənsɪ/ n area f elettorale di un deputato nel Regno Unito

constituent /kən'stɪtjʊənt/ n costituente m; (Pol) elettore, -trice f

constitut|e /'kɒnstɪtjuːt/ vt costituire. **~ion** n costituzione f; **~ional** adj costituzionale

construct /kən'strʌkt/ vt costruire. **~ion** n costruzione f; under **~ion** in costruzione. **~ive** adj costruttivo

consul /'kɒnsl/ n console m. **~ar** adj consolare. **~ate** n consolato m

consult /kən'sʌlt/ vt consultare. **~ant** n consulente mf; (Med) specialista mf. **~ation** n consultazione f; (Med) consulto m

consume /kən'sjuːm/ vt consumare. **~r** n consumatore, -trice mf. **~r goods** npl beni mpl di consumo. **~r organization** n organizzazione f per la tutela dei consumatori

consummate /'kɒnsəmeɪt/ vt consumare

consumption /kən'sʌmpʃn/ n consumo m

contact /'kɒntækt/ n contatto m; (person) conoscenza f ● vt mettersi in contatto con. **~ lenses** npl lenti fpl a contatto

contagious /kən'teɪdʒəs/ adj contagioso

contain /kən'teɪn/ vt contenere; **~** oneself controllarsi. **~er** n recipiente m; (for transport) container m inv

contaminat|e /kən'tæmɪneɪt/ vt contaminare. **~ion** n contaminazione f

contemplat|e /'kɒntəmpleɪt/ vt contemplare; (consider) considerare; **~e** doing sth considerare di fare qcsa. **~ion** n contemplazione f

contemporary /kən'tempərərɪ/ adj & n contemporaneo, -a mf

contempt /kən'tempt/ n disprezzo m; beneath **~** più che vergognoso; **~** of court oltraggio m alla Corte. **~ible** adj sprezzevole. **~uous** adj sprezzante

contend /kən'tend/ vi **~** with occuparsi di ● vt (assert) sostenere. **~er** n concorrente mf

content[1] /'kɒntent/ n contenuto m

content[2] /kən'tent/ adj soddisfatto ● vt **~** oneself accontentarsi (with di). **~ed** adj soddisfatto. **~edly** adv con aria soddisfatta

contentment /kən'tentmənt/ n soddisfazione f

contents /'kɒntents/ npl contenuto m

contest[1] /'kɒntest/ n gara f

contest[2] /kən'test/ vt contestare (statement); impugnare (will); (Pol) (candidates:) contendersi; (one candidate:) aspirare a. **~ant** n concorrente mf

context /'kɒntekst/ n contesto m

continent /'kɒntɪnənt/ n continente m; the C**~** l'Europa f continentale

continental /kɒntɪ'nentl/ adj continentale. **~** breakfast n prima colazione f a base di pane, burro, marmellata, croissant, ecc. **~** quilt n piumone m

contingency /kən'tɪndʒənsɪ/ n eventualità f inv

continual /kən'tɪnjʊəl/ adj

continuo

continuation /kəntɪnjuˈeɪʃn/ n continuazione f

continue /kənˈtɪnjuː/ vt continuare; ∼ to do sth continuare a fare qcsa; to be ∼d continua ● vi continuare. ∼d adj continuo

continuity /kɒntɪˈnjuːətɪ/ n continuità f

continuous /kənˈtɪnjʊəs/ adj continuo

contort /kənˈtɔːt/ vt contorcere. ∼ion n contorsione f. ∼ionist n contorsionista mf

contour /ˈkɒntʊə(r)/ n contorno m; (line) curva f di livello

contraband /ˈkɒntrəbænd/ n contrabbando m

contracep|tion /kɒntrəˈsepʃn/ n contraccezione f. ∼tive n contraccettivo m

contract[1] /ˈkɒntrækt/ n contratto m

contract[2] /kənˈtrækt/ vi (get smaller) contrarsi ● vt contrarre (illness). ∼ion n contrazione f. ∼or n imprenditore, -trice mf

contradict /kɒntrəˈdɪkt/ vt contraddire. ∼ion n contraddizione f. ∼ory adj contraddittorio

contraption /kənˈtræpʃn/ n 🔲 aggeggio m

contrary[1] /ˈkɒntrərɪ/ adj contrario ● adv ∼ to contrariamente a ● n contrario m; on the ∼ al contrario

contrary[2] /kənˈtreərɪ/ adj disobbediente

contrast[1] /ˈkɒntrɑːst/ n contrasto m

contrast[2] /kənˈtrɑːst/ vt confrontare ● vi contrastare. ∼ing adj contrastante

contraven|e /kɒntrəˈviːn/ vt trasgredire. ∼tion n trasgressione f

contribut|e /kənˈtrɪbjuːt/ vt/i contribuire. ∼ion n contribuzione f; (what is contributed) contributo m. ∼or

n contributore, -trice mf

contrive /kənˈtraɪv/ vt escogitare; ∼ to do sth riuscire a fare qcsa

control /kənˈtrəʊl/ n controllo m; ∼s pl (of car, plane) comandi mpl; get out of ∼ sfuggire al controllo ● vt (pt/pp controlled) controllare; ∼ oneself controllarsi

controvers|ial /kɒntrəˈvɜːʃl/ adj controverso. ∼y n controversia f

convalesce /kɒnvəˈles/ vi essere in convalescenza

convector /kənˈvektə(r)/ n ∼ [heater] convettore m

convene /kənˈviːn/ vt convocare ● vi riunirsi

convenience /kənˈviːnɪəns/ n convenienza f; [public] ∼ gabinetti mpl pubblici; with all modern ∼s con tutti i comfort

convenient /kənˈviːnɪənt/ adj comodo; be ∼ for sb andar bene per qcno; if it is ∼ [for you] se ti va bene. ∼ly adv comodamente; ∼ly located in una posizione comoda

convent /ˈkɒnvənt/ n convento m

convention /kənˈvenʃn/ n convenzione f; (assembly) convegno m. ∼al adj convenzionale

converge /kənˈvɜːdʒ/ vi convergere

conversation /kɒnvəˈseɪʃn/ n conversazione f. ∼al adj di conversazione. ∼alist n conversatore, -trice mf

converse[1] /kənˈvɜːs/ vi conversare

converse[2] /ˈkɒnvɜːs/ n inverso m. ∼ly adv viceversa

conversion /kənˈvɜːʃn/ n conversione f

convert[1] /ˈkɒnvɜːt/ n convertito, -a mf

convert[2] /kənˈvɜːt/ vt convertire (into in); sconsacrare (church). ∼ible adj convertibile ● n (Auto) macchina f decappottabile

convex /ˈkɒnveks/ adj convesso

convey /kən'veɪ/ vt portare; trasmettere (idea, message). ~**or belt** n nastro m trasportatore

convict[1] /'kɒnvɪkt/ n condannato, -a mf

convict[2] /kən'vɪkt/ vt giudicare colpevole. ~**ion** n condanna f; (belief) convinzione f; **previous** ~**ion** precedente m penale

convinc|e /kən'vɪns/ vt convincere. ~**ing** adj convincente

convoluted /'kɒnvəluːtɪd/ adj contorto

convoy /'kɒnvɔɪ/ n convoglio m

convuls|e /kən'vʌls/ vt sconvolgere; **be** ~**ed with laughter** contorcersi dalle risa. ~**ion** n convulsione f

coo /kuː/ vi tubare

cook /kʊk/ n cuoco, -a mf • vt cucinare; **is it** ~**ed**? è cotto?; ~ **the books** 🈲 truccare i libri contabili • vi (food:) cuocere; (person:) cucinare. ~**book** n libro m di cucina

cooker /'kʊkə(r)/ n cucina f; (apple) mela f da cuocere. ~**y** n cucina f. ~**y book** n libro m di cucina

cookie /'kʊkɪ/ n Am biscotto m

cool /kuːl/ adj fresco; (calm) calmo; (unfriendly) freddo • n fresco m • vt rinfrescare • vi rinfrescarsi. ~**-box** n borsa f termica. ~**ness** n freddezza f

coop /kuːp/ n stia f • vt ~ **up** rinchiudere

co-operat|e /kəʊ'ɒpəreɪt/ vi cooperare. ~**ion** n cooperazione f

co-operative /kəʊ'ɒpərətɪv/ adj cooperativo • n cooperativa f

co-opt /kəʊ'ɒpt/ vt eleggere

co-ordinat|e /kəʊ'ɔːdɪneɪt/ vt coordinare. ~**ion** n coordinazione f

cop /kɒp/ n 🈲 poliziotto m

cope /kəʊp/ vi 🈲 farcela; **can she** ~ **by herself?** ce la fa da sola?; ~ **with** farcela con

copious /'kəʊpɪəs/ adj abbondante

copper[1] /'kɒpə(r)/ n rame m; ~**s** pl monete fpl da uno o due pence • attrib di rame

copper[2] n 🈲 poliziotto m

copy /'kɒpɪ/ n copia f • vt (pt/pp -ied) copiare

copyright n diritti mpl d'autore

coral /'kɒrəl/ n corallo m

cord /kɔːd/ n corda f; (thinner) cordoncino m; (fabric) velluto m a coste; ~**s** pl pantaloni mpl di velluto a coste

cordial /'kɔːdɪəl/ adj cordiale • n analcolico m

cordon /'kɔːdn/ n cordone m (di persone) • **cordon off** vt mettere un cordone (di persone) intorno a

core /kɔː(r)/ n (of apple, pear) torsolo m; (fig of organization) cuore m; (of problem, theory) nocciolo m

cork /kɔːk/ n sughero m; (for bottle) turacciolo m. ~**screw** n cavatappi m inv

corn[1] /kɔːn/ n grano m; (Am: maize) granturco m

corn[2] n (Med) callo m

corned beef /kɔːnd'biːf/ n manzo m sotto sale

corner /'kɔːnə(r)/ n angolo m; (football) calcio m d'angolo, corner m inv • vt fig bloccare; (Comm) accaparrarsi (market)

cornet /'kɔːnɪt/ n (Mus) cornetta f; (for ice-cream) cono m

corn: ~**flour** n, Am ~**starch** n farina f di granturco

corny /'kɔːnɪ/ adj (-ier, -iest) (🈲: joke, film) scontato; (person) banale; (sentimental) sdolcinato

coronary /'kɒrənrɪ/ adj coronario • n ~ **[thrombosis]** trombosi f coronarica

coronation /kɒrə'neɪʃn/ n incoronazione f

coroner /'kɒrənə(r)/ n coroner m inv (nel diritto britannico, ufficiale incaricato delle indagini su morti sospette)

corporal[1] /'kɔːpərəl/ n (Mil)

caporale m

corporal[2] adj corporale; ~ punishment punizione f corporale

corporate /'kɔ:parat/ adj (decision, policy, image) aziendale; ~ life la vita in un'azienda

corporation /kɔ:pa'reɪʃn/ n ente m; (of town) consiglio m comunale

corps /kɔ:(r)/ n (pl corps /kɔ:z/) corpo m

corpse /kɔ:ps/ n cadavere m

corpulent /'kɔ:pjʊlant/ adj corpulento

correct /ka'rekt/ adj corretto; be ~ (person:) aver ragione; ~! esatto! • vt correggere. ~ion n correzione f. ~ly adv correttamente

correspond /kɒrɪ'spɒnd/ vi corrispondere (to a); (two things:) corrispondere; (write) scriversi. ~ence n corrispondenza f. ~ent n corrispondente mf. ~ing adj corrispondente. ~ingly adv in modo corrispondente

corridor /'kɒrɪdɔ:(r)/ n corridoio m

corro|de /ka'raʊd/ vt corrodere • vi corrodersi. ~sion n corrosione f

corrugated /'kɒrageɪtɪd/ adj ondulato. ~ iron n lamiera f ondulata

corrupt /ka'rʌpt/ adj corrotto • vt corrompere. ~ion n corruzione f

corset /'kɔ:sɪt/ n & -s pl busto m

Corsica /'kɔ:sɪka/ n Corsica f. ~n adj & n corso, -a mf

cosmetic /kɒz'metɪk/ adj cosmetico • n ~s pl cosmetici mpl

cosmic /'kɒzmɪk/ adj cosmico

cosmopolitan /kɒzma'pɒlɪtan/ adj cosmopolita

cosmos /'kɒzmɒs/ n cosmo m

cosset /'kɒsɪt/ vt coccolare

cost /kɒst/ n costo m; ~s pl (Jur) spese fpl processuali; at all ~s a tutti i costi; I learnt to my ~ ho imparato a mie spese • vt (pt/pp cost) costare; it ~ me £20 mi è costato 20 sterline • vt (pt/pp costed)

~ [out] stabilire il prezzo di

costly /'kɒstlɪ/ adj (-ier, -iest) costoso

costume /'kɒstju:m/ n costume m. ~ jewellery n bigiotteria f

cosy /'kəʊzɪ/ adj (-ier, -iest) (pub, chat) intimo; it's nice and ~ in here si sta bene qui

cot /kɒt/ n lettino m; (Am: camp-bed) branda f

cottage /'kɒtɪdʒ/ n casetta f. ~ 'cheese n fiocchi mpl di latte

cotton /'kɒtn/ n cotone m • attrib di cotone • cotton on vi 🔲 capire

cotton 'wool n cotone m idrofilo

couch /kaʊtʃ/ n divano m. ~ potato n pantofolaio, -a mf

cough /kɒf/ n tosse f • vi tossire. □ ~ **up** vt/i sputare; (🔲: pay) sborsare

'cough mixture n sciroppo m per la tosse

could /kʊd/, atono /kəd/ v aux (see also **can**[2]) ~ I have a glass of water? potrei avere un bicchier d'acqua?; I ~n't do it even if I wanted to non potrei farlo nemmeno se lo volessi; I ~n't care less non potrebbe importarmene di meno; he ~n't have done it without help non avrebbe potuto farlo senza aiuto; you ~ have phoned avresti potuto telefonare

council /'kaʊnsl/ n consiglio m. ~ house n casa f popolare

councillor /'kaʊnsəla(r)/ n consigliere, -a mf

counsel /'kaʊnsl/ n consigli mpl; (Jur) avvocato m • vt (pt/pp counselled) consigliare a (person). ~lor n consigliere, -a mf

count[1] /kaʊnt/ n (nobleman) conte m

count[2] n conto m; keep ~ tenere il conto • vt/i contare. □ ~ **on** vt contare su

countdown /'kauntdaun/ n conto m alla rovescia

counter¹ /'kauntə(r)/ n banco m; (in games) gettone m

counter² adv ~ to contro, in trasto a; go ~ to sth andare contro qcsa • vt/i opporre (measure, effect); parare (blow)

counter'act vt neutralizzare

'counter-attack n contrattacco m

'counterfeit /-fɪt/ adj contraffatto • n contraffazione f • vt contraffare

'counterfoil n matrice f

counter-pro'ductive adj controproduttivo

countess /'kauntɪs/ n contessa f

countless /'kauntlɪs/ adj innumerevole

country /'kʌntrɪ/ n nazione f, paese m; (native land) patria f; (countryside) campagna f; in the ~ in campagna; go to the ~ andare in campagna; (Pol) indire le elezioni politiche. ~man n uomo m di campagna; (fellow ~man) compatriota m. ~side n campagna f

county /'kauntɪ/ n contea f (unità amministrativa britannica)

coup /ku:/ n (Pol) colpo m di stato

couple /'kʌpl/ n coppia f; a ~ of un paio di

coupon /'ku:pɒn/ n tagliando m; (for discount) buono m sconto

courage /'kʌrɪdʒ/ n coraggio m. ~ous adj coraggioso

courgette /kʊə'ʒet/ n zucchino m

courier /'kʊrɪə(r)/ n corriere m; (for tourists) guida f

course /kɔ:s/ n (Sch) corso m; (Naut) rotta f; (Culin) portata f; (for golf) campo m; ~ of treatment (Med) serie f inv di cure; of ~ naturalmente; in the ~ of durante; in due ~ a tempo debito

court /kɔ:t/ n tribunale m; (Sport)

campo m; take sb to ~ citare qcno in giudizio • vt fare la corte a (woman); sfidare (danger); ~ing couples coppiette fpl

courteous /'kɜ:tɪəs/ adj cortese

courtesy /'kɜ:təsɪ/ n cortesia f

court: ~ 'martial (pl ~s martial) corte f marziale. ~-martial vt (pt ~-martialled) portare davanti alla corte marziale; ~yard n cortile m

cousin /'kʌzn/ n cugino, -a mf

cove /kəʊv/ n insenatura f

cover /'kʌvə(r)/ n copertura f; (of cushion, to protect sth) fodera f; (of book, magazine) copertina f; take ~ mettersi al riparo; under separate ~ a parte • vt coprire; foderare (cushion) (Journ) fare un servizio su. □ ~ up vt coprire; fig soffocare (scandal)

coverage /'kʌvərɪdʒ/ n (Journ) it got a lot of ~ i media gli hanno dedicato molto spazio

cover: ~ charge n coperto m. ~ing n copertura f; (for floor) rivestimento m; ~ing letter lettera f d'accompagnamento

covet /'kʌvɪt/ vt bramare

cow /kaʊ/ n vacca f, mucca f

coward /'kaʊəd/ n vigliacco, -a mf. ~ice n vigliaccheria f; (of deed) vigliacco. ~ly adj da vigliacco

'cowboy n cowboy m inv; [] buffone m

cower /'kaʊə(r)/ vi acquattarsi

coy /kɔɪ/ adj falsamente timido; (flirtatiously) civettuolo; be ~ about sth essere evasivo su qcsa

crab /kræb/ n granchio m

crack /kræk/ n (in wall) crepa f; (in china, glass, bone) incrinatura f; (noise) scoppio m; ([]: joke) battuta f; have a ~ (try) fare un tentativo • adj ([]: best) di prim'ordine • vt incrinare (china, glass); schiacciare (nut); decifrare (code); [] risolvere (problem); ~ a joke [] fare una battuta • vi (china, glass:) incrinarsi; (whip:) schioccare. □~ **down** vt ① prendere seri provvedimenti. □~ **down on** vt ① prendere seri provvedimenti contro

cracker /'krækə(r)/ n (biscuit) cracker m inv; (firework) petardo m; [Christmas] ~ tubo m di cartone colorato contenente una sorpresa

crackle /'krækl/ vi crepitare

cradle /'kreɪdl/ n culla f

craft[1] /krɑːft/ n inv (boat) imbarcazione f

craft[2] n mestiere m; (technique) arte f. ~**sman** n artigiano m

crafty /'krɑːftɪ/ adj (-ier, -iest) astuto

cram /kræm/ v (pt/pp crammed) ●vt stipare (into in) ●vi (for exams) sgobbare

cramp /kræmp/ n crampo m. ~**ed** adj (room) stretto; (handwriting) appiccicato

cranberry /'krænbərɪ/ n (Culin) mirtillo m rosso

crane /kreɪn/ n (at docks, bird) gru f inv ●vt ~ one's neck allungare il collo

crank[1] /kræŋk/ n tipo, -a mf strampalato, -a

crank[2] n (Techn) manovella f. ~**shaft** n albero m a gomiti

cranky /'kræŋkɪ/ adj strampalato; (Am: irritable) irritabile

cranny /'krænɪ/ n fessura f

crash /kræʃ/ n (noise) fragore m; (Aeron, Auto) incidente m; (Comm) crollo m ●vi schiantarsi (into contro); (plane:) precipitare ●vt schiantare (car)

crash: ~ **course** n corso m intensivo. ~**helmet** n casco m

crate /kreɪt/ n (for packing) cassa f

crater /'kreɪtə(r)/ n cratere m

crav|e /kreɪv/ vt morire dalla voglia di. ~**ing** n voglia f smodata

crawl /krɔːl/ n (swimming) stile m libero; do the ~ nuotare a stile libero; at a ~ a passo di lumaca ●vi andare carponi; ~ with brulicare di. ~**er lane** n (Auto) corsia f riservata al traffico lento

crayon /'kreɪən/ n pastello m a cera; (pencil) matita f colorata

craze /kreɪz/ n mania f

crazy /'kreɪzɪ/ adj (-ier, -iest) matto; be ~ about andar matto per

creak /kriːk/ n scricchiolio m ●vi scricchiolare

cream /kriːm/ n crema f; (fresh) panna f ●adj (colour) [bianco] panna inv ●vt (Culin) sbattere. ~ 'cheese n formaggio m cremoso. ~**y** adj cremoso

crease /kriːs/ n piega f ●vt stropicciare ●vi stropicciarsi. ~**-resistant** adj che non si stropiccia

creat|e /kriː'eɪt/ vt creare. ~**ion** n creazione f. ~**ive** adj creativo. ~**or** n creatore, -trice mf

creature /'kriːtʃə(r)/ n creatura f

crèche /kreʃ/ n asilo m nido

credibility /kredə'bɪlətɪ/ n credibilità f

credible /'kredəbl/ adj credibile

credit /'kredɪt/ n credito m; (honour) merito m; take the ~ for prendersi il merito di ●vt (pt/pp credited) accreditare; ~ **sb with** (Comm) accreditare qcsa a qcno; fig attribuire qcsa a qcno. ~**able** adj lodevole

credit: ~ **card** n carta f di credito. ~**or** n creditore, -trice mf

creed /kriːd/ n credo m inv

creek /kriːk/ n insenatura f; (Am: stream) torrente m

creep /kriːp/ vi (pt/pp crept) muoversi furtivamente ●n ① tipo m viscido. ~**er** n pianta f rampicante. ~**y** adj che fa venire i brividi

cremat|e /krɪ'meɪt/ vt cremare. ~**ion** n cremazione f

crematorium /kremə'tɔːrɪəm/ n

crematorio m

crept /krept/ ▷CREEP

crescent /'kresənt/ n mezzaluna f

crest /krest/ n cresta f; (coat of arms) cimiero m

Crete /kri:t/ n Creta f

crevice /'krevɪs/ n crepa f

crew /kru:/ n equipaggio m; (gang) équipe f inv. ~ cut n capelli mpl a spazzola. ~ neck n girocollo m

crib¹ /krɪb/ n (for baby) culla f

crib² vt/i (pt/pp cribbed) 🗓 copiare

crick /krɪk/ n ~ in the neck torcicollo m

cricket¹ /'krɪkɪt/ n (insect) grillo m

cricket² n cricket m. ~er n giocatore m di cricket

crime /kraɪm/ n crimine m; (criminality) criminalità f

criminal /'krɪmɪnl/ adj criminale; (law, court) penale ● n criminale m

crimson /'krɪmzn/ adj cremisi inv

cringe /krɪndʒ/ vi (cower) acquattarsi; (at bad joke etc) fare una smorfia

crinkle /'krɪŋkl/ vt spiegazzare ● vi spiegazzarsi

cripple /'krɪpl/ n storpio, -a mf ● vt storpiare; fig danneggiare. ~d adj (person) storpio; (ship) danneggiato

crisis /'kraɪsɪs/ n (pl -ses /-si:z/) crisi f inv

crisp /krɪsp/ adj croccante; (air) frizzante; (style) incisivo. ~bread n crostini mpl di pane. ~s npl patatine fpl

criterion /kraɪ'tɪərɪən/ n (pl -ria /-rɪə/) criterio m

critic /'krɪtɪk/ n critico, -a mf. ~al adj critico. ~ally adv in modo critico; ~ally ill gravemente malato

criticism /'krɪtɪsɪzm/ n critica f; he doesn't like ~ non ama le critiche

criticize /'krɪtɪsaɪz/ vt criticare

croak /krəʊk/ vi gracchiare; (frog:) gracidare

Croatia /krəʊ'eɪʃə/ n Croazia f

crochet /'krəʊʃeɪ/ n lavoro m all'uncinetto ● vt fare all'uncinetto. ~-hook n uncinetto m

crockery /'krɒkərɪ/ n terrecotte fpl

crocodile /'krɒkədaɪl/ n coccodrillo m. ~ tears lacrime fpl di coccodrillo

crocus /'krəʊkəs/ n (pl -es) croco m

crook /krʊk/ n (🗓: criminal) truffatore, -trice mf

crooked /'krʊkɪd/ adj storto; (limb) storpiato; (🗓: dishonest) disonesto

crop /krɒp/ n raccolto m; fig quantità f inv ● v (pt/pp cropped) ● vt coltivare. □ ~ up vi 🗓 presentarsi

croquet /'krəʊkeɪ/ n croquet m

croquette /krəʊ'ket/ n crocchetta f

cross /krɒs/ adj (annoyed) arrabbiato; talk at ~ purposes fraintendersi ● n croce f; (Bot, Zool) incrocio m ● vt sbarrare (cheque); incrociare (road, animals); ~ oneself farsi il segno della croce; ~ one's arms incrociare le braccia; ~ one's legs accavallare le gambe; keep one's fingers ~ed for sb tenere le dita incrociate per qcno; it ~ed my mind mi è venuto in mente ● vi (go across) attraversare; (lines:) incrociarsi. □ ~ out vt depennare

cross: ~bar n (of goal) traversa f; (on bicycle) canna f. ~ex'amine vt sottoporre a controinterrogatorio. ~-'eyed adj strabico. ~fire n fuoco m incrociato. ~ing n (for pedestrians) passaggio m pedonale; (sea journey) traversata f. ~'reference n rimando m. ~roads n incrocio m. ~-'section n sezione f; (of community) campione m. ~word n ~word [puzzle] parole fpl crociate

crouch /kraʊtʃ/ vi accovacciarsi

crow /krəʊ/ n corvo m; as the ~ flies in linea d'aria ● vi cantare. ~bar n piede m di porco

crowd /kraʊd/ n folla f ● vt affollare ● vi affollarsi. ~ed adj affollato

crown /kraʊn/ n corona f ● vt incoronare; incapsulare (tooth)

crucial /'kru:ʃl/ adj cruciale

crucifix /'kru:sɪfɪks/ n crocifisso m

crucif|ixion /kru:sɪ'fɪkʃn/ n crocifissione f. **~y** vt (pt/pp -ied) crocifiggere

crude /kru:d/ adj (oil) greggio; (language) crudo; (person) rozzo

cruel /kru:əl/ adj (crueller, cruellest) crudele (to verso). **~ly** adv con crudeltà. **~ty** n crudeltà f

cruis|e /kru:z/ n crociera f ● vi fare una crociera; (car:) andare a velocità di crociera. **~er** n (Mil) incrociatore m; (motor boat) motoscafo m. **~ing speed** n velocità f inv di crociera

crumb /krʌm/ n briciola f

crumb|le /'krʌmbl/ vt sbriciolare ● vi sbriciolarsi; (building, society:) sgretolarsi. **~ly** adj friabile

crumple /'krʌmpl/ vt spiegazzare ● vi spiegazzarsi

crunch /krʌntʃ/ n 🆄 when it comes to the **~** quando si viene al dunque ● vt sgranocchiare ● vi (snow:) scricchiolare

crusade /kru:'seɪd/ n crociata f. **~r** n crociato m

crush /krʌʃ/ n (crowd) calca f; have a **~** on sb essersi preso una cotta per qcno ● vt schiacciare; sgualcire (clothes)

crust /krʌst/ n crosta f

crutch /krʌtʃ/ n gruccia f; (Anat) inforcatura f

crux /krʌks/ n fig punto m cruciale

cry /kraɪ/ n grido m; have a **~** farsi un pianto; a far **~** from fig tutta un'altra cosa rispetto a ● vi (pt/pp cried) (weep) piangere; (call) gridare

crypt /krɪpt/ n cripta f. **~ic** adj criptico

crystal /'krɪstl/ n cristallo m; (glassware) cristalli mpl. **~lize** vi (become clear) concretizzarsi

cub /kʌb/ n (animal) cucciolo m; C**~**

[Scout] lupetto m

Cuba /'kju:bə/ n Cuba f

cubby-hole /'kʌbɪ-/ n (compartment) scomparto m; (room) ripostiglio m

cub|e /kju:b/ n cubo m. **~ic** adj cubico

cubicle /'kju:bɪkl/ n cabina f

cuckoo /'kuku:/ n cuculo m. **~ clock** n orologio m a cucù

cucumber /'kju:kʌmbə(r)/ n cetriolo m

cuddl|e /'kʌdl/ vt coccolare ● vi **~e up to** starsene accoccolato insieme a ● n have a **~e** (child:) farsi coccolare; (lovers:) abbracciarsi. **~y** adj tenerone; (wanting cuddles) coccolone. **~y 'toy** n peluche m inv

cue¹ /kju:/ n segnale m; (Theat) battuta f d'entrata

cue² n (in billiards) stecca f. **~ ball** n pallino m

cuff /kʌf/ n polsino m; (Am: turn-up) orlo m; (blow) scapaccione m; off the **~** improvvisando ● vt dare una pacca a. **~-link** n gemello m

cul-de-sac /'kʌldəsæk/ n vicolo m cieco

culinary /'kʌlɪnərɪ/ adj culinario

cull /kʌl/ vt scegliere (flowers); (kill) selezionare e uccidere

culminat|e /'kʌlmɪneɪt/ vi culminare. **~ion** n culmine m

culprit /'kʌlprɪt/ n colpevole mf

cult /kʌlt/ n culto m

cultivate /'kʌltɪveɪt/ vt coltivare; fig coltivarsi (person)

cultural /'kʌltʃərəl/ adj culturale

culture /'kʌltʃə(r)/ n cultura f. **~d** adj colto

cumbersome /'kʌmbəsəm/ adj ingombrante

cunning /'kʌnɪŋ/ adj astuto ● n astuzia f

cup /kʌp/ n tazza f; (prize, of bra) coppa f

cupboard /'kʌbəd/ n armadio m.

~love ① amore m interessato

curator /kjʊəˈreɪtə(r)/ n direttore, -trice mf (di museo)

curb /kɜːb/ vt tenere a freno

curdle /ˈkɜːdl/ vi coagularsi

cure /kjʊə(r)/ n cura f ● vt curare; (salt) mettere sotto sale; (smoke) affumicare

curfew /ˈkɜːfjuː/ n coprifuoco m

curiosity /kjʊərɪˈɒsətɪ/ n curiosità f

curious /ˈkjʊərɪəs/ adj curioso. ~ly adv (strangely) curiosamente

curl /kɜːl/ n ricciolo m ● vt arricciare ● vi arricciarsi. □ ~ up vi raggomitolarsi

curler /ˈkɜːlə(r)/ n bigodino m

curly /ˈkɜːlɪ/ adj (-ier, -iest) riccio

currant /ˈkʌrənt/ n (dried) uvetta f

currency /ˈkʌrənsɪ/ n valuta f; (of word) ricorrenza f; foreign ~ valuta f estera

current /ˈkʌrənt/ adj corrente ● n corrente f. ~ affairs or events npl attualità fsg. ~ly adv attualmente

curriculum /kəˈrɪkjʊləm/ n programma m di studi. ~ vitae n curriculum vitae m inv

curry /ˈkʌrɪ/ n curry m inv; (meal) piatto m cucinato nel curry ● vt (pt/pp -ied) ~ favour with sb cercare di ingraziarsi qcno

curse /kɜːs/ n maledizione f; (oath) imprecazione f ● vt maledire ● vi imprecare

cursory /ˈkɜːsərɪ/ adj sbrigativo

curt /kɜːt/ adj brusco

curtain /ˈkɜːtn/ n tenda f; (Theat) sipario m

curtsy /ˈkɜːtsɪ/ n inchino m ● vi (pt/pp -ied) fare l'inchino

curve /kɜːv/ n curva f ● vi curvare; ~ to the right/left curvare a destra/sinistra. ~d adj curvo

cushion /ˈkʊʃn/ n cuscino m ● vt attutire; (protect) proteggere

cushy /ˈkʊʃɪ/ adj (-ier, -iest) ①

facile

custard /ˈkʌstəd/ n (liquid) crema f pasticcera

custody /ˈkʌstədɪ/ n (of child) custodia f; (imprisonment) detenzione f preventiva

custom /ˈkʌstəm/ n usanza f; (Jur) consuetudine f; (Comm) clientela f. ~ary adj (habitual) abituale; it's ~ary to... è consuetudine.... ~er n cliente mf

customs /ˈkʌstəmz/ npl dogana f. ~ officer n doganiere m

cut /kʌt/ n (with knife etc, of clothes) taglio m; (reduction) riduzione f; (in public spending) taglio m ● vt/i (pt/pp cut, pres p cutting) tagliare; (reduce) ridurre; ~ one's finger tagliarsi il dito; (with cards) alzare. □ ~ back vt tagliare (hair); potare (hedge); (reduce) ridurre. □ ~ down vt abbattere (tree); (reduce) ridurre. □ ~ off vt tagliar via; (disconnect) interrompere; fig isolare; I was ~ off (Teleph) la linea è caduta. □ ~ out vt ritagliare; (delete) eliminare; be ~ out for ① essere tagliato per; ~ it out! ① dacci un taglio!. □ ~ up vt (slice) tagliare a pezzi

cute /kjuːt/ adj ① (in appearance) carino; (clever) acuto

cutlery /ˈkʌtlərɪ/ n posate fpl

cutlet /ˈkʌtlɪt/ n cotoletta f

'cut-price adj a prezzo ridotto; (shop) che fa prezzi ridotti

'cut-throat adj spietato

cutting /ˈkʌtɪŋ/ adj (remark) tagliente ● n (from newspaper) ritaglio m; (of plant) talea f

CV n abbr curriculum vitae

cycl|e /ˈsaɪkl/ n ciclo m; (bicycle) bicicletta f, bici f inv ① ● vi andare in bicicletta. ~ing n ciclismo m. ~ist n ciclista mf

cylind|er /ˈsɪlɪndə(r)/ n cilindro m. ~rical adj cilindrico

cynic /'sɪnɪk/ n cinico, -a mf • **~al** adj cinico. **~ism** n cinismo m

Cyprus /'saɪprəs/ n Cipro m

Czech /tʃek/ adj ceco; **~ Republic** Repubblica f Ceca • n ceco, -a mf

Dd

dab /dæb/ n colpetto m; a **~** of un pochino di • vt (pt/pp dabbed) toccare leggermente. □ **~ on** vt mettere un po' di (paint etc)

daddy-'long-legs n zanzarone m [dei boschi]; (Am: spider) ragno m

daffodil /'dæfədɪl/ n giunchiglia f

daft /dɑːft/ adj sciocco

dagger /'dægə(r)/ n stiletto m

dahlia /'deɪlɪə/ n dalia f

Dáil Éireann Dáil Éireann è la camera bassa del Parlamento della Repubblica di Irlanda. È composto da 166 deputati (o TD) in rappresentanza di 41 collegi elettorali. I deputati sono infatti eletti col sistema proporzionale e la Costituzione ne prevede uno per ogni 20.000–30.000 cittadini.

daily /'deɪlɪ/ adj giornaliero • adv giornalmente • n (newspaper) quotidiano m; (**T**: cleaner) donna f delle pulizie

dainty /'deɪntɪ/ adj (-ier, -iest) grazioso; (movement) delicato

dairy /'deərɪ/ n caseificio m; (shop) latteria f. **~ cow** n mucca f da latte. **~ products** npl latticini mpl

daisy /'deɪzɪ/ n margheritina f; (larger) margherita f

dam /dæm/ n diga f • vt (pt/pp dammed) costruire una diga su

damag|e /'dæmɪdʒ/ n danno m (to a); **~es** pl (Jur) risarcimento msg • vt danneggiare; fig nuocere a. **~ing** adj dannoso

dame /deɪm/ n liter dama f; Am 🅇 donna f

damn /dæm/ adj 🅣 maledetto • adv (lucky, late) maledettamente • n I don't give a **~** 🅣 non me ne frega un accidente • vt dannare. **~ation** n dannazione f • int 🅣 accidenti!

damp /dæmp/ adj umido • n umidità f • vt inumidire

dance /dɑːns/ n ballo m • vt/i ballare. **~-hall** n sala f da ballo. **~ music** n musica f da ballo

dancer /'dɑːnsə(r)/ n ballerino, -a mf

dandelion /'dændɪlaɪən/ n dente m di leone

dandruff /'dændrʌf/ n forfora f

Dane /deɪn/ n danese mf; **Great ~** danese m

danger /'deɪndʒə(r)/ n pericolo m; in/out of **~** in/fuori pericolo. **~ous** adj pericoloso. **~ously** adv pericolosamente; **~ously ill** in pericolo di vita

dangle /'dæŋgl/ vi penzolare • vt far penzolare

Danish /'deɪnɪʃ/ adj & n danese m. **~ 'pastry** n dolce m a base di pasta sfoglia contenente pasta di mandorle, mele ecc

dare /deə(r)/ vt/i osare; (challenge) sfidare (to a); **~ [to]** do sth osare fare qcsa; I **~** say! molto probabilmente! • n sfida f. **~devil** n spericolato, -a mf

daring /'deərɪŋ/ adj audace • n audacia f

dark /dɑːk/ adj buio; **~ blue/brown** blu/marrone scuro; it's getting **~** sta cominciando a fare buio; **~ horse** fig (in race, contest) vincitore m imprevisto; (not much known about) misterioso m; **keep sth ~** fig tenere qcsa nascosto • n after **~** col buio;

in the ~ al buio; keep sb in the ~ *fig* tenere qcno all'oscuro

dark|en /'dɑːkn/ vt oscurare •vi oscurarsi. ~**ness** n buio m

'**dark-room** n camera f oscura

darling /'dɑːlɪŋ/ adj adorabile; my ~ Joan carissima Joan •n tesoro m

darn /dɑːn/ vt rammendare. ~**ing-needle** n ago m da rammendo

dart /dɑːt/ n dardo m; (*in sewing*) pince f inv; ~**s** sg (*game*) freccette fpl •vi lanciarsi

dartboard /'dɑːtbɔːd/ n bersaglio m [per freccette]

dash /dæʃ/ n (Typ) trattino m; (*in Morse*) linea f; a ~ of milk un goccio di latte; make a ~ for lanciarsi verso •vi I must ~ devo scappare •vt far svanire (hopes). □ ~ **off** vi scappar via •vt (*write quickly*) buttare giù. □ ~ **out** vi uscire di corsa

'**dashboard** n cruscotto m

data /'deɪtə/ npl & sg dati mpl. ~**base** n base [di] dati f, database m inv. ~**comms** n telematica f. ~ **processing** n elaborazione f [di] dati

date[1] /deɪt/ n (*fruit*) dattero m

date[2] n data f; (*meeting*) appuntamento m; to ~ fino ad oggi; out of ~ (*not fashionable*) fuori moda; (*expired*) scaduto; (*information*) non aggiornato; make a ~ with sb dare un appuntamento a qcno; be up to ~ essere aggiornato •vt/i datare; (*go out with*) uscire con. □ ~ **back to** vi risalire a

dated /'deɪtɪd/ adj fuori moda; (language) antiquato

daub /dɔːb/ vt imbrattare (walls)

daughter /'dɔːtə(r)/ n figlia f. ~-**in-law** n (pl ~**s-in-law**) nuora f

dawdle /'dɔːdl/ vi bighellonare; (*over work*) cincischiarsi

dawn /dɔːn/ n alba f; at ~ all'alba •vi albeggiare; it ~**ed** on me *fig* mi è apparso chiaro

day /deɪ/ n giorno m; (*whole day*) gior-

nata f; (*period*) epoca f; these ~**s** oggigiorno; in those ~**s** a quei tempi; it's had its ~ 🔲 ha fatto il suo tempo

day: ~**break** n at ~**break** allo spuntar del giorno. ~-**dream** n sogno m ad occhi aperti •vi sognare ad occhi aperti. ~**light** n luce f del giorno. ~**time** n giorno m; in the ~**time** di giorno

daze /deɪz/ n in a ~ stordito; *fig* sbalordito. ~**d** adj stordito; *fig* sbalordito

dazzle /'dæzl/ vt abbagliare

dead /ded/ adj morto; (*numb*) intorpidito; ~ **body** morto m; ~ **centre** pieno centro m •adv ~ **tired** stanco morto; ~ **slow/easy** lentissimo/facilissimo; you're ~ **right** hai perfettamente ragione; stop ~ fermarsi di colpo; be ~ **on time** essere in perfetto orario •n the ~ pl i morti; in the ~ **of night** nel cuore della notte

deaden /'dedn/ vt attutire (sound); calmare (pain)

dead: ~ **'end** n vicolo m cieco. ~**line** n scadenza f. ~**lock** n reach ~**lock** *fig* giungere a un punto morto

deadly /'dedlɪ/ adj (-ier, -iest) mortale; (🔲: dreary) barboso; ~ **sins** peccati mpl capitali

deaf /def/ adj sordo; ~ **and dumb** sordomuto. ~-**aid** n apparecchio m acustico

deaf|en /'defn/ vt assordare; (*permanently*) render sordo. ~**ening** adj assordante. ~**ness** n sordità f

deal /diːl/ n (*agreement*) patto m; (*in business*) accordo m; whose ~? (*in cards*) a chi tocca dare le carte?; a good or great ~ molto; get a raw ~ [1] ricevere un trattamento ingiusto •vt (pt/pp dealt /delt/) (*in cards*) dare; ~ **sb a blow** dare un colpo a qcno. □ ~ **in** vt trattare in. □ ~ **out** vt (hand out) distribuire. □ ~ **with** vt (handle) occuparsi di; trattare con (company); (be about) trattare di; that's been ∼t with è stato risolto

deal|er /'di:lə(r)/ n commerciante mf; (in drugs) spacciatore, -trice mf. ∼ings npl have ∼ings with avere a che fare con

dean /di:n/ n decano m; (Univ) ≈ preside mf di facoltà

dear /dɪə(r)/ adj caro; (in letter) Caro; (formal) Gentile ● n caro, -a mf ● int oh ∼! Dio mio!. ∼ly adv (love) profondamente; (pay) profumatamente

death /deθ/ n morte f. ∼ certificate n certificato m di morte. ∼ duty n tassa f di successione

death trap n trappola f mortale

debatable /dɪ'beɪtəbl/ adj discutibile

debate /dɪ'beɪt/ n dibattito m ● vt discutere; (in formal debate) dibattere ● vi ∼ whether to... considerare se...

debauchery /dɪ'bɔ:tʃərɪ/ n dissolutezza f

debit /'debɪt/ n debito m ● vt (pt/pp debited) (Comm) addebitare (sum)

debris /'debri:/ n macerie fpl

debt /det/ n debito m; be in ∼ avere dei debiti. ∼or n debitore, -trice mf

decade /'dekeɪd/ n decennio m

decaden|ce /'dekədəns/ n decadenza f. ∼t adj decadente

decay /dɪ'keɪ/ n (also fig) decadenza f; (rot) decomposizione f; (of tooth) carie f inv ● vi imputridire; (rot) decomporsi; (tooth:) cariarsi

deceased /dɪ'si:st/ adj defunto ● n the ∼d il defunto; la defunta

deceit /dɪ'si:t/ n inganno m. ∼ful adj falso

deceive /dɪ'si:v/ vt ingannare

December /dɪ'sembə(r)/ n dicembre m

decency /'di:sənsɪ/ n decenza f

decent /'di:sənt/ adj decente; (respectable) rispettabile; very ∼ of you molto gentile da parte tua. ∼ly adv decentemente; (kindly) gentilmente

decept|ion /dɪ'sepʃn/ n inganno m. ∼ive adj ingannevole. ∼ively adv ingannevolmente; it looks ∼ively easy sembra facile, ma non lo è

decibel /'desɪbel/ n decibel m inv

decide /dɪ'saɪd/ vt decidere ● vi decidere (on di)

decided /dɪ'saɪdɪd/ adj risoluto. ∼ly adv risolutamente; (without doubt) senza dubbio

decimal /'desɪml/ adj decimale ● n numero m decimale. ∼ 'point n virgola f

decipher /dɪ'saɪfə(r)/ vt decifrare

decision /dɪ'sɪʒn/ n decisione f

decisive /dɪ'saɪsɪv/ adj decisivo

deck[1] /dek/ vt abbigliare

deck[2] n (Naut) ponte m; on ∼ in coperta; top ∼ (of bus) piano m di sopra; ∼ of cards mazzo m. ∼-chair n [sedia f a] sdraio f inv

declaration /deklə'reɪʃn/ n dichiarazione f

declare /dɪ'kleə(r)/ vt dichiarare; anything to ∼? niente da dichiarare?

decline /dɪ'klaɪn/ n declino m ● vt also (Gram) declinare ● vi (decrease) diminuire; (health:) deperire; (say no) rifiutare

decode /di:'kəʊd/ vt decifrare; (Comput) decodificare

decompose /di:kəm'pəʊz/ vi decomporsi

décor /'deɪkɔ:(r)/ n decorazione f; (including furniture) arredamento m

decorat|e /'dekəreɪt/ vt decorare; (paint) pitturare; (wallpaper) tappezzare. ∼ion n decorazione f. ∼ive adj decorativo. ∼or n painter and ∼or imbianchino m

decoy[1] /'di:kɔɪ/ n esca f

decoy² /dɪˈkɔɪ/ vt adescare
decrease¹ /ˈdiːkriːs/ n diminuzione f
decrease² /dɪˈkriːs/ vt/i diminuire
decree /dɪˈkriː/ n decreto m • vt (pt/pp decreed) decretare
decrepit /dɪˈkrepɪt/ adj decrepito
dedicat|e /ˈdedɪkeɪt/ vt dedicare. ~ed adj (person) scrupoloso. ~ion n dedizione f; (in book) dedica f
deduce /dɪˈdjuːs/ vt dedurre (from da)
deduct /dɪˈdʌkt/ vt dedurre
deduction /dɪˈdʌkʃn/ n deduzione f
deed /diːd/ n azione f; (Jur) atto m di proprietà
deem /diːm/ vt ritenere
deep /diːp/ adj profondo; go off the ~ end 🔢 arrabbiarsi
deepen /ˈdiːpn/ vt approfondire; scavare più profondamente (trench) • vi approfondirsi; (fig: mystery:) infittirsi
deep-'freeze n congelatore m
deeply /ˈdiːplɪ/ adv profondamente
deer /dɪə(r)/ n inv cervo m
deface /dɪˈfeɪs/ vt sfigurare (picture); deturpare (monument)
default /dɪˈfɔːlt/ n (non-payment) morosità f; (failure to appear) contumacia f; win by ~ (Sport) vincere per abbandono dell'avversario; in ~ of per mancanza di • adj ~ drive (Comput) lettore m di default • vi (not pay) venir meno a un pagamento
defeat /dɪˈfiːt/ n sconfitta f • vt sconfiggere; (frustrate) vanificare (attempts); that ~s the object questo fa fallire l'obiettivo
defect¹ /dɪˈfekt/ vi (Pol) fare defezione
defect² /ˈdiːfekt/ n difetto m. ~ive adj difettoso
defence /dɪˈfens/ n difesa f. ~less adj indifeso

defend /dɪˈfend/ vt difendere; (justify) giustificare. ~ant n (Jur) imputato, -a mf
defensive /dɪˈfensɪv/ adj difensivo • n difensiva f; on the ~ sulla difensiva
defer /dɪˈfɜː(r)/ v (pt/pp deferred) • vt (postpone) rinviare • vi ~ to sb rimettersi a qcno
deferen|ce /ˈdefərəns/ n deferenza f. ~tial adj deferente
defian|ce /dɪˈfaɪəns/ n sfida f; in ~ce of sfidando. ~t adj (person) ribelle; (gesture, attitude) di sfida. ~tly adv con aria di sfida
deficien|cy /dɪˈfɪʃnsɪ/ n insufficienza f. ~t adj insufficiente; be ~t in mancare di
deficit /ˈdefɪsɪt/ n deficit m inv
define /dɪˈfaɪn/ vt definire
definite /ˈdefɪnɪt/ adj definito; (certain) (answer, yes) definitivo; (improvement, difference) netto; he was ~ about it è stato chiaro in proposito. ~ly adv sicuramente
definition /defɪˈnɪʃn/ n definizione f
definitive /dɪˈfɪnɪtɪv/ adj definitivo
deflate /dɪˈfleɪt/ vt sgonfiare. ~ion n (Comm) deflazione f
deflect /dɪˈflekt/ vt deflettere
deform|ed /dɪˈfɔːmd/ adj deforme. ~ity n deformità f inv
defrost /diːˈfrɒst/ vt sbrinare (fridge); scongelare (food)
deft /deft/ adj abile
defuse /diːˈfjuːz/ vt disinnescare; calmare (situation)
defy /dɪˈfaɪ/ vt (pt/pp -ied) (challenge) sfidare; resistere a (attempt); (not obey) disobbedire a
degenerate¹ /dɪˈdʒenəreɪt/ vi degenerare; ~ into fig degenerare in
degenerate² /dɪˈdʒenərət/ adj degenerato
degree /dɪˈɡriː/ n grado m; (Univ)

laurea f; 20 ~s 20 gradi; not to the same ~ non allo stesso livello

deign /deɪn/ vi ~ to do sth degnarsi di fare qcsa

deity /ˈdiːɪti/ n divinità f inv

dejected /dɪˈdʒektɪd/ adj demoralizzato

delay /dɪˈleɪ/ n ritardo m; without ~ senza indugio ● vt ritardare; be ~ed (person:) essere trattenuto; (train, aircraft:) essere in ritardo ● vi indugiare

delegate¹ /ˈdelɪɡət/ n delegato, -a mf

delegat|e² /ˈdelɪɡeɪt/ vt delegare. ~ion n delegazione f

delet|e /dɪˈliːt/ vt cancellare. ~ion n cancellatura f

deliberate¹ /dɪˈlɪbərət/ adj deliberato; (slow) posato. ~ly adv deliberatamente; (slowly) in modo posato

deliberat|e² /dɪˈlɪbəreɪt/ vt/i deliberare. ~ion n deliberazione f

delicacy /ˈdelɪkəsi/ n delicatezza f; (food) prelibatezza f

delicate /ˈdelɪkət/ adj delicato

delicatessen /delɪkəˈtesn/ n negozio m di specialità gastronomiche

delicious /dɪˈlɪʃəs/ adj delizioso

delight /dɪˈlaɪt/ n piacere m ● vt deliziare ● vi ~ in dilettarsi con. ~ed adj lieto. ~ful adj delizioso

deli|rious /dɪˈlɪrɪəs/ adj be ~rious delirare; (fig: very happy) essere pazzo di gioia. ~rium n delirio m

deliver /dɪˈlɪvə(r)/ vt consegnare; recapitare (post, newspaper); tenere (speech); dare (message); tirare (blow); (set free) liberare; ~ a baby far nascere un bambino. ~ance n liberazione f. ~y n consegna f; (of post) distribuzione f; (Med) parto m; cash on ~y pagamento m alla consegna

delude /dɪˈluːd/ vt ingannare; ~ oneself illudersi

deluge /ˈdeljuːdʒ/ n diluvio m ● vt

(fig: with requests etc) inondare

delusion /dɪˈluːʒn/ n illusione f

de luxe /dəˈlʌks/ adj di lusso

delve /delv/ vi ~ into (into pocket etc) frugare in; (into notes, the past) fare ricerche in

demand /dɪˈmɑːnd/ n richiesta f; (Comm) domanda f; in ~ richiesto; on ~ a richiesta ● vt esigere (of/ from sb). ~ing adj esigente

demented /dɪˈmentɪd/ adj demente

demister /diːˈmɪstə(r)/ n (Auto) sbrinatore m

demo /ˈdeməʊ/ n (pl ~s) 🔲 manifestazione f; ~ disk (Comput) demo disk m inv

democracy /dɪˈmɒkrəsi/ n democrazia f

democrat /ˈdeməkræt/ n democratico, -a mf. ~ic adj democratico

demo|lish /dɪˈmɒlɪʃ/ vt demolire. ~lition n demolizione f

demon /ˈdiːmən/ n demonio m

demonstrat|e /ˈdemənstreɪt/ vt dimostrare; fare una dimostrazione sull'uso di (appliance) ● vi (Pol) manifestare. ~ion n dimostrazione f; (Pol) manifestazione f

demonstrator /ˈdemənstreɪtə(r)/ n (Pol) manifestante mf; (for product) dimostratore, -trice mf

demoralize /dɪˈmɒrəlaɪz/ vt demoralizzare

demote /dɪˈməʊt/ vt retrocedere di grado; (Mil) degradare

demure /dɪˈmjʊə(r)/ adj schivo

den /den/ n tana f; (room) rifugio m

denial /dɪˈnaɪəl/ n smentita f

denim /ˈdenɪm/ n (tessuto m) jeans m; ~s pl (blue)jeans mpl

Denmark /ˈdenmɑːk/ n Danimarca f

denounce /dɪˈnaʊns/ vt denunciare

dens|e /dens/ adj denso; (crowd, forest) fitto; (stupid) ottuso. ~ely adv (populated) densamente; ~ely wooded fittamente ricoperto di alberi. ~ity n densità f inv; (of forest) fittezza f

dent /dent/ n ammaccatura f ● vt ammaccare; ~ed adj ammaccato

dental /'dentl/ adj dei denti; (treatment) dentistico; (hygiene) dentale. ~ surgeon n odontoiatra mf, medico m dentista

dentist /'dentist/ n dentista mf. ~ry n odontoiatria f

dentures /'dentʃəz/ npl dentiera fsg

deny /dɪ'naɪ/ vt (pt/pp -ied) negare; (officially) smentire; ~ sb sth negare qcsa a qcno

deodorant /di:'əʊdərənt/ n deodorante m

depart /dɪ'pɑːt/ vi (plane, train): partire; (liter: person) andare via; (deviate) allontanarsi (from da)

department /dɪ'pɑːtmənt/ n reparto m; (Pol) ministero m; (of company) sezione f; (Univ) dipartimento m. ~ store n grande magazzino m

departure /dɪ'pɑːtʃə(r)/ n partenza f; (from rule) allontanamento m; new ~ svolta f

depend /dɪ'pend/ vi dipendere (on da); (rely) contare (on su); it all ~s dipende; ~ing on what he says a seconda di quello che dice. ~able adj fidato. ~ant n persona f a carico. ~ence n dipendenza f. ~ent adj dipendente (on da)

depict /dɪ'pɪkt/ vt (in writing) dipingere; (with picture) rappresentare

deplete /dɪ'pliːt/ vt ridurre; totally ~d completamente esaurito

deplor|able /dɪ'plɔːrəbl/ adj deplorevole. ~e vt deplorare

deploy /dɪ'plɔɪ/ vt (Mil) spiegare ● vi schierarsi

deport /dɪ'pɔːt/ vt deportare. ~ation n deportazione f

depose /dɪ'pəʊz/ vt deporre

deposit /dɪ'pɒzɪt/ n deposito m;

(against damage) cauzione f; (first instalment) acconto m ● vt (pt/pp deposited) depositare. ~ account n libretto m di risparmio; (without instant access) conto m vincolato

depot /'depəʊ/ n deposito m; Am (Rail) stazione f ferroviaria

depress /dɪ'pres/ vt deprimere; (press down) premere. ~ed adj depresso; ~ed area zona f depressa. ~ing adj deprimente. ~ion n depressione f

deprivation /deprɪ'veɪʃn/ n privazione f

deprive /dɪ'praɪv/ vt ~ sb of sth privare qcno di qcsa. ~d adj (area, childhood) disagiato

depth /depθ/ n profondità f inv; in ~ (study, analyse) in modo approfondito; in the ~s of winter in pieno inverno; be out of one's ~ (in water) non toccare il fondo; fig sentirsi in alto mare

deputize /'depjʊtaɪz/ vi ~ for fare le veci di

deputy /'depjʊtɪ/ n vice mf; (temporary) sostituto, -a mf ● attrib ~ leader ≈ vicesegretario, -a mf; ~ chairman vicepresidente mf

derail /dɪ'reɪl/ vt be ~ed (train:) essere deragliato. ~ment n deragliamento m

derelict /'derəlɪkt/ adj abbandonato

deri|de /dɪ'raɪd/ vt deridere. ~sion n derisione f

derisory /dɪ'raɪsərɪ/ adj (laughter) derisorio; (offer) irrisorio

derivation /derɪ'veɪʃn/ n derivazione f

derivative /dɪ'rɪvətɪv/ adj derivato ● n derivato m

derive /dɪ'raɪv/ vt (obtain) derivare; be ~d from (word:) derivare da

derogatory /dɪ'rɒgətrɪ/ adj (comments) peggiorativo

descend /dɪ'send/ vi scendere ● vt scendere da; be ~ed from discendere da. **~ant** *n* discendente *mf*

descent /dɪˈsent/ *n* discesa *f*; (*lineage*) origine *f*

describe /dɪˈskraɪb/ *vt* descrivere

descrip|tion /dɪˈskrɪpʃn/ *n* descrizione *f*; **they had no help of any ~tion** non hanno avuto proprio nessun aiuto. **~tive** *adj* descrittivo; (*vivid*) vivido

desecrat|e /ˈdesɪkreɪt/ *vt* profanare. **~ion** *n* profanazione *f*

desert[1] /ˈdezət/ *n* deserto *m* ● *adj* deserto; **~ island** isola *f* deserta

desert[2] /dɪˈzɜːt/ *vt* abbandonare ● *vi* disertare. **~ed** *adj* deserto. **~er** *n* (*Mil*) disertore *m*. **~ion** *n* (*Mil*) diserzione *f*; (*of family*) abbandono *m*

deserts /dɪˈzɜːts/ *npl* **get one's just ~** ottenere ciò che ci si merita

deserv|e /dɪˈzɜːv/ *vt* meritare. **~ing** *adj* meritevole; **~ing cause** opera *f* meritoria

design /dɪˈzaɪn/ *n* progettazione *f*; (*fashion ~*, *appearance*) design *m inv*; (*pattern*) modello *m*; (*aim*) proposito *m* ● *vt* progettare; disegnare (*clothes*, *furniture*, *model*); **be ~ed for** essere fatto per

designat|e /ˈdezɪɡneɪt/ *vt* designare. **~ion** *n* designazione *f*

designer /dɪˈzaɪnə(r)/ *n* progettista *mf*; (*of clothes*) stilista *mf*; (*Theat: of set*) scenografo, -a *mf*

desirable /dɪˈzaɪərəbl/ *adj* desiderabile

desire /dɪˈzaɪə(r)/ *n* desiderio *m* ● *vt* desiderare

desk /desk/ *n* scrivania *f*; (*in school*) banco *m*; (*in hotel*) reception *f inv*; (*cash ~*) cassa *f*. **~top 'publishing** *n* desktop publishing *m*, editoria *f* da tavolo

desolat|e /ˈdesələt/ *adj* desolato. **~ion** *n* desolazione *f*

despair /dɪˈspeə(r)/ *n* disperazione *f*; **in ~** disperato; (*say*) per disperazione ● *vi* **I ~ of that boy** quel ra-

gazzo mi fa disperare

desperat|e /ˈdespərət/ *adj* disperato; **be ~e** (*criminal:*) essere un disperato; **be ~e for sth** morire dalla voglia di. **~ely** *adv* disperatamente; **he said ~ely** ha detto, disperato. **~ion** *n* disperazione *f*; **in ~ion** per disperazione

despicable /dɪˈspɪkəbl/ *adj* disprezzevole

despise /dɪˈspaɪz/ *vt* disprezzare

despite /dɪˈspaɪt/ *prep* malgrado

despondent /dɪˈspɒndənt/ *adj* abbattuto

despot /ˈdespɒt/ *n* despota *m*

dessert /dɪˈzɜːt/ *n* dolce *m*. **~ spoon** *n* cucchiaio *m* da dolce

destination /destɪˈneɪʃn/ *n* destinazione *f*

destiny /ˈdestɪnɪ/ *n* destino *m*

destitute /ˈdestɪtjuːt/ *adj* bisognoso

destroy /dɪˈstrɔɪ/ *vt* distruggere. **~er** *n* (*Naut*) cacciatorpediniere *m*

destruc|tion /dɪˈstrʌkʃn/ *n* distruzione *f*. **~tive** *adj* distruttivo; (*fig:* criticism*) negativo

detach /dɪˈtætʃ/ *vt* staccare. **~able** *adj* separabile. **~ed** *adj fig* distaccato; **~ed house** villetta *f*

detachment /dɪˈtætʃmənt/ *n* distacco *m*; (*Mil*) distaccamento *m*

detail /ˈdiːteɪl/ *n* particolare *m*, dettaglio *m*; **in ~** particolareggiatamente ● *vt* esporre con tutti i particolari; (*Mil*) assegnare. **~ed** *adj* particolareggiato, dettagliato

detain /dɪˈteɪn/ *vt* (*police:*) trattenere; (*delay*) far ritardare. **~ee** *n* detenuto, -a *mf*

detect /dɪˈtekt/ *vt* individuare; (*perceive*) percepire. **~ion** *n* scoperta *f*

detective /dɪˈtektɪv/ *n* investigatore, -trice *mf*. **~ story** *n* racconto *m* poliziesco

detector /dɪˈtektə(r)/ *n* (*for metal*) metal detector *m inv*

detention /dɪ'tenʃn/ n detenzione f; (Sch) punizione f

deter /dɪ'tɜ:(r)/ vt (pt/pp deterred) impedire; ~ sb from doing sth impedire a qcno di fare qcsa

detergent /dɪ'tɜ:dʒənt/ n detersivo m

deteriorat|e /dɪ'tɪərɪəreɪt/ vi deteriorarsi. ~ion n deterioramento m

determination /dɪtɜ:mɪ'neɪʃn/ n determinazione f

determine /dɪ'tɜ:mɪn/ vt (ascertain) determinare; ~ to (resolve) decidere di. ~d adj deciso

deterrent /dɪ'terənt/ n deterrente m

detest /dɪ'test/ vt detestare. ~able adj detestabile

detonat|e /'detəneɪt/ vt far detonare ● vi detonare. ~or n detonatore m

detour /'di:tʊə(r)/ n deviazione f

detract /dɪ'trækt/ vi ~ from sminuire (merit); rovinare (pleasure, beauty)

detriment /'detrɪmənt/ n to the ~ of a danno di. ~al adj dannoso

de'value vt svalutare (currency)

devastat|e /'devəsteɪt/ vt devastare. ~ed adj 🔲 sconvolto. ~ing adj devastante; (news) sconvolgente. ~ion n devastazione f

develop /dɪ'veləp/ vt sviluppare; contrarre (illness); (add to value of) valorizzare (area) ● vi svilupparsi; ~ into divenire. ~er n [property] ~er imprenditore, -trice m edile

development /dɪ'veləpmənt/ n sviluppo m; (of vaccine etc) messa f a punto

deviant /'di:vɪənt/ adj deviato

deviat|e /'di:vɪeɪt/ vi deviare. ~ion n deviazione f

device /dɪ'vaɪs/ n dispositivo m

devil /'devl/ n diavolo m

devious /'di:vɪəs/ adj (person) sub-

dolo; (route) tortuoso

devise /dɪ'vaɪz/ vt escogitare

devoid /dɪ'vɔɪd/ adj ~ of privo di

devolution /di:və'lu:ʃn/ n (of power) decentramento m

devot|e /dɪ'vəʊt/ vt dedicare. ~ed adj (daughter etc) affezionato; be ~ed to sth consacrarsi a qcsa. ~ee n appassionato, -a mf

devotion /dɪ'vəʊʃn/ n dedizione f; ~s pl (Relig) devozione fsg

devour /dɪ'vaʊə(r)/ vt divorare

devout /dɪ'vaʊt/ adj devoto

dew /dju:/ n rugiada f

dexterity /dek'sterətɪ/ n destrezza f

diabet|es /daɪə'bi:ti:z/ n diabete m. ~ic adj diabetico ● n diabetico, -a mf

diabolical /daɪə'bɒlɪkl/ adj diabolico

diagnose /daɪəg'nəʊz/ vt diagnosticare

diagnosis /daɪəg'nəʊsɪs/ n (pl -oses /-si:z/) diagnosi f inv

diagonal /daɪ'ægənl/ adj diagonale ● n diagonale f

diagram /'daɪəgræm/ n diagramma m

dial /'daɪəl/ n (of clock, machine) quadrante m; (Teleph) disco m combinatore ● vi (pt/pp dialled) ● vi (Teleph) fare il numero; ~ direct chiamare in teleselezione ● vt fare (number)

dialect /'daɪəlekt/ n dialetto m

dialling /'daɪəlɪŋ/ ~ code n prefisso m. ~ tone n segnale m di linea libera

dialogue /'daɪəlɒg/ n dialogo m

'dial tone n Am (Teleph) segnale m di linea libera

diameter /daɪ'æmɪtə(r)/ n diametro m

diamond /'daɪəmənd/ n diamante m, brillante m; (shape) losanga f; ~s pl (in cards) quadri mpl

diaper /'daɪəpə(r)/ n Am pannolino m

diaphragm /'daɪəfræm/ n diaframma m

diarrhoea /daɪə'rɪːə/ n diarrea f

diary /'daɪərɪ/ n (for appointments) agenda f; (for writing in) diario m

dice /daɪs/ n inv dadi mpl ● vt (Culin) tagliare a dadini

dictat|e /dɪk'teɪt/ vt/i dettare. ~ion n dettato m

dictator /dɪk'teɪtə(r)/ n dittatore m. ~ial adj dittatoriale. ~ship n dittatura f

dictionary /'dɪkʃənrɪ/ n dizionario m

did /dɪd/ ▷DO

didn't /'dɪdnt/ = did not

die /daɪ/ vi (pres p dying) morire (of di); be dying to do sth 🄸 morire dalla voglia di fare qcsa. □ ~ down vi calmarsi; (fire, flames:) spegnersi. □ ~ out vi estinguersi; (custom:) morire

diesel /'diːzl/ n diesel m

diet /'daɪət/ n regime m alimentare; (restricted) dieta f; be on a ~ essere a dieta ● vi essere a dieta

differ /'dɪfə(r)/ vi differire; (disagree) non essere d'accordo

difference /'dɪfrəns/ n differenza f; (disagreement) divergenza f

different /'dɪfrənt/ adj diverso, differente; (various) diversi; be ~ from essere diverso da

differently /'dɪfrəntlɪ/ adv in modo diverso; ~ from diversamente da

difficult /'dɪfɪkəlt/ adj difficile. ~y n difficoltà f inv

diffuse[1] /dɪ'fjuːs/ adj diffuso; (wordy) prolisso

diffuse[2] /dɪ'fjuːz/ vt (Phys) diffondere

dig /dɪg/ n (poke) spinta f; (remark) frecciata f; (Archaeol) scavo m; ~s pl 🄸 camera fsg ammobiliata ● vt/i (pt/pp dug, pres p digging) scavare

(hole); vangare (garden); (thrust) conficcare; ~ sb in the ribs dare una gomitata a qcno. □ ~ out vt fig tirar fuori. □ ~ up vt scavare (garden, street, object); sradicare (plant); (fig: find) scovare

digest[1] /'daɪdʒest/ n compendio m

digest[2] /daɪ'dʒest/ vt digerire. ~ible adj digeribile. ~ion n digestione f

digger /'dɪgə(r)/ n (Techn) scavatrice f

digit /'dɪdʒɪt/ n cifra f; (finger) dito m

digital /'dɪdʒɪtl/ adj digitale; ~ camera fotocamera f digitale. ~ clock orologio m digitale

digitize /'dɪdʒɪtaɪz/ vt digitalizzare

dignified /'dɪgnɪfaɪd/ adj dignitoso

dignitary /'dɪgnɪtərɪ/ n dignitario m

dignity /'dɪgnɪtɪ/ n dignità f

digress /daɪ'gres/ vi divagare. ~ion n digressione f

dike /daɪk/ n diga f

dilapidated /dɪ'læpɪdeɪtɪd/ adj cadente

dilate /daɪ'leɪt/ vi dilatarsi

dilemma /dɪ'lemə/ n dilemma m

dilute /daɪ'luːt/ vt diluire

dim /dɪm/ adj (dimmer, dimmest) debole (light); (dark) scuro; (prospect, chance) scarso; (indistinct) impreciso; (🄸: stupid) tonto ● vt/i (pt/pp dimmed) affievolire. ~ly adv (see, remember) indistintamente; (shine) debolmente

dime /daɪm/ n Am moneta f da dieci centesimi

dimension /daɪ'menʃn/ n dimensione f

diminish /dɪ'mɪnɪʃ/ vt/i diminuire

dimple /'dɪmpl/ n fossetta f

din /dɪn/ n baccano m

dine /daɪn/ vi pranzare. ~r n (Am: restaurant) tavola f calda; the last ~r in the restaurant l'ultimo cliente nel ristorante

dinghy /'dɪŋgɪ/ n dinghy m; (inflatable) canotto m pneumatico

dingy /'dɪndʒɪ/ adj (-ier, -iest) squallido e tetro

dinner /'dɪnə(r)/ n cena f; (at midday) pranzo m. ~-jacket n smoking m inv

dinosaur /'daɪnəsɔ:(r)/ n dinosauro m

dint /dɪnt/ n by ~ of a forza di

dip /dɪp/ n (in ground) inclinazione f; (Culin) salsina f; go for a ~ andare a fare una nuotata ● v (pt/pp dipped) ● vt (in liquid) immergere; abbassare (head, headlights) ● vi (land:) formare un avvallamento. □ ~ **into** vt scorrere (book)

diphthong /'dɪfθɒŋ/ n dittongo m

diploma /dɪ'pləʊmə/ n diploma m

diplomacy /dɪ'pləʊməsɪ/ n diplomazia f

diplomat /'dɪpləmæt/ n diplomatico, -a mf. ~ic adj diplomatico. ~ically adv con diplomazia

'dip-stick n (Auto) astina f dell'olio

dire /'daɪə(r)/ adj (situation, consequences) terribile

direct /dɪ'rekt/ adj diretto ● adv direttamente ● vt (aim) rivolgere (attention, criticism); (control) dirigere; fare la regia di (film, play); ~ **sb** (show the way) indicare la strada a qcno; ~ **sb to do sth** ordinare a qcno di fare qcsa. ~ 'current n corrente f continua

direction /dɪ'rekʃn/ n direzione f; (of play, film) regia f; ~**s** pl indicazioni fpl

directly /dɪ'rektlɪ/ adv direttamente; (at once) immediatamente ● conj [non] appena

director /dɪ'rektə(r)/ n (Comm) direttore, -trice mf; (of play, film) regista mf

directory /dɪ'rektərɪ/ n elenco m; (Teleph) elenco m [telefonico]; (of streets) stradario m

dirt /dɜ:t/ n sporco m; ~ **cheap** 1 a [un] prezzo stracciato

dirty /'dɜ:tɪ/ adj (-ier, -iest) sporco; ~ **trick** brutto scherzo m; ~ **word** parolaccia f ● vt (pt/pp -ied) sporcare

disa'bility /dɪs-/ n infermità f inv. ~**abled** adj invalido

disad'vantage n svantaggio m; **at a** ~**tage** in una posizione di svantaggio. ~**taged** adj svantaggiato. ~**tageous** adj svantaggioso

disa'gree vi non essere d'accordo; ~ **with** (food:) far male a

disa'greeable adj sgradevole

disa'greement n disaccordo m; (quarrel) dissidio m

disap'pear vi scomparire. ~**ance** n scomparsa f

disap'point vt deludere; I'm ~**ed** sono deluso. ~**ing** adj deludente. ~**ment** n delusione f

disap'proval n disapprovazione f

disap'prove vi disapprovare; ~ **of sb/sth** disapprovare qcno/qcsa

dis'arm vt disarmare ● vi (Mil) disarmarsi. ~**ament** n disarmo m. ~**ing** adj (frankness etc) disarmante

disar'ray n in ~ in disordine

disast|er /dɪ'zɑ:stə(r)/ n disastro m. ~**rous** adj disastroso

dis'band vt sciogliere; smobilitare (troops) ● vi sciogliersi; (regiment:) essere smobilitato

disbe'lief n incredulità f; **in** ~ con incredulità

disc /dɪsk/ n disco m; (CD) compact disc m inv

discard /dɪ'skɑ:d/ vt scartare; (throw away) eliminare; scaricare (boyfriend)

discern /dɪ'sɜ:n/ vt discernere. ~**ible** adj discernibile. ~**ing** adj perspicace

'discharge¹ n (Electr) scarica f; (dismissal) licenziamento m; (Mil) congedo m; (Med: of blood) emissione f; (of cargo) scarico m

dis'charge² vt scaricare (battery, cargo); (dismiss) licenziare; (Mil) congedare; (Jur) assolvere (accused); dimettere (patient) ● vi (Electr) scaricarsi

disciple /dɪ'saɪpl/ n discepolo m

disciplinary /'dɪsɪplɪnərɪ/ adj disciplinare

discipline /'dɪsɪplɪn/ n disciplina f ● vt disciplinare; (punish) punire

'disc jockey n disc jockey m inv

dis'claim vt disconoscere. ~er n rifiuto m

dis'clos|e vt svelare. ~ure n rivelazione f

disco /'dɪskəʊ/ n discoteca f

dis'colour vt scolorire ● vi scolorirsi

dis'comfort n scomodità f; fig disagio m

disconcert /dɪskən'sɜːt/ vt sconcertare

discon'nect vt disconnettere

disconsolate /dɪs'kɒnsələt/ adj sconsolato

discon'tent n scontentezza f. ~ed adj scontento

discon'tinue vt cessare, smettere; (Comm) sospendere la produzione di; ~d line linea f serie

'discord n discordia f; (Mus) dissonanza f. ~ant adj ~ant note nota f discordante

'discount¹ n sconto m

dis'count² vt (not believe) non credere a; (leave out of consideration) non tener conto di

dis'courage vt scoraggiare; (dissuade) dissuadere

dis'courteous adj scortese

dis'cover /dɪs'kʌvə(r)/ vt scoprire. ~y n scoperta f

dis'credit n discredito m ● vt (pt/pp discredited) screditare

discreet /dɪ'skriːt/ adj discreto

discrepancy /dɪ'skrepənsɪ/ n discrepanza f

discretion /dɪ'skreʃn/ n discrezione f

discriminat|e /dɪ'skrɪmɪneɪt/ vi discriminare (against contro); ~e between distinguere tra. ~ing adj esigente. ~ion n discriminazione f; (quality) discernimento m

discus /'dɪskəs/ n disco m

discuss /dɪ'skʌs/ vt discutere; (examine critically) esaminare. ~ion n discussione f

disdain /dɪs'deɪn/ n sdegno f ● vt sdegnare. ~ful adj sdegnoso

disease /dɪ'ziːz/ n malattia f. ~d adj malato

disem'bark vi sbarcare

disen'tangle vt districare

dis'figure vt deformare

dis'grace n vergogna f; I am in ~ sono caduto in disgrazia; it's a ~ è una vergogna ● vt disonorare. ~ful adj vergognoso

disgruntled /dɪs'grʌntld/ adj malcontento

disguise /dɪs'gaɪz/ n travestimento m; in ~ travestito ● vt contraffare (voice); dissimulare (emotions); ~d as travestito da

disgust /dɪs'gʌst/ n disgusto m; in ~ con aria disgustata ● vt disgustare. ~ing adj disgustoso

dish /dɪʃ/ n piatto m; do the ~es lavare i piatti ● dish out vt (serve) servire; (distribute) distribuire. □ ~ up vt servire

'dishcloth n strofinaccio m

dis'honest adj disonesto. ~y n disonestà f

dis'honour n disonore m ● vt disonorare (family); non onorare (cheque). ~able adj disonorevole. ~ably adv in modo disonorevole

'dishwasher n lavapiatti f inv

disil'lusion vt disilludere. ~ment n disillusione f

disin'fect vt disinfettare. ~ant n

d

disinfettante *m*

dis'integrate *vi* disintegrarsi

dis'interested *adj* disinteressato

dis'jointed *adj* sconnesso

disk /dɪsk/ *n* (Comput) disco *m*; (*diskette*) dischetto *m*

dis'like *n* avversione *f*; your likes and ~s i tuoi gusti ● *vt* I ~ him/it non mi piace; I don't ~ him/it non mi dispiace

dislocate /'dɪsləkeɪt/ *vt* slogare; ~ one's shoulder slogarsi una spalla

dis'lodge *vt* sloggiare

dis'loyal *adj* sleale. ~ty *n* slealtà *f*

dismal /'dɪzməl/ *adj* (person) abbacchiato; (news, weather) deprimente; (performance) mediocre

dismantle /dɪs'mæntl/ *vt* smontare (tent, machine); *fig* smantellare

dis'may *n* sgomento *m*. ~ed *adj* sgomento

dis'miss *vt* licenziare (employee); (*reject*) scartare (idea, suggestion). ~al *n* licenziamento *m*

dis'mount *vi* smontare

diso'bedien|ce *n* disubbidienza *f*. ~t *adj* disubbidiente

diso'bey *vt* disubbidire a (rule) ● *vi* disubbidire

dis'order *n* disordine *m*; (Med) disturbo *m*. ~ly *adj* disordinato; (crowd) turbolento; ~ly conduct turbamento *m* della quiete pubblica

dis'organized *adj* disorganizzato

dis'orientate *vt* disorientare

dis'own *vt* disconoscere

disparaging /dɪ'spærɪdʒɪŋ/ *adj* sprezzante

dispatch /dɪ'spætʃ/ *n* (Comm) spedizione *f*; (Mil, report) dispaccio *m*; with ~ con prontezza ● *vt* spedire; (*kill*) spedire al creatore

dispel /dɪ'spel/ *vt* (*pt/pp* dispelled) dissipare

dispensable /dɪ'spensəbl/ *adj* dispensabile

dispense /dɪ'spens/ *vt* distribuire; ~ with fare a meno di; **dispensing chemist** farmacista *mf*; (shop) farmacia *f*. ~e vt dispenser *m* (in device) distributore *m*

dispers|al /dɪ'spɜːsl/ *n* dispersione *f*. ~e vt disperdere ● vi disperdersi

dispirited /dɪ'spɪrɪtɪd/ *adj* scoraggiato

display /dɪ'spleɪ/ *n* mostra *f*; (Comm) esposizione *f*; (of feelings) manifestazione *f*; *pej* ostentazione *f*; (Comput) display *m inv* ● *vt* mostrare; esporre (goods); manifestare (feeling); (Comput) visualizzare

dis'please *vt* non piacere a; be ~d with essere scontento di

dis'pleasure *n* malcontento *m*

disposable /dɪ'spəʊzəbl/ *adj* (throwaway) usa e getta; (income) disponibile

disposal /dɪ'spəʊzl/ *n* (getting rid of) eliminazione *f*; be at sb's ~ essere a disposizione di qcno

disproportionate /dɪsprə'pɔːʃə·nət/ *adj* sproporzionato

dis'prove *vt* confutare

dispute /dɪ'spjuːt/ *n* disputa *f*; (industrial) contestazione *f* ● *vt* contestare (statement)

disqualifi'cation *n* squalifica *f*; (from driving) ritiro *m* della patente

dis'qualify *vt* (*pt/pp* -ied) escludere; (Sport) squalificare; ~ sb from driving ritirare la patente a qcno

disre'gard *n* mancanza *f* di considerazione ● *vt* ignorare

dis'reputable *adj* malfamato

disre'spect *n* mancanza *f* di rispetto. ~ful *adj* irrispettoso

disrupt /dɪs'rʌpt/ *vt* creare scompiglio in; sconvolgere (plans). ~ion *n* scompiglio *m*; (of plans) sconvolgimento *m*. ~ive *adj* (person, behaviour) indisciplinato

dissatis'faction *n* malcontento *m*

dis'satisfied *adj* scontento

dissect /dɪˈsekt/ vt sezionare. ~ion n dissezione f

dissent /dɪˈsent/ n dissenso m ● vi dissentire

dissertation /dɪsəˈteɪʃn/ n tesi f inv

dissident /ˈdɪsɪdənt/ n dissidente mf

dis'similar adj dissimile (to da)

dissolute /ˈdɪsəluːt/ adj dissoluto

dissolve /dɪˈzɒlv/ vt dissolvere ● vi dissolversi

dissuade /dɪˈsweɪd/ vt dissuadere

distance /ˈdɪstəns/ n distanza f; it's a short ~ from here to the station la stazione non è lontana da qui; in the ~ in lontananza; from a ~ da lontano

distant /ˈdɪstənt/ adj distante; (relative) lontano

dis'taste n avversione f. ~ful adj spiacevole

distil /dɪˈstɪl/ vt (pt/pp distilled) distillare. ~lation n distillazione f. ~lery n distilleria f

distinct /dɪˈstɪŋkt/ adj chiaro; (different) distinto. ~ion n distinzione f; (Sch) massimo m dei voti. ~ive adj caratteristico. ~ly adv chiaramente

distinguish /dɪˈstɪŋgwɪʃ/ vt/i distinguere; ~ oneself distinguersi. ~ed adj rinomato; (appearance) distinto; (career) brillante

distort /dɪˈstɔːt/ vt distorcere. ~ion n distorsione f

distract /dɪˈstrækt/ vt distrarre. ~ed adj assente; (fam: worried) preoccupato. ~ing adj che distoglie. ~ion n distrazione f; (despair) disperazione f; drive sb to ~ portare qcno alla disperazione

distraught /dɪˈstrɔːt/ adj sconvolto

distress /dɪˈstres/ n angoscia f; (pain) sofferenza f; (danger) difficoltà f ● vt sconvolgere; (sadden) affliggere. ~ing adj penoso; (shocking) sconvolgente. ~ signal n segnale m di richiesta di soccorso

distribut|e /dɪˈstrɪbjuːt/ vt distribuire. ~ion n distribuzione f. ~or n distributore m

district /ˈdɪstrɪkt/ n regione f; (Admin) distretto m. ~ nurse n infermiere, -a mf che fa visite a domicilio

dis'trust n sfiducia f ● vt non fidarsi di. ~ful adj diffidente

disturb /dɪˈstɜːb/ vt disturbare; (emotionally) turbare; spostare (papers). ~ance n disturbo m; ~ances (pl: rioting etc) disordini mpl. ~ed adj turbato; [mentally] ~ed malato di mente. ~ing adj inquietante

dis'used adj non utilizzato

ditch /dɪtʃ/ n fosso m ● vt (fam: abandon) abbandonare (plan, car); piantare (lover)

dither /ˈdɪðə(r)/ vi titubare

divan /dɪˈvæn/ n divano m

dive /daɪv/ n tuffo m; (Aeron) picchiata f; (fam: place) bettola f ● vi tuffarsi; (when in water) immergersi; (Aeron) scendere in picchiata; (fam: rush) precipitarsi

diver /ˈdaɪvə(r)/ n (from board) tuffatore, -trice mf; (scuba) sommozzatore, -trice mf; (deep sea) palombaro m

diverge /daɪˈvɜːdʒ/ vi divergere. ~gent adj divergente

diverse /daɪˈvɜːs/ adj vario

diversify /daɪˈvɜːsɪfaɪ/ vt/i (pt/pp -ied) diversificare

diversion /daɪˈvɜːʃn/ n deviazione f; (distraction) diversivo m

diversity /daɪˈvɜːsəti/ n varietà f

divert /daɪˈvɜːt/ vt deviare (traffic); distogliere (attention)

divide /dɪˈvaɪd/ vt dividere (by per); six ~d by two sei diviso due ● vi dividersi

dividend /ˈdɪvɪdend/ n dividendo m; pay ~s fig ripagare

divine /dɪˈvaɪn/ adj divino

diving /'daɪvɪŋ/ n (from board) tuffi mpl; (scuba) immersione f. ~-board n trampolino m. ~ mask n maschera f [subacquea]. ~-suit n muta f; (deep sea) scafandro m

division /dɪ'vɪʒn/ n divisione f; (in sports league) serie f

divorce /dɪ'vɔːs/ n divorzio m • vt divorziare da. ~d adj divorziato; get ~d divorziare

divorcee /dɪvɔː'siː/ n divorziato, -a mf

divulge /daɪ'vʌldʒ/ vt rendere pubblico

DIY n abbr do-it-yourself

dizziness /'dɪzɪnɪs/ n giramenti mpl di testa

dizzy /'dɪzɪ/ adj (-ier, -iest) vertiginoso; I feel ~ mi gira la testa

do¹ /duː/

3 sing pres tense **does**; past tense **did**; past participle **done**

• vt fare; (🅸: cheat) fregare; be done (Culin) essere cotto; well done bravo; (Culin) ben cotto; do the flowers sistemare i fiori; do the washing up lavare i piatti; do one's hair farsi i capelli

• vi (be suitable) andare; (be enough) bastare; this will do questo va bene; that will do! basta così; do well/badly cavarsela bene/male; how is he doing? come sta?

• v aux (used to form questions and negatives; often not translated) do you speak Italian? parli italiano?; you don't like him, do you? non ti piace, vero?; (expressing astonishment) non dirmi che ti piace!; yes, I do si; (emphatic) invece sì; I don't no; I don't smoke non fumo; don't

you/doesn't he? vero?; so do I anch'io; do come in, John entra, John; how do you do? piacere. □ ~ away with vt abolire (rule). □ ~ for vt done for 🅸 rovinato. □ ~ in vt (🅸: kill) uccidere; farsi male a (back); done in 🅸 esausto. □ ~ up vt (fasten) abbottonare; (renovate) rimettere a nuovo; (wrap) avvolgere. □ ~ with vt I could do with a spanner mi ci vorrebbe una chiave inglese. □ ~ without vt fare a meno di

do² /duː/ n (pl dos or do's) 🅸 festa f

docile /'dəʊsaɪl/ adj docile

dock¹ /dɒk/ n (Jur) banco m degli imputati

dock² n (Naut) bacino m • vi entrare in porto; (spaceship) congiungersi. ~er n portuale m. ~s npl porto m. ~yard n cantiere m navale

doctor /'dɒktə(r)/ n dottore m, dottoressa f • vt alterare (drink); castrare (cat). ~ate n dottorato m

doctrine /'dɒktrɪn/ n dottrina f

document /'dɒkjʊmənt/ n documento m. ~ary adj documentario • n documentario m

dodge /dɒdʒ/ n 🅸 trucco m • vt schivare (blow); evitare (person) • vi scansarsi; ~ out of the way scansarsi

dodgems /'dɒdʒəmz/ npl autoscontro msg

dodgy /'dɒdʒɪ/ adj (-ier, -iest) (🅸: dubious) sospetto

doe /dəʊ/ n femmina f (di daino, renna, lepre); (rabbit) coniglia f

does /dʌz/ ▷ **do**

doesn't /'dʌznt/ = does not

dog /dɒg/ n cane m • vt (pt/pp dogged) (illness, bad luck) perseguitare

dogged /'dɒgɪd/ adj ostinato

'dog house n in the ~ 🅸 in disgrazia

dogma /'dɒɡmə/ n dogma m. ~**tic**
adj dogmatico

do-it-yourself /'du:ɪtjə'self/ n fai
da te m, bricolage m. ~ **shop** n negozio m di bricolage

dole /dəʊl/ n sussidio m di disoccupazione; **be on the** ~ essere disoccupato • **dole out** vt distribuire

doleful /'dəʊlfl/ adj triste

doll /dɒl/ n bambola f • **doll oneself
up** vt 🔲 mettersi in ghingheri

dollar /'dɒlə(r)/ n dollaro m

dollop /'dɒləp/ n 🔲 cucchiaiata f

dolphin /'dɒlfɪn/ n delfino m

dome /dəʊm/ n cupola f

domestic /də'mestɪk/ adj domestico; (Pol) interno; (Comm) nazionale

domesticated /də'mestɪkeɪtɪd/ adj
(animal) addomesticato

domestic flight n volo m nazionale

dominant /'dɒmɪnənt/ adj dominante

dominat|e /'dɒmɪneɪt/ vt/i domi-
nare. ~**ion** n dominio m

domineering /dɒmɪ'nɪərɪŋ/ adj
autoritario

dominion /də'mɪnjən/ n Br (Pol)
dominion m inv

donat|e /dəʊ'neɪt/ vt donare. ~**ion**
n donazione f

done /dʌn/ ▷**DO**

donkey /'dɒŋkɪ/ n asino m; ~'s
years 🔲 secoli mpl. ~-**work** n sgobbata f

donor /'dəʊnə(r)/ n donatore,
-trice mf

doodle /'du:dl/ vi scarabocchiare

doom /du:m/ n fato m; (ruin) rovina f
• vt **be** ~**ed** [to failure] essere destinato al fallimento; ~**ed** (ship) destinato ad affondare

door /dɔ:(r)/ n porta f; (of car) portiera f; **out of** ~**s** all'aperto

door: ~**mat** n zerbino m. ~**step** n
gradino m della porta. ~**way** n vano

m della porta

dope /dəʊp/ n 🔲 (drug) droga f legge-
gera; (information) indiscrezioni fpl;
(idiot) idiota mf • vt drogare; (Sport)
dopare

dormant /'dɔ:mənt/ adj latente;
(volcano) inattivo

dormitory /'dɔ:mɪtərɪ/ n dormitorio m

dormouse /'dɔ:-/ n ghiro m

dosage /'dəʊsɪdʒ/ n dosaggio m

dose /dəʊs/ n dose f

dot /dɒt/ n punto m; **at 8 o'clock on
the** ~ alle 8 in punto

dot-com /dɒt'kɒm/ n azienda f le-
gata a Internet

dote /dəʊt/ vi ~ **on** stravedere per

dotty /'dɒtɪ/ adj (-ier, -iest) 🔲
tocco; (idea) folle

double /'dʌbl/ adj doppio • adv **cost**
~ costare il doppio; **see** ~ vedere
doppio; **the** ~ **the amount** la quantità
doppia • n doppio m; (person) sosia m
inv; ~**s** pl (Tennis) doppio m; **at the** ~
di corsa • vt raddoppiare; (fold) piegare in due • vi raddoppiare. □ ~
back vi (go back) tornare indietro.
□ ~ **up** vi (bend) piegarsi in due
(with per); (share) dividere una
stanza

double: ~-**bass** n contrabbasso m.
~ '**bed** n letto m matrimoniale.
'~-**chin** n doppio mento m. ~-'**click**
vt/i cliccare due volte, fare doppio
clic (on su). ~-'**cross** vt ingannare.
~-'**decker** n autobus m inv a due
piani. ~ '**Dutch** n 🔲 ostrogoto m.
~ '**glazing** n doppiovetro m

doubly /'dʌblɪ/ adv doppiamente

doubt /daʊt/ n dubbio m • vt dubi-
tare di. ~**ful** adj dubbio; (having
doubts) in dubbio. ~**fully** adv con aria
dubbiosa. ~**less** adv indubbiamente

dough /dəʊ/ n pasta f; (for bread)
impasto m; (🔲 money) quattrini mpl.
~**nut** n bombolone m, krapfen m inv

dove /dʌv/ n colomba f. ~**tail** n

(*Techn*) incastro *m* a coda di rondine

down[1] /daun/ *n* (*feathers*) piumino *m*

down[2] *adv* giù; go/come ~ scendere; ~ there laggiù; sales are ~ le vendite sono diminuite; £50 ~ 50 sterline d'acconto; ~ 10% ridotto del 10%; ~ with...! abbasso...! • *prep* walk ~ the road camminare per strada; ~ the stairs giù per le scale; fall ~ the stairs cadere giù dalle scale; get that ~ you! ① butta giù!; be ~ the pub ① essere al pub • *vt* bere tutto d'un fiato (drink)

down: ~-and-'out *n* spiantato, -a *mf*. ~cast *adj* abbattuto. ~fall *n* caduta *f*. (*of person*) rovina *f*. ~-'hearted *adj* scoraggiato. ~hill *adv* in discesa; go ~hill essere in declino. ~load *vt* scaricare. ~ payment *n* deposito *m*. ~pour *n* acquazzone *m*. ~right *adj* (*absolute*) totale; (*lie*) bell'e buono; (*idiot*) perfetto • *adv* (*completely*) completamente. ~stairs *adv* al piano di sotto • *adj* del piano di sotto. ~stream *adv* a valle. ~-to-'earth *adj* (person) con i piedi per terra. ~town *adv Am* in centro. ~ward[s] *adj* verso il basso; (*slope*) in discesa • *adv* verso il basso

> *i* **Downing Street** È una via del centro di Londra, nel quartiere di Westminster. Al numero 10 si trova la residenza ufficiale del Primo Ministro britannico e al numero 11 quella del *Chancellor of the Exchequer* (il Cancelliere dello Scacchiere, equivalente del Ministro delle Finanze e del Tesoro). Le espressioni *Downing Street* e *Number 10* sono spesso usate dalla stampa per indicare il Primo Ministro.

dowry /'dauri/ *n* dote *f*

doze /dəuz/ *n* sonnellino *m* • *vi* sonnecchiare. □ ~ off *vi* assopirsi

dozen /'dʌzn/ *n* dozzina *f*; ~s of books libri a dozzine

Dr *abbr* doctor

drab /dræb/ *adj* spento

draft[1] /drɑːft/ *n* abbozzo *m*; (*Comm*) cambiale *f*; *Am* (*Mil*) leva *f* • *vt* abbozzare; *Am* (*Mil*) arruolare

draft[2] *n Am* = draught

drag /dræg/ *n* ① scocciatura *f*; in ~ ① (man) travestito da donna • *vt* (*pt/pp* dragged) trascinare; dragare (river). □ ~ on *vi* (time, meeting:) trascinarsi

dragon /'drægən/ *n* drago *m*. ~-fly *n* libellula *f*

drain /dreɪn/ *n* tubo *m* di scarico; (*grid*) tombino *m* f; the ~s *pl* le fognature; be a ~ on sb's finances prosciugare le finanze di qcno • *vt* drenare (land, wound); scolare (liquid, vegetables); svuotare (tank, glass, person) • *vi* ~ [away] andar via

drama /'drɑːmə/ *n* arte *f* drammatica; (*play*) opera *f* teatrale; (*event*) dramma *m*

dramatic /drə'mætɪk/ *adj* drammatico

dramat|ist /'dræmətɪst/ *n* drammaturgo, -a *mf*. ~ize *vt* adattare per il teatro; *fig* drammatizzare

drank /dræŋk/ ▷DRINK

drape /dreɪp/ *n Am* tenda *f* • *vt* appoggiare (over su)

drastic /'dræstɪk/ *adj* drastico; ~ally *adv* drasticamente

draught /drɑːft/ *n* corrente *f* [d'aria]; ~s *sg* (*game*) [gioco *m* della] dama *fsg*

draught beer *n* birra *f* alla spina

draughty /'drɑːftɪ/ *adj* pieno di correnti d'aria; it's ~ c'è corrente

draw /drɔː/ *n* (*attraction*) attrazione *f*; (*Sport*) pareggio *m*; (*in lottery*) sorteggio *m* • *v* (*pt* drew, *pp* drawn) • *vt* tirare; (*attract*) attirare; disegnare (picture); tracciare (line); ritirare (money); ~ lots tirare a sorte • *vi* (tea:) essere in infusione; (*Sport*) pareggiare; ~ **near** avvicinarsi. □ ~ **back** *vt* tirare indietro; ritirare (hand); tirare (curtains) ● *vi* (*recoil*) tirarsi indietro. □ ~ **in** *vt* ritrarre (claws etc) ● *vi* (train:) arrivare; (days:) accorciarsi. □ ~ **out** *vt* (*pull out*) tirar fuori; ritirare (money) ● *vi* (train:) partire; (days:) allungarsi. □ ~ **up** *vt* redigere (document); accostare (chair); ~ oneself up to one's full height farsi grande ● *vi* (*stop*) fermarsi

draw: ~**back** *n* inconveniente *m*. ~**bridge** *n* ponte *m* levatoio

drawer /drɔ:(r)/ *n* cassetto *m*

drawing /'drɔ:ɪŋ/ *n* disegno *m*

drawing: ~ **pin** *n* puntina *f*. ~ **room** *n* salotto *m*

drawl /drɔ:l/ *n* pronuncia *f* strascicata

drawn /drɔ:n/ ▷**DRAW**

dread /dred/ *n* terrore *m* ● *vt* aver il terrore di

dreadful /'dredfʊl/ *adj* terribile. ~**ly** *adv* terribilmente

dream /dri:m/ *n* sogno *m* ● *attrib* di sogno ● *vt/i* (*pt/pp dreamt* /dremt/ *or dreamed*) sognare (about/di di)

dreary /'drɪərɪ/ *adj* (-ier, -iest) tetro; (*boring*) monotono

dredge /dredʒ/ *vt/i* dragare

dregs /dregz/ *npl* feccia *fsg*

drench /drentʃ/ *vt* get ~ed inzupparsi; ~ed zuppo

dress /dres/ *n* (*woman's*) vestito *m*; (*clothing*) abbigliamento *m* ● *vt* vestire; (*decorate*) adornare; (*Culin*) condire; (*Med*) fasciare; ~ oneself, get ~ed vestirsi ● *vi* vestirsi. □ ~ **up** *vi* mettersi elegante; (*in disguise*) travestirsi (as da)

dress circle *n* (*Theat*) prima galleria *f*

dressing /'dresɪŋ/ *n* (*Culin*) condimento *m*; (*Med*) fasciatura *f*

dressing: ~-**gown** *n* vestaglia *f*.

~-**room** *n* (*in gym*) spogliatoio *m*; (*Theat*) camerino *m*. ~-**table** *n* toilette *f* inv

dress: ~**maker** *n* sarta *f*. ~ **rehearsal** *n* prova *f* generale

drew /dru:/ ▷**DRAW**

dribble /'drɪbl/ *vi* gocciolare; (baby:) sbavare; (*Sport*) dribblare

dried /draɪd/ *adj* (food) essiccato

drier /'draɪə(r)/ *n* asciugabiancheria *m inv*

drift /drɪft/ *n* movimento *m* lento; (*of snow*) cumulo *m*; (*meaning*) senso *m* ● *vi* (*off course*) andare alla deriva; (snow:) accumularsi; (fig: person:) procedere senza meta. □ ~ **apart** *vi* (people:) allontanarsi l'uno dall'altro

drill /drɪl/ *n* trapano *m*; (*Mil*) esercitazione *f* ● *vt* trapanare; (*Mil*) fare esercitare ● *vi* (*Mil*) esercitarsi; ~ **for** oil trivellare in cerca di petrolio

drink /drɪŋk/ *n* bevanda *f*; (*alcoholic*) bicchierino *m*; have a ~ bere qualcosa; a ~ of water un po' d'acqua ● *vt/i* (*pt drank*, *pp drunk*) bere. □ ~ **up** *vt* finire ● *vi* finire il bicchiere

drink|able /'drɪŋkəbl/ *adj* potabile. ~**er** *n* bevitore, -trice *mf*

'drinking-water *n* acqua *f* potabile

drip /drɪp/ *n* gocciolamento *m*; (*drop*) goccia *f*; (*Med*) flebo *f* inv; (🔲: *person*) mollaccione, -a *mf* ● *vi* (*pt/pp* dripped) gocciolare. ~-'**dry** *adj* che non si stira. ~**ping** *n* (*from meat*) grasso *m* d'arrosto ● *adj* ~**ping** [wet] fradicio

drive /draɪv/ *n* (*in car*) giro *m*; (*entrance*) viale *m*; (*energy*) grinta *f*; (*Psych*) pulsione *f*; (*organized effort*) operazione *f*; (*Techn*) motore *m*; (*Comput*) lettore *m* ● *v* (*pt drove*, *pp driven*) ● *vt* portare (person by car); guidare (car); (*Sport: hit*) mandare; (*Techn*) far funzionare; ~ **sb mad** far diventare matto qcno ● *vi* guidare. □ ~ **at** *vt* what are you driving at? dove vuoi arrivare? **drive away** *vt* portare via in macchina; (*chase*) cacciare ● *vi* andare via in macchina. □ ~ **in** *vt* piantare (nail) ● *vi* arrivare [in macchina]. □ ~ **off** *vt* portare via in macchina; (*chase*) cacciare ● *vi* andare via in macchina. □ ~ **on** *vi* proseguire (in macchina). □ ~ **up** *vi* arrivare (in macchina).

drivel /'drɪvl/ *n* 🇮🇹 sciocchezze *fpl*

driver /'draɪvə(r)/ *n* guidatore, -trice *mf*; (of train) conducente *mf*

driving /'draɪvɪŋ/ (rain) violento; (force) motore ● *n* guida *f*

driving: ~ licence *n* patente *f* di guida. ~ **test** *n* esame *m* di guida

drizzle /'drɪzl/ *n* pioggerella *f* ● *vi* piovigginare

drone /drəʊn/ *n* (bee) fuco *m*; (sound) ronzio *m*

droop /druːp/ *vi* abbassarsi; (flowers:) afflosciarsi

drop /drɒp/ *n* (of liquid) goccia *f*; (fall) caduta *f*; (in price, temperature) calo *m* ● *v* (pt/pp dropped) ● *vt* far cadere; sganciare (bomb); (omit) omettere; (give up) abbandonare ● *vi* cadere; (price, temperature, wind:) calare; (ground:) essere in pendenza. □ ~ **in** *vi* passare. □ ~ **off** *vt* depositare (person) ● *vi* cadere; (fall asleep) assopirsi. □ ~ **out** *vi* cadere; (of race, society) ritirarsi; ~ **out of school** lasciare la scuola

'drop-out *n* persona *f* contro il sistema sociale

drought /draʊt/ *n* siccità *f*

drove /drəʊv/ ▷ **DRIVE**

drown /draʊn/ *vi* annegare ● *vt* annegare; coprire (noise); **he was ~ed** è annegato

drowsy /'draʊzɪ/ *adj* sonnolento

drudgery /'drʌdʒərɪ/ *n* lavoro *m* pesante e noioso

drug /drʌg/ *n* droga *f*; (Med) farmaco *m*; **take ~s** drogarsi ● *vt* (pt/pp drugged) drogare

drug: ~ addict *n* tossicomane, -a

mf. ~ **dealer** *n* spacciatore, -trice *mf* [di droga]. ~**gist** *n* Am farmacista *mf*. ~**store** *n* Am negozio *m* di generi vari, inclusi medicinali, che funge anche da bar; (dispensing) farmacia *f*

drum /drʌm/ *n* tamburo *m*; (for oil) bidone *m*; ~**s** (pl: in pop-group) batteria *f* ● *v* (pt/pp drummed) ● *vi* suonare il tamburo; (in pop-group) suonare la batteria ● *vt* ~ **sth into sb** ripetere qcsa a qcno cento volte. ~**mer** *n* percussionista *mf*; (in pop-group) batterista *mf*. ~**stick** *n* bacchetta *f*; (of chicken, turkey) coscia *f*

drunk /drʌŋk/ ▷ **DRINK** ● *adj* ubriaco; **get** ~ ubriacarsi ● *n* ubriaco, -a *mf*

drunkard /'drʌŋkəd/ *n* ubriacone, -a *mf*. ~**en** *adj* ubriaco; ~**en driving** guida *f* in stato di ebbrezza

dry /draɪ/ *adj* (drier, driest) asciutto; (climate, country) secco ● *vt/i* (pt/pp dried) asciugare; ~ **one's eyes** asciugarsi le lacrime. □ ~ **up** *vi* seccarsi; (fig: source) prosciugarsi; (🇮🇹: be quiet) stare zitto; (do dishes) asciugare i piatti

dry: ~'clean *vt* pulire a secco. ~**-'cleaner's** *n* (shop) tintoria *f*. ~**ness** *n* secchezza *f*

DTD *n abbr* (digital type definition) DTD *f*

dual /'djuːəl/ *adj* doppio

dual 'carriageway *n* strada *f* a due carreggiate

dub /dʌb/ *vt* (pt/pp dubbed) doppiare (film); (name) soprannominare

dubious /'djuːbɪəs/ *adj* dubbio; **be ~ about** avere dei dubbi riguardo

duchess /'dʌtʃɪs/ *n* duchessa *f*

duck /dʌk/ *n* anatra *f* ● *vt* (in water) immergere; ~ **one's head** abbassare la testa ● *vi* abbassarsi. ~**ling** *n* anatroccolo *m*

duct /dʌkt/ *n* condotto *m*; (Anat) dotto *m*

dud /dʌd/ 🇮🇹 *adj* (Mil) disattivato; (coin) falso; (cheque) a vuoto ● *n*

(*banknote*) banconota *f* falsa

due /dju:/ *adj* dovuto; be ~ (*train:*) essere previsto; the baby is ~ next week il bambino dovrebbe nascere la settimana prossima; ~ to (*owing to*) a causa di; be ~ to (*causally*) essere dovuto a; I'm ~ to... dovrei...; in ~ course a tempo debito ● *adv* ~ north direttamente a nord

duel /'dju:əl/ *n* duello *m*

dues /dju:z/ *npl* quota *f* [di iscrizione]

duet /dju:'et/ *n* duetto *m*

dug /dʌg/ ▷DIG

duke /dju:k/ *n* duca *m*

dull /dʌl/ *adj* (*overcast, not bright*) cupo; (*not shiny*) opaco; (*sound*) soffocato; (*boring*) monotono; (*stupid*) ottuso ● *vt* intorpidire (mind); attenuare (pain)

dumb /dʌm/ *adj* muto; (🆊: *stupid*) ottuso. ~**founded** *adj* sbigottito. □ ~ **down** *vt* semplificare il livello di

dummy /'dʌmɪ/ *n* (*tailor's*) manichino *m*; (*for baby*) succhiotto *m*; (*model*) riproduzione *f*

dump /dʌmp/ *n* (*for refuse*) scarico *m*; (🆊: *town*) mortorio *m*; be down in the ~s 🆊 essere depresso ● *vt* scaricare; (🆊: *put down*) lasciare; (🆊: *get rid of*) liberarsi di

dumpling /'dʌmplɪŋ/ *n* gnocco *m*

dunce /dʌns/ *n* zuccone, -a *mf*

dung /dʌŋ/ *n* sterco *m*

dungarees /dʌŋgə'ri:z/ *npl* tuta *fsg*

dungeon /'dʌndʒən/ *n* prigione *f* sotterranea

duplicate[1] /'dju:plɪkət/ *adj* doppio ● *n* duplicato *m*; (*document*) copia *f*; in ~ in duplicato

duplicat|e[2] /'dju:plɪkeɪt/ *vt* fare un duplicato di; (*research:*) essere una ripetizione di (work)

durable /'djuərəbl/ *adj* resistente; durevole (basis, institution)

duration /djuə'reɪʃn/ *n* durata *f*

duress /djuə'res/ *n* costrizione *f*; under ~ sotto minaccia

during /'djuərɪŋ/ *prep* durante

dusk /dʌsk/ *n* crepuscolo *m*

dust /dʌst/ *n* polvere *f* ● *vt* spolverare; (*sprinkle*) cospargere (cake) (with di) ● *vi* spolverare

dust: ~**bin** *n* pattumiera *f*. ~**er** *n* strofinaccio *m*. ~**jacket** *n* sopraccoperta *f*. ~**man** *n* spazzino *m*. ~**pan** *n* paletta *f* per la spazzatura

dusty /'dʌstɪ/ *adj* (-ier, -iest) polveroso

Dutch /dʌtʃ/ *adj* olandese; go ~ 🆊 fare alla romana ● *n* (*language*) olandese *m*; the ~ *pl* gli olandesi. ~**man** *n* olandese *m*

duty /'dju:tɪ/ *n* dovere *m*; (*task*) compito *m*; (*tax*) dogana *f*; be on ~ essere di servizio. ~-**free** *adj* esente da dogana

duvet /'du:veɪ/ *n* piumone *m*

DVD *n* DVD *m inv*

dwarf /dwɔ:f/ *n* (*pl* -s or dwarves) nano, -a *mf* ● *vt* rimpicciolire

dwell /dwel/ *vi* (*pt/pp* dwelt) *liter* dimorare. □ ~ **on** *vt fig* soffermarsi su. ~**ing** *n* abitazione *f*

dwindle /'dwɪndl/ *vi* diminuire

dye /daɪ/ *n* tintura *f* ● *vt* (*pres p* dyeing) tingere

dying /'daɪɪŋ/ ▷DIE[2]

dynamic /daɪ'næmɪk/ *adj* dinamico

dynamite /'daɪnəmaɪt/ *n* dinamite *f*

dynamo /'daɪnəməʊ/ *n* dinamo *f inv*

dynasty /'dɪnəstɪ/ *n* dinastia *f*

. . . .

Ee

. . . .

each /i:tʃ/ *adj* ogni ● *pron* ognuno; £1 ~ una sterlina ciascuno; they love/hate ~ other si amano/odiano; we lend ~ other money ci prestiamo i soldi

eager /'iːgə(r)/ adj ansioso (to do of fare); (pupil) avido di sapere. ~ly adv (wait) ansiosamente; (offer) premurosamente. ~ness n premura f

eagle /'iːgl/ n aquila f

ear[1] /ɪə(r)/ n (of corn) spiga f

ear[2] n orecchio m. ~ache n mal m d'orecchi. ~-drum n timpano m

earl /ɜːl/ n conte m

early /'ɜːlɪ/ adj (-ier, -iest) (before expected time) in anticipo; (spring) prematuro; (reply) pronto; (works, writings) primo; be here ~! sii puntuale!; you're ~! sei in anticipo!; ~ morning walk passeggiata f mattutina; in the ~ morning la mattina presto; in the ~ spring all'inizio della primavera; ~ retirement prepensionamento m ● adv presto; (ahead of time) in anticipo; ~ in the morning la mattina presto

earn /ɜːn/ vt guadagnare; (deserve) meritare

earnest /'ɜːnɪst/ adj serio ● n in ~ sul serio. ~ly adv con aria seria

earnings /'ɜːnɪŋz/ npl guadagni mpl; (salary) stipendio m

ear-~phones npl cuffia fsg. ~-ring n orecchino m. ~shot n within ~shot a portata d'orecchio; he is out of ~shot non può sentire

earth /ɜːθ/ n terra f; where/what on ~ do? dove/che diavolo? ● vt (Electr) mettere a terra

'earthquake n terremoto m

earwig /'ɪəwɪg/ n forbicina f

ease /iːz/ n at ~ a proprio agio; at ~! (Mil) riposo!; ill at ~ a disagio; with ~ con facilità ● vt calmare (pain); alleviare (tension, shortage); (slow down) rallentare; (loosen) allentare ● vi (pain, situation, wind:) calmarsi

easel /'iːzl/ n cavalletto m

easily /'iːzɪlɪ/ adv con facilità; ~ the best certamente il meglio

east /iːst/ n est m; to the ~ of a est

di ● adj dell'est ● adv verso est

Easter /'iːstə(r)/ n Pasqua f. ~ egg n uovo m di Pasqua

east|**erly** /'iːstəlɪ/ adj da levante. ~ern adj orientale. ~ward[s] /-wəd[z]/ adv verso est

easy /'iːzɪ/ adj (-ier, -iest) facile; take it or things ~ prendersela con calma; take it ~! (don't get excited) calma!; go ~ with andarci piano con

easy: ~ **chair** n poltrona f. ~**'going** adj conciliante; too ~**going** troppo accomodante

eat /iːt/ vt/i (pt ate, pp eaten) mangiare. □ ~ **into** vt intaccare. □ ~ **up** vt mangiare tutto (food); fig inghiottire (profits)

eaves /iːvz/ npl cornicione msg. ~**drop** vi (pt/pp ~**dropped**) origliare; ~**drop on** ascoltare di nascosto

ebb /eb/ n (tide) riflusso m; at a low ~ fig a terra ● vi rifluire; fig declinare

ebony /'ebənɪ/ n ebano m

eccentric /ɪk'sentrɪk/ adj & n eccentrico, -a mf

echo /'ekəʊ/ n (pl -es) eco f or m ● v (pt/pp echoed, pres p echoing) ● vt echeggiare; ripetere (words) ● vi risuonare (with di)

eclipse /ɪ'klɪps/ n (Astr) eclissi f inv ● vt fig eclissare

ecological /iːkə'lɒdʒɪkl/ adj ecologico. ~**y** n ecologia f

e-commerce /'iː'kɒmɜːs/ n e-commerce m inv, commercio m elettronico

economic /iːkə'nɒmɪk/ adj economico; ~ refugee rifugiato, -a mf economico, -a. ~**al** adj economico. ~**ally** adv economicamente; (thriftily) in economia. ~**s** n economia f

economist /ɪ'kɒnəmɪst/ n economista mf

economize /ɪ'kɒnəmaɪz/ vi economizzare (on su)

economy /ɪˈkɒnəmɪ/ n economia f

ecstasy /ˈekstəsɪ/ n estasi f inv; (drug) ecstasy f

eczema /ˈeksɪmə/ n eczema m

edge /edʒ/ n bordo m; (of knife) filo m; (of road) ciglio m; on ~ con i nervi tesi; have the ~ on 🔢 avere un vantaggio su • vt bordare. □ ~ **forward** vi avanzare lentamente

edgeways /ˈedʒweɪz/ adv di fianco; I couldn't get a word in ~ non ho potuto infilare neanche mezza parola nel discorso

edgy /ˈedʒɪ/ adj nervoso

edible /ˈedɪbl/ adj commestibile; this pizza's not ~ questa pizza è immangiabile

> **Edinburgh Festival** La più *i* importante manifestazione culturale britannica, fondata nel 1947 e tenuta annualmente nella capitale scozzese, in agosto. Il festival offre spettacoli di musica, teatro, danza, ecc. e attira ogni anno moltissimi visitatori. Un settore sempre molto interessante è quello del cosiddetto *Fringe*, ossia gli eventi fuori dal programma ufficiale.

edit /ˈedɪt/ vt (pt/pp edited) far la revisione di (text); curare l'edizione di (anthology, dictionary); dirigere (newspaper); montare (film); editare (tape); ~ed by a cura di

edition /ɪˈdɪʃn/ n edizione f

editor /ˈedɪtə(r)/ n (of anthology, dictionary) curatore, -trice mf; (of newspaper) redattore, -trice mf; (of film) responsabile mf del montaggio

editorial /edɪˈtɔːrɪəl/ adj redazionale • n (Journ) editoriale m

educate /ˈedjʊkeɪt/ vt istruire; educare (mind); be ~d at Eton essere educato a Eton. ~d adj istruito

education /edjʊˈkeɪʃn/ n istru-

zione f; (culture) cultura f, educazione f. ~al adj istruttivo; (visit) educativo; (publishing) didattico

eel /iːl/ n anguilla f

eerie /ˈɪərɪ/ adj (-ier, -iest) inquietante

effect /ɪˈfekt/ n effetto m; in ~ in effetti; take ~ (law:) entrare in vigore; (medicine:) fare effetto • vt effettuare

effective /ɪˈfektɪv/ adj efficace; (striking) che colpisce; (actual) di fatto; ~ from in vigore a partire da. ~ly adv efficacemente; (actually) di fatto. ~ness n efficacia f

effeminate /ɪˈfemɪnət/ adj effeminato

efficiency /ɪˈfɪʃənsɪ/ n efficienza f; (of machine) rendimento m

efficient /ɪˈfɪʃənt/ adj efficiente. ~ly adv efficientemente

effort /ˈefət/ n sforzo m; make an ~ sforzarsi. ~less adj facile. ~lessly adv con facilità

e.g. abbr (exempli gratia) per es.

egg[1] /eg/ vt ~ on 🔢 incitare

egg[2] n uovo m. ~-cup n portauovo m inv. ~-head n 🔢 intellettuale mf. ~shell n guscio m d'uovo. ~timer n clessidra f per misurare il tempo di cottura delle uova

ego /ˈiːgəʊ/ n ego m. ~centric adj egocentrico. ~ism n egoismo m. ~ist n egoista mf. ~tism n egotismo m. ~tist n egotista mf

Egypt /ˈiːdʒɪpt/ n Egitto m. ~ian adj & n egiziano, -a mf

EHIC n abbr (European Health Insurance Card) TEAM f

eiderdown /ˈaɪdə-/ n (quilt) piumino m

eigh|t /eɪt/ adj otto • n otto m. ~**teen** adj diciotto. ~**teenth** adj diciottesimo

eighth /eɪtθ/ adj ottavo • n ottavo m

eightieth /ˈeɪtɪɪθ/ adj ottantesimo

eighty /ˈeɪtɪ/ adj ottanta

either /ˈaɪðə(r)/ adj & pron [of

them] l'uno o l'altro; I don't like ~ [of them] non mi piace né l'uno né l'altro; on ~ side da tutte e due le parti ● adv I don't ~ nemmeno io; I don't like John or his brother ~ non mi piace John e nemmeno suo fratello ● conj ~ John or his brother will be there ci saranno o John o suo fratello; I don't like ~ John or his brother non mi piacciono né John né suo fratello; ~ you go to bed or else... o vai a letto o altrimenti ...

eject /ɪ'dʒekt/ vt eiettare (pilot); espellere (tape, drunk)

eke /iːk/ vt ~ out far bastare; (increase) arrotondare; ~ out a living arrangiarsi

elaborate[1] /ɪ'læbərət/ adj elaborato

elaborate[2] /ɪ'læbəreɪt/ vi entrare nei particolari (on di)

elapse /ɪ'læps/ vi trascorrere

elastic /ɪ'læstɪk/ adj elastico ● n elastico m. ~ 'band n elastico m

elated /ɪ'leɪtɪd/ adj esultante

elbow /'elbəʊ/ n gomito m

elder[1] /'eldə(r)/ n (tree) sambuco m

eld|er[2] adj maggiore ● n the ~ il/la maggiore. ~erly adj anziano. ~est adj maggiore ● n the ~est il/la maggiore

elect /ɪ'lekt/ adj the president ~ il futuro presidente ● vt eleggere; ~ to do sth decidere di fare qcsa. ~ion n elezione f

elector /ɪ'lektə(r)/ n elettore, -trice mf. ~al adj elettorale; ~al roll liste fpl elettorali. ~ate n elettorato m

electric /ɪ'lektrɪk/ adj elettrico

electrical /ɪ'lektrɪkl/ adj elettrico; ~ engineering elettrotecnica f

electric 'blanket n termocoperta f

electrician /ɪlek'trɪʃn/ n elettricista m

electricity /ɪlek'trɪsəti/ n

elettricità f

electrify /ɪ'lektrɪfaɪ/ vt (pt/pp -ied) elettrificare; fig elettrizzare. ~ing adj fig elettrizzante

electrocute /ɪ'lektrəkjuːt/ vt fulminare; (execute) giustiziare sulla sedia elettrica

electrode /ɪ'lektrəʊd/ n elettrodo m

electron /ɪ'lektrɒn/ n elettrone m

electronic /ɪlek'trɒnɪk/ adj elettronico. ~ mail n posta f elettronica. ~s n elettronica f

elegance /'elɪgəns/ n eleganza f

elegant /'elɪgənt/ adj elegante

element /'elɪmənt/ n elemento m. ~ary adj elementare

elephant /'elɪfənt/ n elefante m

elevat|e /'elɪveɪt/ vt elevare. ~ion n elevazione f; (height) altitudine f; (angle) alzo m

elevator /'elɪveɪtə(r)/ n Am ascensore m

eleven /ɪ'levn/ adj undici ● n undici m. ~th adj undicesimo; at the ~th hour 🅵 all'ultimo momento

elf /elf/ n (pl elves) elfo m

eligible /'elɪdʒəbl/ adj eleggibile; be ~ for aver diritto a

eliminate /ɪ'lɪmɪneɪt/ vt eliminare

élite /er'liːt/ n fior fiore m

ellip|se /ɪ'lɪps/ n ellisse f. ~tical adj ellittico

elm /elm/ n olmo m

elope /ɪ'ləʊp/ vi fuggire [per sposarsi]

eloquen|ce /'eləkwəns/ n eloquenza f. ~t adj eloquente. ~tly adv con eloquenza

else /els/ adv altro; who ~? e chi altro?; he did of course, who ~? l'ha fatto lui e chi, se no?; nothing ~ nient'altro; or ~ altrimenti; someone ~ qualcun altro; somewhere ~ da qualche altra parte; anyone ~ chiunque altro; (as ques-

tion) nessun'altro?; anything ~ qualunque altra cosa; *(as question)* altro?. ~where *adv* altrove

elude /ɪˈluːd/ *vt* eludere; *(avoid)* evitare; the name ~s me il nome mi sfugge

elusive /ɪˈluːsɪv/ *adj* elusivo

emaciated /ɪˈmeɪsɪeɪtɪd/ *adj* emaciato

e-mail /ˈiːmeɪl/ *n* posta *f* elettronica ● *vt* spedire via posta elettronica. ~ **address** *n* indirizzo *m* e-mail

embankment /ɪmˈbæŋkmənt/ *n* argine *m*; *(Rail)* massicciata *f*

embargo /ɪmˈbɑːgəʊ/ *n* (*pl* -es) embargo *m*

embark /ɪmˈbɑːk/ *vi* imbarcarsi; ~ **on** intraprendere. ~ation *n* imbarco *m*

embarrass /emˈbærəs/ *vt* imbarazzare. ~ed *adj* imbarazzato. ~ing *adj* imbarazzante. ~ment *n* imbarazzo *m*

embassy /ˈembəsɪ/ *n* ambasciata *f*

embedded /ɪmˈbedɪd/ *adj* *(in concrete)* cementato; *(traditions, feelings)* radicato

embellish /ɪmˈbelɪʃ/ *vt* abbellire

embers /ˈembəz/ *npl* braci *fpl*

embezzle /ɪmˈbezl/ *vt* appropriarsi indebitamente di. ~ment *n* appropriazione *f* indebita

emblem /ˈembləm/ *n* emblema *m*

embrace /ɪmˈbreɪs/ *n* abbraccio *m* ● *vt* abbracciare ● *vi* abbracciarsi

embroider /ɪmˈbrɔɪdə(r)/ *vt* ricamare *(design)*; *fig* abbellire. ~y *n* ricamo *m*

embryo /ˈembrɪəʊ/ *n* embrione *m*

emerald /ˈemərəld/ *n* smeraldo *m*

emer|ge /ɪˈmɜːdʒ/ *vi* emergere; *(come into being: nation)* nascere; *(sun, flowers)* spuntare fuori. ~gence *n* emergere *m*; *(of new country)* nascita *f*

emergency /ɪˈmɜːdʒənsɪ/ *n* emergenza *f*; in an ~ in caso di emer-

genza. ~ **exit** *n* uscita *f* di sicurezza

emigrant /ˈemɪgrənt/ *n* emigrante *mf*

emigrat|e /ˈemɪgreɪt/ *vi* emigrare. ~ion *n* emigrazione *f*

eminent /ˈemɪnənt/ *adj* eminente. ~ly *adv* eminentemente

emission /ɪˈmɪʃn/ *n* emissione *f*; *(of fumes)* esalazione *f*

emit /ɪˈmɪt/ *vt* *(pt/pp* emitted) emettere; esalare *(fumes)*

emotion /ɪˈməʊʃn/ *n* emozione *f*. ~al *adj* denso di emozione; *(person, reaction)* emotivo; become ~al avere una reazione emotiva

emotive /ɪˈməʊtɪv/ *adj* emotivo

emperor /ˈempərə(r)/ *n* imperatore *m*

emphasis /ˈemfəsɪs/ *n* enfasi *f*; put the ~ on sth accentuare qcsa

emphasize /ˈemfəsaɪz/ *vt* accentuare *(word, syllable)*; sottolineare *(need)*

emphatic /emˈfætɪk/ *adj* categorico

empire /ˈempaɪə(r)/ *n* impero *m*

empirical /emˈpɪrɪkl/ *adj* empirico

employ /ɪmˈplɔɪ/ *vt* impiegare; *fig* usare *(tact)*. ~ee *n* impiegato, -a *mf*. ~er *n* datore *m* di lavoro. ~ment *n* occupazione *f*; *(work)* lavoro *m*. ~ment **agency** *n* ufficio *m* di collocamento

empower /ɪmˈpaʊə(r)/ *vt* autorizzare; *(enable)* mettere in grado

empress /ˈemprɪs/ *n* imperatrice *f*

empty /ˈemptɪ/ *adj* vuoto; *(promise, threat)* vano ● *v* *(pt/pp* -ied) ● *vt* vuotare *(container)* ● *vi* vuotarsi

emulate /ˈemjʊleɪt/ *vt* emulare

emulsion /ɪˈmʌlʃn/ *n* emulsione *f*

enable /ɪˈneɪbl/ *vt* ~ **sb** to mettere qcno in grado di

enact /ɪˈnækt/ *vt* *(Theat)* rappresentare; decretare *(law)*

enamel /ɪˈnæml/ *n* smalto *m* ● *vt* *(pt/pp* enamelled) smaltare

enchant /ɪn'tʃɑːnt/ vt incantare. ∼ing adj incantevole. ∼ment n incanto m

encircle /ɪn'sɜːkl/ vt circondare

enclave /'enkleɪv/ n enclave f inv; fig territorio m

enclos|e /ɪn'kləʊz/ vt circondare (land); (in letter) allegare (with a). ∼ed adj (in space) chiuso; (in letter) allegato. ∼ure n (at zoo) recinto m; (in letter) allegato m

encore /'ɒŋkɔː(r)/ n & int bis m inv

encounter /ɪn'kaʊntə(r)/ n incontro m; (battle) scontro m ● vt incontrare

encourage /ɪn'kʌrɪdʒ/ vt incoraggiare; promuovere (the arts, independence). ∼ment n incoraggiamento m; (of the arts) promozione f. ∼ing adj incoraggiante; (smile) di incoraggiamento

encroach /ɪn'krəʊtʃ/ vi ∼ on invadere (land, privacy); abusare di (time); interferire con (rights)

encyclop[a]ed|ia /ɪnsaɪklə'piː,dɪə/ n enciclopedia f. ∼ic adj enciclopedico

end /end/ n fine f; (of box, table, piece of string) estremità f; (of town, room) parte f; (purpose) fine m; in the ∼ alla fine; at the ∼ of May alla fine di maggio; at the ∼ of the street/ garden in fondo alla strada/al giardino; on ∼ (upright) in piedi; for days on ∼ per giorni e giorni; for six days on ∼ per sei giorni di fila; put an ∼ to sth mettere fine a qcsa; make ∼s meet 🔢 sbarcare il lunario; no ∼ of 🔢 un sacco di ● vt/i finire; ∼ up doing sth finire col fare qcsa

endanger /ɪn'deɪndʒə(r)/ vt rischiare (one's life); mettere a repentaglio (sb else, success of sth)

endear|ing /ɪn'dɪərɪŋ/ adj accattivante. ∼ment n term of ∼ment vezzeggiativo m

endeavour /ɪn'devə(r)/ n tentativo m ● vi sforzarsi (to di)

ending /'endɪŋ/ n fine f; (Gram) desinenza f

endless /'endlɪs/ adj interminabile; (patience) infinito. ∼ly adv continuamente; (patient) infinitamente

endorse /ɪn'dɔːs/ vt girare (cheque); (sports personality:) fare pubblicità a (product); approvare (plan). ∼ment n (of cheque) girata f; (of plan) conferma f; (on driving licence) registrazione f su patente di un'infrazione

endur|e /ɪn'djʊə(r)/ vt sopportare ● vi durare. ∼ing adj duraturo

enemy /'enəmɪ/ n nemico, -a mf ● attrib nemico

energetic /enə'dʒetɪk/ adj energico

energy /'enədʒɪ/ n energia f

enforce /ɪn'fɔːs/ vt far rispettare (law). ∼d adj forzato

engage /ɪn'geɪdʒ/ vt assumere (staff); (Theat) ingaggiare; (Auto) ingranare (gear) ● vi (Techn) ingranare; ∼ in impegnarsi in. ∼d adj (in use, busy) occupato; (person) impegnato; (to be married) fidanzato; get ∼d (of couple) fidanzarsi; (toilet, phone:) diventare occupato; ∼d tone (Teleph) segnale m di occupato. ∼ment n fidanzamento m; (appointment) appuntamento m; (Mil) combattimento m; ∼ment ring anello m di fidanzamento

engine /'endʒɪn/ n motore m; (Rail) locomotrice f. ∼-driver n macchinista m

engineer /endʒɪ'nɪə(r)/ n ingegnere m; (service, installation) tecnico m; (Naut, Am Rail) macchinista m ● vt fig architettare. ∼ing n ingegneria f

England /'ɪŋglənd/ n Inghilterra f

English /'ɪŋglɪʃ/ adj inglese; the ∼ Channel la Manica ● n (language) inglese m; the ∼ pl gli inglesi. ∼man n inglese m. ∼woman n inglese f

engrave /ɪn'greɪv/ vt incidere.

~ing n incisione f

engulf /ɪnˈɡʌlf/ vt (fire, waves:) inghiottire

enhance /ɪnˈhɑːns/ vt accrescere (beauty, reputation); migliorare (performance)

enigma /ɪˈnɪɡmə/ n enigma m. ~tic adj enigmatico

enjoy /ɪnˈdʒɔɪ/ vt godere di (good health); ~ oneself divertirsi; I ~ cooking/painting mi piace cucinare/dipingere; ~ your meal buon appetito. ~able adj piacevole. ~ment n piacere m

enlarge /ɪnˈlɑːdʒ/ vt ingrandire ●vi ~ upon dilungarsi su. ~ment n ingrandimento m

enlighten /ɪnˈlaɪtn/ vt illuminare. ~ed adj progressista. ~ment n The E~ment l'Illuminismo m

enlist /ɪnˈlɪst/ vt (Mil) reclutare; ~ sb's help farsi aiutare da qcno ●vi (Mil) arruolarsi

enliven /ɪnˈlaɪvn/ vt animare

enormity /ɪˈnɔːmətɪ/ n enormità f

enormous /ɪˈnɔːməs/ adj enorme. ~ly adv estremamente; (grateful) infinitamente

enough /ɪˈnʌf/ adj & n abbastanza; I didn't bring ~ clothes non ho portato abbastanza vestiti; have you had ~? (to eat/drink) hai mangiato/bevuto abbastanza?; I've had ~! 🔢 ne ho abbastanza!; is that ~? basta?; that's ~! basta così; £50 isn't ~ 50 sterline non sono sufficienti ●adv abbastanza; you're not working fast ~ non lavori abbastanza in fretta; funnily ~ stranamente

enquir|e /ɪnˈkwaɪə(r)/ vi domandare; ~e about chiedere informazioni su. ~y n domanda f; (investigation) inchiesta f

enrage /ɪnˈreɪdʒ/ vt fare arrabbiare

enrol /ɪnˈrəʊl/ vi (pt/pp -rolled) (for exam, in club) iscriversi (for, in a).

~ment n iscrizione f

ensu|e /ɪnˈsjuː/ vi seguire; the ~ing discussion la discussione che ne è seguita

ensure /ɪnˈʃʊə(r)/ vt assicurare; ~ that (person:) assicurarsi che; (measure:) garantire che

entail /ɪnˈteɪl/ vt comportare; what does it ~? in che cosa consiste?

entangle /ɪnˈtæŋɡl/ vt get ~d in rimanere impigliato in; fig rimanere coinvolto in

enter /ˈentə(r)/ vt entrare in; iscrivere (horse, runner in race); cominciare (university); partecipare a (competition); (Comput) immettere (data); (write down) scrivere ●vi entrare; (Theat) entrare in scena; (register as competitor) iscriversi; (take part) partecipare (in a)

enterpris|e /ˈentəpraɪz/ n impresa f; (quality) iniziativa f. ~ing adj intraprendente

entertain /entəˈteɪn/ vt intrattenere; (invite) ricevere; nutrire (ideas, hopes); prendere in considerazione (possibility) ●vi intrattenersi; (have guests) ricevere. ~er n artista mf. ~ing adj (person) di gradevole compagnia; (evening, film, play) divertente. ~ment n (amusement) intrattenimento m

enthral /ɪnˈθrɔːl/ vt (pt/pp enthralled) be ~led essere affascinato (by da)

enthusiasm /ɪnˈθjuːzɪæzm/ n entusiasmo m. ~t n entusiasta mf. ~tic adj entusiastico

entice /ɪnˈtaɪs/ vt attirare. ~ment n (incentive) incentivo m

entire /ɪnˈtaɪə(r)/ adj intero. ~ly adv del tutto; I'm not ~ly satisfied non sono completamente soddisfatto. ~ty n in its ~ty nell'insieme

entitlement /ɪnˈtaɪtlmənt/ n diritto m

entity /ˈentətɪ/ n entità f

entrance[1] /'entrəns/ n entrata f; (Theat) entrata f in scena; (right to enter) ammissione f; 'no ~' 'ingresso vietato'. ~ examination n esame m di ammissione. ~ fee n how much is the ~ fee? quanto costa il biglietto di ingresso?

entrance[2] /ɪn'trɑːns/ vt estasiare

entrant /'entrənt/ n concorrente m

entreat /ɪn'triːt/ vt supplicare

entrenched /ɪn'trentʃt/ adj (ideas, views) radicato

entrust /ɪn'trʌst/ vt ~ sb with sth, ~ sth to sb affidare qcsa a qcno

entry /'entrɪ/ n ingresso m; (way in) entrata f; (in directory etc) voce f; (in appointment diary) appuntamento m; no ~ ingresso vietato; (Auto) accesso vietato. ~ form n modulo m di ammissione. ~ visa n visto m di ingresso

enumerate /ɪ'njuːməreɪt/ vt enumerare

envelop /ɪn'veləp/ vt (pt/pp enveloped) avviluppare

envelope /'envələʊp/ n busta f

enviable /'envɪəbl/ adj invidiabile

envious /'envɪəs/ adj invidioso. ~ly adv con invidia

environment /ɪn'vaɪrənmənt/ n ambiente m

environmental /ɪnvaɪrən'mentl/ adj ambientale. ~ist n ambientalista mf. ~ly adv ~ly friendly che rispetta l'ambiente

envisage /ɪn'vɪzɪdʒ/ vt prevedere

envoy /'envɔɪ/ n inviato, -a mf

envy /'envɪ/ n invidia f • vt (pt/pp -ied) ~ sb sth invidiare qcno per qcsa

enzyme /'enzaɪm/ n enzima m

epic /'epɪk/ adj epico • n epopea f

epidemic /epɪ'demɪk/ n epidemia f

epilepsy /'epɪlepsɪ/ n epilessia f. ~tic adj & n epilettico, -a mf

epilogue /'epɪlɒg/ n epilogo m

episode /'epɪsəʊd/ n episodio m

epitaph /'epɪtɑːf/ n epitaffio m

epitome /ɪ'pɪtəmɪ/ n epitome f. ~ize vt essere il classico esempio di

epoch /'iːpɒk/ n epoca f

equal /'iːkwl/ adj (parts, amounts) uguale; of ~ height della stessa altezza; be ~ to the task essere all'altezza del compito • n pari m inv • vt (pt/pp equalled) (be same in quantity as) essere pari a; (rival) uguagliare; 5 plus 5 ~s 10 5 più 5 [è] uguale a 10. ~ity n uguaglianza f

equalize /'iːkwəlaɪz/ vi (Sport) pareggiare. ~r n (Sport) pareggio m

equally /'iːkwəlɪ/ adv (divide) in parti uguali; ~ intelligent della stessa intelligenza; ~.... allo stesso tempo...

equator /ɪ'kweɪtə(r)/ n equatore m

equilibrium /iːkwɪ'lɪbrɪəm/ n equilibrio m

equinox /'iːkwɪnɒks/ n equinozio m

equip /ɪ'kwɪp/ vt (pt/pp equipped) equipaggiare; attrezzare (kitchen, office). ~ment n attrezzatura f

equivalent /ɪ'kwɪvələnt/ adj equivalente; be ~ to equivalere a • n equivalente m

equivocal /ɪ'kwɪvəkl/ adj equivoco

era /'ɪərə/ n età f; (geological) era f

eradicate /ɪ'rædɪkeɪt/ vt eradicare

erase /ɪ'reɪz/ vt cancellare. ~r n gomma f [da cancellare]; (for blackboard) cancellino m

erect /ɪ'rekt/ adj eretto • vt erigere. ~ion n erezione f

erode /ɪ'rəʊd/ vt (water:) erodere; (acid:) corrodere. ~sion n erosione f; (by acid) corrosione f

erotic /ɪ'rɒtɪk/ adj erotico.

err /ɜː(r)/ vi errare; (sin) peccare

errand /'erənd/ n commissione f

erratic /ɪ'rætɪk/ adj irregolare; (person, moods) imprevedibile; (exchange rate) incostante

erroneous /ɪˈrəʊnɪəs/ adj erroneo

error /ˈerə(r)/ n errore m; in ~ per errore

erudite /ˈerʊdaɪt/ adj erudito. ~ion n erudizione f

erupt /ɪˈrʌpt/ vi eruttare; (spots:) spuntare; (fig: in anger) dare in escandescenze. ~ion n eruzione f; fig scoppio m

escalate /ˈeskəleɪt/ vi intensificarsi ● vt intensificare. ~ion n escalation f inv. ~or n scala f mobile

escapade /eskəpeɪd/ n scappatella f

escape /ɪˈskeɪp/ n fuga f; (from prison) evasione f; have a narrow ~ cavarsela per un pelo ● vi (prisoner:) evadere (from sb); sfuggire (from sb alla sorveglianza di qcno); (animal:) scappare; (gas:) fuoriuscire ● vt ~ notice passare inosservato; the name ~s me mi sfugge il nome

escapism /ɪˈskeɪpɪzm/ n evasione f [dalla realtà]

escort[1] /ˈeskɔːt/ n accompagnatore, -trice mf; (Mil etc) scorta f

escort[2] /ɪˈskɔːt/ vt accompagnare; (Mil etc) scortare

Eskimo /ˈeskɪməʊ/ n esquimese mf

especial /ɪˈspeʃl/ adj speciale. ~ly adv specialmente; (kind) particolarmente

espionage /ˈespɪənɑːʒ/ n spionaggio m

essay /ˈeseɪ/ n saggio m; (Sch) tema f

essence /ˈesns/ n essenza f; in ~ in sostanza

essential /ɪˈsenʃl/ adj essenziale ● npl the ~s l'essenziale m. ~ly adv essenzialmente

establish /ɪˈstæblɪʃ/ vt stabilire (contact, lead); fondare (firm); (prove) accertare; ~ oneself as affermarsi come. ~ment n (firm) azienda f; the E~ment l'ordine m costituito

estate /ɪˈsteɪt/ n tenuta f; (possessions) patrimonio m; (housing) quartiere m residenziale. ~ agent n agente m immobiliare. ~ car n giardiniera f

esteem /ɪˈstiːm/ n stima f ● vt stimare; (consider) giudicare

estimate[1] /ˈestɪmət/ n valutazione f; (Comm) preventivo m; at a rough ~ a occhio e croce

estimate[2] /ˈestɪmeɪt/ vt stimare. ~ion n (esteem) stima f; in my ~ion (judgement) a mio giudizio

estuary /ˈestjʊərɪ/ n estuario m

etc /et'setərə/ abbr (et cetera) ecc

etching /ˈetʃɪŋ/ n acquaforte f

eternal /ɪˈtɜːnl/ adj eterno

eternity /ɪˈtɜːnətɪ/ n eternità f

ethic /ˈeθɪk/ n etica f. ~al adj etico. ~s n etica f

ethnic /ˈeθnɪk/ adj etnico

etiquette /ˈetɪket/ n etichetta f

EU n abbr (European Union) UE f

euphemism /ˈjuːfəmɪzm/ n eufemismo m. ~tic adj eufemistico

euphoria /juːˈfɔːrɪə/ n euforia f

euro /ˈjʊərəʊ/ n euro m inv

Euro- /ˈjʊərəʊ/ pref ~cheque n eurochèque m inv. ~dollar n eurodollaro m

Europe /ˈjʊərəp/ n Europa f

European /jʊərəˈpɪən/ adj europeo; ~ Union Unione f Europea ● n europeo, -a mf

Euro-sceptic /jʊərəʊˈskeptɪk/ adj euroscettico ● n euroscettico, -a mf

evacuate /ɪˈvækjʊeɪt/ vt evacuare (building, area). ~ion n evacuazione f

evade /ɪˈveɪd/ vt evadere (taxes); evitare (the enemy, authorities); ~ the issue evitare l'argomento

evaluate /ɪˈvæljʊeɪt/ vt valutare. ~ion /-ˈeɪʃn/ n valutazione f

evangelical /iːvænˈdʒelɪkl/ adj evangelico. ~list n evangelista m

evaporate /ɪˈvæpəreɪt/ vi evaporare; fig svanire. ~ion n evaporazione f

evasion /ɪ'veɪʒn/ n evasione f

evasive /ɪ'veɪsɪv/ adj evasivo

eve /iːv/ n liter vigilia f

even /'iːvn/ adj (level) piatto; (same, equal) uguale; (regular) regolare; (number) pari; get ~ with vendicarsi di; now we're ~ adesso siamo pari ● adv anche, ancora; ~ if anche se; ~ so con tutto ciò; not ~ nemmeno; ~ bigger/hotter ancora più grande/caldo ● vt ~ the score (Sport) pareggiare. □ ~ out vi livellarsi. □ ~ up vi livellare

evening /'iːvnɪŋ/ n sera f; (whole evening) serata f; this ~ stasera; in the ~ la sera. ~ class n corso m serale. ~ dress n abito m scuro; (woman's) abito m da sera

event /ɪ'vent/ n avvenimento m; (function) manifestazione f; (Sport) gara f; in the ~ of nell'eventualità di; in the ~ alla fine. ~ful adj movimentato

eventual /ɪ'ventjʊəl/ adj the ~ winner was... alla fine il vincitore è stato.... ~ity n eventualità f. ~ly adv alla fine; I'll ~ly finally. ~ly finalmente!

ever /'evə(r)/ adv mai; I haven't ~... non ho mai...; for ~ per sempre; hardly ~ quasi mai; ~ since da quando; (since that time) da allora; ~ so ⊺ veramente

'evergreen n sempreverde m

ever'lasting adj eterno

every /'evrɪ/ adj ogni; ~ one ciascuno; ~ other day un giorno sì un giorno no

every: ~body pron tutti pl. ~day adj quotidiano, di ogni giorno. ~one pron tutti pl; ~thing pron tutto; ~where adv dappertutto; (wherever) dovunque

evict /ɪ'vɪkt/ vt sfrattare. ~ion n sfratto m

eviden|ce /'evɪdəns/ n evidenza f; (Jur) testimonianza f; give ~ce te-

stimoniare. ~t adj evidente. ~tly adv evidentemente

evil /'iːvl/ adj cattivo ● n male m

evocative /ɪ'vɒkətɪv/ adj evocativo; be ~ of evocare

evoke /ɪ'vəʊk/ vt evocare

evolution /iːvə'luːʃn/ n evoluzione f

evolve /ɪ'vɒlv/ vt evolvere ● vi evolversi

ewe /juː/ n pecora f

exact /ɪg'zækt/ adj esatto ● vt esigere. ~ing adj esigente. ~itude n esattezza f. ~ly adv esattamente; not ~ly non proprio. ~ness n precisione f

exaggerat|e /ɪg'zædʒəreɪt/ vt/i esagerare. ~ion n esagerazione f

exam /ɪg'zæm/ n esame m

examination /ɪgzæmɪ'neɪʃn/ n esame m; (of patient) visita f

examine /ɪg'zæmɪn/ vt esaminare; visitare (patient). ~r n (Sch) esaminatore, -trice mf

example /ɪg'zɑːmpl/ n esempio m; for ~ per esempio; make an ~ of sb punire qcno per dare un esempio; be an ~ to sb dare il buon esempio a qcno

exasperat|e /ɪg'zæspəreɪt/ vt esasperare. ~ion n esasperazione f

excavat|e /'ekskəveɪt/ vt scavare; (Archaeol) fare gli scavi di. ~ion n scavo m

exceed /ɪk'siːd/ vt eccedere. ~ingly adv estremamente

excel /ɪk'sel/ v (pt/pp excelled) ● vi eccellere ● vt ~ oneself superare se stessi

excellen|ce /'eksələns/ n eccellenza f. E~cy n (title) Eccellenza f. ~t adj eccellente

except /ɪk'sept/ prep eccetto, tranne; ~ for eccetto, tranne; ~ that... eccetto che... ● vt eccettuare. ~ing prep eccetto, tranne

exception /ɪkˈsepʃn/ n eccezione f; take ~ to fare obiezioni a. ~al adj eccezionale. ~ally adv eccezionalmente

excerpt /ˈeksɜːpt/ n estratto m

excess /ɪkˈses/ n eccesso m; in ~ di oltre. ~ baggage n bagaglio m in eccedenza. ~ ˈfare n supplemento m

excessive /ɪkˈsesɪv/ adj eccessivo. ~ly adv eccessivamente

exchange /ɪksˈtʃeɪndʒ/ n scambio m; (Teleph) centrale f; (Comm) cambio m; in ~ in cambio (for di) • vt scambiare (for con); cambiare (money). ~ rate n tasso m di cambio

excise¹ /ˈeksaɪz/ n dazio m; ~ duty dazio m

excise² /ekˈsaɪz/ vt recidere

excitable /ɪkˈsaɪtəbl/ adj eccitabile

excite|e /ɪkˈsaɪt/ vt eccitare. ~ed adj eccitato; get ~ed eccitarsi. ~edly adv tutto eccitato. ~ement n eccitazione f. ~ing adj eccitante; (story, film) appassionante; (holiday) entusiasmante

exclaim /ɪkˈskleɪm/ vt/i esclamare

exclamation /ekskləˈmeɪʃn/ n esclamazione f. ~ mark n, Am ~ point n punto m esclamativo

exclu|de /ɪkˈskluːd/ vt escludere. ~ding prep escluso. ~sion n esclusione f

exclusive /ɪkˈskluːsɪv/ adj (rights, club) esclusivo; (interview) in esclusiva; ~ of... ...escluso. ~ly adv esclusivamente

excruciating /ɪkˈskruːʃɪeɪtɪŋ/ adj atroce (pain); (🔲: very bad) spaventoso

excursion /ɪkˈskɜːʃn/ n escursione f

excusable /ɪkˈskjuːzəbl/ adj perdonabile

excuse¹ /ɪkˈskjuːs/ n scusa f

excuse² /ɪkˈskjuːz/ vt scusare; ~ from esonerare da; ~ me! (to get attention) scusi!; (to get past) permesso!,

scusi!; (indignant) come ha detto?

ex-diˈrectory adj be ~ non figurare nell'elenco telefonico

execute /ˈeksɪkjuːt/ vt eseguire; (put to death) giustiziare; attuare (plan)

execution /eksɪˈkjuːʃn/ n esecuzione f; (of plan) attuazione f. ~er n boia m inv

executive /ɪgˈzekjʊtɪv/ adj esecutivo • n dirigente mf; (Pol) esecutivo m

executor /ɪgˈzekjʊtə(r)/ n (Jur) esecutore, -trice mf

exempt /ɪgˈzempt/ adj esente • vt esentare (from da). ~ion n esenzione f

exercise /ˈeksəsaɪz/ n esercizio m; (Mil) esercitazione f; physical ~s ginnastica f; take ~ fare del moto • vt esercitare (muscles, horse); portare a spasso (dog); mettere in pratica (skills) • vi esercitarsi. ~ book n quaderno m

exert /ɪgˈzɜːt/ vt esercitare; ~ oneself sforzarsi. ~ion n sforzo m

exhale /eksˈheɪl/ vt/i esalare

exhaust /ɪgˈzɔːst/ n (Auto) scappamento m; (pipe) tubo m di scappamento; ~ fumes fumi mpl di scarico m • vt esaurire. ~ed adj esausto. ~ing adj estenuante; (climate, person) sfibrante. ~ion n esaurimento m. ~ive adj fig esauriente

exhibit /ɪgˈzɪbɪt/ n oggetto m esposto; (Jur) reperto m • vt esporre; fig dimostrare

exhibition /eksɪˈbɪʃn/ n mostra f; (of strength, skill) dimostrazione f. ~ist n esibizionista mf

exhibitor /ɪgˈzɪbɪtə(r)/ n espositore, -trice mf

exhort /ɪgˈzɔːt/ vt esortare

exile /ˈeksaɪl/ n esilio m; (person) esule m • vt esiliare

exist /ɪgˈzɪst/ vi esistere. ~ence n esistenza f; in ~ esistente; be in

~ence esistere. ~ing adj attuale

exit /'eksɪt/ n uscita f; (Theat) uscita f di scena • vi (Theat) uscire di scena; (Comput) uscire

exorbitant /ɪg'zɔːbɪtənt/ adj esorbitante

exotic /ɪg'zɒtɪk/ adj esotico

expand /ɪk'spænd/ vt espandere • vi espandersi; (Comm) svilupparsi; (metal): dilatarsi; ~ on (fig: explain better) approfondire

expans|e /ɪk'spæns/ n estensione f. ~ion n espansione f; (Comm) sviluppo m; (of metal) dilatazione f. ~ive adj espansivo

expatriate /eks'pætrɪət/ n espatriato, -a m f

expect /ɪk'spekt/ vt aspettare (letter, baby); (suppose) pensare; (demand) esigere; I ~ so penso di sì; ~ing adj in stato interessante

expectan|cy /ɪk'spektənsɪ/ n aspettativa f. ~t adj in attesa; ~t mother donna f incinta. ~tly adv con impazienza

expectation /ekspek'teɪʃn/ n aspettativa f, speranza f

expedient /ɪk'spiːdɪənt/ adj conveniente • n espediente f

expedition /ekspɪ'dɪʃn/ n spedizione f. ~ary adj (Mil) di spedizione

expel /ɪk'spel/ vt (pt/pp expelled) espellere

expend /ɪk'spend/ vt consumare. ~able adj sacrificabile

expenditure /ɪk'spendɪtʃə(r)/ n spesa f

expense /ɪk'spens/ n spesa f; business ~s pl spese fpl; at my ~ a mie spese; at the ~ of fig a spese di

expensive /ɪk'spensɪv/ adj caro, costoso. ~ly adv costosamente

experience /ɪk'spɪərɪəns/ n esperienza f • vt provare (sensation); avere (problem). ~d adj esperto

experiment /ɪk'sperɪmənt/ n esperimento • vi sperimentare. ~al

adj sperimentale

expert /'ekspɜːt/ adj & n esperto, -a m f. ~ly adv abilmente

expertise /ekspɜː'tiːz/ n competenza f

expire /ɪk'spaɪə(r)/ vi scadere

expiry /ɪk'spaɪərɪ/ n scadenza f. ~ date n data f di scadenza

explain /ɪk'spleɪn/ vt spiegare

explana|tion /eksplə'neɪʃn/ n spiegazione f. ~tory adj esplicativo

explicit /ɪk'splɪsɪt/ adj esplicito. ~ly adv esplicitamente

explode /ɪk'spləʊd/ vi esplodere • vt fare esplodere

exploit¹ /'eksplɔɪt/ n impresa f

exploit² /ɪk'splɔɪt/ vt sfruttare. ~ation n sfruttamento m

explora|tion /eksplə'reɪʃn/ n esplorazione f. ~tory adj esplorativo

explore /ɪk'splɔː(r)/ vt esplorare; fig studiare (implications). ~r n esploratore, -trice m f

explos|ion /ɪk'spləʊʒn/ n esplosione f. ~ive adj & n esplosivo m

export /'ekspɔːt/ n esportazione f • vt /-'spɔːt/ esportare. ~er n esportatore, -trice m f

expos|e /ɪk'spəʊz/ vt esporre; (reveal) svelare; smascherare (traitor etc). ~ure n esposizione f; (Med) esposizione f prolungata al freddo; caldo; (of crimes) smascheramento m; 24 ~ures (Phot) 24 pose

express /ɪk'spres/ adj espresso • adv (send) per espresso • n (train) espresso m • vt esprimere; ~ oneself esprimersi. ~ion n espressione f. ~ive adj espressivo. ~ly adv espressamente

expulsion /ɪk'spʌlʃn/ n espulsione f

exquisite /ek'skwɪzɪt/ adj squisito

extend /ɪk'stend/ vt prolungare (visit, road); prorogare (visa, contract); ampliare (building, knowledge); (*stretch out*) allungare; tendere (hand) ● *vi* (garden, knowledge:) estendersi

extension /ɪkˈstenʃn/ *n* prolungamento *m*; (*of visa, contract*) proroga *f*; (*of treaty*) ampliamento *m*; (*part of building*) annesso *m*; (*length of cable*) prolunga *f*; (*Teleph*) interno *m*; ➤ 226 interno 226

extensive /ɪkˈstensɪv/ *adj* ampio, vasto. ~**ly** *adv* ampiamente

extent /ɪkˈstent/ *n* (*scope*) portata *f*; to a certain ~ fino a un certo punto; to such an ~ that... fino al punto che...

exterior /ɪkˈstɪərɪə(r)/ *adj* & *n* esterno *m*

exterminat|e /ɪkˈstɜːmɪneɪt/ *vt* sterminare. ~**ion** *n* sterminio *m*

external /ɪkˈstɜːnl/ *adj* esterno; for ~ use only (*Med*) per uso esterno. ~**ly** *adv* esternamente

extinct /ɪkˈstɪŋkt/ *adj* estinto. ~**ion** *n* estinzione *f*

extinguish /ɪkˈstɪŋgwɪʃ/ *vt* estinguere. ~**er** *n* estintore *m*

extort /ɪkˈstɔːt/ *vt* estorcere. ~**ion** *n* estorsione *f*

extortionate /ɪkˈstɔːʃənət/ *adj* esorbitante

extra /ˈekstrə/ *adj* in più; (train) straordinario; an ~ £10 10 sterline extra, 10 sterline in più ● *adv* in più, (*especially*) più; pay ~ pagare in più, pagare extra; ~ **strong**/**busy** fortissimo/occupatissimo *m* (*in* (*Theat*) comparsa *f*; ~**s** *pl* extra *mpl*

extract[1] /ˈekstrækt/ *n* estratto *m*

extract[2] /ɪkˈstrækt/ *vt* estrarre (tooth, oil); strappare (secret); ricavare (truth). ~**or** *n* [fan] ~ aspiratore *m*

extradit|e /ˈekstrədaɪt/ *vt* (*Jur*) estradare. ~**ion** *n* estradizione *f*

extraordinar|y /ɪkˈstrɔːdɪnərɪ/ *adj* straordinario. ~**ly** *adv* straordinariamente

extravagan|ce /ɪkˈstrævəgəns/ *n* (*with money*) prodigalità *f*; (*of behaviour*) stravaganza *f*. ~**t** *adj* spendaccione; (*bizarre*) stravagante; (claim) esagerato

extrem|e /ɪkˈstriːm/ *adj* estremo ● *n* estremo *m*; in the ~e al massimo. ~**ely** *adv* estremamente. ~**ist** *n* estremista *mf*

extricate /ˈekstrɪkeɪt/ *vt* districare

extrovert /ˈekstrəvɜːt/ *n* estroverso, -a *mf*

exuberant /ɪgˈzjuːbərənt/ *adj* esuberante

exude /ɪgˈzjuːd/ *vt also fig* trasudare

exult /ɪgˈzʌlt/ *vi* esultare

eye /aɪ/ *n* occhio *m*; (*of needle*) cruna *f*; keep an ~ on tener d'occhio; see ~ to ~ aver le stesse idee ● *vt* (*pt*/ *pp* eyed, *pres p* ey[e]ing) guardare

eye: ~**ball** *n* bulbo *m* oculare. ~ **brow** *n* sopracciglio *m* (*pl* sopracciglia *f*). ~**lash** *n* ciglio *m* (*pl* ciglia *f*). ~**lid** *n* palpebra *f*. ~**opener** *n* rivelazione *f*. ~**shadow** *n* ombretto *m*. ~**sight** *n* vista *f*. ~**sore** *n* ① pugno *m* nell'occhio. ~**witness** *n* testimone *mf* oculare

• •

Ff

• •

fable /ˈfeɪbl/ *n* favola *f*

fabric /ˈfæbrɪk/ *n* also *fig* tessuto *m*

fabulous /ˈfæbjʊləs/ *adj* ① favoloso

façade /fəˈsɑːd/ *n* (*of building, person*) facciata *f*

face /feɪs/ *n* faccia *f*, viso *m*; (grimace) smorfia *f*; (*surface*) faccia *f*; (*of clock*) quadrante *m*; pull ~**s** far boccacce; in the ~ of di fronte a; on the ~ of it in apparenza ● *vt* essere di fronta a; (*confront*) affrontare; ~

north (house:) dare a nord; ~ **the fact that** arrendersi al fatto che. □~ **up to** vt accettare (facts); affrontare (person)

face: ~**-flannel** n ≈ guanto m di spugna. ~**less** adj anonimo. ~**-lift** n plastica f facciale

facetious /fə'si:ʃəs/ adj spiritoso. ~ **remarks** spiritosaggini mpl

facial /'feɪʃl/ adj facciale ● n trattamento m di bellezza al viso

facile /'fæsaɪl/ adj semplicistico

facilitate /fə'sɪlɪteɪt/ vt rendere possibile; (make easier) facilitare

facility /fə'sɪlɪtɪ/ n facilità f; ~**ies** pl (of area, in hotel etc) attrezzature fpl

fact /fækt/ n fatto m; **in** ~ infatti

faction /'fækʃn/ n fazione f

factor /'fæktə(r)/ n fattore m

factory /'fæktərɪ/ n fabbrica f

factual /'fæktʃʊəl/ adj **be** ~ attenersi ai fatti. ~**ly** adv (inaccurate) dal punto di vista dei fatti

faculty /'fækəltɪ/ n facoltà f inv

fad /fæd/ n capriccio m

fade /feɪd/ vi sbiadire; (sound, light:) affievolirsi; (flower:) appassire. □~ **in** vt cominciare in dissolvenza (picture). □~ **out** vt finire in dissolvenza (picture)

fag /fæg/ n (chore) fatica f; (🔲: cigarette) sigaretta f; (Am 🔲: homosexual) frocio m. ~ **end** n 🔲 cicca f

Fahrenheit /'færənhaɪt/ adj Fahrenheit

fail /feɪl/ vi **without** ~ senz'altro ● vi (attempt:) fallire; (eyesight, memory:) indebolirsi; (engine, machine:) guastarsi; (marriage:) andare a rotoli; (in exam) essere bocciato; ~ **to do sth** non fare qcsa; **I tried but I** ~**ed** ho provato ma non ci sono riuscito ● vt non superare (exam); bocciare (candidate); (disappoint) deludere; **words** ~ **me** mi mancano le parole

failing /'feɪlɪŋ/ n difetto m ● prep ~ **that** altrimenti

failure /'feɪljə(r)/ n fallimento m; (mechanical) guasto m; (person) incapace mf

faint /feɪnt/ adj leggero; (memory) vago; **feel** ~ sentirsi mancare ● n svenimento m ● vi svenire

faint: ~**-'hearted** adj timido. ~**ly** adv (slightly) leggermente

fair¹ /feə(r)/ n fiera f

fair² adj (hair, person) biondo; (skin) chiaro; (weather) bello; (just) giusto; (quite good) discreto; (Sch) abbastanza bene; **a** ~ **amount** abbastanza ● adv **play** ~ fare un gioco pulito. ~**ly** adv con giustizia; (rather) discretamente, abbastanza. ~**ness** n giustizia f. ~ **play** n fair play m inv. ~ **trade** n commercio m equo e solidale

fairy /'feərɪ/ n fata f; ~ **story**, ~**-tale** n fiaba f

faith /feɪθ/ n fede f; (trust) fiducia f; **in good/bad** ~ in buona/mala fede

faithful /'feɪθfl/ adj fedele. ~**ly** adv fedelmente; **yours** ~**ly** distinti saluti. ~**ness** n fedeltà f

fake /feɪk/ adj falso ● n falsificazione f; (person) impostore m ● vt falsificare; (pretend) fingere

falcon /'fɔ:lkən/ n falcone m

fall /fɔ:l/ n caduta f; (in prices) ribasso m; (Am: autumn) autunno m; **have a** ~ fare una caduta ● vi (pt fell, pp fallen) cadere; (night:) scendere; ~ **in love** innamorarsi. □~ **about** vi (with laughter) morire dal ridere. □~ **back on** vt ritornare su. □~ **for** vt 🔲 innamorarsi di (person); cascarci (sth, trick). □~ **down** vi cadere; (building:) crollare. □~ **in** vi caderci dentro; (collapse) crollare; (Mil) mettersi in riga; ~ **in with** concordare con (plan). □~ **off** vi cadere; (diminish) diminuire. □~ **out** vi (quarrel) litigare; **his hair is** ~**ing out** perde i capelli. □~ **over** vi cadere. □~ **through** vi (plan:) andare a monte

fallacy /'fæləsɪ/ n errore m

fallible /ˈfæləbl/ adj fallibile

'fall-out n pioggia f radioattiva

false /fɔːls/ adj falso; ~ bottom doppio fondo m; ~ start (Sport) falsa partenza f. ~hood n menzogna f. ~ness n falsità f

false 'teeth npl dentiera f

falsify /ˈfɔːlsɪfaɪ/ vt (pt/pp -ied) falsificare

falter /ˈfɔːltə(r)/ vi vacillare; (making speech) esitare

fame /feɪm/ n fama f

familiar /fəˈmɪljə(r)/ adj familiare; be ~ with (know) conoscere. ~ity n familiarità f. ~ize vt familiarizzare; ~ize oneself with familiarizzarsi con

family /ˈfæməlɪ/ n famiglia f

family: ~ 'planning n pianificazione f familiare. ~ 'tree n albero m genealogico

famine /ˈfæmɪn/ n carestia f

famished /ˈfæmɪʃt/ adj be ~ 🗊 avere una fame da lupo

famous /ˈfeɪməs/ adj famoso

fan[1] /fæn/ n ventilatore m; (handheld) ventaglio m ● vt (pt/pp fanned) far vento a; ~ oneself sventagliarsi; fig ~ the flames soffiare sul fuoco. □ ~ out vi spiegarsi a ventaglio

fan[2] n (admirer) ammiratore, -trice mf; (Sport) tifoso m; (of Verdi etc) appassionato, -a mf

fanatic /fəˈnætɪk/ n fanatico, -a mf. ~al adj fanatico. ~ism n fanatismo m

'fan belt n cinghia f per ventilatore

fanciful /ˈfænsɪfl/ adj fantasioso

fancy /ˈfænsɪ/ n fantasia f; I've taken a real ~ to him mi è molto simpatico; as the ~ takes you come ti pare ● adj [a] fantasia ● vt (pt/pp -ied) (believe) credere; (🗊: want) aver voglia di; he fancies you 🗊 gli piaci; ~ that! ma guarda un po'! ~ 'dress n costume m (per maschera)

fanfare /ˈfænfeə(r)/ n fanfara f

fang /fæŋ/ n zanna f; (of snake) dente m

fantas|ize /ˈfæntəsaɪz/ vi fantasticare. ~tic adj fantastico. ~y n fantasia f

far /fɑː(r)/ adv lontano; (much) molto; by ~ di gran lunga; ~ away lontano; as ~ as the church fino alla chiesa; how ~ is it from here? quanto dista da qui? as ~ as I know per quanto io sappia ● adj (end, side) altro; the F~ East l'Estremo Oriente m

farc|e /fɑːs/ n farsa f. ~ical adj ridicolo

fare /feə(r)/ n tariffa f; (food) vitto m. ~-dodger n passeggero, -a mf senza biglietto

farewell /feəˈwel/ int liter addio! ● n addio m

far-'fetched adj improbabile

farm /fɑːm/ n fattoria f ● vi fare l'agricoltore ● vt coltivare (land). ~er n agricoltore m

farm: ~house n casa f colonica. ~ing n agricoltura f. ~yard n aia f

far: ~-'reaching adj di larga portata. ~-'sighted adj fig prudente; (Am: long-sighted) presbite

farther /ˈfɑːðə(r)/ adv più lontano ● adj at the ~ end all'altra estremità di

fascinat|e /ˈfæsɪneɪt/ vt affascinare. ~ing adj affascinante. ~ion n fascino m

fascis|m /ˈfæʃɪzm/ n fascismo m. ~t n fascista mf ● adj fascista

fashion /ˈfæʃn/ n moda f; (manner) maniera f ● vt modellare. ~able adj di moda; be ~able essere alla moda. ~ably adv alla moda

fast[1] /fɑːst/ adj veloce; (colour) indelebile; be ~ (clock:) andare avanti ● adv velocemente; (firmly) saldamente; ~er! più in fretta!; be ~ asleep dormire profondamente

fast² n digiuno m • vi digiunare

fasten /'fɑːsn/ vt allacciare; chiudere (window); (stop flapping) mettere un fermo a • vi allacciarsi. ~er n, ~ing n chiusura f

fat /fæt/ adj (fatter, fattest) (person, cheque) grasso • n grasso m

fatal /'feɪtl/ adj mortale; (error) fatale. ~ism n fatalismo m. ~ist mf. ~ity n morte f. ~ly adv mortalmente

fate /feɪt/ n destino m. ~ful adj fatidico

father /'fɑːðə(r)/ n padre m; F~ Christmas Babbo m Natale • vt generare (child)

father|hood n paternità f. ~-in-law n (pl ~s-in-law) suocero m. ~ly adj paterno

fathom /'fæð(ə)m/ n (Naut) braccio m • vt ~ [out] comprendere

fatigue /fə'tiːg/ n fatica f

fatten /'fætn/ vt ingrassare (animal). ~ing adj cream is ~ing la panna fa ingrassare

fatty /'fæti/ adj grasso • n (fam) ciccione, -a mf

fatuous /'fætjuəs/ adj fatuo

faucet /'fɔːsɪt/ n Am rubinetto m

fault /fɔːlt/ n difetto m; (Geol) faglia f; (Tennis) fallo m; be at ~ avere torto; find ~ with trovare da ridire su; it's your ~ è colpa tua • vt criticare. ~less adj impeccabile

faulty /'fɔːltɪ/ adj difettoso

favour /'feɪvə(r)/ n favore m; be in ~ of sth essere a favore di qcsa; do sb a ~ fare un piacere a qcno • vt (prefer) preferire. ~able adj favorevole

favourit|e /'feɪvərɪt/ adj preferito • n amico, -a mf; (Sport) favorito, -a mf. ~ism n favoritismo m

fawn /fɔːn/ adj fulvo • n (animal) cerbiatto m

fax /fæks/ n (document, machine) fax m inv; by ~ per fax • vt faxare. ~ ma-

chine n fax m inv. ~-modem n modem-fax m inv, fax-modem m inv

fear /fɪə(r)/ n paura f; no ~! [fam] vai tranquillo! • vt temere • vi ~ for sth temere per qcsa

fear|ful /'fɪəfl/ adj pauroso; (awful) terribile. ~less adj impavido. ~some adj spaventoso

feas|ibility /fiːzə'bɪlɪtɪ/ n praticabilità f. ~ible adj fattibile; (possible) probabile

feast /fiːst/ n festa f; (banquet) banchetto m • vi banchettare; ~ on godersi

feat /fiːt/ n impresa f

feather /'feðə(r)/ n piuma f

feature /'fiːtʃə(r)/ n (quality) caratteristica f; (Journ) articolo m; ~s (pl: of face) lineamenti mpl • vt (film:) avere come protagonista • vi (on a list etc) comparire. ~ film n lungometraggio m

February /'februərɪ/ n febbraio m

fed /fed/ ▶FEED • adj be ~ up [fam] essere stufo (with di)

federal /'fed(ə)rəl/ adj federale

federation /fedə'reɪʃn/ n federazione f

fee /fiː/ n tariffa f; (lawyer's, doctor's) onorario m; (for membership, school) quota f

feeble /'fiːbl/ adj debole; (excuse) fiacco

feed /fiːd/ n mangiare m; (for baby) pappa f • v (pt/pp fed) • vt dar da mangiare a (animal); (support) nutrire; ~ sth into sth inserire qcsa in qcsa • vi mangiare

'feedback n controreazione f; (of information) risposta f, feedback m

feel /fiːl/ v (pt/pp felt) • vt sentire; (experience) provare; (think) pensare; (touch: searching) tastare; (touch: for texture) toccare • vi ~ soft/hard essere duro/morbido al tatto; ~ hot/hungry aver caldo/fame; ~ ill sentirsi male; I don't ~ like it non ne ho voglia; how do you ~ about it? (*opinion*) che te ne pare?; it doesn't ~er right non mi sembra giusto. ~er n (*of animal*) antenna f; put out ~ers *fig* tastare il terreno. ~ing n sentimento m; (*awareness*) sensazione f

feet /fiːt/ ▷ **FOOT**

feign /feɪn/ vt simulare

fell[1] /fel/ vt (*knock down*) abbattere

fell[2] ▷ **FALL**

fellow /ˈfeləʊ/ n (*of society*) socio m; (🛈: *man*) tipo m

fellow 'countryman n compatriota n

felony /ˈfeləni/ n delitto m

felt[1] /felt/ ▷ **FEEL**

felt[2] /felt/ n feltro m. ~-tipped 'pen /[-tɪpt/ n pennarello m

female /ˈfiːmeɪl/ adj femminile; the ~ antelope l'antilope femmina ● n femmina f

femin|ine /ˈfemɪnɪn/ adj femminile ● n (*Gram*) femminile m. ~inity n femminilità f. ~ist adj & n femminista mf

fenc|e /fens/ n recinto m; (🛈: *person*) ricettatore m ● vi (*Sport*) tirar di scherma. ⬜ ~ **in** vt chiudere in un recinto. ~er n schermidore m. ~ing n steccato m; (*Sport*) scherma f

fend /fend/ vi ~ **for oneself** badare a se stesso. ⬜ ~ **off** vt parare; difendersi da (*criticisms*)

fender /ˈfendə(r)/ n parafuoco m inv; (*Am: on car*) parafango m

fennel /ˈfenl/ n finocchio m

ferment[1] /ˈfɜːment/ n fermento m

ferment[2] /fəˈment/ vi fermentare ● vt far fermentare. ~ation n fermentazione f

fern /fɜːn/ n felce f

feroc|ious /fəˈrəʊʃəs/ adj feroce. ~ity n ferocia f

ferret /ˈferɪt/ n furetto m ● ferret out vt scovare

ferry /ˈferi/ n traghetto m ● vt

traghettare

fertil|e /ˈfɜːtaɪl/ adj fertile. ~ity n fertilità f

fertilize /ˈfɜːtɪlaɪz/ vt fertilizzare (land, ovum). ~r n fertilizzante m

fervent /ˈfɜːvənt/ adj fervente

fervour /ˈfɜːvə(r)/ n fervore m

fester /ˈfestə(r)/ vi suppurare

festival /ˈfestɪvl/ n (*Mus, Theat*) festival m; (*Relig*) festa f

festiv|e /ˈfestɪv/ adj festivo; ~e season periodo m delle feste natalizie. ~ities vt andare/venire a prendere; (*be sold for*) raggiungere [il prezzo di]

fetch /fetʃ/ vt andare/venire a prendere; (*be sold for*) raggiungere [il prezzo di]

fetching /ˈfetʃɪŋ/ adj attraente

fête /feɪt/ n festa f ● vt festeggiare

fetish /ˈfetɪʃ/ n feticcio m

fetter /ˈfetə(r)/ vt incatenare

feud /fjuːd/ n faida f

feudal /ˈfjuːdl/ adj feudale

fever /ˈfiːvə(r)/ n febbre f. ~ish adj febbricitante; *fig* febbrile

few /fjuː/ adj pochi; every ~ days ogni due o tre giorni; a ~ people alcuni; ~er reservations meno prenotazioni; the ~est number il numero più basso ● pron pochi; ~ of us pochi di noi; a ~ alcuni; quite a ~ parecchi; ~er than last year meno dell'anno scorso

fiancé /fɪˈɒnseɪ/ n fidanzato m. ~e n fidanzata f

fiasco /fɪˈæskəʊ/ n fiasco m

fib /fɪb/ n storia f; tell a ~ raccontare una storia

fibre /ˈfaɪbə(r)/ n fibra f. ~glass n fibra f di vetro

fickle /ˈfɪkl/ adj incostante

fiction /ˈfɪkʃn/ n (works of ~) narrativa f; (*fabrication*) finzione f. ~al adj immaginario

fictitious /fɪkˈtɪʃəs/ adj fittizio

fiddle /'fɪdl/ n ① violino m; (cheating) imbroglio m • vi gingillarsi (with con) • vt ① truccare (accounts)

fidget /'fɪdʒɪt/ vi agitarsi. ~y adj agitato

field /fiːld/ n campo m

field: ~-glasses npl binocolo msg. F~ 'Marshal n feldmaresciallo m. ~work n ricerche fpl sul terreno

fiend /fiːnd/ n demonio m

fierce /fɪəs/ adj feroce. ~ness n ferocia f

fiery /'faɪərɪ/ adj (-ier, -iest) focoso

fifteen /fɪf'tiːn/ adj & n quindici m. ~th adj quindicesimo

fifth /fɪfθ/ adj quinto

fiftieth /'fɪftɪɪθ/ adj cinquantesimo

fifty /'fɪftɪ/ adj cinquanta

fig /fɪg/ n fico m

fight /faɪt/ n lotta f; (brawl) zuffa f; (argument) litigio m; (boxing) incontro m • v (pt/pp fought) • vt also fig combattere • vi combattere; (argue) litigare; (argue) litigare. ~er n combattente mf; (Aeron) caccia m inv. ~ing n combattimento m

figment /'fɪgmənt/ n it's a ~ of your imagination questo è solo una tua invenzione

figurative /'fɪgjʊrətɪv/ adj (sense) figurato; (art) figurativo

figure /'fɪgə(r)/ n (digit) cifra f; (carving, sculpture, illustration, form) figura f; (body shape) linea f; ~ of speech modo m di dire • vi (appear) figurare • vt (Am: think) pensare. □ ~ out vt dedurre; capire (person)

figurehead n figura f simbolica

file[1] /faɪl/ n scheda f; (set of documents) incartamento m; (folder) cartellina f; (Comput) file m inv • vt archiviare (documents)

file[2] n (line) fila f; in single ~ in fila

file[3] n (Tech) lima f • vt limare

filing cabinet /'faɪlɪŋkæbɪnət/ n schedario m, classificatore m

fill /fɪl/ n eat one's ~ mangiare a sazietà • vt riempire; otturare (tooth) • vi riempirsi. □ ~ in vt compilare (form). □ ~ out vt compilare (form). □ ~ up vi (room, tank): riempirsi; (Auto) far il pieno • vt riempire

fillet /'fɪlɪt/ n filetto m • vt (pt/pp filleted) disossare

filling /'fɪlɪŋ/ n (Culin) ripieno m; (of tooth) piombatura f. ~ station n stazione f di rifornimento

film /fɪlm/ n (Cinema) film m inv; (Phot) pellicola f; (cling) ~ pellicola f per alimenti • vt/i filmare. ~ star n star f inv, divo, -a mf

filter /'fɪltə(r)/ n filtro m • vt filtrare. □ ~ through vi (news:) trapelare. ~ tip n filtro m; (cigarette) sigaretta f col filtro

filth /fɪlθ/ n sudiciume m. ~y adj (-ier, -iest) sudicio; (word) sconcio

fin /fɪn/ n pinna f

final /'faɪnl/ adj finale; (conclusive) decisivo • n (Sport) finale f; ~s pl (Univ) esami mpl finali

finale /fɪ'nɑːlɪ/ n finale m

final|ist /'faɪnəlɪst/ n finalista mf. ~ity n finalità f

final|ize /'faɪnəlaɪz/ vt mettere a punto (text); definire (agreement). ~ly adv at (last) finalmente; (at the end) alla fine; (to conclude) per finire

finance /'faɪnæns/ n finanza f • vt finanziare

financial /faɪ'nænʃl/ adj finanziario

find /faɪnd/ n scoperta f • vt (pt/pp found) trovare; (establish) scoprire; ~ sb guilty (Jur) dichiarare qcno colpevole. □ ~ out vt scoprire • vi (enquire) informarsi

findings /'faɪndɪŋz/ npl conclusioni fpl

fine[1] /faɪn/ n (penalty) multa f • vt multare

fine[2] adj bello; (slender) fine; he's ~ (in health) sta bene. ~ arts npl belle arti fpl. • adv bene; that's cutting it

~ non ci lascia molto tempo ● *int*
[va] bene. ~ly *adv* (cut) finemente

finger /'fɪŋgə(r)/ *n* dito *m* (*pl* dita *f*)
● *vt* tastare

finger: ~**nail** *n* unghia *f*. ~**print** *n*
impronta *f* digitale. ~**tip** *n* punta *f*
del dito; have sth at one's ~**tips**
sapere qcsa a menadito; (*close at
hand*) avere qcsa a portata di mano

finish /'fɪnɪʃ/ *n* fine *f*; (*finishing line*)
traguardo *m*; (*of product*) finitura *f*;
have a good ~ (runner:) avere un
buon finale ● *vt* finire; ~ **reading**
finire di leggere ● *vi* finire

finite /'faɪnaɪt/ *adj* limitato

Finland /'fɪnlənd/ *n* Finlandia *f*

Finn /fɪn/ *n* finlandese *mf*. ~**ish** *adj*
finlandese ● *n* (*language*) finnico *m*

fiord /fjɔːd/ *n* fiordo *m*

fir /fɜː(r)/ *n* abete *m*

fire /'faɪə(r)/ *n* fuoco *m*; (*forest, house*)
incendio *m*; be on ~ bruciare; catch
~ prendere fuoco; set ~ to dar
fuoco a; under ~ sotto il fuoco ● *vt*
cuocere (pottery); sparare (shot); tirare (gun); (ⅈ: *dismiss*) buttar
fuori ● *vi* sparare (at a)

fire: ~ **alarm** *n* allarme *m* antincen-
dio. ~**arm** *n* arma *f* da fuoco. ~
brigade *n* vigili *mpl* del fuoco.
~**engine** *n* autopompa *f*.
~**escape** *n* uscita *f* di sicurezza. ~
extinguisher *n* estintore *m*. ~**man**
n pompiere *m*, vigile *m* del fuoco.
~**place** *n* caminetto *m*. ~**side** *n* by
or at the ~**side** accanto al fuoco.
~**wood** *n* legna *f* (da ardere). ~**work**
n fuoco *m* d'artificio

firm¹ /fɜːm/ *n* ditta *f*, azienda *f*

firm² *adj* fermo; (soil) compatto;
(*stable, properly fixed*) solido; (*resolute*)
risoluto. ~**ly** *adv* (hold) stretto; (say)
con fermezza

first /fɜːst/ *adj & n* primo, -a *mf*; at ~
all'inizio; who's ~? chi è il primo?;
from the ~ [in] dall'inizio ● *adv* (arrive, leave) per primo; (*beforehand*)

prima; (*in listing*) prima di tutto, in-
nanzitutto

first: ~ **'aid** *n* pronto soccorso *m*.
~**'aid kit** *n* cassetta *f* di pronto
soccorso. ~**class** *adj* di prim'ordine;
(Rail) di prima classe ● *adv* (travel) in
prima classe. ~ **'floor** *n* primo piano
m; (Am: *ground floor*) pianterreno *m*.
~**ly** *adv* in primo luogo. ~ **name** *n*
nome *m* di battesimo. ~**rate** *adj*
ottimo

fish /fɪʃ/ *n* pesce *m* ● *vt/i* pescare.
□ ~ **out** *vt* tirar fuori

fish: ~**erman** *n* pescatore *m*. ~
'**finger** *n* bastoncino *m* di pesce

fishing /'fɪʃɪŋ/ *n* pesca *f*. ~ **boat** *n*
peschereccio *m*. ~**rod** *n* canna *f*
da pesca

fish: ~**monger** /-mʌŋgə(r)/ *n* pesci-
vendolo *m*. ~**y** *adj* (ⅈ: *suspicious*) sospetto

fission /'fɪʃn/ *n* (Phys) fissione *f*

fist /fɪst/ *n* pugno *m*

fit¹ /fɪt/ *n* (*attack*) attacco *m*; (*of rage*)
accesso *m*; (*of generosity*) slancio *m*

fit² *adj* (fitter, fittest) (*suitable*)
adatto; (*healthy*) in buona salute;
(Sport) in forma; be ~ to do sth essere in grado di fare qcsa; ~ to eat
buono da mangiare; keep ~ tenersi
in forma

fit³ *n* (*of clothes*) taglio *m*; it's a good
~ (coat) etc: ti/le sta bene ● *v* (pt/pp
fitted) ● *vi* (be the right size) andare
bene; it won't ~ (no room) non ci
sta ● *vt* (*fix*) applicare (to a); (*install*)
installare; it doesn't ~ me (coat
etc:) non mi va bene; ~ with fornire
di. □ ~ **in** *vi* (person:) adattarsi; it
won't ~ **in** (no room) non ci sta ● *vt*
(*in schedule, vehicle*) trovare un
buco per

fit: ~**ful** /'fɪtfl/ *adj* irregolare. ~**fully**
adv (sleep) a sprazzi. ~**ments** *npl* (in
house) impianti *mpl* fissi. ~**ness** *n*
(*suitability*) capacità *f*; [physical]
~**ness** forma *f*, fitness *m*

fitting /'fɪtɪŋ/ adj appropriato ● n (of clothes) prova f; (Techn) montaggio m; ~s pl accessori mpl. ~ room n camerino m

five /faɪv/ adj & n cinque m. ~r n Ⓔ biglietto m da cinque sterline

fix /fɪks/ n (Ⓧ: drugs) pera f; be in a ~ Ⓔ essere nei guai ● vt fissare; (repair) aggiustare; preparare (meal). □~ up vt fissare (meeting)

fixed /fɪkst/ adj fisso

fixture /'fɪkstʃə(r)/ n (Sport) incontro m; ~s and fittings impianti mpl fissi

fizz /fɪz/ vi frizzare

fizzle /'fɪzl/ vi ~ out finire in nulla

fizzy /'fɪzɪ/ adj gassoso. ~ drink n bibita f gassata

flabbergasted /'flæbəgɑːstɪd/ adj be ~ rimanere a bocca aperta

flabby /'flæbɪ/ adj floscio

flag[1] /flæg/ n bandiera f ● flag down vt (pt/pp flagged) far segno di fermarsi a (taxi)

flag[2] n (pt/pp flagged) cedere

'flag-pole n asta f della bandiera

flagrant /'fleɪgrənt/ adj flagrante

flair /fleə(r)/ n (skill) talento m; (style) stile m

flake /fleɪk/ n fiocco m ● vi ~ [off] cadere in fiocchi

flaky /'fleɪkɪ/ adj a scaglie. ~ pastry n pasta f sfoglia

flamboyant /flæm'bɔɪənt/ adj (personality) brillante; (tie) sgargiante

flame /fleɪm/ n fiamma f

flammable /'flæməbl/ adj infiammabile

flan /flæn/ n [fruit] ~ crostata f

flank /flæŋk/ n fianco m ● vt fiancheggiare

flannel /'flæn(ə)l/ n flanella f; (for washing) ≈ guanto m di spugna; ~s (trousers) pantaloni mpl di flanella

flap /flæp/ n (of pocket, envelope) risvolto m; (of table) ribalta f; in a ~ Ⓔ in grande agitazione ● v (pt/pp flapped) ● vi sbattere; Ⓔ agitarsi ● vt ~ its wings battere le ali

flare /fleə(r)/ n fiammata f; (device) razzo m ● flare up vi (rash:) venire fuori; (fire:) fare una fiammata; (person, situation:)) esplodere. ~d adj (garment) svasato

flash /flæʃ/ n lampo m; in a ~ Ⓔ in un attimo ● vi lampeggiare; ~ past passare come un bolide ● vt lanciare (smile); ~ one's head-lights lampeggiare; ~ a torch at puntare una torcia su

flash: ~back n scena f retrospettiva. ~light n (Phot) flash m inv; (Am: torch) torcia f [elettrica]. ~y adj vistoso

flask /flɑːsk/ n fiasco m; (vacuum ~) termos m inv

flat /flæt/ adj (flatter, flattest) piatto; (refusal) reciso; (beer) sgassato; (battery) scarico; (tyre) a terra; A ~ (Mus) la bemolle ● n appartamento m; (Mus) bemolle m; (puncture) gomma f a terra

flat: ~ly adv (refuse) categoricamente. ~ rate n tariffa f unica

flatten /'flætn/ vt appiattire

flatter /'flætə(r)/ vt adulare. ~ing adj (comments) lusinghiero; (colour, dress) che fa sembrare più bello. ~y n adulazione f

flaunt /flɔːnt/ vt ostentare

flavour /'fleɪvə(r)/ n sapore m ● vt condire; chocolate ~ed al sapore di cioccolato. ~ing n condimento m

flaw /flɔː/ n difetto m. ~less adj perfetto

flea /fliː/ n pulce m. ~ market n mercato m delle pulci

fleck /flek/ n macchiolina f

fled /fled/ ▷FLEE

flee /fliː/ vt/i (pt/pp fled) fuggire (from da)

fleece /fliːs/ n pelliccia f ● vt Ⓔ

spennare. ~y adj (lining) felpato

fleet /fliːt/ n flotta f; (of cars) parco m

fleeting /ˈfliːtɪŋ/ adj catch a ~ glance of sth intravedere qcsa; for a ~ moment per un attimo

flesh /fleʃ/ n carne f; in the ~ in persona. ~y adj carnoso

flew /fluː/ ▷ FLY¹

flex¹ /fleks/ vt flettere (muscle)

flex² n (Electr) filo m

flexib|ility /fleksɪˈbɪlətɪ/ n flessibilità f. ~le adj flessibile

'flexitime /ˈfleksɪ-/ n orario m flessibile

flick /flɪk/ vt dare un buffetto a; ~ sth off sth togliere qcsa da qcsa con un colpetto. □ ~ **through** vt sfogliare

flicker /ˈflɪkə(r)/ vi tremolare

flight¹ /flaɪt/ n (fleeing) fuga f; take ~ darsi alla fuga

flight² n (flying) volo m; ~ of stairs rampa f

'flight recorder n registratore m di volo

flimsy /ˈflɪmzɪ/ adj (-ier, -iest) (material) leggero; (shelves) poco robusto; (excuse) debole

flinch /flɪntʃ/ vi (wince) sussultare; (draw back) ritirarsi; ~ from a task fig sottrarsi a un compito

fling /flɪŋ/ n have a ~ (🔲: affair) aver un'avventura ● vt (pt/pp flung) gettare

flint /flɪnt/ n pietra f focaia; (for lighter) pietrina f

flip /flɪp/ v (pt/pp flipped) ● vt dare un colpetto a; buttare in aria (coin) ● vi 🔲 uscire dai gangheri; (go mad) impazzire. □ ~ **through** vt sfogliare

flippant /ˈflɪpənt/ adj irriverente

flipper /ˈflɪpə(r)/ n pinna f

flirt /flɜːt/ n civetta f ● vi flirtare

flit /flɪt/ vi (pt/pp flitted) volteggiare

float /fləʊt/ n galleggiante m; (in pro-

cession) carro m; (money) riserva f di cassa ● vi galleggiare; (Fin) fluttuare

flock /flɒk/ n gregge m; (of birds) stormo m ● vi affollarsi

flog /flɒg/ vt (pt/pp flogged) bastonare; (🔲: sell) vendere

flood /flʌd/ n alluvione f; (of river) straripamento m; (fig: of replies, letters, tears) diluvio m; be in a ~ (river:) essere straripato ● vt allagare ● vi (river:) straripare

'floodlight n riflettore m ● vt (pt/pp floodlit) illuminare con riflettori

floor /flɔː(r)/ n pavimento m; (storey) piano m; (for dancing) pista f ● vt (baffle) confondere; (knock down) stendere (person)

'floor polish n cera f per il pavimento

flop /flɒp/ n 🔲 (failure) tonfo m; (Theat) fiasco m ● vi (pt/pp flopped) (🔲: fail) far fiasco. □ ~ **down** vi accasciarsi

floppy /ˈflɒpɪ/ adj floscio. ~ 'disk n floppy disk m inv. ~ [disk] drive n lettore di floppy m

floral /ˈflɔːrəl/ adj floreale

florid /ˈflɒrɪd/ adj (complexion) florido; (style) troppo ricercato

florist /ˈflɒrɪst/ n fioraio, -a mf

flounder¹ /ˈflaʊndə(r)/ vi dibattersi; (speaker:) impappinarsi

flounder² n (fish) passera f di mare

flour /ˈflaʊə(r)/ n farina f

flourish /ˈflʌrɪʃ/ n gesto m drammatico; (scroll) ghirigoro m ● vi prosperare ● vt brandire

flout /flaʊt/ vt fregarsene di (rules)

flow /fləʊ/ n flusso m ● vi scorrere; (hang loosely) ricadere

flower /ˈflaʊə(r)/ n fiore m ● vi fiorire

flower: ~-bed n aiuola f. ~y adj fiorito

flown /fləʊn/ ▷ FLY²

flu /fluː/ n influenza f

fluctuat|e /'flʌktjʊeɪt/ vi fluttuare. **~ion** n fluttuazione f

fluent /'fluːənt/ adj spedito; speak **~** Italian parlare correntemente l'italiano. **~ly** adv speditamente

fluff /flʌf/ n peluria f. **~y** adj (-ier, -iest) vaporoso; (toy) di peluche

fluid /'fluːɪd/ adj fluido• n fluido m

flung /flʌŋ/ ▷ **FLING**

fluorescent /flʊə'resnt/ adj fluorescente

flush /flʌʃ/ n (blush) [vampata di] rossore m • vi arrossire • vt lavare con un getto d'acqua; **~** the toilet tirare l'acqua • adj a livello (with di); (🗆: affluent) a soldi

flute /fluːt/ n flauto m

flutter /'flʌtə(r)/ n battito m • vi svolazzare

flux /flʌks/ n in a state of **~** in uno stato di flusso

fly¹ /flaɪ/ n (pl flies) mosca f

fly² v (pt flew, pp flown) • vi volare; (go by plane) andare in aereo; (flag) sventolare; (rush) precipitarsi; **~ open** spalancarsi • vt pilotare (plane); trasportare [in aereo] (troops, supplies); volare con (Alitalia etc)

fly³ n & flies pl (on trousers) patta f

flying /'flaɪɪŋ/: **~ 'buttress** n arco m rampante. **~ 'colours**: with **~ colours** a pieni voti. **~ 'saucer** n disco m volante. **~ 'start** n get off to a **~ start** fare un'ottima partenza. **~ 'visit** n visita f lampo

fly: **~ leaf** n risguardo m. **~over** n cavalcavia m inv

foal /fəʊl/ n puledro m

foam /fəʊm/ n schiuma f; (synthetic) gommapiuma® f • vi spumare; **~** at the mouth far la bava alla bocca. **~ 'rubber** n gommapiuma® f

fob /fɒb/ vt (pt/pp fobbed) **~** sth off affibbiare qcsa (on sb a qcno); **~** sb off liquidare qcno

focal /'fəʊkl/ adj focale

focus /'fəʊkəs/ n fuoco m; in **~** a fuoco; out of **~** sfocato • v (pt/pp focused or focussed) • vt concentrare (on su) • vi (Phot) **~** on mettere a fuoco; fig concentrarsi (on su)

fodder /'fɒdə(r)/ n foraggio m

foe /fəʊ/ n nemico, -a mf

foetus /'fiːtəs/ n (pl -tuses) feto m

fog /fɒg/ n nebbia f

foggy /'fɒgɪ/ adj (foggier, foggiest) nebbioso; it's **~** c'è nebbia

'fog-horn n sirena f da nebbia

foil¹ /fɔɪl/ n lamina f di metallo

foil² vt (thwart) frustrare

foil³ n (sword) fioretto m

foist /fɔɪst/ vt appioppare (on sb a qcno)

fold¹ /fəʊld/ n (for sheep) ovile m

fold² n piega f• vt piegare; **~** one's arms incrociare le braccia • vi piegarsi; (fail) crollare. □ **~ up** vt ripiegare (chair) • vi essere pieghevole; (business:) collassare

fold|er /'fəʊldə(r)/ n cartella f. **~ing** adj pieghevole

folk /fəʊk/ npl gente f; my **~s** (family) i miei; hello there **~s** ciao a tutti

folklore n folclore m

follow /'fɒləʊ/ vt/i seguire; it doesn't **~** non è necessariamente così; **~** suit fig fare lo stesso; as **~s** come segue. □ **~ up** vt seguire a (letter)

follow|er /'fɒləʊə(r)/ n seguace mf. **~ing** adj seguente • n seguito m; (supporters) seguaci mpl • prep in seguito a

folly /'fɒlɪ/ n follia f

fond /fɒnd/ adj affezionato di; (hope) vivo; be **~** of essere appassionato di (music); I'm **~** of... (food, person) mi piace moltissimo...

fondle /'fɒndl/ vt coccolare

fondness /'fɒndnɪs/ n affetto m; (for things) amore m

font /fɒnt/ n fonte f battesimale; (Typ) carattere m di stampa

food /fuːd/ n cibo m; (for animals, groceries) mangiare m; let's buy some ∼ compriamo qualcosa da mangiare

food processor n tritatutto m inv elettrico

fool[1] /fuːl/ n sciocco, -a mf; she's no ∼ non è una stupida; make a ∼ of oneself rendersi ridicolo ● vt prendere in giro ● vi ∼ around giocare; (husband, wife): avere l'amante

fool[2] n (Culin) crema f

fool|**hardy** adj temerario; ∼ish adj stolto. ∼ishly adv scioccamente. ∼ishness n sciocchezza f. ∼proof adj facilissimo

foot /fʊt/ n (pl **feet**) piede m; (of animal) zampa f; (measure) piede m (= 30,48 cm); on ∼ a piedi; on one's feet in piedi; put one's ∼ in it 🄘 fare una gaffe

foot: ∼**-and-**'**mouth disease** n afta f epizootica. ∼**ball** n calcio m; (ball) pallone m. ∼**baller** n giocatore m di calcio. ∼**bridge** n passerella f. ∼**hills** npl colline fpl pedemontane. ∼**hold** n punto m d'appoggio. ∼**ing** n I lose one's ∼ing perdere l'appiglio; on an equal ∼ing in condizioni di parità. ∼**man** n valletto m. ∼**note** n nota f a piè di pagina. ∼**path** n sentiero m. ∼**print** n orma f. ∼**step** n passo m; follow in sb's ∼**steps** fig seguire l'esempio di qcno. ∼**wear** n calzature fpl

for /fə(r), accentato /fɔː(r)/

● prep per; ∼ this reason per questa ragione; I have lived here ∼ ten years vivo qui da dieci anni; ∼ supper per cena; ∼ all that nonostante questo; what ∼? a che scopo?; send ∼ a doctor chiamare un dottore; fight ∼ a cause lottare per una causa; go ∼ a walk

andare a fare una passeggiata; there's no need ∼ you to go non c'è bisogno che tu vada; it's not ∼ me to say non sta a me dirlo; now you're ∼ it ora sei nei pasticci

● conj poiché, perché

forage /ˈfɒrɪdʒ/ n foraggio m ● vi ∼ for cercare

forbade /fəˈbæd/ ▷**FORBID**

forbear|**ance** /fɔːˈbeərəns/ n pazienza f. ∼**ing** adj tollerante

forbid /fəˈbɪd/ vt (pt **forbade**, pp **forbidden**) proibire. ∼**ding** adj (prospect) che spaventa; (stern) severo

force /fɔːs/ n forza f; in ∼ in vigore; (in large numbers) in massa; come into ∼ entrare in vigore; the [armed] ∼**s** pl le forze armate ● vt forzare; ∼ sth on sb (decision) imporre qcsa a qcno; (drink) costringere qcno a fare qcsa

forced /fɔːst/ adj forzato

force: ∼'**feed** vt (pt/pp **-fed**) nutrire a forza. ∼'**ful** adj energico

forceps /ˈfɔːseps/ npl forcipe m

forcible /ˈfɔːsɪbl/ adj forzato

ford /fɔːd/ n guado m ● vt guadare

fore /fɔː(r)/ n to the ∼ in vista; come to the ∼ salire alla ribalta

fore: ∼**arm** n avambraccio m. ∼**boding** /-ˈbəʊdɪŋ/ n presentimento m. ∼**cast** n previsione f ● vt (pt/pp **-cast**) prevedere. ∼**court** n cortile m anteriore. ∼**finger** n [dito m] indice m. ∼**front** n be in the ∼front essere all'avanguardia. ∼**gone** adj be a ∼gone conclusion essere una cosa scontata. ∼**ground** n primo piano m. ∼**head** /ˈfɔːhed/, /ˈfɒrɪd/ n fronte f

foreign /ˈfɒrən/ adj straniero; (trade) estero; (not belonging) estraneo; he is ∼ è uno straniero. ∼ **currency** n valuta f estera. ∼**er** n straniero, -a mf. ∼ **language** n lingua *f* straniera

fore: ~**man** *n* caporeparto *m*. ~**most** *adj* principale ● *adv* first and in primo luogo

'forerunner *n* precursore *m*

fore'see *vt* (*pt* -saw, *pp* -seen) prevedere. ~**able** *adj* in the ~able future in futuro per quanto si possa prevedere

'foresight *n* previdenza *f*

forest /'fɒrɪst/ *n* foresta *f*. ~**er** *n* guardia *f* forestale

fore'stall *vt* prevenire

forestry /'fɒrɪstrɪ/ *n* silvicoltura *f*

'foretaste *n* pregustazione *f*

fore'tell *vt* (*pt*/*pp* -told) predire

forever /fə'rɛvə(r)/ *adv* per sempre; he's ~ complaining si lamenta sempre

fore'warn *vt* avvertire

foreword /'fɔːwɜːd/ *n* prefazione *f*

forfeit /'fɔːfɪt/ *n* (*in game*) pegno *m*; (*Jur*) penalità *f* ● *vt* perdere

forgave /fə'geɪv/ ▷FORGIVE

forge[1] /fɔːdʒ/ *vi* ~ ahead (*runner:*) lasciarsi indietro gli altri; *fig* farsi strada

forge[2] *n* fucina *f* ● *vt* fucinare; (*counterfeit*) contraffare. ~**r** *n* contraffattore *m*. ~**ry** *n* contraffazione *f*

forget /fə'gɛt/ *vt*/*i* (*pt* -got, *pp* -gotten, *pres p* -getting) dimenticare; dimenticarsi di (*language, skill*). ~**ful** *adj* smemorato. ~**fulness** *n* smemoratezza *f*, ~**me-not** *n* non-ti-scordar-di-mé *m inv*. ~**table** *adj* (*day, film*) da dimenticare

forgive /fə'gɪv/ *vt* (*pt* -gave, *pp* -given) ~ sb for sth perdonare qcno per qcsa. ~**ness** *n* perdono *m*

forgo /fɔː'gəʊ/ *vt* (*pt* -went, *pp* -gone) rinunciare a

forgot(ten) /fə'gɒt(n)/ ▷FORGET

fork /fɔːk/ *n* forchetta *f*; (*for digging*) forca *f*; (*in road*) bivio *m* ● *vi* (*road:*) biforcarsi; ~ right prendere a de-

stra. □ ~ **out** *vt* 🄵 sborsare

fork-lift 'truck *n* elevatore *m*

forlorn /fə'lɔːn/ *adj* (*look*) perduto; (*place*) derelitto; ~ **hope** speranza *f* vana

form /fɔːm/ *n* forma *f*; (*document*) modulo *m*; (*Sch*) classe *f* ● *vt* formare; formulare (*opinion*) ● *vi* formarsi

formal /'fɔːml/ *adj* formale. ~**ity** *f inv*. ~**ly** *adv* in modo formale; (*officially*) ufficialmente

format /'fɔːmæt/ *n* formato *m* ● *vt* formattare (*disk, page*)

formation /fɔː'meɪʃn/ *n* formazione *f*

former /'fɔːmə(r)/ *adj* precedente; (*PM, colleague*) ex; the ~, the latter il primo, l'ultimo. ~**ly** *adv* precedentemente; (*in olden times*) in altri tempi

formidable /'fɔːmɪdəbl/ *adj* formidabile

formula /'fɔːmjʊlə/ *n* (*pl* -ae /-liː/ o -s) formula *f*

formulate /'fɔːmjʊleɪt/ *vt* formulare

forsake /fə'seɪk/ *vt* (*pt* -sook /-sʊk/, *pp* -saken) abbandonare

fort /fɔːt/ *n* (*Mil*) forte *m*

forth /fɔːθ/ *adv* back and ~ avanti e indietro; and so ~ e così via

forth: ~'**coming** *adj* prossimo; (*communicative*) communicativo; no response was ~ non arrivava nessuna risposta. ~'**right** *adj* schietto. ~'**with** *adv* immediatamente

fortieth /'fɔːtɪɪθ/ *adj* quarantesimo

fortnight /'fɔːt-/ *Br n* quindicina *f*. ~**ly** *adj* bimensile ● *adv* ogni due settimane

fortress /'fɔːtrɪs/ *n* fortezza *f*

fortunate /'fɔːtʃənət/ *adj* fortunato; that's ~! meno male!. ~**ly** *adv* fortunatamente

fortune /'fɔːtʃuːn/ *n* fortuna *f*. ~-**teller** *n* indovino, -a *mf*

forty /ˈfɔːtɪ/ adj & n quaranta m

forum /ˈfɔːrəm/ n foro m

forward /ˈfɔːwəd/ adv avanti; (towards the front) in avanti ● adj in avanti; (presumptuous) sfacciato ● n (Sport) attaccante m ● vt inoltrare (letter); spedire (goods). ~s adv avanti

fossil /ˈfɒsl/ n fossile m. ~ized adj fossile; (ideas) fossilizzato

foster /ˈfɒstə(r)/ vt allevare (child). ~-child n figlio, -a m/f in affidamento. ~-mother n madre f affidataria

fought /fɔːt/ ▷FIGHT

foul /faʊl/ adj (smell, taste) cattivo; (air) viziato; (language) osceno; (mood, weather) orrendo; ~ play n (Sport) fallo m ● n (Sport) fallo m ● vt inquinare (water); (Jur) delitto m ● n (Sport) fallo m ● vt commettere un fallo contro; (nets, rope:) impigliarsi in. ~-smelling adj puzzo

found¹ /faʊnd/ ▷FIND

found² vt fondare

foundation /faʊnˈdeɪʃn/ n (basis) fondamento m; (charitable) fondazione f; ~s pl (of building) fondamenta fpl; lay the ~-stone porre la prima pietra

founder¹ /ˈfaʊndə(r)/ n fondatore, -trice mf

founder² vi (ship:) affondare

fountain /ˈfaʊntɪn/ n fontana f. ~-pen n penna f stilografica

four /fɔː(r)/ adj & n quattro m

four: ~some /ˈfɔːsəm/ n quartetto m. ~teen adj & n quattordici m. ~teenth adj quattordicesimo

fourth /fɔːθ/ adj quarto

fowl /faʊl/ n pollame m

fox /fɒks/ n volpe f ● vt (puzzle) ingannare

foyer /ˈfɔɪeɪ/ n (Theat) ridotto m; (in hotel) salone m d'ingresso

fraction /ˈfrækʃn/ n frazione f

fracture /ˈfræktʃə(r)/ n frattura f ● vt fratturare ● vi fratturarsi

fragile /ˈfrædʒaɪl/ adj fragile

fragment /ˈfrægmənt/ n frammento m. ~ary adj frammentario

fragran|ce /ˈfreɪgrəns/ n fragranza f. ~t adj fragrante

frail /freɪl/ adj gracile

frame /freɪm/ n (of picture, door, window) cornice f; (of spectacles) montatura f; (Anat) ossatura f; (structure, of bike) telaio m; ~ of mind stato m d'animo ● vt incorniciare (picture); fig formulare; (🔲: incriminate) montare. ~work n struttura f

France /frɑːns/ n Francia f

frank¹ /fræŋk/ vt affrancare (letter)

frank² adj franco. ~ly adv francamente

frantic /ˈfræntɪk/ adj frenetico; be ~ with worry essere agitatissimo. ~ally adv freneticamente

fraternal /frəˈtɜːnl/ adj fraterno

fraud /frɔːd/ n frode f; (person) impostore m. ~ulent adj fraudolento

fraught /frɔːt/ adj ~ with pieno di

fray¹ /freɪ/ n mischia f

fray² vi sfilacciarsi

freak /friːk/ n fenomeno m; (person) scherzo m di natura; (🔲: weird person) tipo m strambo ● adj anormale. ~ish adj strambo

freckle /ˈfrekl/ n lentiggine f. ~d adj lentigginoso

free /friː/ adj (freer, freest) libero; (ticket, copy) gratuito; (lavish) generoso; ~ of charge gratuito; set ~ liberare ● vt (pt/pp freed) liberare

free: ~dom n libertà f. ~hold n proprietà f [fondiaria] assoluta. ~ 'kick n calcio m di punizione. ~lance adj & adv indipendente. ~ly adv liberamente; (generously) generosamente; I ~ly admit that... devo ammettere che.... f~mason n massone m. ~-range n ~-range egg uovo m di gallina ruspante. ~style n stile m libero. ~way n Am autostrada f

freez|e /friːz/ vt (pt froze, pp frozen) gelare; bloccare (wages) ● vi (water:) gelare; it's ~ing si gela; my hands are ~ing ho le mani congelate

freez|er /ˈfriːzə(r)/ n freezer m inv, congelatore m. ~ing adj gelido ● n below ~ing sotto zero

freight /freɪt/ n carico m. ~er n nave f da carico. ~ train n Am treno m merci

French /frentʃ/ adj francese ● n (language) francese m; the ~ pl i francesi mpl

French: ~ 'fries n patate fpl fritte. ~man n francese m. ~ 'window n porta-finestra f. ~woman n francese f

frenzied /ˈfrenzɪd/ adj frenetico

frenzy /ˈfrenzɪ/ n frenesia f

frequency /ˈfriːkwənsɪ/ n frequenza f

frequent[1] /ˈfriːkwənt/ adj frequente. ~ly adv frequentemente

frequent[2] /frɪˈkwent/ vt frequentare

fresh /freʃ/ adj fresco; (new) nuovo; (Am: cheeky) sfacciato. ~ly adv di recente

freshen /ˈfreʃn/ vi (wind:) rinfrescare. □ ~ up vt dare una rinfrescata a ● vi rinfrescarsi

freshness /ˈfreʃnɪs/ n freschezza f

fret /fret/ vi (pt/pp fretted) inquietarsi. ~ful adj irritabile

friction /ˈfrɪkʃn/ n frizione f

Friday /ˈfraɪdeɪ/ n venerdì m inv

fridge /frɪdʒ/ n frigo m

fried /fraɪd/ ▷ FRY ● adj fritto; ~ egg uovo m fritto

friend /frend/ n amico, -a mf. ~ly adj (-ier, -iest) (relations, meeting, match) amichevole; (neighbourhood, smile) piacevole; (software) di facile uso; be ~ly with essere amico di. ~ship n amicizia f

frieze /friːz/ n fregio m

fright /fraɪt/ n paura f; take ~ spaventarsi

frighten /ˈfraɪtn/ vt spaventare. ~ed adj spaventato; be ~ed aver paura (of di). ~ing adj spaventoso

frightful /ˈfraɪtfl/ adj terribile

frigid /ˈfrɪdʒɪd/ adj frigido. ~ity n freddezza f; (Psych) frigidità f

frill /frɪl/ n volant m inv. ~y adj (dress) con tanti volant

fringe /frɪndʒ/ n frangia f; (of hair) frangetta f; (fig: edge) margine m. ~ benefits npl benefici mpl supplementari

fritter /ˈfrɪtə(r)/ n frittella f ● fritter away vt sprecare

frivol|ity /frɪˈvɒlətɪ/ n frivolezza f. ~ous adj frivolo

fro /frəʊ/ ▷ TO

frock /frɒk/ n abito m

frog /frɒg/ n rana f. ~man n uomo m rana

frolic /ˈfrɒlɪk/ vi (pt/pp frolicked) (lambs:) sgambettare; (people:) folleggiare

from /frɒm/ prep da; ~ Monday da lunedì; ~ that day da quel giorno; he's ~ London è di Londra; this is a letter ~ my brother questa è una lettera di mio fratello; documents ~ the 16th century documenti del XVI secolo; made ~ fatto con; she felt ill ~ fatigue si sentiva male dalla stanchezza; ~ now on d'ora in poi

front /frʌnt/ n parte f anteriore; (fig: organization etc) facciata f; (of garment) davanti m; (sea-) lungomare m; (Mil, Pol, Meteorol) fronte m; in ~ of davanti a; in or at the ~ davanti; to the ~ avanti ● adj davanti; (page, row, wheel) anteriore

frontal /ˈfrʌntl/ adj frontale

front 'door n porta f d'entrata

frontier /ˈfrʌntɪə(r)/ n frontiera f

frost /frɒst/ n gelo m; (hoar~) brina f

~**bite** *n* congelamento *m*. ~**bitten** *adj* congelato

frost|ed /'frɒstɪd/ *adj* ~ed glass vetro *m* smerigliato. ~**ily** *adv* gelidamente. ~**ing** *n* Am (Culin) glassa *f*. ~**y** *adj also fig* gelido

froth /frɒθ/ *n* schiuma *f* • *vi* far schiuma. ~**y** *adj* schiumoso

frown /fraʊn/ *n* cipiglio *m* • *vi* aggrottare le sopracciglia. □ ~ **on** *vt* disapprovare

froze /frəʊz/ ▷**FREEZE**

frozen /'frəʊzn/ ▷**FREEZE** • *adj* (corpse, hand) congelato; (wastes) gelido; (Culin) surgelato; I'm ~ sono gelato. ~ **food** *n* surgelati *mpl*

frugal /'fru:gl/ *adj* frugale

fruit /fru:t/ *n* frutto *m*; (collectively) frutta *f*; eat more ~ mangia più frutta. ~ **cake** *n* dolce *m* con frutta candita

fruition /fru:'ɪʃn/ *n* come to ~ dare dei frutti

fruit: ~**less** *adj* infruttuoso. ~'**salad** *n* macedonia *f* [di frutta]

frustrat|e /frʌ'streɪt/ *vt* frustrare; rovinare (plans). ~**ing** *adj* frustrante. ~**ion** *n* frustrazione *f*

fry[1] *vt/i* (pt/pp fried) friggere

fry[2] /fraɪ/ *n inv* small ~ *fig* pesce *m* piccolo

frying pan *n* padella *f*

fudge /fʌdʒ/ *n* caramella *f* a base di zucchero, burro e latte

fuel /'fju:əl/ *n* carburante *m*; *fig* nutrimento *m* • *vt fig* alimentare

fugitive /'fju:dʒɪtɪv/ *n* fuggiasco, -a *mf*

fulfil /fʊl'fɪl/ *vt* (pt/pp -filled) soddisfare (conditions, need); realizzare (dream, desire); ~ **oneself** realizzarsi. ~**ling** *adj* soddisfacente. ~**ment** *n* sense of ~ment senso *m* di appagamento

full /fʊl/ *adj* pieno (of di); (detailed) esauriente; (bus, hotel) completo;

(skirt) ampio; at ~ speed a tutta velocità; in ~ swing in pieno fervore • *n* in ~ per intero

full: ~ '**moon** *n* luna *f* piena. ~**scale** *adj* (model) in scala reale; (alert) di massima gravità. ~ '**stop** *n* punto *m*. ~**time** *adj & adv* a tempo pieno

fully /'fʊlɪ/ *adv* completamente; (in detail) dettagliatamente; ~ **booked** (hotel, restaurant) tutto prenotato

fumble /'fʌmbl/ *vi* ~ in rovistare in; ~ **with** armeggiare con; ~ **for one's keys** rovistare alla ricerca delle chiavi

fume /fju:m/ *vi* (be angry) essere furioso

fumes /fju:mz/ *npl* fumi *mpl*; (from car) gas *mpl* di scarico

fumigate /'fju:mɪgeɪt/ *vt* suffumicare

fun /fʌn/ *n* divertimento *m*; for ~ per ridere; make ~ of prendere in giro; have ~ divertirsi

function /'fʌŋkʃn/ *n* funzione *f*; (event) cerimonia *f* • *vi* funzionare; ~ **as** (serve as) funzionare da. ~**al** *adj* funzionale

fund /fʌnd/ *n* fondo *m*; *fig* pozzo *m*; ~**s** *pl* fondi *mpl* • *vt* finanziare

fundamental /fʌndə'mentl/ *adj* fondamentale

funeral /'fju:nərəl/ *n* funerale *m*

funeral directors *n* impresa *f* di pompe funebri

'**funfair** *n* luna park *m inv*

fungus /'fʌŋgəs/ *n* (pl -gi /-gaɪ/ or -gai /-gaɪ/) fungo *m*

funnel /'fʌnl/ *n* imbuto *m*; (on ship) ciminiera *f*

funnily /'fʌnɪlɪ/ *adv* comicamente; (oddly) stranamente; ~ **enough** strano a dirsi

funny /'fʌnɪ/ *adj* (-ier, -iest) buffo; (odd) strano. ~ **business** *n* affare *m* losco

fur /fɜ:(r)/ n pelo m; (for clothing) pelliccia f; (in kettle) deposito m. ~ 'coat n pelliccia f

furious /ˈfjʊərɪəs/ adj furioso

furnace /ˈfɜːnɪs/ n fornace f

furnish /ˈfɜːnɪʃ/ vt ammobiliare (flat); fornire (supplies). ~ed adj ~ed room stanza f ammobiliata. ~ings npl mobili mpl

furniture /ˈfɜːnɪtʃə(r)/ n mobili mpl

furrow /ˈfʌrəʊ/ n solco m

furry /ˈfɜːrɪ/ adj (animal) peloso; (toy) di peluche

further /ˈfɜːðə(r)/ adj (additional) ulteriore; at the ~ end all'altra estremità; until ~ notice fino a nuovo avviso ● adv più lontano; ~,... inoltre,...; ~ off più lontano ● vt promuovere

further'more adv per di più

furthest /ˈfɜːðɪst/ adj più lontano ● adv più lontano

furtive /ˈfɜːtɪv/ adj furtivo

fury /ˈfjʊərɪ/ n furore m

fuse[1] /fjuːz/ n (of bomb) detonatore m; (cord) miccia f

fuse[2] n (Electr) fusibile m ● vt fondere; (Electr) far saltare ● vi fondersi; (Electr) saltare; the lights have ~d sono saltate le luci. ~box n scatola f dei fusibili

fuselage /ˈfjuːzəlɑːʒ/ n (Aeron) fusoliera f

fusion /ˈfjuːʒn/ n fusione f

fuss /fʌs/ n storie fpl; make a ~ fare storie; make a ~ of colmare di attenzioni ● vi fare storie

fussy /ˈfʌsɪ/ adj (-ier, -iest) (person) difficile da accontentare; (clothes etc) pieno di fronzoli

futil|e /ˈfjuːtaɪl/ adj inutile. ~ity n futilità f

future /ˈfjuːtʃə(r)/ adj & n futuro; in ~ in futuro. ~ perfect futuro m anteriore

futuristic /fjuːtʃəˈrɪstɪk/ adj futuristico

fuzz /fʌz/ n the ~ (※: police) la pula

fuzzy /ˈfʌzɪ/ adj (-ier, -iest) (hair) crespo; (photo) sfuocato

Gg

gab /gæb/ n ① have the gift of the ~ avere la parlantina

gabble /ˈgæb(ə)l/ vi parlare troppo in fretta

gad /gæd/ vi (pt/pp gadded) ~ about andarsene in giro

gadget /ˈgædʒɪt/ n aggeggio m

Gaelic /ˈgeɪlɪk/ adj & n gaelico m

gaffe /gæf/ n gaffe f inv

gag /gæg/ n bavaglio m; (joke) battuta f ● vt (pt/pp gagged) imbavagliare

gaily /ˈgeɪlɪ/ adv allegramente

gain /geɪn/ n guadagno m; (increase) aumento m ● vt acquisire; ~ weight aumentare di peso; ~ access accedere ● vi (clock): andare avanti. ~ful adj ~ful employment lavoro m remunerativo

gait /geɪt/ n andatura f

gala /ˈgɑːlə/ n gala f; swimming ~ manifestazione f di nuoto ● attrib di gala

galaxy /ˈgæləksɪ/ n galassia f

gale /geɪl/ n bufera f

gall /gɔːl/ n (impudence) impudenza f

gallant /ˈgælənt/ adj coraggioso; (chivalrous) galante. ~ry n coraggio m

gall-bladder n cistifellea f

gallery /ˈgælərɪ/ n galleria f

galley /ˈgælɪ/ n (ship's kitchen) cambusa f; ~ [proof] bozza f in colonna

gallivant /'gælɪvænt/ vi 🔲 andare in giro

gallon /'gælən/ n gallone m (= 4,5 l; Am = 3,7 l)

gallop /'gæləp/ n galoppo m ● vi galoppare

gallows /'gæləʊz/ n forca f

galore /gə'lɔ:(r)/ adv a bizzeffe

galvanize /'gælvənaɪz/ vt (Techn) galvanizzare; fig stimolare (into a)

gambl|e /'gæmbl/ n (risk) azzardo m ● vi giocare; (on Stock Exchange) speculare; ~e on (rely) contare su. ~er n giocatore, -trice mf [d'azzardo]. ~ing n gioco m [d'azzardo]

game /geɪm/ n gioco m; (match) partita f; (animals, birds) selvaggina f; ~s (Sch) ≈ ginnastica f ● adj (brave) coraggioso; are you ~? ti va?; be ~ for essere pronto per. ~keeper n guardacaccia m inv

gammon /'gæmən/ n coscia f di maiale

gamut /'gæmət/ n fig gamma f

gander /'gændə(r)/ n oca f maschio

gang /gæŋ/ n banda f; (of workmen) squadra f ● **gang up** vi far comunella (on contro)

gangling /'gæŋglɪŋ/ adj spilungone

gangmaster /'gæŋmɑːstə(r)/ n caporale m (di manodopera abusiva)

gangrene /'gæŋgriːn/ n cancrena f

gangster /'gæŋstə(r)/ n gangster m inv

gangway /'gæŋweɪ/ n passaggio m; (Aeron, Naut) passerella f

gaol /dʒeɪl/ n carcere m ● vt incarcerare. ~er n carceriere m

gap /gæp/ n spazio m; (in ages, between teeth) scarto m; (in memory) vuoto m; (in story) punto m oscuro

gap|e /geɪp/ vi stare a bocca aperta; (be wide open) spalancarsi; ~e at guardare a bocca aperta. ~ing adj aperto

gap year In Gran Bretagna il gap year è l'anno di intervallo che gli studenti si prendono tra la fine della scuola secondaria e l'università. Molti studenti utilizzano questo periodo sabbatico per intraprendere attività completamente diverse da ciò che hanno studiato o che studieranno e alcuni lo utilizzano per lavorare e mettere da parte qualche risparmio. Altri, infine, ne approfittano per viaggiare all'estero e conoscere il mondo.

garage /'gærɑːʒ/ n garage m inv; (for repairs) meccanico m; (for petrol) stazione f di servizio

garbage /'gɑːbɪdʒ/ n immondizia f; (nonsense) idiozie fpl. ~ can n Am bidone m dell'immondizia

garden /'gɑːdn/ n giardino m; [public] ~s pl giardini mpl pubblici ● vi fare giardinaggio. ~ centre n negozio m di piante e articoli da giardinaggio. ~er n giardiniere, -a mf. ~ing n giardinaggio m

gargle /'gɑːgl/ n gargarismo m ● vi fare gargarismi

gargoyle /'gɑːgɔɪl/ n gargouille f inv

garish /'geərɪʃ/ adj sgargiante

garland /'gɑːlənd/ n ghirlanda f

garlic /'gɑːlɪk/ n aglio m. ~ bread n pane m condito con aglio

garment /'gɑːmənt/ n indumento m

garnish /'gɑːnɪʃ/ n guarnizione f ● vt guarnire

garrison /'gærɪsn/ n guarnigione f

garter /'gɑːtə(r)/ n giarrettiera f; (for socks) reggicalze m inv da uomo

gas /gæs/ n gas m inv; (Am 🔲: petrol) benzina f ● v (pt/pp gassed) ● vt assfissiare ● vi 🔲 blaterare. ~ cooker n cucina f a gas. ~ 'fire n stufa f a gas

gash /gæʃ/ n taglio m ● vt tagliare

gasket /'gæskɪt/ n (Techn) guarnizione f

gas: ~ **mask** n maschera f antigas. ~**-meter** n contatore m del gas

gasoline /ˈɡæsəliːn/ n Am benzina f

gasp /ɡɑːsp/ vi avere il fiato mozzato

'gas station n Am distributore m di benzina

gastric /ˈɡæstrɪk/ adj gastrico. ~ **flu** n influenza f gastro-intestinale. ~ **'ulcer** n ulcera f gastrica

gate /ɡeɪt/ n cancello m; (at airport) uscita f

gate: ~**crash** vt entrare senza invito a. ~**crasher** n intruso, -a mf. ~**way** n ingresso m

gather /ˈɡæðə(r)/ vt raccogliere; (conclude) dedurre; (in sewing) arricciare; ~ **speed** acquistare velocità; ~ **together** radunare (people, belongings); (obtain gradually) acquistare ● vi (people:) radunarsi. ~**ing** n family ~**ing** ritrovo m di famiglia

gaudy /ˈɡɔːdɪ/ adj (-ier, -iest) pacchiano

gauge /ɡeɪdʒ/ n calibro m; (Rail) scartamento m; (device) indicatore m ● vt misurare; fig stimare

gaunt /ɡɔːnt/ adj (thin) smunto

gauze /ɡɔːz/ n garza f

gave /ɡeɪv/ ▷GIVE

gawky /ˈɡɔːkɪ/ adj (-ier, -iest) sgraziato

gawp /ɡɔːp/ vi ~ [at] ▢ guardare con aria da ebete

gay /ɡeɪ/ adj gaio; (homosexual) omosessuale; (bar, club) gay

gaze /ɡeɪz/ n sguardo m fisso ● vi guardare; ~ **at** fissare

GB abbr (Great Britain) GB

gear /ɡɪə(r)/ n equipaggiamento m; (Techn) ingranaggio m; (Auto) marcia f; in ~ con la marcia innestata; change ~ cambiare marcia ● vt finalizzare (to a)

gearbox n (Auto) scatola f del cambio

geese /ɡiːs/ ▷GOOSE

gel /dʒel/ n gel m inv

gelatine /ˈdʒelətɪn/ n gelatina f

gelignite /ˈdʒelɪɡnaɪt/ n gelatina f esplosiva f

gem /dʒem/ n gemma f

Gemini /ˈdʒemɪnaɪ/ n (Astr) Gemelli mpl

gender /ˈdʒendə(r)/ n (Gram) genere m

gene /dʒiːn/ n gene m

genealogy /dʒiːnɪˈælədʒɪ/ n genealogia f

general /ˈdʒenrəl/ adj generale ● n generale m; in ~ in generale. ~ **e'lection** n elezioni fpl politiche

generaliz|ation /dʒenrəlaɪˈzeɪʃn/ n generalizzazione f. ~**e** vi generalizzare

generally /ˈdʒenrəlɪ/ adv generalmente

general prac'titioner n medico m generico

generate /ˈdʒenəreɪt/ vt generare

generation /dʒenəˈreɪʃn/ n generazione f

generator /ˈdʒenəreɪtə(r)/ n generatore m

generosity /dʒenəˈrɒsɪtɪ/ n generosità f

generous /ˈdʒenərəs/ adj generoso. ~**ly** adv generosamente

genetic /dʒɪˈnetɪk/ adj genetico. ~ **engineering** n ingegneria f genetica. ~**s** n genetica f

Geneva /dʒɪˈniːvə/ n Ginevra f

genial /ˈdʒiːnɪəl/ adj gioviale

genitals /ˈdʒenɪtlz/ npl genitali mpl

genitive /ˈdʒenɪtɪv/ adj & n ~ [case] genitivo m

genius /ˈdʒiːnɪəs/ n (pl -uses) genio m

genocide /ˈdʒenəsaɪd/ n genocidio m

genre /ˈʒãːɡrə/ n genere m [letterario]

gent /dʒent/ n ▢ signore m; the ~**s**

sg il bagno per uomini

genteel /dʒenˈtiːl/ adj raffinato

gentle /ˈdʒentl/ adj delicato; (breeze, tap, slope) leggero

gentleman /ˈdʒentlmən/ n signore m; (well-mannered) gentiluomo m

gent|leness /ˈdʒentlnɪs/ n delicatezza f. ~**ly** adv delicatamente

genuine /ˈdʒenjʊm/ adj genuino. ~**ly** adv (sorry) sinceramente

geograph|ical /dʒɪəˈgræfɪkl/ adj geografico. ~**y** n geografia f

geological /dʒɪəˈlɒdʒɪkl/ adj geologico

geolog|ist /dʒɪˈɒlədʒɪst/ n geologo, -a mf. ~**y** n geologia f

geranium /dʒəˈreɪnɪəm/ n geranio m

geriatric /dʒerɪˈætrɪk/ adj geriatrico; ~ **ward** n reparto m geriatria. ~**s** n geriatria f

germ /dʒɜːm/ n germe m; ~**s** pl microbi mpl

German /ˈdʒɜːmən/ n & adj tedesco, -a mf; (language) tedesco m

Germanic /dʒɜːˈmænɪk/ adj germanico

German 'measles n rosolia f

Germany /ˈdʒɜːmənɪ/ n Germania f

germinate /ˈdʒɜːmɪneɪt/ vi germogliare

gesticulate /dʒeˈstɪkjʊleɪt/ vi gesticolare

gesture /ˈdʒestʃə(r)/ n gesto m

get /get/ verb

past tense/past participle **got**, past participle Am **gotten**, pres participle **getting**

● vt (receive) ricevere; (obtain) ottenere; trovare (job); (buy, catch, fetch) prendere; (transport, deliver to airport etc) portare; (reach on

telephone) trovare; (⊤: understand) comprendere; preparare (meal); ~ **sb to do sth** far fare qcsa a qcno

● vi (become) ~ **tired/bored/angry** stancarsi/annoiarsi/arrabbiarsi; **I'm** ~**ting hungry** mi sta venendo fame; ~ **dressed/married** vestirsi/sposarsi; ~ **sth ready** preparare qcsa; ~ **nowhere** non concludere nulla; **this is** ~**ting us nowhere** questo non ci è di nessun aiuto; ~ **to** (reach) arrivare a. ▫ ~ **at** vi (criticize) criticare; **I see what you're** ~**ting at** ho capito cosa vuoi dire; **what are you** ~**ting at?** dove vuoi andare a parare?. ▫ ~ **away** vi (leave) andarsene; (escape) scappare. ▫ ~ **back** vi tornare ● vt (recover) riavere; ~ **one's own back** rifarsi. ▫ ~ **by** vi passare; (manage) cavarsela. ▫ ~ **down** vi scendere; ~ **down to work** mettersi al lavoro ● vt (depress) buttare giù. ▫ ~ **in** vi entrare ● vt mettere dentro (washing); far venire (plumber). ▫ ~ **off** vi scendere; (from work) andarsene; (Jur) essere assolto; ~ **off the bus/one's bike** scendere dal pullman/dalla bici ● vt (remove) togliere. ▫ ~ **on** vi salire; (be on good terms) andare d'accordo; (make progress) andare avanti; (in life) riuscire; ~ **on the bus/one's bike** salire sul pullman/sulla bici; **how are you** ~**ting on?** come va?. ▫ ~ **out** vi uscire; (of car) scendere; ~ **out!** fuori!. ● vt (avoid doing) evitare ● vt togliere (cork, stain). ▫ ~ **over** vi andare di là ● vt fig riprendersi da (illness). ▫ ~ **round** vt aggirare (rule); rigirare (person) ● vi **I never** ~ **round to it** non mi sono mai deciso a farlo. ▫ ~ **through** vi (on telephone) prendere

g

la linea. □~ **up** vi alzarsi; (climb)
salire; ~ **up a hill** salire su una
collina

geyser /ˈgiːzə(r)/ n scaldabagno m;
(Geol) geyser m inv

ghastly /ˈgɑːstlɪ/ adj (-ier, -iest) terribile; **feel** ~ sentirsi da cani

gherkin /ˈgɜːkɪn/ n cetriolino m

ghetto /ˈgetəʊ/ n ghetto m

ghost /ɡəʊst/ n fantasma m. ~**ly** adj
spettrale

giant /ˈdʒaɪənt/ n gigante m ● adj
gigante

gibberish /ˈdʒɪbərɪʃ/ n stupidaggini fpl

gibe /dʒaɪb/ n malignità f inv

giblets /ˈdʒɪblɪts/ npl frattaglie fpl

giddiness /ˈɡɪdɪnɪs/ n vertigini fpl

giddy /ˈɡɪdɪ/ adj (-ier, -iest) vertiginoso; **feel** ~ avere le vertigini

gift /ɡɪft/ n dono m; (to charity) donazione f. ~**ed** adj dotato. ~**wrap** vt
impacchettare in carta da regalo

gig /ɡɪɡ/ n (Mus) [T] concerto m

gigantic /dʒaɪˈɡæntɪk/ adj gigantesco

giggle /ˈɡɪɡl/ n risatina f ● vi ridacchiare

gild /ɡɪld/ vt dorare

gills /ɡɪlz/ npl branchia fsg

gilt /ɡɪlt/ adj dorato ● n doratura f.
~**-edged stock** n investimento m
sicuro

gimmick /ˈɡɪmɪk/ n trovata f

gin /dʒɪn/ n gin m inv

ginger /ˈdʒɪndʒə(r)/ adj rosso fuoco
inv; (cat) rosso ● n zenzero m. ~ **ale**
n, ~ **beer** n bibita f allo zenzero.
~**bread** n panpepato m

gipsy /ˈdʒɪpsɪ/ n = gypsy

giraffe /dʒɪˈrɑːf/ n giraffa f

girder /ˈɡɜːdə(r)/ n (Techn) trave f

girl /ɡɜːl/ n ragazza f; (female child)
femmina f. ~ **band** n girl band f inv.
~**friend** n amica f; (of boy) ragazza f.

~**ish** adj da ragazza

giro /ˈdʒaɪərəʊ/ n bancogiro m;
(cheque) sussidio m di disoccupazione

girth /ɡɜːθ/ n circonferenza f

gist /dʒɪst/ n the ~ la sostanza

give /ɡɪv/ n elasticità f ● v t (pt gave,
pp given) ● vt dare; (as present) regalare (to a); fare (lecture, present,
shriek); donare (blood); ~ **birth** partorire ● vi (to charity) fare delle donazioni; (yield) cedere. □~ **away** vt dare
via; (betray) tradire; (distribute) assegnare; ~ **away the bride** portare la
sposa all'altare. □~ **back** vt restituire. □~ **in** vt consegnare ● vi
(yield) arrendersi. □~ **off** vt emanare. □~ **over** vi ~ over! piantala!.
□~ **up** vt rinunciare a; ~ **oneself**
up arrendersi ● vi rinunciare. □~
way vi cedere; (Auto) dare la precedenza; (collapse) crollare

given /ˈɡɪvn/ ▷GIVE ● adj ~ **name**
nome m di battesimo

glacier /ˈɡlæsɪə(r)/ n ghiacciaio m

glad /ɡlæd/ adj contento (of di).
~**den** vt rallegrare

gladly /ˈɡlædlɪ/ adv volentieri

glamour /ˈɡlæmə(r)/ n fascino m

glance /ɡlɑːns/ n sguardo m ● vi ~
at dare un'occhiata a. □~ **up** vi alzare gli occhi

gland /ɡlænd/ n glandola f

glare /ɡleə(r)/ n bagliore m; (look)
occhiataccia f ● vi ~ **at** dare un'occhiataccia a

glaring /ˈɡleərɪŋ/ adj sfolgorante;
(mistake) madornale

glass /ɡlɑːs/ n vetro m; (for drinking)
bicchiere m; ~**es** (pl: spectacles) occhiali mpl. ~**y** adj vitreo

glaze /ɡleɪz/ n smalto m ● vt mettere
i vetri a (door, window); smaltare
(pottery); (Culin) spennellare. ~**d** adj
(eyes) vitreo

gleam /gli:m/ n luccichio m • vi luccicare

glean /gli:n/ vt racimolare (information)

glee /gli:/ n gioia f. ~**ful** adj gioioso

glib /glɪb/ adj pej insincero

glide /glaɪd/ vi scorrere; (through the air) planare. ~**er** n aliante m

glimmer /'glɪmə(r)/ n barlume m • vi emettere un barlume

glimpse /glɪmps/ n catch a ~ of intravedere • vt intravedere

glint /glɪnt/ vi luccicare

glisten /'glɪsn/ vi luccicare

glitter /'glɪtə(r)/ vi brillare

gloat /gləʊt/ vi gongolare (over su)

global /'gləʊbl/ adj mondiale. ~**ization** n globalizzazione f

globe /gləʊb/ n globo m; (map) mappamondo m

gloom /glu:m/ n oscurità f; (sadness) tristezza f. ~**ily** adv (sadly) con aria cupa

gloomy /'glu:mɪ/ adj (-ier, -iest) cupo

glorify /'glɔ:rɪfaɪ/ vt (pt/pp -ied) glorificare; a ~ied waitress niente più che una cameriera

glorious /'glɔ:rɪəs/ adj splendido; (deed, hero) glorioso

glory /'glɔ:rɪ/ n gloria f; (splendour) splendore m; (cause for pride) vanto m • vi (pt/pp -ied) ~ in vantarsi di

gloss /glɒs/ n lucentezza f. ~ paint n vernice f lucida • gloss over vt sorvolare su

glossary /'glɒsərɪ/ n glossario m

glossy /'glɒsɪ/ adj (-ier, -iest) lucido; ~ [magazine] rivista f femminile

glove /glʌv/ n guanto m. ~ compartment n (Auto) cruscotto m

glow /gləʊ/ n splendore m; (in cheeks) rossore m; (of candle) luce f soffusa • vi risplendere; (candle): brillare; (person): avvampare. ~**ing** adj ardente; (account) entusiastico.

~**-worm** n lucciola f

glucose /'glu:kəʊs/ n glucosio m

glue /glu:/ n colla f • vt (pres p gluing) incollare

glum /glʌm/ adj (glummer, glummest) tetro

glutton /'glʌtən/ n ghiottone, -a mf. ~**ous** adj ghiotto. ~**y** n ghiottoneria f

gnarled /nɑ:ld/ adj nodoso

gnash /næʃ/ vt ~ one's teeth digrignare i denti

gnaw /nɔ:/ vt rosicchiare

go[1] /gəʊ/ n (pl goes) energia f; (attempt) tentativo m; on the go in movimento; at one go in una sola volta; it's your go tocca a te; make a go of it riuscire

---

go[2] /gəʊ/

3 sing pres tense **goes**, past tense **went**, past participle **gone**

• vi andare; (leave) andar via; (vanish) sparire; (become) diventare; (be sold) vendersi; go and see andare a vedere; go swimming/shopping andare a nuotare/fare spese; where's the time gone? come ha fatto il tempo a volare così?; it's all gone è finito; be going to do stare per fare; I'm not going to non ne ho nessuna intenzione; to go (hamburgers etc) da asporto; a coffee to go un caffè da portar via. □ ~ **about** vi andare in giro. □ ~ **away** vi andarsene. □ ~ **back** vi ritornare. □ ~ **by** vi passare. □ ~ **down** vi scendere; (sun): tramontare; (ship): affondare; (swelling): diminuire. □ ~ **for** vt andare a prendere; andare a cercare (doctor); (choose) optare per; (attack) aggredire; he's not the kind I go for non è il genere che mi attira. □ ~ **in** vi entrare. □ ~ **in for** vt partecipare a (competition); darsi a (tennis). □ ~ **off** vi andarsene; (alarm:) scattere; (gun, bomb:) esplodere; (food, milk:) andare a male; go off well riuscire. □ ~ **on** vi andare avanti; what's going on? cosa succede? go on at vt 🗊 scocciare. □ ~ **out** vi uscire; (light, fire:) spegnersi. □ ~ **over** vi andare • vt (check) controllare. □ ~ **round** vi andare in giro; (visit) andare; (turn) girare; is there enough to go round? ce n'è abbastanza per tutti? go through vi (bill, proposal:) passare • vt (suffer) subire; (check) controllare; (read) leggere. □ ~ **under** vi passare sotto; (ship, swimmer:) andare sott'acqua; (fail) fallire. □ ~ **up** vi salire; (Theat: curtain:) aprirsi. □ ~ **with** vt accompagnare. □ ~ **without** vt fare a meno di (supper, sleep) • vi fare senza

goad /gəʊd/ vt spingere (into a); (taunt) spronare

'**go-ahead** adj (person, company) intraprendente • n okay m

goal /gəʊl/ n porta f; (point scored) gol m inv; (in life) obiettivo m; score a ~ segnare. ~ie n 🗊, ~keeper n portiere m. ~post n palo m

goat /gəʊt/ n capra f.

gobble /'gɒbl/ vt ~ [down, up] tranguggiare

God, god /gɒd/ n Dio m, dio m

god: ~**child** n figlioccio m. ~**daughter** n figlioccia f. ~**dess** n dea f. ~**father** n padrino m. ~**forsaken** adj dimenticato da Dio. ~**mother** n madrina f. ~**send** n manna f. ~**son** n figlioccio m

going /'gəʊɪŋ/ adj (price, rate) corrente; ~ **concern** azienda f florida

• n it's hard ~ è una faticaccia; while the ~ is good finché si può. ~**s-'on** npl avvenimenti mpl

gold /gəʊld/ n oro m • adj d'oro

golden /'gəʊldn/ adj dorato. ~ '**handshake** n buonuscita f (al termine di un rapporto di lavoro). ~ **mean** n giusto mezzo m. ~ '**wedding** n nozze fpl d'oro

gold: ~**fish** n inv pesce m rosso. ~**-mine** n miniera f d'oro. ~**-plated** adj placcato d'oro. ~**smith** n orefice m

golf /gɒlf/ n golf m

golf: ~**-club** n circolo m di golf; (implement) mazza f da golf. ~**-course** n campo m di golf. ~**er** n giocatore, -trice mf di golf

gondo|la /'gɒndələ/ n gondola f. ~**lier** n gondoliere m

gone /gɒn/ ▷**go**

gong /gɒŋ/ n gong m inv

good /gʊd/ adj (better, best) buono; (child, footballer, singer) bravo; (holiday, film) bello; ~ **at** bravo in; a ~ deal of anger molta rabbia; as ~ as (almost) quasi; ~ **morning**, ~ **afternoon** buon giorno; ~ **evening** buona sera; ~ **night** buonanotte; have a ~ time divertirsi • n bene m; for ~ per sempre; do ~ far del bene; do sb ~ far bene a qcno; it's no ~ è inutile; be up to no ~ combinare qualcosa

goodbye /gʊd'baɪ/ int arrivederci

good: ~**-for-nothing** n buono, -a mf a nulla. G~ '**Friday** n Venerdì m Santo

good-'looking adj bello

goodness /'gʊdnɪs/ n bontà f; my ~! santo cielo!; thank ~! grazie al cielo!

goods /gʊdz/ npl prodotti mpl. ~ **train** n treno m merci

good'will n buona volontà f; (Comm) avviamento m

goody /'gʊdɪ/ n (🔢: person) buono m. ~-**goody** n santarellino, -a mf

gooey /'guː:ɪ/ adj 🔢 appiccicaticcio; fig sdolcinato

google /'guːgl/ vt/i googlare

goose /guːs/: ~-**flesh** n, ~-**pimples** npl pelle fsg d'oca

gooseberry /'gʊzbərɪ/ n uva f spina

gore¹ /gɔː(r)/ n sangue m

gore² vt incornare

gorge /gɔːdʒ/ n (Geog) gola f ● vt ~ oneself ingozzarsi

gorgeous /'gɔːdʒəs/ adj stupendo

gorilla /gə'rɪlə/ n gorilla m inv

gorse /gɔːs/ n ginestrone m

gory /'gɔːrɪ/ adj (-ier, -iest) cruento

gosh /gɒʃ/ int 🔢 caspita

gospel /'gɒspl/ n vangelo m. ~ **truth** n sacrosanta verità f

gossip /'gɒsɪp/ n pettegolezzi mpl; (person) pettegolo, -a mf ● vi pettegolare. ~y adj pettegolo

got /gɒt/ ▷**GET**: have ~ avere; have ~ to do sth dover fare qcsa

gotten /'gɒtn/ Am see **get**

gouge /gaʊdʒ/ vt ~ **out** cavare

gourmet /'gʊəmeɪ/ n buongustaio, -a mf

govern /'gʌv(ə)n/ vt/i governare; (determine) determinare

government /'gʌvnmənt/ n governo m. ~al adj governativo

governor /'gʌvənə(r)/ n governatore m; (of school) membro m del consiglio di istituto; (of prison) direttore, -trice mf; (🔢: boss) capo m

gown /gaʊn/ n vestito m; (Jur, Univ) toga f

GP n abbr general practitioner

GPS abbr (Global Positioning System) GPS m

grab /græb/ vt (pt/pp grabbed) ~ [hold of] afferrare

grace /greɪs/ n grazia f; (before meal)

benedicite m inv; with good ~ volentieri; three days' ~ tre giorni di proroga. ~**ful** adj aggraziato. ~**fully** adv con grazia

gracious /'greɪʃəs/ adj cortese; (elegant) lussuoso

grade /greɪd/ n livello m; (Comm) qualità f; (Sch) voto m; (Am Sch: class) classe f; Am = **gradient** ● vt (Comm) classificare; (Sch) dare il voto a. ~ **crossing** n Am passaggio m a livello

gradient /'greɪdɪənt/ n pendenza f

gradual /'grædʒʊəl/ adj graduale. ~**ly** adv gradualmente

graduate¹ /'grædʒʊət/ n laureato, -a mf

graduate² /'grædʒʊeɪt/ vi (Univ) laurearsi

graduation /grædʒʊ'eɪʃn/ n laurea f

graffiti /grə'fiːti/ npl graffiti mpl

graft /grɑːft/ n (Bot, Med) innesto m; (Med: organ) trapianto m; (🔢: hard work) duro lavoro m; (🔢: corruption) corruzione f ● vt innestare; trapiantare (organ)

grain /greɪn/ n (of sand, salt) granello m; (of rice) chicco m; (cereals) cereali mpl; (in wood) venatura f; it goes against the ~ fig è contro la mia/sua natura

gram /græm/ n grammo m

grammar /'græmə(r)/ n grammatica f. ~ **school** n ≈ liceo m

grammatical /grə'mætɪkl/ adj grammaticale

grand /grænd/ adj grandioso; 🔢 eccellente

'grandchild n nipote mf

'granddaughter n nipote f

grandeur /'grændʒə(r)/ n grandiosità f

'grandfather n nonno m. ~ **clock** n pendolo m (che poggia a terra)

grandiose /'grændɪəʊs/ adj

grandioso

grand: ~**mother** n nonna f. ~**parents** npl nonni mpl. ~ **pi'ano** n pianoforte m a coda. ~**son** n nipote m. ~**stand** n tribuna f

granite /'grænɪt/ n granito m

granny /'grænɪ/ n 🔟 nonna f

grant /grɑːnt/ n (money) sussidio m; (Univ) borsa f di studio ● vt accordare; (admit) ammettere; take sth for ~ed dare per scontato qcsa

granule /'grænjuːl/ n granello m

grape /greɪp/ n acino m; ~s pl uva fsg

grapefruit /'greɪp-/ n inv pompelmo m

graph /grɑːf/ n grafico m

graphic /'græfɪk/ adj grafico; (vivid) vivido. ~s n grafica f

grapple /'græpl/ vi ~ with also fig essere alle prese con

grasp /grɑːsp/ n stretta f; (understanding) comprensione f ● vt afferrare. ~ing adj avido

grass /grɑːs/ n erba f; at the ~ roots alla base. ~**hopper** n cavalletta f. ~**land** n prateria f

grassy /'grɑːsɪ/ adj erboso

grate¹ /greɪt/ n grata f

grate² /greɪt/ vt (Culin) grattugiare ● vi stridere

grateful /'greɪtfl/ adj grato. ~ly adv con gratitudine

grater /'greɪtə(r)/ n (Culin) grattugia f

gratif|y /'grætɪfaɪ/ vt (pt/pp -ied) appagare. ~**ied** adj appagato. ~**ying** adj appagante

grating /'greɪtɪŋ/ n grata f

gratitude /'grætɪtjuːd/ n gratitudine f

gratuitous /grə'tjuːɪtəs/ adj gratuito

gratuity /grə'tjuːɪtɪ/ n gratifica f

grave¹ /greɪv/ adj grave

grave² n tomba f

gravel /'grævl/ n ghiaia f

grave: ~**stone** n lapide f. ~**yard** n cimitero m

gravitate /'grævɪteɪt/ vi gravitare

gravity /'grævɪtɪ/ n gravità f

gravy /'greɪvɪ/ n sugo m della carne

gray /greɪ/ adj Am = grey

graze¹ /greɪz/ vi (animal:) pascolare

graze² n escoriazione f ● vt (touch lightly) sfiorare; (scrape) escoriare; sbucciarsi (knee)

grease /griːs/ n grasso m ● vt ungere. ~-**proof 'paper** n carta f oleata

greasy /'griːsɪ/ adj (-ier, -iest) untuoso; (hair, skin) grasso

great /greɪt/ adj grande; (🔟: marvellous) eccezionale

great: G~ **'Britain** n Gran Bretagna f. ~'**grandfather** n bisnonno m. ~'**grandmother** n bisnonna f

great|ly /'greɪtlɪ/ adv enormemente. ~**ness** n grandezza f

Greece /griːs/ n Grecia f

greed /griːd/ n avidità f; (for food) ingordigia f

greedy /'griːdɪ/ adj (-ier, -iest) avido; (for food) ingordo

Greek /griːk/ adj & n greco, -a mf; (language) greco m

green /griːn/ adj verde; (fig: inexperienced) immaturo ● n verde m; ~s pl verdura f; the G~s pl (Pol) i verdi. ~ **belt** n zona f verde intorno a una città. ~ **card** n (Auto) carta f verde

> **Green Card** Negli Stati i
> Uniti è un documento ufficiale che concede a qualsiasi persona priva della cittadinanza americana il permesso di risiedere e lavorare indefinitivamente negli Stati Uniti. Nel Regno Unito, invece, è un documento che dei conducenti o proprietari di

autoveicoli devono richiedere alla propria compagnia di assicurazione per convalidare la polizza in occasione di viaggi all'estero.

greenery /ˈgriːnəri/ n verde m

green: ~**grocer** n fruttivendolo, -a mf. ~**ing** n saluto m; (welcome) accoglienza f. ~**ings card** n biglietto m d'auguri

greet /griːt/ vt salutare; (welcome) accogliere. ~**ing** n saluto m; (welcome) accoglienza f. ~**ings card** n biglietto m d'auguri

gregarious /grɪˈgeərɪəs/ adj gregario; (person) socievole

grenade /grɪˈneɪd/ n granata f

grew /gruː/ ▷GROW

grey /greɪ/ adj grigio; (hair) bianco ● n grigio m. ~**hound** n levriero m

grid /grɪd/ n griglia f; (on map) reticolato m; (Electr) rete f

grief /griːf/ n dolore m; come to ~ (plans) naufragare

grievance /ˈgriːvəns/ n lamentela f

grieve /griːv/ vt addolorare ● vi essere addolorato

grill /grɪl/ n graticola f; (for grilling) griglia f; mixed ~ grigliata f mista ● vt/i cuocere alla griglia; (interrogate) sottoporre al terzo grado

grille /grɪl/ n grata f

grim /grɪm/ adj (grimmer, grimmest) arcigno; (determination) accanito

grimace /grɪˈmeɪs/ n smorfia f ● vi fare una smorfia

grime /graɪm/ n sudiciume m

grimy /ˈgraɪmɪ/ adj (-ier, -iest) sudicio

grin /grɪn/ n sorriso m ● vi (pt/pp grinned) fare un gran sorriso

grind /graɪnd/ n (🄸: hard work) sfacchinata f ● vt (pt/pp ground) macinare; affilare (knife); (Am: mince) tritare; ~ one's teeth digrignare i denti

grip /grɪp/ n presa f; fig controllo m; (bag) borsone m; get a ~ on oneself controllarsi ● vt (pt/pp gripped) afferrare; far presa su; tenere avvinto (attention)

grisly /ˈgrɪzlɪ/ adj (-ier, -iest) raccapricciante

gristle /ˈgrɪsl/ n cartilagine f

grit /grɪt/ n graniglia f; (for roads) sabbia f; (courage) coraggio m ● vt (pt/pp gritted) spargere sabbia su (road); ~ one's teeth serrare i denti

groan /grəʊn/ n gemito m ● vi gemere

grocer /ˈgrəʊsə(r)/ n droghiere, -a mf; ~'s [shop] drogheria f. ~**ies** npl generi mpl alimentari

groggy /ˈgrɒgɪ/ adj (-ier, -iest) stordito; (unsteady) barcollante

groin /grɔɪn/ n (Anat) inguine m

groom /gruːm/ n sposo m; (for horse) stalliere m ● vt strigliare (horse); fig preparare; well-~ed ben curato

groove /gruːv/ n scanalatura f

grope /grəʊp/ vi brancolare; ~ for cercare a tastoni

gross /grəʊs/ adj obeso; (coarse) volgare; (glaring) grossolano; (salary, weight) lordo ● n inv grossa f. ~**ly** adv (very) enormemente

grotesque /grəʊˈtesk/ adj grottesco

ground¹ /graʊnd/ ▷GRIND

ground² n terra f; (Sport) terreno m; (reason) ragione f; ~**s** pl (park) giardini mpl; (of coffee) fondi mpl ● vi (ship) arenarsi ● vt bloccare a terra (aircraft); Am (Electr) mettere a terra

ground: ~**floor** n pianterreno m. ~**ing** n base f. ~**less** adj infondato. ~**sheet** n telone m impermeabile. ~**work** n lavoro m di preparazione

group /gruːp/ n gruppo m ● vt raggruppare ● vi raggrupparsi

grouse¹ /graʊs/ n inv gallo m

cedrone

grouse² vi 🔲 brontolare

grovel /ˈɡrɒvl/ vi (pt/pp grovelled) strisciare. ~ling adj leccapiedi inv

grow /ɡrəʊ/ v (pt grew, pp grown) ● vi crescere; (become) diventare; (unemployment, fear:) aumentare; (town:) ingrandirsi ● vt coltivare; ~ one's hair farsi crescere i capelli. □ ~ up vi crescere; (town:) svilupparsi

growl /ɡraʊl/ n grugnito m ● vi ringhiare

grown /ɡrəʊn/ ▷GROW ● adj adulto. ~-up adj & n adulto, -a m f

growth /ɡrəʊθ/ n crescita f; (increase) aumento m; (Med) tumore m

grub /ɡrʌb/ n larva f; (🔲: food) mangiare m

grubby /ˈɡrʌbɪ/ adj (-ier, -iest) sporco

grudge /ɡrʌdʒ/ n rancore m; bear sb a ~e portare rancore a qcno ● vt dare a malincuore. ~ing adj reluttante. ~ingly adv a malincuore

gruelling /ˈɡruːəlɪŋ/ adj estenuante

gruesome /ˈɡruːsəm/ adj macabro

gruff /ɡrʌf/ adj burbero

grumble /ˈɡrʌmbl/ vi brontolare (at contro)

grumpy /ˈɡrʌmpɪ/ adj (-ier, -iest) scorbutico

grunt /ɡrʌnt/ n grugnito m ● vi fare un grugnito

guarant|ee /ɡærənˈtiː/ n garanzia f ● vt garantire. ~or n garante m f

guard /ɡɑːd/ n guardia f; (security) guardiano m; (on train) capotreno m; (Techn) schermo m protettivo; be on ~ essere di guardia ● vt sorvegliare; (protect) proteggere. □ ~ against vt guardarsi da. ~-dog n cane m da guardia

guarded /ˈɡɑːdɪd/ adj guardingo

guardian /ˈɡɑːdɪən/ n (of minor) tutore, -trice m f

guerrilla /ɡəˈrɪlə/ n guerrigliero, -a m f. ~ warfare n guerriglia f

guess /ɡes/ n supposizione f ● vt indovinare ● vi indovinare; (Am: suppose) supporre. ~work n supposizione f

guest /ɡest/ n ospite m f; (in hotel) cliente m f. ~-house n pensione f

guffaw /ɡʌˈfɔː/ n sghignazzata f ● vi sghignazzare

guidance /ˈɡaɪdəns/ n guida f; (advice) consigli mpl

guide /ɡaɪd/ n guida f; [Girl] G~ giovane esploratrice f ● vt guidare. ~book n guida f turistica

guide: ~-dog n cane m per ciechi. ~-lines npl direttive fpl

guild /ɡɪld/ n corporazione f

guile /ɡaɪl/ n astuzia f

guillotine /ˈɡɪlətiːn/ n ghigliottina f; (for paper) taglierina f

guilt /ɡɪlt/ n colpa f. ~ily adv con aria colpevole

guilty /ˈɡɪltɪ/ adj (-ier, -iest) colpevole; have a ~ conscience avere la coscienza sporca

guinea-pig /ˈɡɪnɪ-/ n porcellino m d'India; (fig: used for experiments) cavia f

guitar /ɡɪˈtɑː(r)/ n chitarra f. ~ist n chitarrista m f

gulf /ɡʌlf/ n (Geog) golfo m; fig abisso m

gull /ɡʌl/ n gabbiano m

gullet /ˈɡʌlɪt/ n esofago m; (throat) gola f

gullible /ˈɡʌlɪbl/ adj credulone

gully /ˈɡʌlɪ/ n burrone m; (drain) canale m di scolo

gulp /ɡʌlp/ n azione f di deglutire; (of food) boccone m; (of liquid) sorso m ● vi deglutire. □ ~ down vt tranguggiare (food); scolarsi (liquid)

gum¹ /ɡʌm/ n (Anat) gengiva f

gum² n gomma f; (chewing gum) gomma f da masticare, chewing gum m inv ● vt (pt/pp gummed) ingommare (to a)

gun /gʌn/ n pistola f; (rifle) fucile m; (cannon) cannone m • **gun down** vt (pt/pp gunned) freddare

gun: ~**fire** n spari mpl; (of cannon) colpi mpl [di cannone]. ~**man** uomo m armato

gun: ~**powder** n polvere f da sparo. ~**shot** n colpo m [di pistola]

gurgle /'gɜːgl/ vi gorgogliare; (baby:) fare degli urletti

gush /gʌʃ/ vi sgorgare; (enthuse) parlare con troppo entusiasmo (over di). □ ~ **out** vi sgorgare. ~**ing** adj eccessivamente entusiastico

gust /gʌst/ n (of wind) raffica f

gusto /'gʌstəʊ/ n **with** ~ con trasporto

gusty /'gʌstɪ/ adj ventoso

gut /gʌt/ n intestino m; ~s pl pancia f; (🔲: courage) fegato m • vt (pt/pp gutted) svuotare delle interiora; ~**ted by fire** sventrato da un incendio

gutter /'gʌtə(r)/ n canale m di scolo; (on roof) grondaia f; fig bassifondi mpl

guttural /'gʌtərəl/ adj gutturale

guy /gaɪ/ n 🔲 tipo m, tizio m

guzzle /'gʌzl/ vt ingozzarsi con (food); he's ~d the lot si è sbafato tutto

gym /dʒɪm/ n 🔲 palestra f; (gymnastics) ginnastica f

gymnasium /dʒɪm'neɪzɪəm/ n palestra f

gymnast /'dʒɪmnæst/ n ginnasta mf. ~**ics** n ginnastica f

gymslip /(Sch)/ ≈ grembiule m (da bambina)

gynaecolog|ist /gaɪnɪ'kɒlədʒɪst/ n ginecologo, -a mf. ~**y** n ginecologia f

gypsy /'dʒɪpsɪ/ n zingaro, -a mf

gyrate /dʒaɪ'reɪt/ vi roteare

Hh

haberdashery /hæbə'dæʃərɪ/ n merceria f; Am negozio m d'abbigliamento da uomo

habit /'hæbɪt/ n abitudine f; (Relig: costume) tonaca f; **be in the** ~ **of doing sth** avere l'abitudine di fare qcsa

habitable /'hæbɪtəbl/ adj abitabile

habitat /'hæbɪtæt/ n habitat m inv

habitation /hæbɪ'teɪʃn/ n **unfit for human** ~ inagibile

habitual /hə'bɪtjʊəl/ adj abituale; (smoker, liar) inveterato. ~**ly** adv regolarmente

hack¹ /hæk/ n (writer) scribacchino, -a mf

hack² vt tagliare; ~ **to pieces** tagliare a pezzi

hackneyed /'hæknɪd/ adj trito [e ritrito]

had /hæd/ ▷**HAVE**

haddock /'hædək/ n inv eglefino m

haemorrhage /'hemərɪdʒ/ n emorragia f

haemorrhoids /'hemərɔɪdz/ npl emorroidi fpl

hag /hæg/ n **old** ~ vecchia befana f

haggard /'hægəd/ adj sfatto

hail¹ /heɪl/ vt salutare; far segno a (taxi) • vi ~ **from** provenire da

hail² /heɪl/ n grandine f • vi grandinare. ~**stone** n chicco m di grandine. ~**storm** n grandinata f

hair /heə(r)/ n capelli mpl; (on body, of animal) pelo m

hair: ~**brush** n spazzola f per capelli. ~**cut** n taglio m di capelli; **have a** ~**cut** farsi tagliare i capelli. ~**do** n 🔲 pettinatura f. ~**dresser** n parrucchiere, -a mf. ~**dryer** n fon m

hairy | handy

inv; (*with hood*) casco *m* [asciugacapelli]. ~-**grip** *n* molletta *f.* ~-**pin** *n* forcina *f.* ~-**pin 'bend** *n* tornante *m*, curva *f* a gomito. ~-**raising** *adj* terrificante. ~-**style** *n* acconciatura *f*

hairy /'heəri/ *adj* (-ier, -iest) peloso; (⊞ *frightening*) spaventoso

half /hɑ:f/ *n* (*pl* halves) metà *f inv*; cut in ~ tagliare a metà; one and a ~ uno e mezzo; a dozen mezza dozzina; ~ an hour mezz'ora ● *adj* mezzo; [at] ~ price [a] metà prezzo ● *adv* a metà; ~ past two le due e mezza

half: ~-'hearted *adj* esitante. ~-'mast *n* at ~ a mast a mezz'asta. ~-'term *n* vacanza *f* di metà trimestre. ~-'time *n* (*Sport*) intervallo *m*. ~-way *adj* the ~way mark/stage il livello intermedio ● *adv* a metà strada; get ~way *fig* arrivare a metà

hall /hɔ:l/ *n* (*entrance*) ingresso *m*; (*room*) sala *f*; (*mansion*) residenza *f* di campagna; ~ of residence (*Univ*) casa *f* dello studente

'**hallmark** *n* marchio *m* di garanzia; *fig* marchio *m*

hallo /hə'ləʊ/ *int* ciao!; (*on telephone*) pronto!; say ~ to salutare

Hallowe'en /hæləʊ'i:n/ *n* vigilia *f* d'Ognissanti e notte delle streghe, celebrata soprattutto dai bambini

hallucination /həlu:sɪ'neɪʃn/ *n* allucinazione *f*

halo /'heɪləʊ/ *n* (*pl* -es) aureola *f*; (*Astr*) alone *m*

halt /hɔ:lt/ *n* alt *m inv*; come to a ~ fermarsi; (*traffic*) bloccarsi ● *vi* fermarsi; ~! alt! ● *vt* fermare. ~-ing *adj* esitante

halve /hɑ:v/ *vt* dividere a metà; (*reduce*) dimezzare

ham /hæm/ *n* prosciutto *m*; (*Theat*) attore, -trice *mf* da strapazzo

hamburger /'hæmbɜ:gə(r)/ *n* hamburger *m inv*

hammer /'hæmə(r)/ *n* martello *m*

● *vt* martellare ● *vi* ~ at/on picchiare a

hammock /'hæmək/ *n* amaca *f*

hamper[1] /'hæmpə(r)/ *n* cesto *m*; [gift] ~ cestino *m*

hamper[2] *vt* ostacolare

hamster /'hæmstə(r)/ *n* criceto *m*

hand /hænd/ *n* mano *f*; (*of clock*) lancetta *f*; (*writing*) scrittura *f*; (*worker*) manovale *m*; at ~, to ~ a portata di mano; on the one ~ da un lato; on the other ~ d'altra parte; out of ~ incontrollabile; (*summarily*) su due piedi; give sb a ~ dare una mano a qcno ● *vt* porgere. □ ~ **down** *vt* tramandare. □ ~ **in** *vt* consegnare. □ ~ **out** *vt* distribuire. □ ~ **over** *vt* passare; (*to police*) consegnare

hand: ~**bag** *n* borsa *f* (*da signora*). ~**brake** *n* freno *m* a mano. ~**cuffs** *npl* manette *fpl.* ~**ful** *n* manciata *f*; be [quite] a ~ful ⊞ essere difficile da tenere a freno

handicap /'hændɪkæp/ *n* handicap *m inv.* ~**ped** *adj* mentally/physically ~**ped** mentalmente/fisicamente handicappato

handi|**craft** /'hændɪkrɑ:ft/ *n* artigianato *m.* ~**work** *n* opera *f*

handkerchief /'hæŋkətʃɪf/ *n* (*pl* ~s & -chieves) fazzoletto *m*

handle /'hændl/ *n* manico *m*; (*of door*) maniglia *f*; fly off the ~ ⊞ perdere le staffe ● *vt* maneggiare; occuparsi di (*problem, customer*); prendere (*difficult person*); trattare (*subject*). ~**bars** *npl* manubrio *m*

hand: ~**out** *n* (*at lecture*) foglio *m* informativo; (⊞ *money*) elemosina *f.* ~**shake** *n* stretta *f* di mano

handsome /'hænsəm/ *adj* bello; (*fig* *generous*) generoso

handwriting *n* calligrafia *f*

handy /'hændɪ/ *adj* (-ier, -iest) utile (*person*) abile; have/keep ~ avere/ tenere a portata di mano. ~**man** *n* tuttofare *m inv*

hang /hæŋ/ vt (pt/pp hung) appendere (picture); (pt/pp hanged) impiccare (criminal); ~ oneself impiccarsi • vi (pt/pp hung) pendere; (hair:) scendere • n get the ~ of it 🔢 wit afferrare. □~ **about** vi gironzolare. □~ **on** vi tenersi stretto; (🔢 wait) aspettare; (Teleph) restare in linea. □~ **on to** vt tenersi stretto a; (keep) tenere. □~ **out** vi spuntare; where does he usually ~ out? 🔢 dove bazzica di solito? • vt stendere (washing). □~ **up** vt appendere; (Teleph) riattaccare • vi essere appeso; (Teleph) riattaccare

hangar /ˈhæŋə(r)/ n (Aeron) hangar m inv

hanger /ˈhæŋə(r)/ n gruccia f. ~-**on** n leccapiedi mf

hang: ~-**glider** n deltaplano m. ~**over** n 🔢 postumi mpl da sbornia. ~-**up** n 🔢 complesso m

hanky /ˈhæŋkɪ/ n 🔢 fazzoletto m

haphazard /hæpˈhæzəd/ adj a casaccio

happen /ˈhæpn/ vi capitare, succedere; as it ~s per caso; I ~ed to meet him mi è capitato di incontrarlo; what has ~ed to him? cosa gli è capitato?; (become of) che fine ha fatto? ~**ing** n avvenimento m

happily /ˈhæpɪlɪ/ adv felicemente; (fortunately) fortunatamente. ~**ness** n felicità f

happy /ˈhæpɪ/ adj (-ier, -iest) contento, felice. ~-**go-lucky** adj spensierato

harass /ˈhærəs/ vt perseguitare. ~**ed** adj stressato. ~**ment** n persecuzione f; sexual ~**ment** molestie fpl sessuali

harbour /ˈhaːbə(r)/ n porto m • vt dare asilo a; nutrire (grudge)

hard /haːd/ adj duro; (question, problem) difficile; ~ of hearing duro d'orecchi; be ~ on sb (person:) essere duro con qcno • adv (work) duramente; (pull, hit, rain,

snow) forte; ~ hit by unemployment duramente colpito dalla disoccupazione; take sth ~ non accettare qcsa; think ~! pensaci bene!; try ~ mettercela tutta; try ~er metterci più impegno; ~ done by 🔢 trattato ingiustamente

hard: **hard-boiled** adj (egg) sodo. ~ **disk** n hard disk m inv, disco m rigido

harden /ˈhaːdn/ vi indurirsi

hard: ~-**headed** adj (businessman) dal sangue freddo. ~**line** adj duro

hardly /ˈhaːdlɪ/ adv appena; ~ ever quasi mai. ~**ness** n durezza f. ~**ship** n avversità f inv

hard: ~ **shoulder** n (Auto) corsia f d'emergenza. ~**ware** n ferramenta fpl; (Comput) hardware m inv. ~-**working** adj be ~-**working** essere un gran lavoratore

hardy /ˈhaːdɪ/ adj (-ier, -iest) dal fisico resistente; (plant) che sopporta il gelo

hare /heə(r)/ n lepre f. ~-**brained** adj 🔢 (scheme) da scervellati

hark /haːk/ vi ~ **back to** fig ritornare su

harm /haːm/ n male m; (damage) danni mpl; out of ~'s way in un posto sicuro; it won't do any ~ non farà certo male • vt far male a; (damage) danneggiare. ~**ful** adj dannoso. ~**less** adj innocuo

harmonica /haːˈmɒnɪkə/ n armonica f (a bocca)

harmonious /haːˈməʊnɪəs/ adj armonioso. ~**ly** adv in armonia

harness /ˈhaːnɪs/ n finimenti mpl; (of parachute) imbracatura f • vt bardare (horse); sfruttare (resources)

harp /haːp/ n arpa f • **harp on** vi 🔢 insistere (about su). ~**ist** n arpista mf

harpoon /haːˈpuːn/ n arpione m

harpsichord /ˈhaːpsɪkɔːd/ n clavicembalo m

harrowing /ˈhærəʊɪŋ/ adj straziante

harsh /hɑːʃ/ adj duro; (light) abbagliante. ~ness n durezza f

harvest /ˈhɑːvɪst/ n raccolta f; (of grapes) vendemmia f; (crop) raccolto m • vt raccogliere

has /hæz/ ▷HAVE

hassle /ˈhæsl/ ① n rottura f • vt rompere le scatole a

haste /heɪst/ n fretta f

hasty /ˈheɪstɪ/ adj (-ier, -iest) frettoloso; (decision) affrettato. ~ily adv frettolosamente

hat /hæt/ n cappello m

hatch[1] /hætʃ/ n (for food) sportello m passavivande; (Naut) boccaporto m

hatch[2] vi ~[out] rompere il guscio; (egg:) schiudersi • vt covare; tramare (plot)

'hatchback n tre/cinque porte m inv; (door) porta f del bagagliaio

hatchet /ˈhætʃɪt/ n ascia f

hate /heɪt/ n odio m • vt odiare. ~ful adj odioso

hatred /ˈheɪtrɪd/ n odio m

haughty /ˈhɔːtɪ/ adj (-ier, -iest) altezzoso. ~ily adv altezzosamente

haul /hɔːl/ n (fish) pescata f; (loot) bottino m; (pull) tirata f • vt tirare; trasportare (goods) • vi ~ on tirare. ~age n trasporto m. ~ier n autotrasportatore m

haunt /hɔːnt/ n ritrovo m • vt frequentare; (linger in the mind) perseguitare; this house is ~ed questa casa è abitata da fantasmi

---

have /hæv/

• vt (3 sg pres tense has; pt/pp had) avere; fare (breakfast, bath, walk etc); ~ a drink bere qualcosa; ~ lunch/dinner pranzare/cenare; ~ a rest riposarsi; I had my hair cut mi sono tagliata i capelli; we had a

house painted abbiamo fatto tinteggiare la casa; I had it made l'ho fatto fare; ~ to do sth dover fare qcsa; ~ him telephone me tomorrow digli di telefonarmi domani; he has or he's got two houses ha due case; you've got the money, ~n't you? hai i soldi, no?

• v aux avere; (with verbs of motion & some others) essere; I ~ seen him l'ho visto; he has never been there non ci è mai stato. □ ~ on vt (be wearing) portare; (dupe) prendere in giro; I've got something on tonight ho un impegno stasera. □ ~ out vt ~ it out with sb chiarire le cose con qcno

• npl the ~s and the ~-nots i ricchi e i poveri

---

haven /ˈheɪvn/ n fig rifugio m

haversack /ˈhævə-/ n zaino m

havoc /ˈhævək/ n strage f; play ~ with fig scombussolare

hawk /hɔːk/ n falco m

hay /heɪ/ n fieno m. ~ fever n raffreddore m da fieno. ~stack n pagliaio m

'haywire adj ① go ~ dare i numeri; (plans:) andare all'aria

hazard /ˈhæzəd/ n (risk) rischio m • vt rischiare; ~ a guess azzardare un'ipotesi. ~ous adj rischioso. ~ [warning] lights npl (Auto) luci fpl d'emergenza

haze /heɪz/ n foschia f

hazel /ˈheɪz(ə)l/ n nocciolo m; (colour) [color m] nocciola m inv. ~nut n nocciola f

hazy /ˈheɪzɪ/ adj (-ier, -iest) nebbioso; (fig: person) confuso; (memories) vago

he /hiː/ pron lui; he's tired è stanco; I'm going but he's not io vengo, ma lui no

head /hed/ n testa f; (of firm) capo

m; (of primary school) direttore, -trice mf; (of secondary school) preside mf; (on beer) schiuma f; be off one's ~ essere fuori di testa; have a good ~ for business avere il senso degli affari; have a good ~ for heights non soffrire di vertigini; 10 pounds a ~ 10 sterline a testa; 20 ~ of cattle 20 capi di bestiame; ~ first a capofitto; ~ over heels in love innamorato pazzo; ~s or tails? testa o croce? ● vt essere a capo di; (lead) essere in testa a (list); colpire di testa (ball) ● vi ~ for dirigersi verso.

head: ~ache n mal m di testa. ~er /'hedə(r)/ n rinvio m di testa; (dive) tuffo m di testa. ~ing (in list etc) titolo m. ~lamp n (Auto) fanale m. ~land n promontorio m. ~line n titolo m. ~long adj & adv a capofitto. ~'master n (of primary school) direttore m; (of secondary school) preside m. ~'mistress n (of primary school) direttrice f; (of secondary school) preside f. ~-on adj (collision) frontale ● adv frontalmente. ~phones npl cuffie fpl. ~quarters npl sede fsg; (Mil) quartier m generale msg. ~strong adj testardo

heady /'hedɪ/ adj che dà alla testa

heal /hiːl/ vt/i guarire

health /helθ/ n salute f

health|y /'helθɪ/ adj (-ier, -iest) sano. ~ily adv in modo sano

heap /hiːp/ n mucchio m; ~s of 🗊 un sacco di ● vt ~ [up] ammucchiare; ~ed teaspoon un cucchiaino abbondante

hear /hɪə(r)/ vt/i (pt/pp heard) sentire; ~, ~! bravo! ~ from vi aver notizie di. □ ~ of vi sentir parlare di; he would not ~ of it non ne ha voluto sentir parlare

hearing /'hɪərɪŋ/ n udito m; (Jur) udienza f. ~-aid n apparecchio m acustico

hearsay n from ~ per sentito dire

hearse /hɜːs/ n carro m funebre

heart /hɑːt/ n cuore m; ~s pl (in cards) cuori mpl; by ~ a memoria

heart: ~ache n pena f. ~ attack n infarto m. ~break n afflizione f. ~-breaking adj straziante. ~burn n mal m di stomaco. ~felt adj di cuore

hearth /hɑːθ/ n focolare m

heart|ily /'hɑːtɪlɪ/ adv di cuore; (eat) con appetito; be ~ily sick of sth non poterne più di qcsa. ~less adj spietato. ~-searching n esame m di coscienza. ~-to-~ n conversazione f a cuore aperto ● adj a cuore aperto. ~y adj caloroso; (meal) copioso; (person) gioviale

heat /hiːt/ n calore m; (Sport) prova f eliminatoria ● vt scaldare ● vi scaldarsi. ~ed adj (swimming pool) riscaldato; (discussion) animato. ~er n (for room) stufa f; (for water) boiler m inv; (Auto) riscaldamento m

heath /hiːθ/ n brughiera f

heathen /'hiːðn/ adj & n pagano, -a mf

heather /'heðə(r)/ n erica f

heating /'hiːtɪŋ/ n riscaldamento m

heat: ~-stroke n colpo m di sole. ~ wave n ondata f di calore

heave /hiːv/ vt tirare; (lift) tirare su; (🗊: throw) gettare; emettere (sigh) ● vi tirare

heaven /'hev(ə)n/ n paradiso m; ~ help you if... Dio ti scampi se...; H~s! santo cielo!. ~ly adj celeste; 🗊 delizioso

heav|y /'hevɪ/ adj (-ier, -iest) pesante; (traffic) intenso; (rain, cold) forte; be a ~y smoker/drinker essere un gran fumatore/bevitore. ~ily adv pesantemente; (smoke, drink etc) molto. ~yweight n peso m massimo

Hebrew /'hiːbruː/ adj ebreo

heckle /'hekl/ vt interrompere di continuo. ~r n disturbatore, -trice mf

hectic /'hektɪk/ adj frenetico

hedge /hedʒ/ n siepe f ● vi fig essere

evasivo. ~hog n riccio m

heed /hiːd/ n pay ~ to prestare ascolto a • vt prestare ascolto a. ~less adj noncurante

heel[1] /hiːl/ n tallone m, (of shoe) tacco m; take to one's ~s 🅃 darsela a gambe

heel[2] vi ~ over (Naut) inclinarsi

hefty /'heftɪ/ adj (-ier, -iest) massiccio

heifer /'hefə(r)/ n giovenca f

height /haɪt/ n altezza f; (of plane) altitudine f; (of season, fame) culmine m. ~en vt fig accrescere

heir /eə(r)/ n erede mf. ~ess n ereditiera f. ~loom n cimelio m di famiglia

held /held/ ▷HOLD[2]

helicopter /'helɪkɒptə(r)/ n elicottero m

hell /hel/ n inferno m; go to ~! 🅇 va' al diavolo! • int porca miseria!

hello /hə'ləʊ/ int & n = hallo

helm /helm/ n timone m; at the ~ fig al timone

helmet /'helmɪt/ n casco m

help /help/ n aiuto m; (employee) aiuto m domestico; that's no ~ non è d'aiuto • vt aiutare; ~ oneself to sth servirsi di qcsa; ~ yourself (at table) serviti pure; I could not ~ laughing non ho potuto trattenermi dal ridere; it cannot be ~ed non c'è niente da fare; I can't ~ it non ci posso far niente • vi aiutare

help|er /'helpə(r)/ n aiutante mf. ~ful adj (person) di aiuto; (advice) utile. ~ing n porzione f. ~less adj (unable to manage) incapace; (powerless) impotente

hem /hem/ n orlo m • vt (pt/pp hemmed) orlare. ~ in vt intrappolare

hemisphere /'hemɪ-/ n emisfero m

hen /hen/ n gallina f; (any female bird) femmina f

hence /hens/ adv (for this reason) quindi. ~forth adv d'ora innanzi

henpecked adj tiranneggiato dalla moglie

her /hɜː(r)/ poss adj il suo m, la sua f, i suoi mpl, le sue fpl; ~ mother/father sua madre/suo padre • pers pron (direct object) la; (indirect object) le; (after prep) lei; I know ~ la conosco; give ~ the money dalle i soldi; give it to ~ daglielo; I came with ~ sono venuto con lei; it's ~ è lei; I've seen ~ l'ho vista; I've seen ~, but not him ho visto lei, ma non lui

herb /hɜːb/ n erba f

herbal /'hɜːb(ə)l/ adj alle erbe; ~ tea tisana f

herd /hɜːd/ n gregge m • vt (tend) sorvegliare; (drive) far muovere; fig ammassare

here /hɪə(r)/ adv qui, qua; in ~ qui dentro; come/bring ~ vieni/porta qui; ~ is..., ~ are... ecco...; ~ you are! ecco qua!. ~'after adv in futuro. ~'by adv con la presente

heredit|ary /hə'redɪtərɪ/ adj ereditario. ~y n eredità f

here|sy /'herəsɪ/ n eresia f. ~tic n eretico, -a mf

here'with adv (Comm) con la presente

heritage /'herɪtɪdʒ/ n eredità f. ~ 'tourism n turismo m culturale

hernia /'hɜːnɪə/ n ernia f

hero /'hɪərəʊ/ n (pl -es) eroe m

heroic /hɪ'rəʊɪk/ adj eroico

heroin /'herəʊɪn/ n eroina f (droga)

hero|ine /'herəʊɪn/ n eroina f. ~ism n eroismo m

heron /'herən/ n airone m

herring /'herɪŋ/ n aringa f

hers /hɜːz/ poss pron il suo m, la sua f, i suoi mpl, le sue fpl; a friend of ~ un suo amico; friends of ~ dei suoi amici; that is ~ quello è suo; (as opposed to mine) quello è il suo

her'self *pers pron* (*reflexive*) si; (*emphatic*) lei stessa; (*after prep*) sé, se stessa; she poured ~ a drink si è versata da bere; she told me so ~ me lo ha detto lei stessa; she's proud of ~ è fiera di sé; by ~ da sola

hesitant /ˈhezɪtənt/ *adj* esitante. ~ly *adv* con esitazione

hesitat|e /ˈhezɪteɪt/ *vi* esitare. ~ion *n* esitazione *f*

hetero'sexual /hetərəʊ-/ *adj* eterosessuale

hexagon /ˈheksəgən/ *n* esagono *m*. ~al *adj* esagonale

hey /heɪ/ *int* ehi

heyday /ˈheɪ-/ *n* tempi *mpl* d'oro

hi /haɪ/ *int* ciao!

hibernat|e /ˈhaɪbəneɪt/ *vi* andare in letargo. ~ion *n* letargo *m*

hiccup /ˈhɪkʌp/ *n* singhiozzo *m*; (🔲: *hitch*) intoppo *m* ● *vi* fare un singhiozzo

hide¹ /haɪd/ *n* (*leather*) pelle *f* (*di animale*)

hide² *vt* (*pt* hid, *pp* hidden) nascondere ● *vi* nascondersi. ~-and-'seek *n* play ~-and-seek giocare a nascondino

hideous /ˈhɪdɪəs/ *adj* orribile

'hide-out *n* nascondiglio *m*

hiding¹ /ˈhaɪdɪŋ/ *n* (🔲: *beating*) bastonata *f*; (*defeat*) batosta *f*

hiding² *n* go into ~ sparire dalla circolazione

hierarchy /ˈhaɪərɑːkɪ/ *n* gerarchia *f*

hieroglyphics /haɪərəˈɡlɪfɪks/ *npl* geroglifici *mpl*

hi-fi /ˈhaɪfaɪ/ *n* 🔲 stereo *m*, hi-fi *m* *inv* ● *adj* 🔲 ad alta fedeltà

high /haɪ/ *adj* alto; (*meat*) che comincia ad andare a male; (*wind*) forte; (*on drugs*) fatto; it's ~ time we did something about it è ora di fare qualcosa in proposito ● *adv* in alto; ~ and low in lungo e in largo

● *n* massimo *m*; (*temperature*) massima *f*; be on a ~ 🔲 essere fatto

high: ~er education *n* formazione *f* universitaria. ~'-handed *adj* dispotico. ~ heels *npl* tacchi *mpl* alti

highlight /ˈhaɪlaɪt/ *n* fig momento *m* clou; ~s *pl* (*in hair*) mèche *fpl* ● *vt* (*emphasize*) evidenziare. ~er *n* (*marker*) evidenziatore *m*

highly /ˈhaɪlɪ/ *adv* molto; speak ~ of lodare; think ~ of avere un'alta opinione di. ~'-strung *adj* nervoso

high: ~-rise *adj* (*building*) molto alto ● *n* edificio *m* molto alto. ~ school *n* ≈ scuola *f* superiore. ~ street *n* strada *f* principale. ~way code *n* codice *m* stradale

---

High School Negli Stati Uniti indica la scuola superiore, generalmente per studenti di età compresa tra i 14 e i 18 anni. In Gran Bretagna il termine è usato solo nella denominazione di alcune scuole.

---

hijack /ˈhaɪdʒæk/ *vt* dirottare ● *n* dirottamento *m*. ~er *n* dirottatore, -trice *mf*

hike /haɪk/ *n* escursione *f* a piedi ● *vi* fare un'escursione a piedi. ~r *n* escursionista *mf*

hilarious /hɪˈleərɪəs/ *adj* esilarante

hill /hɪl/ *n* collina *f*; (*mound*) collinetta *f*; (*slope*) altura *f*

hill: ~side *n* pendio *m*. ~y *adj* collinoso

hilt /hɪlt/ *n* impugnatura *f*; to the ~ (*support*) fino in fondo; (*mortgaged*) fino al collo

him /hɪm/ *pers pron* (*direct object*) lo; (*indirect object*) gli; (*with prep*) lui; I know ~ lo conosco; give ~ the money dagli i soldi; give it to ~ daglielo; I spoke to ~ gli ho parlato; it's ~ è lui; she loves ~ lo ama; she loves ~, not you ama lui, non te. ~'self *pers pron* (*reflexive*) si;

(emphatic) lui stesso; (after prep) sé, se stesso; he poured ~ a drink si è versato da bere; he told me so ~self me lo ha detto lui stesso; he's proud of ~self è fiero di sé; by ~self da solo

hind|er /'hɪndə(r)/ vt intralciare. ~rance n intralcio m

hindsight /'haɪnd-/ n with ~ con il senno del poi

Hindu /'hɪndu:/ n indù m f inv ● adj indù. ~ism n induismo m

hinge /hɪndʒ/ n cardine m ● vi ~ on fig dipendere da

hint /hɪnt/ n (clue) accenno m; (advice) suggerimento m; (indirect suggestion) allusione f; (trace) tocco m ● vt ~ that... far capire che... ● vi ~ at alludere a

hip /hɪp/ n fianco m

hippie /'hɪpɪ/ n hippy m f inv

hippopotamus /hɪpə'pɒtəməs/ n (pl -muses or -mi /-maɪ/) ippopotamo m

hire /'haɪə(r)/ vt affittare; assumere (person); ~ [out] affittare ● n noleggio m; 'for ~' 'affittasi'. ~ car n macchina f a noleggio. ~ purchase n acquisto m rateale

his /hɪz/ poss adj il suo m, la sua f, i suoi mpl, le sue fpl; ~ mother/father sua madre/suo padre ● poss pron il suo m, la sua f, i suoi mpl, le sue fpl; a friend of ~ un suo amico; friends of ~ dei suoi amici; that is ~ questo è suo; (as opposed to mine) questo è il suo

hiss /hɪs/ n sibilo m; (of disapproval) fischio m ● vt fischiare ● vi sibilare; (in disapproval) fischiare

historian /hɪ'stɔ:rɪən/ n storico, -a mf

history /'hɪstərɪ/ n storia f; make ~ passare alla storia

hit /hɪt/ n (blow) colpo m; (fig: success) successo m; score a direct ~ (missile:) colpire in pieno ● vt/i (pt/pp hit,

pres p hitting) colpire; ~ one's head on the table battere la testa contro il tavolo; the car ~ the wall la macchina ha sbattuto contro il muro; ~ the roof 🅵 perdere le staffe. □~ off vt ~ it off andare d'accordo. □~ on vt fig trovare

hitch /hɪtʃ/ n intoppo m; technical ~ problema m tecnico ● vt attaccare; ~ a lift chiedere un passaggio. □~ up vt tirarsi su (trousers). ~hike vi fare l'autostop. ~hiker n autostoppista mf

hither /'hɪðə(r)/ adv ~ and thither di qua e di là. ~to adv finora

hit-or-miss adj on a very ~ basis all'improvvista

hive /haɪv/ n alveare m; ~ of industry fucina f di lavoro ● hive off vt (Comm) separare

hoard /hɔːd/ n provvista f; (of money) gruzzolo m ● vt accumulare

hoarding /'hɔːdɪŋ/ n palizzata f; (with advertisements) tabellone m per manifesti pubblicitari

hoarse /hɔːs/ adj rauco. ~ly adv con voce rauca. ~ness n raucedine f

hoax /həʊks/ n scherzo m; (false alarm) falso allarme m. ~er n burlone, -a mf

hob /hɒb/ n piano m di cottura

hobble /'hɒbl/ vi zoppicare

hobby /'hɒbɪ/ n hobby m inv. ~-horse n fig fissazione f

hockey /'hɒkɪ/ n hockey m

hoe /həʊ/ n zappa f

hog /hɒg/ n maiale m ● vt (pt/pp hogged) 🅵 monopolizzare

hoist /hɔɪst/ n montacarichi m inv; (🅵: push) spinta f in su ● vt sollevare; innalzare (flag); levare (anchor)

hold[1] /həʊld/ n (Aeron, Naut) stiva f

hold[2] /həʊld/ n presa f; (fig: influence) ascendente m; get ~ of trovare; procurarsi (information) ● v (pt/pp held) ● vt tenere; (container:) contenere; essere titolare di (licence, passport);

trattenere (breath, suspect); mantenere vivo (interest); (civil servant etc:) occupare (position); (retain) mantenere; ~ sb's hand tenere qcno per mano; ~ one's tongue tenere la bocca chiusa; ~ sb responsible considerare qcno responsabile; ~ that (believe) ritenere che ● vi tenere; (weather, luck:) durare; (offer:) essere valido; (Teleph) restare in linea; I don't ~ with the idea that... 🛈 non sono d'accordo sul fatto che... □~ **back** vt rallentare ● vi esitare. □~ **down** vt tenere a bada (sb). □~ **on** vi (wait) attendere; (Teleph) restare in linea. □~ **on to** vt aggrapparsi a; (keep) tenersi. □~ **out** vt porgere (hand); fig offrire (possibility) ● vi (resist) resistere. □~ **up** vt tenere su; (delay) rallentare; (rob) assalire; ~ one's head up fig tenere la testa alta

hold: ~**all** n borsone m. ~**er** n titolare m; (of record) detentore, -trice mf; (container) astuccio m. ~**-up** n ritardo m; (attack) rapina f a mano armata

hole /həʊl/ n buco m

holiday /'hɒlɪdeɪ/ n vacanza f; (public) giorno m festivo; (day off) giorno m di ferie; go on ~ andare in vacanza ● vi andare in vacanza. ~**-maker** n vacanziere f

holiness /'həʊlɪnəs/ n santità f; Your H~ Sua Santità

Holland /'hɒlənd/ n Olanda f

hollow /'hɒləʊ/ adj cavo; (promise) a vuoto; (voice) assente; (cheeks) infossato ● n cavità f inv; (in ground) affossamento m

holly /'hɒlɪ/ n agrifoglio m

holocaust /'hɒləkɔːst/ n olocausto m

holster /'həʊlstə(r)/ n fondina f

holy /'həʊlɪ/ adj (-ier, -est) santo; (water) benedetto. H~ Ghost or Spirit n Spirito m Santo. H~ Scriptures npl sacre scritture fpl. H~ Week n settimana f santa

homage /'hɒmɪdʒ/ n omaggio m; pay ~ to rendere omaggio a

home /həʊm/ n casa f; (for children) istituto m; (for old people) casa f di riposo; (native land) patria f ● adv at ~ a casa; (football) in casa; feel at ~ sentirsi a casa propria; come/go venire/andare a casa; drive a nail ~ piantare un chiodo a fondo ● adj domestico; (movie, video) casalingo; (team) ospitante; (Pol) nazionale

home: ~ **ad'dress** n indirizzo m di casa. ~**land** n patria f; ~**land se'curity** n sicurezza f delle frontiere. ~**less** adj senza tetto

homely /'həʊmlɪ/ adj (-ier, -iest) semplice; (atmosphere) familiare; (Am: ugly) bruttino

home: ~**-'made** adj fatto in casa. H~ **Office** n Br ministero m degli interni. ~**sick** adj be ~sick avere nostalgia (for di). ~ **town** n città f inv natia. ~**work** n (Sch) compiti mpl

homicide /'hɒmɪsaɪd/ n (crime) omicidio m

homoeopath|ic /həʊmɪəʊˈpæθɪk/ adj omeopatico. ~**y** n omeopatia f

homogeneous /həmədʒɪˈnɪəs/ adj omogeneo

homo'sexual adj & n omosessuale mf

honest /'ɒnɪst/ adj onesto; (frank) sincero. ~**ly** adv onestamente; (frankly) sinceramente; ~ly! ma insommal. ~**y** n onestà f; (frankness) sincerità f

honey /'hʌnɪ/ n miele m; (🛈: darling) tesoro m

honey: ~**comb** n favo m. ~**moon** n luna f di miele. ~**suckle** n caprifoglio m

honorary /'ɒnərərɪ/ adj onorario

honour /'ɒnə(r)/ n onore m ● vt onorare. ~**able** adj onorevole. ~**ably** adv con onore. ~ **degree** n ≈ diploma m di laurea

hood /hʊd/ n cappuccio m; (of pram)

tettuccio m; (over cooker) cappa f; Am (Auto) cofano m

hoodlum /ˈhuːdləm/ n teppista m

'hoodwink vt 🔟 infinocchiare

hoof /huːf/ n (pl ∼s or hooves) zoccolo m

hook /huk/ n gancio m; (for fishing) amo m; off the ∼ (Teleph) staccato; fig fuori pericolo ● vt agganciare ● vi agganciarsi

hook|ed /hukt/ adj (nose) adunco ∼ed on (🗓: drugs) dedito a; be ∼ed on skiing essere un fanatico dello sci. ∼er n Am 🗓 battona f

hookey /ˈhuki/ n play ∼ Am 🗓 marinare la scuola

hooligan /ˈhuːlɪgən/ n teppista mf. ∼ism n teppismo m

hoop /huːp/ n cerchio m

hooray /huˈreɪ/ int & n = hurrah

hoot /huːt/ n colpo m di clacson; (of siren) ululato m; (of owl) grido m ● vi (owl:) gridare; (car:) clacsonare; (siren:) ululare; (jeer) fischiare. ∼er n (of factory) sirena f; (Auto) clacson m inv

hoover® /ˈhuːvə(r)/ n aspirapolvere m inv ● vt passare l'aspirapolvere su (carpet); passare l'aspirapolvere in (room)

hop /hɒp/ n saltello m ● vi (pt/pp hopped) saltellare; ∼ it! 🗓 tela!. □ ∼ in vi 🗓 saltar su

hope /həup/ n speranza f ● vi sperare (for sth); I ∼ so/not spero di sì/ no ● vt ∼ that sperare che

hope|ful /ˈhəupfl/ adj pieno di speranza; (promising) promettente; be ∼ful that avere molte buone speranze che. ∼fully adv con speranza; (it is hoped) se tutto va bene. ∼less adj senza speranze; (useless) impossibile; (incompetent) incapace. ∼lessly adv disperatamente; (inefficient, lost) completamente. ∼lessness n disperazione f

horde /hɔːd/ n orda f

horizon /həˈraɪzn/ n orizzonte m

horizontal /hɒrɪˈzɒntl/ adj orizzontale

hormone /ˈhɔːməun/ n ormone m

horn /hɔːn/ n corno m; (Auto) clacson m inv

horoscope /ˈhɒrəskəup/ n oroscopo m

horribl|e /ˈhɒrɪbl/ adj orribile. ∼y adv spaventosamente

horrid /ˈhɒrɪd/ adj orrendo

horrific /həˈrɪfɪk/ adj raccapricciante; (accident, prices, story) terrificante

horrify /ˈhɒrɪfaɪ/ vt (pt/pp -ied) far inorridire; I was horrified ero sconvolto. ∼ing adj terrificante

horror /ˈhɒrə(r)/ n orrore m. ∼ film n film m dell'orrore

horse /hɔːs/ n cavallo m

horse: ∼back n on ∼back a cavallo. ∼power n cavallo m [vapore]. ∼-racing n corse fpl di cavalli. ∼shoe n ferro m di cavallo

horti'cultural /hɔːtɪ-/ adj di orticoltura

'horticulture n orticoltura f

hose /həuz/ n (pipe) manichetta f ● hose down vt lavare con la manichetta

hospice /ˈhɒspɪs/ n (for the terminally ill) ospedale m per i malati in fase terminale

hospitabl|e /hɒˈspɪtəbl/ adj ospitale. ∼y adv con ospitalità

hospital /ˈhɒspɪtl/ n ospedale m

hospitality /hɒspɪˈtælətɪ/ n ospitalità f

host¹ /həust/ n a ∼ of una moltitudine di

host² n ospite m

host³ n (Relig) ostia f

hostage /ˈhɒstɪdʒ/ n ostaggio m; hold sb ∼ tenere qcno in ostaggio

hostel /ˈhɒstl/ n ostello m

hostess /ˈhəustɪs/ n padrona f di

casa; (Aeron) hostess f inv

hostile /ˈhɒstaɪl/ adj ostile

hostilit|y /hɒˈstɪlətɪ/ n ostilità f; ~ies pl ostilità fpl

hot /hɒt/ adj (hotter, hottest) caldo; (spicy) piccante; I am or feel ~ ho caldo; it is ~ fa caldo

hotbed n fig focolaio m

hotchpotch /ˈhɒtʃpɒtʃ/ n miscuglio m

hot-dog n hot dog m inv

hotel /həʊˈtel/ n albergo m. ~ier n albergatore, -trice mf

hot: ~**house** n serra f. ~**plate** n piastra f riscaldante ~-**water bottle** n borsa f dell'acqua calda

hound /haʊnd/ n cane m da caccia ● vt fig perseguire

hour /ˈaʊə(r)/ n ora f. ~ly adj ad ogni ora; (pay, rate) a ora ● adv ogni ora

house¹ /haʊs/: ~**boat** n casa f galleggiante. ~**breaking** n furto m con scasso. ~**hold** n casa f, famiglia f. ~**holder** n capo m di famiglia. ~**keeper** n governante f di casa. ~**keeping** n governo m della casa; (money) soldi mpl per le spese di casa. ~**plant** n pianta f da appartamento. ~**trained** adj che non sporca in casa. ~-**warming party** n festa f di inaugurazione della nuova casa. ~**wife** n casalinga f. ~**work** n lavoro m domestico

house¹ /haʊs/ n casa f; (Pol) camera f; (Theat) sala f; at my ~ a casa mia, da me

house² /haʊz/ vt alloggiare (person)

housing /ˈhaʊzɪŋ/ n alloggio m. ~ estate n zona f residenziale

hovel /ˈhɒvl/ n tugurio m

hover /ˈhɒvə(r)/ vi librarsi; (linger) indugiare. ~**craft** n hovercraft m inv

how /haʊ/ adv come; ~ are you? come stai?; ~ about a coffee/going on holiday? che ne diresti di un caffè/di andare in vacanza?; ~

do you do? molto lieto!; ~ old are you? quanti anni hai?; ~ long quanto tempo; ~ many quanti; ~ much quanto; ~ often ogni quanto; and ~! eccome!; ~ odd! che strano!

how'ever adv (nevertheless) comunque; ~ small per quanto piccolo

howl /haʊl/ n ululato m ● vi ululare; (cry, with laughter) singhiozzare. ~**er** n 🛈 strafalcione m

HP n abbr hire purchase; n abbr (horse power) C.V.

hub /hʌb/ n mozzo m; fig centro m

'hub-cap n coprimozzo m

huddle /ˈhʌdl/ vi ~ together rannicchiarsi

hue¹ /hjuː/ n colore m

hue² n ~ and cry clamore m

huff /hʌf/ n be in/go into a ~ fare il broncio

hug /hʌg/ n abbraccio m ● vt (pt/pp hugged) abbracciare; (keep close to) tenersi vicino a

huge /hjuːdʒ/ adj enorme

hull /hʌl/ n (Naut) scafo m

hullo /hʌˈləʊ/ int = hallo

hum /hʌm/ n ronzio m ● v (pt/pp hummed) ● vt canticchiare ● vi (motor:) ronzare; fig fervere (di attività); ~ and haw esitare

human /ˈhjuːmən/ adj umano ● n essere m umano. ~ 'being n essere m umano

humane /hjuːˈmeɪn/ adj umano

humanitarian /hjuːmænɪˈteərɪən/ adj & n umanitario, -a mf

humanit|y /hjuːˈmænɪtɪ/ n umanità f; ~ies pl (Univ) dottrine fpl umanistiche

humbl|e /ˈhʌmbl/ adj umile ● vt umiliare

'humdrum adj noioso

humid /ˈhjuːmɪd/ adj umido. ~ifier n umidificatore m. ~ity /-ˈmɪdətɪ/ n umidità f

h

humiliat|e /hjuːˈmɪlɪeɪt/ vt umiliare. **~ion** n umiliazione f

humility /hjuːˈmɪlətɪ/ n umiltà f

humorous /ˈhjuːmərəs/ adj umoristico. **~ly** adv con spirito

humour /ˈhjuːmə(r)/ n umorismo m; (mood) umore m; have a sense of ~ avere il senso dell'umorismo ● vt compiacere

hump /hʌmp/ n protuberanza f; (of camel, hunchback) gobba f

hunch /hʌntʃ/ n (idea) intuizione f

'hunch|back n gobbo, -a mf. **~ed** adj ~ed up incurvato

hundred /ˈhʌndrəd/ adj one/a ~ cento ● n cento m; ~s of centinaia di. **~th** adj centesimo ● n centesimo m. **~weight** n cinquanta chili m

hung /hʌŋ/ ▷ HANG

Hungarian /hʌŋˈgeərɪən/ n & adj ungherese mf; (language) ungherese m

Hungary /ˈhʌŋgərɪ/ n Ungheria f

hunger /ˈhʌŋgə(r)/ n fame f. **~-strike** n sciopero m della fame m

hungr|y /ˈhʌŋgrɪ/ adj (-ier, -iest) affamato; be ~y aver fame. **~ily** adv con appetito

hunk /hʌŋk/ n (grosso) pezzo m

hunt /hʌnt/ n caccia f ● vt andare a caccia di (animal); dare la caccia a (criminal) ● vi andare a caccia; ~ for cercare. **~er** n cacciatore m. **~ing** n caccia f

hurl /hɜːl/ vt scagliare

hurrah /hʊˈrɑː/, **hurray** /hʊˈreɪ/ int urrà ● n urrà m

hurricane /ˈhʌrɪkən/ n uragano m

hurried /ˈhʌrɪd/ adj affrettato; (job) fatto in fretta. **~ly** adv in fretta

hurry /ˈhʌrɪ/ n fretta f; be in a ~ aver fretta ● vi (pt/pp -ied) affrettarsi. **□ ~ up** vi sbrigarsi ● vt fare sbrigare (person); accelerare (things)

hurt /hɜːt/ v (pt/pp hurt) ● vt far male a; (offend) ferire ● vi far male; my leg ~s mi fa male la gamba.

~ful adj fig offensivo

hurtle /ˈhɜːtl/ vi ~ along andare a tutta velocità

husband /ˈhʌzbənd/ n marito m

hush /hʌʃ/ n silenzio m ● hush up vt mettere a tacere. **~ed** adj (voice) sommesso. **~-'hush** adj 🔲 segretissimo

husky /ˈhʌskɪ/ adj (-ier, -iest) (voice) rauco

hustle /ˈhʌsl/ vt affrettare ● n attività f incessante; ~ and bustle trambusto m

hut /hʌt/ n capanna f

hybrid /ˈhaɪbrɪd/ adj ibrido ● n ibrido m

hydrant /ˈhaɪdrənt/ n [fire] ~ idrante m

hydraulic /haɪˈdrɔːlɪk/ adj idraulico

hydroe'lectric /haɪdrəʊ-/ adj idroelettrico

hydrofoil /ˈhaɪdrə-/ n aliscafo m

hydrogen /ˈhaɪdrədʒən/ n idrogeno m

hyena /haɪˈiːnə/ n iena f

hygien|e /ˈhaɪdʒiːn/ n igiene f. **~ic** adj igienico

hymn /hɪm/ n inno m. **~-book** n libro m dei canti

hypermarket /ˈhaɪpəmɑːkɪt/ n ipermercato m

hyphen /ˈhaɪfn/ n lineetta f. **~ate** vt unire con lineetta

hypno|sis /hɪpˈnəʊsɪs/ n ipnosi f. **~tic** adj ipnotico

hypno|tism /ˈhɪpnətɪzm/ n ipnotismo m. **~tist** n ipnotizzatore, -trice mf. **~tize** vt ipnotizzare

hypochondriac /haɪpə-ˈkɒndrɪæk/ adj ipocondriaco ● n ipocondriaco, -a mf

hypocrisy /hɪˈpɒkrəsɪ/ n ipocrisia f

hypocrit|e /ˈhɪpəkrɪt/ n ipocrita mf. **~ical** adj ipocrita

hypodermic /haɪpəˈdɜːmɪk/ adj & n ~ [syringe] siringa f ipodermica

hypothe|sis /haɪˈpɒθəsɪs/ n ipotesi f inv. ~**tical** adj ipotetico. ~**tically** adv in teoria; (speak) per ipotesi

hyster|ia /hɪˈstɪərɪə/ n isterismo m. ~**ical** adj isterico. ~**ically** adv istericamente; ~**ically funny** da morir dal ridere. ~**ics** npl attacco m isterico

· · · · · · · · · · · · · · · · · · · ·

Ii

· · · · · · · · · · · · · · · · · · · ·

I /aɪ/ pron io; **I'm tired** sono stanco; **he's going, but I'm not** lui va, ma io no

ice /aɪs/ n ghiaccio m ● vt glassare (cake). □ ~ **over/up** vi ghiacciarsi

ice: ~**-axe** n piccozza f per il ghiaccio. ~**berg** /-bɜ:g/ n iceberg m inv. ~**box** n Am frigorifero m. ~'**cream** n gelato m. ~**-cube** n cubetto m di ghiaccio

Iceland /ˈaɪslənd/ n Islanda f. ~**er** n islandese mf; ~**ic** /-ˈlændɪk/ adj & n islandese m

ice: ~**-lolly** n ghiacciolo m. ~ **rink** n pista f di pattinaggio. ~ **skater** pattinatore, -trice mf sul ghiaccio. ~ **skating** pattinaggio m su ghiaccio

icicle /ˈaɪsɪkl/ n ghiacciolo m

icing /ˈaɪsɪŋ/ n glassa f. ~ **sugar** n zucchero m a velo

icon /ˈaɪkɒn/ n icona f

ic|y /ˈaɪsɪ/ adj (-ier, -iest) ghiacciato; fig gelido. ~**ily** adv gelidamente

idea /aɪˈdɪə/ n idea f; **I've no** ~! non ne ho idea!

ideal /aɪˈdɪəl/ adj ideale ● n ideale m. ~**ism** n idealismo m. ~**ist** n idealista mf. ~**istic** adj idealistico. ~**ize** vt idealizzare. ~**ly** adv idealmente

identical /aɪˈdentɪkl/ adj identico

identi|fication /aɪdentɪfɪˈkeɪʃn/ n identificazione f; (proof of identity) documento m di riconoscimento. ~**fy** vt (pt/pp -ied) identificare

identity /aɪˈdentətɪ/ n identità f inv. ~ **card** n carta f d'identità. ~ **theft** n furto m d'identità

ideolog|ical /aɪdɪəˈlɒdʒɪkl/ adj ideologico. ~**y** n ideologia f

idiom /ˈɪdɪəm/ n idioma f. ~**atic** adj idiomatico

idiot /ˈɪdɪət/ n idiota mf. ~**ic** adj idiota

idl|e /ˈaɪd(ə)l/ adj (lazy) pigro, ozioso; (empty) vano; (machine) fermo ● vi oziare; (engine): girare a vuoto. ~**eness** n ozio m. ~**y** adv oziosamente

idol /ˈaɪdl/ n idolo m. ~**ize** vt idolatrare

idyllic /ɪˈdɪlɪk/ adj idillico

i.e. abbr (id est) cioè

if /ɪf/ conj se; **as if** come se

ignite /ɪgˈnaɪt/ vt dar fuoco a ● vi prender fuoco

ignition /ɪgˈnɪʃn/ n (Auto) accensione f. ~ **key** n chiave f d'accensione

ignoramus /ɪgnəˈreɪməs/ n ignorante mf

ignoran|ce /ˈɪgnərəns/ n ignoranza f. ~**t** adj (lacking knowledge) ignaro; (rude) ignorante

ignore /ɪgˈnɔ:(r)/ vt ignorare

ill /ɪl/ adj ammalato; **feel** ~ sentirsi a disagio ● adv male ● n male m. ~**-advised** adj avventato. ~**-bred** adj maleducato

illegal /ɪˈli:gl/ adj illegale

illegibl|e /ɪˈledʒɪbl/ adj illeggibile

illegitima|cy /ɪlɪˈdʒɪtɪməsɪ/ n illegittimità f. ~**te** adj illegittimo

illitera|cy /ɪˈlɪtərəsɪ/ n analfabetismo m. ~**te** adj & n analfabeta mf

illness /ˈɪlnɪs/ n malattia f

illogical /ɪˈlɒdʒɪkl/ adj illogico

h
i

illuminat|e /ɪˈluːmɪneɪt/ vt illuminare. ~ing adj chiarificatore. ~ion n illuminazione f

illusion /ɪˈluːʒn/ n illusione f; be under the ~ that avere l'illusione che

illustrat|e /ˈɪləstreɪt/ vt illustrare. ~ion n illustrazione f. ~or n illustratore, -trice mf

illustrious /ɪˈlʌstrɪəs/ adj illustre

ill 'will n malanimo m

image /ˈɪmɪdʒ/ n immagine f; (exact likeness) ritratto m

imagin|able /ɪˈmædʒɪnəbl/ adj immaginabile. ~ary adj immaginario

imaginat|ion /ɪmædʒɪˈneɪʃn/ n immaginazione f, fantasia f; it's your ~ion è solo una tua idea. ~ive adj fantasioso. ~ively adv con fantasia or immaginazione

imagine /ɪˈmædʒɪn/ vt immaginare; (wrongly) inventare

im'balance n squilibrio m

imbecile /ˈɪmbəsiːl/ n imbecille mf

imitat|e /ˈɪmɪteɪt/ vt imitare. ~ion n imitazione f. ~or n imitatore, -trice mf

immaculate /ɪˈmækjʊlət/ adj immacolato. ~ly adv immacolatamente

imma'ture adj immaturo

immediate /ɪˈmiːdɪət/ adj immediato; (relative) stretto; in the ~ vicinity nelle immediate vicinanze. ~ly adv immediatamente; ~ly next to subito accanto a ● conj [non] appena

immense /ɪˈmens/ adj immenso

immers|e /ɪˈmɜːs/ vt immergere; be ~ed in fig essere immerso in. ~ion n immersione f. ~ion heater n scaldabagno m elettrico

immigrant /ˈɪmɪɡrənt/ n immigrante m

imminent /ˈɪmɪnənt/ adj imminente

immobil|e /ɪˈməʊbaɪl/ adj immobile. ~ize vt immobilizzare

immoderate /ɪˈmɒdərət/ adj smodato

immoral /ɪˈmɒrəl/ adj immorale. ~ity n immoralità f

immortal /ɪˈmɔːtl/ adj immortale. ~ity n immortalità f. ~ize vt immortalare

immune /ɪˈmjuːn/ adj immune (to/from da). ~ system n sistema m immunitario

immunity /ɪˈmjuːnətɪ/ n immunità f

immuniz|e /ˈɪmjʊnaɪz/ vt immunizzare

imp /ɪmp/ n diavoletto m

impact /ˈɪmpækt/ n impatto m

impair /ɪmˈpeə(r)/ vt danneggiare

impale /ɪmˈpeɪl/ vt impalare

impart /ɪmˈpɑːt/ vt impartire

im'partial adj imparziale. ~ality n imparzialità f

im'passable adj impraticabile

im'passive adj impassibile

im'patien|ce n impazienza f. ~t adj impaziente. ~tly adv impazientemente

impeccabl|e /ɪmˈpekəbl/ adj impeccabile. ~y adv in modo impeccabile

impede /ɪmˈpiːd/ vt impedire

impediment /ɪmˈpedɪmənt/ n impedimento m; (in speech) difetto m

impending /ɪmˈpendɪŋ/ adj imminente

impenetrable /ɪmˈpenɪtrəbl/ adj impenetrabile

imperative /ɪmˈperətɪv/ adj imperativo ● n (Gram) imperativo m

imper'ceptible adj impercettibile

im'perfect adj imperfetto; (faulty) difettoso ● n (Gram) imperfetto m. ~ion n imperfezione f

imperial /ɪmˈpɪərɪəl/ adj imperiale. ~ism n imperialismo m. ~ist n imperialista mf

im'personal *adj* impersonale
impersonat|e /ɪm'pɜːsəneɪt/ *vt* impersonare. ~or *n* imitatore, -trice *mf*
impertinen|ce /ɪm'pɜːtɪnəns/ *n* impertinenza *f*. ~t *adj* impertinente
impervious /ɪm'pɜːvɪəs/ *adj* ~ to *fig* indifferente a
impetuous /ɪm'petjuəs/ *adj* impetuoso. ~ly *adv* impetuosamente
impetus /'ɪmpɪtəs/ *n* impeto *m*
implacable /ɪm'plækəbl/ *adj* implacabile
im'plant¹ *vt* trapiantare; *fig* inculcare
'implant² *n* trapianto *m*
implement¹ /'ɪmplɪmənt/ *n* attrezzo *m*
implement² /'ɪmplɪment/ *vt* mettere in atto. ~ation /-'eɪʃn/ *n* attuazione *f*
implicat|e /'ɪmplɪkeɪt/ *vt* implicare. ~ion *n* implicazione *f*; by ~ion implicitamente
implicit /ɪm'plɪsɪt/ *adj* implicito; (absolute) assoluto
implore /ɪm'plɔː(r)/ *vt* implorare
imply /ɪm'plaɪ/ *vt* (pt/pp -ied) implicare; what are you ~ing? che cosa vorresti insinuare?
impo'lite *adj* sgarbato
import¹ /'ɪmpɔːt/ *n* (Comm) importazione *f*
import² /ɪm'pɔːt/ *vt* importare
importan|ce /ɪm'pɔːtəns/ *n* importanza *f*. ~t *adj* importante
importer /ɪm'pɔːtə(r)/ *n* importatore, -trice *mf*
impos|e /ɪm'pəʊz/ *vt* imporre (on a) • *vi* imporsi; ~e on abusare di. ~ing *adj* imponente. ~ition *n* imposizione *f*
impossi'bility *n* impossibilità *f*
im'possibl|e *adj* impossibile
impostor /ɪm'pɒstə(r)/ *n* impostore, -trice *mf*

impoten|ce /'ɪmpətəns/ *n* impotenza *f*. ~t *adj* impotente
impound /ɪm'paʊnd/ *vt* confiscare
impoverished /ɪm'pɒvərɪʃt/ *adj* impoverito
im'practical *adj* non pratico
impregnable /ɪm'pregnəbl/ *adj* imprendibile
impregnate /'ɪmpregneɪt/ *vt* impregnare (with di); (Biol) fecondare
im'press *vt* imprimere; *fig* colpire (positivamente); ~ sth on sb fare capire qcsa a qcno
impression /ɪm'preʃn/ *n* impressione *f*; (imitation) imitazione *f*. ~able *adj* (child, mind) influenzabile. ~ism *n* impressionismo *m*. ~ist *n* imitatore, -trice *mf*; (artist) impressionista *mf*
impressive /ɪm'presɪv/ *adj* imponente
imprint¹ *n* impressione *f*
im'print² *vt* imprimere; ~ed on my mind impresso nella mia memoria
im'prison *vt* incarcerare. ~ment *n* reclusione *f*
im'probable *adj* improbabile
impromptu /ɪm'prɒmptjuː/ *adj* improvvisato
im'proper *adj* (use) improprio; (behaviour) scorretto. ~ly *adv* scorrettamente
improve /ɪm'pruːv/ *vt/i* migliorare. improve on *vt* perfezionare. ~ment *n* miglioramento *m*
improvis|e /'ɪmprəvaɪz/ *vt/i* improvvisare
impuden|ce /'ɪmpjʊdəns/ *n* sfrontatezza *f*. ~t *adj* sfrontato
impuls|e /'ɪmpʌls/ *n* impulso *m*; on [an] ~e impulsivamente. ~ive *adj* impulsivo
im'pur|e *adj* impuro. ~ity *n* impurità *f inv*; ~ities *pl* impurità *fpl*
in /ɪn/ *prep* in; (with names of towns) a;

in the garden in giardino; in the street in *or* per strada; in bed/hospital a letto/all'ospedale; in the world nel mondo; in the rain sotto la pioggia; in the sun al sole; in this heat con questo caldo; in summer/winter in estate/inverno; in 1995 nel 1995; in the evening la sera; he's arriving in two hours time arriva fra due ore; deaf in one ear sordo da un orecchio; in the army nell'esercito; in English/Italian in inglese/italiano; in ink/pencil a penna/matita; in red (dressed, circled) di rosso; the man in the raincoat l'uomo con l'impermeabile; in a soft/loud voice a voce bassa/alta; one in ten people una persona su dieci; in doing this, he... nel far questo,...; in itself in sé; in that in quanto ● adv (*at home*) a casa; (*indoors*) dentro; he's not in yet non è ancora arrivato; in there/here lì/qui dentro; ten in all dieci in tutto; day in, day out giorno dopo giorno; have it in for sb 🇮🇹 avercela con qcno; send him in fallo entrare; come in entrare; bring in the washing portare dentro i panni ● adj (🇮🇹: *in fashion*) di moda ● n the ins and outs i dettagli

ina'bility n incapacità f

inac'cessible adj inaccessibile

in'accuracy n inesattezza f. ~te adj inesatto

in'ac|tive adj inattivo. ~'tivity n inattività f

in'adequate adj inadeguato. ~ly adv inadeguatamente

inadvertently /ɪnəd'vɜːtəntlɪ/ adv inavvertitamente

inad'visable adj sconsigliabile

inane /ɪ'neɪn/ adj stupido

in'animate adj esanime

inap'propriate adj inadatto

inar'ticulate adj inarticolato

inat'tentive adj disattento

in'audible adj impercettibile

inaugurate /ɪ'nɔːɡjʊreɪt/ vt inaugurare. ~ion n inaugurazione f

inborn /'ɪnbɔːn/ adj innato

inbred /ɪn'bred/ adj congenito

incalculable /ɪn'kælkjʊləbl/ adj incalcolabile

in'capable adj incapace

incapacitate /ɪnkə'pæsɪteɪt/ vt rendere incapace

incarnate /ɪn'kɑːnət/ adj the devil ~e il diavolo in carne e ossa

incendiary /ɪn'sendɪərɪ/ adj incendiario

incense[1] /'ɪnsens/ n incenso m

incense[2] /ɪn'sens/ vt esasperare

incentive /ɪn'sentɪv/ n incentivo m

incessant /ɪn'sesənt/ adj incessante

incest /'ɪnsest/ n incesto m

inch /ɪntʃ/ n pollice m (= 2.54 cm) ● vi ~ forward avanzare gradatamente

inciden|ce /'ɪnsɪdəns/ n incidenza f. ~t n incidente m

incidental /ɪnsɪ'dentl/ adj incidentale; ~ expenses spese fpl accessorie. ~ly adv incidentalmente; (*by the way*) a proposito

incinerate /ɪn'sɪnəreɪt/ vt incenerire. ~or n inceneritore m

incision /ɪn'sɪʒn/ n incisione f

incite /ɪn'saɪt/ vt incitare. ~ment n incitamento m

inclination /ɪnklɪ'neɪʃn/ n inclinazione f

incline[1] /ɪn'klaɪn/ vt inclinare; be ~d to do sth essere propenso a fare qcsa

incline[2] /'ɪnklaɪn/ n pendio m

include /ɪn'kluːd/ vt includere. ~ding prep incluso. ~sion n inclusione f

inclusive /ɪn'kluːsɪv/ adj incluso; ~ of comprendente; be ~ of comprendere ● adv incluso

incognito /ɪnkɒɡ'niːtəʊ/ adv incognito

inco'herent adj incoerente; (be-

cause drunk etc) incomprensibile

income /'mkʌm/ n reddito m. ~ **tax** n imposta f sul reddito

incoming adj in arrivo. ~ **tide** n marea f montante

incomparable adj incomparabile

incompatible adj incompatibile

incompeten|ce n incompetenza f. ~t adj incompetente

incomplete adj incompleto

incomprehensible adj incomprensibile

inconceivable adj inconcepibile

inconclusive adj inconcludente

incongruous /m'kɒŋgrʊəs/ adj contrastante

inconsiderate adj trascurabile

inconsistency n incoerenza f

inconsistent adj incoerente; be ~ with non essere coerente con. ~ly adv in modo incoerente

inconspicuous adj non appariscente. ~ly adv modestamente

inconvenien|ce n scomodità f; (drawback) inconveniente m; put sb to ~ce dare disturbo a qcno. ~t adj scomodo; (time, place) inopportuno. ~tly adv in modo inopportuno

incorporate /m'kɔ:pərət/ vt incorporare; (contain) comprendere

incorrect adj incorretto. ~ly adv scorrettamente

increase¹ /'ɪŋkri:s/ n aumento m; on the ~ in aumento

increase² /ɪŋ'kri:s/ vt/i aumentare. ~ing adj (impatience etc) crescente; (numbers) in aumento. ~ingly adv sempre più

incredible adj incredibile

incredulous /m'kredjʊləs/ adj incredulo

incriminate /m'krɪmɪneɪt/ vt (Jur) incriminare

incubat|e /'ɪŋkjʊbeɪt/ vt incubare. ~ion n incubazione f. ~ion period n (Med) periodo m di incubazione.

~**or** n (for baby) incubatrice f

incur /m'kɜ:(r)/ vt (pt/pp incurred) incorrere; contrarre (debts)

incurable adj incurabile

indebted /m'detɪd/ adj obbligato (to verso)

indecent adj indecente

indecision n indecisione f

indecisive adj indeciso. ~ness n indecisione f

indeed /m'di:d/ adv (in fact) difatti; yes ~! sì, certamente!; ~ I am/do veramente!; very much ~ moltissimo; thank you very much ~ grazie infinite; ~? davvero?

indefinable adj indefinibile

indefinite adj indefinito. ~ly adv indefinitamente; (postpone) a tempo indeterminato

indelible /m'delɪbl/ adj indelebile

indemnity /m'demnɪtɪ/ n indennità f inv

indent¹ /'ɪndent/ n (Typ) rientranza f dal margine

indent² /m'dent/ vt (Typ) fare rientrare dal margine. ~ation n (notch) intaccatura f

independen|ce n indipendenza f. ~t adj indipendente. ~tly adv indipendentemente

indescribable /ɪndɪ'skraɪbəbl/ adj indescrivibile

indestructible /ɪndɪ'strʌktɪbl/ adj indistruttibile

indeterminate /ɪndɪ'tɜːmɪnət/ adj indeterminato

index /'ɪndeks/ n indice m

index: ~ **finger** n dito m indice. ~-'**linked** adj (pension) legato al costo della vita

India /'ɪndɪə/ n India f. ~n adj indiano; (American) indiano [d'America] ● n indiano, -a mf; (American) indiano, -a mf [d'America]

indicat|e /'ɪndɪkeɪt/ vt indicare; (register) segnare ● vi (Auto) mettere la freccia. ~ion n indicazione f.

indicative /ɪnˈdɪkətɪv/ adj be ~ of essere indicativo di ●n (Gram) indicativo m

indicator /ˈɪndɪkeɪtə(r)/ n (Auto) freccia f.

indict /ɪnˈdaɪt/ vt accusare. ~ment n accusa f.

in'differen|ce n indifferenza f. ~t adj indifferente; (not good) mediocre

indi'gestible adj indigesto. ~ion n indigestione f

indigna|nt /ɪnˈdɪgnənt/ adj indignato. ~ntly adv con indignazione. ~tion n indignazione f

indi'rect adj indiretto. ~ly adv indirettamente

indi'screet adj indiscreto

indis'cretion n indiscrezione f

indiscriminate /ɪndɪˈskrɪmɪnət/ adj indiscriminato. ~ly adv senza distinzione

indi'spensable adj indispensabile

indisposed /ɪndɪˈspəʊzd/ adj indisposto

indisputable /ɪndɪˈspjuːtəbl/ adj indisputabile

indistinguishable /ɪndɪˈstɪŋgwɪʃəbl/ adj indistinguibile

individual /ɪndɪˈvɪdjʊəl/ adj individuale ●n individuo m. ~ity n individualità f

indoctrinate /ɪnˈdɒktrɪneɪt/ vt indottrinare

indomitable /ɪnˈdɒmɪtəbl/ adj indomito

indoor /ˈɪndɔː(r)/ adj interno; (shoes) per casa; (plant) da appartamento; (swimming pool etc) coperto. ~s adv dentro

induce /ɪnˈdjuːs/ vt indurre (to a); (produce) causare. ~ment n (incentive) incentivo m

indulge /ɪnˈdʌldʒ/ vt soddisfare; viziare (child) ●vi ~ in concedersi. ~nce n lusso m; (leniency) indulgenza

f. ~nt adj indulgente

industrial /ɪnˈdʌstrɪəl/ adj industriale; take ~ action scioperare. ~ist n industriale mf. ~ized adj industrializzato

industr|ious /ɪnˈdʌstrɪəs/ adj industrioso. ~y n industria f; (zeal) operosità f

inebriated /ɪˈniːbrɪeɪtɪd/ adj ebbro

in'edible adj immangiabile

inef'fective adj inefficace

ineffectual /ɪnɪˈfektʃʊəl/ adj inutile; (person) inconcludente

inef'ficien|cy n inefficienza f. ~t adj inefficiente

in'eligible adj inadatto

inept /ɪˈnept/ adj inetto

ine'quality n ineguaglianza f

inert /ɪˈnɜːt/ adj inerte. ~ia n inerzia f

inescapable /ɪnɪˈskeɪpəbl/ adj inevitabile

inevitabl|e /ɪnˈevɪtəbl/ adj inevitabile. ~y adv inevitabilmente

ine'xact adj inesatto

inex'cusable adj imperdonabile

inex'pensive adj poco costoso

inex'perience n inesperienza f. ~d adj inesperto

inexplicable /ɪnɪkˈsplɪkəbl/ adj inesplicabile

in'fallible adj infallibile

infam|ous /ˈɪnfəməs/ adj infame; (person) infamato. ~y n infamia f

infan|cy /ˈɪnfənsɪ/ n infanzia f; in its ~cy fig agli inizi. ~t n bambino, -a mf piccolo, -a. ~tile adj infantile

infantry /ˈɪnfəntrɪ/ n fanteria f

infatuat|ed /ɪnˈfætʃʊeɪtɪd/ adj infatuato (with di). ~ion n infatuazione f

infect /ɪnˈfekt/ vt infettare; become ~ed (wound:) infettarsi. ~ion adj infettivo

infer /ɪnˈfɜː(r)/ vt (pt/pp inferred) dedurre (from da); (imply) implicare.

~ence n deduzione f

inferior /ɪnˈfɪərɪə(r)/ adj inferiore; (goods) scadente; (in rank) subalterno ● n inferiore mf; (in rank) subalterno, -a mf

inferiority /ɪnfɪərɪˈɒrətɪ/ n inferiorità f. ~ **complex** n complesso m di inferiorità

in'fertile adj sterile. ~'tility n sterilità f

infest /ɪnˈfest/ vt be ~ed with essere infestato di

infidelity n infedeltà f

infiltrate /ˈɪnfɪltreɪt/ vt infiltrare; (Pol) infiltrarsi in

infinite /ˈɪnfɪnət/ adj infinito

infinitive /ɪnˈfɪnətɪv/ n (Gram) infinito m

infinity /ɪnˈfɪnətɪ/ n infinità f

infirm /ɪnˈfɜːm/ adj debole. ~**ary** n infermeria f. ~**ity** n debolezza f

inflame /ɪnˈfleɪm/ vt infiammare. ~d adj infiammato; become ~d infiammarsi

in'flammable adj infiammabile

inflammation /ɪnfləˈmeɪʃn/ n infiammazione f

inflat|e /ɪnˈfleɪt/ vt gonfiare. ~**ion** n inflazione f. ~**ionary** adj inflazionario

in'flexible adj inflessibile

inflict /ɪnˈflɪkt/ vt infliggere (on a)

influen|ce /ˈɪnflʊəns/ n influenza f ● vt influenzare. ~**tial** adj influente

influenza /ɪnflʊˈenzə/ n influenza f

influx /ˈɪnflʌks/ n affluenza f

inform /ɪnˈfɔːm/ vt informare; keep sb ~ed tenere qcno al corrente ● vi ~ against denunziare

in'formal adj informale; (agreement) ufficioso. ~**mally** adv in modo informale. ~**mality** n informalità f inv

nformation /ɪnfəˈmeɪʃn/ n informazioni fpl; a piece of ~ un'informazione. ~**ion highway** n autostrada f telematica. ~**ion**

technology n informatica f. ~**ive** adj informativo; (film, book) istruttivo

informer /ɪnˈfɔːmə(r)/ n informatore, -trice mf; (Pol) delatore, -trice mf

infra-'red /ɪnfrə-/ adj infrarosso

infringe /ɪnˈfrɪndʒ/ vt ~ on usurpare. ~**ment** n violazione f

infuriat|e /ɪnˈfjʊərɪeɪt/ vt infuriare. ~**ing** adj esasperante

ingenious /ɪnˈdʒiːnɪəs/ adj ingegnoso

ingenuity /ɪndʒɪˈnjuːətɪ/ n ingegnosità f

ingot /ˈɪŋgət/ n lingotto m

ingrained /ɪnˈgreɪnd/ adj (in person) radicato; (dirt) incrostato

ingratiate /ɪnˈgreɪʃɪeɪt/ vt ~ oneself with sb ingraziarsi qcno

in'gratitude n ingratitudine f

ingredient /ɪnˈgriːdɪənt/ n ingrediente m

ingrowing /ˈɪngrəʊɪŋ/ adj (nail) incarnito

inhabit /ɪnˈhæbɪt/ vt abitare. ~**ant** n abitante mf

inhale /ɪnˈheɪl/ vt aspirare; (Med) inalare ● vi inspirare; (when smoking) aspirare. ~**r** n (device) inalatore m

inherent /ɪnˈhɪərənt/ adj inerente

inherit /ɪnˈherɪt/ vt ereditare. ~**ance** n eredità f inv

inhibit /ɪnˈhɪbɪt/ vt inibire. ~**ed** adj inibito. ~**ion** n inibizione f

inho'spitable adj inospitale

initial /ɪˈnɪʃl/ adj iniziale ● n iniziale f ● vt (pt/pp initialled) siglare. ~**ly** adv all'inizio

initiat|e /ɪˈnɪʃɪeɪt/ vt iniziare. ~**ion** n iniziazione f

initiative /ɪˈnɪʃətɪv/ n iniziativa f

inject /ɪnˈdʒekt/ vt iniettare. ~**ion** n iniezione f

injur|e /ˈɪndʒə(r)/ vt ferire; (wrong) nuocere. ~**y** n ferita f; (wrong) torto m

i

in'justice n ingiustizia f; do sb an ~ giudicare qcno in modo sbagliato

ink /ɪŋk/ n inchiostro m

inland /'ɪnlənd/ adj interno ● adv all'interno. **I~ Revenue** n fisco m

in-laws /'ɪnlɔːz/ npl [] parenti mpl acquisiti

inlay /'ɪnleɪ/ n intarsio m

inlet /'ɪnlet/ n insenatura f; (Techn) entrata f

inmate /'ɪnmeɪt/ n (of hospital) degente m; (of prison) carcerato, -a mf

inn /ɪn/ n locanda f

innate /ɪ'neɪt/ adj innato

inner /'ɪnə(r)/ adj interno. **~most** adj il più profondo. **~ tube** camera f d'aria

innocen|ce /'ɪnəsəns/ n innocenza f. **~t** adj innocente

innocuous /ɪ'nɒkjʊəs/ adj innocuo

innovat|e /'ɪnəveɪt/ vi innovare. **~ion** n innovazione f. **~ive** adj innovativo. **~or** n innovatore, -trice mf

innuendo /ɪnjʊ'endəʊ/ n (pl -es) insinuazione f

innumerable /ɪ'njuːmərəbl/ adj innumerevole

inoculat|e /ɪ'nɒkjʊleɪt/ vt vaccinare. **~ion** n vaccinazione f

inof'fensive adj inoffensivo

in'opportune adj inopportuno

input /'ɪnpʊt/ n input m inv, ingresso m

inquest /'ɪnkwest/ n inchiesta f

inquir|e /ɪn'kwaɪə(r)/ vi informarsi (about su); **~e into** far indagini su ● vt domandare. **~y** n domanda f; (investigation) inchiesta f

inquisitive /ɪn'kwɪzətɪv/ adj curioso

in'sane adj pazzo; fig insensato

in'sanity n pazzia f

insatiable /ɪn'seɪʃəbl/ adj insaziabile

inscri|be /ɪn'skraɪb/ vt iscrivere. **~ption** n iscrizione f

inscrutable /ɪn'skruːtəbl/ adj impenetrabile

insect /'ɪnsekt/ n insetto m. **~icide** n insetticida m

inse'cur|e adj malsicuro; (fig: person) insicuro. **~ity** n mancanza f di sicurezza

in'sensitive adj insensibile

in'separable adj inseparabile

insert [1] /'ɪnsɜːt/ n inserto m

insert [2] /ɪn'sɜːt/ vt inserire. **~ion** n inserzione f

inside /ɪn'saɪd/ n interno m. **~s** npl [] pancia f ● attrib (Auto) **~ lane** n corsia f interna ● adv dentro; **~ out** a rovescio; (thoroughly) a fondo ● prep dentro; (of time) entro

insight /'ɪnsaɪt/ n intuito m (into per); **an ~ into** uno quadro di

insig'nificant adj insignificante

insin'cer|e adj poco sincero. **~ity** n mancanza f di sincerità

insinuat|e /ɪn'sɪnjʊeɪt/ vt insinuare. **~ion** n insinuazione f

insipid /ɪn'sɪpɪd/ adj insipido

insist /ɪn'sɪst/ vi insistere (on per) ● vt **~ that** insistere che. **~ence** n insistenza f. **~ent** adj insistente

insolen|ce /'ɪnsələns/ n insolenza f. **~t** adj insolente

in'soluble adj insolubile

insomnia /ɪn'sɒmnɪə/ n insonnia f

inspect /ɪn'spekt/ vt ispezionare; controllare (ticket). **~ion** n ispezione f; (of ticket) controllo m. **~or** n ispettore, -trice mf; (of tickets) controllore m

inspiration /ɪnspə'reɪʃn/ n ispirazione f

inspire /ɪn'spaɪə(r)/ vt ispirare

insta'bility n instabilità f

install /ɪn'stɔːl/ vt installare. **~ation** n installazione f

instalment /ɪn'stɔːlmənt/ n (Comm) rata f; (of serial) puntata f; (of publication) fascicolo m

instance /'ɪnstəns/ n (case) caso m; (example) esempio m; in the first ~ in primo luogo; for ~ per esempio

instant /'ɪnstənt/ adj immediato; (Culin) espresso ● n istante m. ~aneous adj istantaneo

instead /ɪn'sted/ adv invece; ~ of doing anziché fare; ~ of me al mio posto; ~ of going invece di andare

instigat|e /'ɪnstɪgeɪt/ vt istigare. ~ion n istigazione f; at his ~ion dietro suo suggerimento. ~or n istigatore, -trice mf

instinct /'ɪnstɪŋkt/ n istinto m. ~ive adj istintivo

institut|e /'ɪnstɪtjuːt/ n istituto m ● vt istituire (scheme); iniziare (search); intentare (legal action). ~ion n istituzione f; (home for elderly) istituto m per anziani; (for mentally ill) istituto m per malati di mente

instruct /ɪn'strʌkt/ vt istruire; (order) ordinare. ~ion n istruzione f; ~s (orders) ordini mpl. ~ive adj istruttivo. ~or n istruttore, -trice mf

instrument /'ɪnstrʊmənt/ n strumento m. ~al adj strumentale; be ~al in contribuire a. ~alist n strumentista mf

insu'bordin|ate adj insubordinato. ~nation n insubordinazione f

in'sufferable adj insopportabile

insuf'ficient adj insufficiente

insular /'ɪnsjʊlə(r)/ adj fig gretto

insulat|e /'ɪnsjʊleɪt/ vt isolare. ~ing tape n nastro m isolante. ~ion n isolamento m

insulin /'ɪnsjʊlɪn/ n insulina f

insult[1] /'ɪnsʌlt/ n insulto m

insult[2] /ɪn'sʌlt/ vt insultare

insur|ance /ɪn'ʃʊərəns/ n assicurazione f. ~e vt assicurare

intact /ɪn'tækt/ adj intatto

integral /'ɪntɪgrəl/ adj integrale

integrat|e /'ɪntɪgreɪt/ vt integrare ● vi integrarsi. ~ion n integrazione f

integrity /ɪn'tegrətɪ/ n integrità f

intellect /'ɪntəlekt/ n intelletto m. ~ual adj & n intellettuale m

intelligen|ce /ɪn'telɪdʒəns/ n intelligenza f; (Mil) informazioni fpl. ~t adj intelligente

intelligible /ɪn'telɪdʒəbl/ adj intelligibile

intend /ɪn'tend/ vt destinare; (have in mind) aver intenzione di; be ~ed for essere destinato a. ~ed (effect) voluto ● my ~ed 🅸 il mio/la mia fidanzato, -a

intense /ɪn'tens/ adj intenso; (person) dai sentimenti intensi. ~ly adv intensamente; (very) estremamente

intensity /ɪn'tensətɪ/ n intensità f

intensive /ɪn'tensɪv/ adj intensivo. ~ care (for people in coma) rianimazione f; ~ care [unit] terapia f intensiva

intent /ɪn'tent/ adj intento; ~ on (absorbed in) preso da; be ~ on doing sth essere intento a fare qcsa ● n intenzione f; to all ~s and purposes a tutti gli effetti. ~ly adv attentamente

intention /ɪn'tenʃn/ n intenzione f. ~al adj intenzionale. ~ally adv intenzionalmente

inter'act|ion n cooperazione f. ~ve adj interattivo

intercept /ɪntə'sept/ vt intercettare

'interchange n scambio m; (Auto) raccordo m [autostradale]

inter'changeable adj interscambiabile

'intercourse n (sexual) rapporti mpl [sessuali]

interest /'ɪntrəst/ n interesse m; have an ~ in (Comm) essere cointeressato in; be of ~ essere interessante; ~ rate n tasso m di interesse ● vt interessare. ~ed adj interessato. ~ing adj interessante

interface /'ɪntəfeɪs/ n interfaccia f ● vt interfacciare ● vi interfacciarsi

interfere /ɪntəˈfɪə(r)/ vi interferire; ~ **with** interferire con. ~**nce** n interferenza f

interior /ɪnˈtɪərɪə(r)/ adj interiore ● n interno m. ~ **designer** n arredatore, -trice mf

interlude /ˈɪntəluːd/ n intervallo m

intermediary /ɪntəˈmiːdɪərɪ/ n intermediario, -a mf

interminable /ɪnˈtɜːmɪnəbl/ adj interminabile

intermittent /ɪntəˈmɪtənt/ adj intermittente

intern /ɪnˈtɜːn/ vt internare

internal /ɪnˈtɜːnl/ adj interno. I~ 'Revenue (Am) n fisco m. ~**ly** adv internamente; (deal with) all'interno

inter'national adj internazionale ● n (game) incontro m internazionale; (player) competitore, -trice mf in gare internazionali. ~**ly** adv internazionalmente

Internet /ˈɪntənet/ n Internet m

interpret /ɪnˈtɜːprɪt/ vt interpretare ● vi fare l'interprete. ~**ation** n interpretazione f. ~**er** n interprete mf

interrogate /ɪnˈterəɡeɪt/ vt interrogare. ~**ion** n interrogazione f; (by police) interrogatorio m

interrogative /ɪntəˈrɒɡətɪv/ adj & n [~ pronoun] interrogativo m

interrupt /ɪntəˈrʌpt/ vt/i interrompere. ~**ion** n interruzione f

intersect /ɪntəˈsekt/ vi intersecarsi ● vt intersecare. ~**ion** n intersezione f; (of street) incrocio m

inter'twine vi attorcigliarsi

interval /ˈɪntəvl/ n intervallo m; bright ~**s** pl schiarite fpl

interven|e /ɪntəˈviːn/ vi intervenire. ~**tion** n intervento m

interview /ˈɪntəvjuː/ n (Journ) intervista f; (for job) colloquio m [di lavoro] ● vt intervistare. ~**er** n intervistatore, -trice mf

intestin|e /ɪnˈtestɪn/ n intestino m.

~**al** adj intestinale

intimacy /ˈɪntɪməsɪ/ n intimità f

intimate¹ /ˈɪntɪmət/ adj intimo. ~**ly** adv intimamente

intimate² /ˈɪntɪmeɪt/ vt far capire; (imply) suggerire

intimidat|e /ɪnˈtɪmɪdeɪt/ vt intimidire. ~**ion** n intimidazione f

into /ˈɪntə/, di fronte a una vocale /ˈɪntʊ/ prep dentro, in; go ~ the house andare dentro [casa] o in casa; be ~ (🄐: like) essere appassionato di; I'm not ~ that questo non mi piace; 7 ~ 21 goes 3 il 7 nel 21 ci sta 3 volte; translate ~ French tradurre in francese; get ~ trouble mettersi nei guai

in'tolerable adj intollerabile

in'toleran|ce n intolleranza f. ~**t** adj intollerante

intoxicat|ed /ɪnˈtɒksɪkeɪtɪd/ adj inebriato. ~**ion** n ebbrezza f

in'transitive adj intransitivo

intravenous /ɪntrəˈviːnəs/ adj endovenoso. ~**ly** adv per via endovenosa

intrepid /ɪnˈtrepɪd/ adj intrepido

intricate /ˈɪntrɪkət/ adj complesso

intrigu|e /ɪnˈtriːɡ/ n intrigo m ● vt intrigare ● vi tramare. ~**ing** adj intrigante

intrinsic /ɪnˈtrɪnsɪk/ adj intrinseco

introduce /ɪntrəˈdjuːs/ vt presentare; (bring in, insert) introdurre

introduct|ion /ɪntrəˈdʌkʃn/ n introduzione f; (to person) presentazione f; (to book) prefazione f. ~**ory** adj introduttivo

introvert /ˈɪntrəvɜːt/ n introverso, -a mf

intru|de /ɪnˈtruːd/ vi intromettersi. ~**der** n intruso, -a mf. ~**sion** n intrusione f

intuit|ion /ɪntjuːˈɪʃn/ n intuito m. ~**ive** adj intuitivo

inundate /ˈɪnəndeɪt/ vt (flood)

inondare (with di)

invade /ɪnˈveɪd/ vt invadere. ~r n invasore m

invalid¹ /ˈɪnvəlɪd/ n invalido, -a af

invalid² /ɪnˈvælɪd/ adj non valido. ~ate vt invalidare

in'valuable adj prezioso; (priceless) inestimabile

in'variabl|e adj invariabile. ~y adv invariabilmente

invasion /ɪnˈveɪʒn/ n invasione f

invent /ɪnˈvent/ vt inventare. ~ion n invenzione f. ~ive adj inventivo. ~or n inventore, -trice mf

inventory /ˈɪnvəntrɪ/ n inventario m

invest /ɪnˈvest/ vt investire ● vi fare investimenti; ~ in (ⅈ: buy) comprarsi

investigat|e /ɪnˈvestɪgeɪt/ vt investigare. ~ion n investigazione f

invest|ment /ɪnˈvestmənt/ n investimento m. ~or n investitore, -trice mf

inveterate /ɪnˈvetərət/ adj inveterato

invidious /ɪnˈvɪdɪəs/ adj ingiusto; (position) antipatico

invincible /ɪnˈvɪnsəbl/ adj invincibile

in'visible adj invisibile

invitation /ɪnvɪˈteɪʃn/ n invito m

invit|e /ɪnˈvaɪt/ vt invitare; (attract) attirare. ~ing adj invitante

invoice /ˈɪnvɔɪs/ n fattura f ● vt ~ sb emettere una fattura a qcno

in'voluntar|y adj involontario

involve /ɪnˈvɒlv/ vt comportare; (affect, include) coinvolgere; (entail) implicare; get ~d with sb legarsi a qcno; (romantically) legarsi sentimentalmente a qcno. ~d adj complesso. ~ment n coinvolgimento m

inward /ˈɪnwəd/ adj interno; (thoughts etc) interiore; ~ investment (Comm) investimento m stra-

niero. ~ly adv interiormente. ~[s] adv verso l'interno

iodine /ˈaɪədiːn/ n iodio m

iota /aɪˈəʊtə/ n briciolo m

IOU n abbr (I owe you) pagherò m inv

IQ n abbr (intelligence quotient) Q.I.

Iran /ɪˈrɑːn/ n Iran m. ~ian adj & n iraniano, -a mf

Iraq /ɪˈrɑːk/ n Iraq m. ~i adj & n iracheno, -a mf

irate /aɪˈreɪt/ adj adirato

Ireland /ˈaɪələnd/ n Irlanda f

iris /ˈaɪrɪs/ n (Anat) iride f; (Bot) iris f inv

Irish /ˈaɪrɪʃ/ adj irlandese ● n the ~ pl gli irlandesi mpl. ~man n irlandese m. ~woman n irlandese f

iron /ˈaɪən/ adj di ferro. I~ Curtain n cortina f di ferro ● n ferro m; (appliance) ferro m [da stiro] ● vt/i stirare. □ ~ out vt eliminare stirando; fig appianare

'ironmonger /-mʌŋgə(r)/ n ~'s [shop] negozio m di ferramenta

irony /ˈaɪrənɪ/ n ironia f

irrational /ɪˈræʃənl/ adj irrazionale

irrefutable /ɪrɪˈfjuːtəbl/ adj irrefutabile

irregular /ɪˈreɡjʊlə(r)/ adj irregolare. ~ity n irregolarità f inv

irrelevant /ɪˈreləvənt/ adj non pertinente

irreparabl|e /ɪˈrepərəbl/ adj irreparabile. ~y adv irreparabilmente

irreplaceable /ɪrɪˈpleɪsəbl/ adj insostituibile

irresistible /ɪrɪˈzɪstəbl/ adj irresistibile

irrespective /ɪrɪˈspektɪv/ adj ~ of senza riguardo per

irresponsible /ɪrɪˈspɒnsɪbl/ adj irresponsabile

irreverent /ɪˈrevərənt/ adj irreverente

irrevocabl|e /ɪˈrevəkəbl/ adj irrevocabile. ~y adv irrevocabilmente

irrigat|e /'ɪrɪgeɪt/ vt irrigare. ~**ion** n irrigazione f

irritable /'ɪrɪtəbl/ adj irritabile

irritat|e /'ɪrɪteɪt/ vt irritare. ~**ing** adj irritante. ~**ion** n irritazione f

is /ɪz/ ▷BE

Islam /'ɪzlɑːm/ n Islam m. ~**ic** adj islamico

island /'aɪlənd/ n isola f; (in road) isola f spartitraffico. ~**er** n isolano, -a mf

isolat|e /'aɪsəleɪt/ vt isolare. ~**ed** adj isolato. ~**ion** n isolamento m

Israel /'ɪzreɪl/ n Israele m. ~**i** adj & n israeliano, -a mf

issue /'ɪʃuː/ n (outcome) risultato m; (of magazine) numero m; (of stamps etc) emissione f; (offspring) figli mpl; (matter, question) questione f; at ~ in questione; take ~ with sb prendere posizione contro qcno ● vt distribuire (supplies); rilasciare (passport); emettere (stamps, order); pubblicare (book); be ~d with sth ricevere qcsa ● vi ~ from uscire da

it /ɪt/ pron (direct object) lo m, la f; (indirect object) gli m, le f; it's broken è rotto/rotta; will it be enough? basterà?; it's hot fa caldo; it's raining piove; it's me sono io; who is it? chi è?; it's two o'clock sono le due; I doubt it ne dubito; take it with you prendilo con te; give it a wipe dagli una pulita

Italian /ɪ'tæljən/ adj & n italiano, -a mf; (language) italiano m

Italy /'ɪtəlɪ/ n Italia f

itch /ɪtʃ/ n prurito m ● vi avere prurito, prudere; be ~**ing** to 🔢 avere una voglia matta di. ~**y** adj che prude; my foot is ~**y** ho prurito al piede

item /'aɪtəm/ n articolo m; (on agenda, programme) punto m; (on invoice) voce f; ~ [of news] notizia f. ~**ize** vt dettagliare (bill)

itinerary /aɪ'tɪnərərɪ/ n itinerario m

itself /ɪt'self/ pron (reflexive) si; (emphatic) essa stessa; the baby looked at ~ in the mirror il bambino si è guardato nello specchio; by ~ da solo; the machine in ~ is simple la macchina di per sé è semplice

ITV n abbr (Independent Television) stazione f televisiva privata britannica

ivory /'aɪvərɪ/ n avorio m

ivy /'aɪvɪ/ n edera f

The Ivy League Il gruppo delle più antiche e rinomate università statunitensi, situate nel nordest del paese: Harvard, Yale, Columbia University, Cornell University, Dartmouth College, Brown University, Princeton University e la University of Pennsylvania. L'espressione deriva dall'edera che cresce sugli antichi edifici universitari.

Jj

jab /dʒæb/ n colpo m secco; (🔢 injection). puntura f ● vt (pt/pp jabbed) punzecchiare

jack /dʒæk/ n (Auto) cric m inv; (in cards) fante m, jack m inv ● **jack up** vt (Auto) sollevare [con il cric]

jackdaw /'dʒækdɔː/ n taccola f

jacket /'dʒækɪt/ n giacca f; (of book) sopraccoperta f. ~ po'tato n patata f cotta al forno con la buccia

'jackpot n premio m (di una lotteria); win the ~ vincere alla lotteria; hit the ~ fig fare un colpo grosso

jade /dʒeɪd/ n giada f ● attrib di giada

jagged /'dʒægɪd/ adj dentellato

jail /dʒeɪl/ = gaol

jam[1] /dʒæm/ n marmellata f

jam[2] n (Auto) ingorgo m; (fig: difficulty) guaio m • v (pt/pp jammed) • vt (cram) pigiare; disturbare (broadcast); inceppare (mechanism, drawer etc); be ~med (roads:) essere congestionato • vi (mechanism:) incepparsi; (window, drawer:) incastrarsi

Jamaica /dʒəˈmeɪkə/ n Giamaica f. ~n adj & n giamaicano, -a mf

jangle /ˈdʒæŋgl/ vt far squillare • vi squillare

janitor /ˈdʒænɪtə(r)/ n (caretaker) custode m; (in school) bidello, -a f

January /ˈdʒænjʊərɪ/ n gennaio m

Japan /dʒəˈpæn/ n Giappone m. ~ese adj & n giapponese mf; (language) giapponese m

jar[1] /dʒɑ:(r)/ n (glass) barattolo m

jar[2] vi (pt/pp jarred) (sound:) stridere

jargon /ˈdʒɑ:gən/ n gergo m

jaundice /ˈdʒɔ:ndɪs/ n itterizia f. ~d adj fig inacidito

jaunt /dʒɔ:nt/ n gita f

jaunty /ˈdʒɔ:ntɪ/ adj (-ier, -iest) sbarazzino

jaw /dʒɔ:/ n mascella f; (bone) mandibola f

jay-walker /ˈdʒeɪwɔ:kə(r)/ n pedone m distratto

jazz /dʒæz/ n jazz m • jazz up vt ravvivare. ~y adj vistoso

jealous /ˈdʒeləs/ adj geloso. ~y n gelosia f

jeans /dʒi:nz/ npl [blue] jeans mpl

jeep /dʒi:p/ n jeep f inv

jeer /dʒɪə(r)/ n scherno m • vi schernire; ~ at prendersi gioco di • vt (boo) fischiare

jelly /ˈdʒelɪ/ n gelatina f. ~fish n medusa f

jeopardize /ˈdʒepədaɪz/ vt mettere in pericolo. ~dy n in ~dy in pericolo

jerk /dʒɜ:k/ n scatto m, scossa f • vt scattare • vi sobbalzare; (limb,

muscle:) muoversi a scatti. ~ily adv a scatti. ~y adj traballante

jersey /ˈdʒɜ:zɪ/ n maglia f; (Sport) maglietta f; (fabric) jersey m

jest /dʒest/ n scherzo m; in ~ per scherzo • vi scherzare

Jesus /ˈdʒi:zəs/ n Gesù m

jet[1] /dʒet/ n (stone) giaietto m

jet[2] n (of water) getto m; (nozzle) becco m; (plane) aviogetto m, jet m inv

jet: ~-**black** adj nero ebano. ~**lag** n scombussolamento da fuso orario. ~-**pro'pelled** adj a reazione

jettison /ˈdʒetɪsn/ vt gettare a mare; fig abbandonare

jetty /ˈdʒetɪ/ n molo m

Jew /dʒu:/ n ebreo m

jewel /ˈdʒu:əl/ n gioiello m. ~ler n gioielliere m; ~ler's [shop] gioielleria f. ~lery n gioielli mpl

jiffy /ˈdʒɪfɪ/ n [I] in a ~ in un batter d'occhio

jigsaw /ˈdʒɪgsɔ:/ n ~ [puzzle] puzzle m inv

jilt /dʒɪlt/ vt piantare

jingle /ˈdʒɪŋgl/ n (rhyme) canzoncina f pubblicitaria • vi tintinnare

job /dʒɒb/ n lavoro m; this is going to be quite a ~ [I] (questa) non sarà un'impresa facile; it's a good ~ that... meno male che.... ~ **cen**tre n ufficio m statale di collocamento. ~**less** adj senza lavoro

jockey /ˈdʒɒkɪ/ n fantino m

jocular /ˈdʒɒkjʊlə(r)/ adj scherzoso

jog /dʒɒg/ n colpetto m; at a ~ in un balzo; (Sport) go for a ~ andare a fare jogging • v (pt/pp jogged) • vt (hit) urtare; ~ sb's memory farlo ritornare in mente a qcno • vi (Sport) fare jogging. ~**ging** n jogging m

join /dʒɔɪn/ n giuntura f • vt raggiungere, unire; raggiungere (person); (become member of) iscriversi a; entrare in (firm) • vi (roads:) congiungersi. □~ **in** vi partecipare. □~ **up** vi (Mil) arruolarsi ●vt unire

joiner /'dʒɔɪnə(r)/ n falegname m

joint /dʒɔɪnt/ adj comune ●n articolazione f; (in wood, brickwork) giuntura f; (Culin) arrosto m; (🔢 bar) bettola f; (🔢 drug) spinello m. ~ly adv unitamente

joist /dʒɔɪst/ n travetto m

jok|e /dʒəʊk/ n (trick) scherzo m; (funny story) barzelletta f ●vi scherzare. ~er n burlone, -a mf; (in cards) jolly m inv. ~ing n ~ing apart scherzi a parte. ~ingly adv per scherzo

jolly /'dʒɒlɪ/ adj (-ier, -iest) allegro ●adv 🔢 molto

jolt /dʒəʊlt/ n scossa f, sobbalzo m ●vt far sobbalzare ●vi sobbalzare

jostle /'dʒɒsl/ vt spingere

jot /dʒɒt/ n nulla f ●jot down vt (pt/pp jotted) annotare. ~ter n taccuino m

journal /'dʒɜːnl/ n giornale m; (diary) diario m. ~ese n gergo m giornalistico. ~ism n giornalismo m. ~ist n giornalista mf

journey /'dʒɜːnɪ/ n viaggio m

jovial /'dʒəʊvɪəl/ adj gioviale

joy /dʒɔɪ/ n gioia f. ~ful adj gioioso. ~ride n 🔢 giro m con una macchina rubata. ~stick n (Comput) joystick m inv

jubil|ant /'dʒuːbɪlənt/ adj giubilante. ~ation n giubilo m

jubilee /'dʒuːbɪliː/ n giubileo m

judge /dʒʌdʒ/ n giudice m ●vt giudicare; (estimate) valutare; (consider) ritenere ●vi giudicare (by da). ~ment n giudizio m; (Jur) sentenza f

judic|ial /dʒuː'dɪʃl/ adj giudiziario. ~iary n magistratura f. ~ious adj giudizioso

judo /'dʒuːdəʊ/ n judo m

jug /dʒʌg/ n brocca f; (small) bricco m

juggernaut /'dʒʌgənɔːt/ n 🔢 grosso autotreno m

juggle /'dʒʌgl/ vi fare giochi di destrezza. ~r n giocoliere, -a mf

juice /dʒuːs/ n succo m

juicy /'dʒuːsɪ/ adj (-ier, -iest) succoso; (🔢 story) piccante

juke-box /'dʒuːk-/ n juke-box m inv

July /dʒʊ'laɪ/ n luglio m

jumble /'dʒʌmbl/ n accozzaglia f ●vt ~ (up) mischiare. ~ sale n vendita f di beneficenza

jumbo /'dʒʌmbəʊ/ n ~ [jet] jumbo jet m inv

jump /dʒʌmp/ n salto m; (in prices) balzo m; (in horse racing) ostacolo m ●vi saltare; (with fright) sussultare; (prices:) salire rapidamente; ~ to conclusions saltare alle conclusioni ●vt saltare; ~ the gun fig precipitarsi; ~ the queue non rispettare la fila. □~ **at** vt fig accettare con entusiasmo (offer). □~ **up** vi rizzarsi in piedi

jumper /'dʒʌmpə(r)/ n (sweater) golf m inv

jumpy /'dʒʌmpɪ/ adj nervoso

junction /'dʒʌŋkʃn/ n (of roads) incrocio m; (of motorway) uscita f; (Rail) nodo m ferroviario

June /dʒuːn/ n giugno m

jungle /'dʒʌŋgl/ n giungla f

junior /'dʒuːnɪə(r)/ adj giovane; (in rank) subalterno; (Sport) junior inv ●n the ~s (Sch) i più giovani. ~ schoo
l n scuola f elementare

junk /dʒʌŋk/ n cianfrusaglie fpl. ~ food n 🔢 cibo m poco sano, porcherie fpl. ~ mail posta f spazzatura

junkie /'dʒʌŋkɪ/ n 🔢 tossico, -a mf

'**junk-shop** n negozio m di rigattiere

jurisdiction /dʒʊərɪs'dɪkʃn/ n giurisdizione f

juror /'dʒʊərə(r)/ n giurato, -a mf

jury /'dʒʊərɪ/ n giuria f

just /dʒʌst/ adj giusto ●adv (barely)

appena; (*simply*) solo; (*exactly*) esattamente; ~ **as tall** altrettanto alto; ~ **as I was leaving** proprio quando stavo andando via; **I've** ~ **seen her** l'ho appena vista; **it's** ~ **as well** meno male; ~ **at that moment** proprio in quel momento; ~ **listen!** ascolta!; **I'm** ~ **going** sto andando proprio ora

justice /'dʒʌstɪs/ *n* giustizia *f*; **do** ~ **to** rendere giustizia a; **J**~ **of the Peace** giudice *m* conciliatore

justifiabl|e /'dʒʌstɪfaɪəbl/ *adj* giustificabile

justi|fication /dʒʌstɪfɪ'keɪʃn/ *n* giustificazione *f*. **~fy** *vt* (*pt/pp* -ied) giustificare

jut /dʒʌt/ *vi* (*pt/pp* jutted) ~ **out** sporgere

juvenile /'dʒuːvənaɪl/ *adj* giovanile; (*childish*) infantile; (*for the young*) per i giovani ● *n* giovane *mf*. ~ **delinquency** *n* delinquenza *f* giovanile

Kk

kangaroo /kæŋgə'ruː/ *n* canguro *m*

karate /kə'rɑːtɪ/ *n* karate *m*

keel /kiːl/ *n* chiglia *f* ● **keel over** *vi* capovolgersi

keen /kiːn/ *adj* (*intense*) acuto; (*interest*) vivo; (*eager*) entusiastico; (*competition*) feroce; (*wind, knife*) tagliente; ~ **on** entusiasta di; **she's** ~ **on him** le piace molto; **be** ~ **to do sth** avere voglia di fare qcsa. ~**ness** *n* entusiasmo *m*

keep /kiːp/ *n* (*maintenance*) mantenimento *m*; (*of castle*) maschio *m*; **for** ~**s** per sempre ● *v* (*pt/pp* kept) ● *vt* tenere; (*not throw away*) conservare; (*detain*) trattenere; mantenere (family,

promise); avere (shop); allevare (animals); rispettare (law, rules); ~ **sth hot** tenere qcsa in caldo; ~ **sb from doing sth** impedire a qcno di fare qcsa; ~ **sb waiting** far aspettare qcno; ~ **sth to oneself** tenere qcsa per sè; ~ **sth from sb** tenere nascosto qcsa a qcno ● *vi* (*remain*) rimanere; (*food*) conservarsi; ~ **calm** rimanere calmo; ~ **left/right** tenere la destra/la sinistra; ~ **[on]** doing sth continuare a fare qcsa. □ ~ **back** *vt* trattenere (person); ~ **sth back from sb** tenere nascosto qcsa a qcno ● *vi* tenersi indietro. □ ~ **in with** *vt* mantenersi in buoni rapporti con. □ ~ **on** *vi* 🅸 assillare (**at sb** qcno). □ ~ **up** *vi* stare al passo ● *vt* (*continue*) continuare

kennel /'kenl/ *n* canile *m*; ~**s** *pl* (*boarding*) canile *m*; (*breeding*) allevamento *m* di cani

Kenya /'kenjə/ *n* Kenia *m*. ~**n** *adj* & *n* keniota *mf*

kept /kept/ ▷KEEP

kerb /kɜːb/ *n* bordo *m* del marciapiede

kerosene /'kerəsiːn/ *n* *Am* cherosene *m*

ketchup /'ketʃʌp/ *n* ketchup *m*

kettle /'ket(ə)l/ *n* bollitore *m*; **put the** ~ **on** mettere l'acqua a bollire

key /kiː/ *n* anche (Mus) chiave *f*; (*of piano, typewriter*) tasto *m* ● *vt* ~ **[in]** digitare (character); **could you** ~ **this?** puoi battere questo?

key: ~**board** *n* (Comput, Mus) tastiera *f*. ~**hole** *n* buco *m* della serratura. ~**ring** *n* portachiavi *m inv*

khaki /'kɑːkɪ/ *adj* cachi *inv* ● *n* cachi

kick /kɪk/ *n* calcio *m*; (🅸: *thrill*) piacere *m*; **for** ~**s** 🅸 per spasso ● *vt* dar calci a; ~ **the bucket** 🅸 crepare ● *vi* (*animal*: *also*) dare calci; (*person*:) dare calci. □ ~ **off** *vi* (Sport) dare il calcio d'inizio; 🅸 iniziare. □ ~ **up** *vt* ~ **up**

a row fare una scenata

'kick-off n (Sport) calcio m d'inizio

kid /kɪd/ n capretto m; (①: child) ragazzino, -a mf ● v (pt/pp kidded) ● vt ① prendere in giro ● vi ① scherzare

kidnap /'kɪdnæp/ vt (pt/pp -napped) rapire, sequestrare. **~per** n sequestratore, -trice mf, rapitore, -trice mf. **~ping** n rapimento m, sequestro m [di persona]

kidney /'kɪdnɪ/ n rene m; (Culin) rognone m. **~ machine** n rene m artificiale

kill /kɪl/ vt uccidere; fig metter fine a; ammazzare (time). **~** n assassino, -a mf. **~ing** n uccisione f; (murder) omicidio m; **make a ~ing** fig fare un colpo grosso

kiln /kɪln/ n fornace f

kilo /'kiːlə/: **~byte** n kilobyte m inv. **~gram** n chilogrammo m. **~metre** n chilometro m. **~watt** n chilowatt m inv

kilt /kɪlt/ n kilt m inv (gonnellino degli scozzesi)

kin /kɪn/ n congiunti mpl; **next of ~** parente m stretto; parenti mpl stretti

kind[1] /kaɪnd/ n genere m, specie f; (brand, type) tipo m; **~ of** ① alquanto; **two of a ~** due della stessa specie

kind[2] adj gentile, buono; **~ to animals** amante degli animali; **~ regards** cordiali saluti

kindergarten /'kɪndəgɑːtn/ n asilo m infantile

kindle /'kɪndl/ vt accendere

kind|ly /'kaɪndlɪ/ adj (-ier, -iest) benevolo ● adv gentilmente; (if you please) per favore. **~ness** n gentilezza f

king /kɪŋ/ n re m inv. **~dom** n regno m

king: **~fisher** n martin m inv pescatore. **~-sized** adj (cigarette) kingsize inv, lungo; (bed) matrimoniale

grande

kink /kɪŋk/ n nodo m. **~y** adj ①

kiosk /'kiːɒsk/ n chiosco m; (Teleph) cabina f telefonica

kipper /'kɪpə(r)/ n aringa f affumicata

kiss /kɪs/ n bacio m; **~ of life** respirazione f bocca a bocca ● vt baciare ● vi baciarsi

kit /kɪt/ n equipaggiamento m, kit m inv; (tools) attrezzi mpl; (construction ~) pezzi mpl da montare, kit m inv ● **kit out** vt (pt/pp kitted) equipaggiare. **~bag** n sacco m a spalla

kitchen /'kɪtʃɪn/ n cucina f ● attrib di cucina. **~ette** n cucinino m

kitchen towel Scottex® m inv

kite /kaɪt/ n aquilone m

kitten /'kɪtn/ n gattino m

knack /næk/ n tecnica f; **have the ~ for doing sth** avere la capacità di fare qcsa

knead /niːd/ vt impastare

knee /niː/ n ginocchio m. **~cap** n rotula f

kneel /niːl/ vi (pt/pp knelt) **~ [down]** inginocchiarsi; **be ~ing** essere inginocchiato

knelt /nelt/ ▷**KNEEL**

knew /njuː/ ▷**KNOW**

knickers /'nɪkəz/ npl mutandine fpl

knife /naɪf/ n (pl knives) coltello m ● vt ① accoltellare

knight /naɪt/ n cavaliere m; (in chess) cavallo m ● vt nominare cavaliere

knit /nɪt/ vt/i (pt/pp knitted) lavorare a maglia; **~ one, purl one** un diritto, un rovescio; **~ting** n lavorare m a maglia; (work) lavoro m a maglia. **~ting-needle** n ferro m da calza. **~wear** n maglieria f

knives /naɪvz/ ▷**KNIFE**

knob /nɒb/ n pomello m; (of stick) pomo m; (of butter) noce f. **~bly** adj nodoso; (bony) spigoloso

knock /nɒk/ n colpo m; there was a ~ at the door hanno bussato alla porta ● vt bussare a (door); (🗊: criticize) denigrare; ~ a hole in sth fare un buco in qcsa; ~ one's head battere la testa (on contro) ● vi (at door) bussare. □ ~ **about** vt malmenare ● vi 🗊 girovagare. □ ~ **down** vt far cadere; (with fist) stendere con un pugno; (in car) investire; (demolish) abbattere; (🗊: reduce) ribassare (price). □ ~ **off** vt (🗊: steal) fregare; (🗊: complete quickly) fare alla bell'e meglio ● vi (🗊: cease work) staccare. □ ~ **out** vt eliminare; (make unconscious) mettere K.O.; (🗊: anaesthetize) addormentare. □ ~ **over** vt rovesciare; (in car) investire

knock: ~**er** n battente m. ~**-kneed** /-'niːd/ adj con gambe storte. ~**-out** n (in boxing) knock-out m inv

knot /nɒt/ n nodo m ● vt (pt/pp knotted) annodare

know /nəʊ/ v (pt knew, pp known) ● vt sapere; conoscere (person, place); (recognize) riconoscere; get to ~ sb conoscere qcno; ~ how to swim sapere nuotare ● vi sapere; did you ~ about this? lo sapevi? ● n in the ~ 🗊 al corrente

know: ~**-all** n 🗊 sapientone, -a mf. ~**-how** n abilità f. ~**ingly** adv (intentionally) consapevolmente; (smile etc) con un'aria d'intesa

knowledge /'nɒlɪdʒ/ n conoscenza f. ~**able** adj ben informato

known /nəʊn/ ▷KNOW ● adj noto

knuckle /'nʌkl/ n nocca f ● **knuckle down** vi darci sotto (to con). □ ~ **under** vi sottomettersi

Koran /kɔ'rɑːn/ n Corano m

Korea /kə'rɪə/ n Corea f. ~**n** adj & n coreano, -a m

kosher /'kəʊʃə(r)/ adj kasher inv

kudos /'kjuːdɒs/ n 🗊 gloria f

Ll

lab /læb/ n laboratorio m

label /'leɪbl/ n etichetta f ● vt (pt/pp labelled) mettere un'etichetta a; fig etichettare (person)

laboratory /lə'bɒrətrɪ/ n laboratorio m

laborious /lə'bɔːrɪəs/ adj laborioso

labour /'leɪbə(r)/ n lavoro m; (workers) manodopera f; (Med) doglie fpl; be in ~ avere le doglie; L~ (Pol) partito m laburista ● attrib (Pol) laburista ● vi lavorare ● vt ~ the point fig ribadire il concetto. ~**er** n manovale m

lace /leɪs/ n pizzo m; (of shoe) laccio m ● attrib di pizzo ● vt allacciare (shoes); correggere (drink)

lacerate /'læsəreɪt/ vt lacerare

lack /læk/ n mancanza f ● vt mancare di; I ~ the time mi manca il tempo ● vi be ~ing mancare; be ~ing in sth mancare di qcsa

lad /læd/ n ragazzo m

ladder /'lædə(r)/ n scala f; (in tights) sfilatura f

laden /'leɪdn/ adj carico (with di)

ladle /'leɪdl/ n mestolo m ● vt ~ [out] versare (col mestolo)

lady /'leɪdɪ/ n signora f; (title) Lady; ladies [room] bagno m per donne

lady: ~**bird** n, Am ~**bug** n coccinella f. ~**like** adj signorile

lag¹ /læg/ vi (pt/pp lagged) ~ behind restare indietro

lag² vt (pt/pp lagged) isolare (pipes)

lager /'lɑːgə(r)/ n birra f chiara

lagoon /lə'guːn/ n laguna f

laid /leɪd/ ▷LAY³

lain /leɪn/ ▷LIE²

lair /leə(r)/ n tana f

lake /leɪk/ n lago m

lamb /læm/ n agnello m

lame /leɪm/ adj zoppo; fig (argument) zoppicante; (excuse) traballante

lament /lə'ment/ n lamento m • vi lamentare • vi lamentarsi

lamentable /'læməntəbl/ adj deplorevole

lamp /læmp/ n lampada f; (in street) lampione m. ∼post n lampione m. ∼shade n paralume m

lance /lɑːns/ n fiocina f • vt (Med) incidere. ∼-corporal n appuntato m

land /lænd/ n terreno m; (country) paese m; (as opposed to sea) terra f; plot of ∼ pezzo m di terreno • vt (Naut) sbarcare; (fam: obtain) assicurarsi; be ∼ed with sth 🔢 ritrovarsi fra capo e collo qcsa • vi (Aeron) atterrare; (fall) cadere. □ ∼ up vi 🔢 finire

landing /'lændɪŋ/ n (Naut) sbarco m; (Aeron) atterraggio m; (top of stairs) pianerottolo m. ∼-stage n pontile da sbarco. ∼-strip n pista f d'atterraggio di fortuna

land: ∼lady n proprietaria f; (of flat) padrona f di casa. ∼lord n proprietario m; (of flat) padrone m di casa. ∼mark n punto m di riferimento; fig pietra f miliare. ∼scape -skeɪp/ n paesaggio m. ∼slide n frana f; (Pol) valanga f di voti

lane /leɪn/ n sentiero m; (Auto, Sport) corsia f

language /'læŋgwɪdʒ/ n lingua f; (speech, style) linguaggio m. ∼ laboratory n laboratorio m linguistico

lank /læŋk/ adj (hair) diritto

lanky /'læŋkɪ/ adj (-ier, -iest) allampanato

lantern /'læntən/ n lanterna f

lap¹ /læp/ n grembo m

lap² n (of journey) tappa f; (Sport) giro m • v (pt/pp lapped) • vi (water:) ∼ against lambire • vt (Sport) doppiare

lap³ vt (pt/pp lapped) ∼ up bere avidamente; bersi completamente (lies); credere ciecamente a (praise)

lapel /lə'pel/ n bavero m

lapse /læps/ n sbaglio m; (moral) sbandamento m [morale]; (of time) intervallo m • vi (expire) scadere; (morally) scivolare; ∼ into cadere in

laptop /'læptɒp/ n ∼ [computer] computer m inv portatile, laptop m inv

lard /lɑːd/ n strutto m

larder /'lɑːdə(r)/ n dispensa f

large /lɑːdʒ/ adj grande; (number, amount) grande, grosso; by and ∼ in complesso; at ∼ in libertà; (in general) ampiamente. ∼ly adv ampiamente; ∼ly because of in gran parte a causa di

lark¹ /lɑːk/ n (bird) allodola f

lark² n (joke) burla f • **lark about** vi giocherellare

larva /'lɑːvə/ n (pl -vae /-viː/) larva f

laser /'leɪzə(r)/ n laser m inv. ∼ printer n stampante f laser

lash /læʃ/ n frustata f; (eyelash) ciglio m • vt (whip) frustare; (tie) legare fermamente. □ ∼ out vi attaccare; (spend) sperperare (on in)

lashings /'læʃɪŋz/ npl ∼ of 🔢 una marea di

lass /læs/ n ragazzina f

lasso /lə'suː/ n lazo m

last /lɑːst/ adj (final) ultimo; (recent) scorso; ∼ year l'anno scorso; at ∼ alla fine; at ∼! finalmente; that's the ∼ straw 🔢 questa è l'ultima goccia • n ultimo, -a m/f; the ∼ but one il penultimo • adv per ultimo; (last time) l'ultima volta • vi durare. ∼ing adj durevole. ∼ly adv infine

late /leɪt/ adj (delayed) in ritardo; (at a late hour) tardo; (deceased) defunto; it's ∼ (at night) è tardi; in ∼ November alla fine di Novembre • adv tardi; stay up ∼ stare alzati fino a tardi.

~comer n ritardatario, -a mf; (to political party etc) nuovo, -a arrivato, -a mf. ~ly adv recentemente. ~ness n ora f tarda; (delay) ritardo m

atent /'leɪtnt/ adj latente

ater /'leɪtə(r)/ adj (train) che parte più tardi; (edition) più recente. -a mf. più tardi; ~ on più tardi, dopo

ateral /'lætərəl/ adj laterale

atest /'leɪtɪst/ adj ultimo; (most recent) più recente; the ~ [news] le ultime notizie. ~ at six o'clock at the ~ alle sei al più tardi

athe /leɪð/ n tornio m

ather /'lɑːðə(r)/ n schiuma f • vt insaponare • vi far schiuma

atin /'lætɪn/ adj latino • n latino m. ~ A'merica n America f Latina. ~ A'merican adj & n latino-americano,

atitude /'lætɪtjuːd/ n (Geog) latitudine f; fig libertà f d'azione

atter /'lætə(r)/ adj ultimo • the ~ quest'ultimo. ~ly adv ultimamente

atvia /'lætvɪə/ n Lettonia f. ~n adj & n lettone mf

augh /lɑːf/ n risata f • vi ridere (at/ about di); ~ at sb (mock) prendere in giro qcno. ~able adj ridicolo. ~ing-stock n zimbello m

aughter /'lɑːftə(r)/ n risata f

aunch¹ /lɔːntʃ/ n (boat) varo m

aunch² n lancio m; (of ship) varo m • vt lanciare (rocket, product); varare (ship); sferrare (attack)

aunder /'lɔːndə(r)/ vt lavare e stirare; ~ money fig riciclare denaro sporco. ~ette n lavanderia f automatica

aundry /'lɔːndrɪ/ n lavanderia f; (clothes) bucato m

ava /'lɑːvə/ n lava f

avatory /'lævətrɪ/ n gabinetto m

avish /'lævɪʃ/ adj copioso; (wasteful) prodigo; on a ~ scale su vasta scala

• vt ~ sth on sb ricoprire qcno di qcsa. ~ly adv copiosamente

law /lɔː/ n legge f; study ~ studiare giurisprudenza, studiare legge; ~ and order ordine m pubblico

lawcourt n tribunale m

lawn /lɔːn/ n prato m [all'inglese]. ~-mower n tosaerbe m inv

'law suit n causa f

lawyer /'lɔːjə(r)/ n avvocato m

lax /læks/ adj negligente; (morals etc) lassista

laxative /'læksətɪv/ n lassativo m

lay¹ /leɪ/ adj laico; fig profano

lay² ▸LIE²

lay³ vt (pt/pp laid) porre, mettere; apparecchiare (table) • vi (hen:) fare le uova. □ ~ down vt posare; stabilire (rules, conditions). □ ~ off vt licenziare (workers) • vi (🎘: stop) ~ off! smettila! lay out vt (display, set forth) esporre; (plan) pianificare (garden); (spend) sborsare; (Typ) impaginare

lay: ~about n fannullone, -a mf. ~-by n corsia f di sosta

layer /'leɪə(r)/ n strato m

lay: ~man n profano m. ~out n disposizione f; (Typ) impaginazione f, layout m inv

laze /leɪz/ vi ~ [about] oziare

laziness /'leɪzɪnɪs/ n pigrizia f

lazy /'leɪzɪ/ adj (-ier, -iest) pigro. ~-bones n poltrone, -a mf

lead¹ /led/ n piombo m; (of pencil) mina f

lead² /liːd/ n guida f; (leash) guinzaglio m; (flex) filo m; (clue) indizio m; (Theat) parte f principale; (distance ahead) distanza f (over su); in the ~ in testa • v (pt/pp led) • vt condurre; dirigere (expedition, party etc); (induce) indurre; ~ the way mettersi in testa • vi (be in front) condurre; (in race, competition) essere in testa; (at cards) giocare (per primo). □ ~ away vt portar via. □ ~ to vt portare a.

□ ~ **up to** vt preludere; what's this ~ing up to? dove porta questo?

leader /'li:də(r)/ n capo m; (of orchestra) primo violino m; (in newspaper) articolo m di fondo. ~ship n direzione f, leadership f inv; show ~ship mostrare capacità di comando

leading /'li:dɪŋ/ adj principale; ~ lady/man attrice f/attore m principale; ~ question domanda f tendenziosa

leaf /li:f/ n (pl leaves) foglia f; (of table) asse f ● leaf through vt sfogliare. ~let n dépliant m inv; (advertising) dépliant m inv pubblicitario; (political) manifestino m

league /li:g/ n lega f; (Sport) campionato m; be in ~ with essere in combutta con

leak /li:k/ n (hole) fessura f; (Naut) falla f; (of gas & fig) fuga f ● vi colare; (ship) fare acqua; (liquid, gas) fuoriuscire ● vt ~ sth to sb fig far trapelare qcsa a qcno. ~y adj che perde; (Naut) che fa acqua

lean¹ /li:n/ adj magro

lean² v (pt/pp leaned or leant /lent/) ● vt appoggiare (against/on contro/su) ● vi appoggiarsi (against/on contro/su); (not be straight) pendere; be ~ing against essere appoggiato contro; ~ on sb (depend on) appoggiarsi a qcno; (⊞: exert pressure on) stare alle calcagne di qcno. □ ~ **back** vi sporgersi indietro. □ ~ **forward** vi piegarsi in avanti. □ ~ **out** vi sporgersi. □ ~ **over** vi piegarsi

leaning /'li:nɪŋ/ adj pendente; the L~ Tower of Pisa la torre di Pisa, la torre pendente ● n tendenza f

leap /li:p/ n salto m ● vi (pt/pp leapt /lept/ or leaped) saltare; he leapt at it ⊞ l'ha preso al volo. ~-frog n cavallina f. ~ year n anno m bisestile

learn /lɜ:n/ v (pt/pp learnt or learned) ● vt imparare; ~ to swim imparare a nuotare; I have ~ed that... (heard) sono venuto a sapere

che... ● vi imparare

learn|ed /'lɜ:nɪd/ adj colto. ~er n also (Auto) principiante mf. ~ing n cultura f. ~ing curve n curva f d'apprendimento

lease /li:s/ n contratto m d'affitto; (rental) affitto m ● vt affittare

leash /li:ʃ/ n guinzaglio m

least /li:st/ adj più piccolo; (amount) minore; you've got ~ luggage hai meno bagagli di tutti ● n the ~ il meno; at ~ almeno; not in the ~ niente affatto ● adv meno; the ~ expensive wine il vino meno caro

leather /'leðə(r)/ n pelle f; (of soles) cuoio m ● attrib di pelle/cuoio. ~y adj (meat, skin) duro

leave /li:v/ n (holiday) congedo m; (Mil) licenza f; on ~ in congedo/licenza ● v (pt/pp left) ● vt lasciare; uscire da (house, office); (forget) dimenticare; there is nothing left non è rimasto niente ● vi andare via (train, bus); partire. □ ~ **behind** vt lasciare; (forget) dimenticare. □ ~ **out** vt omettere; (not put away) lasciare fuori

leaves /li:vz/ ▷ **LEAF**

Leban|on /'lebənən/ n Libano m. ~ese /-'ni:z/ adj & n libanese mf

lecture /'lektʃə(r)/ n conferenza f; (Univ) lezione f; (reproof) ramanzina f ● vi fare una conferenza (on su); (Univ) insegnare (on sth qcsa) ● vt ~ sb rimproverare qcno. ~r n conferenziere, -a mf; (Univ) docente mf universitario, -a

led /led/ ▷ **LEAD**²

ledge /ledʒ/ n cornice f; (of window) davanzale m

leek /li:k/ n porro m

leer /lɪə(r)/ n sguardo m libidinoso ● vi ~ [at] guardare in modo libidinoso

left¹ /left/ ▷ **LEAVE**

left² adj sinistro ● adv a sinistra ● n also (Pol) sinistra f; on the ~

a sinistra;

left: ~-'handed adj mancino. ~-'luggage office n deposito m bagagli. ~overs npl rimasugli mpl. ~-'wing adj (Pol) di sinistra

leg /leg/ n gamba f; (of animal) zampa f; (of journey) tappa f; (Culin: of chicken) coscia f; (: of lamb) cosciotto m

legacy /'legəsɪ/ n lascito m

legal /'li:gl/ adj legale; take ~ action intentare un'azione legale. ~ly adv legalmente

legality /lɪ'gælətɪ/ n legalità f

legalize /'li:gəlaɪz/ vt legalizzare

legend /'ledʒənd/ n leggenda f. ~ary adj leggendario

legib|le /'ledʒəbl/ adj leggibile. ~ly adv in modo leggibile

legislat|e /'ledʒɪsleɪt/ vi legiferare. ~ion n legislazione f

legitima|te /lɪ'dʒɪtɪmət/ adj legittimo; (excuse) valido

leisure /'leʒə(r)/ n tempo m libero; at your ~ con comodo. ~ly adj senza fretta

lemon /'lemən/ n limone m. ~ade n limonata f

lend /lend/ vt (pt/pp lent) prestare; ~ a hand fig dare una mano. ~ing library n biblioteca f per il prestito

length /leŋθ/ n lunghezza f; (piece) pezzo m; (of wallpaper) parte f; (of visit) durata f; at ~ a lungo; (at last) alla fine

length|en /'leŋθən/ vt allungare ● vi allungarsi. ~ways adv per lungo

lengthy /'leŋθɪ/ adj (-ier, -iest) lungo

lens /lenz/ n lente f; (Phot) obiettivo m; (of eye) cristallino m

lent /lent/ ▷ LEND

Lent n Quaresima f

Leo /'li:əʊ/ n (Astr) Leone m

leopard /'lepəd/ n leopardo m

leotard /'li:ətɑ:d/ n body m inv

lesbian /'lezbɪən/ adj lesbico ● n lesbica f

less /les/ adj meno di; ~ and ~ sempre meno ● adv & prep meno ● n meno m

lessen /'lesn/ vt/i diminuire

lesson /'lesn/ n lezione f

lest /lest/ conj liter per timore che

let /let/ vt (pt/pp let, pres p letting) lasciare, permettere; (rent) affittare; ~ alone (not to mention) tanto meno; 'to ~' 'affittasi'; ~ us go andiamo; ~ sb do sth lasciare fare qcsa a qcno, permettere a qcno di fare qcsa; ~ me know fammi sapere; just ~ him try! che ci provi solamente!; ~ oneself in for sth 🔝 impelagarsi in qcsa. □ ~ down vt sciogliersi (hair); abbassare (blinds); (lengthen) allungare; (disappoint) deludere; don't ~ me down conto su di te. □ ~ in vt far entrare. □ ~ off vt far partire; (not punish) perdonare; ~ sb off doing sth far abbonare qcsa a qcno. □ ~ out vt far uscire; (make larger) allargare; emettere (scream, groan). □ ~ through vt far passare. □ ~ up vi 🔝 diminuire

'**let-down** n delusione f

lethal /'li:θl/ adj letale

letharg|ic /lɪ'θɑ:dʒɪk/ adj apatico. ~y n apatia f

letter /'letə(r)/ n lettera f. ~-box n buca f per le lettere. ~-head n carta f intestata. ~ing n caratteri mpl

lettuce /'letɪs/ n lattuga f

'**let-up** n 🔝 pausa f

leukaemia /lu:'ki:mɪə/ n leucemia f

level /'levl/ adj piano; (in height, competition) allo stesso livello; (spoonful) raso; draw ~ with sb affiancare qcno ● n livello m; on the ~ 🔝 giusto ● vt (pt/pp levelled) livellare; (aim) puntare (at su)

level 'crossing n passaggio m a livello

lever /'li:va(r)/ n leva f ● **lever up** vt sollevare (con una leva). ~**age** n azione f (di una leva); fig influenza f

levy /'levi/ vt (pt/pp levied) imporre (tax)

lewd /lju:d/ adj osceno

liabilit|y /laɪə'bɪlətɪ/ n responsabilità f; (🔲: burden) peso m; ~**ies** pl debiti mpl

liable /'laɪəbl/ adj responsabile (for di); be ~ to (rain, break etc) rischiare di; (tend to) tendere a

liaise /lɪ'eɪz/ vi 🔲 essere in contatto

liaison /lɪ'eɪzɒn/ n contatti mpl; (Mil) collegamento m; (affair) relazione f

liar /'laɪə(r)/ n bugiardo, -a mf

libel /'laɪbl/ n diffamazione f ● vt (pt/pp libelled) diffamare. ~**lous** adj diffamatorio

liberal /'lɪb(ə)rəl/ adj (tolerant) di larghe vedute; (generous) generoso. L~ (Pol) liberale ● n liberale mf

liberat|e /'lɪbəreɪt/ vt liberare. ~**ed** adj (woman) emancipata. ~**ion** n liberazione f; (of women) emancipazione f. ~**or** n liberatore, -trice mf

liberty /'lɪbətɪ/ n libertà f; take the ~ of doing sth prendersi la libertà di fare qcsa; be at ~ to do sth essere libero di fare qcsa

Libra /'li:brə/ n (Astr) Bilancia f

librarian /laɪ'breərɪən/ n bibliotecario, -a mf

library /'laɪbrərɪ/ n biblioteca f

Libya /'lɪbɪə/ n Libia f. ~**n** adj & n libico, -a mf

lice /laɪs/ ▷LOUSE

licence /'laɪsns/ n licenza f; (for TV) canone m televisivo; (for driving) patente f; (freedom) sregolatezza f. ~**plate** n targa f

license /'laɪsns/ vt autorizzare; be ~**d** (car:) avere il bollo; (restaurant:) essere autorizzato alla vendita di alcolici

lick /lɪk/ n leccata f; a ~ of paint una passata leggera di pittura ● vt leccare; (🔲: defeat) battere; leccarsi (lips)

lid /lɪd/ n coperchio m; (of eye) palpebra f

lie¹ /laɪ/ n bugia f; tell a ~ mentire ● vi (pt/pp lied, pres p lying) mentire

lie² vi (pt lay, pp lain, pres p lying) (person:) sdraiarsi; (object:) stare; (remain) rimanere; leave sth lying about or around lasciare qcsa in giro. □ ~ **down** vi sdraiarsi

lie-in n have a ~ restare a letto fino a tardi

lieutenant /lef'tenənt/ n tenente m

life /laɪf/ n (pl lives) vita f

life|-belt n salvagente m. ~**-boat** n lancia f di salvataggio; (on ship) scialuppa f di salvataggio. ~**-buoy** n salvagente m. ~ **coach** n life coach m/f inv. ~**guard** n bagnino m. ~**jacket** n giubbotto m di salvataggio. ~**less** adj inanimato. ~**like** adj realistico. ~**long** adj di tutta la vita. ~**size[d]** adj in grandezza naturale. ~**time** n vita f; the chance of a ~**time** un'occasione unica

lift /lɪft/ n ascensore m; (Auto) passaggio m ● vt sollevare; revocare (restrictions); (🔲: steal) rubare ● vi (fog:) alzarsi. □ ~ **up** vt sollevare

'lift-off n decollo m (di razzo)

light¹ /laɪt/ adj (not dark) luminoso; ~ green verde chiaro ● n luce f; (lamp) lampada f; in the ~ of fig alla luce di; have you got a ~? ha da accendere?; come to ~ essere rivelato ● vt (pt/pp lit or lighted) accendere; (illuminate) illuminare. □ ~ **up** vi (face:) illuminarsi

light² adj (not heavy) leggero ● adv travel ~ viaggiare con poco bagaglio

'light-bulb n lampadina f

lighten¹ /'laɪtn/ vt illuminare

lighten² vt alleggerire (load)

lighter /'laɪtə(r)/ n accendino m

light: ~-'hearted adj spensierato. ~house n faro m. ~ly adv leggermente; (accuse) con leggerezza; (without concern) senza dare importanza alla cosa; get off ~ly cavarsela a buon mercato

lightning /'laɪtnɪŋ/ n lampo m, fulmine m. ~-conductor n parafulmine m

lightweight adj leggero • n (in boxing) peso m leggero

like¹ /laɪk/ adj simile • prep come; ~ this/that così; what's he ~? com'è? • conj (: as) come; (Am: as if) come se

like² vt piacere, gradire; I should/would ~ vorrei, gradirei; I ~ him mi piace; I ~ this car mi piace questa macchina; I ~ dancing mi piace ballare; I ~ that! [] questa mi è piaciuta! • n ~s and dislikes pl gusti mpl

like|able /'laɪkəbl/ adj simpatico. ~lihood n probabilità f. ~ly adj (-ier, -iest) probabile • adv probabilmente; not ~ly!! [] neanche per sogno!

liken /'laɪkən/ vt paragonare (to a)

like|ness /'laɪknɪs/ n somiglianza f. ~wise adv lo stesso

liking /'laɪkɪŋ/ n gusto m; is it to your ~? è di suo gusto?; take a ~ to sb prendere qcno in simpatia

lilac /'laɪlək/ n lillà m • adj color lillà

lily /'lɪlɪ/ n giglio m. ~ of the valley n mughetto m

limb /lɪm/ n arto m

lime¹ /laɪm/ n (fruit) cedro m; (tree) tiglio m

lime² n calce f. '~light n be in the ~light essere molto in vista. ~stone n calcare m

limit /'lɪmɪt/ n limite m; that's the ~! [] questo è troppo! • vt limitare (to a). ~ation n limite m. ~ed adj ristretto; ~ed company società f

anonima

limousine /'lɪməziːn/ n limousine f inv

limp¹ /lɪmp/ n andatura f zoppicante; have a ~ zoppicare • vi zoppicare

limp² adj floscio

line¹ /laɪn/ n linea f; (length of rope, cord) filo m; (of writing) riga f; (of poem) verso m; (row) fila f; (wrinkle) ruga f; (of business) settore m; (Am: queue) coda f; in ~ with in conformità con • vt segnare; fiancheggiare (street). □ ~ up vi allinearsi • vt allineare

line² vt foderare (garment)

lined¹ /laɪnd/ adj (face) rugoso; (paper) a righe

lined² adj (garment) foderato

linen /'lɪnɪn/ n lino m; (articles) biancheria f • attrib di lino

liner /'laɪnə(r)/ n nave f di linea

linger /'lɪŋɡə(r)/ vi indugiare

lingerie /'læ:ɪ.ʒərɪ/ n biancheria f intima (da donna)

linguist /'lɪŋɡwɪst/ n linguista mf

linguistic /lɪŋ'ɡwɪstɪk/ adj linguistico. ~s n linguistica fsg

lining /'laɪnɪŋ/ n (of garment) fodera f; (of brakes) guarnizione f

link /lɪŋk/ n (of chain) anello m; fig legame m • vt collegare. □ ~ up vi unirsi (with a); (TV) collegarsi

lino /'laɪnəʊ/ n, **linoleum** /lɪ'nəʊlɪəm/ n linoleum m

lint /lɪnt/ n garza f

lion /'laɪən/ n leone m. ~ess n leonessa f

lip /lɪp/ n labbro m (pl labbra f); (edge) bordo m

lip: ~-read vi leggere le labbra; ~-service n pay ~-service to approvare soltanto a parole. ~salve n burro m [di] cacao. ~stick n rossetto m

liqueur /lɪ'kjʊə(r)/ n liquore m

liquid /'lɪkwɪd/ n liquido m • adj

liquido

liquidat|e /'lɪkwɪdeɪt/ vt liquidare. **~ion** n liquidazione f; (Comm) go into **~ion** andare in liquidazione

liquidize /'lɪkwɪdaɪz/ vt rendere liquido. **~r** n (Culin) frullatore m

liquor /'lɪkə(r)/ n bevanda f alcoolica

liquorice /'lɪkərɪs/ n liquirizia f

liquor store n Am negozio m di alcolici

lisp /lɪsp/ n pronuncia f con la lisca ● vi parlare con la lisca

list¹ /lɪst/ n lista f ● vt elencare

list² vi (ship): inclinarsi

listen /'lɪsn/ vi ascoltare; **~** to ascoltare; **~er** n ascoltatore, -trice mf

listless /'lɪstlɪs/ adj svogliato

lit /lɪt/ ▷LIGHT

literacy /'lɪtərəsɪ/ n alfabetizzazione f

literal /'lɪtərəl/ adj letterale. **~ly** adv letteralmente

literary /'lɪtərərɪ/ adj letterario

literate /'lɪtərət/ adj be **~** saper leggere e scrivere

literature /'lɪtrətʃə(r)/ n letteratura f

Lithuania /lɪθjʊ'eɪnɪə/ n Lituania f. **~n** adj & n lituano, -a f

litre /'liːtə(r)/ n litro m

litter /'lɪtə(r)/ n immondizie fpl; (Zool) figliata f ● vt be **~ed** with essere ingombrato di. **~-bin** n bidone m della spazzatura

little /'lɪtl/ adj piccolo; (not much) poco ● adv & n poco m; **a ~** un po'; **a ~** water un po' d'acqua; **a ~** better un po' meglio; **~** by **~** a poco a poco

live¹ /laɪv/ adj vivo; (ammunition) carico; **~** broadcast trasmissione f in diretta; be **~** (Electr) essere sotto tensione; **~** wire n fig persona f dinamica ● adv (broadcast) in diretta

live² /lɪv/ vi vivere; (reside) abitare; **~** with convivere con. □ **~** down vt far dimenticare. □ **~** off vt vivere alle spalle di. □ **~** on vt vivere di ● vi sopravvivere. □ **~** up vt it up far la bella vita. □ **~** up to vt essere all'altezza di

livelli|hood /'laɪvlɪhʊd/ n mezzi mpl di sostentamento. **~ness** n vivacità f

lively /'laɪvlɪ/ adj (-ier, -iest) vivace

liver /'lɪvə(r)/ n fegato m

lives /laɪvz/ ▷LIFE

livestock /'laɪv-/ n bestiame m

livid /'lɪvɪd/ adj ① livido

living /'lɪvɪŋ/ adj vivo ● n earn one's **~** guadagnarsi da vivere; the **~** pl i vivi. **~-room** n soggiorno m

lizard /'lɪzəd/ n lucertola f

load /ləʊd/ n carico m; **~s of** ① un sacco di ● vt caricare. **~ed** adj carico; (①: rich) ricchissimo

loaf¹ /ləʊf/ n (pl loaves) pagnotta f

loaf² vi oziare

loan /ləʊn/ n prestito m; on **~** in prestito ● vt prestare

loath|e /ləʊð/ vt detestare. **~ing** n disgusto m. **~some** adj disgustoso

lobby /'lɒbɪ/ n atrio m; (Pol) gruppo m di pressione, lobby m inv

lobster /'lɒbstə(r)/ n aragosta f

local /'ləʊkl/ adj locale; I'm not **~** non sono del posto ● n abitante mf del luogo; (①: public house) pub m locale. **~ au'thority** n autorità f locale. **~ call** n (Teleph) telefonata f urbana. **~ government** n autorità f inv locale

locality /ləʊ'kælətɪ/ n zona f

local|ization /ləʊklaɪ'zeɪʃn/ n localizzazione f. **~ized** adj localizzato

locally /'ləʊkəlɪ/ adv localmente; (live, work) nei paraggi

locat|e /ləʊ'keɪt/ vt situare; trovare (person); be **~ed** essere situato. **~ion** n posizione f; filmed on ~ion girato in esterni

lock¹ /lɒk/ n (hair) ciocca f.

lock² n (on door) serratura f; (on canal) chiusa f ● vt chiudere a chiave; bloccare (wheels) ● vi chiudersi. □ ~ **in** vt chiudere dentro. □ ~ **out** vt chiudere fuori. □ ~ **up** vt (in prison) mettere dentro ● vi chiudere

locker /'lɒkə(r)/ n armadietto m

locket /'lɒkɪt/ n medaglione m

lock: ~**out** n serrata f. ~**smith** n fabbro m

locomotive /laukə'məutɪv/ n locomotiva f

lodge /lɒdʒ/ n (porter's) portineria f; (masonic) loggia f ● vt presentare (claim, complaint); (with bank, solicitor) depositare; **be** ~**d** essersi conficcato ● vi essere a pensione (with da); (become fixed) conficcarsi. ~**r** n inquilino, -a m f

lodgings /'lɒdʒɪŋz/ npl camere fpl in affitto

loft /lɒft/ n soffitta f

lofty /'lɒftɪ/ adj (-ier, -iest) alto; (haughty) altezzoso

log /lɒg/ n ceppo m; (Naut) giornale m di circolazione; (Naut) giornale m di bordo ● vt (pt logged) registrare. □ ~ **on to** vt (Comput) connettersi a

logarithm /'lɒgərɪðm/ n logaritmo m

'log-book n (Naut) giornale m di bordo; (Auto) libretto m di circolazione

loggerheads /'lɒgə-/ npl **be at** ~ 🄘 essere in totale disaccordo

logic /'lɒdʒɪk/ n logica f. ~**al** adj logico. ~**ally** adv logicamente

logistics /lə'dʒɪstɪks/ npl logistica f

logo /'ləugəu/ n logo m inv

loin /lɔɪn/ n (Culin) lombata f

loiter /'lɔɪtə(r)/ vi gironzolare

loll|ipop /'lɒlɪpɒp/ n lecca-lecca m inv. ~**y** n lecca-lecca m, (🄘: money)

quattrini mpl

London /'lʌndən/ n Londra f ● attrib londinese, di Londra. ~**er** n londinese mf

lone /ləun/ adj solitario. ~**liness** n solitudine f

lonely /'ləunlɪ/ adj (-ier, -iest) solitario; (person) solo

lone|r /'ləunə(r)/ n persona f solitaria. ~**some** adj solo

long¹ /lɒŋ/ adj lungo; **a** ~ **time** molto tempo; **a** ~ **way** distante; **in the** ~ **run** a lungo andare; (in the end) alla fin fine ● adv a lungo, lungamente; **how** ~ **is?** quanto è lungo?; (in time) quanto dura?; **all day** ~ tutto il giorno; **not** ~ **ago** non molto tempo fa; **before** ~ fra breve; **he's no** ~**er here** non è più qui; **as or so** ~ **as** finché; (provided that) purché; **so** ~! 🄘 ciao!; **will you be** ~? [ti] ci vuole molto?

long² vi ~ **for** desiderare ardentemente

long-'distance adj a grande distanza; (Sport) di fondo; (call) interurbano

longing /'lɒŋɪŋ/ adj desideroso ● n brama f. ~**ly** adv con desiderio

longitude /'lɒŋgɪtjuːd/ n (Geog) longitudine f

long: ~ **jump** n salto m in lungo. ~-**range** adj (Aeron, Mil) a lunga portata; (forecast) a lungo termine. ~-**sighted** adj presbite. ~-**term** adj a lunga scadenza. ~-**winded** /-'wɪndɪd/ adj prolisso

loo /luː/ n 🄘 gabinetto m

look /lʊk/ n occhiata f; (appearance) aspetto m; [**good**] ~**s** pl bellezza f; **have a** ~ **at** dare un'occhiata a ● vi guardare; (seem) sembrare; ~ **here!** mi ascolti bene!; ~ **at** guardare; ~ **for** cercare; ~ **like** (resemble) assomigliare a. □ ~ **after** vt badare a. ~ **down** vi guardare in basso; ~ **down on sb** fig guardare dall'alto in basso qcno. ◻ ~ **forward to** vt essere impaziente di. ◻ ~ **in on** vt passare da. ◻ ~ **into** vt (examine) esaminare. ◻ ~ **on to** vt (room): dare su. ◻ ~ **out** vi guardare fuori; (take care) fare attenzione; ~ out for cercare; ~ out! attento! look round vi girarsi; (in shop, town etc) dare un'occhiata. ◻ ~ **through** vt dare un'occhiata a (script, notes). ◻ ~ **up** vi guardare in alto; ~ up to sb fig rispettare qcno ● vt cercare [nel dizionario] (word); (visit) andare a trovare

'look-out n guardia f; (prospect) prospettiva f; be on the ~ for tenere gli occhi aperti per

loom /luːm/ vi apparire; fig profilarsi

loony /'luːnɪ/ adj & n 🗊 matto, -a mf. ~ **bin** n manicomio m

loop /luːp/ n cappio m; (on garment) passante m. ~**hole** n (in the law) scappatoia f

loose /luːs/ adj libero; (knot) allentato; (page) staccato; (clothes) largo; (morals) dissoluto; (inexact) vago; be at a ~ end non sapere cosa fare; come ~ (knot): sciogliersi; set ~ liberare. ~ **change** n spiccioli mpl. ~**ly** adv scorrevolmente; (defined) vagamente

loosen /'luːsn/ vt sciogliere

loot /luːt/ n bottino m ● vt/i depredare. ~**er** n predatore, -trice mf. ~**ing** n saccheggio m

lop /lɒp/ ~ **off** vt (pt/pp lopped) potare

lop'sided adj sbilenco

lord /lɔːd/ n signore m; (title) Lord m; House of L~s Camera f dei Lords; the L~'s Prayer il Padrenostro; good L~! Dio mio!

lorry /'lɒrɪ/ n camion m inv; ~ **driver** camionista m

lose /luːz/ v (pt/pp lost) ● vt perdere ● vi perdere; (clock): essere indietro; get lost perdersi; get lost! 🗊 va a quel paese! ~**r** n perdente mf

loss /lɒs/ n perdita f; (Comm) ~**es** perdite fpl; be at a ~ essere perplesso; be at a ~ **for words** non trovare le parole

lost /lɒst/ ▷LOSE ● adj perduto. ~ **'property office** n ufficio m oggetti smarriti

lot[1] /lɒt/ (at auction) lotto m; draw ~s tirare a sorte

lot[2] n the ~ il tutto; a ~ of, ~s of molto/i; the ~ of you tutti voi; it has changed a ~ è cambiato molto

lotion /'ləʊʃn/ n lozione f

lottery /'lɒtərɪ/ n lotteria f. ~ **ticket** n biglietto m della lotteria

loud /laʊd/ adj sonoro, alto; (colours) sgargiante ● adv forte; out ~ ad alta voce. ~ **'hailer** n megafono m. ~**ly** adv forte. ~ **'speaker** n altoparlante m

lounge /laʊndʒ/ n salotto m; (in hotel) salone m ● vi poltrire. ~ **suit** n vestito m da uomo, completo m da uomo

louse /laʊs/ n (pl lice) pidocchio m

lousy /'laʊzɪ/ adj (-ier, -iest) 🗊 schifoso

lout /laʊt/ n zoticone m. ~**ish** adj rozzo

lovable /'lʌvəbl/ adj adorabile

love /lʌv/ n amore m; (Tennis) zero m; in ~ innamorato (with di) ● vt amare (person, country); I ~ watching tennis mi piace molto guardare il tennis. ~**affair** n relazione f [sentimentale]. ~ **letter** n lettera f d'amore

lovely /'lʌvlɪ/ adj (-ier, -iest) bello; (in looks) bello, attraente; (in character) piacevole; (meal) delizioso; have a ~ time divertirsi molto

lover /'lʌvə(r)/ n amante mf

loving /'lʌvɪŋ/ adj affettuoso

low /ləʊ/ adj basso; (depressed) giù inv ● adv basso; feel ~ sentirsi giù ● n minimo m; (Meteorol) depressione f;

at an all-time ~ (prices etc) al livello minimo

lower /'ləʊə(r)/ adj & adv ▷**LOW** ●vt abbassare; ~ **oneself** abbassarsi

loyal /'lɔɪəl/ adj leale. ~**ty** n lealtà f; ~ **card** carta f fedeltà

lozenge /'lɒzɪndʒ/ n losanga f; (tablet) pastiglia f

LP n abbr long-playing record

Ltd abbr (Limited) s.r.l.

lubricat|e /'lu:brɪkeɪt/ vt lubrificare. ~**ion** n lubrificazione f

lucid /'lu:sɪd/ adj (explanation) chiaro; (sane) lucido. ~**ity** n lucidità f; (of explanation) chiarezza f

luck /lʌk/ n fortuna f; **bad** ~ sfortuna f; **good** ~! buona fortuna! ~**ily** adv fortunatamente

lucky /'lʌkɪ/ adj (-ier, -iest) fortunato; **be** ~ essere fortunato; (thing:) portare fortuna. ~ **charm** n portafortuna m inv

lucrative /'lu:krətɪv/ adj lucrativo

ludicrous /'lu:dɪkrəs/ adj ridicolo. ~**ly** adv (expensive, complex) eccessivamente

lug /lʌg/ vt (pt/pp lugged) 🗓 trascinare

luggage /'lʌgɪdʒ/ n bagaglio m; ~-**rack** n portabagagli m inv. ~-**trolley** n carrello m portabagagli. ~-**van** n bagagliaio m

lukewarm /'lu:k-/ adj tiepido; fig poco entusiasta

lull /lʌl/ n pausa f ●vt ~ **to sleep** cullare

lullaby /'lʌləbaɪ/ n ninna nanna f

lumber /'lʌmbə(r)/ n cianfrusaglie fpl; (Am: timber) legname m ●vt 🗓 ~ **sb with sth** affibbiare qcsa a qcno. ~-**jack** n tagliaboschi m inv

luminous /'lu:mɪnəs/ adj luminoso

lump¹ /lʌmp/ n (of sugar) zolletta f; (swelling) gonfiore m; (in breast) nodulo m; (in sauce) grumo m ●vt ~

together ammucchiare

lump² vt ~ **it** 🗓 **you'll just have to** ~ **it** che ti piaccia o no è così

lump sum n somma f globale

lumpy /'lʌmpɪ/ adj (-ier, -iest) grumoso

lunacy /'lu:nəsɪ/ n follia f

lunar /'lu:nə(r)/ adj lunare

lunatic /'lu:nətɪk/ n pazzo, -a mf

lunch /lʌntʃ/ n pranzo m ●vi pranzare

luncheon /'lʌntʃn/ n (formal) pranzo m. ~ **meat** n carne f in scatola. ~ **voucher** n buono m pasto

lung /lʌŋ/ n polmone m. ~ **cancer** n cancro m al polmone

lunge /lʌndʒ/ vi lanciarsi (at su)

lurch¹ /lɜ:tʃ/ n **leave in the** ~ 🗓 lasciare nei guai

lurch² vi barcollare

lure /lʊə(r)/ n esca f; fig lusinga f ●vt adescare

lurid /'lʊərɪd/ adj (gaudy) sgargiante; (sensational) sensazionalistico

lurk /lɜ:k/ vi appostarsi

luscious /'lʌʃəs/ adj saporito; fig sexy inv

lush /lʌʃ/ adj lussureggiante

lust /lʌst/ n lussuria f ●vi ~ **after** desiderare [fortemente]. ~**ful** adj lussurioso

lute /lu:t/ n liuto m

luxuriant /lʌg'ʒʊərɪənt/ adj lussureggiante

luxurious /lʌg'ʒʊərɪəs/ adj lussuoso

luxury /'lʌkʃərɪ/ n lusso m ●attrib di lusso

lying /'laɪɪŋ/ ▷**LIE¹** & ² ●n mentire m

lynch /lɪntʃ/ vt linciare

lyric /'lɪrɪk/ adj lirico. ~**al** adj lirico; (🗓: enthusiastic) entusiasta. ~**s** npl parole fpl

Mm

mac /mæk/ n 🔲 impermeabile m

macaroni /mækəˈrəʊni/ n maccheroni mpl

mace¹ /meɪs/ n (staff) mazza f

mace² n (spice) macis m o f

machine /məˈʃiːn/ n macchina f • vt (sew) cucire a macchina; (Techn) lavorare a macchina. ~-gun n mitragliatrice f

machinery /məˈʃiːnəri/ n macchinario m

mackerel /ˈmækr(ə)l/ n inv sgombro m

mackintosh /ˈmækɪntɒʃ/ n impermeabile m

mad /mæd/ adj (madder, maddest) pazzo, matto; (🔲: angry) furioso (at con); like ~ 🔲 come un pazzo; be ~ about sb/sth (🔲: keen on) andare matto per qcno/qcsa

madam /ˈmædəm/ n signora f

mad cow disease n morbo m della mucca pazza

madden /ˈmædən/ vt (make angry) far diventare matto

made /meɪd/ ▷ MAKE; ~ to measure [fatto] su misura

mad|ly /ˈmædli/ adv 🔲 follemente. ~ly in love innamorato follemente. ~man n pazzo m. ~ness n pazzia f

madonna /məˈdɒnə/ n madonna f

magazine /mægəˈziːn/ n rivista f; (Mil, Phot) magazzino m

maggot /ˈmægət/ n verme m

magic /ˈmædʒɪk/ n magia f; (tricks) giochi mpl di prestigio • adj magico; (trick) di prestigio. ~al adj magico

magician /məˈdʒɪʃn/ n mago, -a mf; (entertainer) prestigiatore, -trice m

magistrate /ˈmædʒɪstreɪt/ n magistrato m

magnet /ˈmægnɪt/ n magnete m, calamita f. ~ic adj magnetico. ~ism n magnetismo m

magnification /mægnɪfɪˈkeɪʃn/ n ingrandimento m

magnificen|ce /mægˈnɪfɪsəns/ n magnificenza f. ~t adj magnifico

magnify /ˈmægnɪfaɪ/ vt (pt/pp -ied) ingrandire; (exaggerate) ingigantire. ~ing glass n lente f d'ingrandimento

magnitude /ˈmægnɪtjuːd/ n grandezza f; (importance) importanza f

magpie /ˈmægpaɪ/ n gazza f

mahogany /məˈhɒgəni/ n mogano m • attrib di mogano

maid /meɪd/ n cameriera f; old ~ pej zitella f

maiden /ˈmeɪdn/ n (liter) fanciulla f • adj (speech, voyage) inaugurale. ~ aunt n zia f zitella. ~ name n nome m da ragazza

mail /meɪl/ n posta f • vt impostare. ~bag n sacco m postale. ~box n Am cassetta f delle lettere; (e-mail) casella f di posta elettronica. ~ing list n elenco m d'indirizzi per un mailing. ~man n Am postino m. ~ order n vendita f per corrispondenza. ~order firm n ditta f di vendita per corrispondenza. ~shot n mailing m inv

maim /meɪm/ vt menomare

main¹ /meɪn/ n (water, gas, electricity) conduttura f principale

main² adj principale; the ~ thing is to... la cosa essenziale è di... • n in the ~ in complesso

main: ~land /-lənd/ n continente m. ~ly adv principalmente. ~ street n via f principale

maintain /meɪnˈteɪn/ vt mantenere; (keep in repair) curare la manutenzione di; (claim) sostenere

maintenance /ˈmeɪntənəns/ n mantenimento m; (care) manutenzione f; (allowance) alimenti mpl

maisonette /meɪzə'net/ n appartamento m a due piani

majestic /mə'dʒestɪk/ adj maestoso

majesty /'mædʒəstɪ/ n maestà f; His/Her M~ Sua Maestà

major /'meɪdʒə(r)/ adj maggiore; ~ road strada f con diritto di precedenza ●n (Mil, Mus) maggiore m ●vi Am ~ in specializzarsi in

Majorca /mə'jɔ:kə/ n Maiorca f

majority /mə'dʒɒrətɪ/ n maggioranza f; be in the ~ avere la maggioranza

make /meɪk/ n (brand) marca f ●v t (pt/pp made) ●v t fare; (earn) guadagnare; rendere (happy, clear); prendere (decision); ~ sb laugh far ridere qcno; ~ sb do sth far fare qcsa a qcno; ~ it (to party, top of hill etc) farcela; what time do you ~ it? che ore fai? ●v i ~ as if to fare per. □ ~ **do** vi arrangiarsi. □ ~ **for** vt dirigersi verso. □ ~ **off** vi fuggire. □ ~ **out** vt (distinguish) distinguere; (write out) rilasciare (cheque); compilare (list); (claim) far credere. □ ~ **over** vt cedere. □ ~ **up** vt (constitute) comporre; (complete) completare; (invent) inventare; (apply cosmetics to) truccare (face, parcel); ~ up one's mind decidersi; ~ it up (after quarrel) riconciliarsi ●v i (after quarrel) fare la pace; ~ up for compensare; ~ up for lost time recuperare il tempo perso

make-believe n finzione f

maker /'meɪkə(r)/ n fabbricante mf; M~ Creatore m

make: ~ **shift** adj di fortuna ●n espediente m. ~-**up** n trucco m; (character) natura f

making /'meɪkɪŋ/ n have the ~s of aver la stoffa di

maladjust|ed /mælə'dʒʌstɪd/ adj disadattato

malaria /mə'leərɪə/ n malaria f

Malaysia /mə'leɪzɪə/ n Malesia f

male /meɪl/ adj maschile ●n maschio m. ~ **nurse** n infermiere m.

malfunction /mæl'fʌŋkʃn/ n funzionamento m imperfetto ●v i funzionare male

malice /'mælɪs/ n malignità f; bear sb ~ voler del male a qcno

malicious /mə'lɪʃəs/ adj maligno

mallet /'mælɪt/ n martello m di legno

malnu'trition /mæl-/ n malnutrizione f

mal'practice n negligenza f

malt /mɔ:lt/ n malto m

Malta /'mɔ:ltə/ n Malta f. ~**ese** adj & n maltese mf

mammal /'mæml/ n mammifero m

mammoth /'mæməθ/ adj mastodontico ●n mammut m inv

man /mæn/ n (pl men) uomo m; (chess, draughts) pedina f ●v t (pt/pp manned) equipaggiare; essere di servizio a (counter, telephones)

manage /'mænɪdʒ/ vt dirigere; gestire (shop, affairs); (cope with) farcela; ~ to do sth riuscire a fare qcsa ●v i riuscire; (cope) farcela (on con). ~**able** adj (hair) docile; (size) maneggevole. ~**ment** n gestione f; the ~**ment** la direzione

manager /'mænɪdʒə(r)/ n direttore m; (of shop, bar) gestore m; (Sport) manager m inv. ~**ess** n direttrice f. ~**ial** adj ~ial staff personale m direttivo

mandat|e /'mændeɪt/ n mandato m. ~**ory** adj obbligatorio

mane /meɪn/ n criniera f

mangle /'mæŋgl/ vt (damage) maciullare

man: ~**handle** vt malmenare. ~**hole** n botola f. ~**hood** n età f adulta; (quality) virilità f. ~-**hour** n ora f lavorativa. ~-**hunt** n caccia f all'uomo

man|ia /'meɪnɪə/ n mania f. ~**iac** n maniaco, -a mf

m

manicure /'mænɪkjʊə(r)/ n manicure f • vt fare la manicure a

manifest /'mænɪfest/ adj manifesto • vt ~ itself manifestarsi. ~ly adv palesemente

manifesto /mænɪ'festəʊ/ n manifesto m

manipulat|e /mə'nɪpjʊleɪt/ vt manipolare. ~ion n manipolazione f

man'kind n genere m umano

manly /'mænlɪ/ adj virile

'man-made adj artificiale. ~ fibre n fibra f sintetica

manner /'mænə(r)/ n maniera f; in this ~ in questo modo; have no ~s avere dei pessimi modi; good/bad ~s buone/cattive maniere fpl. ~ism n affettazione f

manor /'mænə(r)/ n maniero m

'manpower n manodopera f

mansion /'mænʃn/ n palazzo m

'manslaughter n omicidio m colposo

mantelpiece /'mæntl-/ n mensola f di caminetto

manual /'mænjʊəl/ adj manuale • n manuale m

manufacture /mænjʊ'fæktʃə(r)/ vt fabbricare • n manifattura f. ~r n fabbricante m

manure /mə'njʊə(r)/ n concime m

manuscript /'mænjʊskrɪpt/ n manoscritto m

many /'menɪ/ adj & pron molti; there are as ~ boys as girls ci sono tanti ragazzi quante ragazze; as ~ as 500 ben 500; as ~ as that così tanti; as ~ altrettanti; very ~, a good/great ~ moltissimi; ~ a time molte volte

map /mæp/ n carta f geografica; (of town) mappa f • map out vt (pt/pp mapped) fig programmare

mar /mɑ:(r)/ vt (pt/pp marred) rovinare

marathon /'mærəθən/ n maratona f

marble /'mɑ:bl/ n marmo m; (for game) pallina f • attrib di marmo

march n marcia f; (protest) dimostrazione f • vi marciare • vt far marciare; ~ sb off scortare qcno fuori

March /mɑ:tʃ/ n marzo m

mare /meə(r)/ n giumenta f

margarine /mɑ:dʒə'ri:n/ n margarina f

margin /'mɑ:dʒɪn/ n margine m. ~al adj marginale. ~ally adv marginalmente

marijuana /mærʊ'wɑ:nə/ n marijuana f

marina /mə'ri:nə/ n porticciolo m

marine /mə'ri:n/ adj marino • n (sailor) soldato m di fanteria marina

marionette /mærɪə'net/ n marionetta f

mark¹ /mɑ:k/ n (currency) marco m

mark² n (stain) macchia f; (sign, indication) segno m; (Sch) voto m • vt segnare; (stain) macchiare; (Sch) correggere; (Sport) marcare; ~ time (Mil) segnare il passo; fig non far progressi; ~ my words ricordati quello che dico. ▫ ~ out vt delimitare; fig designare

marked /mɑ:kt/ adj marcato. ~ly adv notevolmente

marker /'mɑ:kə(r)/ n (for highlighting) evidenziatore m; (Sport) marcatore m; (of exam) esaminatore, -trice mf

market /'mɑ:kɪt/ n mercato m • vt vendere al mercato; (launch) commercializzare; on the ~ sul mercato. ~ing n marketing m. ~ re'search n ricerca f di mercato

marksman /'mɑ:ksmən/ n tiratore m scelto

marmalade /'mɑ:məleɪd/ n marmellata f d'arance

maroon /mə'ru:n/ adj marrone rossastro

marquee /mɑ:'ki:/ n tendone m

marriage /'mærɪdʒ/ n

matrimonio m

married /ˈmærɪd/ adj sposato; (life) coniugale

marrow /ˈmærəʊ/ n (Anat) midollo m; (vegetable) zucca f

marr|y /ˈmærɪ/ vt (pt/pp married) sposare; get ~ied sposarsi ● vi sposarsi

marsh /mɑːʃ/ n palude f

marshal /ˈmɑːʃl/ n (steward) cerimoniere m ● vt (pt/pp marshalled) fig organizzare (arguments)

marshy /ˈmɑːʃɪ/ adj paludoso

martial /ˈmɑːʃl/ adj marziale

martyr /ˈmɑːtə(r)/ n martire mf ● vt martoriare. ~dom n martirio m. ~ed adj 🔢 da martire

marvel /ˈmɑːvl/ n meraviglia f ● vi (pt/pp marvelled) meravigliarsi (at di). ~lous adj meraviglioso

Marxis|m /ˈmɑːksɪzm/ n marxismo m. ~t adj & n marxista mf

marzipan /ˈmɑːzɪpæn/ n marzapane m

mascara /mæˈskɑːrə/ n mascara m inv

mascot /ˈmæskət/ n mascotte f inv

masculin|e /ˈmæskjʊlɪn/ adj maschile ● n (Gram) maschile m. ~ity n mascolinità f

mash /mæʃ/ vt impastare. ~ed potatoes npl purè m inv di patate

mask /mɑːsk/ n maschera f ● vt mascherare

masochis|m /ˈmæsəkɪzm/ n masochismo m. ~t n masochista mf

mason /ˈmeɪsn/ n muratore m. **Mason** n massone m. ~ic adj massonico

masonry /ˈmeɪsnrɪ/ n massoneria f

masquerade /mæskəˈreɪd/ n fig mascherata f ● vi ~ as (pose) farsi passare per

mass¹ /mæs/ n (Relig) messa f

mass² n massa f; ~es of 🔢 un sacco di ● vi ammassarsi

massacre /ˈmæsəkə(r)/ n massacro m ● vt massacrare

massage /ˈmæsɑːʒ/ n massaggio m ● vt massaggiare; fig manipolare (statistics)

masseu|r /mæˈsɜː(r)/ n massaggiatore m. ~se n massaggiatrice f

massive /ˈmæsɪv/ adj enorme

mass: ~ **media** npl mezzi mpl di comunicazione di massa, mass media mpl. ~-**pro·duce** vt produrre in serie

mast /mɑːst/ n (Naut) albero m; (for radio) antenna f

master /ˈmɑːstə(r)/ n maestro m, padrone m; (teacher) professore m; (of ship) capitano m; M~ (boy) signorino m

master: ~-**key** n passe-partout m inv. ~-**mind** n cervello m ● vt ideare e dirigere. ~**piece** n capolavoro m. ~-**stroke** n colpo m da maestro. ~**y** n (of subject) padronanza f

masturbat|e /ˈmæstəbeɪt/ vi masturbarsi. ~**ion** n masturbazione f

mat /mæt/ n stuoia f; (on table) sottopiatto m

match¹ /mætʃ/ n (Sport) partita f; (equal) uguale mf; (marriage) matrimonio m; (person to marry) partito m; be a good ~ (colours): intonarsi bene; be no ~ for non essere dello stesso livello di ● vt (equal) uguagliare; (be like) andare bene con ● vi intonarsi

match² n fiammifero m. ~**box** n scatola f di fiammiferi

matching /ˈmætʃɪŋ/ adj intonato

mate¹ /meɪt/ n compagno, -a mf; (assistant) aiuto m; (Naut) secondo m; (🔢: friend) amico, -a mf ● vi accoppiarsi ● vt accoppiare

mate² n (in chess) scacco m matto

material /məˈtɪərɪəl/ n materiale m; (fabric) stoffa f; raw ~s materie fpl prime ● adj materiale

maternal /məˈtɜːnl/ adj materno

maternity /məˈtɜːnətɪ/ n maternità f. ~ **clothes** npl abiti mpl premaman.

~ ward n maternità f inv

mathematic|al /mæθə'mætɪkl/ adj matematico. ~ian n matematico, -a mf

mathematics /mæθə'mætɪks/ n matematica fsg

maths /mæθs/ n ① matematica fsg

matinée /'mætɪneɪ/ n (Theat) matinée n

matriculat|e /mə'trɪkjʊleɪt/ vi immatricolarsi. ~ion n immatricolazione f

matrix /'meɪtrɪks/ n (pl matrices /-si:z/) n matrice f

matted /'mætɪd/ adj ~ hair capelli mpl tutti appiccicati tra loro

matter /'mætə(r)/ n (affair) faccenda f; (question) questione f; (pus) pus m; (phys: substance) materia f; as a ~ of fact a dire la verità; what is the ~? che cosa c'è? ● vi importare; ~ to sb essere importante per qcno; it doesn't ~ non importa. ~-of-fact adj pratico

mattress /'mætrɪs/ n materasso m

matur|e /mə'tʃʊə(r)/ adj maturo; (Comm) in scadenza ● vi maturare ● vt far maturare. ~ity n maturità f; (Fin) maturazione f

maul /mɔːl/ vt malmenare

mauve /məʊv/ adj malva

maxim /'mæksɪm/ n massima f

maximum /'mæksɪməm/ adj massimo; ten minutes ~ dieci minuti al massimo ● n (pl -ima) massimo m

may /meɪ/ v.aux (solo al presente) potere; ~ I come in? posso entrare? if I ~ say so se mi posso permettere; ~ you both be very happy siate felici; I ~ as well stay potrei anche rimanere; it ~ be true potrebbe esser vero; she ~ be old, but... sarà anche vecchia, ma...

May /meɪ/ n maggio m

maybe /'meɪbiː/ adv forse, può darsi

'May Day n il primo maggio

mayonnaise /meɪə'neɪz/ n maionese f

mayor /'meə(r)/ n sindaco m. ~ess n sindaco m; (wife of mayor) moglie f del sindaco

maze /meɪz/ n labirinto m

me /miː/ pron (object) mi; (with preposition) me; she called me mi ha chiamato; she called me, not you no te; give me the money dammi i soldi; give it to me dammelo; he gave it to me me lo ha dato; it's ~ sono io

meadow /'medəʊ/ n prato m

meagre /'miːɡə(r)/ adj scarso

meal¹ /miːl/ n pasto m

meal² /n (grain) farina f

mean¹ /miːn/ adj avaro; (unkind) meschino

mean² adj medio ● n (average) media f; Greenwich ~ time ora f media di Greenwich

mean³ vt (pt/pp meant) voler dire; (signify) significare; (intend) intendere; I ~ it lo dico seriamente; ~ well avere buone intenzioni; be meant for (present:) essere destinato a; (remark:) essere riferito a

meander /mɪ'ændə(r)/ vi vagare

meaning /'miːnɪŋ/ n significato m. ~ful adj significativo. ~less adj senza senso

means /miːnz/ n mezzo m; ~ of transport mezzo m di trasporto; by ~ of per mezzo di; by all ~! certamente!; by no ~ niente affatto ● npl (resources) mezzi mpl

meant /ment/ ▷MEAN³

'meantime n in the ~ nel frattempo ● adv intanto

'meanwhile adv intanto

measles /'miːzlz/ n morbillo m

measly /'miːzlɪ/ adj ① misero

measure /'meʒə(r)/ n misura f ● vt/i misurare. □ ~ up to vt fig essere all'altezza di. ~d adj misurato.

~ment n misura f

meat /mi:t/ n carne f. ~ **ball** n (Culin) polpetta f di carne. ~ **loaf** n polpettone m

mechan|ic /mɪˈkænɪk/ n meccanico m. ~**ical** adj meccanico; ~**ical engineering** ingegneria f meccanica. ~**ically** adv meccanicamente. ~**ics** n meccanica f ● npl meccanismo msg

mechan|ism /ˈmekənɪzm/ n meccanismo m. ~**ize** vt meccanizzare

medal /ˈmedl/ n medaglia f

medallist /ˈmedəlɪst/ n vincitore, -trice mf di una medaglia

meddle /ˈmedl/ vi immischiarsi (in di); (tinker) armeggiare (with con)

media /ˈmiːdɪə/ ▷MEDIUM ● npl the ~ i mass media

mediat|e /ˈmiːdɪeɪt/ vi fare da mediatore. ~**ion** n mediazione f. ~**or** n mediatore, -trice mf

medical /ˈmedɪkl/ adj medico ● n visita f medica. ~ **insurance** n assicurazione f sanitaria. ~ **student** n studente, -essa mf di medicina

medicat|ed /ˈmedɪkeɪtɪd/ adj medicato. ~**ion** n (drugs) medicinali mpl

medicinal /mɪˈdɪsɪnl/ adj medicinale

medicine /ˈmedsən/ n medicina f

medieval /medɪˈiːvl/ adj medievale

mediocr|e /miːdɪˈəʊkə(r)/ adj mediocre. ~**ity** n mediocrità f

meditat|e /ˈmedɪteɪt/ vi meditare (on su). ~**ion** n meditazione f

Mediterranean /medɪtəˈreɪnɪən/ n the ~ [Sea] il [mare m] Mediterraneo m ● adj mediterraneo

medium /ˈmiːdɪəm/ adj medio; (Culin) di media cottura ● n (pl media) mezzo m; (pl -s) (person) medium mf inv

medium-sized adj di taglia media

medley /ˈmedlɪ/ n miscuglio m; (Mus) miscellanea f

meek /miːk/ adj mite, mansueto.

~**ly** adv docilmente

meet /miːt/ v (pt/pp met) ● vt incontrare; (at station, airport) andare incontro a; (for first time) fare la conoscenza di; pagare (bill); soddisfare (requirements) ● vi incontrarsi; (committee:) riunirsi; ~ **with** incontrare (problem); incontrarsi con (person) ● n raduno m [sportivo]

meeting /ˈmiːtɪŋ/ n riunione f, meeting m inv; (large) assemblea f; (by chance) incontro m

megabyte /ˈmegəbaɪt/ n megabyte m

megaphone /ˈmegəfəʊn/ n megafono m

melancholy /ˈmelənkəlɪ/ adj malinconico ● n malinconia f

mellow /ˈmeləʊ/ adj (wine) generoso; (sound, colour) caldo; (person) dolce ● vi (person:) addolcirsi

melodrama /ˈmelə-/ n melodramma m. ~**tic** adj melodrammatico

melody /ˈmelədɪ/ n melodia f

melon /ˈmelən/ n melone m

melt /melt/ vt sciogliere ● vi sciogliersi. □ ~ **down** vt fondere. ~**ing-pot** n fig crogiuolo m

member /ˈmembə(r)/ n membro m; ~ **countries** paesi mpl membri; M~ **of Parliament** deputato, -a mf; M~ **of the European Parliament** eurodeputato, -a mf. ~**ship** n iscrizione f; (members) soci mpl

membrane /ˈmembreɪn/ n membrana f

memo /ˈmeməʊ/ n promemoria m inv

memorable /ˈmemərəbl/ adj memorabile

memorandum /meməˈrændəm/ n promemoria m inv

memorial /mɪˈmɔːrɪəl/ n monumento m. ~ **service** n funzione f commemorativa

memorize /ˈmemərɑɪz/ vt

m

memorizzare

memory /'meməri/ n also (Comput) memoria f; (thing remembered) ricordo m; from ~ a memoria; in ~ of in ricordo di

men /men/ ▷ **MAN**

menac|e /'menəs/ n minaccia f; (nuisance) piaga f ● vt minacciare. ~**ing** adj minaccioso

mend /mend/ vt riparare; (darn) rammendare ● n on the ~ in via di guarigione

'**menfolk** n uomini mpl

menial /'mi:nɪəl/ adj umile

meningitis /menɪn'dʒaɪtɪs/ n meningite f

menopause /'menə-/ n menopausa f

menstruat|e /'menstrʊeɪt/ vi mestruare. ~**ion** n mestruazione f

mental /'mentl/ adj mentale; (🔲: mad) pazzo. ~ a'rithmetic n calcolo m mentale. ~ 'illness n malattia f mentale

mental|ity /men'tælətɪ/ n mentalità f inv. ~**ly** adv mentalmente; ~**ly** ill malato di mente

mention /'menʃn/ n menzione f ● vt menzionare; don't ~ it non c'è di che

menu /'menju:/ n menu m inv

MEP n abbr Member of the European Parliament

mercenary /'mɜːsɪnərɪ/ adj mercenario ● n mercenario m

merchandise /'mɜːtʃəndaɪz/ n merce f

merchant /'mɜːtʃənt/ n commerciante mf. ~ **bank** n banca f d'affari. ~ '**navy** n marina f mercantile

merci|ful /'mɜːsɪfl/ adj misericordioso. ~**fully** adv 🔲 grazie a Dio. ~**less** adj spietato

mercury /'mɜːkjʊrɪ/ n mercurio m

mercy /'mɜːsɪ/ n misericordia f; be at sb's ~ essere alla mercè di qcno,

essere in balia di qcno

mere /mɪə(r)/ adj solo. ~**ly** adv solamente

merge /mɜːdʒ/ vi fondersi

merger /'mɜːdʒə(r)/ n fusione f

meringue /mə'ræŋ/ n meringa f

merit /'merɪt/ n merito m; (advantage) qualità f ● vt meritare

mermaid /'mɜːmeɪd/ n sirena f

merri|ly /'merɪlɪ/ adv allegramente. ~**ment** n baldoria f

merry /'merɪ/ adj (-ier, -iest) allegro; ~ Christmas! Buon Natale!

merry: ~-**go-round** n giostra f. ~-**making** n festa f

mesh /meʃ/ n maglia f

mesmerize /'mezməraɪz/ vt ipnotizzare. ~**d** adj fig ipnotizzato

mess /mes/ n disordine m, casino m 🔲; (trouble) guaio m; (something spilt) sporco m; (Mil) mensa f; make a ~ of (botch) fare un pasticcio di ● **mess about** vi perder tempo; ~ **about** with armeggiare con ● vt prendere in giro (person). □ ~ **up** vt mettere in disordine, incasinare 🔲; (botch) mandare all'aria

message /'mesɪdʒ/ n messaggio m

messenger /'mesɪndʒə(r)/ n messaggero m

Messiah /mɪ'saɪə/ n Messia m

Messrs /'mesəz/ npl (on letter) ~ Smith Spett. ditta Smith

messy /'mesɪ/ adj (-ier, -iest) disordinato; (in dress) sciatto

met /met/ ▷ **MEET**

metal /'metl/ n metallo m ● adj di metallo. ~**lic** adj metallico

metaphor /'metəfə(r)/ n metafora f. ~**ical** adj metaforico

meteor /'mi:tɪə(r)/ n meteora f. ~**ic** adj fig fulmineo

meteorological /mi:tɪərə'lɒdʒɪkl/ adj meteorologico

meteo|rologist /mi:tɪə'rɒlədʒɪst/ n meteorologo, -a mf. ~**rology** n meteorologia f

meter[1] /ˈmiːtə(r)/ n contatore m

meter[2] n Am = **metre**

method /ˈmeθəd/ n metodo m

methodical /mɪˈθɒdɪkl/ adj metodico. **~ly** adv metodicamente

methylated /ˈmeθɪleɪtɪd/ adj **~ spirit[s]** alcol m denaturato

meticulous /mɪˈtɪkjʊləs/ adj meticoloso. **~ly** adv meticolosamente

metre /ˈmiːtə(r)/ n metro m

metric /ˈmetrɪk/ adj metrico

metropolis /mɪˈtrɒpəlɪs/ n metropoli f inv

mew /mjuː/ n miao m ●vi miagolare

Mexican /ˈmeksɪkən/ adj & n messicano, -a mf. **'Mexico** n Messico m

miaow /mɪˈaʊ/ n miao m ●vi miagolare

mice /maɪs/ ▷ MOUSE

mickey /ˈmɪkɪ/ n take the **~** out of prendere in giro

micro /ˈmaɪkrəʊ/: **~chip** n microchip m. **~computer** n microcomputer m. **~film** n microfilm m. **~phone** n microfono m. **~processor** n microprocessore m. **~scope** n microscopio m. **~scopic** adj microscopico. **~wave** n microonda f. **(oven)** forno m a microonde

microbe /ˈmaɪkrəʊb/ n microbo m

mid /mɪd/ adj **~ May** metà maggio; in **~** air a mezz'aria

midday /mɪdˈdeɪ/ n mezzogiorno m

middle /ˈmɪdl/ adj di centro; the M**~** Ages il medioevo; the **~** class[es] la classe media; the M**~** East il Medio Oriente ●n mezzo m; in the **~** of (room, floor etc) nel mezzo di; in the **~** of the night nel pieno della notte, a notte piena

middle: **~-aged** adj di mezza età. **~-class** adj borghese. **~man** n (Comm) intermediario m

middling /ˈmɪdlɪŋ/ adj discreto

midge /mɪdʒ/ n moscerino m

midget /ˈmɪdʒɪt/ n nano, -a mf

Midlands /ˈmɪdləndz/ npl the **~** l'Inghilterra fsg centrale

midnight /ˈmɪdnaɪt/ n mezzanotte f

midriff /ˈmɪdrɪf/ n diaframma m

midst /mɪdst/ n in the **~** of in mezzo a; in our **~** fra di noi, in mezzo a noi

mid: **~summer** n mezza estate f **~way** adv a metà strada. **~wife** n ostetrica f. **~'winter** n pieno inverno m

might[1] /maɪt/ v aux I **~** potrei; will you come? – I **~** vieni? – può darsi; it **~** be true potrebbe essere vero; I **~** as well stay potrei anche restare; you **~** have drowned avresti potuto affogare; you **~** have said so! avresti potuto dirlo!

might[2] n potere m

mighty /ˈmaɪtɪ/ adj (-ier, -iest) potente ●adv 🔲 molto

migraine /ˈmiːɡreɪn/ n emicrania f

migrant /ˈmaɪɡrənt/ adj migratore ●n (bird) migratore, -trice mf; (person: for work) emigrante m

migrat|e /maɪˈɡreɪt/ vi migrare. **~ion** n migrazione f

Milan /mɪˈlæn/ n Milano f

mild /maɪld/ adj (weather) mite; (person) dolce; (flavour) delicato; (illness) leggero

mildew /ˈmɪldjuː/ n muffa f

mild|ly /ˈmaɪldlɪ/ adv moderatamente; (say) dolcemente; to put it **~ly** a dir poco, senza esagerazione. **~ness** n (of person, words) dolcezza f; (of weather) mitezza f

mile /maɪl/ n miglio m (= 1,6 km); **~s** nicer 🔲 molto più bello

mileage /-ɪdʒ/ n chilometraggio m. **~stone** n pietra f miliare

militant /ˈmɪlɪtənt/ adj & n militante mf

military /ˈmɪlɪtrɪ/ adj militare. **~ service** n servizio m militare

m

militia /mɪˈlɪʃə/ n milizia f

milk /mɪlk/ n latte m ● vt mungere

milk: ~man n lattaio m. **~ shake** n frappé m inv

milky /ˈmɪlkɪ/ adj (-ier, -iest) latteo; (tea etc) con molto latte. **M~ Way** n (Astr) Via f Lattea

mill /mɪl/ n mulino m; (factory) fabbrica f; (for coffee etc) macinino m ● vt macinare (grain). **mill about, mill around** vi brulicare

millennium /mɪˈlenɪəm/ n millennio m

miller /ˈmɪlə(r)/ n mugnaio m

million /ˈmɪljən/ n milione m; **a ~ pounds** un milione di sterline. **~aire** n miliardario, -a mf

'millstone n fig peso m

mime /maɪm/ n mimo m ● vt mimare

mimic /ˈmɪmɪk/ n imitatore, -trice mf ● vt (pt/pp mimicked) imitare. **~ry** n mimetismo m

mince /mɪns/ n carne f tritata ● vt (Culin) tritare; **not ~ one's words** parlare senza mezzi termini

mince 'pie n pasticcino m a base di frutta secca

mincer /ˈmɪnsə(r)/ n tritacarne m inv

mind /maɪnd/ n mente f; (sanity) ragione f; **to my ~** a mio parere; **give sb a piece of one's ~** dire chiaro e tondo a qcno quello che si pensa; **make up one's ~** decidersi; **have sth in ~** avere qcsa in mente; **bear sth in ~** tenere presente qcsa; **have something on one's ~** essere preoccupato; **have a good ~ to** avere una gran voglia di; **I have changed my ~** ho cambiato idea; **in two ~s** indeciso; **are you out of your ~?** sei diventato matto? ● vt (look after) occuparsi di; **I don't ~ the noise** il rumore non mi dà fastidio; **I don't ~ what we do** non mi importa quello che facciamo; **~ the**

step! attenzione al gradino! ● vi **I don't ~** non mi importa; **never ~!** non importa!; **do you ~ if...?** ti dispiace se...? **mind out** vi **~ out!** [fai] attenzione!

mind|ful adj **~ful of** attento a. **~less** adj noncurante

mine[1] /maɪn/ poss pron **il mio** m, **la mia** f, **i miei** mpl, **le mie** fpl; **a friend of ~** un mio amico; **friends of ~** dei miei amici; **that is ~** questo è mio; (as opposed to yours) questo è **il mio**

mine[2] n miniera f; (explosive) mina f ● vt estrarre; (Mil) minare. **~ detector** n rivelatore m di mine. **~field** n campo m minato

mineral /ˈmɪnərəl/ n minerale m ● adj minerale. **~ water** n acqua f minerale

mingle /ˈmɪŋgl/ vi **~ with** mescolarsi a

mini /ˈmɪnɪ/ n (skirt) mini f

miniature /ˈmɪnɪtʃə(r)/ adj in miniatura ● n miniatura f

mini|bus /ˈmɪnɪ-/ n minibus m, pulmino m. **~cab** n taxi m inv

minim|al /ˈmɪnɪməl/ adj minimo. **~ize** vt minimizzare. **~um** n (pl -ima) minimo m ● adj minimo; **ten minutes ~um** dieci minuti

mining /ˈmaɪnɪŋ/ n estrazione f ● adj estrattivo

miniskirt /ˈmɪnɪ-/ n minigonna f

minist|er /ˈmɪnɪstə(r)/ n ministro m; (Relig) pastore m. **~erial** adj ministeriale

ministry /ˈmɪnɪstrɪ/ n (Pol) ministero m; **the ~** (Relig) il ministero sacerdotale

mink /mɪŋk/ n visone m

minor /ˈmaɪnə(r)/ adj minore ● n minorenne mf

minority /maɪˈnɒrətɪ/ n minoranza f; (age) minore età f

mint[1] /mɪnt/ n **1** patrimonio m ● adj **in ~ condition** in condizione perfetta

mint² n (herb) menta f

minus /'maɪnəs/ prep meno; (⊞: without) senza ● n ≈ [sign] meno m

minute¹ /'mɪnɪt/ n minuto m; in a ~ (shortly) in un minuto; ~s pl (of meeting) verbale msg

minute² /maɪ'njuːt/ adj minuto; (precise) minuzioso

mirac|le /'mɪrəkl/ n miracolo m. ~**ulous** adj miracoloso

mirage /'mɪrɑːʒ/ n miraggio m

mirror /'mɪrə(r)/ n specchio m ● vt rispecchiare

mirth /mɜːθ/ n ilarità f

misappre'hension n malinteso m; be under a ~ avere frainteso

misbe'have vi comportarsi male

mis'calcu|late vt/i calcolare male. ~'**lation** n calcolo m sbagliato

miscarriage n aborto m spontaneo; ~ of justice errore m giudiziario. **mis'carry** vi abortire

miscellaneous /mɪsə'leɪnɪəs/ adj assortito

mischief /'mɪstʃɪf/ n malefatta f; (harm) danno m

mischievous /'mɪstʃɪvəs/ adj (naughty) birichino; (malicious) dannoso

miscon'ception n concetto m erroneo

mis'conduct n cattiva condotta f

misde'meanour n reato m

miser /'maɪzə(r)/ n avaro m

miserab|le /'mɪzrəbl/ adj (unhappy) infelice; (wretched) miserabile; (fig: weather) deprimente. ~**ly** adv (live, fail) miseramente; (say) tristemente

miserly /'maɪzəlɪ/ adj avaro; (amount) ridicolo

misery /'mɪzərɪ/ n miseria f; (⊞: person) piagnone, -a mf

mis'fire vi (gun:) far cilecca; (plan etc:) non riuscire

misfit n disadattato, -a mf

mis'fortune n sfortuna f

mis'guided adj fuorviato

mishap /'mɪshæp/ n disavventura f

misin'terpret vt fraintendere

mis'judge vt giudicar male; (estimate wrongly) valutare male

mis'lay vt (pt/pp -laid) smarrire

mis'lead vt (pt/pp -led) fuorviare. ~**ing** adj fuorviante

mis'manage vt amministrare male. ~**ment** n cattiva amministrazione f

'misprint n errore m di stampa

miss /mɪs/ n colpo m mancato ● vt (fail to hit or find) mancare; perdere (train, bus, class); (feel the loss of) sentire la mancanza di; I ~ed that part (failed to notice) mi è sfuggita quella parte ● vi but he ~ed (failed to hit) ma l'ha mancato. □ ~ **out** vt saltare, omettere

Miss n (pl -es) signorina f

misshapen /mɪs'ʃeɪpən/ adj malformato

missile /'mɪsaɪl/ n missile m

missing /'mɪsɪŋ/ adj mancante; (person) scomparso; (Mil) disperso; be ~ essere introvabile

mission /'mɪʃn/ n missione f

missionary /'mɪʃənrɪ/ n missionario, -a mf

mist /mɪst/ n (fog) foschia f ● mist up vi appannarsi, annebbiarsi

mistake /mɪ'steɪk/ n sbaglio m; by ~ per sbaglio ● vt (pt mistook, pp mistaken) sbagliare (road, house); fraintendere (meaning, words); ~ for prendere per

mistaken /mɪ'steɪkən/ adj sbagliato; be ~ sbagliarsi; ~ identity errore m di persona. ~**ly** adv erroneamente

mistletoe /'mɪsltəʊ/ n vischio m

mistress /'mɪstrɪs/ n padrona f; (teacher) maestra f; (lover) amante f

mis'trust n sfiducia f ● vt non aver fiducia in

m

misty /'mɪstɪ/ adj (-ier, -iest)
nebbioso

misunder'stand vt (pt/pp -stood)
fraintendere. ~ing n malinteso m

misuse¹ /mɪs'juːz/ vt usare male

misuse² /mɪs'juːs/ n cattivo uso m

mite /maɪt/ n (child) piccino, -a mf

mitten /'mɪtn/ n manopola f, muffola m

mix /mɪks/ n (combination) mescolanza
f; (Culin) miscuglio m; (ready-made)
preparato m ● vt mischiare ● vi mischiarsi; (person): inserirsi; ~ with
(associate with) frequentare. □ ~ up vt
mescolare (papers); (confuse, mistake
for) confondere

mixed /mɪkst/ adj misto; ~ up
(person) confuso

mixer /'mɪksə(r)/ n (Culin) frullatore
m, mixer m inv; he's a good ~ è un
tipo socievole

mixture /'mɪkstʃə(r)/ n mescolanza
f; (medicine) sciroppo m; (Culin) miscela f

'mix-up n (confusion) confusione f;
(mistake) pasticcio m

moan /məʊn/ n lamento m ● vi lamentarsi; (complain) lagnarsi

moat /məʊt/ n fossato m

mob /mɒb/ n folla f; (rabble) gentaglia f; (🔲: gang) banda f ● vt (pt/pp
mobbed) assalire

mobile /'məʊbaɪl/ adj mobile ● n
composizione f mobile. ~ 'home n
casa f roulotte. ~ [phone] n [telefono m] cellulare m, telefonino m

mock /mɒk/ adj finto ● vt canzonare.
~ery n derisione f

model /'mɒdl/ n modello m;
[fashion] ~ indossatore, -trice mf,
modello, -a ● adj (yacht, plane) in
miniatura; (pupil, husband) esemplare, modello ● v (pt/pp modelled)
● vt indossare (clothes) ● vi fare l'indossatore, -trice mf; (for artist) posare

modem /'məʊdem/ n modem m inv

moderate¹ /'mɒdəreɪt/ vt mode-

rare ● vi moderarsi

moderate² /'mɒdərət/ adj moderato ● n (Pol) moderato, -a mf. ~ly
adv (drink, speak etc) moderatamente; (good, bad etc) relativamente

moderation /mɒdə'reɪʃn/ n moderazione f; in ~ con moderazione

modern /'mɒdn/ adj moderno.
~ize vt modernizzare

modest /'mɒdɪst/ adj modesto. ~y
n modestia f

modification /mɒdɪfɪ'keɪʃn/ n
modificazione f. ~fy vt (pt/pp -fied)
modificare

module /'mɒdjuːl/ n modulo m

moist /mɔɪst/ adj umido

moisten /'mɔɪsn/ vt inumidire

moisture /'mɔɪstʃə(r)/ n umidità f.
~izer n [crema f] idratante m

mole¹ /məʊl/ n (on face etc) neo m

mole² n (Zool) talpa f

molecule /'mɒlɪkjuːl/ n molecola f

molest /mə'lest/ vt molestare

mollycoddle /'mɒlɪkɒdl/ vt tenere
nella bambagia

molten /'məʊltən/ adj fuso

mom /mɒm/ n Am 🔲 mamma f

moment /'məʊmənt/ n momento
m; at the ~ in questo momento.
~arily adv momentaneamente.
~ary adj momentaneo

momentous /mə'mentəs/ adj
molto importante

momentum /mə'mentəm/ n impeto m

monarch /'mɒnək/ n monarca m.
~y n monarchia f

monastery /'mɒnəstrɪ/ n monastero m. ~ic adj monastico

Monday /'mʌndeɪ/ n lunedì m inv

money /'mʌnɪ/ n denaro m

money-box n salvadanaio m

mongrel /'mʌŋgrəl/ n bastardo m

monitor /'mɒnɪtə(r)/ n (Techn) monitor *m inv* • *vt* controllare

monk /mʌŋk/ *n* monaco *m*

monkey /ˈmʌŋkɪ/ *n* scimmia *f*. ∼-**nut** *n* nocciolina *f* americana. ∼-**wrench** *n* chiave *f* inglese a rullino

mono /ˈmɒnəʊ/ *n* mono *m*

monologue /ˈmɒnəlɒg/ *n* monologo *m*

monopol|ize /məˈnɒpəlaɪz/ *vt* monopolizzare. ∼**y** *n* monopolio *m*

monotone /ˈmɒnətəʊn/ *n* speak in a ∼ parlare con tono monotono

monoton|ous /məˈnɒtənəs/ *adj* monotono. ∼**y** *n* monotonia *f*

monsoon /mɒnˈsuːn/ *n* monsone *m*

monster /ˈmɒnstə(r)/ *n* mostro *m*

monstrous /ˈmɒnstrəs/ *adj* mostruoso

Montenegro /mɒntɪˈniːgrəʊ/ *n* Montenegro *m*

month /mʌnθ/ *n* mese *m*. ∼**ly** *adj* mensile • *adv* mensilmente • *n* (*periodical*) mensile *m*

monument /ˈmɒnjʊmənt/ *n* monumento *m*. ∼**al** *adj fig* monumentale

moo /muː/ *n* muggito *m* • *vi* (*pt/pp* mooed) muggire

mood /muːd/ *n* umore *m*; be in a good/bad ∼ essere di buon/cattivo umore; be in the ∼ for essere in vena di

moody /ˈmuːdɪ/ *adj* (-ier, -iest) (*variable*) lunatico; (*bad-tempered*) di malumore

moon /muːn/ *n* luna *f*; over the ∼ 🔢 al settimo cielo

moon: ∼**light** *n* chiaro *m* di luna • *vi* 🔢 lavorare in nero. ∼**lit** *adj* illuminato dalla luna

moor¹ /mʊə(r)/ *n* brughiera *f*

moor² *vt* (*Naut*) ormeggiare

mop /mɒp/ *n* straccio *m* (*per i pavimenti*); ∼ of hair zazzera *f* • *vt* (*pt/pp* mopped) lavare con lo straccio. ▫ ∼ **up** *vt* (*dry*) asciugare con lo

straccio; (*clean*) pulire con lo straccio

mope /məʊp/ *vi* essere depresso

moped /ˈməʊped/ *n* ciclomotore *m*

moral /ˈmɒrəl/ *adj* morale • *n* morale *f*. ∼**ly** *adv* moralmente. ∼**s** *pl* moralità *f*

morale /məˈrɑːl/ *n* morale *m*

morality /məˈrælətɪ/ *n* moralità *f*

more /mɔː(r)/ *adj* più; a few ∼ books un po' più di libri; some ∼ tea? ancora un po' di tè?; there's no ∼ bread non c'è più pane; there are no ∼ apples non ci sono più mele; one ∼ word and... ancora una parola e... • *pron* di più; would you like some ∼? ne vuoi ancora?; no ∼, thank you non ne voglio più, grazie • *adv* più; ∼ interesting più interessante; ∼ and ∼ quickly sempre più veloce; ∼ than più di; I don't love him any ∼ non lo amo più; once ∼ ancora una volta; ∼ or less più o meno; the ∼ I see him, the ∼ I like him più lo vedo, più mi piace

moreover /mɔːrˈəʊvə(r)/ *adv* inoltre

morgue /mɔːg/ *n* obitorio *m*

morning /ˈmɔːnɪŋ/ *n* mattino *m*, mattina *f*; in the ∼ del mattino; (*tomorrow*) domani mattina

Morocc|o /məˈrɒkəʊ/ *n* Marocco *m* • *adj* ∼**an** *adj* & *n* marocchino, -a *mf*

moron /ˈmɔːrɒn/ *n* 🔢 deficiente *mf*

morose /məˈrəʊs/ *adj* scontroso

Morse /mɔːs/ *n* ∼ [code] [codice *m*] Morse *m*

morsel /ˈmɔːsl/ *n* (*food*) boccone *m*

mortal /ˈmɔːtl/ *adj* & *n* mortale *mf*. ∼**ity** *n* mortalità *f*. ∼**ly** *adv* (*wounded, offended*) a morte; (*afraid*) da morire

mortar /ˈmɔːtə(r)/ *n* mortaio *m*

mortgage /ˈmɔːgɪdʒ/ *n* mutuo *m*; (*on property*) ipoteca *f* • *vt* ipotecare

mortuary /ˈmɔːtjʊərɪ/ *n* camera *f* mortuaria

m

mosaic /məʊˈzeɪɪk/ n mosaico m

Moslem /ˈmʊzlɪm/ adj & n musulmano, -a m f

mosque /mɒsk/ n moschea f

mosquito /mɒsˈkiːtəʊ/ n (pl -es) zanzara f

moss /mɒs/ n muschio m. ~y adj muschioso

most /məʊst/ adj (majority) la maggior parte di; for the ~ part per lo più ● adv più, maggiormente; (very) estremamente, molto; the ~ interesting day la giornata più interessante; a ~ interesting day una giornata estremamente interessante; the ~ beautiful woman in the world la donna più bella del mondo; ~ unlikely improbabile ● pron ~ of them la maggior parte di loro; at [the] ~ al massimo; make the ~ of sfruttare al massimo; ~ of the time la maggior parte del tempo. ~ly adv per lo più

MOT n revisione f obbligatoria di autoveicoli

motel /məʊˈtel/ n motel m inv

moth /mɒθ/ n falena f; [clothes-] ~ tarma f

mother /ˈmʌðə(r)/ n madre f; M~'s Day la festa della mamma ● vt fare da madre a

mother: ~-in-law n (pl ~s-in-law) suocera f. ~ly adj materno. ~-of-pearl n madreperla f. ~-to-be n futura mamma f. ~ tongue n madrelingua f

motif /məʊˈtiːf/ n motivo m

motion /ˈməʊʃn/ n moto m; (proposal) mozione f; (gesture) gesto m ● vt/i ~ [to] sb to come in fare segno a qcno di entrare. ~less adj immobile. ~lessly adv senza alcun movimento

motivat|e /ˈməʊtɪveɪt/ vt motivare. ~ion n motivazione f

motive /ˈməʊtɪv/ n motivo m

motley /ˈmɒtlɪ/ adj disparato

motor /ˈməʊtə(r)/ n motore m; (car) macchina f adj a motore; (Anat) motore ● vi andare in macchina

motor: ~ bike n 🗓 moto f inv. ~ boat n motoscafo m. ~ car n automobile f. ~ cycle n motocicletta f. ~-cyclist n motociclista mf. ~ing n automobilismo m. ~ist n automobilista mf. ~way n autostrada f

motto /ˈmɒtəʊ/ n (pl -es) motto m

mould¹ /məʊld/ n (fungus) muffa f

mould² n stampo m ● vt foggiare; fig formare. ~ing n (Archit) cornice f

mouldy /ˈməʊldɪ/ adj ammuffito; (🗓: worthless) ridicolo

moult /məʊlt/ vi (bird:) fare la muta; (animal:) perdere il pelo

mound /maʊnd/ n mucchio m; (hill) collinetta f

mount /maʊnt/ n (horse) cavalcatura f; (of jewel, photo, picture) montatura f ● vt montare a (horse); salire su (bicycle); incastonare (jewel); incorniciare (photo, picture) ● vi aumentare. □ ~ up vi aumentare

mountain /ˈmaʊntɪn/ n montagna f; ~ bike n mountain bike f inv

mountaineer /maʊntɪˈnɪə(r)/ n alpinista mf. ~ing n alpinismo m

mountainous /ˈmaʊntɪnəs/ adj montagnoso

mourn /mɔːn/ vt lamentare ● vi ~ for piangere la morte di. ~er n persona f che partecipa a un funerale. ~ful adj triste. ~ing n in ~ing in lutto

mouse /maʊs/ n (pl mice) topo m; (Comput) mouse m inv. ~trap n trappola f [per topi]

mousse /muːs/ n (Culin) mousse f inv

moustache /məˈstɑːʃ/ n baffi mpl

mouth¹ /maʊð/ vt ~ sth dire qcsa silenziosamente muovendo solamente le labbra

mouth² /maʊθ/ n bocca f; (of river) foce f

mouth: ~ful n boccone m

~-**organ** n armonica f [a bocca].
~-**wash** n acqua f dentifricia

move /muːv/ n mossa f; (moving house) trasloco m; on the ~ in movimento; get a ~ on 🔁 darsi una mossa ● vt muovere; (emotionally) commuovere; spostare (car); (transfer) trasferire; (propose) proporre; ~ house traslocare ● vi muoversi; (move house) traslocare. □ ~ **along** vi andare avanti ● vt muovere in avanti. □ ~ **away** vi allontanarsi; (move house) trasferirsi ● vt allontanare. □ ~ **forward** vi avanzare ● vt spostare avanti. □ ~ **in** vi (to a house) trasferirsi. □ ~ **off** vi muoversi. □ ~ **out** vi andare via. □ ~ **over** vi spostarsi ● vt spostare. □ ~ **up** vi muoversi; (advance) avanzare

movement /ˈmuːvmənt/ n movimento m

movie /ˈmuːvɪ/ n film m inv; go to the ~s andare al cinema

moving /ˈmuːvɪŋ/ adj mobile; (touching) commovente

mow /məʊ/ vt (pt mowed, pp mown or mowed) tagliare (lawn). □ ~ **down** vt (destroy) sterminare

mower /ˈməʊə(r)/ n tosaerba m inv

MP n abbr Member of Parliament

MP3 player n lettore m MP3

Mr /ˈmɪstə(r)/ n (pl **Messrs**) Signor m

Mrs /ˈmɪsɪz/ n Signora f

Ms /mɪz/ n Signora f (modo in formale di rivolgersi ad una donna quando non si vuole connotarsi come sposata o nubile)

much /mʌtʃ/ adj, adv & pron molto; ~ as per quanto; I love you just as ~ as before/him ti amo quanto prima/lui; as ~ as £5 million ben cinque milioni di sterline; as ~ as that così tanto; very ~ tantissimo, moltissimo; ~ the same quasi uguale

muck /mʌk/ n (dirt) sporcizia f; (farming) letame m; (🔁: filth) porcheria f. □ ~ **about** vi 🔁 perder tempo; ~

about with trafficare con. □ ~ **up** vt 🔁 rovinare; (make dirty) sporcare

mud /mʌd/ n fango m

muddle /ˈmʌdl/ n disordine m; (mix-up) confusione f ● vt ~ [up] confondere (dates)

muddy /ˈmʌdɪ/ adj (-ier, -iest) (path) fangoso; (shoes) infangato

muesli /ˈmuːzlɪ/ n muesli m inv

muffle /ˈmʌfl/ vt smorzare (sound). **muffle up** vt (for warmth) imbacuccare

muffler /ˈmʌflə(r)/ n sciarpa f; Am (Auto) marmitta f

mug[1] /mʌg/ n tazza f; (for beer) boccale m; (🔁: face) muso m; (🔁: simpleton) pollo m

mug[2] vt (pt/pp mugged) aggredire e derubare. ~**ger** n assalitore, -trice mf. ~**ging** n aggressione f per furto

muggy /ˈmʌgɪ/ adj (-ier, -iest) afoso

mule /ˈmjuːl/ n mulo m

mull /mʌl/ vt ~ over rimuginare su

multiple /ˈmʌltɪpl/ adj multiplo

multiplication /ˌmʌltɪplɪˈkeɪʃn/ n moltiplicazione f

multiply /ˈmʌltɪplaɪ/ v (pt/pp -ied) ● vt moltiplicare (by per) ● vi moltiplicarsi

mum[1] /mʌm/ adj keep ~ 🔁 non aprire bocca

mum[2] n 🔁 mamma f

mumble /ˈmʌmbl/ vt/i borbottare

mummy[1] /ˈmʌmɪ/ n 🔁 mamma f

mummy[2] n (Archaeol) mummia f

mumps /mʌmps/ n orecchioni mpl

munch /mʌntʃ/ vt/i sgranocchiare

mundane /mʌnˈdeɪn/ adj (everyday) banale

municipal /mjuːˈnɪsɪpl/ adj municipale

mural /ˈmjʊərəl/ n dipinto m murale

murder /ˈmɜːdə(r)/ n assassinio m ● vt assassinare; (🔁: ruin) massacrare. ~**er** n assassino, -a mf. ~**ous** adj omicida

m

murky /'mɜːkɪ/ adj (-ier, -iest) oscuro

murmur /'mɜːmə(r)/ n mormorio m • vt/i mormorare

muscle /'mʌsl/ n muscolo m • **muscle in** vi 🖾 intromettersi (on in)

muscular /'mʌskjʊlə(r)/ adj muscolare; (strong) muscoloso

muse /mjuːz/ vi meditare (on su)

museum /mjuː'zɪəm/ n museo m

mushroom /'mʌʃrʊm/ n fungo m • vi fig spuntare come funghi

music /'mjuːzɪk/ n musica f; (written) spartito m.

musical /'mjuːzɪkl/ adj musicale; (person) dotato di senso musicale • n commedia f musicale. ~ **box** n carillon m inv. ~ **instrument** n strumento m musicale

musician /mjuː'zɪʃn/ n musicista mf

Muslim /'mʊzlɪm/ adj & n musulmano, -a mf

mussel /'mʌsl/ n cozza f

must /mʌst/ v aux (solo al presente) dovere; you ~ not be late non devi essere in ritardo; she ~ have finished by now (probability) deve aver finito ormai • n a ~ 🅣 una cosa da non perdere

mustard /'mʌstəd/ n senape f

musty /'mʌstɪ/ adj (-ier, -iest) stantio

mutation /mjuː'teɪʃn/ n (Biol) mutazione f

mute /mjuːt/ adj muto

mutilate /'mjuːtɪleɪt/ vt mutilare. ~**ion** n mutilazione f

mutter /'mʌtə(r)/ vt/i borbottare

mutton /'mʌtn/ n carne f di montone

mutual /'mjuːtjʊəl/ adj reciproco; (🅣: common) comune. ~**ly** adv reciprocamente

muzzle /'mʌzl/ n (of animal) muso m; (of firearm) bocca f; (for dog) muse-

ruola f • vt fig mettere il bavaglio a

my /maɪ/ adj il mio m, la mia f, i miei mpl, le mie fpl; **my mother/father** mia madre/mio padre

myself /maɪ'self/ pron (reflexive) mi; (emphatic) me stesso; (after prep) me; I've seen it ~ l'ho visto io stesso; by ~ da solo; I thought to ~ ho pensato tra me e me; I'm proud of ~ sono fiero di me

mysterious /mɪ'stɪərɪəs/ adj misterioso. ~**ly** adv misteriosamente

mystery /'mɪstərɪ/ n mistero m; ~ [story] racconto m del mistero

mystic[**al**] /'mɪstɪk[l]/ adj mistico. ~**cism** n misticismo m

mystify /'mɪstɪfaɪ/ vt (pt/pp -ied) disorientare

mystique /mɪ'stiːk/ n mistica f

myth /mɪθ/ n mito m. ~**ical** adj mitico

mythology /mɪ'θɒlədʒɪ/ n mitologia f

Nn

nab /næb/ vt (pt/pp nabbed) 🅣 beccare

nag[1] /næg/ n (horse) ronzino m

nag[2] /næg/ (pt/pp nagged) vt assillare • vi essere insistente • n (person) brontolone, -a mf. ~**ging** adj (pain) persistente

nail /neɪl/ n chiodo m; (of finger, toe) unghia f • **nail down** vt inchiodare; ~ **sb down** to a time/price far fissare a qcno un'ora/un prezzo

nail polish n smalto m [per unghie]

naked /'neɪkɪd/ adj nudo; with the ~ **eye** a occhio nudo

name /neɪm/ n nome m; what's

your ∼? come ti chiami?; my ∼ is Matthew mi chiamo Matthew; I know her by ∼ la conosco di nome; by the ∼ of Bates di nome Bates; call sb ∼s 🔲 insultare qcno ● vt (to position) nominare; chiamare (baby); (identify) citare; be ∼d after essere chiamato col nome di. ∼less adj senza nome. ∼ly adv cioè

namesake n omonimo, -a mf

nanny /'næni/ n bambinaia f. ∼-goat n capra f

nap /næp/ n pisolino m; have a ∼ fare un pisolino ● vi (pt/pp napped) catch sb ∼ping cogliere qcno alla sprovvista

napkin /'næpkɪn/ n tovagliolo m

Naples /'neɪplz/ n Napoli f

nappy /'næpi/ n pannolino m

narcotic /nɑː'kɒtɪk/ adj & n narcotico m

narrat|e /nə'reɪt/ vt narrare. ∼ion n narrazione f

narrative /'nærətɪv/ adj narrativo ● n narrazione f

narrator /nə'reɪtə(r)/ n narratore, -trice mf

narrow /'nærəʊ/ adj stretto; (fig: views) ristretto; (margin, majority) scarso ● vi restringersi. ∼ly adv ∼ly escape death evitare la morte per un pelo. ∼-'minded adj di idee ristrette

nasal /'neɪzl/ adj nasale

nasty /'nɑːstɪ/ adj (-ier, -iest) (smell, person, remark) cattivo; (injury, situation, weather) brutto; turn ∼ (person:) diventare cattivo

nation /'neɪʃn/ n nazione f

national /'næʃənl/ adj nazionale ● n cittadino, -a mf

national 'anthem n inno m nazionale

nationalism /'næʃənəlɪzm/ n nazionalismo m

nationality /næʃə'næləti/ n nazionalità f inv

'nation-wide adj su scala nazionale

native /'neɪtɪv/ adj nativo; (innate) innato ● n nativo, -a mf; (local inhabitant) abitante mf del posto; (outside Europe) indigeno, -a mf; she's a ∼ of Venice è originaria di Venezia

native: ∼ **land** n paese m nativo. ∼ **language** n lingua f madre

Nativity /nə'tɪvəti/ n the ∼ la Natività f. ∼ **play** n rappresentazione f sulla nascita di Gesù

natter /'nætə(r)/ vi 🔲 chiacchierare

natural /'nætʃrəl/ adj naturale

natural 'history n storia f naturale

naturalist /'nætʃ(ə)rəlɪst/ n naturalista mf

naturally /'nætʃ(ə)rəlɪ/ adv (of course) naturalmente; (by nature) per natura

nature /'neɪtʃə(r)/ n natura f; by ∼ per natura. ∼ **reserve** n riserva f naturale

naughty /'nɔːti/ adj (-ier, -iest) monello; (slightly indecent) spinto

nausea /'nɔːzɪə/ n nausea f

nautical /'nɔːtɪkl/ adj nautico. ∼ **mile** n miglio m marino

naval /'neɪvl/ adj navale

nave /neɪv/ n navata f centrale

navel /ˈneɪvl/ n ombelico m

navigable /ˈnævɪgəbl/ adj navigabile

navigat|e /ˈnævɪgeɪt/ vi navigare; (Auto) fare da navigatore • vt navigare su (river). ~ion n navigazione f. ~or n navigatore m

navy /ˈneɪvɪ/ n marina f • ~ [blue] adj blu marine inv • n blu m inv marine

Neapolitan /nɪəˈpɒlɪtn/ adj & n napoletano, -a mf

near /nɪə(r)/ adj vicino; (future) prossimo; the ~est bank la banca più vicina • adv vicino; draw ~ avvicinarsi; ~ at hand a portata di mano • prep vicino a; he was ~ to tears aveva le lacrime agli occhi • vt avvicinarsi a

near: ~by adj & adv vicino. ~ly adv quasi; it's not ~ly enough non è per niente sufficiente. ~-sighted adj Am miope

neat /niːt/ adj (tidy) ordinato; (clever) efficace; (undiluted) liscio. ~ly adv ordinatamente; (cleverly) efficacemente. ~ness n (tidiness) ordine m

necessarily /nesəˈserɪlɪ/ adv necessariamente

necessary /ˈnesəsərɪ/ adj necessario

necessit|ate /nɪˈsesɪteɪt/ vt rendere necessario. ~y n necessità f

neck /nek/ n collo m; (of dress) colletto m; ~ and ~ testa a testa

necklace /ˈneklɪs/ n collana f

neckline n scollatura f

need /niːd/ n bisogno m; be in ~ of avere bisogno di; if ~ be se ce ne fosse bisogno; there is a ~ for c'è bisogno di; there is no ~ for that non ce n'è bisogno; there is no ~ for you to go non c'è bisogno che tu vada • vt aver bisogno di; I ~ to know devo saperlo; it ~s to be done bisogna farlo • v aux you ~ not go non c'è bisogno che tu vada;

~ I come? devo [proprio] venire?

needle /ˈniːdl/ n ago m; (for knitting) uncinetto m; (of record player) puntina f • vt (fig: annoy) punzecchiare

needless /ˈniːdlɪs/ adj inutile

needlework n cucito m

needy /ˈniːdɪ/ adj (-ier, -iest) bisognoso

negative /ˈnegətɪv/ adj negativo • n negazione f; (Phot) negativo m; in the ~ (Gram) alla forma negativa

neglect /nɪˈglekt/ n trascuratezza f; state of ~ stato m di abbandono • vt trascurare; he ~ed to write non si è curato di scrivere. ~ed adj trascurato. ~ful adj negligente; be ~ful of trascurare

negligen|ce /ˈneglɪdʒəns/ n negligenza f. ~t adj negligente

negligible /ˈneglɪdʒəbl/ adj trascurabile

negotiable /nɪˈgəʊʃəbl/ adj (road) transitabile; (Comm) negoziabile; not ~ (cheque) non trasferibile

negotiat|e /nɪˈgəʊʃɪeɪt/ vt negoziare; (Auto) prendere (bend) • vi negoziare. ~ion n negoziato m. ~or n negoziatore, -trice mf

neigh /neɪ/ vi nitrire

neighbour /ˈneɪbə(r)/ n vicino, -a mf. ~hood n vicinato m; in the ~hood of nei dintorni di; fig circa. ~ing adj vicino. ~ly adj amichevole

neither /ˈnaɪðə(r)/ adj & pron nessuno dei due, né l'uno né l'altro • adv ~... nor né... né • conj nemmeno, neanche; ~ do/did I nemmeno io

neon /ˈniːɒn/ n neon m. ~ light n luce f al neon

nephew /ˈnevjuː/ n nipote m

nerve /nɜːv/ n nervo m; (fig: courage) coraggio m; (fig: impudence) faccia f tosta; lose one's ~ perdersi d'animo. ~-racking adj logorante

nervous /ˈnɜːvəs/ adj nervoso; he makes me ~ mi mette in agitazione; be a ~ wreck avere i nervi a pezzi. ~ 'breakdown n esaurimento m nervoso. ~ness n nervosismo m; (before important event) tensione f

nervy /'nɜːvɪ/ adj (-ier, -iest) nervoso; (Am: impudent) sfacciato

nest /nest/ n nido m ● vi fare il nido. ~-egg n gruzzolo m

nestle /'nesl/ vi accoccolarsi

net[1] /net/ n rete f ● vt (pt/pp netted) (catch) prendere (con la rete)

net[2] adj netto ● vt (pt/pp netted) incassare un utile netto di

netball n sport m inv femminile, simile a pallacanestro

Netherlands /'neðələndz/ npl the ~ i Paesi mpl Bassi

netting /'netɪŋ/ n (wire) ~ reticolato m

nettle /'netl/ n ortica f

network n rete f

neur|osis /njʊə'rəʊsɪs/ n (pl -oses /-siːz/) nevrosi f inv. ~**otic** adj nevrotico

neuter /'njuːtə(r)/ adj (Gram) neutro ● n (Gram) neutro m ● vt sterilizzare

neutral /'njuːtrəl/ adj neutro; (country, person) neutrale ● n in ~ (Auto) in folle. ~**ity** n neutralità f. ~**ize** vt neutralizzare

never /'nevə(r)/ adv [non...] mai; (I: expressing disbelief) ma va; ~ again mai più; well I ~! chi l'avrebbe detto!. ~-**ending** adj interminabile

nevertheless /nevəðə'les/ adv tuttavia

new /njuː/ adj nuovo

new: ~-**born** adj neonato. ~**comer** n nuovo, -a arrivato, -a mf. ~**fangled** /-'fæŋgld/ adj pej modernizzante

newly adv (recently) di recente; ~-**built** costruito di recente. ~-**weds** npl sposini mpl

news /njuːz/ n notizie fpl; (TV) tele-

giornale m; (Radio) giornale m radio; piece of ~ notizia f

news: ~**agent** n giornalaio, -a mf. ~**caster** n giornalista mf televisivo, -a/radiofonico, -a. ~**flash** n notizia f flash. ~**letter** n bollettino m d'informazione. ~**paper** n giornale m; (material) carta f di giornale. ~**reader** n giornalista mf televisivo, -a/radiofonico, -a

new: ~ **year** n (next year) anno m nuovo; N~ Year's Day n Capodanno m. N~ Year's Eve n vigilia f di Capodanno. N~ **Zealand** /'ziːlənd/ n Nuova Zelanda f

next /nekst/ adj prossimo; (adjoining) vicino; who's ~? a chi tocca?; ~ door accanto; ~ to nothing quasi niente; the ~ day il giorno dopo; ~ week la settimana prossima; the week after ~ fra due settimane ● adv dopo; when will you see him ~? quando lo rivedi la prossima volta?; ~ to accanto a ● n seguente mf; ~ of kin parente m prossimo

nib /nɪb/ n pennino m

nibble /'nɪbl/ vt/i mordicchiare

nice /naɪs/ adj (day, weather, holiday) bello; (person) gentile, simpatico; (food) buono; it was ~ meeting you è stato un piacere conoscerla. ~**ly** adv gentilmente; (well) bene. ~**ties** n nicchia f

niche /niːʃ/ n nicchia f

nick /nɪk/ n tacca f; (on chin etc) taglietto m; (I: prison) galera f; (I: police station) centrale f [di polizia]; in the ~ of time I appena in tempo ● vt intaccare; (I: steal) fregare; (I: arrest) beccare; ~ one's chin farsi un taglietto nel mento

nickel /'nɪkl/ n nichel m; Am moneta f da cinque centesimi

nickname n soprannome m ● vt soprannominare

nicotine /'nɪkətiːn/ n nicotina f

niece /niːs/ n nipote f

niggling /'nɪglɪŋ/ adj (detail) insignificante; (pain) fastidioso; (doubt) persistente

night /naɪt/ n notte f; (evening) sera f; at ~ la notte, di notte; (in the evening) la sera, di sera; Monday ~ lunedì notte/sera ● adj di notte

night: ~cap n papalina f; (drink) bicchierino m bevuto prima di andare a letto. ~-club n locale m notturno; night[-club] m inv. ~-dress n camicia f da notte. ~fall n crepuscolo m. ~-gown, ⓉⒺ ~ie /'naɪtɪ/ n camicia f da notte

night: ~-life n vita f notturna. ~ly adj di notte, di sera ● adv ogni notte, ogni sera. ~mare n incubo m. ~-school n scuola f serale. ~-time n at ~-time di notte, la notte. ~'watchman n guardiano m notturno

nil /nɪl/ n nulla m; (Sport) zero m

nimble /'nɪmbl/ adj agile. ~y adv agilmente

nine /naɪn/ adj nove inv ● n nove m. ~'teen adj diciannove inv ● n diciannove. ~'teenth adj & n diciannovesimo, -a mf

ninetieth /'naɪntɪθ/ adj & n novantesimo, -a

ninety /'naɪntɪ/ adj novanta inv ● n novanta m

ninth /naɪnθ/ adj & n nono, -a mf

nip /nɪp/ n pizzicotto m; (bite) morso m ● vt pizzicare; (bite) mordere; ~ in the bud fig stroncare sul nascere ● vi (Ⓣ: run) fare un salto

nipple /'nɪpl/ n capezzolo m; (Am: on bottle) tettarella f

nippy /'nɪpɪ/ adj (-ier, -iest) ⓉⒺ (cold) pungente; (quick) svelto

nitrogen /'naɪtrədʒn/ n azoto m

no /nəʊ/ adv no ● n (pl noes) no m inv ● adj nessuno; I have no time non ho tempo; in no time in un baleno; 'no parking' 'sosta vietata'; 'no smoking' 'vietato fumare'; no one

nessuno v. nobody

noble /'nəʊbl/ adj nobile. ~man n nobile m

nobody /'nəʊbədɪ/ pron nessuno; he knows ~ non conosce nessuno ● n he's a ~ non è nessuno

nocturnal /nɒk'tɜːnl/ adj notturno

nod /nɒd/ n cenno m del capo● vi (pt/pp nodded) fare un cenno col capo; (in agreement) fare di sì col capo ● vt ~ one's head fare di sì col capo. □ ~ off vi assopirsi

noise /nɔɪz/ n rumore m; (loud) rumore m, chiasso m. ~less adj silenzioso. ~lessly adv silenziosamente

noisy /'nɔɪzɪ/ adj (-ier, -iest) rumoroso

nomad /'nəʊmæd/ n nomade mf. ~ic adj nomade

nominate /'nɒmɪneɪt/ vt proporre come candidato; (appoint) designare. ~ion n nomina f; (person nominated) candidato, -a mf

nonchalant /'nɒnʃələnt/ adj disinvolto

non-com'mittal adj che non si sbilancia

nondescript /'nɒndɪskrɪpt/ adj qualunque

none /nʌn/ pron (person) nessuno; (thing) niente; ~ of us nessuno di noi; ~ of this niente di questo; there's ~ left non ce n'è più ● adv she's ~ too pleased non è per niente soddisfatta; I'm ~ the wiser non ne so più di prima

nonentity /nɒ'nentətɪ/ n nullità f

non-ex'istent adj inesistente

nonplussed /nɒn'plʌst/ adj perplesso

nonsense /'nɒnsəns/ n sciocchezze fpl. ~ical adj assurdo

non-'smoker n non fumatore, -trice mf; (compartment) scompartimento m non fumatori

non-'stop adj ~ 'flight volo m diretto ● adv senza sosta; (fly) senza scalo

noodles /'nuːdlz/ npl taglierini mpl

nook /nʊk/ n cantuccio m

noon /nuːn/ n mezzogiorno m; at ~ a mezzogiorno

noose /nuːs/ n nodo m scorsoio

nor /nɔː(r)/ adv & conj né; ~ do I neppure io

norm /nɔːm/ n norma f

normal /'nɔːml/ adj normale. **~ity** n normalità f. **~ly** adv (usually) normalmente

north /nɔːθ/ n nord m; to the ~ of a nord di ● adj del nord, settentrionale ● adv a nord

north: N~ America n America f del Nord. **~-east** adj di nord-est, nordorientale ● n nord-est m ● adv a nord-est; (travel) verso nord-est

norther|ly /'nɔːðəlɪ/ adj (direction) nord; (wind) del nord. **~n** adj del nord, settentrionale. **N~n Ireland** n Irlanda f del Nord

north: N~ 'Sea n Mare m del Nord. **~ward[s]** /-wəd[z]/ adv verso nord. **~-west** adj di nord-ovest, nordoccidentale ● n nord-ovest m ● adv a nord-ovest; (travel) verso nord-ovest

Nor|way /'nɔːweɪ/ n Norvegia f. **~wegian** adj & n norvegese mf

nose /nəʊz/ n naso m

nose: ~bleed n emorragia f nasale. **~dive** n (Aeron) picchiata f

nostalg|ia /nɒ'stældʒɪə/ n nostalgia f. **~ic** adj nostalgico

nostril /'nɒstrəl/ n narice f

nosy /'nəʊzɪ/ adj (-ier, -iest) 🄵 ficcanaso inv

not /nɒt/ adv non; he is ~ Italian non è italiano; I hope ~ spero di no; ~ all of us have been invited non siamo stati tutti invitati; if ~ se no; ~ at all niente affatto; ~ a bit per niente; ~ even neanche; ~ yet non ancora; ~ only... but also... non solo... ma anche...

notab|le /'nəʊtəbl/ adj (remarkable) notevole. **~y** adv (in particular) in particolare

notary /'nəʊtərɪ/ n notaio m; ~ 'public notaio m

notch /nɒtʃ/ n tacca f ● **notch up** vt (score) segnare

note /nəʊt/ n nota f; (short letter, banknote) biglietto m; (memo, written comment etc) appunto m; of ~ (person) di spicco; (comments, event) degno di nota; make a ~ of prendere nota di; take ~ of (notice) prendere nota di ● vt (notice) notare; (write) annotare. □ **~ down** vt annotare

'notebook n taccuino m; (Comput) notebook m inv

noted /'nəʊtɪd/ adj noto, celebre (for per)

notepaper n carta f da lettere

nothing /'nʌθɪŋ/ pron niente, nulla ● adv niente affatto. for ~ (free, in vain) per niente; (with no reason) senza motivo; ~ but nient'altro che; ~ much poco o nulla; ~ interesting niente di interessante; it's ~ to do with you non ti riguarda

notice /'nəʊtɪs/ n (on board) avviso m; (review) recensione f; (termination of employment) licenziamento m; [advance] ~ preavviso m; two months' ~ due mesi di preavviso; at short ~ con breve preavviso; until further ~ fino nuovo avviso; hand in one's ~ (employee) dare le dimissioni; give an employee ~ dare il preavviso a un impiegato; take no ~ of non fare caso a; take no ~! non farci caso! ● vt notare. **~able** adj evidente. **~ably** adv sensibilmente. **~board** n bacheca f

noti|fication /nəʊtɪfɪ'keɪʃn/ n notifica f. **~fy** vt (pt/pp -ied) notificare

notion /'nəʊʃn/ n idea f, nozione f; **~s** pl (Am: haberdashery) merceria f

notorious /nəʊ'tɔːrɪəs/ adj famigerato; be ~ for essere tristemente famoso per

n

notwith'standing prep malgrado ● adv ciononostante

nougat /'nu:ɡɑ:/ n torrone m

nought /nɔ:t/ n zero m

noun /naʊn/ n nome m, sostantivo m

nourish /'nʌrɪʃ/ vt nutrire. ~ing adj nutriente. ~ment n nutrimento m

novel /'nɒvl/ adj insolito ● n romanzo m. ~ist n romanziere, -a mf. ~ty n novità f; ~ties pl (objects) oggettini mpl

November /nəʊ'vembə(r)/ n novembre m

novice /'nɒvɪs/ n novizio, -a mf

now /naʊ/ adv ora, adesso; by ~ ormai; just ~ proprio ora; right ~ subito; ~ and again, ~ and then ogni tanto; ~, ~! su! ● conj ~ [that] ora che, adesso che

'nowadays adv oggigiorno

nowhere /'nəʊ-/ adv in nessun posto, da nessuna parte

nozzle /'nɒzl/ n bocchetta f

nuance /'nju:ɑ̃:s/ n sfumatura f

nuclear /'nju:klɪə(r)/ adj nucleare

nucleus /'nju:klɪəs/ n (pl -lei /-lɪaɪ/) nucleo m

nude /nju:d/ adj nudo ● n nudo m; in the ~ nudo

nudge /nʌdʒ/ n colpetto m di gomito ● vt dare un colpetto col gomito a

nudism /'nju:dɪzm/ n nudismo m

nud|ist /'nju:dɪst/ n nudista mf. ~ity n nudità f

nuisance /'nju:sns/ n seccatura f; (person) piaga f; what a ~! che seccatura!

null /nʌl/ adj ~ and void nullo

numb /nʌm/ adj intorpidito; ~ with cold intirizzito dal freddo

number /'nʌmbə(r)/ n numero m; a ~ of people un certo numero di persone ● vt numerare; (include) annoverare. ~-plate n targa f

numeral /'nju:mərəl/ n numero m, cifra f

numerical /nju:'merɪkl/ adj numerico; in ~ order in ordine numerico

numerous /'nju:mərəs/ adj numeroso

nun /nʌn/ n suora f

nurse /nɜ:s/ n infermiere, -a mf; children's ~ bambinaia f ● vt curare

nursery /'nɜ:sərɪ/ n stanza f dei bambini; (for plants) vivaio m; [day] ~ asilo m. ~ rhyme n filastrocca f. ~ school n scuola f materna

nut /nʌt/ n noce f; (Techn) dado m; (🖫: head) zucca f; ~s npl frutta f secca; be ~s 🖫 essere svitato. ~crackers npl schiaccianoci m inv. ~meg n noce f moscata

nutrit|ion /nju:'trɪʃn/ n nutrizione f. ~ious adj nutriente

'nutshell n in a ~ fig in parole povere

nylon /'naɪlɒn/ n nailon m; ~s pl calze fpl di nailon ● attrib di nailon

Oo

oaf /əʊf/ n (pl oafs) zoticone, -a mf

oak /əʊk/ n quercia f ● attrib di quercia

OAP n abbr (old-age pensioner) pensionato, -a mf

oar /ɔ:(r)/ n remo m. ~sman n vogatore m

oasis /əʊ'eɪsɪs/ n (pl oases /-si:z/) oasi f inv

oath /əʊθ/ n giuramento m; (swear-word) bestemmia f

oatmeal /'əʊt-/ n farina f d'avena

oats /əʊts/ npl avena fsg; (Culin) [rolled] ~ fiocchi mpl di avena

obedien|ce /əˈbiːdɪəns/ n ubbidienza f. **~t** adj ubbidiente

obes|e /əˈbiːs/ adj obeso. **~ity** n obesità f

obey /əˈbeɪ/ vt ubbidire a; osservare (instructions, rules) ● vi ubbidire

obituary /əˈbɪtjʊərɪ/ n necrologio m

object¹ /ˈɒbdʒɪkt/ n oggetto m; (Gram) complemento m oggetto; money is no **~** i soldi non sono un problema

object² /əbˈdʒekt/ vi (be against) opporsi (to a); **~** that... obiettare che...

objection /əbˈdʒekʃn/ n obiezione f; have no **~** non avere niente in contrario. **~able** adj discutibile; (person) sgradevole

objectiv|e /əbˈdʒektɪv/ adj oggettivo ● n obiettivo m. **~ely** adv obiettivamente. **~ity** n oggettività f

obligation /ɒblɪˈɡeɪʃn/ n obbligo m; be under an **~** avere un obbligo; without **~** senza impegno

obligatory /əˈblɪɡətrɪ/ adj obbligatorio

oblig|e /əˈblaɪdʒ/ vt (compel) obbligare; much **~ed** grazie mille. **~ing** adj disponibile

oblique /əˈbliːk/ adj obliquo; fig indiretto ● n **~** [stroke] barra f

obliterate /əˈblɪtəreɪt/ vt obliterare

oblivion /əˈblɪvɪən/ n oblio m

oblivious /əˈblɪvɪəs/ adj be **~** essere dimentico (of, to di)

oblong /ˈɒblɒŋ/ adj oblungo ● n rettangolo m

obnoxious /əbˈnɒkʃəs/ adj detestabile

oboe /ˈəʊbəʊ/ n oboe m inv

obscen|e /əbˈsiːn/ adj osceno; (profits, wealth) vergognoso. **~ity** n oscenità f inv

obscur|e /əbˈskjʊə(r)/ adj oscuro ● vt oscurare; (confuse) mettere in

ombra. **~ity** n oscurità f

obsequious /əbˈsiːkwɪəs/ adj ossequioso

observatory /əbˈzɜːvətrɪ/ n osservatorio m

observe /əbˈzɜːv/ vt osservare; (notice) notare; (keep, celebrate) celebrare. **~r** n osservatore, -trice mf

obsess /əbˈses/ vt be **~ed** by essere fissato con. **~ion** n fissazione f. **~ive** adj ossessivo

obsolete /ˈɒbsəliːt/ adj obsoleto; (word) desueto

obstacle /ˈɒbstəkl/ n ostacolo m

obstinacy /ˈɒbstɪnəsɪ/ n ostinazione f. **~te** adj ostinato

obstruct /əbˈstrʌkt/ vt ostruire; (hinder) ostacolare. **~ion** n ostruzione f; (obstacle) ostacolo m. **~ive** adj be **~ive** (person): creare dei problemi

obtain /əbˈteɪn/ vt ottenere. **~able** adj ottenibile

obtrusive /əbˈtruːsɪv/ adj (object) stonato

obtuse /əbˈtjuːs/ adj ottuso

obvious /ˈɒbvɪəs/ adj ovvio. **~ly** adv ovviamente

occasion /əˈkeɪʒn/ n occasione f; (event) evento m; on **~** talvolta; on the **~** of in occasione di

occasional /əˈkeɪʒənl/ adj saltuario; he has the **~** glass of wine ogni tanto beve un bicchiere di vino. **~ly** adv ogni tanto

occult /ɒˈkʌlt/ adj occulto

occupant /ˈɒkjʊpənt/ n occupante mf; (of vehicle) persona f a bordo

occupation /ɒkjʊˈpeɪʃn/ n occupazione f; (job) professione f. **~al** adj professionale

occupier /ˈɒkjʊpaɪə(r)/ n residente mf

occupy /ˈɒkjʊpaɪ/ vt (pt/pp occupied) occupare; (keep busy) tenere occupato

occur /əˈkɜː(r)/ vi (pt/pp occurred)

accadere; (*exist*) trovarsi; it ~red to me that mi è venuto in mente che. ~rence *n* (*event*) fatto *m*

ocean /ˈəʊʃn/ *n* oceano *m*

octave /ˈɒktɪv/ *n* (*Mus*) ottava *f*

October /ɒkˈtəʊbə(r)/ *n* ottobre *m*

octopus /ˈɒktəpəs/ *n* (*pl* -puses) polpo *m*

odd /ɒd/ *adj* (*number*) dispari, (*not of set*) scompagnato; (*strange*) strano; forty ~ quaranta e rotti; ~ jobs lavoretti *mpl*; the ~ one out l'eccezione; at ~ moments a tempo perso; have the ~ glass of wine avere un bicchiere di vino ogni tanto

odd|**ity** /ˈɒdɪti/ *n* stranezza *f*. ~ly *adv* stranamente; ~ly enough stranamente. ~ment *n* (*of fabric*) scampolo *m*

odds /ɒdz/ *npl* (*chances*) probabilità *fpl*; at ~ in disaccordo; ~ and ends cianfrusaglie *fpl*; it makes no ~ non fa alcuna differenza

odour /ˈəʊdə(r)/ *n* odore *m*. ~less *adj* inodore

of /ɒv/, /əv/ *prep* di; a cup of tea/ coffee una tazza di tè/caffè; the hem of my skirt l'orlo della mia gonna; the summer of 1989 l'estate del 1989; the two of us noi due; made of di; that's very kind of you è molto gentile da parte tua; a friend of mine un mio amico; a child of three un bambino di tre anni; the fourth of January il quattro gennaio; within a year of their divorce a circa un anno dal loro divorzio; half of it la metà; the whole of the room tutta la stanza

off /ɒf/ *prep* da; (*distant from*) lontano da; take £10 ~ the price ridurre il prezzo di 10 sterline; ~ the coast presso la costa; a street ~ the main road una traversa della via principale; (*near*) una strada vicino alla via principale; get ~ the ladder scendere dalla scala; get off the bus uscire dall'autobus; leave the lid ~

the saucepan lasciare la pentola senza il coperchio ● *adv* (*button, handle*) staccato; (*light, machine*) spento; (*brake*) tolto; (*tap*) chiuso; 'off' (*on appliance*) 'off'; 2 kilometres ~ a due chilometri di distanza; a long way ~ molto distante; (*time*) lontano; ~ and on di tanto in tanto; with his hat/coat ~ senza il cappello/cappotto; with the light ~ a luce spenta; 20% ~ 20% di sconto; be ~ (*leave*) andar via; (*Sport*) essere partito; (*food*) essere andato a male; (*all gone*) essere finito; (*wedding, engagement*) essere cancellato; I'm ~ alcohol ho smesso di bere; be ~ one's food non avere appetito; she's ~ today (*on holiday*) è in ferie oggi; (*ill*) è malata oggi; I'm ~ home vado a casa; you'd be better ~ doing... faresti meglio a fare...; have a day ~ avere un giorno di vacanza; drive/sail ~ andare via

'**off-beat** *adj* insolito

'**off-chance** *n* possibilità *f* remota

offence /əˈfens/ *n* (*illegal act*) reato *m*; give ~ offendere; take ~ offendersi (at per)

offend /əˈfend/ *vt* offendere. ~er *n* (*Jur*) colpevole *mf*

offensive /əˈfensɪv/ *adj* offensivo ● *n* offensiva *f*

offer /ˈɒfə(r)/ *n* offerta *f* ● *vt* offrire; opporre (*resistance*); ~ sb sth offrire qcsa a qcno; ~ to do sth offrirsi di fare qcsa. ~ing *n* offerta *f*

off'hand *adj* (*casual*) spiccio ● *adv* su due piedi

office /ˈɒfɪs/ *n* ufficio *m*; (*post, job*) carica *f*. ~ hours *pl* orario *m* d'ufficio

officer /ˈɒfɪsə(r)/ *n* ufficiale *m*; (*police*) agente *m* [di polizia]

official /əˈfɪʃl/ *adj* ufficiale ● *n* funzionario, -a *mf*; (*Sport*) dirigente *m*. ~ly *adv* ufficialmente

'**offing** *n* in the ~ in vista

'off-licence n negozio m per la vendita di alcolici

'offset vt (pt/pp -set, pres p -setting) controbilanciare

'offshore ●adj (wind) di terra; (company, investment) offshore. ●adv (sail) al largo; (relocate) all'estero (in paesi dove la manodopera costa meno); ~ **rig** n piattaforma f petrolifera, off-shore m inv

off'side adj (Sport) [in] fuori gioco; (wheel etc) (left) sinistro; (right) destro

'offspring n prole m

off'stage adv dietro le quinte

often /'ɒfn/ adv spesso; how ~ ogni quanto; every so ~ una volta ogni tanto

oh /əʊ/ int oh!; ~ **dear** oh Dio!

oil /ɔɪl/ n olio m; (petroleum) petrolio m; (for heating) nafta f ● vt oliare

oil: ~**field** n giacimento m di petrolio. ~**painting** n pittura f a olio. ~ **refinery** n raffineria f di petrolio. ~ **rig** piattaforma f per trivellazione subacquea

oily /'ɔɪlɪ/ adj (-ier, -iest) unto; fig untuoso

ointment /'ɔɪntmənt/ n pomata f

OK /əʊ'keɪ/ int va bene, o.k. ●adj if that's OK with you se ti va bene; she's OK (well) sta bene; is the milk still OK? il latte è ancora buono? ●adv (well) bene ●vt (anche okay) (pt/pp okayed) dare l'o.k.

old /əʊld/ adj vecchio; (girlfriend) ex; how ~ is she? quanti anni ha?; she is ten years ~ ha dieci anni

old: ~ **'age** n vecchiaia f. ~**'fashioned** adj antiquato

olive /'ɒlɪv/ n (fruit, colour) oliva f; (tree) olivo m ●adj d'oliva; (colour) olivastro. ~ **branch** n fig ramoscello m d'olivo. ~ **oil** n olio m di oliva

Olympic /ə'lɪmpɪk/ adj olimpico; ~**s,** ~ **Games** Olimpiadi fpl

omelette /'ɒmlɪt/ n omelette f inv

omission /ə'mɪʃn/ n omissione f

omit /ə'mɪt/ vt (pt/pp omitted) omettere

on /ɒn/ prep su; (on horizontal surface) su, sopra; ~ **Monday** lunedì; ~ **Mondays** di lunedì; ~ **the first of May** il primo maggio; ~ **arriving** all'arrivo; ~ **foot** a piedi; ~ **the right/left** a destra/sinistra; ~ **the radio/television** alla radio/televisione; ~ **the bus/train** in autobus/treno ● adv (further on) dopo; (switched on) acceso; (in operation) in funzione; he had his hat/coat ~ portava il cappello/cappotto; be ~ (event) esserci; ~ **and** ~ senza sosta; go ~ continuare

once /wʌns/ adv una volta; (formerly) un tempo; ~ **upon a time there was** c'era una volta; at ~ subito; (at the same time) contemporaneamente; ~ **and for all** una volta per tutte ● conj [non] appena. ~

one | /wʌn/

● adj uno, una; not ~ **person** nemmeno una persona

● n uno m

● pron uno; (impersonal) si; ~ **another** l'un l'altro; ~ **by** ~ [a] uno a uno; ~ **never knows** non si sa mai

one: ~**self** pron (reflexive) si; (emphatic) sé, se stesso; by ~**self** da solo; be proud of ~**self** essere fieri di sé. ~**way** adj (street) a senso unico; (ticket) di sola andata

onion /'ʌnjən/ n cipolla f

on-'line adj/adv su Internet

'onlooker n spettatore, -trice mf

only /'əʊnlɪ/ adj solo; ~ **child** figlio, -a mf unico, -a ● adv & conj solo, solamente; ~ **just** appena

'onset n (beginning) inizio m

onslaught /'ɒnslɔːt/ n attacco m

ooze /uːz/ vi fluire

opaque /əʊ'peɪk/ adj opaco

open /'əʊpən/ adj aperto; (free to all) pubblico; (job) vacante; in the ~ air all'aperto • n in the ~ all'aperto; fig alla luce del sole • vt aprire • vi aprirsi; (shop:) aprire; (flower:) sbocciare. □~ up vt aprire • vi aprirsi

opening /'əʊpənɪŋ/ n apertura f; (beginning) inizio m; (job) posto m libero; ~ hours npl orario m d'apertura

openly /'əʊpənlɪ/ adv apertamente

open: ~-'minded adj aperto; (broadminded) di vedute larghe. ~-plan adj a pianta aperta

Open University Fondata nel 1969, è il sistema di università a distanza del Regno Unito. L'insegnamento viene impartito con vari mezzi: per corrispondenza, attraverso programmi radiotelevisivi trasmessi dalla BBC e anche via Internet. Gli studenti inviano per posta i compiti svolti a un tutore. Generalmente si seguono corsi part time della durata di quattro o cinque anni, anche se non ci sono limiti di tempo per completare gli studi.

opera /'ɒpərə/ n opera f

opera-house n teatro m lirico

operate /'ɒpəreɪt/ vt far funzionare (machine, lift); azionare (lever, brake); mandare avanti (business) • vi (Techn) funzionare; (be in action) essere in funzione; (Mil, fig) operare; ~ on (Med) operare

operatic /ɒpə'rætɪk/ adj lirico, operistico

operation /ɒpə'reɪʃn/ n operazione f; (Techn) funzionamento m; in ~ (Techn) in funzione; come into ~ fig entrare in funzione; (law:) entrare in vigore; have an ~ (Med) subire un'operazione. ~al adj operativo; (law etc) in vigore

operative /'ɒpərətɪv/ adj operativo

operator /'ɒpəreɪtə(r)/ n (user) operatore, -trice mf; (Teleph) centralinista mf

opinion /ə'pɪnjən/ n opinione f; in my ~ secondo me. ~ated adj dogmatico

opponent /ə'pəʊnənt/ n avversario, -a m

opportun|e /'ɒpətjuːn/ adj opportuno. ~ist n opportunista mf. ~istic adj opportunistico

opportunity /ɒpə'tjuːnətɪ/ n opportunità f inv

oppos|e /ə'pəʊz/ vt opporsi a; be ~ed to sth essere contrario a qcsa; as ~ed to al contrario di. ~ing adj avversario; (opposite) opposto

opposite /'ɒpəzɪt/ adj opposto; (house) di fronte; ~ number fig controparte f; the ~ sex l'altro sesso • n contrario m • adv di fronte • prep di fronte a

opposition /ɒpə'zɪʃn/ n opposizione f

oppress /ə'pres/ vt opprimere. ~ion n oppressione f. ~ive adj oppressivo; (heat) opprimente. ~or n oppressore m

opt /ɒpt/ vi ~ for optare per; ~ out dissociarsi (of da)

optical /'ɒptɪkl/ adj ottico; ~ illusion illusione f ottica

optician /ɒp'tɪʃn/ n ottico, -a mf

optimis|m /'ɒptɪmɪzm/ n ottimismo m. ~t n ottimista mf. ~tic adj ottimistico

option /'ɒpʃn/ n scelta f; (Comm) opzione f. ~al adj facoltativo; ~al extras pl optional m inv

or /ɔ:(r)/ conj o, oppure; (after negative) né; or [else] se no; in a year or two fra un anno o due

oral /'ɔːrəl/ adj orale • n 🆃 esame m orale. ~ly adv oralmente

orange /'ɒrɪndʒ/ n arancia f; (colour) arancione m • adj arancione. ~ade n

aranciata f. ~ juice n succo m d'a-
rancia

orbit /'ɔːbɪt/ n orbita f ● vt orbitare.
~al adj ~al road tangenziale f

orchard /'ɔːtʃəd/ n frutteto m

orches|tra /'ɔːkɪstrə/ n orchestra f.
~tral adj orchestrale. ~trate vt or-
chestrare

orchid /'ɔːkɪd/ n orchidea f

ordain /ɔː'deɪn/ vt decretare; (Relig)
ordinare

ordeal /ɔː'diːl/ n fig terribile esperienza f

order /'ɔːdə(r)/ n ordine m; (Comm)
ordinazione f; out of ~ (machine)
fuori servizio; in ~ that affinché; in
~ to per ● vt ordinare

orderly /'ɔːdəlɪ/ adj ordinato ● n
(Mil) attendente m; (Med) inser-
viente m

ordinary /'ɔːdɪnərɪ/ adj ordinario

ore /ɔː(r)/ n minerale m grezzo

organ /'ɔːgən/ n (Anat, Mus)
organo m

organic /ɔː'gænɪk/ adj organico;
(without chemicals) biologico. ~ally adv
organicamente; ~ally grown colti-
vato biologicamente

organism /'ɔːgənɪzm/ n organismo m

organist /'ɔːgənɪst/ n organista mf

organization /ɔːgənaɪ'zeɪʃn/ n organizzazione f

organize /'ɔːgənaɪz/ vt organizzare.
~r n organizzatore, -trice mf

orgasm /'ɔːgæzm/ n orgasmo m

orgy /'ɔːdʒɪ/ n orgia f

Orient /'ɔːrɪənt/ n Oriente m. o~al
adj orientale ● n orientale mf

orient|ate /'ɔːrɪenteɪt/ vt ~ate
oneself orientarsi. ~ation n orientamento m

origin /'ɒrɪdʒɪn/ n origine f

original /ə'rɪdʒɪn(ə)l/ adj originario;
(not copied, new) originale ● n originale
m; in the ~ in versione originale

~ity n originalità f. ~ly adv origina-
riamente

originat|e /ə'rɪdʒɪneɪt/ vi ~e in
avere origine in. ~or n ideatore,
-trice mf

ornament /'ɔːnəmənt/ n ornamento m; (on mantelpiece etc) sopram-
mobile m. ~al adj ornamentale.
~ation n decorazione f

ornate /ɔː'neɪt/ adj ornato

orphan /'ɔːfn/ n orfano, -a mf ● vt
rendere orfano; be ~ed rimanere
orfano. ~age n orfanotrofio m

orthodox /'ɔːθədɒks/ adj ortodosso

oscillate /'ɒsɪleɪt/ vi oscillare

osteopath /'ɒstɪəpæθ/ n osteo-
pata mf

ostracize /'ɒstrəsaɪz/ vt bandire

ostrich /'ɒstrɪtʃ/ n struzzo m

other /'ʌðə(r)/ adj, pron & n altro, -a
mf; the ~ [one] l'altro, -a mf; the ~
two gli altri due; two ~s altri due;
~ people gli altri; any ~ questions? altre domande?; every ~
day (alternate days) a giorni alterni;
the ~ day l'altro giorno; the ~
evening l'altra sera; someone/
something or ~ qualcuno/qualcosa
● adv ~ than tranne lui; somehow or ~ in qualche modo; somewhere or ~ da qualche parte

'otherwise adv altrimenti; (differently) diversamente

otter /'ɒtə(r)/ n lontra f

ouch /aʊtʃ/ int ahi!

ought /ɔːt/ v aux I/we ~ to stay
dovrei/dovremmo rimanere; he ~
not to have done it non avrebbe
dovuto farlo; that ~ to be enough
questo dovrebbe bastare

ounce /aʊns/ n oncia f (= 28,35 g)

our /aʊə(r)/ adj il nostro m, la nostra
f, i nostri mpl, le nostre fpl; ~
mother/father nostra madre/
nostro padre

ours /'aʊəz/ poss pron il nostro m, la
nostra f, i nostri mpl, le nostre fpl; a

friend of ~ un nostro amico; friends of ~ dei nostri amici; that is ~ quello è nostro; (as opposed to yours) quello è il nostro

ourselves /aʊə'selvz/ pron (reflexive) ci; (emphatic) noi, noi stessi; we poured ~ a drink ci siamo versati da bere; we heard it ~ l'abbiamo sentito noi stessi; we are proud of ~ siamo fieri di noi; by ~ da soli

out /aʊt/ adv fuori; (not alight) spento; be ~ (flower:) essere sbocciato; (workers:) essere in sciopero; (calculation:) essere sbagliato; (Sport) essere fuori; (unconscious) aver perso i sensi; (fig: not feasible) fuori questione; the sun is ~ è uscito il sole; ~ and about in piedi; get ~! 🔢 fuori!; you should get ~ more dovresti uscire più spesso; ~ with it! 🔢 sputa il rospo!; • prep ~ of fuori da; ~ of date non aggiornato; (passport) scaduto; ~ of order guasto; ~ of print/stock esaurito; ~ of bed/the room fuori dal letto/dalla stanza; ~ of breath senza fiato; ~ of danger fuori pericolo; ~ of work disoccupato; nine ~ of ten nove su dieci; be ~ of sugar/bread rimanere senza zucchero/pane; go ~ of the room uscire dalla stanza

'outbreak n (of war) scoppio m; (of disease) insorgenza f

'outburst n esplosione f

'outcome n risultato m

'outcry n protesta f

out'dated adj sorpassato

out'do vt (pt -did, pp -done) superare

'outdoor adj (life, sports) all'aperto; ~ clothes pl vestiti per uscire; ~ swimming pool piscina f scoperta

out'doors adv all'aria aperta; go ~ uscire [all'aria aperta]

'outer adj esterno

'outfit n equipaggiamento m; (clothes) completo m; (🔢: organization)

organizzazione. ~ter n men's ~ter's negozio m di abbigliamento maschile

'outgoing adj (president) uscente; (mail) in partenza; (sociable) estroverso. ~s npl uscite fpl

out'grow vi (pt -grew, pp -grown) diventare troppo grande per

outing /'aʊtɪŋ/ n gita f

outlandish /aʊt'lændɪʃ/ adj stravagante

'outlaw n fuorilegge mf inv • vt dichiarare illegale

'outlay n spesa f

'outlet n sbocco m; fig sfogo m; (Comm) punto m [di] vendita

'outline n contorno m; (summary) sommario m • vt tracciare il contorno di; (describe) descrivere

out'live vt sopravvivere a

'outlook n vista f; (future prospect) prospettiva f; (attitude) visione f

'outlying adj ~ areas pl zone fpl periferiche

out'number vt superare in numero

'out-patient n paziente mf esterno, -a; ~s' department ambulatorio m

'output n produzione f

'outright¹ adj completo; (refusal) netto

out'right² adv completamente; (at once) immediatamente; (frankly) francamente

'outset n inizio m; from the ~ fin dall'inizio

'outside¹ adj esterno • n esterno m; from the ~ dall'esterno; at the ~ al massimo

out'side² adv all'esterno, fuori; (out of doors) fuori; go ~ andare fuori • prep fuori da; (in front of) davanti a

'outskirts npl sobborghi mpl

out'spoken adj schietto

out'standing adj eccezionale;

(landmark) prominente; (not settled) in sospeso

out'stretched adj allungato

out'strip vt (pt/pp -stripped) superare

'outward /-wəd/ adj esterno; (journey) di andata ● adv verso l'esterno. **~ly** adv esternamente. **~s** adv verso l'esterno

out'weigh vt aver maggior peso di

out'wit vt (pt/pp -witted) battere in astuzia

oval /'əʊvl/ adj ovale ● n ovale m

ovary /'əʊvərɪ/ n (Anat) ovaia f

ovation /əʊ'veɪʃn/ n ovazione f

oven /'ʌvn/ n forno m. **~-ready** adj pronto da mettere in forno

over /'əʊvə(r)/ prep sopra; (across) al di là di; (during) durante; (more than) più di; **~ the phone** al telefono; **~ the page** alla pagina seguente; **all ~ Italy** in tutta [l']Italia; (travel) per l'Italia ● adv (Math) col resto di; (ended) finito; **~ again** un'altra volta; **~ and ~** più volte; **~ and above** oltre a; **~ here/there** qui/là; **all ~** (everywhere) dappertutto; **it's all ~** è tutto finito; **I ache all ~** ho male dappertutto; **come/bring ~** venire/portare; **turn ~** girare

over- pref (too) troppo

overall¹ /'əʊvərɔːl/ n grembiule m; **~s** pl tuta fsg [da lavoro]

overall² /əʊvər'ɔːl/ adj complessivo; (general) generale ● adv complessivamente

over'balance vi perdere l'equilibrio

over'bearing adj prepotente

'overboard adv (Naut) in mare

'overcast adj coperto

over'charge vt **~ sb** far pagare più del dovuto a qcno ● vi far pagare più del dovuto

'overcoat n cappotto m

over'come vt (pt -came, pp -come)

vincere; **be ~ by** essere sopraffatto da

over'crowded adj sovraffollato

over'do vt (pt -did, pp -done) esagerare; (cook too long) stracuocere; **~ it** (ⓘ: do too much) strafare

'overdose n overdose f inv

'overdraft n scoperto m; **have an ~** avere il conto scoperto

over'draw vt (pt -drew, pp -drawn) **~ one's account** andare allo scoperto; **be ~n** by (account:) essere [allo] scoperto di

over'due adj in ritardo

over'estimate vt sopravvalutare

'overflow¹ n (water) acqua f che deborda; (people) pubblico m in eccesso; (outlet) scarico m; **~ car park** parcheggio m supplementare

over'flow² vi debordare

over'grown adj (garden) coperto di erbacce

'overhaul¹ n revisione f

over'haul² vt (Techn) revisionare

over'head¹ adv in alto

'overhead² adj aereo; (railway) sopraelevato; (lights) da soffitto. **~s** npl spese fpl generali

over'hear vt (pt/pp -heard) sentire per caso (conversation)

over'joyed adj felicissimo

'overland adj & adv via terra; **~ route** via f terrestre

over'lap v (pt/pp -lapped) ● vi sovrapporsi ● vt sovrapporre

'overleaf adv sul retro

over'load vt sovraccaricare

over'look vt dominare; (fail to see, ignore) lasciarsi sfuggire

over'night¹ adv per la notte; **stay ~** fermarsi a dormire

'overnight² adj notturno; **~ bag** piccola borsa f da viaggio; **~ stay** sosta f per la notte

'overpass n cavalcavia m inv

over'pay vt (pt/pp -paid) strapagare

o

over'power vt sopraffare. ~ing adj insostenibile

over'priced adj troppo caro

overre'act vi avere una reazione eccessiva. ~ion n reazione f eccessiva

over'rid|e vt (pt -rode, pp -ridden) passare sopra a. ~ing adj prevalente

over'rule vt annullare (decision)

over'run vt (pt -ran, pp -run, pres p -running) invadere; oltrepassare (time); be ~ with essere invaso da

over'seas[1] adv oltremare

'overseas[2] adj d'oltremare

over'see vt (pt -saw, pp -seen) sorvegliare

over'shadow vt adombrare

over'shoot vt (pt/pp -shot) oltrepassare

'oversight n disattenzione f; an ~ una svista

over'sleep vi (pt/pp -slept) svegliarsi troppo tardi

over'step vt (pt/pp -stepped) ~ the mark oltrepassare ogni limite

overt /əʊ'vɜːt/ adj palese

over'tak|e vt/i (pt -took, pp -taken) sorpassare. ~ing n sorpasso m; no ~ing divieto di sorpasso

'overthrow[1] n (Pol) rovesciamento m

over'throw[2] vt (pt -threw, pp -thrown) (Pol) rovesciare

'overtime n lavoro m straordinario ● adv work ~ fare lo straordinario

overture /'əʊvətjʊə(r)/ n (Mus) preludio m; ~s pl fig approccio msg

over'turn vt ribaltare ● vi ribaltarsi

over'weight adj sovrappeso

overwhelm /-'welm/ vt sommergere (with di); (with emotion) confondere. ~ing adj travolgente; (victory, majority) schiacciante

over'work n lavoro m eccessivo ● vt far lavorare eccessivamente ● vi lavorare eccessivamente

ow|e /əʊ/ vt also fig dovere ([to] sb a qcno); ~e sth to sb dovere qcsa a qcno. ~ing adj be ~ing (money): essere da pagare ● prep ~ing to a causa di

owl /aʊl/ n gufo m

own[1] /əʊn/ adj proprio ● pron a car of my ~ una macchina per conto mio; on one's ~ da solo; hold one's ~ with tener testa a; get one's ~ back 🄣 prendersi una rivincita

own[2] vt possedere; (confess) ammettere; I don't ~ it non mi appartiene. □ ~ up vi confessare (to sth qcsa)

owner /'əʊnə(r)/ n proprietario, -a mf. ~ship n proprietà f

oxygen /'ɒksɪdʒən/ n ossigeno m; ~ mask maschera f a ossigeno

oyster /'ɔɪstə(r)/ n ostrica f

ozone /'əʊzəʊn/ n ozono m. ~-'friendly adj che non danneggia l'ozono. ~ layer n fascia f d'ozono

Pp

pace /peɪs/ n passo m; (speed) ritmo m; keep ~ with camminare di pari passo con ● vi ~ up and down camminare avanti e indietro. ~-maker n (Med) pacemaker m; (runner) battistrada m

Pacific /pə'sɪfɪk/ adj & n the ~ [Ocean] l'oceano m Pacifico, il Pacifico

pacifist /'pæsɪfɪst/ n pacifista mf

pacify /'pæsɪfaɪ/ vt (pt/pp -ied) placare (person); pacificare (country)

pack /pæk/ n (of cards) mazzo m; (of hounds) muta f; (of wolves, thieves) branco m; (of cigarettes etc) pacchetto *m*; a ~ of lies un mucchio di bugie ● *vt* impacchettare (article); fare (suitcase); mettere in valigia (swimsuit etc); (*press down*) comprimere; ~ed [out] (*crowded*) pieno zeppo ● *vi* fare i bagagli; send sb ~ing 🔤 mandare qcno a stendere. □ ~ up *vt* impacchettare ● *vi* 🔤 (machine:) piantare in asso

package /'pækɪdʒ/ *n* pacco *m* ● *vt* impacchettare. ~ **deal** offerta *f* tutto compreso. ~ **holiday** *n* vacanza *f* organizzata. ~ **tour** viaggio *m* organizzato

packet /'pækɪt/ *n* pacchetto *m*; cost a ~ 🔤 costare un sacco

pact /pækt/ *n* patto *m*

pad[1] /pæd/ *n* imbottitura *f*; (*for writing*) bloc-notes *m*, taccuino *m*; (🔤: *home*) [piccolo] appartamento *m* ● *vt* (*pt/pp* padded) imbottire. □ ~ **out** *vt* gonfiare

pad[2] *vi* (*pt/pp* padded) camminare con passo felpato

paddle[1] /'pæd(ə)l/ *n* pagaia *f* ● *vt* (*row*) spingere remando

paddle[2] *vi* (*wade*) squazzare

paddock /'pædək/ *n* recinto *m*

padlock /'pædlɒk/ *n* lucchetto *m* ● *vt* chiudere con lucchetto

paediatrician /pi:dɪə'trɪʃn/ *n* pediatra *mf*

page[1] /peɪdʒ/ *n* pagina *f*

page[2] *n* (*boy*) paggetto *m*; (*in hotel*) fattorino *m* ● *vt* far chiamare (person)

pager /'peɪdʒə(r)/ *n* cercapersone *m inv*

paid /peɪd/ ▷PAY ● *adj* ~ employment lavoro *m* remunerato; put ~ to mettere un termine a

pail /peɪl/ *n* secchio *m*

pain /peɪn/ *n* dolore *m*; be in ~ soffrire; take ~ darsi un gran d'affare; ~ in the neck 🔤 spina *f* nel fianco

pain: ~**ful** *adj* doloroso; (*laborious*) penoso. ~**killer** *n* calmante *m*. ~**less** *adj* indolore

painstaking /'peɪnsteɪkɪŋ/ *adj* minuzioso

paint /peɪnt/ *n* pittura *f*; ~s colori *mpl* ● *vt/i* pitturare; (artist:) dipingere. ~**brush** *n* pennello *m*. ~**er** *n* pittore, -trice *mf*; (*decorator*) imbianchino *m*. ~**ing** *n* pittura *f*; (*picture*) dipinto *m*. ~**work** *n* pittura *f*

pair /peə(r)/ *n* paio *m*; (*of people*) coppia *f*; ~ of trousers paio *m* di pantaloni; ~ of scissors paio *m* di forbici

pajamas /pə'dʒɑːməz/ *npl* Am pigiama *msg*

Pakistan /pɑːkɪ'stɑːn/ *n* Pakistan *m*. ~**i** *adj* pakistano ● *n* pakistano, -a *mf*

pal /pæl/ *n* 🔤 amico, -a *mf*

palace /'pælɪs/ *n* palazzo *m*

palatable /'pælətəbl/ *adj* gradevole (*al gusto*)

palate /'pælət/ *n* palato *m*

pale /peɪl/ *adj* pallido

Palestin|e /'pæləstaɪn/ *n* Palestina *f*. ~**ian** *adj* palestinese ● *n* palestinese *mf*

palette /'pælɪt/ *n* tavolozza *f*

palm /pɑːm/ *n* palmo *m*; (*tree*) palma *f*; P~ Sunday *n* Domenica *f* delle Palme ● **palm off** *vt* ~ sth off on sb rifilare qcsa a qcno

palpable /'pælpəbl/ *adj* palpabile; (*perceptible*) tangibile

palpitate /'pælpɪteɪt/ *vi* palpitare. ~**ions** *npl* palpitazioni *fpl*

pamper /'pæmpə(r)/ *vt* viziare

pamphlet /'pæmflɪt/ *n* opuscolo *m*

pan /pæn/ *n* tegame *m*, pentola *f*; (*for frying*) padella *f*; (*of scales*) piatto *m* ● *vt* (*pt/pp* panned) (🔤: *criticize*) stroncare

pancake *n* crêpe *f inv*, frittella *f*

panda /'pændə/ *n* panda *m inv*. ~ **car** *n* macchina *f* della polizia

pandemonium /pændɪ'məʊnɪəm/ *n* pandemonio *m*

pander /'pændə(r)/ *vi* ~ to sb

compiacere qcno

pane /peɪn/ n ~ [of glass] vetro m

panel /ˈpænl/ n pannello m; (group of people) giuria f; ~ of experts gruppo m di esperti. ~ling n pannelli mpl

pang /pæŋ/ n ~s of hunger morsi mpl della fame; ~s of conscience rimorsi mpl di coscienza

panic /ˈpænɪk/ n panico m ● vi (pt/pp panicked) lasciarsi prendere dal panico. ~-stricken adj in preda al panico

panoram|a /pænəˈrɑːmə/ n panorama m. ~ic adj panoramico

pansy /ˈpænzɪ/ n viola f del pensiero; (🔲: effeminate man) finocchio m

pant /pænt/ vi ansimare

panther /ˈpænθə(r)/ n pantera f

panties /ˈpæntɪz/ npl mutandine fpl

pantomime /ˈpæntəmaɪm/ n pantomima f

pantry /ˈpæntrɪ/ n dispensa f

pants /pænts/ npl (underwear) mutande fpl; (woman's) mutandine fpl; (trousers) pantaloni mpl

pantyhose n Am collant m inv

paper /ˈpeɪpə(r)/ n carta f; (wallpaper) carta f da parati; (newspaper) giornale m; (exam) esame m; (treatise) saggio m; ~s (documents) documenti mpl; (for identification) documento m [d'identità]; on ~ in teoria; put down on ~ mettere per iscritto ● attrib di carta ● vt tappezzare

paper: ~back n edizione f economica. ~-clip n graffetta f. ~weight n fermacarte m inv. ~work n lavoro m d'ufficio

parable /ˈpærəbl/ n parabola f

parachut|e /ˈpærəʃuːt/ n paracadute m ● vi lanciarsi col paracadute. ~ist n paracadutista m

parade /pəˈreɪd/ n (military) parata f militare ● vi sfilare ● vt (show off) far sfoggio di

paradise /ˈpærədaɪs/ n paradiso m

paraffin /ˈpærəfɪn/ n paraffina f

paragraph /ˈpærəɡrɑːf/ n paragrafo m

parallel /ˈpærəlel/ adj & adv parallelo. ~ bars npl parallele fpl. ~ port n (Comput) porta f parallela ● n (Geog), fig parallelo m; (line) parallela f ● vt essere paragonabile a

Paralympics /pærəˈlɪmpɪks/ npl the P~ le Paraolimpiadi fpl

paralyse /ˈpærəlaɪz/ vt also fig paralizzare

paralysis /pəˈræləsɪs/ n (pl -ses /-siːz/) paralisi f inv

paramedic /pærəˈmedɪk/ n paramedico, -a mf

parameter /pəˈræmɪtə(r)/ n parametro m

paranoia /pærəˈnɔɪə/ n paranoia f

paranoid /ˈpærənɔɪd/ adj paranoico, -a mf

paraphernalia /pærəfəˈneɪlɪə/ n armamentario m

paraplegic /pærəˈpliːdʒɪk/ adj paraplegico ● n paraplegico, -a mf

parasite /ˈpærəsaɪt/ n parassita mf

paratrooper /ˈpærətruːpə(r)/ n paracadutista m

parcel /ˈpɑːsl/ n pacco m

parch /pɑːtʃ/ vt disseccare; be ~ed (person): morire dalla sete

pardon /ˈpɑːdn/ n perdono m; (Jur) grazia f; ~? prego?; I beg your ~? fml chiedo scusa?; I do beg your ~ (sorry) chiedo scusa! ● vt perdonare; (Jur) graziare

parent /ˈpeərənt/ n genitore, -trice mf; ~s pl genitori mpl. ~al adj dei genitori

parenthesis /pəˈrenθəsɪs/ n (pl -ses /-siːz/) parentesi f inv

Paris /ˈpærɪs/ n Parigi f

parish /ˈpærɪʃ/ n parrocchia f. ~ioner n parrocchiano, -a mf

park /pɑːk/ n parco m ● vt/i (Auto) posteggiare, parcheggiare; ~ oneself 🔲 installarsi

park-and-'ride n park

and ride *m inv*

parking /'pɑːkɪŋ/ *n* parcheggio *m*, posteggio *m*; 'no ~' 'divieto di sosta'. ~-lot *n Am* posteggio *m*, parcheggio *m*. ~-meter *n* parchimetro *m*. ~ space *n* posteggio *m*, parcheggio *m*

parliament /'pɑːləmənt/ *n* parlamento *m*. ~ary *adj* parlamentare

> **Parliament** Il Parlamento britannico è l'organo legislativo del paese, suddiviso in due Camere: *House of Commons* e *House of Lords*. La prima è composta di 650 parlamentari, o *MPs (Members of Parliament)*, eletti a suffragio popolare; la seconda è formata da oltre 1000 membri, tra i quali esponenti dell'aristocrazia, ex primi ministri e cittadini che si sono in qualche modo distinti. Ogni anno è il capo della monarchia ad aprire ufficialmente il Parlamento e l'anno legislativo.

parlour /'pɑːlə(r)/ *n* salotto *m*

parochial /pə'rəʊkɪəl/ *adj* parrocchiale; *fig* ristretto

parody /'pærədɪ/ *n* parodia *f* ● *vt* (*pt/pp* -ied) parodiare

parole /pə'rəʊl/ *n* on ~ in libertà condizionale ● *vt* mettere in libertà condizionale

parrot /'pærət/ *n* pappagallo *m*

parsley /'pɑːslɪ/ *n* prezzemolo *m*

parsnip /'pɑːsnɪp/ *n* pastinaca *f*

part /pɑːt/ *n* parte *f*; (*of machine*) pezzo *m*; for my ~ per quanto mi riguarda; on the ~ of da parte di; take sb's ~ prendere le parti di qcno; take ~ in prendere parte a ● *adv* in parte ● *vt* ~ one's hair farsi la riga ● *vi* (*people*) separarsi; ~ with separarsi da

partial /'pɑːʃl/ *adj* parziale; be ~ to aver un debole per. ~ly *adv* parzialmente

particip|ant /pɑː'tɪsɪpənt/ *n* partecipante *mf*. ~ate *vi* partecipare (in a). ~ation *n* partecipazione *f*

particle /'pɑːtɪkl/ *n* (*Gram, Phys*) particella *f*

particular /pə'tɪkjʊlə(r)/ *adj* particolare; (*precise*) meticoloso; *pej* noioso; in ~ in particolare. ~ly *adv* particolarmente. ~s *npl* particolari *mpl*

parting /'pɑːtɪŋ/ *n* separazione *f*; (*in hair*) scriminatura *f* ● *attrib* di commiato

partisan /pɑːtɪ'zæn/ *n* partigiano, -a *mf*

partition /pɑː'tɪʃn/ *n* (*wall*) parete *f* divisoria; (*Pol*) divisione *f* ● *vt* dividere (*in parti*). □ ~ **off** *vt* separare

partly /'pɑːtlɪ/ *adv* in parte

partner /'pɑːtnə(r)/ *n* (*Comm*) socio, -a *mf*; (*in relationship*) compagno, -a *mf*. ~ship *n* (*Comm*) società *f*

partridge /'pɑːtrɪdʒ/ *n* pernice *f*

part-time *adj & adv* part time; be or work ~ lavorare part time

party /'pɑːtɪ/ *n* ricevimento *m*, festa *f*; (*group*) gruppo *m*; (*Pol*) partito *f*; (*Jur*) parte *f* (*in causa*); be ~ to essere parte attiva in

pass /pɑːs/ *n* lasciapassare *m inv*; (*in mountains*) passo *m*; (*Sport*) passaggio *m*; (*Sch: mark*) [voto *m*] sufficiente *m*; make a ~ at 🆃 fare delle avances a ● *vt* passare; (*overtake*) sorpassare; (*approve*) far passare; fare (*remark*); (*Jur*) pronunciare (*sentence*); ~ the time passare il tempo ● *vi* passare; (*in exam*) essere promosso. □ ~ **away** *vi* mancare. □ ~ **down** *vt* passare; *fig* trasmettere. □ ~ **out** *vi* 🆃 svenire. □ ~ **round** *vt* far passare. □ ~ **through** *vt* attraversare. □ ~ **up** *vt* passare; (🆃: *miss*) lasciarsi scappare

passable /'pɑːsəbl/ *adj* (*road*) praticabile; (*satisfactory*) passabile

passage /'pæsɪdʒ/ *n* passaggio *m*; (*corridor*) corridoio *m*; (*voyage*)

P

traversata f

passenger /'pæsɪndʒə(r)/ n passeggero, -a mf. ~ seat n posto m accanto al guidatore

passer-by /pɑːsə'baɪ/ n (pl ~sby) passante m

passion /'pæʃn/ n passione f. ~ate adj appassionato

passive /'pæsɪv/ adj passivo ● n passivo m. ~ness n passività f

Passover /'pɑːsəʊvə(r)/ n Pasqua f ebraica

pass: ~port n passaporto m. ~word n parola f d'ordine

past /pɑːst/ adj passato; (former) ex; in the ~ few days nei giorni scorsi; that's all ~ tutto questo è passato; the ~ week la settimana scorsa ● n passato m ● prep oltre; at ten ~ two alle due e dieci ● adv oltre; go/come ~ passare

pasta /'pæstə/ n pasta(sciutta) f

paste /peɪst/ n pasta f; (dough) impasto m; (adhesive) colla f ● vt incollare

pastel /'pæstl/ n pastello m ● attrib pastello

pasteurize /'pɑːstʃəraɪz/ vt pastorizzare

pastime /'pɑːstaɪm/ n passatempo m

pastry /'peɪstrɪ/ n pasta f; ~ies pl pasticcini mpl

pasture /'pɑːstʃə(r)/ n pascolo m

pasty[1] /'peɪstɪ/ n ≈ pasticcio m

pasty[2] /'peɪstɪ/ adj smorto

pat /pæt/ n buffetto m; (of butter) pezzetto m ● adv have sth off ~ conoscere qcsa a menadito ● vt (pt/pp patted) dare un buffetto a; ~ sb on the back fig congratularsi con qcno

patch /pætʃ/ n toppa f; (spot) chiazza f; (period) periodo m; not a ~ on [T] molto inferiore a ● vt mettere una toppa su. □ ~ up vt riparare alla bell'e meglio; appianare (quarrel)

pâté /'pæteɪ/ n pâté m inv

patent /'peɪtnt/ adj palese ● n brevetto m ● vt brevettare. ~ leather shoes npl scarpe fpl di vernice. ~ly adv in modo palese

patern|al /pə'tɜːnl/ adj paterno. ~ity n paternità f inv

path /pɑːθ/ n (pl ~s /pɑːðz/) sentiero m; (orbit) traiettoria m; fig strada f

pathetic /pə'θetɪk/ adj patetico; (T: very bad) penoso

patience /'peɪʃns/ n pazienza f; (game) solitario m

patient /'peɪʃnt/ adj paziente ● n paziente mf. ~ly adv pazientemente

patio /'pætɪəʊ/ n terrazza f

patriot /'pætrɪət/ n patriota mf. ~ic adj patriottico. ~ism n patriottismo m

patrol /pə'trəʊl/ n pattuglia f ● vt/i pattugliare. ~ car n autopattuglia f

patron /'peɪtrən/ n patrono m; (of charity) benefattore, -trice mf; (of the arts) mecenate mf; (customer) cliente mf

patroniz|e /'pætrənaɪz/ vt frequentare abitualmente; fig trattare con condiscendenza. ~ing adj condiscendente. ~ingly adv con condiscendenza

pattern /'pætn/ n disegno m (stampato); (for knitting, sewing) modello m

paunch /pɔːntʃ/ n pancia f

pause /pɔːz/ n pausa f ● vi fare una pausa

pave /peɪv/ vt pavimentare; ~ the way preparare la strada (for a). ~ment n marciapiede m

paw /pɔː/ n zampa f ● vt [T] mettere le zampe addosso a

pawn[1] /pɔːn/ n (in chess) pedone m; fig pedina f

pawn[2] vt impegnare ● n in ~ in pegno. ~broker n prestatore, -trice mf su pegno. ~shop n monte m di pietà

pay /peɪ/ n paga f; in the ~ of al soldo di ● v (pt/pp **paid**) ● vt pagare; prestare (attention); fare (compliment, visit); fare pagare in contanti ● vi pagare; (be profitable) rendere; it doesn't ~ to... fig è fatica sprecata...; ~ for sth pagare per qcsa. □ ~ **back** vt ripagare. □ ~ **in** vt versare. □ ~ **off** vt saldare (debt) ● vi fig dare dei frutti. □ ~ **up** vi pagare

payable /ˈpeɪəbl/ adj pagabile; make ~ to intestare a

payment /ˈpeɪmənt/ n pagamento m

PC n abbr (personal computer) PC m inv

pea /piː/ n pisello m

peace /piːs/ n pace f; ~ of mind tranquillità f

peach /piːtʃ/ n pesca f; (tree) pesco m

peacock /ˈpiːkɒk/ n pavone m

peak /piːk/ n picco m; fig culmine m. ~ed 'cap n berretto m a punta. ~ hours npl ore fpl di punta

peal /piːl/ n (of bells) scampanio m; ~s of laughter fragore m di risate

peanut n nocciolina f [americana]; ~s [T] miseria f

pear /peə(r)/ n pera f; (tree) pero m

pearl /pɜːl/ n perla f

peasant /ˈpeznt/ n contadino, -a mf

pebble /ˈpebl/ n ciottolo m

peck /pek/ n beccata f; (kiss) bacetto m ● vt beccare; (kiss) dare un bacetto a. ~ing order n gerarchia f. ~ **at** vt beccare

peculiar /prˈkjuːlɪə(r)/ adj strano; (special) particolare; ~ to tipico di. ~ity n stranezza f; (feature) particolarità f inv

pedal /ˈpedl/ n pedale m ● vi pedalare. ~ **bin** n pattumiera f a pedale

pedantic /prˈdæntɪk/ adj pedante

pedestal /ˈpedɪstl/ n piedistallo m

pedestrian /prˈdestrɪən/ n pedone m ● adj fig scadente. ~ **'crossing** n passaggio m pedonale. ~ **'precinct** n zona f pedonale

pedigree /ˈpedɪgriː/ n pedigree m inv; (of person) lignaggio m ● attrib (animal) di razza, con pedigree

peek /piːk/ vi [T] sbirciare

peel /piːl/ n buccia f ● vt sbucciare ● vi (nose) etc: spellarsi; (paint:) staccarsi

peep /piːp/ n sbirciata f ● vi sbirciare

peer[1] /pɪə(r)/ vi ~ **at** scrutare

peer[2] n nobile m; his ~s pl (in rank) i suoi pari mpl; (in age) i suoi coetanei mpl. ~age n nobiltà f

peg /peg/ n (hook) piolo m; (for tent) picchetto m; (for clothes) molletta f; off the ~ [T] prêt-à-porter

pejorative /prˈdʒɒrətɪv/ adj peggiorativo

pelican /ˈpelɪkən/ n pellicano m

pellet /ˈpelɪt/ n pallottola f

pelt /pelt/ vt bombardare ● vi ([T]: run fast) catapultarsi; ~ **down** (rain:) venir giù a fiotti

pelvis /ˈpelvɪs/ n (Anat) bacino m

pen[1] /pen/ n (for animals) recinto m

pen[2] n penna f; (ball-point) penna f a sfera

penal /ˈpiːnl/ adj penale. ~ize vt penalizzare

penalty /ˈpenltɪ/ n sanzione f; (fine) multa f; (in football) ~ [kick] [calcio m di] rigore m; ~ **area** or **box** area f di rigore

penance /ˈpenəns/ n penitenza f

pence /pens/ ▷PENNY

pencil /ˈpensl/ n matita f. ~-sharpener n temperamatite m inv

pendulum /ˈpendjʊləm/ n pendolo m

penetrate /ˈpenɪtreɪt/ vt/i penetrare. ~ing adj acuto; (sound, stare) penetrante. ~ion n penetrazione f

penguin /ˈpeŋgwɪn/ n pinguino m

P

penicillin /penɪˈsɪlɪn/ n penicillina f

peninsula /pɪˈnɪnsjʊlə/ n penisola f

penis /ˈpiːnɪs/ n pene m

pen: ~**knife** n temperino m. ~**name** n pseudonimo m

penniless /ˈpenɪlɪs/ adj senza un soldo

penny /ˈpenɪ/ n (pl pence; single coins pennies) penny m; Am centesimo m; spend a ~ 🚽 andare in bagno

pension /ˈpenʃn/ n pensione f. ~**er** n pensionato, -a mf

pensive /ˈpensɪv/ adj pensoso

Pentecost /ˈpentɪkɒst/ n Pentecoste f

pent-up /ˈpentʌp/ adj represso

penultimate /pɪˈnʌltɪmət/ adj penultimo

people /ˈpiːpl/ npl persone fpl, gente fsg; (citizens) popolo msg; a lot of ~ una marea di gente; the ~ la gente; English ~ gli inglesi; ~ say si dice; for four ~ per quattro ● vt popolare

pepper /ˈpepə(r)/ n pepe m; (vegetable) peperone m ● vt (season) pepare

pepper: ~**corn** n grano m di pepe. ~ **mill** macinapepe m inv. ~**mint** n menta f peperita; (sweet) caramella f alla menta. ~**pot** n pepiera f

per /pɜː(r)/ prep per; ~ annum all'anno; ~ cent percento

perceive /pəˈsiːv/ vt percepire; (interpret) interpretare

percentage /pəˈsentɪdʒ/ n percentuale f

perceptible /pəˈseptəbl/ adj percettibile; (difference) sensibile

percept|ion /pəˈsepʃn/ n percezione f. ~**ive** adj perspicace

perch /pɜːtʃ/ n pertica f ● vi (bird:) appollaiarsi

percolator /ˈpɜːkəleɪtə(r)/ n caffettiera f a filtro

percussion /pəˈkʌʃn/ n percussione f. ~ **instrument** n strumento m a percussione

perfect[1] /ˈpɜːfɪkt/ adj perfetto ● n (Gram) passato m prossimo

perfect[2] /pəˈfekt/ vt perfezionare. ~**ion** n perfezione f; to ~**ion** alla perfezione. ~**ionist** n perfezionista mf

perfectly /ˈpɜːfɪktlɪ/ adv perfettamente

perform /pəˈfɔːm/ vt compiere, fare; eseguire (role); (operation, sonata); recitare (role); mettere in scena (play) ● vi (Theat) recitare; (Techn) funzionare. ~**ance** n esecuzione f; (at theatre, cinema) rappresentazione f; (Techn) rendimento m. ~**er** n artista mf

perfume /ˈpɜːfjuːm/ n profumo m

perhaps /pəˈhæps/ adv forse

peril /ˈperɪl/ n pericolo m. ~**ous** adj pericoloso

perimeter /pəˈrɪmɪtə(r)/ n perimetro m

period /ˈpɪərɪəd/ n periodo m; (menstruation) mestruazioni fpl; (Sch) ora f di lezione; (full stop) punto m fermo ● attrib (costume) d'epoca; (furniture) in stile. ~**ic** adj periodico. ~**ical** n periodico m, rivista f

peripher|al /pəˈrɪfərəl/ adj periferico. ~**y** n periferia f

perish /ˈperɪʃ/ vi (rot) deteriorarsi; (die) perire. ~**able** adj deteriorabile

perjur|e /ˈpɜːdʒə(r)/ vt ~ oneself spergiurare. ~**y** n spergiuro m

perk /pɜːk/ n 🚽 vantaggio m

perm /pɜːm/ n permanente f ● vt ~ sb's hair fare la permanente a qno

permanent /ˈpɜːmənənt/ adj permanente; (job, address) stabile. ~**ly** adv stabilmente

permissible /pəˈmɪsəbl/ adj ammissibile

permission /pəˈmɪʃn/ n permesso m

permit[1] /pəˈmɪt/ vt (pt/pp -mitted) permettere; ~ sb to do sth permet

permit | philistine

permit² /ˈpɜːmɪt/ n autorizzazione f

perpendicular /pɜːpənˈdɪkjʊlə(r)/ adj perpendicolare ● n perpendicolare f

perpetual /pəˈpetjʊəl/ adj perenne. ~ly adv perennemente

perpetuate /pəˈpetjʊeɪt/ vt perpetuare

perplex /pəˈpleks/ vt lasciare perplesso. ~ed adj perplesso. ~ity n perplessità f inv

persecute /ˈpɜːsɪkjuːt/ vt perseguitare. ~ion n persecuzione f

perseverance /pɜːsɪˈvɪərəns/ n perseveranza f

persever|e /pɜːsɪˈvɪə(r)/ vi perseverare. ~ing adj assiduo

Persian /ˈpɜːʃn/ adj persiano

persist /pəˈsɪst/ vi persistere; ~ in doing sth persistere nel fare qcsa. ~ence n persistenza f. ~ent adj persistente. ~ently adv persistentemente

person /ˈpɜːsn/ n persona f; in ~ di persona

personal /ˈpɜːsənl/ adj personale. ~ 'hygiene n igiene f personale. ~ organizer n (Comput) agenda f elettronica. ~ly adv personalmente.

personality /pɜːsəˈnælətɪ/ n personalità f inv; (on TV) personaggio m

personnel /pɜːsəˈnel/ n personale m

perspective /pəˈspektɪv/ n prospettiva f

persp|iration /pɜːspɪˈreɪʃn/ n sudore m. ~ire vi sudare

persua|de /pəˈsweɪd/ vt persuadere. ~sion n persuasione f; (belief) convinzione f

persuasive /pəˈsweɪsɪv/ adj persuasivo. ~ly adv in modo persuasivo

pertinent /ˈpɜːtɪnənt/ adj pertinente (to a)

perturb /pəˈtɜːb/ vt perturbare

peruse /pəˈruːz/ vt leggere

pervers|e /pəˈvɜːs/ adj irragionevole. ~ion n perversione f

pervert /ˈpɜːvɜːt/ n pervertito, -a m f

pessimis|m /ˈpesɪmɪzm/ n pessimismo m. ~t n pessimista m f. ~tic adj pessimistico. ~tically adv in modo pessimistico

pest /pest/ n piaga f; (🄸: person) peste f

pester /ˈpestə(r)/ vt molestare

pesticide /ˈpestɪsaɪd/ n pesticida m

pet /pet/ n animale m domestico; (favourite) cocco, -a m f ● adj prediletto ● v (pt/pp petted) ● vt coccolare ● vi (couple:) praticare il petting

petal /ˈpetl/ n petalo m

petition /pəˈtɪʃn/ n petizione f

pet 'name n vezzeggiativo m

petrol /ˈpetrəl/ n benzina f

petroleum /pɪˈtrəʊlɪəm/ n petrolio m

petrol: ~-pump n pompa f di benzina. ~ station n stazione f di servizio. ~ tank n serbatoio m della benzina

petticoat /ˈpetɪkəʊt/ n sottoveste f

petty /ˈpetɪ/ adj (-ier, -iest) insignificante; (mean) meschino. ~ 'cash n cassa f per piccole spese

petulant /ˈpetjʊlənt/ adj petulante

pew /pjuː/ n banco m (di chiesa)

phantom /ˈfæntəm/ n fantasma m

pharmaceutical /fɑːməˈsjuːtɪkl/ adj farmaceutico

pharmac|ist /ˈfɑːməsɪst/ n farmacista m f. ~y n farmacia f

phase /feɪz/ n fase f ● vt phase in/out introdurre/eliminare gradualmente

pheasant /ˈfeznt/ n fagiano m

phenomen|al /fɪˈnɒmɪnl/ adj fenomenale; (incredible) incredibile. ~ally adv incredibilmente. ~on n (pl -na) fenomeno m

philistine /ˈfɪlɪstaɪn/ n filisteo, -a m f

philosoph|er /fɪ'lɒsəfə(r)/ *n* filosofo, -a *mf.* ~ical *adj* filosofico. ~ically *adv* con filosofia. ~y *n* filosofia *f*

phlegm /flem/ *n* (*Med*) flemma *f*

phlegmatic /fleg'mætɪk/ *adj* flemmatico

phobia /'fəʊbɪə/ *n* fobia *f*

phone /fəʊn/ *n* telefono *m*; be on the ~ avere il telefono; (*be phoning*) essere al telefono ● *vt* telefonare a ● *vi* telefonare. □ ~ **back** *vt/i* richiamare. ~ **book** *n* guida *f* del telefono. ~ **box** *n* cabina *f* telefonica. ~ **call** telefonata *f.* ~ **card** *n* scheda *f* telefonica. ~**-in** *n* trasmissione *f* con chiamate in diretta. ~ **number** *n* numero *m* telefonico

phonetic /fə'netɪk/ *adj* fonetico. ~**s** *n* fonetica *f*

phoney /'fəʊnɪ/ *adj* (-ier, -iest) fasullo

phosphorus /'fɒsfərəs/ *n* fosforo *m*

photo /'fəʊtəʊ/ *n* foto *f*; ~ **album** album *m inv* di fotografie. ~**copier** *n* fotocopiatrice *f.* ~**copy** *n* fotocopia *f* ● *vt* fotocopiare

photogenic /fəʊtəʊ'dʒenɪk/ *adj* fotogenico

photograph /'fəʊtəgrɑːf/ *n* fotografia *f* ● *vt* fotografare

photograph|er /fə'tɒgrəfə(r)/ *n* fotografo, -a *mf.* ~**ic** *adj* fotografico. ~**y** *n* fotografia *f*

phrase /freɪz/ *n* espressione *f* ● *vt* esprimere. ~**-book** *n* libro *m* di fraseologia

physical /'fɪzɪkl/ *adj* fisico. ~ e**ducation** *n* educazione *f* fisica. ~**ly** *adv* fisicamente

physician /fɪ'zɪʃn/ *n* medico *m*

physic|ist /'fɪzɪsɪst/ *n* fisico, -a *mf.* ~**s** *n* fisica *f*

physiology /fɪzɪ'ɒlədʒɪ/ *n* fisiologia *f*

physio'therap|ist /fɪzɪəʊ-/ *n* fisioterapista *mf.* ~**y** *n* fisioterapia *f*

physique /fɪ'ziːk/ *n* fisico *m*

pianist /'pɪənɪst/ *n* pianista *mf*

piano /pɪ'ænəʊ/ *n* piano *m*

pick¹ /pɪk/ *n* (*tool*) piccone *m*

pick² *n* scelta *f*; take your ~ prendi quello che vuoi ● *vt* (*select*) scegliere; cogliere (flowers); scassinare (lock); borseggiare (pockets); ~ and choose fare il difficile; ~ one's nose mettersi le dita nel naso; ~ a quarrel attaccar briga; ~ holes in 🔲 criticare; ~ at one's food spilluzzicare. □ ~ **on** *vt* (🔲: *nag*) assillare; he always ~s on me ce l'ha con me. □ ~ **out** *vt* (*identify*) individuare. □ ~ **up** *vt* sollevare; (*off the ground, information*) raccogliere; prendere in braccio (baby); (*learn*) imparare; prendersi (illness); (*buy*) comprare; captare (signal); (*collect*) andare/venire a prendere; prendere (passengers, habit); (*police*): arrestare (criminal); 🔲 rimorchiare (girl); ~ **oneself up** riprendersi ● *vi* (*improve*) recuperare; (weather): rimettersi

'pickaxe *n* piccone *m*

picket /'pɪkɪt/ *n* picchettista *mf* ● *vt* picchettare. ~ **line** *n* picchetto *m*

pickle /'pɪkl/ *n* ~**s** *pl* sottaceti *mpl*; in a ~ *fig* nei pasticci ● *vt* mettere sottaceto

pick: ~**pocket** *n* borsaiolo *m.* ~**-up** *n* (*truck*) furgone *m*; (*on record-player*) pickup *m inv*

picnic /'pɪknɪk/ *n* picnic *m* ● *vi* (*pt/pp* -nicked) fare un picnic

picture /'pɪktʃə(r)/ *n* (*painting*) quadro *m*; (*photo*) fotografia *f*; (*drawing*) disegno *m*; (*film*) film *m inv*; put sb in the ~ *fig* mettere qcno al corrente; the ~**s** il cinema ● *vt* (*imagine*) immaginare. ~**sque** *adj* pittoresco

pie /paɪ/ *n* torta *f*

piece /piːs/ *n* pezzo *m*; (*in game*) pedina *f*; a ~ of bread/paper un pezzo di pane/carta; a ~ of news/ advice una notizia/un consiglio; take to ~s smontare. ~meal *adv* un po' alla volta. ~work *n* lavoro *m* a cottimo ● **piece together** *vt* montare; *fig* ricostruire

pier /pɪə(r)/ *n* molo *m*; (*pillar*) pilastro *m*

pierce /pɪəs/ *vt* perforare; ~e a hole in sth fare un buco in qcsa. ~ing *n* [body] ~ piercing *m inv* ● *adj* penetrante

pig /pɪg/ *n* maiale *m*

pigeon /ˈpɪdʒɪn/ *n* piccione *m*. ~hole *n* casella *f*

piggy /ˈpɪgɪ/ ~back *n* give sb a ~back portare qcno sulle spalle. ~ bank *n* salvadanaio *m*

pigheaded *adj* 🅸 cocciuto

pigtail *n* (*plait*) treccina *f*

pile /paɪl/ *n* (*heap*) pila *f* ● *vt* ~ sth on to sth appilare qcsa su qcsa. □ ~ up *vt* accatastare ● *vi* ammucchiarsi

piles /paɪlz/ *npl* emorroidi *fpl*

pile-up *n* tamponamento *m* a catena

pilgrim /ˈpɪlgrɪm/ *n* pellegrino, -a *mf*. ~age *n* pellegrinaggio *m*

pill /pɪl/ *n* pillola *f*

pillar /ˈpɪlə(r)/ *n* pilastro *m*. ~-box *n* buca *f* delle lettere

pillow /ˈpɪləʊ/ *n* guanciale *m*. ~case *n* federa *f*

pilot /ˈpaɪlət/ *n* pilota *mf* ● *vt* pilotare. ~-light *n* fiamma *f* di sicurezza

pimple /ˈpɪmpl/ *n* foruncolo *m*

pin /pɪn/ *n* spillo *m*; (*Electr*) spinotto *m*; (*Med*) chiodo *m*; I have ~s and needles in my leg 🅸 mi formicola una gamba ● *vt* (*pt/pp* pinned) appuntare (to/on su); (*sewing*) fissare con gli spilli; (*hold down*) immobilizzare; ~ sb down to a date ottenere un appuntamento da qcno; ~ sth on sb 🅸 addossare a qcno la colpa di qcsa. □ ~ up *vt* appuntare; (*on wall*) affiggere

pinafore /ˈpɪnəfɔː(r)/ *n* grembiule *m*. ~ dress *n* scamiciato *m*

pincers /ˈpɪnsəz/ *npl* tenaglie *fpl*

pinch /pɪntʃ/ *n* pizzicotto *m*; (*of salt*) presa *f*; at a ~ in caso di bisogno ● *vt* pizzicare; (🅸: *steal*) fregare ● *vi* (*shoe*) stringere

pine[1] /paɪn/ *n* (*tree*) pino *m*

pine[2] /paɪn/ *vi* she is pining for you le manchi molto. □ ~ away *vi* deperire

pineapple /ˈpaɪn-/ *n* ananas *m inv*

ping-pong *n* ping-pong *m*

pink /pɪŋk/ *adj* rosa *m*

pinnacle /ˈpɪnəkl/ *n* guglia *f*

PIN number *n* codice *m* segreto

pin: ~point *vt* definire con precisione. ~stripe *adj* gessato

pint /paɪnt/ *n* pinta *f* (= 0,571, *Am*: 0,47 l); a ~ 🅸 una birra media

pioneer /paɪəˈnɪə(r)/ *n* pioniere, -a *mf* ● *vt* essere un pioniere di

pious /ˈpaɪəs/ *adj* pio

pip /pɪp/ *n* (*seed*) seme *m*

pipe /paɪp/ *n* tubo *m*; (*for smoking*) pipa *f*; the ~s (*Mus*) la cornamusa ● *vt* far arrivare con tubature (water, gas etc). □ ~ down *vi* abbassare la voce

pipe: ~dream *n* illusione *f*. ~line *n* conduttura *f*; in the ~line 🅸 in cantiere

piping /ˈpaɪpɪŋ/ *adj* ~ hot bollente

pirate /ˈpaɪrət/ *n* pirata *m*

Pisces /ˈpaɪsiːz/ *n* (*Astr*) Pesci *mpl*

piss /pɪs/ *vi* ⊠ pisciare

pistol /ˈpɪstl/ *n* pistola *f*

piston /ˈpɪstn/ *n* (*Techn*) pistone *m*

pit /pɪt/ *n* fossa *f*; (*mine*) miniera *f*; (*for orchestra*) orchestra *f* ● *vt* (*pt/pp* pitted) *fig* opporre (against a)

pitch[1] /pɪtʃ/ *n* (tone) tono *m*; (level) altezza *f*; (in sport) campo *m*; (*fig: degree*) grado *m* ● *vt* montare (tent). □ ~ in *vi* 🅸 mettersi sotto

pitch[2] *n* ~-black *adj* nero come la pece. ~-dark *adj* buio pesto

'pitfall n fig trabocchetto m

pith /pɪθ/ n (of lemon, orange) interno m della buccia

piti|ful /'pɪtɪfl/ adj pietoso. **~less** adj spietato

pittance /'pɪtns/ n miseria f

pity /'pɪtɪ/ n pietà f; what a **~** I che peccato!; take **~** on avere compassione di ● vt aver pietà di

pivot /'pɪvət/ n perno m; fig fulcro m ● vi imperniarsi (on su)

pizza /'piːtsə/ n pizza f

placard /'plækɑːd/ n cartellone m

placate /plə'keɪt/ vt placare

place /pleɪs/ n posto m; (🏠: house) casa f; (in book) segno m; feel out of **~** sentirsi fuori posto; take **~** aver luogo; all over the **~** dappertutto ● vt collocare; (remember) identificare; **~** an order fare un'ordinazione; be **~**d (in race) piazzarsi. **~-mat** n sottopiatto m

placid /'plæsɪd/ adj placido

plague /pleɪg/ n peste f

plaice /pleɪs/ n inv platessa f

plain /pleɪn/ adj chiaro; (simple) semplice; (not pretty) scialbo; (not patterned) normale; (chocolate) fondente; in **~** clothes in borghese ● adv (simply) semplicemente ● n pianura f. **~ly** adv francamente; (simply) semplicemente; (obviously) chiaramente

plaintiff /'pleɪntɪf/ n (Jur) parte f lesa

plait /plæt/ n treccia f ● vt intrecciare

plan /plæn/ n progetto m, piano m ● vt (pt/pp planned) progettare; (intend) prevedere

plane¹ /pleɪn/ n (tree) platano m

plane² n aeroplano m

plane³ n (tool) pialla f ● vt piallare

planet /'plænɪt/ n pianeta m

plank /plæŋk/ n asse f

planning /'plænɪŋ/ n pianificazione f. **~** permission n licenza f edilizia

plant /plɑːnt/ n pianta f; (machinery) impianto m; (factory) stabilimento m ● vt piantare. **~ation** n piantagione f

plaque /plɑːk/ n placca f

plasma /'plæzmə/ n plasma m

plaster /'plɑːstə(r)/ n intonaco m; (Med) gesso m; (sticking **~**) cerotto m; **~** of Paris gesso m ● vt intonacare (wall); (cover) ricoprire. **~ed** adj 🗷 sbronzo. **~er** n intonacatore m

plastic /'plæstɪk/ n plastica f ● adj plastico

plastic surgery n chirurgia f plastica

plate /pleɪt/ n piatto m; (flat sheet) placca f; (gold and silverware) argenteria f; (in book) tavola f [fuori testo] ● vt (cover with metal) placcare

platform /'plætfɔːm/ n (stage) palco m; (Rail) marciapiede m; (Pol) piattaforma f; **~** 5 binario 5

platinum /'plætɪnəm/ n platino m ● attrib di platino

platitude /'plætɪtjuːd/ n luogo m comune

platonic /plə'tɒnɪk/ adj platonico

plausible /'plɔːzəbl/ adj plausibile

play /pleɪ/ n gioco m; (Theat, TV) rappresentazione f; (Radio) sceneggiato m radiofonico; **~** on words gioco m di parole ● vt giocare a; (act) recitare; suonare (instrument); giocare (card) ● vi giocare; (Mus) suonare; **~** safe non prendere rischi. **□ ~ down** vt minimizzare. **□ ~ up** 🗓 fare i capricci

play: ~er n giocatore, -trice mf. **~ful** adj scherzoso. **~ground** n (Sch) cortile m (per la ricreazione). **~group** n asilo m

playing: ~-card n carta f da gioco. **~-field** n campo m da gioco

play: ~-pen n box m inv. **~wright** /-raɪt/ n drammaturgo, -a mf

plc n abbr (public limited company) s.r.l.

plea /pliː/ n richiesta f; make a **~**

for fare un appello a

plead /pliːd/ *vi* fare appello (for a); ~ **guilty** dichiararsi colpevole; ~ **with** sb implorare qcno

pleasant /ˈplez(ə)nt/ *adj* piacevole. ~**ly** *adv* piacevolmente; (say, smile) cordialmente

pleas|e /pliːz/ *adv* per favore; ~**e do** prego ● *vt* far contento; ~**e self** fare il proprio comodo; ~**e yourself!** come vuoi!; *pej* fai come ti parel. ~**ed** *adj* lieto; ~**ed with/about** contento di. ~**ing** *adj* gradevole

pleasure /ˈpleʒə(r)/ *n* piacere *m*; **with** ~ con piacere, volentieri

pleat /pliːt/ *n* piega *f* ● *vt* pieghettare. ~**ed 'skirt** *n* gonna *f* a pieghe

pledge /pledʒ/ *n* pegno *m*; (promise) promessa *f* ● *vt* impegnarsi a; (pawn) impegnare

plentiful /ˈplentɪfl/ *adj* abbondante

plenty /ˈplentɪ/ *n* abbondanza *f*; ~ **of money** molti soldi; ~ **of people** molta gente; I've got ~ ne ho in abbondanza

pliable /ˈplaɪəbl/ *adj* flessibile

pliers /ˈplaɪəz/ *npl* pinze *fpl*

plight /plaɪt/ *n* condizione *f*

plimsolls /ˈplɪmsəlz/ *npl* scarpe *fpl* da ginnastica

plod /plɒd/ *vi* (pt/pp plodded) trascinarsi; (work hard) sgobbare

plot /plɒt/ *n* complotto *m*; (of novel) trama *f*; ~ **of land** appezzamento *m* [di terreno] ● *vt/i* complottare

plough /plaʊ/ *n* aratro *m*; ~**man's lunch** piatto *m* di formaggi e sottaceti, servito con pane. ● *vt/i* arare. □ ~ **back** *vt* (Comm) reinvestire

ploy /plɔɪ/ *n* 🔢 manovra *f*

pluck /plʌk/ *n* fegato *m* ● *vt* strappare; depilare (eyebrows); spennare (bird); cogliere (flower). □ ~ **up** *vt* ~ **up courage** farsi coraggio

plucky /ˈplʌkɪ/ *adj* (-ier, -iest) coraggioso

plug /plʌg/ *n* tappo *m*; (Electr) spina *f*; (Auto) candela *f*; (🔢: advertisement) pubblicità *f inv* ● *vt* (pt/pp plugged) tappare; (🔢: advertise) pubblicizzare con insistenza. □ ~ **in** *vt* (Electr) inserire la spina di

plum /plʌm/ *n* prugna *f*; (tree) prugno *m*

plumage /ˈpluːmɪdʒ/ *n* piumaggio *m*

plumb|er /ˈplʌmə(r)/ *n* idraulico *m*. ~**ing** *n* impianto *m* idraulico

plume /pluːm/ *n* piuma *f*

plump /plʌmp/ *adj* paffuto ● **plump for** *vt* scegliere

plunge /plʌndʒ/ *n* tuffo *m*; take the ~ 🔢 buttarsi ● *vt* tuffare; *fig* sprofondare ● *vi* tuffarsi

plural /ˈplʊərəl/ *adj* plurale ● *n* plurale *m*

plus /plʌs/ *prep* più ● *adj* in più; 500 ~ più di 500 ● *n* più *m*; (advantage) extra *m inv*

plush /plʌʃ/ *adj* lussuoso

plutonium /pluːˈtəʊnɪəm/ *n* plutonio *m*

ply /plaɪ/ *vt* (pt/pp plied) ~ sb with drink continuare a offrire da bere a qcno. ~**wood** *n* compensato *m*

p.m. *abbr* (post meridiem) del pomeriggio

PM *n abbr* Prime Minister

pneumonia /njuːˈməʊnɪə/ *n* polmonite *f*

P.O. *abbr* Post Office

poach /pəʊtʃ/ *vt* (Culin) bollire; cacciare di frodo (deer); pescare di frodo (salmon); ~**ed egg** uovo *m* in camicia. ~**er** *n* bracconiere *m*

pocket /ˈpɒkɪt/ *n* tasca *f*; be out of ~ rimetterci ● *vt* intascare. ~**book** *n* taccuino *m*; (wallet) portafoglio *m*. ~**-money** *n* denaro *m* per le piccole spese

pod /pɒd/ *n* baccello *m*

poem /ˈpəʊɪm/ *n* poesia *f*

poet /'pəʊɪt/ n poeta m. **~ic** adj poetico

poetry /'pəʊɪtrɪ/ n poesia f

poignant /'pɔɪnjənt/ adj emozionante

point /pɔɪnt/ n punto m; (sharp end) punta f; (meaning, purpose) senso m; (Electr) presa f [di corrente]; **~s** pl (Rail) scambio m; **~ of view** punto di vista; good/bad **~s** aspetti mpl positivi/negativi; **what is the ~?** a che scopo?; **the ~ is** il fatto è; **I don't see the ~** non vedo il senso; **up to a ~** fino a un certo punto; **be on the ~ of doing sth** essere sul punto di fare qcsa ● vt puntare (at verso) ● vi (with finger) puntare il dito; **~ at/to** (person): mostrare col dito; (indicator): indicare. □ **~ out** vt far notare (fact); **~ sth out to sb** far notare qcsa a qcno

point-'blank adj a bruciapelo

point|ed /'pɔɪntɪd/ adj appuntito; (question) diretto. **~ers** npl (advice) consigli mpl. **~less** adj inutile

poise /pɔɪz/ n padronanza f. **~d** adj in equilibrio; **~d to** sul punto di

poison /'pɔɪzn/ n veleno m ● vt avvelenare. **~ous** adj velenoso

poke /pəʊk/ n [piccola] spinta f ● vt spingere; (fire) attizzare; (put) ficcare; **~ fun at** prendere in giro. □ **~ about** vi frugare

poker[1] n attizzatoio m

poker[2] n (Cards) poker m

poky /'pəʊkɪ/ adj (-ier, -iest) angusto

Poland /'pəʊlənd/ n Polonia f

polar /'pəʊlə(r)/ adj polare. **~ 'bear** n orso m bianco. **~ize** vt polarizzare

pole[1] n palo m

pole[2] n (Geog, Electr) polo m

Pole /pəʊl/ n polacco, -a mf

police /pə'liːs/ npl polizia f ● vt pattugliare (area)

police: ~man n poliziotto m. **~ station** n commissariato m

~woman n donna f poliziotto

policy[1] /'pɒlɪsɪ/ n politica f

policy[2] n (insurance) polizza f

polio /'pəʊlɪəʊ/ n polio f

polish /'pɒlɪʃ/ n lucentezza f; (substance) lucido m; (for nails) smalto m; fig raffinatezza f ● vt lucidare; fig smussare. □ **~ off** vt ① finire in fretta; spazzolare (food)

Polish /'pəʊlɪʃ/ adj polacco ● n (language) polacco m

polished /'pɒlɪʃt/ adj (manner) raffinato; (performance) senza sbavature

polite /pə'laɪt/ adj cortese. **~ly** adv cortesemente. **~ness** n cortesia f

politic|al /pə'lɪtɪkl/ adj politico. **~ally** adv dal punto di vista politico. **~ian** n politico m

politics /'pɒlɪtɪks/ n politica f

poll /pəʊl/ n votazione f; (election) elezioni fpl; opinion **~** sondaggio m d'opinione; **go to the ~s** andare alle urne ● vt ottenere (votes)

pollen /'pɒlən/ n polline m

pollut|e /pə'luːt/ vt inquinare. **~ion** n inquinamento m

polo /'pəʊləʊ/ n polo m. **~-neck** n collo m alto. **~ shirt** n dolcevita f

polythene /'pɒlɪθiːn/ n politene m. **~ bag** n sacchetto m di plastica

polyun'saturated adj polinsaturo

pomp /pɒmp/ n pompa f

pompous /'pɒmpəs/ adj pomposo

pond /pɒnd/ n stagno m

ponder /'pɒndə(r)/ vt/i ponderare

pony /'pəʊnɪ/ n pony m. **~-tail** n coda f di cavallo. **~-trekking** n escursioni fpl col pony

poodle /'puːdl/ n barboncino m

pool[1] /puːl/ n (of water, blood) pozza f; [swimming] **~** piscina f

pool[2] n (common fund) cassa f comune; (in cards) piatto m; (game) biliardo m a buca. **~s** npl ≈ totocalcio msg ● vt mettere insieme

oor /pʊə(r)/ adj povero; (not good) scadente; in ~ health in cattiva salute ● npl the ~ i poveri. ~ly adj be ~ly non stare bene ● adv male

op¹ /pɒp/ n botto m; (drink) bibita f gasata ● v (pt/pp popped) ● vt (🄘: put) mettere; (burst) far scoppiare ● vi (burst) scoppiare. □ ~ **in/out** vi 🄘 fare un salto/un salto fuori

op² n 🄘 musica f pop ● attrib pop

opcorn n popcorn m inv

ope /pəʊp/ n papa m

oplar /ˈpɒplə(r)/ n pioppo m

oppy /ˈpɒpɪ/ n papavero m

opular /ˈpɒpjʊlə(r)/ adj popolare; (belief) diffuso. ~**ity** n popolarità f

opulat|e /ˈpɒpjʊleɪt/ vt popolare. ~**ion** n popolazione f

op-up n popup m inv

orcelain /ˈpɔːsəlɪn/ n porcellana f

orch /pɔːtʃ/ n portico m; Am veranda f

orcupine /ˈpɔːkjʊpaɪn/ n porcospino m

ore¹ /pɔː(r)/ n poro m

ore² vi ~ over immergersi in

ork /pɔːk/ n carne f di maiale

orn /pɔːn/ n 🄘 porno m. ~**o** adj 🄘 porno inv

ornograph|ic /pɔːnəˈɡræfɪk/ adj pornografico. ~**y** n pornografia f

orpoise /ˈpɔːpəs/ n focena f

orridge /ˈpɒrɪdʒ/ n farinata f di fiocchi d'avena

ort¹ /pɔːt/ n porto m

ort² n (Naut: side) babordo m

ort³ n (wine) porto m

ortable /ˈpɔːtəbl/ adj portatile

orter /ˈpɔːtə(r)/ n portiere m; (for luggage) facchino m

orthole n oblò m inv

ortion /ˈpɔːʃn/ n parte f; (of food) porzione f

ortrait /ˈpɔːtrɪt/ n ritratto m

portray /pɔːˈtreɪ/ vt ritrarre; (represent) descrivere; (actor:) impersonare. ~**al** n ritratto m

Portug|al /ˈpɔːtjʊɡl/ n Portogallo m. ~**uese** adj portoghese ● n portoghese mf

pose /pəʊz/ n posa f ● vt porre (problem, question) ● vi (for painter) posare; ~ **as** atteggiarsi a

posh /pɒʃ/ adj lussuoso; (people) danaroso

position /pəˈzɪʃn/ n posizione f; (job) posto m; (status) ceto m [sociale] ● vt posizionare

positive /ˈpɒzɪtɪv/ adj positivo; (certain) sicuro; (progress) concreto ● n positivo m. ~**ly** adv positivamente; (decidedly) decisamente

possess /pəˈzes/ vt possedere. ~**ion** n possesso m; ~**ions** pl beni mpl

possess|ive /pəˈzesɪv/ adj possessivo. ~**iveness** n carattere m possessivo. ~**or** n possessore, -ditrice mf

possibility /pɒsəˈbɪlətɪ/ n possibilità f inv

possib|le /ˈpɒsɪbl/ adj possibile. ~**ly** adv possibilmente; I couldn't ~**ly** accept non mi è possibile accettare; he can't ~**ly** be right non è possibile che abbia ragione; could you ~**ly**...? potrebbe per favore...?

post¹ /pəʊst/ n (pole) palo m ● vt affiggere (notice)

post² n (place of duty) posto m ● vt appostare; (transfer) assegnare

post³ n (mail) posta f; by ~ per posta ● vt spedire; (put in letter-box) imbucare; (as opposed to fax) mandare per posta; keep sb ~**ed** tenere qcno al corrente

post- pref dopo

postage /ˈpəʊstɪdʒ/ n affrancatura f. ~ **stamp** n francobollo m

postal /ˈpəʊstl/ adj postale. ~ **order** n vaglia m postale

post: ~**box** n cassetta f delle lettere. ~**card** n cartolina f. ~**code** n

p

codice m postale

poster /'pəʊstə(r)/ n poster m inv; (advertising, election) cartellone m

posterity /pɒ'sterətɪ/ n posterità f

posthumous /'pɒstjʊməs/ adj postumo. **~ly** adv dopo la morte

post: **~man** n postino m. **~mark** n timbro m postale

post-mortem /-'mɔːtəm/ n autopsia f

post office n ufficio m postale

postpone /pəʊst'pəʊn/ vt rimandare. **~ment** n rinvio m

posture /'pɒstʃə(r)/ n posizione f

pot /pɒt/ n vaso m; (for tea) teiera f; (for coffee) caffettiera f; (for cooking) pentola f; **~s of money** [] un sacco di soldi; go to **~** [] andare in malora

potato /pə'teɪtəʊ/ n (pl -es) patata f

poten|t /'pəʊtənt/ adj potente. **~tate** n potentato m

potential /pə'tenʃl/ adj potenziale ● n potenziale m. **~ly** adv potenzialmente

pot: **~hole** n cavità f inv; (in road) buca f. **~shot** n take a **~shot** at sparare a casaccio a

potter¹ /'pɒtə(r)/ vi **~ about** gingillarsi

potter² n vasaio, -a mf. **~y** n lavorazione f della ceramica; (articles) ceramiche fpl; (place) laboratorio m di ceramiche

potty /'pɒtɪ/ adj (-ier, -iest) [] matto ● n vasino m

pouch /paʊtʃ/ n marsupio m

poultry /'pəʊltrɪ/ n pollame m

pounce /paʊns/ vi balzare; **~ on** saltare su

pound¹ /paʊnd/ n libbra f (= 0,454 kg); (money) sterlina f

pound² vt battere ● vi (heart:) battere forte; (run heavily) correre pesantemente

pour /pɔː(r)/ vt versare ● vi riversarsi; (with rain) piovere a dirotto. □ **~ ou** vi riversarsi fuori ● vt versare (drink) sfogare (troubles)

pout /paʊt/ vi fare il broncio ● n broncio m

poverty /'pɒvətɪ/ n povertà f

powder /'paʊdə(r)/ n polvere f; (cosmetic) cipria f ● vt polverizzare; (face) incipriare. **~y** adj polveroso

power /'paʊə(r)/ n potere m; (Elect) corrente f [elettrica]; (Math) potenza f. **~ cut** n interruzione f di corrente. **~ed** adj **~ed by electricity** dotato di corrente [elettrica]. **~ful** adj potente. **~less** adj impotente. **~-station** n centrale f elettrica

PR n abbr public relations

practicable /'præktɪkəbl/ adj praticabile

practical /'præktɪkl/ adj pratico. **~ joke** n burla f. **~ly** adv praticamente

practice /'præktɪs/ n pratica f; (custom) usanza f; (habit) abitudine f; (exercise) esercizio m; (Sport) allenamento m; in **~** (in reality) in pratica; out of **~** fuori esercizio; put into **~** mettere in pratica

practise /'præktɪs/ vt fare pratica in; (carry out) mettere in pratica; esercitare (profession) ● vi esercitarsi; (doctor:) praticare. **~d** adj esperto

praise /preɪz/ n lode f ● vt lodare. **~worthy** adj lodevole

pram /præm/ n carrozzella f

prank /præŋk/ n tiro m

prawn /prɔːn/ n gambero m. **~ cocktail** n cocktail m inv di gamberetti

pray /preɪ/ vi pregare. **~er** n preghiera f

preach /priːtʃ/ vt/i predicare. **~er** n predicatore, -trice mf

pre-ar'range /priː-/ vt predisporre

precarious /prɪ'keərɪəs/ adj precario. **~ly** adv in modo precario

precaution /prɪ'kɔːʃn/ n precauzione f; as a **~** per precauzione.

~ary adj preventivo

recede /prɪ'si:d/ vt precedere

receden|ce /'presɪdəns/ n precedenza f. ~t n precedente m

receding /prɪ'si:dɪŋ/ adj precedente

recinct /'pri:sɪŋkt/ n (traffic-free) zona f pedonale; (Am: district) circoscrizione f

recious /'preʃəs/ adj prezioso; (style) ricercato ● adv Ⓣ ~ little ben poco

recipice /'presɪpɪs/ n precipizio m

recipitate /prɪ'sɪpɪteɪt/ vt precipitare

recis|e /prɪ'saɪs/ adj preciso. ~ely adv precisamente. ~ion n precisione f

recursor /pri:'kɜ:sə(r)/ n precursore m

redator /'predətə(r)/ n predatore, -trice mf. ~y adj rapace

redecessor /'pri:dɪsesə(r)/ n predecessore m

redicament /prɪ'dɪkəmənt/ n situazione f difficile

redict /prɪ'dɪkt/ vt predire. ~able adj prevedibile. ~ion n previsione f

reen /pri:n/ vt lisciarsi; ~ oneself fig farsi bello

re|fab /'pri:fæb/ n Ⓣ casa f prefabbricata. ~'fabricated adj prefabbricato

reface /'prefɪs/ n prefazione f

refect /'pri:fekt/ n (Sch) studente, -tessa mf della scuola superiore con responsabilità disciplinari, ecc

refer /prɪ'fɜ:(r)/ vt (pt/pp referred) preferire

refera|ble /'prefərəbl/ adj preferibile (to a). ~bly adv preferibilmente

referen|ce /'prefərəns/ n preferenza f. ~tial adj preferenziale

regnan|cy /'pregnənsɪ/ n gravidanza f. ~t adj incinta

rehi'storic /pri:-/ adj preistorico

prejudice /'predʒʊdɪs/ n pregiudizio m ● vt influenzare (against contro); (harm) danneggiare. ~d adj prevenuto

preliminary /prɪ'lɪmɪnərɪ/ adj preliminare

prelude /'prelju:d/ n preludio m

premature /'premətjʊə/ adj prematuro

pre'meditated /pri:-/ adj premeditato

premier /'premɪə(r)/ adj primario ● n (Pol) primo ministro m, premier m inv

première /'premɪeə(r)/ n prima f

premises /'premɪsɪz/ npl locali mpl; on the ~ sul posto

premium /'pri:mɪəm/ n premio m; be at a ~ essere una cosa rara

premonition /premə'nɪʃn/ n presentimento m

preoccupied /pri:'ɒkjʊpaɪd/ adj preoccupato

preparation /prepə'reɪʃn/ n preparazione f. ~s preparativi mpl

preparatory /prɪ'pærətrɪ/ adj preparatorio ● adv ~ to per

prepare /prɪ'peə(r)/ vt preparare ● vi prepararsi (for per); ~d to disposto a

preposition /prepə'zɪʃn/ n preposizione f

preposterous /prɪ'pɒstərəs/ adj assurdo

prerequisite /pri:'rekwɪzɪt/ n condizione f sine qua non

prescribe /prɪ'skraɪb/ vt prescrivere

prescription /prɪ'skrɪpʃn/ n (Med) ricetta f

presence /'prezns/ n presenza f; ~ of mind presenza f di spirito

present[1] /'preznt/ adj presente ● n presente m; at ~ attualmente

present[2] n (gift) regalo m; give sb sth as a ~ regalare qcsa a qcno

P

present³ /prɪ'zent/ vt presentare; ~ sb with an award consegnare un premio a qcno. ~able adj be ~able essere presentabile

presentation /prezn'teɪʃn/ n presentazione f

presently /'prezntlɪ/ adv fra poco; (Am: now) attualmente

preservation /prezə'veɪʃn/ n conservazione f

preservative /prɪ'zɜ:vətɪv/ n conservante m

preserve /prɪ'zɜ:v/ vt preservare; (maintain, Culin) conservare ● n (in hunting & fig) riserva f; (jam) marmellata f

preside /prɪ'zaɪd/ vi presiedere (over a)

presidency /'prezɪdənsɪ/ n presidenza f

president /'prezɪdənt/ n presidente m. ~ial adj presidenziale

press /pres/ n (machine) pressa f; (newspapers) stampa f ● vt premere; pressare (flower); (iron) stirare; (squeeze) stringere ● vi (urge) incalzare. □ ~ for vi fare pressione per; be ~ed for essere a corto di. □ ~ on vi andare avanti

press: ~ conference n conferenza f stampa. ~ cutting n ritaglio m di giornale. ~ing adj urgente. ~-up n flessione f

pressure /'preʃə(r)/ n pressione f ● vt = **pressurize**. ~-cooker n pentola f a pressione. ~ group n gruppo m di pressione

pressurize /'preʃəraɪz/ vt far pressione su. ~d adj pressurizzato

prestige /pre'sti:ʒ/ n prestigio m. ~ious adj prestigioso

presumably /prɪ'zju:məblɪ/ adv presumibilmente

presume /prɪ'zju:m/ vt presumere; ~ to do sth permettersi di fare qcsa

presuppose /pri:-/ vt presupporre

pretence /prɪ'tens/ n finzione f; (pretext) pretesto m; it's all ~ è tutt una scena

pretend /prɪ'tend/ vt fingere; (claim pretendere ● vi fare finta

pretentious /prɪ'tenʃəs/ adj pretenzioso

pretext /'pri:tekst/ n pretesto m

pretty /'prɪtɪ/ adj (-ier, -iest) carino ● adv (II: fairly) abbastanza

prevail /prɪ'veɪl/ vi prevalere; ~ on sb to do sth convincere qcno a fare qcsa. ~ing adj prevalente

prevalen|ce /'prevələns/ n diffusione f. ~t adj diffuso

prevent /prɪ'vent/ vt impedire; ~ sb [from] doing sth impedire a qcno di fare qcsa. ~ion n prevenzione f. ~ive adj preventivo

preview /'pri:vju:/ n anteprima f

previous /'pri:vɪəs/ adj precedente. ~ly adv precedentemente

prey /preɪ/ n preda f; bird of ~ uc cello m rapace ● vi ~ on far preda di; ~ on sb's mind attanagliare qcno

price /praɪs/ n prezzo m ● vt (Comm) fissare il prezzo di. ~less adj inestimabile; (II: amusing) spassosissimo. ~y adj II caro

prick /prɪk/ n puntura f ● vt pungere. □ ~ up vi ~ up one's ears rizzare le orecchie

prickl|e /'prɪkl/ n spina f; (sensation) formicolio m. ~y adj pungente; (person) irritabile

pride /praɪd/ n orgoglio m ● vt ~ oneself on vantarsi di

priest /pri:st/ n prete m

prim /prɪm/ adj (primmer, primmest) perbenino

primarily /'praɪmərɪlɪ/ adv in primo luogo

primary /'praɪmərɪ/ adj primario; (chief) principale. ~ school n scuola elementare

prime¹ /praɪm/ adj principale, primo; (*first-rate*) eccellente ● be in one's ~ essere nel fiore degli anni

prime² vt preparare (surface, person)

Prime Minister n Primo m Ministro

primeval /praɪˈmiːvl/ adj primitivo

primitive /ˈprɪmɪtɪv/ adj primitivo

primrose /ˈprɪmrəʊz/ n primula f

prince /prɪns/ n principe m

princess /prɪnˈses/ n principessa f

principal /ˈprɪnsəpl/ adj principale ● n (Sch) preside m

principally /ˈprɪnsəpl/ adv principalmente

principle /ˈprɪnsəpl/ n principio m; in ~ in teoria; on ~ per principio

print /prɪnt/ n (mark, trace) impronta f; (Phot) copia f; (picture) stampa f; in ~ (printed out) stampato; (book) in commercio; out of ~ esaurito ● vt stampare; (write in capitals) scrivere in stampatello. ~ed matter n stampe fpl

print|er /ˈprɪntə(r)/ n stampante f; (Typ) tipografo, -a mf. ~er port n (Comput) porta f per la stampante. ~ing n tipografia f

printout n (Comput) stampa f

prior /ˈpraɪə(r)/ adj precedente. ~ to prep prima di

priority /praɪˈɒrɪtɪ/ n precedenza f; (matter) priorità f

prise /praɪz/ vt ~ open/up forzare

prison /ˈprɪz(ə)n/ n prigione f. ~er n prigioniero, -a mf

privacy /ˈprɪvəsɪ/ n privacy f inv

private /ˈpraɪvət/ adj privato; (car, secretary, letter) personale ● n (Mil) soldato m semplice; in ~ in privato. ~ly adv (funded, educated etc) privatamente; (in secret) in segreto; (confidentially) in privato; (inwardly) interiormente

privation /praɪˈveɪʃn/ n privazione

f; ~s npl stenti mpl

privilege /ˈprɪvɪlɪdʒ/ n privilegio m. ~d adj privilegiato

prize /praɪz/ n premio m ● adj (idiot etc) perfetto ● vt apprezzare. ~-giving n premiazione f. ~-winner n vincitore, -trice mf. ~-winning adj vincente

pro /prəʊ/ n ([] professional) professionista mf; the ~s and cons il pro e il contro

probability /prɒbəˈbɪlətɪ/ n probabilità f inv

probabl|e /ˈprɒbəbl/ adj probabile. ~y adv probabilmente

probation /prəˈbeɪʃn/ n prova f; (Jur) libertà f vigilata. ~ary adj in prova; ~ary period periodo m di prova

probe /prəʊb/ n sonda f; (fig: investigation) indagine f ● vt sondare; (investigate) esaminare a fondo

problem /ˈprɒbləm/ n problema m ● adj difficile. ~atic adj problematico

procedure /prəˈsiːdʒə(r)/ n procedimento m

proceed /prəˈsiːd/ vi procedere ● vt ~ to do sth proseguire facendo qcsa

proceedings /prəˈsiːdɪŋz/ npl (report) atti mpl; (Jur) azione fsg legale

proceeds /ˈprəʊsiːdz/ npl ricavato msg

process /ˈprəʊses/ n processo m; (procedure) procedimento m; in the ~ nel far ciò ● vt trattare; (Admin) occuparsi di; (Phot) sviluppare

procession /prəˈseʃn/ n processione f

processor /ˈprəʊsesə(r)/ n (Comput) processore m; (for food) robot m inv da cucina

proclaim /prəˈkleɪm/ vt proclamare

procure /prəˈkjʊə(r)/ vt ottenere

prod /prɒd/ n colpetto m ● vt (pt/pp prodded) punzecchiare; fig incitare

P

produce[1] /ˈprɒdjuːs/ n prodotti mpl; ~ of Italy prodotto in Italia

produce[2] /prəˈdjuːs/ vt produrre; (bring out) tirar fuori; (cause) causare; (🔲: give birth to) fare. ~r n produttore m

product /ˈprɒdʌkt/ n prodotto m. ~ion n produzione f; (Theat) spettacolo m

productiv|e /prəˈdʌktɪv/ adj produttivo. ~ity n produttività f

profession /prəˈfeʃn/ n professione f. ~al adj professionale; (not amateur) professionista; (piece of work) da professionista; (man) di professione ● n professionista mf. ~ally adv professionalmente

professor /prəˈfesə(r)/ n professore m [universitario]

proficien|cy /prəˈfɪʃnsɪ/ n competenza f. ~t adj be ~t in essere competente in

profile /ˈprəʊfaɪl/ n profilo m

profit /ˈprɒfɪt/ n profitto m ● vi ~ from trarre profitto da. ~able adj proficuo. ~ably adv in modo proficuo

profound /prəˈfaʊnd/ adj profondo. ~ly adv profondamente

profus|e /prəˈfjuːs/ adj ~e apologies/flowers una profusione di scuse/fiori. ~ion n profusione f; in ~ion in abbondanza

prognosis /prɒɡˈnəʊsɪs/ n (pl -oses) prognosi f inv

program /ˈprəʊɡræm/ n programma m ● vt (pt/pp programmed) programmare

programme /ˈprəʊɡræm/ n Br programma m. ~r n (Comput) programmatore, -trice mf

progress[1] /ˈprəʊɡres/ n progresso m; in ~ in corso; make ~ fig fare progressi

progress[2] /prəˈɡres/ vi progredire; fig fare progressi

progressive /prəˈɡresɪv/ adj pro-

gressivo; (reforming) progressista. ~ly adv progressivamente

prohibit /prəˈhɪbɪt/ vt proibire. ~ive adj proibitivo

project[1] /ˈprɒdʒekt/ n progetto m; (Sch) ricerca f

project[2] /prəˈdʒekt/ vt proiettare (film, image) ● vi (jut out) sporgere

projector /prəˈdʒektə(r)/ n proiettore m

prolific /prəˈlɪfɪk/ adj prolifico

prologue /ˈprəʊlɒɡ/ n prologo m

prolong /prəˈlɒŋ/ vt prolungare

promenade /prɒməˈnɑːd/ n lungomare m inv

prominent /ˈprɒmɪnənt/ adj prominente; (conspicuous) di rilievo

promiscu|ity /prɒmɪˈskjuːətɪ/ n promiscuità f. ~ous adj promiscuo

promis|e /ˈprɒmɪs/ n promessa f ● vt promettere; ~e sb that promettere a qcno che; I ~ed to ho promesso. ~ing adj promettente

promot|e /prəˈməʊt/ vt promuovere; be ~ed (Sport) essere promosso. ~ion n promozione f

prompt /prɒmpt/ adj immediato; (punctual) puntuale ● adv in punto ● vt incitare (to a); (Theat) suggerire a ● vi suggerire. ~er n suggeritore, -trice mf. ~ly adv puntualmente

Proms /prɒmz/ npl rassegna f di concerti estivi di musica classica presso l'Albert Hall a Londra

> **Proms** I Proms sono una
> serie di concerti di musica
> classica che ogni estate,
> per otto settimane, si tengono
> giornalmente all'Albert Hall di
> Londra. Istituiti nel 1895 per
> iniziativa di Sir Henry Wood, il loro
> nome è l'abbreviazione di *promenade
> concerts*, concerti durante i quali a
> parte dei pubblico in sala sono
> riservati posti in piedi.

prone /prəʊn/ adj be ~ to do sth essere incline a fare qcsa

pronoun /ˈprəʊnaʊn/ n pronome m

pronounce /prəˈnaʊns/ vt pronunciare; (declare) dichiarare. ~d adj (noticeable) pronunciato

pronunciation /prənʌnsɪˈeɪʃn/ n pronuncia f

proof /pruːf/ n prova f; (Typ) bozza f, prova f ● adj ~ against a prova di

propaganda /prɒpəˈgændə/ n propaganda f

propel /prəˈpel/ vt (pt/pp propelled) spingere. ~ler n elica f

proper /ˈprɒpə(r)/ adj corretto; (suitable) adatto; (fam: real) vero [e proprio]. ~ly adv correttamente. ~ 'name, ~ 'noun n nome m proprio

property /ˈprɒpətɪ/ n proprietà f inv. ~ developer n agente m immobiliare. ~ market n mercato m immobiliare

prophecy /ˈprɒfəsɪ/ n profezia f

prophesy /ˈprɒfəsaɪ/ vt (pt/pp -ied) profetizzare

prophet /ˈprɒfɪt/ n profeta m. ~ic adj profetico

proportion /prəˈpɔːʃn/ n proporzione f; (share) parte f; ~s pl (dimensions) proporzioni fpl. ~al adj proporzionale. ~ally adv in proporzione

proposal /prəˈpəʊzl/ n proposta f; (of marriage) proposta f di matrimonio

propose /prəˈpəʊz/ vt proporre; (intend) proporsi ● vi fare una proposta di matrimonio

proposition /prɒpəˈzɪʃn/ n proposta f; (fam: task) impresa f

proprietor /prəˈpraɪətə(r)/ n proprietario, -a mf

prose /prəʊz/ n prosa f

prosecut|e /ˈprɒsɪkjuːt/ vt intentare azione contro. ~ion n azione f giudiziaria; the ~ion l'accusa f. ~or n [Public] P~or il Pubblico Ministero m

prospect[1] /ˈprɒspekt/ n (expectation) prospettiva f

prospect[2] /prəˈspekt/ vi ~ for cercare

prospect|ive /prəˈspektɪv/ adj (future) futuro; (possible) potenziale. ~or n cercatore m

prospectus /prəˈspektəs/ n prospetto m

prosper /ˈprɒspə(r)/ vi prosperare; (person:) stare bene finanziariamente. ~ity n prosperità f

prosperous /ˈprɒspərəs/ adj prospero

prostitut|e /ˈprɒstɪtjuːt/ n prostituta f. ~ion n prostituzione f

prostrate /ˈprɒstreɪt/ adj prostrato; ~ with grief fig prostrato dal dolore

protagonist /prəʊˈtægənɪst/ n protagonista mf

protect /prəˈtekt/ vt proteggere (from da). ~ion n protezione f. ~ive adj protettivo. ~or n protettore, -trice mf

protein /ˈprəʊtiːn/ n proteina f

protest[1] /ˈprəʊtest/ n protesta f

protest[2] /prəˈtest/ vt/i protestare

Protestant /ˈprɒtɪstənt/ adj protestante ● n protestante mf

protester /prəˈtestə(r)/ n contestatore, -trice mf

protocol /ˈprəʊtəkɒl/ n protocollo m

protrude /prəˈtruːd/ vi sporgere

proud /praʊd/ adj fiero (of di). ~ly adv fieramente

prove /pruːv/ vt provare ● vi ~ to be a lie rivelarsi una bugia. ~n adj dimostrato

proverb /ˈprɒvɜːb/ n proverbio m. ~ial adj proverbiale

provide /prəˈvaɪd/ vt fornire; ~ sb with sth fornire qcsa a qcno ● vi ~ for (law:) prevedere

provided /prəˈvaɪdɪd/ conj ~ [that] purché

providen|ce /'prɒvɪdəns/ n providenza f. ~tial adj providenziale

providing /prə'vaɪdɪŋ/ conj = provided

provinc|e /'prɒvɪns/ n provincia f; fig campo m. ~ial adj provinciale

provision /prə'vɪʒn/ n (of food, water) approvvigionamento m (of di); (of law) disposizione f; ~s pl provviste fpl. ~al adj provvisorio

provocat|ion /prɒvə'keɪʃn/ n provocazione f. ~ive adj provocatorio; (sexually) provocante. ~ively adv in modo provocatorio

provoke /prə'vəʊk/ vt provocare

prow /praʊ/ n prua f

prowess /'praʊɪs/ n abilità f inv

prowl /praʊl/ vi aggirarsi ● n on the ~ in cerca di preda. ~er n tipo m sospetto

proximity /prɒk'sɪmətɪ/ n prossimità f

proxy /'prɒksɪ/ n procura f; (person) persona f che agisce per procura

prude /pruːd/ n be a ~ essere eccessivamente pudico

pruden|ce /'pruːdəns/ n prudenza f. ~t adj prudente; (wise) oculatezza f

prudish /'pruːdɪʃ/ adj eccessivamente pudico

prune[1] /pruːn/ n prugna f secca

prune[2] vt potare

pry /praɪ/ vi (pt/pp pried) ficcare il naso

psalm /sɑːm/ n salmo m

psychiatric /saɪkɪ'ætrɪk/ adj psichiatrico

psychiatr|ist /saɪ'kaɪətrɪst/ n psichiatra mf. ~y n psichiatria f

psychic /'saɪkɪk/ adj psichico; I'm not ~ non sono un indovino

psychological /saɪkə'lɒdʒɪkl/ adj psicologico

psycholog|ist /saɪ'kɒlədʒɪst/ n psicologo, -a mf. ~y n psicologia f

pub /pʌb/ n 🅸 pub m inv

puberty /'pjuːbətɪ/ n pubertà f

public /'pʌblɪk/ adj pubblico ● n the ~ il pubblico; in ~ in pubblico. ~ly adv pubblicamente

publican /'pʌblɪkən/ n gestore, -trice mf/proprietario, -a mf di un pub

publication /pʌblɪ'keɪʃn/ n pubblicazione f

public: ~ 'holiday n festa f nazionale. ~ 'house n pub m

publicity /pʌb'lɪsətɪ/ n pubblicità f

publicize /'pʌblɪsaɪz/ vt pubblicizzare

public: ~ relations pubbliche relazioni fpl. ~ 'school n scuola f privata; Am scuola f pubblica

publish /'pʌblɪʃ/ vt pubblicare. ~er n editore m; (firm) editore m, casa f editrice. ~ing n editoria f

pudding /'pʊdɪŋ/ n dolce m cotto al vapore; (course) dolce m

puddle /'pʌdl/ n pozzanghera f

puff /pʌf/ n (of wind) soffio m; (of

(smoke) tirata *f*; (*for powder*) piumino *m*
• *vt* sbuffare. puff at *vt* tirare boccate da (pipe). □ ~ **out** *vi* lasciare senza fiato (person); spegnere (candle). ~ed *adj* (*out of breath*) senza fiato. ~ **pastry** *n* pasta *f* sfoglia

uffy /'pʌfɪ/ *adj* gonfio

ull /pʊl/ *n* trazione *f*; (*fig*: *attraction*) attrazione *f*; (☐: *influence*) influenza *f* • *vt* tirare; estrarre (tooth); stirarsi (muscle); ~ **faces** far boccace; ~ **oneself together** controllarsi; ~ **one's weight** mettercela tutta; ~ **sb's leg** ☐ prendere in giro qcno. □ ~ **down** *vt* (*demolish*) demolire. □ ~ **in** *vi* (Auto) accostare. □ ~ **off** *vt* togliere; ☐ azzeccare. □ ~ **out** *vt* tirar fuori • *vi* (Auto) sporstarsi; (*of competition*) ritirarsi. □ ~ **through** *vi* (*recover*) farcela. □ ~ **up** *vt* sradicare (plant); (*reprimand*) rimproverare • *vi* (Auto) fermarsi

ullover /'pʊləʊvə(r)/ *n* pullover *m*

ulp /pʌlp/ *n* poltiglia *f*; (*of fruit*) polpa *f*; (*for paper*) pasta *f*

ulpit /'pʊlpɪt/ *n* pulpito *m*

ulse /pʌls/ *n* polso *m*

ummel /'pʌml/ *vt* (*pt/pp* pummelled) prendere a pugni

ump /pʌmp/ *n* pompa *f* • *vt* pompare; ☐ cercare di estorcere da. □ ~ **up** (*inflate*) gonfiare

umpkin /'pʌmpkɪn/ *n* zucca *f*

un /pʌn/ *n* gioco *m* di parole

unch¹ /pʌntʃ/ *n* pugno *m*; (*device*) pinza *f* per forare • *vt* dare un pugno a; forare (ticket); perforare (hole)

unch² *n* (*drink*) ponce *m inv*

unctual /'pʌŋktjʊəl/ *adj* puntuale. ~**ity** *n* puntualità *f*. ~**ly** *adv* puntualmente

unctuate /'pʌŋktjʊeɪt/ *vt* punteggiare. ~**ion** *n* punteggiatura *f*. ~**ion mark** *n* segno *m* di interpunzione

uncture /'pʌŋktʃə(r)/ *n* foro *m*;

(tyre) foratura *f* • *vt* forare

punish /'pʌnɪʃ/ *vt* punire. ~**able** *adj* punibile. ~**ment** *n* punizione *f*

punk /pʌŋk/ *n* punk *m inv*

punt /pʌnt/ *n* (*boat*) barchino *m*

punter /'pʌntə(r)/ *n* (*gambler*) scommettitore, -trice *mf*; (*client*) consumatore, -trice *mf*

puny /'pjuːnɪ/ *adj* (-ier, -iest) striminzito

pup /pʌp/ *n* = puppy

pupil /'pjuːpl/ *n* alunno, -a *mf*; (*of eye*) pupilla *f*

puppet /'pʌpɪt/ *n* marionetta *f*; (*glove ~*, *fig*) burattino *m*

puppy /'pʌpɪ/ *n* cucciolo *m*

purchase /'pɜːtʃəs/ *n* acquisto *m*; (*leverage*) presa *f* • *vt* acquistare. ~**r** *n* acquirente *m*

pure /pjʊə(r)/ *adj* puro. ~**ly** *adv* puramente

purgatory /'pɜːgətrɪ/ *n* purgatorio *m*

purge /pɜːdʒ/ (Pol) *n* epurazione *f* • *vt* epurare

puri|fication /pjʊərɪfɪ'keɪʃn/ *n* purificazione *f*. ~**fy** *vt* (*pt/pp* -ied) purificare

puritan /'pjʊərɪtən/ *n* puritano, -a *mf*. ~**ical** *adj* puritano

purity /'pjʊərɪtɪ/ *n* purità *f*

purple /'pɜːpl/ *adj* viola

purpose /'pɜːpəs/ *n* scopo *m*; (*determination*) fermezza *f*; **on** ~ apposta. ~**-built** *adj* costruito ad hoc. ~**ful** *adj* deciso. ~**fully** *adv* con decisione. ~**ly** *adv* apposta

purr /pɜː(r)/ *vi* (cat:) fare le fusa

purse /pɜːs/ *n* borsellino *m*; (Am: *handbag*) borsa *f* • *vt* increspare (lips)

pursue /pə'sjuː/ *vt* inseguire; *fig* proseguire. ~**r** *n* inseguitore, -trice *mf*

pursuit /pə'sjuːt/ *n* inseguimento *m*; (*fig*: *of happiness*) ricerca *f*; (*pastime*) attività *f inv*; **in** ~ all'inseguimento

pus /pʌs/ n pus m

push /pʊʃ/ n spinta f; (fig: effort) sforzo m; (drive) iniziativa f; at a ~ in caso di bisogno; get the ~ 🅸 essere licenziato ● vt spingere; premere (button); (pressurize) far pressione su; be ~ed for time 🅸 non aver tempo ● vi spingere. □ ~ **aside** vt scostare. □ ~ **back** vt respingere. □ ~ **off** vt togliere ● vi (🅸: leave) levarsi dai piedi. □ ~ **on** vi (continue) continuare. □ ~ **up** vt alzare (price)

push: ~**-chair** n passeggino m. ~**up** n flessione f

pushy /'pʊʃɪ/ adj 🅸 troppo intraprendente

put /pʊt/ vt (pt/pp put, pres p putting) mettere; ~ the cost of sth at valutare il costo di qcsa ● vi ~ to sea salpare. □ ~ **aside** vt mettere da parte. □ ~ **away** vt mettere via. □ ~ **back** vt rimettere; mettere indietro (clock). □ ~ **by** vt mettere da parte. □ ~ **down** vt mettere giù; (suppress) reprimere; (kill) sopprimere; (write) annotare; ~ one's foot down 🅸 essere fermo; (Auto) dare un'accelerata; ~ down to (attribute) attribuire. □ ~ **forward** vt avanzare; mettere avanti (clock). □ ~ **in** vt (insert) introdurre; (submit) presentare ● vi ~ in for far domanda di. □ ~ **off** vt spegnere (light); (postpone) rimandare; ~ sb off tenere a bada qcno; (deter) smontare qcno; (disconcert) distrarre qcno; ~ sb off sth (disgust) disgustare qcno di qcsa. □ ~ **on** vt mettersi (clothes); mettere (brake); (Culin) mettere su; accendere (light); mettere in scena (play); prendere (accent); ~ **on weight** mettere su qualche chilo. □ ~ **out** vt spegnere (fire, light); tendere (hand); (inconvenience) creare degli inconvenienti a. □ ~ **through** vt far passare; (Teleph) I'll ~ you through to him glielo passo. □ ~ **up** vt alzare; erigere (building); montare (tent); aprire

(umbrella); affiggere (notice); aumentare (price); ospitare (guest); ~ sb up to sth mettere qcsa in testa qcno ● vi (at hotel) stare; ~ up with sopportare ● adj stay ~! rimani lì!

puzzle /'pʌzl/ n enigma m; (jigsaw) puzzle m inv ● vt lasciare perplesso ● vi ~e over scervellarsi su. ~**ing** adj inspiegabile

pygmy /'pɪgmɪ/ n pigmeo, -a mf

pyjamas /pə'dʒɑːməz/ npl pigiama msg

pylon /'paɪlən/ n pilone m

pyramid /'pɪrəmɪd/ n piramide f

python /'paɪθn/ n pitone m

Qq

quack[1] /kwæk/ n qua qua m inv ● vi fare qua qua

quack[2] n (doctor) ciarlatano m

quadrangle /'kwɒdræŋgl/ n quadrangolo m; (court) cortile m quadrangolare

quadruped /'kwɒdruped/ n quadrupede m

quadruple /'kwɒdrʊpl/ adj quadruplo ● vt quadruplicare ● vi quadruplicarsi. ~**ts** npl quattro gemelli mpl

quagmire /'kwɒgmaɪə(r)/ n pantano m

quaint /kweɪnt/ adj pittoresco; (odd) bizzarro

quake /kweɪk/ n 🅸 terremoto m ● vi tremare

qualification /kwɒlɪfɪ'keɪʃn/ n qualifica f. ~**ied** adj qualificato; (limited) con riserva

qualify /'kwɒlɪfaɪ/ v (pt/pp -ied) ~ (course): dare la qualifica a (as di); (entitle) dare diritto a; (limit) precisare

• vi ottenere la qualifica; (*Sport*) qualificarsi

uality /'kwɒlətɪ/ n qualità f inv

ualm /kwɑːm/ n scrupolo m

uandary /'kwɒndərɪ/ n dilemma m

uantity /'kwɒntɪtɪ/ n quantità f inv; in ∼ in grande quantità

uarantine /'kwɒrəntiːn/ n quarantena f

uarrel /'kwɒrəl/ n lite f ● vi (pt/pp quarrelled) litigare. ∼some adj litigioso

uarry[1] /'kwɒrɪ/ n (*prey*) preda f

uarry[2] n cava f

uart /kwɔːt/ n 1.14 litro

uarter /'kwɔːtə(r)/ n quarto m; (of year) trimestre m; Am 25 centesimi mpl; ∼s pl (Mil) quartiere msg; at [a] ∼ to six alle sei meno un quarto ● vt dividere in quattro. ∼-'final n quarto m di finale

uarterly /'kwɔːtəlɪ/ adj trimestrale ● adv trimestralmente

uartz /kwɔːts/ n quarzo m. ∼ watch n orologio m al quarzo

uay /kiː/ n banchina f

ueasy /'kwiːzɪ/ adj I feel ∼ ho la nausea

ueen /kwiːn/ n regina f. ∼ mother n regina f madre

ueer /kwɪə(r)/ adj strano; (dubious) sospetto; (I: homosexual) finocchio ● n I finocchio m

uench /kwentʃ/ vt ∼ one's thirst dissetarsi

uery /'kwɪərɪ/ n domanda f; (question mark) punto m interrogativo ● vt (pt/pp -ied) interrogare; (doubt) mettere in dubbio

uest /kwest/ n ricerca f (for di)

uestion /'kwestʃn/ n domanda f; (for discussion) questione f; out of the ∼ fuori discussione; without ∼ senza dubbio; in ∼ in questione ● vt

interrogare; (doubt) mettere in dubbio. ∼able adj discutibile. ∼ mark n punto m interrogativo

questionnaire /kwestʃə'neə(r)/ n questionario m

queue /kjuː/ n coda f, fila f ● vi ∼ [up] mettersi in coda (for per)

quick /kwɪk/ adj veloce; be ∼ sbrigati!; have a ∼ meal fare uno spuntino ● adv in fretta ● n be cut to the ∼ fig essere punto sul vivo. ∼ly adv in fretta. ∼-tempered adj collerico

quid /kwɪd/ n inv I sterlina f

quiet /'kwaɪət/ adj (calm) tranquillo; (silent) silenzioso; (voice, music) basso; keep ∼ about I non raccontare a nessuno ● n quiete f; on the ∼ di nascosto. ∼ly adv (peacefully) tranquillamente; (say) a bassa voce

quiet|en /'kwaɪətn/ vt calmare. □ ∼ down vi calmarsi. ∼ness n quiete f

quilt /kwɪlt/ n piumino m. ∼ed adj trapuntato

quintet /kwɪn'tet/ n quintetto m

quirk /kwɜːk/ n stranezza f

quit /kwɪt/ v (pt/pp quitted, quit) ● vt lasciare; (give up) smettere (doing di fare) ● vi (I: resign) andarsene; (Comput) uscire; give sb notice to ∼ (of landlord:) dare a qcno il preavviso di sfratto

quite /kwaɪt/ adv (fairly) abbastanza; (completely) completamente; (really) veramente; ∼ [so]! proprio così!; ∼ a few parecchi

quits /kwɪts/ adj pari

quiver /'kwɪvə(r)/ vi tremare

quiz /kwɪz/ n (game) quiz m inv ● vt (pt/pp quizzed) interrogare

quota /'kwəʊtə/ n quota f

quotation /kwəʊ'teɪʃn/ n citazione f; (price) preventivo m; (of shares) quota f. ∼ marks npl virgolette fpl

quote /kwəʊt/ n I = quotation; ∼s tra virgolette ● vt citare; quotare (price)

q

Rr

rabbi /ˈræbaɪ/ n rabbino m; (title) rabbi

rabbit /ˈræbɪt/ n coniglio m

rabies /ˈreɪbiːz/ n rabbia f

race[1] /reɪs/ n (people) razza f

race[2] n corsa f • vi correre • vt ga- reggiare con; fare correre (horse)

race: ~course n ippodromo m. ~horse n cavallo m da corsa. ~track n pista f

racial /ˈreɪʃl/ adj razziale. ~ism n razzismo m

racing /ˈreɪsɪŋ/ n corse fpl; (horse-) corse fpl dei cavalli. ~ car n macchina f da corsa. ~ driver n corridore m automobilistico

racis|m /ˈreɪsɪzm/ n razzismo m. ~t adj razzista n razzista mf

rack[1] /ræk/ n (for bikes) rastrelliera f; (for luggage) portabagagli m inv; (for plates) scolapiatti m inv • vt ~ one's brains scervellarsi

rack[2] n go to ~ and ruin andare in rovina

racket[1] /ˈrækɪt/ n (Sport) racchetta f

racket[2] n (din) chiasso m; (swindle) truffa f; (crime) racket m inv, giro m

radar /ˈreɪdɑː(r)/ n radar m

radian|ce /ˈreɪdɪəns/ n radiosità f inv. ~t adj raggiante

radiat|e /ˈreɪdɪeɪt/ vt irradiare • vi (heat:) irradiarsi. ~ion n radiazione f

radiator /ˈreɪdɪeɪtə(r)/ n radiatore m

radical /ˈrædɪkl/ adj radicale • n radicale mf. ~ly adv radicalmente

radio /ˈreɪdɪəʊ/ n radio f inv

radio|active /reɪdɪəʊ-/ adj radioattivo. ~ac'tivity n radioattività f

radish /ˈrædɪʃ/ n ravanello m

radius /ˈreɪdɪəs/ n (pl -dii /-dɪaɪ/) raggio m

raffle /ˈræfl/ n lotteria f

raft /rɑːft/ n zattera f

rafter /ˈrɑːftə(r)/ n trave f

rag /ræg/ n straccio m; (pej: newspaper) giornalaccio m; in ~s stracciato

rage /reɪdʒ/ n rabbia f; all the ~ 🔲 all'ultima moda • vi infuriarsi; (storm:) infuriare; (epidemic:) imperversare

ragged /ˈrægɪd/ adj logoro; (edge) frastagliato

raid /reɪd/ n (by thieves) rapina f; (Mil) incursione f, raid m inv; (police) irruzione f • vt (Mil) fare un'incursione in (police, burglars:) fare irruzione in. ~er n (of bank) rapinatore, -trice mf

rail /reɪl/ n ringhiera f; (hand~) ringhiera f; (Naut) parapetto m; by ~ per ferrovia

railroad n Am = railway

railway n ferrovia f. ~man n ferro viere m. ~ station n stazione f ferro viaria

rain /reɪn/ n pioggia f • vi piovere

rain: ~bow n arcobaleno m. ~coa n impermeabile m. ~fall n precipita zione f [atmosferica]

rainy /ˈreɪnɪ/ adj (-ier, -iest) piovos

raise /reɪz/ n Am aumento m • vt alzare; levarsi (hat); allevare (children, animals); sollevare (question); ottenere (money)

raisin /ˈreɪzn/ n uva f passa

rake /reɪk/ n rastrello m • vt rastrellare. □ ~ up vt raccogliere col rastrello; 🔲 rivangare

rally /ˈrælɪ/ n raduno m; (Auto) rally m inv; (Tennis) scambio m • vt (pt/pp -ied) radunare • vi radunarsi; (recover strength) riprendersi

ram /ræm/ n montone m; (Astr) Ariete m • vt (pt/pp rammed) cozzar contro

RAM | ravenous

RAM /ræm/ n [memoria f] RAM f

rambl|e /'ræmbl/ n escursione f • vi gironzolare; (in speech) divagare. ~er n escursionista mf; (rose) rosa f rampicante. ~ing adj (in speech) sconnesso; (club) escursionistico

ramp /ræmp/ n rampa f; (Aeron) scaletta f mobile (di aerei)

rampage /ræmpeɪdʒ/ n be/go on the ~ scatenarsi • vi • through the streets scatenarsi per le strade

ramshackle /'ræmʃækl/ adj sgangherato

ran /ræn/ ▷RUN

ranch /rɑːntʃ/ n ranch m

random /'rændəm/ adj casuale; ~ sample campione m a caso • n at ~ a casaccio

rang /ræŋ/ ▷RING²

range /reɪndʒ/ n serie f; (Comm, Mus) gamma f; (of mountains) catena f; (distance) raggio m; (for shooting) portata f; (stove) cucina f economica; at a ~ of a una distanza di • vi estendersi; ~ from... to... andare da... a.... ~r n guardia f forestale

rank /ræŋk/ n (row) riga f; (Mil) grado m; (social position) rango m; the ~ and file la base f; the ~s (Mil) i soldati mpl semplici • vt (place) annoverare (among tra) • vi (be placed) collocarsi

ransack /'rænsæk/ vt rovistare; (pillage) saccheggiare

ransom /'rænsəm/ n riscatto m; hold sb to ~ tenere qcno in ostaggio (per il riscatto)

rant /rænt/ vi inveire; what's he ~ing on about? cosa sta blaterando?

rap /ræp/ n colpo m [secco]; (Mus) rap m • v (pt/pp rapped) • vt dare colpetti a • vi • at bussare a

rape /reɪp/ n (sexual) stupro m • vt violentare, stuprare

rapid /'ræpɪd/ adj rapido. ~ity n rapidità f. ~ly adv rapidamente

rapids /'ræpɪdz/ npl rapida fsg

rapist /'reɪpɪst/ n violentatore m

raptur|e /'ræptʃə(r)/ n estasi f. ~ous adj entusiastico

rare¹ /rea(r)/ adj raro. ~ly adv raramente

rare² adj (Culin) al sangue

rarefied /'reərɪfaɪd/ adj rarefatto

rarity /'reərətɪ/ n rarità f inv

rascal /'rɑːskl/ n mascalzone m

rash¹ /ræʃ/ n (Med) eruzione f

rash² adj avventato. ~ly adv avventatamente

rasher /'ræʃə(r)/ n fetta f di pancetta

rasp /rɑːsp/ n (noise) stridio m. ~ing adj stridente

raspberry /'rɑːzbərɪ/ n lampone m

rat /ræt/ n topo m; (ℑ: person) carogna f; smell a ~ ℑ sentire puzzo di bruciato

rate /reɪt/ n (speed) velocità f; (of payment) tariffa f; (of exchange) tasso m; ~s pl (taxes) imposte fpl comunali sui beni immobili; at any ~ in ogni caso; at this ~ di questo passo • vt stimare; ~ among annoverare tra • vi ~ as essere considerato

rather /'rɑːðə(r)/ adv piuttosto; ~! eccomi!; ~ too... un po' troppo...

rating /'reɪtɪŋ/ n ~s pl (Radio, TV) indice m d'ascolto, audience f inv

ratio /'reɪʃɪəʊ/ n rapporto m

ration /'ræʃn/ n razione f • vt razionare

rational /'ræʃnəl/ adj razionale. ~ize vt/i razionalizzare

rattle /'rætl/ n tintinnio m; (toy) sonaglio m • vi tintinnare • vt (shake) scuotere; ℑ innervosire. □ ~ off ℑ sciorinare

raucous /'rɔːkəs/ adj rauco

rave /reɪv/ vi vaneggiare; ~ about andare in estasi per

raven /'reɪvn/ n corvo m imperiale

ravenous /'rævənəs/ adj (person)

affamato

ravine /rə'viːn/ n gola f

raving /'reɪvɪŋ/ adj ~ **mad** 🔲 matto da legare

ravishing /'rævɪʃɪŋ/ adj incantevole

raw /rɔː/ adj crudo; (not processed) grezzo; (weather) gelido; (inexperienced) inesperto; **get a ~ deal** 🔲 farsi fregare. ~ **ma'terials** npl materie fpl prime

ray /reɪ/ n raggio m; ~ **of hope** barlume m di speranza

raze /reɪz/ vt ~ **to the ground** radere al suolo

razor /'reɪzə(r)/ n rasoio m. ~ **blade** n lametta f da barba

re /riː/ prep con riferimento a

reach /riːtʃ/ n portata f; **within** ~ a portata di mano; **out of** ~ of fuori dalla portata di; **within easy** ~ facilmente raggiungibile ● vt arrivare a (place, decision); (contact) contattare; (pass) passare; **I can't** ~ **it** non ci arrivo ● vi arrivare (to a); **for** allungare la mano per prendere

re'act /rɪ-/ vi reagire

re'action /rɪ-/ n reazione f. ~**ary** adj reazionario, -a mf

reactor /rɪ'æktə(r)/ n reattore m

read /riːd/ vt (pt/pp read /red/) leggere; (Univ) studiare ● vi leggere; (instrument:) indicare. □ ~ **out** vt leggere ad alta voce

readable /'riːdəbl/ adj piacevole a leggersi; (legible) leggibile

reader /'riːdə(r)/ n lettore, -trice mf; (book) antologia f

readily /'redɪlɪ/ adv volentieri; (easily) facilmente. ~**ness** n disponibilità f inv; in ~**ness** pronto

reading /'riːdɪŋ/ n lettura f

rea'djust /riː-/ vt regolare di nuovo ● vi riabituarsi (to a)

ready /'redɪ/ adj (-ier, -iest) pronto; (quick) veloce; **get** ~ prepararsi

ready-'made adj confezionato

real /rɪəl/ adj vero; (increase) reale ● adv Am 🔲 veramente. ~ **estate** n beni mpl immobili

realism /'rɪəlɪzm/ n realismo m. ~**t** n realista mf. ~**tic** adj realistico

reality /rɪ'ælətɪ/ n realtà f inv; ~ **TV** n reality TV f

realization /rɪəlaɪ'zeɪʃn/ n realizzazione f

realize /'rɪəlaɪz/ vt realizzare

really /'rɪəlɪ/ adv davvero

realm /relm/ n regno m

realtor /'rɪəltə(r)/ n Am agente mf immobiliare

reap /riːp/ vt mietere

reap'pear /riː-/ vi riapparire

rear¹ /rɪə(r)/ adj posteriore; (Auto) di dietro; ~ **end** 🔲 didietro m ● n the ~ (of building) il retro m; (of bus, plane:) la parte f posteriore; **from the** ~ da dietro

rear² vt allevare ● vi ~ [up] (horse:) impennarsi

rear'range /riː-/ vt cambiare la disposizione di

reason /'riːzn/ n ragione f; **within** ~ nei limiti del ragionevole ● vi ragionare; ~ **with** cercare di far ragionare. ~**able** adj ragionevole. ~**ably** adv (in reasonable way, fairly) ragionevolmente

reas'sur|ance /riː-/ n rassicurazione f. ~**e** vt rassicurare; ~ **sb of** sth rassicurare qcno su qcsa. ~**ing** adj rassicurante

rebate /'riːbeɪt/ n rimborso m; (discount) deduzione f

rebel¹ /'rebl/ n ribelle mf

rebel² /rɪ'bel/ vi (pt/pp rebelled) ribellarsi. ~**lion** n ribellione f. ~**lious** adj ribelle

re'bound¹ /rɪ-/ vi rimbalzare; fig ricadere

'rebound² /riː-/ n rimbalzo m

rebuff /rɪ'bʌf/ n rifiuto m

re'build /ri:-/ vt (pt/pp -built) ricostruire

rebuke /rɪ'bjuːk/ vt rimproverare

re'call /rɪ-/ n richiamo m; beyond ~ irrevocabile • vt richiamare; riconcocare (diplomat, parliament); (remember) rievocare

recap /'riːkæp/ vt/i 🔢 = recapitulate • n ricapitolazione f

recapitulate /riːkə'pɪtjʊleɪt/ vt/i ricapitolare

re'capture /riː-/ vt riconquistare; ricatturare (person, animal)

reced|e /rɪ'siːd/ vi allontanarsi. ~ing adj (forehead, chin) sfuggente; have ~ing hair essere stempiato

receipt /rɪ'siːt/ n ricevuta f; (receiving) ricezione f; ~s pl (Comm) entrate fpl

receive /rɪ'siːv/ vt ricevere. ~r n (Teleph) ricevitore m; (Radio, TV) apparecchio m ricevente; (of stolen goods) ricettatore, -trice mf

recent /'riːsnt/ adj recente. ~ly adv recentemente

reception /rɪ'sepʃn/ n ricevimento m; (welcome) accoglienza f; (Radio) ricezione f; ~ [desk] (in hotel) reception f inv. ~ist n persona f alla reception

receptive /rɪ'septɪv/ adj ricettivo

recess /rɪ'ses/ n rientranza f; (holiday) vacanza f; Am (Sch) intervallo m

recession /rɪ'seʃn/ n recessione f

re'charge /riː-/ vt ricaricare

recipe /'resəpɪ/ n ricetta f

recipient /rɪ'sɪpɪənt/ n (of letter) destinatario, -a mf; (of money) beneficiario, -a mf

recital /rɪ'saɪtl/ n recital m inv

recite /rɪ'saɪt/ vt recitare; (list) elencare

reckless /'reklɪs/ adj (action, decision) sconsiderato; be a ~ driver guidare in modo spericolato. ~ly adv in modo sconsiderato. ~ness n

sconsideratezza f

reckon /'rekən/ vt calcolare; (consider) pensare. □ ~ on/with vt fare i conti con

re'claim /rɪ-/ vt reclamare; bonificare (land)

reclin|e /rɪ'klaɪn/ vi sdraiarsi. ~ing adj (seat) reclinabile

recluse /rɪ'kluːs/ n recluso, -a mf

recognition /rekəg'nɪʃn/ n riconoscimento m; beyond ~ irriconoscibile

recognize /'rekəgnaɪz/ vt riconoscere

re'coil /rɪ-/ vi (in fear) indietreggiare

recollect /rekə'lekt/ vt ricordare. ~ion n ricordo m

recommend /rekə'mend/ vt raccomandare. ~ation n raccomandazione f

recon|cile /'rekənsaɪl/ vt riconciliare; conciliare (facts); ~cile oneself to rassegnarsi a. ~ciliation n riconciliazione f

reconnaissance /rɪ'kɒnɪsns/ n (Mil) ricognizione f

reconnoitre /rekə'nɔɪtə(r)/ vi (pres p -tring) fare una ricognizione

recon'sider /riː-/ vt riconsiderare

recon'struct /riː-/ vt ricostruire. ~ion n ricostruzione f

record[1] /rɪ'kɔːd/ vt registrare; (make a note of) annotare

record[2] /'rekɔːd/ n (file) documentazione f; (Mus) disco m; (Sport) record m inv; ~s pl (files) schedario msg; keep a ~ of tener nota di; off the ~ in via ufficiosa; have a [criminal] ~ avere la fedina penale sporca

recorder /rɪ'kɔːdə(r)/ n (Mus) flauto m dolce

recording /rɪ'kɔːdɪŋ/ n registrazione f

'record-player n giradischi m inv

recount /rɪ'kaʊnt/ vt raccontare

re-'count[1] /riː-/ vt ricontare

're-count² /'ri:-/ n (Pol) nuovo conteggio m

recover /rɪ'kʌvə(r)/ vt/i recuperare. **~y** n recupero m; (of health) guarigione m

re-'cover /ri:-/ vt rifoderare

recreation /rekrɪ'eɪʃn/ n ricreazione f. **~al** adj ricreativo

recruit /rɪ'kru:t/ n (Mil) recluta f; new **~** (member) nuovo, -a adepto, -a mf; (worker) neoassunto, -a mf ● vt assumere (staff). **~ment** n assunzione f

rectang|le /'rektæŋgl/ n rettangolo m. **~ular** adj rettangolare

rectify /'rektɪfaɪ/ vt (pt/pp -ied) rettificare

recuperate /rɪ'ku:pəreɪt/ vt/i ristabilirsi

recur /rɪ'kɜ:(r)/ vi (pt/pp recurred) ricorrere; (illness:) ripresentarsi

recurren|ce /rɪ'kʌrəns/ n ricorrenza f; (of illness) ricomparsa f. **~t** adj ricorrente

recycle /ri:'saɪkl/ vt riciclare

red /red/ adj (redder, reddest) rosso ● n rosso m; in the **~** (account) scoperto. R**~** Cross n Croce f rossa

redd|en /'redn/ vt arrossare ● vi arrossire. **~ish** adj rossastro

re'decorate /ri:-/ vt (paint) ridipingere; (wallpaper) ritappezzare

redeem /rɪ'di:m/ vt **~ing** quality unico aspetto m positivo

redemption /rɪ'dempʃn/ n riscatto m

red: ~-haired adj con i capelli rossi. **~-handed** adj catch sb **~-**handed cogliere qcno con le mani nel sacco. **~ 'herring** n diversione f. **~-hot** adj rovente

red: ~ 'light n (Auto) semaforo m rosso

re'double /ri:-/ vt raddoppiare

red 'tape n 🆃 burocrazia f

reduc|e /rɪ'dju:s/ vt ridurre; (Culin)

far consumare. **~tion** n riduzione f

redundan|cy /rɪ'dʌndənsɪ/ n licenziamento m; (payment) cassa f integrazione. **~t** adj superfluo; make **~t** licenziare; be made **~t** essere licenziato

reed /ri:d/ n (Bot) canna f

reef /ri:f/ n scogliera f

reek /ri:k/ vi puzzare (of di)

reel /ri:l/ n bobina f ● vi (stagger) vacillare. □ **~ off** vt fig snocciolare

refectory /rɪ'fektərɪ/ n refettorio m; (Univ) mensa f universitaria

refer /rɪ'fɜ:(r)/ v (pt/pp referred) ● vt rinviare (matter) (to a); indirizzare (person) ● vi **~ to** fare allusione a; (consult) rivolgersi a (book)

referee /refə'ri:/ n arbitro m; (for job) garante mf ● vt/i (pt/pp refereed) arbitrare

reference /'refərəns/ n riferimento m; (in book) nota f bibliografica; (for job) referenza f; (Comm) 'your **~**' 'riferimento'; with **~ to** con riferimento a; make [a] **~ to** fare riferimento a. **~ book** n libro m di consultazione. **~ number** n numero m di riferimento

referendum /refə'rendəm/ n referendum m inv

re'fill¹ /ri:-/ vt riempire di nuovo; ricaricare (pen, lighter)

'refill² /ri:-/ n (for pen) ricambio m

refine /rɪ'faɪn/ vt raffinare. **~d** adj raffinato. **~ment** n raffinatezza f; (Techn) raffinazione f. **~ry** n raffineria f

reflect /rɪ'flekt/ vt riflettere; be **~ed** in essere riflesso in ● vi (think) riflettere (on su); **~ badly on sb** fig mettere in cattiva luce qcno. **~ion** n riflessione f; (image) riflesso m; on **~ion** dopo riflessione. **~ive** adj riflessivo. **~or** n riflettore m

reflex /'ri:fleks/ n riflesso m ● attrib di riflesso

reflexive /rɪ'fleksɪv/ adj riflessivo

reform /rɪˈfɔːm/ n riforma f ● vt riformare ● vi correggersi. R~ation n (Relig) riforma f. ~er n riformatore, -trice mf

refrain¹ /rɪˈfreɪn/ n ritornello m

refrain² vi astenersi (from da)

refresh /rɪˈfreʃ/ vt rinfrescare. ~ing adj rinfrescante. ~ments npl rinfreschi mpl

refrigerat|e /rɪˈfrɪdʒəreɪt/ vt conservare in frigo. ~or n frigorifero m

re'fuel /riː-/ vt (pt/pp -fuelled) ● vt rifornire (di carburante) ● vi fare rifornimento

refuge /ˈrefjuːdʒ/ n rifugio m; take ~ rifugiarsi

refugee /refjʊˈdʒiː/ n rifugiato, -a mf

refund¹ /ˈriː-/ n rimborso m

re'fund² /rɪ-/ vt rimborsare

refusal /rɪˈfjuːzl/ n rifiuto m

refuse¹ /rɪˈfjuːz/ vt/i rifiutare; ~ to do sth rifiutare di fare qcsa

refuse² /ˈrefjuːs/ n rifiuti mpl. ~ collection n raccolta f dei rifiuti

refute /rɪˈfjuːt/ vt confutare

re'gain /rɪ-/ vt riconquistare

regal /ˈriːgl/ adj regale

regatta /rɪˈɡætə/ n regata f

regime /reɪˈʒiːm/ n regime m

regiment /ˈredʒɪmənt/ n reggimento m. ~al adj reggimentale. ~ation n irreggimentazione f

region /ˈriːdʒən/ n regione f; in the ~ of fig approssimativamente. ~al adj regionale

register /ˈredʒɪstə(r)/ n registro m ● vt registrare; mandare per raccomandata (letter); assicurare (luggage); immatricolare (vehicle); mostrare (feeling) ● vi (instrument:) funzionare; (student:) iscriversi (for a); ~ with iscriversi nella lista del (doctor)

registrar /redʒɪˈstrɑː(r)/ n ufficiale m di stato civile

registration /redʒɪˈstreɪʃn/ n (of vehicle) immatricolazione f; (of letter) raccomandazione f; (of luggage) assicurazione f; (for course) iscrizione f. ~ number n (Auto) targa f

registry office /ˈredʒɪstrɪ-/ n anagrafe f

regret /rɪˈgret/ n rammarico m ● vt (pt/pp regretted) rimpiangere; I ~ that mi rincresce che. ~fully adv con rammarico

regrettab|le /rɪˈgretəbl/ adj spiacevole. ~ly adv spiacevolmente; (before adjective) deplorevolmente

regular /ˈregjʊlə(r)/ adj regolare; (usual) abituale ● n cliente mf abituale. ~ity n regolarità f. ~ly adv regolarmente

regulat|e /ˈregjʊleɪt/ vt regolare. ~ion n (rule) regolamento m

rehearsal /rɪˈhɜːsl/ n (Theat) prova f. ~e vt/i provare

reign /reɪn/ n regno m ● vi regnare

reinforce /riːmˈfɔːs/ vt rinforzare. ~d 'concrete n cemento m armato. ~ment n rinforzo m

reiterate /riːˈɪtəreɪt/ vt reiterare

reject /rɪˈdʒekt/ vt rifiutare. ~ion n rifiuto m; (Med) rigetto m

rejoic|e /rɪˈdʒɔɪs/ vi liter rallegrarsi. ~ing n gioia f

rejuvenate /rɪˈdʒuːvəneɪt/ vt ringiovanire

relapse /rɪˈlæps/ n ricaduta f ● vi ricadere

relate /rɪˈleɪt/ vt (tell) riportare; (connect) collegare ● vi ~ to riferirsi a; identificarsi con (person). ~d adj imparentato (to a); (ideas etc) affine

relation /rɪˈleɪʃn/ n rapporto m; (person) parente mf. ~ship n rapporto m (blood tie) parentela f; (affair) relazione f

relative /ˈrelətɪv/ n parente mf • adj relativo. ~ly adv relativamente

relax /rɪˈlæks/ vt rilassare; allentare (pace, grip) • vi rilassarsi. ~ation n rilassamento m, relax m inv; (recreation) svago m. ~ing adj rilassante

relay¹ /riːˈleɪ/ vt ritrasmettere; (Radio, TV) trasmettere

relay² /ˈriːleɪ/ n (Electr) relais m inv; work in ~s fare i turni. ~ [race] n [corsa f a] staffetta f

release /rɪˈliːs/ n rilascio m; (of film) distribuzione f • vt liberare; lasciare (hand); togliere (brake); distribuire (film); rilasciare (information etc)

relegate /ˈrelɪɡeɪt/ vt relegare; be ~d (Sport) essere retrocesso

relent /rɪˈlent/ vi cedere. ~less adj inflessibile; (unceasing) incessante. ~lessly adv incessantemente

relevan|ce /ˈreləvəns/ n pertinenza f. ~t adj pertinente (to a)

reliab|ility /rɪlaɪəˈbɪlətɪ/ n affidabilità f. ~le adj affidabile a. ~ly adv in modo affidabile; be ~ly informed sapere da fonte certa

relian|ce /rɪˈlaɪəns/ n fiducia f (on in). ~t adj fiducioso (on in)

relic /ˈrelɪk/ n (Relig) reliquia f; ~s npl resti mpl

relief /rɪˈliːf/ n sollievo m; (assistance) soccorso m; (distraction) diversivo m; (replacement) cambio m; (in art) rilievo m; in ~ in rilievo. ~ map n carta f in rilievo. ~ train n treno m supplementare

relieve /rɪˈliːv/ vt alleviare; (take over from) dare il cambio a; ~ of liberare da (burden)

religion /rɪˈlɪdʒən/ n religione f

religious /rɪˈlɪdʒəs/ adj religioso. ~ly adv (conscientiously) scrupolosamente

relinquish /rɪˈlɪŋkwɪʃ/ vt abbandonare; ~ sth to sb rinunciare a qcsa in favore di qcno

relish /ˈrelɪʃ/ n gusto m; (Culin) salsa f • vt apprezzare

reluctan|ce /rɪˈlʌktəns/ n riluttanza f. ~t adj riluttante. ~tly adv a malincuore

rely /rɪˈlaɪ/ vi (pt/pp -ied) ~ on dipendere da; (trust) contare su

remain /rɪˈmeɪn/ vi restare. ~der n resto m. ~ing adj restante. ~s npl resti mpl; (dead body) spoglie fpl

remand /rɪˈmɑːnd/ n on ~ in custodia cautelare • vt ~ in custody rinviare con detenzione provvisoria

remark /rɪˈmɑːk/ n osservazione f • vt osservare. ~able adj notevole. ~ably adv notevolmente

remarry /riːˈ-/ vi risposarsi

remedy /ˈremədɪ/ n rimedio m (for contro) • vt (pt/pp -ied) rimediare a

remember /rɪˈmembə(r)/ vt ricordare, ricordarsi; ~ to do sth ricordarsi di fare qcsa; ~ me to him salutamelo • vi ricordarsi

remind /rɪˈmaɪnd/ vt ~ sb of sth ricordare qcsa a qcno. ~er n ricordo m; (memo) promemoria m; (letter) lettera f di sollecito

reminisce /remɪˈnɪs/ vi rievocare il passato. ~nces npl reminiscenze fpl. ~nt adj be ~ of richiamare alla memoria

remnant /ˈremnənt/ n resto m; (of material) scampolo m; (trace) traccia f

remorse /rɪˈmɔːs/ n rimorso m. ~ful adj pieno di rimorso. ~less adj spietato. ~lessly adv senza pietà

remote /rɪˈməʊt/ adj remoto; (slight) minimo. ~ access n (Comput) accesso m remoto. ~ con'trol n telecomando m. ~-con'trolled adj telecomandato. ~ly adv lontanamente; be not ~ly... non essere lontanamente...

re'movable /riː-/ adj rimovibile

removal /rɪˈmuːvl/ n rimozione f;

(*from house*) trasloco *m*. ~ **van** *n* camion *m inv* da trasloco

remove /rɪˈmuːv/ *vt* togliere; togliersi (*clothes*); eliminare (*stain, doubts*)

render /ˈrendə(r)/ *vt* rendere (*service*)

renegade /ˈrenɪɡeɪd/ *n* rinnegato, -a *mf*

renew /rɪˈnjuː/ *vt* rinnovare (*contract*). ~al *n* rinnovo *m*

renounce /rɪˈnaʊns/ *vt* rinunciare a

renovat|e /ˈrenəveɪt/ *vt* rinnovare. ~ion *n* rinnovo *m*

renown /rɪˈnaʊn/ *n* fama *f*. ~ed *adj* rinomato

rent /rent/ *n* affitto *m* ● *vt* affittare; (*take*) [out] dare in affitto. ~al *n* affitto *m*

renunciation /rɪnʌnsɪˈeɪʃn/ *n* rinuncia *f*

re|open /riː-/ *vt*/*i* riaprire

re'organize /riː-/ *vt* riorganizzare

rep /rep/ *n* (*Comm*) ≈ rappresentante *mf*; (*Theat*) ≈ teatro *m* stabile

repair /rɪˈpeə(r)/ *n* riparazione *f*; in good/bad ~ in cattive/buone condizioni ● *vt* riparare

repatriat|e /riːˈpætrɪeɪt/ *vt* rimpatriare. ~ion *n* rimpatrio *m*

re'pay /riː-/ *vt* (*pt*/*pp* -paid) ripagare. ~ment *n* rimborso *m*

repeal /rɪˈpiːl/ *n* abrogazione *f* ● *vt* abrogare

repeat /rɪˈpiːt/ *n* (*TV*) replica *f* ● *vt*/*i* ripetere; ~ oneself ripetersi. ~ed *adj* ripetuto. ~edly *adv* ripetutamente

repel /rɪˈpel/ *vt* (*pt*/*pp* repelled) respingere; *fig* ripugnare. ~lent *adj* ripulsivo

repent /rɪˈpent/ *vi* pentirsi. ~ance *n* pentimento *m*. ~ant *adj* pentito

repertoire /ˈrepətwɑː(r)/ *n* repertorio *m*

repetit|ion /repɪˈtɪʃn/ *n* ripetizione

f. ~ive *adj* ripetitivo

re'place /rɪ-/ *vt* (*put back*) rimettere a posto; (*take the place of*) sostituire; ~ **sth with sth** sostituire qcsa con qcsa. ~ment *n* sostituzione *m*; (*person*) sostituto, -a *mf*. ~ment part *n* pezzo *m* di ricambio

'**replay** /ˈriː-/ *n* (*Sport*) partita *f* ripetuta; [action] ~ replay *m inv*

replenish /rɪˈplenɪʃ/ *vt* rifornire (*stocks*); (*refill*) riempire di nuovo

replica /ˈreplɪkə/ *n* copia *f*

reply /rɪˈplaɪ/ *n* risposta *f* (to a) ● *vt*/*i* (*pt*/*pp* replied) rispondere

report /rɪˈpɔːt/ *n* rapporto *m*; (*TV, Radio*) servizio *m*; (*Journ*) cronaca *f*; (*Sch*) pagella *f*; (*rumour*) diceria *f* ● *vt* riportare; ~ **sb to the police** denunciare qcno alla polizia ● *vi* riportare; (*present oneself*) presentarsi (to a). ~edly *adv* secondo quanto si dice. ~er *n* cronista *mf*, reporter *mf inv*

reprehensible /reprɪˈhensəbl/ *adj* riprovevole

represent /reprɪˈzent/ *vt* rappresentare

representative /reprɪˈzentətɪv/ *adj* rappresentativo ● *n* rappresentante *mf*

repress /rɪˈpres/ *vt* reprimere. ~ion *n* repressione *f*. ~ive *adj* repressivo

reprieve /rɪˈpriːv/ *n* commutazione *f* della pena capitale; (*postponement*) sospensione *f* della pena capitale; *fig* tregua *f* ● *vt* sospendere la sentenza a; *fig* risparmiare

reprimand /ˈreprɪmɑːnd/ *n* rimprovero *m* ● *vt* rimproverare

reprisal /rɪˈpraɪzl/ *n* rappresaglia *f*; in ~ for per rappresaglia contro

reproach /rɪˈprəʊtʃ/ *n* ammonimento *m* ● *vt* ammonire. ~ful *adj* riprovevole. ~fully *adv* con aria di rimprovero

repro'duc|e /riː-/ *vt* riprodurre ● *vi*

riprodursi. ~tion n riproduzione f.
~tive adj riproduttivo

reprove /rɪ'pruːv/ vt rimproverare

reptile /'reptail/ n rettile m

republic /rɪ'pʌblɪk/ n repubblica f.
~an adj repubblicano ● n repubblicano, -a mf

repugnan|ce /rɪ'pʌɡnəns/ n ripugnanza f. ~t adj ripugnante

repuls|ion /rɪ'pʌlʃn/ n repulsione f.
~ive adj ripugnante

reputable /'repjʊtəbl/ adj affidabile

reputation /repjʊ'teɪʃn/ n reputazione f

request /rɪ'kwest/ n richiesta f ● vt richiedere. ~ stop n fermata f a richiesta

require /rɪ'kwaɪə(r)/ vt (need) necessitare di; (demand) esigere. ~d adj richiesto; I am ~d to do so si esige che io faccia. ~ment n esigenza f; (condition) requisito m

rescue /'reskjuː/ n salvataggio m ● vt salvare. ~r n salvatore, -trice mf

research /rɪ'sɜːtʃ/ n ricerca f ● vt fare ricerche su; (Journ) fare un'inchiesta su ● vi ~ into fare ricerche su. ~er n ricercatore, -trice mf

resem|blance /rɪ'zembləns/ n rassomiglianza f. ~ble vt rassomigliare a

resent /rɪ'zent/ vt risentirsi per.
~ful adj pieno di risentimento.
~fully adv con risentimento. ~ment n risentimento m

reservation /rezə'veɪʃn/ n (booking) prenotazione f; (doubt, enclosure) riserva f

reserve /rɪ'zɜːv/ n riserva f; (shyness) riserbo m ● vt riservare; riservarsi (right). ~d adj riservato

reservoir /'rezəvwɑː(r)/ n bacino m idrico

re'shuffle /riː-/ n (Pol) rimpasto m ● vt (Pol) rimpastare

residence /'rezɪdəns/ n residenza f; (stay) soggiorno m. ~ permit n permesso m di soggiorno

resident /'rezɪdənt/ adj residente ● n residente mf. ~ial adj residenziale

residue /'rezɪdjuː/ n residuo m

resign /rɪ'zaɪn/ vt dimettersi da; ~ oneself to rassegnarsi a ● vi dare le dimissioni. ~ation n rassegnazione f; (from job) dimissioni fpl. ~ed adj rassegnato

resilient /rɪ'zɪliənt/ adj elastico; fig con buone capacità di ripresa

resin /'rezɪn/ n resina f

resist /rɪ'zɪst/ vt resistere a ● vi resistere. ~ance n resistenza f. ~ant adj resistente

resolute /'rezəluːt/ adj risoluto.
~ely adv con risolutezza. ~ion n risolutezza f

resolve /rɪ'zɒlv/ vt ~ to do decidere di fare

resort /rɪ'zɔːt/ n (place) luogo m di villeggiatura; as a last ~ come ultima risorsa ● vi ~ to ricorrere a

resource /rɪ'sɔːs/ n ~s pl risorse fpl. ~ful adj pieno di risorse; (solution) ingegnoso. ~fulness n ingegnosità f inv

respect /rɪ'spekt/ n rispetto m; (aspect) aspetto m; with ~ to per quanto riguarda ● vt rispettare

respect|able /rɪ'spektəbl/ adj rispettabile. ~ably adv rispettabilmente. ~ful adj rispettoso

respective /rɪ'spektɪv/ adj rispettivo. ~ly adv rispettivamente

respiration /respɪ'reɪʃn/ n respirazione f

respite /'respaɪt/ n respiro m

respond /rɪ'spɒnd/ vi rispondere; (react) reagire (to a); (patient:) rispondere (to a)

response /rɪ'spɒns/ n risposta f; (reaction) reazione f

responsibility /rɪspɒnsɪ'bɪlətɪ/ n responsabilità f inv

responsib|le /rɪ'spɒnsəbl/ adj responsabile; (job) impegnativo

responsive /rɪˈspɒnsɪv/ adj be ~ (audience etc.) reagire; (brakes:) essere sensibile

rest¹ /rest/ n riposo m; (Mus) pausa f; have a ~ riposarsi ● vt riposare; (lean) appoggiare (on su); (place) appoggiare ● vi riposarsi; (elbows:) appoggiarsi; (hopes:) riposare

rest² n the ~ il resto m; (people) gli altri mpl ● vi it ~s with you sta a te

restaurant /ˈrestərɒnt/ n ristorante m. ~ car n vagone m ristorante

restful /ˈrestfl/ adj riposante

restive /ˈrestɪv/ adj irrequieto

restless /ˈrestlɪs/ adj nervoso

restoration /restəˈreɪʃn/ n (of building) restauro m

restore /rɪˈstɔː(r)/ vt ristabilire; restaurare (building); (give back) restituire

restrain /rɪˈstreɪn/ vt trattenere; ~ oneself controllarsi. ~ed adj controllato. ~t n restrizione f; (moderation) ritegno m

restrict /rɪˈstrɪkt/ vt limitare; ~ to limitarsi a. ~ion n limite m; (restraint) restrizione f. ~ive adj limitativo

rest room n Am toilette f inv

result /rɪˈzʌlt/ n risultato m; as a ~ a causa (of di) ● vi ~ from risultare da; ~ in portare a

resume /rɪˈzjuːm/ vt/i riprendere

résumé /ˈreɪzjumeɪ/ n riassunto m; Am curriculum vitae m inv

resurrect /rezəˈrekt/ vt fig risuscitare. ~ion n the R~ion (Relig) la Risurrezione

resuscitat|e /rɪˈsʌsɪteɪt/ vt rianimare. ~ion n rianimazione f

retail /ˈriːteɪl/ n vendita f al minuto o al dettaglio ● adj & adv al minuto ● vt vendere al minuto ● vi ~ at essere venduto al pubblico al prezzo di. ~er n dettagliante mf

retain /rɪˈteɪn/ vt conservare; (hold back) trattenere

retaliat|e /rɪˈtælɪeɪt/ vi vendicarsi. ~ion n rappresaglia f; in ~ion for per rappresaglia contro

retarded /rɪˈtɑːdɪd/ adj ritardato

rethink /riːˈθɪŋk/ vt (pt/pp rethought) ripensare

reticen|ce /ˈretɪsəns/ n reticenza f. ~t adj reticente

retina /ˈretɪnə/ n retina f

retinue /ˈretɪnjuː/ n seguito m

retire /rɪˈtaɪə(r)/ vi andare in pensione; (withdraw) ritirarsi ● vt mandare in pensione (employee). ~d adj in pensione. ~ment n pensione f; since my ~ment da quando sono andato in pensione

retiring /rɪˈtaɪərɪŋ/ adj riservato

retort /rɪˈtɔːt/ n replica f ● vt ribattere

re'trace /riː-/ vt ripercorrere; ~ one's steps ritornare sui propri passi

retract /rɪˈtrækt/ vt ritirare; ritrattare (statement, evidence) ● vi ritrarsi

re'train /riː-/ vt riqualificare ● vi riqualificarsi

retreat /rɪˈtriːt/ n ritirata f; (place) ritiro m ● vi ritirarsi; (Mil) battere in ritirata

re'trial /riː-/ n nuovo processo m

retrieval /rɪˈtriːvl/ n recupero m

retrieve /rɪˈtriːv/ vt recuperare

retrograde /ˈretrəgreɪd/ adj retrogrado

retrospect /ˈretrəspekt/ n in ~ guardando indietro. ~ive adj retrospettivo; (legislation) retroattivo ● n retrospettiva f

return /rɪˈtɜːn/ n ritorno m; (giving back) restituzione f; (Comm) profitto m; (ticket) biglietto m di andata e ritorno; by ~ [of post] a stretto giro di posta; in ~ in cambio (for di); many happy ~s! cento di questi

r

giorni; ● vi ritornare ● vt (give back) restituire; ricambiare (affection, invitation); (put back) rimettere; (send back) mandare indietro; (elect) eleggere

return: ~ **match** n rivincita f. ~ **ticket** n biglietto m di andata e ritorno

reunion /riːˈjuːnjən/ n riunione f

reunite /riːjuːˈnaɪt/ vt riunire

rev /rev/ n (Auto), 🔟 giro m (di motore) ● v (pt/pp revved) ● vt ~ [up] far andare su di giri ● vi andare su di giri

reveal /rɪˈviːl/ vt rivelare; (dress:) scoprire. ~**ing** adj rivelatore; (dress) osé

revel /ˈrevl/ vi (pt/pp revelled) ~ **in** sth godere di qcsa

revelation /revəˈleɪʃn/ n rivelazione f

revelry /ˈrevlrɪ/ n baldoria f

revenge /rɪˈvendʒ/ n vendetta f; (Sport) rivincita f; take ~ vendicarsi ● vt vendicare

revenue /ˈrevənjuː/ n reddito m

revere /rɪˈvɪə(r)/ vt riverire. ~**nce** n riverenza f

Reverend /ˈrevərənd/ adj reverendo

reverent /ˈrevərənt/ adj riverente

reverse /rɪˈvɜːs/ adj opposto; in ~ **order** in ordine inverso ● n contrario m; (back) rovescio m; (Auto) marcia indietro ● vt invertire; ~ **the car into the garage** entrare in garage a marcia indietro; ~ **the charges** (Teleph) fare una telefonata a carico ● vi (Auto) fare marcia indietro

revert /rɪˈvɜːt/ vi ~ **to** tornare a

review /rɪˈvjuː/ n (survey) rassegna f; (re-examination) riconsiderazione f; (Mil) rivista f; (of book, play) recensione f ● vt riesaminare (situation); (Mil) passare in rivista; recensire (book, play). ~**er** n critico, -a mf

revise /rɪˈvaɪz/ vt rivedere; (for exam) ripassare. ~**ion** n revisione f;

(for exam) ripasso m

revive /rɪˈvaɪv/ vt resuscitare; rianimare (person) ● vi riprendersi; (person:) rianimarsi

revolt /rɪˈvəʊlt/ n rivolta f ● vi ribellarsi ● vt rivoltare. ~**ing** adj rivoltante

revolution /revəˈluːʃn/ n rivoluzione f; (Auto) ~**s per minute** giri mpl al minuto. ~**ary** adj & n rivoluzionario, -a mf. ~**ize** vt rivoluzionare

revolve /rɪˈvɒlv/ vi ruotare; ~ **around** girare intorno

revolver /rɪˈvɒlvə(r)/ n rivoltella f, revolver m inv. ~**ing** adj ruotante

revue /rɪˈvjuː/ n rivista f

revulsion /rɪˈvʌlʃn/ n ripulsione f

reward /rɪˈwɔːd/ n ricompensa f ● vt ricompensare. ~**ing** adj gratificante

re'write /riː-/ vt (pt rewrote, pp rewritten) riscrivere

rhetoric /ˈretərɪk/ n retorica f. ~**al** adj retorico

rhinoceros /raɪˈnɒsərəs/ n rinoceronte m

rhubarb /ˈruːbɑːb/ n rabarbaro m

rhyme /raɪm/ n rima f; (poem) filastrocca f ● vi rimare

rhythm /ˈrɪðm/ n ritmo m. ~**ic[al]** adj ritmico. ~**ically** adv con ritmo

rib /rɪb/ n costola f

ribbon /ˈrɪbən/ n nastro m; in ~**s** a brandelli

rice /raɪs/ n riso m

rich /rɪtʃ/ adj ricco; (food) pesante ● n the ~ pl i ricchi mpl; ~**es** pl ricchezze fpl. ~**ly** adv riccamente; (deserve) largamente

ricochet /ˈrɪkəʃeɪ/ vi rimbalzare ● n rimbalzo m

rid /rɪd/ vt (pt/pp rid, pres p ridding) sbarazzare (of di); get ~ **of** sbarazzarsi di

riddance /ˈrɪdns/ n good ~! che liberazione!

ridden /ˈrɪdn/ ▸RIDE

riddle /ˈrɪdl/ n enigma m

ride /raɪd/ n (on horse) cavalcata f; (in vehicle) giro m; (journey) viaggio m; **take sb for a ~** 🔢 prendere qcno in giro • v (pt rode, pp ridden) • vt montare (horse); andare su (bicycle) • vi andare a cavallo; (jockey:) cavalcare; (cyclist:) andare in bicicletta; (in vehicle) viaggiare. **~r** n cavallerizzo, -a mf; (in race) fantino m; (on bicycle) ciclista mf; (in document) postilla f

ridge /rɪdʒ/ n spigolo m; (on roof) punta f; (of mountain) cresta f

ridicule /ˈrɪdɪkjuːl/ n ridicolo m • vt mettere in ridicolo

ridiculous /rɪˈdɪkjʊləs/ adj ridicolo

rife /raɪf/ adj **be ~** essere diffuso; **~ with** pieno di

rifle /ˈraɪfl/ n fucile m; **~-range** tiro m al bersaglio • vt **~ [through]** mettere a soqquadro

rift /rɪft/ n fessura f; fig frattura f

rig[1] /rɪg/ n equipaggiamento m; (at sea) piattaforma f per trivellazioni subacquee • **rig out** vt (pt/pp rigged) equipaggiare. □ **~ up** vt allestire

rig[2] /rɪg/ vt (pt/pp rigged) manovrare (election)

right /raɪt/ adj giusto; (not left) destro; **be ~** (person:) aver ragione; (clock:) essere giusto; **put ~** mettere all'ora (clock); correggere (person); rimediare a (situation); **that's ~!** proprio così! • adv (correctly) bene; (not left) a destra; (directly) proprio; (completely) completamente; **~ away** immediatamente • n angolo m; (not left) destra f; (what is due) diritto m; **on/to the ~** a destra; **be in the ~** essere nel giusto; **know ~ from wrong** distinguere il bene dal male; **by ~s** secondo giustizia; **the R~** (Pol) la destra f • vt raddrizzare; **a wrong** fig riparare a un torto. **~ angle** n angolo m retto

rightful /ˈraɪtfl/ adj legittimo

right: **~-handed** adj che usa la mano destra. **~-hand 'man** n fig braccio m destro

rightly /ˈraɪtlɪ/ adv giustamente

right: **~ of way** n diritto m di transito; (path) passaggio m; (Auto) precedenza f. **~-wing** adj (Pol) di destra • n (Sport) ala f destra

rigid /ˈrɪdʒɪd/ adj rigido. **~ity** n rigidità f inv

rigorous /ˈrɪgərəs/ adj rigoroso

rim /rɪm/ n bordo m; (of wheel) cerchione m

rind /raɪnd/ n (on fruit) scorza f; (on cheese) crosta f; (on bacon) cotenna f

ring[1] /rɪŋ/ n (circle) cerchio m; (on finger) anello m; (boxing) ring m inv; (for circus) pista f; **stand in a ~** essere in cerchio

ring[2] n suono m; **give sb a ~** (Teleph) dare un colpo di telefono a qcno • v (pt rang, pp rung) • vt suonare; **~ [up]** (Teleph) telefonare a • vi suonare; (Teleph) **~ [up]** telefonare. □ **~ back** vt/i (Teleph) richiamare. □ **~ off** vi (Teleph) riattaccare

ring: **~leader** n capobanda m. **~ road** n circonvallazione f. **~tone** n suoneria f

rink /rɪŋk/ n pista f di pattinaggio

rinse /rɪns/ n risciacquo m; (hair colour) cachet m inv • vt sciacquare

riot /ˈraɪət/ n rissa f; (of colour) accozzaglia f; **~s** pl disordini mpl; **run ~** impazzare • vi creare disordini. **~er** n dimostrante mf. **~ous** adj chiassoso

rip /rɪp/ n strappo m • vt (pt/pp ripped) strappare; **~ open** aprire con uno strappo. □ **~ off** vt 🔢 fregare

ripe /raɪp/ adj maturo; (cheese) stagionato

ripen /ˈraɪpn/ vi maturare; (cheese:) stagionarsi • vt far maturare; stagionare (cheese)

'rip-off n 🔢 frode f

ripple /ˈrɪpl/ n increspatura f; (sound) mormorio m •

rise /raɪz/ n (of sun) levata f; (fig: to fame, power) ascesa f; (increase)

r

aumento m; **give ~ to** dare adito a ● vi (*pt* rose, *pp* risen) alzarsi; (sun:) sorgere; (dough:) lievitare; (prices, water level:) aumentare; (*to power, position*) arrivare (*to* a). **~r** n early **~r** persona f mattiniera

rising /'raɪzɪŋ/ adj (sun) levante; (*generation*) nuova generazione f ● n (*revolt*) sollevazione f

risk /rɪsk/ n rischio m; **at one's own ~** a proprio rischio e pericolo ● vt rischiare

risky /'rɪskɪ/ adj (-ier, -iest) rischioso

rite /raɪt/ n rito m; **last ~s** estrema unzione f

ritual /'rɪtjʊəl/ adj rituale ● n rituale m

rival /'raɪvl/ adj rivale ● n rivale m/f; **~s** pl (Comm) concorrenti mpl ● vt (*pt/pp* rivalled) rivaleggiare con. **~ry** n rivalità f inv; (Comm) concorrenza f

river /'rɪvə(r)/ n fiume m. **~-bed** n letto m del fiume

rivet /'rɪvɪt/ n rivetto m ● vt rivettare; **~ed** by fig inchiodato da

road /rəʊd/ n strada f, via f; **be on the ~** viaggiare

road: ~-map n carta f stradale. **~side** n bordo m della strada. **~works** npl lavori mpl stradali. **~worthy** adj sicuro

roam /rəʊm/ vi girovagare

roar /rɔː(r)/ n ruggito m; **~s of** laughter scroscio msg di risa ● vi ruggire; (lorry, thunder:) rombare; **~ with laughter** ridere fragorosamente. **~ing** adj do a **~ing trade** 🔲 fare affari d'oro

roast /rəʊst/ adj arrosto; **~ pork** arrosto m di maiale ● n arrosto m ● vt arrostire (meat) ● vi arrostirsi

rob /rɒb/ vt (*pt/pp* robbed) derubare (*of* di); svaligiare (bank). **~ber** n rapinatore m. **~bery** n rapina f

robe /rəʊb/ n tunica f; (*Am: bathrobe*) accappatoio m

robin /'rɒbɪn/ n pettirosso m

robot /'rəʊbɒt/ n robot m inv

robust /rəʊ'bʌst/ adj robusto

rock¹ /rɒk/ n roccia f; (*in sea*) scoglio m; (*sweet*) zucchero m candito. **on the ~s** (ship) incagliato; (marriage) finito; (drink) con ghiaccio

rock² vt cullare (baby); (shake) far traballare; (shock) scuotere ● vi dondolarsi

rock³ n (Mus) rock m inv

rock-'bottom adj bassissimo ● n livello m più basso

rocket /'rɒkɪt/ n razzo m ● vi salire alle stelle

rocky /'rɒkɪ/ adj (-ier, -iest) roccioso; fig traballante

rod /rɒd/ n bacchetta f; (*for fishing*) canna f

rode /rəʊd/ ▷RIDE

rodent /'rəʊdnt/ n roditore m

rogue /rəʊg/ n farabutto m

role /rəʊl/ n ruolo m

roll /rəʊl/ n rotolo m; (bread) panino m; (list) lista f; (of ship, drum) rullio m ● vi rotolare; **be ~ing in money** 🔲 nuotare nell'oro ● vt spianare (lawn, pastry). **~ over** vi rigirarsi. **~ up** vt arrotolare; rimboccarsi (sleeves) ● vi 🔲 arrivare

'roll-call n appello m

roller /'rəʊlə(r)/ n rullo m; (*for hair*) bigodino m. **~ blades** npl pattini npl in linea. **~ blind** n tapparella f. **~-coaster** n montagne fpl russe. **~-skate** n pattino m a rotelle

'rolling-pin n mattarello m

Roman /'rəʊmən/ adj romano ● n romano, -a m/f. **~ Catholic** adj cattolico ● n cattolico, -a m/f

romance /rəʊ'mæns/ n (love affair) storia f d'amore; (book) romanzo m rosa

Romania /rəʊ'meɪnɪə/ n Romania f. **~n** adj rumeno ● n rumeno, -a m/f

romantic /rəʊ'mæntɪk/ adj roman-

tico. ~**ally** adv romanticamente.
~**ism** n romanticismo m.

Rome /rəʊm/ n Roma f

romp /rɒmp/ n gioco m rumoroso
● vi giocare rumorosamente. ~**ers**
npl pagliaccetto msg

roof /ruːf/ n tetto m; (of mouth) palato m ● vt mettere un tetto su.
~-**rack** n portabagagli m inv. ~-**top**
n tetto m

rook /rʊk/ n corvo m; (in chess)
torre f

room /ruːm/ n stanza f; (bedroom)
camera f; (for functions) sala f; (space)
spazio m. ~**y** adj spazioso;
(clothes) ampio

roost /ruːst/ vi appollaiarsi

root[1] /ruːt/ n radice f; take ~ metter radici ● root out vt fig scovare

root[2] vi ~ about grufolare; ~ for
sb Am 1 fare il tifo per qcno

rope /rəʊp/ n corda f; know the ~s
1 conoscere i trucchi del mestiere
● rope in vt 1 coinvolgere

rose[1] /rəʊz/ n rosa f; (of watering-can)
bocchetta f

rose[2] ▷**RISE**

rosé /ˈrəʊzeɪ/ n [vino m] rosé m inv

rot /rɒt/ n marciume m; (1: nonsense) sciocchezze fpl ● vi (pt/pp rot-
ted) marcire

rota /ˈrəʊtə/ n tabella f dei turni

rotary /ˈrəʊtərɪ/ adj rotante

rotat|**e** /rəʊˈteɪt/ vt far ruotare; avvi-
cendare (crops) ● vi ruotare. ~**ion**
n rotazione f; in ~**ion** a turno

rote /rəʊt/ n by ~ meccanicamente

rotten /ˈrɒtn/ adj marcio; 1 schifoso; (person) penoso

rough /rʌf/ adj (not smooth) ruvido;
(ground) accidentato; (behaviour) rozzo;
(sport) violento; (area) malfamato;
(crossing, time) brutto; (estimate)
approssimativo ● adv (play) grossola-
namente; sleep ~ dormire sotto i

ponti ● vt ~ it vivere senza confort.
□ ~ **out** vt abbozzare

roughage /ˈrʌfɪdʒ/ n fibre fpl

rough|**ly** /ˈrʌflɪ/ adv rozzamente;
(more or less) pressappoco. ~**ness** n
ruvidità f; (of behaviour) rozzezza f

roulette /ruːˈlet/ n roulette f inv

round /raʊnd/ adj rotondo ● n
tondo m; (slice) fetta f; (of visits, drinks)
giro m; (of competition) partita f; (boxing) ripresa f, round m inv; do one's
~s (doctor:) fare il giro delle visite
● prep intorno a; open ~ the clock
aperto ventiquattr'ore ● adv all ~
tutt'intorno; ask sb ~ invitare qcno
da; (turn/look ~ girarsi; ~ **about**
(approximately) intorno a ● vt arrotondare; (girare (corner). □ ~ **down** vt
arrotondare (per difetto). □ ~ **off** vt
(end) terminare. □ ~ **on** vt aggredire.
□ ~ **up** vt radunare; arrotondare
(prices)

roundabout /ˈraʊndəbaʊt/ adj indiretto ● n giostra f; (for traffic) ro-
tonda f

round: ~ **trip** n viaggio m di andata e ritorno

rous|**e** /raʊz/ vt svegliare; risvegliare
(suspicion, interest). ~**ing** adj di incoraggiamento

route /ruːt/ n itinerario m; (Aeron,
Naut) rotta f; (of bus) percorso m

routine /ruːˈtiːn/ adj di routine ● n
routine f inv; (Theat) numero m

row[1] /rəʊ/ n (line) fila f; three years
in a ~ tre anni di fila

row[2] vi (in boat) remare

row[3] /raʊ/ n 1 (quarrel) litigata f;
(noise) baccano m ● vi 1 litigare

rowdy /ˈraʊdɪ/ adj (-ier, -iest)
chiassoso

rowing boat /ˈrəʊɪŋ-/ n barca f
a remi

royal /ˈrɔɪəl/ adj reale

royalt|**y** /ˈrɔɪəltɪ/ n appartenenza f

r

alla famiglia reale; (persons) i membri mpl della famiglia reale. ~es npl (payments) diritti mpl d'autore

rub /rʌb/ n give sth a ~ dare una sfregata a qcsa ●vt (pt/pp rubbed) sfregare. □ ~ **in** vt don't ~ it in 🔢 non rigirare il coltello nella piaga. □ ~ **off** vt mandar via sfregando (stain); (from blackboard) cancellare ●vi andar via; ~ off on essere trasmesso a. □ ~ **out** vt cancellare

rubber /'rʌbə(r)/ n gomma f; (eraser) gomma f [da cancellare]. ~ **band** n elastico m. ~y adj gommoso

rubbish /'rʌbɪʃ/ n immondizie fpl; (🔢: nonsense) idiozie fpl; (🔢: junk) robaccia f ●vt 🔢 fare a pezzi. ~ **bin** n pattumiera f. ~ **dump** n discarica f; (official) discarica f comunale

rubble /'rʌbl/ n macerie fpl

ruby /'ru:bɪ/ n rubino m ●attrib di rubini; (lips) scarlatta

rucksack /'rʌksæk/ n zaino m

rudder /'rʌdə(r)/ n timone m

rude /ru:d/ adj scortese; (improper) spinto. ~ly adv scortesemente. ~ness n scortesia f

ruffian /'rʌfɪən/ n farabutto m

ruffle /'rʌfl/ n gala f ●vt scompigliare (hair)

rug /rʌg/ n tappeto m; (blanket) coperta f

rugby /'rʌgbɪ/ n [football] rugby m

rugged /'rʌgɪd/ adj (coastline) roccioso

ruin /'ru:ɪn/ n rovina f; in ~s in rovina ●vt rovinare. ~ous adj estremamente costoso

rule /ru:l/ n regola f; (control) ordinamento m; (for measuring) metro m; ~s regolamento m; as a ~ generalmente ●vt governare; dominare (colony, behaviour); ~ that stabilire che ●vi governare. □ ~ **out** vt escludere

ruler /'ru:lə(r)/ n capo m di Stato; (sovereign) sovrano, -a mf; (measure) righello m, regolo m

ruling /'ru:lɪŋ/ adj (class) dirigente; (party) di governo ●n decisione f

rum /rʌm/ n rum m inv

rumble /'rʌmbl/ n rombo m; (of stomach) brontolio m ●vi rombare; (stomach:) brontolare

rummage /'rʌmɪdʒ/ vi rovistare (in/through in)

rumour /'ru:mə(r)/ n diceria f ●vt is ~ed that si dice che

run /rʌn/ n (on foot) corsa f; (distance to be covered) tragitto m; (outing) giro m; (Theat) rappresentazioni fpl; (in skiing) pista f; (Am: ladder) smagliatura f (in calze); at a ~ di corsa; ~ of bad luck periodo m sfortunato; on the ~ in fuga; have the ~ of avere a disposizione; in the long ~ a lungo termine ●v (pt ran, pp run, pres p running) ●vi correre; (river:) scorrere; (nose, make-up:) colare; (bus:) fare servizio; (play:) essere in cartellone; (colours:) sbiadire; (in election) presentarsi [come candidato] ●vt (manage) dirigere; tenere (house); (drive) dare un passaggio a; correre (risk); (Comput) lanciare; (Journ) pubblicare (article); (pass) far scorrere (eyes, hand); ~ a bath far scorrere l'acqua per il bagno. □ ~ **across** vi (meet, find) imbattersi in. □ ~ **away** vi scappare [via]. □ ~ **down** vi scaricarsi; (clock:) scaricarsi; (stocks:) esaurirsi ●vt (Auto) investire; (reduce) esaurire; (🔢: criticize) denigrare. □ ~ **in** vi entrare di corsa. □ ~ **into** vi (meet) imbattersi in; (knock against) urtare. □ ~ **off** vi andare via di corsa ●vt stampare (copies). □ ~ **out** vi uscire di corsa; (supplies, money:) esaurirsi; ~ **out of** rimanere senza. □ ~ **over** vi correre; (overflow) traboccare ●vt (Auto) investire. □ ~ **through** vi scorrere. □ ~ **up** vi salire di corsa; (towards) arrivare di corsa ●vt accumulare (debts, bill);

(sew) cucire

runaway n fuggitivo, -a mf

un-'down adj (area) in abbandono; (person) esaurito ● n analisi f

rung[1] /rʌŋ/ n (of ladder) piolo m

rung[2] ▷**RING**[2]

runner /'rʌnə(r)/ n podista mf; (in race) corridore, -trice mf; (on sledge) pattino m. ~ bean n fagiolino m. ~-up n secondo, -a mf classificato, -a

running /'rʌnɪŋ/ adj in corsa; (water) corrente; four times ~ quattro volte di seguito ● n corsa f; (management) direzione f; be in the ~ essere in lizza. ~ **commentary** n cronaca f

runny /'rʌnɪ/ adj semiliquido; ~ nose naso che cola

unway n pista f

rupture /'rʌptʃə(r)/ n rottura f; (Med) ernia f ● vt rompere; ~ oneself farsi venire l'ernia ● vi rompersi

rural /'rʊərəl/ adj rurale

ruse /ruːz/ n astuzia f

rush[1] /rʌʃ/ n (Bot) giunco m

rush[2] n fretta f; in a ~ di fretta ● vi precipitarsi ● vt far premura a; ~ sb to hospital trasportare qcno di corsa all'ospedale. ~-**hour** n ora f di punta

Russia /'rʌʃə/ n Russia f. ~n adj & n russo, -a mf; (language) russo m

rust /rʌst/ n ruggine f ● vi arrugginirsi

rustle /'rʌsl/ vi frusciare ● vt far frusciare; Am rubare (cattle). □ ~ **up** vt ☐ rimediare

rustproof adj a prova di ruggine

rusty /'rʌstɪ/ adj (-ier, -iest) arrugginito

rut /rʌt/ n solco m; in a ~ ☐ nella routine

ruthless /'ruːθlɪs/ adj spietato. ~**ness** n spietatezza f

ye /raɪ/ n segale f

Ss

sabot|age /'sæbətɑːʒ/ n sabotaggio m ● vt sabotare. ~**eur** n sabotatore, -trice mf

saccharin /'sækərɪn/ n saccarina f

sachet /'sæʃeɪ/ n bustina f; (scented) sacchetto m profumato

sack[1] /sæk/ vt (plunder) saccheggiare

sack[2] n sacco m; get the ~ ☐ essere licenziato ● vt ☐ licenziare. ~**ing** n tela f per sacchi; (☐: dismissal) licenziamento m

sacrament /'sækrəmənt/ n sacramento m

sacred /'seɪkrɪd/ adj sacro

sacrifice /'sækrɪfaɪs/ n sacrificio m ● vt sacrificare

sacrilege /'sækrɪlɪdʒ/ n sacrilegio m

sad /sæd/ adj (sadder, saddest) triste. ~**den** vt rattristare

saddle /'sædl/ n sella f ● vt sellare; I've been ~d with... fig mi hanno affibbiato...

sad|ly /'sædlɪ/ adv tristemente; (unfortunately) sfortunatamente. ~**ness** n tristezza f

safe /seɪf/ adj sicuro; (out of danger) salvo; (object) al sicuro; ~ and sound sano e salvo ● n cassaforte f. ~**guard** n protezione f ● vt proteggere. ~**ly** adv in modo sicuro; (arrive) senza incidenti; (assume) con certezza

safety /'seɪftɪ/ n sicurezza f. ~-**belt** n cintura f di sicurezza. ~-**deposit box** n cassetta f di sicurezza. ~-**pin** n spilla f di sicurezza o da balia. ~-**valve** n valvola f di sicurezza

sag /sæg/ vi (pt/pp sagged) abbassarsi

saga /'sɑːgə/ n saga f

sage /seɪdʒ/ n (herb) salvia f

Sagittarius /sædʒɪˈteərɪəs/ n Sagittario m

said /sed/ ▷ SAY

sail /seɪl/ n vela f; (trip) giro m in barca a vela ● vi navigare; (Sport) praticare la vela; (leave) salpare ● vt pilotare

sailing /ˈseɪlɪŋ/ n vela f. ~-boat n barca f a vela. ~-ship n veliero m

sailor /ˈseɪlə(r)/ n marinaio m

saint /seɪnt/ n santo, -a mf. ~ly adj da santo

sake /seɪk/ n for the ~ of (person) per il bene di; (peace) per amor di; for the ~ of it per il gusto di farlo

salad /ˈsæləd/ n insalata f. ~ bowl n insalatiera f. ~ cream n salsa f per condire l'insalata. ~-dressing n condimento m per insalata

salary /ˈsælərɪ/ n stipendio m

sale /seɪl/ n vendita f (at reduced prices) svendita f; for/on ~ in vendita

sales|man /ˈseɪlzmən/ n venditore m; (traveller) rappresentante m. ~-woman n venditrice f

saliva /səˈlaɪvə/ n saliva f

salmon /ˈsæmən/ n salmone m

saloon /səˈluːn/ n (Auto) berlina f; (Am: bar) bar m

salt /sɔːlt/ n sale m ● adj salato; (fish, meat) sotto sale ● vt salare; (cure) mettere sotto sale. ~-cellar n saliera f. ~ 'water n acqua f di mare. ~y adj salato

salute /səˈluːt/ n (Mil) n saluto m ● vt salutare ● vi fare il saluto

salvage /ˈsælvɪdʒ/ n (Naut) recupero m ● vt recuperare

salvation /sælˈveɪʃn/ n salvezza f. S~ 'Army n Esercito m della Salvezza

same /seɪm/ adj stesso (as di) ● pron the ~ lo stesso; be all the ~ essere tutti uguali ● adv the ~ nello stesso

modo; all the ~ (however) lo stesso; the ~ to you altrettanto

sample /ˈsɑːmpl/ n campione m ● vt testare

sanction /ˈsæŋkʃn/ n (approval) autorizzazione f; (penalty) sanzione f ● vt autorizzare

sanctuary /ˈsæŋktjʊərɪ/ n (Relig) santuario m; (refuge) asilo m; (for wild-life) riserva f

sand /sænd/ n sabbia f ● vt ~ [down] carteggiare

sandal /ˈsændl/ n sandalo m

sandpaper /ˈsændpeɪpə(r)/ n carta f vetrata ● vt cartavetrare

sandwich /ˈsænwɪdʒ/ n tramezzino m ● vt ~ed between schiacciato tra

sandy /ˈsændɪ/ adj (-ier, -iest) (beach, soil) sabbioso; (hair) biondiccio

sane /seɪn/ adj (not mad) sano di mente; (sensible) sensato

sang /sæŋ/ ▷ SING

sanitary /ˈsænɪtərɪ/ adj igienico; (system) sanitario. ~ napkin n Am, ~ towel n assorbente m igienico

sanitation /sænɪˈteɪʃn/ n impianti mpl igienici

sanity /ˈsænɪtɪ/ n sanità f inv di mente; (common sense) buon senso m

sank /sæŋk/ ▷ SINK

sapphire /ˈsæfaɪə(r)/ n zaffiro m ● adj blu zaffiro

sarcas|m /ˈsɑːkæzm/ n sarcasmo m. ~tic adj sarcastico

sardine /sɑːˈdiːn/ n sardina f

sash /sæʃ/ n fascia f; (for dress) fusciacca f

sat /sæt/ ▷ SIT

satchel /ˈsætʃl/ n cartella f

satellite /ˈsætəlaɪt/ n satellite m. ~ dish n antenna f parabolica. ~ television n televisione f via satellite

satin /ˈsætɪn/ n raso m ● attrib di raso

satire /ˈsætaɪə(r)/ n satira f

satirical /səˈtɪrɪkl/ adj satirico

satisfaction /sætɪsˈfækʃn/ n soddisfazione f; be to sb's ∼ soddisfare qcno

satisfactor|y /sætɪsˈfæktərɪ/ adj soddisfacente. ∼ily adv in modo soddisfacente

satisf|y /ˈsætɪsfaɪ/ vt (pt/pp -fied) soddisfare; (convince) convincere; be ∼ied essere soddisfatto. ∼ying adj soddisfacente

satphone /ˈsætfəʊn/ n telefono m satellitare

saturat|e /ˈsætʃəreɪt/ vt inzuppare (with di); (Chem), fig saturare (with di). ∼ed adj saturo

Saturday /ˈsætədeɪ/ n sabato m

sauce /sɔːs/ n salsa f; (cheek) impertinenza f. ∼pan n pentola f

saucer /ˈsɔːsə(r)/ n piattino m

saucy /ˈsɔːsɪ/ adj (-ier, -iest) impertinente

Saudi Arabia /saʊdɪəˈreɪbɪə/ n Arabia f Saudita

sauna /ˈsɔːnə/ n sauna f

saunter /ˈsɔːntə(r)/ vi andare a spasso

sausage /ˈsɒsɪdʒ/ n salsiccia f; (dried) salame m

savage /ˈsævɪdʒ/ adj feroce; (tribe, custom) selvaggio ● n selvaggio, -a mf ● vt fare a pezzi. ∼ry n ferocia f

save /seɪv/ n (Sport) parata f ● vt salvare (from da); (keep, collect) tenere; risparmiare (time, money); (avoid) evitare; (Sport) parare (goal); (Comput) salvare, memorizzare ● vi ∼ [up] risparmiare ● prep salvo

saver /ˈseɪvə(r)/ n risparmiatore, -trice mf

savings /ˈseɪvɪŋz/ npl (money) risparmi mpl. ∼ account n libretto m di risparmio. ∼ bank n cassa f di risparmio

saviour /ˈseɪvjə(r)/ n salvatore m

savour /ˈseɪvə(r)/ n sapore m ● vt

assaporare. ∼y adj salato; fig rispettabile

saw[1] /sɔː/ see see[1]

saw[2] n sega f ● vt/i (pt sawed, pp sawn or sawed) segare. ∼dust n segatura f

saxophone /ˈsæksəfəʊn/ n sassofono m

say /seɪ/ n have one's ∼ dire la propria; have a ∼ avere voce in capitolo ● vt/i (pt/pp said) dire; that is to ∼ cioè; that goes without ∼ing questo è ovvio; when all is said and done alla fine dei conti. ∼ing n proverbio m

scab /skæb/ n crosta f; pej crumiro m

scald /skɔːld/ vt scottare; (milk) scaldare ● n scottatura f

scale[1] /skeɪl/ n (of fish) scaglia f

scale[2] n scala f; on a grand ∼ su vasta scala ● vt (climb) scalare. □ ∼ down vt diminuire

scales /skeɪlz/ npl (for weighing) bilancia fsg

scalp /skælp/ n cuoio m capelluto

scamper /ˈskæmpə(r)/ vi ∼ away sgattaiolare via

scan /skæn/ n (Med) scanning m inv, scansioscintigrafia f ● vt (pt/pp scanned) scrutare; (quickly) dare una scorsa a; (Med) fare uno scanning di

scandal /ˈskændl/ n scandalo m; (gossip) pettegolezzi mpl. ∼ize vt scandalizzare. ∼ous adj scandaloso

Scandinavia /skændɪˈneɪvɪə/ n Scandinavia f. ∼n adj & n scandinavo, -a mf

scanner /ˈskænə(r)/ n (Comput) scanner m inv

scant /skænt/ adj scarso

scant|y /ˈskæntɪ/ adj (-ier, -iest) scarso; (clothing) succinto. ∼ily adv scarsamente; (clothed) succintamente

scapegoat /ˈskeɪp-/ n capro m

espiatorio

scar /skɑː(r)/ n cicatrice f ● vt (pt/pp **scarred**) lasciare una cicatrice a

scarc|e /skeəs/ adj scarso; fig raro; **make oneself ~e** ① svignarsela. **~ely** adv appena; **~ely anything** quasi niente. **~ity** n scarsezza f

scare /skeə(r)/ n spavento m; (panic) panico m ● vt spaventare; **be ~d** aver paura (**of** di)

'scarecrow n spaventapasseri m inv

scarf /skɑːf/ n (pl **scarves**) sciarpa f; (square) foulard m inv

scarlet /'skɑːlət/ adj scarlatto. **~ fever** n scarlattina f

scary /'skeərɪ/ adj **be ~** far paura

scathing /'skeɪðɪŋ/ adj mordace

scatter /'skætə(r)/ vt spargere; (disperse) disperdere ● vi disperdersi. **~-brained** adj ① scervellato. **~ed** adj sparso

scavenge /'skævɪndʒ/ vi frugare nella spazzatura. **~r** n persona f che fruga nella spazzatura

scenario /sɪ'nɑːrɪəʊ/ n scenario m

scene /siːn/ n scena f; (quarrel) scenata f; **behind the ~s** dietro le quinte

scenery /'siːnərɪ/ n scenario m

scenic /'siːnɪk/ adj panoramico

scent /sent/ n odore m; (trail) scia f; (perfume) profumo m. **~ed** adj profumato (**with** di)

sceptic|al /'skeptɪkl/ adj scettico. **~ism** n scetticismo m

schedule /'ʃedjuːl/ n piano m, programma m; (of work) programma m; (timetable) orario m; **behind ~** in indietro; **on ~** nei tempi previsti; **according to ~** secondo i tempi previsti ● vt prevedere. **~d flight** n volo m di linea

scheme /skiːm/ n (plan) piano m; (plot) macchinazione f ● vi pej macchinare

scholar /'skɒlə(r)/ n studioso, -a m. **~ly** adj erudito. **~ship** n erudizione f; (grant) borsa f di studio

school /skuːl/ n scuola f; (in university) facoltà f; (of fish) branco m

school: **~boy** n scolaro m. **~girl** n scolara f. **~ing** n istruzione f. **~-teacher** n insegnante mf

sciatica /saɪ'ætɪkə/ n sciatica f

scien|ce /'saɪəns/ n scienza f; **~ce fiction** fantascienza f. **~tific** adj scientifico. **~tist** n scienziato, -a mf

scissors /'sɪzəz/ npl forbici fpl

scoff¹ /skɒf/ vi **~ at** schernire

scoff² vt ① divorare

scold /skəʊld/ vt sgridare. **~ing** n sgridata f

scoop /skuːp/ n paletta f; (Journ) scoop m inv ● **scoop out** vt svuotare. □ **~ up** vt tirare su

scope /skəʊp/ n portata f; (opportunity) opportunità f inv

scorch /skɔːtʃ/ vt bruciare. **~er** n ① giornata f torrida. **~ing** adj caldissimo

score /skɔː(r)/ n punteggio m; (individual) punteggio m; (Mus) partitura f; (for film, play) musica f; **a ~ [of]** (twenty) una ventina [di]; **keep [the] ~** tenere il punteggio; **on that ~** a questo proposito ● vt segnare (goal); (cut) incidere ● vi far punti; (in football etc) segnare; (keep score) tenere il punteggio. **~r** n segnapunti m inv; (of goals) giocatore, -trice mf che segna

scorn /skɔːn/ n disprezzo m ● vt disprezzare. **~ful** adj sprezzante

Scorpio /'skɔːpɪəʊ/ n Scorpione m

scorpion /'skɔːpɪən/ n scorpione m

Scot /skɒt/ n scozzese mf

scotch vt far cessare

Scotch /skɒtʃ/ adj scozzese ● n (whisky) whisky m [scozzese]

Scot|land /'skɒtlənd/ n Scozia f. **~s**, **~tish** adj scozzese

scoundrel /ˈskaʊndrəl/ n mascalzone m

scour¹ /ˈskaʊə(r)/ vt *(search)* perlustrare

scour² vt *(clean)* strofinare

scourge /skɜːdʒ/ n flagello m

scout /skaʊt/ n esploratore m • vi ~ for andare in cerca di

Scout n [Boy] ~ [boy]scout m inv

scowl /skaʊl/ n sguardo m torvo • vi guardare [di] storto

scram /skræm/ vi 🖪 levarsi dai piedi

scramble /ˈskræmbl/ n *(climb)* arrampicata f • vi *(clamber)* arrampicarsi; ~ for azzuffarsi per un *(Teleph)* creare delle interferenze in; *(eggs)* strapazzare

scrap¹ /skræp/ n *(🖪: fight)* litigio m

scrap² n pezzetto m; *(metal)* ferraglia f; ~s pl *(of food)* avanzi mpl • vt *(pt/pp scrapped)* buttare via

scrap-book n album m inv

scrape /skreɪp/ vt raschiare; *(damage)* graffiare. □ ~ through vi passare per un pelo. □ ~ together vt racimolare

scraper /ˈskreɪpə(r)/ n raschietto m

scrap-yard n deposito m di ferraglia; *(for cars)* cimitero m delle macchine

scratch /skrætʃ/ n graffio m; *(to relieve itch)* grattata f; start from ~ partire da zero; up to ~ *(work)* all'altezza • vt graffiare; *(to relieve itch)* grattare • vi grattarsi. ~ card n gratta e vinci m inv

scrawl /skrɔːl/ n scarabocchio m • vt/i scarabocchiare

scream /skriːm/ n strillo m • vt/i strillare

screech /skriːtʃ/ n stridore m • vi stridere • vt strillare

screen /skriːn/ n paravento m; *(Cinema, TV)* schermo m • vt proteggere; *(conceal)* riparare; proiettare *(film)*; *(candidates)* passare al setaccio; *(Med)* sottoporre a visita medica. ~ing n *(Med)* visita f medica; *(of film)* proiezione f. ~play n sceneggiatura f

screw /skruː/ n vite f • vt avvitare. □ ~ up vt *(crumple)* accartocciare; strizzare *(eyes)*; storcere *(face)*; *(🖫: bungle)* mandare all'aria. ~driver n cacciavite m

scribble /ˈskrɪbl/ n scarabocchio m • vt/i scarabocchiare

script /skrɪpt/ n scrittura f *(a mano)*; *(of film)* sceneggiatura f

scroll /skrəʊl/ n rotolo m *(di pergamena)*; *(decoration)* voluta f. □ ~ down vi scorrere in giù

scrounge /skraʊndʒ/ vt/i scroccare. ~r n scroccone, -a mf

scrub¹ /skrʌb/ n *(land)* boscaglia f

scrub² vt/i *(pt/pp scrubbed)* strofinare; *(🖫: cancel)* cancellare *(plan)*

scruff /skrʌf/ n by the ~ of the neck per la collottola

scruffy /ˈskrʌfi/ adj *(-ier, -iest)* trasandato

scruple /ˈskruːpl/ n scrupolo m

scrupulous /ˈskruːpjʊləs/ adj scrupoloso

scrutin|ize /ˈskruːtɪnaɪz/ vt scrutinare. ~y n *(look)* esame m minuzioso

scuffle /ˈskʌfl/ n tafferuglio m

sculpt /skʌlpt/ vt/i scolpire. ~or n scultore m. ~ure n scultura f

scum /skʌm/ n schiuma f; (people) feccia f

scurry /'skʌri/ vi (pt/pp -ied) affrettare il passo

scuttle /'skʌtl/ vi (hurry) ~ away correre via

sea /siː/ n mare m; at ~ in mare; fig confuso; by ~ via mare. ~board n costiera f. ~food n frutti mpl di mare. ~gull n gabbiano m.

seal¹ /siːl/ n (Zool) foca f

seal² n sigillo m; (Techn) chiusura f ermetica ● vt sigillare; (Techn) chiudere ermeticamente. □ ~ off vt bloccare (area)

'sea-level n livello m del mare

seam /siːm/ n cucitura f; (of coal) strato m

'seaman n marinaio m

seamy /'siːmi/ adj sordido; (area) malfamato

seance /'seɪɑːns/ n seduta f spiritica

search /sɜːtʃ/ n ricerca f; (official) perquisizione f; in ~ of alla ricerca di ● vt frugare (for alla ricerca di); perlustrare (area); (officially) perquisire ● vi ~ for cercare. ~ing adj penetrante

search: ~light n riflettore m. ~-party n squadra f di ricerca

sea: ~sick adj be/get ~ avere il mal di mare. ~side n at/to the ~side al mare

season /'siːzn/ n stagione f ● vt (flavour) condire. ~able adj, ~al adj stagionale. ~ing n condimento m

'season ticket n abbonamento m

seat /siːt/ n (chair) sedia f; (in car) sedile m; (place to sit) posto m [a sedere]; (bottom) didietro m; (of government) sede f; take a ~ sedersi ● vt mettere a sedere; (have seats for) aver posti [a sedere] per; remain ~ed mantenere il proprio posto. ~-belt n cintura f di sicurezza

sea: ~weed n alga f marina. ~worthy adj in stato di navigare

seclu|ded /sɪ'kluːdɪd/ adj appartato. ~sion n isolamento m

second¹ /sɪ'kɒnd/ vt (transfer) distaccare

second² /'sekənd/ adj secondo; on ~ thoughts ripensandoci meglio ● secondo m; ~s pl (goods) merce fsg di seconda scelta; have ~s (at meal) fare il bis; John the S~ Giovanni Secondo ● adv (in race) al secondo posto ● vt assistere; appoggiare (proposal)

secondary /'sekəndri/ adj secondario. ~ school n ≈ scuola f media (inferiore e superiore)

second: ~ class adv (travel, send) in seconda classe. ~-class adj di seconda classe

'second hand n (on clock) lancetta f dei secondi

second-'hand adj & adv di seconda mano

secondly /'sekəndli/ adv in secondo luogo

second-'rate adj di second'ordine

secrecy /'siːkrəsi/ n segretezza f; in ~ in segreto

secret /'siːkrɪt/ adj segreto ● n segreto m

secretarial /sekrə'teəriəl/ adj (work, staff) di segreteria

secretary /'sekrətəri/ n segretario, -a mf

secretive /'siːkrətɪv/ adj riservato. ~ness n riserbo m

sect /sekt/ n setta f. ~arian /sek'teəriən/ adj settario

section /'sekʃn/ n sezione f

sector /'sektə(r)/ n settore m

secular /'sekjʊlə(r)/ adj secolare; (education) laico

secure /sɪ'kjʊə(r)/ adj sicuro ● vt proteggere; chiudere bene (door); rendere stabile (ladder); (obtain) assicurarsi. ~ly adv saldamente

security /sɪ'kjʊərəti/ n sicurezza f;

(*for loan*) garanzia *f.* ~ies *npl* titoli *mpl*

sedate[1] /sɪ'deɪt/ *adj* posato

sedate[2] *vt* somministrare sedativi a

sedation /sɪ'deɪʃn/ *n* somministrazione *f* di sedativi; **be under ~** essere sotto l'effetto di sedativi

sedative /'sedətɪv/ *adj* sedativo ● *n* sedativo *m*

sediment /'sedɪmənt/ *n* sedimento *m*

seduce /sɪ'djuːs/ *vt* sedurre

seduct|ion /sɪ'dʌkʃn/ *n* seduzione *f*. ~**ive** *adj* seducente

see[1] /siː/ *v* (*pt* saw, *pp* seen) ● *vt* vedere; (*understand*) capire; (*escort*) accompagnare; **go and ~** andare a vedere; (*visit*) andare a trovare; ~ **you!** ci vediamo!; ~ **you later!** a più tardi!; ~**ing that** visto che ● *vi* vedere; (*understand*) capire; ~ **that** (*make sure*) assicurarsi che; ~ **about** occuparsi di. □ ~ **off** *vt* veder partire; (*chase away*) mandar via. □ ~ **through** *vi* vedere attraverso; *fig* non farsi ingannare da ● *vt* portare a buon fine. □ ~ **to** *vi* occuparsi di

seed /siːd/ *n* seme *m*; (*Tennis*) testa *f* di serie; **go to ~** fare seme; *fig* lasciarsi andare. ~**ed player** *n* (*Tennis*) testa *f* di serie. ~**ling** *n* pianticella *f*

seedy /'siːdɪ/ *adj* (-ier, -iest) squallido

seek /siːk/ *vt* (*pt/pp* sought) cercare

seem /siːm/ *vi* sembrare. ~**ingly** *adv* apparentemente

seen /siːn/ ▷**SEE**[1]

seep /siːp/ *vi* filtrare

see-saw /'siːsɔː/ *n* altalena *f*

seethe /siːð/ *vi* ~ **with anger** ribollire di rabbia

'see-through *adj* trasparente

segment /'segmənt/ *n* segmento *m*; (*of orange*) spicchio *m*

segregat|e /'segrɪgeɪt/ *vt* segregare. ~**ion** *n* segregazione *f*

seize /siːz/ *vt* afferrare; (*Jur*) confi-

scare. □ ~ **up** *vi* (*Techn*) bloccarsi

seizure /'siːʒə(r)/ *n* (*Jur*) confisca *f*; (*Med*) colpo *m* [apoplettico]

seldom /'seldəm/ *adv* raramente

select /sɪ'lekt/ *adj* scelto; (*exclusive*) esclusivo ● *vt* scegliere; selezionare (team). ~**ion** *n* selezione *f*. ~**ive** *adj* selettivo. ~**or** *n* (*Sport*) selezionatore, -trice *mf*

self /self/ *n* io *m*

self: ~-**ad'dressed** *adj* con il proprio indirizzo. ~'**catering** *adj* in appartamento attrezzato di cucina. ~'**centred** *adj* egocentrico. ~'**confidence** *n* fiducia *f* in se stesso. ~'**confident** *adj* sicuro di sé. ~'**conscious** *adj* impacciato. ~-**con'tained** *adj* (flat) con ingresso indipendente. ~-**con'trol** *n* autocontrollo *m*. ~-**de'fence** *n* autodifesa *f*; (*Jur*) legittima difesa *f*. ~-**em'ployed** *adj* che lavora in proprio. ~-'**evident** *adj* ovvio. ~-**in'dulgent** *adj* indulgente con se stesso. ~-'**interest** *n* interesse *m* personale

self|ish /'selfɪʃ/ *adj* egoista. ~**ishness** *n* egoismo *m*. ~**less** *adj* disinteressato

self: ~-**pity** *n* autocommiserazione *f*. ~-**portrait** *n* autoritratto *m*. ~-**re'spect** *n* amor *m* proprio. ~-'**righteous** *adj* presuntuoso. ~-'**sacrifice** *n* abnegazione *f*. ~-'**satisfied** *adj* compiaciuto di sé. ~-'**service** *n* self-service *m inv* ● *attrib* self-service. ~-**suf'ficient** *adj* autosufficiente

sell /sel/ *v* (*pt/pp* sold) ● *vt* vendere; **be sold out** essere esaurito ● *vi* vendersi. □ ~ **off** *vt* liquidare

seller /'selə(r)/ *n* venditore, -trice *mf*

Sellotape® /'seləʊ-/ *n* nastro *m* adesivo, scotch® *m*

'sell-out *n* (①: *betrayal*) tradimento *m*; **be a ~** (*concert*:) fare il tutto esaurito

s

semblance /'semblǝns/ n parvenza f

semester /sɪ'mestǝ(r)/ n Am semestre m

semi /'semɪ/: ~**breve** /'semɪbriːv/ n semibreve f. ~**circle** n semicerchio m. ~**circular** adj semicircolare. ~**colon** n punto e virgola f. ~**de'tached** adj gemella • n casa f gemella. ~**'final** n semifinale f

seminar /'semɪnɑː(r)/ n seminario m. ~**y** n seminario m

senate /'senǝt/ n senato m. ~**or** n senatore m

send /send/ vt/i (pt/pp sent) mandare; ~ **for** mandare a chiamare (person); far venire (thing). ~**er** n mittente mf. ~**off** n commiato m

senil|**e** /'siːnaɪl/ adj arteriosclerotico; (Med) senile. ~**ity** n senilismo m

senior /'siːnɪǝ(r)/ adj più vecchio; (in rank) superiore • n (in rank) superiore mf; (in sport) senior mf; **she's two years my** ~ è più vecchia di me di due anni. ~ **'citizen** n anziano, -a mf

seniority /siːnɪ'ɒrǝtɪ/ n anzianità f inv di servizio

sensation /sen'seɪʃn/ n sensazione f. ~**al** adj sensazionale. ~**ally** adv in modo sensazionale

sense /sens/ n senso m; (common ~) buon senso m; **in a** ~ in un certo senso; **make** ~ aver senso • vt sentire. ~**less** adj insensato; (unconscious) privo di sensi

sensib|**le** /'sensǝbl/ adj sensato; (suitable) appropriato. ~**y** adv in modo appropriato

sensitiv|**e** /'sensǝtɪv/ adj sensibile; (touchy) suscettibile. ~**ely** adv con sensibilità. ~**ity** n sensibilità f inv

sensual /'sensjʊǝl/ adj sensuale. ~**ity** n sensualità f inv

sensuous /'sensjʊǝs/ adj voluttuoso

sent /sent/ ▷**SEND**

sentence /'sentǝns/ n frase f; (Jur) sentenza f; (punishment) condanna f • vt ~ **to** condannare a

sentiment /'sentɪmǝnt/ n sentimento m; (opinion) opinione f; (sentimentality) sentimentalismo m. ~**al** adj sentimentale; pej sentimentalista. ~**ality** n sentimentalità f inv

sentry /'sentrɪ/ n sentinella f

separable /'sepǝrǝbl/ adj separabile

separate[1] /'sepǝrǝt/ adj separato. ~**ly** adv separatamente

separat|**e**[2] /'sepǝreɪt/ vt separare • vi separarsi. ~**ion** n separazione f

September /sep'tembǝ(r)/ n settembre m

septic /'septɪk/ adj settico; **go** ~ infettarsi. ~ **tank** n fossa f biologica

sequel /'siːkwǝl/ n seguito m

sequence /'siːkwǝns/ n sequenza f

Serbia /'sɜːbɪǝ/ n Serbia f

serenade /serǝ'neɪd/ n serenata f • vt fare una serenata a

seren|**e** /sɪ'riːn/ adj sereno. ~**ity** n serenità f

sergeant /'sɑːdʒǝnt/ n sergente m

serial /'sɪǝrɪǝl/ n racconto m a puntate; (TV) sceneggiato m a puntate; (Radio) commedia f radiofonica. ~**ize** vt pubblicare a puntate; (Radio, TV) trasmettere a puntate. ~ **killer** n serial killer mf inv. ~ **number** n numero m di serie. ~ **port** n (Comput) porta f seriale

series /'sɪǝriːz/ n serie f inv

serious /'sɪǝrɪǝs/ adj serio; (illness, error) grave. ~**ly** adv seriamente; (ill) gravemente; **take** ~**ly** prendere sul serio. ~**ness** n serietà f inv; (of situation) gravità f inv

sermon /'sɜːmǝn/ n predica f

serum /'sɪǝrǝm/ n siero m

servant /'sɜːvǝnt/ n domestico, -a mf

serve /sɜːv/ n (Tennis) servizio m • vt servire; scontare (sentence); ~ **its purpose** servire al proprio scopo; **it** ~**s you right!** ben ti sta!; ~**s two**

per due persone ●vi prestare servizio; (Tennis) servire; ~ as servire da. ~r n (Comput) server m inv

service /'sɜ:vɪs/ n servizio m; (Relig) funzione f; (maintenance) revisione f; ~s pl forze fpl armate; (on motorway) area f di servizio; **in the ~s** sotto le armi; **of ~ to** utile a; **out of ~** (machine:) guasto ●vt (Techn) revisionare. **~able** adj utilizzabile; (hard-wearing) resistente; (practical) pratico

service: ~ **charge** n servizio m. ~ **station** n stazione f di servizio

serviette /sɜ:vɪ'et/ n tovagliolo m

servile /'sɜ:vaɪl/ adj servile

session /'seʃn/ n seduta f; (Jur) sessione f; (Univ) anno m accademico

set /set/ n serie f, set m inv; (of crockery, cutlery) servizio m; (Radio, TV) apparecchio m; (Math) insieme m; (Theat) scenario m; (Cinema, Tennis) set m inv; (of people) circolo m; (of hair) messa f in piega ●adj (ready) pronto; (rigid) fisso; (book) in programma; **be ~ on doing sth** essere risoluto a fare qcsa; **be ~ in one's ways** essere abitudinario ●v (pt/pp set, pres p setting) ●vt mettere, porre; mettere (alarm clock); assegnare (task, homework); fissare (date, limit); chiedere (questions); montare (gem); assestare (bone); apparecchiare (table); ~ **fire to** dare fuoco a; ~ **free** liberare ●vi (sun:) tramontare; (jelly, concrete:) solidificarsi; **about doing sth** mettersi a fare qcsa. □ ~ **back** vt mettere indietro; (hold up) ritardare; (🄵: cost) costare a. □ ~ **off** vi partire ●vt avviare; mettere (alarm); fare esplodere (bomb). □ ~ **out** vi partire ●vt ~ **out to do sth** proporsi di fare qcsa ●vt disporre; (state) esporre. □ ~ **to** vi mettersi all'opera. □ ~ **up** vt fondare (company); istituire (committee)

'**set-back** n passo m indietro

settee /se'ti:/ n divano m

setting /'setɪŋ/ n scenario m; (position) posizione f; (of sun) tramonto m; (of jewel) montatura f

settle /'setl/ vt (decide) definire; risolvere (argument); fissare (date); calmare (nerves); saldare (bill) ●vi (to live) stabilirsi; (snow, dust, bird:) posarsi; (subside) assestarsi; (sediment:) depositarsi. □ ~ **down** vi sistemarsi; (stop making noise) calmarsi. □ ~ **for** vt accontentarsi di. □ ~ **up** vi regolare i conti

settlement /'setlmənt/ n (agreement) accordo m; (of bill) saldo m; (colony) insediamento m

settler /'setlə(r)/ n colonizzatore, -trice m/f

'**set-to** n 🄵 zuffa f; (verbal) battibecco m

'**set-up** n situazione f

seven /'sevn/ adj sette. ~**teen** adj diciassette. ~**teenth** adj diciassettesimo

seventh /'sevnθ/ adj settimo

seventieth /'sevntɪɪθ/ adj settantesimo

seventy /'sevntɪ/ adj settanta

sever /'sevə(r)/ vt troncare (relations)

several /'sevrəl/ adj & pron parecchi

sever|e /sɪ'vɪə(r)/ adj severo; (pain) violento; (illness) grave; (winter) rigido. ~**ely** adv severamente; (ill) gravemente. ~**ity** /-'verətɪ/ n severità f; (of pain) violenza f; (of illness) gravità f; (of winter) rigore m

sew /səʊ/ vt/i (pt sewed, pp sewn or sewed) cucire. □ ~ **up** vt ricucire

sewage /'su:ɪdʒ/ n acque fpl di scolo

sewer /'su:ə(r)/ n fogna f

sewing /'səʊɪŋ/ n cucito m; (work) lavoro m di cucito. ~ **machine** n macchina f da cucire

sewn /səʊn/ ▷SEW

sex /seks/ n sesso m; **have ~** avere rapporti sessuali. ~**ist** adj sessista. ~ **offender** n colpevole mf di delitti a sfondo sessuale

sexual /'seksjʊəl/ adj sessuale. ~ **intercourse** n rapporti mpl sessuali. ~**ity** n sessualità f inv. ~**ly** adv sessualmente

sexy /'seksɪ/ adj (-ier, -iest) sexy

shabb|y /'ʃæbɪ/ adj (-ier, -iest) scialbo; (treatment) meschino. ~**iness** n trasandatezza f; (of treatment) meschinità f inv

shack /ʃæk/ n catapecchia f ● **shack up with** vi 🗓 vivere con

shade /ʃeɪd/ n ombra f; (of colour) sfumatura f; (for lamp) paralume m; (Am: for window) tapparella f; a ~ better un tantino meglio ● vt riparare dalla luce; (draw lines on) ombreggiare. ~s npl 🗓 occhiali mpl da sole

shadow /'ʃædəʊ/ n ombra f; S~ Cabinet governo m ombra ● vt (follow) pedinare. ~**y** adj ombroso

shady /'ʃeɪdɪ/ adj (-ier, -iest) ombroso; (🗓: disreputable) losco

shaft /ʃɑːft/ n (Techn) albero m; (of light) raggio m; (of lift, mine) pozzo m; ~**s** pl (of cart) stanghe fpl

shaggy /'ʃægɪ/ adj (-ier, -iest) irsuto; (animal) dal pelo arruffato

shake /ʃeɪk/ n scrollata f ● v (pt shook, pp shaken) ● vt scuotere; agitare (bottle); far tremare (building); ~ **hands** with stringere la mano a ● vi tremare. □ ~ **off** vt scrollarsi di dosso. ~**up** n (Pol) rimpasto m; (Comm) ristrutturazione f

shaky /'ʃeɪkɪ/ adj (-ier, -iest) tremante; (table etc) traballante; (unreliable) vacillante

shall /ʃæl/ v aux I ~ go andrò; we ~ see vedremo; what ~ I do? cosa faccio?; I'll come too, ~ I? vengo anch'io, no?; thou shalt not kill liter non uccidere

shallow /'ʃæləʊ/ adj basso, poco profondo; (dish) poco profondo; fig superficiale

sham /ʃæm/ adj falso ● n finzione f;

(person) spaccone, -a mf ● vt (pt/pp shammed) simulare

shambles /'ʃæmblz/ n baraonda fsg

shame /ʃeɪm/ n vergogna f; **it's a** ~ **that** è un peccato che; **what a** ~! che peccato! ~**-faced** adj vergognoso

shame|ful /'ʃeɪmfl/ adj vergognoso. ~**less** adj spudorato

shampoo /ʃæm'puː/ n shampoo m inv ● vt fare uno shampoo a

shape /ʃeɪp/ n forma f; (figure) ombra f; **take** ~ prendere forma; **get back in** ~ ritornare in forma ● vt dare forma a (into di) ● vi ~ **[up]** mettere la testa a posto; ~ **up** nicely mettersi bene. ~**less** adj informe

share /ʃeə(r)/ n porzione f; (Comm) azione f ● vt dividere; condividere (views) ● vi dividere. ~**holder** n azionista mf

shark /ʃɑːk/ n squalo m, pescecane m; fig truffatore, -trice mf

sharp /ʃɑːp/ adj (knife etc) tagliente; (pencil) appuntito; (drop) a picco; (reprimand) severo; (outline) marcato; (alert) acuto; (unscrupulous) senza scrupoli; ~ **pain** fitta f ● adv a punto; (Mus) fuori tono; **look** ~! sbrigati! n (Mus) diesis m inv. ~**en** vt affilare (knife); appuntire (pencil)

shatter /'ʃætə(r)/ vt frantumare; fig mandare in frantumi; ~**ed** (🗓: exhausted) a pezzi ● vi frantumarsi

shav|e /ʃeɪv/ n rasatura f; **have a** ~ farsi la barba ● vt radere ● vi radersi. ~**er** n rasoio m elettrico. ~**ing-brush** n pennello m da barba; ~**ing foam** n schiuma f da barba; ~**ing soap** n sapone m da barba

shawl /ʃɔːl/ n scialle m

she /ʃiː/ pron lei

sheaf /ʃiːf/ n (pl sheaves) fascio m

shear /ʃɪə(r)/ vt (pt sheared, pp shorn or sheared) tosare

shears /ʃɪəz/ npl (for hedge) cesoie fpl

shed¹ /ʃed/ n baracca f; (for cattle) stalla f

shed² vt (pt/pp shed, pres p shedding) perdere; versare (blood, tears); ~ **light on** far luce su

sheep /ʃiːp/ n inv pecora f. ~**-dog** n cane m da pastore

sheepish /ˈʃiːpɪʃ/ adj imbarazzato. ~**ly** adv con aria imbarazzata

sheer /ʃɪə(r)/ adj puro; (steep) a picco; (transparent) trasparente ● adv a picco

sheet /ʃiːt/ n lenzuolo m; (of paper) foglio m; (of glass, metal) lastra f

shelf /ʃelf/ n (pl shelves) ripiano m; (set of shelves) scaffale m

shell /ʃel/ n conchiglia f; (of egg, snail, tortoise) guscio m; (of crab) corazza f; (of unfinished building) ossatura f; (Mil) granata f ● vt sgusciare (peas); (Mil) bombardare. □ ~ **out** vi 🎫 sborsare

'shellfish n inv mollusco m; (Culin) frutti mpl di mare

shelter /ˈʃeltə(r)/ n rifugio m; (air raid) ~ rifugio m antiaereo ● vt riparare (from da); fig mettere al riparo; (give lodging to) dare asilo a ● vi rifugiarsi. ~**ed** adj (spot) riparato; (life) ritirato

shelve /ʃelv/ vt accantonare (project)

shelving /ˈʃelvɪŋ/ n (shelves) ripiani mpl

shepherd /ˈʃepəd/ n pastore m ● vt guidare. ~**'s pie** n pasticcio m di carne tritata e patate

sherry /ˈʃeri/ n sherry m

shield /ʃiːld/ n scudo m; (for eyes) maschera f; (Techn) schermo m ● vt proteggere (from da)

shift /ʃɪft/ n cambiamento m; (in position) spostamento m; (at work) turno m ● vt spostare; (take away) togliere; riversare (blame) ● vi spostarsi; (wind) cambiare; (🎫: move quickly) darsi una mossa

shifty /ˈʃɪfti/ adj (-ier, -iest) pej losco; (eyes) sfuggente

shimmer /ˈʃɪmə(r)/ n luccichio m ● vi luccicare

shin /ʃɪn/ n stinco m

shine /ʃaɪn/ n lucentezza f; give sth a ~ dare una lucidata a qcsa ● vi (pt/pp shone) ● vi splendere; (reflect light) brillare; (hair, shoes:) essere lucido ● vt a ~ **a light on** puntare una luce su

shingle /ˈʃɪŋgl/ n (pebbles) ghiaia f

shiny /ˈʃaɪni/ adj (-ier, -iest) lucido

ship /ʃɪp/ n nave f ● vt (pt/pp shipped) spedire; (by sea) spedire via mare

ship: ~**ment** n spedizione f; (consignment) carico m. ~**ping** n trasporto m; (traffic) imbarcazioni fpl. ~**shape** adj & adv in perfetto ordine. ~**wreck** n naufragio m. ~**wrecked** adj naufragato. ~**yard** n cantiere m navale

shirk /ʃɜːk/ vt scansare. ~**er** n scansafatiche mf inv

shirt /ʃɜːt/ n camicia f; in ~**-sleeves** in maniche di camicia

shit /ʃɪt/ 🎫 n & int merda f ● vi (pt/pp shit) cagare

shiver /ˈʃɪvə(r)/ n brivido m ● vi rabbrividire

shoal /ʃəʊl/ n (of fish) banco m

shock /ʃɒk/ n (impact) urto m; (Electr) scossa f [elettrica]; fig colpo m, shock m inv; (Med) shock m inv; **get a** ~ (Electr) prendere la scossa ● vt scioccare. ~**ing** adj scioccante; (🎫: weather, handwriting etc) tremendo

shod /ʃɒd/ ▷ SHOE

shoddy /ˈʃɒdi/ adj (-ier, -iest) scadente

shoe /ʃuː/ n scarpa f; (of horse) ferro m ● vt (pt/pp shod, pres p shoeing) ferrare (horse)

shoe: ~**horn** n calzante m. ~**lace** n laccio m da scarpa

shone /ʃɒn/ ▷ SHINE

shoo /ʃuː/ vt ~ away cacciar via ● int sciò

shook /ʃʊk/ ▷ SHAKE

shoot /ʃuːt/ n (Bot) germoglio m; (hunt) battuta f di caccia ● v (pt/pp shot) ● vt sparare; girare (film) ● vi (hunt) andare a caccia. □ ~ **down** vt abbattere. □ ~ **out** vi (rush) precipitarsi fuori. □ ~ **up** vi (grow) crescere in fretta; (prices): salire di colpo

shop /ʃɒp/ n negozio m; (workshop) officina f; talk ~ 🔢 parlare di lavoro ● vi (pt/pp shopped) far compere; **go** ~**ping** andare a fare compere. □ ~ **around** vi confrontare i prezzi

shop: ~**assistant** n commesso, -a mf. ~**keeper** n negoziante mf. ~**lifter** n taccheggiatore, -trice mf. ~**lifting** n taccheggio m; ~**per** n compratore, -trice mf.

shopping /ʃɒpɪŋ/ n compere fpl; (articles) acquisti mpl; **do the** ~ fare la spesa. ~ **bag** n borsa f per la spesa. ~ **centre** n centro m commerciale. ~ **trolley** n carrello m

shop: ~**steward** n rappresentante mf sindacale. ~**'window** n vetrina f

shore /ʃɔː(r)/ n riva f

shorn /ʃɔːn/ ▷ SHEAR

short /ʃɔːt/ adj corto; (not lasting) breve; (person) basso; (curt) brusco; **a** ~ **time ago** poco tempo fa; **be** ~ **of sth** essere a corto di; **be in** ~ **supply** essere scarso; fig essere raro; **Mick is** ~ **for Michael** Mick è il diminutivo di Michael ● adv bruscamente; **in** ~ in breve; ~ **of doing** a meno di fare; **go** ~ essere privato (**of** di); **stop** ~ **of doing sth** non arrivare fino a fare qcsa; **cut** ~ interrompere (meeting, holiday); **to cut a long story** ~ per farla breve

shortage /ʃɔːtɪdʒ/ n scarsità f inv

short: ~**bread** n biscotto m di pasta frolla. ~'**circuit** n corto m circuito. ~'**coming** n difetto m. ~ '**cut** n scorciatoia f

shorten /ʃɔːtn/ vt abbreviare; accorciare (garment)

shorthand n stenografia f

short|ly /ʃɔːtlɪ/ adv presto; ~**ly before/after** poco prima/dopo. ~**ness** n brevità f inv; (of person) bassa statura f

shorts /ʃɔːts/ npl calzoncini mpl corti

short-'sighted adj miope

shot /ʃɒt/ ▷ SHOOT ● n colpo m; (person) tiratore m; (Phot) foto f; (injection) puntura f; (🔢 attempt) prova f; **like a** ~ 🔢 come un razzo. ~**gun** n fucile m da caccia

should /ʃʊd/ v aux I ~ **go** dovrei andare; I ~ **have seen him** avrei dovuto vederlo; I ~ **like** mi piacerebbe; **this** ~ **be enough** questo dovrebbe bastare; **if he** ~ **come** se dovesse venire

shoulder /ʃəʊldə(r)/ n spalla f ● vt mettersi in spalla; fig accollarsi. ~**bag** n borsa f a tracolla. ~**blade** n scapola f. ~**strap** n spallina f; (of bag) tracolla f

shout /ʃaʊt/ n grido m ● vt/i gridare. □ ~ **at** vi alzar la voce con. □ ~ **down** vt azzittire gridando

shove /ʃʌv/ n spintone m ● vt spingere; (🔢 put) ficcare ● vi spingere. □ ~ **off** vi 🔢 togliersi di torno

shovel /ʃʌvl/ n pala f ● vt (pt/pp shovelled) spalare

show /ʃəʊ/ n (display) manifestazione f; (exhibition) mostra f; (ostentation) ostentazione f; (Theat), (TV) spettacolo m; (programme) programma m; **on** ~ esposto ● v (pt showed, pp shown) ● vt mostrare; (put on display) esporre; proiettare (film) ● vi (film): essere proiettato; **your slip is** ~**ing** ti si vede la sottoveste. □ ~ **in** vt fare accomodare. □ ~ **off** vi 🔢 mettersi in mostra ● vt mettere in mostra. □ ~ **up** vi risaltare; (🔢 arrive) farsi vedere ● vt (🔢 embarrass) far fare una brutta figura a '**show-down** n regolamento m dei conti

shower /ˈʃaʊə(r)/ n doccia f; (of rain) acquazzone m; have a ∼ fare la doccia ●vt ∼ with coprire di ●vi fare la doccia. ∼**proof** adj impermeabile. ∼**y** adj da acquazzoni

'**show-jumping** n concorso m ippico

shown /ʃəʊn/ ▷**SHOW**

'**show-off** n esibizionista mf

showy /ˈʃəʊɪ/ adj appariscente

shrank /ʃræŋk/ ▷**SHRINK**

shred /ʃred/ n brandello m; fig briciolo m ●vt (pt/pp shredded) fare a brandelli; (Culin) tagliuzzare. ∼**der** n distruttore m di documenti

shrewd /ʃruːd/ adj accorto. ∼**ness** n accortezza f

shriek /ʃriːk/ n strillo m ●vt/i strillare

shrift /ʃrɪft/ n give sb short ∼ liquidare qcno rapidamente

shrill /ʃrɪl/ adj penetrante

shrimp /ʃrɪmp/ n gamberetto m

shrine /ʃraɪn/ n (place) santuario m

shrink /ʃrɪŋk/ vi (pt shrank, pp shrunk) restringersi; (draw back) ritrarsi (from da)

shrivel /ˈʃrɪvl/ vi (pt/pp shrivelled) raggrinzare

shroud /ʃraʊd/ n sudario m; fig manto m

Shrove /ʃrəʊv/ n ∼ Tuesday martedì m grasso

shrub /ʃrʌb/ n arbusto m

shrug /ʃrʌg/ n scrollata f di spalle ●vt/i (pt/pp shrugged) ∼ [one's shoulders] scrollare le spalle

shrunk /ʃrʌŋk/ ▷**SHRINK**. ∼**en** adj rimpicciolito

shudder /ˈʃʌdə(r)/ n fremito m ●vi fremere

shuffle /ˈʃʌfl/ vi strascicare i piedi ●vt mescolare (cards)

shun /ʃʌn/ vt (pt/pp shunned)

rifuggire

shunt /ʃʌnt/ vt smistare

shush /ʃʊʃ/ int zitto!

shut /ʃʌt/ v (pt/pp shut, pres p shutting) ●vt chiudere ●vi chiudersi; (shop:) chiudere. □ ∼ **down** vt/i chiudere. □ ∼ **up** vt chiudere; **T** far tacere □ ∼ **up!** stai zitto!

shutter /ˈʃʌtə(r)/ n serranda f; (Phot) otturatore m

shuttle /ˈʃʌtl/ n navetta f ●vi far la spola

shuttle: ∼**cock** n volano m. ∼ **service** n servizio m pendolare

shy /ʃaɪ/ adj (timid) timido. ∼**ness** n timidezza f

Sicily /ˈsɪsɪlɪ/ n Sicilia f. ∼**ian** adj & n siciliano, -a m

sick /sɪk/ adj ammalato; (humour) macabro; be ∼ (vomit) vomitare; be ∼ of sth **T** essere stufo di qcsa; feel ∼ aver la nausea

sickly /ˈsɪklɪ/ adj (-ier, -iest) malaticcio. ∼**ness** n malattia f; (vomiting) nausea f. ∼**ness benefit** n indennità f di malattia

side /saɪd/ n lato m; (of person, mountain) fianco m; (of road) bordo m; on the ∼ (as sideline) come attività secondaria; ∼ **by** ∼ fianco a fianco; take ∼s immischiarsi; take sb's ∼ prendere le parti di qcno; be on the safe ∼ andare sul sicuro ●attrib laterale ●vi ∼ with parteggiare per

side: ∼**board** n credenza f. ∼**effect** n effetto m collaterale. ∼**lights** npl luci fpl di posizione. ∼**line** n attività f inv complementare. ∼**show** n attrazione f. ∼**step** vt schivare. ∼**track** vt sviare. ∼**walk** n Am marciapiede m. ∼**ways** adv obliquamente

siding /ˈsaɪdɪŋ/ n binario m di raccordo

sidle /ˈsaɪdl/ vi camminare furtivamente (up to verso)

siege /siːdʒ/ n assedio m

sieve /sɪv/ n setaccio m ● vt setacciare

sift /sɪft/ vt setacciare; ~ [through] fig passare al setaccio

sigh /saɪ/ n sospiro m ● vi sospirare

sight /saɪt/ n vista f; (on gun) mirino m; the ~s pl le cose da vedere; at first ~ a prima vista; be within/out of ~ essere/non essere in vista; lose ~ of perdere di vista; know by ~ conoscere di vista. have bad ~ vederci male ● vt avvistare

'sightseeing n go ~ andare a visitare posti

sign /saɪn/ n segno m; (notice) insegna f ● vt/i firmare. □ ~ on vi (as unemployed) presentarsi all'ufficio di collocamento; (Mil) arruolarsi

signal /ˈsɪɡnl/ n segnale m ● v (pt/pp signalled) ● vt segnalare ● vi fare segnali; ~ to sb far segno a qcno (to di). ~-box n cabina f di segnalazione

signature /ˈsɪɡnətʃə(r)/ n firma f. ~ tune n sigla f [musicale]

significance /sɪɡˈnɪfɪkəns/ n significato m. ~t adj significativo

signify /ˈsɪɡnɪfaɪ/ vt (pt/pp -ied) indicare

signpost /ˈsaɪn-/ n segnalazione f stradale

silence /ˈsaɪləns/ n silenzio m● vt far tacere. ~r n (on gun) silenziatore m; (Auto) marmitta f

silent /ˈsaɪlənt/ adj silenzioso; (film) muto; remain ~ rimanere in silenzio. ~ly adv silenziosamente

silhouette /sɪluˈet/ n sagoma f, silhouette f inv ● vt be ~d profilarsi

silicon /ˈsɪlɪkən/ n silicio m. ~ chip piastrina f di silicio

silk /sɪlk/ n seta f ● attrib di seta. ~worm n baco m da seta

silky /ˈsɪlkɪ/ adj (-ier, -iest) come la seta

silly /ˈsɪlɪ/ adj (-ier, -iest) sciocco

silt /sɪlt/ n melma f

silver /ˈsɪlvə(r)/ adj d'argento; (paper) argentato ● n argento m; (silverware) argenteria f

silver: ~-plated adj placcato d'argento. ~ware n argenteria f

SIM card /ˈsɪmkɑːd/ n carta f SIM

similar /ˈsɪmɪlə(r)/ adj simile. ~ity n somiglianza f. ~ly adv in modo simile

simile /ˈsɪmɪlɪ/ n similitudine f

simmer /ˈsɪmə(r)/ vi bollire lentamente ● vt far bollire lentamente. □ ~ down vi calmarsi

simple /ˈsɪmpl/ adj semplice; (person) sempliciotto. ~-minded adj sempliciotto

simplicity /sɪmˈplɪsətɪ/ n semplicità f inv

simply /ˈsɪmplɪ/ adv semplicemente

simulate /ˈsɪmjʊleɪt/ vt simulare. ~ion n simulazione f

simultaneous /sɪmlˈteɪnɪəs/ adj simultaneo

sin /sɪn/ n peccato m ● vi (pt/pp sinned) peccare

---

since /sɪns/

● prep da I've been waiting ~ Monday aspetto da lunedì

● adv da allora

● conj da quando; (because) siccome

---

sincere /sɪnˈsɪə(r)/ adj sincero. ~ly adv sinceramente; Yours ~ly distinti saluti

sincerity /sɪnˈserətɪ/ n sincerità f inv

sinful /ˈsɪnfl/ adj peccaminoso

sing /sɪŋ/ vt/i (pt sang, pp sung) cantare

singe /sɪndʒ/ vt (pres p singeing) bruciacchiare

singer /ˈsɪŋə(r)/ n cantante mf

single /ˈsɪŋgl/ adj solo; (not double) semplice; (unmarried) celibe; (woman) nubile; (room) singolo; (bed) a una piazza ●n (ticket) biglietto m di sola andata; (record) singolo m; ∼s pl (Tennis) singolo m ●**single out** vt scegliere; (distinguish) distinguere

single-handed adj & adv da solo

singular /'sɪŋɡjʊlə(r)/ adj (Gram) singolare ●n singolare m. ∼**ly** adv singolarmente

sinister /'sɪnɪstə(r)/ adj sinistro

sink /sɪŋk/ n lavandino m ●v (pt sank, pp sunk) ●vi affondare ●vt affondare (ship); scavare (shaft); investire (money). □ ∼ **in** vi penetrare; **it took a while to ∼ in** (🄵: be understood) c'è voluto un po' a capirlo

sinner /'sɪnə(r)/ n peccatore, -trice mf

sip /sɪp/ n sorso m ●vt (pt/pp sipped) sorseggiare

siphon /'saɪfn/ n (bottle) sifone m ●**siphon off** vt travasare (con sifone)

sir /sɜː(r)/ n signore m; S∼ (title) Sir m; **Dear S∼s** Spettabile ditta

siren /'saɪrən/ n sirena f

sister /'sɪstə(r)/ n sorella f; (nurse) [infermiera f] caposala f. ∼**-in-law** (pl ∼**s-in-law**) cognata f. ∼**ly** adj da sorella

sit /sɪt/ v (pt/pp **sat**, pres p **sitting**) ●vi essere seduto; (sit down) sedersi; (committee:) riunirsi ●vt sostenere (exam). □ ∼ **back** vi fig starsene con le mani in mano. □ ∼ **up** vi mettersi a sedere. □ ∼ **up** vi mettersi seduto; (not slouch) star seduto diritto; (stay up) stare alzato

site /saɪt/ n posto m; (Archaeol) sito m; (building ∼) cantiere m ●vt collocare

sit-in /'sɪtɪn/ n occupazione f (di fabbrica, ecc.)

sitting /'sɪtɪŋ/ n seduta f; (for meals) turno m. ∼**-room** n salotto m

situat|e /'sɪtjʊeɪt/ vt situare. ∼**ed** adj situato. ∼**ion** n situazione f; (location) posizione f; (job) posto m

six /sɪks/ adj sei. ∼**teen** adj sedici.

∼**teenth** adj sedicesimo

sixth /sɪksθ/ adj sesto

sixtieth /'sɪkstɪɪθ/ adj sessantesimo

sixty /'sɪkstɪ/ adj sessanta

size /saɪz/ n dimensioni fpl; (of clothes) taglia f, misura f; (of shoes) numero m; **what ∼ is the room?** che dimensioni ha la stanza? ●**size up** vt 🄵 valutare

sizzle /'sɪzl/ vi sfrigolare

skate[1] /skeɪt/ n inv (fish) razza f

skate[2] /skeɪt/ n pattino m ●vi pattinare

skateboard /'skeɪtbɔːd/ n skateboard m inv

skater /'skeɪtə(r)/ n pattinatore, -trice mf

skating /'skeɪtɪŋ/ n pattinaggio m. ∼**-rink** n pista f di pattinaggio

skeleton /'skelɪtn/ n scheletro m. ∼ **'key** n passe-partout m inv. ∼ **'staff** n personale m ridotto

sketch /sketʃ/ n schizzo m; (Theat) sketch m inv ●vt fare uno schizzo di

sketch|y /'sketʃɪ/ adj (-ier, -iest) abbozzato. ∼**ily** adv in modo abbozzato

ski /skiː/ n sci m inv ●vi (pt/pp **skied**, pres p **skiing**) sciare; **go ∼ing** andare a sciare

skid /skɪd/ n slittata f ●vi (pt/pp **skidded**) slittare

skier /'skiːə(r)/ n sciatore, -trice mf

skiing /'skiːɪŋ/ n sci m

skilful /'skɪlfl/ adj abile

'ski-lift n impianto m di risalita

skill /skɪl/ n abilità f inv. ∼**ed** adj dotato; (worker) specializzato

skim /skɪm/ vt (pt/pp **skimmed**) schiumare; scremare (milk). □ ∼ **off** vt togliere. □ ∼ **through** vt scorrere

skimp /skɪmp/ vi ∼ **on** lesinare su

skimpy /'skɪmpɪ/ adj (-ier, -iest) succinto

skin /skɪn/ n pelle f; (on fruit) buccia f ●vt (pt/pp **skinned**) spellare

skin: ∼**-deep** adj superficiale.

∼-diving n nuoto m subacqueo

skinny /'skɪnɪ/ adj (-ier, -iest) molto magro

skip[1] /skɪp/ n (container) benna f

skip[2] n salto m ● v (pt/pp skipped) ● vi saltellare; (with rope) saltare la corda ● vt omettere.

skipper /'skɪpə(r)/ n skipper m inv

skipping-rope /'skɪpɪŋrəʊp/ n corda f per saltare

skirmish /'skɜːmɪʃ/ n scaramuccia f

skirt /skɜːt/ n gonna f ● vt costeggiare

skittle /'skɪtl/ n birillo m

skulk /skʌlk/ vi aggirarsi furtivamente

skull /skʌl/ n cranio m

sky /skaɪ/ n cielo m. ∼light n lucernario m. ∼ marshal n guardia f armata a bordo di un aereo. ∼scraper n grattacielo m

slab /slæb/ n lastra f; (slice) fetta f; (of chocolate) tavoletta f

slack /slæk/ adj lento; (person) fiacco e fig fiacco o fa scansafatiche. □ ∼ off vi rilassarsi

slacken /'slækn/ vi allentare; ∼ [off] (trade): rallentare; (speed, rain): diminuire ● vt allentare; diminuire (speed)

slain /sleɪn/ ▷ SLAY

slam /slæm/ n (pt/pp slammed) ● vt sbattere; (fam: criticize) stroncare ● vi sbattere

slander /'slɑːndə(r)/ n diffamazione f ● vt diffamare. ∼ous adj diffamatorio

slang /slæŋ/ n gergo m. ∼y adj gergale

slant /slɑːnt/ n pendenza f; (point of view) angolazione f; on the ∼ in pendenza ● vt pendere; fig distorcere (report) ● vi pendere

slap /slæp/ n schiaffo m ● vt (pt/pp slapped) schiaffeggiare; (put) schiaffare ● adv in pieno

slap: ∼-dash adj [⏻] frettoloso

slash /slæʃ/ n taglio m ● vt tagliare; ridurre drasticamente (prices)

slat /slæt/ n stecca f

slate /sleɪt/ n ardesia f ● vt [⏻] fare a pezzi

slaughter /'slɔːtə(r)/ n macello m; (of people) massacro m ● vt macellare; massacrare (people). ∼house n macello m

slave /sleɪv/ n schiavo, -a mf ● vi ∼ [away] lavorare come un negro. ∼-driver n schiavista mf

slav|ery /'sleɪvərɪ/ n schiavitù f inv. ∼ish adj servile

slay /sleɪ/ vt (pt slew, pp slain) ammazzare

sleazy /'sliːzɪ/ adj (-ier, -iest) sordido

sledge /sledʒ/ n slitta f. ∼-hammer n martello m

sleek /sliːk/ adj liscio, lucente; (wellfed) pasciuto

sleep /sliːp/ n sonno m; go to ∼ addormentarsi; put to ∼ far addormentare ● v (pt/pp slept) ● vi dormire ● vt ∼ six ha sei posti letto. ∼er n (Rail) treno m con vagoni letto; (compartment) vagone m letto; be a light/heavy ∼er avere il sonno leggero/pesante

sleeping: ∼-bag n sacco m a pelo. ∼-car n vagone m letto. ∼-pill n sonnifero m

sleepless adj insonne

sleepy /'sliːpɪ/ adj (-ier, -iest) assonnato; be ∼ aver sonno

sleet /sliːt/ n nevischio m ● vi it is ∼ing nevischia

sleeve /sliːv/ n manica f; (for record) copertina f. ∼less adj senza maniche

sleigh /sleɪ/ n slitta f

slender /'slendə(r)/ adj snello; (fingers, stem) affusolato; fig scarso; (chance) magro

slept /slept/ ▷ SLEEP

slew¹ /sluː/ vi girare

slew² ▷SLAY

slice /slaɪs/ n fetta f ● vt affettare; ~d bread pane m a cassetta

slick /slɪk/ adj liscio; (cunning) astuto ● n (of oil) chiazza f di petrolio

slid|e /slaɪd/ n scivolata f; (in playground) scivolo m; (for hair) fermaglio m (per capelli); (Phot) diapositiva f ● v (pt/pp slid) ● vi scivolare ● vt far scivolare. ~-rule n regolo m calcolatore. ~ing adj scorrevole; (door, seat) scorrevole; ~ing scale scala f mobile

slight /slaɪt/ adj leggero; (importance) poco; (slender) esile. ~est adj minimo; not in the ~est niente affatto ● vt offendere ● n offesa f. ~ly adv leggermente

slim /slɪm/ adj (slimmer, slimmest) snello; fig scarso; (chance) magro ● vi dimagrire

slim|e /slaɪm/ n melma f. ~y adj melmoso; fig viscido

sling /slɪŋ/ n (Med) benda f al collo ● vt (pt/pp slung) 🔲 lanciare

slip /slɪp/ n scivolata f; (mistake) lieve errore m; (petticoat) sottoveste f; (for pillow) federa f; (paper) scontrino m; give sb the ~ 🔲 sbarazzarsi di qcno; ~ of the tongue lapsus m inv ● v (pt/pp slipped) ● vi scivolare; (go quickly) sgattaiolare; (decline) retrocedere ● vt he ~ped it into his pocket se l'è infilato in tasca; ~ sb's mind sfuggire di mente a qcno. □ ~ away vi sgusciar via; (time:) sfuggire. □ ~ into vi infilarsi (clothes). □ ~ up vi 🔲 sbagliare

slipper /ˈslɪpə(r)/ n pantofola f

slippery /ˈslɪpərɪ/ adj scivoloso

slip-road n bretella f

slipshod /ˈslɪpʃɒd/ adj trascurato

'slip-up n 🔲 sbaglio m

slit /slɪt/ n spacco m; (tear) strappo m; (hole) fessura f ● vt (pt/pp slit) tagliare

slither /ˈslɪðə(r)/ vi scivolare

slobber /ˈslɒbə(r)/ vi sbavare

slog /slɒg/ n [hard] ~ sgobbata f ● vi (pt/pp slogged) (work) sgobbare

slogan /ˈsləʊgən/ n slogan m inv

slop /slɒp/ v (pt/pp slopped) ● vt versare. □ ~ over vi versarsi

slop|e /sləʊp/ n pendenza f; (ski-) pista f ● vi essere inclinato, inclinarsi. ~ing adj in pendenza

sloppy /ˈslɒpɪ/ adj (-ier, -iest) (work) trascurato; (worker) negligente; (in dress) sciatto; (sentimental) sdolcinato

slosh /slɒʃ/ vi 🔲 (person, feet:) squazzare; (water:) scrosciare ● vt 🔲 (hit) colpire

slot /slɒt/ n fessura f; (time-) spazio m ● v (pt/pp slotted) ● vt infilare. □ ~ in vi incastrarsi

'slot-machine n distributore m automatico; (for gambling) slot-machine f inv

slouch /slaʊtʃ/ vi (in chair) stare scomposto

Slovakia /sləˈvækɪə/ n Slovacchia f

Slovenia /sləˈviːnɪə/ n Slovenia f

sloven|ly /ˈslʌvnlɪ/ adj sciatto. ~iness n sciatteria f

slow /sləʊ/ adj lento; be ~ (clock:) essere indietro; in ~ motion al rallentatore ● adv lentamente ● ~ down/up vt/i rallentare

slowly adv lentamente

sludge /slʌdʒ/ n fanghiglia f

slug /slʌg/ n lumacone m; (bullet) pallottoia f. ~gish adj lento

slum /slʌm/ n (house) tugurio m; ~s pl bassifondi mpl

slumber /ˈslʌmbə(r)/ vi dormire

slump /slʌmp/ n crollo m; (economic) depressione f ● vi crollare

slung /slʌŋ/ ▷SLING

slur /slɜː(r)/ n (discredit) calunnia f ● vt (pt/pp slurred) biascicare

slush /slʌʃ/ n pantano m nevoso; fig sdolcinatezza f. ~ fund n fondi mpl neri. ~y adj fangoso; (sentimental) sdolcinato

sly /slaɪ/ adj (-er, -est) scaltro ● on the ~ di nascosto

smack¹ /smæk/ n (on face) schiaffo m; (on bottom) sculaccione m ● vt (on face) schiaffeggiare; (on bottom) sculacciare; ~ one's lips far schioccare le labbra ● adv 🔢 in pieno

smack² vi ~ of fig sapere di

small /smɔːl/ adj piccolo; be out/ work etc until the ~ hours fare le ore piccole ● adv chop up ~ fare a pezzettini ● n the ~ of the back le reni fpl

small: ~ ads npl annunci mpl (commerciali). ~ 'change n spiccioli mpl. ~pox n vaiolo m. ~ talk n chiacchiere fpl

smart /smɑːt/ adj elegante; (clever) intelligente; (brisk) svelto; be ~ (🔢 cheeky) fare il furbo ● vi (hurt) bruciare

smash /smæʃ/ n fragore m; (collision) scontro m; (Tennis) schiacciata f ● vt spaccare; (Tennis) schiacciare ● vi spaccarsi; (crash) schiantarsi (into contro). ~ [hit] n successo m. ~ing adj 🔢 fantastico

smattering /'smætərɪŋ/ n infarinatura f

smear /smɪə(r)/ n macchia f; (Med) striscio m ● vt imbrattare; (coat) spalmare (with di); fig calunniare

smell /smel/ n odore m; (sense) odorato m ● v (pt/pp smelt or smelled) ● vt odorare; (sniff) annusare ● vi odorare (of di)

smelly /'smelɪ/ adj (-ier, -iest) puzzolente

smelt¹ /smelt/ ▷ **SMELL**

smelt² vt fondere

smile /smaɪl/ n sorriso m ● vi sorridere; ~ at sorridere a (sb); sorridere di (sth)

smirk /smɜːk/ n sorriso m compiaciuto

smithereens /smɪðə'riːnz/ npl

to/in ~ in mille pezzi

smock /smɒk/ n grembiule m

smog /smɒg/ n smog m inv

smoke /sməʊk/ n fumo m ● vt/i fumare. ~less adj senza fumo; (fuel) che non fa fumo

smoker /'sməʊkə(r)/ n fumatore, -trice mf; (Rail) vagone m fumatori

smoky /'sməʊkɪ/ adj (-ier, -iest) fumoso; (taste) di fumo

smooth /smuːð/ adj liscio; (movement) scorrevole; (sea) calmo; (manners) mellifluo ● vt lisciare. □ ~ out vt lisciare. ~ly adv in modo scorrevole

smother /'smʌðə(r)/ vt soffocare

smoulder /'sməʊldə(r)/ vi fumare; (with rage) consumarsi

smudge /smʌdʒ/ n macchia f ● vt/i imbrattare

smug /smʌg/ adj (smugger, smuggest) compiaciuto. ~ly adv con aria compiaciuta

smuggle /'smʌgl/ vt contrabbandare. ~r n contrabbandiere, a mf. ~ing n contrabbando m

snack /snæk/ n spuntino m. ~-bar n snack bar m inv

snag /snæg/ n (problem) intoppo m

snail /sneɪl/ n lumaca f; at a ~'s pace a passo di lumaca

snake /sneɪk/ n serpente m

snap /snæp/ n colpo m secco; (photo) istantanea f ● attrib (decision) istantaneo ● v (pt/pp snapped) ● vi (break) spezzarsi; ~ at (dog): cercare di azzannare; (person:) parlare seccamente a ● vt (break) spezzare; (say) dire seccamente; (Phot) fare un'istantanea di. □ ~ up vt afferrare

snappy /'snæpɪ/ adj (-ier, -iest) scorbutico; (smart) elegante; make it ~! sbrigati!

'snapshot n istantanea f

snare /sneə(r)/ n trappola f

snarl /snɑːl/ n ringhio m ● vi

ringhiare

snatch /snætʃ/ n strappo m; (*fragment*) brano m; (*theft*) scippo m; **make a ~ at** cercare di afferrare qcsa • vt strappare [di mano] (**from** a); (*steal*) scippare; rapire (*child*)

sneak /sniːk/ n 🔲 spia mf • vi (🔲: *tell tales*) fare la spia • vt (*take*) rubare; **~ a look at** dare una sbirciata a. □ **~ in/out** vi sgattaiolare dentro/fuori

sneakers /'sniːkəz/ npl Am scarpe fpl da ginnastica

sneaky /'sniːkɪ/ adj sornione

sneer /snɪə(r)/ n ghigno m • vi sogghignare; (*mock*) ridere di

sneeze /sniːz/ n starnuto m • vi starnutire

snide /snaɪd/ adj 🔲 insinuante

sniff /snɪf/ n (*of dog*) annusata f • vi tirare su col naso • vt odorare (*flower*) sniffare (*glue, cocaine*); (*dog:*) annusare

snigger /'snɪgə(r)/ n risatina f soffocata • vi ridacchiare

snip /snɪp/ n taglio m; (🔲: *bargain*) affare m • vt/i (*pt/pp* snipped) **~** [**at**] tagliare

snippet /'snɪpɪt/ n **a ~ of** information/news una breve notizia/informazione

snivel /'snɪvl/ vi (*pt/pp* snivelled) piagnucolare. **~ling** adj piagnucoloso

snob /snɒb/ n snob mf. **~bery** n snobismo m. **~bish** adj da snob

snooker /'snuːkə(r)/ n snooker m

snoop /snuːp/ n spia f • vi 🔲 curiosare

snooze /snuːz/ n sonnellino m • vi fare un sonnellino

snore /snɔː(r)/ vi russare

snorkel /'snɔːkl/ n respiratore m

snort /snɔːt/ n sbuffo m • vi sbuffare

snout /snaʊt/ n grugno m

snow /snəʊ/ n neve f • vi nevicare; **~ed under with** fig sommerso di

snow: **~ball** n palla f di neve • vi fare a palle di neve. **~board** n snowboard m. **~drift** n cumulo m di neve. **~fall** n nevicata f. **~flake** n fiocco m di neve. **~man** n pupazzo m di neve. **~plough** n spazzaneve m. **~storm** n tormenta f. **~y** adj nevoso

snub /snʌb/ n sgarbo m • vt (*pt/pp* snubbed) snobbare

'snub-nosed adj dal naso all'insù

snug /snʌg/ adj (snugger, snuggest) comodo; (*tight*) aderente

so /səʊ/
• adv così; **so far** finora; **so am I** anch'io; **so I see** così pare; **that is so** è così; **so much** così tanto; **so much the better** tanto meglio; **so it is** proprio così; **if so** se è così; **so as to** in modo così; **so long!** 🔲 a presto!

• pron **I hope/think/am afraid so** spero/penso/temo di sì; **I told you so** te l'ho detto; **because I say so** perché lo dico io; **I did so!** è vero!; **so saying/doing,...** così dicendo/facendo,...; **or so** circa; **very much so** sì, molto; **and so forth** or **on** e così via

• conj (*therefore*) perciò; (*in order that*) così; **so that** affinché; **so there!** ecco!; **so what!** e allora?; **so where have you been?** allora, dove sei stato?

soak /səʊk/ vt mettere a bagno • vi stare a bagno; **~ in** (liquid:) penetrare. □ **~ up** vt assorbire

soaking /'səʊkɪŋ/ n ammollo m • adj & adv **~** [**wet**] 🔲 inzuppato

so-and-so /'səʊənsəʊ/ n Tal dei Tali mf; (*euphemism*) specie f di imbecille

soap /səʊp/ n sapone m. **~ opera** n telenovela f. **~ powder** n detersivo m in polvere

soapy /'səʊpɪ/ adj (-ier, -iest) insaponato

soar /sɔ:(r)/ vi elevarsi; (prices:) salire alle stelle

sob /sɒb/ n singhiozzo m • vi (pt/pp sobbed) singhiozzare

sober /ˈsəʊbə(r)/ adj sobrio; (serious) serio • **sober up** vi ritornare sobrio

'so-called adj cosiddetto

soccer /ˈsɒkə(r)/ n calcio m

sociable /ˈsəʊʃəbl/ adj socievole

social /ˈsəʊʃl/ adj sociale; (sociable) socievole

socialis|m /ˈsəʊʃəlɪzm/ n socialismo m. ~**t** adj socialista • n socialista mf

socialize /ˈsəʊʃəlaɪz/ vi socializzare

social: ~ **se'curity** n previdenza f sociale. ~ **worker** n assistente mf sociale

society /səˈsaɪətɪ/ n società f inv

sociolog|ist /səʊsɪˈɒlədʒɪst/ n sociologo, -a mf. ~**y** n sociologia f

sock¹ /sɒk/ n calzino m; (kneelength) calza f

sock² n 🎵 pugno m • vt 🎵 dare un pugno a

socket /ˈsɒkɪt/ n (wall plug) presa f [di corrente]; (for bulb) portalampada m inv

soda /ˈsəʊdə/ n soda f; Am gazzosa f. ~ **water** n seltz m inv

sodium /ˈsəʊdɪəm/ n sodio m

sofa /ˈsəʊfə/ n divano m. ~ **bed** n divano m letto

soft /sɒft/ adj morbido, soffice; (voice) sommesso; (light, colour) tenue; (not strict) indulgente; (🎵: silly) stupido; have a ~ **spot for** sb avere un debole per qcno. ~ **drink** n bibita f analcolica

soften /ˈsɒfn/ vt ammorbidire; fig attenuare • vi ammorbidirsi

softly /ˈsɒftlɪ/ adv (say) sottovoce; (treat) con indulgenza; (play music) in sottofondo

software n software m

soggy /ˈsɒgɪ/ adj (-ier, -iest) zuppo

soil¹ /sɔɪl/ n suolo m

soil² vt sporcare

solar /ˈsəʊlə(r)/ adj solare

sold /səʊld/ ▷**SELL**

solder /ˈsəʊldə(r)/ n lega f da saldatura • vt saldare

soldier /ˈsəʊldʒə(r)/ n soldato m • **soldier on** vi perseverare

sole¹ /səʊl/ n (of foot) pianta f; (of shoe) suola f

sole² n (fish) sogliola f

sole³ adj unico, solo. ~**ly** adv unicamente

solemn /ˈsɒləm/ adj solenne. ~**ity** n solennità f inv

solicitor /səˈlɪsɪtə(r)/ n avvocato m

solid /ˈsɒlɪd/ adj solido; (oak, gold) massiccio • n (figure) solido m; ~**s** pl (food) cibi mpl solidi

solidarity /sɒlɪˈdærətɪ/ n solidarietà f inv

solidify /səˈlɪdɪfaɪ/ vi (pt/pp -ied) solidificarsi

solitary /ˈsɒlɪtərɪ/ adj solitario; (sole) solo. ~ **con'finement** n cella f di isolamento

solitude /ˈsɒlɪtju:d/ n solitudine f

solo /ˈsəʊləʊ/ n (Mus) assolo m • adj (flight) in solitario • adv in solitario. ~**ist** n solista mf

solstice /ˈsɒlstɪs/ n solstizio m

soluble /ˈsɒljəbl/ adj solubile

solution /səˈlu:ʃn/ n soluzione f

solve /sɒlv/ vt risolvere

solvent /ˈsɒlvənt/ adj solvente • n solvente m

sombre /ˈsɒmbə(r)/ adj tetro; (clothes) scuro

some /sʌm/ adj (a certain amount of) del; (a certain number of) qualche, alcuni; ~ **day** un giorno o l'altro; I need ~ **money/books** ho bisogno di soldi/libri; do ~ **shopping** fare qualche acquisto • pron (a certain amount) un po'; (a certain number) alcuni; I want ~ ne voglio

some: ~**body** /-bədɪ/ *pron & n* qualcuno *m*. ~**how** *adv* in qualche modo; ~**how or other** in un modo o nell'altro. ~**one** *pron & n* = somebody

somersault /'sʌməsɔːlt/ *n* capriola *f*; turn a ~ fare una capriola

'**something** *pron* qualche cosa, qualcosa; ~ **different** qualcosa di diverso; ~ **like** un po' come; (*approximately*) qualcosa come; see ~ **of sb** vedere qcno un po'

some: ~**time** *adv* un giorno o l'altro; ~**times** *adv* qualche volta. ~**what** *adv* piuttosto. ~**where** *adv* da qualche parte ●*pron* ~**where to** eat un posto in cui mangiare

son /sʌn/ *n* figlio *m*

sonata /sə'nɑːtə/ *n* sonata *f*

song /sɒŋ/ *n* canzone *f*

sonic /'sɒnɪk/ *adj* sonico. ~ '**boom** *n* bang *m inv* sonico

'**son-in-law** *n* (*pl* ~**s-in-law**) genero *m*

sonnet /'sɒnɪt/ *n* sonetto *m*

soon /suːn/ *adv* presto; (*in a short time*) tra poco; **as** ~ **as** [non] appena; **as** ~ **as possible** il più presto possibile; ~**er or later** prima o poi; **the** ~**er the better** prima è, meglio è; **no** ~**er had I arrived than...** ero appena arrivato quando...; **I would** ~**er go** preferirei andare; ~ **after** subito dopo

soot /sʊt/ *n* fuliggine *f*

soothe /suːð/ *vt* calmare

sooty /'sʊtɪ/ *adj* fuligginoso

sophisticated /sə'fɪstɪkeɪtɪd/ *adj* sofisticato

sopping /'sɒpɪŋ/ *adj & adv* **be** ~ [**wet**] essere bagnato fradicio

soppy /'sɒpɪ/ *adj* (-ier, -iest) 🔢 svenevole

soprano /sə'prɑːnəʊ/ *n* soprano *m*

sordid /'sɔːdɪd/ *adj* sordido

sore /sɔː(r)/ *adj* dolorante; (*Am:*

vexed) arrabbiato; **it's** ~ **fa male;** **have a** ~ **throat** avere mal di gola ●*n* piaga *f*. ~**ly** *adv* (tempted) seriamente

sorrow /'sɒrəʊ/ *n* tristezza *f*. ~**ful** *adj* triste

sorry /'sɒrɪ/ *adj* (-ier, -iest) (sad) spiacente; (wretched) pietoso; **you'll be** ~**!** te ne pentirai!; **I am** ~ mi dispiace; **be or feel** ~ **for** provare compassione per; ~**!** scusa!; (more polite) scusi!

sort /sɔːt/ *n* specie *f*; (🔢: person) tipo *m*; **it's a** ~ **of fish** è un tipo di pesce; **be out of** ~**s** (🔢: unwell) stare poco bene ●*vt* classificare. □ ~ **out** *vt* selezionare (papers); *fig* risolvere (problem); occuparsi di (person)

'**so-so** *adj & adv* così così

sought /sɔːt/ ▷ SEEK

soul /səʊl/ *n* anima *f*

sound¹ /saʊnd/ *adj* sano; (sensible) saggio; (secure) solido; (thrashing) clamoroso ●*adv* ~ **asleep** profondamente addormentato

sound² *n* suono *m*; (noise) rumore *m*; **I don't like the** ~ **of it** 🔢 non mi suona bene ●*vi* suonare; (seem) aver l'aria ●*vt* (pronounce) pronunciare; (Med) auscultare (chest). ~ **barrier** *n* muro *m* del suono. ~ **card** *n* (Comput) scheda *f* sonora. ~**less** *adj* silenzioso. □ ~ **out** *vt fig* sondare

soundly /'saʊndlɪ/ *adv* (sleep) profondamente; (defeat) clamorosamente

'**sound:** ~**proof** *adj* impenetrabile al suono. ~**track** *n* colonna *f* sonora

soup /suːp/ *n* minestra *f*. ~**ed-up** *adj* 🔢 (engine) truccato

sour /'saʊə(r)/ *adj* agro; (not fresh & fig) acido

source /sɔːs/ *n* fonte *f*

south /saʊθ/ *n* sud *m*; **to the** ~ **of** a sud di ●*adj* del sud, meridionale

● adv verso il sud

south: S~ 'Africa n Sudafrica m. S~ A'merica n America f del Sud. S~ American adj & n sudamericano, -a mf. ~-'east n sudest m

southerly /'sʌðəlɪ/ adj del sud

southern /'sʌðən/ adj del sud, meridionale; ~ Italy il Mezzogiorno m. ~er n meridionale mf

'southward[s] /-wəd[z]/ adv verso sud

souvenir /su:və'nɪə(r)/ n ricordo m, souvenir m inv

sovereign /'sɒvrɪn/ adj sovrano ● n sovrano, -a mf. ~ty n sovranità f inv

Soviet /'səʊvɪət/ adj sovietico; ~ Union Unione f Sovietica

sow¹ /saʊ/ n scrofa f

sow² /səʊ/ vt (pt sowed, pp sown or sowed) seminare

soya /'sɔɪə/ n ~ bean soia f

spa /spɑ:/ n stazione f termale

space /speɪs/ n spazio m ● adj (research etc) spaziale ● vt ~ [out] distanziare

space: ~ship n astronave f. ~shuttle n navetta f spaziale

spade /speɪd/ n vanga f; (for child) paletta f; ~s pl (in cards) picche fpl. ~work n lavoro m preparatorio

Spain /speɪn/ n Spagna f

spam /spæm/ n spam m

span¹ /spæn/ n spanna f; (of arch) luce f; (of time) arco m; (of wings) apertura f ● vt (pt/pp spanned) estendersi su

span² ▷SPICK

Spaniard /'spænjəd/ n spagnolo, -a mf. ~ish adj spagnolo ● n (language) spagnolo m; the ~ish pl gli spagnoli

spank /spæŋk/ vt sculacciare. ~ing n sculacciata f

spanner /'spænə(r)/ n chiave f inglese

spare /speə(r)/ adj (surplus) in più;

(additional) di riserva ● n (part) ricambio m ● vt risparmiare; (do without) fare a meno di; **can you ~ five minutes?** avresti cinque minuti?; **to ~** (surplus) in eccedenza. ~ **part** n pezzo m di ricambio. ~ **time** n tempo m libero. ~-'wheel n ruota f di scorta

spark /spɑ:k/ n scintilla f. ~ing-plug n (Auto) candela f

sparkle /'spɑ:kl/ n scintillio m ● vi scintillare. ~ing adj frizzante; (wine) spumante

sparrow /'spærəʊ/ n passero m

sparse /spɑ:s/ adj rado. ~ly adv scarsamente; ~ly populated a bassa densità di popolazione

spasm /'spæzm/ n spasmo m. ~odic adj spasmodico

spat /spæt/ ▷SPIT¹

spate /speɪt/ n (series) successione f; **be in full ~** essere in piena

spatial /'speɪʃl/ adj spaziale

spatter /'spætə(r)/ vt schizzare

spawn /spɔ:n/ n uova fpl (di pesci, rane, ecc.) ● vi deporre le uova ● vt fig generare

speak /spi:k/ v (pt spoke, pp spoken) ● vi parlare (to a); ~ing! (Teleph) sono io! ● vt dire; ~ one's mind dire quello che si pensa. □ ~ **for** vi parlare a nome di. □ ~ **up** vi parlare più forte; ~ **up for oneself** parlare a favore di

speaker /'spi:kə(r)/ n parlante m/f; (in public) oratore, -trice mf; (of stereo) cassa f

spear /spɪə(r)/ n lancia f

special /'speʃl/ adj speciale. ~ist n specialista mf. ~ity n specialità f inv

specialize /'speʃəlaɪz/ vi specializzarsi. ~ly adv specialmente; (particularly) particolarmente

species /'spi:ʃi:z/ n specie f inv

specific /spə'sɪfɪk/ adj specifico. ~ally adv in modo specifico

specify /'spesɪfaɪ/ vt (pt/pp -ied)

specificare

specimen /'spesɪmən/ n campione m

speck /spek/ n macchiolina f; (*particle*) granello m

specs /speks/ npl 🔢 occhiali mpl

spectacle /'spektəkl/ n (*show*) spettacolo m. ~s npl occhiali mpl

spectacular /spek'tækjʊlə(r)/ adj spettacolare

spectator /spek'teɪtə(r)/ n spettatore, -trice mf

spectre /'spektə(r)/ n spettro m

spectrum /'spektrəm/ n (pl -tra) spettro m; fig gamma f

speculat|e /'spekjʊleɪt/ vi speculare. ~ion n speculazione f. ~ive adj speculativo. ~or n speculatore, -trice mf

sped /sped/ ▷SPEED

speech /spiːtʃ/ n linguaggio m; (*address*) discorso m. ~less adj senza parole

speed /spiːd/ n velocità f inv; (*gear*) marcia f; at ~ a tutta velocità ● vi (pt/pp sped) andare veloce; (pt/pp speeded) (*go too fast*) andare a velocità eccessiva. □ ~ up (pt/pp speeded up) vt/i accelerare

speed: ~boat n motoscafo m. ~camera n Autovelox® m inv. ~dating n speed dating m. ~ limit n limite m di velocità

speedometer /spiː'dɒmɪtə(r)/ n tachimetro m

speed|y /'spiːdɪ/ adj (-ier, -iest) rapido. ~ily adv rapidamente

spell¹ /spel/ n (turn) turno m; (of weather) periodo m

spell² /spel/ v (pt/pp spelled, spelt) ● vt how do you ~...? come si scrive...?; could you ~ that for me? me lo può compitare?; ~ disaster essere disastroso ● vi he can't ~ fa molti errori d'ortografia

spell³ /spel/ n (magic) incantesimo m. ~bound adj affascinato

spelling /'spelɪŋ/ n ortografia f

spelt /spelt/ ▷SPELL²

spend /spend/ vt/i (pt/pp spent) spendere; passare (time)

sperm /spɜːm/ n spermatozoo m; (semen) sperma m

spew /spjuː/ vt/i vomitare

spher|e /sfɪə(r)/ n sfera f. ~ical adj sferico

spice /spaɪs/ n spezia f; fig pepe m

spick /spɪk/ adj ~ and span lindo

spicy /'spaɪsɪ/ adj piccante

spider /'spaɪdə(r)/ n ragno m

spik|e /spaɪk/ n punta f; (Bot, Zool) spina f; (on shoe) chiodo m. ~y adj (plant) pungente

spill /spɪl/ v (pt/pp spilt or spilled) ● vt versare (blood) ● vi rovesciarsi

spin /spɪn/ v (pt/pp spun, pres p spinning) ● vt far girare; filare (wool); centrifugare (washing) ● vi girare; (washing machine:) centrifugare ● n rotazione f; (short drive) giretto m. □ ~ out vt far durare

spinach /'spɪnɪdʒ/ n spinaci mpl

spin-drier n centrifuga f

spine /spaɪn/ n spina f dorsale; (of book) dorso m; (Bot, Zool) spina f. ~less adj fig smidollato

spin-off n ricaduta f

spiral /'spaɪrəl/ adj a spirale ● n spirale f ● vi (pt/pp spiralled) formare una spirale. ~ 'staircase n scala f a chiocciola

spire /spaɪə(r)/ n guglia f

spirit /'spɪrɪt/ n spirito m; (courage) ardore m; ~s pl (alcohol) liquori mpl; in good ~s di buon umore; in low ~s abbattuto

spirited /'spɪrɪtɪd/ adj vivace; (courageous) pieno d'ardore

spiritual /'spɪrɪtjʊəl/ adj spirituale ● n spiritual m. ~ism n spiritismo m. ~ist n spiritista mf

spit¹ /spɪt/ n (for roasting) spiedo m

spit² /spɪt/ n sputo m ● vt/i (pt/pp spat, pres

p spitting) sputare; (cat:) soffiare; (fat:) sfrigolare; it's ~ting [with rain] piovviggina; the ~ting image of il ritratto spiccicato di

spite /spaɪt/ n dispetto m; in ~ of malgrado ● vt far dispetto a. ~**ful** adj indispettito

spittle /'spɪtl/ n saliva f

splash /splæʃ/ n schizzo m; (of colour:) macchia f; (🗉: drop) goccio m ● vt schizzare; ~ sb with sth schizzare qcno il qcsa ● vi schizzare. □ ~ **about** vi schizzarsi. □ ~ **down** vi (spacecraft:) ammarare

splendid /'splendɪd/ adj splendido

splendour /'splendə(r)/ n splendore m

splint /splɪnt/ n (Med) stecca f

splinter /'splɪntə(r)/ n scheggia f ● vi scheggiarsi

split /splɪt/ n fessura f; (quarrel:) rottura f; (division) scissione f; (tear) strappo m ● v (pt/pp split, pres p splitting) ● vt spaccare; (share, divide) dividere; (tear) strappare ● vi spaccarsi; (tear) strapparsi; (divide) dividersi; ~ **on sb** 🗉 denunciare qcno ● adj a ~ **second** una frazione f di secondo. □ ~ **up** vi dividersi ● vi (couple:) separarsi

splutter /'splʌtə(r)/ vi farfugliare

spoil /spɔɪl/ n ~s pl bottino msg ● v (pt/pp spoilt or spoiled) ● vt rovinare; viziare (person) ● vi andare a male. ~**sport** n guastafeste mf inv

spoke[1] /spəʊk/ n raggio m

spoke[2], **spoken** /'spəʊkn/ ▷SPEAK

'**spokesman** n portavoce m inv

sponge /spʌndʒ/ n spugna f ● vt pulire (con la spugna) ● vi ~ **on** scroccare da. ~**cake** n pan di Spagna

sponsor /'spɒnsə(r)/ n garante m; (Radio, TV) sponsor m inv; (god-parent) padrino m, madrina f; (for membership) socio, -a mf garante ● vt sponsorizzare. ~**ship** n sponsorizzazione f

spontaneous /spɒn'teɪnɪəs/ adj spontaneo

spoof /spu:f/ n 🗉 parodia f

spooky /'spu:kɪ/ adj (-ier, -iest) 🗉 sinistro

spool /spu:l/ n bobina f

spoon /spu:n/ n cucchiaio m ● vt mettere col cucchiaio. ~**feed** vt (pt/ pp -fed) fig imboccare. ~**ful** n cucchiaiata f

sporadic /spə'rædɪk/ adj sporadico

sport /spɔ:t/ n sport m in ● vt sfoggiare. ~**ing** adj sportivo. ~**ing chance** possibilità f inv

sports: ~**car** n automobile f sportiva. ~**man** n sportivo m. ~**woman** n sportiva f

spot /spɒt/ n macchia f; (pimple) brufolo m; (place) posto m; (in pattern) pois m inv; (of rain) goccia f; (of water) goccio m; ~s pl (rash) sfogo msg; a ~ of 🗉 un po' di; a ~ of bother qualche problema; on the ~ sul luogo; (immediately) immediatamente; in a [tight] ~ 🗉 in difficoltà ● vt (pt/pp spotted) macchiare; (🗉: notice) individuare

spot: ~ **check** n (without warning) controllo m a sorpresa; do a ~ check on sth dare una controllata a qcsa. ~**less** adj immacolato. ~**light** n riflettore m

spotted /'spɒtɪd/ adj (material) a pois

spotty /'spɒtɪ/ adj (-ier, -iest) (pimply) brufoloso

spouse /spaʊz/ n consorte mf

spout /spaʊt/ n becco m ● vi zampillare (from da)

sprain /spreɪn/ n slogatura f ● vt slogare

sprang /spræŋ/ ▷SPRING[2]

spray /spreɪ/ n spruzzo m; (preparation) spray m inv; (container) spruzzatore m inv ● vt spruzzare. ~**gun** n pistola f a spruzzo

spread /spred/ n estensione f; (of

disease) diffusione f; (paste) crema f; (🗎: feast) banchetto m ● v (pt/pp spread) ● vt spargere; spalmare (butter, jam); stendere (cloth, arms); diffondere (news, disease); dilazionare (payments); ~ sth with spalmare qcsa di ● vi spargersi; (butter:) spalmarsi; (disease:) diffondersi. ~-sheet n (Comput) foglio m elettronico. □ ~ out vi sparpagliare ● vi sparpagliarsi

spree /spriː/ n 🗎 go on a ~ far baldoria; go on a shopping ~ fare spese folli

sprightly /ˈspraɪtlɪ/ adj (-ier, -iest) vivace

spring¹ /sprɪŋ/ n primavera f ● attrib primaverile

spring² n (jump) balzo m; (water) sorgente f; (device) molla f; (elasticity) elasticità f inv ● v (pt sprang, pp sprung) ● vi balzare; (arise) provenire (from da) ● vt he just sprang it on me me l'ha detto a cose fatte compiuto. □ ~ up balzare; fig spuntare

spring: ~board n trampolino m. ~time n primavera f

sprinkl|e /ˈsprɪŋkl/ vt (scatter) spruzzare (liquid); spargere (flour, cocoa); ~ sth with spruzzare qcsa di (liquid); cospargere qcsa di (flour, cocoa). ~er n sprinkler m inv; (for lawn) irrigatore m. ~ing n (of liquid) spruzzatina f; (of pepper, salt) pizzico m; (of flour, sugar) spolverata f; (of knowledge) infarinatura f; (of people) pugno m

sprint /sprɪnt/ n sprint m inv ● vi fare uno sprint; (Sport) sprintare. ~er n sprinter mf inv

sprout /spraʊt/ n germoglio m; [Brussels] ~s pl cavolini mpl di Bruxelles ● vi germogliare

sprung /sprʌŋ/ ▷SPRING² ● adj molleggiato

spud /spʌd/ n 🗎 patata f

spun /spʌn/ ▷SPIN

spur /spɜː(r)/ n sperone m; (stimulus)

stimolo m; (road) svincolo m; on the ~ of the moment su due piedi ● vt (pt/pp spurred) ~ [on] fig spronare [a]

spurn /spɜːn/ vt sdegnare

spurt /spɜːt/ n getto m; (Sport) scatto m; put on a ~ fare uno scatto ● vi sprizzare; (increase speed) scattare

spy /spaɪ/ n spia f ● v (pt/pp spied) ● vi spiare ● vt (🗎: see) spiare. □ ~ on vi spiare

squabble /ˈskwɒbl/ n bisticcio m ● vi bisticciare

squad /skwɒd/ n squadra f; (Sport) squadra

squadron /ˈskwɒdrən/ n (Mil) squadrone m; (Aeron, Naut) squadriglia f

squalid /ˈskwɒlɪd/ adj squallido

squalor /ˈskwɒlə(r)/ n squallore m

squander /ˈskwɒndə(r)/ vt sprecare

square /skweə(r)/ adj quadrato; (meal) sostanzioso; (🗎: old-fashioned) vecchio stampo; all ~ 🗎 pari ● n quadrato m; (in city) piazza f; (on chessboard) riquadro m ● vt (settle) far quadrare; (Math) elevare al quadrato ● vi (agree) armonizzare

squash /skwɒʃ/ n (drink) spremuta f; (sport) squash m; (vegetable) zucca f ● vt schiacciare; soffocare (rebellion)

squat /skwɒt/ adj tarchiato ● n 🗎 edificio m occupato abusivamente ● vi (pt/pp squatted) accovacciarsi; ~ in occupare abusivamente. ~ter n occupante mf abusivo, -a

squawk /skwɔːk/ n gracchio m ● vi gracchiare

squeak /skwiːk/ n squittio m; (of hinge, brakes) scricchiolio m ● vi squittire; (hinge, brakes:) scricchiolare

squeal /skwiːl/ n strillo m; (of brakes) cigolio m ● vi strillare; (brakes:) cigolare

squeamish /ˈskwiːmɪʃ/ adj dallo stomaco delicato

squeeze /skwiːz/ n stretta f; (crush)

s

pigia pigia m inv ● vt premere; (to get juice) spremere; stringere (hand); (force) spingere a forza; (🔲: extort) estorcere (out of da). □~ **in/out** vi sguisciare dentro/fuori. □~ **up** vi stringersi

squid /skwɪd/ n calamaro m

squiggle /'skwɪgl/ n scarabocchio m

squint /skwɪnt/ n strabismo m ● vi essere strabico

squirm /skwɜ:m/ vi contorcersi; (feel embarrassed) sentirsi imbarazzato

squirrel /'skwɪrəl/ n scoiattolo m

squirt /skwɜ:t/ n spruzzo m; (🔲: person) presuntuoso m ● vt/i spruzzare

St abbr (Saint) S; abbr Street

stab /stæb/ n pugnalata f, coltellata f; (sensation) fitta f; (🔲: attempt) tentativo m ● vt (pt/pp stabbed) pugnalare, accoltellare

stability /stə'bɪlətɪ/ n stabilità f inv

stabilize /'steɪbɪlaɪz/ vt stabilizzare ● vi stabilizzarsi

stable¹ /'steɪbl/ adj stabile

stable² n stalla f; (establishment) scuderia f

stack /stæk/ n catasta f; (of chimney) comignolo m; (chimney) ciminiera f; (🔲: large quantity) montagna f ● vt accatastare

stadium /'steɪdɪəm/ n stadio m

staff /stɑ:f/ n (stick) bastone m; (employees) personale m; (teachers) corpo m insegnante; (Mil) Stato m Maggiore ● vt fornire di personale. ~-**room** n (Sch) sala f insegnanti

stag /stæg/ n cervo m

stage /steɪdʒ/ n palcoscenico m; (profession) teatro m; (in journey) tappa f; (in process) stadio m; go on the ~ darsi al teatro; by or in ~s a tappe ● vt mettere in scena; (arrange) organizzare

stagger /'stægə(r)/ vi barcollare ● vt sbalordire; scaglionare (holidays etc); I was ~ed sono rimasto sbalordito

~n vacillamento m. ~**ing** adj sbalorditivo

stagnant /'stægnənt/ adj stagnante

stagnat|e /stæg'neɪt/ vi fig [ri]stagnare. ~**ion** n fig inattività f

'**stag party** n addio m al celibato

staid /steɪd/ adj posato

stain /steɪn/ n macchia f; (for wood) mordente m ● vt macchiare; (wood) dare il mordente a; ~**ed glass** vetro m colorato; ~**ed-glass window** vetrata f colorata. ~**less** adj senza macchia; (steel) inossidabile. ~ **remover** n smacchiatore m

stair /steə(r)/ n gradino m; ~s pl scale fpl. ~**case** n scale fpl

stake /steɪk/ n palo m; (wager) posta f; (Comm) partecipazione f; at ~ in gioco ● vt puntellare; (wager) scommettere

stale /steɪl/ adj stantio; (air) viziato; (uninteresting) trito [e ritrito]. ~**mate** n (in chess) stallo m; (deadlock) situazione f di stallo

stalk¹ /stɔ:k/ n gambo m

stalk² vt inseguire ● vi camminare impettito

stall /stɔ:l/ n box m inv; (in market) bancarella f; ~s pl (Theat) platea f ● vi (engine:) spegnersi; fig temporeggiare ● vt far spegnere (engine); tenere a bada (person)

stallion /'stæljən/ n stallone m

stalwart /'stɔ:lwət/ adj fedele

stamina /'stæmɪnə/ n [capacità f inv di] resistenza f

stammer /'stæmə(r)/ n balbettio m ● vt/i balbettare

stamp /stæmp/ n (postage ~) francobollo m; (instrument) timbro m; (fig impronta f ● vt affrancare (letter); timbrare (bill); battere (feet). □~ **out** vt spegnere; fig soffocare

stampede /stæm'pi:d/ n fuga f precipitosa; (🔲: fuggi-fuggi m ● vi fuggire precipitosamente

stance /stɑ:ns/ n posizione f

stand /stænd/ n (for bikes) rastrelliera f; (at exhibition) stand m inv; (in market) bancarella f; (in stadium) gradinata f (nr pl); fig posizione f • vi (pt/pp stood) • vi stare in piedi; (rise) alzarsi [in piedi]; (be) trovarsi; (be candidate) essere candidato f per a); (stay valid) rimanere valido; ~ still non muoversi; I don't know where I ~ non so qual'è la mia posizione; ~ firm fig tener duro; ~ together essere solidali; ~ to lose/gain rischiare di perdere/vincere; ~ to reason essere logico • vt (withstand) resistere a; (endure) sopportare; (place) mettere; ~ a chance avere una possibilità; ~ one's ground tener duro; ~ the test of time superare la prova del tempo; ~ sb a beer offrire una birra a qcno. □ ~ by vi stare a guardare; (be ready) essere pronto • vt (support) appoggiare. □ ~ down vi (retire) ritirarsi. □ ~ for vt (mean) significare; (tolerate) tollerare. □ ~ in for vt sostituire. □ ~ out vi spiccare. □ ~ up vi alzarsi [in piedi]. □ ~ up for vt prendere le difese di; ~ up for oneself farsi valere. □ ~ up to vt affrontare

standard /'stændəd/ adj standard; be ~ practice essere pratica corrente • n standard m inv; (Techn) norma f; (level) livello m; (quality) qualità f inv; (flag) stendardo m; ~s pl (morals) valori mpl; ~ of living tenore m di vita. ~ize vt standardizzare

'**standard lamp** n lampada f a stelo

'**stand-by** n riserva f; on ~ (at airport) in lista d'attesa

'**stand-in** n controfigura f

standing /'stændɪŋ/ adj (erect) in piedi; (permanent) permanente • n posizione f; (duration) durata f. ~ -room n posti mpl in piedi

stand: ~**point** n punto m di vista. ~**still** n come to a ~**still** fermarsi; at a ~**still** in un periodo di stasi

stank /stæŋk/ ▷ **STINK**

staple¹ /'steɪpl/ n (product) prodotto m principale

staple² n graffa f • vt pinzare. ~**r** n pinzatrice f, cucitrice f

star /stɑː(r)/ n stella f; (asterisk) asterisco m; (Cinema, Sport, Theat) divo, -a mf, stella f • vi (pt/pp starred) essere l'interprete principale

starboard /'stɑːbəd/ n tribordo m

starch /stɑːtʃ/ n amido m • vt inamidare. ~**y** adj ricco di amido; fig compito

stare /steə(r)/ n sguardo m fisso • vi it's rude to ~ è da maleducati fissare la gente; ~ at fissare; ~ into space guardare nel vuoto

'**starfish** n stella f di mare

stark /stɑːk/ adj austero; (contrast) forte • adv completamente; ~ naked completamente nudo

starling /'stɑːlɪŋ/ n storno m

starry /'stɑːrɪ/ adj stellato

start /stɑːt/ n inizio m; (departure) partenza f; (jump) sobbalzo m; from the ~ [fin] dall'inizio; for a ~ tanto per cominciare; give sb a ~ (Sport) dare un vantaggio a qcno • vi [in]cominciare; (set out) avviarsi; (engine, car:) partire; (jump) trasalire; to ~ with,... tanto per cominciare,... • vt [in]cominciare; (cause) dare inizio a; (found) mettere su; mettere in moto (car); mettere in giro (rumour). ~**er** n (Culin) primo m [piatto m]; (in race: giving signal) starter m inv; (participant) concorrente m f; (Auto) motorino m d'avviamento. ~**ing-point** n punto m di partenza

startle /'stɑːtl/ vt far trasalire; (news:) sconvolgere

starvation /stɑːˈveɪʃn/ n fame f

starve /stɑːv/ vi morire di fame • vt far morire di fame

state /steɪt/ n stato m; (grand style) pompa f; ~ of play punteggio m; be in a ~ (person:) essere agitato;

lie in ∼ essere esposto ● *attrib* di Stato; (*Sch*) pubblico; (*with ceremony*) di gala ● *vt* dichiarare; (*specify*) precisare. ∼less *adj* apolide

stately /'steɪtlɪ/ *adj* (-ier, -iest) maestoso. ∼ '**home** *n* dimora *f* signorile

statement /'steɪtmənt/ *n* dichiarazione *f*; (*Jur*) deposizione *f*; (*in banking*) estratto *m* conto; (*account*) rapporto *m*

'**statesman** *n* statista *mf*

static /'stætɪk/ *adj* statico

station /'steɪʃn/ *n* stazione *f*; (*police*) commissariato *m* ● *vt* appostare (guard); **be** ∼**ed in** Germany essere di stanza in Germania. ∼**ary** *adj* immobile

'**station-wagon** *n* *Am* familiare *f*

statistic|al /stə'tɪstɪkl/ *adj* statistico. ∼**s** *n* & *pl* statistica *f*

statue /'stætjuː/ *n* statua *f*

stature /'stætʃə(r)/ *n* statura *f*

status /'steɪtəs/ *n* condizione *f*; (*high rank*) alto rango *m*. ∼ **symbol** *n* status symbol *m inv*

statut|e /'stætjuːt/ *n* statuto *m*. ∼**ory** *adj* statutario

staunch /stɔːntʃ/ *adj* fedele. ∼**ly** *adv* fedelmente

stave /steɪv/ *vt* ∼ **off** tenere lontano

stay /steɪ/ *n* soggiorno *m* ● *vi* restare, rimanere; (*reside*) alloggiare; ∼ **the night** passare la notte; ∼ **put** non muoversi ● *vt* ∼ **the course** resistere fino alla fine. □ ∼ **away** *vi* stare lontano. □ ∼ **behind** *vi* non andare con gli altri. □ ∼ **in** *vi* (*at home*) stare in casa; (*Sch*) restare a scuola dopo le lezioni. □ ∼ **up** *vi* stare su; (*person*): stare alzato

stead /sted/ *n* in his ∼ in sua vece; **stand sb in good** ∼ tornare utile a qcno. ∼**fast** *adj* fedele; (*refusal*) fermo

steadily /'stedɪlɪ/ *adv* (*continually*) continuamente

steady /'stedɪ/ *adj* (-ier, -iest) saldo, fermo; (*breathing*) regolare; (*job, boyfriend*) fisso; (*dependable*) serio

steak /steɪk/ *n* (*for stew*) spezzatino *m*; (*for grilling, frying*) bistecca *f*

steal /stiːl/ *v* (*pt* stole, *pp* stolen) ● *vt* rubare (from da). □ ∼ **in/out** *vi* entrare/uscire furtivamente

stealth /stelθ/ *n* by ∼ di nascosto. ∼**y** *adj* furtivo

steam /stiːm/ *n* vapore *m*; **under one's own** ∼ 🅵 da solo ● *vt* (*Culin*) cucinare a vapore ● *vi* fumare. □ ∼ **up** *vi* appannarsi

'**steam-engine** *n* locomotiva *f*

steamer /'stiːmə(r)/ *n* piroscafo *m*; (*saucepan*) pentola *f* a vapore

'**steamroller** *n* rullo *m* compressore

steamy /'stiːmɪ/ *adj* appannato

steel /stiːl/ *n* acciaio *m* ● *vt* ∼ **oneself** temprarsi

steep[1] /stiːp/ *vt* (soak) lasciare a bagno

steep[2] /stiːp/ *adj* ripido; (🅵: price) esorbitante. ∼**ly** *adv* ripidamente

steeple /'stiːpl/ *n* campanile *m*. ∼**chase** *n* corsa *f* ippica a ostacoli

steer /stɪə(r)/ *vt/i* guidare; ∼ **clear of** stare alla larga da. ∼**ing** *n* (*Auto*) sterzo *m*. ∼**ing-wheel** *n* volante *m*

stem[1] /stem/ *n* stelo *m*; (*of glass*) gambo *m*; (*of word*) radice *f* ● *vi* (*pt/pp* stemmed) ∼ **from** derivare da

stem[2] *vt* (*pt/pp* stemmed) contenere

stench /stentʃ/ *n* fetore *m*

step /step/ *n* passo *m*; (*stair*) gradino *m*; ∼**s** *pl* (*ladder*) scala *f* portatile; in

~ al passo; be out of ~ non stare al passo; ~ by ~ un passo alla volta ●vi (pt/pp stepped) □ ~ into entrare in; □ ~ out of uscire da; ~ out of line sgarrare. □ ~ **down** vi fig dimettersi. □ ~ **forward** vi farsi avanti. □ ~ **in** vi fig intervenire. □ ~ **up** vt (increase) aumentare

step: ~**brother** n fratellastro m. ~**daughter** n figliastra f. ~**father** n patrigno m. ~**ladder** n scala f portatile. ~**mother** n matrigna f

'**stepping-stone** n pietra f per guadare; fig trampolino m

step: ~**sister** n sorellastra f. ~**son** n figliastro m

stereo /'steriəʊ/ n stereo m; in ~ in stereofonia. ~**phonic** adj stereofonico

stereotype /'steriətaip/ n stereotipo m. ~**d** adj stereotipato

steril|e /'sterail/ adj sterile. ~**ity** n sterilità f inv

sterling /'stɜːlɪŋ/ adj fig apprezzabile; ~ **silver** argento m pregiato ●n sterlina f

stern[1] /stɜːn/ adj severo

stern[2] n (of boat) poppa f

stethoscope /'steθəskəʊp/ n stetoscopio m

stew /stjuː/ n stufato m; in a ~ fig agitato ●vt/i cuocere in umido; ~**ed fruit** frutta f cotta

steward /'stjuːəd/ n (at meeting) organizzatore, -trice mf; (on ship, aircraft) steward m inv. ~**ess** n hostess f inv

stick[1] /stɪk/ n bastone m; (of celery, rhubarb) gambo m; (Sport) mazza f

stick[2] v (pt/pp stuck) ●vt (stab) [con]ficcare; (glue) attaccare; (□: put) mettere; (□: endure) sopportare ●vi (adhere) attaccarsi (to a); (jam) bloccarsi; ~ **to** attenersi a (facts); mantenere (story); perseverare in (task); ~ **at it** □ tener duro; ~ **at nothing** □ non fermarsi di fronte a niente; be stuck (vehicle, person:)

---

stepping-stone | stink

essere bloccato; (drawer:) essere incastrato; be stuck with sth □ farsi incastrare con qcsa. □ ~ **out** vi (project) sporgere; (□: catch the eye) risaltare ●vt □ fare (tongue). □ ~ **up for** vt □ difendere

sticker /'stɪkə(r)/ n autoadesivo m

'**sticking plaster** n cerotto m

stickler /'stɪklə(r)/ n be a ~ **for** tenere molto a

sticky /'stɪkɪ/ adj (-ier, -iest) appiccicoso; (adhesive) adesivo; (fig: difficult) difficile

stiff /stɪf/ adj rigido; (brush, task) duro; (person) controllato; (drink) forte; (penalty) severo; (price) alto; bored ~ □ annoiato a morte; ~ **neck** torcicollo m. ~**en** vt irrigidire ●vi irrigidirsi. ~**ness** n rigidità f inv

stifl|e /'staifl/ vt soffocare. ~**ing** adj soffocante

still[1] /stɪl/ n distilleria f

still[2] adj fermo; (drink) non gasato; keep/stand ~ stare fermo ●n quiete f; (photo) posa f ●adv ancora; (nevertheless) nondimeno, comunque; I'm ~ **not sure** non sono ancora sicuro

'**stillborn** adj nato morto

still 'life n natura f morta

stilted /'stɪltɪd/ adj artificioso

stilts /stɪlts/ npl trampoli mpl

stimulant /'stɪmjʊlənt/ n eccitante m

stimulat|e /'stɪmjʊleit/ vt stimolare. ~**ion** n stimolo m

stimulus /'stɪmjʊləs/ n (pl -li /-lai/) stimolo m

sting /stɪŋ/ n puntura f; (from nettle, jellyfish) sostanza f irritante; (organ) pungiglione m ●v (pt/pp stung) ●vt pungere; (jellyfish:) pizzicare ●vi (insect:) pungere. ~**ing nettle** n ortica f

stingy /'stɪndʒɪ/ adj (-ier, -iest) tirchio

stink /stɪŋk/ n puzza f ●vi (pt stank,

pp stunk) puzzare

stipulate /'stɪpjʊleɪt/ *vt* porre come condizione; ~**ion** *n* condizione *f*

stir /stɜː(r)/ *n* mescolata *f*; (*commotion*) trambusto *m* ● *v* (*pt/pp* stirred) ● *vt* muovere; (*mix*) mescolare ● *vi* muoversi

stirrup /'stɪrəp/ *n* staffa *f*

stitch /stɪtʃ/ *n* punto *m*; (*in knitting*) maglia *f*; (*pain*) fitta *f*; have sb in ~es 🔢 far ridere qcno a crepapelle ● *vt* cucire

stock /stɒk/ *n* (*for use or selling*) scorta *f*, stock *m inv*; (*livestock*) bestiame *m*; (*lineage*) stirpe *f*; (*Fin*) titoli *mpl*; (*Culin*) brodo *m*; in ~ disponibile; out of ~ esaurito; take ~ *fig* fare il punto ● *adj* solito ● *vt* (*shop*:) vendere; approvvigionare (shelves). ~ **up** *vi* far scorta (with di)

stock: ~**broker** *n* agente *m* di cambio. S~ **Exchange** *n* Borsa *f* Valori

stocking /'stɒkɪŋ/ *n* calza *f*

stock: ~**pile** *vt* far scorta di ● *n* riserva *f*. ~'**still** *adj* immobile. ~**taking** *n* (*Comm*) inventario *m*

stocky /'stɒkɪ/ *adj* (-ier, -iest) tarchiato

stodgy /'stɒdʒɪ/ *adj* indigesto

stoke /stəʊk/ *vt* alimentare

stole[1] /stəʊl/ *n* stola *f*

stole[2], **stolen** /'stəʊln/ ▷**STEAL**

stomach /'stʌmək/ *n* pancia *f*; (*Anat*) stomaco *m* ● *vt* 🔢 reggere. ~**ache** *n* mal *m* di pancia

stone /stəʊn/ *n* pietra *f*; (*in fruit*) nocciolo *m*; (*Med*) calcolo *m*; (*weight*) 6,348 *kg* ● *adj* di pietra; (wall, Age) della pietra ● *vt* snocciolare (fruit). ~**cold** *adj* gelido. ~-'**deaf** *adj* 🔢 sordo come una campana

stony /'stəʊnɪ/ *adj* pietroso; (glare) glaciale

stood /stʊd/ ▷**STAND**

stool /stuːl/ *n* sgabello *m*

stoop /stuːp/ *n* curvatura *f* ● *vi* stare curvo; (*bend down*) chinarsi; *fig* abbassarsi

stop /stɒp/ *n* (*break*) sosta *f*; (*for bus, train*) fermata *f*; (*Gram*) punto *m*; come to a ~ fermarsi; put a ~ to sth mettere fine a qcsa ● *v* (*pt/pp* stopped) ● *vt* fermare; arrestare (machine); (*prevent*) impedire; ~ sb doing sth impedire a qcno di fare qcsa; ~ doing sth smettere di fare qcsa; ~ that! smettila! ● *vi* fermarsi; (rain:) smettere ● *int* fermo!. □ ~ **off** *vi* fare una sosta. □ ~ **up** *vt* otturare (sink); tappare (hole). □ ~ **with** *vi* (🔢: *stay with*) fermarsi da

stop: ~**gap** *n* palliativo *m*; (*person*) tappabuchi *m inv*. ~-**over** *n* sosta *f*; (*Aeron*) scalo *m*

stoppage /'stɒpɪdʒ/ *n* ostruzione *f*; (*strike*) interruzione *f*; (*deduction*) trattenute *fpl*

stopper /'stɒpə(r)/ *n* tappo *m*

stop-watch *n* cronometro *m*

storage /'stɔːrɪdʒ/ *n* deposito *m*; (*in warehouse*) immagazzinaggio *m*; (*Comput*) memoria *f*

store /stɔː(r)/ *n* (*stock*) riserva *f*; (*shop*) grande magazzino *m*; (*depot*) deposito *m*; in ~ in deposito; what the future has in ~ for me cosa mi riserva il futuro; set great ~ by tenere in gran conto ● *vt* tenere; (*in warehouse*, *Comput*:) immagazzinare. ~**room** *n* magazzino *m*

storey /'stɔːrɪ/ *n* piano *m*

stork /stɔːk/ *n* cicogna *f*

storm /stɔːm/ *n* temporale *m*; (*with thunder*) tempesta *f* ● *vt* prendere d'assalto. ~**y** *adj* tempestoso

story /'stɔːrɪ/ *n* storia *f*; (*in newspaper*) articolo *m*

stout /staʊt/ *adj* (shoes) resistente; (*fat*) robusto; (defence) strenuo

stove /stəʊv/ *n* stufa *f*; (*for cooking*) cucina *f* [economica]

stow /stəʊ/ *vt* metter via. ~**away** *n*

passeggero, -a *mf* clandestino, -a

straggl|e /'strægl/ *vi* crescere disordinatamente; (*dawdle*) rimanere indietro. ~**er** *n* persona *f* che rimane indietro. ~**y** *adj* in disordine

straight /streɪt/ *adj* diritto, dritto; (*answer, question, person*) diretto; (*tidy*) in ordine; (*drink, hair*) liscio ● *adv* diritto, dritto; (*directly*) direttamente; ~ **away** immediatamente; ~ **on** or **ahead** diritto; ~ **out** *fig* apertamente; **go** Ⓣ rigare diritto; **put** sth ~ mettere qcsa in ordine; **sit/stand up** ~ stare diritto

straighten /'streɪtn/ *vt* raddrizzare ● *vi* raddrizzarsi; ~ **[up]** (*person:*) mettersi diritto. □ ~ **out** *vt fig* chiarire (*situation*)

straight'forward *adj* franco; (*simple*) semplice

strain[1] /streɪn/ *n* (*streak*) vena *f*; (*Bot*) varietà *f inv*; (*of virus*) forma *f*

strain[2] *n* tensione *f*; (*injury*) stiramento *m*; ~**s** *pl* (*of music*) note *fpl* ● *vt* tirare; sforzare (*eyes, voice*); stirarsi (*muscle*); (*Culin*) scolare ● *vi* sforzarsi. ~**ed** *adj* (*relations*) teso. ~**er** *n* colino *m*

strait /streɪt/ *n* stretto *m*; **in dire** ~**s** in serie difficoltà. ~**-jacket** *n* camicia *f* di forza. ~**-laced** *adj* puritano

strand[1] /strænd/ *n* (*of thread*) gugliata *f*; (*of beads*) filo *m*; (*of hair*) capello *m*

strand[2] *vt* **be** ~**ed** rimanere bloccato

strange /streɪndʒ/ *adj* strano; (*not known*) sconosciuto; (*unaccustomed*) estraneo. ~**ly** *adv* stranamente; ~**ly enough** curiosamente. ~**r** *n* estraneo, -a *mf*

strangle /'stræŋgl/ *vt* strangolare; *fig* reprimere

strap /stræp/ *n* cinghia *f* (*to grasp in vehicle*) maniglia *f*; (*of watch*) cinturino *m*; (*shoulder* ~) bretella *f*, spallina *f* ● *vt*

(*pt/pp* **strapped**) legare; ~ **in** or **down** assicurare

strategic /strə'tiːdʒɪk/ *adj* strategico

strategy /'strætɪdʒɪ/ *n* strategia *f*

straw /strɔː/ *n* paglia *f*; (*single piece*) fuscello *m*; (*for drinking*) cannuccia *f*; **the last** ~ l'ultima goccia

strawberry /'strɔːbərɪ/ *n* fragola *f*

stray /streɪ/ *adj* (*animal*) randagio ● *n* randagio *m* ● *vi* andarsene per conto proprio; (*deviate*) deviare (**from** da)

streak /striːk/ *n* striatura *f*; (*fig: trait*) vena *f* ● *vi* sfrecciare. ~**y** *adj* striato; (*bacon*) grasso

stream /striːm/ *n* ruscello *m*; (*current*) corrente *f*; (*of blood, people*) flusso *m*; (*Sch*) classe *f* ● *vi* scorrere. □ ~ **in/out** *vi* entrare/uscire a fiotti

streamer /'striːmə(r)/ *n* (*paper*) stella *f* filante; (*flag*) pennone *m*

'streamline *vt* rendere aerodinamico; (*simplify*) snellire. ~**d** *adj* aerodinamico

street /striːt/ *n* strada *f*. ~**car** *n* *Am* tram *m inv*. ~**lamp** *n* lampione *m*

strength /streŋθ/ *n* forza *f*; (*of wall, bridge etc*) solidità *f inv*; ~**s** punti *mpl* forti; **on the** ~ **of** grazie a. ~**en** *vt* rinforzare

strenuous /'strenjʊəs/ *adj* faticoso; (*attempt, denial*) energico

stress /stres/ *n* (*emphasis*) insistenza *f*; (*Gram*) accento *m* tonico; (*mental*) stress *m inv*; (*Mech*) spinta *f* ● *vt* (*emphasize*) insistere su; (*Gram*) mettere l'accento [tonico] su. ~**ed** *adj* (*mentally*) stressato. ~**ful** *adj* stressante

stretch /stretʃ/ *n* stiramento *m*; (*period*) periodo *m* di tempo; (*of road*) estensione *f*; (*elasticity*) elasticità *f inv*; **at a** ~ di fila; **have a** ~ stirarsi ● *vt* tirare; allargare (*shoes, arms etc*); (*person:*) allungare ● *vi* (*become wider*) allargarsi; (*extend*) estendersi; (*person:*) stirarsi. ~**er** *n* barella *f*

strict /strɪkt/ *adj* severo; (*precise*)

preciso. ~ly adv severamente; ~ly
speaking in senso stretto

stride /straɪd/ n [lungo] passo m;
take sth in one's ~ accettare qcsa
con facilità ● vi (pt strode, pp strid-
den) andare a gran passi

strident /'straɪdənt/ adj stridente;
(colour) vistoso

strife /straɪf/ n conflitto m

strike /straɪk/ n sciopero m; (Mil) attacco m; on ~ in sciopero ● v (pt/pp
struck) ● vt colpire; accendere
(match); trovare (oil, gold); (delete)
depennare; (occur to) venire in mente
a; (Mil) attaccare ● vi (lightning:)
cadere; (clock:) suonare; (Mil) attaccare; (workers:) scioperare; ~ lucky
azzeccarla. □~ **off**, strike out vt eliminare. □~ **up** vt fare (friendship);
attaccare (conversation). ~**breaker**
n persona f che non aderisce a uno sciopero

striker /'straɪkə(r)/ n scioperante mf

striking /'straɪkɪŋ/ adj impressio-
nante; (attractive) affascinante

string /strɪŋ/ n spago m; (of musical
instrument, racket) corda f; (of pearls) filo
m; (of lies) serie f; the ~s (Mus) gli
archi; pull ~s 🔢 usare le proprie
conoscenze ● vt (pt/pp strung)
(thread) infilare (beads). ~ed adj (instrument) a corda

stringent /'strɪndʒənt/ adj rigido

strip /strɪp/ n striscia f ● v (pt/pp
stripped) ● vt spogliare; togliere le
lenzuola a (bed); scrostare (wood,
furniture); smontare (machine); (deprive) privare del (of); (undress) spogliarsi. ~ **cartoon** n striscia f. ~
club n locale m di strip-tease

stripe /straɪp/ n striscia f; (Mil) gallone m. ~d adj a strisce

strip-'tease n spogliarello m, strip-
tease m inv

strive /straɪv/ vi (pt strove, pp
striven) sforzarsi (to di); ~ for sforzarsi di ottenere

strode /strəʊd/ ▷STRIDE

stroke[1] /strəʊk/ n colpo m; (of pen)
tratto m; (in swimming) bracciata f;
(Med) ictus m inv; ~ **of luck** colpo m
di fortuna; put sb off his ~ far perdere il filo a qcno

stroke[2] vt accarezzare

stroll /strəʊl/ n passeggiata f ● vi
passeggiare. ~**er** n (Am: push-chair)
passeggino m

strong /strɒŋ/ adj (-er /-gə(r)/, -est
/-gɪst/) forte; (argument) valido

strong: ~**hold** n roccaforte f. ~**ly**
adv fortemente. ~**room** n camera f
blindata

stroppy /'strɒpɪ/ adj scorbutico

strove /strəʊv/ ▷STRIVE

struck /strʌk/ ▷STRIKE

structural /'strʌktʃərəl/ adj strut-
turale. ~**ly** adv strutturalmente

structure /'strʌktʃə(r)/ n
struttura f

struggle /'strʌgl/ n lotta f; with a
~ lottare con ● vi lottare; ~ **for**
breath respirare per fatica; ~ to do
sth fare fatica a fare qcsa; ~ to
one's feet alzarsi con fatica

strum /strʌm/ vt/i (pt/pp
strummed) strimpellare

strung /strʌŋ/ ▷STRING

strut[1] /strʌt/ n (component) pun-
tello m

strut[2] vi (pt/pp strutted) camminare
impettito

stub /stʌb/ n mozzicone m; (counterfoil) matrice f ● vt (pt/pp stubbed) ~
one's toe sbattere il dito del piede
(on contro). □~ **out** vt spegnere
(cigarette)

stubb|le /'stʌbl/ n barba f ispida.
~**ly** adj ispido

stubborn /'stʌbən/ adj testardo;
(refusal) ostinato

stuck /stʌk/ ▷STICK[2]. ~**-'up** adj
🔢 snob

stud[1] /stʌd/ n (on boot) tacchetto m;

(on jacket) borchia f; (for ear) orecchino m [a bottone]

stud² /stʌd/ n (of horses) scuderia f

student /'stjuːdənt/ n studente m, studentessa f; (school child) scolaro, -a mf. ~ **nurse** n studente, studentessa infermiere, -a

studio /'stjuːdɪəʊ/ n studio m

studious /'stjuːdɪəs/ adj studioso; (attention) studiato

study /'stʌdɪ/ n studio m • vt/i (pt/pp studied) studiare

stuff /stʌf/ n materiale m; (🔢: things) roba f • vt riempire; (with padding) imbottire; (Culin) farcire; ~ **sth into a drawer/one's pocket** ficcare qcsa alla rinfusa in un cassetto/in tasca. ~**ing** n (padding) imbottitura f; (Culin) ripieno m

stuffy /'stʌfɪ/ adj (-ier, -iest) che sa di chiuso; (old-fashioned) antiquato

stumble /'stʌmbl/ vi inciampare; ~**e across** or on imbattersi in. ~**ing-block** n ostacolo m

stump /stʌmp/ n ceppo m; (of limb) moncone m. ~**ed** adj 🔢 perplesso • **stump up** vt/i 🔢 sganciare

stun /stʌn/ vt (pt/pp stunned) stordire; (astonish) sbalordire

stung /stʌŋ/ ▷**STING**

stunk /stʌŋk/ ▷**STINK**

stunning /'stʌnɪŋ/ adj 🔢 favoloso; (blow, victory) sbalorditivo

stunt¹ /stʌnt/ n 🔢 trovata f pubblicitaria

stunt² vt arrestare lo sviluppo di. ~**ed** adj stentato

stupendous /stjuːˈpendəs/ adj stupendo. ~**ly** adv stupendamente

stupid /'stjuːpɪd/ adj stupido. ~**ity** n stupidità f. ~**ly** adv stupidamente

stupor /'stjuːpə(r)/ n torpore m

sturdy /'stɜːdɪ/ adj (-ier, -iest) robusto; (furniture) solido

stutter /'stʌtə(r)/ n balbuzie f • vt/i balbettare

sty, stye /staɪ/ n (pl styes) (Med) orzaiolo m

style /staɪl/ n stile m; (fashion) moda f; (sort) tipo m; (hair~) pettinatura f; **in** ~ in grande stile

stylish /'staɪlɪʃ/ adj elegante. ~**ly** adv con eleganza

stylist /'staɪlɪst/ n stilista mf; (hair~) parrucchiere, -a mf. ~**ic** adj stilistico

stylus /'staɪləs/ n (on record player) puntina f

suave /swɑːv/ adj dai modi garbati

sub'conscious /sʌb-/ adj subcosciente n subcosciente m. ~**ly** adv in modo inconscio

'subdivi|de vt suddividere. ~**sion** n suddivisione f

subject¹ /'sʌbdʒɪkt/ adj ~ **to** soggetto a; (depending on) subordinato a; ~ **to availability** nei limiti della disponibilità • n soggetto m; (of ruler) suddito, -a mf; (Sch) materia f

subject² /səbˈdʒekt/ vt (to attack, abuse) sottoporre; assoggettare (country)

subjective /səbˈdʒektɪv/ adj soggettivo. ~**ly** adv soggettivamente

subjunctive /səbˈdʒʌŋktɪv/ adj & n congiuntivo m

sublime /səˈblaɪm/ adj sublime. ~**ly** adv sublimamente

subma'rine n sommergibile m

submerge /səbˈmɜːdʒ/ vt immergere; **be** ~**d** essere sommerso • vi immergersi

submission /səbˈmɪʃn/ n sottomissione f. ~**ive** adj sottomesso

submit /səbˈmɪt/ v (pt/pp -mitted, pres p -mitting) • vt sottoporre • vi sottomettersi

subordinate /səbˈbɔːdɪmeɪt/ vt subordinare (to a)

subscribe /səbˈskraɪb/ vi contribuire; ~ **to** abbonarsi a (newspaper); sottoscrivere (fund); fig aderire a. ~**r** n abbonato, -a mf

s

subscription /səb'skrɪpʃn/ n (to club) sottoscrizione f; (to newspaper) abbonamento m

subsequent /'sʌbsɪkwənt/ adj susseguente. ~ly adv in seguito

subside /səb'saɪd/ vi sprofondare; (ground:) avvallarsi; (storm:) placarsi

subsidiary /səb'sɪdɪərɪ/ adj secondario ● n ~ [company] filiale f

subsid|ize /'sʌbsɪdaɪz/ vt sovvenzionare. ~y n sovvenzione f

substance /'sʌbstəns/ n sostanza f

sub'standard adj di qualità inferiore

substantial /səb'stænʃl/ adj solido; (meal) sostanzioso; (considerable) notevole. ~ly adv notevolmente; (essentially) sostanzialmente

substitut|e /'sʌbstɪtjuːt/ n sostituto m ● vt ~e A for B sostituire B con A ● vi ~e for sb sostituire qcno. ~ion n sostituzione f

subterranean /sʌbtə'reɪnɪən/ adj sotterraneo

'subtitle n sottotitolo m

sub|tle /'sʌtl/ adj sottile; (taste, perfume) delicato. ~tlety n sottigliezza f. ~tly adv sottilmente

subtract /səb'trækt/ vt sottrarre. ~ion n sottrazione f

suburb /'sʌbɜːb/ n sobborgo m; in the ~s in periferia. ~an adj suburbano. ~ia n i sobborghi mpl

subversive /səb'vɜːsɪv/ adj sovversivo

'subway n sottopassaggio m; (Am: railway) metropolitana f

succeed /sək'siːd/ vi riuscire; (follow) succedere a; ~ in doing riuscire a fare ● vt succedere a (king). ~ing adj successivo

success /sək'ses/ n successo m; be a ~ (in life) aver successo. ~ful adj riuscito; (businessman, artist etc) di successo. ~fully adv con successo

succession /sək'seʃn/ n successione f; in ~ di seguito

successive /sək'sesɪv/ adj successivo. ~ly adv successivamente

successor /sək'sesə(r)/ n successore m

succulent /'sʌkjʊlənt/ adj succulento

succumb /sə'kʌm/ vi soccombere (to a)

such /sʌtʃ/ adj tale; ~ a book un libro di questo genere; ~ a thing una cosa di questo genere; ~ a long time ago talmente tanto tempo fa; there is no ~ thing non esiste una cosa così; there is no ~ person non esiste una persona così ● pron as ~ come tale; ~ as chi; and ~ e simili; ~ as it is così com'è. ~like pron I di tal genere

suck /sʌk/ vt succhiare. □ ~ up vt assorbire. □ ~ up to vt I fare il lecchino con

sucker /'sʌkə(r)/ n (Bot) pollone m; (I: person) credulone, -a mf

suction /'sʌkʃn/ n aspirazione f

sudden /'sʌdn/ adj improvviso ● n all of a ~ all'improvviso. ~ly adv improvvisamente

sue /suː/ vt (pres p suing) fare causa a (for per) ● vi fare causa

suede /sweɪd/ n pelle f scamosciata

suet /'suːɪt/ n grasso m di rognone

suffer /'sʌfə(r)/ vi soffrire (from per) ● vt soffrire; subire (loss etc); (tolerate) subire. ~ing n sofferenza f

suffice /sə'faɪs/ vi bastare

sufficient /sə'fɪʃnt/ adj sufficiente. ~ly adv sufficientemente

suffix /'sʌfɪks/ n suffisso m

suffocat|e /'sʌfəkeɪt/ vt/i soffocare. ~ion n soffocamento m

sugar /'ʃʊɡə(r)/ n zucchero m ● vt zuccherare. ~ basin, ~bowl n zuccheriera f. ~y adj zuccheroso; fig sdolcinato

suggest /sə'dʒest/ vt suggerire; (indicate, insinuate) fare pensare a. ~ion n suggerimento m; (trace) traccia f.

~ive adj allusivo. ~ively adv in modo allusivo

suicidal /su:ɪˈsaɪdl/ adj suicida

suicide /ˈsu:ɪsaɪd/ n suicidio m; (person) suicida mf; **commit** ~ suicidarsi

suit /su:t/ n vestito m; (woman's) tailleur m inv; (in cards) seme m; (Jur) causa f; **follow** ~ fig fare lo stesso ● vt andar bene a; (adapt) adattare (to a); (be convenient for) andare bene per; **be** ~**ed to** or **for** essere adatto a; ~ **yourself!** fa' come vuoi!

suitabl|e /ˈsu:təbl/ adj adatto. ~**y** adv convenientemente

'suitcase n valigia f

suite /swi:t/ n suite f inv; (of furniture) divano m e poltrone fpl assortiti

sulk /sʌlk/ vi fare il broncio. ~**y** adj imbronciato

sullen /ˈsʌlən/ adj svogliato

sulphur /ˈsʌlfə(r)/ n zolfo m. ~**ic acid** n acido m solforico

sultana /sʌlˈtɑːnə/ n uva f sultanina

sultry /ˈsʌltrɪ/ adj (-ier, -iest) (weather) afoso; fig sensuale

sum /sʌm/ n somma f; (Sch) addizione f ● ~ **up** (pt/pp summed) vi riassumere ● vt valutare

summar|ize /ˈsʌməraɪz/ vt riassumere. ~**y** n sommario m ● adj sommario; (dismissal) sbrigativo

summer /ˈsʌmə(r)/ n estate f. ~**house** n padiglione m. ~**time** n (season) estate f

> **Summer camp** Negli Stati Uniti indica il campeggio estivo cui moltissimi ragazzi si recano per socializzare e praticare attività ricreative e sportive all'aria aperta; tra queste il nuoto, il canottaggio, l'arrampicata e i corsi di sopravvivenza. ⓘ

summery /ˈsʌmərɪ/ adj estivo

summit /ˈsʌmɪt/ n cima f. ~ **conference** n vertice m

summon /ˈsʌmən/ vt convocare; (Jur) citare. □ ~ **up** vt raccogliere (strength); rievocare (memory)

summons /ˈsʌmənz/ n (Jur) citazione f ● vt citare in giudizio

sumptuous /ˈsʌmptjʊəs/ adj sontuoso. ~**ly** adv sontuosamente

sun /sʌn/ n sole m ● vt (pt/pp sunned) ~ **oneself** prendere il sole

sun: ~**bathe** vi prendere il sole. ~**burn** n scottatura f (solare). ~**burnt** adj scottato (dal sole)

Sunday /ˈsʌndeɪ/ n domenica f

'sunflower n girasole m

sung /sʌŋ/ ▷ **SING**

'sun-glasses npl occhiali mpl da sole

sunk /sʌŋk/ ▷ **SINK**

sunken /ˈsʌŋkn/ adj incavato

'sunlight n luce f del sole m

sunny /ˈsʌnɪ/ adj (-ier, -iest) assolato

sun: ~**rise** n alba f. ~**roof** n (Auto) tettuccio m apribile. ~**set** n tramonto m. ~**shine** n luce f del sole m. ~**stroke** n insolazione f. ~**tan** n abbronzatura f. ~**tan oil** n olio m solare

super /ˈsuːpə(r)/ adj 🔟 fantastico

superb /sʊˈpɜːb/ adj splendido

supercilious /suːpəˈsɪlɪəs/ adj altezzoso

superficial /suːpəˈfɪʃl/ adj superficiale. ~**ly** adv superficialmente

superfluous /sʊˈpɜːflʊəs/ adj superfluo

super'human adj sovrumano

superintendent /suːpərɪnˈtendənt/ n (of police) commissario m di polizia

superior /suːˈpɪərɪə(r)/ adj superiore ● n superiore, -a mf. ~**ity** n superiorità f

superlative /suːˈpɜːlətɪv/ adj eccellente ● n superlativo m

'supermarket n supermercato m

s

super'natural *adj* soprannaturale

'superpower *n* superpotenza *f*

super'sede /suːpə'siːd/ *vt* rimpiazzare

super'sonic *adj* supersonico

superstiti|on /suːpə'stɪʃn/ *n* superstizione *f*. **~ous** *adj* superstizioso

supervis|e /'suːpəvaɪz/ *vt* supervisionare. **~ion** *n* supervisione *f*. **~or** *n* supervisore *m*

supper /'sʌpə(r)/ *n* cena *f*

supple /'sʌpl/ *adj* slogato

supplement /'sʌplɪmənt/ *n* supplemento *m* ● *vt* integrare. **~ary** *adj* supplementare

supplier /sə'plaɪə(r)/ *n* fornitore, -trice *mf*

supply /sə'plaɪ/ *n* fornitura *f*; (*in economics*) offerta *f*; **supplies** *pl* (*Mil*) approvvigionamenti *mpl* ● *vt* (*pt/pp -ied*) fornire; **~ sb with sth** fornire qcsa a qcno

support /sə'pɔːt/ *n* sostegno *m*; (*base*) supporto *m*; (*keep*) sostentamento *m* ● *vt* sostenere; mantenere (*family*); (*give money to*) mantenere finanziariamente; (*Sport*) fare il tifo per. **~er** *n* sostenitore, -trice *mf*; (*Sport*) tifoso, -a *mf*. **~ive** *adj* incoraggiante

suppose /sə'pəʊz/ *vt* (*presume*) supporre; (*imagine*) pensare; **be ~d to** do dover fare; **not be ~d to** 🔢 non avere il permesso di; **I ~ so** suppongo di sì. **~dly** *adv* presumibilmente

suppress /sə'pres/ *vt* sopprimere. **~ion** *n* soppressione *f*

supremacy /suː'preməsɪ/ *n* supremazia *f*

supreme /suː'priːm/ *adj* supremo

sure /ʃʊə/ *adj* sicuro, certo; make **~** accertarsi; **be ~ to do** lo mi raccomando di farlo ● *adv* Am 🔢 certamente; **~ enough** infatti. **~ly** *adv* certamente; (*Am: gladly*) volentieri

surety /'ʃʊərətɪ/ *n* garanzia *f*; **stand**

~ for garantire

surf /sɜːf/ *n* schiuma *f* ● *vt* (*Comput*) **~ the Net** surfare in Internet

surface /'sɜːfɪs/ *n* superficie *f*; **on the ~** *fig* in apparenza ● *vi* (*emerge*) emergere. **~ mail** *n* by **~** mail per posta ordinaria

'surfboard *n* tavola *f* da surf

surfing /'sɜːfɪŋ/ *n* surf *m* *inv*

surge /sɜːdʒ/ *n* (*of sea*) ondata *f*; (*of interest*) aumento *m*; (*in demand*) impennata *f*; (*of anger, pity*) impeto *m* ● *vi* riversarsi; **~ forward** buttarsi in avanti

surgeon /'sɜːdʒən/ *n* chirurgo *m*

surgery /'sɜːdʒərɪ/ *n* chirurgia *f*; (*place, consulting room*) ambulatorio *m*; (*hours*) ore *fpl* di visita; **have ~** subire un'intervento [chirurgico]

surgical /'sɜːdʒɪkl/ *adj* chirurgico

surly /'sɜːlɪ/ *adj* (*-ier, -iest*) scontroso

surmise /sə'maɪz/ *vt* supporre

surmount /sə'maʊnt/ *vt* sormontare

surname /'sɜːneɪm/ *n* cognome *m*

surpass /sə'pɑːs/ *vt* superare

surplus /'sɜːpləs/ *adj* d'avanzo ● *n* sovrappiù *m*

surpris|e /sə'praɪz/ *n* sorpresa *f* ● *vt* sorprendere; **be ~d** essere sorpreso (at da). **~ing** *adj* sorprendente. **~ingly** *adv* sorprendentemente

surrender /sə'rendə(r)/ *n* resa *f* ● *vi* arrendersi ● *vt* cedere

surreptitious /sʌrəp'tɪʃəs/ *adj* & *adv* di nascosto

surround /sə'raʊnd/ *vt* circondare. **~ing** *adj* circostante. **~ings** *npl* dintorni *mpl*

surveillance /sə'veɪləns/ *n* sorveglianza *f*

survey[1] /'sɜːveɪ/ *n* sguardo *m*; (*poll*) sondaggio *m*; (*investigation*) indagine *f*; (*of land*) rilevamento *m*; (*of house*) perizia f

survey[2] /səˈveɪ/ vt esaminare; fare un rilevamento di (land); fare una perizia di (building). ~or n perito m; (of land) topografo, -a mf

survival /səˈvaɪvl/ n sopravvivenza f; (relic) resto m

surviv|e /səˈvaɪv/ vt sopravvivere a ●vi sopravvivere. ~or n superstite mf; be a ~or 🔲 riuscire sempre a cavarsela

susceptible /səˈseptəbl/ adj influenzabile; ~ to sensibile a

suspect[1] /səˈspekt/ vt sospettare; (assume) supporre

suspect[2] /ˈsʌspekt/ adj & n sospetto, -a mf

suspend /səˈspend/ vt appendere; (stop, from duty) sospendere. ~er belt n reggicalze m inv. ~ders npl giarrettiere fpl; (Am: braces) bretelle mpl

suspense /səˈspens/ n tensione f; (in book etc) suspense f

suspension /səˈspenʃn/ n (Auto) sospensione f. ~ bridge n ponte m sospeso

suspici|on /səˈspɪʃn/ n sospetto m; (trace) pizzico m; under ~on sospettato. ~ous adj sospettoso; (arousing suspicion) sospetto. ~ously adv sospettosamente; (arousing suspicion) in modo sospetto

sustain /səˈsteɪn/ vt sostenere; mantenere (life); subire (injury)

swab /swɒb/ n (Med) tampone m

swagger /ˈswægə(r)/ vi pavoneggiarsi

swallow[1] /ˈswɒləʊ/ vt/i inghiottire. □ ~ up vt divorare; (earth, crowd:) inghiottire

swallow[2] n (bird) rondine f

swam /swæm/ ▷SWIM

swamp /swɒmp/ n palude f ●vt fig sommergere. ~y adj paludoso

swan /swɒn/ n cigno m

swap /swɒp/ n 🔲 scambio m ●vt (pt/pp swapped) 🔲 scambiare (for con) ●vi fare cambio

swarm /swɔːm/ n sciame m ●vi sciamare; be ~ing with brulicare di

swarthy /ˈswɔːðɪ/ adj (-ier, -iest) di carnagione scura

swat /swɒt/ vt (pt/pp swatted) schiacciare

sway /sweɪ/ n fig influenza f ●vi oscillare; (person:) ondeggiare ●vt (influence) influenzare

swear /sweə(r)/ v (pt swore, pp sworn) ●vt giurare ●vi giurare; (curse) dire parolacce; ~ at sb imprecare contro qcno; ~ by 🔲 credere ciecamente in. ~-word n parolaccia f

sweat /swet/ n sudore m ●vi sudare

sweater /ˈswetə(r)/ n golf m inv

swede /swiːd/ n rapa f svedese

Swede|e n svedese mf. ~en n Svezia f. ~ish adj svedese

sweep /swiːp/ n scopata f, spazzata f; (curve) curva f; (movement) movimento m ampio; make a clean ~ fig fare piazza pulita ●v (pt/pp swept) ●vt scopare, spazzare; (wind:) spazzare ●vi (go swiftly) andare rapidamente; (wind:) soffiare. □ ~ away vt fig spazzare via. □ ~ up vt spazzare

sweeping /ˈswiːpɪŋ/ adj (gesture) ampio; (statement) generico; (changes) radicale

sweet /swiːt/ adj dolce; have a ~ tooth essere goloso ●n caramella f; (dessert) dolce m. ~ corn n mais m

sweeten /ˈswiːtn/ vt addolcire. ~er n dolcificante m

sweetheart n innamorato, -a mf; hi, ~ ciao, tesoro

swell /swel/ ●v (pt swelled, pp swollen or swelled) ●vi gonfiarsi; (increase) aumentare ●vt gonfiare; (increase) far salire. ~ing n gonfiore m

swept /swept/ ▷SWEEP

swerve /swɜːv/ vi deviare bruscamente

s

swift /swɪft/ *adj* rapido. ~**ly** *adv* rapidamente

swig /swɪg/ *n* 🄸 sorso *m* ● *vt* (*pt/pp* swigged) 🄸 scolarsi

swim /swɪm/ *n* have a ~ fare una nuotata ● *v* (*pt* swam, *pp* swum) ● *vi* nuotare; (*room:*) girare; **my head is** ~**ming** mi gira la testa ● *vt* percorrere a nuoto. ~**mer** *n* nuotatore, -trice *mf*

swimming /'swɪmɪŋ/ *n* nuoto *m*. ~-**baths** *npl* piscina *fsg*. ~ **costume** *n* costume *m* da bagno. ~-**pool** *n* piscina *f*. ~ **trunks** *npl* calzoncini *mpl* da bagno

'**swim-suit** *n* costume *m* da bagno

swindle /'swɪndl/ *n* truffa *f* ● *vt* truffare. ~**r** *n* truffatore, -trice *mf*

swine /swaɪn/ *n* 🄸 porco *m*

swing /swɪŋ/ *n* oscillazione *f*; (*shift*) cambiamento *m*; (*seat*) altalena *f*; (*Mus*) swing *m*; **in full** ~ in piena attività ● *v* (*pt/pp* swung) ● *vi* oscillare; (*on swing, sway*) dondolare; (*dangle*) penzolare; (*turn*) girare ● *vt* oscillare; far deviare (vote). ~-'**door** *n* porta *f* a vento

swipe /swaɪp/ *n* 🄸 botta *f* ● *vt* 🄸 colpire; (*steal*) rubare; far passare nella macchinetta (credit card); ~ **card** *n* pass *m* inv magnetico

Swiss /swɪs/ *adj & n* svizzero, -a *mf*; **the** ~ *pl* gli svizzeri. ~ '**roll** *n* rotolo *m* di pan di Spagna ripieno di marmellata

switch /swɪtʃ/ *n* interruttore *m*; (*change*) mutamento *m* ● *vt* cambiare; (*exchange*) scambiare ● *vi* cambiare; ~ **to** passare a. □ ~ **off** *vt* spegnere. □ ~ **on** *vt* accendere

switchboard *n* centralino *m*

Switzerland /'swɪtsələnd/ *n* Svizzera *f*

swivel /'swɪvl/ *v* (*pt/pp* swivelled) ● *vt* girare ● *vi* girarsi

swollen /'swəʊlən/ ▷SWELL ● *adj* gonfio. ~-'**headed** *adj* presuntuoso

swoop /swuːp/ *n* (*by police*) incursione *f* ● *vi* ~ [**down**] (bird:) piombare; *fig* fare un'incursione

sword /sɔːd/ *n* spada *f*

swore /swɔː(r)/ ▷SWEAR

sworn /swɔːn/ ▷SWEAR

swot /swɒt/ *n* 🄸 sgobbone, -a *mf* ● *vt* (*pt/pp* swotted) 🄸 sgobbare

swum /swʌm/ ▷SWIM

swung /swʌŋ/ ▷SWING

syllable /'sɪləbl/ *n* sillaba *f*

syllabus /'sɪləbəs/ *n* programma *m* [dei corsi]

symbol /'sɪmbl/ *n* simbolo *m* (of di). ~**ic** *adj* simbolico. ~**ism** *n* simbolismo *m*. ~**ize** *vt* simboleggiare

symmetr|**ical** /sɪ'metrɪkl/ *adj* simmetrico. ~**y** *n* simmetria *f*

sympathetic /sɪmpə'θetɪk/ *adj* (*understanding*) comprensivo; (*showing pity*) compassionevole. ~**ally** *adv* con comprensione/compassione

sympathize /'sɪmpəθaɪz/ *vi* capire; (*in grief*) solidarizzare; ~ **with sb** capire qcno/solidarizzare con qcno. ~**r** *n* (*Pol*) simpatizzante *mf*

sympathy /'sɪmpəθɪ/ *n* comprensione *f*; (*pity*) compassione *f*; (*condolences*) condoglianze *fpl*; **in** ~ **with** (*strike*) per solidarietà con

symphony /'sɪmfənɪ/ *n* sinfonia *f*

symptom /'sɪmptəm/ *n* sintomo *m*. ~**atic** *adj* sintomatico (of di)

synagogue /'sɪnəgɒg/ *n* sinagoga *f*

synchronize /'sɪŋkrənaɪz/ *vt* sincronizzare

syndicate /'sɪndɪkət/ *n* gruppo *m*

synonym /'sɪnənɪm/ *n* sinonimo *m*. ~**ous** *adj* sinonimo

syntax /'sɪntæks/ *n* sintassi *f inv*

synthesize /'sɪnθəsaɪz/ *vt* sintetizzare. ~**r** *n* (*Mus*) sintetizzatore *m*

synthetic /sɪn'θetɪk/ *adj* sintetico ● *n* fibra *f* sintetica

syringe /sɪ'rɪndʒ/ *n* siringa *f*

syrup /'sɪrəp/ *n* sciroppo *m*; *treacle* tipo *m* di melassa

system | take

system /ˈsɪstəm/ n sistema m. **∼atic** adj sistematico

Tt

tab /tæb/ n linguetta f; (with name) etichetta f; **keep ∼s on** □ sorvegliare; **pick up the ∼** □ pagare il conto

table /ˈteɪbl/ n tavolo m; (list) tavola f; **at [the] ∼** a tavola; **∼ of contents** tavola f delle materie ● vt proporre. **∼-cloth** n tovaglia f. **∼-spoon** n cucchiaio m da tavola. **∼spoon[ful]** n cucchiaiata f

tablet /ˈtæblɪt/ n pastiglia f; (slab) lastra f; **∼ of soap** saponetta f

table tennis n tennis m da tavolo; (everyday level) ping pong m

tabloid /ˈtæblɔɪd/ n [giornale m formato] tabloid m inv; pej giornale m scandalistico

taboo /təˈbuː/ adj tabù inv ● n tabù m inv

tacit /ˈtæsɪt/ adj tacito

taciturn /ˈtæsɪtɜːn/ adj taciturno

tack /tæk/ n (nail) chiodino m; (stitch) imbastitura f; (Naut) virata f; fig linea f di condotta ● vt inchiodare; (sew) imbastire ● vi (Naut) virare

tackle /ˈtækl/ n (equipment) attrezzatura f; (football etc) contrasto m, tackle m inv ● vt affrontare

tacky /ˈtækɪ/ adj (paint) non ancora asciutto; (glue) appiccicoso; fig pacchiano

tact /tækt/ n tatto m. **∼ful** adj pieno di tatto; (remark) delicato. **∼fully** adv con tatto

tactic|al /ˈtæktɪkl/ adj tattico. **∼s** npl tattica fsg

tactless /ˈtæktlɪs/ adj privo di tatto.

∼ly adv senza tatto. **∼ness** n mancanza f di tatto; (of remark) indelicatezza f

tadpole /ˈtædpəʊl/ n girino m

tag[1] /tæg/ n (label) etichetta f ● vt (pt/pp tagged) attaccare l'etichetta a. □ **∼ along** vi seguire passo passo

tag[2] n (game) acchiapparello m

tail /teɪl/ n coda f; **∼s** pl (tailcoat) frac m inv ● vt (①: follow) pedinare. □ **∼ off** vi diminuire

tail light n fanalino m di coda

tailor /ˈteɪlə(r)/ n sarto m. **∼-made** adj fatto su misura

taint /teɪnt/ vt contaminare

take /teɪk/ n (Cinema) ripresa f ● v (pt took, pp taken) ● vt prendere; (to a place) portare (person, object); (contain) contenere (passengers etc); (endure) sopportare; (require) occorrere; (teach) insegnare; (study) studiare (subject); fare (exam, holiday, photograph, walk, bath); sentire (pulse); misurare (sb's temperature); **∼ sb prisoner** fare prigioniero qcno; **be ∼n ill** ammalarsi; **∼ sth calmly** prendere con calma qcsa ● vi (plant:) attecchire. □ **∼ after** vt assomigliare a. □ **∼ away** vt (with one) portare via; (remove) togliere; (subtract) sottrarre; **'to ∼ away'** 'da asporto'. □ **∼ back** vt riprendere; ritirare (statement); (return) riportare [indietro]. □ **∼ down** vt portare giù; (remove) tirare giù; (write down) prendere nota di. □ **∼ in** vt (bring indoors) portare dentro; (to sb's home) ospitare; (understand) capire; (deceive) ingannare; riprendere (garment); (include) includere. □ **∼ off** vt togliersi (clothes); (deduct) togliere; (mimic) imitare; **∼ time off** prendere delle vacanze; **∼ oneself off** andarsene ● vi (Aeron) decollare. □ **∼ on** vt farsi carico di; assumere (employee); (as opponent) prendersela con. □ **∼ out** vt portare fuori; togliere (word, stain); (withdraw) ritirare (money, books); **∼**

s
t

out a subscription to sth abbonarsi a qcsa; ~ it out on sb ⚠ prendersela con qcno. □ ~ **over** vt assumere il controllo di (firm) ● vi ~ over from sb sostituire qcno; (permanently) succedere a qcno. □ ~ **to** vt (as a habit) darsi a; I took to her (liked) mi è piaciuta. □ ~ **up** vt portare su; accettare (offer); intraprendere (profession); dedicarsi a (hobby); prendere (time); occupare (space); tirare su (floor-boards); accorciare (dress); ~ sth up with sb discutere qcsa con qcno ● vi ~ up with sb legarsi a qcno

take: ~-**off** n (Aeron) decollo m. ~-**over** n rilevamento m

takings /'teɪkɪŋz/ npl incassi mpl

tale /teɪl/ n storia f; pej fandonia f

talent /'tælənt/ n talento m. ~ed adj [ricco] di talento

talk /tɔːk/ n conversazione f; (lecture) conferenza f; (gossip) chiacchere fpl; make small ~ parlare del più e del meno ● vi parlare ● vt parlare di (politics etc); ~ sb into sth convincere qcno di qcsa. □ ~ **over** vt discutere

talkative /'tɔːkətɪv/ adj loquace

tall /tɔːl/ adj alto. ~boy n cassettone m. ~ order n impresa f difficile. ~ 'story n frottola f

tally /'tælɪ/ n conteggio m; keep a ~ of tenere il conto di ● vi coincidere

tambourine /tæmbə'riːn/ n tamburello m

tame /teɪm/ adj (animal) domestico; (dull) insulso ● vt domare. ~ly adv docilmente. ~r n domatore, -trice mf

tamper /'tæmpə(r)/ vi ~ with manomettere

tampon /'tæmpon/ n tampone m

tan /tæn/ adj marrone rossiccio ● n marrone m rossiccio; (from sun) abbronzatura f ● v (pt/pp tanned) ● vt conciare (hide) ● vi abbronzarsi

tang /tæŋ/ n sapore m forte; (smell)

odore m penetrante

tangent /'tændʒənt/ n tangente f

tangible /'tændʒɪbl/ adj tangibile

tangle /'tæŋgl/ n groviglio m; (in hair) nodo m ● vt ~ [up] aggrovigliare ● vi aggrovigliarsi

tango /'tæŋgəʊ/ n tango m inv

tank /tæŋk/ n contenitore m; (for petrol) serbatoio m; (fish ~) acquario m; (Mil) carro m armato

tanker /'tæŋkə(r)/ n nave f cisterna; (lorry) autobotte f

tantrum /'tæntrəm/ n scoppio m d'ira

tap /tæp/ n rubinetto m; (knock) colpo m; on ~ a disposizione ● v (pt/pp tapped) ● vt dare un colpetto a; sfruttare (resources); mettere sotto controllo (telephone) ● vi picchiettare. ~-**dance** n tip tap m ● vi ballare il tip tap

tape /teɪp/ n nastro m; (recording) cassetta f ● vt legare con nastro; (record) registrare

tape-measure n metro m [a nastro]

taper /'teɪpə(r)/ n candela f sottile ● taper off vi assottigliarsi

tape recorder n registratore m

tapestry /'tæpɪstrɪ/ n arazzo m

tar /tɑː(r)/ n catrame m ● vt (pt/pp tarred) incatramare

target /'tɑːgɪt/ n bersaglio m; fig obiettivo m

tarnish /'tɑːnɪʃ/ vi ossidarsi ● vt ossidare; fig macchiare

tart[1] /tɑːt/ adj aspro; fig acido

tart[2] n crostata f; (individual) crostatina f; (🔲: prostitute) donnaccia f ● tart up vt ⚠ ~ oneself up agghindarsi

tartan /'tɑːtn/ n tessuto m scozzese tartan m inv ● attrib di tessuto scozzese

task /tɑːsk/ n compito m; take sb to ~ riprendere qcno. ~ force n (Pol) commissione *f*; (Mil) task-force *f inv*

tassel /'tæsl/ *n* nappa *f*

taste /teɪst/ *n* gusto *m*; (sample) assaggio *m*; **get a** ~ **of sth** *fig* assaporare il gusto di qcsa ● *vt* sentire il sapore di; (sample) assaggiare ● *vi* sapere (**of** di); **it** ~**s lovely** è ottimo. ~**ful** *adj* di [buon] gusto. ~**fully** *adv* con gusto. ~**less** *adj* senza gusto. ~**lessly** *adv* con cattivo gusto

tasty /'teɪstɪ/ *adj* (-ier, -iest) saporito

tat /tæt/ ▷ **TIT²**

tatter|ed /'tætəd/ *adj* cencioso; (pages) stracciato. ~**s** *npl* **in** ~**s** a brandelli

tattoo¹ /tæ'tu:/ *n* tatuaggio *m* ● *vt* tatuare

tattoo² *n* (Mil) parata *f* militare

tatty /'tætɪ/ *adj* (-ier, -iest) (clothes, person) trasandato; (book) malandato

taught /tɔːt/ ▷ **TEACH**

taunt /tɔːnt/ *n* scherno *m* ● *vt* schernire

Taurus /'tɔːrəs/ *n* Toro *m*

taut /tɔːt/ *adj* teso

tax /tæks/ *n* tassa *f*; (on income) imposte *fpl*; **before** ~ (price) tasse escluse; (salary) lordo ● *vt* tassare; *fig* mettere alla prova; ~ **with** accusare di. ~**able** *adj* tassabile. ~**ation** *n* tasse *fpl*. ~ **evasion** *n* evasione *f* fiscale. ~-**free** *adj* esentasse. ~ **haven** *n* paradiso *m* fiscale

taxi /'tæksɪ/ *n* taxi *m inv* ● *vi* (*pt/pp* taxied, *pres p* taxiing) (aircraft:) rullare. ~ **driver** *n* tassista *mf*. ~ **rank** *n* posteggio *m* per taxi

taxpayer *n* contribuente *mf*

tea /ti:/ *n* tè *m inv*. ~-**bag** *n* bustina *f* di tè. ~-**break** *n* intervallo *m* per il tè

teach /ti:tʃ/ *vt/i* (*pt/pp* taught) insegnare; ~ **sb sth** insegnare qcsa a qcno. ~**er** *n* insegnante *mf*; (primary)

maestro, -a *mf*. ~**ing** *n* insegnamento *m*

teacup *n* tazza *f* da tè

team /ti:m/ *n* squadra *f*; *fig* équipe *f inv* ● **team up** *vi* unirsi

team-work *n* lavoro *m* di squadra; *fig* lavoro *m* d'équipe

teapot *n* teiera *f*

tear¹ /teə(r)/ *n* strappo *m* ● *v* (*pt* tore, *pp* torn) ● *vt* strappare ● *vi* strappare; (material:) strapparsi; (run) precipitarsi. □ ~ **apart** *vt* (*fig*: criticize) fare a pezzi; (separate) dividere. □ ~ **away** *vt* ~ **oneself away** andare via; ~ **oneself away from** staccarsi da (television). □ ~ **open** *vt* aprire strappando. □ ~ **up** *vt* strappare; rompere (agreement)

tear² /tɪə(r)/ *n* lacrima *f*. ~**ful** *adj* (person) in lacrime; (farewell) lacrimevole. ~**fully** *adv* in lacrime. ~-**gas** *n* gas *m* lacrimogeno

tease /ti:z/ *vt* prendere in giro (person); tormentare (animal)

tea: ~-**set** *n* servizio *m* da tè. ~-**spoon** *n* cucchiaino *m* [da tè]

teat /ti:t/ *n* capezzolo *m*; (on bottle) tettarella *f*

tea-towel *n* strofinaccio *m* [per i piatti]

technical /'teknɪkl/ *adj* tecnico. ~**ity** *n* tecnicismo *m*; (Jur) cavillo *m* giuridico. ~**ly** *adv* tecnicamente; (strictly) strettamente

technician /tek'nɪʃn/ *n* tecnico, -a *mf*

technique /tek'ni:k/ *n* tecnica *f*

technological /teknə'lɒdʒɪkl/ *adj* tecnologico

technology /tek'nɒlədʒɪ/ *n* tecnologia *f*

tedious /'ti:dɪəs/ *adj* noioso

tedium /'ti:dɪəm/ *n* tedio *m*

teem /ti:m/ *vi* (rain) piovere a dirotto; **be** ~**ing with** (full of) pullulare di

t

teenage /ˈtiːneɪdʒ/ adj per ragazzi; ~ **boy/girl** adolescente mf. ~**r** n adolescente mf

teens /tiːnz/ npl the ~ l'adolescenza fsg; **be in one's** ~ essere adolescente

teeny /ˈtiːnɪ/ adj (-ier, -iest) piccolissimo

teeter /ˈtiːtə(r)/ vi barcollare

teeth /tiːθ/ ▷**TOOTH**

teeth|e /tiːð/ vi mettere i [primi] denti. ~**ing troubles** npl fig difficoltà fpl iniziali

telecommunications /ˌtelɪkəmjuːnɪˈkeɪʃnz/ npl telecomunicazioni fpl

telegram /ˈtelɪɡræm/ n telegramma m

telepathy /tɪˈlepəθɪ/ n telepatia f

telephone /ˈtelɪfəʊn/ n telefono m; **be on the** ~ avere il telefono; (be telephoning) essere al telefono ● vt telefonare a ● vi telefonare

telephone: ~ **booth** n, ~ **box** n cabina f telefonica. ~ **directory** n elenco m telefonico

telephonist /tɪˈlefənɪst/ n telefonista mf

telescop|e /ˈtelɪskəʊp/ n telescopio m. ~**ic** adj telescopico

televise /ˈtelɪvaɪz/ vt trasmettere per televisione

television /ˈtelɪvɪʒn/ n televisione f; **watch** ~ guardare la televisione. ~ **set** n televisore m

teleworking /ˈtelɪwɜːkɪŋ/ n telelavoro m

telex /ˈteleks/ n telex m inv

tell /tel/ vt (pt/pp **told**) dire; raccontare (story); (distinguish) distinguere (from da); ~ **sb sth** dire qcsa a qcno; ~ **the time** dire l'ora; I couldn't ~ **why**... non sapevo perché... ● vi (produce an effect) avere effetto; **time will** ~ il tempo ce lo dirà; **his age is beginning to** ~ l'età comincia a farsi sentire [per

lui]; **you mustn't** ~ non devi dire niente. □ ~ **off** vt sgridare

teller /ˈtelə(r)/ n (in bank) cassiere, -a mf

telling /ˈtelɪŋ/ adj significativo; (argument) efficace

telly /ˈtelɪ/ n 🔲 tv f inv

temp /temp/ n 🔲 impiegato, -a mf temporaneo, -a

temper /ˈtempə(r)/ n (disposition) carattere m; (mood) umore m; (anger) collera f; **lose one's** ~ arrabbiarsi; **be in a** ~ essere arrabbiato; **keep one's** ~ mantenere la calma

temperament /ˈtemprəmənt/ n temperamento m. ~**al** adj (moody) capriccioso

temperate /ˈtempərət/ adj (climate) temperato

temperature /ˈtemprətʃə(r)/ n temperatura f; **have a** ~ avere la febbre

temple[1] /ˈtempl/ n tempio m

temple[2] n (Anat) tempia f

tempo /ˈtempəʊ/ n ritmo m; (Mus) tempo m

temporar|y /ˈtempərərɪ/ adj temporaneo; (measure, building) provvisorio. ~**ily** adv temporaneamente; (introduced, erected) provvisoriamente

tempt /tempt/ vt tentare; sfidare (fate); ~ **sb to** indurre qcno a; be ~**ed** essere tentato (to di); I am ~**ed by** the offer l'offerta mi tenta. ~**ation** n tentazione f. ~**ing** adj allettante; (food, drink) invitante

ten /ten/ adj dieci

tenaci|ous /tɪˈneɪʃəs/ adj tenace. ~**ty** n tenacia f

tenant /ˈtenənt/ n inquilino, -a mf; (Comm) locatario, -a mf

tend /tend/ vi **to do sth** tendere a far qcsa

tendency /ˈtendənsɪ/ n tendenza f

tender[1] /ˈtendə(r)/ n (Comm) offerta

f: be legal ∼ avere corso legale ● vt offrire; presentare (resignation)

tender² /adj/ tenero; (painful) dolorante. ∼ly adv teneramente. ∼ness n tenerezza f; (painfulness) dolore m

tendon /'tendən/ n tendine m

tennis /'tenɪs/ n tennis m. ∼-court n campo m da tennis. ∼ player n tennista mf

tenor /'tenə(r)/ n tenore m

tense¹ /tens/ n (Gram) tempo m

tense² adj teso ● vt tendere (muscle). □ ∼ up vi tendersi

tension /'tenʃn/ n tensione f

tent /tent/ n tenda f

tentacle /'tentəkl/ n tentacolo m

tentative /'tentətɪv/ adj provvisorio; (smile, gesture) esitante. ∼ly adv timidamente; (accept) provvisoriamente

tenterhooks /'tentəhʊks/ npl be on ∼ essere sulle spine

tenth /tenθ/ adj decimo ● n decimo, -a mf

tenuous /'tenjʊəs/ adj fig debole

tepid /'tepɪd/ adj tiepido

term /tɜ:m/ n periodo m; (Sch) (Univ) trimestre m; (expression) termine m; ∼s pl (conditions) condizioni fpl; ∼ of office carica f; in the short/long ∼ a breve/lungo termine; be on good/bad ∼s essere in buoni/cattivi rapporti; come to ∼s with accettare (past, fact); easy ∼s facilità f di pagamento

terminal /'tɜ:mɪn(ə)l/ adj finale; (Med) terminale ● n (Aeron) terminal m inv; (Rail) stazione f di testa; (of bus) capolinea m; (on battery) morsetto m; (Comput) terminale m. ∼ly adv be ∼ly ill essere in fase terminale

terminate /'tɜ:mɪneɪt/ vt terminare; rescindere (contract); interrompere (pregnancy) ● vi terminare; ∼e in finire in. ∼ion n termine m; (Med) interruzione f di gravidanza

terminology /tɜ:mɪ'nɒlədʒɪ/ n terminologia f

terrace /'terəs/ n terrazza f; (houses) fila f di case a schiera; the ∼s (Sport) le gradinate. ∼d house n casa f a schiera

terrain /te'reɪn/ n terreno m

terrible /'terəbl/ adj terribile

terrific /tə'rɪfɪk/ adj ① (excellent) fantastico; (huge) enorme. ∼ally adv ① terribilmente

terri|fy /'terɪfaɪ/ vt (pt/pp -ied) atterrire; be ∼fied essere terrorizzato. ∼fying adj terrificante

territorial /terɪ'tɔ:rɪəl/ adj territoriale

territory /'terɪtərɪ/ n territorio m

terror /'terə(r)/ n terrore m. ∼ism n terrorismo m. ∼ist n terrorista mf. ∼ize vt terrorizzare

terse /tɜ:s/ adj conciso

test /test/ n esame m; (in laboratory) esperimento m; (of friendship, machine) prova m; (of intelligence, aptitude) test m inv; put to the ∼ mettere alla prova ● vt esaminare; provare (machine)

testament /'testəmənt/ n testamento m; Old/New T∼ Antico/Nuovo Testamento m

testicle /'testɪkl/ n testicolo m

testify /'testɪfaɪ/ vt/i (pt/pp -ied) testimoniare

testimonial /testɪ'məʊnɪəl/ n lettera f di referenze

testimony /'testɪmənɪ/ n testimonianza f

'test: ∼ match n partita f internazionale. ∼-tube n provetta f

tether /'teðə(r)/ n be at the end of one's ∼ non poterne più

text /tekst/ n testo m. ∼book n manuale m

textile /'tekstaɪl/ adj tessile ● n stoffa f

text message n sms m inv, breve messaggio m di testo

texture /'tekstʃə(r)/ n (of skin)

t

grana *f*; (*of food*) consistenza *f*; of a smooth ~ (*to the touch*) soffice al tatto

Thames /temz/ *n* Tamigi *m*

than /ðan/, *accentato* /ðæn/ *conj* che; (*with numbers, names*) di; older ~ me più vecchio di me

thank /θæŋk/ *vt* ringraziare; ~ you [very much] grazie [mille]. ~ful *adj* grato. ~fully *adv* con gratitudine; (*happily*) fortunatamente. ~less *adj* ingrato

thanks /θæŋks/ *npl* ringraziamenti *mpl*; ~! □ grazie!; ~ to grazie a

that /ðat/
● *adj & pron* (*pl* those) quel, quei *pl*; (*before s + consonant, gn, ps and z*) quello, quegli *pl*; (*before vowel*) quell' *mf*, quegli *mpl*, quelle *fpl*; ~ one quello; I don't like those quelli non mi piacciono; ~ is cioè; is ~ you? sei tu?; who is ~? chi è?; what did you do after ~? cosa hai fatto dopo?; like ~ in questo modo, così; a man like ~ un uomo così; ~ is why ecco perché; ~'s it! (*you've understood*) ecco!; (*I've finished*) ecco fatto!; (*I've had enough*) basta così!; (*there's nothing more*) tutto qui!; ~'s ~! (*with job*) ecco fatto!; (*with relationship*) è tutto finito!; and ~'s ~! punto e basta! all ~ I know tutto quello che so
● *adv* così; it wasn't ~ good non era poi così buono
● *rel pron* che; the man ~ I spoke to l'uomo con cui ho parlato; the day ~ I saw him il giorno in cui l'ho visto; all ~ I know tutto quello che so
● *conj* che; I think ~… penso che…

thaw /θɔː/ *n* disgelo *m* ● *vt* fare scongelare (*food*) ● *vi* (*food:*) scon-

gelarsi; it's ~ing sta sgelando

the /ðə/, *di fronte a una vocale* /ðiː/
● *def art* il, la *f*; i *mpl*, le *fpl*; (*before s + consonant, gn, ps and z*) lo, gli *mpl*; (*before vowel*) l' *mf*, gli *mpl*, le *fpl*; at ~ cinema/station al cinema/alla stazione; from ~ cinema/station dal cinema/ dalla stazione
● *adv* ~ more ~ better più ce n'è meglio è; (*with reference to pl*) più ce ne sono, meglio è; all ~ better tanto meglio

theatre /'θɪətə(r)/ *n* teatro *m*; (*Med*) sala *f* operatoria

theatrical /θɪ'ætrɪkl/ *adj* teatrale; (*showy*) melodrammatico

theft /θeft/ *n* furto *m*

their /ðeə(r)/ *adj* il loro *m*, la loro *f*, i loro *mpl*, le loro *fpl*; ~ mother/ father la loro madre/il loro padre

theirs /ðeəz/ *poss pron* il loro *m*, la loro *f*, i loro *mpl*, le loro *fpl*; a friend of ~ un loro amico; friends of ~ dei loro amici; those are ~ quelli sono loro; (*as opposed to ours*) quelli sono i loro

them /ðem/ *pron* (*direct object*) li *m*, le *f*; (*indirect object*) gli, loro *fml*; (*after prep. with people*) loro; (*after preposition: with things*) essi; we haven't seen ~ non li/le abbiamo visti/viste; give ~ the money dai loro or dagli i soldi; give it to ~ daglielo; I've spoken to ~ ho parlato con loro; it's ~ sono loro

theme /θiːm/ *n* tema *m*. ~ park *n* parco *m* a tema. ~ song *n* motivo *m* conduttore

themselves *pron* (*reflexive*) si; (*emphatic*) se stessi; they poured ~ a drink si sono versati da bere; they said so ~ lo hanno detto loro stessi; they kept it to ~ se lo sono tenuti per sé; by ~ da soli

then /ðen/ *adv* allora; (*next*) poi; by

~ (in the past) ormai; (in the future) per allora; since ~ sin da allora; before ~ prima di allora; from ~ on da allora in poi; now and ~ ogni tanto; there and ~ all'istante ●adj di allora

theoretical /θɪəˈretɪkl/ adj teorico

theory /ˈθɪərɪ/ n teoria f; in ~ in teoria

therapeutic /θerəˈpjuːtɪk/ adj terapeutico

therapist /ˈθerəpɪst/ n terapista mf. ~y n terapia f

there /ðeə(r)/ adv là, lì; down/up ~ laggiù/lassù; ~ is/are c'è/ci sono; he/she is eccolo/eccola ●int ~, ~! dai, su!

there: ~abouts adv [or] ~abouts (roughly) all'incirca. ~fore /-fɔː(r)/ adv perciò

thermometer /θəˈmɒmɪtə(r)/ n termometro m

thermostat /ˈθɜːməstæt/ n termostato m

thesaurus /θɪˈsɔːrəs/ n dizionario m dei sinonimi

these /ðiːz/ ▷THIS

thesis /ˈθiːsɪs/ n (pl -ses /-siːz/) tesi f inv

they /ðeɪ/ pron loro; ~ are tired sono stanchi; we're going, but ~ are not noi andiamo, ma loro no; ~ say (generalizing) si dice; ~ are building a new road stanno costruendo una nuova strada

thick /θɪk/ adj spesso; (forest) fitto; (liquid) denso; (hair) folto; (fig: stupid) ottuso; (I: close) molto unito; be 5 mm ~ essere 5 mm di spessore ●adv densamente ●n the ~ of nel mezzo di. ~en vi ispessire (sauce) ●vi infittirsi; (fog) infittirsi. ~ly adv densamente; (cut) a fette spesse. ~ness n spessore m

thief /θiːf/ n (pl thieves) ladro, -a m

thigh /θaɪ/ n coscia f

thimble /ˈθɪmbl/ n ditale m

thin /θɪn/ adj (thinner, thinnest) sottile; (shoes, sweater) leggero; (liquid) liquido; (person) magro; (fig: excuse, plot) inconsistente ●adv = thinly ●v (pt/pp thinned) ●vt diluire (liquid) ●vi diradarsi. □ ~ out vi diradarsi. ~ly adv (populated) scarsamente; (disguised) leggermente; (cut) a fette sottili

thing /θɪŋ/ n cosa f; ~s pl (belongings) roba fsg; for one ~ in primo luogo; the right ~ la cosa giusta; just the ~! proprio quel che ci vuole!; how are ~s? come vanno le cose?; the latest ~ I l'ultima cosa; the best ~ would be la cosa migliore sarebbe; poor ~! poveretto!

think /θɪŋk/ vt/i (pt/pp thought) pensare; (believe) credere; I ~ so credo di sì; what do you ~? (what is your opinion?) cosa ne pensi?; ~ of/about pensare a; what do you ~ of it? cosa ne pensi di questo?. □ ~ over vt riflettere su. □ ~ up vt escogitare

third /θɜːd/ adj & n terzo, -a mf. ~ly adv terzo. ~-rate adj scadente

thirst /θɜːst/ n sete f. ~ily adv con sete. ~y adj assetato; be ~y aver sete

thirteen /θɜːˈtiːn/ adj tredici. ~th adj tredicesimo

thirtieth /ˈθɜːtɪɪθ/ adj trentesimo

thirty /ˈθɜːtɪ/ adj trenta

this /ðɪs/ adj (pl these) questo; ~ man/woman quest'uomo/questa donna; these men/women questi uomini/queste donne; ~ one questo; ~ morning/evening stamattina/stasera ●pron (pl these) questo; we talked about ~ and that abbiamo parlato del più e del meno; like ~ così; ~ is Peter questo è Peter; (Teleph) sono Peter; who is ~ chi è?; (Teleph) chi parla? ●adv così; ~ big così grande

thistle /ˈθɪsl/ n cardo m

thorn /θɔːn/ n spina f. ~y adj

spinoso

thorough /ˈθʌrə/ adj completo; (knowledge) profondo; (clean, search, training) a fondo; (person) scrupoloso

thorough∼bred n purosangue m inv. ∼**fare** n via f principale; 'no ∼**fare**' 'strada non transitabile'

thorough∣ly /ˈθʌrəlɪ/ adv (clean, search, know sth) a fondo; (extremely) estremamente. ∼**ness** n completezza f

those /ðəʊz/ ▷THAT

though /ðəʊ/ conj sebbene; as ∼ come se ● adv 🆃 tuttavia

thought /θɔːt/ ▷THINK ● n pensiero m; (idea) idea f. ∼**ful** adj pensieroso; (considerate) premuroso. ∼**fully** adv pensierosamente; (considerately) premurosamente. ∼**less** adj (inconsiderate) sconsiderato. ∼**lessly** adv con non curanza

thousand /ˈθaʊznd/ adj one/a ∼ mille m inv ● a ∼ mille m inv; ∼s of migliaia fpl di. ∼**th** adj millesimo ● n millesimo, -a f

thrash /θræʃ/ vt picchiare; (defeat) sconfiggere. □ ∼ **out** vt mettere a punto

thread /θred/ n filo m; (of screw) filetto m ● vt infilare (beads); ∼ one's way through farsi strada fra. ∼**bare** adj logoro

threat /θret/ n minaccia f

threaten /ˈθretn/ vt minacciare (to do di fare) ● vi fig incalzare. ∼**ing** adj minaccioso; (sky, atmosphere) sinistro

three /θriː/ adj tre. ∼**fold** adj & adv triplo. ∼**some** n trio m

threshold /ˈθreʃəʊld/ n soglia f

threw /θruː/ ▷THROW

thrift /θrɪft/ n economia f. ∼**y** adj parsimonioso

thrill /θrɪl/ n emozione f; (of fear) brivido m ● vt entusiasmare; be ∼**ed** with essere entusiasta di. ∼**er** n

(book) [romanzo m] giallo m; (film) [film m] giallo m. ∼**ing** adj eccitante

thrive /θraɪv/ vi (pt thrived or throve, pp thrived or thriven /ˈθrɪvn/) (business): prosperare; (child, plant): crescere bene; I ∼ on pressure mi piace essere sotto tensione

throat /θrəʊt/ n gola f; sore ∼ mal di gola

throb /θrɒb/ n pulsazione f; (of heart) battito m ● vi (pt/pp throbbed) (vibrate) pulsare; (heart): battere

throes /θrəʊz/ npl in the ∼ of fig alle prese con

throne /θrəʊn/ n trono m

throng /θrɒŋ/ n calca f

throttle /ˈθrɒtl/ n (on motorbike) manopola f di accelerazione ● vt strozzare

through /θruː/ prep attraverso; (during) durante; (by means of) tramite; (thanks to) grazie a; Saturday ∼ Tuesday Am da sabato a martedì incluso ● adv attraverso; ∼ and ∼ fino in fondo; wet ∼ completamente bagnato; read sth ∼ dare una lettura a qcsa; let ∼ lasciare passare (sb) ● adj (train) diretto; be ∼ (finished) aver finito; (Teleph) avere la comunicazione

throughout /θruːˈaʊt/ prep per tutto ● adv completamente; (time) per tutto il tempo

throw /θrəʊ/ n tiro m ● vt (pt threw, pp thrown) lanciare; (throw away) gettare; azionare (switch); disarcionare (rider); 🆃 disconcert) disorientare; fam dare (party). □ ∼ **away** vt gettare via. □ ∼ **out** vt gettare via; rigettare (plan); buttare fuori (person). □ ∼ **up** vt alzare ● vi (vomit) vomitare

thrush /θrʌʃ/ n tordo m

thrust /θrʌst/ n spinta f ● vt (pt/pp thrust) (push) spingere; (insert) conficcare; ∼ [up]on imporre a

thud /θʌd/ n tonfo m

thug /θʌg/ n delinquente m

thumb /θʌm/ n pollice m; as a rule of ∼ come regola generale; under sb's ∼ succube di qcno ● vt a ∼ a lift fare l'autostop. ∼-index n indice m a rubrica. ∼tack n Am puntina f da disegno

thump /θʌmp/ n colpo m; (noise) tonfo m ● vt battere su (table, door); battere (fist); colpire (person) ● vi battere (on su); (heart:) battere forte. □ ∼ about vi camminare pesantemente

thunder /ˈθʌndə(r)/ n tuono m; (loud noise) rimbombo m ● vi tuonare; (make loud noise) rimbombare. ∼clap n rombo m di tuono. ∼storm n temporale m. ∼y adj temporalesco

Thursday /ˈθɜːzdeɪ/ n giovedì m inv

thus /ðʌs/ adv così

thwart /θwɔːt/ vt ostacolare

Tiber /ˈtaɪbə(r)/ n Tevere m

tick /tɪk/ n (sound) ticchettio m; (mark) segno m; (fam: instant) attimo m ● vi ticchettare. □ ∼ off vt spuntare; (fam) sgridare. □ ∼ over vi (engine:) andare al minimo

ticket /ˈtɪkɪt/ n biglietto m; (for item deposited, library) tagliando m; (label) cartellino m; (fine) multa f. ∼-collector n controllore m. ∼-office n biglietteria f

tick|le /ˈtɪkl/ n solletico m ● vt fare il solletico a; (amuse) divertire ● vi fare prurito. ∼lish adj che soffre il solletico

tide /taɪd/ n marea f; (of events) corso m; the ∼ is in/out c'è alta/bassa marea ● tide over vt ∼ sb over aiutare qcno a andare avanti

tidily /ˈtaɪdɪlɪ/ adv in modo ordinato

tidiness /ˈtaɪdɪnɪs/ n ordine m

tidy /ˈtaɪdɪ/ adj (-ier, -iest) ordinato; (fam: amount) bello ● vt (pt/pp -ied) ∼ [up] ordinare; ∼ oneself up mettersi in ordine

tie /taɪ/ n cravatta f; (cord) legaccio m; (fig: bond) legame m; (restriction) im-

pedimento m; (Sport) pareggio m ● v (pres p tying) vt legare; fare (knot); be ∼d (in competition) essere in parità ● vi pareggiare. □ ∼ in with vi corrispondere a. □ ∼ up vt legare; vincolare (capital); be ∼d up (busy) essere occupato

tier /tɪə(r)/ n fila f; (of cake) piano m; (in stadium) gradinata f

tiger /ˈtaɪgə(r)/ n tigre f

tight /taɪt/ adj stretto; (taut) teso; (fam: drunk) sbronzo; (fam: mean) spilorcio; ∼ corner f brutta situazione f ● adv strettamente; (hold) forte; (closed) bene

tighten /ˈtaɪtn/ vt stringere; avvitare (screw); intensificare (control) ● vi stringersi

tight: ∼-fisted adj tirchio. ∼ly adv strettamente; (hold) forte; (closed) bene. ∼rope n fune f (da funambulo)

tile /taɪl/ n mattonella f; (on roof) tegola f ● vt rivestire di mattonelle (wall)

till¹ /tɪl/ prep & conj = until

till² n cassa f

tilt /tɪlt/ n inclinazione f; at full ∼ a tutta velocità ● vt inclinare ● vi inclinarsi

timber /ˈtɪmbə(r)/ n legname m

time /taɪm/ n tempo m; (occasion) volta f; (by clock) ora f; two ∼s four due volte quattro; at any ∼ in qualsiasi momento; this ∼ questa volta; at ∼s, from ∼ to ∼ ogni tanto; ∼ and again cento volte; two at a ∼ due alla volta; on ∼ in orario; in ∼ in tempo; (eventually) col tempo; in no ∼ al velocemente; in a year's ∼ fra un anno; behind ∼ in ritardo; behind the ∼s antiquato; for the ∼ being per il momento; what is the ∼? che ora è?; by the ∼ we arrive quando arriviamo; did you have a nice ∼? ti sei divertito?; have a good ∼! divertiti! ● vt

scegliere il momento per; cronome‐
trare (race); to be well ~d essere ben
calcolato

time: ~ **bomb** n bomba f a orolo‐
geria. ~ly adj opportuno. ~‐**table** n
orario m

timid /'tımıd/ adj (shy) timido; (fear‐
ful) timoroso

tin /tın/ n stagno m; (container) barat‐
tolo m ● vt (pt/pp tinned) inscatolare.
~ **foil** n [carta f] stagnola f

tinge /tındʒ/ n sfumatura f ● vt ~d
with fig misto a

tingle /'tıŋgl/ vi pizzicare

tinker /'tıŋkə(r)/ vi armeggiare

tinkle /'tıŋkl/ n tintinnio m; (🕾:
phone call) colpo m di telefono ● vi tin‐
tinnare

tinned /tınd/ adj in scatola

'tin opener n apriscatole m inv

tint /tınt/ n tinta f ● vt tingersi (hair)

tiny /'taını/ adj (-ier, -iest) mi‐
nuscolo

tip[1] /tıp/ n punta f

tip[2] n (money) mancia f; (advice) consi‐
glio m; (for rubbish) discarica f ● v (pt/
pp tipped) ● vt (tilt) inclinare; (overturn)
capovolgere; (pour) versare; (reward)
dare una mancia a ● vi inclinarsi;
(overturn) capovolgersi. □ ~ **off** vt ~
sb off (inform) fare una soffiata a
qcno. □ ~ **out** vt rovesciare. □ ~
over vt capovolgere ● vi capovolgersi

tipped /tıpt/ adj (cigarette) col filtro

tipsy /'tıpsı/ adj 🕾 brillo

tiptoe /'tıptəʊ/ n on ~ in punta
di piedi

tiptop /tıp'tɒp/ adj 🕾 in condizioni
perfette

tire /'taıə(r)/ vt stancare ● vi stan‐
carsi. ~d adj stanco; ~d **of** stanco
di; ~d **out** stanco morto. ~**less** adj
instancabile. ~**some** adj fastidioso

tiring /'taıərıŋ/ adj stancante

tissue /'tıʃuː/ n tessuto m; (handker‐
chief) fazzolettino m di carta.

~‐**paper** n carta f velina

tit[1] /tıt/ n (bird) cincia f

tit[2] n ~ **for tat** pan per focaccia

title /'taıtl/ n titolo m. ~‐**deed** n
atto m di proprietà. ~‐**role** n ruolo
m principale

---

to /tuː/, atono /tə/

● prep a; (to countries) in; (towards)
verso; (up to, until) fino a; **I'm
going to John's**/the butcher's
vado da John/dal macellaio;
come/go to sb venire/andare
da qcno; **to Italy**/Switzerland
in Italia/Svizzera; **I've never
been to Rome** non sono mai
stato a Roma; **go to the mar‐
ket** andare al mercato; **to the
toilet**/my room in bagno/
camera mia; **to an exhibition** a
una mostra; **to university** all'u‐
niversità; **twenty**/quarter to
eight le otto meno venti/un
quarto; **5 to 6 kilos** da 5 a 6
chili; **to the end** alla fine; **to
this day** fino a oggi; **to the
best of my recollection** per
quanto mi possa ricordare;
give/say sth to sb dare/dire
qcsa a qcno; **give it to me**
dammelo; **there's nothing to it**
è una cosa da niente

● verbal constructions to go andare;
learn to swim imparare a nuo‐
tare; **I want to/have to go**
voglio/devo andare; **it's easy to
forget** è facile da dimenticare;
too ill/tired to go troppo
malato/stanco per andare; **you
have to** devi; **I don't want to**
non voglio; **live to be 90** vivere
fino a 90 anni; **he was the last
to arrive** è stato l'ultimo ad ar‐
rivare; **to be honest,...** per es‐
sere sincero,...

● adv **pull to** chiudere; **to and fro**
avanti e indietro

toad /təʊd/ n rospo m. ~**stool** n fungo m velenoso

toast /təʊst/ n pane m tostato; (drink) brindisi m ● vt tostare (bread); (drink a ~ to) brindare a. ~**er** n tostapane m inv

tobacco /təˈbækəʊ/ n tabacco m. ~**nist's** [**shop**] n tabaccheria f

toboggan /təˈbɒgən/ n toboga m ● vi andare in toboga

today /təˈdeɪ/ adj & adv oggi m; a week ~ una settimana a oggi; ~'s paper il giornale di oggi

toddler /ˈtɒdlə(r)/ n bambino, -a mf ai primi passi

toe /təʊ/ n dito m del piede; (of footwear) punta f; **big** ~ alluce m ● vt ~ **the line** rigar diritto. ~**nail** n unghia f del piede

toffee /ˈtɒfɪ/ n caramella f al mou

together /təˈgeðə(r)/ adv insieme; (at the same time) allo stesso tempo; ~ **with** insieme a

toilet /ˈtɔɪlɪt/ n (lavatory) gabinetto m. ~ **paper** n carta f igienica

toiletries /ˈtɔɪlɪtrɪz/ npl articoli mpl da toilette

toilet roll n rotolo m di carta igienica

token /ˈtəʊkən/ n segno m; (counter) gettone m; (voucher) buono m ● attrib simbolico

told /təʊld/ ▷**TELL** ● adj **all** ~ in tutto

tolerab|le /ˈtɒl(ə)rəbl/ adj tollerabile; (not bad) discreto. ~**y** adv discretamente

toleran|ce /ˈtɒl(ə)r(ə)ns/ n tolleranza f. ~**t** adj tollerante. ~**tly** adv con tolleranza

tolerate /ˈtɒləreɪt/ vt tollerare

toll[1] /təʊl/ n pedaggio m; **death** ~ numero m di morti

toll[2] vi suonare a morto

tomato /təˈmɑːtəʊ/ n (pl -es) pomodoro m. ~ **ketchup** n ketchup m.

~ **purée** n concentrato m di pomodoro

tomb /tuːm/ n tomba f

'tombstone n pietra f tombale

tomorrow /təˈmɒrəʊ/ adj & adv domani m; ~ **morning** domani mattina; **the day after** ~ dopodomani; **see you** ~! a domani!

ton /tʌn/ n tonnellata f (= 1,016 kg.); ~**s of** 🔢 un sacco di

tone /təʊn/ n tono m; (colour) tonalità f inv ● **tone down** vt attenuare. □ ~ **up** vt tonificare (muscles)

tongs /tɒŋz/ npl pinze fpl

tongue /tʌŋ/ n lingua f; ~ **in cheek** (say) ironicamente. ~-**twister** n scioglilingua m inv

tonic /ˈtɒnɪk/ n tonico m; (for hair) lozione f per i capelli; fig toccasana m inv; ~ [**water**] acqua f tonica

tonight /təˈnaɪt/ adv stanotte; (evening) stasera ● n questa notte f; (evening) questa sera f

tonne /tʌn/ n tonnellata f metrica

tonsil /ˈtɒnsl/ n (Anat) tonsilla f. ~**litis** n tonsillite f

too /tuː/ adv troppo; (also) anche; ~ **many** troppi; ~ **much** troppo; ~ **little** troppo poco

took /tʊk/ ▷**TAKE**

tool /tuːl/ n attrezzo m

tooth /tuːθ/ n (pl **teeth**) dente m

tooth: ~**ache** n mal m di denti. ~**brush** n spazzolino m da denti. ~**paste** n dentifricio m. ~**pick** n stuzzicadenti m

top[1] /tɒp/ n (toy) trottola f

top[2] n **cima** f; (Sch) primo, -a mf; (upper part or half) parte f superiore; (of rage, list, road) inizio m; (upper surface) superficie f; (lid) coperchio m; (of bottle) tappo m; (garment) maglia f; (blouse) camicia f; (Auto) marcia f più alta; **at the** ~ fig al vertice; **at the** ~ **of one's voice** a squarciagola; **on** ~/**on** ~ **of** sopra; **on** ~ **of that** (besides) per di più; **from** ~ **to bottom**

t

da cima a fondo ● adj in alto; (official, floor) superiore; (pupil, musician etc) migliore; (speed) massimo ● vt (pt/pp topped) essere in testa a (list); (exceed) sorpassare; ~ped with ice-cream ricoperto di gelato. □ ~ up vt riempire

top: ~ 'floor n ultimo piano m. ~ hat n cilindro m. ~-heavy adj con la parte superiore sovraccarica

topic /'tɒpɪk/ n soggetto m; (of conversation) argomento m. ~al adj d'attualità

topless adj & adv topless

topple /'tɒpl/ vt rovesciare ● vi rovesciarsi. □ ~ off vi cadere

top-'secret adj segretissimo, top secret inv

torch /tɔːtʃ/ n torcia f [elettrica]; (flaming) fiaccola f

tore /tɔː(r)/ ▷ TEAR¹

torment¹ /'tɔːment/ n tormento m

torment² /tɔː'ment/ vt tormentare

torn /tɔːn/ ▷ TEAR¹ ● adj bucato

tornado /tɔː'neɪdəʊ/ n (pl -es) tornado m inv

torpedo /tɔː'piːdəʊ/ n (pl -es) siluro m ● vt silurare

torrent /'tɒrənt/ n torrente m. ~ial adj (rain) torrenziale

tortoise /'tɔːtəs/ n tartaruga f

torture /'tɔːtʃə(r)/ n tortura f ● vt torturare

Tory /'tɔːrɪ/ adj & n [T] conservatore, -trice mf

toss /tɒs/ vt gettare; (into the air) lanciare in aria; (shake) scrollare; (horse:) disarcionare; mescolare (salad); rivoltare facendo saltare in aria (pancake); ~ a coin fare testa o croce ● vi ~ and turn (in bed) rigirarsi; let's ~ for it facciamo testa o croce

tot¹ /tɒt/ n bimbetto, -a mf; (T: of liquor) goccio m

tot² vt (pt/pp totted) □ ~ up [T] fare la somma di

total /'təʊtl/ adj totale ● n totale m ● vt (pt/pp totalled) ammontare a; (add up) sommare

totalitarian /təʊtælɪ'teərɪən/ adj totalitario

totally /'təʊtəlɪ/ adv totalmente

totter /'tɒtə(r)/ vi barcollare; (government:) vacillare

touch /tʌtʃ/ n tocco m; (sense) tatto m; (contact) contatto m; (trace) traccia f; (of irony, humour) tocco m; get/be in ~ mettersi/essere in contatto ● vt toccare; (lightly) sfiorare; (equal) eguagliare; (fig: move) commuovere ● vi toccarsi. □ ~ down vi (Aeron) atterrare. □ ~ on vt fig accennare a. touch down vt ritoccare (painting). ~ing adj commovente. ~screen n touch screen inv. ~-tone adj a tastiera. ~y adj permaloso; (subject) delicato

tough /tʌf/ adj duro; (severe, harsh) severo; (durable) resistente; (resilient) forte

toughen /'tʌfn/ vt rinforzare. □ ~ up vt rendere più forte (person)

tour /tʊə(r)/ n giro m; (of building, town) visita f; (Theat, Sport) tournée inv; (of duty) servizio m ● vt visitare ● fare un giro turistico; (Theat) essere in tournée

tourism /'tʊərɪzm/ n turismo m. ~t n turista mf ● attrib turistico. ~t office n ufficio m turistico

tournament /'tʊənəmənt/ n torneo m

tousle /'taʊzl/ vt spettinare

tout /taʊt/ n (ticket ~) bagarino m; (horse-racing) informatore m ● vi ~ for sollecitare

tow /təʊ/ n rimorchio m; 'on ~' 'a rimorchio'; in ~ al seguito ● vt rimorchiare. □ ~ away vt portare via col carro attrezzi

toward[s] /tə'wɔːd(z)/ prep verso (with respect to) nei riguardi di

towel /'taʊəl/ n asciugamano m.

~ling *n* spugna *f*

tower /'taʊə(r)/ *n* torre *f* ● *vi* ~ **above** dominare. ~ **block** *n* palazzone *m*. ~ing *adj* torreggiante; (rage) violento

town /taʊn/ *n* città *f inv*. ~ 'hall *n* municipio *m*

toxic /'tɒksɪk/ *adj* tossico

toy /tɔɪ/ *n* giocattolo *m*. ~shop *n* negozio *m* di giocattoli. □ ~ **with** *vt* giocherellare con

trace /treɪs/ *n* traccia *f* ● *vt* seguire le tracce di; (find) rintracciare; (draw) tracciare; (with tracing-paper) ricalcare

track /træk/ *n* traccia *f*; (path, (Sport)) pista *f*; (Rail) binario *m*; **keep ~ of** tenere d'occhio ● *vt* seguire le tracce di. □ ~ **down** *vt* scovare

tracksuit *n* tuta *f* da ginnastica

tractor /'træktə(r)/ *n* trattore *m*

trade /treɪd/ *n* commercio *m*; (line of business) settore *m*; (craft) mestiere *m*; **by** ~ di mestiere ● *vt* commerciare; ~ **sth for sth** scambiare qcsa per qcsa ● *vi* commerciare. □ ~ **in** *vt* (give in part exchange) dare in pagamento parziale

trade mark *n* marchio *m* di fabbrica

trader /'treɪdə(r)/ *n* commerciante *mf*

trades 'union *n* sindacato *m*

tradition /trə'dɪʃn/ *n* tradizione *f*. ~al *adj* tradizionale. ~ally *adv* tradizionalmente

traffic /'træfɪk/ *n* traffico *m* ● *vi* (pt/ pp trafficked) trafficare

traffic: ~ **circle** *n Am* isola *f* rotatoria. ~ **jam** *n* ingorgo *m*. ~ **lights** *npl* semaforo *msg*. ~ **warden** *n* vigile *m* [urbano]; (woman) vigilessa *f*

tragedy /'trædʒədɪ/ *n* tragedia *f*

tragic /'trædʒɪk/ *adj* tragico. ~ally *adv* tragicamente

trail /treɪl/ *n* traccia *f*; (path) sentiero *m* ● *vi* strisciare; (plant:) arrampicarsi; ~ **[behind]** rimanere indietro; (in

competition) essere in svantaggio ● *vt* trascinare

trailer /'treɪlə(r)/ *n* (Auto) rimorchio *m*; (Am: caravan) roulotte *f inv*; (film) presentazione *f* (di un film)

train /treɪn/ *n* treno *m*; ~ **of thought** filo *m* dei pensieri ● *vt* formare professionalmente; (Sport) allenare; (aim) puntare; educare (child); addestrare (animal, soldier) ● *vi* fare il tirocinio; (Sport) allenarsi. ~ed *adj* (animal) addestrato (to do a fare)

trainee /treɪ'niː/ *n* apprendista *mf*

train|er /'treɪnə(r)/ *n* (Sport) allenatore, -trice *mf*; (in circus) domatore, -trice *mf*; (of dog, race-horse) addestratore, -trice *mf*; ~ers *pl* scarpe *fpl* da ginnastica. ~ing *n* tirocinio *m*; (Sport) allenamento *m*; (of animal, soldier) addestramento *m*

trait /treɪt/ *n* caratteristica *f*

traitor /'treɪtə(r)/ *n* traditore, -trice *mf*

tram /træm/ *n* tram *m inv*. ~-lines *npl* rotaie *fpl* del tram

tramp /træmp/ *n* (hike) camminata *f*; (vagrant) barbone, -a *mf*; (of feet) calpestio *m* ● *vi* camminare con passo pesante; (hike) percorrere a piedi

trample /'træmpl/ *vt/i* ~ **[on]** calpestare

trampoline /'træmpəliːn/ *n* trampolino *m*

trance /trɑːns/ *n* trance *f inv*

tranquil /'træŋkwɪl/ *adj* tranquillo. ~lity *n* tranquillità *f*

tranquillizer /'træŋkwɪlaɪzə(r)/ *n* tranquillante *m*

transatlantic /trænzət'læntɪk/ *adj* transatlantico

transcend /træn'send/ *vt* trascendere

transfer[1] /'trænsfɜː(r)/ *n* trasferimento *m*; (Sport) cessione *f*; (design) decalcomania *f*

transfer[2] /træns'fɜː(r)/ *v* (pt/pp

transferred) • vt trasferire; (Sport) cedere • vi trasferirsi; (when travelling) cambiare. ~able adj trasferibile

transform /træns'fɔːm/ vt trasformare. ~ation n trasformazione f. ~er n trasformatore m

transfusion /træns'fjuːʒn/ n trasfusione f

transient /'trænzɪənt/ adj passeggero

transistor /træn'zɪstə(r)/ n transistor m inv; (radio) radiolina f a transistor

transit /'trænzɪt/ n transito m; in ~ (goods) in transito

transition /træn'zɪʃn/ n transizione f. ~al adj di transizione

transitive /'trænzɪtɪv/ adj transitivo

translat|e /trænz'leɪt/ vt tradurre. ~ion n traduzione f. ~or n traduttore, -trice mf

transmission /trænz'mɪʃn/ n trasmissione f

transmit /trænz'mɪt/ vt (pt/pp transmitted) trasmettere. ~ter n trasmettitore m

transparen|cy /træn'spærənsɪ/ n (Phot) diapositiva f. ~t adj trasparente

transplant¹ /'trænsplɑːnt/ n trapianto m

transplant² /træns'plɑːnt/ vt trapiantare

transport¹ /'trænspɔːt/ n trasporto m

transport² /træn'spɔːt/ vt trasportare. ~ation n trasporto m

trap /træp/ n trappola f; (□: mouth) boccaccia f • vt (pt/pp trapped) intrappolare; schiacciare (finger in door). ~'door n botola f

trapeze /trə'piːz/ n trapezio m

trash /træʃ/ n robaccia f; (rubbish) spazzatura f; (nonsense) schiocchezze fpl. ~can n Am secchio m della spazzatura. ~y adj scadente

travel /'trævl/ n viaggi mpl • v (pt/pp travelled) • vi viaggiare; (to work) andare • vt percorrere (distance). ~ agency n agenzia f di viaggi. ~ agent n agente mf di viaggio

traveller /'trævələ(r)/ n viaggiatore, -trice mf; (Comm) commesso m viaggiatore; ~s pl (gypsies) zingari mpl. ~'s cheque n traveller's cheque m inv

trawler /'trɔːlə(r)/ n peschereccio m

tray /treɪ/ n vassoio m; (for baking) teglia f; (for documents) vaschetta f sparticarta; (of printer, photocopier) vassoio m

treacher|ous /'tretʃərəs/ adj traditore; (weather, currents) pericoloso. ~y n tradimento m

treacle /'triːkl/ n melassa f

tread /tred/ n andatura f; (step) gradino m; (of tyre) battistrada m inv • v (pt trod, pp trodden) • vi (walk) camminare. □ ~ on vt calpestare (grass), pestare (foot)

treason /'triːzn/ n tradimento m

treasure /'treʒə(r)/ n tesoro m • vt tenere in gran conto. ~r n tesoriere -a mf

treasury /'treʒərɪ/ n the T~ il Ministero del Tesoro

treat /triːt/ n piacere m; (present) regalo m; give sb a ~ fare una sorpresa a qcno • vt trattare; (Med) curare; ~ sb to sth offrire qcsa a qcno

treatise /'triːtɪz/ n trattato m

treatment /'triːtmənt/ n trattamento m; (Med) cura f

treaty /'triːtɪ/ n trattato m

treble /'trebl/ adj triplo • n (Mus: voice) voce f bianca • vt triplicare • vi triplicarsi. ~ clef n chiave f di violino

tree /triː/ n albero m

trek /trek/ n scarpinata f; (as holiday) trekking m inv • vi (pt/pp trekked) farsi una scarpinata; (on holiday) fare trekking

tremble /'trembl/ vi tremare

tremendous /trɪ'mendəs/ adj (huge) enorme; (🄸: excellent) formidabile. ~ly adv (very) straordinariamente; (adj lot) enormemente

tremor /'tremə(r)/ n tremito m; [earth] ~ scossa f [sismica]

trench /trentʃ/ n fosso m; (Mil) trincea f. ~ coat n trench m inv

trend /trend/ n tendenza f; (fashion) moda f. ~y adj (-ier, -iest) 🄸 di o alla moda

trepidation /trepɪ'deɪʃn/ n trepidazione f

trespass /'trespəs/ vi ~ on introdursi abusivamente in; fig abusare di. ~er n intruso, -a mf

trial /'traɪəl/ n (Jur) processo m; (test, ordeal) prova f; on ~ in prova; (Jur) in giudizio; by ~ and error per tentativi

triangle /'traɪæŋgl/ n triangolo m. ~ular adj triangolare

tribe /traɪb/ n tribù f inv

tribulation /trɪbjʊ'leɪʃn/ n tribolazione f

tribunal /traɪ'bjuːnl/ n tribunale m

tributary /'trɪbjʊtərɪ/ n affluente m

tribute /'trɪbjuːt/ n tributo m; pay ~ rendere omaggio

trick /trɪk/ n trucco m; (joke) scherzo m; (in cards) presa f; do the ~ 🄸 funzionare; play a ~ on fare uno scherzo a ● vt imbrogliare

trickle /'trɪkl/ vi colare

trick|ster /'trɪkstə(r)/ n imbroglione, -a mf. ~y adj (-ier, -iest) adj (operation) complesso; (situation) delicato

tricycle /'traɪsɪkl/ n triciclo m

tried /traɪd/ ▷TRY

trifl|e /'traɪfl/ n inezia f; (Culin) zuppa f inglese. ~ing adj insignificante

trigger /'trɪgə(r)/ n grilletto m ● vt ~ [off] scatenare

trim /trɪm/ adj (trimmer, trimmest) curato; (figure) snello ● n (of hair, hedge) spuntata f; (decoration) rifinitura f; in good ~ in buono stato; (person) in forma ● vt (pt/pp trimmed) spuntare (hair etc); (decorate) ornare; (Naut) orientare. ~ming n bordo m; ~mings pl (decorations) guarnizioni fpl; with all the ~mings (Culin) guarnito

trinket /'trɪŋkɪt/ n ninnolo m

trio /'triːəʊ/ n trio m

trip /trɪp/ n (excursion) gita f; (journey) viaggio m; (stumble) passo m falso ● v (pt/pp tripped) ● vt far inciampare ● vi inciampare (on/over in). □ ~ up vt far inciampare

tripe /traɪp/ n trippa f; (🄸: nonsense) fesserie fpl

triple /'trɪpl/ adj triplo ● vt triplicare ● vi triplicarsi

triplets /'trɪplɪts/ npl tre gemelli mpl

triplicate /'trɪplɪkət/ n in ~ in triplice copia

tripod /'traɪpɒd/ n treppiede m inv

trite /traɪt/ adj banale

triumph /'traɪʌmf/ n trionfo m ● vi trionfare (over su). ~ant adj trionfante. ~antly adv (exclaim) con tono trionfante

trivial /'trɪvɪəl/ adj insignificante. ~ity n banalità f inv

trolley /'trɒlɪ/ n carrello m; (Am: tram) tram m inv. ~ bus n filobus m inv

trombone /trɒm'bəʊn/ n trombone m

troop /truːp/ n gruppo m; ~s pl truppe fpl ● vi ~ in/out entrare/uscire in gruppo

trophy /'trəʊfɪ/ n trofeo m

tropic /'trɒpɪk/ n tropico m; ~s pl tropici mpl. ~al adj tropicale

trot /trɒt/ n trotto m ● vi (pt/pp trotted) trottare

trouble /'trʌbl/ n guaio m; (difficulties) problemi mpl; (inconvenience, Med) disturbo m; (conflict) conflitto

t

m; **be in** ~ essere nei guai; (swimmer, climber:) essere in difficoltà; **get into** ~ finire nei guai; **get sb into** ~ mettere qcno nei guai; **take the** ~ **to do sth** darsi la pena di far qcsa ● *vt* (*worry*) preoccupare; (*inconvenience*) disturbare; (*conscience, old wound:*) tormentare ● **i don't** ~**!** non ti disturbare!. ~**-maker** *n* be a ~**-maker** seminare zizzania. ~**some** *adj* fastidioso

trough /trɒf/ *n* trogolo *m*; (*atmospheric*) depressione *f*

troupe /truːp/ *n* troupe *f inv*

trousers /ˈtraʊzəz/ *npl* pantaloni *mpl*

trout /traʊt/ *n inv* trota *f*

trowel /ˈtraʊəl/ *n* (*for gardening*) paletta *f*; (*for builder*) cazzuola *f*

truant /ˈtruːənt/ *n* **play** ~ marinare la scuola

truce /truːs/ *n* tregua *f*

truck /trʌk/ *n* (*lorry*) camion *m inv*

trudge /trʌdʒ/ *n* camminata *f* faticosa ● *vi* arrancare

true /truː/ *adj* vero; **come** ~ avverarsi

truffle /ˈtrʌfl/ *n* tartufo *m*

truly /ˈtruːlɪ/ *adv* veramente; **Yours** ~ distinti saluti

trump /trʌmp/ *n* (*in cards*) atout *m inv*

trumpet /ˈtrʌmpɪt/ *n* tromba *f*. ~**er** *n* trombettista *m*

truncheon /ˈtrʌntʃn/ *n* manganello *m*

trunk /trʌŋk/ *n* (*of tree, body*) tronco *m*; (*of elephant*) proboscide *f*; (*for travelling, storage*) baule *m*; (*Am: of car*) bagagliaio *m*; ~**s** *pl* calzoncini *mpl* da bagno

truss /trʌs/ *n* (*Med*) cinto *m* erniario

trust /trʌst/ *n* fiducia *f*; (*group of companies*) trust *m inv*; (*organization*) associazione *f*; on ~ sulla parola ● *vt* fidarsi di; (*hope*) augurarsi ● *vi* ~ **in** credere in; ~ **to** affidarsi a. ~**ed** *adj* fidato

trustee /trʌsˈtiː/ *n* amministratore, -trice *mf* fiduciario, -a

'**trust|ful** /ˈtrʌstfl/ *adj* fiducioso. ~**ing** *adj* fiducioso. ~**worthy** *adj* fidato

truth /truːθ/ *n* (*pl* -s /truːðz/) verità *f inv*. ~**ful** *adj* veritiero. ~**fully** *adv* sinceramente

try /traɪ/ *n* tentativo *m*, prova *f*; (*in rugby*) meta *f* ● *v* (*pt/pp* **tried**) ● *vt* provare; (*be a strain on*) mettere a dura prova; (*Jur*) processare (*person*); discutere (*case*); ~ **to do sth** provare a fare qcsa ● *vi* provare. □ ~ **on** *vt* provarsi (*garment*). □ ~ **out** *vt* provare

trying /ˈtraɪɪŋ/ *adj* duro; (*person*) irritante

T-shirt /ˈtiː-/ *n* maglietta *f*

tub /tʌb/ *n* tinozza *f*; (*carton*) vaschetta *f*; (*bath*) vasca *f* da bagno

tuba /ˈtjuːbə/ *n* (*Mus*) tuba *f*

tubby /ˈtʌbɪ/ *adj* (-ier, -iest) tozzo

tube /tjuːb/ *n* tubo *m*; (*of toothpaste*) tubetto *m*; (*Rail*) metro *f*

tuberculosis /tjuːbɜːkjʊˈləʊsɪs/ *n* tubercolosi *f*

tubular /ˈtjuːbjʊlə(r)/ *adj* tubolare

tuck /tʌk/ *n* piega *f* ● *vt* (*put*) infilare. □ ~ **in** *vt* rimboccare; ~ **sb in** rimboccare le coperte a qcno ● *vi* (🔲: *eat*) mangiare con appetito. □ ~ **up** *vt* rimboccarsi (*sleeves*); (*in bed*) rimboccare le coperte a

Tuesday /ˈtjuːzdeɪ/ *n* martedì *m inv*

tuft /tʌft/ *n* ciuffo *m*

tug /tʌg/ *n* strattone *m*; (*Naut*) rimorchiatore *m* ● *v* (*pt/pp* **tugged**) ● *vt* tirare ● *vi* dare uno strattone. ~ **of war** *n* tiro *m* alla fune

tuition /tjuːˈɪʃn/ *n* lezioni *fpl*

tulip /ˈtjuːlɪp/ *n* tulipano *m*

tumble /ˈtʌmbl/ *n* ruzzolone *m* ● *vi* ruzzolare. ~**down** *adj* cadente. ~**-drier** *n* asciugabiancheria *f*

tumbler /ˈtʌmblə(r)/ *n* bicchiere *m*

(senza stelo)

tummy /'tʌmɪ/ *n* 🔲 pancia *f*.

tumour /'tju:mə(r)/ *n* tumore *m*

tumult /'tju:mʌlt/ *n* tumulto *m*. **~uous** *adj* tumultuoso

tuna /'tju:nə/ *n* tonno *m*

tune /tju:n/ *n* motivo *m*; out of/in ~ (instrument) scordato/accordato; (person) stonato/intonato; to the ~ of 🔲 per la modesta somma di • *vt* accordare (instrument); sintonizzare (radio, TV); mettere a punto (engine). □ ~ **in** *vt* sintonizzare • *vi* sintonizzarsi (to su). □ ~ **up** *vi* (orchestra:) accordare gli strumenti

tuneful /'tju:nfl/ *adj* melodioso

tuner /'tju:nə(r)/ *n* accordatore, -trice *mf*; (Radio, TV) sintonizzatore *m*

tunic /'tju:nɪk/ *n* tunica *f*; (Mil) giacca *f*; (Sch) ≈ grembiule *m*

tunnel /'tʌnl/ *n* tunnel *m inv* • *vi* (pt/ pp tunnelled) scavare un tunnel

turban /'tɜ:bən/ *n* turbante *m*

turbine /'tɜ:bam/ *n* turbina *f*

turbulen|ce /'tɜ:bjʊləns/ *n* turbolenza *f*. **~t** *adj* turbolento

turf /tɜ:f/ *n* erba *f*; (segment) zolla *f* erbosa • **turf out** *vt* 🔲 buttar fuori

Turin /tju:'rm/ *n* Torino *f*

Turk /tɜ:k/ *n* turco, -a *mf*

turkey /'tɜ:kɪ/ *n* tacchino *m*

Turk|ey /'tɜ:kɪ/ *n* Turchia *f*. **~ish** *adj* turco

turmoil /'tɜ:mɔɪl/ *n* tumulto *m*

turn /tɜ:n/ *n* (rotation, short walk) giro *m*; (in road) svolta *f*, curva *f*; (development) svolta *f*; (Theat) numero *m*; (attack) crisi *f inv*; a ~ **for** the better/ worse un miglioramento/ peggioramento; do sb a **good** ~ rendere un servizio a qcno; take ~s fare a turno; **in** ~ a turno; **out of** ~ (speak) a sproposito; **it's your** ~ tocca a te • *vt* girare; voltare (back, eyes); dirigere (gun, attention) • *vi* girare; (person:) girarsi; (leaves:) ingiallire; (become) diventare; ~ **right/**

left girare a destra/sinistra; ~ **sour** inacidirsi; ~ **to sb** girarsi verso qcno; fig rivolgersi a qcno. □ ~ **against** *vi* diventare ostile a • *vt* mettere contro. □ ~ **away** *vt* mandare via (people); girare dall'altra parte (head) • *vi* girarsi dall'altra parte. □ ~ **down** *vt* piegare (collar); abbassare (heat, gas, sound); respingere (person, proposal). □ ~ **in** *vt* ripiegare in dentro (edges); consegnare (lost object) • *vi* (🔲: go to bed) andare a letto; ~ **into** the drive entrare nel viale. □ ~ **off** *vt* spegnere; chiudere (tap, water) • *vi* (car:) girare. □ ~ **on** *vt* accendere; aprire (tap, water); (🔲: attract) eccitare • *vi* (attack) attaccare. □ ~ **out** *vt* (expel) mandar via; spegnere (light, gas); (produce) produrre; (empty) svuotare (room, cupboard) • *vi* (transpire) risultare; ~ **out well/badly** (cake, dress:) riuscire bene/male; (situation:) andare bene/male. □ ~ **over** *vt* girare • *vi* girarsi; please ~ **over** vedi retro. □ ~ **round** *vi* girarsi; (car:) girare. □ ~ **up** *vt* tirare su (collar); alzare (heat, gas, sound, radio) • *vi* farsi vedere

turning /'tɜ:nɪŋ/ *n* svolta *f*. **~-point** *n* svolta *f* decisiva

turnip /'tɜ:nɪp/ *n* rapa *f*

turn: **~over** *n* (Comm) giro *m* d'affari; (of staff) ricambio *m*. **~pike** *n* Am autostrada *f*. **~stile** *n* cancelletto *m* girevole. **~table** *n* piattaforma *f* girevole; (on record-player) piatto *m* (di giradischi). **~up** *n* (of trousers) risvolto *m*

turquoise /'tɜ:kwɔɪz/ *adj* (colour) turchese • *n* turchese *m*

turret /'tʌrɪt/ *n* torretta *f*

turtle /'tɜ:tl/ *n* tartaruga *f* acquatica

tusk /tʌsk/ *n* zanna *f*

tussle /'tʌsl/ *n* zuffa *f* • *vi* azzuffarsi

tutor /'tju:tə(r)/ *n* insegnante *mf* privato, -a; (Univ) insegnante *mf* universitario, -a che segue individualmente un ristretto *numero di studenti.* ~**ial** *n* discussione *f* col tutor

tuxedo /tʌkˈsiːdəʊ/ *n Am* smoking *m inv*

TV *n abbr* (television) tv *f inv*, tivù *f inv*

twang /twæŋ/ *n* (in voice) suono *m* nasale *m* ● *vt* far vibrare

tweezers /ˈtwiːzəz/ *npl* pinzette *fpl*

twelfth /twelfθ/ *adj* dodicesimo

twelve /twelv/ *adj* dodici

twentieth /ˈtwentɪɪθ/ *adj* ventesimo

twenty /ˈtwentɪ/ *adj* venti

twice /twaɪs/ *adv* due volte

twiddle /ˈtwɪdl/ *vt* giocherellare con; ~ **one's thumbs** *fig* girarsi i pollici

twig[1] /twɪg/ *n* ramoscello *m*

twig[2] *vt/i* (*pt/pp* **twigged**) 🆑 intuire

twilight /ˈtwaɪ-/ *n* crepuscolo *m*

twin /twɪn/ *n* gemello, -a *m* ● *attrib* gemello. ~ **beds** *npl* letti *mpl* gemelli

twine /twaɪn/ *n* spago *m* ● *vi* intrecciarsi; (plant:) attorcigliarsi ● *vt* intrecciare

twinge /twɪndʒ/ *n* fitta *f*; ~ **of conscience** rimorso *m* di coscienza

twinkle /ˈtwɪŋkl/ *n* scintillio *m* ● *vi* scintillare

twirl /twɜːl/ *vt* far roteare ● *vi* volteggiare ● *n* piroetta *f*

twist /twɪst/ *n* torsione *f*; (curve) curva *f*; (in rope) attorcigliata *f*; (in book, plot) colpo *m* di scena ● *vt* attorcigliare (rope); torcere (metal); girare (knob, cap); (distort) distorcere; ~ **one's ankle** storcersi la caviglia ● *vi* attorcigliarsi; (road:) essere pieno di curve

twit /twɪt/ *n* 🆑 cretino, -a *mf*

twitch /twɪtʃ/ *n* tic *m inv*; (jerk) strattone *m* ● *vi* contrarsi

twitter /ˈtwɪtə(r)/ *n* cinguettio *m* ● *vi* cinguettare; (person:) cianciare

two /tuː/ *adj* due

two: ~**-faced** *adj* falso. ~**-piece** *adj*

(swimsuit) due pezzi *m inv*; (suit) completo *m*. ~**-way** *adj* (traffic) a doppio senso di marcia

tycoon /taɪˈkuːn/ *n* magnate *m*

tying /ˈtaɪɪŋ/ ▷ **TIE**

type /taɪp/ *n* tipo *m*; (printing) carattere *m* [tipografico] ● *vt* scrivere a macchina ● *vi* scrivere a macchina. ~**writer** *n* macchina *f* da scrivere. ~**written** *adj* dattiloscritto

typical /ˈtɪpɪkl/ *adj* tipico. ~**ly** *adv* tipicamente; (as usual) come al solito

typify /ˈtɪpɪfaɪ/ *vt* (*pt/pp* -**ied**) essere tipico di

typing /ˈtaɪpɪŋ/ *n* dattilografia *f*

typist /ˈtaɪpɪst/ *n* dattilografo, -a *f*

tyrannical /tɪˈrænɪkl/ *adj* tirannico

tyranny /ˈtɪrənɪ/ *n* tirannia *f*

tyrant /ˈtaɪrənt/ *n* tiranno, -a *mf*

tyre /ˈtaɪə(r)/ *n* gomma *f*, pneumatico *m*

....

Uu

udder /ˈʌdə(r)/ *n* mammella *f* (di vacca, capra etc)

ugly /ˈʌglɪ/ *adj* (-**ier**, -**iest**) brutto

UK *n abbr* United Kingdom

ultimate /ˈʌltɪmət/ *adj* definitivo; (final) finale; (fundamental) fondamentale. ~**ly** *adv* alla fine

ultimatum /ʌltɪˈmeɪtəm/ *n* ultimatum *m inv*

ultra'violet *adj* ultravioletto

umbrella /ʌmˈbrelə/ *n* ombrello *m*

umpire /ˈʌmpaɪə(r)/ *n* arbitro *m* ● *vt/i* arbitrare

umpteen /ʌmpˈtiːn/ *adj* 🆑 innumerevole. ~**th** *adj* 🆑 ennesimo; **for the** ~**th time** per l'ennesima volta

UN *n abbr* (United Nations) ONU *f*

unable | underfed

un'able /ʌn-/ adj be ~ to do sth non potere fare qcsa; (not know how) non sapere fare qcsa

unac'companied adj non accompagnato; (luggage) incustodito

unac'customed adj insolito; be ~ to non essere abituato a

un'aided adj senza aiuto

unanimous /juːˈnænɪməs/ adj unanime. ~ly adv all'unanimità

un'armed adj disarmato; ~ combat n lotta f senza armi

unat'tended adj incustodito

una'voidable adj inevitabile

una'ware adj be ~ of sth non rendersi conto di qcsa. ~s adv catch sb ~s prendere qcno alla sprovvista

un'bearabl|e adj insopportabile. ~y adv insopportabilmente

unbeat|able /ʌnˈbiːtəbl/ adj imbattibile. ~en adj imbattuto

unbe'lievable adj incredibile

un'biased adj obiettivo

un'block vt sbloccare

un'bolt vt togliere il chiavistello di

un'breakable adj infrangibile

un'button vt sbottonare

uncalled-for /ʌnˈkɔːldfɔː(r)/ adj fuori luogo

un'canny adj sorprendente; (silence, feeling) inquietante

un'certain adj incerto; (weather) instabile; in no ~ terms senza mezzi termini. ~ty n incertezza f

un'charitable adj duro

uncle /ˈʌŋkl/ n zio m

Uncle Sam Personaggio immaginario che rappresenta gli Stati Uniti, il suo governo e i suoi cittadini. Nell'iconografia è tradizionalmente rappresentato con la barba bianca, vestito dei colori nazionali bianco, rosso e azzurro, con un gran cappello a cilindro con le stelle della bandiera americana. Spesso utilizzato quando si fa appello al patriottismo americano.

un'comfortabl|e adj scomodo; imbarazzante (silence, situation); feel ~e fig sentirsi a disagio. ~ly adv (sit) scomodamente; (causing alarm etc) spaventosamente

un'common adj insolito

un'compromising adj intransigente

uncon'ditional adj incondizionato. ~ly adv incondizionatamente

uncon'scious adj privo di sensi; (unaware) inconsapevole; be ~ of sth non rendersi conto di qcsa. ~ly adv inconsapevolmente

uncon'ventional adj poco convenzionale

un'cork vt sturare

uncouth /ʌnˈkuːθ/ adj zotico

un'cover vt scoprire; portare alla luce (buried object)

unde'cided adj indeciso; (not settled) incerto

undeniabl|e /ʌndɪˈnaɪəbl/ adj innegabile. ~y adv innegabilmente

under /ˈʌndə(r)/ prep sotto; (less than) al di sotto di; ~ there lì sotto; ~ repair/construction in riparazione/costruzione; ~ way fig in corso ● adv (~ water) sott'acqua; (unconscious) sotto anestesia

'undercarriage n (Aeron) carrello m

'underclothes npl biancheria fsg intima

under'cover adj clandestino

'undercurrent n corrente f sottomarina; fig sottofondo m

'underdog n perdente m

under'done adj (meat) al sangue

under'estimate vt sottovalutare

under'fed adj denutrito

under'foot adv sotto i piedi; trample ~ calpestare

under'go vt (pt -went, pp -gone) subire (operation, treatment); ~ repair essere in riparazione

under'graduate n studente, -tessa mf universitario, -a

under'ground[1] adv sottoterra

'underground[2] adj sotterraneo; (secret) clandestino ● n (railway) metropolitana f. ~ car park n parcheggio m sotterraneo

'undergrowth n sottobosco m

under'hand adj subdolo

under'lie vt (pt -lay, pp -lain, pres p -lying) fig essere alla base di

under'line vt sottolineare

under'lying adj fig fondamentale

under'mine vt fig minare

underneath /ʌndə'ni:θ/ prep sotto; ~ it sotto ● adv sotto

under'paid adj mal pagato

'underpants npl mutande fpl

'underpass n sottopassaggio m

under'privileged adj non abbiente

under'rate vt sottovalutare

'undershirt n Am maglia f della pelle

under'stand vt (pt/pp -stood) capire; I ~ that... (have heard) mi risulta che... ● vi capire. ~able adj comprensibile. ~ably adv comprensibilmente

under'standing adj comprensivo ● n comprensione f; (agreement) accordo m; on the ~ that a condizione che

'understatement n understatement m inv

under'take vt (pt -took, pp -taken) intraprendere; ~ to do sth impegnarsi a fare qcsa

'undertaker n impresario m di pompe funebri; (firm of) ~s n impresa f di pompe funebri

under'taking n impresa f; (promise) promessa f

'undertone n fig sottofondo m; in an ~ sottovoce

under'value vt sottovalutare

'underwater[1] adj subacqueo

under'water[2] adv sott'acqua

'underwear n biancheria f intima

under'weight adj sotto peso

'underworld n (criminals) malavita f

unde'sirable adj indesiderato; (person) poco raccomandabile

un'dignified adj non dignitoso

un'do vt (pt -did, pp -done) disfare; slacciare (dress, shoes); sbottonare (shirt); fig, (Comput) annullare

un'doubted adj indubbio. ~ly adv senza dubbio

un'dress vt spogliare; get ~ed spogliarsi ● vi spogliarsi

un'due adj eccessivo

un'duly adv eccessivamente

un'earth vt dissotterrare; fig scovare; scoprire (secret). ~ly adj soprannaturale; at an ~ly hour 1 a un'ora impossibile

uneco'nomic adj poco remunerativo

unem'ployed adj disoccupato ● npl the ~ i disoccupati

unem'ployment n disoccupazione f. ~ benefit n sussidio m di disoccupazione

un'ending adj senza fine

un'equal adj disuguale; (struggle) impari; be ~ to a task non essere all'altezza di un compito

unequivocal /ʌnɪ'kwɪvəkl/ adj inequivocabile; (person) esplicito

un'ethical adj immorale

un'even adj irregolare; (distribution) ineguale; (number) dispari

unex'pected adj inaspettato. ~ly adv inaspettatamente

un'fair adj ingiusto. ~ly adv ingiustamente. ~ness n ingiustizia f

un'faithful adj infedele

unfa'miliar adj sconosciuto; be ~ with non conoscere

un'fasten vt slacciare; (detach) staccare

un'favourable adj sfavorevole; (impression) negativo

un'feeling adj insensibile

un'fit adj inadatto; (morally) indegno; (Sport) fuori forma; ~ for work non in grado di lavorare

un'fold vt spiegare; (spread out) aprire; fig rivelare • vi (view:) spiegarsi

unfore'seen adj imprevisto

unfor'gettable /ʌnfə'getəbl/ adj indimenticabile

unfor'givable /ʌnfə'gɪvəbl/ adj imperdonabile

un'fortunate adj sfortunato; (regrettable) spiacevole; (remark, choice) infelice. ~ly adv purtroppo

un'founded adj infondato

un'furl vt spiegare

un'gainly /ʌn'geɪnlɪ/ adj sgraziato

un'grateful adj ingrato. ~ly adv senza riconoscenza

un'happy adj infelice; (not content) insoddisfatto (with di)

un'harmed adj incolume

un'healthy adj poco sano; (insanitary) malsano

un'hurt adj illeso

unification /juːnɪfɪ'keɪʃn/ n unificazione f

uniform /'juːnɪfɔːm/ adj uniforme • n uniforme f. ~ly adv uniformemente

unify /'juːnɪfaɪ/ vt (pt/pp -ied) unificare

uni'lateral /juːnɪ-/ adj unilaterale

uni'maginable adj inimmaginabile

unim'portant adj irrilevante

unin'habited adj disabitato

unin'tentional adj involontario. ~ly adv involontariamente

union /'juːnɪən/ n unione f; (trade ~) sindacato m. U~ Jack n bandiera f del Regno Unito

unique /juː'niːk/ adj unico. ~ly adv unicamente

unison /'juːnɪsn/ n in ~ all'unisono

unit /'juːnɪt/ n unità f inv; (department) reparto m; (of furniture) elemento m

unite /juː'naɪt/ vt unire • vi unirsi

unity /'juːnətɪ/ n unità f; (agreement) accordo m

universal /juːnɪ'vɜːsl/ adj universale. ~ly adv universalmente

universe /'juːnɪvɜːs/ n universo m

university /juːnɪ'vɜːsətɪ/ n università f • attrib universitario

un'just adj ingiusto

un'kind adj scortese. ~ly adv in modo scortese. ~ness n mancanza f di gentilezza

un'known adj sconosciuto

un'lawful adj illecito, illegale

un'leaded /ʌn'ledɪd/ adj senza piombo

un'leash vt fig scatenare

unless /ən'les/ conj a meno che; ~ I am mistaken se non mi sbaglio

un'like adj (not the same) diversi • prep diverso da; that's ~ him non è da lui; ~ me, he... diversamente da me, lui...

un'likely adj improbabile

un'limited adj illimitato

un'load vt scaricare

un'lock vt aprire (con chiave)

un'lucky adj sfortunato; it's ~ to... porta sfortuna...

un'married adj non sposato. ~ 'mother n ragazza f madre

un'mask vt fig smascherare

unmistak'able /ʌnmɪ'steɪkəbl/ adj inconfondibile. ~y adv chiaramente

u

un'natural adj innaturale; pej anormale. ~ly adv in modo innaturale; pej in modo anormale

un'necessar|y adj inutile. ~ily adv inutilmente

un'noticed adj inosservato

unob'tainable adj (product) introvabile; (phone number) non ottenibile

unob'trusive adj discreto. ~ly adv in modo discreto

unof'ficial adj non ufficiale. ~ly adv ufficiosamente

un'pack vi disfare le valigie ● vt svuotare (parcel); spacchettare (books); ~ one's case disfare la valigia

un'paid adj da pagare; (work) non retribuito

un'pleasant adj sgradevole; (person) maleducato. ~ly adv sgradevolmente; (behave) maleducatamente. ~ness n (bad feeling) tensioni fpl

un'plug vt (pt/pp -plugged) staccare

un'popular adj impopolare

un'precedented adj senza precedenti

unpre'dictable adj imprevedibile

unpre'pared adj impreparato

unpro'fessional adj non professionale; it's ~ è una mancanza di professionalità

un'profitable adj non redditizio

un'qualified adj non qualificato; (fig: absolute) assoluto

un'questionable adj incontestabile

unravel /ʌn'rævl/ vt (pt/pp -ravelled) districare; (in knitting) disfare

un'real adj irreale; 🔲 inverosimile

un'reasonable adj irragionevole

unre'lated adj (fact) senza rapporto (to con); (person) non imparentato (to con)

unre'liable adj inattendibile; (person) inaffidabile, che non dà affidamento

un'rest n fermenti mpl

un'rivalled adj ineguagliato

un'roll vt srotolare ● vi srotolarsi

unruly /ʌn'ruːlɪ/ adj indisciplinato

un'safe adj pericoloso

unsatis'factory adj poco soddisfacente

un'savoury adj equivoco

unscathed /ʌn'skeɪðd/ adj illeso

un'screw vt svitare

un'scrupulous adj senza scrupoli

un'seemly adj indecoroso

un'selfish adj disinteressato

un'settled adj in agitazione; (weather) variabile; (bill) non saldato

unshakeable /ʌn'ʃeɪkəbl/ adj categorico

unshaven /ʌn'ʃeɪvn/ adj non rasato

unsightly /ʌn'saɪtlɪ/ adj brutto

un'skilled adj non specializzato. ~ worker n manovale m

unso'ciable adj scontroso

unso'phisticated adj semplice

un'sound adj (building, reasoning) poco solido; (advice) poco sensato; of ~ mind malato di mente

un'stable adj instabile; (mentally) squilibrato

un'steady adj malsicuro

un'stuck adj come ~ staccarsi; (🔲 project) andare a monte

unsuc'cessful adj fallimentare; be ~ (in attempt) non aver successo. ~ly adv senza successo

un'suitable adj (inappropriate) inadatto; (inconvenient) inopportuno

unthinkable /ʌn'θɪŋkəbl/ adj impensabile

un'tidiness n disordine m

un'tidy adj disordinato

un'tie vt slegare

until /ən'tɪl/ prep fino a; not ∼ non prima di; ∼ the evening fino alla sera; ∼ his arrival fino al suo arrivo ● conj finché, fino a quando; no ∼ you've seen it non prima che tu l'abbia visto

un'told adj (wealth) incalcolabile; (suffering) indescrivibile; (story) inedito

un'true adj falso; that's ∼ non è vero

unused¹ /ʌn'juːzd/ adj non [ancora] usato

unused² /ʌn'juːst/ adj be ∼ to non essere abituato a

un'usual adj insolito. ∼ly adv insolitamente

un'veil vt scoprire

un'wanted adj indesiderato

un'welcome adj sgradito

un'well adj indisposto

unwieldy /ʌn'wiːldɪ/ adj ingombrante

un'willing adj riluttante. ∼ly adv malvolentieri

un'wind v (pt/pp unwound) ● vt svolgere, srotolare ● vi svolgersi, srotolarsi; (🔲: relax) rilassarsi

un'wise adj imprudente

un'worthy adj non degno

un'wrap vt (pt/pp -wrapped) scartare (present, parcel)

un'written adj tacito

up /ʌp/ adv su; (not in bed) alzato; (road) smantellato; (theatre curtain, blinds) alzato; (shelves, tent) montato; (notice) affisso; (building) costruito; prices are up i prezzi sono aumentati; be up for sale essere in vendita; up here/there quassù/lassù; time's up tempo scaduto; what's up? 🔲 cosa è successo?; up to (as far as) fino a; be up to essere all'altezza di (task); what's he up to? 🔲 cosa sta facendo?; (plotting) cosa sta combinando?; I'm up to page 100 sono arrivato a pagina 100; feel up to it sentirsela; be one up on sb 🔲 essere in vantaggio su qcno; go up salire; lift up alzare; up against fig alle prese con ● prep su; the cat ran/is up the tree il gatto è salito di corsa/è sull'albero; further up this road più avanti su questa strada; row up the river risalire il fiume; go up the stairs salire su per le scale; be up the pub 🔲 essere al pub; be up on or in sth essere bene informato su qcsa ● n ups and downs npl alti mpl e bassi

'upbringing n educazione f

up'date¹ vt aggiornare

'update² n aggiornamento m

up'grade vt promuovere (person); modernizzare (equipment)

upheaval /ʌp'hiːvl/ n scompiglio m

up'hill adj in salita; fig arduo ● adv in salita

up'hold vt (pt/pp upheld) sostenere (principle); confermare (verdict)

upholster /ʌp'həʊlstə(r)/ vt tappezzare. ∼er n tappezziere, -a mf. ∼y n tappezzeria f

'upkeep n mantenimento m

up-'market adj di qualità

upon /ə'pɒn/ prep su; ∼ arriving home una volta arrivato a casa

upper /'ʌpə(r)/ adj superiore ● n (of shoe) tomaia f

upper class n alta borghesia f

'upright adj dritto; (piano) verticale; (honest) retto ● n montante m

'uprising n rivolta f

'uproar n tumulto m; be in an ∼ essere in trambusto

up'set¹ vt (pt/pp upset, pres p upsetting) rovesciare; sconvolgere (plan); (distress) turbare; get ∼ about sth prendersela per qcsa; be very ∼ essere sconvolto; have an ∼ stomach avere l'intestino disturbato

'upset² n scombussolamento m

'upshot n risultato m

upside 'down adv sottosopra;
turn ~ ~ capovolgere
up'stairs¹ adv [al piano] di sopra
up'stairs² adj del piano superiore
'upstart n arrivato, -a mf
up'stream adv controcorrente
'uptake n be slow on the ~ essere lento nel capire; be quick on
the ~ capire le cose al volo
up-to-'date adj moderno; (news)
ultimo; (records) aggiornato
'upturn n ripresa f
upward /'ʌpwəd/ adj verso l'alto, in
su; ~ slope salita f ● adv ~[s] verso
l'alto; ~s di oltre
uranium /jʊ'reɪnɪəm/ n uranio m
urban /'ɜːbən/ adj urbano
urge /ɜːdʒ/ n forte desiderio m ● vt
esortare (to a). □ ~ **on** vt spronare
urgen|cy /'ɜːdʒənsɪ/ n urgenza f.
~t adj urgente
urinate /'jʊərɪneɪt/ vi urinare
urine /'jʊərɪn/ n urina f
us /ʌs/ pron ci; (after prep) noi; they
know us ci conoscono; give us the
money dateci i soldi; give it to us
datecelo; they showed it to us ce
l'hanno fatto vedere; they meant
us, not you intendevano noi, non
voi; it's us siamo noi; she hates us
ci odia
US[A] n[pl] abbr (United States [of
America]) U.S.A. mpl
usage /'juːsɪdʒ/ n uso m
use¹ /juːs/ n uso m; be of ~ essere
utile; be of no ~ essere inutile;
make ~ of usare; (exploit) sfruttare;
it is no ~ è inutile; what's the ~?
a che scopo?
use² /juːz/ vt usare. □ ~ **up** vt consumare
used¹ /juːzd/ adj usato
used² /juːst/ pt be ~ to sth essere
abituato a qcsa; get ~ to abituarsi
a; he ~ to live here viveva qui
useful /'juːsfl/ adj utile. ~**ness** n

utilità f
useless /'juːslɪs/ adj inutile; (🔲:
person) incapace
user /'juːzə(r)/ n utente mf.
~-'friendly adj facile da usare
usher /'ʌʃə(r)/ n (Theat) maschera f;
(Jur) usciere m; (at wedding) persona f
che accompagna gli invitati a un matrimonio
ai loro posti in chiesa ● **usher in** vt fare
entrare
usherette /ʌʃə'ret/ n maschera f
usual /'juːʒʊəl/ adj usuale; as ~
come al solito. ~**ly** adv di solito
utensil /juː'tensl/ n utensile m
utilize /'juːtɪlaɪz/ vt utilizzare
utmost /'ʌtməʊst/ adj estremo ● n
one's ~ tutto il possibile
utter¹ /'ʌtə(r)/ adj totale. ~**ly** adv
completamente
utter² vt emettere (sigh, sound);
proferire (word). ~**ance** n dichiarazione f
U-turn /'juː-/ n (Auto) inversione f a
U; fig marcia f in dietro

Vv

vacan|cy /'veɪk(ə)nsɪ/ n (job) posto
m vacante; (room) stanza f disponibile. ~t adj libero; (position) vacante; (look) assente
vacate /və'keɪt/ vt lasciare libero
vacation /və'keɪʃn/ n vacanza f
vaccinat|e /'væksɪmeɪt/ vt vacci-
nare. ~**ion** n vaccinazione f
vaccine /'væksiːn/ n vaccino m
vacuum /'vækjʊəm/ n vuoto m ● vt
passare l'aspirapolvere in/su. ~
cleaner n aspirapolvere m inv. ~
flask n thermos® m inv. ~-packed
adj confezionato sottovuoto

vagina | Venetian

vagina /vəˈdʒaɪnə/ n (Anat) vagina f

vague /veɪg/ adj vago; (outline) impreciso; (absent-minded) distratto; I'm still ~ about it non ho ancora le idee chiare in proposito. ~ly adv vagamente

vain /veɪn/ adj vanitoso; (hope, attempt) vano; in ~ invano. ~ly adv vanamente

valentine /ˈvæləntaɪn/ n (card) biglietto m di San Valentino

valiant /ˈvælɪənt/ adj valoroso

valid /ˈvælɪd/ adj valido. ~ate vt (confirm) convalidare. ~ity n validità f

valley /ˈvælɪ/ n valle f

valour /ˈvælə(r)/ n valore m

valuable /ˈvæljʊəbl/ adj di valore; fig prezioso. ~s npl oggetti mpl di valore

valuation /væljʊˈeɪʃn/ n valutazione f

value /ˈvæljuː/ n valore m; (usefulness) utilità f • vt valutare; (cherish) apprezzare. ~ 'added tax n imposta f sul valore aggiunto

valve /vælv/ n valvola f

vampire /ˈvæmpaɪə(r)/ n vampiro m

van /væn/ n furgone m

vandal /ˈvændl/ n vandalo, -a mf. ~ism n vandalismo m. ~ize vt vandalizzare

vanilla /vəˈnɪlə/ n vaniglia f

vanish /ˈvænɪʃ/ vi svanire

vanity /ˈvænətɪ/ n vanità f. ~ bag or case n beauty-case m inv

vapour /ˈveɪpə(r)/ n vapore m

variable /ˈveərɪəbl/ adj variabile; (adjustable) regolabile

variance /ˈveərɪəns/ n be at ~ essere in disaccordo

variant /ˈveərɪənt/ n variante f

variation /veərɪˈeɪʃn/ n variazione f

varied /ˈveərɪd/ adj vario; (diet) diversificato; (life) movimentato

variety /vəˈraɪətɪ/ n varietà f inv

various /ˈveərɪəs/ adj vario

varnish /ˈvɑːnɪʃ/ n vernice f; (for nails) smalto m • vt verniciare; ~ one's nails mettersi lo smalto

vary /ˈveərɪ/ vt/i (pt/pp -ied) variare. ~ing adj variabile; (different) diverso

vase /vɑːz/ n vaso m

vast /vɑːst/ adj vasto; (difference, amusement) enorme. ~ly adv (superior) di gran lunga; (different, amused) enormemente

vat /væt/ n tino m

VAT /viːeɪˈtiː, /væt/ n abbr (value added tax) I.V.A. f

vault[1] /vɔːlt/ n (roof) volta f; (in bank) caveau m inv; (tomb) cripta f

vault[2] n salto m • vt/i ~ [over] saltare

VDU n abbr (visual display unit) VDU n

veal /viːl/ n carne f di vitello • attrib di vitello

veer /vɪə(r)/ vi cambiare direzione; (Auto, Naut) virare

vegetable /ˈvedʒtəbl/ n (food) verdura f; (when growing) ortaggio m • attrib (oil, fat) vegetale

vegetarian /vedʒɪˈteərɪən/ adj & n vegetariano, -a mf

vehicle /ˈviːɪkl/ n veicolo m; (fig: medium) mezzo m

veil /veɪl/ n velo m • vt velare

vein /veɪn/ n vena f; (mood) umore m; (manner) tenore m. ~ed adj venato

velocity /vɪˈlɒsətɪ/ n velocità f

velvet /ˈvelvɪt/ n velluto m. ~y adj vellutato

vendetta /venˈdetə/ n vendetta f

vending-machine /ˈvendɪŋ-/ n distributore m automatico

veneer /vəˈnɪə(r)/ n impiallacciatura f; fig vernice f. ~ed adj impiallacciato

venereal /vɪˈnɪərɪəl/ adj ~ disease malattia f venerea

Venetian /vəˈniːʃn/ adj & n veneziano, -a mf. v~ blind n persiana f alla veneziana

vengeance /'vendʒəns/ n vendetta f; with a ~ 🔟 a più non posso

venison /'venɪsn/ n (Culin) carne f di cervo

venom /'venəm/ n veleno m. ~ous adj velenoso

vent[1] /vent/ n presa f d'aria; give ~ to fig dar libero sfogo a ● vt fig sfogare (anger)

vent[2] n (in jacket) spacco m

ventilat|e /'ventɪleɪt/ vt ventilare. ~ion n ventilazione f; (installation) sistema m di ventilazione. ~or n ventilatore m

ventriloquist /ven'trɪləkwɪst/ n ventriloquo, -a mf

venture /'ventʃə(r)/ n impresa f ● vt azzardare ● vi avventurarsi

venue /'venju:/ n luogo m (di convegno, concerto, ecc.)

veranda /və'rændə/ n veranda f

verb /vɜ:b/ n verbo m. ~al adj verbale

verdict /'vɜ:dɪkt/ n verdetto m; (opinion) parere m

verge /vɜ:dʒ/ n orlo m; be on the ~ of doing sth essere sul punto di fare qcsa ● verge on vt fig rasentare

verify /'verɪfaɪ/ vt (pt/pp -ied) verificare; (confirm) confermare

vermin /'vɜ:mɪn/ n animali mpl nocivi

versatil|e /'vɜ:sətaɪl/ adj versatile. ~ity n versatilità f

verse /vɜ:s/ n verso m; (of Bible) versetto m; (poetry) versi mpl

versed /vɜ:st/ adj ~ in versato in

versus /'vɜ:səs/ prep contro

vertebra /'vɜ:tɪbrə/ n (pl -brae /-bri:/) (Anat) vertebra f

vertical /'vɜ:tɪkl/ adj & n verticale m

vertigo /'vɜ:tɪgəʊ/ n (Med) vertigine f

verve /vɜ:v/ n verve f

very /'verɪ/ adv molto; ~ much

molto; ~ little pochissimo; ~ many moltissimi; ~ few pochissimi; ~ probably molto probabilmente; ~ well benissimo; at the ~ most tutt'al più al più; at the ~ latest al più tardi ● adj the ~ first il primissimo; the ~ thing proprio ciò che ci vuole; at the ~ end/beginning proprio alla fine/all'inizio; that ~ day proprio quel giorno; the ~ thought la sola idea; only a ~ little solo un pochino

vessel /'vesl/ n nave f

vest /vest/ n maglia f della pelle; (Am: waistcoat) gilè m inv. ~ed interest n interesse m personale

vestige /'vestɪdʒ/ n (of past) vestigio m

vet /vet/ n veterinario, -a mf ● vt (pt/pp vetted) controllare minuziosamente

veteran /'vetərən/ n veterano, -a mf

veterinary /'vetərɪnərɪ/ adj veterinario. ~ surgeon n medico m veterinario

veto /'vi:təʊ/ n (pl -es) veto m ● vt proibire

vex /veks/ vt irritare. ~ation n irritazione f. ~ed adj irritato; ~ed question questione f controversa

via /'vaɪə/ prep via; (by means of) attraverso

viable /'vaɪəbl/ adj (life form, relationship, company) in grado di sopravvivere; (proposition) attuabile

viaduct /'vaɪədʌkt/ n viadotto m

vibrat|e /vaɪ'breɪt/ vi vibrare. ~ion n vibrazione f

vicar /'vɪkə(r)/ n parroco m (protestante). ~age n casa f parrocchiale

vice[1] /vaɪs/ n vizio m

vice[2] n (Techn) morsa f

vice versa /vaɪsɪ'vɜ:sə/ adv viceversa

vicinity /vɪ'sɪnətɪ/ n vicinanza f; in the ~ of nelle vicinanze di

vicious /ˈvɪʃəs/ adj cattivo; (attack) brutale; (animal) pericoloso. ~ 'circle n circolo m vizioso. ~ly adv (attack) brutalmente

victim /ˈvɪktɪm/ n vittima f. ~ize vt fare delle rappresaglie contro

victor /ˈvɪktə(r)/ n vincitore m

victor|ious /vɪkˈtɔːrɪəs/ adj vittorioso. ~y n vittoria f

video /ˈvɪdɪəʊ/ n video m; (cassette) videocassetta f; (recorder) videoregistratore m ●attrib video ● vt registrare

video: ~ recorder n videoregistratore m. ~-tape n videocassetta f

vie /vaɪ/ vi (pres p vying) rivaleggiare

view /vjuː/ n vista f; (photographed, painted) veduta f; (opinion) visione f; look at the ~ guardare il panorama; in my ~ secondo me; in ~ of in considerazione di; on ~ esposto; with a ~ to con l'intenzione di ● vt visitare (house); (consider) considerare ● vi (TV) guardare. ~er n (TV) telespettatore, -trice mf; (Phot) visore m

view: ~finder n (Phot) mirino m. ~point n punto m di vista

vigilan|ce /ˈvɪdʒɪləns/ n vigilanza f. ~t adj vigile

vigorous /ˈvɪɡərəs/ adj vigoroso

vigour /ˈvɪɡə(r)/ n vigore m

vile /vaɪl/ adj disgustoso; (weather) orribile; (temper, mood) pessimo

village /ˈvɪlɪdʒ/ n paese m. ~r n paesano, -a mf

villain /ˈvɪlən/ n furfante m; (in story) cattivo m

vindicate /ˈvɪndɪkeɪt/ vt (from guilt) discolpare; you are ~d ti sei dimostrato nel giusto

vindictive /vɪnˈdɪktɪv/ adj vendicativo

vine /vaɪn/ n vite f

vinegar /ˈvɪnɪɡə(r)/ n aceto m

vineyard /ˈvɪnjəːd/ n vigneto m

vintage /ˈvɪntɪdʒ/ adj (wine) d'an-

nata ●n (year) annata f

viola /vɪˈəʊlə/ n (Mus) viola f

violat|e /ˈvaɪəleɪt/ vt violare. ~ion n violazione f

violen|ce /ˈvaɪələns/ n violenza f. ~t adj violento

violet /ˈvaɪələt/ adj violetto ●n (flower) violetta f; (colour) violetto ●n

violin /vaɪəˈlɪn/ n violino m. ~ist n violinista m

VIP n abbr (very important person) vip mf

virgin /ˈvɜːdʒɪn/ adj vergine ●n vergine f. ~ity n verginità f

Virgo /ˈvɜːɡəʊ/ n Vergine f

virile /ˈvɪraɪl/ adj virile. ~ity n virilità f

virtual /ˈvɜːtjʊəl/ adj effettivo. ~ reality n realtà f virtuale. ~ly adv praticamente

virtue /ˈvɜːtjuː/ n virtù f inv; (advantage) vantaggio m; by or in ~ of a causa di

virtuous /ˈvɜːtjʊəs/ adj virtuoso

virulent /ˈvɪrʊlənt/ adj virulento

virus /ˈvaɪərəs/ n virus m inv

visa /ˈviːzə/ n visto m

visibility /vɪzəˈbɪlɪtɪ/ n visibilità f

visib|le /ˈvɪzəbl/ adj visibile. ~y adv visibilmente

vision /ˈvɪʒn/ n visione f; (sight) vista f

visit /ˈvɪzɪt/ n visita f ● vt andare a trovare (person); andare da (doctor etc); visitare (town, building). ~ing hours npl orario m delle visite. ~or n ospite mf; (of town, museum) visitatore, -trice mf; (in hotel) cliente mf

visor /ˈvaɪzə(r)/ n visiera f; (Auto) parasole m

visual /ˈvɪzjʊəl/ adj visivo. ~ aids npl supporto m visivo. ~ dis'play unit n visualizzatore m. ~ly adv visualmente; ~ly handicapped non vedente

visualize /ˈvɪzjʊəlaɪz/ vt visualizzare

vital /'vaɪtl/ adj vitale. ~ity n vitalità f. ~ly adv estremamente

vitamin /'vɪtəmɪn/ n vitamina f

vivaci|ous /vɪ'veɪʃəs/ adj vivace. ~ty n vivacità f

vivid /'vɪvɪd/ adj vivido. ~ly adv in modo vivido

vocabulary /və'kæbjʊlərɪ/ n vocabolario m; (list) glossario m

vocal /'vəʊkl/ adj vocale; (vociferous) eloquente. ~ cords npl corde fpl vocali

vocalist /'vəʊkəlɪst/ n vocalista mf

vocation /və'keɪʃn/ n vocazione f. ~al adj di orientamento professionale

vociferous /və'sɪfərəs/ adj vociante

vogue /vəʊg/ n moda f; in ~ in voga

voice /vɔɪs/ n voce f ● vt esprimere. ~mail n posta f elettronica vocale

void /vɔɪd/ adj (not valid) nullo; ~ of privo di ● n vuoto m

volatile /'vɒlətaɪl/ adj volatile; (person) volubile

volcanic /vɒl'kænɪk/ adj vulcanico

volcano /vɒl'keɪnəʊ/ n vulcano m

volley /'vɒlɪ/ n (of gunfire) raffica f; (Tennis) volée f inv

volt /vəʊlt/ n volt m inv. ~age n (Electr) voltaggio m

volume /'vɒljuːm/ n volume m; (of work, traffic) quantità f inv. ~ control n volume m

voluntar|y /'vɒləntərɪ/ adj volontario. ~y work n volontariato m. ~ily adv volontariamente

volunteer /vɒlən'tɪə(r)/ n volontario, -a mf ● vt offrire volontariamente (information); ● vi offrirsi volontario; (Mil) arruolarsi come volontario

vomit /'vɒmɪt/ n vomito m ● vt/i vomitare

voracious /və'reɪʃəs/ adj vorace

vot|e /vəʊt/ n voto m; (ballot) votazione f; (right) diritto m di voto; take

a ~e on votare su ● vi votare ● vt ~e sb president eleggere qcno presidente. ~er n elettore, -trice mf. ~ing n votazione f

vouch /vaʊtʃ/ vi ~ for garantire per. ~er n buono m

vow /vaʊ/ n voto m ● vt giurare

vowel /'vaʊəl/ n vocale f

voyage /'vɔɪɪdʒ/ n viaggio m [marittimo]; (in space) viaggio m [nello spazio]

vulgar /'vʌlgə(r)/ adj volgare. ~ity n volgarità f inv

vulnerable /'vʌlnərəbl/ adj vulnerabile

vulture /'vʌltʃə(r)/ n avvoltoio m

vying /'vaɪɪŋ/ ▷VIE

• •

Ww

• •

wad /wɒd/ n batuffolo m; (bundle) rotolo m. ~ding n ovatta f

waddle /'wɒdl/ vi camminare ondeggiando

wade /weɪd/ vi guadare; ~ through 🔢 procedere faticosamente in (book)

wafer /'weɪfə(r)/ n cialda f, wafer m inv; (Relig) ostia f

waffle¹ /'wɒfl/ vi 🔢 blaterare

waffle² n (Culin) cialda f

waft /wɒft/ vt trasportare ● vi diffondersi

wag /wæg/ v (pt/pp wagged) ● vt agitare ● vi agitarsi

wage¹ /weɪdʒ/ vt dichiarare (war); lanciare (campaign)

wage² n, & ~s pl salario msg. ~ packet n busta f paga

waggle /'wægl/ vt dimenare ● vi dimenarsi

wagon /ˈwægən/ n carro m; (Rail) vagone m merci

wail /weɪl/ n piagnucolio m; (of wind) lamento m; (of baby) vagito m ● vi piagnucolare; (wind:) lamentarsi; (baby:) vagire

waist /weɪst/ n vita f. **~coat** n gilè m inv; (of man's suit) panciotto m. **~line** n vita f

wait /weɪt/ n attesa f; **lie in ~ for** appostarsi per sorprendere ● vi aspettare; **~ for** aspettare ● vt **~ one's turn** aspettare il proprio turno. □ **~ on** vt servire

waiter /ˈweɪtə(r)/ n cameriere m

waiting /ˈweɪtɪŋ/ **~-list** n lista f d'attesa. **~-room** n sala f d'aspetto

waitress /ˈweɪtrɪs/ n cameriera f

waive /weɪv/ vt rinunciare a (claim); non tener conto di (rule)

wake¹ /weɪk/ n veglia f funebre ● vt (pt woke, pp woken) **~** [up] ● vt svegliare ● vi svegliarsi

wake² n (Naut) scia f; **in the ~ of** fig nella scia di

Wales /weɪlz/ n Galles m

walk /wɔːk/ n passeggiata f; (gait) andatura f; (path) sentiero m; **go for a ~** andare a fare una passeggiata ● vi camminare; (as opposed to drive etc) andare a piedi; (ramble) passeggiare ● vt portare a spasso (dog); percorrere (streets); □ **~ out** vi lasciare (husband, employee:) andarsene; (workers:) scioperare. □ **~ out on** vt lasciare

walker /ˈwɔːkə(r)/ n camminatore, -trice mf; (rambler) escursionista mf

walk-out n sciopero m

wall /wɔːl/ n muro m; **go to the ~** 🔟 andare a rotoli; **drive sb up the ~** 🔟 far diventare matto qcno ● **wall up** vt murare

wallet /ˈwɒlɪt/ n portafoglio m

wallop /ˈwɒləp/ n 🔟 colpo m ● vt (pt/pp walloped) 🔟 colpire

wallow /ˈwɒləʊ/ vi sguazzare; (in self-pity, grief) crogiolarsi

'wallpaper n tappezzeria f ● vt tappezzare

Wall Street Via di Manhattan, a New York, dove hanno sede la Borsa e altri istituti finanziari. Quando si parla di *Wall Street* ci si riferisce appunto a tali istituti.

walnut /ˈwɔːlnʌt/ n noce f

waltz /wɔːlts/ n valzer m inv ● vi ballare il valzer

wand /wɒnd/ n (magic ~) bacchetta f [magica]

wander /ˈwɒndə(r)/ vi girovagare; (fig: digress) divagare. □ **~ about** vi andare a spasso

wane /weɪn/ n **be on the ~** essere in fase calante ● vi calare

wangle /ˈwæŋgl/ vt 🔟 rimediare (invitation, holiday)

want /wɒnt/ n (hardship) bisogno m; (lack) mancanza f ● vt volere; (need) aver bisogno di; **~** [to have] sth volere qcsa; **~ to do** sth voler fare qcsa; **we ~ to stay** vogliamo rimanere; **I ~ you to go** voglio che tu vada; **it ~s painting** ha bisogno d'essere dipinto; **you ~ to learn to swim** bisogna che impari a nuotare ● vi **~ for** mancare di. **~ed** adj ricercato. **~ing** adj **be ~ing** mancare; **be ~ing in** mancare di

WAP /wæp/ n abbr (wireless application protocol) WAP m inv

war /wɔː(r)/ n guerra f; fig lotta f (on contro); **at ~** in guerra

ward /wɔːd/ n (in hospital) reparto m; (child) minore m sotto tutela ● **ward off** vt evitare; parare (blow)

warden /ˈwɔːdn/ n guardiano, -a mf

warder /ˈwɔːdə(r)/ n guardia f carceraria

wardrobe /ˈwɔːdrəʊb/ n guardaroba m

warehouse /ˈweəhaʊs/ n

w

magazzino m

war: ~**fare** n guerra f. ~**head** n testata f

warm /wɔ:m/ adj caldo; (welcome) caloroso; be ~ (person:) aver caldo; it is ~ (weather) fa caldo ● vt scaldare. □ ~ **up** vt scaldare ● vi scaldarsi; fig animarsi. ~**hearted** adj espansivo. ~**ly** adv (greet) calorosamente; (dress) in modo pesante. ~**th** n calore m

warn /wɔ:n/ vt avvertire. ~**ing** n avvertimento m; (advance notice) preavviso m

warp /wɔ:p/ vt deformare; fig distorcere ● vi deformarsi

warped /wɔ:pt/ adj fig contorto; (sexuality) deviato; (view) distorto

warrant /'wɒrənt/ n (for arrest, search) mandato m ● vt (justify) giustificare; (guarantee) garantire. ~**y** n garanzia f

warrior /'wɒrɪə(r)/ n guerriero, -a mf

'**warship** n nave f da guerra

wart /wɔ:t/ n porro m

'**wartime** n tempo m di guerra

warly /'weərɪ/ adj (-ier, -iest) (careful) cauto; (suspicious) diffidente

was /wɒz/ ▷ BE

wash /wɒʃ/ n lavata f; (clothes) bucato m; (in washing machine) lavaggio m; have a ~ darsi una lavata ● vt lavare; (sea:) bagnare; ~ one's hands lavarsi le mani ● vi lavarsi. □ ~ **out** vt sciacquare (soap); sciacquarsi (mouth). □ ~ **up** vt lavare ● vi lavare i piatti; Am lavarsi

washable /'wɒʃəbl/ adj lavabile

wash-basin n lavandino m

washer /'wɒʃə(r)/ n (Techn) guarnizione f; (machine) lavatrice f

washing /'wɒʃɪŋ/ n bucato m. ~**machine** n lavatrice f. ~**powder** n detersivo m. ~'**up** n do the ~'up lavare i piatti. ~'**up liquid** n detersivo m per i piatti

wash: ~**out** n disastro m. ~**room** n bagno m

wasp /wɒsp/ n vespa f

waste /weɪst/ n spreco m; (rubbish) rifiuto m; ~ **of time** perdita f di tempo ● adj (product) di scarto; (land) desolato; lay ~ devastare ● vt sprecare. □ ~ **away** vi deperire

waste: ~-**disposal unit** n eliminatore m di rifiuti. ~**ful** adj dispendioso. ~-'**paper basket** n cestino m per la carta [straccia]

watch /wɒtʃ/ n guardia f; (period of duty) turno m di guardia; (timepiece) orologio m; be on the ~ stare all'erta ● vt guardare (film, match, television); (be careful of, look after) stare attento a ● vi guardare. □ ~ **out** vi (be careful) stare attento (for a). □ ~ **out for** vt (look for) fare attenzione all'arrivo di (person)

watch: ~-**dog** n cane m da guardia. ~**man** n guardiano m

water /'wɔ:tə(r)/ n acqua f ● vt annaffiare (garden, plant); (dilute) annacquare ● vi (eyes:) lacrimare; my mouth was ~**ing** avevo l'acquolina in bocca. □ ~ **down** vt diluire; fig attenuare

water: ~-**colour** n acquerello m. ~**cress** n crescione m. ~**fall** n cascata f

'**watering-can** n annaffiatoio m

water: ~-**lily** n ninfea f. ~ **logged** adj inzuppato. ~**proof** adj impermeabile. ~-**skiing** n sci m nautico. ~**tight** adj stagno; fig irrefutabile. ~**way** n canale m navigabile

watery /'wɔ:tərɪ/ adj acquoso; (eyes) lacrimoso

watt /wɒt/ n watt m inv

wave /weɪv/ n onda f; (gesture) cenno m; fig ondata f ● vt agitare; ~ one's hand agitare la mano ● vi far segno; (flag:) sventolare. ~**length** n lunghezza f d'onda

waver /'weɪvə(r)/ vi vacillare;

(hesitate) esitare

wavy /'weɪvɪ/ *adj* ondulato

wax¹ /wæks/ *vi* (moon:) crescere; *(fig: become)* diventare

wax² *n* cera *f*; *(in ear)* cerume *m* ● *vt* dare la cera a. ~**works** *n* museo *m* delle cere

way /weɪ/ *n* percorso *m*; *(direction)* direzione *f*; *(manner, method)* modo *m*; ~**s** *pl (customs)* abitudini *fpl*; **be in the** ~ essere in mezzo; **on the** ~ **to Rome** andando a Roma; **I'll do it on the** ~ lo faccio mentre vado; **it's on my** ~ è sul mio percorso; **a long** ~ **off** lontano; **this** ~ da questa parte; *(like this)* così; **by the** ~ a proposito; **by** ~ **of** come; *(via)* via; **either** ~ *(whatever we do)* in un modo o nell'altro; **in some** ~**s** sotto certi aspetti; **in a** ~ in un certo senso; **in a bad** ~ *(person)* molto grave; **out of the** ~ fuori mano; **under** ~ in corso; **lead the** ~ far strada; *(fig)* aprire la strada; **make** ~ far posto *(for a)*; **give** ~ *(Auto)* dare la precedenza; **go out of one's** ~ *fig* scomodarsi *(to per)*; **get one's** [**own**] ~ averla vinta ● *adv* ~ **behind** molto indietro. ~ '**in** *n* entrata *f*

way'lay *vt (pt/pp -laid)* aspettare al varco *(person)*

way 'out *n* uscita *f*; *fig* via *f* d'uscita

way-'out *adj* 🔲 eccentrico

we /wiː/ *pron* noi; **we're the last** siamo gli ultimi; **they're going, but we're not** loro vanno, ma noi no

weak /wiːk/ *adj* debole; *(liquid)* leggero. ~**en** *vt* indebolire ● *vi* indebolirsi. ~**ling** *n* smidollato, -a *mf*. ~**ness** *n* debolezza *f*; *(liking)* debole *m*

wealth /welθ/ *n* ricchezza *f*; *fig* gran quantità *f*. ~**y** *adj* (-ier, -iest) ricco

weapon /'wepən/ *n* arma *f*; ~**s of mass destruction** *npl* armi *mpl* di distruzione di massa

wear /weə(r)/ *n (clothing)* abbigliamento *m*; **for everyday** ~ da portare tutti i giorni; ~ [**and tear**] usura *f* ● *vt (pt wore, pp worn)* ● *vt* portare; *(damage)* consumare; ~ **a hole in sth** logorare qcsa fino a fare un buco; **what shall I** ~? cosa mi metto? ● *vi* consumarsi; *(last)* durare. □ ~ **off** *vi* scomparire; *(effect:)* finire. □ ~ **out** *vt* consumare [fino in fondo]; *(exhaust)* estenuare ● *vi* estenuarsi

wear|y /'wɪərɪ/ *adj* (-ier, -iest) sfinito ● *v (pt/pp wearied)* ● *vt* sfinire ● *vi* ~**y** di stancarsi di. ~**ily** *adv* stancamente

weather /'weðə(r)/ *n* tempo *m*; **in this** ~ con questo tempo; **under the** ~ 🔲 giù di corda ● *vt* sopravvivere a *(a storm)*

weather: ~**-beaten** *adj* (face:) segnato dalle intemperie. ~ **forecast** *n* previsioni *fpl* del tempo

weave¹ /wiːv/ *vi (pt/pp weaved)* *(move)* zigzagare

weave² *n* tessuto *m* ● *vt (pt wove, pp woven)* tessere; intrecciare (flowers etc); intrecciare la fila di (story etc). ~**r** *n* tessitore, -trice *mf*

web /web/ *n* rete *f*; *(spider's)* ragnatela *f*. **W**~ *(Comput)* Web *m inv*, Rete *f*. ~**bed feet** *npl* piedi *mpl* palmati. ~**cam** *n* webcam *f inv*. ~**master** *n* webmaster *m inv*. ~ **page** *n* pagina *f* web. ~ **site** *n* sito *m* web

wed /wed/ *vt (pt/pp wedded)* sposare ● *vi* sposarsi. ~**ding** *n* matrimonio *m*

wedding: ~ **cake** *n* torta *f* nuziale. ~**ring** *n* fede *f*

wedge /wedʒ/ *n* zeppa *f*; *(for splitting wood)* cuneo *m*; *(of cheese)* fetta *f* ● *vt (fix)* fissare

Wednesday /'wenzdeɪ/ *n* mercoledì *m inv*

wee¹ /wiː/ *adj* 🔲 piccolo

wee² *vi* 🔲 fare la pipì

weed /wiːd/ *n* erbaccia *f*; (🔲: *person)*

w

mollusco *m* ● *vt* estirpare le erbacce da. □ ~ **out** *vt fig* eliminare

'weed-killer *n* erbicida *m*

weedy /'wi:dɪ/ *adj* 🔲 mingherlino

week /wi:k/ *n* settimana *f*. ~**day** *n* giorno *m* feriale. ~**end** *n* fine settimana *m*

weekly /'wi:klɪ/ *adj* settimanale ● *n* settimanale *m* ● *adv* settimanalmente

weep /wi:p/ *vi* (*pt/pp* wept) piangere

weigh /weɪ/ *vt/i* pesare; ~ **anchor** levare l'ancora. □ ~ **down** *vt fig* piegare. □ ~ **up** *vt fig* soppesare; valutare (person)

weight /weɪt/ *n* peso *m*; put on/lose ~ ingrassare/dimagrire. ~**ing** *n* (allowance) indennità *f inv*

weight-lifting *n* sollevamento *m* pesi

weir /wɪə(r)/ *n* chiusa *f*

weird /wɪəd/ *adj* misterioso; (bizarre) bizzarro

welcome /'welkəm/ *adj* benvenuto; you're ~! prego!; you're ~ to have it/to come prendilo/vieni pure ● *n* accoglienza *f* ● *vt* accogliere; (appreciate) gradire

weld /weld/ *vt* saldare. ~**er** *n* saldatore *m*

welfare /'welfeə(r)/ *n* benessere *m*; (aid) assistenza *f*. W~ **State** *n* Stato *m* assistenziale

well[1] /wel/ *n* pozzo *m*; (of staircase) tromba *f*

well[2] *adv* (better, best) bene; as ~ anche; as ~ as (in addition) oltre a; ~ done! bravo!; very ~ benissimo ● *adj* he is not ~ non sta bene; get ~ soon! guarisci presto! ● *int* beh!; ~ I never! ma va!

well-behaved *adj* educato

well: ~-**known** *adj* famoso. ~-**off** *adj* benestante. ~-**to-do** *adj* ricco

Welsh /welʃ/ *adj & n* gallese; the ~ *pl* i gallesi. ~**man** *n* gallese *m*. ~ **rabbit** *n* toast *m inv* al formaggio

went /went/ ▷**GO**

wept /wept/ ▷**WEEP**

were /wɜ:(r)/ ▷**BE**

west /west/ *n* ovest *m*; to the ~ of a ovest di; the W~ l'Occidente *m* ● *adj* occidentale ● *adv* verso occidente; go ~ 🔲 andare in malora. ~**erly** *adj* verso ovest; occidentale (wind). ~**ern** *adj* occidentale ● *n* western *m inv*

West: ~ **Indian** *adj & n* antillese *mf*. ~ **Indies** /'ɪndɪz/ *npl* Antille *fpl*

'westward[s] /-wəd[z]/ *adj* verso ovest

wet /wet/ *adj* (wetter, wettest) bagnato; fresco (paint); (rainy) piovoso; (🔲: person) smidollato; get ~ bagnarsi ● *vt* (*pt/pp* wet, wetted) bagnare. ~ '**blanket** *n* guastafeste *mf inv*

whack /wæk/ *n* 🔲 colpo *m* ● *vt* 🔲 dare un colpo a. ~**ed** *adj* 🔲 stanco morto. ~**ing** *adj* (🔲: huge) enorme

whale /weɪl/ *n* balena *f*; have a ~ of a time 🔲 divertirsi un sacco

wham /wæm/ *int* bum

wharf /wɔ:f/ *n* banchina *f*

what /wɒt/ *pron* che, [che] cosa; ~ for? perché?; ~ is that for? a che cosa serve?; ~ is it? (what do you want) cosa c'è?; ~ is it like? com'è?; ~ is your name? come ti chiami?; ~ is the weather like? com'è il tempo?; ~ is the film about? di cosa parla il film?; ~ is he talking about? di cosa sta parlando?; he asked me ~ she had said mi ha chiesto cosa ha detto; ~ about going to the cinema? e se andassimo al cinema?; ~ about the children? (*what will they do*) e i bambini?; ~ if it rains? e se piove? ● adj quale, che; take ~ books you want prendi tutti i libri che vuoi; ~ kind of a che tipo di; at ~ time? a che ora? ● adv che; ~ a lovely day! che bella giornata! ● int ~! [che] cosa!; ~? [che] cosa?

what'ever adj qualunque ● pron qualsiasi cosa; ~ is it? cos'è?; ~ he does qualsiasi cosa faccia; ~ happens qualunque cosa succeda; nothing ~ proprio niente

vhatso'ever adj & pron = whatever

vheat /wi:t/ n grano m, frumento m

vheel /wi:l/ n ruota f; (*steering* ~) volante m; at the ~ al volante ● vt (*push*) spingere ● vi (*circle*) ruotare; ~ [round] ruotare

vheel: ~**barrow** n carriola f. ~**chair** n sedia f a rotelle. ~**clamp** n ceppo m bloccaruote

vheeze /wi:z/ vi ansimare

vhen /wen/ adv & conj quando; the day ~ il giorno in cui; ~ swimming/reading nuotando/leggendo

vhen'ever adv & conj in qualsiasi momento; (*every time that*) ogni volta che; ~ did it happen? quando è successo?

vhere /weə(r)/ adv & conj dove; the street ~ I live la via in cui abito; ~ do you come from? da dove vieni?

vhereabouts[1] /weərə'baʊts/ adv dove

vhereabouts[2] n nobody knows his ~ nessuno sa dove si trova

vhere'as conj dal momento che; (*in contrast*) mentre

vher'ever adv & conj dovunque; ~

is he? dov'è mai?; ~ possible dovunque sia possibile

whet /wet/ vt (pt/pp whetted) aguzzare (appetite)

whether /'weðə(r)/ conj se; ~ you like it or not che ti piaccia o no

which /wɪtʃ/ adj & pron quale; ~ one? quale?; ~ of you? chi di voi?; ~ way? (direction) in che direzione? ● rel pron (object) che; ~ he does vuol dire cosa che fa spesso; after ~ dopo di che; on/in ~ su/in cui

which'ever adj & pron qualunque; ~ it is qualunque sia; ~ one of you chiunque tra voi

while /waɪl/ n a long ~ un bel po'; a little ~ un po' ● conj mentre; (as long as) finché; (although) sebbene ● while away vt passare (time)

whilst /waɪlst/ conj see while

whim /wɪm/ n capriccio m

whimper /'wɪmpə(r)/ vi piagnucolare; (dog): mugolare

whine /waɪn/ n lamento m; (of dog) guaito m ● vi lamentarsi; (dog): guaire

whip /wɪp/ n frusta f; (Pol: person) parlamentare mf incaricato, -a di assicurarsi della presenza dei membri del suo partito alle votazioni ● vt (pt/pp whipped) frustare; (Culin) sbattere; (snatch) afferrare; (**1**: steal) fregare. □ ~ **up** vt (incite) stimolare; **1** improvvisare (meal). ~**ped** 'cream n panna f montata

whirl /wɜ:l/ n (movement) rotazione f; my mind's in a ~ ho le idee confuse ● vi girare rapidamente ● vt far girare rapidamente. ~ **pool** n vortice m. ~ **wind** n turbine m

whirr /wɜ:(r)/ vi ronzare

whisk /wɪsk/ n (Culin) frullino m ● vt (Culin) frullare. □ ~ **away** vt portare via

whisker /'wɪskə(r)/ n ~s (of cat) baffi mpl; (on man's cheek) basette fpl;

by a ~ per un pelo
whisky /'wɪskɪ/ n whisky m inv
whisper /'wɪspə(r)/ n sussurro m; (rumour) diceria f ● vt/i sussurrare
whistle /'wɪsl/ n fischio m; (instrument) fischietto m ● vt fischiettare ● vi fischiettare; (referee) fischiare
white /waɪt/ adj bianco; go ~ (pale) sbiancare ● n bianco m; (of egg) albume m; (person) bianco, -a mf
white: ~ 'coffee n caffè m inv macchiato. ~-'collar worker n colletto m bianco
white 'lie n bugia f pietosa
whiten /'waɪtn/ vt imbiancare ● vi sbiancare
'**whitewash** n intonaco m; fig copertura f ● vt dare una mano d'intonaco a; fig coprire
Whitsun /'wɪtsn/ n Pentecoste f
who /huː/ inter pron chi; rel pron che; the children, ~ were all tired,... i bambini, che erano tutti stanchi,...
who'ever pron chiunque; ~ he is chiunque sia; ~ can that be? chi può mai essere?
whole /həʊl/ adj tutto; (not broken) intatto; the ~ truth tutta la verità; the ~ world il mondo intero; the ~ lot (everything) tutto; (pl) tutti; the ~ lot of you tutti voi ● n tutto m; as a ~ nell'insieme; on the ~ tutto considerato; the ~ of Italy tutta l'Italia
whole: ~-'hearted adj di tutto cuore. ~meal adj integrale
'**wholesale** adj & adv all'ingrosso; fig in massa. ~r n grossista mf
wholesome /'həʊlsəm/ adj sano
wholly /'həʊlɪ/ adv completamente
whom /huːm/ rel pron che; the man I ~ I saw l'uomo che ho visto; to/with ~ a/con cui ● inter pron chi; to ~ did you speak? con chi hai parlato?
whooping cough /'huːpɪŋ/ n pertosse f

whore /hɔː(r)/ n 🔟 puttana f
whose /huːz/ rel pron il cui; people ~ name begins with D le persone i cui nomi cominciano con la D ● inter pron di chi; ~ is that? di chi è quello? ● adj ~ car did you use? di chi è la macchina che hai usato?
why /waɪ/ adv (inter) perché; the reason ~ la ragione per cui; that's ~ per questo ● int diamine
wick /wɪk/ n stoppino m
wicked /'wɪkɪd/ adj cattivo; (mischievous) malizioso
wicker /'wɪkə(r)/ n vimini mpl ● attrib di vimini
wide /waɪd/ adj largo; (experience, knowledge) vasto; (difference) profondo; (far from target) lontano; 10 cm ~ largo 10 cm; how ~ is it? quanto è largo? ● adv (off target) lontano dal bersaglio; ~ awake del tutto sveglio; ~ open spalancato; far and ~ in lungo e in largo. ~ly adv largamente; (known, accepted) generalmente; (different) profondamente
widen /'waɪdn/ vt allargare ● vi allargarsi
'**widespread** adj diffuso
widow /'wɪdəʊ/ n vedova f. ~ed adj vedovo. ~er n vedovo m
width /wɪdθ/ n larghezza f; (of material) altezza f
wield /wiːld/ vt maneggiare; esercitare (power)
wife /waɪf/ n (pl wives) moglie f
wig /wɪg/ n parrucca f
wiggle /'wɪgl/ vi dimenarsi ● vt dimenare
wild /waɪld/ adj selvaggio; (animal, flower) selvatico; (furious) furibondo; (applause) fragoroso; (idea) folle; (with joy) pazzo; (guess) azzardato; be ~ about (keen on) andare pazzo per ● adv run ~ crescere senza controllo ● n in the ~ allo stato naturale; the ~s pl le zone fpl sperdute

wilderness /ˈwɪldənɪs/ n deserto m; (fig: garden) giungla f

wildfire n spread like ~ allargarsi a macchia d'olio

wild: ~-'goose chase n ricerca f inutile. ~life n animali mpl selvatici

will¹ /wɪl/ v aux he ~ arrive tomorrow arriverà domani; I won't tell him non glielo dirò; you ~ be back soon, won't you? tornerai presto, no?; he ~ be there, won't he? sarà là, no?; she ~ be there by now sarà là ormai; ~ you go? (do you intend to go) pensi di andare?; ~ you go to the baker's and buy...? puoi andare dal panettiere a comprare...?; ~ you be quiet! vuoi stare calmo!; ~ you have some wine? vuoi del vino?; the engine won't start la macchina non parte

will² n volontà f inv; (document) testamento m

willing /ˈwɪlɪŋ/ adj disposto; (eager) volonteroso. ~ly adv volentieri. ~ness n buona volontà f

willow /ˈwɪləʊ/ n salice m

will-power n forza f di volontà

wilt /wɪlt/ vi appassire

win /wɪn/ n vittoria f; have a ~ riportare una vittoria ● v (pt/pp won; pres p winning) vt vincere; conquistare (fame) ● vi vincere. □ ~ **over** vt convincere

wince /wɪns/ vi contrarre il viso

winch /wɪntʃ/ n argano m

wind¹ /wɪnd/ n vento m; (breath) fiato m; (□: flatulence) aria f; get/ have the ~ up [T] aver fifa; get ~ of aver sentore di; in the ~ nell'aria ● vt ~ sb lasciare qcno senza fiato

wind² /waɪnd/ v (pt/pp wound) ● vt (wrap) avvolgere; (move by turning) far girare; (clock) caricare ● vi (road:)

serpeggiare. □ ~ **up** vt caricare (clock); concludere (proceedings); [T] prendere in giro (sb)

windfall /ˈwɪndfɔːl/ n fig fortuna f inaspettata

'wind farm n centrale f eolica

winding /ˈwaɪndɪŋ/ adj tortuoso

wind: ~ **instrument** n strumento m a fiato. ~**mill** n mulino m a vento

window /ˈwɪndəʊ/ n finestra f; (of car) finestrino m; (of shop) vetrina f

window: ~-**box** n cassetta f per i fiori. ~-**sill** n davanzale m

'windscreen n, Am **'windshield** n parabrezza m inv. ~ **washer** n getto m d'acqua. ~-**wiper** n tergicristallo m

wine /waɪn/ n vino m

wine: ~**glass** n bicchiere m da vino. ~-**list** n carta f dei vini

'wine-tasting n degustazione f di vini

wing /wɪŋ/ n ala f; (Auto) parafango m; ~s pl (Theat) quinte fpl. ~**er** n (Sport) ala f

wink /wɪŋk/ n strizzata f d'occhio; not sleep a ~ non chiudere occhio ● vi strizzare l'occhio; (light:) lampeggiare

winner /ˈwɪnə(r)/ n vincitore, -trice mf

wint|er /ˈwɪntə(r)/ n inverno m. ~**ry** adj invernale

wipe /waɪp/ n passata f; (to dry) asciugata f ● vt strofinare; (dry) asciugare. □ ~ **off** vt asciugare; (erase) cancellare. □ ~ **out** vt annientare; eliminare (village); estinguere (debt). □ ~ **up** vt asciugare (dishes)

wire /ˈwaɪə(r)/ n fil m di ferro; (electrical) filo m elettrico

wiring /ˈwaɪərɪŋ/ n impianto m elettrico

wisdom /ˈwɪzdəm/ n saggezza f; (of action) sensatezza f. ~ **tooth** n dente

w

m del giudizio

wise /waɪz/ *adj* saggio; (*prudent*) sensato. ~**ly** *adv* saggiamente; (*act*) sensatamente

wish /wɪʃ/ *n* desiderio *m*; make a ~ esprimere un desiderio; with best ~es con i migliori auguri ● *vt* desiderare; ~ sb well fare tanti auguri a qcno; I ~ you every success ti auguro buona fortuna; I ~ you could stay vorrei che tu potessi rimanere ● *vi* ~ for sth desiderare qcsa. ~**ful** *adj* ~**ful thinking** illusione *f*

wistful /'wɪstfl/ *adj* malinconico

wit /wɪt/ *n* spirito *m*; (*person*) persona *f* di spirito; be at one's ~s' end non saper che pesci pigliare

witch /wɪtʃ/ *n* strega *f*. ~**craft** *n* magia *f*. ~**hunt** *n* caccia *f* alle streghe

with /wɪð/ *prep* con; (*fear, cold, jealousy etc*) di; I'm not ~ you ⓘ non ti seguo; can I leave it ~ you? (*task*) puoi occupartene tu?; ~ no regrets/money senza rimpianti/soldi; be ~ it ⓘ essere al passo coi tempi; (*alert*) essere concentrato

with'draw *v* (*pt* -drew, *pp* -drawn) ● *vt* ritirare; prelevare (*money*) ● *vi* ritirarsi. ~**al** *n* ritiro *m*; (*of money*) prelevamento *m*; (*from drugs*) crisi *f inv* di astinenza; (*Psych*) chiusura *f* in se stessi. ~**al symptoms** *npl* sintomi *mpl* da crisi di astinenza

with'drawn ▷**WITHDRAW** ● *adj* (*person*) chiuso in se stesso

wither /'wɪðə(r)/ *vi* (*flower:*) appassire

with'hold *vt* (*pt/pp* -held) rifiutare (*consent*) (from a); nascondere (*information*) (from a); trattenere (*smile*)

with'in *prep* in; (*before the end of*) entro; ~ **the law** legale ● *adv* all'interno

with'out *prep* senza; ~ **stopping** senza fermarsi

with'stand *vt* (*pt/pp* -stood) resistere a

witness /'wɪtnɪs/ *n* testimone *mf* ● *vt* autenticare (*signature*); essere testimone di (*accident*). ~**-box** *n*, *Am* ~**-stand** *n* banco *m* dei testimoni

witticism /'wɪtɪsɪzm/ *n* spiritosaggine *f*

witty /'wɪtɪ/ *adj* (-ier, -iest) spiritoso

wives /waɪvz/ ▷**WIFE**

wizard /'wɪzəd/ *n* mago *m*. ~**ry** *n* stregoneria *f*

wobb|le /'wɒbl/ *vi* traballare. ~**ly** *adj* traballante

woe /wəʊ/ *n* afflizione *f*

woke, woken /wəʊk/, /'wəʊkn/ ▷**WAKE**¹

wolf /wʊlf/ *n* (*pl* **wolves** /wʊlvz/) lupo *m*; (ⓘ: *womanizer*) donnaiolo *m* ● *vt* ~ [**down**] divorare. ~**whistle** *n* fischio *m* ● *vi* ~-**whistle at sb** fischiare dietro a qcno

woman /'wʊmən/ *n* (*pl* **women**) donna *f*. ~**izer** *n* donnaiolo *m*. ~**ly** *adj* femmineo

womb /wuːm/ *n* utero *m*

women /'wɪmɪn/ ▷**WOMAN**. W~'s Libber *n* femminista *f*. W~'s Liberation *n* movimento *m* femminista

won /wʌn/ ▷**WIN**

wonder /'wʌndə(r)/ *n* meraviglia *f*; (*surprise*) stupore *m*; no ~! non c'è da stupirsi; it's a ~ that... è incredibile che... ● *vi* restare in ammirazione; (*be surprised*) essere sorpreso; I ~ è quello che mi chiedo; I ~ whether she is ill mi chiedo se è malata?. ~**ful** *adj* meraviglioso. ~**fully** *adv* meravigliosamente

wood /wʊd/ *n* legno *m*; (*for burning*) legna *f*; (*forest*) bosco *m*; out of the ~ fig fuori pericolo; touch ~! tocca ferro!

wood: ~**ed** /-ɪd/ *adj* boscoso. ~**en** *adj* di legno; *fig* legnoso. ~**wind** *n* strumenti *mpl* a fiato. ~**work** *n* (*wooden parts*) parti *fpl* in legno; (*craft*)

falegnameria f. **~worm** n tarlo m. **~y** adj (hill) boscoso

wool /wʊl/ n lana f ● attrib di lana. **~len** adj di lana. **~lens** n capi mpl di lana

woolly /'wʊlɪ/ adj (-ier, -iest) (sweater) di lana; fig fig confuso

word /wɜːd/ n parola f; (news) notizia f; by ~ of mouth a viva voce; have a ~ with dire due parole a; have ~s bisticciare; in other ~s in altre parole. **~ing** n parole fpl. **~ processor** n programma m di videoscrittura, word processor m inv

wore /wɔː(r)/ ▷WEAR

work /wɜːk/ n lavoro m; (of art) opera f; ~s pl (factory) fabbrica fsg; (mechanism) meccanismo msg; at ~ al lavoro; out of ~ disoccupato ● vi lavorare; (machine, ruse:) funzionare; (study) studiare ● vt far funzionare (machine); far lavorare (employee); far studiare (student). □ ~ off vt sfogare (anger); lavorare per estinguere (debt); fare sport per smaltire (weight). □ ~ out vt elaborare (plan); risolvere (problem); calcolare (bill); I ~ed out how he did it ho capito come l'ha fatto ● vi evolvere. □ ~ up vt I've ~ed up an appetite mi è venuto appetito; don't get ~ed up (anxious) non farti prendere dal panico; (angry) non arrabbiarti

workable /'wɜːkəbl/ adj (feasible) fattibile

worker /'wɜːkə(r)/ n lavoratore, -trice mf; (manual) operaio, -a mf

working /'wɜːkɪŋ/ adj (clothes etc) da lavoro; (day) feriale; in ~ order funzionante. ~ **class** n classe f operaia. ~**-class** adj operaio

work: **~man** n operaio m. **~manship** n lavorazione f. **~shop** n officina f; (discussion) dibattito m

world /wɜːld/ n mondo m; a ~ of difference una differenza abissale; out of this ~ favoloso; think the ~ of sb andare matto per qcno. **~ly** adj materiale; (person) materialista. **~-'wide** adj mondiale ● adv mondialmente

worm /wɜːm/ n verme m ● vt ~ one's way into sb's confidence conquistarsi la fiducia di qcno in modo subdolo. **~-eaten** adj tarlato

worn /wɔːn/ ▷WEAR ● adj sciupato. **~-out** adj consumato; (person) sfinito

worried /'wʌrɪd/ adj preoccupato

worry /'wʌrɪ/ n preoccupazione f ● v (pt/pp worried) ● vt preoccupare; (bother) disturbare ● vi preoccuparsi. **~ing** adj preoccupante

worse /wɜːs/ adj peggiore ● adv peggio ● n peggio m

worsen /'wɜːsn/ vt/i peggiorare

worship /'wɜːʃɪp/ n culto m; (service) funzione f; Your/His W~ (to judge) signor giudice/il giudice ● v (pt/pp -shipped) ● vt venerare ● vi andare a messa

worst /wɜːst/ adj peggiore ● adv peggio [di tutti] ● n the ~ il peggio; get the ~ of it avere la peggio; if the ~ comes to the ~ nella peggiore delle ipotesi

worth /wɜːθ/ n valore m; £10 ~ of petrol 10 sterline di benzina ● adj be ~ valere; be ~ it fig valerne la pena; it's ~ trying vale la pena di provare; it's ~ my while mi conviene. **~less** adj senza valore. **~while** adj che vale la pena; (cause) lodevole

worthy /'wɜːðɪ/ adj degno; (cause, motive) lodevole

would /wʊd/ v aux I ~ do it lo farei; ~ you go? andresti?; ~ you mind if I opened the window? ti dispiace se apro la finestra?; he ~ come if he could verrebbe se potesse; he said he ~n't ha detto di no; ~ you like a drink? vuoi

           w

qualcosa da bere?; what ~ you like to drink? cosa prendi da bere?; you ~n't, ~ you? non lo faresti, vero?

wound[1] /wu:nd/ n ferita f ● vt ferire

wound[2] /waʊnd/ ▷**WIND**[2]

wrangle /ˈræŋgl/ n litigio m ● vi litigare

wrap /ræp/ n (shawl) scialle m ● vt (pt/pp wrapped) ~ [up] avvolgere; (present) incartare; be ~ped up in fig essere completamente preso da ● vi ~ up warmly coprirsi bene. ~per n (for sweet) carta f [di caramella]. ~ping n materiale m da imballaggio. ~ping paper n carta f da pacchi; (for gift) carta f da regalo

wrath /rɒθ/ n ira f

wreak /ri:k/ vt ~ havoc with sth scombussolare qcsa

wreath /ri:θ/ n (pl ~s /-ðz/) corona f

wreck /rek/ n (of ship) relitto m; (of car) carcassa f; (person) rottame m ● vt far naufragare; demolire (car). ~age n rottami mpl; fig brandelli mpl

wrench /rentʃ/ n (injury) slogatura f; (tool) chiave f inglese; (pull) strattone m ● vt (pull) strappare; slogarsi (wrist, ankle etc)

wrestl|e /ˈresl/ vi lottare corpo a corpo; fig lottare. ~er n lottatore, -trice mf. ~ing n lotta f libera; (all-in) catch m

wretch /retʃ/ n disgraziato, -a mf. ~ed odioso; (weather) orribile; feel ~ed (unhappy) essere triste; (ill) sentirsi malissimo

wriggle /ˈrɪgl/ n contorsione f ● vi contorcersi; (move forward) strisciare; ~ out of sth 🛈 sottrarsi a qcsa

wring /rɪŋ/ vt (pt/pp wrung) torcere (sb's neck); strizzare (clothes); ~ one's hands torcersi le mani; ~ing wet inzuppato

wrinkle /ˈrɪŋkl/ n grinza f; (on skin) ruga f ● vt/i raggrinzire. ~d adj (skin,

face) rugoso; (clothes) raggrinzito

wrist /rɪst/ n polso m. ~-watch n orologio m da polso

writ /rɪt/ n (Jur) mandato m

write /raɪt/ vt/i (pt wrote, pp written, pres p writing) scrivere. □ ~ down vt annotare. □ ~ off vt cancellare (debt); distruggere (car)

'write-off n (car) rottame m

writer /ˈraɪtə(r)/ n autore, -trice mf; she's a ~ è una scrittrice

writhe /raɪð/ vi contorcersi

writing /ˈraɪtɪŋ/ n (occupation) scrivere m; (words) scritte fpl; (handwriting) scrittura f; in ~ per iscritto. ~-paper n carta f da lettera

written /ˈrɪtn/ ▷**WRITE**

wrong /rɒŋ/ adj sbagliato; be ~ (person): sbagliare; what's ~? cosa c'è che non va? ● adv (spelt) in modo sbagliato; go ~ (person): sbagliare; (machine): funzionare male; (plan): andar male ● n ingiustizia f; in the ~ dalla parte del torto; know right from ~ distinguere il bene dal male ● vt fare torto a. ~ful adj ingiusto. ~ly adv in modo sbagliato; (accuse, imagine) a torto; (informed) male

wrote /raʊt/ ▷**WRITE**

wrought iron /rɔːt-/ n ferro m battuto ● attrib di ferro battuto

wrung /rʌŋ/ ▷**WRING**

wry /raɪ/ adj (-er, -est) (humour, smile) beffardo

• •

Xx

Xmas /ˈkrɪsməs/ n 🛈 Natale m

'X-ray n (picture) radiografia f; have an ~ farsi fare una radiografia ● vt passare ai raggi X

Yy

yacht /jɒt/ n yacht m inv; (for racing) barca f a vela. **~ing** n vela f

yank /jæŋk/ vt 🗆 tirare

Yank n 🗆 americano, -a mf

yap /jæp/ vi (pt/pp yapped) (dog:) guaire

yard[1] /jɑːd/ n cortile m; (for storage) deposito m

yard[2] n iarda f (= 91,44 cm). **~stick** n fig pietra f di paragone

yarn /jɑːn/ n filo m; (🗆: tale) storia f

yawn /jɔːn/ n sbadiglio m ● vi sbadigliare. **~ing** adj **~ing** gap sbadiglio m

yeah /jeə/ adv sì

year /jɪə(r)/ n anno m; (of wine) annata f; for **~s** 🗆 da secoli. **~book** n annuario m. **~ly** adj annuale ● adv annualmente

yearn /jɜːn/ vi struggersi. **~ing** n desiderio m struggente

yeast /jiːst/ n lievito m

yell /jel/ n urlo m ● vi urlare

yellow /'jeləʊ/ adj & n giallo m

yelp /jelp/ n (of dog) guaito m ● vi (dog:) guaire

yes /jes/ adv sì ● n sì m inv

yesterday /'jestədeɪ/ adj & adv ieri m inv; **~'s** paper il giornale di ieri; the day before **~** l'altroieri

yet /jet/ adv ancora; as **~** fino ad ora; not **~** non ancora; the best **~** il migliore finora ● conj eppure

yield /jiːld/ n produzione f; (profit) reddito m ● vt produrre; (profit) (profit) ● vi cedere; Am (Auto) dare la precedenza

yoga /'jəʊgə/ n yoga m

yoghurt /'jɒgət/ n yogurt m inv

yoke /jəʊk/ n giogo m; (of garment) carré m inv

yokel /'jəʊkl/ n zotico, -a mf

yolk /jəʊk/ n tuorlo m

you /juː/ pron (subject) tu, voi pl; (formal) lei, voi pl; (direct/indirect object) ti, vi pl; (formal direct object) la; (formal indirect object) le; (after prep) te, voi pl; (formal: after prep) lei;

tu is used when speaking to friends, children and animals. lei is used to speak to someone you do not know. voi is used to speak to more than one person. Note that you is often not translated when it is the subject of the sentence

~ are very kind (sg) sei molto gentile; (formal) è molto gentile; (pl & formal) siete molto gentili; **~** can stay, but he has to go (sg) tu puoi rimanere, ma lui deve andarsene; (pl) voi potete rimanere, ma lui deve andarsene; all of **~** tutti voi; I'll give **~** the money (sg) ti darò i soldi; (pl) vi darò i soldi; I'll give it to **~** (sg) te/(pl) ve lo darò; it was **~** (sg) eri tu!; (pl) eravate voi!; **~** have to be careful (one) si deve fare attenzione

young /jʌŋ/ adj giovane ● npl (animals) piccoli mpl; the **~** (people) i giovani mpl. **~** lady n signorina f. **~** man n giovanotto. **~ster** n ragazzo, -a mf; (child) bambino -a m

your /jɔː(r)/ adj il tuo m, la tua f, i tuoi mpl, le tue fpl; (formal) il suo m, la sua f, i suoi mpl, le sue fpl (pl & formal pl) il vostro m, la vostra f, i vostri mpl, le vostre fpl; **~** mother/father tua madre/tuo padre; (formal) sua madre/suo padre; (pl & formal pl) vostra madre/vostro padre

yours /jɔːz/ poss pron il tuo m, la tua f, i tuoi mpl, le tue fpl; (formal) il suo m, la sua f, i suoi mpl, le sue fpl; (pl & formal pl) il vostro m, la vostra f, i vostri mpl, le vostre fpl; a friend of ~ un tuo/suo/vostro amico; friends of ~ dei tuoi/vostri/suoi amici; that is ~ quello è tuo/vostro/suo; (as opposed to mine) quello è il tuo/il vostro/il suo

your'self pron (reflexive) ti; (formal) si; (emphatic) te stesso; (formal) sé, se stesso; do pour ~ a drink versati da bere; (formal) si versi da bere; you said so ~ lo hai detto tu stesso; (formal) lo ha detto lei stesso; you can be proud of ~ puoi essere fiero di te/di sé; by ~ da solo

your'selves pron (reflexive) vi; (emphatic) voi stessi; do pour ~ a drink versatevi da bere; you said so ~ lo avete detto voi stessi; you can be proud of ~ potete essere fieri di voi; by ~ da soli

youth /juːθ/ n (pl youths /-ðːz/) gioventù f inv; (boy) giovanetto m; the ~ (young people) i giovani mpl. ~ful adj giovanile. ~ hostel n ostello m [della gioventù]

Yugoslav /'juːɡəslɑːv/ adj & n jugoslavo, -a mf

Yugoslavia /-'slɑːvɪə/ n jugoslavia f

Zz

zeal /ziːl/ n zelo m

zealous /'zeləs/ adj zelante. ~ly adv con zelo

zebra /'zebrə/ n zebra f. ~·'crossing n passaggio m pedonale, zebre fpl

zero /'zɪərəʊ/ n zero m

zest /zest/ n gusto m

zigzag /'zɪɡzæɡ/ n zigzag m inv ● vi (pt/pp -zagged) zigzagare

zilch /zɪltʃ/ n Ⅰ zero m assoluto

zinc /zɪŋk/ n zinco m

zip /zɪp/ n [fastener] cerniera f [lampo] ● vt (pt/pp zipped) ~ [up] chiudere con la cerniera [lampo]

'Zip code n Am codice m postale

zipper /'zɪpə(r)/ n Am cerniera f [lampo]

zodiac /'zəʊdɪæk/ n zodiaco m

zombie /'zɒmbɪ/ n Ⅰ zombi mf inv

zone /zəʊn/ n zona f

zoo /zuː/ n zoo m inv

zoolog|ist /zəʊ'bɒlədʒɪst/ n zoologo, -a mf. ~y zoologia f

zoom /zuːm/ vi sfrecciare. ~ lens n zoom m inv

Verbi inglese irregolari

Infinito	Passato	Participio passato	Infinito	Passato	Participio passato
be	was	been	**drive**	drove	driven
bear	bore	borne	**eat**	ate	eaten
beat	beat	beaten	**fall**	fell	fallen
become	became	become	**feed**	fed	fed
begin	began	begun	**feel**	felt	felt
bend	bent	bent	**fight**	fought	fought
bet	bet,	bet,	**find**	found	found
	betted	betted	**flee**	fled	fled
bid	bade, bid	bidden, bid	**fly**	flew	flown
bind	bound	bound	**forecast**	forecast,	forecast,
bite	bit	bitten		forecasted	forecasted
bleed	bled	bled	**forget**	forgot	forgotten,
blow	blew	blown			forgot US
break	broke	broken	**freeze**	froze	frozen
breed	bred	bred	**get**	got	got, gotten US
bring	brought	brought	**give**	gave	given
build	built	built	**go**	went	gone
burn	burnt,	burnt,	**grow**	grew	grown
	burned	burned	**hang**	hung,	hung,
burst	burst	burst		hanged	hanged
buy	bought	bought	**have**	had	had
catch	caught	caught	**hear**	heard	heard
choose	chose	chosen	**hide**	hid	hidden
cling	clung	clung	**hit**	hit	hit
come	came	come	**hold**	held	held
cost	cost,	cost,	**hurt**	hurt	hurt
	costed (vt)	costed	**keep**	kept	kept
cut	cut	cut	**kneel**	knelt	knelt
deal	dealt	dealt	**know**	knew	known
dig	dug	dug	**lay**	laid	laid
do	did	done	**lead**	led	led
draw	drew	drawn	**lean**	leaned,	leaned,
dream	dreamt,	dreamt,		leant	leant
	dreamed	dreamed	**leap**	leaped,	leaped,
drink	drank	drunk		leapt	leapt

Infinito	Passato	Participio passato	Infinito	Passato	Participio passato
learn	learnt, learned	learnt, learned	**smell**	smelt, smelled	smelt, smelled
leave	left	left	**speak**	spoke	spoken
lend	lent	lent	**spell**	spelled, spelt	spelled, spelt
let	let	let			
lie	lay	lain	**spend**	spent	spent
lose	lost	lost	**spit**	spat	spat
make	made	made	**spoil**	spoilt, spoiled	spoilt, spoiled
mean	meant	meant			
meet	met	met	**spread**	spread	spread
pay	paid	paid	**spring**	sprang	sprung
put	put	put	**stand**	stood	stood
quit	quitted, quit	quitted, quit	**steal**	stole	stolen
			stick	stuck	stuck
read	read	read	**sting**	stung	stung
ride	rode	ridden	**stride**	strode	stridden
ring	rang	rung	**strike**	struck	struck
rise	rose	risen	**swear**	swore	sworn
run	ran	run	**sweep**	swept	swept
say	said	said	**swell**	swelled	swollen, swelled
see	saw	seen			
seek	sought	sought	**swim**	swam	swum
sell	sold	sold	**swing**	swung	swung
send	sent	sent	**take**	took	taken
set	set	set	**teach**	taught	taught
sew	sewed	sewn, sewed	**tear**	tore	torn
shake	shook	shaken	**tell**	told	told
shine	shone	shone	**think**	thought	thought
shoe	shod	shod	**throw**	threw	thrown
shoot	shot	shot	**thrust**	thrust	thrust
show	showed	shown	**tread**	trod	trodden
shut	shut	shut	**understand**	understood	understood
sing	sang	sung			
sink	sank	sunk	**wake**	woke	woken
sit	sat	sat	**wear**	wore	worn
sleep	slept	slept	**win**	won	won
sling	slung	slung	**write**	wrote	written